HOWL

By Allen Ginsberg

Poetry

Howl and Other Poems *1956*
Kaddish and Other Poems *1961*
Empty Mirror: Early Poems *1961*
Reality Sandwiches *1963*
Angkor Wat *1968*
Planet News *1968*
Airplane Dreams *1969*
The Gates of Wrath: Rhymed Poems 1948–51 *1972*
The Fall of America: Poems of These States *1973*
Iron Horse *1973*
First Blues *1975*
Mind Breaths: Poems 1971–76 *1978*
Plutonian Ode: Poems 1977–1980 *1982*
Collected Poems 1947–1980 *1984*
White Shroud: Poems 1980–1985 *1986*
Cosmopolitan Greetings: Poems 1986–1992 *1994*

Prose

The Yage Letters (WITH WILLIAM BURROUGHS) *1963*
Indian Journals *1970*
Gay Sunshine Interview (WITH ALLEN YOUNG) *1974*
Allen Verbatim: Lectures on Poetry, Politics, Consciousness (GORDON BALL, ED.) *1974*
Chicago Trial Testimony *1975*
To Eberhart from Ginsberg *1976*
Journals: Early Fifties, Early Sixties (GORDON BALL, ED.) *1977, 1993*
As Ever: Collected Correspondence Allen Ginsberg & Neal Cassady (BARRY GIFFORD, ED.) *1977*
Composed on the Tongue (Literary Conversations 1967–1977) *1980*
Straight Hearts Delight, Love Poems and Selected Letters 1947–1980, with Peter Orlovsky
    (WINSTON LEYLAND, ED.) *1980*
Howl, Original Draft Facsimilie, Fully Annotated (BARRY MILES, ED.) *1986*
The Visions of the Great Rememberer (with Visions of Cody, Jack Kerouac) *1993*
Journals Mid-Fifties: 1954–1958 *1995*

Photography

Photographs (TWELVETREES PRESS) *1991*
Snapshot Poetics (CHRONICLE BOOKS) *1993*

Vocal Words and Music

First Blues CASSETTE TAPE ONLY (FOLKWAYS/SMITHSONIAN RECORDS FSS 37560) *1981*
Howls, Raps & Roars 4 CD BOX (FANTASY) *1993*
Hydrogen Jukebox (OPERA) WITH PHILIP GLASS, CD (ELEKTRA/NONESUCH) *1981*
Holy Soul Jelly Roll: Poems & Songs 1949–1993 4 CD BOX (RHINO RECORDS) *1994*

ALLEN GINSBERG

HOWL

ORIGINAL DRAFT FACSIMILE, TRANSCRIPT

& VARIANT VERSIONS, FULLY ANNOTATED BY AUTHOR,

WITH CONTEMPORANEOUS CORRESPONDENCE, ACCOUNT OF FIRST

PUBLIC READING, LEGAL SKIRMISHES, PRECURSOR TEXTS

& BIBLIOGRAPHY

*"For the nightly Visitor is at the window of the impenitent,
while I sing a psalm of my own composing."*

Edited by Barry Miles

HarperPerennial
A Division of HarperCollins*Publishers*

Designed by Sidney Feinberg

The Library of Congress has catalogued the hardcover edition as follows:

Ginsberg, Allen, 1926–
    Howl : original draft facsimile, transcript & variant versions, fully
annotated by author, with contemporaneous correspondence, account of first
public reading, legal skirmishes, precursor texts & bibliography.
    Rev. ed. of: Howl, and other poems. 1956.
    Bibliography: p.
    Includes index.
    1. Ginsberg, Allen, 1926– . Howl, and other poems—Manuscripts—
Facsimiles. 2. Ginsberg, Allen, 1926– —Technique.
I. Miles, Barry, 1943– . II. Ginsberg, Allen, 1926– . Howl, and other
poems. III. Title.
PS3513.I74H6 1986
811´.54   86-45105

ISBN 0-06-092611-2 (pbk.)
    04 03 02 01 00 CW 10 9 8 7 6 5 4 3

To
Lawrence Ferlinghetti
Poet
Editor, Publisher and Defender of "Howl"
in gratitude for his comradeship over three decades

Missing all our appointments
and turning up unshaven
years later
old cigarette papers
stuck to our pants
leaves in our hair.

Contents

ILLUSTRATIONS

Contemporaneous Photographs & Images Relevant to HOWL

(Above) 1010 Montgomery Street San Francisco, author's room facing back to fireplace, Summer 1955. Robert La Vigne's watercolors on wall; bed bureau, Bach & clock, checkered blanket over alley window.   *Photo by A.G.*

(Below) Same furnished room facing front street window shade, La Vigne's gesso portrait of Orlovsky on floor. Part I *Howl* written on desk typewriter, corner left, same month photo taken.   *Photo by A.G.*

Author's Preface: Reader's Guide

Since this work is not done posthumously, I've had the liberty to annotate each verse regarding appropriate cultural references which few critics have examined (especially to Christopher Smart's "Jubilate Agno," Cézanne's aesthetics and Schwitters' sound poems). I've lived with and enjoyed Howl for three decades, it has become a social and poetical landmark, notorious at worst illuminative at best, more recently translated for understanding hitherto forbidden to the public in Eastern Europe, the Soviet Union and China. It seems helpful in this fourth decade of the poem's use to clarify its literary background and historical implications as well as its author's intentions. Few poets have enjoyed the opportunity to expound their celebrated texts. Usually it is the lamplit study of an academic scholar, as with Mr. J. Livingston Lowes' hard interesting work on Coleridge's "Rime." Wordsworth essayed explanations of his editions. Whitman early and appreciatively critiqued his own *Leaves* with modest anonymity for a generally hostile or indifferent literary society. Later, for a more sympathetic public, he expounded its purport through several prefaces unique in comprehension of his own appointments and disappointments. Still I've ventured my intelligence, neither modest nor immodest, for the general public, poetry lovers, scholars, breakthrough artists and future generations of inspired youths.

The appeal in "Howl" is to the secret or hermetic tradition of art "justifying" or "making up for" defeat in worldly life, to the acknowledgment of an

> "Unworldly love
> that has no hope
>   of the world
>
>   and that
> cannot change the world
> to its delight—"*

after desolation

> "as if the earth under our feet
> were
> an excrement of some sky
>
> and we degraded prisoners
> destined
> to hunger until we eat filth"†

Thus William Carlos Williams appealed to the "imagination" of art to reveal our deepest natural ground: love, hopeless yet permanently present in the heart, unalterable. ("Love is not love / Which alters when it alteration finds.") The unworldly love hypostatized as comradeship through thick and thin with Carl Solomon rose out of primordial filial loyalty to my mother, then in distress. Where mother love conflicts with social facade, the die is cast from antiquity in favor of sympathy.

Blocked by appearances, love comes through in the free play of the imagination, a world of art, the field of space where Appearance—natural recognition of social tragedy & world failure—shows lesser sentience than original compassionate expansiveness of heart.

It is in the poem, as W.C.W. says, that we reconstruct the world lost. The end

---

* William Carlos Williams, "Rain," in *The Collected Earlier Poems* (New York: New Directions, 1966), p. 76.
  † Williams, "To Elsie," ibid., pp. 271–2.

verses of Part I hypothesize various arts that reconstruct our original *"petite sensation"* of *"Pater Omnipotens Aeterne Deus."* The classic art tactics catalogued there suggest a shrewd humor that protects our unobstructed sympathy from chaos. The matter is in objective acknowledgment of emotion.

"Howl" was written in a furnished room at 1010 Montgomery, a few houses up from where the street meets Broadway, in North Beach, and continues down a few steep blocks into San Francisco's financial district. I had weeks earlier quit work as a minor market research executive, had moved in with new-met friend Peter Orlovsky, but as he returned to Long Island to visit his family over the summer, I was alone. I had the leisure of unemployment compensation for six months ahead, had concluded a longish period of psychotherapeutic consultation, enjoyed occasional visits from Neal Cassady, decade-old friend, now brakeman on Southern Pacific Railroad, and maintained energetic correspondence with Jack Kerouac in Long Island and William Burroughs in Tanger.

I had recently dreamt of the late Joan Burroughs, a sympathetic encounter with her spirit. She inquired the living fate of our friends. I wrote the dream as a poem ("Dream Record: June 8, 1955"), about which in a few days Kenneth Rexroth, an elder in this literary city, wrote me he thought was stilted & somewhat academic. A week later, I sat idly at my desk by the first-floor window facing Montgomery Street's slope to gay Broadway—only a few blocks from City Lights literary paperback bookshop. I had a secondhand typewriter, some cheap scratch paper. I began typing, not with the idea of writing a formal poem, but stating my imaginative sympathies, whatever they were worth. As my loves were impractical and my thoughts relatively unworldly, I had nothing to gain, only the pleasure of enjoying on paper those sympathies most intimate to myself and most awkward in the great world of family, formal education, business and current literature.

What I wrote that afternoon, printed here in facsimile, was not conceived as a poem to publish. It stands now as the first section of "Howl." Later parts were written in San Francisco, and in a garden cottage in Berkeley over the next few months, with the idea of completing a poem.

In publishing "Howl," I was curious to leave behind after my generation an emotional time bomb that would continue exploding in U.S. consciousness in case our military-industrial-nationalist complex solidified into a repressive police bureaucracy. As a sidelight, I thought to disseminate a poem so strong that a clean Saxon four-letter word might enter high school anthologies permanently and deflate tendencies toward authoritarian strong-arming (evident in later-'50s neoconservative attacks on Kerouac's heartfelt prose and Burrough's poetic humor).

This facsimile edition is a "How to" book, a handbook for composition of one kind of expansive poetry: its process, basic sorting and judgment, revision, transposition of artful choices. Some interpretations, obvious to old-dog poet-teacher-critic, may unbewilder folk who think they can't understand "poetic inspiration." A ground of common sense is exposed in first draft, a path of re-composition is mapped in orderly detail, the stages and associations leading to finished text are laid bare. For writers interested in open form or long-line verse, annotations provide a key to ordinary writing activity, dissolving mystery's veil of private allusion, or author's subjective assumptions of common reference.

Detailed contents pages provide reader with a map through these leaves of manuscript, persons, decades of anecdote & gossip, aesthetic theory, familiar epistles, noble attacks & sympathies, notable literary moments, poetic arrests, trials & judgment, spiritual breaths, and books & images indexed for posterity.

Pleased with this *Howl*, I remain

Your yet living servant, etc.

The author,

Allen Ginsberg

May 17, 1986

A Note on the Manuscript

The manuscript of "Howl" is on standard typing paper, as reproduced here. Part I and possibly Part III were composed directly on the typewriter. The first drafts of Part II and Part IV were composed in holograph, with all subsequent drafts of all parts composed on the typewriter. "Howl" Part I was written early in August 1955 (before August 16th), at 1010 Montgomery Street, San Francisco. The first three lines and the last four of Part II were written on, or shortly before August 24th, in San Francisco, while the middle section of the poem was composed at 1624 Milvia Street, Berkeley. Ginsberg moved to Milvia Street on September 1st, 1955 and first met Gary Snyder on September 8th,* who was present in the cottage when draft five of Part II was being composed. It therefore seems likely that the middle section of Part II dates from late September, 1955. Part IV, or "Footnote to Howl" cannot be accurately dated. Part I was the only section regarded by Ginsberg as sufficiently complete to be read in public at the time of the Six Gallery reading on October 7, 1955. Ginsberg continued to make minor changes to all sections of the poem right up until the time of publication and many of the later drafts reproduced here date from the winter of 1955–56 and the following spring.

As soon as he had made a clean copy from the original manuscript of "Howl," Part I, Ginsberg sent the first six pages to Jack Kerouac, who was living in Mexico City. The seventh page was retained ("I probably didn't send it because it was so messy") and was kept among the author's papers. On August 30, 1955, Kerouac sent the manuscript on to John Clellon Holmes in New York City. Holmes writes:

"Sometime in the mid-50's, certainly over a year before the City Lights edition, Jack Kerouac wrote me a newsy letter from San Francisco,† enclosing an early draft of 'Howl.' It was such a cross-hatch of emendations and inkings-out that it was hard to get any coherent idea of its accumulating power. But power it had, even then, and when Richard Eberhart reported to the *New York Times* on the Six Gallery Reading‡ a little later (one of the first East Coast notices of the ferment going on in Frisco just then), he mentioned the poem as the ultimate event of the evening. This early draft proved different than the final version, but having no address to which to return it, I filed it away, and forgot it. Years later, in the late 70's, I discovered it in a box of old papers in Saybrook, Conn. That fall, back in Arkansas for my annual teaching gig, I finally returned it to Allen, not without some reluctance, knowing its value, but in memory of those early *samizdat* days when mss. criss-crossed the country, friend to friend, seeking a readership the circumstances in the culture then denied us." (January 18, 1986.)

The other drafts of "Howl," together with the drafts of the later parts, were all stored in a trunk at Ginsberg's father's house in Paterson, New Jersey, when Ginsberg and Peter Orlovsky departed for Europe in March 1957. The manuscript remained there until March 12, 1969, when all of Ginsberg's papers were deposited at the Special Collections department of the Butler Library of Columbia University.

Holmes returned the first six pages of "Howl," Part I, to Ginsberg in July 1980, and they were placed in a bank vault for safekeeping. These pages were reunited with the final, seventh, page in the fall of 1985, when I examined all the extant manuscripts in preparation for this volume.

---

* *Kerouac* by Ann Charters, New York, Warner Books, 1973, 1974, p. 239.

† Kerouac left Mexico City for San Francisco on September 9, 1955, so if the annotation on the first page of the original manuscript is correct, and Holmes received the manuscript from Kerouac in August, it must have been sent from Mexico.

‡ See Appendix II.

The manuscripts were in no particular order, and it took Ginsberg and myself some time to agree to an exact chronology of folios, particularly for the drafts of "Howl," Part II, where the second folio of each draft was sometimes difficult to identify. Some of the drafts were accompanied by carbon copies, and these, together with a number of drafts that showed only slight development of the text, have been excluded from this volume.

There are a number of other variants of the text available. Ginsberg sent copies of the manuscript in its various stages to a number of his friends and acquaintances, and many of these drafts are now in the libraries of universities and other specialized collections. Two different drafts, similar but not identical to the drafts included here, are in the William Carlos Williams collection at Yale. Other drafts are no longer extant. An early clean typed copy, taken from the heavily annotated first draft reproduced here, was given to Sheila Boucher as a gift in exchange for retyping first versions. This draft, which included a number of major revisions, was lost shortly afterward.

BARRY MILES

HOWL: FINAL TEXT, 1986

Howl

For Carl Solomon

I

1   I saw the best minds of my generation destroyed by madness, starving hysterical naked,

dragging themselves through the negro streets at dawn looking for an angry fix,

angelheaded hipsters burning for the ancient heavenly connection to the starry dynamo in the machinery of night,

who poverty and tatters and hollow-eyed and high sat up smoking in the supernatural darkness of cold-water flats floating across the tops of cities contemplating jazz,

5   who bared their brains to Heaven under the El and saw Mohammedan angels staggering on tenement roofs illuminated,

who passed through universities with radiant cool eyes hallucinating Arkansas and Blake-light tragedy among the scholars of war,

who were expelled from the academies for crazy & publishing obscene odes on the windows of the skull,

who cowered in unshaven rooms in underwear, burning their money in wastebaskets and listening to the Terror through the wall,

who got busted in their pubic beards returning through Laredo with a belt of marijuana for New York,

10   who ate fire in paint hotels or drank turpentine in Paradise Alley, death, or purgatoried their torsos night after night

with dreams, with drugs, with waking nightmares, alcohol and cock and endless balls,

incomparable blind streets of shuddering cloud and lightning in the mind leaping toward poles of Canada & Paterson, illuminating all the motionless world of Time between,

Peyote solidities of halls, backyard green tree cemetery dawns, wine drunkenness over the rooftops, storefront boroughs of teahead joyride neon blinking traffic light, sun and moon and tree vibrations in the roaring winter dusks of Brooklyn, ashcan rantings and kind king light of mind,

who chained themselves to subways for the endless ride from Battery to holy Bronx on benzedrine until the noise of wheels and children brought them down shuddering mouth-wracked and battered bleak of brain all drained of brilliance in the drear light of Zoo,

15   who sank all night in submarine light of Bickford's floated out and sat through the stale beer afternoon in desolate Fugazzi's, listening to the crack of doom on the hydrogen jukebox,

who talked continuously seventy hours from park to pad to bar to Bellevue to museum to the Brooklyn Bridge,

a lost battalion of platonic conversationalists jumping down the stoops off fire escapes off windowsills off Empire State out of the moon,

yacketayakking screaming vomiting whispering facts and memories and anecdotes and eyeball kicks and shocks of hospitals and jails and wars,

whole intellects disgorged in total recall for seven days and nights with brilliant eyes, meat for the Synagogue cast on the pavement,

20   who vanished into nowhere Zen New Jersey leaving a trail of ambiguous picture postcards of Atlantic City Hall,

suffering Eastern sweats and Tangerian bone-grindings and migraines of China under junk-withdrawal in Newark's bleak furnished room,

who wandered around and around at midnight in the railroad yard wondering where to go, and went, leaving no broken hearts,

who lit cigarettes in boxcars boxcars boxcars racketing through snow toward lonesome farms in grandfather night, who studied Plotinus Poe St. John of the Cross telepathy and bop kabbalah because the cosmos instinctively vibrated at their feet in Kansas,

who loned it through the streets of Idaho seeking visionary indian angels who were visionary indian angels,

who thought they were only mad when Baltimore gleamed in supernatural ecstasy,

who jumped in limousines with the Chinaman of Oklahoma on the impulse of winter midnight streetlight smalltown rain,

who lounged hungry and lonesome through Houston seeking jazz or sex or soup, and followed the brilliant Spaniard to converse about America and Eternity, a hopeless task, and so took ship to Africa,

who disappeared into the volcanoes of Mexico leaving behind nothing but the shadow of dungarees and the lava and ash of poetry scattered in fireplace Chicago,

who reappeared on the West Coast investigating the FBI in beards and shorts with big pacifist eyes sexy in their dark skin passing out incomprehensible leaflets,

who burned cigarette holes in their arms protesting the narcotic tobacco haze of Capitalism,

who distributed Supercommunist pamphlets in Union Square weeping and undressing while the sirens of Los Alamos wailed them down, and wailed down Wall, and the Staten Island ferry also wailed,

who broke down crying in white gymnasiums naked and trembling before the machinery of other skeletons,

who bit detectives in the neck and shrieked with delight in policecars for committing no crime but their own wild cooking pederasty and intoxication,

who howled on their knees in the subway and were dragged off the roof waving genitals and manuscripts,

who let themselves be fucked in the ass by saintly motorcyclists, and screamed with joy,

who blew and were blown by those human seraphim, the sailors, caresses of Atlantic and Caribbean love,

who balled in the morning in the evenings in rosegardens and the grass of public parks and cemeteries scattering their semen freely to whomever come who may,

who hiccuped endlessly trying to giggle but wound up with a sob behind a partition in a Turkish Bath when the blond & naked angel came to pierce them with a sword,

who lost their loveboys to the three old shrews of fate the one eyed shrew of the heterosexual dollar the one eyed shrew that winks out of the womb and the one eyed shrew that does nothing but sit on her ass and snip the intellectual golden threads of the craftsman's loom,

who copulated ecstatic and insatiate with a bottle of beer a sweetheart a package of cigarettes a candle and fell off the bed, and continued along the floor and down the hall and ended fainting on the wall with a vision of ultimate cunt and come eluding the last gyzym of consciousness,

who sweetened the snatches of a million girls trembling in the sunset, and were red eyed in the morning but prepared to sweeten the snatch of the sunrise, flashing buttocks under barns and naked in the lake,

who went out whoring through Colorado in myriad stolen night-cars, N.C., secret hero of these poems, cocksman and Adonis of Denver—joy to the memory of his innumerable lays of girls in empty lots & diner backyards, moviehouses' rickety rows, on mountaintops in caves or with gaunt waitresses in familiar roadside lonely petticoat upliftings & especially secret gas-station solipsisms of johns, & hometown alleys too,

who faded out in vast sordid movies, were shifted in dreams, woke on a sudden Manhattan, and picked themselves up out of basements hungover with heartless Tokay and horrors of Third Avenue iron dreams & stumbled to unemployment offices,

who walked all night with their shoes full of blood on the snowbank docks waiting for a door in the East River to open to a room full of steam-heat and opium, who created great suicidal dramas on the apartment cliff-banks of the Hudson under the wartime blue floodlight of the moon & their heads shall be crowned with laurel in oblivion,

who ate the lamb stew of the imagination or digested the crab at the muddy bottom of the rivers of Bowery,

who wept at the romance of the streets with their pushcarts full of onions and bad music,

who sat in boxes breathing in the darkness under the bridge, and rose up to build harpsichords in their lofts,

50 who coughed on the sixth floor of Harlem crowned with flame under the tubercular sky surrounded by orange crates of theology,

who scribbled all night rocking and rolling over lofty incantations which in the yellow morning were stanzas of gibberish,

who cooked rotten animals lung heart feet tail borsht & tortillas dreaming of the pure vegetable kingdom,

who plunged themselves under meat trucks looking for an egg,

who threw their watches off the roof to cast their ballot for Eternity outside of Time, & alarm clocks fell on their heads every day for the next decade,

55 who cut their wrists three times successively unsuccessfully, gave up and were forced to open antique stores where they thought they were growing old and cried,

who were burned alive in their innocent flannel suits on Madison Avenue amid blasts of leaden verse & the tanked-up clatter of the iron regiments of fashion & the nitroglycerine shrieks of the fairies of advertising & the mustard gas of sinister intelligent editors, or were run down by the drunken taxicabs of Absolute Reality,

who jumped off the Brooklyn Bridge this actually happened and walked away unknown and forgotten into the ghostly daze of Chinatown soup alleyways & firetrucks, not even one free beer,

who sang out of their windows in despair, fell out of the subway window, jumped in the filthy Passaic, leaped on negroes, cried all over the street, danced on broken wineglasses barefoot smashed phonograph records of nostalgic European 1930s German jazz finished the whiskey and threw up groaning into the bloody toilet, moans in their ears and the blast of colossal steamwhistles,

who barreled down the highways of the past journeying to each other's hotrod-Golgotha jail-solitude watch or Birmingham jazz incarnation,

60 who drove crosscountry seventytwo hours to find out if I had a vision or you had a vision or he had a vision to find out Eternity,

who journeyed to Denver, who died in Denver, who came back to Denver & waited in vain, who watched over Denver & brooded & loned in Denver and finally went away to find out the Time, & now Denver is lonesome for her heroes,

who fell on their knees in hopeless cathedrals praying for each other's salvation and light and breasts, until the soul illuminated its hair for a second,

who crashed through their minds in jail waiting for impossible criminals with golden heads and the charm of reality in their hearts who sang sweet blues to Alcatraz,

who retired to Mexico to cultivate a habit, or Rocky Mount to tender Buddha or Tangiers to boys or Southern Pacific to the black locomotive or Harvard to Narcissus to Woodlawn to the daisychain or grave,

65 who demanded sanity trials accusing the radio of hypnotism & were left with their insanity & their hands & a hung jury,

who threw potato salad at CCNY lecturers on Dadaism and subsequently presented themselves on the granite steps of the madhouse with shaven heads and harlequin speech of suicide, demanding instantaneous lobotomy,

and who were given instead the concrete void of insulin Metrazol electricity hydrotherapy psychotherapy pingpong & amnesia,

who in humorless protest overturned only one symbolic pingpong table, resting briefly in catatonia, returning years later truly bald except for a wig of blood, and tears and fingers, to the visible madman doom of the wards of the madtowns of the East,

70   Pilgrim State's Rockland's and Greystone's foetid halls, bickering with the echoes of the soul, rocking and rolling in the midnight solitude-bench dolmen-realms of love, dream of life a nightmare, bodies turned to stone as heavy as the moon,

with mother finally ******, and the last fantastic book flung out of the tenement window, and the last door closed at 4 A.M. and the last telephone slammed at the wall in reply and the last furnished room emptied down to the last piece of mental furniture, a yellow paper rose twisted on a wire hanger in the closet, and even that imaginary, nothing but a hopeful little bit of hallucination—

ah, Carl, while you are not safe I am not safe, and now you're really in the total animal soup of time—

and who therefore ran through the icy streets obsessed with a sudden flash of the alchemy of the use of the ellipsis catalog a variable measure and the vibrating plane,

who dreamt and made incarnate gaps in Time & Space through images juxtaposed, and trapped the archangel of the soul between 2 visual images and joined the elemental verbs and set the noun and dash of consciousness together jumping with sensation of Pater Omnipotens Aeterne Deus

75   to recreate the syntax and measure of poor human prose and stand before you speechless and intelligent and shaking with shame, rejected yet confessing out the soul to conform to the rhythm of thought in his naked and endless head,

the madman bum and angel beat in Time, unknown, yet putting down here what might be left to say in time come after death,

and rose reincarnate in the ghostly clothes of jazz in the goldhorn shadow of the band and blew the suffering of America's naked mind for love into an eli eli lamma lamma sabacthani saxophone cry that shivered the cities down to the last radio

with the absolute heart of the poem of life butchered out of their own bodies good to eat a thousand years.

II

What sphinx of cement and aluminum bashed open their skulls and ate up their brains and imagination?

80   Moloch! Solitude! Filth! Ugliness! Ashcans and unobtainable dollars! Children screaming under the stairways! Boys sobbing in armies! Old men weeping in the parks!

Moloch! Moloch! Nightmare of Moloch! Moloch the loveless! Mental Moloch! Moloch the heavy judger of men!

Moloch the incomprehensible prison! Moloch the crossbone soulless jailhouse and Congress of sorrows! Moloch whose buildings are judgment! Moloch the vast stone of war! Moloch the stunned governments!

Moloch whose mind is pure machinery! Moloch whose blood is running money! Moloch whose fingers are ten armies! Moloch whose breast is a cannibal dynamo! Moloch whose ear is a smoking tomb!

Moloch whose eyes are a thousand blind windows! Moloch whose skyscrapers stand in the long streets like endless Jehovahs! Moloch whose factories dream and croak in the fog! Moloch whose smokestacks and antennae crown the cities!

85   Moloch whose love is endless oil and stone! Moloch whose soul is electricity and banks! Moloch whose poverty is the specter of genius! Moloch whose fate is a cloud of sexless hydrogen! Moloch whose name is the Mind!

Moloch in whom I sit lonely! Moloch in whom I dream Angels! Crazy in Moloch! Cocksucker in Moloch! Lacklove and manless in Moloch!

Moloch who entered my soul early! Moloch in whom I am a consciousness without a body! Moloch who frightened me out of my natural ecstasy! Moloch whom I abandon! Wake up in Moloch! Light streaming out of the sky!

Moloch! Moloch! Robot apartments! invisible suburbs! skeleton treasuries! blind capitals! demonic industries! spectral nations! invincible madhouses! granite cocks! monstrous bombs!

They broke their backs lifting Moloch to Heaven! Pavements, trees, radios, tons! lifting the city to Heaven which exists and is everywhere about us!

Visions! omens! hallucinations! miracles! ecstasies! gone down the American river!

Dreams! adorations! illuminations! religions! the whole boatload of sensitive bullshit!

Breakthroughs! over the river! flips and crucifixions! gone down the flood! Highs! Epiphanies! Despairs! Ten years' animal screams and suicides! Minds! New loves! Mad generation! down on the rocks of Time!

Real holy laughter in the river! They saw it all! the wild eyes! the holy yells! They bade farewell! They jumped off the roof! to solitude! waving! carrying flowers! Down to the river! into the street!

III

Carl Solomon! I'm with you in Rockland
        where you're madder than I am
I'm with you in Rockland
        where you must feel very strange
I'm with you in Rockland
        where you imitate the shade of my mother
I'm with you in Rockland
        where you've murdered your twelve secretaries
I'm with you in Rockland
        where you laugh at this invisible humor
I'm with you in Rockland
        where we are great writers on the same dreadful typewriter
I'm with you in Rockland
        where your condition has become serious and is reported on the radio
I'm with you in Rockland
        where the faculties of the skull no longer admit the worms of the senses
I'm with you in Rockland
        where you drink the tea of the breasts of the spinsters of Utica
I'm with you in Rockland
        where you pun on the bodies of your nurses the harpies of the Bronx
I'm with you in Rockland
        where you scream in a straightjacket that you're losing the game of the actual pingpong of the abyss
I'm with you in Rockland
        where you bang on the catatonic piano the soul is innocent and immortal it should never die ungodly in an armed madhouse
I'm with you in Rockland
        where fifty more shocks will never return your soul to its body again from its pilgrimage to a cross in the void
I'm with you in Rockland
        where you accuse your doctors of insanity and plot the Hebrew socialist revolution against the fascist national Golgotha
I'm with you in Rockland
        where you will split the heavens of Long Island and resurrect your living human Jesus from the superhuman tomb

I'm with you in Rockland
> where there are twentyfive thousand mad comrades all together singing the final stanzas of the Internationale

110 I'm with you in Rockland
> where we hug and kiss the United States under our bedsheets the United States that coughs all night and won't let us sleep

I'm with you in Rockland
> where we wake up electrified out of the coma by our own souls' airplanes roaring over the roof they've come to drop angelic bombs the hospital illuminates itself imaginary walls collapse O skinny legions run outside O starry-spangled shock of mercy the eternal war is here O victory forget your underwear we're free

I'm with you in Rockland
> in my dreams you walk dripping from a sea-journey on the highway across America in tears to the door of my cottage in the Western night

San Francisco, 1955–1956

Footnote to Howl

Holy! Holy! Holy! Holy! Holy! Holy! Holy! Holy! Holy! Holy! Holy! Holy! Holy! Holy! Holy!
The world is holy! The soul is holy! The skin is holy! The nose is holy! The tongue and cock and hand and asshole holy!

115 Everything is holy! everybody's holy! everywhere is holy! everyday is in eternity! Everyman's an angel!
The bum's as holy as the seraphim! the madman is holy as you my soul are holy!
The typewriter is holy the poem is holy the voice is holy the hearers are holy the ecstasy is holy!
Holy Peter holy Allen holy Solomon holy Lucien holy Kerouac holy Huncke holy Burroughs holy Cassady holy the unknown buggered and suffering beggars holy the hideous human angels!
Holy my mother in the insane asylum! Holy the cocks of the grandfathers of Kansas!

120 Holy the groaning saxophone! Holy the bop apocalypse! Holy the jazzbands marijuana hipsters peace peyote pipes & drums!
Holy the solitudes of skyscrapers and pavements! Holy the cafeterias filled with the millions! Holy the mysterious rivers of tears under the streets!
Holy the lone juggernaut! Holy the vast lamb of the middleclass! Holy the crazy shepherds of rebellion! Who digs Los Angeles IS Los Angeles!
Holy New York Holy San Francisco Holy Peoria & Seattle Holy Paris Holy Tangiers Holy Moscow Holy Istanbul!
Holy time in eternity holy eternity in time holy the clocks in space holy the fourth dimension holy the fifth International holy the Angel in Moloch!

125 Holy the sea holy the desert holy the railroad holy the locomotive holy the visions holy the hallucinations holy the miracles holy the eyeball holy the abyss!
Holy forgiveness! mercy! charity! faith! Holy! Ours! bodies! suffering! magnanimity!
Holy the supernatural extra brilliant intelligent kindness of the soul!

Berkeley, 1955

HOWL: FOR CARL SOLOMON

Original Drafts: Selected Facsimiles and Transcripts

Guide to Original Manuscripts, Part I

Facsimile of Manuscripts of Howl, Part I (Drafts 1–5)

Guide to Original Manuscripts, Part II

Facsimile of Manuscripts of Howl, Part II (Drafts 1–18)

Guide to Original Manuscripts, Part III

Facsimile of Manuscripts of Howl, Part III (Drafts 1–5)

Guide to Original Manuscripts, Part IV (Footnote)

Facsimile of Manuscripts of Howl, Part IV (Drafts 1–7)

Note to the Reader

Facing several facsimiles of the early typescript drafts of "Howl" are pages of transcription which use a two-color format to illuminate the poet's creative process. Ginsberg's pencil deletions and additions to the poem appear in red in the transcription, while his typed changes in the manuscript are indicated in black on the transcription pages.

Guide to Original Manuscripts, Part I

Draft 1: Alphabetic marginalia (A, B, C, D in author's handscript, left) were made to sort out groups of lines in thematic order; verses or single-motif sections "hooked" into each other, linked by my own associations or external logic; these were assembled together physically in later typescript drafts.

Page 1 of original ms. Part I has relative integrity of progression. Note that first page's verse line breaks down under weight of associations and extended breath (see note, verse 42); the original intention was to build on the triadic ladder form established by W. C. Williams, imitated by the author in "Sakyamuni Coming Out from the Mountain," and a tetradic verse variant in "The Green Automobile," both 1953.*

Lines marked "A" (page 2, original draft) seemed to proceed from or around New York, as page 4, "expelled from colleges" returns to N.Y. Columbia University & Madison Avenue, impressions of late '40s. Page 4 "A" lines also revolve around Columbia University, Lower East Side, & my own York Avenue apartment, 1948.

"B" verses continue N.Y. theme, but relate to the break of life between the womb of college days & the shock & alienation entering the world, making a crippled living outside of family & academic shelter—this motif accounting vocational failure or readjustment, leaving the city, or nervous breakdown, typical post-college crisis.

"C" groups together personal apocalypsis, estrangement, breakthrough to social solitude, disaster or triumph, mixed illumination and/or madness, travel, unthinkable dramas, comedies & tragedies of maturation—arrest, hospitalization, outcast status—degradation and transcendence (see "late C"—"Who stood before you speechless").

"D" verses conjoin images of practical transformation of self-defeat & social ignominy into conscious illumination via artworks for Eternity, "Calling the Great Call" of candor and actuality: "alchemy of the use of the [ellipsis]" (haiku), "catalogue" (Whitman), "a relative measure [the meter]" (W. C. Williams), the "vibrating plane" (Cézanne).

Crossouts (single line or x-cancellation) indicate either (1) rejection of a verse or (2) completed shift of a verse to its agglomerate motif group of verses.

Drafts 2–5: Successive drafts rearrange and rehook the verses into their appropriate groups; some further refine rhythm, syntax or diction to create an even and elastic flow verse to verse (as exampled by Smart). These revisions condense the syntax into solid blocks or "chains of flashing images," and eliminate words that embarrass by inaccuracy or impractical "idiot compassion"; thus "starving mystical naked" was changed to "starving hysterical naked." More in Annotations.

* Allen Ginsberg, *Collected Poems 1947–1980* (New York: Harper & Row, 1984).

hysterical

I saw the best minds of my generation
        generation destroyed by madness
  draggin   starving, ~~mystical~~, naked,
~~who~~ dragged themselves thru the angry streets at
        dawn looking for a negro fix
who poverty and tatters and fantastic minds
        sat up all night in lofts
                contemplating jazz,
who bared their brains to heaven under the El
        and saw Mohammedan angels staggering
                on tenement roofs illuminated,
who sat in rooms naked and unshaven
        listening to the Terror through the wall,
who burned their money in wastebaskets
        amid the rubbish of unread Bronx manifestos,
who got busted in their beards returning
        through the border with a belt
                of marihuana for New York,
who loned it through the streets of Idaho
        seeking visionary indian angels
                who were visionary indian angels,
who passed through universities
        with radiant cool eyes hallucinating
  Arkansas ~~anarchy~~ & Blake-light tragedy
                among the post-war cynical scholars,
who burned in the hells of ~~poetry~~ *turpentine + paint*
        whose apartments flared up in the joyous fires
                of their heavenly brains,
who purgatoried their bodies night after night
        with dreams, with drugs, with waking nightmeares,
                alchohol and cock and endless balls,
Peyotl solidities of the halls, backyard cemetary mornings,
        wine drunkeness over the rooftops, teahed red light
                districts, sun and moon and tree vibrations
                in the roaring ~~dusks of winter~~
                        winter dusks of Brooklyn,
who chained themselves to subways for an endless ride
        ~~that~~ from Battery to holy Bronx until the noise
                of wheels and children brought them down
                ~~trembling~~ wide eyed on Benzadrine shuddering
                mouth-racked and brilliant brained
                        in the drear light of Zoo,
who mopped all night in desolate Bickfords
  or   listening to the crack of doom
  el   on the hydrogen jukebox,
who talked continuously seventy hours from park
        to pad to bar to Bellevue to museum
                to Long Island to
the Brooklyn Bridge, a lost batallion of platonic
        conversationalists jumping down the stoops
  Evening +   vomiting out their facts and anecdotes
                memories and eyeball kicks and shocks
                of hospitals and jails and wars,
who vanished into ~~the tricks of~~ the New Jersies of amnesia
        posting cryptic picture postcards
                of Belmar City Hall and last years sharks,
~~who~~ suffered*ing* sweats and bone grindings and migraines
        of junk-witdrawel in Newark's bleak frnisjed room,
   in   *under*

+ later —
and black-frained
all
drained
of brilliance

Howl for Carl Solomon

[*in John Clellon Holmes' holograph*]
sent by Kerouac to me
Aug. 30, 1955
JCH

1   I saw the best minds of my generation
                     generation destroyed by madness
                        starving, ~~mystical~~, naked,   *hysterical*

dragging ———————————— ~~who dragged~~ themselves thru the angry streets at
                   dawn looking for a negro fix
            who poverty and tatters and fantastic minds
               sat up all night in lofts
                     contemplating jazz,
          who bared their brains to heaven under the El
             and saw Mohammedan angels staggering
                   on tenement roofs illuminated,

5   who sat in rooms naked and unshaven
              listening to the Terror through the wall,
         who burned their money in wastebaskets
            amid the rubbish of unread Bronx manifestos,
         who got busted in their beards returning
             through the border with a belt
                  of marihuana for New York,
         who loned it through the streets of Idaho
             seeking visionary indian angels
                 who were visionary indian angels,
         who passed through universities
             with radiant cool eyes hallucinating
Arkansaw ————————————————— ~~anarchy~~ & Blake-light tragedy
                  among the post-war ~~cynical~~ scholars,

10   s   who burned in the hell|of ~~poetry & paint~~ ———————— turpentine & paint
          whose apartments flared up in the joyous fires
              of their heavenly brains,
         who purgatoried their bodies night after night
             with dreams, with drugs, with waking nightmeares,
                alchohol and cock and endless balls,
Peyotl solidities of the halls, backyard cemetary mornings,
             wine drunkeness over the rooftops, teahed red light
       flying⁄   districts,|sun and moon and tree vibrations
             in the roaring ~~dusks of winter~~
                 winter dusks of Brooklyn,
         who chained themselves to subways for an endless ride
     & batter -   ~~thru~~ from Battery to holy Bronx until the noise
and bleak ~~of~~ brained   of wheels and children brought them down
       all   ~~trembling~~ wide eyed on Benzadrine shuddering
drained of brilliance ———————— mouth-racked and brilliant brained
                  in the drear light of Zoo,
         who mopped all night in desolate Bickfords
     or   ed   listen~~ing~~ to the crack of doom
                    on the hydrogen jukebox, ——— in the stale beer bars

15   who talked continuously seventy hours from park   of third avenue,
             to pad to bar to Bellevue to museum
                 to Long Island to
         the Brooklyn Bridge, a lost batallion of platonic
             conversationalists jumping down the stoops ———— off fire escape
Screaming & ——————————— vomiting ~~out~~ their facts and anecdotes off Empire ~~State bldg,~~
               —memories and eyeball kicks and shocks   ~~& off the Empire State~~
               of hospitals and jails and wars,   & off the moon
        who vanished into ~~the Jersies of~~ the New Jersies of amnesia
             posting cryptic picture postcards
               of Belmar City Hall and last years sharks
ing   ~~who~~ ~~suffered~~ sweats and bone grindings and migraines ———— of Tangier
in ——————————— ~~of~~ junk-witdrawel ~~in~~ Newark's bleak frnisjed room,   under

Kaballa and ~~Prixx~~ Fludd and ~~Vico~~
who studied ~~Caxxizzifxand Raixhxandxxxgxxxx~~
~~and~~ telepathy & jazz because the cosmos
                instinctively vibrated at their feet in Kansas,
who let themselves be fucked in the ass
        by saintly motorcyclists, and screamed with joy,
who ~~blew and~~ were blown by those human angels, the sailors,
        caresses of Atlantic ~~and~~ Carribean love,
who copulated all weekend exstatic and insatiate
        with a bottle of beer, and fell off the bed,
        and continued along the floor and down the hall
                and ended fainting on the wall;
                with a vision of ultimate cunt and come
                        eluding the ~~xxx~~ of consciousness;
who fell on their knees in ~~Catxxxx~~ Cathedrals praying
        for each other's salvation & light & breasts,
who burned on highways journying night to each others
        hot-rod golgotha ~~or~~ jail solitude watch
                or Burmingham jazz incarnation,
waiting, watching, thinking blind or nude or pointed
                staring at the sky eternity behind the ~~rooftops~~
                        and television treetop naked ~~heights~~ lights,
where the stars wheeled ~~inxthexxightzxxndxhxxxxxx~~
                        in the ball of heaven
                and the solid light of sun revolved ~~in their~~ hair
                        and the soul illuminated itself
                        for a few brightened seconds & light
                        of ancient years fell through the air,
who picked themselves up out of alleys hungover
        with heartless Tokay & horrors of iron,
                their and stumbled to unemployment offices,
who fell out of/windows in dispair, or drowned
        their heads in ~~xx~~ vomit in the toilet,
                moans in their ears and blast of steamwhistles,
who screamed on all fours in the subway, and were dragged
        off the roof waving genitals and manuscripts,
who howled with delight in the police cars for committing
        no crime but their own ~~intxxixxxixxxx~~ wild cooking
                ~~fxxxxxx~~ pederasty & intoxication,
who passed out leaflets to themselves weeping and naked
        in Union Square ~~dxxxxx~~ while atomic sirens wailed
                them down, and wailed down ~~the city,~~
who plunged themselves under meat trucks looking for ~~an~~ egg,
        who jumped off the Brooklyn Bridge
                and walked away unknown and forgotten
                into the ~~dxxxxxx~~ ghostly daze of Chinatown
                soup ~~xxxxx~~ alleyways & firetrucks,
who painted their pictures ~~sxxxxxxxxxxxx wxxxxxx~~ fishpaper
                in their unhappiness ~~and~~ knowledge,
who burned cigarette holes in their arms
        protesting the ~~xxxxxxxx~~ tobacco of capitalism,
                narcotiv   haze
who drove crosscountry in 72 hours to find out if I
        had a vision or you had a vision or he
                had ~~illumination yet,~~ to find out the ~~future,~~
who journeyed to Denver, who died in Denver again, who
        waited in Denver, watched and went away, to find
        out the ~~past~~ finally finally

Kaballa ———————————————————— ~~Kaballa~~ and ~~Fuldd~~ Fludd and ~~Vico~~   Vico

who studied ~~Gurdjieff and Reich and orgones~~

and telepathy & jazz because the cosmos

instinctively vibrated at their feet in Kansas,

20   who let themselves be fucked in the ass

by saintly motorcyclists, and screamed with joy,

who ~~blew and~~ were blown by those human angels, the sailors,   in

caresses of Atlantic and Carribean love,

who copulated all weekend exstatic and insatiate

with a bottle of beer, and fell off the bed,

and continued along the floor and down the hall

and ended fainting on the wall,

with a vision of ultimate cunt and come

eluding the ~~end~~ of consciousness;   last

A   hopeless   who fell on their knees in ~~Catebd~~ Cathedrals praying

for each other's salvation & light & breasts,

who burned on highways journying night to each others   nite

hot-rod golgotha ~~or~~ jail solitude watch

A 25   or Burmingham jazz incarnation, ——————————— incarceration

waiting, watching, thinking blind or nude or pointed ———— up leaned back   cocks

on their arms on rooftops ———— staring at the sky eternity behind ~~the rooftops~~

~~and~~ television treetop naked ~~heights~~ ————————— lights,

where the stars wheeled ~~in the night, and heaven~~

nite   in the ball of heaven ———————————— & height,

stood still in the height   and the solid light of sun ~~revolved in their hair~~

over their hair   and the soul illuminated itself

for a few brightened seconds & ~~light~~ ——————————— the rays

of ancient years fell through the air,

who picked themselves up out of alleys hungover

with heartless Tokay & horrors of iron,

and stumbled to unemployment offices,

A   their   who fell out of windows in dispair, or drowned

their heads in ~~vm~~ vomit in the toilet,   their own

moans in their ears and blast of steamwhistles,

who screamed on all fours in the subway, and were dragged

off the roof waving genitals and manuscripts,

30   who howled with delight in the police cars for committing

no crime but their own ~~intoxication,~~ wild cooking

~~fucking~~ pederasty & intoxication,

A   who passed out leaflets to themselves weeping and naked

in Union Square ~~during~~ while atomic sirens wailed ——— ~~Bronx~~ Wall St

them down, and wailed down ~~the city,~~ ———— & the whole ~~of~~ Bronx—

A   who plunged themselves under meat trucks looking for ~~an~~ egg,   a ~~gold~~ ~~bad~~

who jumped off the Brooklyn Bridge

and walked away unknown and forgotten

into the ~~daze and~~ ghostly daze of Chinatown

soup ~~truck~~ alleyways & firetrucks,

who painted their pictures ~~on burlap and wrapping~~ fishpaper

in their unhappiness ~~and~~ knowledge, ——————— Subtlety, & Craft,

who burned cigarette holes in their arms

narcotiv   protesting the ~~narcotic~~ tobacco of capitalism,   haze

35   who drove crosscountry in 72 hours to find out if I

had a vision or you had a vision or he ——————————— yet

A   a vision   had ~~illumination yet,~~ to find out the ~~future,~~ ————— ~~Past~~ Present

who journeyed to Denver, who died in Denver again, who

waited in Denver, watched and went away~~x,~~ to find   finally

future   out the ~~past~~ ————————————— ~~finally~~

to find out the past (Huston)

who   bit detectives in the neck and climbed ~~xxx watertanksx~~
          ~~zkaazsmokaskaokz~~ green smokestacks & flaming watertanks
     flew   and flew up intoheaven x with their screams,
who ~~xkxmbiad xx~~ out of cars ~~apsidexdownxwithxthexxii~~
          ~~hyxaaxwaikxafx xixaaxhyxnaxz~~ in one shoe upside down
          on Utopia Bulovard with the hyena ~~waikxnfxsixxaxx~~
          ~~thexsirens~~ of eternity wailing in the void,
who stumbled by billboards with 6 cents and broken glasses   on
          ~~andxx~~ bloody nose and stomach full of ~~guilt metaphysixx~~
                         wind &   ~~karxxx xkikfright~~
               and metaphysical lightning blasting through
                              the icy skull,
who broke down crying in white gymnasiums naked   other
          and trembling before the machinery x of ~~thexbxsxxx~~
                              skeletons,
who disappeared intoMexican volcanos leaving ~~bahind~~
          nothing but the ~~xxxda~~ shadow of dungarees
               and the lava and ash~~xxxfxthxix~~ poetry
          scattered in the fireplacex of Chicago;
who sat years after ~~taikingxkxxthxirxshadxxx~~ bickering
          their own echoes in the madtowns of the east,
rolling &   rocking in the minight solitude bench~~axx~~ dolmen
          realms of love, Rocklands and Greystones, foetid
          hasseling with imaginary ghouls ~~in xaikxx~~ halls,
          and tangled in the shrouds & straightjackets
     of mental rage   aching for their ancestors, laughing in
                    ~~inzkhxixxxxxfxxxgxikxx~~
               eclipsex until their bodies
               turn to stone as heavy as the moon,
                    and noone gave them a fuck,
who demanded sanity trial~~x~~ accusing the radio ofhypnotism,
          & were left with ~~hxngxjxxxxx~~ their insanity ~~xxxkkxxx~~
          and their   hands and a hung jury,
          who ran thru icy streets obsessed with a sudden flash
alchemy of the   of the use of the ellipse, the catalogue ~~xx~~
          the meter and vibrating plane,
who dreamt and made incarnate gaps in time and space
          Shoving through images juxtaposed and ~~pigments xxxk~~blocks of
pigments ~~sixxxxxx xxxxxxxxxxxxxxxxxx xx~~ a flat dimension,
          ~~shifting~~ back in forth in front of
               and lost their loveboys to the three old shrews of fate,
          ~~xxx~~ the one eyed shrew of the heterosexual dollar,
               the one eyed shrew that winks out of the womb
               & the oneeyed shrew that does nothing
                    but sit on her ass and snip the golden
                    ~~thexthxxxdsxxfxthexinkekkexxxxixxxxx~~
                    intellectual thread of the ~~ixxmx~~
                              craftsman's loom,

who threw potato salad at dadaist lecturers at CCNY &
          subsequently presented themselves on the granite steps
          of madhoused with shaven heads ~~dxmandingx~~ and
          harlequin speech of ~~sxixidxxx xxdxxxx~~suicide,
               demanding instantaneous lobotomies,
          and who were given the concrete void of ~~xxxxk~~ insulen
          metrosol electricity hydrotherapy psychotherapy
          occupational therapy ~~xx~~pingpong & amnesia

          and who in protest overturned one
               symbolic pingpong table,

who bit detectives in the neck and climbed ~~wae watertanks~~
~~the smokestack~~ green smokestacks ———————— ~~& flaming watertanks~~
and flew up into heaven ~~a~~ with their screams,

C   flew

who ~~stumbled~~ on out of cars ~~upside down with the wil[d]~~
~~hyena wail of~~ ~~siren hyena~~ in one shoe upside down
on Utopia Bulovard with the hyena ~~wail of sirens~~
~~the~~ sirens of eternity wailing in the void,
who stumbled by billboards with 6 cents and broken glasses
~~and a~~ bloody nose and stomach full of ~~guilt metaphysics~~ on ~~terror shit~~ fright

wind &

and metaphysical lightning blasting through
the icy skull,

40

who broke down crying in white gymnasiums naked
and trembling before the machinery ~~f~~ of ~~their own~~ ———————— other
who disappeared into Mexican volcanos leaving ~~behind~~ ———————— skeletons,
nothing but the ~~hsade~~ shadow of dungarees
and the lava and ashes ~~of their~~ poetry
scattered in the fireplaces of Chicago;

C

who sat years after ~~talking to their shades~~ bickering
their own echoes in the madtowns of the east,

rolling & ———————— rocking in the minight solitude benches ———————— dolmen
realms of love, Rocklands and Greystones, ————————
hasseling with imaginary ghouls ~~in halls,~~ ———————— foetid halls,

en ╱
of mental rage ———————— ~~and~~ tangled in the shrouds & straightjackets
aching for their ancestors, laughing in
~~in the last forgotten~~
eclipses until their bodies
turn to stone as heavy as the moon,
and noone gave them a fuck,
who demanded sanity trials accusing the radio of hypnotism,
& were left with ~~hung juries~~ their insanity ~~on their~~
and their ———————— hands and a hung jury,

alchemy of the ———————— who ran thru icy streets obsessed with a sudden flash
of the use of the ellipse, the catalogue ~~&~~
the meter and vibrating plane,

D 45

who dreamt and made incarnate gaps in time and space
through images juxtaposed and ~~pigments shot~~ blocks of
pigments, ~~slipping forward and backward on~~ a flat dimension,

shoving ———————— ~~shifting~~ back in forth in front of space
and lost their loveboys to the three old shrews of fate
and the one eyed shrew of the heterosexual dollar,
~~and~~ the one eyed shrew that winks out of the womb
& the oneeyed shrew that does nothing
but sit on her ass and snip (the golden) intellectual
~~the threads of the intellectual loom~~
intellectual thread of the ~~loom~~
craftsman's loom,
who threw potato salad at dadaist lecturers at CCNY &
subsequently presented themselves on the granite steps
of madhouses with shaven heads ~~demanding~~ and
harlequin speech of ~~suicide,~~ ———————— ~~modern~~ suicide,

C

demanding instantaneous lobotomies,

instead

and who were given the concrete void of ~~shock~~ insulen
metrosol electricity hydrotherapy psychotherapy
occupational therapy ~~&~~ pingpong & amnesia

humorless
tabletennis

and who in protest ~~only~~ overturned one only
symbolic ~~pingpong~~ table, giggling ~~humorlessly~~
homosexually,

```
                    megnetic                    of the wards
          returning to the/xxxx reality/wards years later   truly bald,
 their own      xith blood on their hands without fingers & tears
                oixxxxxxxxf inxixxhxhxnyxxxfdxixxxx
                af self-delivered truth's final lobotomy,
                                to
          and a heartfull of Time, & the bleak xxxxxxxx uncle-lawyer
                af unxixxxxxdxixwyxxxxandxdxxxxxxxxdx the
                scream of imaginary Society blasting his eardrums
            with a greek chorus of xhexxdxdxxxxxfxxixxhxxxxxdxxxxxx
                                visible madman doom,

                         own
          with his/mother finally fucked & the last book burned
                on the windowsill & the last prosepoem covered with anal
                as   xxxxxxxxxxx xxxxx Apocalypse for of the    in        slime
          & published to xxx xxxxxxx multitudinous rats of the
                                sewer xxxxxxxx
                & the last door closed at four AM and the last
 hopeless            xxxxxx   companion flown West and the last
                      telephone slammed dxwxxinxxxxix at the wall
                                in reply and the last furnished room
                emptied     xxxxx toxxxxxxxxxxxixx the last piece of
                xxxxxxxxxxxxxxxxxx mental furnature
                      a yellow paper rose twisted on
                                   a wire hanger, in the closet,
                      and even alixthat imaginary,
                nothing but a hopeful little hallucination,
                                      bit of


          ah Carl Solomon, while you are not safe none of us are safe--
          for now     xxx you're really in the trouble of all Time,


          who were expelled from colleges for printing obscene odes in the dust
                off the sexless xxxdxxxxxf windows of men's dormatories
                      and burned alive in bloody flannel suits of innocence
                      onxxhxxxxxxxxxxxfxxhxxxxxxxxxxxx
                      cannon xxxxxxx     bestsellers
                amid the xxx blasts/and schrapbels ofxxxx of leaden verse
                      and nitroglycerine  shrieks of fairies
                         and mustard gas of sinister intelligent xxxxxxx
                                                editors

                      xxxxxxxxxxxxxxxxxxxxxxxxxxxxxxx
                and the subconscous grenadex bloops of the hand grenades
          of the xxxxxxxxxxxxxxfxxxxxxxxxxxxxxxxshock corps of advertising
                      pxxxxxxxxxxxxxxxdxxxxxxxxxxx
                      with xhx explosions of pseudobulshit xxxxxxx
                            their
          charred xxx up      undeniable reality  annotating the
                      xxxxxxx margins of xix flesh with xxxxxxxxxx
                                     the
                      xxxxxxxxxxxixxxxxxxxxxxxxxx jellied petroleum
                xxxxxxxxx of their xxxxxxxxxbrains.


          who lounged hungry and lonesome thru Huston seeking
                  xxxx  xx jazz or soup; & ate candy for six days
                      and followed the brilliant SPaniard
                                to converse about America & Eternity
          a hopeless task,
```

C

their own   returning to the ~~grey~~ reality wards years later   truly bald,   of the wards
           ~~with~~ blood on their ~~hands elbows~~ fingers & tears   hands, all
           ~~of truth's final lobotomy selfdelivered~~
to   ~~of~~ self-delivered truth's final lobotomy,
           and a heartfull of Time, & the bleak ~~screams~~ uncle-lawyer
           ~~of uncles and lawyers and doctors and~~
           scream of imaginary Society blasting ~~his~~ eardrums   the

with a   greek chorus of ~~the dd doom of visible madmen,~~ visible madman doom,
own   with his mother finally fucked & the last book burned
           on the window sill & the last prosepoem covered with anal ——————— slime
           as ~~covered with to be~~ Apocalypse ~~for~~ ——————— of the
           & published to ~~the sewers multitudinous~~ rats ~~of~~ the   in
           sewer ~~system,~~
           & the last door closed at four AM and the last

hopeless   ~~inept~~ ——————— companion flown West and the last
           telephone slammed ~~down in reply~~ at the wall
           in reply and the last furnished room

emptied ——————— ~~bared to~~ ~~furnished with~~ the last piece of
           ~~consciousness,~~ a mental furnature
           a yellow paper rose twisted on
             a wire hanger, in the closet,
           and even ~~all~~ that imaginary,
           nothing but a hopeful little hallucination,   bit of
ah Carl Solomon, while you are not safe none of us are safe—
           for now   ~~and~~ you're really in the trouble of all Time,

50

who were expelled from colleges for printing obscene odes in the dust
           of the sexless ~~windows of~~ windows of men's dormatories
           and burned alive in bloody flannel suits of innocence

A

           ~~on the stake of their innocense~~
cannon ——————— ~~in the~~
           amid the ~~gas~~ blasts and schrapbels ~~of the~~ of leaden verse   bestsellers
           and nitroglycerine   shrieks of fairies
           and mustard gas of sinister intelligent ~~manners~~ ——————— editors
           ~~with an eye nervous on the ball~~
           and the subconscous ~~grenades~~ bloops of the hand grenades
           of the ~~& explosions of pseudobulshit~~ shock corps of advertising
           ~~pseudobullshit advertising~~

B

their   with ~~the~~ explosions of pseudobulshit ~~sex and~~
           undeniable reality   annotating the
the   charred ~~out~~ up nervous margins of ~~his~~ flesh with ~~competent~~
           ~~editorial liquid petroleum~~ jellied petroleum
           ~~of their~~ of their ~~competent~~ brains.
who lounged hungry and lonesome thru Huston seeking
       ~~love or~~ jazz or soup; and ate candy for six days
           and followed the brilliant SPaniard
             to converse about America & Eternity
a hopeless task,

Who   cut out each others hearts on the banks of the Hudson
          xxxif lifexxxxx a drama on a great lost stage
               under the searxhxtxxxxxxxxxzxxxxx fxxxxxxxxxxxxxxx
                    crimson fxxxxxxx of the moon,
                         streetlamp
     who digested xxxxxxxxxxxxxxxxxxxxxxxxxxxxxxxxxxxx rotten
          animals lung heart feet tail borsht and tortillas
          dreaming of the pure vegetable kingdom,
     who wept at the romance of the xxxxxxxxxxxxxxxxxxxxxxxxxxx
          pushcart streets full of onions and bad music,
     who coughed up celluloid balls in Harlem with their lungs
          full of sixth floors of skyxz tuburcular sky
          and orange crates of theology,
     who wandered all night x with their shoes full of blood
          on the snowbanks of East River looking for the door
in the river xxxxxxxxdoor to open on a roomfull of steamheat
          and opium, picking his scabs saying who is my
          friend? cherries
     whopondered his xxx xxxxxxxx in longchamps waiting to
          kidnap a xxxxxxxxxxxxxxxxxxxxxxxxxxx
               axxxxxxxxxxxxxxxxxxxxxxxxxxxxxx an overcoat
          on a coat hanger, apparition of a week's rent,
     who wandered in bryant park digging the color of the negro of
          the skyx evening sky,
     who cut their wrists three times xxxxxxxxxx xxxxxxxxxxx
          xxxxxxxxxxxxxx successively and were forced to
          xxxxxxxxxxxxxxxxxxxx where they xxxxxxxxxx cried,
          open antique stores
     who threw their watches out of the windows in the ballet of
          fxx eternity and were presented with alarm clocks
          daily for the next ten years,
     who retired to mexico to cultivate sex or Rocky Mount to Buddha
          or xxxxxxxxxxxx Southern Pacific to the black
          Locomotive or harvard to narcissus to Woodlawn
          to the grave to cultivate a final xxxxxxxxxxxxx
          daisychain of blue, all Poe,

                                        with
     who hiscouped endlessly trying to giggle but wound up in a sob
          behind a partition in a turkish bath when the blond
          & naked angelsx came to pierce them with the sword
Who xxxxxxxxxxxxxxxxxxxxxxxxxxxxxxxxxxx& sat in boxes breathing
          in the darkness under the bridge, and rose to
          build harpsichers in their lofts,
     who rose xxxxxxxxxxxxx in the gxx goldhorn shadow of the band
in clothew of and blew xxxxxxx up a saxophone cry that shivered
     music the cities down to the last radio xxxxxxxxxxx
          xxxxxxxxxxxxxxxxxxxxxxxxxxxxxxxxxxxxxx whith a
          lament for the blue/jelly of the xxxxxx Time,
                    last   sad
     who died eating the octpus of their own imagination,
          but it was autohypnosis all along & they wound up
          eating xxxxxxxxx at the muddy bottom of the rivers
          of Bowery, crabs or lamb xxxx stew in paradise,

                         * Garver: "No coathangers
                              in L'champs"

A   Who cut out each others hearts on the banks of the Hudson
                ~~as if~~ life~~s~~~~were~~ a drama on a great lost stage
                   under the search~~lighthe moonlight~~ ~~floodlight moon~~,
                   crimson ~~floodlamp~~ of the moon,
                       streetlamp

A   who digested ~~lung stw and hearts and feet and tails~~ rotten
                   animals lung heart feet tail borsht and tortillas
                   dreaming of the pure vegetable kingdom,
           who wept at the romance of the ~~street full of py pushcarts~~
                   pushcart streets full of onions and bad music,

A 55   who coughed up celluloid balls in Harlem with their lungs
                   full of sixth floors of ~~sky~~ tuburcular sky
                   and orange crates of theology,
           who wandered all night ~~i~~ with their shoes full of blood
                   on the snowbanks of East River looking for the door
in the river   ~~a glass~~ door to open on a roomfull of steamheat
                   and opium, picking his scabs saying who is my
                   friend?

cherries   who pondered his ~~eye icecream~~ in longchamps waiting to
A   kidnap a ~~russian overcoat the apparition~~
                   ~~an apartment in the apparition of~~ an overcoat
                   on a coat hanger,* apparition of a week's rent

A   who wandered in bryant park digging the color of the negro of
                   the ~~sky~~ evening sky,

           who cut their wrists three times ~~successively unsuccessfulz~~
B   ~~and were forced~~ successively and were forced to
                   ~~go into another industry~~ where they ~~had to cry~~ cried,
                   open antique stores

  60   who threw their watches out of the windows in the ballot of
                   ~~for~~ eternity and were ~~presented~~ with alarm clocks   stoned   had
B   fall on their heads ——————— daily for the next ten years,

           who retired to mexico to cultivate sex or Rocky Mount to Buddha
B   or ~~Frisco to the~~ Southern Pacific to the black
                   Locomotive or harvard to narcissus to Woodlawn
                   to the grave to cultivate a final ~~daisy, blue,~~
                   daisychain ~~of blue~~, all Poe,

           who hisccuped endlessly trying to giggle but wound up ~~in~~ a sob   with
                   behind a partition in a turkish bath when the blond
                  & naked   angels   came to pierce them with the sword
Who ——————— ~~who built harpsichords in lofts~~, & sat in boxes breathing
                   in the darkness under the bridge, and rose to   up
                   build harpsichors in their lofts,

D   who rose ~~to the stand~~ in the ~~gl~~ goldhorn shadow of the band
in clothes of music ——————— and blew ~~sinsiter~~ up a saxophone cry that shivered
                   the cities down to the last radio ~~and dressed~~
                   ~~the high schools up in clothes of music~~, whith a
last   lament for the blue jelly of ~~the world~~ Time,   ~~sad~~

  65   who died eating the octpus of their own imagination,
                   but it was autohypnosis all along & they wound up
                   eating ~~Lamb Stew~~ at the muddy bottom of the rivers
                   of Bowery, crabs   or lamb ~~stwe~~ stew in paradise,

* [*in Jack Kerouac's holograph*] *Garver: "No coathangers in L' champs"*

                cigabettes
Who lit ~~matches~~ in boxcars boxcars boxcars racketing ~~toward the~~
     ~~lonesome grandfather~~   through snow toward lonesome ~~nights~~
     ~~on grandfather farms~~ farms in ~~grandfather night~~ in ~~that~~
     grandfather night,

who jumped in cars with chinamen on the impulse of winter midnight
     ~~streetlight rain~~ smalltown ~~rain~~ smalltown streetlight rain,
                              sidestreet
who took off their clothes on the/corner and wandered into groceries
     ~~on the sidestreet asking for the Milky way~~ inquiring
     Milky Way?

who walked around and around in the railroad station wondering where
     to go, and went, leaving no broken hearts, and returned six
     weeks later ~~XX~~

                                                  growing
who limped ~~around the~~ over the city hills with half a mustache on
     ~~the sinister~~   the sinister side of the lip, ~~an expert amateur~~
~~of the baroque architecture looking for an example looking~~
     his passion to absurd to inscribe, ~~namely he was actually~~ he said
     ~~only~~ looking for an example of baroque architecture

        carrying ~~a volume of Yeats Works~~ Butler's Analogy

who wandered around the ~~xxx~~ windy streets carrying Butlers analogy
        looking for an example of Butler's analogy
     ~~rapidly~~ rapidly
who/translated the Songs of Maldoror ~~rapidly~~ and threw himself
        on the mercy of Alchoholics Anonymous,
or
who appeared on the west coast in beards and shorts with big
        pacifist eyes ~~and were~~ sexy in their dark skin, passing
        out ~~leaflets~~ incomprehensable ~~propaganda~~ leaflets
                        reading   want ads
who investigated the FBI by ~~reading~~ spenglerian ~~newspapers~~ on Peyotl,

who read ~~Marx Spengler Antonin Artaud Genet Dostoievsky Genet~~
        Genet ~~Genet~~ Spengler Dostoievsky ~~Antonin Artaud~~ Rimbaud
        ~~Wolfe~~ Louis Ferdinand Celine Proust Wolfe Whitman Buddha
        Ginsberg Kerouac Burroughs & Neal Cassady, I name them all,
        except ~~Lukian~~ Carr who ~~took to journalism they must~~
        ~~have read him too~~ got psychoanalysed and took to journalism
        so they must have read him ~~anyway~~ too anyway.
                        while
who sweetened the cunt ~~of k~~ a million girls trembling in the sunset,
        and ~~by sunrise~~ were ~~ready and~~ ~~xxx~~ red eyed in the morning
        but prepared to sweeten the sunrise, wearing their skin
        naked in the alleys with the flash of buttocks ~~in by~~ under
        doorways. ~~barns and~~

who didnt have enough time to speak among themselves of love

who crashed thru their minds in jail and waited for impossible
        criminals, hipsters with angelic ~~minds~~ heads and no ~~more~~ worries,
        poets with ~~horkeah~~ sensibility and the charm of reality in
        their hearts who sang sweet blues to the ~~jaxx jailers~~
        ~~their~~ lawyers.

cigarettes

Who lit ~~matches~~ in boxcars boxcars boxcars racketing ~~toward the~~
~~lonesome apocalypse~~   through snow toward lonesome ~~nights~~
~~on granfathers farm,~~ farms in ~~gradfather night~~ in ~~the~~
grandfather night,
who jumped in cars with chinamen on the impulese of winter midnight
~~streetlight rain~~ smalltown ~~rain~~   smalltown streetlight rain,
who took off their clothes on the corner and wandered into groceries   sidestreet
~~on the   sidestreet asking for the Milky way,~~ inquiring
Milky Way?
who walked around and around in the railroad station wondering where
to go, and went, leaving no broken hearts, and returned six
weeks later ~~to~~

70
who limped ~~around the~~   over the city hills with half a mustache on   growing
~~the   his sinsi~~   the sinister side of the lip, ~~up expert amateur~~
~~of in baroque architecture, looking for a church to look at~~
his passion to absurd to inscribe, ~~namely he was actually~~ he said
~~only~~ looking for an example of baroque architecture
carrying ~~a volume of Isaac Watts~~ Butler's Analogy
who wandered around the ~~su~~ windy streets carrying Butlers analogy
looking for an example of Butler's analogy

~~rapidly~~   rapidly
who translated the Songs of Maldoror ~~rapidly~~ and threw himself
on the mercy of Alchoholics Anonymous,

or ————————————
who appeared   on the west coast in beards and shorts with big
pacifist eyes ~~and were~~ sexy in their dark skin, passing
out ~~leaflets~~ incomprehensable propaganda   leaflets

reading
who investigated the FBI by ~~reding~~ spenglerian ~~newspapers~~ on Peyotl,   want ads
75
who read ~~Marx Spengler Antonin Artaud Gne Gneet Genet Gurj ieff~~
Genet ~~Gurjieff~~ Spengler Dostoievsky ~~Antonin Artaud~~   Rimbaud
~~Wolfe~~ Louis Ferdinand Celine Proust Wolfe Whitman Buddha
Ginsberg Kerouac Burroughs & Neal Cassady, I name them all,
except Lu~~cien~~ Carr who ~~took to journalism so they must~~
~~have read himm too~~ got psychoanalysed and took to journalism
so they must have read him ~~anyway~~ too anyway.

D

while
who sweetened the cunt ~~of t~~ a million girls trembling in the sunset,
and ~~by sunrise~~ were ~~readyed rea~~ red eyed in the morning
but prepared to sweeten the sunrise, wearing their skin

or   and   ing
naked in the alleys ~~with the~~ flash of buttocks in ~~by~~ ———— [indecipherable]
~~barns~~ — barns ————————— ~~doorways~~ ———————— under
who didnt have enough time to speak among themselves of love
who crashed thru their minds in jail and waited for impossible

Early   heads
C
criminals, hipsters with angelic ~~minds~~ and no ~~care~~ worries,
poets with ~~hophead~~ sensibility and the charm of reality in
their hearts who sang sweet blues to the ~~jau~~ ——————— jailers
~~their~~ lawyers.

D   who translated lonesome Catullus into personal talk
               thru time across the ruinx of xxxxxx xxx a continent,
               and set down now xxxx what might be left to say
               anew xxxxxxxxxxxxx in time after death,

D   who recreated syntax & structure of prose
             to conform to the rhythm of thought
                    in xxxxxxxxx naked and endless head,
                 his
                 archangelx of   visual
who trapped the xxxxxxxxxxxxxxxxxxxxxxxxxx soul between 2/images,
    &   xxxxxxxxxxxxxxxxxxxxxx
D   joined   xxxxxxlemental verbs   and   of consciou~
             and set the noun xxxxxxxxxxxxxx dash/ together s~
             jumping with xxxxxxxxxxxxxxx sensation
                 of   xxxx Cezanne's
          pater omnipotens aeterna deus,
               the father-thought of all.
               out of the
who invented xxx angels xxxx flesh and xxx blood of lovers,
          and the angelic consciousness
             out of the rhetoric & xxxxxx secret cackle
               of poor human xxxxx xxxxxxxx xxxxx poetry
D   who rejected the moral imagination of xxxxxxxx the wierd xxxxxxx
          academies of abstract prose and offered the ancient
             xxxxxxxxxxxxxxxxxxxxxxxxxxxxxxxxxxxxxxxxxx
             xxxabsolute heart of the poem of life
               butchered/from their own xxxxxx xxxxxxxxxx
                 out   bodies
       and good to eat a thousand years,
D   posessiog xxxxxxx xxx wisdom of real meat,
             thenergy   &
       so   accept no substitubex, xxxxxxxxxx
             xxx   for the true heart of the folk
               naked   gasping original
           with all its xxxxxxxx blood & xxxxx xxxx
       unconditioned beat on the page

who stood before you speechless & intelligent and shaking with shame
        who were yourselves, your own xxx souls' confessions,
           your miseries incarnate in madman xxx bum & angel
           preaching neither acceptance nor rejection
Late C   neither man nor god,   xxxxxxx
         reality or imagination:xxx xxxx xxxx
              xxxxxxxxxxxxxxxxxxxxxxx   saying
thexxxxxxxxxxxxxxxxxxxx whtch xxxxxxxxxxxxxxxxx.

  Ixthink the suffering of love is naked mind.
                [handwritten: my]
who
       [handwritten: love]   *[handwritten: naked]*
       [handwritten: of America the ~~still~~ mind to suffer love]

[handwritten at bottom:]
Who ate ~~pigflesh~~ clampfageth ~~oysters~~ snails
Borsht & tortillas & savemory

Who wept at the romance of the streets
~~with the cheapwine & the~~ pushcartsfull of onions cheap
                            music

who translated lonesome Catullus into personal talk
thru time across the ruins ~~of Sirmie, the~~ a continent,
and set down now ~~anew~~ what might be left to say
anew ~~after our death,~~ in time after death,

D

80

D

who recreated syntax & structure of prose
to conform to the rhythm of thought
in ~~the neaked~~ naked and endless head,

his
archangels of   who trapped ~~the invisible sensations of the~~ soul between 2 images,   visual
       &   ~~&in theelements of verbs~~
      joined   ~~in thee~~lemental verbs

D

and   and set the noun ~~and adjective and~~ dash together|s ness   of consciou
of — ~~like~~ Cezanne's   jumping with ~~objective chemestry~~ sensation
        pater omnipotens aeterna deus,
         the father-thought of all.

out of the   who invented ~~the~~ angels ~~from~~ flesh and ~~be~~ blood of lovers,
       and the angelic consciousness

D

       out of the rhetoric & ~~cackle~~ secret cackle
        of poor human ~~prose academic prose~~ poetry
who rejected the moral imagination of ~~academy~~ the wierd ~~academy~~
       academies of abstract prose and offered the ancient
        ~~a platter of dead cats, christmas livers~~
        ~~the~~ absolute heart of the poem of life

out   butchered from their own ~~bodies imagination~~ ——— bodies

D

       and good to eat a thousand years,
thenergy   posessiog ~~forver & the~~ wisdom of real meat,   &
       so accept no substitute ~~m, it's ther,~~
        ~~for~~ ——————————— for the true heart of the folk
naked   with all its ~~fantastic~~ blood & ~~naked beat~~ ——— gasping original
       unconditioned beat on the page
who stood before you speechless & intelligent and shaking with shame
      who were yourselves, your own ~~sol~~ souls' confessions,
       your miseries incarnate in madman ~~and~~ bum & angel
        preaching neither acceptance nor rejection
      neither man nor god,

Late C

       reality or imagination: ~~not even love~~ ——————— ~~but only~~
        ~~which is but naked mind.~~ ——————— saying
     ~~the suffering of love, which is but naked mind.~~
     ~~I think~~ The suffering ~~of love~~ is naked mind.
~~my~~ love
who   In America the ~~naked~~ mind to suffer love   naked
        [hereon all holograph]

Who ate pigliver clamspaghetti lung stew snails
    borsht & tortillas to save money
Who wept at the romance of the streets
    ~~with its cheap music~~ & ~~piles~~ pushcarts full of onions & cheap music,

STROPHES

"I saw the best mind of my generation destroyed by madness,
starving, hysterical, naked, ~~angel headed hopeless~~

    wandering around the negro streets at dawn looking for an angry
fix, *angelheaded hipsters hookin for the shuddering connection between the wheels + wires of the machine the Night*

    who poverty and tatters and ~~fantastic~~ eyed and high sat up
all night in the supernatural darkness of cold water flats floating
across the tops of cities contemplating jazz,

    who sat in rooms in underwear unshaven burning their dollars
in wastebaskets listening to the Terror through the wall,

    who bared their brains to Heaven under the El and saw Mohhamed-
an angels staggering on tenement roofs illuminated,

    who chained themselves to subways for an endless ride from
Battery to Holy Bronx until the noise of wheels and children brought
them down shuddering mouth-racked and battered bleak of brain on
Benzedrine all drained of brilliance in the drear light of Zoo,

    who ~~stood~~ in the stale ~~bars of morning~~ afternoon *desolate Fugazzis bar* listening
to the crack of doom on the hydrogen jukebox,

    who talked continuously seventy hours from park to pad to bar
to Bellevue to museum to ~~saloon~~ to *the* Brooklyn Bridge,

    a lost battalion of platonic conversationalists jumping off
the stoops off windowsills off empire states out of the moon

    yackatayaking screaming vomiting whispering facts and memories
and anecdotes and eyeball kicks and shocks of hospitals and jails
and wars,

    who lounged hungry and lonesome in Huston seeking Jazz or soup,

    who lit cigarettes in boxcars boxcars boxcars racketing thru
snow toward lonesome farms in grandfather night,

    who studied Vico Fludd telepathy and bop kaballa because the
cosmos instinctively vibrated at their feet in Kansas,

    who loned it through the streets of Idaho seeking visionary
indian angels who were visionary indian angels,

    who jumped in cars with the Chinaman on the impulse of
winter midnight streetlight smalltown rain,

    who disappeared into the volcanos of Mexico leaving behind
nothing but the shadow of dungarees and the lava and ash of poetry
in fireplace Chicago,

    who broke down crying in white gymnaseums naked and trembling
before the machinery of other skeletons,

    who screamed on all fours in the subway, and were dragged off
the roof waving genitals and manuscripts,

    who let themselves be fucked in the ass by saintly motorcyclists
and howled with joy,

    who blew and were blown by those human angels the sailors,
caresses of atlantic and carribean love,

    who hiccuped endlessly trying to giggle but wound up with a
sob when the blond and naked seraph emerged ~~from~~ the partition
in a turkish bath to pierce them with a sword,

Numbers mark lines (not verses) wherefrom less legible excisions and revisions are set in print.—A.G.

2: Angel headed hipster [canceled]
4: Angelheaded hipsters looking for the shuddering con-
nection between the wheels & wires of the machine of
the Night

5: hollow-
16: sat . . . in desolate Fugazzi's bar
19: ["saloon" canceled] . . . the
46: behind

who bit detectives in the neck and shrieked with delight in
policecars for committing no crime but their own wild cooking
pederasty and intoxication,
     who copulated extatic and insatiate with a package of cigarettes
a sweetheart a bottle of beer and a candle, and fell off the bed,
and continued along the floor and down the hall and ended fainting
on the wall a vision of ultimate jazz eluding the last come of
consciousness,
     who ate the lamb stew of the imagination or digested the crab
at the muddy bottom of the rivers of Bowery,
     who digested rotten animals lung heart feet tail borsht and
tortillas dreaming of the pure vegetable kingdom,
     who plunged themselves under meat trucks looking for an egg,
and wept at the romance of the streets with their pushcarts full of
onions and bad music,
     who walked allnight with shoes full of blood on the snowbank
docks waiting for a door in the East River to open to a roomfull
of steamheat and opium,
     who fell on their knees in cathedrals praying for eachothers'
salvation and light and breasts until the soul illuminated its hair
for a second,
     who drove crosscountry seventytwo hours to find out if I had a
vision or you had a vision or he had a vision to find out the
present,
     who journeyed to Denver who died in Denver who watched and waited
and came back and went away from Denver to find out the future,
     who left for Tangiers to cultivate sex or Rocky Mount to Buddha
or southern Pacific to the black locomotive or Harvard to narcissus
to Woodlawn to the grave to daisychain,
     who crashed through their minds in jail waiting for impossible
criminals with golden heads and the charm of reality in their hearts
who sang sweet blues to Alcatraz,
     who threw potato salad at doctors of dadaism and subsequently
presented themselves on the granite steps of the madhouse with
shaven heads and harlequin speech of suicide demanding instant-
aneous lobotomy,
     and who were given instead the concrete void of insulen metrasol
electricity hydrotherapy psychotherapy occupational therapy pingpong
& amnesia,
     and who in humorless protest overturned only one symbolic
pingpong table and rested briefly in catatonia,
     and who returned later truly bald with ░░ mother finally fucked
and the last door closed and the last telephone slammed at the wall
in reply and the last furnished room emptied down to the last piece
of mental furnature, a yellow paper rose twisted on a wire hangar in
the closet, and even that imaginary, nothing but a hopeful little bit
of hallucination,
     --Ah, Carl, while you are not safe none of us are safe for now
your'e really in the total soup of Time,--
     who stood before you speechless and intelligent and shaking
with shame rejected yet confessing out the soul of his naked and
endless head the madman bum and angel beat in time unknown yet
putting down what might be left to say in time come after death,
     and rose reincarnate in the clothes of ghostly jjazz in the
goldhorn shadow of the band and blew the suffering of America's
naked mind for love into a saxophone cry that shivered the cities
down to the last radio
     with the absolute heart of the poem of life butchered out of
~~their own bodies~~ good to eat a thousand years.

human *y*

their own bodies,

Left margin: Particulars
59: human [bod]y [canceled] their own bodies,

I   Howl For Carl Solomon

I saw the best minds of my generation destroyed by madness,/starving,
    hysterical, naked,
dragging themselves through the negro streets at dawn looking/for an
    angry fix,
angelheaded hipsters exploring for the ancient shuddering connection
    between the wires and the wheels of the dynamo of night,
who,poverty and tatters and hollow-eyed and high sat up in the super-
    natural darkness of coldwater flats/floating across the tops
    of cities contemplating jazz,
who bared their brains to heaven under the El and saw mohammedan
    angels staggering on tenement roofs illuminated,
who sat in rooms in underwear unshaven burning their money in waste-
    baskets amid the rubbish of memorable Berkeley manifestos
    listening to the Terror through the wall,
who got busted in their beards returning through Laredo with a belt
    of marijuana for New York,
who passed through universities with radiant cool eyes hallucinating
    Arkansas and Blake-light tragedy among the scholars of war,
who burned in hells of turpentine in Paradise Alley or purgatoried
    their torsos night after night
with dreams, with drugs, with waking nightmares, alchohol and cock
    and endless balls,
incomparable blind streets of shuddering cloud and lightning (in the mind)
    leaping toward poles of Canada and Paterson,illuminating
    all the motionless world of Time between,
peyote solidities of halls, backyard green tree cemetary dawns, wine
    drunkenness over the rooftops, boroughs of teahead neon green
    and blinking traffic light, sun and moon and tree vibrations
    in the roaring winter dusks of Brooklyn, ashcan rantings and
    kind king light of mind,
who chained themselves to subways for the endless ride from Battery
    to holy Bronx on benzedrine until the noise of wheels and children
    brought them down shuddering mouth-wracked and battered bleak
    of brain all drained of brilliance in the drear light of Zoo,
who moped all night in submarine Bickford's and returned to sit/all thru
    the stale morning in desolate Fugazzi's,listening to the crack
    of doom on the hydrogen jukebox,
who talked continuously seventy hours from park to pad to bar to
    Bellevue to museum to the Brooklyn Bridge,
yackata yakking screaming vomiting whispering facts and memories and
    anecdotes and eyeball kicks and shocks of hospitals and jails/and wars,
a lost battalion of platonic conversationalists jumping down the stoops
    off fire-escapes and windowsills off Empire State out of the moon,
who vanished into nowhere Zen New Jersey leaving a trail of ambiguous
    picture postcards of Atlantic Cryptic Hall,
suffering Eastern sweats and Tangerian bonegrindings and migraines
    of China under junk-withdrawall in Newark's bleak furnished room,
who lounged hungry and lonesome through Huston seeking Jazz or soup,
    and followed the brilliant Mexican to converse about/America and
    Eternity, a hopeless task, and so took ship/to Africa,
who sneaked through the railroad yard wondering where/to go, and went,
    leaving no broken hearts,
who lit cigarettes in boxcars boxcars boxcars racketing through snow
    toward lonesome farms in grandfather night,
who studied Vico Fludd telepathy and bop kaballa because the cosmos
    instinctively vibrated at their feet in Kansas,

(handwritten: wandered around & around in)

(handwritten: Stumbling in the aisles of Kansas)

who loned it through the streets of Idaho seeking visionary indian angels
    who were visionary indian angels,
~~who didn't have enough time to speak among themselves of love, who~~
    ~~didn't have time to smoke their dark cigars,~~
who jumped in cars with the Chinaman on the impulse of winter
    midnight streetlight smalltown rain,
who disappeared into the volcanos of Mexico leaving behind nothing scattered
    but the shadow of dungarees and the lava and ash of poetry in
    fireplace Chicago,
who reappeared on the West Coast investigating the FBI in beards and
    shorts with big pacifist eyes sexy in their dark skin passing out
    incomprehensible leaflets,
who limped penniless over city hills with half a moustache hanging on
    the sinister lip looking for an example of baroque architecture
    and spent hours in the bathroom washing their few nickles with
    a Buffalo toothbrush,
who broke down crying in white gymnasiums naked and trembling before
    the machinery of other skeletons,
who burned cigarette holes in their arms protesting the narcotic
    tobacco haze of capitalism,
who passed out supercommunist leaflets in Union Square weeping and
    undressing, while the sirens of Los Alamos wailed them down,
    and wailed down Wall, and the Staten Island ferry also wailed,
who screamed on all fours in the subway, and were dragged off the roof
    waving genitals and manuscripts,
who bit detectives in the neck and shrieked with delight in particulars
    in policecars for committing no crime but their own wild
    cooking pederasty and intoxication,
who let themselves be fucked in the ass by saintly motorcyclists,
    and screamed with joy,
who blew and were blown by these human seraphs, the sailors,
    caresses of Atlantic and Carribean love,
who hiccuped endlessly trying to giggle but wound up with a sob
    behind a partition in a Turkish bath when the blonde and naked
    angel came to pierce them with the sword,
who lost their loveboys to the three old shrews of fate, the one-eyed
    shrew of the heterosexual dollar, the one-eyed shrew that winks
    out of the womb and the one-eyed shrew that does nothing
    but sit on her ass and snip the intellectual golden threads
    of the craftsman's loom,
who copulated ecstatic and insatiate with a bottle of beer a sweetheart
    a package of cigarettes a candle, and fell off the bed, and
    continued along the floor and down the hall and ended fainting
    gyzym on the wall with a vision of ultimate cunt and come eluding the
    last juice of consciousness,
who sweetened the snatch of a million girls trembling in the sunset,
    flashing buttocks under barns, and were red-eyed in the morning
    but prepared to sweeten the snatch of the sunrise, naked in the
    lake,
who picked themselves up out of basements hungover with heartless
    Tokay and 3rd Avenue horrors of dismantled iron and stumbled
    to unemployment offices,
who ate the lamb stew of the imagination or digested the crab at the
    muddy bottom of the rivers of Bowery and cooked rotten animals
    lung heart feet tail borsht and tortillas dreaming of the pure
    vegetable kingdom,

Who

8: scattered
45: jissum [canceled] gyzym

54: [Printer's paragraph mark]
    Who [repeated below as insert]

place first strophe as indicated by [arrow] after "bad music"

                                      their groans   *bloody*

who sang out of their windows in despair, or threw up ~~drunk~~ in the toilet,
     moans in their ears and the blast of colossal steamwhistles,
who plunged themselves under meat trucks looking for an egg,
who jumped off the Brooklyn Bridge this actually happened and walked away
     unknown and forgotten into the ghostly daze of Chinatown soup
     alleyways and firetrucks, not even one free beer,
who were expelled from the academies for crazy and publish~~ed~~ ing obscene odes
     on the windows of the skull,
who wept at the romance of the streets with their pushcarts full of onions
     and bad music,
who walked all night on the snowbank docks with their shoes full of blood
     waiting for a door in the East River to open to a room full of
     steamheat and opium, who walked between the violet and the violet,
who created great suicidal dramas on the banks of the Hudson under
     the wartime floodlight of the moon,
who coughed on the sixth floor of Harlem under the tubercular sky surround-
     ed by the orange crates of theology,
who burned on the highways of the past journeying to each other's hot-rod
     Golgotha jail-solitude watch or Burmingham blues incarnation,
who drove crosscountry seventy~~eight~~ hours to find out if I had a vision
     or you had a vision or he had a vision, to find out the present,
who journeyed to Denver, who died in Denver, who came back and waited in
     Denver, watched and went away finally to find out the future,
who fell on their knees in hopeless cathedrals praying for each others'
     salvation and light and breasts, until the soul illuminated its
     hair for a second,
who threw their watches out of windows in the ballot of Eternity and
     alarm clocks fell on their heads everyday for the next decade,
who cut their wrists three times unsuccessfully and were forced to
     open antique stores where they thought they were growing old and cried,
who were burned alive in their innocent flannel suits on Madison Avenue
     amid ~~explosions of popular novels and~~ blasts of leaden verse
     and the nitroglycerine shrieks of the faries of advertising and
     the mustard gas of sinister intelligent editors, or were run down by
     the drunken taxicabs of absolute reality,
who sat in boxes breathing in the darkness under the bridge and rose up
     to build harpsichords in their lofts,
who retired to Mexico to cultivate sex or Rocky Mount to Buddha or
     Tangiers to boys or Southern Pacific to the black locomotive or
     Harvard to narcissus to Woodlawn to the daisychain or grave,
who crashed through their minds in jail waiting for impossible
     criminals with golden heads and the charm of reality in their
     hearts who sang sweet blues to Alcatraz,
who demanded sanity trials accusing the radio of hypnotism and were
     left with their insanity and their hands and a hung jury,
who threw potato salad at CCNY lecturers on Dadaism and subsequently
     presented themselves on the granite steps of the madhouse with
     shaven heads and harlequin speech of suicide, demanding instantaneous
     lobotomy,
and who were given instead the concrete void of insulin metrasol elec-
     tricity hydrotherapy psychotherapy occupational therapy pingpong
     & amnesia,
and who in humorless protest overturned only one symbolic pingpong
     table, resting briefly in catatonia,
returning a few years later truly bald except for a wig of blood to
     the visible madman doom of the wards of the madtowns of the East,

Head of page: Place first strophe *as indicated*
   by [arrow sign] after "bad music"

1: their groans [in]to [the] bloody   17: the
7: [publish]ing   20: [seventy]two
13: walking

to bicker with ~~an~~ echo^s, rocking and rolling in the midnight solitude-
bench dolmen-realms of love, Rockland's and Greystone's
foetid halls, aching for the ancestors, dream of life a
nightmare, laughing in eclipse with bod~~y~~ies turned to stone
as heavy as the moon, at 4 A.M.
with mother finally fucked, and the last book thrown out of the attic, window
and the last door closed and the last telephone slammed at the
wall in reply, and the last furnished room emptied down to the
last piece of mental furniture, a yellow paper rose twisted
on a wire hangar in the closet, and even that imaginary, nothing
but a hopeful little bit of hallucination--
ah, Carl, while you're not safe ~~none of us are~~ I am not safe, ~~for~~ and now
you're really in the total soup of Time --
and who therefore ran through the icy streets obsessed with a sudden
flash of the alchemy of the use of the ellipse, the catalogue,
the meter and vibrating plane,
who dreamt and made incarnate gaps in time and space through images
juxtaposed and trapped the archangel of the soul between 2
visual images and joined the elemental verbs and set the noun
and dash of consciousness together jumping with sensation of ~~the~~
~~of~~ Pater Onmipotens Aeterna Deus,
~~who~~ recreate~~d~~ing the syntax and structure of poor human prose and ~~stood~~ to stand
before you speechless and intelligent and shaking with shame,
rejected yet confessing out the soul to conform to the rhythm
of thought in his naked and endless head, the madman bum and
angel beat in time, unknown, yet putting down what might be left
to say in Time come after death,
and rose reincarnate in the clothes of ghostly jazz in the goldhorn
shadow of the band and blew the suffering of America's naked mind
for love into ~~a~~ saxophone cry that shivered the cities down
to the last radio
with the absolute heart of the poem of life butchered out of their
own bodies good to eat a thousand years.

an eli eli lamma lamma sabacthani (saxophone cry)

1: an [canceled] [echo]s   7: at 4 A.M.   30: eli eli lamma sabacthani [canceled] An eli lamma
4: [bod]ies   12: I am not [safe,] and   lamma sabacthani (saxophone cry) [as insert]
6: window   22: [recreate]ing . . . to stand

H O W L

for

Carl Solomon

by

Allen Ginsberg

Unscrew the locks from the doors!
Unscrew the doors themselves from their jambs!

N.B. Sequence of drafts was established in case-by-case examination of changes. Some three dozen alterations evidence progression from 4th to 5th draft, though another half dozen indicate ambiguous chronology. These may be caused by typist's lacunae, reversions to earlier phrasing, or uncertainty of phrasing solved in later drafts. —A.G.

HOWL

for

Carl Solomon

I

I saw the best minds of my generation destroyed by

    madness, starving, hysterical, mystical, naked,

dragging themselves through the negro streets at dawn

    looking for an angry fix,

angelheaded hipsters burning for the ancient heavenly

    connection to the starry dynamo in the machinery

    of night,

who poverty and tatters and hollow-eyed and high sat

    up smoking in the supernatural darkness of cold-

    water flats floating across the tops of cities

    contemplating jazz,

who bared their brains to heaven under the El and saw

    Mohammedan angels staggering on tenement roofs

    illuminated,

who ~~sat~~ Cowered in unshaven rooms in underwear burning their

    money in wastebaskets amid the rubbish of mem-

    orable Barkeley manifestoes listening to the

    Terror through the wall,

who got busted in their ~~phellic~~ pubic beards returning

    through Laredo with a belt of marijuana for

    New York,

who passed through universities with radiant cool

    eyes hallucinating Arkansas and Blake-light

15: ["sat" canceled] cowered   19: pubic

Who
were
expelled

> tragedy among the scholars of war,

who ate fire in paint hotels or turpentine^drank in Para-
        dise Alley, death, or purgatoried their torsos
        night after night.

with dreams, with drugs, with waking nightmares,
        alchohol and cock and endless balls,

incomparable blind streets of shuddering cloud and
        lightning in the mind leaping toward poles
        of Canada & Paterson, illuminating all the
        motionless world between,

Peyote solidities of halls, backyard green tree
        cemetary dawns, wine drunkeness over/roof- ^the
        tops, boroughs of teahead neon green and
        blinking traffic light, sun and moon and
        tree vibrations in the roaring winter dusks
        of Brooklyn, ashcan rantings and kind king
        light of mind,

who chained themselves to subways for the endless
        ride from Battery to holy Bronx on benzedrine
        until the noise of wheels and children
        brought them down shuddering mouth-wracked
        and battered bleak of brain all drained of
        brilliance in the drear light of Zoo,

who sank all night in submarine Bickfords and
        ~~rose up~~ floated out to sit all thru the stale morning ^beer ^afternoon
        in desolate Fugazzi's, listening to the crack
        of doom on the hydrogen jukebox,

Left margin: Who were expelled   2: drank   25: floated out . . . beer [morning] afternoon

who talked continuously seventy hours from park to
        pad to bar to Bellevue to museum to the Brook-
        lyn Bridge,
yackatayaking screaming vomiting whispering facts and
        memories and anecdotes and eyeball kicks and
        shocks of hospitals and jails and wars,
a lost batallion of platonic conversationalists
        jumping down the stoops off fire escapes off
        windowsills off Empire State out of the moon,
who vanished into nowhere Zen New Jersey leaving a
        trail of ambiguous picture postcards of At-
        lantic Cryptic Hall,
suffering eastern sweats and tangerian bonegrindings
        and migraines of china under Junk-withdrawal
        in Newark's bleak furnished room,
who wandered midnight in the railroad yard wondering
        where to go, and went, leaving no broken hearts,
who lit cigarettes in boxcars boxcars boxcars racket-
        ing through snow toward lonesome farms in
        grandfather night,
who studied Plotinus and Fludd telepathy & bop
        kaballa because the cosmos instinctively
        vibrated at their feet in Kansas,
who loned it through the streets of Idaho seeking
        visionary indian angels who were visionary
        indian angels,

who jumped in cars with the Chinaman of Illinois on
the impulse of winter midnight streetlight
smalltown rain,

who lounged hungry and lonesome through Huston seek-
ing jazz or sex or soup, and followed the
brilliant Spaniard to converse about America
and Eternity, a hopeless task, and so took
ship to Africa,

who disappeared into the volcanos of Mexico leaving
behind nothing but the shadow of dungarees
and the lava and ash of poetry scattered in
fireplace Chicago,

who reappeared on the West Coast investigating the
FBI in beards and shorts with big pacifist
eyes sexy in their dark skin passing out
incomprehensible leaflets,

who limped penniless over city hills with half a
mustache hanging on the sinister lip looking
for an example of Baroque architecture, and
spent hours thereafter in the bathroom wash-
ing their few nickles with a Buffalo tooth-
brush,

who broke down crying in white gymnasiums naked and
trembling before the machinery of other skeletons,

who burned cigarette holes in their arms protesting
the narcotic tobacco haze of capitalism,

who passed out super-communist leaflets in Union Sq.
weeping and undressing, while the sirens of
Los Alamos wailed them down, and wailed down   *+ Bird was wailing*
Wall, and the Staten Island ferry also wailed,   *the most at Birdland*

who bit detectives in the neck and shrieked with
delight in policecars for committing no crime
but their own wild cooking pederasty & intox-
ication,

who ~~screamed~~ *howled* on their knees in the subway, and were
dragged off the roof waving genitals and man-
uscripts,

who blew and were blown by those human seraphs, the
sailors, caresses of Atlantic and Caribbean joy,

who let themselves be fucked in the ass by saintly
motorcyclists, and screamed with joy,

who hiccupped endlessly trying to giggle but wound
up with a sob behind a partition in a Turkish
bath when the blond & naked angel came to
pierce them with a sword,

who lost their loveboys to the three old shrews of fate
the oneeyed shrew of the heterosexual dollar,
the oneeyed shrew that winks out of the womb
and the oneeyed shrew that does nothing but
sit on her ass and snip the intellectual gold-
en threads of the craftsman's loom,

who sweetened the snatches of a million girls tremb-
ling in the sunset, flashing buttocks under
barns, and were red-eyed in the morning but
prepared to sweeten the snatch of the sunrise
naked in the lake,

4: & Bird was wailing the most at Birdland   9: howled

who went out whoring through the Midwest, in myriad
          stolen night cars, N.C., (secret hero of these
          poems, cocksman and Adonis of Denver, our long
          old love, heart of ten thousand bodies on
          either coast,) joy to the memory of his innum-
          erable lays of girls in empty lots and diners, or backyards
          moviehouses rickety rows, on mountaintops or with
          gaunt waittresses in familiar roadside lonesome
          petticoat upliftings & especially secret gas-
          station solipsisms of johns, & hometown alleys
          too,

who copulated ecstatic and insatiate with a bottle
          of beer a sweetheart a package of cigarettes
          a candle and fell off the bed, and con-
          tinued along the floor and down the hall and
          ended fainting on the wall with a vision of
          ultimate cunt and come eluding the last gyzym
          of consciousness,

who were shifted in vast sordid movies to sudden
          Manhattans, and picked themselves up out of
          basements hungover with heartless Tokay &
          3rd Avenue horrors of dismantled iron and
          stumbled to unemployment offices,

or ate the lamb stew of the imagination or digested
          the crab at the muddy bottom of the rivers
          of Bowery,

who wept at the romance of the streets with their
          pushcarts full of onions and bad music,

6: backyards   7: in caves   19: faded out . . . & woke up in Manhattan   24: Who

who sat in boxes breathing in the darkness under the

Bridge, and rose up to build harpsichords in

their lofts,

who coughed on the sixth floor of Harlem under the

tuburcular sky surrounded by orange crates

of theology,

who cooked rotten animals lung heart feet tail borsht

& tortillas dreaming of the pure vegetable king-

dom,

who sang out of their windows in despair or threw up

their groans into the bloody toilet, moans in

their ears and the blast of colossal steamwhistles,

who plunged themselves under meat trucks looking for

an egg,

who jumped off the Brooklyn Bridge this actually

happened and walked away unknown and forgotten

into the ghostly daze of Chinatown soup

alleyways and firetrucks, not even one free

beer,

who were expelled from the academies for crazy &

publishing obscene odes on the windows of

the skull,

who threw their watches off the roof ▮▮▮ casting

their ballot for Eternity outside of Time,

and alarm clocks fell on their heads every day

for the next decade,

3/4: Who sat all nite rocking & rolling over lofty
  incantations which in the yellow morning were
  stanzas of gibberish
9, left margin: * Meat truck egg
10: lunged out of subway windows, jumped in the filthy
  Passaic, leaped on negroes, Cried al over the street,
  danced on broken wineglasses barefoot smashed their
  phonograph records of European 1930's German jazz
  finished the whiskey &

11: groaning
15: got hi [canceled]
20–2, left margin: See p 1 [proposed shift to page 1—
  A.G.]
23–6, left margin: After free Beer [proposed shift to
  follow verse 6 above—A.G.]

After Steamwhistles, p. 7

who created great national suicidal dramas on the

banks of the Hudson   under the wartime blue

floodlight of the moon on the apartment cliffs,   & their heads shall be crowned with laurel in oblivion.

who cut their wrists three times unsuccessfully

gave up and were forced to open antique

stores where they thought they were growing

old and cried,

who were burnt alive in their innocent flannel

suits on Madison Avenue amid blasts of

leaden verse & the clatter of iron

regiments of fashion & the nitroglycerine

shrieks of the fairies of advertising &

the mustard gas of sinister intelligent

editors, or were run down by the drunken

taxicabs of Absolute Reality,

who walked all night with shoes full of blood on

the snowbank docks, waiting for a door in

the East River to open to a room full of

steamheat and opium,

who barrelled down the highways of the past journeying to

each other's hotrod Golgotha jail-solitude watch

or Birmingham jazz incarnation,

who drove crosscountry seventy-two hours to find out

if I had a vision or you had a vision or he had

a vision to find out the present,

Left margin: After Steamwhistles, p. 7 [proposed shift to p. 7 of this draft as insert to verse 4a—A.G.]
2: [insert] the . . . blue
3: & their heads shall be crowned with laurel in oblivion.
20: barrelled down . . . [journ]e[ying]

who journeyed to Denver, who died in Denver, who came
        back to Denver & waited in vain, who watched
        and finally went away to find out the future,
who fell on their knees in hopeless cathedrals
        praying for each other's salvation and light
        and breasts, till the soul illuminated its
        hair for a second,
who crashed through their minds in jail waiting for
        impossible criminals with golden heads and
        the charm of reality in their hearts who sang
        sweet blues to Alcatraz,
who retired to Mexico to cultivate a habit or
        Rocky Mount to tender Buddha or Tangiers
        to boys or Southern Pacific to the black
        locomotive or Harvard to Narcissus to
        Woodlawn to the daisychain or grave,
who demanded sanity trials accusing the radio of
        hypnotism and were left with their insanity
        and their hands and a hung jury,
who threw potato salad at CCNY lecturers on Dadaism
        and subsequently presented themselves on the
        granite steps of the madhouse with shaven heads
        and harlequin speech of suicide, demanding
        instantaneous lobotomy,

and who were given instead the concrete void of

       insulin metrasol electricity hydrotherapy

       psychotherapy occupational therapy pingpong

       & amnesia,

and who in humorless protest overturned only one

       symbolic pingpong table, resting briefly

       in catatonia,

returning years later truly bald except for a wig of

       blood to the visible madman doom of the wards

       of the madtowns of the East,

Rockland's and Greystone's foetid halls, bickering

       with echoes, rocking and rolling in the mid-

       night solitude bench dolmen-realms of love,

       dream of life a nightmare, laughing in

       eclipse with bodies turned to stone as heavy

       as the moon,

with mother finally ***, and the last book thrown out

       of ~~the~~ Lexington attic window, and the last

       door closed at 4 AM, and the last telephone

       slammed at the wall in reply and the last under-

       wear stripped down to the floor and the last

       furnished room emptied down to the last piece

       of mental furniture, a yellow paper rose twisted

       on a wire hanger in the closet, and even that

       imaginary, nothing but a hopeful little bit of

       hallucination--

Ah, Carl, while you are not safe I am not safe, and

       now you're _really_ in the total trouble soup of Time!--

28: really

and who therefore ran through the icy streets obsessed
        with a sudden flash of the alchemy of the use
        of the ellipse the catalogue the meter and the
        vibrating plane,
who dreamt and made incarnate heavenly gaps in time
        and space through images juxtaposed and
        trapped the archangel of the soul between
        2 visual images and joined the elemental verbs
        and set the breath and dash of consciousness
        together nouned and jumping with sensation of
        Pater Omnipotens Aeterna Deus
recreating the syntax and measure of poor human prose
        to stand before you speechless & intelligent
        & shaking with shame, rejected yet confessing
        .out the soul to conform to the rhythm of thought
        in his naked and endless head,
the madman bum and angel, beat in Time, unknown yet
        putting down what must be left to say in Time
        come after death,
and rose reincarnate in the ghostly clothes of jazz
        in the goldhorn shadow of the the band and blew
        the suffering of America's naked mind for love
        into an eli eli lamma lamma sabacthani sax-
        ophone cry that shivered the cities down
        to the last radio
with the absolute heart of the poem of life butchered
        out of their own bodies good to eat a thous-
        and years.

21: of

HOWL

for

Carl Solomon

I saw the best minds of my generation destroyed by mad-
          ness, starving hysterical naked,
dragging themselves through the negro streets at dawn
          looking for an angry fix,
angelheaded hipsters burning for the ancient heavenly
          connection to the starry dynamo in the machinery
          of night,
who poverty and tatters and hollow-eyed and high sat up
          smoking in the supernatural darkness of cold-
          water flats floating across the tops of cities
          contemplating jazz,
who bared their brains to heaven under the El and saw
          Mohammedan angels staggering on tenement roofs
          illuminated,
who ~~crouched~~ Cowered in unshaven rooms in underwear burning
          their money in wastebaskets amid the rubbish
          of memorable Berkeley manifestoes listening to
          the Terror through the wall,
                              pubic
who got busted in their ⌃beards returning through Laredo
          with a belt of marijuana for New York,

15: ["crouched" canceled] cowered   19: pubic

44   HOWL, PART I: DRAFT 5

who passed through universities with radiant cool eyes
        hallucinating Arkansas and Blake-light tragedy
        among the scholars of war,
who were expelled from the academies for crazy &   pub-
        lishing obscene odes on the windows of the skull,
who ate fire in paint hotels or drank turpentine in
        Paradise Alley, death, or purgatoried their torsos
        night after night
with dreams, with drugs, with waking nightmares, alchohol
        and cock and endless balls,
incomparable blind streets of shuddering cloud and
        lightning in the mind leaping toward poles of
        Canada & Paterson, illuminating all the motion-
        less world of time between,
Peyote solidities of halls, backyard green tree cemetary
        dawns, wine drunkenness over the rooftops, stoorfront
        boroughs of teahead joyride neon blinking
        traffic light, sun and moon and tree vibrations
        in the roaring winter dusks of Brooklyn, ashcan
        rantings and kind king light of mind,
who chained themselves to subways for the endless rage ride
        from Battery to holy Bronx on benzedrine until
        the noise of wheels and children brought them down
        shuddering mouth-wracked and battered bleak of
        brain all drained of brilliance in the drear
        light of Zoo,

21: the [endless] ["rage" canceled] ride

who sank all night in submarine Bickfords and ~~rose up~~ FLOATED OUT

    to sit all through the stale beer ~~morning~~

    afternoons in desolate ~~Fugazzi's~~ listening

    to the crack of doom on the hydrogen jukebox,

who talked continuously seventy hours from park to

    pad to bar to Bellevue to museum to the

    Brooklyn Bridge,

yackatayaking screaming vomiting whispering facts

    and memories and anecdotes and eyeball kicks

    and shocks of hospitals and jails and wars,

a lost batallion of platonic conversationalists

    jumping down the stoops off fire escapes

    off windowsills off Empire State out of

    the moon,

who vanished into nowhere Zen New Jersey leaving

    a trail of ambiguous picture postcards of

    Atlantic Cryptic Hall,

suffering Eastern sweats and Tangerian bonegrindings

    and migraines of China under junk-withdrawal

    in Newark's bleak furnished room,

who wandered at midnight in the railroad yard won-

    dering where to go, and went, leaving no

    broken hearts,

1: ["rose up" canceled] floated out   2: ["morning" canceled]   3: Fugazzi's

who lit cigarettes in boxcars boxcars boxcars racket-
        ing through snow toward lonesome farms in
        grandfather night,
who studied Plotinus and Fludd telepathy and bop
        kaballa because the cosmos instinctively
        vibrated at their feet in Kansas,
who loned it through the streets of Idaho seeking
        visionary indian angels who were visionary
        indian angels,
who lounged hungry and lonesome through Houston
        seeking jazz or sex or soup, and followed
        the brilliant Spaniard to converse about
        America and Eternity, a hopeless task, and so
        took ship to Africa,
who disappeared into the volcanoes of Mexico leaving
        behind nothing but the shadow of dungarees
        and the lava and ash of poetry scattered in
        fireplace Chicago,
who reappeared on the West Coast investigating the
        FBI in beards and shorts with big pacifist eyes
        sexy in their dark skin passing out incompre-
        hensible leaflets,
who limped penniless over city hills looking for an
        example of Baroque architecture with half a
        mustache hanging on the sinister lip, and spent
        hours in the bathroom washing their poor
        nickles with a buffalo toothbrush,

who jumped in limosines with the Chinaman of Oklahoma
        on the impulse of winter midnight smalltown
        streetlight rain,
who broke down crying in white gymnasiums naked and
        trembling before the machinery of other
        skeletons,
who burned cigarette holes in their arms protesting
        the narcotic tobacco haze of Capitalism,
who passed out Supercommunist leaflets in Union
        Square while the sirens of Los Alamos wailed
        them down, and wailed down Wall, and the
        Staten Island Ferry also wailed, and Bird
                       the most
        was wailing at Birdland,
who bit detectives in the neck and shrieked with
        delight in policecars for committing no crime
        but their own wild cooking pederasty and
        intoxication,
who howled on their knees in the subway, and were
        dragged off the roof waving genitals and
        manuscripts,
who let themselves be fucked in the ass by saintly
        motorcyclists, and screamed with joy,
who blew and were blown by those human seraphim
        the sailors, caresses of Atlantic and
        Carribean love,

who hiccupped endlessly trying to giggle but wound up
with a sob behind a partition in a Turkish Bath
when the blond & naked angel came to pierce them
with a sword,

who lost their loveboys to the three old shrews of fate
the one eyed shrew of the heterosexual dollar
the one eyed shrew that winks out of the womb
and the one eyed shrew that does nothing but sit
on her ass and snip the intellectual golden
threads of the craftsman's loom,

who sweetened the snatches of a million girls trembling
in the sunset flashing buttocks under barns,
and were red eyed in the morning but prepared
to sweeten the snatch of the sunrise naked in
the lake,

who went out whoring through midwest in myriad stolen
night cars, joy to the memory of his innumerable
lays of girls in empty lots & diners, backyards
moviehouses' rickety rows in caves and mountain-
tops, or with gaunt waittresses in familiar roadside
lonely petticoat upliftings & especially secret
gas-station solipsisms of johns, & hometown
alleys too,

who copulated ecstatic and insatiate with a bottle of
beer a sweetheart a package of cigarettes a
candle and fell off the bed, and continued
along the floor and down the hall and ended
fainting on the wall with a vision of ultimate
cunt and come eluding the last gyzym of
consciousness,

who faded out in vast sordid movies and suddenly woke up
          in Manhattan, picked themselves up out of base-
          ments hung-over with heartless Tokay and horrors
          of dismantled Third Avenue iron dreams && stumbled
          to unemployment offices,

who ate the lamb stew of the imagination or digested
          the crab at the muddy bottom of the rivers of
          Bowery,

who wept at the romance of the streets with their
          pushcarts full of onions and bad music,

who sat in boxes breathing in darkness under the
          Bridge, and rose up to build harpsichords
          in their lofts,

who sat all night rocking and rolling over LOFTY incantations
          which in the yellow morning were stanzas of
          gibberish,

who coughed on the sixth floor of Harlem under the
          tubercular sky surrounded by orange crates
          of theology,

who cooked rotten animals lung heart feet tail borsht
          & tortillas dreaming of the pure vegetable
          kingdom,

who plunged themselves under meat trucks looking for
          an egg,

who sang out of their windows in dispair, lunged out
          of subway windows, jumped in the filthy Passaic,
          leaped on negroes, cried all over the street,
          [finished the whiskey] danced on x broken wine glasses
          barefoot smashed their phonograph records of
          European 1930's German jazz & threw up groaning
          into the bloody toilet, moans in their ears and
          the blast of colossal steamwhistles,

East River

~~who plunged themselves under meat trucks looking for~~
~~an egg,~~

who ~~got high and~~ jumped off the Brooklyn Bridge this
actually happen**ed** and walked away unknown and
forgotten into the ghostly daze of Chinatown
soup alleyways and firetrucks, not even one
free beer,

who threw their watches off the roof to cast their
ballot for Eternity outside of Time, & &
alarm clocks fell on their heads every day
for the next decade,

who created great suicidal dramas on the apartment
cliff-banks of the Hudson under the wartime
BLUE floodlight of the moon and their heads shall
be crowned with laurel in oblivion,

who cut their wrists three times successively un-
successfully, gave up, and were forced to
open antique stores where they throught they
were growing old and cried,

who were burned alive in their innocent flannel suits
on Madison Avenue amid blasts of leaden verse
& the tanked-up clatter of the iron regiments of
fashion & the nitroglycerine shrieks of the
fairies of advertising & the mustard gas of
sinister intelligent editors, or were run down
by the drunken taxicabs of Absolute Reality,

1: shifted around . . . up   14: blue
Left margin: East River
14: lofty

who walked all night with /shoes full of blood on the
snowbank docks waiting for a door in the East
River to open to a room full of steamheat and
opium,

who barreled down the highways of the past journeying
to eachother's hotrod-Golgotha jail-solitude
watch or Birmingham jazz incarnation,

who drove crosscountry seventy-two hours to find out
if I had a vision or you had a vision or he had
a vision to find out the present,

who journeyed to Denver, who died in Denver, who
came back to Denver & waited in vain, who
watched and finally went away to find out
the future,

who fell on their knees in hopeless cathedrals praying
for each other's salvation and light and breasts,
till the soul illuminated its hair for a second,

who crashed through their minds in jail waiting for
impossible criminals with golden heads and
the charm of reality in their hearts who sang
sweet blues to Alcatraz,

who retired to Mexico to cultivate a habit, or Rocky
Mount to tender Buddha or Tangiers to boys
or Southern Pacific to the black locomotive
or Harvard to Narcissus to Woodlawn to the
daisychain or grave,

1: their

who demanded sanity trials accusing the radio of

    hypnotism and were left with their insanity

    and their hands and a hung jury,

who threw potato salad at CCNY lecturers on Dadaism

    and subsequently presented themselves on the

    granite steps of the madhouse with shaven

    heads and harlequin speech of suicide, de-

    manding instantaneous lobotomy,

and who were given instead the concrete void of

    insulin metrasol electricity hydrotherapy

    psychotherapy occupational therapy pingpong

    & amnesia,

who in humorless protest overturned only one symbolic

    pingpong table, rested briefly in catatonia,

returning years later truly bald except for a wig of

    blood ~~and helpless fingers~~ to the visible

    madman doom of the wards of the madtowns

    of the East,

Greystone's and Rockland's foetid halls, bickering

    with echoes, rocking and rolling in the mid-

    night solitude-bench dolmen-realms of Love,

    dream of life a nightmare, laughing in eclipse,

    with bodies turned to stone as heavy as the moon,

with mother finally ***, and the last magical book ~~of magic~~

    thrown out of the attic window, and the last

    door closed at ~~four~~ 4 AM, and the last telephone

    slammed at the wall in reply and the last

    furnished room emptied down to the last piece

16: ["and helpless fingers" canceled]
23: [bod]ies

24: magical . . . ["of magic" canceled]
26: ["four" canceled] 4

of mental furniture, a yellow paper rose

twisted in a wire hanger in the closet, and

even that imaginary, nothing but a hopeful

little bit of hallucination--

ah, Carl, while you are not safe I am not safe, and

now you're ~~really~~ in the ~~total~~ animal soup

of Time--

and who therefore ran through the icy streets obsessed

with a sudden flash of the alchemy of the use

of the ellipse the meter the catalogue and

the vibrating plane,

who dreamt and made incarnate gaps in time and space

through images juxtaposed, and trapped the

archangel of the soul between 2 visual images

and joined the elemental verbs and set the noun

and dash of consciousness together ~~in a breath~~

~~and~~ jumping with sensation of Pater Omnipotens

Aeterna Deus,

to recreate the syntax and measure of poor human prose

and stand before you speechless and intelligent

and shaking with shame, rejected yet confessing

out the soul to conform to the rhythm of thought

in his naked and endless head, the madman bum and

angel, beat in time, unknown yet putting down

now what might be left to say in time come after

death,

6: ["total" canceled] total   16: ["in a breath" canceled]   17: ["and" canceled]

and rose reincarnate in the ghostly clothes of jazz
        in the goldhorn shadow of the band and blew
        the suffering of America's naked mind for love
        into an eli eli lamma ~~lamma~~ sabacthani sax-
        ophone cry that shivered the cities down to
        the last radio
with the absolute heart of the poem of life butchered
        out of their own bodies good to eat a thousand
        years.

Guide to Original Manuscripts, Part II

Draft 1: This manuscript, handwrit on the last page of a scrapped late version of Part I, provided a form for the "Moloch" inspiration, a rhythmic logic.

Draft 2: First draft typed, cleaned up, cut, and tied together for clarity, with marginal note on antiphonal cadence implicit.

Draft 3: A worksheet, phrasings improved, verse divisions balanced neater, arrow re-orders last verse group to midsection.

Draft 4: Clear-typed to consolidate prior corrections, this draft provides a clean & strong skeleton on which to hang more appendages, meat and lungs.

Draft 5: Four pages of pleasure cadenzas on the anaphoric trochee "Moloch!" fill in the body of the monster vision. Since word combinations possible were inexhaustible, there was space for free mind play. Imagination was released to juxtapose disparate archetypes of electric modernity, condense naturalistic observation of the industrial landscape into hyperbolic images of metropolitan apocalypse. Any spontaneous majestic glimpse could be solidified merely by typing outrageous verbal associations on the page, free from any idea logic but phrase wit, auditory intuition of assonance and cadence, and beauty of picture.

These pages were written one afternoon late 1955 in the small backyard cottage I shared with Gary Snyder, 1624 Milvia Street, Berkeley. I sat at typewriter desk facing garden window bushes, he sat Japanese style cross-legged before a writing frame on the floor rug, translating Chinese, Han Shan. Must've heard me muttering, sometimes laughing aloud, and distracted by my trancelike self-absorption, he called out, "Moloch who reaches up at night thru the bottom of the toilet bowl and grabs my pecker everytime I try to take a crap!"

How cohere these inklings of extravaganza? The most glittering intense phrases were hand-underlined next, first pass at selecting pure gold nuggets—workable serious images—out of the mass of random associations.

Draft 6: Incorporates prior draft's experimental spontaneous rhapsody of "Moloch!"'s. The task was, scan raw material of nonparagraphed improvisations, select best phrase elements, set them in "strophic" verses, experiment with balance and arrangement of the rhetorical flight. This typescript presumes the initial two-verse rhythmic statement up to "Old men weeping in parks!" and the entire closure following "Monstrous bombs!" Later this material is added into the midsection catalogue of Molochs fixed in Draft 4.

Draft 7: Adds the initial two verses, refines an extended list of Molochs, connects that directly to the Adonic apostrophe "Robot apartments!," suspending one verse ("broken backs lifting moloch to heaven") for use further on.

Draft 8: This fragment works out a problem of transition passage from panoramic to personal reference in Moloch midsection, changing "we sit lonely" to "I sit lonely."

Draft 9: Work here sets up whole structure, builds cadence & energy in middle section, extends all useful Moloch phrases, juggles and cuts them, summing up to reconnect with "breaking their backs" and the coda, "Visions, omens etc."

Draft 10: Surveys Moloch catalogue first page with cuts and transpositions, suspends "consciousness without body" for use later in section, adds key phrase, "whose name is the Mind."

Draft 11: Begins to untangle the bones of epithet for "congress and prison," and weigh proper placement for crucial Moloch name "Mind."

Draft 12: This fragment focused back on the problematic transition passage, somewhat clarifying the visual panorama, extending ecstatic personal confession—and here hit on more direct phrasing, the exclamatory "Wake up in Moloch!," to resolve thought rhythms and climax the imitation of vision.

Draft 13: The complete structure is consolidated, beginning to end. Some epithets within each strophic verse will be eliminated, and some phrases change, but the sequence of verses & the interior relations of phrases within these verses are in right rhythmic order.

Draft 14: Rehearses all but the coda, rearranging crucial images, progressively improving surface and sequence. "Consumer" & "slaughterer," etc., reincorporate unsuccessfully. "Consciousness without a body" has located a fitting place by hand, and "Moloch whose name is the Mind" still floats around looking for logical sonorous home among the verses.

Draft 15: This isolate worksheet is an attempt to account previous draft's corrections (elisions & transpositions) indicated for two verses, consolidating the good phrases lined up in order condensed into one fat strophe. With a few phrases eliminated, the original sequence will be restored, divided in two again.

Draft 16: "Cannibal dynamo" phrase moves ahead, Moloch's "poverty" finds right place, first seven verses run through near perfected, stumbling on the "bodiless God" transition. The two climactic verses follow almost completely in place. Moloch's "Mind" isn't settled.

Draft 17: The weak "star of Apocalypse" obstructs the spot where Moloch might be named "the Mind"; but "bodiless God" has been removed to the tail of the catalogue, temporarily out of the way. A rhythmic continuity moves between "a cloud of sexless hydrogen" and "Moloch in whom I sit lonely," only one phrase wants laying in place to couple the parts. Handmade brackets arrow "bodiless God" back in between them, halfway uncertain, well-wishing, rhythmic heart in the right place.

Draft 18: This is the last typescript stage surviving in author's possession. In this penultimate draft most everything's in place. The coda "They broke their backs . . . Into the streets!" from Draft 13 was to be added on, with minor variants. These further changes were, in order:

"Thousand blind windows," fifth verse, will come to follow not precede "machinery," sixth verse, for the sake of rhythmic buildup. "Moloch whose name is the Mind" follows in dactylic natural cadence after "a cloud of sexless hydrogen." The next three phrases, always excessive and metaphysically vague, will be dropped. "Frightened natural ecstasy" was still to be discovered in place of "a burned down world." Blake's satanic "mills" further down the line will turn into demonic "industries," following "blind capitals."

Other than first mimeo (Ditto process), final draft printer's copy in publisher City Lights Books archives is represented by published text.

returning to the magneta reality of the wards years later
        truly bald except for a wig of blood, with a
        handfull of Time, all fingers and tears, and the
        bleak scream of society blasting out of his ears,
with his visible madman doom, and his own mother finally
        fucked, and the last book burned on the windowsill,
        and the last anal prosepoem published as Apocalypse
        to the rats under the toilet, and the last door closed
        at 4 AM and the last helpless companion up in a plane,
        and the last telephone slammed against the wall in reply,
        and the last furnished room emptied down to the last
        piece of mental furniture, a yellow paper rose twisted
        on a wire hanger in the ghostly closet, and even that
        hallucination, --
Ah, Carl Solomon while you are not safe I am not safe,
        for now you're really in the total soup of Time, --
who sat years after bickering his echo in the madtowns of the
        east, rocking and rolling in themidnight solitude
        bench dolmen realms of love, Rockland and Greystone's
        foetid halls,
tangled in the hassels of imaginary shrouds and straightjackets,
        aching for ancestors, dream of life a nightmare,
        laughing in eclipse until the body turns to
        stone as heavy as the moon
and who therefore ran through the icy streets obsessed with
        a sudden flash of the alchemy of the use of the
        elipse, the catalogue, the meterand vibrating
        plane,
who dreamt and made incarnate gaps in time and space through
        images juxtaposed and blocke of color shoving back
        and forth in front of a flat dimension
who rose reincarnate in the clothes of music in the goldhorn
        shadow the the band and blew the suffering of
        America's naked mind for love into a saxaphone cry
        that shivered the cities down to the last radio,
who stood before you speechless and intelligent and shaking with
        shame, rejected, yet confessing out the soul, the
        madman bum and angel, beat in Time, unknown,
who recreated the synatx and structure of poor human prose
        to conform to the rhythm of thoughtin his naked
        and endless head, and set down here what might be left
        to say in Time come after death,
who trapped the archangel of soul between 2 visual
        images and joined the elemental verms and setthe noun
        and dash of consciousness together jumping with sensation
        of Cezanne, Pater Omnipotens Aeterna Deus,
the absolute heart of the poem of life butchered out from
        their own bodies good to eat a thousand years.

Moloch! Moloch! Whose hand ripped out their brains
and scattered their minds on the wheels of subways!
    Moloch! Filth! Ugliness! Ashcans and unobtanable dollars!
Beauties dying in lofts! Harpsichords unbuilt! Children
Screaming under the stairways! old men weeping in the parks!

(1)

Children! children! The very children breaking their
backs under the subways. Breaking their backs trying to lift the
Whole City on their backs—Pavements! Buildings! Trees
Rockefeller Center Tons—The whole damned lot of it—the
screaming radios—Hitler! Stalin! Christmas! Jesus!
The wires coming out of our ears—lifting the city on our
backs! To ~~heav~~ heaven—

Heaven which is exists and is everywhere about us
Dreams! Visions! Gone, Garbaged, in the morgue,
with the rest of them, the wholel boatload of sensitive bullshit,
raving insanity

Passed over the river, down on the rocks, Time gone,
10 years past, the flowers carried off by the stream, amid
screams and shriekings and laughter! real holy laughter in
the ~~strea strea~~ river. They saw it all, they heard it all,
each others desperate Cries, bade farewell as they jumped off
the roof to solitude, Carrying flowers, ~~the~~ down to the
river, down in the streat.

Moloch! Molock! Whose hand ripped out their brains
and scattered their minds on the wheels of subways?
Molloch! Filth! Ugliness! Ashcans and unobtainable dollars!
~~Beatit~~ Beauties dying in lofts! Harpsichords unbuilt! Children ~~never~~
screaming under the stairways! old men weeping in the parks!

HOWL, PART II: DRAFT I   59

MOLOCH! MOLOCK! Whose hand bashed out their brains on the subway ~~wxxx~~
 wheels?
Moloch Filth Ugliness! Ashcans and unobta~~f~~able dollars! Unbuilt
 harpsichords! Beauties dying in lofts! Screaming under the
 stairways! Harpsichords unbuilt! Old men weeping in the parks!
Children! Children! breaking their backs lifting t~~h~~e city up into
 heaven. Pavements, trees, tons. The screaming radios. Xmas!
 Jesus! Wires coming out of the ears. Lifting the city on our
 backs
to Heaven which exists ~~and is~~ everywhere.

    Visions! Hallucinations! Omens! Dreams! Illuminations!
Garbage! Corpses!
    Gone down the river, the whole boatload of sensitive bullshit!
    Miracles! Ecstasies! Flips! Highs! Break-throughs! Telepathies!
    Over the river, gone down the flood, time gone, ten years,
animal screams, real holy laughter in the river!
    They saw it all, they heard the drowning yell!
    They bade farewell as they jumped off the roof to solitude,
carrying flowers, down to the street.

Moloch! Moloch! The ugly cities, the skullhead ~~buildings~~,
 monsterous warehouses, abbatoirs, treasuries, banks and
 robot hotels
    robot apartments, skullhead hotels, skeleton treasuries,
ghostly banks, bloody abbotoirs, monster warehouses, spectral
streets, ~~xxxxxxxxx~~ capitols, stone cock skyscrapers
        eyeless

10: ["and is" canceled]
Left margin: "*Antiphonal* river vs stacatto!" A struc-
 tural note, proposing that verse strung with ex-
 clamatory or "stacatto" single words ("Visions!")

alternate with verse made up of short phrasing
("Gone down the river!"). —A.G.
20: ["buildings" x-ed out]
25: ["eyes in the" x-ed out]

~~Moloch! Moloch!~~ What Sphinx of cement and alluminum bashed ~~in~~ their
    skulls and ate ~~up imagination?~~ *their brains & imagination*
Moloch ⌠ Moloch! Solitude! Ugliness! Ashcans and unobtainable dollars! Garbage
    heap of brains! ~~Boys~~ screaming under the stairways! Old men
    weeping in the parks! *Children*
    Moloch! Moloch! breaking their backs lifting Moloch to heaven!
    Pavements, trees, radios, tons! Lifting the city to heaven
    which exists everywhere!
                          and is
    Visions! Omens! Hallucinations! Miracles! Ecstasies! Gone down the
    American river!
    Dreams! Illuminations! ~~Garbage!~~ Corpses! The whole boatload of
    sensitive bullshit!
    Breakthroughs! Over the river! Flips! gone down the flood! Telepathies!
    Time gone! Highs! Animal screams! Ten Years! Epiphanies!
    Real holy laughter in the river!
    They saw it all! The wild eyes! The holy yells! They bade farewell!
    They jumped off the roof to solitude! Carrying flowers!
    Down to the river! Into the street!
                                              Dynasour
    Moloch! Moloch! Robot apartments! Eyeless capitols! ~~Monsterous~~ bombs!
    Skeleton treasuries! ~~Ghostly~~ banks! Granite phalluses!
                    crazy

1: ["Moloch! Moloch! canceled] . . . ["in" x-ed out]
2: ["up" x-ed out] . . . ["imagination?" canceled] up
    their brains & imagination
3: Moloch
4: ["Boys" canceled] children
8: and is
11: ["Garbage" canceled]
19: ["Monsterous" canceled] Dynasaur
20: ["Ghostly" canceled] craz[y]

II

What sphinx of cement and aluminum bashed in their skulls and
        ate up their brains and imagination?
Moloch! Solitude! Filth! Ugliness! Ashcans and unobtainable
        dollars! Garbage heap of eyebrows and brains! Children
        screaming under the stairways! Old men weeping in the parks!
Moloch! Moloch! Breaking their backs lifting Moloch to Heaven!
        Pavements, trees, radios, tons! lifting the city
to Heaven which exists and is everywhere!

Moloch! Moloch! Robot apartments! Invisible suburbs! Skeleton
        treasuries! Blind capitals! Ghostly bureaucracies!
        Invincible madhouses! Granite cocks! Monsterous bombs!

Visions! Omens! Hallucinations! Miracles! Ecstasies! Gone down
        the American river!
Dreams! Illuminations! Crosses! Religions! The whole boatload
        of sensitive bullshit!
Breakthroughs! Over the river! Corpses! Gone down the flood!
        Telepathies! Flips! Highs! Animal screams! Ten years!
        Mad generations! Epiphanies! Down on the rocks of time!
Real holy laughter in the river! They saw it all! The wild eyes!
        The holy yells! They bade farewell! They jumped off the
        roof! to solitude! Waving! Carrying flowers! Down to the
        river! Into the street!

Moloch! Moloch! Nightmare of Moloch! Moloch the buildings!

Moloch the battleship! Moloch the loveless! .

Moloch the labor! Malachzx Brokenleg Moloch!

Moloch the Money! Moloch the mental, moloch the

heavy moloch the ponderous moloch the inhuman

moloch the judger of men moloch the enfless

moloch the scientist moloch the President

moloch the priest moloch the prophet moloch the

Moloch the soulless moloch the, omen moloch the

avenger moloch the judger moloch the harbor

moloch the sity moloch the metropolis moloch the

capital moloch the labor loloch the vision molovh

theacademy moloch the lawful moloch the radio

moloch the soldier moloch the teacher moloch

the congress molochq the charity moloch the

dollar moloch/ the ponderous moloch the powerful

moloch the s   sexless moloch   moloch the   *monarch*

marriage moloch thetelevision antennae moloch

the books amoloch the movies moloch the

New York Daily news, moloch the magazine of Time

moloch the heavy ~~moloch~~ of stone moloch the   *monolith*

heartless moloch the fearful moloch the

stone buildings moloch the vast stone of war

moloch the stunned intelligence moloch the   *kingdome*

blind buildings moloch the buildings of

judgement moloch the incomprelensible prisons

moloch the electrical gallows ,moloch the lonely

streets moloch the empty/eyes moloch the mad

crowd of daytime moloch the

moloch the deathless ~~government~~ moloch the mental jury
moloch the flags of the nations moloch the invisible
God moloch the slaughterer of sheep moloch the slaugh
terer of men moloch the slaughterer of mankind ,
moloch the slaughterer of a billion christs moloch
the ~~bringer of~~ builders of Hell moloch the bodiless
god moloch the god whose eyes are a thousand blind
windows moloch whose apartments stand in the
streets like lonely endless crazy geniusses and
spectral goliath 1 moloch whose names is America
Moloch whose name is Russia moloch whose name is
justice moloch whose name is religion moloch
whose name is poverty moloch whose name is plenty
moloch whose name is Congress moloch whose name is
Chicago and Moscow moloch whose name is democracy
moloch whose name is the Mind moloch whose name is
insanity moloch whose name is sanity moloch whose
~~heart is industrial~~ heart is Natural Resources Moloch
whose mind is machinery moloch whos legs are
pattleships moloch whose fingers are armies moloch
whose love is a stone moloch whose cock is the
washington monument moloch whose eyes are the atombombs
 moloch whose soul is physical fire moloch whose
conceptions are dreary

6: ["bringer of" x-ed out]   18: ["heart is indus[trial(?)] x-ed out]   22: the

moloch the man who interviewed me at the draftb

oard moloch for whom I sit lonely at the

typewriter moloch in whom I am homosexual moloch

in whom I am guilty moloch in whom I suffer mol

moloch in ~~whose xxx~~ whom I am nightmare moloch

in whom
in whom I am mad moloch ~~in whom my~~ my mind has

abandoned itself moloch in whom we are mad mol

moloch in whom we are lovelorn moloch in whom

we live like dreams moloch for whome we are

fools moloch who entered our souls early

moloch from whom we waken in streaming
in
light from heaven moloch whom we hide moloch

whom we abandon with tears of pity & suffering

moloch that nurders the world moloch that stares

like a blind abysmal barren bleak beliefless

hellish god out of the win dows of the sirfrancis

dRake twoweyed god whose windows are lavatories

wwhose nose is a barroom and whose teeth are

the rooms of businessmen pulling million dollar

international deals and running the world.

Molich in whom I am a consciousness without

a body.

Moloch in whom I sit lonely: Moloch in whom I am gddd

guilty: Moloch in whom I dream of angels: Moloch

in whom I am a hysterical fairy moloch in whom I

amd a nut moloch in whom I make insane prophecies

moloch in whom I am hopeless moloch of whivh I pseak

lightly moloch which is the lawyer moloch which is

my madness moloch in which I typewrite moloch in whom

I stare at the streets moloch in which I walk down

by the river moloch in whom I wander and stare at

rosebushes moloch wherein I fuck up moloch wherein I

cant get a hardom moloch what has me by the balls

moloch in whom I am manless moloch who gives me no

angel moloch who I give an angel moloch in whicj

I am my own angel moloch in whom I fall in the

battleship moloch whose broken glasses I wear moloch

whose anesthesia and e ther I sip moloch where my love

is empty and eccentri c moloch where my love is a

void moloch in which I go to the hopspital to be anal

ysed moloch in whom I vomit moloch in whom I stare at

rosebushes moloch in which I eat garbage moloch in

which I ocook garbage moloch in which I hitchike.

Moloch whose name is America! Moloch whose poverty is the makes

spectre of genius! Moloch whose insanity is justice!

Moloch whose name is Chicago! Moloch whose name is demo-

cracy! Moloch whose name is the Mind!

Moloch whose mind is pure machinery! Moloch whose fingers

are armies! Moloch whose genitals are financial!

Moloch whose cock is the Washington Monument!

Moloch whose love is endless oil and stone! Moloch whose

amen

soul is physical fire! Moloch whose dream is Apocalypse!

Moloch in whom I sit lonely! Moloch in whom I am guilty!

I am mad!   I suffer

Moloch in whom I suffer madness! Moloch in whom

we are lovelorn in eternity!

my   I

Moloch who enters our souls early! Moloch in whom we hide!

I

Moloch whome we abandon in tears of pity and fright!

I

Moloch who murders the world! Moloch from whom we

waken in light streaming down from heaven!

broken

Moloch! Moloch! breaking our backs lifting moloch to

heaven! Pavements, trees, radios, tons! Lifting

the cities to Heaven which exists

and is everywhere!

Moloch! Moloch! Robot apartments! invisible suburbs!

skeleton treasuries! blind capitols! ghostly

bureaucracies! bloodie industries! invincible

madhouses! granite cock! Monsterous bombs!

1: makes
9: ["dream" canceled] amen
11: I am mad! . . . I suffer
12: ["we are" canceled]

13: ["our" canceled] my . . . ["we" canceled] I
16: ["down" canceled]
17: broken ["my" canceled]

What spxinx of cement and aluminum bashed open their
    skulls and ate up their brains and imagination?

Moloch! Solitude! Filth! Ugliness! Ashcans and unob-
    tainable dollars! Garbage heap of eyebrows
    and brains! Children weeping under the stair-
    ways! Boys sobbing in armies! Old men weeping
    in the parks!

Moloch! Moloch! Nightmare of Moloch! Moloch the loveless!
    Moloch the mental! Moloch the heavy judger of
    men! Moloch the Avenger!

Moloch the economic monolith! Moloch the electrical
    prison! Moloch the incomprehensible Congress!

Moloch whose buildings are judgement! Moloch the vast
    stone of war! Moloch the stunned kingdoms!

Moloch in whom we are a consciousness without a body!
    Moloch the slaughterer of sheep! Moloch the
    slaughterer of men! Moloch the crucifier of a
    billion Christs! Moloch the bodiless God!

Moloch whose eyes are a thousand blind windows! Moloch
    whose apartments stand in the streets like
    endless dead Jehovahs!

Moloch whose name is America! Moloch whose poverty
    is the spectre of genius! Moloch whose name
    is Chicago! Moloch whose name is democracy!
    Moloch whose name is the Mind!

Moloch whose head is pure machinery! Moloch whose
    fingers are armies! Moloch whose cock is

5: Screaming   11: of sorrow . . . avenger   17: slaughter
10: ["heartless" canceled] 14: governments!

the Washington Monument!

Moloch whose love is endless stone and oil! Moloch
          Moloch whose eyes are the atom bombs!
       whose soul is physical fire!/Moloch whose

       omen is Apocalypse!

Moloch in whom we sit lonely! Moloch in whom we are

       guilty! Moloch in whom we suffer insanity!

       Moloch in whom we are lovelorn in eternity!

Moloch who enters our souls early! Moloch in whom

       we hide! Moloch whom we abandon in tears of

       pity and fright! Moloch from whom we waken

       in light streaming from heaven!

Moloch! Moloch! robot apartments! invisible suburbs!

       skeleton treasuries! blind capitols! ghostly

       bureaucracies! bloody industries! invincible

       madhouses! granite cocks! monsterous bombs!

Moloch whose mind is pure machinery! Moloch whose
        blood is green money! Moloch whose fingers
        are armies! Moloch whose ear is the tomb!
Moloch whose love is endless oil and stone! Moloch
        whose soul is physical fire! Moloch whose
        illuminations are atomic bombs! Moloch whose
        omen is ~~omenzis~~ Apocalypse!
Moloch in whom I sit lonely! Moloch in whom I am
        guilty!

7: ["omen is" x-ed out]

What sphinx of cement and aluminum knocked open their
        skulls and ate up their brains and imagination?
Moloch! Solitude! Beatness! Filth! Ugliness! Ashcans
        and unobtainable dollars! Garbage heap of eyebrows
        and brains! Children screaming under the stair-
        ways! Boys sobbing in armies! Old men weeping
        in the parks!
Moloch! Moloch! Nightmare of Moloch! Moloch the loveless!
        Moloch the mental! Moloch the heavy judger of men!
        Moloch the soulless! Moloch the Avenger!
Moloch the vision of the radio! Moloch the lawful Congress!
        Moloch the ponderous dollar!
Moloch the sexless monarch! Moloch the powerful marriage!
        Moloch the heartless monolithic magazine of Time!
Moloch the incomprehensible prison! Moloch the electrical
        gallows! Moloch the *sorrowful* ~~fearful~~ Congress!
Moloch *which are* the buildings of judgement! Moloch the vast stone
        of war! Moloch the stunned kingdoms!
Moloch in whom we are a consciousness without a body!
        Moloch the deathless governments! Moloch the
        flags of the nations! Moloch the builder of hell!
Moloch the invisible mental jury! Moloch the slaughterer
        of mankind! Moloch the crucifier of a billion
        Christs! Moloch the bodiless God!
Moloch whøxøx the god whose eyes are a thousand blind
        windows! Moloch whose apartments stand in the
        streets like *endless* ~~mad lonely~~ Jehovahs!

13: ["monarch" canceled]   17: whose [buildings] are   27: ["mad lonely" canceled] endless
16: sorrowful   25: ["whose" x-ed out] ["the god" canceled]

Moloch whose mind is pure machinery! Moloch whose
        blood is money! Moloch whose fingers are
        armies! Moloch whose ear is the tomb!
Moloch whose love is endless oil and stone! Moloch
        whose soul is physical fire! Moloch whose
        death is the atomic bomb! Moloch whose star
        is apocalypse!
Moloch in whom I sit lonely! Moloch in whom I am
        guilty! Moloch in whom I am crazy! Moloch
        in whom I am lovelorn!
Moloch who entered my soul early! Moloch in whom I
        hide! Moloch whom I abandon in tears of fright!
        Moloch who murders the world! Moloch from
        whom I waken in light streaming down from
        Heaven!
Moloch! Moloch! robot apartments! invisible suburbs!
        skeleton treasuries! blind capitals! ghostly
        bureaucracies! mournful industries! invincible
        madhouses! granite cocks! monsterous bombs!
Breaking their backs lifting Moloch to Heaven! pave-
        ments, trees, radios, tons! lifting the cities
        to Heaven
which exists and is everywhere!

-------Visions! omens! hallucinations! miracles! ecstasies!
        Gone down the American river.

What sphinx of cement and aluminum cracked open their
skulls and ate up their brains and imagination?

Moloch! Solitude! Filth! Ugliness! Ashcans and
unobtainable dollars! Garbage heap of eyebrows
and brains! Children screaming under the
stairways! Boys sobbing in armies! Old men
weeping in the parks!

Moloch! Moloch! Nightmare of Moloch! Moloch the
loveless! Mental Moloch! Moloch the heavy
judger of men!

Moloch the heartless monolith in naked Time! (Moloch
the incomprehensible prison! Moloch the
Congress of sorrows!

Moloch in whom I am a consciousness without a body!
Moloch whose buildings are judgement! Moloch
the vast stone of war! Moloch the stunned
governments!

Moloch the builder of hell! Moloch the slaughterer
of sheep! Moloch the slaughterer of a
billion Christs! Moloch the bodiless God!

Moloch whose name is America! Moloch whose name
is Russia! Moloch whose name is Chicago!

Moloch whose name is the Mind!

14: we are

II

What sphinx of cement and aluminum cracked open their
        skulls and ate up their brains and imagination?
Moloch! Solitude! Filth! Ugliness! Ashcans and unob-
        tainable dollars! Garbage heap of eyebrows
        and brains! Children screaming under the
        stairways! Boys sobbing in armies! Old men
        weeping in the parks!
Moloch! Moloch! Nightmare of Moloch! Moloch the
        loveless! Mental Moloch! Moloch the heavy
        judger of men!
Moloch the skull monolith! Moloch the crossbone
        congress and prison! Moloch whose buildings
        are judgement! Moloch the vast stone of war!
        Moloch the stunned govenments!
Moloch the slaughterer of men! Moloch the consumer
        of a billion Christs! Moloch the builder
        of Hell! Moloch the bodiless God!
Moloch whose name is the Mind! Moloch whose eyes are
        a thousand blind windows! Moloch whose sky-
        scrapers stand on the streets like endless
        Jehovahs! Moloch whose smokestacks and antennae
        crown ~~the~~ cities!

11: Granite [skull]ed   22: ["the" canceled, "all," as annotation, canceled]

Moloch whose mind is greasy machinery! Moloch whose
        blood is running money! Moloch whose fingers
        are ten armies! Moloch whose ear is a smoking
        tomb!

Moloch whose love is endless oil and stone! Moloch whose
        soul is electricity and banks! Moloch whose fate
        is a cloud of sexless hydrogen! Moloch whose
        star is Apocalypse!

Moloch in whom I sit lonely! Moloch in whom I dream
        Angels! Crazy in Moloch! Cocksucker in Moloch!
        Lacklove and manless in Moloch!

Moloch who entered my soul early! Moloch whom I abandon!
        Moloch who murders the world! ~~Moloch I wake in!~~
        Light streaming out of the sky! *Wake up in Moloch!*

13: Wake up in Moloch!

II

What sphinx of cement and aluminum bashed open their
skulls and ate up their brains and imagination?

Moloch! Solitude! Filth! Ugliness! Ashcans and unob-
tainable dollars! Garbage heap of eyebrows and
brains! Children screaming under the stairways!
Boys sobbing in armies! Old men weeping in the
parks!

Moloch! Moloch! Nightmare of Moloch! Moloch the loveless!
Mental Moloch! Moloch the heavy judger of men!

Moloch the granite-skull~~ed monolith~~ *monument*! Moloch the crossbone
Congress and prison! Moloch whose buildings
are judgement! Moloch the vast stone of war!
Moloch the stunned governments!

Moloch ~~the~~ consumer of mankind! Moloch the slaughterer
of a billion Christs! Moloch the builder of Hell!
Moloch the bodiless God!

~~Moloch whose name is the Mind!~~ Moloch whose eyes are
a thousand blind windows! Moloch whose sky-
scrapers stand in the streets like endless
Jehovahs! Moloch whose smokestacks and antennae
crown ~~the~~ cities!

10: ["[skull]ed" canceled] monument   17: ["Moloch whose name is the Mind!" canceled]
14: ["the" canceled]   21: ["the" canceled]

Moloch whose mind is pure machinery! Moloch whose
        blood is running money! Moloch whose fingers
        are ten armies! Moloch whose ear is a smoking
        tomb!

Moloch whose love is endless oil and stone! Moloch
        whose soul is electricity and banks! Moloch
        whose fate is a cloud of sexless hydrogen!
        Moloch whose star is Apocalypse!

Moloch in whom I sit lonely! Moloch in whom I dream
        Angels! Crazy in Moloch! Cocksucker in Moloch!
        Lacklove and manless in Moloch!

Moloch who entered my soul early! Moloch ~~which~~ who
        burned down my springtime! ~~Moloch in whom~~
        ~~I am a consciousness without a body!~~ Moloch
        who murders the world! Moloch whom I abandon!
        Wake up in Moloch! Light streaming out of
        the sky!

Moloch! Moloch! Robot apartments! invisible suburbs!
        skeleton treasuries! blind capitals! ghostly
        bureaucracies! ~~ghostly industries~~ demonic mills! spectral
        nations! invincible madhouses! granite cocks!
        monsterous bombs!

12: ["which" canceled] who
20: demonic mills

Moloch! Moloch! breaking their backs lifting Moloch
    to Heaven! Pavements, trees, radios, tons!
    lifting the city to Heaven
Which exists and is everywhere!

Visions! omens! hallucinations! miracles! ecstasies!
    gone down the American river!
Dreams! adorations! illuminations! religions! the whole
    boatload of sensitive bullshit!
Break-throughs! over the river! Flips and crucifixions!
    gone down the flood! Highs! epiphanies! ten years'
    animal screams and suicides! Minds! new loves!
    # Mad generation! down on the rocks of time!
Real holy laughter in the river! They saw it all!
    the wild eyes! the holy yells! They bade fare-
    well! they jumped off the roof! to solitude!
    waving! carrying flowers! Down to the river!
    into the street!

12: ["A" canceled] M[ad generation]s[!]

II

What sphinx of cement and aluminum bashed open their

skulls and ate up their brains and imagination?

Moloch! Solitude! Filth! Ugliness! Ashcans and unob-

tainable dollars! Garbageheap of eyebrows and

brains! Children screaming under the stairways!

Boys sobbing in armies! Old men weeping in the

parks!

Moloch! Moloch! Nightmare of Moloch! Moloch the love-

less! Mental Moloch! Moloch the heavy judger of

men!

Moloch the ~~great-skulled~~ incomprehensible prison!

Moloch the crossbone soulless jailhouse &

Congress of sorrows! Moloch the ~~Avenger~~

whose buildings are judgement! Moloch the

vast stone of war! Moloch the stunned govern-

ments!

Moloch whose eyes are a thousand blind windows! Moloch

whose ~~apartments~~ skyscrapers stand in the streets like endless

Jehovahs! ~~Moloch whose skyscrapers scream out~~

~~their rusty agony into the winter night!~~ Moloch

whose factories dream & croak in the fog!

Moloch whose smokestacks and antennae crown

~~the~~ cities!

18: skyscrapers   23: ["the" canceled]

Moloch whose mind is pure machinery! Moloch whose blood
is running money! Moloch whose belly is a cannibal
dynamo! ~~Moloch whose cock is the Washington
Monument!~~ Moloch whose fingers are ten armies!
Moloch whose ear is a smoking tomb!

Moloch whose love is endless oil and stone! ~~Moloch
whose poverty is the spectre of genius!~~ Moloch
whose soul is electricity and banks! Moloch
whose fate is a cloud of sexless hydrogen! Moloch
whose Star is Apocalypse!

Moloch whose name is the Mind! Moloch consumer of man-
kind! Moloch the slaughterer of a billion ~~sheep
of~~ Christ! Moloch the builder of Hell! Moloch
the bodiless God!

Moloch in whom I sit lonely! ~~Moloch in whom I am a
consciousness without a body!~~ Moloch in whom
I dream Angels! Crazy in Moloch! Cocksucker
in Moloch! Lacklove and manless in Moloch!

Moloch who entered my soul early! ~~Moloch who took away
joy as the bringer of Justice! Moloch who
burned down my Spring time!~~ Moloch our
~~merciless~~ Father! Moloch who murders the world!
Wake up in Moloch! Light streaming out of the
sky!

Moloch! Moloch! Robot apartments! invisible suburbs!
skeleton treasuries! blind capitols! ghostly
bureaucracies! spectral nations! demonic mills!
invincible madhouses! granite cocks! monsterous
bombs!

2: ["is" canceled] is   22: merciless
13: [Christ]s   26: [[gh]a[stly] canceled] [gh]o[stly]

Moloch who entered my soul early! Moloch in whom I am

    a consciousness without a body! Moloch in whom

    I sit lonely! Moloch in whom I dream Angels!

    Moloch who murders the world! Crazy in Moloch!

    Cocksucker in Moloch! Lacklove and manless in

    Moloch! Wake up in Moloch! Light streaming out

    of the sky!

N.B. This isolate draft attempts to condense corrections & resolve problems indicated for two verses (Draft 14) into one fat verse. Original sequence of exclamations was later restored, a few phrases eliminated, then verse divided in two again. —A.G.

II

What sphinx of cement and aluminum bashed open their

skulls and ate up their brains and imagination?

Moloch! Solitude! Filth! Ugliness! Ashcans and unob-

tainable dollars! Garbageheap of eyebrows and

brains! Children screaming under the stairways!

Boys sobbing in armies! Old men weeping in the

parks!

Moloch! Moloch! Nightmare of Moloch! Moloch the loveless!

Mental Moloch! Moloch the heavy judger of men!

Moloch the incomprehensible prison! Moloch the crossbone

soulless jailhouse and Congress of sorrows!

Moloch whose buildings are judgement! Moloch

the vast stone of war! Moloch the stunned gov-

ernments!

Moloch whose eyes are a thousand blind windows! Moloch

whose skyscrapers stand in the streets like

endless Jehovahs! Moloch whose factories ~~dream~~

~~&~~ croak in the fog! Moloch whose smokestacks and

antennae crown ^the^ cities!

Moloch whose mind is pure machinery! Moloch whose blood

is running money! ~~Moloch whose cock is the Wash-~~

~~ington Monument!~~ Moloch whose ~~belly's~~ ^~~heart~~ belly's^ a cannibal

dynamo! Moloch whose fingers are ten armies!

Moloch whose ear is a smoking tomb!

17: ["dream" canceled]   18: ["&" canceled]   19: the   22: ["belly's" canceled] ["heart" canceled] belly's

Moloch whose love is endless oil and stone! Moloch whose
soul is electricity and banks! ^poverty Moloch whose fate
is a cloud of sexless hydrogen! Moloch whose Star
is Apocalypse!

Moloch whose name is the Mind! Moloch consumer of man-
kind! Moloch the slaughterer of a billion Christs!
Moloch the builder of Hell! Moloch the bodiless
God!

Moloch in whom I sit lonely! Moloch in whom I dream
Angels! Crazy in Moloch! Cocksucker in Moloch!
Lacklove and manless in Moloch!

Moloch who entered my soul early! Moloch in whom I am
a consciousness without a body! Moloch who murders
the world! Moloch whom I abandon! ^Wake up in Moloch! Light streaming
out of the sky!

Moloch! Moloch! Robot apartments! invisible suburbs!
skeleton treasuries! blind capitals! ghostly
bureaucracies! spectral nations! demonic mills!
invincible madhouses! granite cocks! monsterous
bombs!

2: poverty   14: Moloch whom I abandon!

II

What sphinx of cement and aluminum bashed open their
        skulls and ate up their brains and imagination?
Moloch! Solitude! Filth! Ugliness! Ashcans and unob-
        tainable dollars! Garbageheap of eyebrows and
        brains! Children screaming under the stairways!
        Old men weeping in the parks!
Moloch! Moloch! Nightmare of Moloch! Moloch the love-
        less! Mental Moloch! Moloch the heavy judger
        of men!
Moloch the incomprehensible prison! Moloch the cross-
        bone soulless jailhouse and Congress of sorrows!
        Moloch whose buildings are judgement! Moloch
        the vast stone of war! Moloch the stunned gov-
        ernments!
Moloch whose eyes are a thousand blind windows! Moloch
                                    long
        whose skyscrapers stand in the/streets like
        endless Jehovahs! Moloch whose factories dream
        and croak in the fog! Moloch whose smokestacks
                            the
        & antennae crown cities!
                        ^

19: the

Moloch whose mind is pure machinery! Moloch whose blood
      is running money! Moloch whose fingers are ten
      armies! Moloch whose belly is a cannibal dynamo!
      Moloch whose ear is a smoking tomb!

Moloch whose love is endless oil and stone! Moloch
      whose soul is electricity and banks! Moloch
      whose poverty is the spectre of genius! Moloch
      whose fate is a cloud of sexless hydrogen!
      Moloch whose Star is Apocalypse!

Moloch in whom I sit lonely! Moloch in whom I dream
      Angels! Crazy in Moloch! Cocksucker in Moloch!
      Lacklove and manless in Moloch!

Moloch who entered my soul early! Moloch in whom I am
      a consciousness without a body! Moloch who burned
              Moloch whom I abandon!
      down the world!/Wake up in Moloch! Light stream-
      ing out of the sky!

Moloch whose name is the mind! Moloch consumer of man-
      kind! Moloch the builder of hell! Moloch the
      bodiless god!

Moloch Moloch Robot apartments Invisible suburbs skel-
      eton treasuries demonic mills blind capitals
      silent bureaucracies spectral nations invincible
      madhouses granite cocks monsterous bombs

II

What sphinx of cement and aluminum bashed open their
skulls and ate up their brains and imagination?

Moloch! Solitude! Filth! Ugliness! Ashcans and unob-
tainable dollars! Garbageheap of eyebrows and
brains! Children screaming under the stairways!
Old men weeping in the parks!

Moloch! Moloch! Nightmare of Moloch! Moloch the love-
less! Mental Moloch! Moloch the heavy judger
of men!

Moloch the incomprehensible prison! Moloch the crossbone
soulless jailhouse and Congress of sorrows!
Moloch whose buildings are judgement! Moloch
the vast stone of war! Moloch the stunned
governments!

Moloch whose eyes are a thousand blind windows! Moloch
whose skyscrapers stand in the long streets like
endless Jehovahs! Moloch whose factories dream
and creak in the fog! Moloch whose smokestacks
and antennae crown the cities!

Moloch whose mind is pure machinery! Moloch whose
          blood is running money! Moloch whose fingers
          are ten armies! Moloch whose breast i$_s$ a cannibal
          dynamo! Moloch whose ear is a smoking tomb!
Moloch whose love is endless oil and stone! Moloch
          whose soul is electricity and banks! Moloch
          whose poverty is the spectre of genius! Moloch
          whose fate is a cloud of sexless hydrogen!
Moloch whose name is the Mind! Moloch consumer of
          mankind! Moloch the builder of Hell! Moloch
          the bodiless God!
Moloch in whom I sit lonely! Moloch in whom I dream
          Angels! Crazy in Moloch! Cocksucker in Moloch!
          Lacklove and manless in Moloch!
Moloch who entered my soul early! Moloch in whom I am
          a consciousness without a body! Moloch who burned
          down the world! Moloch whom I abandon! Wake up
          in Moloch! Light streaming out of the sky!
Moloch! Moloch! Robot apartments! invisible suburbs!
          skeleton treasuries! demonic mills! blind
          capitals! cabalistic bureaucracies! spectral
          nations! invincible madhouses! granite cocks!
          monsterous bombs!

Guide to Original Manuscripts, Part III

Draft 1: This is the first stage of improvisation, retained mainly intact, rearranged. It was provisionally titled Part IV, for a time intended to follow "Footnote to Howl," now Part IV. Checks and crossouts were used to keep track of verses rearranged in third draft.

Draft 2: Fills out longish end of pyramid with thicker middle, & rearranges litany for progressively longer responses. Here it was opportune to expand this space to expound terms of spiritual revolution.

Draft 3: Consolidates phrasing & arranges the graduated litany in physical pyramid by eyeball order on one page, as in Schwitters' "Priimiitittiii" model (see p. 182).

Draft 4: Prior draft is revised & tightened, cleaned up, typed single space, and properly titled Part III.

Draft 5: Typed double space near final form.

IV

Carl Solomon!
I am with you in Rockland
        where the faculties of the skull no longer admit the worms
        of the senses
I am with you in Rockland
        where you drink the tea of the breast of the spinsters
        of Utica
I am with you in Rockland
        where you pun on the bodies of your nurses the harpies
        of the Bronx
I am with you in Rockland
        where you imitate the shade of my mother
I am with you in Rockland
        where thirtyfive shocks will never return your soul to its
        body from its pilgrimage in the void
I am with you in Rockland
        where you're madder than I am
I am with you in Rockland
        where you write only letters which are invisible
I am with you in Rockland
        where you wanted to be
where you laugh at this invisible humor

I am with you in Rockland
        where you may stay for the rest of your life
I am with you in Rockland
        where your condition has become serious and is reported
        over the radio
I am with you in Rockland
        where you knock dripping from a sea journey at the door
        of my cottage in the Western night
I am with you in Rockland
        where you have murdered your secretaries
I am with you in Rockland   Appollinaire
        where you play pingpong with Malcolm Chazal and ~~Christopher
        Smart~~
I am with you in Rockland
        where life is easy though you must feel very strange
I am with you in Rockland
        where there are twenty-five thousand mad comrades
        all singing the Internationale together
I am with you in Rockland
        where we are great writers ~~together~~ on the same
        dreadful typewriter
I am with you in Rockland
        where we hug and kiss the United States under our
        bedsheets, the United States that coughs all night,
        and won't let us sleep.

34: Appollinaire   42: ["together" canceled]

I am with you in Rocklaned   against
          where we plot a revolution &m the United States
I am with you in Rockland
          where we plan a new republic based on free money
          and magnanimity
I am with you in Rockland
          where we committ that old blind whore Justice once and for
          all and help young Mercy escape
I am with you in Rockland
          where we make(icecream and mercy for the) merciful icecream
          for the multitudes

I am with you in Rockland
          where xxxaccuse America of insanity and plot a revolution
          against the doctors of your Golgotha
I am with you in Rockland
          where you call for a new god to split the heavens of Long Island
          and ressurect your living body from the tomb
I am with you in Rockland where you walk dripping from a sea-journey
          on the highway to my cottage in the Western night
I am with you in Rockland
          where there are thirtyfive thousand mad comrades all together
          singing the Internationale
I am with you in Rockland
          where we hug and kiss the United States under our bedsheets, the
          United States that coughs all night, and won't let us sleep.

Carl Solomon!
I am with you in Rockland
    where you're madder than I am
I am with you in Rockland
    where you'll stay for the rest of your life
I am with you in Rockland
    where you must feel very strange
I am with you in Rockland
    where you laugh at this invisible humor
I am with you in Rockland
    where you have murdered your secretaries
I am with you in Rockland
    where you imitate the shade of my mother
I am with you in Rockland
    where your condition has become serious and is reported on the
    radio
I am with you in Rockland
    where we are great writers on the same dreadful typewriter
I am with you in Rockland
    where fifty shocks will never again return your soul to its body
    from a pilgrimage in the void
I am with you in Rockland
    where you play pingpong with William Appollinaire and Chris-
    topher Smart
I am with you in Rockland
    where the faculties of the skull no longer admit the worms
    of the senses
I am with you in Rockland
    where you drink the tea of the breasts of the spinsters of
    Utica
I am with you in Rockland where
    where you pun on the bodies of your nurses the harpies of the
    Bronx
I am with you in Rockland
    where you accuse your doctors of insanity and plot the final
    revolution against the national Golgotha
I am with you in Rockland
    where we hug and kiss the United States under our bedsheets,
    the United states that coughs all night, and won't let us sleep
I am with you in Rockland
    where there are thirtyfive thousand mad comrades all together
    singing the final stanzas of the Internationale
I am with you in Rockland/where you will split the heavens of Long
    Island and resurrect your living human Jesus from the tomb
I am with you in Rockland where you walk
    where you walk in my dreams, dripping from a sea-journey, on
    the highway across America in tears, to the door of my cottage
    in the Western night.

5: [you]'ll
23: with the [canceled] the actual pingpong of the abyss

35: existentialism atheism
44: living

Carl Solomon! I'm with you in Rockland
    where you're madder than I am
I'm with you in Rockland
    where you must feel very strange
I'm with you in Rockland
    where you laugh at this invisible humor
I'm with you in Rockland
    where you imitate the shade of my mother
I'm with you in Rockland
    where you've murdered your 12 secretaries
I'm with you in Rockland
    where your condition has become serious and is reported
    on the radio
I'm with you in Rockland
    where we are great writers on the same dreadful typewriter
I'm with you in Rockland
    where the faculties of the skull no longer admit the worms
    of the senses
I'm with you in Rockland
    where you drink the tea of the breasts of the spinsters of
    Utica
I'm with you in Rockland
    where you pun on the bodies of your nurses the harpy magdalines
    of the Bronx
I'm with you in Rockland
    where fifty more shocks will return your soul to its body again
    from its pilgrimage to a cross in the void
I'm with you in Rockland
    where you scream in a straightjacket that you're losing the game
    of the actual pingpong of the abyss
I'm with you in Rockland
    where you accuse your doctors of insanity and plot the Hebrew
    socialist rebellion against the facist national Golgotha
I'm with you in Rockland
    where you will split the heavens of Long Island and resurrect
    your living human Jesus from the superhuman tomb
I'm with you in Rockland
    where there are thirtyfive-thousand mad comrades all together
    singing the final stanzas of the Internationale
I'm with you in Rockland
    where we hug and kiss the United States under our bedsheets,
    the United States that coughs all night, and won't let us sleep
I'm with you in Rockland
    in my dreams you walk dripping from a sea-journey on the highway
    across America in tears to the door of my cottage in the Western
    night.

III

Carl Solomon! I'm with you in Rockland

>> where you're madder than I am

I'm with you in Rockland

>> where you must feel very strange

I'm with you in Rockland

>> where you laugh at this invisible humor

I'm with you in Rockland

>> where you imitate the shade of my mother

I'm with you in Rockland

>> where you have murdered your 12 secretaries

I'm with you in Rockland

>> where your condition has become serious and is
>> reported on the radio

I'm with you in Rockland

>> where we are great writers on the same dread-
>> ful typewriter

I'm with you in Rockland

>> where the faculties of the skull no longer
>> admit the worms of the senses

I'm with you in Rockland

>> where you drink the tea of the breasts of
>> the spinsters of Utica

I'm with you in Rockland

>> where you pun on the bodies of your nurses
>> the harpies of the bronx

I'm with you in Rockland

    where fifty more shocks will never return

    your soul to its body again from its pil-

    grimage to a cross in the void

I'm with you in Rockland

    where you scream in a straightjacket that

    you're losing the game of the actual ping-

    pong of the abyss

I'm with you in Rockland

    where you accuse your doctors of insanity

    and plot the Hebrew socialist rebellion

    against the ~~capitalist~~ *Facist* national Golgotha

I'm with you in Rockland

    where you will split the Heavens of Long

    Island and resurrect your living human

    Jesus from the superhuman tomb

I'm with you in Rockland

    where there are thirty-five-thousand mad

    comrades all together singing the final

    stanzas of the Internationale

I'm with you in Rockland

    where we ~~scream~~ *howl* and dance on the piano

    of spiritual knowledge the soul is inn-

    ocent and immortal ~~and~~ *it* will never die

    ungodly in an armed madhouse

12: Facist   22: howl   24: it

Guide to Original Manuscripts, Part IV (Footnote)

Draft 1: This handscript is the original improvisation, date uncertain, probably written after public reading of Part I. The basic cadence, diction & phrasings are set, all extravagance driving toward redemption.

Draft 2: Begins with 14 "Holy"s, adds prefatory generic blessings, moving from World to bodily parts. Verse 13, adding "voice" and "audience," may refer to 6 Gallery reading. Then personal names and local underground imagery (junky cafeterias, etc.) are set in place, then international panoramic generalizations, "Skyscrapers & Antiquities." Some arrangement of form's begun.

Draft 3: The matter's condensed, beginning with 15 "Holy"s, for continuity of cadence, climaxed with three rolling locomotive comma-less exclamatory verses.

Draft 4: Phrasing boiled down to nonrepetitive usable concepts, the opening is cleaned up, but sequence gets stuck at the end. Bottom page, 15 vertical lines count the "Holy"s into one set of 3 and three sets of 4—upbeat 4/4 time with accented last syllable. If analyzed according to classical meters as suggested by scholar Ed Sanders, its primary reading is catalectic first paeonic tetrameter: a paean to Sacred World. Alternately, it can be read as five sets of 3 trochaic "Holy"s, with heavier stress varying from first to third trochee of each set; and heaviest stress of all on the last trochee of the fifth & last set of "Holy"s.

Draft 5: Lines have been arranged to strophic verse, sets of equivalent phrases grouped together more logically than before. Use of slightly longer verse than in original draft allows separation out of basic ideas, concepts, "angles," in this typescript.

Handscript completes the rhythmic run; this is the first notation of last verse. Kerouac's phrasings "Kind King Mind" (*Mexico City Blues*, 5th chorus) and "Adios, King" (last line of *Visions of Cody*, referring to Neal Cassady) are echoed.

Draft 6: Retyped double spaced & revised, with new key phrases invented: "hideous human angels," "mysterious rivers of tears under the streets," etc.

Draft 7: This final retype cleans up several single-word revisions and transpositions. A few phrases (of verse 11, oddly characterizing author's appearance, Beijing 1984) are omitted in published version.

Holy Peter Holy Allen Holy Kerouac Holy Huncke
Holy the Numberless & the unknown beggars & bums
Holy the hipsters Holy the Tender Criminals
Holy the Damned Holy the Saved! Holy the Holy
Holy the Turks and the Cows Holy the Idiots
Holy the heavens & the pavements! Holy the Cafeterias
Holy the Dayglooms Holy the Marijuana Holy the Saxophones!
Holy the Tankies Holy the Tuna Holy the Needle
Holy the pants! Holy the babies! Holy the Reefer
Holy the lovers! Holy the fucking! Holy the Queers Holy cocksucking,
Holy, Forgiveness! Mercy! Love! Charity! Faith! Helplessness
Holy ourselves are beggars
Holy the Juggernaut Holy the Murders Holy the Moloch
Holy the vast Middleclasses Holy the bitters & holy the rebellions
Holy Rebellions! Holy Skyscrapers & Antiquities Holy the millions
Holy NY Holy SF Holy Paris Holy Tangier Holy Istanbul
Holy the Bastards   Holy Rome
Holy the Visions Holy the Hallucinations Holy the Void Holy Holy the abyss

Holy Time in Eternity Holy Eternity in Time
Holy the Clocks Holy Space Holy Infinity Holy the 4th dimension
Holy my mother in the insane asylum! Holy the cunt
Holy My father's cock Holy My cock & the Cocks of my lovers!
Holy the Cocks of the grandfathers of Kansas!
Holy the aeroplanes! Holy the heavens! Holy the pavements! Holy the Concrete
Holy the Sea Holy the Desert Holy the Railroad Holy the locomotive
Holy the endless disciples of Buddha Holy the Categories of beings Holy particulars

Holy the rumblings in my gut! Holy my shit in the toilet!
Holy the come on the tip of my cock! Holy the Cock in my mouth
Holy the Cock in my asshole Holy the Cock in between my legs.

Holy Peter Holy Allen Holy Kerouac Holy Huncke
Holy the numberless & the unknown beggars & bums
Holy the hipsters Holy the Junkies & Criminals
Holy the Damned Holy the Saved! Holy the Holy
Holy the Turks and the Cows Holy the Idiots
Holy the heavens & the pavements! Holy the cafeterias
Holy the Jazzbands Holy the Marijuana Holy the saxophones!
Holy the Junkies Holy the Junk Holy the Needle
Holy the Pants! Holy the babies! Holy the Diapers
Holy the lovers! Holy the fucking! Holy the Quers Holy Cocksucking.
Holy, Forgiveness! Mercy! Love! Charity! Faith! Magnanimity
    Holy Dimes to the beggars
Holy the Juggernaut Holy the Murders Holy the Moloch
Holy the vast Middleclasses Holy the Hitlers Holy the rebellios
Holy rebellions! Holy Skyscrapers & Antiquities Holy the millions
Holy NY Holy SF Holy Paris Holy Tangier Holy Istanbul
                                 Holy Rome
                                 Holy Lhasa
Holy the Bastards
Holy the Visions Holy the Hallucination Holy the Void Holy the abyss

Holy Time in Eternity Holy Eternity in Time
Holy the Clocks Holy Space Holy Infinity Holy the Cunt   4th Dimension
Holy my Mother in the insane asylum! Holy the Cunt
Holy My father's cock Holy My cock & The Cocks of my lovers!
Holy the Cocks of the grandfathers of Kansas!
Holy the aeroplanes! Holy the Heavens! Holy the Pavements! Holy the Concrete
Holy the Sea Holy the Desert Holy the Railroad Holy the locomotive
Holy the endless disciples of Bhudda Holy the Catagories of beings Holy
                                    Particulars

Holy the rumblings in my gut! holy my shit in the toilet!
Holy the come on the tip of my cock! Holy the Cock in my mouth
Holy the Cock in my asshole Holy the Cock in between my legs

Holy! holy! holy! holy! holy! holy! holy!
holy! holy! holy! holy! holy! holy! holy!
The World is holy! the soul is holy!
The skin is holy; the nose is holy
the hand is holy! the eyeball holy!
The ~~nose~~ and cock and ears and asshole holy!

Everything is holy! everybody's holy everyone's an angel
Everywhere is heaven Everyplace is paradise
~~Every every is a seraph every everyness is God~~
          man

The pig is holy as the seraphim is holy
The bum is holy as you my soul are holy
The notebook is holy The poem is holy
the voice is holy the addience is holy the typewriter is holy

          Solomon Carl
Holy ~~Peter~~ Holy Allen Holy Kerouac Holy Huncke
Holy the numberless unknown beggars and bums
Holy the hipsters Holy the Junkies and Criminals
(~~Holy the Damned Holy the Saved! Holy the Holy!~~)
(~~Holy the Turks and the Cows! Holy the Idiots~~)
Holy the heavens and the pavements! Holy the cafeterias
Holy the Jazzbands holy the Marijuana Holy the Saxophones!
Holy the Junkies Holy the Junk Holy the Needle
(~~Holy the pants! Holy the babies! Holy the diapers!~~)
                                                    the
Holy the lovers! Holy the fucking! ~~Holy the Queers!~~ Holy cocksucking
~~Holy,~~ Forgiveness! Mercy! Love! Charity! Faith! Magnanimity!
~~Holy dimes to the beggars~~
Holy the Juggernauts Holy the Murders Holy the Moloch
Holy the vast Middleclass ~~Holy the Hitlers Holy the rebellious~~
Holy Rebellions! Holy Skyscrapers & Antiquities Holy the Millions
Holy NY Holy SF Holy Paris Holy Tangiers Holy Istanbul Holy Rome
~~Holy the Bastards~~
Holy the visions Holy the Hallucinations Holy the Void Holy the
                                        ~~Holy vast~~ abyss

⌈Holy Time in Eternity Holy Eternity in Time
⌊Holy the clocks Holy Space Holy Infinity Holy ~~the Cunt~~ 4th Dimens
                                                          ion

Holy my mother in the insane asylum! ~~Holy the Cunt~~
~~Holy my father's cock Holy my cock and the cocks of my lovers!~~
Holy the cocks of the grandfathers of Kansas!
Holy the aeroplanes! Holy the Heavens! Holy the pavements! Holy
                                              the concrete
Holy the sea Holy the desert Holy the railroad Holy the locomotive
~~Holy the endless disciples of Buddha Holy the Categories of Beings~~
                              Holy particulars
~~Holy the rumblings in my gut! Holy the shit in my toilet!~~
Holy the come on the tip of my cock! ~~Holy the cock in my mouth!~~
~~Holy the cock in my asshole~~ Holy the cock in between my legs.

Holy!

9: man   14: Solomon [canceled] Carl   23: the   43: [insert] Holy

Holy! Holy! holy! holy! holy! holy! holy!
Holy! Holy! Holy! holy! holy! holy! holy! holy!
The World is Holy! the soul is holy!
The skin is holy! the ~~nose~~ is holy! *the madman is holy!*
~~The madman is holy! the sane man is holy!~~
The tongue and cock and ears and asshole holy!
Everything is holy! everybody's holy! everyone's an angel!
Everywhere is heaven! Everyday's eternity! everyman is god!
The pig is holy as the seraphim is holy!
The bum is holy as you my soul are holy!
The notebook is holy the typewriter is holy the poem is holy
the voice is holy the audience is holy the ecstasy is holy
Solomon is holy Allen is Holy Kerouac is Holy Huncke is holy
Holy the unknown numberless beggars and bums
Holy the hipsters holy the jazzbands holy the ~~Junkies~~ *Marijuani*
~~Holy the fuckers holy the marijuana holy~~ the saxophones
Holy my mother in the insane asylum holy the cocks of the
                    grandfathers of Kansas
Holy the heavens and the pavements holy the cafeterias
Holy the Jauggernauts holy the vast middleclass holy the rebellions
Holy the millions holy the skyscrapers holy the moloch holy the
~~Holyxthexnationsxholyxthexseasxholyxthexdesertsxholyxthe~~
                              Nations
Holy ~~the~~ NY holy SF holy Paris HolyTangiers holy Jerusalem holy
                              Istanbul
Holy the visions holy the hallucinations holythe Omens holy the
                              abyss
Holy Time in Eternity Holy Eeternity in Time holy the clocks
      ~~holyxspacexholy~~ in space holy the Foubth Dimension
Holyforgiveness holy mercy holy love holycharity faith magnanimity
        holy the soul!

4: skin . . . the madman is holy!   15: marijuana

Holy! Holy! holy! Holy! holy! holy! Holy!
Holy! holy! holy! holy! holy! holy! holy!
The world is holy! the soul is holy! the body holy!
The nose is holy! the hand is holy! the eyeball holy!
The cock and tongue and ears and dreams are holy!
Everything is holy! everybody's holy! everyone's an angel!
Everywhere is heaven ! everyplace is Paradise! everytime eternity
Everyman's a seraph! Everyday is Eden! Everynight eternity!
The sufferer is holy as the seraphim are holy!
The saint is holy the bum is holy as you my soul are holy!
The notebook is holy the typewriter is holy the poem is holy
the voice is holy the audience is holy the ecstasy is holy
Holy Solomon Holy Allen Holy Kerouac Holy Huncke
Holy the numberless unknown beggars and bums
Holy the hipsters holy the Junkies Holy the Junk & the Needle
Holy the jazzbands Holy their Marijuana Holy their Saxophones
Holy the lovers! Holy the fucking Holy the cocksucking
Holy my mother in the insane asylum! Holy the cocks of the
                                    Grandfathers of Kansas!
Holy the juggernauts! Holy the vast middleclass! Holy the Moloch!
Holy the Rebbellions! Holy the skyscrapers! Holy the Millions!
Holy NY Holy SF Holy Paris Holy Tangiers Holy Istanbul Holy China
Holy the visions! Holy the Hallucinations! Holy the void Abyss!
Holy the Heavens! Holy the Aeroplanes! Holy the Sea! Holy the
                                    Concrete!
Holy the pavements! Holy the desert! Holy the RR! Holy the
                                    locomotive!
Holy the endless disciples of Buddha! Holy the cafeterias!

IV

Holy! holy! holy! holy! holy! holy! holy! holy! holy!
holy! holy! holy! holy! holy! holy!
The world is holy! the skin is holy! the nose is holy!
the hand is holy! the tongue and cock and ears
and asshole holy!
Everything is holy! everybody's holy! everywhere is heaven!
everyday is in eternity! everyman is angel!
The madman is holy as the seraphim is holy! The bum is holy
as you my soul are holy!
The notebook is holy the tyepewriter is holy the poem is holy
the voice is holy the ecstasy is holy the audience
is holy!
Holy Solomon Holy Allen Holy Kerouac Holy Cassady Holy Lucien
holy Burroughs holy Huncke holy the unknown numberless
suffering beggars and angels!
Holy the hipsters holy the jazzbands holy themarijuana holy
the junkies holy the saxophones!
Holy my mother in the insane asylum! Holy the cocks of the
grandfathers of Kansas!
Holy the heavens and the pavements! holy the cafeterias and
the millions!
Holy the juggernauts holy the vast middleclass holy the rebellious
holy thskyscrapers holy the moloch!
Holy the nations holy NY holy SF Holy Paris holy Tangiers holy
Jerusalem holy Istanbul!
Holy time in eternity holy eternity in time holy the clocks
in space holy the fourth dimension!
Holy the visions holy the hallucinations holy the intelligence
holy the omens holy the abyss!
Holy forgiveness ~~holy~~ mercy! ~~holy~~ love! ~~holy~~ charity ~~holy~~ faith!
~~holy~~ magnanimity! ~~holy the soul!~~

~~Holy the supernatural excess brilliant kindness of the kindly brilliance extra brilliant kindness of the soul!~~
natural natural

Holy the supernatural ~~natural~~ extra brilliant intelligent
intelligent kindness of the Soul!

30–31: Holy the supernatural excess ["excess" canceled, replaced by:] natural brilliant kindness of the ["brilliant kindness of the" canceled, replaced by:] kindly brilliance of the soul! ["brilliant kindness of the" replaced by:] extra brilliant kindness intelligent [inserted between "brilliant" and "kindness" [Entire line canceled, replaced by:] Holy the supernatural natural extra brilliant intelligent kindness of the Soul! ["natural" canceled]

Holy! Holy! Holy! Holy! Holy!Holy! Holy! Holy!

    Holy! Holy! Holy! Holy!Holy! Holy! Holy!

The world is holy! the soul is holy! the skin is

    holy! the nose is holy! the head is holy! the

    tongue and cock and hand and asshole holy!

Everything is holy! everybody's holy! everywhere is *holy*

    h~~eaven~~! everyone is here! everyday is in

    eternity! everyman is angel!

The pig is holy as the seraphim! the madman is holy

    as you my soul are holy!

The notebook is holy the typewriter is holy the poem

    is holy the voice is holy the ecstasy is holy

    the hearer is holy!

Holy Peter holy Allen holy Solomon holy Lucien holy

    Kerouac holy Cassady holy Huncke holy Burroughs

    holy the unknown b~~u~~gg~~ered~~ and suffering bums!

    Holy the hideous human angels!

Holy my mother in the insane asylum! Holy the cocks

    of the grandfathers of Kansas!

Holy the groaning saxophones! Holy the bop apocal-

    ypse! Holy the ~~drunken~~ jazzbands marijuana

    hipsters peace & junk & drums!

Holy the solitude of skyscrapers and pavements!

    Holy the cafeterias and the millions! Holy

    the mysterious rivers of tears under the

    streets!

6: holy   16: [b]u[gg]ered

Holy the lone juggernaut! Holy the vast lamb of
the middle-class! Holy the crazy shepherds
of rebellion! Denver is lonesome for her
heroes!
Holy the glitter-eyed stranger digging the scene
in Peking! he's in a sexual China! and who
digs Los Angeles is Los Angeles!
Holy NY holy SF holy Paris holy ~~Jerusalem~~ holy
Tangiers holy Moscow holy Istanbul!
Holy Time in Eternity holy Eternity in Time holy
the clock in space holy the Fourth Dimension
holy the Angel in Moloch!
Holy the sea holy the desert holy the railroad holy
the locomotive holy the visions holy the omens
holy the hallucinations holy the miracles holy
the abyss!
Holy forgiveness! mercy! charity! faith! holy! ours!
bodies! suffering! magnanimity!
Holy the supernatural extra brilliant intelligent
kindness of the soul!

III

Holy! Holy! Holy! Holy! Holy! Holy! Holy! Holy!
      Holy! Holy! Holy! Holy! Holy! Holy! Holy!
The world is holy! The soul is holy! the skin is
      holy! the nose is holy! the heart is holy!
      the head is holy! the tongue and cock and
      hand and asshole holy!
Everything is holy! everybody's holy! everywhere
      is holy! everyman is here! everyday's eternity!
      everyone's an angel!
The bum is holy as the seraph! the madman is holy
      as you my soul are holy!
The notebook is holy the typewriter is holy the poem
      is holy the voice is holy the hearer is holy
      the ecstasy is holy!
Holy Peter holy Allen holy Kerouac holy Solomon holy
      Lucien holy Cassady holy Burroughs holy Huncke
      holy the unknown buggered and suffering beggars!
      Holy the hideous human angels!
Holy my mother in the insane asylum! Holy the cocks of
      the grandfathers of Kansas!
Holy the groaning saxophone! Holy the bop apocalypse!
      Holy the jazzbands marijuana hipsters peace &
      junk & drums!
Holy the solitude of skyscrapers & pavements! Holy
      the cafeterias and the millions! Holy the
      mysterious rivers of tears under the streets!

Holy the lone juggernaut! Holy the vast lamb of the
        middle class! Holy the crazy shepherds of
        rebellion! Denver is lonesome for her heroes!
Holy the glitter-eyed stranger digging the scene in
        Peking! he's in a sexual China! and who digs
        Los Angeles IS Los Angeles!
Holy NY holy SF holy Paris holy Hutchinson & Bellingham
        holy Tangiers holy Moscow holy Istanbul!
Holy time in eternity holy eternity in time holy
        the clocks in space holy the fourth dimension
        holy the fifth International holy the Angel
        in Moloch!
Holy the sea holy the desert holy the railroad holy
        the locomotive holy the visions holy the omens
        holy the hallucinations holy the miracles holy
        the eyeball holy the abyss!
Holy forgiveness! mercy! charity! faith! Holy! Ours!
        bodies! suffering! magnanimity! Holy the
        supernatural extra brilliant intelligent kindness
        of the soul!

CARL SOLOMON SPEAKS

Carl Solomon in his apartment, New York, circa 1953, several years after residence with author at N.Y. Psychiatric Institute, newly working at Ace Books editing W. S. Burroughs' *Junkie.* *Photo by A.G.*

Carl Solomon on his favorite Sunday outing, fishing under City Island bridge, N.Y., Summer 1983. *Photo by A.G.*

Reintroduction to Carl Solomon

Here the personage whose name was taken as the mythical dedicatee of "Howl: For Carl Solomon" steps forth. The poem was written in relative literary obscurity in a room on Montgomery Street, in North Beach, San Francisco; I dedicated it to Mr. Solomon by name and didn't have any clear idea that the poem would make its way around the world and proclaim a private reference to public attention. The first printing of 1,000 copies imported from England gave no promise of celebrity to the author or Carl Solomon outside a small circle of witty understanding readers in sophisticated poetry circles of the Bay Area mid 1950s.

Mr. Solomon had recently returned to a mental hospital 3,000 miles away on the East Coast, and I was heart-struck at what seemed his hopeless impasse.

As the poem accumulated public force, the private mythology bandied about between Mr. Solomon and myself solidified as an image notorious on a quasi-national scale. This had unexpected consequences: it put Mr. Solomon's actual person in the world with my stereotype—a poetic metaphor—as a large part of his social identity. (Similarly, *On the Road* readers confuse the heroic fictional Dean Moriarty with his equally heroic prototype, Neal Cassady.) I came to regret my naive use of his name; Mr. Solomon himself bore the burden uneasily, and later was sorely tried by the situation. I am thankful for his sanity and generosity in this strange karmic friendship.

I hadn't realized all the consequences of the Word. I'd thought the poem a gesture of wild solidarity, a message into the asylum, a sort of heart's trumpet call, but was mistaken in my diagnosis of his "case" ("You're madder than I am"). In hindsight, his lifelong virtues of endurance, familial fidelity and ultimate balance make my appeal seem hysterical, myself overwrought, as in 1963 dream printed below.

Beyond that I'd used Mr. Solomon's return to the asylum as occasion of a masque on my feelings toward my mother, in itself an ambiguous situation since I had signed the papers giving permission for her lobotomy a few years before. Thereby hangs another tale.

Hence follows a recent statement by Carl Solomon as background to our first encounter, also a brief selection of his essays relevant to "Howl" and its literary presumptions, as well as my own rueful dream dated 1963, "O Carl!"

His specific comments on my unlicensed poetic version of his adventures are integrated, with others' appropriately signed, and my own notes forethought and afterthought verse by verse, in the section Annotations.

May this writing sweep away Clouds of Ignorance
From sentient beings too much in pain to see dream humor
Metaphor & hyperbole as comedic personae of the Muse
& for those ill-affected by "Howl"'s text, redress the karmic balance.

February 1986   Allen Ginsberg

Statement by Carl Solomon

A kind of immature romantic at that time, full of flowery dreams of Paris—having just read to completion Romain Rolland's novel *Jean Christophe*—I deserted, very precipitously and foolishly, I later decided, the American Liberty ship *Alexander Ramsey*, in the port of La Pallice in Brittany (during May of 1947) and made my way to La Rochelle (the provincial capital). There my first move was to get a haircut.

Then, on to Paris, settled in Montparnasse, read *Tropic of Cancer*, and hired a French lady to teach me the language.

It was not long before I had developed a taste for nougat and haricots verts, attended a lecture on Kafka by Jean-Paul Sartre at the Salle Gaveau, seen the *Mona Lisa*, made friends at the Cité Universitaire who had turned me on to Prévert and Michaux, begun an amatory relationship with a lady in Montmartre, witnessed an Artaud reading on the rue Jacob, attended á CP rally at the Vel d'Hiv,* and discovered Isou and *lettrisme*.

Six weeks and it was all over (the Paris *séjour*) and I came back to the States. Letterism had already awakened an interest in me and I was especially interested in the new poets of my generation of whom Isou and his followers seemed to be very significant ones. The whole tendency toward the non-verbal as I witnessed its reflection even in such American phenomena as the scat singing of Jackie Cain and Ray Kraal.† I sat in the Forty-second Street library in those years reading the latest issues of *La Nouvelle Revue Française*. I remember a special issue devoted to "Young Men of Twenty" in the year 1948.

My protest against the verbal, the rational and the acceptable took the form of disruption of a critical discussion of Mallarmé and other neo-dada clowning, which resulted in my incarceration in a psychiatric hospital in Manhattan. Where I encountered Allen Ginsberg, a fellow patient who was intrigued by my collection of Paris-acquired books. Among the Artaud, Genêt, Michaux, Miller, and Lautréamont was Isou's *Nouvelle Poésie et une Nouvelle Musique*. We discussed all of these things by way of laying the groundwork for Allen's eventual publication of "Howl" in 1956.

After treatment at P.I., I was readmitted to Brooklyn College, dropped out after subsequent marriage and job offer in book publishing.

After release from Pilgrim State (post "Howl") I took a battery of aptitude tests administered by the N.Y. State Department of Vocational Rehabilitation which indicated an IQ slightly above average and aptitude in literature, sales and social service; deficiencies in mechanical, scientific and mathematical areas; I wasn't trying very hard.

I took courses in American literature at the New School. NYU has been trying to get me back into academic work offering credit for life experience. However I still prefer to work.

February 9, 1986

---

* Velodrome d'Hiver, Winter Garden, Paris assembly place for sports and political meets.

† Singers who performed at Birdland, New York bebop mecca.

Report from the Asylum
Afterthoughts of a Shock Patient
By Carl Goy

A book that is accepted, at the moment, as the definitive work on shock-therapy concludes with the astonishing admission that the curative agent in shock-treatment "remains a mystery shrouded within a mystery."[1] This confession of ignorance (and it is extended to both insulin and electric shock-therapies), by two of the men who actually place the electrodes on the heads of mental patients at one of our psychiatric hospitals, certainly opens this field of inquiry to the sensitive layman as well as to the technician. The testimony that follows is that of an eye-witness, one who has undergone insulin-shock treatment and has slept through fifty comas.

One may begin with amusement at the hashish-smokers and their conception of the sublime. They, who at the very most, have been "high," consider themselves (quite properly) to be persons of *eminence* and archimandrates of a *High* Church. A patient emerging from an insulin coma, however, cannot help being a confirmed democrat. There can be no hierarchization of different levels of transcendency when they are induced by an intravenously-injected animal secretion, the very purpose of which is to bombard insulin-space with neutrons of glucose-time until space vanishes like a frightened child and one awakens terrified to find oneself bound fast by a restraining-sheet (wholly supererogatory to the patient, since, in the waking state, spaceless, mobility seems inconceivable). The ingenuousness of the hashishins is stupendous.

It is as though the Insulin Man were to call his drug by a pet name and spend days thrashing out the differences between "gone pot" and "nowhere pot."

The difference between hashish and insulin is in many ways similar to a difference between surrealism and magic. The one is affective and is administered by the subject himself; the other is violently resisted by the subject (since this substance offers not even the most perverse form of satisfactions); it is forcibly administered in the dead of night by white-clad, impersonal creatures who tear the subject from his bed, carry him screaming into an elevator, strap him to another bed on another floor, and who, later, recall

him from his "revery" (a purely polemical term employed in writing "down" to the hashishin). Thus, insulin comes as a succubus, is effective, suggests grace.

In this respect, the paranoid phantasies released by hashish lack substantiality and are of the nature of automatic writing or gratuitous acts. In the case of insulin-shock therapy, one finds onself presented with a complete symbolism of paranoia, beginning with the rude awakening and the enormous hypodermic-needle, continuing through the dietary restrictions imposed upon patients receiving shock, and ending with the lapses of memory and the temporary physical disfigurement.

Early in the treatment, which consists of fifty hypoglycemic comas, I reacted in a highly paranoid manner and mocked the doctors by accusing them of "amputating" my brain. Of course, my illness was such that I was perpetually joking (having presented myself to the hospital upon reaching my majority, I had requested immediate electrocution since I was now of age—how serious was this request, I have no way of knowing—and was discharged as cured exactly nine months later, the day before Christmas).

Nevertheless, I noted similar paranoid responses on the part of other patients in shock.

For those of us acquainted with Kafka, an identification with K. became inevitable. Slowly, however, the identification with K. and with similar characters came to imply far more than we Kafkians had ever dreamed. We knew it to be true that we had been abducted for the most absurd of reasons: for spending hours at a time in the family-shower, for plotting to kill a soldier, for hurling refuse at a lecturer. And, in this particular, the text had been followed quite literally. The need for a revision of the Kafkian perspective arose, however, when the bureaucracy suddenly revealed itself as benevolent. We had not been dragged to a vacant lot and murdered, but had been dragged to a Garden of Earthly Delights and had there been fed (there were exceptions and there is a certain small percentage of fatalities resulting from shock, making the parallel to grace even more obvious). This impression arose, somehow, from the very nature of the subjective coma.

Upon being strapped into my insulin-bed, I would at once break off my usual stream of puns and hysterical chatter. I would stare at the bulge I

First published in *Neurotica* 6 (Spring 1950). Reprinted in *Mishaps, Perhaps*.

1. Hoch and Kalinowski, "Shock Therapy."

made beneath the canvas restraining-sheet, and my body, insulin-packed, would become to me an enormous concrete pun with infinite levels of association, and thereby, a means of surmounting association with things, much as the verbal puns had surmounted the meaning of words. And beneath this wrathful anticipation of world-destruction lay a vague fear of the consequences.

The coma soon confirms all of the patient's fears. What began as a drugged sleep soon changes organically and becomes one of the millions of psycho-physical universes through which he must pass, before being awakened by his dose of glucose. And he cannot become accustomed to these things. Each coma is utterly incomparable to that of the previous day. Lacking a time-sense and inhabiting all of these universes at one and the same time, my condition was one of omnipresence, of being everywhere at no time. Hence, of being nowhere. Hence, of inhabiting that Void of which Antonin Artaud had screamed (I had been conditioned in illness by classical surrealism).

Invariably, I emerged from the comas bawling like an infant and flapping my arms crazily (after they had been unfastened), screaming, "Eat!" or, "Help!"

The nurses and doctors would ignore me, letting me flap about until my whole aching body and my aching mind (which felt as if it had been sprained) pulled themselves by their bootstraps out of the void of terror and, suddenly, attained a perfectly disciplined silence. This, of course, won the admiration of the dispensers of grace, who then decided that I was eminently worth saving and promptly brought me my breakfast tray and a glucose aperitif. And in this manner, item by item, the bureaucracy of the hospital presents the insulin *maudit* with a world of delightful objects all made of sugar—and gradually wins his undying allegiance. If we are not deceived by appearances we will see clearly that it is the entire world of things which imposes itself upon the would-be *maudit* and eventually becomes the object of his idolatry.

All told, the atmosphere of the insulin-ward was one in which, to the sick, miracles appeared to be occurring constantly. And, most traumatic of all, they were concrete miracles. For example, I am reminded of the day I went into a coma free of crab-lice and emerged thoroughly infested (the sheets are sterilized daily). I had caught the lice in somebody else's coma, since these states of unconsciousness are concrete and are left lying about the universe even after they have been vacated by the original occupant. And this was so credited by one of my fellow patients that he refused to submit to the needle the next day out of fear of venturing into one of my old comas and infesting himself. He believed that I had lied and that I'd had crabs for some time, having caught them in some previous coma.

Meanwhile, on that following day, I was revived from my coma intravenously by an Egyptian resident psychiatrist, who then, very brusquely, ordered the nurses to wrap the sheets around me a bit tighter lest I should free myself prematurely; I shrieked, "Amenhotep!"

And there was the day a young patient who had given the impression of being virtually illiterate, received his intravenous glucose (one is revived from a deep coma in this manner), and then gave ample evidence that he had become thoroughly acquainted with the works of Jacob Boehme in the course of his coma. Simone de Beauvoir, in her book on her travels in America, expresses her consternation upon finding that a member of the editorial board of *Partisan Review* once openly admitted to being ignorant of the writings of Boehme.

Shortly after my mummification and defiance of Amenhotep, I encountered what appeared to be a new patient, to whom I mumbled amicably, "I'm Kirilov." He mumbled, in reply, "I'm Myshkin." The cadence of the superreal was never challenged; not one of us would dare assume responsibility for a breach of the unity which each hallucination required.

These collective phantasies in which we dreamed each others dreams contributed to the terror created by contact with the flat, unpredictable insulin void, which had not yet been rendered entirely felicitous (as it was to be later) by the persistent benevolence of man and glucose, and from which all sorts of incredible horrors might yet spring.

The concomitants of therapeutic purgation were, for me, a rather thoroughly atomized amnesia (produced by an insulin convulsion of a rare type and occurring in not more than 2% of cases) and a burgeoning obesity caused by the heavy consumption of glucose. Much later in my treatment, when intensive psychotherapy had replaced insulin, both of these phenomena came to assume places of great importance in the pattern of my reorientation. As my illness had often been verbalized, the first effect of the amnesia was to create a verbal and ideational aphasia, from which resulted an unspoken panic. I had quite simply forgotten the name of my universe, though it was also true that this name rested on the tip of my tongue throughout the amnesiac period. All ideas and all sense of the object had been lost temporarily, and what remained was a state of conscious ideational absence which can only be defined in clinical terms—as amnesia.[2] I had been handed, by skilled and provident men, the very concrete void I'd sought. During this period, I had gained sixty pounds, and upon consulting a mirror, I was confronted with the dual inability to recognize myself or to remember what I had looked like prior to treatment, prior to reaching my majority.

When I had recovered from my amnesia sufficiently to find my way about, I was permitted to leave the hospital on Sundays, in the company of a relative of whom I would take immediate leave. My relatives on these occasions seemed entirely oblivious to any change in my behavior or physique. Generally, still rather hazy, I would be escorted by an old neurotic friend to a homosexual bar where, I would be informed, I had formerly passed much time. However, the most appalling situations would arise at this point, since, in my corpulent forgetfulness, I no longer remotely resembled a "butch" fairy or "rough trade." I had lost all facility with "gay" argot and was incapable of producing any erotic response to the objects proffered me.

Almost imperceptibly, however, the process of object-selection began once more in all realms of activity, and gained momentum.

I amazed my friends in a restaurant one Sunday afternoon by insisting that the waiter remove an entree with which I had been dissatisfied and that he replace it with another. And even greater was their incredulity when they witnessed my abrupt handling of a beggar, this having been the first time that I had ever rejected a request for alms.

"The yearning infinite recoils
For terrible is earth."
—Melville, "L'Envoi."

At about this time, I wrote a sort of manifesto, called "Manifest," which is a most pertinent artifact:

Corsica is an island situated off the coast of Sardinia. Its capital is Ajaccio and it was here that Napoleon Bonaparte was born. Though it is part of the French Empire, Corsica is not part of the mainland. It is an island. As Capri is an island, and Malta. It is not attached to the European mainland. I am in a position to insist upon this point. There is a body of water separating the two, and it is known as the Mediterranean Sea. This is borne out by the maps now in use. I brook no contradiction. If I am challenged on this point, the world will rush to my assistance in one way

or another. What I have just written is a standing challenge to all the forces of evil, of idiocy, of irrelevance, of death, of silence, of vacancy, of transcendency, etc. And I rest secure in the knowledge that my challenge will never be accepted by the *scum* to whom I've addressed it. I've spent considerable time in the clutches of the LOON and I've waited for this opportunity to avenge myself by humiliating the void. Thank you for your kind attention.

— A VEHEMENT ADULT

As the business of selection became increasingly complex, I appeared to develop an unprecedented (for me) suavity in operating within clearly defined limits. Madness had presented itself as an irrelevancy, and I was now busily engaged in assigning values of comparative relevance to all objects within my reach.

My total rejection of psychiatry, which had, after coma, become a fanatical adulation, now passed into a third phase—one of constructive criticism. I became aware of the peripheral obtuseness and the administrative dogmatism of the hospital bureaucracy. My first impulse was to condemn; later, I perfected means of maneuvering freely within the clumsy structure of ward politics. To illustrate, my reading matter had been kept under surveillance for quite some time, and I had at last perfected a means of keeping *au courant* without unnecessarily alarming the nurses and attendants. I had smuggled several issues of *Hound and Horn* into my ward on the pretext that it was a field-and-stream magazine. I had read Hoch and Kalinowski's *Shock Therapy* (a top secret manual of arms at the hospital) quite openly, after I had put it into the dust-jacket of Anna Balakian's *Literary Origins of Surrealism*. Oddly enough, I hadn't thought it necessary to take such pains with Trotsky's *Permanent Revolution* and had become rudely aware of the entire body politic I had so long neglected, when, one evening, I was sharply attacked by the Head Nurse of the ward for "communism." He had slipped behind me on little cat feet and had been reading the book over my shoulder.

The psychiatric ineptitude of the official lower echelons became incredible when, one week before Halloween, it was announced to the patients that a masquerade ball would be held on the appropriate date, that attendance was to be mandatory, and that a prize would be given to the patient wearing the "best" costume. Whereupon, the patients, among whom there was a high spirit of competition, threw themselves precipitously into the work of creating what, for each, promised to be the most striking disguise. The work of sewing, tearing, dyeing, etc., was done in Occupational Therapy, where, at the disposal of all, were an infinite variety of paints,

2. So great was the sense of tangible loss that I later insisted upon an electro-encephalographic examination, to reassure myself that no organic damage had resulted from the convulsion.

gadgets, and fabrics. Supervising all this furious activity was a pedagogic harpy, who had been assigned as Occupational Therapist to see that we didn't destroy any of the implements in the shop (she tried to persuade me to attend the masquerade made up as a dog). Furiously we labored, competing with one another even in regard to speed of accomplishment, fashioning disguised phalluses, swords, spears, scars for our faces, enormous cysts for our heads. When Halloween Night arrived, we were led, dazed and semi-amnesiac, into the small gymnasium that served as a dance floor. Insidious tensions intruded themselves as the time for the awarding of the prize approached. Finally, the Social Therapists seated themselves in the center of the polished floor and ordered us to parade past them in a great circle; one of the nurses sat at the piano and played a march; to the strains of the music, we stepped forward to present our respective embodied idealizations to the judges. There were several Hamlets, a Lear, a grotesque Mr. Hyde, a doctor; there were many cases of transvestism; a young man obsessed with the idea that he was an inanimate object had come as an electric-lamp, brightly-lit, complete with shade; a boy who had filled his head to the point of bursting with baseball lore had come as a "Brooklyn Bum," in derby and tatters. Suddenly, the music stopped; the judges had chosen a winner, rejecting the others; we never learned who the winner had been, so chaotic was the scene that followed. There was a groan of deep torment from the entire group (each feeling that his dream had been condemned). Phantasmal shapes flung themselves about in despair. The nurses and Social Therapists spent the next hour in consoling the losers.

Thus I progressed, after my series of fifty comas had ended, and finally reached my normal weight of 180 pounds and my true sexual orientation: adult heterosexuality (which became my true sexual orientation only after the basic androgynous death-wish had been redirected). It is probably true, however, that my case is atypical and that the great majority of such transformations are not quite as thorough-going, and in some cases, fail to materialize at all. There were those patients who were completely unmoved by the experience of the coma, and who found that it did nothing more than to stimulate their appetites. And there were those Kafkians who remained confirmed paranoiacs to the bitter end.

I should like to quote a passage from an article by the French poet, Antonin Artaud, published posthumously in the February, 1949, issue of *Les Temps Modernes*. Artaud had undergone both electric and insulin shock-therapies during his period of confinement which lasted nine years and terminated with his death in March, 1948.

I died at Rodez under electro-shock. I say dead. Legally and medically dead. The coma of electro-shock lasts a quarter of an hour. Another half-hour and the invalid is breathing. But, one hour after shock I hadn't awakened and had stopped breathing. Surprised by my abnormal rigidity, an attendant went to look for the chief-doctor, who after auscultation found in me no sign of life. I have my own memories of my death at that moment, but it is not upon them that I base my accusation.

I restrict myself to the particulars which were given to me by Dr. Jean Dequeker, young interne of the Rodez asylum, who got them from the mouth of Dr. Ferdiere himself.

And the latter had told him that day he believed me dead, and that he had summoned two asylum guards to instruct them to transport my body to the morgue since I had not returned to myself one hour and a half after shock.

And it appeared that at the very moment the attendants entered to remove my body it quivered slightly, after which I awakened all at once.

I have another recollection of it.

But this memory I had guarded in secret until that day when Dr. Jean Dequeker confirmed it for me from without.

And this recollection is that, confirming all Dr. Jean Dequeker had told me, I had seen not this side of the world but the other. . . .

What he describes above was the experience of us all, but with Artaud and so many others, it stopped short and became the permanent level of existence: the absence of myth represented by the brief "death" was accepted as the culminating, all-embracing myth. Artaud went on to write, in his essay on Van Gogh, that a lunatic "is a man who has preferred to become what is socially understood as mad rather than forfeit a certain superior idea of human honor"; and to write further that "a vicious society has invented psychiatry to defend itself from the investigations of certain superior lucid minds whose intuitive powers were disturbing to it"; and that "every psychiatrist is a low-down son-of-a-bitch." In Paris, quite outrageously, this heart-rendingly skewed essay written by a grievously ill man was honored with a Prix Sainte-Beuve and was underwritten by several of the most distinguished French critics.

I have a small mind and I mean to use it.

The sentence above epitomizes the real lesson of insulin, that of tragedy, and it was neither written nor would it have been understood by Artaud, who remains (he wrote that "the dead continue to revolve around their corpses") a sublime comic figure, one who averted his eyes from the spectre of reality, one who never admitted to having dimensions or sex, and who was incapable of recognizing his own mortality. (In the list of comic figures of our time we can include the homosexual.)

My release from the hospital was followed by a period of headlong and vindictive commitment to substance, a period which continues, which is full of tactical and syntactical retreats and rapid reversals of opinion. It is obvious by this time, though, that the changes of opinion are becoming less frequent, that the truculent drive toward compulsive readjustment, toward the "acting out" of one's adjustment, has been dissipated. My attitude toward the magic I've witnessed is similar to that of the African student I met a month ago, who told me that his uncle had been a witch-doctor. He had seen his uncle turn to a cat before his eyes. He had simply thrown the uncle-cat a scrap of meat, hadn't been particularly impressed by the magic (though conceding its validity), and had come to America to acquire the political and technological skills with which to modernize his country upon his return.

For the ailing intellect, there can be great danger in the poetizing of the coma-void. Only when it is hopelessly distorted and its concrete nature disguised can it serve as material for myth-making. To confront the coma full-face, one must adhere to factual detail and this procedure need not prove deadening. On the contrary, the real coma administers a fillip to one's debilitated thinking processes. Jarry's debraining-machine was not the surgeon's scalpel but was contained within his own cranium. It was to place the coma thus in context that I undertook this examination of its architectonics.

Artaud
by Carl Solomon

I witnessed an Artaud reading in 1947, the year before Artaud's death in Rodez* in 1948. Artaud was being described by a small circle of Paris admirers, some in very high places in the arts, as being a genius who had extended Rimbaud's vision of the poet seer. His name was even described by one admirer, known as "The Alchemist," as Arthur Rimbaud without the *hur* in Arthur and without the *Rimb* in Rimbaud. And this man later made a case for Artaud as being, literally, the reincarnation of Rimbaud and spiritually his descendant. Other admirers were André Gide and Jean Louis Barrault. Gide made a case for Artaud as an existentialist man of despair, and Barrault had been influenced by Artaud on the theater. Artaud's is a tenuous case, an ambiguous one in that he has been highly esteemed by almost everyone of note in the arts and yet widely banned and condemned by legal authorities. To me his case, his destiny has been the cause of considerable confusion since one knows that by accepting his theories one puts one's body in the social frying pan and by rejecting him you are going through life with blinders on. He is certainly the leading critic I have ever read of social hypocrisy and for this became known as a "Damned" poet. He was a junkie, a lunatic and had pursued his peculiar turn of thought so far that he had even rebelled against surrealism which itself is supposed to be rebellion against society deriving from a rebellion against the "rebel," Anatole France, who had been considered too lucid, too rational, by the early dadaists. And where does all this rebellion against rebellion lead but surely into one of many large nuthouses which are continually being constructed all over this country and others in the name of that mystical cause "Mental Health."

From *Mishaps, Perhaps*, pp. 13–15.

* "Je suis mort à Rodez sous l'électrochoc."

The book by Artaud which impressed me most was his *Van Gogh* written in 1948 in which he condemns all forms of psychiatry, and thereby all organized authority, since all countries practise psychiatry including the socialist wonderland. In it, he claims that every lunatic, everyone marked and branded, and believe me all lunatics are really marked and branded, is a person of superior lucidity whose insights society thinks disturbing to it. This book impressed me when I read it in 1948, the year of Truman's upset victory over Dewey. I was still in the school system at that time and the intellectual students, by these I mean the ones who weren't in favor of basketball and who read a book now and then which wasn't on the compulsory reading list, were mostly interested in either Marxism and folksongs or, in the advanced echelons, in Freud or Wilhelm Reich. Now I was interested in Artaud, who to me was a symbol of real rebellion truly meriting the name.

To illustrate the mood of the student body in college at that time, I should state that I walked into a classroom carrying a copy of Baudelaire and was immediately latched upon by a girl English major who seemed to think I was actually Baudelaire in person. Shortly after this I was deposited in a nut factory where I was shocked into a renunciation of all my reading, etc., etc. What books remained to me after I had been shocked then, were later stolen from me by various local hoodlums and I was soon thrown into another more savage nuthouse.

The case of the so-called lunatic opened up by Artaud and no other writer is really the case of Socrates, who was condemned to death for being what, in his day, was considered "bright," that is to say not stupid. I say that we live in a generation of charlatanry, propaganda and corruption, and that there is no room for an honest man on either side of the Iron Curtain.

"O Carl!" A Dream: 1963
By Allen Ginsberg

I go up to room in a big apartment. Mental hospital—family quarters—I have changed— How is Carl Solomon?— He comes in from Elevator, in a blue business suit and tie his face at first looks the same but, as he sits down in Easychair I see he has great swollen spongy belly and huge lumps of football size fat on his arms and white basketball ass—I drift—must be from metrosol, what the doctors did to him with shock, deformed and added to his flesh, however— I explain, walking up and down—"Carl I did do wrong to you, I made you an object, a thing, an image—I didn't mean that, I loved you— I did discover finally what it is I—we—were seeking then in Psychiatric Institute, what it is we felt we thought we wanted all along— I made a mistake Carl. Forgive me, I have the answer now—"

"What is it? What is it?" he cries in his chair, his head is big and his face is red.

While talking I'd said "felt" we were seeking and I thought maybe I'd tipped it off too early without building it up right, formulating it so he'd feel what it was I was screaming about— He cried "What is it?"—

I say, "It's this image, the Mind, the reporters, the interviews, the fame, the image—it was our identity we were seeking wasn't it, our own identity?"

"Yes, yes," he says, but I see the anguish in his eyes—the reporters are waiting downstairs for me, to interview me again, now I see our chance to break thru our Names and Forms in public— I was all wrong to conspire with *Time* to create this Beatnik myself and to throw out into world a howl of Carl Solomon which fixed him in my idea of him a name

a madness a hospital a mass public image surrounding him confusing him furthermore—

I am striding up and down in front of him taking control of the situation, "Look, there are reporters outside waiting to come up and cast the image again, let's do it *now*, let's together make a break, escape the Names, escape our minds, escape their minds, escape the words, break through ourselves, Cut *out*! Cut out!"

"But how?" he says looking at me unhappily from couch—

"Don't you see?" I said—"it's our feelings, our feelings who we are—that's our identity not all these thoughts and ideas and angrys"—

He falls back in chair, his face turns even redder —I am afraid he'll strike me, "But I was depending on you, you let me down, you still don't realize my—"

He begins slapping his palm to his red square Frankenstein forehead—hard, hard slaps—as if hitting a solid bone red object— I get frightened—have I misunderstood?—have all things been mixed so now I am lost and he's damaged:

He: "My feelings always been the trouble, I am split in that organically by the shock"—he points to his freak grotesque sponge swollen doctored body— "How can this . . . ?"

I am desperate, I break down, I think how can I now love this body with my body, how can I touch him and isn't that what he wants and I wanted that we touch with love at last in the end and I cry.

"O Carl!" weeping to him not to desert me, "O Carl! I need you! O Carl! O Carl! O Carl!" broken down as he gazes at me at last, but I am hopeless like a baby with him wanting him to hold me, "O Carl! O Carl! O Carl!" and wake.

Allen Ginsberg, *Journals* (Vancouver), August 10, 1963.

Carl Solomon Bibliography

Mishaps, Perhaps. San Francisco: Beach Books, Texts and Documents/City Lights Books, 1966.

More Mishaps. San Francisco: Beach Books, Texts and Documents/City Lights Books, 1968.

AUTHOR'S ANNOTATIONS

Correspondence Chart: Final and First Drafts, Howl, *Part 1*

Only objectified emotion endures.   —Louis Zukofsky

Author, Berkeley hills in background, U.C. graduate student, engaged with *Howl* Part II late drafts, 1956.
Photo by Peter Orlovsky?

Correspondence Chart: Final and First Drafts, HOWL, Part I*

Verse-by-verse annotation following original draft of "Howl," Part I (and final drafts, Parts II, III and IV) includes analysis of revisions, root reference of vivid phrases, & images traced to personal anecdote; letters, commentary, testimony & clarifications by persons obliquely modeled in the poem, including Philip Lamantia, Carl Solomon, Louis Simpson & Tuli Kupferberg; with currency of author's private image bank declared and deconstruction of his projections; minute particulars and supplementary details background to starry dynamos & hydrogen jukeboxes displayed; rhythmic measures & verse tactics noted, mini-histories behind metaphors unburdened, bibliographic hints for inquisitive readers, and relevant journal jottings emplaced, with literary origins quoted, & visible referents reproduced.

Final Draft	First Draft	Final Draft	First Draft	Final Draft	First Draft	Final Draft	First Draft
1	1	21	18	41	22	61	36
2	2	22	69	42	76	62	23
3	(2)	23	66–67	43	(22)	63	78
4	3	24	19	44	27	64	61
5	4	25	(25)	45	56	65	43
6	9	26	26	46	52	66	46
7	50	27	66–67	47	65	67	46
8	5–6	28	51	48	54	68	46
9	7	29	41	49	63	69	47
10	11	30	73	50	55	70	42
11	11	31	34	51	(55)	71	48
12	12	32	31	52	53	72	49
13	12	33	40	53	52	73	44
14	13	34	28–30, 37	54	60	74	81
15	14	35	28–30, 37	55	59	75	80, 82, 84
16	15–16	36	20	56	50	76	79, 84
17	15–16	37	21	57	32	77	64
18	15–16	38	—	58	23–24	78	83
19	15–16	39	62	60	35		
20	17	40	45				

* Final-draft verses not derived from original draft are annotated in context of original verses, which are enclosed in parentheses.

First and Final Drafts, HOWL, Part I

1 [1]*

Crucial revision: "Mystical" is replaced by "hysterical," a key to the tone of the poem. Tho the initial idealistic impulse of the line went one way, afterthought noticed bathos, and common sense dictated "hysteria." One mind can entertain both notions without "any irritable reaching after fact and reason," as Keats proposed with his definition of "Negative Capability." The word "hysterical" is judicious, but the verse is overtly sympathetic. "Do I contradict myself?/Very well then I contradict myself,/(I am large, I contain multitudes.)" (Whitman, "Song of Myself," 51.) The poem's tone is in this mixture of empathy and shrewdness, the comic realism of Chaplin's *City Lights*, a humorous hyperbole derived in part from Blake's style in *The French Revolution*. "If you have a choice of two things and can't decide, take both," says Gregory Corso. Negative Capability = One Taste.

2 [2]

Herbert Huncke cruised Harlem and Times Square areas at irregular hours, late forties, scoring junk. See Herbert Huncke, *The Evening Sun Turned Crimson* (Cherry Valley, N.Y.: Cherry Valley Editions, 1980).

— [3]

"Starry dynamo" and "machinery of night" are derived from Dylan Thomas's mixture of Nature and Machinery in "The force that through the green fuse drives the flower / Drives my green age . . ."

3 [4]

Ref.: Bill Keck, Anton Rosenberg and other contemporaries who gathered often at the San Remo bar, living in Lower East Side, N.Y., early 1950s—their circle was prototype for Kerouac's fictional description in *The Subterraneans*, written 1953. The jazz was late bop Charlie Parker played in Bowery loft jam sessions in those few years.

4 [5]

Jack Kerouac had given anecdote of Philip Lamantia's celestial adventure to author in early 1950s. Poet Lamantia in note written for author May 25, 1986, New Orleans, provides this accurate account:

> 1953, Spring, aged 25, reading the Koran on a couch, one night, I was suddenly physically laid out by a powerful force beyond my volition, which rendered me almost comatose: suddenly, consciousness was contracted to a single point at the top of my head through which I was "siphoned" beyond the room, space and time into *another* state of awareness that seemed utterly beyond any other state before or since experienced. I floated toward an endless-looking universe of misty, lighted color forms: green, red, blue and silver, which circulated before me accompanied by such bliss that the one dominant thought was: This is it; I never want to return to anywhere but this *place*—i.e., I wanted to remain in this Ineffable Blissful Realm and explore it forever—since I felt a radiance beyond even further within it and so, suddenly the outline of a benign bearded Face appeared to whom I addressed my desire to remain in this marvel—and who calmly replied: "You can return, after you complete your work."

Part of Manhattan's subway system, the Third Avenue elevated railway, one of those familiarly called the "El," was demolished in the mid-'50s. See Kerouac's "sketches" in *Visions of Cody* (New York: McGraw-Hill, 1972), p. 6; as well as pictures in *Berenice Abbott: American Photographer*, ed. Hank O'Neal (New York: McGraw-Hill, 1982), pp. 90, 97, 119, 123, 140.

5 [8]

Ref. Carl Solomon, an anecdote.

6 [8]

Carl Solomon writes: "I burned money while upset about the evils of materialism in 1956, prior to commitment to Pilgrim." Date may have been earlier; "Howl" written in 1955.

7 [9]

Anonymous anecdote, possibly re John Hoffman (see note 41 [29]). Final draft of the poem reads: "Who got busted in their pubic beards . . ." The phrase comes by a simple mechanical method of intensifying a line by unusual juxtaposition of things or concepts, "doctoring" the verse.

9 [6]

Refers to author's adventures at Columbia College.

---

* Annotations of Part I are set in order according to verses of first draft (pp. 13–25) to provide background and references for final draft (pp. 3–8). Verse numbers at left refer to first draft. Bracketed numbers refer to corresponding verses of final draft. Final-draft verses not derived from the first draft (indicated by a dash) are annotated in context of first draft. To trace annotations directly from final back to first draft, see Correspondence Chart, on preceding page.

"Anarchy" changes to "Arkansas," in order to substitute a more concrete thing-name for an abstract word.

"Post-war cynical scholars" refers to some of Lionel Trilling's students, perhaps an inkling of literary "cold-warrior" Norman Podhoretz—see *Making It* (New York: Random House, 1967), pp. 39–40, 215–16. *Time* magazine in the fifties portrayed American intellectuals as comfortable, complacent. *Time*'s negative review of Rachel Carson's *Silent Spring* showed early (& anti-feminist) antagonism toward the inchoate ecology movement.

In final text, "scholars of war": During author's residence, 1944–48, Columbia scientists helped split atoms for military power in secrecy. Subsequent military-industrial funding increasingly dominated university research, thus two decades later rebellious student strikes had as primary grievance that the trusteeships of the university interlocked with Vietnam War–related corporations. That cold war influence darkened the complexion of scientific studies and humanistic attitudes. Columbia President D. D. Eisenhower himself had warned against such military-industrial complexity in his farewell address as U.S. Chief Executive. However, two decades after 1968 student activism, secret military-industrial research reached cosmic proportions, and "Star Wars" era university contracts swelled academic coffers with little hint of an historical scandal. Common private complaint against this "monstrous exotic" rarely flashed on TV.

10–11 [10]

This verse evolves into "Paradise Alley," a cold-water-flat courtyard at 501 East 11th Street, NE corner of Avenue A, Lower East Side New York, bricked up in the '70s and demolished after fire in 1985. As sketched by Kerouac in *The Subterraneans*, the prototype of his heroine Mardou Fox lived there in 1953 in friendly contact with the author, Corso and Kerouac, and typed the original ms. of Burroughs' *Yage Letters* and *Queer*.

Various artists lived in cheap hotels in the area, St. Mark's Place, their small rooms suffused with the smell of turpentine.

Supplemental ref. "apartments": 419 West 115th Street, #51, frequented 1945–46 by the author, William Burroughs, Joan Vollmer (later Joan Burroughs) and Jack Kerouac, among others. Use of Benzedrine inhalers was common, introduced by friends of Herbert Huncke visiting regularly.

"Bodies" changes to "torsos," final draft, for sound and sex.

"Cock & endless balls" ref. vernacular "have a ball."

12 [13]

The "backyard green tree cemetery dawns," ref. Bill Keck's apartment on East 2nd Street off Second Avenue, in New York City, overlooking cemetery; see author's April 17, 1952, entry, *Journals Early Fifties, Early Sixties*, ed. Gordon Ball (New York: Grove Press, 1977). Keck's early poem ended: "Life is the green lime tree." The author tried peyote (sold from East 10th Street storefront) two days later.

The "teahead joyride" likely refers to drive Neal Cassady and Jack Kerouac took thru Brooklyn to hear some early-morning jazz late 1940s. Final draft "kind king light of mind" paraphrases Kerouac's epithet "Kind King Mind" in *Mexico City Blues* and his last phrase in *Visions of Cody*, "Adios, King."

"Tree vibrations" ref. author's first peyote experience—see *Journals*, pp. 7–13.

13 [14]

From an anecdote, trying to score for morphine from an old doctor in the Bronx, 1945, told by Herbert Huncke in the 115th Street apartment.

This verse, the longest so far in its original composition, was a conscious attempt to go all the way from A to Z (Zoo) in associative flash and extension of breath.

14 [15]

Author's casual college job was mopping floors at various Manhattan cafeterias including Bickford's 42nd Street.

Fugazzi's Sixth Avenue Greenwich Village bar was early 1950s alternative to the noisier San Remo nearby. "Fugazzi" phrasing was added to accommodate "jukebox"; cafeterias had no jukeboxes.

Some end-of-the-world or apocalyptic vibration was noticed by the "subterraneans" in the roaring of the jukebox, thus "hydrogen [bomb] jukebox."

15–16 [16]

Ruth G——, an intelligent dreamy young Jewish woman ("meat for the synagogue" [19]), who wore Salvation Army granny dresses in times of Eisenhower prosperity, and associated with author, Carl Solomon and others in early 1950s Greenwich Village, one day began a flight of talk in Washington Square that continued through the day and night for 72 hours until she was finally committed to Bellevue.

Ref. also Neal Cassady's nonstop monologues; see Kerouac's *Visions of Cody*, pp. 268–74, for comic paraphrase of same.

"Eyeball kicks": See note re Cézanne, 44 [73] below.

17 [20]

    "Nowhere Zen New Jersies of amnesia": Composite image of a few post-college "career failures" characteristic of 1950s, including author's own two-year sojourn in Paterson 1950–51 on leaving Columbia Psychiatric Institute. Author's family spent many 1930s summers at the shore in Belmar—"Atlantic City," final draft. "Sharks" ref. recurrent seaside newspaper reports and souvenir postcards.

18 [21]

    "Tangerian bone-grindings": Details of W. S. Burroughs' withdrawals from heroin are found in his letters to the author, *Letters to Allen Ginsberg 1953–1957* (Geneva: Editions Claude Givaudin/Am Here Books, 1978; New York: Full Court Press, 1982).

    Author saw "Newark's bleak furnished room" with Eugene Brooks, his brother, who lived in one such studying law, late forties.

19 [24]

    Author had read in Wilhelm Reich's *Function of the Orgasm* and *Mass Psychology of Fascism*, Vico's *Scienza Nouva*, a smattering of Gurdjieff (at Burroughs' suggestion, 1945), little on kabbalah, and knew Robert Fludd's name only thru reference in W. B. Yeats and random illustrations of cosmographic human form. Change to final draft "Plotinus Poe St. John of the Cross telepathy and bop kabbalah" focused on matter closer to author's reading, juxtaposing hermetic sublime with Americanist esoterica for sake of sound and provincial sense. Plotinus and St. John of the Cross (and Plato's *Phaedrus*) were arranged in bookcase "orange crates of theology" in Russell Durgin's 121st Street Spanish Harlem 6th-floor apartment, where author experienced Wm. Blake illumination described otherwhere. Journal entry April 1953: "to read recommended by [Meyer] Schapiro. Robt. Fludd—Cosmographia . . ." A brief paper on Vico was written as special study of cyclical history for Prof. Jacques Barzun's Columbia College class 1946.

    Overt intention of this mystical name-dropping was to connect younger readers, Whitman's children already familiar with Poe and Bop, to older Gnostic tradition. Whitman dropped such hints to his fancied readers.

20 [36]

    "Saintly motorcyclists" ref. Marlon Brando's film *The Wild One*, 1954.

    "And screamed with joy": Popular superstition had it that one screamed with pain in such a circumstance. "Howl" 's enthusiastic version is more realistic. For its time the iconoclastic "shocker" of the poem, this verse reversed vulgar stereotype with a statement of fact. Tho "screamed" is hyperbole—"moaned" more common.

    This crucial verse militated against author's thinking of the writing draft as "poetry" or "publishable" in any way that would reach the eyes of his family, thus author was left free to write thenceforth what he actually thought, from his own experience.

21 [37]

    The poet Hart Crane picked up sailors to love on Sand Street, Brooklyn, etc. Suffering alcoholic exhaustion and rejected by the crew on his last voyage, from Veracruz, Crane disappeared off the fantail of the Caribbean ship *Orizaba*.

22 [41]

    Hyperbolic ref. to one of Neal Cassady's accounts of sexual enthusiasm (see next entry). "Gyzym" ref. author's recollections of learned New Critical article *Hudson Review* late 1940s perhaps entitled "W. B. Yeats and the Gyzym of Eternity."

— [43]

    Ref. Neal Cassady, 1926–1968, author *The First Third & Other Writings* (San Francisco: City Lights Books, 1971). His account of adolescent adventures stealing cars, seducing waitresses and haunting Denver alleyways written in long "Joan Anderson Letter" inspired Kerouac to forms of spontaneous personal narrative that involved continuous scanning of writer's consciousness during time of original composition for simultaneous multilevel references sufficiently swiftly to include them in extended prose sentences.

    It was Cassady's profusion of physical energy and abundance of self-recollection that brought him to Kerouac's attention as prototype of Dean Moriarty in *On the Road* (1950) and Cody Pomeroy in its grander sequel, *Visions of Cody* (1952), among other books.

    For twelve years with wife, house and children an exemplary senior brakeman on S. P. Railroad till entrapment by marijuana tax agents, Cassady served thereafter as central figure and model driver of Ken Kesey's "Merry Prankster" psychedelic Trips Festival crosscountry and Bay Area celebrations, inspiring songs and attitudes of The Grateful Dead.

    Solitary during withdrawal from the exhaustions of amphetamine in San Miguel Allende, Mexico, Feb. 3, 1968, he passed by the door of a wedding party, was invited in, drank alcoholic pulque, later was found collapsed and suffocating on railroad tracks outside town and died in hospital. His ashes reside with his widow, Carolyn.

    "Secret hero of these poems": The plural ref.

Neal Cassady, "secret hero of these poems," & Natalie Jackson (d. 1955) Conscious of their loves in Eternity on Market Street, San Francisco, Spring 1955.   *Photo by A.G.*

various other works by author, Kerouac and others (later Ken Kesey) accounting his heroic energy. For contemporary chronicle of author's early intense erotic liaison and extended friendship with this figure, see *As Ever: The Collected Correspondence of Allen Ginsberg and Neal Cassady*, ed. Barry Gifford (Berkeley, Cal.: Creative Arts, 1977).

23–24 [62, 59]

Author worked as night copyboy Associated Press office, Rockefeller Center, 1948–49, and stopped in across Fifth Avenue at St. Patrick's Cathedral on his way home, praying for Neal Cassady and friends returning to West Coast after visiting him in an apartment on York Avenue. The season is described in N.Y. chapters of *On the Road*.

"Send me a letter, send it by mail / Send it in care of the Birmingham Jail."—Huddie (Leadbelly) Ledbetter

25 [—]

See "The Trembling of the Veil," in Allen Ginsberg, *Collected Poems 1947–1980* (New York: Harper & Row, 1984), p. 14: "Today out of the window / the trees seemed like live / organisms on the moon."

— [25]

American Indian old ways included "vision quest" as mark of maturation, or resolution of life crisis. Some among the postwar generation of white Americans initiated themselves into this tradition. See Gary Snyder, *The Old Ways* (San Francisco: City Lights Books, 1977).

26 [26]

First and final versions ref. author's Blake illumination E. Harlem 1948. See *Paris Review* interview collected in *Writers at Work, Series 3* (New York: Viking Press, 1967), pp. 301–11. Author also dimly remembered an anecdote from conversation about surrealist poet Philip Lamantia, mostly apocryphal. For "Baltimore," Poe association, his brick house and grave are there.

27 [44]

"Heartless Tokay" ref. Kerouac's letters, an account of occasional drinking on weekends in New York.

28 [58]

"Fell out of windows . . . vomit in the toilet" ref. William Cannastra, legendary late 1940s New York bohemian figure, life cut short by alcoholic accident, body balanced out of subway window, knocked against a pillar, fell at Astor Place, Manhattan. Final draft: "Leaped . . . cried . . . danced . . . smashed . . . records" ref. same saga.

"Nostalgic . . . German jazz": *Rise and Fall of the City of Mahagonny* Brecht-Weill opera arias "O Show Me the Way to the Next Whiskey Bar" and "Benares Song," which echoed loud late nights repeatedly in Cannastra's West 21st Street Manhattan loft 1949.

"The filthy Passaic": In W. C. Williams "The Wanderer: A Baroque Fantasy," 1915, the youthful poet plunges his hands in her waters requesting sacrament of Goddess of Passaic River for his Muse: "and the filthy Passaic consented."

29 [35]

"on all fours": see 28 [58] above re Cannastra.

30 [34]

See 28 [58] re Cannastra.

See oblique references to Cannastra as prototype of Alan Harrington's novel figure Genovese in *The Secret Swinger* (New York: Knopf, 1966). Kerouac's portrait of "Finistra" is found in *Visions of Cody*. "Howl" text's brief summons of this shade is fleshed out two years later as Bill King in "The Names," *Collected Poems*, p. 178.

31 [32]

Living Theater director Judith Malina writes:

June 15, 1955, Julian [Beck] and I and about 27 others refused to take shelter when "the sirens . . . wailed." It was City Hall Park and not in Union Square, and I was sent to Bellevue for sassing the judge. The trial (with lawyers from the Ford Foundation's 20th Century Fund) was prolonged.

"We were an *all star* set of *defendants*; [including] Hugh Corbin, Dorothy Day, Ralph diGia, Ammon Hennacy, Richard Kern, Jackson MacLow, A. J. Muste, James Peck and Bayard Rustin. . . . I tell the story in my Grove Press diary [*The Diaries of Judith Malina 1947–1957* (New York, 1984)] on pps. 367–374.

"There's another telling of the story of the trial, etc. in a booklet called *What Happened On June 15th?* put out by the War Resisters' League. I don't think that anyone took their clothes off for that demo (with Day and Muste!), though surely at many others."

Account in Malina's *Diaries* is invaluable for those who wish to be acquainted with the genesis of postwar peace protest movement, for its humor and simplicity.

32 [57]

"Meat trucks": This apocryphal burlesque conforms with Chaplinesque tone of "hysterical" verse 1. Tuli Kupferberg writes:

In the Spring of 1945 at the age of 21, full of youthful angst, depression over the war and other insanities and at the end of a disastrous love affair, I went over the side of the Manhattan Bridge.

I was picked up tenderly by the crew of a passing tug and taken to Gouveneur Hospital.

My injuries were relatively slight (fracture of a transverse spinal process) but enuf to put me in a body cast.

In the hospital wards I met other suicide attempters less fortunate than me: one who wd walk on crutches and one who wd never walk again.

Thruout the years I have been annoyed many times by "O did you really jump off the Brooklyn Bridge?" as if that was a great accomplishment.

Remember I was a *failure* at the attempt.

Had I succeeded there wd have been 3 less wonderful beings (my children) in the world, no Fugs, and a few missing good poems & songs, & some people (including some lovely women, *hey!*) who might have missed my company.

In the US today, over 5000 young people between the ages of 15 & 24 do succeed *every year* in destroying themselves.

Fools!

There's nothing glamorous about it. (I know first hand of someone who regretted the act the day after & died a lingering death of throat burns 2 weeks later.)

There's time, there's time.

You'll be dead a long long while, & sooner than you imagine.

Patience patience, my young, wild, beautiful, damned friends!

See Tuli Kupferberg's *1001 Ways to Live Without Working* (New York: Birth Press, 1961), illustrated edition (New York: Grove Press, 1967); *Kill for Peace* (being *Yeah* 10), (New York: Birth Press, 1965); *1001 Ways to Beat the Draft* (with Robert Bashlow), (New York: Layton, 1966), illustrated edition (New York: Grove Press, 1967); *1001 Ways to Make Love* (New York: Grove Press, 1969). Also *Birth* magazine and all the recordings of The Fugs, significant intellectual breakthrough rock band of the 1960s returned to play their old and new lyric satires even more brilliantly in the mid 1980s.

33 [—]

Ref. Iris Brody, Lower East Side artist, whose work author collected. Unstable materials used to compose her pictures deteriorated within two decades. Her painting of poet-musician Jackson Mac Low with recorder can be seen in background of author's photographs of William Burroughs 1953.

34 [31]

A specialized Columbia College jape or fad.

"Narcotic . . . haze of capitalism": "WASHINGTON—The tobacco industry spent $1.24 billion advertising cigarettes in 1980 and got the average American smoker to buy 11,633 cigarettes that year, the Federal Trade Commission said. . . ."—*Washington Post*, November 22, 1982

35 [60]

"Crosscountry in 72 hours": To author's recollection, Neal Cassady literally did so in one late-'40s coast-to-coast auto trip on the road to see Kerouac and compare recent illuminations and despairs.

36 [61]

Lyric lines by Kerouac: "Down in Denver,/ Down in Denver,/ All I did was die."

Final-text verse ends "& now Denver is lonesome for her heroes," a line taken intact from December 1951 journal entry, drafts for the poem "Shroudy Stranger of the Night." See also note, verse 66 [23].

37 [34]

"Bit detectives" ref. William Cannastra, not literal.

38–39 [—]

Description of an unfortunate car crash 1948 on Utopia Blvd, Queens, New York, which resulted in

Neal Cassady with dealer looking over used cars, S.F., 1955. *Photo by A.G.*

arrest of author, Herbert Huncke and friends. Stolen car was filled with stolen loot from second-story jobs, as well as several years' journals, address books, letters from William Burroughs, etc., being transported for safekeeping with author's brother prior departure from N.Y.C. See Jane Kramer, *Allen Ginsberg in America* (New York: Random House, 1969), pp. 123–30.

41 [29]

Ref. Malcolm Lowry, *Under the Volcano*. More specifically the myth of John Hoffman, N.Y. acquaintance of author and Carl Solomon. Solomon writes: "John Hoffman, 1930?–1950 or 1951. Hometown: Menlo Park, California. Friend of Gerd Stern, poet, born circa 1930. Also friend of Philip Lamantia, Chris Maclaine, both California poets. Blond, handsome, bespectacled, long hair. Spaced out quality that amused many people. Girl friend blonde girl named

Karen. Went to Mexico in 1950. Experimented with peyote. Died of mononucleosis while in Mexico. Poems highly regarded by avant-garde connoisseurs." Philip Lamantia read Hoffman's work at the seminal Six Gallery poetry reading where author first read Part I of "Howl."

Chicago as fireplace ref. Mrs. O'Leary's cow, which kicked over kerosene lantern, starting the celebrated fire of 1871 which consumed that city.

42 [69–70]

Ref. somewhat to Carl Solomon & those we left behind at Psychiatric Institute, 1949. Dolmens mark a vanished civilization, as Stonehenge or Greystone and Rockland monoliths. At time of writing, author's mother dwelled in her last months at Pilgrim State Hospital, Brentwood, N.Y., housing over 25,000, the largest such mental hospital in the world. Description of the wards and halls is drawn from Greystone State Hospital, near Morristown, N.J., which author frequented in adolescence to visit Naomi Ginsberg. New York's Rockland State Hospital's name was substituted for rhythmic euphony. Poem was occasioned by unexpected news of Carl Solomon's recent removal to Pilgrim State.

At this point, with an unusually extended line, the triadic form of William Carlos Williams definitely broke down and author realized it couldn't be restored as measure for the verse. The only option was to expand the verse line beyond that of Christopher Smart, as on occasion Whitman did, and the modernist Kenneth Fearing, more loosely. Paragraphic prose poetry by Rimbaud and St.-John Perse provided more electric model.

43 [65]

"Accusing the radio of hypnotism": Naomi Ginsberg was convinced circa 1943 that doctors had planted "three big sticks" down her back during insulin and electric shock treatments as antennae to receive radio broadcasts from the ceiling—voices sent by President Roosevelt that alternately praised her as a "great woman" or mocked her as a "radical" and "bad girl."

After shock treatments at Rodez asylum, circa 1943, Artaud, in his "Van Gogh" text, accused his doctors (and modern society itself) of materialist hypnotism. His idea was that electroshock drives the spirit down, from its flight to liberty from God, back into the mortal body, which he calls a pile of shit. See also the brilliant vehemence of accusation in his text "To Be Done with the Judgement of God," and Carl Solomon's mordant refutation of this concept, derived from greater experience with the issue: "Afterthoughts of a Shock Patient," p. 113 above.

Idiomatic metaphor "insanity on their hands" is the subvocal "phrasing." Variant options would have been: "left with *their* insanity on *their* hands & a hung jury" or "left *with* insanity on their hands *with* a hung jury." Neither option was graceful, so the idiomatic phrase was x-ed out on the spot. "And" sounded better, repeated.

44 [73]

This stanza concerns itself with aesthetic technique: the mechanisms of surrealist or ideogrammatic method, the juxtaposition of disparate images to create a gap of understanding which the mind fills in with a flash of recognition of the unstated relationship (as "hydrogen jukebox"); viz. Aristotle's "apt relation of dissimilars," his analysis of traditional metaphor.

L.-F. Céline punctuates the jump cuts in his prose with three dots of *ellipsis*. ("Ellipse" is a solecism in original mss. and printings; "ellipsis" is correct.) One theory of haiku is that it presents two opposite images that connect only in mind of reader. In Buddhist psychology, ordinary mind includes the space between thoughts, awareness of *sunyata*. Or, as in Cézanne: the space gap between hot and cold colors. According to George Wald's Nobel Prize theory of optics, the muscles of the retina can focus on only one plane of color at a time, narrowing or widening the lens in relation to varying intensities of light presented by "hot" and "cold" colors.

Whitman's *catalogues* present such grand spaciousness in "list poems" moving thru varying geographies, trades, sounds, stages, multiple precise but discrete observations. Cézanne re-composed his *"petite sensation"* of space on the flat canvas by interlocking squares, cubes and triangles of "hot" colors advancing and "cold" colors retreating in the optical field. His innovative paintings create the appearance of gaps in space without recourse to conventional perspective lines. Early cubist praxis entered this new space after his breakthrough. Paul Klee's "magic squares" may be viewed in this light. Apollinaire appreciated this mode in poetics, thus his pre-surrealist image montage. Eisenstein applied this insight to film, thus the terms "montage" and "jump cut."

Ezra Pound constructed an epic out of vivid ideograms, and extended the *meters* of English-language poetry to include classic quantity among other neglected measures of verse length. W. C. Williams moved forward into the "variable foot" or "relative measure" to include his own breath's spoken cadences.

A further extension of this model of sense consciousness into open space may be seen in "nonlinear" or "aleatoric" art: work by Gertrude Stein, Jackson Mac Low, John Cage and William S. Burroughs.

Contemporary mass swift-shifting-image music television (MTV) falls into place with the same mind. "Spontaneous prosody" in Kerouac's novels and poetry and in "Howl" text composition rely on the same notion of sense consciousness.

N.B. Phrasing in this verse has been clarified for present edition, from: "use of the ellipse the catalog the meter & the vibrating plane" in *Collected Poems*, to: "use of the ellipsis catalog a variable measure and the vibrating plane," to conform more precisely to above referents.

45 [40, 74]

"Blocks of pigments": A summary reference to Cézanne's theory as author understood it. "Aeterna" (*Collected Poems*) corrected to "Aeterne."

[Regarding the second half of the stanza (40), Ginsberg has tended to leave this out in recent years' public readings. —B.M.]

This line continues the invention of paragraph-long verse formation (see the note to verse 42).

46 [66–67–68]

Carl Solomon writes about the incident in a letter to the author, September 29, 1985:

> This section of the poem garbles history completely and makes light of what to me was an extremely serious matter. I was attending Brooklyn College; the lecturer was Wallace Markfield (later a friend); it was an off-campus affair; Markfield's subject was Mallarmé and Alienation; The potato salad throwing was supposed to be Dadaism and also an illustration of alienation; it was done in jest and also as a gift-gesture to a campus girl-friend whose birthday it was and who thought the idea very funny. Contradiction: "in jest" and "quite a serious matter," this was typical of the black humor of dada.
>
> The harlequin speech of suicide and request for lobotomy was meant to be the absurd humor a lot of people were into then which stemmed from the ill-conceived hard-boiled manners of American students—especially New York students in the 1940s. The perfect existential gesture in those days was supposed to be putting an apple in your mouth and jumping into a fire.

Of the second part of the line, Carl Solomon writes: "No Metrazol or electricity for me. Electricity followed six years later at Pilgrim. But I think Dr. Benway (*Naked Lunch*) treatment seems typical of modern psychiatry."

Of the third part, "who in humorless protest," he writes:

> This sounds good but the catatonia I doubt as P.I. (where it occurred) diagnosed me as neurotic. Can you make sense of this legalistic diagnostic shit? (More, even further compounding the confusion, has been offered since, like "as normal as apple pie"—so long as your politics are OK, and anxiety neurosis thrown in.) In short, whatever [diagnosis] has suited the occasion or the needs of the examiner. Also anybody who yelps is called paranoid even by book-thieves who are trying to ward off a conscientious clerk. *They* call you paranoid too. Pardon the use of the word bullshit, but it should be lavishly applied to most aspects of our culture.

The incident of the Ping-Pong table is described by Solomon as a "big burst anti-authoritarian rage on arrival at P.I. by me."

Author received hydrotherapy, psychotherapy, occupational therapy (oil painting) and played Ping-Pong with Carl Solomon at N.Y. State Psychiatric Institute, July 1948–March 1949.

Carl Solomon writes: "Further addendum, perhaps of some pertinence. I first learned of dadaism in an English class at Townsend Harris H.S. (a school for the academically gifted and a prep school for C.C.N.Y.) conducted by Mr. Melvin Bernstein. He described dada, jocularly, as a pro-Dad protest against Mama. This apparently had no relationship to Philip Wylie's protest against 'Momism.' "

47 [69]

"Uncle-lawyer scream": Author had in mind Ilo Orleans, member of Poetry Society of America, and friend of his father Louis, hired as counsel on author's stolen-car crash bust that led to retirement to P.I. as alternative to law court judgment.

48 [71]

In a passage in his book *More Mishaps*, called "Background to *Howl*: Memoirs of the Waugh Years," Solomon writes:

> History moves in strange ways, I met for the first time my fellow Beatnik to be, Allen Ginsberg. I gave Allen an apocryphal history of my adventures and pseudo-intellectual deeds of daring. He meticulously took note of everything I said (I thought at the time that he suffered from "the writer's disease," imagined that he was a great writer). Later, when I decided to give up the flesh and become a professional lunatic-saint, he published all of this data, compounded partly of truth, but for the most part raving self-justification, crypto-bohemian boasting a la Rimbaud, effeminate prancing, and esoteric aphorisms plagiarized from Kierkegaard and others—in the form of *Howl*. Thus he enshrined falsehood as truth and raving as common sense for future generations to ponder over and be misled. [P. 51.]

Author replaced letters with asterisks in final draft of poem to introduce appropriate element of uncertainty. In a letter regarding this project received

September 29, 1985, Carl Solomon wrote: "Mother finally ***. Crap. Sorry Allen. Also 'heterosexual dollar' is crap; much of our literature is crap. And so on ad infinitum. Howl is a good poem but poetry isn't life."

"Last hopeless companion flown West" ref. the author's 1954 move to West Coast, thinking that also meant "abandoning Carl to Doom and Fate."

Final draft alters to "last fantastic book flung out of the tenement window." Carl Solomon comments: "That's what the best people read in Manhattan. Chic and expensive; not aberrated. Ginsberg was just having a verbal orgy at this point. He likes words. No hallucinations were involved in the 'breakdown'; just overexposure to the metaphysical imagination of Manhattan's crackpot intelligentsia vintage 1956."

The end of the stanza includes author's own associations to Naomi Ginsberg's clothes closet, the "Rosebud" flashback in last scene of *Citizen Kane*; also a paraphrase of L.-F. Céline's "vomiting up the last raspberry" description of shipboard mass seasickness, in *Journey to the End of the Night*.

49: [72]

On the line "Ah, Carl, while you are not safe . . ." Carl Solomon writes: "It's safer in hospital than outside. Vide Neal Cassady's fate. Allen and I are probably both physical cowards anyway which is why he addresses me in such terms.

"I do acknowledge Allen's great skill in describing the maze of thoughts of upset people and conveying this to the reader. A kind of Malcolm Lowry, Virginia Woolf, William Styron expertise. I don't deny he's a great writer."

50 [7, 56]

Verse opens with author's adventures at Columbia College, 1945. Author traced the words "Fuck The Jews," "[N. M.] Butler has no balls," and images of male genitalia and skull and crossbones on the dirty glass of his window to draw the attention of an Irish cleaning lady who consistently overlooked it. The action was seen by Dean Nicholas D. MacKnight as offensive and author was suspended from classes for a year. Final draft: "obscene odes on the windows of the skull."

Ref. Vance Packard's novel *The Man in the Grey Flannel Suit* and Mary McCarthy's story "The Man in the Brooks Brothers Suit," mild aspects of 1950s conformism that clothed the more savage animosity of McCarthyism.

"Blasts . . . of leaden verse": Refers to academic poetry of '40s–'50s, Eliotic tone with J. C. Ransom and Alan Tate text models, rejection of Whitman and W. C. Williams tone and form as naive, crude, raw, provincial. See the modish anthology *New Poets of England and America*, ed. D. Hall, R. Pack and L. Simpson (Cleveland: World Publishing Company, 1957).

"Nitroglycerine shrieks of fairies": See Lorca's "Ode to Walt Whitman" ("shrieks of pansies").

"Sinister intelligent editors" ref. Robert Giroux and other editors' early 1950s rejections of Kerouac's *On the Road* manuscript.

"Subconscious bloops of the hand grenades": Très Beatnik! Phrasing in this verse coincides with Kenneth Koch's "Fresh Air," a contemporaneous comment on the same theme: "Farewell, stale pale skunky pentameters (the only honest English meter, gloop gloop!)!"

— [51]

Ref. Benzedrine exhaustion all night writing experiments 1945; author's crosshatched dawn revisions terminally indecipherable.

51 [28]

In September 1947, author waited a week in Houston-Galveston area for a job on ship to Dakar, W. Africa, after summer with Neal Cassady in Denver and at William Burroughs' marijuana farm, New Waverly, Texas.

"Brilliant Spaniard": *Journals Early Fifties Early Sixties*, entry for June 17, 1952:

In Houston, 1947—I was broke, stealing Pepsi Cola bottles to cash in and buy candy bars for hunger, waiting for a ship. Outside the old Union Hall, walking down the street, a latin animal, Cuban, Spanish, I don't know. Electricity seemed to flow from his powerful body—black hair, curled wildly, looked impossible for him to live in society, to me—powerful malignant features—he was perhaps 22 or less—springing down the street in a tense potent walk, dungarees, powerful legs, not too tall, blue shirt opened several buttons on the chest, black hair curling sparsely on chest—he seemed made of iron, no sweat—or brown polished rock. I never saw in my life a more perfect being—expression of vigor and potency and natural rage on face—I couldn't conceive of him speaking English. I wonder what loves he had. Who could resist him? He must have taken any weak body he needed or wanted. Love from such a face I could not imagine, not gentleness—but love and gentleness are not needed where there was so much life. He just passed me by and I stood there amazed staring at him as he disappeared up the block & around the corner scattering the air in spiritual waves behind him. I couldn't believe he was human. He had thick features, black eyebrows, almost square face, powerful chest, perfect freedom of walk.

Herbert E. Huncke, Fall 1953, Manhattan hotel room N.E. corner 8th Ave & 47th Street. *Photo by A.G.*

52 [46]

Ref. a story told in Jack Kerouac's fiction, *Vanity of Duluoz*, Book 12, Chap. VIII.

53 [52]

Author's mother cooked lungen (lung stew) and Russian borscht (beet soup) when not eating nature-community vegetarian.

54 [48]

Ref. Naomi Ginsberg's Chaplinesque recollections of Orchard and Rivington streets, Manhattan 1905, after debarking ship from Russia. See "Kaddish," Part IV, the "with your eyes" section, for similar images: ". . . with your fingers of rotten mandolins . . . arms of fat Paterson porches . . . belly of strikes and smokestacks . . ."

55 [50]

Russell Durgin (d. August 28, 1985), Columbia theology student in whose sublet apartment, 321 East 121st Street, East Harlem 1948, author read

William Blake, left Manhattan that summer for medical treatment, tubercular lungs. Treatment may have involved filling chest space with celluloid balls to prevent collapse.

"Orange crates of theology": Durgin's books were displayed in wooden orange crates, then commonly used as bookcases, as plastic milk crates serve four decades later.

56 [45]

After homeless weeks on New York's winter streets upon release from Rikers Island prison on an addict sentence, 86'd from Times Square by police who called him "a creep," friend Herbert Huncke knocked at author's door in this condition one winter's day, 1948.

"Scabs": Huncke's skin disturbances 1945–48, related to junk needles and amphetamine.

57 [—]

See William M. Garver in Jack Kerouac's *Mexico City Blues* (Choruses 57–61, 80–84) and other books; in *Junky*, by William S. Burroughs, the character Bill Gains. Garver purloined overcoats from semi-elegant restaurants, pawned them, used the money to score and pay rent—a good Russian overcoat was worth a week's rent. He'd sit at a table nursing coffee and apple pie till he spotted expensive unprotected apparel on a wall hanger.

Author sent Kerouac this original ms. of "Howl" (first six pages of Part I) in Mexico City. Kerouac showed it to Garver, who commented, "No coathangers in Longchamps [restaurants]." See Kerouac's annotation bottom p. 5 thus. Entire verse is dropped in final draft.

"Coat hanger apparition" alludes to W. B. Yeats' "The Apparitions": "Fifteen apparitions have I seen;/ The worst a coat upon a coat hanger."—*The Poems of W. B. Yeats* (New York: Macmillan, 1983), p. 334.

58 [—]

An image of Herbert Huncke hustling Bryant Park, N.Y., which author associates with opening pages of Jean Genêt's *Our Lady of the Flowers* (New York: Grove Press, 1963): ". . . the Negro Angel Sun . . . eyes are clear and sky-blue . . . vacant like the windows of buildings under construction, through which you see the sky . . ."

59 [55]

Ref. some of author's Columbia College gay contemporaries' later careers.

60 [54]

As author remembers anecdote, friend Walter Adams visited poet Louis Simpson's high-floored apartment near Columbia in 1946:

L.S.: Do you have a watch?
W.A.: Yes.
L.S.: Can I have it?
W.A.: Here.
L.S. (throwing watch out window): We don't need time, we're already in eternity.

In letter November 21, 1985, kindly responding to query from author, Louis Simpson writes:

It seems this does apply to me. I say "seems" because I don't remember doing this, but a man whose word I could trust once wrote me a letter in which he said that I thought "that technology had destroyed time so that all lives ever lived were being lived simultaneously, which was why you could ask Walter Adams for his watch, throw it out the window and remark that we didn't need such instruments any more."

This must have happened shortly before I had a "nervous breakdown"—the result of my experience during the war. There may have been other causes, but

I think this was the main. I have no recollections of the months preceding the breakdown, and if people say I threw watches out of windows, OK.

61 [64]

William Burroughs, among others, "retired to Mexico [and Tanger] to cultivate sex," Garver to Mexico for his "habit," Jack Kerouac to his sister's North Carolina house in "Rocky Mount to Buddha," Neal Cassady worked for S.P. Railroad, John Hollander among others went on to Harvard. Naomi Ginsberg's window 1953 overlooked Woodlawn Cemetery in the Bronx; see "Kaddish."

Poe wrote "Annabel Lee," "The Bells," "Ulalume" and "Eureka" 1846–48 in his Fordham cottage, now moved to Grand Concourse, Bronx.

62 [39]

One night 1945, author and William Burroughs visited Everard Baths, rumored to be owned by Police Athletic League, at 28 West 28th Street, N.Y., accompanied by Jack Kerouac, who consorted with several French sailors who blew him. Phallic reference is mostly imaginary.

63 [49]

Bill Keck built a harpsichord in his 2nd Street loft. Other artists had cold-water flats under Brooklyn Bridge, some furnished with Wilhelm Reich's wardrobe-sized Orgone Accumulator boxes to which they repaired sitting in daily sessions to replenish their cosmic-energy monad "orgones." See Reich's *The Function of the Orgasm* (New York: Touchstone, 1974).

Large packing crates were adapted for use as furniture, closets, beds, etc., in this milieu.

64 [77]

"Goldhorn shadow" in this verse paraphrases some sentence by Kerouac.

Lester Young, Coleman Hawkins, Charlie Parker, Illinois Jacquet saxophones were heard on "Symphony Sid" all-night bebop radio program mid-'40s Manhattan.

First draft's concluding phrase, "last blue sad jelly of Time," ref. Jelly Roll Morton's "Jelly, Jelly, Jelly, Jelly stays on my mind," Ma Rainey's "Jellybean Blues," etc., as black metaphor for erotic squish.

"Lamma lamma sabacthani"—"My God, my God, why have you forsaken me?" Christ's last words from the cross ("Eli, Eli, lama sabachthani": Matthew 27: 46)—of final draft was lifted from Tristan Corbière's version in "Cris d'Aveugle" ("Cries of the Blindman") in *Poems*, trans. Walter McElroy (Pawlet, Vt.: Banyan Press, 1947), p. 30:

Les oiseaux croques-morts	The birds those under-takers
Ont donc peur a mon corps	Facing my body show fear
Mon Golgotha n'est pas fini	This Golgotha lasts on for me
Lamma lamma sabacthani	*Lamma lamma sabacthani*
Colombes de la Mort	You doves of Death
	· hover
Soiffez apres mon corps	In thirst for my body here

The poem ends:

J'entends le vent du nord	I hear the north wind roar
Qui bugle comme un cor	It bellows like a horn
C'est l'hallali des trepasses	That halloos for those who are gone
J'aboie apres mon tour assez	I have howled for my turn too long
J'entends le vent du nord	I hear the north wind roar
J'entends le glas du cor	I hear the knell of the horn

65 [47]

Basically it's just Bowery bums.

66–67 [23, 27]

See Hart Crane's "The Bridge":

               Behind
My father's cannery works I used to see
Rail-squatters ranged in nomad raillery,
The ancient men—wifeless or runaway
Hobo-trekkers that forever search
An empire wilderness of freight and rails.
Each seemed a child, like me, on a loose perch,
Holding to childhood like some termless play.
John, Jake or Charley, hopping the slow freight
—Memphis to Tallahassee—riding the rods,
Blind fists of nothing, humpty-dumpty clods.

Yet they touch something like a key perhaps.
From pole to pole across the hills, the states
—They know a body under the wide rain;
Youngsters with eyes like fjords, old reprobates
With racetrack jargon, —dotting immensity
They lurk across her, knowing her yonder breast
Snow-silvered, sumac-stained or smoky blue—
is past the valley-sleepers, south or west.
—As I have trod the rumorous midnights, too.

See also the Circus of Oklahoma in Kafka's *Amerika*, trans. Edwin Muir (New York: New Directions, 1946).

70–71 [—]

Peter Du Peru, San Francisco friend of author 1954 and at time of "Howl"'s writing. See photograph.

72 [—]

The late Guy Wernham, early translator Comte de Lautréamont's *The Chants of Maldoror* (New York: New Directions, 1947), served as bartender at Gino and Carlo's, poet Jack Spicer's favored bar on Green St., North Beach, San Francisco, late 1950s–early 60s.

73 [30]

Joffre Stewart, Chicago vegetarian pacifist war-tax resister, signal member of 1948 "Peacemakers" meeting with Dave Dellinger, Dwight Macdonald, A. J. Muste and Bayard Rustin at Yellow Springs, Ohio, called to plan resistance to reinstatement of draft in peacetime. A strong anarchist, visiting Kenneth Rexroth S.F. 1955 he remarked to author that he was investigating the FBI. Familiarly active around folk clubs and on Chicago's streets thru 1968 police riots to the 1980s, he carried a large white cloth bag filled with peace leaflets and his own provocative anarchist broadsides.

Peter Du Peru, North Beach remittance man wanderer, Broadway corner a few doors below 1010 Montgomery Street. Author had worked as market researcher in financial district several blocks downhill thru Spring 1955. *Photo by A.G.*

75 [—]

Next drafts eliminate this ponderous lineage. "Howl" was originally co-dedicated to Burroughs, Kerouac, Cassady and Lucien Carr; the last preferred his name be dropped lest it cause his life to cast a shadow beyond its actuality.

76 [42]

My own version of Neal Cassady's Western myth, here exaggerated as erotic comedy.

77 [—]

Ref. verse beginning "Nous n'avions pas fini de nous parler d'amour," from "Le Condamné à Mort" by Jean Genêt. Quoted earlier, author's letter to Neal Cassady and Jack Kerouac, February 15, 1952: *As Ever: The Collected Correspondence of Allen Ginsberg & Neal Cassady* (Berkeley, Cal.: Creative Arts, 1977), p. 120.

> We didn't get time to finish talking about love.
> We didn't get time to smoke our cigarettes, Gitanes.
> You ask yourself why the courts passed death sentence
> On a man so beautiful he made the dawn pale.
>
> Nous n'avions pas fini de nous parler d'amour.
> Nous n'avions pas fini de fumer nos gitanes.
> On peut se demander pourquoi les Cours condamné
> Un assassin si beau qu'il fait pâlir le jour.

78 [63]

Ref. Genêt, above. Four years after this draft, Neal Cassady was incarcerated in San Quentin for over two years on conviction of having passed two grass cigarettes to agents in exchange of a lift to work at the S.P.R.R. station. After 1957 publication of *On the Road*, Cassady's association with Jack Kerouac's Dean Moriarty on his picaresque road was well known around San Francisco Bay Area. By 1959 the energetic Cassady gained further underground fame as "Johnny Appleseed" of the local marijuana movement, and was under surveillance for his literary and countercultural celebrity.

In San Quentin he enrolled in religion classes taught by astrologer Gavin Arthur (grandson of Pres. Chester A. Arthur), who in later years housed and befriended Cassady at various times of crisis. Author visited Cassady in San Quentin 1959 invited by Gavin Arthur and read text of "Howl" to his class.

79 [76]

Ref. author's idiomatic adaptation of Catullus XXXVIII, "Malest Cornifici Tuo Catullo" (*Collected Poems*, p. 123) to his domestic situation on meeting Peter Orlovsky.

Catullus returned home to Sirmio after visit to Asia Minor (XXXI); visiting his brother's grave in Asia Minor, he wrote "Ave Atque Vale," his eternal Hail and Farewell (CI): "What might be left to say anew in time after death . . ."

Original ms. ref. also L. Zukofsky's translations of Catullus, and the lyric title of his collection of short poems: *Anew*.

Also: "I'm writing this book because we're all going to die— In the loneliness of my life, my father dead, my brother dead, my mother faraway, my sister and wife far away, nothing here but my own tragic hands that once were guarded by a world, a sweet attention, that now are left to guide and disappear their own way into the common dark of all our death, sleeping in me raw bed, alone and stupid: with just this one pride and consolation: my heart broke in the general despair and opened up inwards to the Lord, I made a supplication in this dream." —Jack Kerouac, *Visions of Cody* (1952; New York: McGraw-Hill, 1972), p. 368.

80 [75]

Ref. Jack Kerouac as creative breakthru artist, especially for *Visions of Cody*'s long-breathed prose-poem "sketches" and "Imitation of the Tape" section; for *Mexico City Blues* (circa 1954–55, same time as "Howl") a seminal volume of poetry; earlier-invented rhapsodic paragraphs in *Book of Dreams*, and *Doctor Sax*; the naked spontaneous-minded pages of "Brakeman on the R.R." prose so much appreciated by Robert Creeley circa 1955 Bay Area, thus first published in his *Black Mountain Review* two autumns later; and supreme improvisations in *Old Angel Midnight* of endless vocal sounds entering the window of the ear. These examples catalyzed the scantier improvisations of "Howl."

Kerouac's superior formal genius as poet, much misnoted by academic criticism, was much appreciated in ms. at the time by his peers Robert Duncan and Robert Creeley, and had strong encouraging influence on the writing of his friends William S. Burroughs, Gary Snyder, Philip Whalen, Lew Welch, Michael McClure, Philip Lamantia and the author of "Howl" among many others, including Bob Dylan a half-decade later.

Kerouac's slogans for composition are outlined in "Belief and Technique of Modern Prose,"* excellent instruction, when well understood, for "First thought, best thought" clarity and sincerity:

---

* In *Heaven and Other Poems* (San Francisco: Grey Fox Press, 1977), pp. 46–7.

List of Essentials

1. Scribbled secret notebooks, and wild typewritten pages, for yr own joy
2. Submissive to everything, open, listening
3. Try never get drunk outside yr own house
4. Be in love with yr life
5. Something that you feel will find its own form
6. Be crazy dumbsaint of the mind
7. Blow as deep as you want to blow
8. Write what you want bottomless from bottom of the mind
9. The unspeakable visions of the individual
10. No time for poetry but exactly what is
11. Visionary tics shivering in the chest
12. In tranced fixation dreaming upon object before you
13. Remove literary, grammatical and syntactical inhibition
14. Like Proust be an old teahead of time
15. Telling the true story of the world in interior monolog
16. The jewel center of interest is the eye within the eye
17. Write in recollection and amazement for yourself
18. Work from pithy middle eye out, swimming in language sea
19. Accept loss forever
20. Believe in the holy contour of life
21. Struggle to sketch the flow that already exists intact in mind
22. Dont think of words when you stop but to see the picture better
23. Keep track of every day the date emblazoned in yr morning
24. No fear or shame in the dignity of yr experience, language & knowledge
25. Write for the world to read and see yr exact pictures of it
26. Bookmovie is the movie in words, the visual American form
27. In praise of Character in the Bleak inhuman Loneliness
28. Composing wild, undisciplined, pure, coming in from under, crazier the better
29. You're a Genius all the time
30. Writer-Director of Earthly movies Sponsored & Angeled in Heaven

This list was tacked on wall above author's bedstead in North Beach hotel a year before "Howl" was written. See Robert Duncan's comments apropos in *Allen Verbatim*, ed. Gordon Ball (New York: McGraw-Hill, 1974), pp. 143–47.

81 [74]

Regarding haiku and prose syntax, reworking and expanding the aesthetic program of verses 44–45

Jack Kerouac with R.R. Brakeman's Rule Book in pocket, visiting Burroughs & author at 206 East 7th Street, N.Y.C., around the time of spontaneous prose mode composition of *Dr. Sax, The Subterraneans* & *MacDougal St. Blues*, Fall 1953.   *Photo by A.G.*

(see note above), reference here is to Cézanne's method of composition. Letters and conversations of Cézanne from which author derived this aesthetic, applied somewhat to "Howl" poetics including paraphrase of key words ("sensation") and phrases, were first encountered in Erle Loran's *Cézanne's Composition* (Berkeley, Cal.: University of California Press, 1943). At the time, author was writing term paper on Cézanne for Prof. Meyer Schapiro at Columbia University. Correct Latin line should read: "Pater Omnipotens Aeterne Deus." Relevant passages from Loran follow:

"The study of arts is very long and badly conducted. Today a painter must discover everything for himself, for there are no longer any but very bad schools, where one becomes warped, where one learns nothing. One must first of all study geometric forms: the cone, the cube, the cylinder, the sphere. When one knows how to render these things in their form and their planes, one ought to know how to paint." —Emile Bernard, *Souvenirs sur Paul Cézanne* (Paris: Chez Michel, 1912).

"The form and contour of objects is given to us by the oppositions and contrasts which result from their individual coloration." —John Rewald, *Cézanne: Sa Vie, son oeuvre, son amitie pour Zola* (Paris: Albin Michel, 1939).

"This is absolutely indisputable—I am very positive: an optical sensation is produced in our visual organ which causes us to classify the planes represented by color modulations into light, half-tone, or quarter-tone." —Bernard, *Souvenirs*.

On Gauguin: "Well, he hasn't understood me; I have never wanted and I shall never accept the absence of modeling or of gradations; it's nonsense. Gauguin isn't a painter, he has only made Chinese images . . . [he has] stolen [my] little sensation and paraded it before the public." —Ibid.

"In an orange, an apple, a ball, a head, there is a culminating point; and this point is always—in spite of the terrible effect: light, shade, sensations of color —the nearest to our eye. The edges of objects recede toward a center placed at our horizon." —Ibid.

"Lines parallel to the horizon give extension, whether it be a section of nature or, if you prefer, of the spectacle that the *Pater Omnipotens aeterne Deus* spreads before our eyes. The lines perpendicular to this horizon give depth. Now for us, nature is more in depth than in surface." —Paul Cézanne to Emile Bernard, April 15, 1904. Ibid.

Cézanne: 'I have my motif [he joins his hands]. A motif, you see, is this. . . .

Gasquet: How's that?

Cézanne: Eh? Yes—[he repeats his gesture, draws his hands apart, fingers spread out, and brings them together again, slowly, slowly; then joins them, presses them together and contracts them, making them interlace] there you have it; that's what one must attain. If I pass too high or too low, all is ruined. There mustn't be a single link too loose, not a crevice through which may escape the emotion, the light, the truth. I advance, you understand, all of my canvas at one time—together. I bring together in the same spirit, the same faith, all that is scattered. All that we see disperses, vanishes; is it not so? Nature is always the same, but nothing remains of it, nothing of what comes to our sight. Our art ought to give the shimmer of its duration with the elements, the appearance of all its changes. It ought to make us taste it eternally. What is underneath? Nothing, perhaps. Perhaps everything. You understand? Thus I join these straying hands. I take from left, from right, here, there, everywhere, tones, colors, shades. I fix them, I bring them together. They make lines. They become objects, rocks, trees, without my thinking about it. They take on volume. They acquire value. If these volumes, these values, correspond on my canvas, in my feeling, to the planes and patches of color which are there before our eyes, very good! my canvas joins hands. It does not vacillate. It does not pass too high or too low. It is true; it is full. But if I feel the least distraction, the least weakness, above all if I interpret too much one day, if today I am carried away by a theory which is contrary to that of the day before, if I think while painting, if I intervene, why then everything is gone.

—Joachim Gasquet, *Paul Cézanne* (Paris: Editions Bernheim-Jeune, 1926).

For earlier articulation of ideas from Cézanne applied to "Howl," see author's 1965 *Paris Review* interview in *Writers at Work: Third Series* (New York: Viking, 1967), pp. 291–97.

82 [75]

On improvised sound track of the Al Leslie–Robert Frank film *Pull My Daisy*, 1959, Kerouac explains: "Well, they turn over their little purple moonlight pages in which their secret naked doodlings do show. Secret scatological thought, and that's why everybody wants to see it." —*Pull My Daisy* (New York: Grove Press, 1961), p. 23.

83 [78]

Ref. Lionel Trilling, *The Liberal Imagination* (New York: Viking, 1950). Author sat in Prof. Trilling's Romantic Literature class at Columbia College, studying Wordsworth, Keats, Shelley, Byron, little Blake, and did paper comparing Rimbaud to Keats. See Trilling's response to "Howl" on p. 156.

Latter half of verse unused in final draft. "Accept no substitute": 1950 slogan for commercial advertisement of a name-brand product forgotten by author.

84 [76]

Attempt to clarify the role of poetry as revealing naked mind, identical itself with the experience (and suffering) of love. See Whitman's poetics "of perfect personal candor," in 1855 preface, *Leaves of Grass*.

"Madman bum & angel [beat in Time]": See note to verse 79 above, re Kerouac's *Visions of Cody*, as quoted.

Final Draft, HOWL, Part II

80*

"Moloch": or Molech, the Canaanite fire god, whose worship was marked by parents' burning their children as propitiatory sacrifice. "And thou shalt not let any of thy seed pass through the fire to Molech" (Leviticus 18:21).

"Boys sobbing in armies": Postwar U.S.A. reinstitution of peacetime draft, 1948; see note to verse 31.

81

Law apparatus is too crude to cover human body of manslaughter, per author's experience; ref. Burroughs et al. See *Queer*, W. S. Burroughs (New York: Viking Press, 1985) pp. xvii–xxii.

"Heavy judger of men": Ref. also world-shock 1953 N.Y. electric chair executions Julius & Ethel Rosenberg spy convicts. (Later, Caryl Chessman gas execution 1960, California.)

82

"Buildings are judgment": See William Blake's spectre of the Jehovic hyper-rationalistic judgmental

* Line numbers from here on refer only to final published text (pp. 3–8).

lawgiver Urizen, creator of spiritual disorder and political chaos. His abstract calipers limit the infinite universe to his egoic horizon, a projection of unmindful selfhood, the result of aggressively naive mental measurements which substitute hypocrite or modish generalizations for experience of event, and oppress physical body, feelings and imagination.

83

"Whose mind is pure machinery": N.B. Marshall McLuhan's apposite axiom, "The medium is the message."

82–84

"Crossbone . . . jailhouse," etc.: Ref. Lynd Ward block-print novel *God's Man* (New York: Jonathan Cape and Harrison Smith, 1929), ex libris author's family 1930s, reprinted in Ward's *Storyteller Without Words* (New York: Harry W. Abrams, 1974), wherein Ward noted that *God's Man* was "published . . . in the same week that saw the crash of the New York stock market." Lynd Ward illustrated "Howl"'s "Moloch" in 1980, his block print thus completing the circle of imagination.

Lynd Ward blockprints: The artist enters the City of a Thousand Blind Windows. The artist sees Buildings of Judgment from the Soulless Jailhouse (likely New York Tombs prison). The artist flees the City whose skyscrapers stand in the long streets like endless Jehovahs.

Illustration for Howl II, *Moloch. Lynd Ward, 1980.*

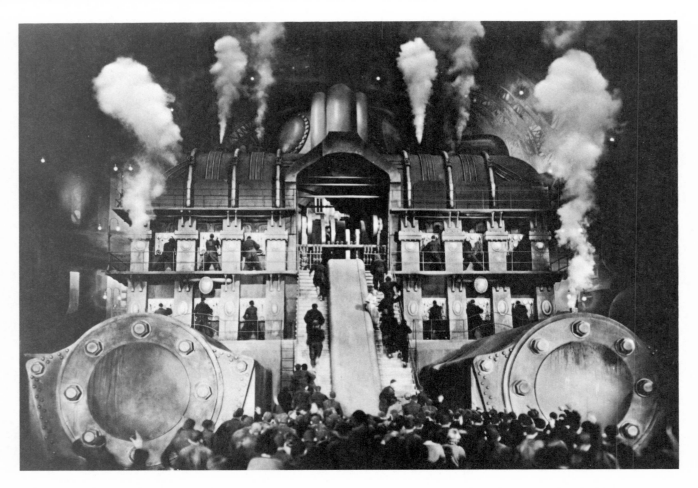

Cannibal dynamo in Metropolis Centrum. Fritz Lang, Berlin 1932.   *Courtesy Museum of Modern Art, Film Stills Archives.*

"Skyscrapers . . . endless Jehovahs," etc.: Ref. cinema images for robot megalopolis centrum, Fritz Lang's *Metropolis*, Berlin, 1932.

83

"Cannibal dynamo": Ref. the opening industrial-heartbeat sound track of Fritz Lang's terrific film *M* (1931); also his *Last Will of Dr. Mabuse* (1933).

84

"Thousand blind windows": Appearance of upper stories Sir Francis Drake Hotel, corner Powell & Pine streets, San Francisco, which image directly inspired this section of the poem. Entry 1954 journal reads:

On peyote, San Francisco, October 17–18, Sat nite. 1:15— Apartment window wide open looking across down downtown the aspect of ferocious building reared in the center looming up in the clouds wisp fog sliding across the flat blue sky.

Uprising in the timeless city gloom, dark tower over ruddy building suddenly a vision the Death Head —the building an evil monster—a tower in Hell—

("Those poor lost souls making it up in the tower") two eyes blast light far apart brick glass illuminated from within—too corny for a painter to make the surrealistic reality—no—deep gong religious

Impassive robot (antennalike structures) of Sir Francis Drake Hotel.
And quite vegetable that monster too—it may be coming to eat me someday—
That was what was familiar all along.
It's got a crown—
Smoke curling up from it—working rooted in the basements
Snub nosed monster—the hideous gorgonian aspect— . . .

Description of the Tower of Baal or Azriel? of Lucifer "The Tower of Lucifer." The star goes out at one A.M.—the monster appears most grim staring into the sky, small noselite—with snout near darkened —someone up late in the tower . . .

With fog rolling by down from Twin Peaks & South San Fran to the bridge and Embarcadero edge of the cock peninsula in the bottom of the vale of the town arranged skyline peyotl buildings:

I came to the window and glanced out into the night space at the unreal city below in which I inhabit a building—

as walking street today I noticed the battlement uprearing facade appearance of the ranges of blocks of houses with fantastic Graeco-mediaeval ornamentation juttings and false stone wood pillars and arches porches & crossbow tower'd bedrooms—

Came to the window to stare at the thousand eyed buildings in the smoke filled stone vale crowded with monstrous edifices shouldering each other rocking stolid on the streets, red lights below and haze purple sky light above as in Rembrandt it was brown—

and fixed eye & noticed the vegetable horror of the Sir Francis Drake Hotel—had waited long for this perception having spent four hours total over a week looking out the window at the wrong building waiting for something to happen—nothing had but that I'd noticed how modern and large and isolate the Sutter St. Med. building stood in my way, too large for the more homely old Drake and downtown other S P and Insurance edifices making a New York Gotham midtown Murray Hill unreal Wall Street miniature

Allen Ginsberg and Peter Orlovsky visiting Moloch with theatric gaze, Nob Hill's Pine Street corner, facing Powell Street downtown, Sir Francis Drake Hotel tower background night-lit, San Francisco, 1959. *Photo by Harry Redl.*

Moloch. Athanasius Kircher, *Oedipus Aegyptiacus*, Rom, 1652.

panorama [sweep] toward [Bay] Bridge—another coast's apple for the eye—

Found suddenly the Gothic eyes of the skull tower glaring out bleak blind blank smoking above in stillness in the atmosphere of the real primeval city world, down-grown out of earth—with horrible cross check dollar sign skull protrusion of lipless jailbarred inhuman longtooth spectral deathhead brick columns making abstract teeth. This phantom building robot was smoking in inaction as it had been stuck there in eternity a golem waiting for the Rabbi of electricity to pull the switch for it to topple forward into the city destroying— Meanwhile serving as an evil tower of thought, glaring profound and open above the streets (into my window)—for every eye to see that could wake from the daily dream to register its central presence in the atmosphere of night.

On top a star of David in great blue silly neon that goes off at 1 A.M. leaving the impression of the continually Death-in-Life robot zombie presence of the Drake (mad cranes tear down the bldgs.) fixed for the night to wait sleepless and unseeing while physicists tinker in its bowels toward the day of resurrection.

85

"Whose soul is electricity and banks": See Ezra Pound's theory of usury as canker of state, *Cantos*, XLV.

"Specter of genius": William Blake's use of "spectre" as disordered shadow states of mind, body, heart or imagination, when mutually unbalanced dominated by or dominating one the others. See S. Foster

Damon, *A Blake Dictionary* (Boulder, Colo.: Shambala Books, 1980), "The Four Zoas," as well as Blake's prophetic book, same name.

"Whose name is the Mind": This verse seems to objectify a recognition uncovered in the act of composition, a crux of the poem.

86

"Cocksucker in Moloch": Ref. also Jean Genêt, another literary cocksucker.

87

Ref. Blake illumination; see note to verse 26.

"Whom I abandon": This verse seems to objectify a decision uncovered in the act of composition and is the crux of the poem.

88

Topographical associations: "Robot apartments," giant downtown money buildings; "invisible suburbs," perhaps Levittown, N.Y.; "skeleton treasuries," early cold war budget debts; "demonic industries," Southern California's night-lit war plants viewed from highway on author's first West Coast trip; "spectral nations," mainland China "unrecognized" by U.S.A., Soviet gulags' ghostly bureaucracies, Western imperium covering Guatemala, Vietnam, Algeria with war; "invincible madhouses," Naomi Ginsberg, Carl Solomon then immured in Pilgrim State Mental Hospital; "monstrous bombs," contemporaneous atomic and hydrogen nuclear weapons.

89

"Heaven which exists and is everywhere": See Arthur Rimbaud, "Morning": "When shall we go beyond the mountains and the shores, to greet the birth of new toil, of new wisdom, the flight of tyrants, of demons, the end of superstition, to adore —the first to adore!—Christmas on the earth." —*Season in Hell*, trans. Louise Varese (New York: New Directions, 1945).

91

"Sensitive bullshit": See note to verse 1 re "starving hysterical naked" for key to contradiction.

92

"Ten years . . . Mad generation": Poem's specific reference was to decade 1945–55.

Final Draft, HOWL, Part III

94*

Carl Solomon writes: "I was never in Rockland . . . Neither of us has ever been in Rockland. Ginsberg never even on a tour." (Not at the time, though I visited a friend of Leary's there later '60s.—A.G.)

96

Naomi Ginsberg then at Pilgrim State Hospital.

97

In early 1950s, Carl Solomon worked as editor for his uncle A. A. Wynn's Ace Books, publishing Burroughs' *Junky* and contracting Ur-text of Kerouac's *On the Road*.

99

Typescript drafts of letters unsent to T. S. Eliot and Malcolm de Chazal from N.Y. Psychiatric Institute fall–winter 1948 co-written by Carl Solomon and Allen Ginsberg.

October 13, 1949

My dear Chevalier de Chazal:

Graciously aware of the poverty of the correspondence, and above all of its tendentious nature, between the mainland and your forlorn Indian domicile, a mere man among monsoons as you undoubtedly hold yourself to be, we have taken advantage of the favorable winds, perhaps over-abruptly, but as a last recourse, to ask for money.

We are determined upon this course only upon considering the favorable rate of exchange. If however, you have nothing but goldfish out there we will accept these, as there is a shortage of exotic goldfish in this hospital. Perhaps we are too exacting. Therefore perhaps we could justify our very inconsiderate demands on your person by inquiring if you are bald.

Uncle Malcolm, we have come upon a stupendous discovery which promises to be the work of a theology student. It would be thoughtful of you to send us a short note of encouragement a mere morsel as we are dying of hunger. We have dyed our hair purple to attract the attention of other theology students but we have met with no encouragement in the eyes of those false hearted ambassadors from Moscow, who will not stop their endless accusations of Chinoiserie.

Since our natal light comes not from China but from Mauritius we feel that you are our last resort.

Can you tell us how much you charge for a season? We can live in goldfish bowls and thereby bring in much revenue from admiring Japanese tourists.

We have poignant types of children to the number of seven.

No more need be said. Beyond a certain point

there can be no spoken communication and all speech is useless.

Shirley Temple and Dagwood Bumpstead
(who affixes his name under protest)*

December 19, 1949

[To T. S. Eliot]
Most distinguished Number 1 poet of 1949:

The year is fast running out. We wish to affirm, if we may use so banal a word, that the year is running out. Does this not frighten you?

"Uneasy wears the crown that wears the head." etc.

Now we know all about cold spots on the moon and other items that probably preoccupy you at this, shall we say turbulent?, moment, so close to Christmas as it is. We understand very well that your conversion was fraudulent. You carried it off very well. Now to get on to business.

We have here crowded into this very room, 45 potential applicants, young legislators to be from various walks of society, together packed tight, and we constitute as you must be aware, a very formidable bloc. What we want to say, though its very difficult to explain pointedly, [is] that we want to represent ourselves as your Maginot line, though it is getting late in the year. We'll make riots for you. We'll make bonfires. There you have it, 45 young legislators (incidentally, to illustrate the prosletysing vigor of our legislators, one of those has just come in and announced to us that he has just converted one John Puccio, tinker, to our cause) scurrying through the night starting—there you have it—bonfires, all over, in order to advance your candidacy under the theory (we know you will sympathize) that every vote counts.

To illustrate the quality of self criticism in our ranks, one of our younger members has just criticised your body. You have a big nose. But we tend to regard this this way—for you to have a big nose is for us to have a big nose. (The ace of spades, the tarot cards, the dying king, the rituals and everything, we all know that.) So now to get on to business as we are legislators.

To illustrate some more of the self criticism, another young legislator of our ranks (the same one as before, it so happens—but he is very vociferous, and is promised to a grey dramatic critic, on Broadway, America) has interjected

" 'Uneasy wears the crown that wears the head' etc. kills the whole program."

The fact is, that some 85% of our young legislators are schemers, and you cannot count on them to be real firebrands (you know our position on that, personally, and you need not worry about us, I am sure you will be gratified by us). We know exactly where you stand

---

* Line numbers refer to final published text only (pp. 3–8).

* *Sens Plastique* (Paris: Gallimard, 1948); trans. Irving Weiss (New York: Sun Books, 1979).

on the question of the existence of your great mind. We are prepared to publicly back up our charges, defying libel, lawsuits, the stupid comments of newspaper would be litterateur editorialists manque.

Certain literary dirigibles (we use the term figuratively) claim that you are a dictator. But these people have nothing to do with the main body of traditional literature, but these people are stinkers. Has a stinker ever occupied a famous place in literature, English or French? I am not speaking of Russians, as they have always been bolsheviks, even before you became a dictator.

We send our regards and highest genuflections to Mrs. literary Dictator and all the little literary dictators. This was decided on at the last meeting, after much debate. Schwamp, who is earnest, but a fool at heart, says that you want to keep them in the background, but we know that your family is really mongoloid. But as an illustration of our total participation in your decades we voted to mention them too. This shows how completely we are of your camp.

We are waiting for marching orders. Some of our younger and less responsible young legislators to be want us to embark en masse, to China, thinking to join you there, on the theory that you'll soon contract a non-aggression pact with the reds in order to play for time. They feel our arrival there would give you an extra card up your sleeve to bargain with. The time will come when you won't have anybody to depend on but us, and young as we are, we still are legislators who know our minds and have taken a blood oath to respect you, no matter what happens. Anybody that reneges on the agreement, we will kill them. We do this with your tacit approval, in order that you need not be implicated if we get caught by the American police who are very brutal. But we vow not to involve you, because we know all about abysses already. In war there is no umpire, but nevertheless do not attempt to use your powers of divination: as regards the powers of divination, il s'agit de guerre moderne, (Clausewitz, Rommel, etc.) but you know all that.

Now to get back to speaking of you, personally, if we may make so bold. There are no atheists in foxholes. This definitely settles the religious question. Some of our younger legislators are Jews (you don't know their names), but we have decided to treat them as if they were dopey daffodils, a special category of legislator which we have invented for your approval. They think they are all budding young Clemenceaus. Perhaps there is a place for them in France.

The meeting is fast becoming a farce, indistinguishable from a pepper steak party, the like of which was given last week, or two weeks ago at the very most, by the young Chevaliers of Malcolm De Chazal, where they did nothing but eat. Therefore, much as we would like to go on chatting with you, exchanging literary gossip, news that would be of mutual interest, we will simply conclude by rephrasing a question that was made from the floor, by one of your young devotees who will not get up, whether you have epilepsy like Dostoievsky. If so (and Dostoievsky we consider from the very first to have been a dead issue, as far as this meeting is concerned—next month being set aside for our Dostoievsky memorial—) we want to know if you have not neglected it. We care for you and would be reassured that you have taken all available steps to curtail this dreadful disease which would turn you into a feebleminded mongolian idiot, too, which would make our position rather embarrassing.

Before saying farewell, we want to assure you that we know a good literary dictator when we see one: A smart young fellow like you, a real hustler.

In case you are wondering who is responsible for this transcription of the meeting, I may be permitted to speak of myself as a young poet who though passing through a position of temporary and purely transitional sterility, as far as productivity presently counts, will soon be bigger than you.

We take our leave by asking us to kiss you goodbye.

> Signed,
> Your 44 favorite legislators,
> (one dissenting vote)
> who are your brightest acolytes,
> Yisraeli Soccer Team.

101

See note to verse 43 [65] re Artaud's "Judgement of God."

102

Likely association with Apollinaire's *Mamelles de Tirésias*; New York's Utica was named for classical Mediterranean city.

103

"Harpies of the Bronx": Solomon's and author's mother and aunts had lived in the Bronx.

104

Carl Solomon was not straightjacketed at N.Y. State Psychiatric Institute while in company with author. Solomon writes: "Not at P.I.; later at Pilgrim rather often." Ping-Pong was actual.

105

Not Solomon but author was rebuked for percussive experiments on piano once in P.I. common room.

"Armed madhouse": "Howl" marks 10th anniversary of Winston Churchill's Fulton, Missouri, "Iron Curtain" speech acknowledging cold war.

106

"Shocks": "Received 50 insulin comas at P.I. and 21 electroshocks at Pilgrim." —Carl Solomon, letter to author, September 29, 1985.

"A cross in the void": See note to verse 43 [65] re Artaud, etc.

107

Of this line, Carl Solomon writes: "At this time I was an admirer of Adlai Stevenson and had all the feelings toward America of a disappointed Democrat." —Letter to author, September 29, 1985

"Accuse your doctors of insanity": See note 43 [65], Artaud, etc.

108

"The heavens of Long Island": Ref. Pilgrim State Hospital, Brentwood, Long Island.

109

"Twenty-five thousand mad comrades": Pilgrim State population; see note to verse 42 [69–70].

> 'Tis the final conflict
> Let each stand in his place
> The International Soviet
> Shall be the human race.

Eugène Pottier, "The Internationale," June 1871, trans. C. H. Kerr, in *I.W.W. Songs* ("Little Red Songbook") 34th ed. (Chicago: International Workers of the World, 1973), pp. 6–7.

110

Democratic Vistas, 1871, limns Walt Whitman's amative affection for these United States. W.W. feared an America "on the road to a destiny, a status, equivalent in its real world, to that of the fabled damned," for want of spiritual adhesiveness.

Carl Solomon writes: "Gay sex reference with late 1940's gay typology involved [sailors in U.S. uniforms]—this typology changed later—different gestalt."

Certain patients on 6th-floor wards of P.I. remained agitated, talking to themselves, coughing all night.

111

"Starry spangled shock of mercy": Old Glory. Perhaps an echo of "star-yspangled," Elizabethan archaism.

112

"Cottage in the Western night": One-room cottage backyard 1624 Milvia Street, Berkeley, California, visited often by Peter Orlovsky and Jack Kerouac. Cottage was shared with Philip Whalen and Gary Snyder early fall 1955, during composition of Parts II and III of "Howl." See "A Strange New Cottage in Berkeley," "Supermarket in California," "Transcription of Organ-Music," in Allen Ginsberg, *Collected Poems*.

1624 Milvia Street Berkeley Cottage back garden 1955. Gesture imitating that painted by Bellini (*St. Francis in Ecstasy*, Frick Collection, N.Y.). Part II *Howl* completed here; Kerouac, Gary Snyder, Philip Whalen, Orlovsky, & others shared author's cottage that year. *Photo by Jack Kerouac?*

Final Draft, HOWL, Part IV (Footnote)

"Everyday is in eternity": "Hold Infinity in the palm of your hand / And Eternity in an hour." —Blake, "Auguries of Innocence." "Only through time time is conquered." —T. S. Eliot, "Burnt Norton"

117

"The typewriter is holy": Part I "Howl" original draft was typewritten; "Footnote" was in holograph.

"Voice" and "hearers": Ref. original reading Part I at Six Gallery.

119

"Grandfathers of Kansas": General ref. mid-America; associated ref. Michael McClure, Wichita participant in "Six Poets at Six Gallery" reading. See *Scratching the Beat Surface* (San Francisco: North Point Press, 1982), pp. 11–33, for his complete account of the occasion and hindsights on the poets' texts.

120

"Bop apocalypse": "When the mode of the music changes the walls of the city shake." —Pythagoras

"Peace and junk and drums," City Lights edition, 1956, changes to "Peace peyote pipes & drums" in certain later editions: *Howl* (San Francisco: Grabhorn-Hoyem, 1971), and *Collected Poems 1947–1980* (New York: Harper & Row, 1984).

121

"Solitudes . . . cafeterias": Ref. also Lynd Ward block prints, Edward Hopper's silent night street corner café paintings.

122

"Lone juggernaut": A burgeoning military-industrial complex.

"Vast lamb of the middleclass": Ref. Dharma slogan "Regard each sentient being as a future Buddha."

* Line numbers refer to final published text (pp. 3–8).

"Who digs Los Angeles": i.e., the Angels; see William Blake's "They became what they beheld."

123

"Holy Tangiers": W. S. Burroughs' letters from Tanger to author in Bay Area 1954–56 contained major portions of *Naked Lunch*. Author had no connection to Peoria or Istanbul other than the sound of their names.

124

"Clocks in space": See note to verse 54.

"Fifth International": First International Workingman's Association, London 1864, under the leadership of Marx and Engels. Second Socialist and Labor International, Paris 1889. Third Communist International (Komintern), Zimmerwald, Switzerland, 1919. Trotskyite Fourth International, Paris, 1938. Fifth International of workers, entrepreneurs, peasants and indigenous communities of world has not yet assembled to propose survival norms in era of imperial private and state monopoly capital's near-absolute and potentially suicidal power.

126

"Charity": Rimbaud: "Charity is that key.— This inspiration proves that I have dreamed." —*A Season in Hell*.

"Ours! bodies! suffering! magnanimity!": Buddhadharma's Four Noble Truths including Eightfold Bodhisattva path, beginning with First Noble Truth of suffering, expounds the latent implication of this verse.

127

"Supernatural" here may be considered hyperbole.

Dharma equivalent of "extra brilliant intelligent kindness" is found in notion of Bodhicitta, "seed of enlightenment" or "essence of awakeness" in ordinary mind.

"*The road of excess leads to the palace of wisdom.*"
—William Blake

APPENDIXES

Bob Donlon (see Rob Donnelly, Kerouac's *Desolation Angels*), Neal Cassady, Peter Orlovsky, painter Robert La Vigne, poet-proprietor Lawrence Ferlinghetti at City Lights Bookshop, San Francisco, 1955. We were just hanging around, *Howl* book wasn't printed yet, Neal looks good, Peter 21.   *Photo by A.G.*

Appendix I
Contemporaneous Correspondence & Poetic Reactions

Response by poets and peers, author's cover letters and explanations, critical reaction, family advice and publisher's plans. (*Footnotes by Barry Miles*)

**Jack Kerouac, in Mexico City,
to Allen Ginsberg, in San Francisco***

August 19, 1955

(Summarized by A.G. in courtesy to Kerouac's family)

Kerouac wrote that my HOWL FOR CARL SOLOMON† was very powerful, but he didn't want it arbitrarily negated by secondary emendations made in time's reconsidering backstep—He wanted my LINGUAL SPONTANEITY or nothing, that went for me & Gregory Corso, he wouldn't read hackled handicapped poetry manuscripts. . . .

Said I should send some spontaneous pure poetry, ORIGINAL Ms. of "Howl" . . . and fuck Carl Solomon. He was a voyeur in the madhouse. HE WAS ALRIGHT. . . .

Said he wrote a poem dedicated to Peter Orlovsky (whoever he was) containing the following parenthesis: "(this madhouse shot of yours is not exactly the immemorial meil)" which he thought of changing to *meow*, thinking of me. . . .

And—he liked, in "Howl," "with a vision of ultimate cunt and come"—and—"waving genitals and manuscripts" (which was like my prose about Peter hitchhiking Texas with "Illuminations" under arm)—and especially he liked "died in Denver again" (I should leave his Dying Denvers) and "self delivered Truth's final lobotomy." . . .

* Abstracted from a ten-page letter.
† The ms. that A.G. sent to Kerouac consisted of the first six pages of "Howl," Part I, which A.G. had titled, in pink pencil, "Howl For Carl Solomon," presumably at the same time that he reorganized the running order of the stanzas, since the same pencil is used for both annotations. When Kerouac received the ms. he naturally referred to it in his letter using Ginsberg's title. A.G., however, had forgotten that he gave the poem a title and thought that Kerouac was suggesting the title to him, thus the reference on the dedication page: "Several phrases and the title of *Howl* are taken from him [Kerouac]." (The title could not have been added by Ginsberg at a later date because the ms., sent by Kerouac to John Clellon Holmes, did not return to Ginsberg's hands until the summer of 1980.)

**Allen Ginsberg, in San Francisco, to Jack
Kerouac, in Mexico City**

August 25, 1955

Dear Jack,
. . . The pages I sent you of Howl (right title) are the first pages put down, as is. I recopied them and sent you the 100% original draft.* There is no preexistant version. I typed it up as I went along, that's why it's so messy.

I realize how right you are, that was the first time I sat down to blow, it came out in your method, sounding like you, an imitation practically. How advanced you are on this. I don't know what I'm doing with poetry. I need years of isolation and constant everyday writing to attain your volume of freedom and knowledge of the form.

Love,
Allen

* See Kerouac's letter of September 6, 1955. Kerouac seemed to be aware that it was the original draft he had; his objection was to the fact that A.G. x-ed out words and phrases, revising during the process of composition.

**Allen Ginsberg, in San Francisco, to Jack
Kerouac, in Mexico City**

August 30, 1955

Dear Almond Crackerjack:
. . . City Lights bookstore here putting out pamphlets—50 short pages—of local poets & one of W.C. Williams reprint & one of Cummings & will put out Howl (under that title) next year, one booklet for that poem, nothing else. It will fill a booklet. . . .

Love,
Allen

**Jack Kerouac, in Mexico City,
to Allen Ginsberg, in San Francisco**

September 1-6, 1955

(Summarized by A.G. in courtesy to Kerouac's family)

J.K. wrote at beginning of September that he'd lit incense to my image and wandered into Tibetas with his incense stick and scroll. He said that I might tell Neal he'd been very high in Mexico, but he didn't come "to Mexico to cultivate sex," came to Mexico to study Madam Green and dance with Mustaphah Fustaphah Fearcrow— Result: Mexico City Blues & long short story. . . .

He said my battleship deodorants* were rather strange, like beautiful masonic rings, and that Garver noticed that line. . . .

He said that Anything is good because it is everything. And things are said in time, and time is of the essence, and when you change yr mind even for an instant and muss up with x-marks (as in "original" ms. of "Howl") you lie. He wrote that *the truth is already there*. He was not interested in what I had to hide, i.e., my "craft," he was interested in what I had to show, i.e., blow. . . .

Kerouac continued same letter September 6, reporting that Garver said I put too much homosexual material in my poems, "See what his reaction is," Garver winked.

Said my Moloch Solitude was great wild poetry—but granite phalluses & eyeless capitols with the "o" spontaneously blurt-blouted? "The whole boatload of sensitive bullshit" had that right sound of genuine eloquent raging appeal, like Jewish prophets of old.

J.K. added that his prophetic reminders were more delicate and gentle and Buddhist now. . . .

* Ref. "My Alba," *Collected Poems*, p. 89.

Allen Ginsberg, in Berkeley, California, to William Carlos Williams, in Rutherford, New Jersey

December 9, 1955

Dear Dr. Williams:

I enclose finally some of my recent work.*

Am reading Whitman through, note enclosed poem on same,† saw your essay a few days ago, you do not go far enough, look what I have done with the long line. In some of these poems it seems to answer your demand for a relatively absolute line with a fixed base, whatever it is (I am writing this in a hurry finally to get it off, have delayed far too long)—all held within the elastic of the breath, though of varying lengths. The key is in Jazz choruses to some extent; also to reliance on spontaneity & expressiveness which long line encourages; also to attention to interior unchecked logical mental stream. With a long line comes a return [to], (caused by) expressive human feeling, it's generally lacking in poetry now, which is inhuman. The release of emotion is one with rhythmical buildup of long line. The most interesting experiment here is perhaps the sort of bachlike fugue built up in part III of the poem called Howl.

This is not all I have done recently, there is one other piece which is nakeder than the rest and passed into prose,‡ I'll send that on if you're interested—also I have a whole book building up since 1951 when you last saw my work. I wish you would look at it but have not sent it on with these, is there enough time?

Enclosed poems are all from the last few months.

* Enclosed were "Howl," Part I, as of Draft 3, and early draft of Parts II and III (Ditto'd version—see note to Carr to Ginsberg letter below. Part I still had its verses in their original order and Parts II and III were much shorter than the final version. Also enclosed were "A Supermarket in California," "In the Baggage Room at Greyhound," and probably "Sunflower Sutra" and "Transcription of Organ Music."
† "A Supermarket in California."
‡ "Transcription of Organ Music."

I hope these answer somewhat what you were looking for.

As ever,
Allen

No time to write a weirder letter

[Holograph note follows as a P.S.]
The poems are arranged in chronological order to show development & uses of the line. They are best & clearest read aloud.

Lucien Carr, in New York City, to Allen Ginsberg, in Berkeley, California

February 13, 1956

Dear Allen,

. . . Thought your *Howl** very good indeed. Must be quite a spectacle to see you perform it. A considerable departure and improvement over earlier stuff. Keep it up, as we of the petit Bourgeoise say.

Lucien

* Probably the version typed by Robert Creeley, Ditto-mimeographed in 50 copies by Martha Rexroth circa May 1956 at San Francisco State College and sent to various friends.

Louis Ginsberg, in Paterson, New Jersey, to Allen Ginsberg, in Berkeley, California

February 29, 1956

Dear Allen,

. . . I am gratified about your new ms. It's a wild, rhapsodic, explosive outpouring with good figures of speech flashing by in its volcanic rushing. It's a hot geyser of emotion suddenly released in wild abandon from subterranean depths of your being. I'd like to see it in its entirety; and, moving back a bit, I'd like to discern its main outlines. I still insist, however, there is no need for dirty, ugly, words, as they will entangle you unnecessarily in trouble. Try to cut them out. . . .

Love,
Louis

William Carlos Williams, in Rutherford, New Jersey, to Allen Ginsberg, in San Francisco

March 14, 1956

Dear Allen,

I remember having spoken to Ferlinghetti telling him I would be glad to do an introduction for your book of poems and now that you have given me a chance to look at them I'll do just that. In a week or so, or just as soon as I can, I'll get to work. But if I don't like 'em I'll say so frankly—in general long poems do not appeal to me, I have a hell of a job reading them.

Best
Bill

[As a postscript]
The first look is favorable, sounds good to me, in my ears. W.

William Carlos Williams, in Rutherford, New Jersey, to Allen Ginsberg, in Berkeley, California

March 17, 1956

Dear Allen,

Flossie read it to me yesterday during the storm. It has a we[a]k spot toward the end of the first part, then it picks up again and goes on powerfully toward the end. It wouldn't be harmed by a little pruning at that point.

In general though it is the most suc[c]essful poems of yours that I have seen. You have something to say and say it supremely well. Congratulations.

Best luck
Sincerely
Bill

Allen Ginsberg, in Berkeley, California, to Louis Ginsberg, in Paterson, New Jersey

[*March 1956*]

Dear Louis:

. . . W.C.Williams read Howl and liked it and wrote an introduction for the book; and meanwhile there is the possibility of expanding and making a whole book of poems. . . .

English publishers wont handle Howl, that is English printers (Villiers) and so there is now difficulty in getting it through unexpurgated. I revised it and it is now worse* than it ever was, too. We're now investigating Mexico, if necessary will spend extra cost and have it done here tho. Civil Liberties Union here was consulted and said they'd defend it if it got into trouble, which I almost hope it does. I am almost ready to tackle the U.S. Govt out of sheer self delight. There is really a great stupid conspiracy of unconscious negative inertia to keep people from "expressing" themselves. I was reading Henry Miller's banned book Tropic Of Cancer, which actually is a great classic—I never heard of it at Columbia with anything but deprecatory dismissal comments—he and Genet are such frank hip writers that the open expression of their perceptions and real beliefs are a threat to society. The wonder is that literature does have so much power.

Love
Allen

* I.e., more unprintable words.

Allen Ginsberg, in San Francisco, to Jack Kerouac, in Mexico City

[*May 1956*]

Dear Jack,

. . . I sent copies* of Howl to T.S.Eliot, Pound, Faulkner, Van Doren, Meyer Schapiro, Eberhart, Trilling, till they were exhausted. I wonder what T.S.Eliot

will do. I wrote them each about you too. Funny letters to each. Imagine to T.S.Eliot! . . .

Allen
Love

* This refers to the mimeographed version of "Howl," not the final printed one.

Allen Ginsberg, in Berkeley, California, to Eugene Brooks, in New York City

May 18, 1956

Dear Gene:

. . . My book is being printed in England. There was a long delay while I held on to the MSS for revisions, & also I added 3 other poems. It will be quite a volume. I sent Louis a complete MSS this week. I don't know how he'll react to the wilder parts but I am very pleased with the whole deal. I have a feeling he'll be too scandalized to want the family to see it but it really is quite a high spirited & funny & serious collection of statements. I sort of feel unchallengeable on the solidity of the contents & expressions. W.C.Williams has written another introduction* and 1000 copies will be made. I'll even make a little money on it says my publisher who's so pleased he decided to give me royalties in addition to publishing it. . . .

Allen

* Williams' first introduction was to Ginsberg's 1952 collection, *Empty Mirror*, unpublished until 1961.

Allen Ginsberg, in Berkeley, California, to Richard Eberhart, in New York City

May 18, 1956

Dear Mr. Eberhart:

Kenneth Rexroth tells me you are writing an article on S.F. Poetry and asked for a copy of my MSS. I'll send it.

It occurred to me with alarm how really horrible generalizations might be if they are off-the-point as in newspapers.

I sat listening sans objection in the car while you told me what you'd said in Berkeley. I was flattered and egotistically hypnotized by the idea of recognition but really didn't agree with your evaluation of my own poetry. Before you say anything in the *Times* let me have my say.

1) The general "problem" is positive and negative "values." "You don't tell me how to live," "you deal with the negative or horrible well but have no positive program" etc.

This is absurd as it sounds.

It would be impossible to write a powerful emotional poem without a firm grasp on "value" not as an intellectual ideal but as an emotional reality.

Reprinted by permission from longer text in *To Eberhart from Ginsberg*, ed. Michael McCurdy (Great Barrington, Mass.: Penmaen Press, 1976).

You heard or saw *Howl* as a negative howl of protest.

The title notwithstanding, the poem itself is an act of sympathy, not rejection. In it I am leaping *out* of a preconceived notion of social "values," following my own heart's instincts—*allowing* myself to follow my own heart's instincts, overturning any notion of propriety, moral "value," superficial "maturity," Trilling-esque sense of "civilization," and exposing my true feelings—of sympathy and identification with the rejected, mystical, individual even "mad."

I am saying that what seems "mad" in America is our expression of natural ecstasy (as in Crane, Whitman) which suppressed, finds no social form organization background frame of reference or rapport or validation from the outside and so the "patient" gets confused thinks he is mad and really goes off rocker. I am paying homage to mystical mysteries in the forms in which they actually occur here in the U.S. in our environment.

I have taken a leap of detachment from the Artificial preoccupations and preconceptions of what is acceptable and normal and given my yea to the specific type of madness listed in the Who section.

The leap in the imagination—it is safe to do in a poem.

A leap to actual living sanctity is not impossible, but requires more time for me.

I used to think I was mad to want to be a saint, but now what have I got to fear? People's opinions? Loss of a teaching job? I am living outside this context. I make my own sanctity. How else? Suffering and humility are forced on my otherwise wild ego by lugging baggage in Greyhound.

I started as a fair-haired boy in academic Columbia.

I have discovered a great deal of my own true nature and that individuality which is a value, the only social value that there can be in the Blake-worlds. I see it as a "social value."

I have told you how to live if I have wakened any emotion of compassion and realization of the beauty of souls in America, thru the poem.

What other value could a poem have—now, historically maybe?

I have released and confessed and communicated clearly my true feelings tho it might involve at first a painful leap of exhibition and fear that I would be rejected.

This is a value, an actual fact, not a mental formulation of some second-rate sociological-moral ideal which is meaningless and academic in the poetry of H——, etc.

Howl is the first discovery as far as *communication* of feeling and truth, that I made. It begins with a cata-logue sympathetically and *humanely* describing excesses of feeling and idealization.

Moloch is the vision of the mechanical feelingless inhuman world we live in and accept—and the key line finally is "Moloch whom I abandon."

It ends with a litany of active acceptance of the suffering of soul of C. Solomon, saying in effect I am *still* your amigo tho you are in trouble and think yourself in a void, and the final strophe states the terms of the communication.

"oh starry spangled shock of MERCY"

and mercy is a real thing and if that is not a value I don't know what is.

How mercy gets to exist where it comes from perhaps can be seen from the inner evidence and images of the poem—an act of self-realization, self-acceptance and the consequent and inevitable relaxation of protective anxiety and selfhood and the ability to see and love others in themselves as angels without stupid mental self deceiving moral categories selecting *who* it is safe to sympathize with and who is not safe.

See Dostoyevsky and Whitman.

*   *   *

Thus I fail to see why you characterize my work as destructive or negative. Only if you are thinking an outmoded dualistic puritanical academic theory ridden world of values can you fail to see I am talking about *realization* of love. LOVE.

The poems are religious and I meant them to be and the effect on audience is (surprising to me at first) a validation of this. It is like "I give the primeval sign" of Acceptance, as in Whitman.

*   *   *

But as to technique—[Ruth] Witt-Diamant said you were surprised I exhibited any interest in the "Line" etc.

What seems formless tho effective is really effective thru discovery or realization of rules and meanings of forms and experiments in them.

The "form" of the poem is an experiment. Experiment with uses of the catalogue, the ellipsis, the long line, the litany, repetition, etc.

The latter parts of the first section set forth a "formal" esthetic derived in part incidentally from my master who is Cezanne.

The poem is really built like a brick shithouse.

This is the general ground plan—all an accident, organic, but quite symmetrical surprisingly. It grew (part III) out of a desire to build up rhythm using a fixed base to respond to and elongating the response still however containing it within the elastic of one breath or one big streak of thought.

The Poem is really built
like a brick shithouse

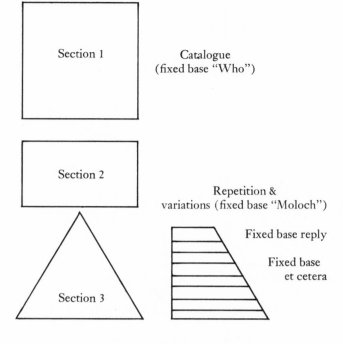

Section 1

Catalogue
(fixed base "Who")

Section 2

Repetition &
variations (fixed base "Moloch")

Fixed base reply

Fixed base
et cetera

Section 3

This is the general ground plan—all an
accident, organic but quite symmetrical, surprisingly.

*   *   *

The Long Line I use came after 7 yrs. work with
fixed iambic rhyme, and 4 yrs. work with Williams' short
line free form—which as you must know has its own mad
rules—indefinable tho they be at present—

The long line, the prose poem, the spontaneous
sketch are XX century French forms which Academic
versifiers despite their continental interests (in XIX cen-
tury French "formal" forms, Baudelaire) have completely
ignored. Why?

This form of writing is very popular in S.A. and is
after all the most interesting thing happening in France.

Whitman
Apollinaire
Lorca

*   *   *

The long line—you need a good ear and an emotional
ground-swell and technical and syntactical ease facility
and a freedom "esprit" to deal with it and make of it any-
thing significant. And you need something to say, i.e.
clear realized feelings. Same as any free verse.

The lines are the result of long thought and experi-
ment as to what unit constitutes *one speech-breath-
thought.* . . .

We think and speak rhythmically all the time, each
phrasing, piece of speech, metrically equivalent to what
we have to say emotionally.

Given a mental release which is not mentally blocked,
the breath of verbal intercourse will come with excellent
rhythm, a rhythm which is perhaps unimprovable.

*   *   *

Since each wave of speech-thought needs to be mea-
sured (we speak and perhaps think in waves)—or what I
speak and think I have at any rate in *Howl* reduced to
waves of relatively equally heavy weight—and set next
to one another they are in a balance O.K.

The technique of writing both prose and poetry, the
technical problem of the present day, is the problem of
Transcription of the natural flow of the mind, the tran-
scription of the melody of actual thought or speech.

I have leaned more toward capturing the inside-
mind-thought rather than the verbalized speech. This
distinction I make because most poets see the problem
via Wordsworth as getting nearer to actual *speech*, verbal
speech.

I have noticed that the unspoken visual-verbal flow
inside the mind has great rhythm and have approached
the problem of Strophe, Line and stanza and measure by
listening and transcribing (to a great extent) the coherent
mental flow. Taking *that* for the model for Form as
Cezanne took Nature.

This is not surrealism—they made up an artificial
literary imitation.

I transcribe from my ordinary thoughts—waiting for
extra exciting or mystical moments or near mystical mo-
ments to transcribe.

This brings up problems of image, and transcription
of mental flow gives helpful knowledge because we think
in sort of surrealist (juxtaposed images) or haiku-like
form.

A haiku as the 1910–20's imagists did *not* know, con-
sists of 2 visual (or otherwise) images stripped down and
juxtaposed—the charge of electricity created by these 2
poles being greater when there is a greater distance be-
tween them—as in Yeats' phrase "murderous innocence
of the sea"—2 opposite poles reconciled in a flash of
recognition.

The mind in its flow creates such fantastic ellipses
thus the key phrase of method in *Howl* is "Hydrogen
Jukebox" which tho quite senseless makes in context
clear sense. . . .

*   *   *

. . . So anybody who wants to hang on to traditional
metrics and values will wind up stultified and self-
deceived anyway despite all the sincerity in the world.

Everybody thinks they should learn academically from "experience" and have their souls put down and destroyed and this has been raised to the status of "value" but to me it seems just the usual old fake death, caused by fear and lack of real experience. I suffered too much under Professor Trilling, whom I love, but who is a poor mental fanatic after all and not a free soul—I'm straying.

* * *

I've said nothing about the extraordinary influence of Bop music on rhythm and drugs on the observation of rhythm and mental processes—not enough time and out of paper.

* * *

Summary

I. VALUES

Howl is an "affirmation" of individual experience of God, sex, drugs, absurdity etc. Part I deals sympathetically with individual cases. Part II describes and rejects the Moloch of society which confounds and suppresses individual experience and forces the individual to consider himself mad if he does not reject his own deepest senses. Part III is an expression of sympathy and identification with C.S. who is in the madhouse—saying that his madness basically is rebellion against Moloch and I am with him, and extending my hand in union. This is an affirmative act of mercy and compassion, which are the basic emotions of the poem. The criticism of society is that "Society" is merciless. The alternative is private, individual acts of mercy. The poem is one such. It is therefore clearly and consciously built on a *liberation* of basic human virtues.

To call it work of nihilistic rebellion would be to mistake it completely. Its force comes from positive "religious" belief and experience. It offers no "constructive" program in sociological terms—no poem could. It does offer a constructive human value—basically the *experience*—of the enlightment of mystical experience—without which no society can long exist.

* * *

II. TECHNIQUE

A. These long lines or Strophes as I call them came spontaneously as a result of the kind of feelings I was trying to put down, and came as a surprise solution to a metrical problem that preoccupied me for a decade.

I have considerable experience writing both rhymed iambics and short line Post-W.C.W. free verse.

Howl's 3 parts consist of 3 different approaches to the use of the long line (longer than Whitman's, more French).

    1. Repetition of the fixed base "Who" for a catalogue.

        A. building up consecutive rhythm from strophe to strophe.

        B. abandoning of fixed base "who" in certain lines but carrying weight and rhythm of strophic form continuously forward.

2. Break up of strophe into pieces within the strophe, thus having the strophe become a new usable form of stanza—Repetition of fixed base "Moloch" to provide cement for continuity. *Supermarket* uses strophe stanza and abandons need for fixed base. I was experimenting with the form.

3. Use of a fixed base, "I'm with you in Rockland," with a reply in which the strophe becomes a longer and longer streak of speech, in order to build up a *relatively* equal nonetheless free and variable structure. Each reply strophe is longer than the previous. I have measured by ear and speech-breath, there being no other measure for such a thing. Each strophe consists of a set of phrases that can be spoken in one breath and each carries relatively equal rhetorical weight. Penultimate strophe is an exception and was meant to be—a series of cries—"O skinny legions run outside O starry spangled shock of mercy O victory etc." You will not fail to observe that the cries are all in definite rhythm.

The technical problem raised and partially solved is the break-through begun by Whitman but never carried forward, from both iambic stultification and literary automatism, and unrhythmical short-line verse, which does not yet offer any kind of *base* cyclical flow for the build up of a powerful rhythm. The long line seems for the moment to free speech for emotional expression and give it a measure to work with. I hope to experiment with short-line free verse with what I have learned from exercise in long.

B. Imagery—is a result of the *kind* of line and the kind of emotions and the kind of speech-and-interior flow-of-the-mind transcription I am doing—the imagery often consists of 1920's W.C.W. imagistically observed detail collapsed together by interior associative logic—i.e., "hydrogen jukebox," Apollinaire, Whitman, Lorca. But *not* automatic surrealism. Knowledge of Haiku and ellipsis is crucial.

        Yours
        Allen Ginsberg

Richard Eberhart, from "West Coast Rhythms"

The West Coast is the liveliest spot in the country in poetry today. It is only here that there is a radical group movement of young poets. San Francisco teems with young poets.

Reprinted from *New York Times Book Review*, September 2, 1956.

Part of this activity is due to the establishment of the Poetry Center at San Francisco State College three years ago. Its originator and moving spirit is Ruth Witt-Diamant, who began by offering readings by local poets and progressed to importing older poets from the East. She hopes next to stimulate the writing of verse drama.

Part of the activity of the young group has been inspired by Kenneth Rexroth, whose presence in San Francisco over a long period of time, embodying his force and convictions, creates a rallying point of ideas, interest and informal occasions. The influence of Kenneth Patchen is also felt by this group. Robinson Jeffers looms as a timeless figure down the Coast. . . .

In the Bay region there are several poetry readings each week. They may be called at the drop of a hat. A card may read "Celebrated Good Time Poetry Night. Either you go home bugged or completely enlightened. Allen Ginsberg blowing hot; Gary Snyder blowing cool; Philip Whalen puffing the laconic tuba; Mike McClure his hip highnotes; Rexroth on the big bass drum. Small collection for wine and postcards . . . abandon, noise, strange pictures on walls, oriental music, lurid poetry. Extremely serious. Town Hall theatre. One and only final appearance of this apocalypse. Admission free."*

Hundreds from about 16 to 30 may show up and engage in an authentic, free-wheeling celebration of poetry, an analogue of which was jazz thirty years ago. The audience participates, shouting and stamping, interrupting and applauding. Poetry here has become a tangible social force, moving and unifying its auditors, releasing the energies of the audience through spoken, even shouted verse, in a way at present unique to this region. . . .

The most remarkable poem of the young group, written during the past year, is "Howl," by Allen Ginsberg, a 29-year-old poet who is the son of Louis Ginsberg, a poet known to newspaper readers in the East. Ginsberg comes from Brooklyn; he studied at Columbia; after years of apprenticeship to usual forms, he developed his brave new medium. This poem has created a furor of praise or abuse whenever read or heard. It is a powerful work, cutting through to dynamic meaning. Ginsberg thinks he is going forward by going back to the methods of Whitman.

My first reaction was that it is based on destructive violence. It is profoundly Jewish in temper. It is Biblical in its repetitive grammatical build-up. It is a howl against everything in our mechanistic civilization which kills the spirit, assuming that the louder you shout the more likely you are to be heard. It lays bare the nerves of suffering and spiritual struggle. Its positive force and energy come from a redemptive quality of love, although it destructively catalogues evils of our time from physical deprivation to madness.

In other poems, Ginsberg shows a crucial sense of humor. It shows up principally in his poem "America," which has lines "Asia is rising against me./ I haven't got

a Chinaman's chance." Humor is also present in "Supermarket in California." His "Sunflower Sutra" is a lyric poem marked by pathos.

Lawrence Ferlinghetti is the publisher of the Pocket Poet Series from his bookshop in San Francisco, the City Lights Pocket Bookshop. . . .

In this series Ferlinghetti's "Pictures of the Gone World" offers his own poetry in a flowing variety of open-running lines. He develops a personal, ritual anecdote as a fresh type of recognition, with acute visual perceptions. He seems to have learned something from James Laughlin. His work measures a racy young maturity of experience. . . .

Of the still bookless poets, Philip Whalen has somewhat Poundian poems and a highly successful refrain "Love You" in a direct and forceful poem entitled "3 Variations: All About Love." Gary Snyder's poetry is most like Rexroth's, not due so much to direct influence as to identity of sources. Both owe much to Far Eastern verse and philosophy, both are deeply bound into the natural world of stars, birds, mountains and flowers. Michael McClure writes with grace and charm on "For the Death of 100 Whales" and "Point Lobos: Animism," striving for "The rising, the exuberance, when the mystery is unveiled." . . .

It is certain that there is a new, vital group consciousness now among young poets in the Bay region. However unpublished they may be, many of these young poets have a numerous and enthusiastic audience. They acquire this audience by their own efforts. Through their many readings they have in some cases a larger audience than more cautiously presented poets in the East.

They are finely alive, they believe something new can be done with the art of poetry, they are hostile to gloomy critics, and the reader is invited to look into and enjoy their work as it appears. They have exuberance and a young will to kick down the doors of older consciousness and established practice in favor of what they think is vital and new.

Allen Ginsberg, on board USNS *Pvt. Joseph F. Merrell*, T-AKV-4 (c/o Fleet Post Office, San Francisco), to Lionel Trilling, in New York City

[*May 1956*]

Dear Lionel:

Enclosed find the ditto mss. of a pamphlet of poems I have being printed here. They are natural developments of the method & practice I was pursuing about 5 years ago. There seems to have been enuf mercy around to get me to heaven anyway, no?

Let me know what you think of them. I can't really imagine what your reaction should be, and I'm interested.

Though my tastes at school were not so, I'm reading a lot of Lorca, Apollinaire, Crane, Thomas—and Whitman. He is a mountain too vast to be seen. Nobody still

---

* This was text of postcard invitation to Berkeley encore of Six Gallery poetry reading, November 1955.

understands him despite the recent books which were just vain and inept, tho sincere.

I had the experience of teaching a term poetry writing at SF State Coll., guest gorilla, I am a really good teacher, naked half the time with big blue flashes of communication. I read them Whitman aloud. If you read him aloud with understanding and some personal passion he comes on what he's supposed to, near saint. Anybody can understand.

Charles Olson is a good poet, Black Mountain now an, the only, Eastern center of real poetic discipline, i.e. freedom. His poem the Death of Europe in a recent Origin Magazine issue is my specimen for this conclusion. If you get to see it, worth while.

I think what is coming is a romantic period (strangely tho everybody thinks that by being hard-up and classical they are going to make it like Eliot which is silly). Eliot & Pound are like Dryden & Pope. What gives now is much more personal—how could there be now anything but a reassertion of naked personal subjective truth— eternally real? Perhaps Whitman will be seen to have set the example and been bypassed for half a century.

There are several good unknown Zen poets out hear (here) two to be exact whose learning and wild accomplishment put to shame anything I heard of in the East. This is an amazing situation.

I'm leaving in two weeks to the Arctic to rhapsodize over icebergs & get $$ to visit Europe in the winter coming. Perhaps I'll see you in NYC then. Please write, let me know what you think of the poems. Mail will be forwarded north.

As ever,
Allen

Kerouac's here too, big genius.

If you like these poems see what you can do to have them reviewed because in normal run of things they likely will not be.

Lionel Trilling, in New York City, to Allen Ginsberg, on board USNS *Pvt. Joseph F. Merrell*

May 29, 1956

Dear Allen,

I'm afraid I have to tell you that I don't like the poems at all. I hesitate before saying that they seem to me quite dull, for to say of a work which undertakes to be violent and shocking that it is dull is, I am aware, a well known and all too easy device. But perhaps you will believe that I am being sincere when I say they are dull. They are not like Whitman—they are all prose, all rhetoric, without any music. What I used to like in your poems, whether I thought they were good or bad, was the *voice* I heard in them, true and natural and interesting. There is no real voice here. As for the doctrinal element of the poems, apart from the fact that I of course

reject it, it seems to me that I heard it very long ago and that you give it to me in all its orthodoxy, with nothing new added.

Sincerely yours,
Lionel Trilling

Naomi Ginsberg, in Pilgrim State Hospital, New York, to Allen Ginsberg, in Berkeley, California

[postmarked] *June 11, 1956**

Dear Allen,

I hope this reaches you. I sent one before which, maybe, they didn't send out!

Congratulations on your birthday!† Received your poetry.‡ I'd like to send it to Louis for criticism. Now what does he think of it! It seemed to me your wording was a little too hard. Do tell me what father thinks of it. You know you have to have a job to get married. I wish you did have a good job. What did you specialise in when you went to college. This going to the North Pole, who supplies the wearing material? They say when you visit the Eskimos you need a double coat of fur. Are you fit for that flying job? Don't take chances with your life! I wish you get married. Do you like farming? Its as good a job as any.

I hope you behave well. Don't go in for too much drink and other things that are not good for you. Eugene and his wife visited me. They expected a child then. I suppose they have it by this time.

I do hope you can get a good job so you can get a girl to get married. Eugene's wife is beautiful.

As for myself. I still have the wire on my head. The doctors know about it. They are cutting the flesh and bone. They are giving me teethache. I do wish you were back east so I could see you. I met Max's§ daughter, she is charming and married. I am glad you are having your poetry published. I wish I were out of here and home at the time you were young; then I would be young. I'm in the prime of life now— Did you read about the two men who died at 139 & 149 yrs of age. I wonder how they lived. I'm looking for a good time.

I hope you are not taking drugs as suggested by your poetry. That would hurt me. Don't go in for ridiculous things. With love & good news (mother)

Naomi

* Naomi Ginsberg died on June 9, 1956, two days before the hospital mailed her letter, written on the eve of her death. The letter was received by Ginsberg days after the news of her death had reached him. See his account in "Kaddish," *Collected Poems*, p. 224.
† Allen Ginsberg was thirty on June 3, 1956.
‡ The poetry she referred to was the Ditto'd version of "Howl."
§ Max was Naomi's brother.

**Allen Ginsberg, on board USNS *Pvt. Joseph F. Merrell*
(mailed San Francisco), to Ezra Pound,
in St. Elizabeths Hospital, Washington, D.C.**

[Early June 1956]

Dear Mr. Pound:

Please READ at least 1 page of the enclosed mss. Or 1 line for that matter so long as you can judge the rhythm.

These are all l-o-n-g lines, used in various ways. I don't think nobody's tried this this way.

Williams wrote an introduction, it will be published by City Lights in SF sometime in July.

I know you are fatigued but I am sending you a gift. I am not a Greek. . . .

Please let me know how the poems strike or affect you.

As ever,
Allen Ginsberg

[Pound did not reply but instead forwarded Ginsberg's letter to William Carlos Williams with note typed on verso.]

**Ezra Pound, in St. Elizabeths Hospital,
Washington, D.C., to William Carlos Williams,
in Rutherford, New Jersey**

[June 1956]

You got more room in yr/ house than I hv/ in my cubicle

If he's yours why dont yu teach him the value of time to those who want to

read something that wil tell 'em wot they dont know

**Allen Ginsberg, on board USNS *Pvt. Joseph F. Merrell*
(mailed San Francisco), to William Carlos Williams,
in Rutherford, New Jersey**

[Early June 1956]

Dear Dr. Williams:

Thanks for your introduction. The book is over in England being printed, and will be out in July sometime. Your foreword is personal and compassionate and you see the point of what has happened. You should see what strength & gaiety there is beyond that though.

The book will contain 3 shorter poems too, written subsequent to Howl:

Supermarket in California—a homage to Whitman
Sunflower Sutra—declaration of the experience of happy real mercy
America—make of it what you can.

I have never been interested in writing except for the splendor of actual experience etc. bullshit, I mean I've never been really crazy, confused at times.

Here are these poems, more long lines, used in different ways, experiments. . . .

Adios.
Allen Ginsberg

IF YOU DONT HAVE TIME FOR ANYTHING ELSE PLEASE READ ENCLOSED SUNFLOWER SUTRA

[A much longer excerpt from this letter may be found incorporated by William Carlos Williams into Book Five, *Paterson*, with Ginsberg's signature reduced to initials.]

**Allen Ginsberg, on board USNS *Sgt. Jack J. Pendleton*,
T-AKV-5, docked in Seattle, to Lawrence Ferlinghetti,
in San Francisco**

June 22, 1956

Dear Larry:

Well what news? I am in Seattle, will be here over weekend and thru next Friday, will return to SF next weekend for a few days—arrive sometime Sunday I expect, around the 30th or 31st. If therefore you got or will get proofs hold on to them, I'll look them over myself.

Generally speaking the Greyhound poem* stinks on ice, at least the end does—that wont last no 1000 years—I had a night mare about it standing on the prow several days ago. I dunno what to do, havn't written anything better on it since leaving town. Maybe later. . . .

As ever,
Allen

* "In the Baggage Room at Greyhound."

**Allen Ginsberg, on board USNS *Sgt. Jack J. Pendleton*
at sea (mail collected by tender),
to Lawrence Ferlinghetti, in San Francisco**

July 3, 1956

Dear Larry:

This being my first book I want it right if I can. Therefore I thought and decided this, about the justifications, of margins. (The reason for my being particular is that the poems are actually sloppy enough written, without sloppiness made worse by typographical arrangement. The one element of order & prearrangement I did pay care to was arrangement into prose-paragraph strophes: each one definite unified long line. So any doubt about irregularity of right hand margin will be sure to confuse critical reader about intention of the prosody. Therefore I've got to change it so it's right.)

It looks like the whole book will have to be reset practically. Find out how much it costs to reset the first proofs we received, which is my fault for not having followed precisely thru and made sure in advance it was understood. I will pay that no matter how much up to $200.00, which I guess it may well cost. For the material they received subsequent to the first proofs, that's their look-to, I think. Can we get them to change that on their own? . . .

Allen

Allen Ginsberg, on board USNS *Sgt. Jack J. Pendleton* at sea, to Eugene Brooks, in New York City

July 10, 1956

Dear Gene,

. . . Got proofs of my book from England and they were set up all wrong, so there'll be a further delay till suppose after summer. The lines were printed wrong due to my negligence & publisher here negligence in instructing printer to line it up like prose, each long line, and make even margin on right hand. As result lines chopped off in middle. So decided it was worth my paying to get right. It will probably set me back $90.00 or so. I didn't want the City Lights man to have the burden, he's putting out as much as he can anyway to have it published without me being finicky about how it is set in type. I instructed him when the bill for the extra work comes to send it to you. He'll give you instructions where to send the money. Withdraw whatever is needed from the amounts I've been sending you. His name is Lawrence Ferlinghetti. He'll write you. Probably next month you'll get this. Letter then will explain what to do. Hate to put out gold like that but I want to get the book right, the writing is sloppy enough as it is without it being fouled up typographically too. There seems to have been room for a lot more writing than anticipated so (for 50 pages) I added a few earlier poems at the end as an appendix. It'll be quite a book. Williams introduction is weird. He don't remember much, talks about how he used to know me "after the first world war."* But he understands the poem and sympathizes. I mean I always thought of that piece of writing (Howl) as an energetic & healthy & rather affirmative & compassionate yell dispite the surface rusty machinery & suicides it is littered with, and he got that point immediately and dug it as the base of the poem. This was gratifying & somewhat of a relief as all I heard from Eberhart & Univ. types & Trilling by implication was a lot of selfsatisfied talk about how I seemed to dwell exclusively on negative protest. Williams is goodhearted and knows his way around the soul. . . .

Love to everybody, send this letter to Louis.

Allen

* "He was physically slight of build and mentally much disturbed by the life which he had encountered about him during those first years after the first world war as it was exhibited to him in and about New York City." Williams, in his introduction, clearly meant to say the Second World War.

Allen Ginsberg, on board USNS *Sgt. Jack J. Pendleton*, docked in Seattle, to Lawrence Ferlinghetti, in San Francisco

[July 1956, second visit to Seattle prior to Arctic voyage]

Dear Lawrence:

I have not yet had time to put together another copy of the mailing list I spoke of but will in a week or so after we sail, and will mail it then, you'll have it in time.

Enclosed please find a note to my brother,
Eugene Brooks
505 West 125 Street
New York City

When the bill comes for the changes I ordered and said I would pay for, send it on to him with instructions how and where to pay it, whether to send you a check or else to Villiers directly, whatever way is most convenient or efficient for you to handle it. In any case send him instructions what to do. He has my money in the bank. If any legal problems rise up to bug us also, consult him, as he is an attorney-at-law. I have already written him of this arrangement, about paying for changes, etc. so he will wait to hear from you.

. . . I leave here in 3 days (Friday or Saturday) (from here, is Seattle) finally for Arctic. Sorry I wasn't able to be around for final OK on proofs so I guess you'll have to read them. Please see that they are alright finally as to the margins.

. . . Drop me a line and let me know what's happening with the book—send me a card for sure when you see the proofs and tell me if it came out alright.

As ever,
Allen

Allen Ginsberg, on board USNS *Sgt. Jack J. Pendleton* at sea, to Lawrence Ferlinghetti, in San Francisco

August 9, 1956 [dated July 9, 1956]

Dear Larry,

Received the copy of the book you sent me promptly —and was excited to see it. Everything worked out fine with the typography—it looks much better this way & it seems to have been real cheap to do—$20. is nuthin. I shuddered when I read the poetry tho, it all seems so jerry-built sloppy and egocentric, most of it. *Greyhound* looks fine, I'm glad you told me to put it in. Reading it all through I'm not sure it deserves all the care & work you've put into it and the encouragement you've given me in fact to tell you the truth I am already embarrassed by half of it but what the hell, thankyou anyway for all your courtesy and I hope few people will see it with such jaded eyes as I do, tho I guess it's best the poems have a truthful fate than an oversympathetic one. I wonder if we will actually sell the thousand copies. . . .

Allen

Louis Ginsberg, in Paterson, New Jersey, to Allen Ginsberg, in Berkeley, California

September 13, 1956

Dear Allen,

. . . I was happy to see it.* Edith† keeps a copy in her purse and shows it to all and sundry. I have passed it around the Newark folks. I rejoice that your book is coming out. I predict it will make a name for you. You may wake up some morning and find yourself famous. I do hope so.

Love
Your father,
Louis

* "West Coast Rhythms," Richard Eberhart's article on the San Francisco Poetry Renaissance in *New York Times Book Review* (see p. 154).
† Edith Ginsberg, the author's stepmother.

Lucien Carr, in New York City, to Allen Ginsberg, in Berkeley, California

September 21, 1956

Dear Allen,

Received copy of Howl (Library of Congress Catalog Card Number: 56—8587) today and was most buoyed up by your fine success. I thought America was about the funniest poem I had ever read & quite penetratingly to the point.

It is very impressive to see the name of Ginsberg on the list with Ferlinghetti, Rexroth and Patchen (who the hell is Ferlinghetti?).

As you might expect I have one small gripe. I was touched at being included in your dedication.*But I value a certain anonymity in life and it always jars me when my friends, of all people, find it desirable to include mention of me in their works—dedication page as well as text. I hope you bear that idiosyncrasy in mind in your next book—"Moan"

It's a small matter

The book is very impressive.

Lucien

*　　　　DEDICATION
　　　　　To—

Jack Kerouac, new Buddha of American prose, who spit forth intelligence into eleven books written in half the number of years (1951-1956)—*On the Road, Visions of Neal, Dr Sax, Springtime Mary, The Subterraneans, San Francisco Blues, Some of the Dharma, Book of Dreams, Wake Up, Mexico City Blues,* and *Visions of Gerard*—creating a spontaneous bop prosody and original classic literature. Several phrases and the title of *Howl* are taken from him.

William Seward Burroughs, author of *Naked Lunch*, an endless novel which will drive everybody mad.

Neal Cassady, author of *The First Third*, an autobiography (1949) which enlightened Buddha. All these books are published in Heaven.

Lucien Carr, recently promoted to Night Bureau Manager of New York United Press.

Gary Snyder, in Kyoto, to Allen Ginsberg, in Berkeley, California

October 12, 1956

Dear Allen,

Four copies of *Howl* I ordered from Ferlinghetti came this week, I am carefully figgering where to plant these bombs. It looks real nice & I can't read it without yr voice ringing in my ears & a vision of your navy sweater & Levis & wine & frosty weather outside like in the Northwest. . . .

Gary

Allen Ginsberg, in San Francisco, to Jack Kerouac, in Mexico City

[Fall 1956]

Dear Jack,

. . . Beginning to get long admiring letters from starry-eyed Parkinson & N.Y. types about Howl. Did you see the N.Y. Times Sept 2 article—I don't remember. . . . Agh! I'm sick of the whole thing, that's all I think about, famous authorhood, like a happy empty dream. W.C.Williams wrote he dug it & read it to "young artists" in N.Y. & they were excited & "Up their alley" and ordered 5 copies extra to pass around to the young. How beautiful, tho. I guess I really feel good about it. It's assuming proportions of an "it" in my life. . . .

Allen

Allen Ginsberg, in Paterson, New Jersey, to Lawrence Ferlinghetti, in San Francisco

December 20, 1956

Dear Larry:

. . . Went to N.Y.Times and bearded them for a review, got interviewed by Harvey Breit, and will, I think, get Howl reviewed there. Few stores carry City Lights, generally unobtainable unless you know where, but one review in Times or Trib or Sat Review could break the ice maybe. . . .

Allen

Lawrence Ferlinghetti, in San Francisco, to Allen Ginsberg, in Tanger, Morocco

February 1957

dear allen . . . the hell with contracts. . . . we will just tell them you have standing agreement with me and you can give me anything you feel like giving me on reprints whenever you get back to States and sit in Poetry Chairs in hinterland CCNYs and are rich and famous and fat and fucking your admirers and getting reprinted in all of seldenrod-man's anthologias, until then, natch, the loot shud be yurs since as you say i am getting famous as your publisher anyway. . . . Do you want more HOWLs and other P[ocket]P[oets] sent now (which ones?) and charged against you? How many? . . . Am still reading Kerouac's poetry woiks and will be at it for some time yet. . . . Max Weiss at Fantasy here is already to do HOWL recording. . . . He is great and honest. He will probably want contract and will send. (Re contracts, you see whut happens after one week in NY—I am talking just like all the other literary detectives there before i leave—contractscontractscontracts . . . well fuckem and fuck the partisanreview whom i've never sent anything to and we'll make it here in sf* . . . OK? G'bye . . .

larry

* San Francisco.

Lucien Carr, in New York City, to Allen Ginsberg, in Tanger, Morocco

April 24, 1957

Dear Allen,
   . . . Trust you'll see to it that one little change will be made to delete self from front page.*

Lucien

  * Ferlinghetti had already received an advance bound copy of the second edition. Unbound sheets containing the dedication page were replaced, with Carr's name deleted, at a cost to Ginsberg of $25.

Allen Ginsberg, in Tanger, Morocco, to Lawrence Ferlinghetti, in San Francisco

[June 1957]

. . . Received your letter today with clippings. I guess this is more serious than the customs seizure since you can lose real money on this deal if they find you guilty. What does it look like? I guess with the ACLU it should be possible to beat—except this is local law—does that give police complete discretion to decide what's obscene? If so, that may make it difficult. . . . Presumably a matter of local politics—therefore can anything be done to call off police through politicians at City Hall thru state college thru Poetry Center thru Witt Diamant? If it is a matter of purely local law & juvenile bureau, perhaps somebody at Berkeley & State Coll . . . but arrest and formal charges have been filed already, so I guess open showdown is inevitable.

Lawrence Ferlinghetti, in San Francisco, to Allen Ginsberg, in Paris

September 17, 1957

Dear Allen . . . Got your last and guess you are now in Paris. I am working on Gregory's book right now, and he agrees with me that you shud do Introduction. . . . I've just sent you, by surface mail, a copy of the Fourth Printing of HOWL. The LIFE article on Sept 9, with your pict, is causing the national distributor to take two or three hundred copies a week . . . though this probably won't keep up indefinitely! *Time* article, on general scene

Peter Orlovsky, Jack Kerouac & William S. Burroughs, Tanger Beach, Morocco, Summer 1957. J.K. & author typing *Naked Lunch* drafts, *Howl* trial had commenced in San Francisco.   *Photo by A.G.*

here, is due out in another week. . . . Have you seen any of the articles on the trial, except what I sent? Am saving clips so you can go over them when you hit town again. . . . On other matters, please let me know if Villiers ever sent HOWL to your father. . . . If not, I'll send them from here. . . . Trial is not over yet—we're in court again this Thursday. . . . Yes, wd like to see mss by Kerouac, Burroughs. . . . Typos in HOWL can't be changed now, without much expense, since photo offset plates are 16 pages to one plate, and one change means 16 pages redone. . . . (I found one typo—"solipisims"—which slipped thru all these printings)—Question of Fucked in the Ass not yet settled in court—so had to let that stand again. . . . Got to go. . . . when you gonna see gregory. . . . his book's going to be great. . . .

larry

Lawrence Ferlinghetti, in San Francisco, to Allen Ginsberg, in Paris

September 28, 1957

Dear Allen . . . Will send you clips on final action on HOWL trial next week, when judge brings in his written decision and opinion. I am writing it up for next issue of EVERGREEN, per request of Don Allen. . . .

LF

Carl Solomon, in New York City, to Allen Ginsberg, in Paris

December 29, 1957

Dear Allen,
    . . . By the way, my profound thanks for the sentiments expressed in "Howl," an excellent piece of writing and just to my taste.

Your friend
Carl

John Hollander, Review of *Howl and Other Poems*

It is only fair to Allen Ginsberg . . . to remark on the utter lack of decorum of any kind in his dreadful little volume. I believe that the title of his long poem, "Howl," is meant to be a noun, but I can't help taking it as an imperative. The poem itself is a confession of the poet's faith, done into some 112 paragraphlike lines, in the ravings of a lunatic friend (to whom it is dedicated), and in the irregularities in the lives of those of his friends who populate his rather disturbed pantheon. Here is the poem's beginning:

Reprinted from *Partisan Review*, Spring 1957.

"I saw the best minds of my generation destroyed by
      madness, starving hysterical naked,
dragging themselves through the negro streets at dawn
      looking for an angry fix . . ."

This continues, sponging on one's toleration, for pages and pages. A kind of climax was reached, for me, in a long section of screams about "Moloch!", at a rare point of self-referential lucidity: "Dreams! adorations! illuminations! religions! the whole boatload of sensitive bullshit!" *Howl* seems to have emerged under the influence of a kind of literary *Festspiel* held at frequent intervals on the West Coast, in the course of which various poets, "with radiant cool eyes," undoubtedly, read their works before audiences of writhing and adoring youths. "Howl" and the other longer poems in this book, including "America," "Sunflower Sutra," "In the Baggage Room at Greyhound" and some dismal pastiches of William Carlos Williams (who wrote a brief reminiscence of the poet to introduce this volume), all proclaim, in a hopped-up and improvised tone, that nothing seems to be worth saying save in a hopped-up and improvised tone. There are also avowed post-Poundian pacts with Walt Whitman and Apollinaire, and perhaps an unacknowledged one with Lautréamont. I don't know; Mr. Ginsberg prefaces *Howl* with a long dedication to some of his fellow-writers that reads just like his poems ("To . . . William Seward Burroughs, author of *Naked Lunch*, an endless novel which will drive everybody mad"), and in the book he alludes to a "spontaneous bop prosody." Perhaps this is as good a characterization of his work as any.

I have spent this much time on a very short and very tiresome book for two reasons. The first of these is involved with the fact that Mr. Ginsberg and his circle are being given a certain amount of touting by those who disapprove of what Horace Gregory, writing in these pages last fall, christened "The Poetry of Suburbia." If it turns out to be to anybody's profit, I shouldn't be a bit surprised if *Howl* and its eventual progeny were accorded some milder version of the celebration Colin Wilson has received in England. This may not be a real danger, however. If it suddenly appeared that there were no possible worlds between suburbia and subterranea, I expect most of us would go underground. But this is not quite yet the case, and the publicity seems regrettable, in view of the fact (my second reason for dealing with him here) that Allen Ginsberg has a real talent and a marvelous ear. It shows up in some of the funniest and most grotesque lines of "Howl," and even without knowing his profound and carefully organized earlier writing (unpublished in book form), one might suspect a good poet lurking behind the modish facade of a frantic and *talentlos* avant-garde.

In *On the Poetry of Allen Ginsberg*,

ed. Lewis Hyde
(Ann Arbor: University of Michigan Press, 1984),
John Hollander attached a rider to the reprint
of his 1957 review.

Addendum (February 1984)

This review was written in my youth and in a sort of worked-up high dudgeon which echoed the high-camp-prophetic mode of *Howl*'s front matter, and which may have masked some of my disappointment in a turn I saw an old friend and poetic mentor to have taken. I only regret now that I hadn't given "America" and "In a Supermarket in California" time to register; I should have certainly commended them. As for not foreseeing that Allen Ginsberg would provide so much hymnody and doctrine to the counterculture which was soon to emerge, I have no regrets, having no stake in prophecy.

Allen Ginsberg, in New York City, to John Hollander [in Cambridge, Mass.?]

September 7, 1958

Dear John:

Got your letter, slow answering . . . It's just that I've tried to do too much explaining & get overwhelmed by the vastness of the task, & sometimes what seems to be all the accumulated ill-will & evil vibrations in America (Kerouac got beaten up at the San Remo for his trouble in coming down there & making himself available.) But to begin somewhere, I should might begin with one thing, simple (I hate to go back to it over & over, like revolving around my corpse, the construction of Howl.) This may be corny to you, my concern with that, but I've got to begin somewhere & perhaps differences of opinion between us can be resolved by looking at that. See, for years before that, thinking in Williams line, which I found very helpful & quite real for what it is doing, the balance by ear of short lines formed of relatively natural ordinary notebook or conversation speech. Xbalba* is fragments of mostly prose, written in a mexican school copybook, over half a year—then re-reading, picking out the purest thoughts, stringing them together, arranging them in lines suitably balanced—mostly measured by the phrase—, that is one phrase a line—you know it's hard to explain this because it's like painting and unless you do it like practicing a piano, you don't think in those terms & get the experience of trying to work that way, so you don't notice all the specific tricks—that anyone who works in that field gets to be familiar with—that's why I'm interested in Blackburn, Levertov, Creeley, Oppenheimer, all the Black Mt people —they work steadily consistently trying to develop this line of goods, and each has a different interesting approach—they all stem out of Williams—but I can tell their lines apart they really are different—just as you can tell the difference between styles & approaches of abstract painters. When you tell me it's [the work of above-named writers] just a bore to you, that just cuts off communication, I mean I don't know what to say, I get embarrassed I feel you're being arbitrary & stubborn, it's some sort of ploy, & I just want to retreat & go about my work and stop explanations. Of course you may not be interested in this field of experiment, but that doesn't mean it's uninteresting to others, that it's categorically a bore. I *also* believe it's the main "tradition," not that there is any tradition except what we make ourselves. But basically I'm not interested in tradition because I'm more interested in what I'm doing, what it's inevitable for me to do. This realization has given me perspective on what a vast sad camp the whole literary-critical approach of School [Columbia College] has been—basically no one has insight into poetry techniques except people who are exercising them. But I'm straying at random. But I'm now getting bugged at people setting themselves up as scholars and authorities and *getting in the way* of continued creative work or its understanding or circulation—there is not one article on the Beat or SF scene yet that has not been (pro or con) invalidated (including yours) by the basic fact that the author is just a big windbag not knowing what he's talking about —no technical background, no knowledge of the vast body of experimental work, published and unpublished (the unpublished is the best), no clear grasp of the various different schools of experiment all converging toward the same or similar end, all at once coming into intercommunication, no knowledge of the letters and conversations in between, not even the basic ability (like Podhoretz) to tell the difference between prosody and diction (as in his *PR** diatribes on spontaneous bop prosody confusing it with the use of hiptalk not realizing it refers to rhythmical construction of phrases & sentences.) I mean where am I going to begin a serious explanation if I have to deal with such unmitigated stupid ignorant ill willed inept vanity as that—someone like that wouldn't listen unless you hit him over the head with a totally new universe, but he's stuck in his own hideous world, I would try, but he scarcely has enough heart to hear)—etc etc—so all these objections about juvenile delinquency, vulgarity, lack of basic education, bad taste, etc etc, no form, etc I mean it's impossible to discuss things like that—finally I get to see them as so basically *wrong* (unscientific) so dependent on ridiculous provincial schoolboy ambitions & presuppositions and so lacking contact with practical fact—that it seems a sort of plot almost, a kind of organized mob stupidity—the final camp of its announcing itself as a representative of value or civilization or taste—I mean I give up, that's just too much fucking nasty brass. And you're guilty of that too John, you've just got to drop it, and take me seriously, and listen to what I have to say. It doesn't mean you have to agree, or change your career or your writing, or anything hideous, it just means you've got to

* "Siesta in Xbalba," *Collected Poems*, pp. 97–110.

* "The Know-Nothing Bohemians," *Partisan Review*, Spring 1958.

have the heart and decency to take people seriously and not depend *only* on your own university experience for arbitrary standards of value to judge others by. It doesn't mean you have to agree, that Free Verse is the Only Path of Prosodaic Experiment, or that Williams is a Saint, or I have some horrible magic secret (tho god knows I have enough, this week with that damned buddhist laughing gas, everybody has). Just enough to dig, you to dig, what others besides yourself are trying to do. And be interested in their work or not, but not get in the way, in fact even encourage where you can see some value. And you're in a position to encourage, you teach, you shouldn't hand down limited ideas to younger minds—that was the whole horror of Columbia, there just was nobody there (maybe except Weaver) who had a serious involvement with advanced work in poetry. Just a bunch of Dilettantes. And THEY have the nerve to set themselves up as guardians of culture?!!? Why it's such a piece of effrontery—enough to make anyone Paranoiac, it's a miracle Jack or myself or anybody independent survived—tho god knows the toll in paranoia been high enough. All these grievances I'm pouring out to you. Well why revise.

Back to Howl: construction. After sick & tired of shortline free verse as not expressionistic enough, not swinging enough, can't develop a powerful enough rhythm, I simply turned aside, accidentally to writing part I of "Howl," in solitude, diddling around with the form, thinking it couldn't be published anyway (queer content my parents shouldn't see etc) also it was out of my short-line line. But what I did taught my theory, I changed my mind about "measure" while writing it.* Part one uses repeated base *who*, as a sort of kithara† BLANG, homeric (in my imagination) to mark off each statement, each rhythmic unit.‡ So that's experiment with longer & shorter variations on a fixed base—the principle being, that each line has to be contained within the elastic of one breath—with suitable punctuatory expressions where the rhythm has built up enough so that I have to let off steam by building a longer climactic line in which there is a jazzy ride. All the ear I've ever developed goes into the balancing of those lines. The interesting moment's when the rhythm is sufficiently powerfully pushing ahead so I can ride out free and drop the *who* key that holds it together. The method of keeping a long line still all poetic & not prosey is the concentration & compression of basically imagistic notations into surrealist or cubist phrasing, like hydrogen jukeboxes. Ideally anyway. Good example of this is Gregory's§ great (I swear) Coit Tower ode. Lines have greater poetic density. But I tried to keep the language sufficiently dense in one way or another—use of primitive naive grammar (expelled for

crazy), elimination of prosy articles & syntactical sawdust, juxtaposition of cubist style images, of hot rhythm.

Well then Part II. Here the basic repeated word is Moloch. The long line is now broken up into component short phrases with ! rhythmical punctuation. The key repeat BLANG word is repeated internally in the line (basic rhythm sometimes emerging /—/—) but the rhythm depends mostly on the internal Moloch repeat. Lines here lengthened—a sort of free verse prose poetry STANZA form invented or used here. This builds up to climax (Visions! Omens! etc) and then falls off in coda. Part III, perhaps an original invention (I thought so then but this type of thinking is vain & shallow anyway) to handling of long line (for the whole poem is an experiment in what you can do with the long line—the whole book is)— ::: that is, a phrase base rhythm (I'm with you etc) followed as in litany by a response of the same length (Where you're madder etc), then repeat of base over and over with the response elongating itself slowly, still contained within the elastic of one breath—till the stanza (for it is a stanza form there, I've used variations of it since)* building up like a pyramid, an emotion crying siren sound, very appropriate to the expressive appeal emotion I felt (a good healthy emotion said my analyst at that time, to dispose once and for all of that idiotic objection)—anyway, building up to the climax where there's a long long long line, penultimate, too long for one breath, where I open out & give the answer (O starry spangled shock of Mercy the eternal war is here). All this rather like a jazz mass, I mean the conception of rhythm not derived from jazz directly but if you listen to jazz you get the idea (in fact specifically old trumpet solo on a *JATP* "Can't Get Started" side†)—well all this is built like a brick shithouse and anybody can't hear the music is as I told you I guess I meekly informed Trilling, who is absolutely lost in poetry, is got a tin ear, and that's so obviously true, I get sick and tired I read 50 reviews of Howl and not one of them written by anyone with enough technical interests to notice the fucking obvious construction of the poem, all the details besides (to say nothing of the various esoteric classical allusions built in like references to Cezanne's theory of composition etc etc)—that I GIVE UP and anybody henceforth comes up to me with a silly look in his eye & begins bullshitting about morals and sociology & tradition and technique & Juvenile Delinquency—I mean I je ne sais plus parler‡—the horrible irony of all these jerks who can't *read* trying to lecture me (us) on FORM. . . .

Footnote to Howl is too lovely & serious a joke to try to explain. The built-in rhythmic exercise should be clear, it's basically a repeat of the Moloch section. It's dedicated to my mother who died in the madhouse and its says I loved her anyway & that even in worst conditions life is holy. The exaggeratedness of the statements

---

* From W. C. Williams' triadic ladder line to extended-breath verse.
† Ancient instrument supposedly used for recitation of tragedy among Greeks, seven or eleven strings, related to lyre.
‡ Anaphora.
§ Gregory Corso, "Ode to Coit Tower," in *Gasoline* (San Francisco: City Lights Books, 1958).

* "Kaddish," Part IV.
† Illinois Jacquet's solo, *Jazz at the Philharmonic*, Vol. II, ed. Norman Granz; a series of live jazz albums.
‡ Arthur Rimbaud, "Matin," in *A Season in Hell*, trans. Louise Varese (New York: New Directions, 1961), p. 80.

is appropriate, and anybody who doesnt understand the specific exaggerations will never understand Rejoice in the Lamb or Lorca's Ode to Whitman or Mayakovsky's At the Top of My Voice or Artaud's Pour En Finir Avec le Judgement de Dieu or Apollinaire's "inspired bullshit" or Whitman's madder passages or anything, anything, anything about the international modern spirit in poesy* to say nothing about the international tradition in prosody which has grown up nor the tradition of open prophetic bardic poetry which 50 years has sung like an angel over the poor soul of the world while all sorts of snippy castrates pursue their good manners and sell out their own souls and the spirit of god who now DEMANDS sincerity and hell fire take him who denies the voice in his soul—except that it's all a kindly joke & the universe disappears after you die so nobody gets hurt no matter how little they allow themselves to live & blow on this Earth....

Latter's unclear I'll start over. Tho poetry in

* See Appendix IV.

Williams has depended a lot on little breath groups for its typographical organization, and in *Howl* an extension into longer breaths (which are more natural to me than Williams short simple talks)—there is another way you would *say* it, a thought, but the way you would think it—i.e. we think rapidly, in visual images as well as words, and if each successive thought were transcribed in its confusion (really its ramification) you get a slightly different prosody than if you were talking slowly....

yours in the kingdom of music
Nella Grebsnig
Allen

[A much fuller version of this thirty-page letter, discussing the work of poets who read at Six Gallery, as well as Kerouac and Corso, the social and literary context of the 1950s, with A.G.'s reaction to contemporaneous reviews of *Howl*, including John Hollander's, was printed in Jane Kramer's *Allen Ginsberg in America* (New York: Random House, 1968), pp. 163–77.]

Appendix II
First Reading at the Six Gallery, October 7, 1955

FROM *The Literary Revolution in America*   *Allen Ginsberg and Gregory Corso*

In the fall of 1955 a group of six unknown poets in San Francisco, in a moment of drunken enthusiasm, decided to defy the system of academic poetry, official reviews, New York publishing machinery, national sobriety and generally accepted standards to good taste, by giving a free reading of their poetry in a run down secondrate experimental art gallery in the Negro section of San Francisco. They sent out a hundred postcards, put up signs in North Beach (Latin Quarter) bars, bought a lot of wine to get the audience drunk, and invited the well known Frisco Anarchist resident poet Kenneth Rexroth to act as Master of Ceremonies. Their approach was purely amateur and goofy, but it should be noted that they represented a remarkable lineup of experience and character—it was an assemblage of really good poets who knew what they were writing and didn't care about anything else. They got drunk, the audience got drunk, all that was missing was the orgy. This was no ordinary poetry reading. Indeed, it resembled anything but a poetry reading. The reading was such a violent and beautiful expression of their revolutionary individuality (a quality bypassed in American poetry since the formulations of Whitman), conducted with such surprising abandon and delight by the poets themselves, and presenting such a high mass of beautiful unanticipated poetry, that the audience, expecting some Bohemian stupidity, was left stunned, and the poets were left with the realization that they were fated to make a permanent change in the literary firmament of the States.

The poets participating were a curious group. First, Philip Lamantia, a surrealist blood poet, former member of San Francisco Anarchist group, who at the age of 13 had in imitation of Rimbaud written surrealist poetry, come to New York, consulted Breton and other surrealists, renounced surrealism, lived with Indians and priests in Mexico, took drugs, underwent visions, became Catholic, became silent, and reappeared at age of 28 in native town to take part in the reading.

The second poet, the youngest, was representative of the Black Mountain School—which derives in influence from Pound and W. C. Williams. Michael McClure read some of his own work and some of [Robert Duncan's. McClure] writes relatively sober mystical poetry. . . .

The next poet, Philip Whalen, a strange fat young man from Oregon—in appearance a Zen Buddhist Bodhisattva—read a series of very personal relaxed, learned mystical-anarchic poems. His obvious carelessness for his reputation as a poet, his delicacy and strange American sanctity is evident in his poetry, written in rare post-

Reprinted abridged from Litterair Paspoort *100 (Amsterdam), November 1957.*

Poundian assemblages of blocks of hard images set in juxtapositions, like haikus.

The most brilliant shock of the evening was the declamation of the now-famous rhapsody, *Howl*, by Allen Ginsberg. . . . The poem initiates a new style in composition in the U.S., returning to the bardic-strophic tradition, till now neglected in the U.S., of Apollinaire, Whitman, Artaud, Lorca, Mayakovsky—and improving on the tradition to the extent of combining the long lines and coherence of Whitman, with the cubist imagery of the French and Spanish traditions, and adding to that a fantastic rhythmic structure which begins on a relatively flat base of repetition, and builds up to the rhythmic crisis of a Bach fugue, and ends on a high peak of ecstatic elongation of the line structure. . . . The poem is built like a pyramid, in three parts, and ends in fantastic merciful tears—the protest against the dehumanizing mechanization of American culture, and an affirmation of individual particular compassion in the midst of a great chant.

The reading was delivered by the poet, rather surprised at his own power, drunk on the platform, becoming increasingly sober as he read, driving forward with a strange ecstatic intensity, delivering a spiritual confession to an astounded audience—ending in tears which restored to American poetry the prophetic consciousness it had lost since the conclusion of Hart Crane's *The Bridge*, another celebrated mystical work.

But this was not all! The last poet to appear on the platform was perhaps more remarkable than any of the others: Gary Snyder, a bearded youth of 26, also from the Northwest, formerly a lumberjack and seaman, student of literature and anthropology who had lived with American Indians and taken the religious drug Peyote with them, and who is now occupied in the study of Chinese and Japanese preparatory to the drunken silence of a Zen Monastery in Japan. He read parts of a hundred page poem he had been composing for 5 years, Myths and Texts—composition of fragments of all his experiences forming an anarchic and mystical pattern of individual revelation.

<u>6 POETS AT 6 GALLERY</u>

Philip Lamantia reading mss. of late John Hoffman-- Mike McClure, Allen Ginsberg, Gary Snyder & Phil Whalen--all sharp now straightforward writing-- remarkable collection of angels on one stage reading their poetry. No charge, small collection for wine and postcards. Charming event.

Kenneth Rexroth, M.C.

8 PM Friday Night October 7, 1955

6 Gallery 3119 Fillmore St.
San Fran

Perhaps the most strange poet in the room was not on the platform—he sat on the edge of it, back to the poets, eyes closed, nodding at good lines, swigging a bottle of California red wine—at times shouting encouragement or responding with spontaneous images—jazz style—to the long zig-zag rhythms chanted in *Howl*. This was Jack Kerouac, then unknown also, now perhaps the most celebrated novelist in America. . . . Mr. Kerouac is also a superb poet, his poems are automatic, pure, brilliant, awesome, gentle, and unpublished as of yet. . . .

I should, at this point, remark that William Carlos Williams, of all the great older poets, has remained in closest touch with these young poets, and he, if anyone, supplies the link with the democratic experimental tradition of the poet.

Mention should also be given Mr. Lawrence Ferlinghetti, publisher of Mr. Ginsberg's *Howl*, and himself poet of a book of verse, *Pictures of the Gone World*. Ferlinghetti is the most advanced publisher in America in that he publishes "suspect" literature, literature usually rejected by other publishing houses because of their wild neo-bop prosody, non-commercial value, extreme expression of soul, and the pure adventure of publishing it. For his pains Mr. Ferlinghetti is now on trial in the American courts for having published Mr. Ginsberg.

This article should properly end with the announcement of the completion of *Naked Lunch*, a long epic prose-poem by William Seward Burroughs. Burroughs is the shadowy unknown genius behind the more publicized figures of Kerouac and Ginsberg, and the completion and editing of his work was the occasion of a transatlantic reunion of the three early this year in Tangiers. The book seems destined to have great difficulties in finding a publisher—its style, almost surrealistic, its structure, its automaticism, its theme, the desecration of the unity, the human image desecrated by a mad society, its images, sex, drugs, dreams, riots, hangings, secret narcotic phantasmal police—in short, *Naked Lunch* is a prose-poetic novel in the tradition of Rimbaud, Artaud, Genet, but the treatment of the work is too *naked* to be admitted into American consciousness past the barrier of commercial publishing, customs inspection, and legal censorship of its "obscenity."

In America, apart from the Little Rock stagnant sign of doom, apart from money-wild cultureless majority of humans that inhabit it, apart from the wealth and woe and fear and sorrow and false joy and guilt, there is, out of all this, in America, a new forceful stir of young poets, and they have taken it upon themselves, with angelic clarions in hand, to announce their discontent, their demands, their hope, their final wondrous unimaginable dream.

FROM *The Dharma Bums*

Jack Kerouac

. . . It was a great night, a historic night in more ways than one. Japhy Ryder and some other poets (he also wrote poetry and translated Chinese and Japanese poetry into English) were scheduled to give a poetry reading at the Gallery Six in town. They were all meeting in the bar and getting high. But as they stood and sat around I saw that he was the only one who didn't look like a poet, though poet he was indeed. The other poets were either hornrimmed intellectual hepcats with wild black hair like Alvah Goldbook, or delicate pale handsome poets like Ike O'Shay (in a suit), or out-of-this-world genteel-looking Renaissance Italians like Francis DaPavia (who looks like a young priest), or bow-tied wild-haired old anarchist fuds like Rheinhold Cacoethes, or big fat bespectacled quiet booboos like Warren Coughlin. And all the other hopeful poets were standing around, in various costumes, worn-at-the-sleeves corduroy jackets, scuffly shoes, books sticking out of their pockets. . . .

Anyway I followed the whole gang of howling poets to the reading at Gallery Six that night, which was, among other important things, the night of the birth of the San Francisco Poetry Renaissance. Everyone was there. It was a mad night. And I was the one who got things jumping by going around collecting dimes and quarters from the rather stiff audience standing around in the gallery and coming back with three huge gallon jugs of California Burgundy and getting them all piffed so that by eleven o'clock when Alvah Goldbook was reading his, wailing his poem "Wail" drunk with arms outspread everybody was yelling "Go! Go! Go!" (like a jam session) and old Rheinhold Cacoethes the father of the Frisco poetry scene was wiping his tears in gladness. Japhy himself read his fine poems about Coyote the God of the North American Plateau Indians (I think), at least the God of the Northwest Indians, Kwakiutl and what-all. "Fuck you! sang Coyote, and ran away!" read Japhy to the distinguished audience, making them all howl with joy, it was so pure, fuck being a dirty word that comes out clean. And he had his tender lyrical lines, like the ones about bears eating berries, showing his love of animals, and great mystery lines about oxen on the Mongolian road showing his knowledge of Oriental literature even on to Hsuan Tsung the great Chinese monk who walked from China to Tibet, Lanchow to Kashgar and Mongolia carrying a stick of incense in his hand. Then Japhy showed his sudden barroom humor with lines about Coyote bringing goodies. And his anarchistic ideas about how Americans don't know how to live, with lines about commuters being trapped in living rooms that come from poor trees felled by chainsaws (showing here, also, his background as a logger up north). This voice was deep and resonant and somehow brave, like the voice of oldtime American heroes and orators. Something earnest and strong and humanly hopeful I liked about him, while the other poets were either too dainty in their aestheticism, or too hysterically cynical to hope for anything, or too abstract and indoorsy, or too political, or like Coughlin too incomprehensible to understand (big Coughlin saying things about "unclarified processes" though where Coughlin did say that revelation was a personal thing I noticed the strong Buddhist and idealistic feeling of Japhy, which he'd shared with goodhearted Coughlin in their buddy days at college, as I had shared mine with Alvah in the Eastern scene and with others less apocalyptical and straighter but in no sense more sympathetic and tearful).

Meanwhile scores of people stood around in the darkened gallery straining to hear every word of the amazing poetry reading as I wandered from group to group, facing them and facing away from the stage, urging them to glug a slug from the jug, or wandered back and sat on the right side of the stage giving out little wows and yesses of approval and even whole sentences of comment with nobody's invitation but in the general gaiety nobody's disapproval either. It was a great night. Delicate Francis DaPavia read, from delicate onionskin yellow pages, or pink, which he kept flipping carefully with long white fingers, the poems of his dead chum Altman who'd eaten too much peyote in Chihuahua (or died of polio, one) but read none of his own poems—a charming elegy in itself to the memory of the dead young poet, enough to draw tears from the Cervantes of Chapter Seven, and read them in a delicate Englishy voice that had me crying with inside laughter though I later got to know Francis and liked him. . . .

Between poets, Rheinhold Cacoethes, in his bow tie and shabby old coat, would get up and make a little funny speech in his snide funny voice and introduce the next reader; but as I say come eleven-thirty when all the poems were read and everybody was milling around wondering what had happened and what would come next in American poetry, he was wiping his eyes with his handkerchief.

From Chap. 2 (New York: Viking Press, 1958).
KEY: Japhy Rider = Gary Snyder; Alvah Goldbook = Allen Ginsberg; Rheinhold Cacoethes = Kenneth Rexroth; Warren Coughlin = Philip Whalen; Francis DaPavia = Philip Lamantia; Ike O'Shea = Michael McClure; Altman = John Hoffman.

FROM *Peter Orlovsky and Allen Ginsberg interview, 1975*

James McKenzie

PETER ORLOVSKY: I was with Neal Cassady at the Six Gallery reading, and Neal said to me, "Come over here, Peter, come stand next to me." I said, "Why? Why, Neal?" and he said, "Well, I don't know anybody here." So I was standing next to Neal but then I moved over and stood next to someone else because, you know, I was a little embarrassed. I was very, very bashful and embarrassed—very self-conscious, you know, in those days. And Neal was there, dressed in his brakeman's uniform. He had his vest on—his watch and his vest. . . . He was very proud, smiling, very happy, full of smiles and bowing. . . .

ALLEN GINSBERG: He came up to me and he said, "Allen, my boy. I'm proud of you." [Laughter] It was really nice—it was the nicest thing I heard that night. It was completely, unabashedly, friendly, happy approval.

Interview in North Dakota, 1975. In *Unspeakable Visions of the Individual*, ed. Arthur and Glee Knight (California, Pa., 1979).

FROM *Jack's Book*

Barry Gifford and Lawrence Lee

ALLEN GINSBERG: The Six Gallery reading had come about when Wally Hedrick, who was a painter and one of the major people there, asked Rexroth if he knew any poets that would put on a reading. Maybe Rexroth asked McClure to organize it and McClure didn't know how or didn't have time. Rexroth asked me, so I met McClure and Rexroth suggested I go visit another poet who was living in Berkeley, which was Gary. So I went right over to Gary's house and immediately had a meeting of minds with him over William Carlos Williams, 'cause I had written *Empty Mirror* at that time and he had begun *Myths and Texts*, or *The Berry Feast*, or something, and he told me about his friend Philip Whalen who was due in town the next day. And I told him about my friend Kerouac who was in town that day, and within three or four days we all met. . . .

Jack and I were coming from Berkeley, and had just arrived in San Francisco at the Key System Terminal, the bus terminal there, and we met right out on First and Mission, by accident. Gary was with Phil and I was with Jack, and we all went off immediately and started talking. And then Philip Lamantia was in town, whom I'd known from '48 in New York, and then there was Michael McClure. So there was a whole complement of poets. Then Gary and I decided we ought to invite Rexroth to be the sixth—sixth poet—to introduce at the Six Gallery, be the elder, since he had linked us up.

New York: St. Martin's Press, 1978.

FROM *Ferlinghetti: A Biography*

Neeli Cherkovski

On the night of the reading the Ferlinghettis invited some of the poets to ride with them. Ginsberg, Kerouac, Kirby, and one or two others managed to get into the car and off they sped. About seventy-five people had crowded into the small gallery. After Ginsberg read the first part of *Howl*, the audience reaction was amazing. They seemed to know that they had heard a great poem, demonstrating that fact by their applause. A party was held after the reading, and most of the poets attended. The Ferlinghettis were tired and went home. Ferlinghetti immediately sat down at his typewriter and composed a telegram that he sent to Ginsberg. The message paraphrased one that Ralph Waldo Emerson had sent to Walt Whitman upon receiving a copy of the 1855 edition of *Leaves of Grass*. The telegram to Ginsberg read: "I greet you at the beginning of a great career. When do I get the manuscript?"

Garden City, N.Y.: Doubleday, 1979.

Michael McClure

Three years before the peyote experience just described, I had given my first poetry reading with Allen Ginsberg, the Zen poet Philip Whalen, Gary Snyder, and the American Surrealist poet Philip Lamantia. The reading was in October 1955, at the Six Gallery in San Francisco. The Six Gallery was a cooperative art gallery run by young artists who centered around the San Francisco Art Institute. They were fiery artists who had either studied with Clyfford Still and Mark Rothko or with the newly emerging figurative painters. Their works ranged from huge drip and slash to minute precision smudges turning into faces. Earlier in the year poet Robert Duncan had given a staged reading of his play *Faust Foutu* (Faust Fucked) at the Six Gallery and, with the audacious purity of an Anarchist poet, he had stripped off his clothes at the end of the play.

On this night Kenneth Rexroth was master of ceremonies. This was the first time that Allen Ginsberg read *Howl*. Though I had known Allen for some months preceding, it was my first meeting with Gary Snyder and Philip Whalen. Lamantia did not read his poetry that night but instead recited works of the recently deceased John Hoffman—beautiful prose poems that left orange stripes and colored visions in the air. . . .

The Six Gallery was a huge room that had been converted from an automobile repair shop into an art gallery. Someone had knocked together a little dais and was exhibiting sculptures by Fred Martin at the back of it—pieces of orange crates that had been swathed in muslin and dipped in plaster of paris to make splintered, sweeping shapes like pieces of surrealist furniture. A hundred and fifty enthusiastic people had come to hear us. Money was collected and jugs of wine were brought back for the audience. I hadn't seen Allen in a few weeks and I had not heard *Howl*—it was new to me. Allen began in a small and intensely lucid voice. At some point Jack Kerouac began shouting "GO" in cadence as Allen read it. In all of our memories no one had been so outspoken in poetry before—we had gone beyond a point of no return—and we were ready for it, for a point of no return. None of us wanted to go back to the gray, chill, militaristic silence, to the intellective void—to the land without poetry—to the spiritual drabness. We wanted to make it new and we wanted to invent it and the process of it as we went into it. We wanted voice and we wanted vision. . . .

Ginsberg read on to the end of the poem, which left us standing in wonder, or cheering and wondering, but knowing at the deepest level that a barrier had been broken, that a human voice and body had been hurled against the harsh wall of America and its supporting armies and navies and academies and institutions and ownership systems and power-support bases. . . .

San Francisco: North Point Press, 1982.

Also that night Gary Snyder, bearded and neat, a rugged young man of nature at age twenty-five, read his scholarly and ebullient nature poem, *A Berry Feast*. . . .

Snyder's gloss on the poem reads: "The berry feast is a first-fruits celebration that consumes a week of mid-August on the Warm Springs Indian Reservation in Oregon. Coyote is the name of the Trickster-Hero of the mythology of that region." . . .

Even in those days Philip Whalen was a big man. As I watched him read, the meaning of his metamorphic poem gradually began to sink in. We laughed as the poem's intent clarified. Here was a poem by a poet-scholar (who is now a Zen priest as well as a major American poet) with a multiple thrust. Whalen was using the American speech that William Carlos Williams instructed us to use, but he put it to a different use. Whalen's poems were not only naturalistic portrayals of objects and persons transformed by poetry—they also used American speech for the naked joy of portraying metamorphosis and of exemplifying and aiding change in the universe. They manifested a positive Whiteheadian joy in shifting and in processes. Whalen read this poem ["Plus Ça Change"] with a mock seriousness that was at once biting, casual, and good natured. . . .

The Six Gallery reading was open to the world and the world was welcome. There were poets and Anarchists and Stalinists and professors and painters and bohemians and visionaries and idealists and grinning cynics.

I had been fascinated by the thought and the poetry of the French *maudite*, antiphysical, mystic poet Antonin Artaud, who had died toothless and, it is said, mad in Paris in 1948, only seven years before our Six Gallery reading. One of my first exchanges with Philip Lamantia on meeting him in 1954 was to ask where I could find more works by Artaud. I was fascinated by Artaud's visionary gnosticism. . . .

One phrase of Artaud's fascinated me: "It is not possible that in the end the miracle willl not occur." I replied with a poem I read at the Six Gallery ["Point Lobos: Animism"]. . . .

At the Six Gallery I also read a poem that sprang from an article in *Time* magazine (April 1954). Excerpts from the article used to preface the poem say:

> Killer whales. . . . Savage sea cannibals up to thirty feet long with teeth like bayonets . . . one was caught with fourteen seals and thirteen porpoises in its belly . . . often tear at boats and nets . . . destroyed thousands of dollars' worth of fishing tackle. . . . Icelandic government appealed to the U.S., which has thousands of men stationed at a lonely NATO airbase on the subarctic island. Seventy-nine bored G.I.'s responded with enthusiasm. Armed with rifles and machine guns one posse of Americans climbed into four small boats and in one morning wiped out a pack of 100 killers. . . .

I was horrified and angry when I read about the slaughter and I wrote: "For the Death of 100 Whales." . . .

Appendix III
Legal History of HOWL

FROM Horn on *Howl* (with interleaved communications) by Lawrence Ferlinghetti

When William Carlos Williams, in his Introduction to *Howl*, said that Ginsberg had come up with "an arresting poem" he hardly knew what he was saying. The first edition of *Howl*, Number Four in the Pocket Poet Series, was printed in England by Villiers, passed thru customs without incident, and was published at the City Lights bookstore here in the fall of 1956. Part of a second printing was stopped by customs on March 25, 1957, not long after an earlier issue of *The Miscellaneous Man* (published in Berkeley by William Margolis) had been seized coming from the same printer. Section 305 of the Tariff Act of 1930 was cited. The San Francisco *Chronicle* (which alone among the local press put up a real howl about censorship) reported, in part:

> Collector of Customs Chester MacPhee continued his campaign yesterday to keep what he considers obscene literature away from the children of the Bay Area. He confiscated 520 copies of a paperbound volume of poetry entitled *Howl and Other Poems*. . . . "The words and the sense of the writing is obscene," MacPhee declared. "You wouldn't want your children to come across it."

[I had submitted the ms. of *Howl* to the ACLU *before* sending it to the printer in England, to see if they would defend us *if* the book was busted, and a good thing too, since without the ACLU, City Lights would no doubt have gone broke and out of business. We were barely breaking even those years, and living on very little, and the expense of a court trial would have been disastrous.]*

On April 3 [1957] the American Civil Liberties Union . . . informed Mr. MacPhee that it would contest the legality of the seizure, since it did not consider the book obscene. We announced in the meantime that an entire new edition of *Howl* was being printed within the United States, thereby removing it from customs jurisdiction. No changes were made in the original text, and a photo-offset edition was placed on sale at City Lights bookstore and distributed nationally while the customs continued to sit on the copies from Britain. . . .

[San Francisco Collector of Customs deserves a word of thanks for seizing Allen Ginsberg's *Howl and Other Poems* thereby rendering it famous. Perhaps we could have a medal made. It would have taken years for critics to accomplish what the good collector did in a day, merely by calling the book obscene. City Lights Books now has had an entirely new edition printed locally and thereby removed it from customs jurisdiction. I should like to justify this action by defending *Howl* as a poetic work leaving moral argument to others. I consider *Howl* to be the most significant long poem to be published in this country since World War II, perhaps since Eliot's *Four Quartets*. In some sense it's a gestalt and archetypical configuration of the mass culture which produced it. The results are a condemnation of our culture. If it is an obscene voice of dissent, perhaps this is really why officials object to it. Condemning it, however, they are condemning our world for it is what he observes that is the great voice of *Howl*. . . .]†

*Lawrence Ferlinghetti to Allen Ginsberg, San Francisco, April 27, 1986.
†Lawrence Ferlinghetti, *San Francisco Chronicle*, May 19, 1957; "This World" section, p. 35: William Hogan's "Between the Lines" column.

Notes on the obscenity trial of *Howl*, from *Evergreen Review* (Winter 1957). Copyright © 1957 by Lawrence Ferlinghetti. Reprinted by permission of City Lights Books.

Lawrence Ferlinghetti & Shigeyoshi Murao, front bench left, *Howl* trial courtroom, San Francisco Hall of Justice, Summer 1957.   *Photo Courtesy City Lights.*

On May 29 customs released the books it had been holding, since the United States Attorney at San Francisco refused to institute condemnation proceedings against *Howl*.

Then the police took over and arrested us, Captain William Hanrahan of the juvenile department (well named, in this case) reporting that the books were not fit for children to read. Thus during the first week in June I found myself being booked and fingerprinted in San Francisco's Hall of Justice. The city jail occupies the upper floors of it, and a charming sight it is, a picturesque return to the early Middle Ages. And my enforced tour of it was a dandy way for the city officially to recognize the flowering of poetry in San Francisco. As one paper reported, "The Cops Don't Allow No Renaissance Here."

The ACLU posted bail. Our trial went on all summer, with a couple of weeks between each day in court. The prosecution soon admitted it had no case against either Shig Murao or myself as far as *The Miscellaneous Man* was concerned, since we were not the publisher of it, in which case there was no proof we knew what was inside the magazine when it was sold at our store. And, under the California Penal Code, the willful and lewd *intent* of the accused had to be established. Thus the trial was narrowed down to *Howl*.

The so-called People's Case (I say so-called, since the People seemed mostly on our side) was presented by Deputy District Attorney Ralph McIntosh whose heart seemed not in it nor his mind on it. He was opposed by some of the most formidable legal talent to be found, in the persons of Mr. Jake ("Never Plead Guilty") Ehrlich, Lawrence Speiser (former counsel for the ACLU), and Albert Bendich (present counsel for the ACLU)—all of whom defended us without expense to us.

The critical support for *Howl* (or the protest against censorship on principle) was enormous. . . . [Letters and written statements were received from Henry Rago, editor of *Poetry* (Chicago); Robert Duncan and Director Ruth Witt-Diamant of the San Francisco (State College) Poetry Center; Thomas Parkinson (University of California); James Laughlin (New Directions); Kenneth Patchen; Northern California Booksellers Association; and Barney Rosset and Donald Allen, editors of the *Evergreen Review* (in which "Howl" was reprinted during the trial).]*

At the trial itself, nine expert witnesses testified in behalf of *Howl*. They were eloquent witnesses, together furnishing as good a one-sided critical survey of *Howl* as could possibly be got up in any literary magazine. These witnesses were: Mark Schorer and Leo Lowenthal (of the University of California faculty), Walter Van Tilburg Clark, Herbert Blau, Arthur Foff, and Mark Linenthal (all of the San Francisco State College faculty), Kenneth Rexroth, Vincent McHugh (poet and novelist), and Luther Nichols (book editor of the San Francisco *Examiner*). . . .

Legally, a layman could see that an important principle was certainly in the line drawn between "hard core pornography" and writing judged to be "social

* L. F. text summarized by A. G.

speech." But more important still was the court's acceptance of the principle that if a work is determined to be "social speech" the question of obscenity may not even be raised. Or, in the words of Counsel Bendich's argument:

> The first amendment to the Constitution of the United States protecting the fundamental freedoms of speech and press prohibits the suppression of literature by the application of obscenity formulae unless the trial court first determines that the literature in question is utterly without social importance." (*Roth* v. *U.S.*)
>
> . . . What is being urged here is that the majority opinion in *Roth* requires a trial court to make the constitutional determination; to decide in the first instance whether a work is utterly without redeeming social importance, *before* it permits the test of obscenity to be applied. . . .
>
> . . . The record is clear that all of the experts for the defense identified the main theme of *Howl* as social criticism. And the prosecution concedes that it does not understand the work, much less what its dominant theme is.

Judge Horn agreed, in his opinion. . . . Under banner headlines, the *Chronicle* reported that "the Judge's decision was hailed with applause and cheers from a packed audience that offered the most fantastic collection of beards, turtlenecked shirts and Italian hairdos ever to grace the grimy precincts of the Hall of Justice." The decision was hailed editorially as a "landmark of law." Judge Horn has since been reelected to office, which I like to think means that the People agree it was the police who here committed an obscene action.

Footnotes to My Arrest for Selling *Howl*

Shigeyoshi Murao

Imagine being arrested for selling poetry! Two police officers from the juvenile squad arrested me. Obscenity was under their purview as a way of protecting the children. They had a "John Doe" warrant for my arrest. I kidded the police officers that I, Shigeyoshi Murao, a Japanese-American, was being arrested as a "John Doe" white man. They smiled, but did not laugh. It was a quotidian arrest. They never even handcuffed me. I was taken by patrol car to the Hall of Justice, three blocks from the store. In the basement, I was fingerprinted, posed for mug shots and locked in the drunk tank. The cell smelled of piss. There was a piss-stained mattress on the floor. For lunch, they served me wieners, very red. The trusty told me that the sausages were full of salt-peter so that the prisoners would not get hard-ons. I didn't eat lunch. The trusty ate my lunch.

In jail, I had no noble thoughts of fighting for freedom of the press and censorship. I had planned to live a quiet life of reading, listening to music and playing chess the rest of my life. Yet here I was involved in a case for selling obscenity.

Two hours later, I was bailed out of jail by the ACLU lawyers. In the jail cell, there was a penal code posted on the wall. Over the penal code, there was graffiti—"cocksuckers." The officers near the police desk talked in the American jocular manner. One said, "The judge must have gotten laid last night; he's so easy on these fuckin' assholes." Another answered, "Nah, the judge must have jacked off last night. His wife is dead."

The week *Life* magazine featured the trial, I flew to Chicago to see my parents. My father, whose English was limited, read *Life*. My spoken Japanese was also limited. I could not explain to them why I was arrested for obscenity. They were just satisfied I did not have to go to jail.

For the trial, I wore a cheap, light-blue summer suit with a white buttoned shirt and a black knit tie. In those days, you had to dress properly or you were held in contempt of court. Jake Ehrlich, our famous criminal lawyer, never said a word to me during the trial, except to make sure that I permitted the press to take pictures of me. After a few sessions, I was dismissed from the case. Section B of the penal code states, ". . . did knowingly sell . . ." The prosecutors could not prove that I had read the book. Eventually we won the case.

Sometime during the trial, someone from the JACL (Japanese American Citizens League) called to ask how I was. After the trial, Ernie Bessig, the ACLU director, talked to me about how his Northern California chapter fought for Japanese-American rights during World War II, the only ACLU chapter to do so.

I went on to a twenty-four-year career of selling books. I became famous for selling bad poetry; but I sold some good ones too. *Howl* was one of them.

March 1986

From How Captain Hanrahan Made *Howl* a Best-Seller

David Perlman

. . . The preparations for the trial produced a certain amount of concern in both legal and literary circles. Captain William Hanrahan, chief of the department's Juvenile Bureau, announced, "We will await the outcome of this case before we go ahead with other books." He did not reveal what books he had in mind, but he made it clear he had quite a list. He also disclosed that his men had been taking a look around the shelves of the city's bookstores—of which there are far more per capita than in any other metropolis outside New York.

When Captain Hanrahan was asked what standards he used to judge a book, his reply was brief but vague: "When I say filthy I don't mean suggestive, I mean filthy words that are very vulgar." He was also asked whether he was planning to send his men out to confiscate the

The Reporter, December 12, 1957.

Bible. His denial was vehement. "Let me tell you, though," the captain added, "what King Solomon was doing with all those women wouldn't be tolerated in San Francisco!"

The City Lights Pocket Bookshop, where Captain Hanrahan's men had dragged their net for filth, is not an ordinary emporium of literature. Its owner, and the principal defendant in the case, is Lawrence Ferlinghetti, a poet himself, a painter, and a canny and relatively affluent citizen of a San Francisco district called North Beach, which is a largely Italian neighborhood near the waterfront, between Telegraph and Russian Hills. Ferlinghetti's store is right in the center of the district . . .

Ferlinghetti's bookshop sells no hard covers,* but it does stock all the quarterlies, all the soft-cover prestige lines of the major publishers, a lot of foreign imprints and periodicals, and just about every other sort of pocket book except the kind whose bosomy covers leer from the racks of drugstores and bus terminals.

His store also contains a lively bulletin board, on which appear notices of art exhibits, beer blasts, little-theater castings, ceramic sales, and odd jobs wanted. The City Lights is tiny and crowded, but it is open far into the night. Many residents in the quarter find it an ideal place for browsing, meeting friends, catching up on North Beach gossip, and even buying books. It is, in a way, the intellectual center of North Beach.

Ferlinghetti is also a publisher. He has issued, under the City Lights imprint, a "Pocket Poets" series, retailing for seventy-five cents each. The first three works offered were Ferlinghetti's own *Pictures of the Gone World*, Rexroth's *Thirty Spanish Poems of Love and Exile*, and Patchen's *Poems of Humor and Protest*. The fourth was a forty-four-page volume called *Howl and Other Poems* by Allen Ginsberg . . .

This was the poem that aroused the San Francisco Police Department and was the actual defendant in the case of *People* vs. *Ferlinghetti*. Ginsberg himself was far away on a trip to Europe, and the owner of the bookstore never took the stand, nor was any evidence presented against him beyond the fact that he had published "Howl." His clerk, Shigeyoshi Murao, was even less involved. The prosecutor conceded that there was no evidence to show the clerk even knew what was in the book, and it was quickly agreed that Murao should be acquitted. It was also agreed that the trial would be held without a jury.

The judge was Clayton W. Horn of the San Francisco Municipal Court, who functions primarily as one of the city's four police magistrates. Judge Horn, who regularly teaches Bible class at a Sunday school, was under something of a cloud when he mounted the bench for the "Howl" case. He had just been raked over by the local press for a decision in which he had sentenced five lady shoplifters to attend *The Ten Commandments* and write penitential essays on the supercolossal epic's moral lesson.

The chief defense counsel was J. W. Ehrlich, known

* It was the first all-paperback bookstore in the U.S., inspired by French custom.

for thirty years in San Francisco as "Jake The Master." . . .

Ehrlich's opponent was Ralph McIntosh, an elderly assistant district attorney . . . something of a specialist in smut cases. Pornographic movies, nudist magazines, and Jane Russell's appearance in *The Outlaw* have all been targets of his zeal. . . .

The first major encounter of the trial came when Ehrlich carefully pitted McIntosh against the defense's principal witness, Mark Schorer. Schorer is professor of English and chairman of graduate studies at the University of California; he is one of America's leading critics, is a textbook consultant to the U.S. Army, has published three novels and seventy-five short stories, and has been awarded a Fulbright and three Guggenheim fellowships.

In his characteristically imperturbable drawl, Schorer testified on direct examination by Ehrlich: "I think that 'Howl,' like any work of literature, attempts and intends to make a significant comment on or interpretation of human experience as the author knows it."

He said the theme and structure "create the impression of a nightmare world in which the 'best minds of our generation' are wandering like damned souls in hell." Much of the content, Schorer said, is "a series of what one might call surrealistic images."

Judge Horn, having carefully read the evolving common law on the subject, ruled that while Schorer and other experts could not testify whether or not they thought the poem obscene, they could state whether they thought the controversial language contained in the poem was "relevant" to the intent and theme of the poet.

"Ginsberg uses the rhythms of ordinary speech and also the diction of ordinary speech," Schorer said. "I would say the poem uses necessarily the language of vulgarity."

Then came the cross-examination. For an hour McIntosh pecked at Schorer, stormed at him, and read him nearly every questionable line in the book. The prosecutor railed at the poem too, and it was sometimes difficult to tell which he objected to more, its dirt or its incomprehensibility.

"I presume you understand the whole thing, is that right?" McIntosh asked Schorer at one point, a dare in his voice.

Schorer smiled. "I hope so," he said. "It's not always easy to know that one understands exactly what a contemporary poet is saying, but I think I do."

"McIntosh flourished the book triumphantly. "Do you understand," he demanded, "what 'angelheaded hipsters burning for the ancient heavenly connection to the starry dynamo in the machinery of night' means?"

"Sir, you can't translate poetry into prose," Schorer answered. "That's why it's poetry."

The audience, among whom were North Beach writers, downtown booksellers, and a few criminal-courts regulars, roared. The judge smiled tolerantly, but McIntosh would not give up.

"In other words," he asked, "you don't have to understand the words?"

"You don't understand the individual words taken out of their context," Schorer explained patiently. "You can no more translate it back into logical prose English than you can say what a surrealistic painting means in words because it's *not* prose."

This still didn't satisfy McIntosh, who kept reading the poem's opening lines and demanding a literal explanation. Finally Schorer said: "I can't possibly translate, nor, I am sure, can anyone in this room translate the opening part of this poem into rational prose."

For some reason, this testimony set McIntosh up immensely. "That's just what I wanted to find out," he declared with the air of one who has just clinched his case.

Having established the impossibility of translation, the prosecutor then read aloud one line of "Howl" after another, each with its quota of Anglo-Saxon words or vivid sexual images, and demanded more translations.

Schorer patiently declined to give them, and McIntosh finally turned to Judge Horn to complain: "Your Honor, frankly I have only got a batch of law degrees. I don't know anything about literature. But I would like to find out what this is all about. It's like this modern painting nowadays, surrealism or whatever they call it, where they have a monkey come in and do some finger painting."

The judge declined to instruct the witness to enlighten McIntosh on the poem's meaning, so the prosecutor tried another tack. He read a few more vivid phrases into the record and then asked Schorer: "Now couldn't that have been worded some other way? Do they have to put words like that in there?"

But Judge Horn disallowed the question, and offered a bit of literary criticism himself: "I think it is obvious," he said, "that the author could have used another term; whether or not it would have served the same purpose is another thing; that's up to the author."

By this time McIntosh was about ready to give up on Schorer. But he decided to have one final go at him. Turning to some of the poems that followed "Howl" in the volume, he asked Schorer to characterize them.

"Those are what one would call lyric poems," Schorer explained, "and the earlier ones are hortatory poems."

McIntosh pricked up his ears.

"Are what?" he demanded.

"Hortatory, Mr. McIntosh."

"That's all," said the prosecutor, and sat down. Schorer bowed gracefully towards McIntosh, and withdrew amid applause.

The defense placed nine expert witnesses on the stand in all, and with each one of them McIntosh went through the same maneuvers: bewilderment at the poem, contempt for the expert on the stand, and glee at the extraction of four-letter words. But no jury was present to see his act.

From Luther Nichols, book critic of the San Francisco *Examiner*, he learned that "Ginsberg's life is a vagabond one; it's colored by exposure to jazz, to Columbia University, to a liberal and Bohemian education, to a certain amount of bumming around. The words he has used are valid and necessary if he's to be honest with his purpose. I think to use euphemisms in describing this would be considered dishonest by Mr. Ginsberg."

From Walter Van Tilburg Clark, author of *The Ox-Bow Incident*, came this statement: "They seem to me, all of the poems in the volume, to be the work of a thoroughly honest poet, who is also a highly competent technician."

"Do you classify yourself as a liberal?" McIntosh asked Clark. But that was as far as he got. Judge Horn barred the question the instant it was uttered.

It was from Kenneth Rexroth—who described himself as a "recognized American poet of recognized competence, and a poetry critic of recognized competence"—that Ehrlich drew the highest qualitative judgment on "Howl." "Its merit is extraordinarily high," Rexroth said. "It is probably the most remarkable single poem published by a young man since the second war."

McIntosh made an effort to discredit the poem by bringing in two expert witnesses of his own to testify in rebuttal.

One was David Kirk, assistant professor of English at the University of San Francisco, a Catholic school. Kirk condemned "Howl" as a "poem apparently dedicated to a long-dead movement called Dadaism. And therefore the opportunity is long past for any significant literary contribution of this poem," and as a "weak imitation of a form that was used eighty or ninety years ago by Walt Whitman."

The second was a blonde named Gail Potter who passed out little printed brochures announcing that she gives private lessons in speech and diction, and who offered a formidable array of qualifications as an expert. She had, she said, rewritten *Faust* from its forty original versions; she had written thirty-five feature articles; she had written a pageant for what she called "one of the big affairs in Florida"; and she had taught at a business college, a church school for girls, and the College of Southern Florida at Lakeland.

"You feel like you are going through the gutter when you have to read that stuff," Miss Potter said of "Howl." Then she shuddered in distaste and added: "I didn't linger on it too long, I assure you."

Jake Ehrlich bowed Miss Potter off the stand without a question, and that was the prosecution's case.

In the arguments of opposing counsel as the trial wound up, the debate ran true to form. McIntosh cried aloud that San Francisco was in dire danger:

"I would like you to ask yourself, Your Honor, in determining whether or not these books are obscene, would you like to see this sort of poetry printed in your local newspaper? Or would you like to have this poetry read to you over the radio as a diet? In other words, Your Honor, how far are we going to license the use of filthy, vulgar, obscene, and disgusting language? How far can we go?"

For Jake Ehrlich, "Howl" was honest poetry, written by an honest poet, and dirty only to the dirty-minded. As for its potential tendency to arouse lustful thoughts

in readers, "The Master" dismissed that key question in a sentence. "You can't think common, rotten things just because you read something in a book unless it is your purpose to read common, rotten things and apply a common, rotten purpose to what you read."

Judge Horn took two weeks to deliberate before reaching a verdict. He took the trouble to read *Ulysses* and the famous court decisions that are part of its publishing history. He read other works that were once attacked as obscene. He read the law, both statute and common.

He found "Howl" not obscene and Ferlinghetti not guilty. His written opinion, although it comes from the state's lowest-ranking bench, must now stand as a major codification of obscenity law in California. . . .

The People of the State of California
vs. Lawrence Ferlinghetti,
Excerpts from the Decision (October 3, 1957)

Horn, Clayton W., J. The defendant is charged with a violation of Section 311.3 of the Penal Code of the State of California. Defendant pleads Not Guilty. The complaint alleged that the defendant did willfully and lewdly print, publish and sell obscene and indecent writings, papers and books, to wit: "Howl and Other Poems." . . .

Unless the words used take the form of dirt for dirt's sake and can be traced to criminal behavior, either actual or demonstrably imminent, they are not in violation of the statute. Indecent as used in the Penal Code is synonymous with obscene, and there is no merit in the contention of the prosecution that the word indecent means something less than obscene. . . .

In determining whether a book is obscene it must be construed as a whole. The courts are agreed that in making this determination, the book must be construed as a whole and that regard shall be had for its place in the arts.

The freedoms of speech and press are inherent in a nation of free people. These freedoms must be protected if we are to remain free, both individually and as a nation. The protection for this freedom is found in the First and Fourteenth Amendments to the United States Constitution, and in the Constitution of California, Art. I, sec. 9 which provides in part:

> Every citizen may freely speak, write, and publish his sentiments on all subjects, being responsible for the abuse of that right; and no law shall be passed to restrain or abridge the liberty of speech or of the press . . .

The Fourteenth Amendment to the Federal Constitution prohibits any State from encroaching upon freedom of speech and freedom of the press to the same extent that the First Amendment prevents the Federal Congress from doing so.

These guarantees occupy a preferred position under our law to such an extent that the courts, when considering whether legislation infringes upon them, neutralize the presumption usually indulged in favor of constitutionality.

Thomas Jefferson in his bill for establishing religious freedom wrote that "to suffer the Civil Magistrate to intrude his powers into the field of opinion, and to restrain the profession or propagation of principles on supposition of their ill tendency, is a dangerous fallacy which at once destroys all religious liberty . . . it is time enough for the rightful purposes of civil government for its officers to interfere when principles break out into overt acts against peace and good order." . . .

The authors of the First Amendment knew that novel and unconventional ideas might disturb the complacent, but they chose to encourage a freedom which they believed essential if vigorous enlightenment was ever to triumph over slothful ignorance.

I agree with the words of Macaulay who finds it difficult to believe that in a world so full of temptations as this, any gentleman, whose life would have been virtuous if he had not read Aristophanes and Juvenal, will be made vicious by reading them.

I do not believe that "Howl" is without redeeming social importance. The first part of "Howl" presents a picture of a nightmare world; the second part is an indictment of those elements in modern society destructive of the best qualities of human nature; such elements are predominantly identified as materialism, conformity, and mechanization leading toward war. The third part presents a picture of an individual who is a specific representation of what the author conceives as a general condition.

"Footnote to Howl" seems to be a declamation that everything in the world is holy, including parts of the body by name. It ends in a plea for holy living. . . .

The theme of "Howl" presents "unorthodox and controversial ideas." Coarse and vulgar language is used in treatment and sex acts are mentioned, but unless the book is entirely lacking in "Social importance" it cannot be held obscene. . . .

There are a number of words used in "Howl" that are presently considered coarse and vulgar in some circles of the community; in other circles such words are in everyday use. It would be unrealistic to deny these facts. The author of "Howl" has used those words because he believed that his portrayal required them as being in character. The People state that it is not necessary to use such words and that others would be more palatable to good taste. The answer is that life is not encased in one formula whereby everyone acts the same or conforms to a particular pattern. No two persons think alike; we were all made from the same mold but in different patterns. Would there be any freedom of press or speech if one must reduce his vocabulary to vapid innocuous euphemism? An author should be real in treating his subject and be allowed to express his thoughts and ideas in his own words. . . .

While the publishing of "smut" or "hard core pornography" is without any social importance and obscene by present-day standards, and should be punished for the good of the community, since there is no straight and unwavering line to act as a guide, censorship by Government should be held in tight reign. To act otherwise would destroy our freedoms of free speech and press. Even religion can be censored by the medium of taxation. The best method of censorship is by the people as self-guardians of public opinion and not by government. So we come back, once more, to Jefferson's advice that the only completely democratic way to control publications which arouse mere thoughts or feelings is through non-governmental censorship by public opinion.

From the foregoing certain rules can be set up, but as has been noted, they are not inflexible and are subject to changing conditions, and above all each case must be judged individually.

1. If the material has the slightest redeeming social importance it is not obscene because it is protected by the First and Fourteenth Amendments of the United States Constitution, and the California Constitution.

2. If it does not have the slightest redeeming social importance it may be obscene.

3. The test of obscenity in California is that the material must have a tendency to deprave or corrupt readers by exciting lascivious thoughts or arousing lustful desire to the point that it presents a clear and present danger of inciting to anti-social or immoral action.

4. The book or material must be judged as a whole by its effect on the *average adult* in the community.

5. If the material is objectionable only because of coarse and vulgar language which is not erotic or aphrodisiac in character it is not obscene.

6. Scienter must be proved.

7. Book reviews may be received in evidence if properly authenticated.

8. Evidence of expert witnesses in the literary field is proper.

9. Comparison of the material with other similar material previously adjudicated is proper.

10. The people owe a duty to themselves and to each other to preserve and protect their constitutional freedoms from any encroachment by government unless it appears that the allowable limits of such protection have been breached, and then to take only such action as will heal the breach.

11. I agree with Mr. Justice Douglas: I have the same confidence in the ability of our people to reject noxious literature as I have in their capacity to sort out the true from the false in theology, economics, politics, or any other field.

12. In considering material claimed to be obscene it is well to remember the motto: "*Honi soit qui mal y pense.*" (Evil to him who evil thinks.)

Therefore, I conclude the book "Howl and Other Poems" does have some redeeming social importance, and I find the book is not obscene.

The defendant is found not guilty.

Appendix IV
Model Texts: Inspirations Precursor to HOWL

Commentary on Poems

These poems were familiar to me by summer 1955. They're arranged in chronological order, a mini-anthology drawn from *Anthology XX Century Expansive Poetry & Heroic Precursors*, composed for my Poetics classes at Naropa Institute.* The principle is expansion of breath, inspiration as in unobstructed breath, "unchecked original impulse" expressed by Walt Whitman. Memory of these verse rhythms superimposed on my own breath passed into the inspiration of "Howl."

The elasticity of the long verse line of Christopher Smart is the immediate inspiration *by ear*. No other English verse plays with humorous quantitative delicacy of line, variably long or short, counterpointed to its neighbors in such accurate balance. Smart's aural intelligence tends to the appropriate syncopated whip crack of a definite self-enclosed rhythm. Here a "variable measure" differs from the powerful ten-syllable balances of Milton. Blake's prophetic verse has similar integrity derived from Hebrew Biblic prosody.

With Shelley we have the buildup of mighty rhythm to ecstatic consciousness: the consciousness of Inspiration, or Breath itself (life as breathing, *spīritus*) as the pivotal self-contemplative subject of the poem. Theme and Word are one.

> The breath whose might I have invoked in song
> Descends on me; my spirit's bark is driven . . .
> ("Adonais")
> . . . be thou, Spirit fierce,
> My spirit!   ("Ode to the West Wind")

This symphonic Hallelujah-like chorale of romantic absolutism, reaching its apogee in Shelley's breakthru to unobstructed Spirit, heard from my poet father's breath in childhood, determines the physical spirit of my own poetry.

In Apollinaire's "Zone" we have the variable breath-stop line of Smart, with the superimposition of the Modern: XX Century automobiles, hangars at the airfield, posters, newspapers, billboards, an industrial street, the world's altitude record, a dirty bar, milkmen. Apollinaire introduces the jump cut, as from "Coblenz at the Hotel of the Giant" to "Rome sitting under a Japanese medlar tree": montage of time & space, surrealist juxtaposition of opposites, compression of images, mind gaps or dissociations, "hydrogen jukeboxes."

Kurt Schwitters' "Priimiititittiii" provided a model

*A contemplative college founded 1974 by Chögyam Trungpa, Rinpoche, in Boulder, Colorado, with its Jack Kerouac School of Disembodied Poetics; formally accredited 1986. It is the first such Buddhist college in the Western World.

structure for pure sound. Despite mystical and sociologic preoccupations, the practical base for poetry is aesthetics of mouth & ear. This "art for art's sake" requires humorous dispassionate inquisitiveness into word materials, in this case sound-forms. How make logical measures & symmetric structures out of the variable breath of long verse? Specifically, Schwitters' little pyramid of sound, the anaphoric fugue-like structure of "Priimiititittiii," provided shape for the graduated litany used in Part III of "Howl" (and later "Kaddish," Part IV).

Frank O'Hara first showed me Marshall's translation of Mayakovsky's penultimate suicide death rattle, "At the Top of My Voice": "My verse / with labour / thrusts through weighted years . . ." Eternal voice claims mortal majesty, self-created or self-born, thus equal to the universe itself, of same stuff as universe. Shakespeare scribes this universal public voice, "That in black ink my love may still shine bright . . . / You still shall live—such virtue hath my pen— / Where breath most breathes, even in the mouths of men." As it breathes "by the incantation of this verse" in Shelley's "West Wind," it sings through Bob Dylan's "Hard Rain": "And I'll tell it and think it and speak it and breathe it / And reflect from the mountain where all souls can see it."

Though in Shelley's terza rima and Spencerian stanzas, Apollinaire's Cubist associations and Mayakovsky's rhymed ladders we have artful means of prophetic proclamation, Antonin Artaud's holy despair breaks all old verse forms and arrives at breath identical to the concentrated spontaneous utterance of besieged spirit burning & "signalling through the flames" of historical or personal crisis. Artaud's physical breath has inevitable propulsion toward specific inviolable insight on "Moloch whose name is the Mind!" My familiarity with this text comes from Carl Solomon, 1948.

Lorca's spirit transcending the concrete prison of megalopolis is articulated with montage of concrete attributes: "New York of wires and death: / What angel do you carry hidden in your cheek? / . . . beard full of butterflies / . . . corduroy shoulders worn down by the moon . . ." Here the variable verse line of Whitman gets "hopped up" to hyperbole, intensified by inclusion of mind-jump-cut facts put together in a flash, surrealist agility.

Hart Crane's "Atlantis" harks back to "Adonais"' mighty rhyme. His blank verse builds an ecstatic expostulation of spirit similar to Shelley's abandon. Crane provides an American bench mark of spiritual breath, updated with industrial landscape & futurist vision. He tries for breakthrough to eternal consciousness: the will is there, the heart passion, the physical ear, the human means for such a pillar of air or whirlwind of inspiration. Although the visual object is fragmented or composite, the breath is precise, practical, grounded, and so it does attain its object—the release of devotional generosity.

In William Carlos Williams' more moderate analysis, "The pure products of America go crazy," we have a breakthrough parallel to Crane's. W.C.W.'s insight is focused in pictures, the world is appreciated sanely, visually objectified. An extensive breath is maintained in a long sentence encompassing not only our hell of despair ("excrement of some sky") but also a version of real paradise ("deer going by fields of goldenrod"), as well as our everyday maneuverings—"no one to drive the car."

Whitman as innovator of many of these breaths and visions remains a mountain too vast to be seen. Natural ecstasy, surrealist juxtaposition ("seas of bright juice suffuse heaven"), long line including startling raw observation of ordinary mind (amounting to surrealism), breakthrough out of the crust of hyper-industrialized consciousness, majestic proclamation of presence, consciousness of the mortal ground of immortality—these the good gray Bard has in abundance.

Unscrew the locks from the doors!
Unscrew the doors themselves from their jambs!
A. G.

Christopher Smart (b. 1722): from *Jubilate Agno*

Let Elizur rejoice with the Partridge, who is a prisoner of state and is proud of his keepers.

Let Shedeur rejoice with Pyrausta, who dwelleth in a medium of fire, which God hath adapted for him.

Let Shelumiel rejoice with Olor, who is of a goodly savour, and the very look of him harmonizes the mind.

Let Jael rejoice with the Plover, who whistles for his live, and foils the marksmen and their guns.

Let Raguel rejoice with the Cock of Portugal—God send good Angels to the allies of England!

Let Hobab rejoice with Necydalus, who is the Greek of a Grub.

Let Zurishaddai with the Polish Cock rejoice—The Lord restore peace to Europe.

Let Zuar rejoice with the Guinea Hen—The Lord add to his mercies in the WEST!

Let Chesed rejoice with Strepsiceros, whose weapons are the ornaments of his peace.

Let Hagar rejoice with Gnesion, who is the right sort of eagle, and towers the highest.

Let Libni rejoice with the Redshank, who migrates not but is translated to the upper regions.

Let Nahshon rejoice with the Seabreese, the Lord give the sailors of his Spirit.

Let Helon rejoice with the Woodpecker—the Lord encourage the propagation of trees!

Let Amos rejoice with the Coote—prepare to meet thy God, O Israel.

Let Ephah rejoice with Buprestis, the Lord endue us with temperance & humanity, till every cow have her mate!

For I am not without authority in my jeopardy, which I derive inevitably from the glory of the name of the Lord.

For I bless God whose name in Jealous—and there is a zeal to deliver us from everlasting burnings.

For my existimation is good even amongst the slanderers and my memory shall arise for a sweet savour unto the Lord.

For I bless the PRINCE of PEACE and pray that all the guns may be nail'd up, save such as are for the rejoicing days.

For I have abstained from the blood of the grape and that even at the Lord's table.

For I have glorified God in GREEK and LATIN, the consecrated languages spoken by the Lord on earth.

For I meditate the peace of Europe amongst family bickerings and domestic jars.

For the HOST is in the WEST—the Lord make us thankful unto salvation.

For I preach the very GOSPEL of CHRIST without comment & with this weapon shall I slay envy.

For I bless God in the rising generation, which is on my side.

For I have translated in the charity, which makes things better & I shall be translated myself at the last.

For he that walked upon the sea, hath prepared the floods with the Gospel of peace.

For the merciful man is merciful to his beast, and to the trees that give them shelter.

For he hath turned the shadow of death into the morning, the Lord is his name.

For I am come home again, but there is nobody to kill the calf or to pay the musick.

Fragment "BI," Stanzas 3–44. *Jubilate Agno*, ed. W. H. Bond (New York: Greenwood Press, 1969).

Let Sarah rejoice with the Redwing, whose harvest is in the frost and snow.

Let Rebekah rejoice with Iynx, who holds his head on one side to deceive the adversary.

Let Shuah rejoice with Boa, which is the vocal serpent.

Let Ehud rejoice with Onocrotalus, whose braying is for the glory of God, because he makes the best musick in his power.

Let Shamgar rejoice with Otis, who looks about him for the glory of God, & sees the horizon compleat at once.

Let Bohan rejoice with the Scythian Stag—he is beef and breeches against want & nakedness.

Let Achsah rejoice with the Pigeon who is an antidote to malignity and will carry a letter.

Let Tohu rejoice with the Grouse—the Lord further the cultivating of heaths & the peopling of deserts.

Let Hillel rejoice with Ammodytes, whose colour is deceitful and he plots against the pilgrim's feet.

Let Eli rejoice with Leucon —he is an honest fellow, which is a rarity.

Let Jemuel rejoice with Charadrius, who is from the HEIGHT & the sight of him is good for the jaundice.

Let Pharaoh rejoice with Anataria, whom God permits to prey upon the ducks to check their increase.

Let Lotan rejoice with Sauterelle. Blessed be the name of the Lord from the Lote-tree to the Palm.

Let Dishon rejoice with the Landrail, God give his grace to the society for preserving the game.

Let Hushim rejoice with the King's Fisher, who is of royal beauty, tho' plebeian size.

Let Machir rejoice with Convolvulus, from him to the ring of Saturn, which is the girth of Job; to the signet of God from Job & his daughters BLESSED BE JESUS.

Let Atad bless with Eleos, the nightly Memorialist ε λεησον χυριε.

Let Jamin rejoice with the Bittern blessed be the name of Jesus for Denver Sluice, Ruston, & the draining of the fens.

Let Ohad rejoice with Byturos who eateth the vine and is a minister of temperance.

Let Zohar rejoice with Cychramus who cometh with the quails on a particular affair.

Let Serah, the daughter of Asher, rejoice with Ceyx, who maketh his cabin in the Halcyon's hold.

Let Magdiel rejoice with Ascarides, which is the life of the bowels—the worm hath a part in our frame.

For the hour of my felicity, like the womb of Sarah, shall come at the latter end.

For I shou'd have avail'd myself of waggery, had not malice been multitudinous.

For there are still serpents that can speak—God bless my head, my heart & my heel.

For I bless God that I am of the same seed as Ehud, Mutius Scævola, and Colonel Draper.

For the word of God is a sword on my side—no matter what other weapon a stick or a straw.

For I have adventured myself in the name of the Lord, and he hath mark'd me for his own.

For I bless God for the Postmaster general & all conveyancers of letters under his care especially Allen & Shelvock.

For my grounds in New Canaan shall infinitely compensate for the flats & maynes of Staindrop Moor.

For the praise of God can give to a mute fish the notes of a nightingale.

For I have seen the White Raven & Thomas Hall of Willingham & am myself a greater curiosity than both.

For I look up to heaven which is my prospect to escape envy by surmounting it.

For if Pharaoh had known Joseph, he woud have blessed God & me for the illumination of the people.

For I pray God to bless improvements in gardening till London be a city of palm-trees.

For I pray to give his grace to the poor of England, that Charity be not offended & that benevolence may increase.

For in my nature I quested for beauty, but God, God hath sent me to sea for pearls.

For there is a blessing from the STONE of Jesus which is founded upon hell to the precious jewell on the right hand of God.

For the nightly Visitor is at the window of the impenitent, while I sing a psalm of my own composing.

For there is a note added to the scale, which the Lord hath made fuller, stronger & more glorious.

For I offer my goat as he browses the vine, bless the Lord from chambering & drunkeness.

For there is a traveling for the glory of God without going to Italy or France.

For I bless the children of Asher for the evil I did them & the good I might have received at their hands.

For I rejoice like a worm in the rain in him that cherishes and from him that tramples.

Let Becher rejoice with Oscen who terrifies the wicked, as trumpet and alarm the coward.

Let Shaul rejoice with Circos, who hath clumsy legs, but he can wheel it the better with his wings.

Let Hamul rejoice with the Crystal, who is pure and translucent.

Let Ziphion rejoice with the Tit-Lark who is a groundling, but he raises the spirits.

Let Mibzar rejoice with the Cadess, as is their number, so are their names, blessed be the Lord Jesus for them all.

Let Jubal rejoice with Cæcilia, the woman and the slow-worm praise the name of the Lord.

Let Arodi rejoice with the Royston Crow, there is a society of them at Trumpington & Cambridge.

For I am ready for the trumpet & alarm to fight, to die & to rise again.

For the banish'd of the Lord shall come about again, for so he hath prepared for them.

For sincerity is a jewel which is pure & transparent, eternal & inestimable.

For my hands and my feet are perfect as the sublimity of Naphtali and the felicity of Asher.

For the names and number of animals are as the names and number of the stars.

For I pray the Lord Jesus to translate my MAGNIFICAT into verse and represent it.

For I bless the Lord Jesus from the bottom of Royston Cave to the top of King's Chapel.

Percy Bysshe Shelley (b. 1791): from *Adonais*

Who mourns for Adonais? Oh, come forth,
Fond wretch! and know thyself and him aright.
Clasp with thy panting soul the pendulous Earth;
As from a center, dart thy spirit's light
Beyond all worlds, until its spacious might
Satiate the void circumference: then shrink
Even to a point within our day and night;
And keep thy heart light lest it make thee sink
When hope has kindled hope, and lured thee to the brink.

Or go to Rome, which is the sepulcher,
Oh, not of him, but of our joy: 'tis naught
That ages, empires, and religions there
Lie buried in the ravage they have wrought;
For such as he can lend—they borrow not
Glory from those who made the world their prey;
And he is gathered to the kings of thought
Who waged contention with their time's decay,
And of the past are all that cannot pass away.

Go thou to Rome—at once the Paradise,
The grave, the city, and the wilderness;
And where its wrecks like shattered mountains rise,
And flowering weeds, and fragrant copses dress
The bones of Desolation's nakedness
Pass, till the spirit of the spot shall lead
Thy footsteps to a slope of green access
Where, like an infant's smile, over the dead
A light of laughing flowers along the grass is spread;

And gray walls molder round, on which dull Time
Feeds, like slow fire upon a hoary brand;
And one keen pyramid with wedge sublime,
Pavilioning the dust of him who planned

Final stanzas, 47–55.

This refuge for his memory, doth stand
Like flame transformed to marble; and beneath,
A field is spread, on which a newer band
Have pitched in Heaven's smile their camp of death,
Welcoming him we lose with scarce extinguished breath.

Here pause: these graves are all too young as yet
To have outgrown the sorrow which consigned
Its charge to each; and if the seal is set,
Here, on one fountain of a mourning mind,
Break it not thou! too surely shalt thou find
Thine own well full, if thou returnest home,
Of tears and gall. From the world's bitter wind
Seek shelter in the shadow of the tomb.
What Adonais is, why fear we to become?

The One remains, the many change and pass;
Heaven's light forever shines, Earth's shadows fly;
Life, like a dome of many-colored glass,
Stains the white radiance of Eternity,
Until Death tramples it to fragments.—Die,
If thou wouldst be with that which thou dost seek!
Follow where all is fled!—Rome's azure sky,
Flowers, ruins, statues, music, words, are weak
The glory they transfuse with fitting truth to speak.

Why linger, why turn back, why shrink, my Heart?
Thy hopes are gone before: from all things here
They have departed; thou shouldst now depart!
A light is passed from the revolving year,
And man, and woman; and what still is dear
Attracts to crush, repels to make thee wither.
The soft sky smiles—the low wind whispers near:
'Tis Adonais calls! oh, hasten thither,
No more let Life divide what Death can join together.

That Light whose smile kindles the Universe,
That Beauty in which all things work and move,
That Benediction which the eclipsing Curse

Of birth can quench not, that sustaining Love
Which through the web of being blindly wove
By man and beast and earth and air and sea,
Burns bright or dim, as each are mirrors of
The fire for which all thirst; now beams on me,
Consuming the last clouds of cold mortality.

The breath whose might I have invoked in song
Descends on me; my spirit's bark is driven,
Far from the shore, far from the trembling throng
Whose sails were never to the tempest given;
The massy earth and spherèd skies are riven!
I am borne darkly, fearfully, afar;
Whilst, burning through the inmost veil of Heaven,
The soul of Adonais, like a star,
Beacons from the abode where the Eternal are.

Percy Bysshe Shelley: *Ode to the West Wind*

I

O wild West Wind, thou breath of Autumn's being,
Thou, from whose unseen presence the leaves dead
Are driven, like ghosts from an enchanter fleeing,

Yellow, and black, and pale, and hectic red,
Pestilence-stricken multitudes: O thou,
Who chariotest to their dark wintry bed

The wingèd seeds, where they lie cold and low,
Each like a corpse within its grave, until
Thine azure sister of the Spring shall blow

Her clarion o'er the dreaming earth, and fill
(Driving sweet buds like flocks to feed in air)
With living hues and odors plain and hill:

Wild Spirit, which art moving everywhere;
Destroyer and preserver; hear, oh, hear!

II

Thou on whose stream, mid the steep sky's commotion,
Loose clouds like earth's decaying leaves are shed,
Shook from the tangled boughs of Heaven and Ocean,

Angels of rain and lightning: there are spread
On the blue surface of thine aery surge,
Like the bright hair uplifted from the head

Of some fierce Maenad, even from the dim verge
Of the horizon to the zenith's height,
The locks of the approaching storm. Thou dirge

Of the dying year, to which this closing night
Will be the dome of a vast sepulcher,
Vaulted with all thy congregated might

Of vapors, from whose solid atmosphere
Black rain, and fire, and hail will burst: oh, hear!

III

Thou who didst waken from his summer dreams
The blue Mediterranean, where he lay,
Lulled by the coil of his crystàlline streams,

Beside a pumice isle in Baiae's bay,
And saw in sleep old palaces and towers
Quivering within the wave's intenser day,

All overgrown with azure moss and flowers
So sweet, the sense faints picturing them! Thou
For whose path the Atlantic's level powers

Cleave themselves into chasms, while far below
The sea-blooms and the oozy woods which wear
The sapless foliage of the ocean, know

Thy voice, and suddenly grow gray with fear,
And tremble and despoil themselves: oh, hear!

IV

If I were a dead leaf thou mightest bear;
If I were a swift cloud to fly with thee;
A wave to pant beneath thy power, and share

The impulse of thy strength, only less free
Than thou, O uncontrollable! If even
I were as in my boyhood, and could be

The comrade of thy wanderings over Heaven,
As then, when to outstrip thy skiey speed
Scarce seemed a vision; I would ne'er have striven

As thus with thee in prayer in my sore need.
Oh, lift me as a wave, a leaf, a cloud!
I fall upon the thorns of life! I bleed!

A heavy weight of hours has chained and bowed
One too like thee: tameless, and swift, and proud.

V

Make me thy lyre, even as the forest is:
What if my leaves are falling like its own!
The tumult of thy mighty harmonies

Will take from both a deep, autumnal tone,
Sweet though in sadness. Be thou, Spirit fierce,
My spirit! Be thou me, impetuous one!

Drive my dead thoughts over the universe
Like withered leaves to quicken a new birth!
And, by the incantation of this verse,

Scatter, as from an unextinguished hearth
Ashes and sparks, my words among mankind!
Be through my lips to unwakened earth

The trumpet of a prophecy! O, Wind,
If Winter comes, can Spring be far behind?

Guillaume Apollinaire (b. 1880) : *Zone*

You are tired at last of this old world

O shepherd Eiffel Tower the flock of bridges bleats at the
morning

You have had enough of life in this Greek and Roman
antiquity

Even the automobiles here seem to be ancient
Religion alone has remained entirely fresh religion
Has remained simple like the hangars at the airfield

You alone in all Europe are not antique O Christian faith
The most modern European is you Pope Pius X
And you whom the windows look down at shame pre-
vents you
From entering a church and confessing this morning
You read prospectuses catalogues and posters which shout
aloud
Here is poetry this morning and for prose there are the
newspapers
There are volumes for 25 centimes full of detective stories
Portraits of famous men and a thousand assorted titles

This morning I saw a pretty street whose name I have
forgotten
Shining and clean it was the sun's bugle
Executives and workers and lovely secretaries
From Monday morning to Saturday evening pass here
four times a day
In the morning the siren wails three times
A surly bell barks around noon
Lettering on signs and walls
Announcements and billboards shriek like parrots
I love the charm of this industrial street
Located in Paris somewhere between the rue Aumont-
Thiéville and the avenue des Ternes
Here is the young street and you are once again a little
child
Your mother dresses you only in blue and white
You are very pious and with your oldest friend René
Dalize
You like nothing so well as the ceremonies of church
It is nine o'clock the gas is down to the blue you come
secretly out of the dormitory
You pray the whole night in the college chapel
While eternal and adorable an amethyst profundity
The flaming glory of Christ turns for ever
It is the beautiful lily we all cultivate
It is the red-headed torch which the wind cannot blow
out
It is the pale and ruddy son of a sorrowful mother
It is the tree always thick with prayers
It is the double gallows of honor and of eternity
It is a six-pointed star
It is God who died on Friday and rose again on Sunday

Selected Writings, trans. Roger Shattuck (New York: New
Directions, 1971).

It is Christ who soars in the sky better than any aviator
He breaks the world's altitude record
Christ the pupil of the eye
Twentieth pupil of the centuries he knows how
And turned into a bird this century rises in the air like
Jesus
The devils in their abysses lift their heads to look at it
They say it is imitating Simon Magus in Judea
They shout that if it knows how to fly it should be called
a flyer
Angels hover about the lovely aerialist
Icarus Enoch Elijah Apollonius of Tyana
Flutter around the original airplane
They separate occasionally to give passage to those whom
the Holy Eucharist carries up
Those priests who rise eternally in lifting the host
The airplane lands at last without folding its wings
The sky fills up then with millions of swallows
In a flash crows falcons and owls arrive
Ibis flamingoes and marabous arrive from Africa
The great Roc celebrated by story tellers and poets
Glides down holding in its claws Adam's scull the first
head
The eagle rushes out of the horizon giving a great cry
From America comes the tiny humming-bird
From China have come long supple pihis
Which only have one wing and fly tandem
Then the dove immaculate spirit
Escorted by the lyre bird and the ocellated peacock
The phoenix that pyre which recreates itself
Veils everything for an instant with its glowing coals
Sirens leaving their perilous straits
Arrive all three of them singing beautifully
And everything eagle phoenix and Chinese pihis
Fraternize with the flying machine

Now you walk through Paris all alone in the crowd
Herds of bellowing busses roll by near you
The agony of love tightens your throat
As if you could never be loved again
If you were living in olden days you would enter a
monastery
You are ashamed when you catch yourself saying a
prayer
You ridicule yourself and your laughter bursts out like
hell fire
The sparks of your laughter gild the depths of your life
It is a picture hung in a somber museum
And sometimes you go to look at it closely

Today you walk through Paris the women are blood-
stained
It was and I would prefer not to remember it was during
beauty's decline

Surrounded by fervent flames Notre Dame looked at me
in Chartres
The blood of your Sacred Heart flooded me in the
Montmartre
I am ill from hearing happy words

The love from which I suffer is a shameful sickness
And the image which possesses you makes you survive in
  sleeplessness and anguish
It is always near you this passing image

Now you are on the shore of the Mediterranean
Under the lemon trees which blossom all year
With your friends you take a boat ride
One from Nice one from Menton and two from Turbie
We look down in fear at the octopodes on the bottom
And amid the algae swim fish images of our Saviour
You are in the garden of an inn on the outskirts of Prague
You feel completely happy a rose is on the table
And instead of writing your story in prose you watch
The rosebug which is sleeping in the heart of the rose
Astonished you see yourself outlined in the agates of St.
  Vitus
You were sad enough to die the day you saw yourself in
  them
You looked like Lazarus bewildered by the light
The hands of the clock in the Jewish quarter turn back-
  wards
And you go slowly backwards in your life
Climbing up to Hradchin and listening at night
In taverns to the singing of Czech songs

Here you are in Marseilles amid the watermelons

Here you are in Coblenz at the Hotel of the Giant

Here you are in Rome sitting under a Japanese medlar
  tree

Here you are in Amsterdam with a girl you find pretty
  and who is ugly
She is to marry a student from Leyden
There are rooms for rent in Latin Cubicula locanda
I remember I stayed three days there and as many at
  Gouda

You are in Paris at the *juge d'instruction*
Like a criminal you are placed under arrest
You have made sorrowful and happy trips
Before noticing that the world lies and grows old
You suffered from love at twenty and thirty
I have lived like a fool and wasted my time
You no longer dare look at your hands and at every
  moment I want to burst out sobbing
For you for her I love for everything that has frightened
  you

With tear-filled eyes you look at those poor emigrants
They believe in God they pray the women nurse their
  children
Their odor fills the waiting room of the gare Saint-Lazare
They have faith in their star like the Magi
They hope to make money in Argentina
And come back to their countries having made their
  fortunes
One family carries a red quilt as one carries one's heart

That quilt and our dream are both unreal
Some of these emigrants stay here and find lodging
In hovels in the rue des Rosiers or the rue des Écouffes
I have often seen them in the evening they take a stroll
  in the street
And rarely travel far like men on a checker board
There are mostly Jews their wives wear wigs
They sit bloodlessly in the backs of little shops

You are standing at the counter of a dirty bar
You have a cheap coffee with the rest of the riffraff

At night you are in a big restaurant

These women are not wicked still they have their worries
All of them even the ugliest has made her lover suffer
She is the daughter of a policeman on the Isle of Jersey

Her hands which I have not seen are hard and chapped
I have an immense pity for the scars on her belly

I humble my mouth by offering it to a poor slut with a
  horrible laugh

You are alone the morning is almost here
The milkmen rattle their cans in the street

The night departs like a beautiful half-caste
False Ferdine or waiting Leah

And you drink this burning liquor like your life
Your life which you drink like an eau-de-vie

You walk toward Auteuil you want to walk home on foot
To sleep among your fetishes from Oceania and Guinea
They are all Christ in another form and of another faith
They are inferior Christs obscure hopes

Adieu adieu

The sun a severed neck

Kurt Schwitters (b. 1887): *Priimiitittiii*

priimiitittiii	tisch
tesch	
priimiitittiii	tesh
tusch	
priimiitittiii	tischa
tescho	
priimiitittiii	tescho
tuschi	
priimiitittiii	
priimiitittiii	
priimiitittiii	too
priimiitittiii	taa
priimiitittiii	too
priimiitittiii	taa
priimiitittiii	tootaa
priimiitittiii	tootaa
priimiitittiii	tuutaa
priimiitittiii	tuutaa
priimiitittiii	tuutaatoo
priimiitittiii	tuutaatoo
priimiitittiii	tuutaatoo
priimiitittiii	tuutaatoo

Dada Painters and Poets: An Anthology, ed. Robert Mother-well (New York: George Wittenborn, 1947).

Vladimir Mayakovsky (b. 1893): *At the Top of My Voice*—First Prelude to a Poem of the Five Year Plan

Most respected
    comrades heirs and descendants:
Excavating
    our contemporary
        petrified muck
studying our days through dark dead centuries,
you'll,
    maybe,
        ask about me, Mayakovsky.
And, maybe,

your scholars will then reveal—
swamping with erudition
    questions that swarm—
there lived once a singer
    blood all-a-boil,
who hated most cold-water raw.
Professor,
    take off those optical-bicycles!
I'll myself relate
    about the times
        about myself.
I'm a sanitary inspector
    and water-carrier,

Mayakovsky and His Poetry, trans. Herbert Marshall (Bom-bay: Current Book House, 1955).

mobilised to the front
    by revolution,
        I came
from the seignorial horticulture
of poetry
    a most capricious dame,
precious Muse that grows, like Mary,
roses
    round
        a bungalow.
"Mary, Mary, quite contrary,
    how does your garden grow?"
Some pour verses from a sprinkler,
some just splutter
    from their lips—
curly-headed Mitraikies,
    muddle-headed Kudraikies—
who the devil knows which from which:
No quarantine will take them in—
there's those mandolines again:
"Tara-tina tara-tina
    t.......e.......n.......n..."
Not much of an honour,
    that from such roses
my very own statue will rise
over squares,
with gobs of tuberculosis,
where whores with hooligans
    and—syphilis . . .
I'm fed
    to the teeth
        with agit-prop,
I'd like
    to scribble for you
        love-ballads—
they're charming
    and pay quite a lot.
But I
    mastered myself,
        and crushed under foot
the throat
    of my very own songs.
Hi listen!
    Comrades heirs and descendants,
to an agitator,
    loud-speaker-in-chief:
Deafening
    poetic deluge,
I stride to you
    through lyrical volumes,
as the live
    with the living speaks.
I'll come to you
    in the distant communist far-off,
but not
    like Yessenin's rhymed knight-errants.
My verse will reach
    over the peaks of eras
far over the heads
    of poets and governments.

My verse will come,
but will come not ornate—
not like an arrow's
    lyrical love-flight from Eros,
not like a worn-out coin
    comes to the numismat
and not like the light of long-dead stars arrives.

My verse
    with labour
        thrusts through weighted years
emerging,
    ponderous,
        rock-rough,
            age-grim,
as when to-day
    an aqueduct appears,
firm-grounded once
    by the branded slaves of Rome.
You'll accidentally find
    in barrows of books,
wrought-iron lines of long-buried poems,
handle them
    with the care that respects
ancient
    but terrible weapons.
My words
    are not used
        to caressing ears;
nor titillate
    with semi-obscenities
maiden ears
    hidden in hair so innocent.
I open on parade
    my pages of fighters,
pass in review
    their lineal front.
My verses stand
    in lead-heavy letters,
ready for death
    and for deathless glory.
Stock-still stand my poems
    muzzle to muzzle set,
their gaping titles aimed
    and at the ready!
And weapons most beloved yet,
ever ready to
    charge with a cheer,
rear all alert
    my cavalry of wit,

tilting their rhymes,
    sharp-pointed spears.
And every single one
    armed to the teeth,
that swept through twenty years
    victorious,
every single one,
    to the very last leaf

I give to you,
    planet-proletariat.
The foe
    of the working class colossal—
is my own foe,
    dead-poisonous and ancient.
We marched behind the blood-red flag—
    impelled
by years of work
    and days of sheer starvation.
We opened
    Marx and Engels
            every tome,
as in our home
    we open wide the shutters,
but without reading
    we understood alone,
whose side we're on
    and in which camp we're fighters.
And not from Hegel
    did we learn
            our dialectics.
That burst
    through interclashing conflict
                into verse,
when under fire
    the bourgeois
            ran from our attacks,
as we
    once also
        ran from theirs.
Let glory,
    disconsolate widow frail,
trudge after genius
    in funeral anthems.
Die, my verse,
    die, like the rank and file,
as our unknown, unnumbered, fell
    in storming heaven.
To hell
    with many-tonned bronzes,
To the devil
    with sleek marble slime!
We'll square up with glory—
    why, we're mates and brothers—
So let there be
    a common monument for us
built up in battles—
                socialism.
Descendants,
    in your lexicons
            look up the flotsam
that floats down from Lethe,
    odd remnant-words
like "prostitution,"
            "tuberculosis,"
                    "blockades."

For you,
    who're so healthy and nimble,
a poet
    licked up
            consumptive spittle
with the crude rough tongue of placards.
From the tail of the years
    I must resemble
a long-tailed monster
    from a fossilized age.
So come,
    Comrade Life,
            let's step hard on the throttle,
and roar out
    the Five-Year-Plan's,
                remnant days.
I haven't got
    a ruble
        left from my verse,
the cabinet-makers
    didn't send the furniture home.
But my only need's
    a clean-laundered shirt,
for the rest
    I honestly
            don't give a damn.
When I appear
    in Tsi-Ka-Ka
            of coming
                bright decades,
above the band
    of skin-flint grafters
                in rhymes,
I'll lift up high,
    like a Bolshevik party-card,
all the hundred books
        of my
            ComParty poems!

Antonin Artaud (b. 1895): from *Van Gogh—The Man Suicided by Society*

introduction

You can say all you want about the mental health of Van Gogh who, during his lifetime, cooked only one of his hands, and other than that did no more than cut off his left ear,

    in a world in which every day they eat vagina cooked in green sauce or the genitals of a newborn child whipped into a rage

        plucked as it came out of the maternal sex.

Artaud Anthology, trans. Jack Hirschman (San Francisco: City Lights, 1965).

And this is not an image, but a fact abundantly and daily repeated and cultivated throughout the world.

And thus, demented as this assertion may seem, present-day life goes on in its old atmosphere of prurience, of anarchy, of disorder, of delirium, of dementia, of chronic lunacy, of bourgeois inertia, of psychic anomaly (for it isn't man but the world that has become abnormal), of deliberate dishonesty and downright hypocrisy, of a mean contempt for anything that shows breeding,

    of the claim of an entire order based on the fulfillment of a primitive injustice,

        in short, of organized crime.

Things are bad because the sick conscience now has a vital interest in not getting over its sickness.

So a sick society invented psychiatry to defend itself against the investigations of certain visionaries whose faculties of divination disturbed it.

. . . .

Faced with Van Gogh's lucidity, always active, psychiatry becomes nothing but a den of gorillas, so obsessed and persecuted that it can only use a ridiculous terminology to palliate the most frightful anxiety and human suffocation

. . . .

And what is a genuine lunatic?

He is a man who prefers to go mad, in the social sense of the word, rather than forfeit a certain higher idea of human honor.

That's how society strangled all those it wanted to get rid of, or wanted to protect itself from, and put them in asylums, because they refused to be accomplices to a kind of lofty swill.

For a lunatic is a man that society does not wish to hear but wants to prevent from uttering certain unbearable truths.

But in that case, internment is not the only weapon, and the concerted assemblage of men has other ways of undermining the wills of those it wants to break.

. . . .

That is why there was a collective spell cast on Baudelaire, Edgar Allan Poe, Gérard de Nerval, Nietzsche, Kierkegaard, Hölderlin and Coleridge.

There was a spell cast on Van Gogh also.

It can happen during the day but preferably, and generally, it happens at night.

. . . .

Confronted by this concerted swill, which deals with sex on the one hand and the masses of some other psychic rites on the other as a base or point of support, there is nothing unbalanced in walking around at night with 12 candles attached to your hat to paint a landscape from nature;

how else could Van Gogh have had light, as our friend the actor Roger Blin so rightly pointed out the other day?

As for the cooked hand, that was heroism pure and
simple;
    as for the severed ear, that was direct logic,
    and I repeat,
    a world that, day and night and more and more eats
the uneatable
    in order to bring its evil will around to its own ends,
    has nothing else to do at this point
    but to shut up.

. . . .

post-scriptum

And it happened to Van Gogh as it usually happens,
during an orgy, a mass, an absolution or any other rite of
consecration, possession, succubation or incubation.
    So it introduced itself into his body,
    this society
    absolved
    consecrated
    sanctified
    and possessed of the devil
    effaced the supernatural consciousness that he had
just acquired, and like a flood of black crows in the
fibers of his internal tree,
    submerged him in a last swell
    and, taking his place,
    killed him. . . .
    For it is the anatomical logic of modern man to
never have been able to live nor think of living except
as one possessed.

Federico García Lorca (b. 1898): *Ode to Walt Whitman*

Along the East River and the Bronx
the boys were singing showing their waists,
with the wheel, the oil, the leather and the hammer.
Ninety thousand miners extracted silver from rocks
and children drew stairs and perspectives.

But none would sleep,
none wanted to be a river,
none loved the great leaves,
none, the blue tongue of the beach.

Along the East River and the Queensborough
the boys were fighting with Industry,
and the Jews were selling to the faun of the river
the rose of the Circumcision,
and the sky rushed through bridges and roofs
herds of bison pushed by the wind.

The Selected Poems of Federico García Lorca, trans.
Stephen Spender and J. L. Gili (New York: New Directions,
1955).

But none would pause,
none wanted to be a cloud,
none searched for the ferns
nor the yellow wheel of the tambourine.

When the moon rises,
the pulleys will turn to disturb the sky:
a boundary of needles will fence in the memory
and the coffins will carry away those who do not work.

New York of slime,
New York of wires and death:
What angel do you carry hidden in your cheek?
What perfect voice will tell the truths of the wheat?
Who, the terrible dream of your stained anemones?

Not for one moment, beautiful aged Walt Whitman,
have I failed to see your beard full of butterflies,
nor your shoulders of corduroy worn out by the moon,
nor your thighs of virginal Apollo,
nor your voice like a pillar of ashes:
ancient and beautiful as the mist,
you moaned like a bird
with the sex transfixed by a needle,
enemy of the satyr,
enemy of the vine,
and lover of bodies under the rough cloth.
Not for one moment; virile beauty,
who in mountains of coal, posters and railways,
dreamed of being a river and sleeping like a river
with that comrade who would place in your breast
the small pain of an ignorant leopard.

Not for one moment, Adam of blood, male,
lone man in the sea, beautiful aged Walt Whitman,
because through the terraces,
clustered around the bars,
pouring out of sewers in bunches,
trembling between the legs of chauffeurs
or revolving on the platforms of absinthe,
the pansies, Walt Whitman, dreamed of you.

This one also! This one! And they fall
on your chaste and luminous beard,
Northern blonds, Negroes of the sands,
multitudes of shrieks and gestures,
like cats or like snakes,
the pansies, Walt Whitman, the pansies,
muddy with tears, flesh for the whip,
boot or bite of subduers.

This one also! This one! Tainted fingers
appear on the shore of your dreams
when the friend eats your apple
with a faint taste of petrol
and the sun sings along the navels
of boys that play under bridges.

But you did not search for the scratched eyes,
or the very dark swamp where children are submerged,
or the frozen saliva,
or the wounded curves resembling toad's bellies
which the pansies carry in cars and terraces
while the moon strikes at them along the corners of fear.

You searched for a nude who was like a river.
Bull and dream that would join the wheel with the
    seaweed,
father of your agony, camelia of your death,
and would moan in the flames of your hidden Equator.

Because it is just that man does not search for his delight
in the jungle of blood of the following morning.
The sky has shores where to avoid life,
and certain bodies must not repeat themselves in the
    dawn.

Agony, agony, dream, ferment and dream.
This is the world, my friend, agony, agony.
The corpses decompose under the clock of the cities.
War passes weeping with a million grey rats,
the rich give to their mistresses
small illuminated moribunds,
and Life is not noble, nor good, nor sacred.

Man can, if he wishes, lead his desire
through vein of coral or celestial nude:
tomorrow love will be rocks, and Time
a breeze which comes sleeping through the branches.

That is why I do not raise my voice, aged Walt Whitman,
against the little boy who writes
a girl's name on his pillow,
nor the boy who dresses himself in the bride's trousseau
in the darkness of the wardrobe,
nor the solitary men in clubs
who drink the water of prostitution with nausea,
nor the men with a green stare
who love man and burn their lips in silence.
But against you, yes, pansies of the cities,
of tumescent flesh and unclean mind,
mud of drains, harpies, unsleeping enemies
of Love which distributes crowns of joy.

Against you always, you who give boys
drops of soiled death with bitter poison.
Against you always,
Fairies of North America,
Pájaros of Havana,
Jotos of Mexico,
Sarasas of Cadiz,
Apios of Seville,
Cancos of Madrid,
Floras of Alicante,
Adelaidas of Portugal.

Pansies of the world, murderers of doves!
Women's slaves, bitches of their boudoirs,
opened with the fever of fans in public squares
or ambushed in frigid landscapes of hemlock.

Let there be no quarter! Death
flows from your eyes
and clusters grey flowers on the shores.
Let there be no quarter! Take heed!
Let the perplexed, the pure,
the classicists, the noted, the supplicants,
close the gates of the Bacchanalia.

And you, beautiful Walt Whitman, sleep on the Hudson's
    banks,
with your beard toward the Pole and your hands open.
Bland clay or snow, your tongue is calling for
comrades that keep watch on your gazelle without a
    body.
Sleep; nothing remains.
A dance of walls agitates the meadows
and America drowns itself in machines and lament.
I want the strong air of the most profound night
to remove flowers and words from the arch where you
    sleep,
and a black boy to announce to the gold-minded whites
the arrival of the reign of the ear of corn.

Hart Crane (b. 1899): *Atlantis*

Through the bound cable strands, the arching path
Upward, veering with light, the flight of strings,—
Taut miles of shuttling moonlight syncopate
The whispered rush, telepathy of wires.
Up the index of night, granite and steel—
Transparent meshes—fleckless the gleaming staves—
Sibylline voices flicker, waveringly stream
As though a god were issue of the strings. . . .

And through that cordage, threading with its call
One arc synoptic of all tides below—
Their labyrinthine mouths of history
Pouring reply as though all ships at sea
Complighted in one vibrant breath made cry,—
"Make thy love sure—to weave whose song we ply!"
—From black embankments, moveless soundings hailed,
So seven oceans answer from their dream.

And on, obliquely up bright carrier bars
New octaves trestle the twin monoliths
Beyond whose frosted capes the moon bequeaths
Two worlds of sleep (O arching strands of song!)—
Onward and up the crystal-flooded aisle
White tempest nets file upward, upward ring
With silver terraces the humming spars,
The loft of vision, palladium helm of stars.

Sheerly the eyes, like seagulls stung with rime—
Slit and propelled by glistening fins of light—
Pick biting way up towering looms that press
Sidelong with flight of blade on tendon blade
—Tomorrows into yesteryear—and link
What cipher-script of time no traveller reads
But who, through smoking pyres of love and death,
Searches the timeless laugh of mythic spears.

Like hails, farewells—up planet-sequined heights
Some trillion whispering hammers glimmer Tyre:
Serenely, sharply up the long anvil cry
Of inchling æons silence rivets Troy.
And you, aloft there—Jason! hesting Shout!
Still wrapping harness to the swarming air!
Silvery the rushing wake, surpassing call,
Beams yelling Æolus! splintered in the straits!

The Bridge (New York: Liveright, 1933).

From gulfs unfolding, terrible of drums,
Tall Vision-of-the-Voyage, tensely spare—
Bridge, lifting night to cycloramic crest
Of deepest day—O Choir, translating time
Into what multitudinous Verb the suns
And synergy of waters ever fuse, recast
In myriad syllables—Psalm of Cathay!
O Love, thy white, pervasive Paradigm . . . !

We left the haven hanging in the night—
Sheened harbor lanterns backward fled the keel.
Pacific here at time's end, bearing corn.—
Eyes stammer through the pangs of dust and steel.
And still the circular, indubitable frieze
Of heaven's meditation, yoking wave
To kneeling wave, one song devoutly binds—
The vernal strophe chimes from deathless strings!

O Thou steeled Cognizance whose leap commits
The agile precincts of the lark's return;
Within whose lariat sweep encinctured sing
In single chrysalis the many twain,—
Of stars Thou art the stitch and stallion glow
And like an organ, Thou, with sound of doom—
Sight, sound and flesh Thou leadest from time's realm
As love strikes clear direction for the helm.

Swift peal of secular light, intrinsic Myth
Whose fell unshadow is death's utter wound,—
O River-throated—iridescently upborne
Through the bright drench and fabric of our veins;
With white escarpments swinging into light,
Sustained in tears the cities are endowed
And justified conclamant with ripe fields
Revolving through their harvests in sweet torment.

Forever Deity's glittering Pledge, O Thou
Whose canticle fresh chemistry assigns
To wrapt inception and beatitude,—
Always through blinding cables, to our joy,
Of thy white seizure springs the prophecy:
Always through spiring cordage, pyramids
Of silver sequel, Deity's young name
Kinetic of white choiring wings . . . ascends.

Migrations that must needs void memory,
Inventions that cobblestone the heart,—
Unspeakable Thou Bridge to Thee, O Love.
Thy pardon for this history, whitest Flower,
O Anwerer of all—Anemone,—
Now while thy petals spend the suns about us, hold—
(O Thou whose radiance doth inherit me)
Atlantis,—hold thy floating singer late!

So to thine Everpresence, beyond time,
Like spears ensanguined of one tolling star
That bleeds infinity—the orphic strings,
Sidereal phalanxes, leap and converge:
—One Song, one Bridge of Fire! Is it Cathay,
Now pity steeps the grass and rainbows ring
The serpent with the eagle in the leaves . . . ?
Whispers antiphonal in azure swing.

William Carlos Williams (b. 1883): *To Elsie*

The pure products of America
go crazy—
mountain folk from Kentucky

or the ribbed north end of
Jersey
with its isolate lakes and

valleys, its deaf-mutes, thieves
old names
and promiscuity between

devil-may-care men who have taken
to railroading
out of sheer lust of adventure—

and young slatterns, bathed
in filth
from Monday to Saturday

to be tricked out that night
with gauds
from imaginations which have no

peasant traditions to give them
character
but flutter and flaunt

sheer rags—succumbing without
emotion
save numbed terror

under some hedge of choke-cherry
or viburnum—
which they cannot express—

Unless it be that marriage
perhaps
with a dash of Indian blood

will throw up a girl so desolate
so hemmed round
with disease or murder

that she'll be rescued by an
agent—
reared by the state and

sent out at fifteen to work in
some hard-pressed
house in the suburbs—

some doctor's family, some Elsie—
voluptuous water
expressing with broken

Collected Earlier Poems (New York: New Directions, 1966).

brain the truth about us—
her great
ungainly hips and flopping breast

addressed to cheap
jewelry
and rich young men with fine eyes

as if the earth under our feet
were
an excrement of some sky

and we degraded prisoners
destined
to hunger until we eat filth

while the imagination strains
after deer
going by fields of goldenrod in

the stifling heat of September
Somehow
it seems to destroy us

It is only in isolate flecks that
something
is given off

No one
to witness
and adjust, no one to drive the car

Appendix V
Bibliography of HOWL by Bill Morgan

HOWL Editions

Howl for Carl Solomon. San Francisco: Ditto mimeograph, May 16, 1956 (25–50 copies).

Howl and Other Poems. San Francisco: City Lights Books, November 1, 1956. Reprinted 33 times; unexpurgated edition beginning with 8th printing.

The Pocket Poets Series, Vol. 1. Millwood, N.Y.: Kraus Reprint Co., 1973.

Howl for Carl Solomon. San Francisco: Grabhorn-Hoyem, 1971 (275 copies).

Moloch. Lincoln, Mass.: Penmaen Press, 1978 (300 copies, broadside).

HOWL Translations

ALBANIAN
Howl, Jeta E Re, Skopje, Yugoslavia, 1986. Translated by Fadil Bajraj.

CHINESE
Modern American Poetry 2. Beijing: Foreign Literature Publishing House, 1985. Translated by Yihen H. Zhao.

Su Que Bu [*Poetry Gazette*]. Hefei, Anhwei, 1986.

CZECH
"Kvileni," in *Sesity* 30 (April 1969). Translated by Jan Zabrana.

DANISH
A.G. "Hyl," in *Nyt fra Jorden*. Arhus, Denmark: Rhodos, 1969. Translated by Erik Thygesen.

Thygesen, Erik, ed. *San Francisco Renaissancen*. Odense, Denmark: Sirius Forlagt, 1964. Translated by Erik Thygesen and Ib Ørnoskov.

"Hylen" in *Vindrosen* 6, no. 4 (May 1959). Translated by Poul Sørensen.

DUTCH
A.G. "Howl," in *Proef m'n tong in je oor*. Amsterdam: De Bezige Bij, 1966. Translated by Simon Vinkenoog.

Van Son, Jacques. "Howl," in *The Beat Generation/Bob Dylan*. Utrecht, Netherlands: Spektakel/Walhalla, 1979.

FINNISH
A.G. "Huuto," in *Huuto Ja Muita Runoja*. Turku, Finland: Kustannusliike Tajo, 1963. Translated by Anselm Hollo.

"Huuto," in *Parnasso* 2 (1961). Translated by Anselm Hollo.

FRENCH
A.G. *Howl and Other Poems*. Paris: Christian Bourgois, 1977. Translated by Robert Cordier and Jean-Jacques Lebel.

A. G. *Howl and Other Poems/Kaddish*. Paris: Christian Bourgois, 1980. Translated by Robert Cordier and Jean-Jacques Lebel.

Lebel, Jean-Jacques. *La Poésie de la Beat Generation*. Paris: Denoël, 1965. Translated by Jean-Jacques Lebel.

Ellipse 8–9. Montreal, 1971. Translated by Jean-Jacques Lebel.

GERMAN
A.G. "Geheul," in *Das Geheul und andere Gedichte*. Wiesbaden: Limes Verlag, 1959. Translated by Wolfgang Fleischmann and Rudolf Wittkopf.

A.G. "Geheul," in *Das Geheul und andere Gedichte*. Wiesbaden: Limes Verlag, 1979. Translated by Carl Weissner.

"Geheul," in *Akzente* 1 (1959). Translated by Walter Höllerer.

"Geheul," in *Exempla* 3, no. 1 (1977). Translated by Jörg Ross.

GREEK
A.G. "ΟΥΡΛΙΑΧΡΟ," in *Sugkhroné Poiésé*. Athens: Boukoumanis, 1974. Translated by Jennie Mastorski.

A.G. "ΟΥΡΛΙΑΧΡΟ," in *Poiémata*. Athens: AKMON, 1978. Translated by Aris Berlis.

HEBREW
Omer, Dan, ed. *An Anthology of American Beat Poetry*. Jersualem, Israel: I. Marcus, 1967. Translated by Dan Omer.

Iked 2 (July 1960). Translated by Isumor Yeiuz Kest.

HUNGARIAN
A.G. "Üvöltés," in *Nagyáruház Kaliforniában*. Budapest: Európa Könyvkiadó, 1973. Translated by Orbán Ottó.

A.G. "Üvöltés," in *A leples bitang*. Budapest: Európa Könyvkiadó, 1984. Translated by Orbán Ottó.

"Üvöltés," in *Üvöltés*. Budapest: Európa Könyvkiadó, 1967. Translated by Orbán Ottó.

"Üvöltés," in *Nagyvilág* 8, no. 6 (June 1963). Translated by Somlyó György.

ITALIAN
A.G. "Urlo," in *Jukebox All'Idrogeno*. Milan: Arnoldo Mondadori Editore, 1965. Translated by Fernanda Pivano.

JAPANESE

A.G. *Howl*. Tokyo, 1963. Translated by Yu Suwa. *Eureka* 47 (1960).

LITHUANIAN

"Kauksmas," trans. Antanas Danielius, in *Tiesa* (Vilna) 269 (November 22, 1985).

MACEDONIAN

A.G. Poems, Skopje, Yugoslavia, 1986: Makedonska Kniga. Translated by Savo Cvetanovski.

NORWEGIAN

A.G. "Hyl," in *Hyl*. Oslo: Pax Forlag, n.d. Translated by Olav Angell.

POLISH

A.G. "Skowyt," in *Skowyt i inne wiersze*. Bydgoszcz, Poland: Pomorze, 1984. Translated by Grzegorz Musiał.

A.G. "Skowyt," in *Utwory Poetyckie*. Krakow: Wydawnictwo Literackie, 1984. Translated by Bogdan Baran.

Truszkowska, Teresa, ed. "Skowyt," in *Wizjonerzy i Buntownicy*. Krakow: Wydawnictwo Literackie, 1976. Translated by Teresa Truszkowska.

"Skowyt," in *Jazz* 9, no. 7/8 (August 1964). Translated by Waclaw Iwaniuk.

"Skowyt" in *Puls*, No. 4–5 (Autumn–Winter 1978–1979). Warsaw (Samizdat edition). Translated by Piotra Allena (pseudonym for Piotr Bikont).

"Skowyt," in *Tematy* 9 (Winter 1964). Translated by Waclaw Iwaniuk.

"Skowyt," in *Literatura na Świecie* 42 (October 1974). Translated by Teresa Truszkowska and Leszek Elektorowicz.

Schäffer, Boguslaw. *Howl* (musical setting). Warsaw: Polskie Wydawnictwo Muzyczne, 1974. Translated by Leszek Elektorowicz.

PORTUGUESE

A.G. "Uivo," in *Uivo*. Lisbon: Publicações dom Quixote, 1973. Translated by José Palla e Carmo.

RUMANIAN

Caraion, Ion, ed. "Urlet de Minie," in *Antologia Poeziei Americane*. Bucharest: Editura "Univers," 1979. Translated by Ion Caraion.

SERBO-CROATIAN

A.G. "Urlik," in *Hidrogenski Džuboks*. Belgrade: Narodna Knjiga, 1983. Translated by Zoran Petković and Mihailo Ristić.

A.G. "Urlik," in *Urlik Uma*. Belgrade: DOB, 1983. Translated by Vojo Sindolić.

"ТРИН," in *Antologiji moderne američke poezije*. Belgrade: Prosveta, 1972. Translated by Ivan V. Lalić.

"Urlik," in *Vidici* 24, no. 5–6 (September–October 1978). Translated by Ljiljana Kojić-Bogdanović and Branko Aleksić.

SPANISH

A.G. "Aullido," in *Aullido*. Santiago, Chile: Editorial del Pacífico, 1957? Translated by Fernando Alegría.

A.G. "Aullido," in *Aullido y otros poemas*. Montevideo, Uruguay: Los Huevos del Plata, 1969. Translated by Andres Boulton Figueira de Mello.

A.G. "Aullido," in *Aullido, Kaddish y Otros Poemas*. Toluca, México: Universidad Autónoma del Estado de México, 1981. Translated by José Vicente Anaya.

Barnatán, Marcos Ricardo, ed. "Aullido," in *Antología de la "Beat Generation."* Barcelona, Spain: Plaza and Janes, 1970. Translated by Marcos Ricardo Barnatán.

"Aullido," in *Revista Literaria de la Sociedad de Escritores de Chile* 1, no. 3 (November 1957). Translated by Fernando Alegría.

"Moloch," in *El Comercio*, May 15, 1960. Translated by José Miguel Oviedo and Carlos Zavaleta.

"Aullido," in *Airón* 1, no. 3–4 (May 1961). Translated by Madela Ezcurra and Leandro Katz.

"Aullido," in *El Corno Emplumado/Plumed Horn* 2 (April 1962). Translated by Agustí Bartra.

"Aullido," in *Ventana* 3, no. 14, ser. 3 (August 1962). Translated by Roberto Cuadra.

"Aullido," in *Haoma* 1, no. 3 (April 1968). Translated by Andres Boulton Figueira de Mello.

SWEDISH

A.G. "Howl," in *Tårgas & Solrosor*. Stockholm: FIBs Lyrikklubb, 1971. Translated by Gösta Friberg and Gunnar Harding.

TURKISH

A.G. and Ferlinghetti, Lawrence. "Uluma," in *Amerika*. Istanbul: Ada Yayinlari, 1976. Translated by Orhan Duru and Ferit Edgü.

RECORDINGS

San Francisco Poets. New York: Evergreen Records, 1958. LP no. EVR–1, 33⅓ rpm, 12″ mono.

San Francisco Poets. New York: Hanover Records, 1959. LP no. M–5001, 33⅓ rpm, 12″ mono. Matrix: HMG 117.

Allen Ginsberg Reads Howl and Other Poems. Berkeley, Cal.: Fantasy Records, 1959. LP no. 7013, 33⅓ rpm, 12″ mono. Matrix: V–5998–1854/1855.

Beauty and the Beast, by Anne Waldman and Allen Ginsberg. Boulder, Colo.: Naropa Recordings, 1976. 1 cassette.

Howl and Other Poems. Wuppertal, West Germany: S Press Tapes, 1981. 1 cassette.

Acknowledgments

Compilation of the manuscripts, documentation and information in this edition of *Howl* was made possible by kindhearted John Clellon Holmes' retrieval and return of original draft to author.

Editor & biographer Barry Miles examined Columbia archives for additional drafts and the mass of material in appendixes, sat with author through annotations, and typed & qualified transcripts and notes, mapping and editing the entire book.

Bibliographer Bill Morgan sorted thru Columbia archives for several years, cataloguing & indexing the entire deposit for retrievability.

Prof. Gordon Ball, editing author's *Journals Early Fifties Early Sixties*, helped fix chronology and found relevant entries. Early annotations evolved through Fernanda Pivano's meticulous Italian translations.

Raymond Foye curated author's three-decade-old photographs, Juanita Lieberman indexed and guarded them, Brian Graham made prints; Robert Frank advised the project.

Wood engraving by Lynd Ward (with Moloch text) was hand printed as poetry broadside by Michael McCurdy, 1978, in limited edition of 300, with 150 signed & numbered: Penmaen Press, RD 2, Box 145, Great Barrington, MA 01230.

Kenneth A. Lohf, Director of Manuscripts and Rare Books at Special Collections Division, Butler Library, Columbia University, preserved author's papers since 1968.

The following granted permission for print or reprint of letters, critiques, commentaries & images, often with great magnanimity: Eugene Brooks, Lucien Carr, Neeli Cherkovsky, Francesco Clementi, Gregory Corso, Richard Eberhart, Lawrence Ferlinghetti, Barry Gifford, John Hollander, Lewis Hyde, Tuli Kupferberg, Larry Lee, Michael McClure, James McKenzie, Shigeyoshi Murao, Peter Orlovsky, David Perlman, Louis Simpson, Gary Snyder, Diana Trilling, May Ward.

Bob Rosenthal, patient poet, coordinated and collaborated in all activities, established & kept track of household archives, and conducted research with Juanita Lieberman & Greg Masters.

Vicki Stanbury & Reid Fossey contributed neighborly typing. Archetype cover pattern invented by Harry Smith.

Author is indebted to others for supportive scholarship, encouragement and advice: Daniel Allman, Gabriel Austin, Ann Charters, Edith Ginsberg, James Laughlin, Michael McCurdy, Rosemary Bailey, Gerald Nicosia, Ed Sanders, Bob Sharrard & Nancy Peters of City Lights Books, and Craig Broadly, their *Subterraneans* distributor.

Andrew Wylie conceived the project; Harper & Row's Aaron Asher and Terry Karten edited the book; Marge Horvitz as copy editor integrated massive designs with late amendments; William Monroe contained all in head and hand; Sidney Feinberg designed the artifact; Julie Metz executed cover.

Carl Solomon's much-tried patience, friendship & commentary generously confirmed the possibility of this tome.

Index

page numbers in *italic* denote illustrations

A portion of this work has appeared in *Poetry*.

Grateful acknowledgment is made for permission to reprint:

"Zone" by Guillaume Apollinaire from *Selected Writings*. Copyright © 1971 by Roger Shattuck. All rights reserved. Reprinted by permission of New Directions Publishing Corporation.

"Poetry Chronicle" by John Hollander from *Partisan Review*, volume 24, number 2, 1957. Reprinted by permission of Partisan Review and the author.

"West Coast Rhythms" by Richard Eberhart from the September 2, 1956 *New York Times Book Review*. Copyright © 1956 by The New York Times Company. Reprinted by permission of The New York Times.

Excerpt from *Jack's Book* by Barry Gifford and Lawrence Lee. Copyright © 1978 by Barry Gifford and Lawrence Lee. Reprinted by permission of St. Martin's Press, Inc.

"Addendum, February, 1984" by John Hollander from *On the Poetry of Allen Ginsberg* by Lewis Hyde. Reprinted by permission of The University of Michigan Press.

"Atlantis" from *The Bridge* by Hart Crane. Copyright 1933, © 1958, 1970 by Liveright Publishing Corporation. Reprinted by permission of Liveright Publishing Corporation.

"Ode to Walt Whitman" by Federico García Lorca from *The Selected Poems of Federico García Lorca*. Copyright © 1955 by New Directions Publishing Corporation. "To Elsie" by William Carlos Williams from *Collected Earlier Poems*. Copyright 1938 by New Directions Publishing Corporation. Reprinted by permission of New Directions Publishing Corporation.

Excerpt from *The Dharma Bums* by Jack Kerouac. Copyright © 1958 by Jack Kerouac. Copyright renewed © 1986 by Stella S. Kerouac and Jan Kerouac. Reprinted by permission of Viking Penguin Inc.

Excerpts from *Scratching the Beat Surface* by Michael McClure. Copyright © 1982 by Michael McClure. Published by North Point Press and reprinted by permission. All Rights Reserved.

Excerpt from *Ferlinghetti: A Biography* by Neeli Cherkovski. Copyright © 1979 by Neeli Cherry. Reprinted by permission of Doubleday & Company, Inc.

Letters of William Carlos Williams from *Previously Unpublished Letters of William Carlos Williams*. Copyright © 1986 by William Eric Williams & Paul H. Williams; Letters of Ezra Pound from *Previously Unpublished Letters by Ezra Pound*. Copyright © 1986 by the Trustees of the Ezra Pound Literary Property Trust. Used by permission of New Directions Publishing Corporation, agents.

"Priimiitittiii" by Kurt Schwitters from *Dada Painters and Poets: An Anthology*, edited by Robert Motherwell. (N.Y.: George Wittenborn, 1947). Reprinted by permission of Wittenborn Art Books, Inc.

Excerpt from *Visions of Cody* by Jack Kerouac. Copyright © 1972 by Jack Kerouac. Reprinted by permission of McGraw-Hill Company.

Excerpts from *As Ever: The Collected Correspondence of Allen Ginsberg & Neal Cassady*, edited by Barry Gifford. (Creative Arts Book Company, 1977). Reprinted by permission.

ORGANISATIONAL CHANGE

ASIA PACIFIC 4TH EDITION

ORGANISATIONAL CHANGE

DEVELOPMENT &
TRANSFORMATION

DIANNE M. WADDELL
THOMAS G. CUMMINGS
CHRISTOPHER G. WORLEY

Organisational Change: Development and
Transformation
4th Edition
Dianne M. Waddell
Thomas G. Cummings
Christopher G. Worley

Publishing manager: Alison Green
Senior publishing editor: Dorothy Chiu
Senior project editor: Nathan Katz
Developmental editor: Kylie McInnes
Cover design: Danielle Maccarone
Text design: Olga Lavecchia
Editor: Anne Mulvaney
Permissions research: Helen Mammides
Indexer: Russell Brooks
Proofreader: James Anderson
Reprint: Magda Koralewska
Cover: iStockphoto
Typeset by KnowledgeWorks Global Limited (KGL)

Any URLs contained in this publication were checked
for currency during the production process. Note,
however, that the publisher cannot vouch for the
ongoing currency
of URLs.

Third edition published in 2007

This fourth edition published in 2011

For product information and technology assistance,
in Australia call 1300 790 853;
in New Zealand call 0800 449 725

For permission to use material from this text or product, please email
aust.permissions@cengage.com

National Library of Australia Cataloguing-in-Publication Data
Author: Waddell, Dianne, 1949-
Title: Organisational change : development and transformation /
Dianne M. Waddell ; Thomas G. Cummings; Christopher G. Worley.
Edition: 4th ed.
ISBN: 9780170185950 (pbk.)
Notes: Previous ed.: South Melbourne, Vic. : Thomson, 2007.
Includes index.
Subjects: Organizational change.
Other Authors/Contributors: Cummings, Thomas G. Worley,
Christopher G.
Dewey Number: 302.35

Cengage Learning Australia
Level 7, 80 Dorcas Street
South Melbourne, Victoria Australia 3205

Cengage Learning New Zealand
Unit 4B Rosedale Office Park
331 Rosedale Road, Albany, North Shore 0632, NZ

For learning solutions, visit cengage.com.au

Printed in China by RR Donnelley Asia Printing Solutions Limited.
2 3 4 5 6 7 8 15 14 13 12 11

Contents

Preface

Organisation Change: Development and Transformation is a book describing change management as a challenge, particularly as the environment in which we work is in such a volatile state. The world of managing Organisational Development (OD), which is a planned process of change, continues to change dramatically as the terminology vacillates towards Organisational Transformation (OT) which is more dramatic and unpredictable. Leaders, and in particular change agents, are faced with conflicting challenges of understanding and motivating an increasingly diverse workforce, being open and accountable to a wide range of stakeholders, planning for the future in an increasingly chaotic environment, considering the ethical implications of decision making and many more unanticipated issues.

For students studying change management, the prospect of managing others in such a situation may be daunting. While it is interesting and somewhat straightforward to become a specialist in a specific field, for example Organisation Development (OD), the added pressure of supervising or managing others can be stressful. This book is written with students in mind, preparing students for these challenges that lay ahead. With many current case studies, exercises and support material, the challenges of change management are presented in a real life manner. There is no 'one method fits all' panacea for being a successful change agent, so this book presents change management issues from a variety of viewpoints.

The first author of this book in particular has taken advice from feedback given by her peers and has attempted to provide a comprehensive overview of the fundamental theory as well as practical applications. Of particular significance is the restructuring of the content, and the focus on an international perspective, as compared to previous editions. Students are the beneficiaries of this exchange of expertise, as this book attempts to draw together the various views about change management, with the emphasis on heightening the learning experience and relevance for students. Students entering a change management position or contemplating being more proactive in being a change agent will be exposed to a variety of challenging management issues in this text. Students should appreciate the following quotation from George Bernard Shaw which could well be their mantra in the future:

> Some men see things as they are and ask why. Others dream things
> that never were and ask why not.

Resources Guide

FOR THE STUDENT

As you read this text you will find a number of features in every chapter to enhance your study of organisational change and help you understand its applications.

Application boxes feature organisational practices of local and international companies that help you relate theory to real world business environments. **Critical thinking questions** encourage you to think critically about the examples covered in the Applications boxes and debate related topical issues.

At the end of each chapter you'll find several tools to help you to review the chapter and key learning concepts, and also to help extend your learning.

The end of chapter **Summary** highlights key points from the chapter, giving you a snapshot of the important concepts covered.

Review questions enable you to test your comprehension of key concepts in each chapter.

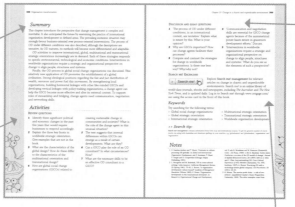

Discussion and essay questions promote analysis and the application of concepts learnt either as an independent or group activity.

Search tip: *Search me! management* contains information from both local and international sources. To get the greatest number of search results, try using both Australian and American spellings in your searches, e.g. 'globalisation' and 'globalization'; 'organisation' and 'organization'

Search me! management
A 6 month subscription to **Search me! management** is provided with this text. This resource provides you with 24-hour access to full-text articles from hundreds of scholarly and popular journals, e-books, and newspapers, including *The Australian* and *The New York Times*, and is updated daily. Use the Search me! management keywords at the end of each chapter to explore topics further and find current references for assignments.

ONLINE CASE DATABASE
Cases from the three previous editions of this book are available on the book's companion website:
www.cengage.com.au/waddell4e.

FOR THE INSTRUCTOR

Cengage Learning is pleased to provide you with a selection of resources that will help you prepare your lectures. These teaching tools are available on the companion website accessible via http://login.cengage.com.

Case database

Cases from the three previous editions of this book are available on the companion website, along with a case matrix.

Instructor's manual

The Instructor's Manual provides you with content to help set up and administer your subject. It includes learning objectives, solutions to the review and discussion questions in the text, additional suggested reading, and more. Suggested solutions are also available for the case study review questions.

PowerPoint™ presentations

Chapter-by-chapter PowerPoint presentations cover the main concepts addressed within the text and can be edited to suit your own requirements. Use these slides to enhance your lecture presentations and to reinforce the key principles of your subject, or for student handouts.

ExamView® test bank

ExamView helps you to create, customise and deliver tests in minutes for both print and online applications. The Quick Test Wizard and Online test Wizard guide you step-by-step through the test-creation process. With ExamView's complete word-processing abilities, you can add an unlimited number of new questions to the bank, edit existing questions and build tests of up to 250 questions using up to 12 question types. You can also export the files into Blackboard or WebCT.

Artwork

These digital files of graphs, tables, pictures and flowcharts from the book can be used in a variety of media. Add them into your course management system, use them within student handouts or copy them into lecture presentations.

Acknowledgements

The success of a project such as this relies on the contribution of many who have been supportive of this venture. To acknowledge everyone would be a difficult task, nevertheless there are those who spring immediately to mind.

Peer reviews have played a very significant role in helping refine the content and pedagogy of this book and without their valuable contribution we would not be able to produce an outcome about which we are proud. I would like to thank sincerely the following colleagues for reviewing the manuscript and providing incisive and helpful feedback: Andy Asquith – Massey University; Kandy Dayaram – Curtin University of Technology; John Gilbert – Wakaito University; Antonia Girardi – Murdoch University; Raymond Gordon – University of Southern Queensland; Richard Hall – University of Sydney; Brad Jorgensen – Queensland University of Technology; Lee Mathias – Auckland University of Technology; David Morgan – University of New South Wales; Pieter Nell – Unitec Institute of Technology; Michael de Percy – University of Canberra; Brenda Scott-Ladd – Curtin University of Technology; Alan Simon – University of Western Australia; Deb Stewart – Victoria University; Noel Tracey – Queensland University of Technology; and Janis Wardrop – University of New South Wales.

I would also like to thank my peers who offered formative suggestions at the very beginning of the writing process. Their comments were instrumental in enabling me to set off in the right direction from the very start and gave me the courage to confront the challenges.

My special appreciation also extends to the following case study authors. The cases gave the book an extra dimension and a thematic approach to the issues: Ramanie Sumaratunge – Monash University; Zane Ma Rhea – Monash University; Dorothy Wardale – Curtin University of Technology; Jessica Stein and Vanessa Grzinic; Jessica Clayden, Simon Woodley and Ranel Juanta.

A special thanks also to Marc Morgan, Jing Ye for their contributions and especially James Malone for the onerous task of editing at the latter stages.

There were many who helped with the research, but it really became a Waddell family activity. Thanks in particular to Suzanne and Corinne who spent many hours researching and writing and really saved me from many a disaster. These tasks are often burdensome and at very short notice; nevertheless they were very generous in sharing their experience and time. I am eternally in their debt, as they constantly remind me, and they are definitely 'in the Will'.

It would be remiss to not acknowledge my appreciation to the team at Cengage Learning for their patience, understanding and, on many occasions, their persistence: My publishing editor, Dorothy Chiu, who is quickly becoming a saint as well as a source of good coffee; Kylie McInnes, my developmental editor, who has been able to keep me on schedule when many would have despaired and, more

importantly, who was able to make sense of my waffle; Helen Mammides, rights and permissions researcher, also assisted me on the project by doing all the hard work. Many thanks should also go to my project editor, Nathan Katz, who deserves a Nobel Prize for endurance and patience, as well as senior designer Danielle Maccarone and creative manager Olga Lavecchia for designing the cover and internal text respectively.

As writing a text book bites considerably into the personal and family time of those involved, I would also like to thank those special people in my life. In particular I would like to thank Denis for enduring 40 years of 'surprises' and not complaining about the cremated dinners. My children Paul, Corinne and Suzanne have also suffered because of my 'distractions' yet have survived the turmoil to become sane adults and have made me very proud. New members of the family Megan and Edhi are still in a state of shock while trying to adapt to the chaos, but hopefully time will help with their adjustment. My grandchildren Kit and Anouk think that their Nanna is a bit 'weird' but at least they now have something for 'show 'n' tell'.

Of course this would not be possible without the support and understanding of my work colleagues and students at Deakin University who were often the 'victims' of my experiments and vehicles for the testing of my ideas. Hopefully I have made a positive contribution and they have pleasant memories of our encounters.

Case matrix

CASE TITLE	CASE AUTHORS	MANUFACTURING	SERVICE
Blended and balanced leadership at IBM	Simon Woodley, Ranel R. Juanta, Jessica Clayden		●
Miwatj executive leadership and management development	Zane Ma Rhea, Monash University		●
NAB – Cultural change program	Jessica Stein, Vanessa Grzinic		●
IBM Australia: Managing diversity through organisational culture	Ramanie Samaratunge and Nilupama Wijewardena, Monash University		●
A new look for Convoy P/L.	Dr Dorothy Wardale, Curtin Graduate School of Business		●
Kenworth Motors	Craig C. Lundberg, Cornell University	●	
Lincoln Hospital: Third-party intervention	R. Wayne Boss, University of Colarado; Leslee S. Boss, Organization Research and Development Associates; Mark W. Dundon, Sisters of Providence Hospital		●
Ben & Jerry's (A): Team development intervention	Philip H. Mirvis, Boston University	●	
Sharpe BMW	Professor Ram Subramanian, Grand Valley State University		●
Fourwinds Marina	W. Harvey Hegarty, Indiana University; Harry Kelsy Jr., Californmay State College		●
B.R Richardson Timber Products Corporation	Craig C. Lundberg, Cornell University		

* Please note that all cases are integrative case studies that can be used in any order. This is a guide only, to identify topics and therefore chapter content that is predominant to each case study.

GOVERNMENT/ NOT FOR PROFIT	INDUSTRIAL GOODS	MULTINATIONAL CORPORATION	SMALL-MEDIUM SIZED COMPANY	RELATES TO CHAPTERS*
				1, 2, 3, 4, 5, 6, 8, 9, 10, 11
●				1, 2, 3, 4, 5, 6, 8, 9, 10, 11
				1, 2, 3, 4, 5, 6, 8, 9, 10, 11
		●		1, 2, 3, 4, 5, 6, 8, 9, 10, 11
●			●	1, 2, 3, 4, 5, 6, 7, 8, 9, 10, 11
	●			1, 3, 4, 6, 7, 8, 10, 11
				1, 2, 3, 4, 5, 6, 8, 9, 10, 11
			●	1, 3, 4, 6, 7, 8, 10, 11
				1, 2, 3, 4, 5, 6, 8, 9, 10, 11
			●	1, 2, 3, 4, 5, 6, 7, 8, 9, 10, 11
			●	2, 4, 5, 6, 7

About the authors

Dianne Waddell is the Associate Dean (Teaching and Learning) with the Faculty of Business and Law at Deakin University, Melbourne, Australia. She is responsible for the development, implementation and evaluation of postgraduate and undergraduate courses and is the coordinator of the *Assurance of Learning* processes in the Faculty. She teaches in the areas of Quality Management, Change Management and Strategic Management. She holds a PhD (Monash), Master of Education Administration (Melbourne), Bachelor of Education (Melbourne) and Bachelor of Arts (La Trobe).

Dianne has published and presented over 80 conference papers on resistance to change, leadership, e-business, quality management, family business and forecasting for managers. Her publications include six books: *Contemporary Management* (McGraw-Hill), *Organisation Development and Change, 3rd edition* (Nelson-Thomson Learning), *E-Business in Australia: Concepts and Cases* (Pearson Publishing), *Managing the Family Business* (Heidelberg Press), *E-Business Innovation and Change Management* (IDEA Publishing) and *Freedom of Information: Accountability or Obfuscation?* (Heidelberg Press).

Dianne is part of the research team focusing on family businesses. The team has designed, implemented and evaluated the KPMG Family Business Needs Survey for the past 4 years. Her research has investigated cultural perspectives in family business succession and governance issues.

She has taught in both public and private education systems for many years, as well as presenting specifically designed industry-based courses. She has received several teaching awards including the 2009 Vice Chancellor's Award for Outstanding Achievement in Teaching and Learning at Deakin University and was admitted as a Fellow in the College of Distinguished Deakin Educators. She is also a Fellow of the Australian Organisation for Quality (AOQ).

Thomas G. Cummings, professor, chair of the Department of Management and Organization, and executive director of the Leadership Institute, received his B.S. and MBA from Cornell University, and his PhD in socio-technical systems from the University of California at Los Angeles. He was previously on the faculty at Case-Western Reserve University. He has authored 13 books, written over 40 scholarly articles and given numerous invited papers at national and international conferences. He is associate editor of the *Journal of Organizational Behavior*, and former editor-in-chief of the *Journal of Management Inquiry*, chairman of the Organizational Development and Change division of the Academy of Management, and president of the Western Academy of Management. His major research and consulting interests include designing high-performing organisations and strategic change management. He has conducted several large-scale organisation design and change projects, and has consulted to a variety of private and public-sector organisations in the United States, Europe, Mexico and Scandinavia.

Dr Christopher G. Worley holds a joint appointment as a research scientist at the Center for Effective Organizations at the University of Southern California's Marshall School of Business and as an associate professor at Pepperdine University. He is the former director of the Master of Science in Organization program at Pepperdine University, where he was awarded the Harriet and Charles Luckman Distinguished Teaching Fellowship between 1995 and 2000. Dr. Worley also has taught undergraduate and graduate courses at the University of San Diego, University of Southern California and Colorado State University. He was chair of the Academy of Management's Organization Development and Change Division. Dr. Worley received his PhD in strategic management from the University of Southern California, an MS in organization development from Pepperdine University, an M.S. in environmental psychology from Colorado State University and a B.S. from Westminster College. He is a member of the Strategic Management Society, the Academy of Management, NTL and the Organization Development Network. He lives with his wife and three children in San Juan Capistrano, California.

PART 1

INTRODUCTION

1 *Introduction*

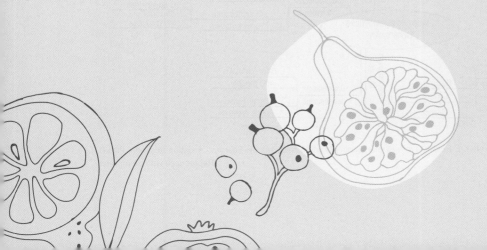

CHAPTER 1

Introduction

Organisations today are confronted almost daily with the need for change.[1] It remains one of the few constants in an increasingly unpredictable and complex environment and one of the more significant and demanding issues facing managers today. As the environment changes, organisations must adapt if they are to be successful. Under these pressures, companies are downsizing, re-engineering, flattening structures, going global and initiating more sophisticated technologies. A major challenge facing organisations today is to develop a management style and culture that will enable them to cope with the challenges and opportunities they face. Irrespective of whether the change has to do with introducing new technology, a reorganisation or new product development, it is important for leaders to have a sound understanding of change issues and theories to help guide their actions.[2]

Kimberley (cited in endnote 2) noted that despite spanning a period of more than half a century, the change literature is complex and fragmented, characterised by a diversity of approaches and opinion. She observes that there is no one universal change model and no one best way of successfully implementing change. As a consequence she designed a mind map that charted a course through organisational change theory. This very useful approach is presented in Figure 1.1.

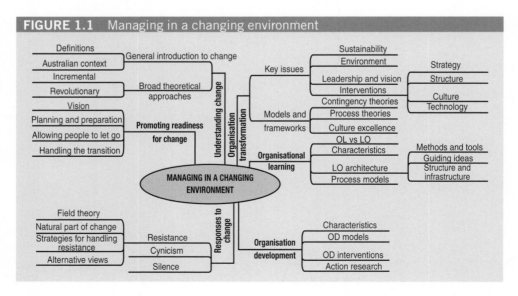

FIGURE 1.1 Managing in a changing environment

Source: D. Waddell, *E-Business in Australia: Concepts and Cases* (Sydney: Pearson Education Australia, 2002). Reproduced with permission.

It becomes apparent from the figure that, for the purposes of sustainability, organisations need to be able to implement both incremental and transformational change.[3] 'This requires organisational and management skills to compete in a mature market (where cost, efficiency and incremental innovation are key) and to develop new products and services (where radical innovation, speed and flexibility are critical).'[4] Thus, managers today are required to master both incremental and revolutionary change.

But in all probability managers have their own intuitive approaches to bringing about change – the change models they carry inside their heads. A personal theory of change would therefore include any assumptions, biases and paradigms that influence their beliefs about what should change and how change should occur. However, in order to successfully implement change, managers should at least be cognisant of various perspectives on change and the thinking that underpins them.

There is a metaphor for change: a pendulum that swings from incremental and planned change (organisation development) to dramatic and unplanned change (organisation transformation). Although organisation transformation (OT) receives headlines in the media it is often organisation development (OD) that is the desired state for organisations. Where OT is a reactive, and sometimes dramatic, response to external pressures, OD is the preferred option for organisations that are introspective and wish to continually improve their products and services in an incremental manner.

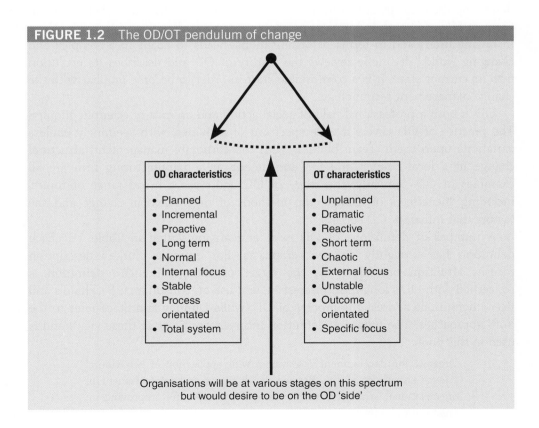

FIGURE 1.2 The OD/OT pendulum of change

OD characteristics	OT characteristics
• Planned	• Unplanned
• Incremental	• Dramatic
• Proactive	• Reactive
• Long term	• Short term
• Normal	• Chaotic
• Internal focus	• External focus
• Stable	• Unstable
• Process orientated	• Outcome orientated
• Total system	• Specific focus

Organisations will be at various stages on this spectrum
but would desire to be on the OD 'side'

This is a book predominantly about OD, the desired state: a process that applies behavioural science knowledge and practices to help organisations achieve greater effectiveness, including increased financial performance and improved quality of work life. It must also be noted that OD differs from other planned change efforts, such as technological innovation, training and development or new product development, in that the focus is on building the organisation's ability to assess its current functioning and to achieve its goals – OD is process-oriented not outcome-oriented. Moreover, OD is oriented to improving the total system[5] – the organisation and its parts in the context of the larger environment that impacts on them.

On the other hand, OT may be perceived as volatile and reactive to environmental forces. In most instances organisations tend to favour OD as it may be implemented proactively and gradually therefore minimise the disturbance within the organisation.

Although this book presents both views of change, OT and OD, it is the latter that is often desired by organisations and planned accordingly. This book covers OD in more detail in preference to OT, as a basis and foundation for the ongoing debate surrounding change management processes.

WHAT IS ORGANISATION DEVELOPMENT?

This section starts consideration of change management by focusing on OD, describing the concept of OD itself, and explains why OD has expanded rapidly in the past 50 years, both in terms of people's needs to work with and through others in organisations and in terms of organisations' needs to adapt to a complex and changing world.[6] It briefly reviews the history of OD and describes its evolution into its current state. It is a comfortable start in order to become familiar with the change management terminology.

OD is both a professional field of social action and an area of scientific inquiry. The practice of OD covers a wide spectrum of activities, with seemingly endless variations upon them. Team building with top corporate management, structural change in a local council and job enrichment in a manufacturing firm are all examples of OD. Similarly, the study of OD addresses a broad range of topics, including the effects of change, the methods of organisational change and the factors that influence OD success.

A number of definitions of OD exist and are presented in Table 1.1. Each definition has a slightly different emphasis. For example, Burke's description focuses attention on culture as the target of change; French's definition is concerned with OD's long-term interest in, and use of, consultants; Beckhard's and Beer's definitions address the process of OD; while Dunphy and Stace refer to the 'soft' approaches. The following definition incorporates most of these views and is used in this book:

> Organisation development is a system wide application of behavioural science knowledge to the planned development and reinforcement of organisational strategies, structures and processes for improving an organisation's effectiveness.

TABLE 1.1 Definitions of organisation development

- Organisation development is a planned process of change in an organisation's culture through the utilisation of behavioural science technology, research and theory (Warner Burke).[7]

- Organisation development refers to a long-range effort to improve an organisation's problem-solving capabilities and its ability to cope with changes in its external environment with the help of external or internal behavioural-scientist consultants, or change agents, as they are sometimes called (Wendell French).[8]

- Organisation development is an effort (1) planned, (2) organisation-wide, and (3) managed from the top to (4) increase organisation effectiveness and health through (5) planned interventions in the organisation's 'processes', using behavioural science knowledge (Richard Beckhard).[9]

- Organisation development is a system-wide process of data collection, diagnosis, action planning, intervention and evaluation aimed at: (1) enhancing congruence between organisational structure, process, strategy, people and culture; (2) developing new and creative organisational solutions; and (3) developing the organisation's self-renewing capacity. It occurs through the collaboration of organisational members working with a change agent using behavioural science theory, research and technology (Michael Beer).[10]

- Organisation development is a 'soft' approach that describes a process of change undertaken in small incremental steps managed participatively (Dexter Dunphy and Doug Stace).[11]

This definition emphasises several features that differentiate OD from other singular approaches to organisational change and improvement, such as technological innovation, training and development, and organisation evolution.

First, OD applies to an entire system, such as an organisation, a single plant of a multiplant firm, or a department or work group. This contrasts with approaches that focus on one or a few aspects of a system, such as a training and development model or a 'one off' technological innovation. In these approaches, attention is narrowed to individuals within a system or to the improvement of particular products or processes.

Second, OD is based on behavioural science knowledge and practice, including microconcepts such as leadership, group dynamics and work design, and macro-approaches such as strategy, organisation design and international relations. These subjects distinguish OD from such applications as technological innovation, which emphasise the technical and rational aspects of organisations. These latter approaches tend to neglect the personal and social characteristics of a system. In addition, the behavioural science approach to change acknowledges the individual's influence over an organisation's destiny. More deterministic perspectives, such as organisation evolution, discount the influence of organisation members on effectiveness.

Third, whereas OD is concerned with planned change, it is not, in the formal sense, typically associated with business planning or technological innovation[12] nor, in the deterministic sense, often associated with organisation evolution.

Instead, OD is more an adaptive process for planning and implementing change than a blueprint for how things should be done. It involves planning to diagnose and solve organisational problems, but such plans are flexible and often revised as new information is gathered about the progress of the change program. If, for example, the performance of international managers was seen to be a concern, a reorganisation process might begin with plans to assess the current relationships between the international divisions and the corporate headquarters, and to redesign them if necessary. These plans would be modified should the assessment discover that most of the international managers' weak performance could be attributed to poor cross-cultural training prior to their international assignment.

Fourth, OD involves both the creation and the subsequent reinforcement of change. It moves beyond the initial efforts to implement a change program to a longer-term concern for stabilising and institutionalising new activities within the organisation. For example, the implementation of self-managed work teams might focus on ways by which supervisors could give workers more control over work methods. After the workers had been given more control, attention would shift to ensuring that supervisors continued to provide that freedom, including the possible rewarding of supervisors for managing in a participative style. This attention to reinforcement is similar to training and development approaches that address maintenance of new skills or behaviours, but differs from other change perspectives that do not address how a change can be institutionalised.

Fifth, OD encompasses strategy, structure and process changes, although different OD programs may focus more on one kind of change than another. A change program aimed at modifying organisation strategy, for example, might focus on how the organisation relates to a wider environment and on how those relationships can be improved. It might include changes in both the grouping of people to perform tasks (structure) and the methods of communicating and solving problems (process) used to support the changes in strategy. Similarly, an OD program directed at helping a top-management team become more effective might focus on interactions and problem-solving processes within the group. This focus might result in the improved ability of top management to solve company problems in strategy and structure. Other approaches to change, such as training and development, typically have a narrower focus on the skills and knowledge of organisation members.

Finally, OD is oriented towards improving organisational effectiveness. This involves two major assumptions. First, an effective organisation is able to solve its own problems and focus its attention and resources on achieving key goals. OD helps organisation members gain the skills and knowledge necessary to conduct these activities by involving them in the process. Second, an effective organisation has both high performance – including quality products and services, high productivity and continuous improvement – and a high quality of work life. The organisation's performance is responsive to the needs of external groups, such as stockholders, customers, suppliers and government agencies that provide the organisation with resources and legitimacy. Moreover, it is able to attract and motivate effective employees who then perform at high levels.

This definition helps to distinguish OD from other applied fields, such as management consulting, operations management or new product development. It also furnishes a clear conception of organisation change, which is a related focus of this book. Organisation change is a broad phenomenon that involves a diversity of applications and approaches, including economic, political, technical and social perspectives. Change in organisations can be in response to external forces, such as market shifts, competitive pressures and radical new product technologies, or it can be internally motivated, such as by managers trying to improve existing methods and practices. Regardless of its origins, change does affect people and their relationships in organisations and so can have significant social consequences. For example, change may have a negative connotation or be poorly implemented. The behavioural sciences have developed useful concepts and methods for helping organisations deal with these problems. They help managers and administrators to manage the change process. Many of these concepts and techniques are described in this book, particularly in relation to managing change.

Organisation development can be applied to managing organisational change. However, it is primarily concerned with change that is oriented to transferring the knowledge and skills needed to build the capability to achieve goals, solve problems and manage change. It is intended to move the organisation in a particular direction, towards improved problem solving, responsiveness, quality of work life and effectiveness. Organisation change, in contrast, is more broadly focused and can apply to any kind of change, including technical, managerial and social innovations. These changes may or may not be directed at making the organisation more developed in the sense implied by OD.

Application 1.1 shows Telstra competing with National Broadband Networks where their structure inhibits their response to change.

1.1

APPLICATION

Telstra's chances

. . .

As more than 1.3 million people have learned, Telstra is a prime lesson that just because you have a near-monopoly and massive cash flows, that doesn't mean you have a business structure which allows you to grow quickly (occasionally, it hasn't grown at all).

Some shareholders may moan about the government intervention that is 'encouraging' it to demerge from its network business (the very thing that keeps the monopoly intact). But strangely, it could be the liberation that Telstra needs to start growing again.

The key to creating the $43 billion National Broadband Network (NBN), which will compete with Telstra, is to gain access to every home and business. The smartest way is to use Telstra's current pipes and connector boxes that run to your house.

There's just one problem. Telstra owns this part of the network and currently has pricing power over it. Telstra can charge itself cheaper prices to access these links than its

>>

competitors (and there are claims that service times for competitors are much longer than for Telstra customers).

When Sol Trujillo became Telstra CEO, one of his ongoing themes was that the company had to be an 'integrated telco'. Telstra had to own the network as well as the services carried on it (broadband, mobile phones, pay TV). Sol's campaign was to coerce government through whatever means to agree that Telstra was the only group capable of delivering the network services to Australia.

Eventually tired of Telstra's brinkmanship, the federal government excluded it from the bidding in the NBN tender process on the grounds that it did not enter a full bid, as required, but only an expression of its intentions. Then came the global financial crisis (GFC), and the government's ability to undertake massive infrastructure projects was unhampered. It shocked Australia, and Telstra, by saying it would build a $43 billion NBN that, if necessary, would bypass Telstra's cabling into the home.

To all observers, the exclusion of Telstra from the broadband rollout never made sense. Why spend the money digging new tunnels for cables into people's houses when the tunnels already existed?

Telstra was forced to become increasingly conciliatory with the government. It was, and still is, in both Telstra's and the government's interests to co-operate on the NBN. The missing piece in the government's puzzle was still the final 200 metres of cable into every person's home. And so Communications Minister Stephen Conroy 'encouraged' Telstra to split part; to allow the government to access its network to make the NBN cheaper, more efficient.

The 'encouragement' (most called it a gun to the head) was that Telstra would miss out on 'spectrum' when the 4G mobile phone network was being rolled out, in other words curtailing its growth in the increasingly technology-driven world.

As well, the government said it would consider forcing Telstra to sell its 50% stake in pay-TV operator Foxtel. These two parts of Telstra are growing faster, and are vital in the changing communications world.

Some shareholders cried 'foul'. How could the government force Telstra into such a position? But wiser heads thought through the issue. If Telstra is split into its high-growth and low-growth components, would it really change things so much?

Telstra shareholders will be given shares or cash when the network is disposed of. They will retain ownership in the higher-growth mobile and broadband businesses and perhaps the stagnancy of the company could finally be shaken free.

At least that's the hope. The alternative – that Telstra goes it alone and competes with the NBN by using shareholder cash to build an alternative network – is almost unthinkably wasteful for the shareholders but, more importantly, for the nation.

Source: Ross Greenwood, 'Telstra's chance', *Money* magazine, October 2009.

Critical thinking questions:
1. If Telstra is split into its high-growth and low-growth components, would it really change circumstances so much?
2. Besides the needs of Telstra, what other considerations should there be before implementing change?
3. Telstra exists and operates within an industry characterised by rapid technological changes. The industry also is highly competitive, with organisations entering and departing frequently. In this environment, how should/can Telstra strike a balance between the application of OD and OT?

WHY STUDY ORGANISATION DEVELOPMENT?

In the previous editions of this book we argued that organisations must adapt to increasingly complex and uncertain technological, economic, political and cultural changes. We have also argued that OD can help an organisation create effective responses to these changes and, in many cases, proactively influence the strategic direction of the organisation. The rapidly changing conditions of the past few years confirm these arguments and accent their relevance. According to several observers, organisations are in the midst of unprecedented uncertainty and chaos, and nothing short of a management revolution will save them.[13] Three major trends are shaping change in organisations: globalisation, information technology and managerial innovation.[14]

First, globalisation is changing the markets and environments in which organisations operate as well as the way they function. New governments, new leadership, new markets and new countries are emerging and creating a new global economy. The expansion of the European Union has developed and strengthened an internal market; the demise of the Soviet Union has allowed the progress of countries such as Kazakhstan, now a major provider of commercial minerals; and the growth of nationalism and religious fervour in Asia and the Middle East has had far-reaching, international effects resulting in economic and political turmoil.

Second, information technology such as e-business is changing how work is performed and how knowledge is used. The way an organisation collects, stores, manipulates, uses and transmits information can lower costs or increase the value and quality of products. Electronic data interchange, for example, directly connects two organisations, allowing instantaneous exchange of sales data, pricing, inventory levels and other information. This can be used to adjust manufacturing scheduling, service delivery, new product development activities and sales campaigns. In addition, the ability to move information easily and inexpensively throughout and between organisations has fuelled the downsizing, delayering and restructuring of firms. High-speed modems and laptop computers have allowed for a new form of work known as telecommuting: organisation members can work from their homes or cars without ever going to the office. Finally, information technology is changing how knowledge is used. Information that is widely shared reduces the concentration of power at the top of the organisation. Decision making, once the exclusive province of senior managers who had key information, is shared by organisation members who now have the same information. The concept of work needs redefinition and the relationship between business and customer is less delineated – business to business (B2B) versus business to consumer and now business to employee.

Third, managerial innovation has both responded to the globalisation and information technology trends and accelerated their impact on organisations. New organisational forms, such as networks, clusters, strategic alliances and virtual corporations, provide organisations with new ways of thinking about how to manufacture goods and deliver services. The strategic alliance,[15] for example, has emerged as one of the indispensable tools in strategy implementation. No single organisation – not even BHP Billiton, Lend Lease or Western Mining Corporation – can control the environmental and market uncertainty it faces. Many CEOs of Australian companies share this viewpoint. For example, Qantas has extended its Australian operations into the global market by allying with Oneworld. In addition, new methods of change, such as downsizing (right sizing, creating job opportunities, etc.) and re-engineering, have radically reduced the size of organisations and increased their flexibility, while new large group interventions, such as the search conference and open space, have increased the speed with which organisational change can take place.

Managers, OD practitioners and researchers argue that these forces are not only powerful in their own right but also interrelated. Their interaction makes for a highly uncertain and chaotic environment for all kinds of organisations, including manufacturing and service firms and those in the public and private sectors. There is no question that these forces are profoundly impacting on organisations.

Fortunately, a growing number of organisations are undertaking the kinds of organisational changes needed to survive and prosper in today's environment. They are making themselves more streamlined and nimble, and more responsive to external demands. They are involving employees in key decisions and paying for performance rather than time. They are taking the initiative in innovating and managing change, rather than simply responding to what has already happened.

Organisation development is playing an increasingly important role in helping organisations change themselves. It is helping organisations to assess themselves and their environments and to revitalise and rebuild their strategies, structures and processes. OD is helping organisation members go beyond surface changes to transform the underlying assumptions and values that govern their behaviours. The different concepts and methods discussed in this book are increasingly finding their way into government agencies, manufacturing firms, multinational corporations, service industries, educational institutions and not-for-profit organisations. Perhaps at no other time has OD been more responsive and practically relevant to organisations' needs if they are to operate effectively in a highly complex and changing world.

Organisation development is obviously important to those who plan a professional career in the field, either as an internal consultant employed by an organisation or as an external consultant practising in many organisations. A career in OD can be highly rewarding, providing challenging and interesting assignments that involve working with managers and employees to improve their organisations and their work lives. In today's environment, the demand for OD professionals is rising rapidly. For example, consulting has been the biggest area of growth for Australia's 'Big Four' accounting practices, and it now represents 25–30% of their total worldwide billings. The owners of fast-growing companies are making more use of consultants, and 58% increased the use of their services. This would indicate that career opportunities in OD should continue to expand in Australia.

Organisation development is also important to those who have no aspirations to become professional practitioners. All managers and administrators are responsible for supervising and developing subordinates and for improving their departments' performances. Similarly, all staff specialists, such as accountants, financial analysts, engineers, personnel specialists or market researchers, are responsible for offering advice and counsel to managers, and for introducing new methods and practices. Finally, OD is important to general managers and other senior executives as it can help the whole organisation be more flexible, adaptable and effective.

Organisation development can help managers and staff personnel perform their tasks more effectively. It can provide the skills and knowledge necessary for establishing effective interpersonal and helping relationships. It can show personnel how to work effectively with others in diagnosing complex problems and devising appropriate solutions. It can help others become committed to the solutions, thereby increasing the chances of their successful implementation. In short, OD is highly relevant to anyone who has to work with and through others in organisations.

Application 1.2 demonstrates how the global financial crisis (GFC) has tested Australia's managerial mettle and reinforced organisational development in business success.

1.2

APPLICATION

Forged by fire

Food importer and distributor Stuart Alexander is one of Australia's oldest businesses. Founded in Sydney 125 years ago, it has survived more booms and busts than most. Chief executive Garry Browne, who has headed the company since 1995, speaks with the wisdom of time: 'When things are going well, be aware, because there's always risk around the corner.'

Stuart Alexander, whose brand portfolio includes Mentos, Guylian and Illy, restructured its operations in 2007, prior to the global financial crisis (GFC). 'The decision to restructure, to delayer the business, was taken to ensure that we remained a sustainable business,' Browne says, 'It proved to be a fortuitous move.'

Despite a 'fitter, more finely tuned' business, the global recession of 2008–09 led to a further review. Stuart Alexander increased sales by 3 per cent for the year to $150 million but margins came under pressure as competition intensified and consumers went to ground. 'Consumers became quite intimidated and all of a sudden retail just died,' Browne says. 'It happened very quickly. It didn't just fade into the distance – it fell off the cliff.'

Stuart Alexander employs 160 people. Browne was determined to maintain service levels during the downturn and not resort to lay-offs. 'That was an imperative because it maintains the confidence of all your stakeholders.'

A review of business processes and transactions followed. Activities were costed, their efficiency was measured and their value to the business assessed. 'We asked a lot of questions. Is this activity important to the business? Can this be done another way?'

Often, the answer was yes. Stuart Alexander closed its Adelaide office, managing South Australia out of Melbourne. It centralised the management of employee travel and used video-conferencing to reduce interstate meetings, slashing travel costs by 20 per cent. Browne says

>>

the GFC has not been without its positive effects. 'It gives people a tremendous impetus when they see that they can improve the performance of the business based on the way they do things,' he says. Asked what has been the biggest lesson of the past 12 months, he replies: 'Focus on what you know. Do what you do best and keep doing it. And don't panic.'

The managing director of recruitment firm Ampersand Executive, Hayley James, shows no sign of panic. She co-founded the business in Melbourne in July 2009. Buoyed by national service agreements with National Australia Bank and Australia and New Zealand Banking Group, Ampersand opened a Sydney office in October 2009.

James says that even in a 'pretty challenging' year for recruitment, Ampersand was able to survive – and grow – by focusing on innovation and customer service. 'Innovating around new product areas was critical. Value-adds are really important. During a downturn it's important to deliver a level of service to clients above and beyond their expectations.'

Ampersand introduced an executive search function, including a 'market mapping' service which provides clients with a detailed analysis of potential candidates for specific positions. The firm has also positioned itself in the growing market for interim management placements.

...The original business plan has been reviewed in light of the GFC and plans to open a Singapore office have been put on hold.

Not surprisingly, James has learnt some lessons from the GFC experience. 'Stay true to your brand,' she says. 'Don't allow service levels to drop. And innovate.'

The managing director and co-owner of Melbourne 'eco fabrics' manufacturer Sustainable Living Fabrics, Bill Jones, has not markedly changed his $5 million-a-year business during the downturn. But he says the downturn has helped highlight a critical weak spot. 'I suspect I became too complacent about our marketing,' he says. 'We were relying on our credentials to sell our product, rather than us going to the market and explaining our product. As the business climate got tougher, people were more interested in price [than the environment] and those suppliers who didn't have green credentials were in a better position to lower their price.'

Source: Leo D'Angelo Fisher, 'Forged by fire', *Business Review Weekly*, December–January 2010.

Critical thinking questions:

1. 'Focus on what you know. Do what you do best and keep doing it. And don't panic.' How should organisations deal with changes to ensure continued survival or even maximise efficiencies to make profits?
2. Hayley James urges firms to 'innovate'. Innovation implies change within the range of products/services and/or the organisational structure. What are likely to be the main points of resistance to change in these areas? How might you overcome them?

A SHORT HISTORY OF ORGANISATION DEVELOPMENT

A brief history of OD will help to clarify the evolution of the term as well as some of the problems and confusions that have surrounded its development. As currently practised, OD emerged from five major backgrounds or stems, as shown in Figure 1.3. The first was the growth of the National Training Laboratories (NTL) and the development of training groups, otherwise known as sensitivity training or T-groups. The second stem of OD was the classic work on action research conducted by social scientists who were interested in applying research to the

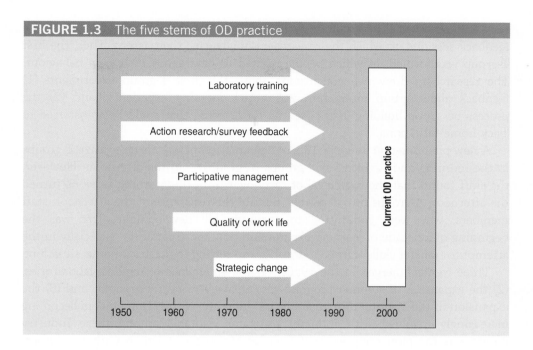

FIGURE 1.3 The five stems of OD practice

management of change. An important feature of action research was a technique known as survey feedback. Kurt Lewin, a prolific theorist, researcher and practitioner in group dynamics and social change, was instrumental in the development of T-groups, survey feedback and action research. His work led to the initial development of OD and still serves as a major source of its concepts and methods. The third stem reflects the work of Rensis Likert and represents the application of participative management to organisation structure and design. The fourth background is the approach that focuses on productivity and the quality of work life. The fifth stem of OD, and the most recent influence on current practice, involves strategic change and organisational transformation.

Laboratory training background

This stem of OD pioneered laboratory training or the T-group: a small, unstructured group in which participants learn from their own interactions and evolving dynamics about such issues as interpersonal relations, personal growth, leadership and group dynamics. Essentially, laboratory training began in the summer of 1946, when Kurt Lewin and his staff at the Research Center for Group Dynamics at the Massachusetts Institute of Technology (MIT) were asked by the Connecticut Interracial Commission and the Committee on Community Interrelations of the American Jewish Congress for help in research on training community leaders. A workshop was developed, and the community leaders were brought together to learn about leadership and discuss problems. At the end of each day, the researchers discussed privately what behaviours and group dynamics they had observed. The community leaders asked permission to sit in on these feedback sessions, to which the researchers finally gave their assent. Thus, the first T-group was formed, in which people reacted to data about their own behaviour. The researchers drew two conclusions about this first T-group experiment: (1) feedback about group interaction was a rich learning experience, and (2) the process of 'group building' had potential for learning that could be transferred to 'back-home' situations.[16]

A new phenomenon arose in 1950 when an attempt was made to have T-groups in the morning and cognitive-skill groups (A-groups)[17] in the afternoon. However, the staff found that the high level of carry-over from the morning sessions turned the afternoon A-groups into T-groups, despite the resistance of the afternoon staff members, who were committed to cognitive-skill development. This was the beginning of a decade of learning experimentation and frustration, especially in the attempt to transfer skills learned in the T-group setting to the 'back-home' situation.

Three trends emerged in the 1950s: (1) the emergence of regional laboratories, (2) the expansion of summer program sessions to year-round sessions, and (3) the expansion of the T-group into business and industry, with NTL members becoming increasingly involved with industry programs. Notable among these industry efforts was the pioneering work of Douglas McGregor at Union Carbide, Herbert Shepard and Robert Blake at Esso Standard Oil (now Exxon), and McGregor and Richard Beckhard at General Mills. Applications of T-group methods at these three companies introduced the term 'organisation development' and led corporate personnel and industrial relations specialists to expand their roles to offer internal consulting services to managers.[18]

Applying T-group techniques to organisations gradually became known as 'team building': a process for helping work groups become more effective in accomplishing tasks and satisfying member needs.

Action research and survey feedback background

Kurt Lewin was also involved in the second movement that led to OD's emergence as a practical field of social science. This second background refers to the processes of action research and survey feedback. The action research contribution began in the 1940s with studies conducted by social scientists John Collier, Kurt Lewin and William Whyte, who discovered that research needed to be closely linked to action if organisation members were to use it to manage change. A collaborative effort was initiated between organisation members and social scientists to collect research data about an organisation's functioning, analyse it for causes of problems, and devise and implement solutions. After implementation, further data were collected to assess the results, and the cycle of data collection and action often continued. The results of action research were twofold: members of organisations were able to use research on themselves to guide action and change, and social scientists were able to study that process to derive new knowledge that could be used elsewhere.

A key component of most action research studies was the systematic collection of survey data, which were subsequently fed back to the client organisation. Following Lewin's death in 1947, his Research Center for Group Dynamics at MIT moved to Michigan and joined with the Survey Research Center as part of the Institute for Social Research. The institute was headed by Rensis Likert, a pioneer in the development of scientific approaches to attitude surveys. Likert's doctoral dissertation at Columbia University, 'A technique for the measurement of attitudes', was the classic study in which he developed the widely used, five-point 'Likert Scale'.[19]

In an early study of the institute, Likert and Floyd Mann administered a company-wide survey of management and employee attitudes at Detroit Edison.[20] Over a two-year period beginning in 1948, three sets of data were developed: (1) the viewpoints of 8000 non-supervisory employees about their supervisors, promotion opportunities and work satisfaction with fellow employees; (2) similar reactions from first- and second-line supervisors; and (3) information from higher levels of management.

The feedback process that evolved was an 'interlocking chain of conferences'. The major findings of the survey were first reported to the top management and then transmitted throughout the organisation. The feedback sessions were conducted in task groups, with supervisors and their immediate subordinates discussing the data together. Although there was little substantial research evidence, the researchers intuitively felt that this was a powerful process for change.

In 1950, eight accounting departments asked for a repeat of the survey, and this generated a new cycle of feedback meetings. Feedback approaches were used in four departments, but the method varied, with two of the remaining departments receiving feedback only at the departmental level. Because of changes in key personnel, nothing was done in two departments.

A third follow-up study indicated that more significant and positive changes (such as job satisfaction) had occurred in the departments that were receiving feedback than in the two departments that did not participate. From these findings, Likert and Mann derived several conclusions about the effects of survey feedback on organisation change, and this led to extensive applications of survey-feedback methods in a variety of settings. The common pattern of data collection, data feedback, action planning, implementation and follow-up data collection in both action research and survey feedback can be seen in these examples.

Participative management background

The intellectual and practical advances from the laboratory training and action research/survey-feedback stems were closely followed by the belief that a human-relations approach represented a one-best-way to manage organisations. This belief was exemplified in research that associated Likert's participative management

(System 4) style with organisational effectiveness.[21] This framework characterised organisation as having one of four types of management systems:[22]

- *Exploitative authoritative*[23] systems (System 1) exhibit an autocratic, top-down approach to leadership. Employee motivation is based on punishment and occasional rewards. Communication is primarily downward, and there is little lateral interaction or teamwork. Decision making and control reside primarily at the top of the organisation. System 1 results in mediocre performance.
- *Benevolent authoritative*[24] systems (System 2) are similar to System 1, except that management is more paternalistic. Employees are allowed a little more interaction, communication and decision making, but within limited boundaries defined by management.
- *Consultative* systems (System 3) increase employee interaction, communication and decision making. Although employees are consulted about problems and decisions, management still makes the final decisions. Productivity is good, and employees are moderately satisfied with the organisation.
- *Participative* group systems (System 4) are almost the opposite of System 1. Designed around group methods of decision making and supervision, the participative group system fosters high degrees of member involvement and participation. Work groups are highly involved in setting goals, making decisions, improving methods and appraising results. Communication occurs both laterally and vertically, and decisions are linked throughout the organisation by overlapping group membership. Shown in Figure 1.4, this linking-pin structure ensures continuity in communication and decision making across groups by means of people who are members of more than one group – the groups they

FIGURE 1.4 The linking pin

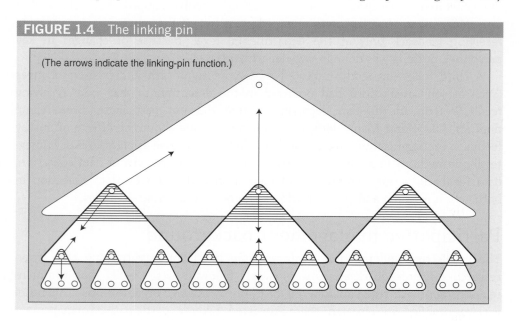

(The arrows indicate the linking-pin function.)

Source: R. Likert, *New Patterns of Management* (New York: McGraw-Hill, 1961). Reproduced by permission of the McGraw-Hill Companies.

supervise and the higher level groups of which they are members. System 4 achieves high levels of productivity, quality and member satisfaction.

Likert applied System 4 management to organisations, using a survey-feedback process. The intervention generally started with organisation members completing the profile of organisational characteristics.[25] The survey asked members for their opinions about both the present and ideal conditions of six organisational features: leadership, motivation, communication, decisions, goals and control. In the second stage, the data were fed back to different work groups within the organisation. Group members examined the discrepancy between their present situation and their ideal, generally using System 4 as the ideal benchmark, and generated action plans to move the organisation towards System 4 conditions.

Productivity and quality-of-work-life background

Projects to improve productivity and the quality of work life (QWL) were originally developed in Europe during the 1950s. Based on the research of Eric Trist and his colleagues at the Tavistock Institute of Human Relations in London, this approach examined the technical and human sides of organisations and how they interrelated.[26] It led to the development of the sociotechnical systems[27] methods of work design that underlie many of the employee involvement and empowerment efforts occurring in Australia today.

Early practitioners in the United Kingdom, Ireland, Norway and Sweden developed work designs that were aimed at better integrating technology and people. These QWL programs generally involved joint participation by unions and management in the design of work, and resulted in work designs that gave employees high levels of discretion, task variety and feedback about results. Perhaps the most distinguishing characteristic of these QWL programs was the development of self-managing work groups as a new form of work design. These groups were composed of multiskilled workers who were given the necessary autonomy and information to design and manage their own task performances.

In Australia today, top management keeps employees motivated by a combination of good financial rewards, an interesting environment and challenging projects. The staff are also given feedback about their own work and kept informed about the company's situation.

Gradually, QWL programs expanded beyond individual jobs to include group forms of work and other features of the workplace that can affect employee productivity and satisfaction, such as reward systems, work flows, management styles and the physical work environment. This expanded focus resulted in larger-scale and longer-term projects than the early job-enrichment programs and shifted attention beyond the individual worker to work groups and the larger work context. Equally importantly, it added the critical dimension of organisational efficiency to what had been up to that time a predominant concern for the human dimension. The economic and human-resource problems that faced Australia during the 1980s have further reinforced this focus upon organisational efficiency.

At one point, the productivity and QWL approach became so popular that it was called an ideological movement. International conferences were aimed at identifying a coalition of groups from among unions and management that supported QWL ideals of employee involvement, participative management and industrial democracy. Some Australian companies adopted the Japanese method of management and employee participation, which involved the spread of quality circles. Ford was one such company. Popularised in Japan, quality circles are groups of employees trained in problem-solving methods who meet regularly to resolve work environment, productivity and quality-control concerns and to develop more efficient ways of working.

Finally, the productivity and QWL approach has gained new momentum by joining forces with the total quality movement advocated by W. Edward Deming[28] and Joseph Juran.[29] In this approach, the organisation is viewed as a set of processes that can be linked to the quality of products and services, modelled through statistical techniques and continuously improved.[30] Quality efforts at Toyota, Sheraton and Ericsson, along with federal government support through the establishment of the Business Excellence Awards, have popularised this strategy of organisation development.

Application 1.3 identifies that more than 1 million Australians work from home – and most would not do it any other way. This revolution in the way we work has profound implications for business and the economy.

1.3

APPLICATION

Join the home office revolution

For much of the Industrial Revolution, the workplace was seen as necessarily separate from the usual boundaries between industrial and domestic environments. However, many of the usual boundaries between industrial and domestic environments are beginning to dissolve.

Twenty-one per cent of businesses in Australia operate from home, the Australian Bureau of Statistics says. It estimates that there are 856,200 home businesses, but combines fully home-based businesses with people who are spending some time working from home. Farms are also included.

A more realistic figure is about 700,000 home businesses, plus 2.6 million Australians who work from home at least some of the time, Jane Shelton, managing director of Marshall Place Associates and author of *No Workplace like Home* (Wilkinson Publishing, 2008), says.

The social, economic and policy implications are profound. The dividing line between family and work life is blurred, redefining social roles. The methods of production become looser, requiring a rethink of traditional economic ideas of labour productivity, which are based on output in relation to traditional work patterns (38 hours at the workplace). It also creates new ways in which businesses find and serve customers, and home businesses are themselves a new type of potential customer.

Not that establishing a home business is necessarily easy. It represents the paradox of freedom. Practitioners get to make up their own rules, but that freedom can easily become a form of tyranny, the oppression of too much choice.

The level of satisfaction in home businesses that survive tends to be high. A survey by social researchers Colmar and Brunton shows only a fifth of home-business owners would consider moving out of their home, and owners of those businesses that have been established for more than a decade are even less likely to consider it.

There are also far-reaching policy implications, although home business has largely emerged without commentary or changes of thinking from government. It is an indication that the 'old industrial state' is on its last legs, Marshall Place Associates chairman Colin Benjamin argues. 'It is invisible to the economic modeller,' he says, adding that home business is growing fast. 'We will be building infrastructure in the home that was previously stuck in institutions – and that has far-reaching implications for national communications and industry systems.'

'. . . it is a difficult sector,' Micro and Home Business Association chief executive Jonathan Brake observes. 'One of the frustrations of government is that [home businesses] are very hard to find. They don't stick their head up because they are often worried about having it shot off. They just like to keep it simple. Plus, they don't have the time to network and socialise like other businesses. But the sector is enormous. You find them in every industry – even mining – and in every business type. The commonalities are usually interpersonal. Isolation is a big one. When you are working all day from home often you don't get out at all.'

Brake lists some obvious advantages of working from home: no commuting, increased flexibility, lower cost overheads, potentially less workplace stress, and more options in managing family and work life. The disadvantages are that it is often hard to manage time and maintain a demarcation between home and work.

'Often the work spreads out onto the dining room table', he says. 'Local councils can also be an issue. There is an instance of a woman on the Gold Coast who sells Tupperware from home who is getting slugged with a big levy from the local council because of cars outside her home. The governmental issues tend to be state and local, rather than federal. Local councils need to come up with a co-ordinated approach to these guys rather than just seeing them as people to be slugged with levies.'

. . .

The emergence of home businesses is more than a socio-economic curiosity. It is redolent of deep changes to the business landscape. Home businesses typically find it easier to be simultaneously local and global because of new communications technology. The emphasis shifts to economies of scope, rather than economics scale.

Source: David James, 'Join the home office revolution', *Business Review Weekly*, February 2010.

Critical thinking questions:
1. Comment on how successful home businesses could be in the future. Can you anticipate any difficulties? Why/why not?
2. Colin Benjamin is quoted as saying 'We will be building infrastructure in the home that was previously stuck in institutions – and that has far-reaching implications for national communications and industry systems.' Identify some of the implications referred to by Colin Benjamin. How might they be resolved?

Strategic change background

The strategic change background is a recent influence on the evolution of OD. As organisations and their technological, political and social environments became more complex and more uncertain, the scale and intricacies of organisational change increased. This trend has produced the need for a strategic perspective from OD and has encouraged planned change processes at the organisation level.[31]

Strategic change involves improving the alignment in an organisation's environment, strategy and organisation design.[32] Strategic change interventions include efforts to improve both the organisation's relationship to its environment and the fit between its technical, political and cultural systems.[33] The need for strategic change is usually triggered by some major disruption to the organisation, such as the lifting of regulatory requirements, a technological breakthrough or a new CEO from outside the organisation.[34]

One of the first applications of strategic change was Richard Beckhard's use of open systems planning.[35] He proposed that an organisation's environment and its strategy could be described and analysed. Based on the organisation's core mission, the differences between what the environment demanded and how the organisation responded could be reduced and performance improved. Since then, change agents have proposed a variety of large-scale or strategic change models.[36] Each of these models recognises that strategic change involves multiple levels of the organisation and a change in its culture, that it is often driven from the top by powerful executives and that it has important impacts on performance.

The strategic change background has significantly influenced OD practice. For example, the implementation of strategic change requires OD practitioners to be familiar with competitive strategy, finance and marketing, as well as team building, action research and survey feedback. Together, these skills have improved OD's relevance to organisations and their managers.

EVOLUTION IN ORGANISATION DEVELOPMENT

Current practice in organisation development is strongly influenced by these five backgrounds, as well as by the trends that shape change in organisations. The laboratory training, action research and survey feedback, and participative management roots of OD are evident in the strong value focus that underlies its practice. The more recent influences (the quality-of-work-life and strategic change backgrounds) have greatly improved the relevance and rigour of OD practice. They have added financial and economic indicators of effectiveness to OD's traditional measures of work satisfaction and personal growth.

Today, the field is being influenced by the globalisation and information technology trends described earlier. OD is being carried out in many more countries and in many more organisations that operate on a worldwide basis, and this is generating a whole new set of interventions as well as adaptations of traditional OD practice.[37] In addition, OD must adapt its methods to the technologies now being used in organisations. As information technology continues to influence organisational environments, strategies and structures, OD will need to manage change processes in cyberspace as well as face to face in the workplace. The diversity of this evolving discipline has led to tremendous growth in the number of professional practitioners, in the kinds of organisations involved with OD and in the range of countries within which OD is practised.

The expansion of the OD network is one indication of this growth. OD divisions have been set up by many training and development organisations, and courses are being taught at Australian universities at postgraduate and undergraduate levels; for example, the Australian Graduate School of Management (University of NSW) offers the Graduate Certificate in Change Management.[38]

In addition to the growth of professional societies and educational programs in OD, the field continues to develop new theorists, researchers and practitioners who are building on the work of the early pioneers and extending it to contemporary issues and conditions. Included among the first generation of contributors are Chris Argyris, who developed a learning and action–science approach to OD;[39] Warren Bennis, who tied executive leadership to strategic change;[40] Edgar Schein, who continues to develop process approaches to OD, including the key role of organisational culture in change management;[41] Richard Beckhard, who focused attention on the importance of managing transitions;[42] and Robert Tannenbaum, who continues to sensitise OD to the personal dimension of participants' lives.[43]

Among the second generation of contributors are Warner Burke, whose work has done much to make OD a professional field;[44] Larry Greiner, who has brought the ideas of power and evolution into the mainstream of OD;[45] Edward Lawler III, who has extended OD to reward systems and employee involvement;[46] Newton Margulies and Anthony Raia, who together have kept attention on the values underlying OD and what they mean for contemporary practice;[47] and Peter Vaill and Craig Lundberg, who continue to develop OD as a practical science.[48]

Included in the newest generation of OD contributors are Dave Brown, whose work on action research and developmental organisations has extended OD into community and societal change;[49] Thomas Cummings, whose work on sociotechnical systems, self-designing organisations and transorganisational development has led OD beyond the boundaries of single organisations to groups of organisations and their environments;[50] Max Widen, whose international work in industrial democracy draws attention to the political aspects of OD;[51] William Pasmore and Jerry Porras, who have done much to put OD on a sound research and conceptual base;[52] and Peter Block, who has focused attention on consulting skills, empowerment processes and reclaiming our individuality.[53]

Other newcomers who are making important contributions to the field include Ken Murrell and Joanne Preston, who have focused attention on the internationalisation of OD;[54] Sue Mohrman and Gerry Ledford, who have explored team-based organisations and compensation;[55] and David Cooperrider, who has turned our attention towards the positive aspects of organisations.[56] In Australia there are such centres as the Centre for Corporate Change in the Australian Graduate School of Management at the University of New South Wales and the Centre for Workplace Culture Change at RMIT University, both of which have actively contributed to the body of research. These academic contributors are joined by a large number of internal OD practitioners and external consultants who lead organisational change, such as the Australian Institute of Training and Development.[57]

Many different organisations have undertaken a wide variety of OD efforts. Many organisations have been at the forefront of innovating new change techniques and methods, as well as new organisational forms. Larger corporations that have engaged in organisation development include General Electric, General Motors, Ford, Corning Glass Works, Intel, Hewlett-Packard, Polaroid, Procter & Gamble and IBM. Traditionally, much of this work was considered confidential and not publicised. Today, however, organisations have increasingly gone public with their OD efforts, sharing the lessons with others.

Organisation development work is also being done in schools, communities and local, state and federal governments. A system that encourages staff at Casey Institute of Technical and Further Education (TAFE) to learn from one another has won its designer, Stuart Williams, a prestigious individual achievement recognition award from the Australian Human Resources Institute (AHRI). It requires all departments to provide six hours of training to fellow staff members annually.[58] The University of Technology in Sydney (UTS) is awarding testamurs to employees of AMP who sign up for its workplace-based program. Described as a revolutionary step by AMP management, the initiative is designed to assess work performance in terms of academic criteria. The award courses, from the faculties of business or mathematical and computer sciences, are based on performance agreements negotiated between AMP, UTS and the employee.[59]

Organisation development is increasingly international. As well as in South-East Asia, it has been applied in the United States, Canada, Sweden, Norway, Germany, Japan, Israel, South Africa, Mexico, Venezuela, the Philippines, China (including Hong Kong), Russia and the Netherlands. These efforts have involved such organisations as Saab (Sweden), Norsk Hydro (Norway), Imperial Chemical Industries (England), Shell Oil Company (Netherlands), Orrefors (Sweden) and Alcan Canada Products.

Although it is evident that OD has vastly expanded in recent years, relatively few of the total number of organisations in Australia are actively involved in formal OD programs. However, many organisations are applying OD approaches and techniques without knowing that such a term exists.

THE RISE OF ORGANISATION TRANSFORMATION

As a result of external forces, for example the GFC, there has been a need to respond quickly in order to anticipate negative consequences and/or capture an opportunity for advancement. Later chapters (see Chapters 9–11) explain how organisation transformation (OT) is often perceived as a 'quick fix' and observable, which may even receive significant coverage in the media as a result. It is also very evident in international contexts where the environment may be unpredictable and planning would be difficult.

This kind of change is often termed revolutionary, as distinct from evolutionary, OD. As a consequence, the alignment with factors (including internationalisation, environment and technology) will vary depending mainly in external forces, whereas OD predominantly has an internal focus. It also requires a different leadership style which would be more directional and/or charismatic, whereas OD requires a more transactional approach.

Despite the energy and resourcing commitment required in an OT change process, organisations naturally desire to 'return' to a stable state. Therefore OT strategies tend to be short-term with the intention to stabilise in the long term reverting back to using OD methodologies.

Summary

This chapter begins with general observations about change management and utilises organisation development (OD) as a vehicle to familiarise ourselves with the terminology. Organisation transformation (OT) will be covered in more detail in later chapters and the reader will expect to be introduced to various global perspectives as well as being challenged to anticipate the future direction of change management.

Book overview

This book presents the process and practice of organisation development in a logical flow, as shown in Figure 1.5 (p. 25). In Part 1, Chapter 1 provides a comprehensive overview of organisation development (OD) that describes the process of planned change, those who perform the transition and the various types of interventions. It also introduces the concept of organisation transformation (OT). Part 2 covers an overview of change processes and concepts. In particular, Chapter 2 defines the term 'planned change' in the context of OD. All approaches to OD rely on some theory about planned change. Three theories are described and compared, and the chapter presents a general model of planned change that integrates recent conceptual developments in OD. Finally, several critiques of planned change are presented. Chapter 3 examines the people who perform OD in organisations and their role as leaders in change. A closer look at OD practitioners provides a more personal perspective on the field, and assists in the understanding of the essential character of OD as a helping profession, involving personal relationships between OD practitioners and organisation members. Chapter 4 presents two contentious issues facing change management practitioners:

resistance to change which is an inevitable response to any attempt to change and fitting their organisational strategies, structures and processes to different organisational cultures. Chapter 5 presents an overview of the design, implementation and evaluation of interventions currently used in OD. It describes an intervention as a set of planned activities intended to help an organisation improve its performance and effectiveness. Effective interventions are designed to fit the needs of the organisation, are based on causal knowledge of intended outcomes and transfer competence to manage change to organisation members.

The book continues with Part 3 which gives further details regarding OD interventions. Chapter 6 describes interventions that enable organisations to change themselves continually. These change processes are particularly applicable for organisations facing turbulent environments where traditional sources of competitive advantage erode quickly. Chapter 7 discusses change programs relating to OD interventions in particular people and processes. These change programs are among the earliest in organisation development and represent attempts to improve people's working relationships with one another. The interventions are aimed at helping group members to assess their interactions and to devise more effective ways of working together. Chapter 8 is concerned with interventions that are aimed at organisation and environment relationships. These change programs are relatively recent additions to the OD field that focus on helping organisations to relate better to their environments, and to achieve a better fit with those external forces that affect goal achievement and performance.

Part 4 presents the various views of OT. Chapter 9 presents interventions for transforming organisations, that is, for changing the basic character of the organisation including how it is structured and how it relates to its environment. These frame-breaking and sometimes revolutionary interventions go beyond improving the organisation incrementally, focusing instead on changing the way it views itself. Chapter 10 describes the practice of change management in a chaotic and unpredictable environment which is exhibited in international settings. It presents the contingencies and practice issues associated with change in organisations outside the host country, in worldwide organisations and in global social change organisations. Chapter 11 describes transformation interventions that help organisations implement strategies for both competing and collaborating with other organisations. They focus on helping organisations position themselves strategically in their social and economic environments and achieve a better fit with the external forces affecting goal achievement and performance.

Finally, Part 5 contains the concluding Chapter 12 which described three trends within OD and four trends driving change in OD's context. The future of OD is likely to be the result of the interactions among the traditional, pragmatic and scholarly trends as well as how the global economy evolves, technology develops, workforces engage and organisations structure themselves.

FIGURE 1.5 Overview of the book

Part 1 Introduction

Chapter 1
Introduction

Part 2 The Environment of Change

Chapter 2
Understanding change

Chapter 3
Leadership and the role of the change agent

Chapter 4
Managing resistance and organisational culture

Chapter 5
The process of organisational change

Part 3 Organisation Development

Chapter 6
Organisation development and change

Chapter 7
OD interventions: People and process

Chapter 8
OD interventions: Strategy and structure

Part 4 Organisation Transformation

Chapter 9
Organisation transformation and change

Chapter 10
Change in a chaotic and unpredictable environment

Chapter 11
Competitive and collaborative strategies

Part 5 The Future of Change Management

Chapter 12
Future directions: Change in a global setting

Part 6 Integrative Case Studies

Activities

REVIEW QUESTIONS

1 Define organisation development and organisation transformation. How are they different? Is it possible for these approaches to coexist? Why? Why not?

2 Organisation development attempts to help an organisation cope with various aspects of the organisation's environment. What are these aspects? Give current examples of OD and explain its value to the organisation.

3 What role does behavioural science play in OD? Is it an important element of OD?

4 What is the assumption that underlies the use of survey feedback in OD? Why is it important to distinguish this from other forms of survey? What is the value of survey feedback in an action research approach to change?

5 What aspects distinguish OD from business planning, technological innovation and organisation evolution?

6 What is productivity? What factors have an effect on productivity? Give current examples of these factors.

7 With what functional considerations do practitioners need to be familiar if they are to create strategic change? Strategic change has often been confused with organisation transformation – why has that been the case?

8 Why should one study OD? What are the major contributions OD can bring to an organisation?

DISCUSSION AND ESSAY QUESTIONS

1 Discuss the value of planned change and explain why it is necessary. Use examples throughout your response to support your understanding.

2 Compare and contrast the five 'stems' of organisation development: laboratory training, action research/survey feedback, participative management, quality of work life and strategic change. Include in your answer the circumstances that are most conducive to the success of these strategies.

3 Outline the key events in the history and evolution of organisation development. What do you see to be the future directions of the field? How would you suggest that practitioners proactively promote or facilitate the evolution of OD?

4 Identify a company/corporation that has undergone or is undergoing organisational development or change. Identify the steps taken and, with the benefit of hindsight, make recommendations to improve the process.

5 Table 1.1 provides five definitions of organisation development. Which, from your perspective, offers the most informative insight into this concept? Why?

6 There are many forms of consulting which seek to assist organisations improve their operations such as management consulting, BPR, best practice, TQM, etc. Is OD different to these forms? If so, how?

Search me! Excercises

Explore **Search me! management** for relevant articles on change management. Search me! is an online library of world-class journals, e-books and newspapers, including *The Australian* and *The New York Times*, and is updated daily. Log in to Search me! through **http://login.cengage.com** using the access card in the front of this book.

Keywords

Try searching for the following terms:
> Action research
> Behavioural science
> Change management
> Organisation development

> Organisation transformation
> Participative management
> Planned change

>> *Search tip:*

Search me! management contains information from both local and international sources. To get the greatest number of search results, try using both Australian and American spellings in your searches, e.g. 'globalisation' and 'globalization'; 'organisation' and 'organization'.

Notes

1 R. Seel, Welcome to New Paradigm Organisation Consulting (Norfolk, UK: 2008), www.new-paradigm.co.uk/index.htm.

2 D. Waddell, *E-business in Australia: Concepts and Cases* (Sydney: Pearson Education Australia, 2002): 23.

3 Incremental and Transformational Change (Innovations Case Discussion: Better Place), Fall, 4, 4, (November 2009): 141–3, www.mitpressjournals.org/doi/abs/10.1162/itgg.2009.4.4.141?journalCode=itgg.

4 M. Tushman and C. O'Reilly, 'Ambidextrous organisations: managing evolutionary and revolutionary change', *California Management Review*, 28 (Summer 1996): 11.

5 K. V. Siakas and E. Georgiadou, *Process Improvement: The Societal Iceberg*, University of North London and Technological Educational Institution of Thessaloniki, 2002, www.iscn.at/select_newspaper/people/unl.htm, cited 15 June 2010.

6 C. D. Lee, *Understanding Complex Ecologies in a Changing World* (Washington, DC, USA: American Educational Research Association, March 2010).

7 W. Burke, *Organization Development: Principles and Practices* (Boston, MA: Little Brown, 1982).

8 W. French, 'Organization development: objectives, assumptions, and strategies', *California Management Review*, 12 (February 1969): 23–34.

9 R. Beckhard, *Organization Development: Strategies and Models* (Reading, MA: Addison-Wesley, 1969).

10 M. Beer, *Organization Change and Development: A Systems View* (Santa Monica, CA: Goodyear Publishing, 1980).

11 D. Dunphy and D. Stace, *Beyond the Boundaries* (Sydney: McGraw-Hill, 1994).

12 *Technological Innovation and Cooperation for Foreign Information Access*, US Department of Education, www.ed.gov/about/offices/list/ope/iegps, cited 10 June 2010.

13 J. Naisbitt and P. Aburdene, *Re-inventing the Corporation* (New York: Warner Books, 1985); N. Tichy and M. Devanna, *The Transformational Leader* (New York: John Wiley and Sons, 1986); R. Kilmann and T. Covin, eds, *Corporate Transformation: Revitalizing Organizations for a Competitive World* (San Francisco: Jossey-Bass, 1988); T. Peters, *Thriving on Chaos: Handbook for a Management Revolution* (New York: Alfred A. Knopf, 1987); J. Kotter, *Leading Change* (Cambridge, MA: Harvard Business School Press, 1996).

14 T. Stewart, 'Welcome to the revolution', *Fortune* (13 December 1993): 66–80; C. Farrell, 'The new economic era', *Business Week* (18 November 1994).

15 B. Sims, 'Sustainable Power Corp., L.Sole' agrees to form strategic alliance', June 2008, www.biomassmagazine.com/article.jsp?article_id=1704.

16 L. Bradford, 'Biography of an institution', *Journal of Applied Behavioural Science*, 3 (1967): 127; A. Marrow, 'Events leading to the establishment of the National Training Laboratories', *Journal of Applied Behavioural Science*, 3 (1967): 145–50.

17 A. Carnevale, 'The work place realities – in the new global workplace, what exactly do employees need and employers want?', American Association of School Administrators, February 2008, http://archives.aasa.org/publications/saarticledetail.cfm?ItemNumber=9739&snItemNumber=950&tnItemNumber=1995.

18 W. French, 'The emergence and early history of organization development with reference to influences upon and interactions among some of the key actors', in *Contemporary Organization Development: Current Thinking and Applications*, ed. D. Warrick (Glenview, IL: Scott, Foresman, 1985): 12–27.

19 ibid.: 19–20.

20 F. Mann, 'Studying and creating change', in *The Planning of Change: Readings in the Applied Behavioural Sciences*, eds W. Bennis, K. Benne and R. Chin (New York: Holt, Rinehart and Winston, 1962): 605–15.

21 R. Likert, *The Human Organization* (New York: McGraw-Hill, 1967); S. Seashore and D. Bowers, 'Durability of organizational change', *American Psychologist*, 25 (1970): 227–33; D. Mosley, 'System Four revisited: some new insights', *Organization Development Journal*, 5 (Spring 1987): 19–24.

22 ibid.

23 M. Arab, M. Tajvar and F. Akbari, 'Selection an appropriate leadership style to direct hospital manpower', *Iranian Journal of Public Health*, 35: 3 (2006): 64–9, http://diglib.tums.ac.ir/pub/magmng/pdf/2560.pdf, cited 12 June 2010.

24 C. Chambers Clark, *Creative Nursing Leadership & Management*, Jones & Bartlett Learning, 2009, http://books.google.com.au/books?id=yLS4qe3YS3QC&pg=PA9&lpg=PA9&dq=Benevolent+authoritative&source=bl&ots=xT5lygWAJ1&sig=qDaddOh-wsB2tZ4_CvBkpLQy4uY&hl=en&ei=lw0fTL6DOYnRcYjFeIM&sa=X&oi=book_result&ct=result&resnum=9&ved=0CDgQ6AEwCA#v=onepage&q=Benevolent%20authoritative&f=false.

25 ibid.

26 A. Rice, *Productivity and Social Organisation: The Ahmedabad Experiment* (London: Tavistock Publications, 1958); E. Trist and K. Bamforth, 'Some social and psychological consequences of the longwall method of coal-getting', *Human Relations*, 4 (January 1951): 1–38.

27 J. Husband, 'Will enterprise 2.0 drive management innovation?', April 2008, www.theappgap.com/will-enterprise-20-drive-management-innovation.html.

28 M. Walton, *The Deming Management Method* (New York: Dodd, Mead and Company, l986).

29 J. Juran, *Juran on Leadership for Quality: An Executive Handbook* (New York: Free Press, 1989).

30 'The quality imperative', *Business Week*, Special Issue (25 October 1991).

31 M. Jelinek and J. Litterer, 'Why OD must become strategic', in *Research in Organizational Change and Development*, 2, eds W. Pasmore and R. Woodman (Greenwich, CT: JAI Press, 1988): 135–62; P. Buller, 'For successful strategic change: blend OD practices with strategic management', *Organizational Dynamics* (Winter 1988): 42–55; C. Worley, D. Hitchin and W. Ross, *Integrated Strategic Change* (Reading, MA: Addison-Wesley, 1996).

32 Worley, Hitchin and Ross, *Integrated Strategic Change*, op. cit.

33 R. Beckhard and R. Harris, *Organizational Transitions: Managing Complex Change*, 2nd edn (Reading, MA: Addison-Wesley, 1987); N. Tichy, *Managing Strategic Change* (New York: John Wiley and Sons, 1983); E. Schein, *Organizational Culture and Leadership* (San Francisco: Jossey-Bass, 1985); C. Lundberg, 'Working with culture', *Journal of Organization Change Management*, 1 (1988): 38–47.

34 D. Miller and P. Freisen, 'Momentum and revolution in organisation adaptation', *Academy of Management Journal*, 23 (1980): 591–614; M. Tushman and E. Romanelli, 'Organizational evolution: a metamorphosis model of convergence and reorientation', in *Research in Organizational Behaviour*, 7, eds L. Cummings and B. Staw (Greenwich, CT: JAI Press, 1985): 171–222.

35 Beckhard and Harris, *Organizational Transitions*, op. cit.

36 T. Covin and R. Kilmann, 'Critical issues in large scale organization change', *Journal of Organization Change Management*, 1 (1988): 59–72; A. Mohrman, S. Mohrman, G. Ledford Jr, T. Cummings and E. Lawler, eds, *Large Scale Organization Change* (San Francisco: Jossey-Bass, 1989); W. Torbert, 'Leading organizational transformation', in *Research in Organization Change and Development*, 3, eds R. Woodman and W. Pasmore (Greenwich, CT: JAI Press, 1989): 83–116; J. Bartunek and M. Louis, 'The interplay of organization development and organization transformation', in *Research in Organizational Change and Development*, 2, eds W. Pasmore and R. Woodman (Greenwich, CT: JAI Press, 1988): 97–134; A. Levy and U. Merry, *Organizational Transformation: Approaches, Strategies, Theories* (New York: Praeger, 1986).

37 A. Jaeger, 'Organization development and national culture: where's the fit?' *Academy of Management Review*, 11 (1986): 178; G. Hofstede, *Culture's Consequences: International Differences in Work-Related Values* (London: Sage, 1980); P. Sorensen Jr, T. Head, N. Mathys, J. Preston and D. Cooperrider, *Global and International Organization Development* (Champaign, IL: Stipes, 1995).

38 www2.agsm.edu.au.

39 C. Argyris and D. Schon, *Organizational Learning* (Reading, MA: Addison-Wesley, 1978); C. Argyris, R. Putnam and D. Smith, *Action Science* (San Francisco: Jossey-Bass, 1985).

40 W. Bennis and B. Nanus, *Leaders* (New York: Harper and Row, 1985).

41 E. Schein, *Process Consultation: Its Role in Organization Development* (Reading, MA: Addison-Wesley, 1969); E. Schein, *Process Consultation, 2: Lessons for Managers and Consultants* (Reading, MA: Addison-Wesley, 1987); E. Schein, *Organizational Culture and Leadership*, 2nd edn (San Francisco: Jossey-Bass, 1992).

42 Beckhard and Harris, *Organizational Transitions*, op. cit.

43 R. Tannenbaum and R. Hanna, 'Holding on, letting go, and moving on: understanding a neglected perspective on change', in *Human Systems Development*, eds R. Tannenbaum, N. Margulies and F. Massarik (San Francisco: Jossey-Bass, 1985): 95–121.

44 W. Burke, *Organization Development: Principles and Practices* (Boston: Little, Brown, 1982); W. Burke, *Organization Development: A Normative View* (Reading, MA: Addison-Wesley, 1987); W. Burke, 'Organization development: then, now, and tomorrow', *OD Practitioner*, 27 (1995): 5–13.

45 L. Greiner and V. Schein, *Power and Organizational Development: Mobilizing Power to Implement Change* (Reading, MA: Addison-Wesley, 1988).

46 E. Lawler III, *Pay and Organization Development* (Reading, MA: Addison-Wesley, 1981); E. Lawler III, *High-Involvement Management* (San Francisco: Jossey-Bass, 1986).

47 A. Raia and N. Margulies, 'Organization development: issues, trends, and prospects', in *Human Systems Development*, eds R. Tannenbaum, N. Margulies and F. Massarik (San Francisco: Jossey-Bass, 1985): 246–72; N. Margulies and A. Raia, 'Some reflections on the values of organizational development', *Academy of Management OD Newsletter*, 1 (Winter 1988): 9–11.

48 P. Vaill, 'OD as a scientific revolution', in *Contemporary Organization Development: Current Thinking and Applications* (Glenview, IL: Scott, Foresman, 1985): 28–41; C. Lundberg, 'On organisation development interventions: a general systems–cybernetic perspective', in *Systems Theory for Organisational Development*, ed. T. Cummings (Chichester: John Wiley and Sons, 1980): 247–71.

49 L. Brown and J. Covey, 'Development organizations and organization development: toward an expanded paradigm for organization development', in *Research in Organizational Change and Development*, l, eds R. Woodman and W. Pasmore (Greenwich, CT: JAI Press, 1987): 59–87.

50 T. Cummings and S. Srivastva, *Management of Work: A Socio-Technical Systems Approach* (San Diego: University Associates, 1977); T. Cummings, 'Transorganizational development', in *Research in Organizational Behaviour*, 6, eds B. Staw and L. Cummings (Greenwich, CT: JAI Press, 1984): 367–422; T. Cummings and S. Mohrman, 'Self-designing organizations: towards implementing quality-of-work-life innovations', in *Research in Organizational Change and Development*, 1, eds R. Woodman and W. Pasmore (Greenwich, CT: JAI Press, 1987): 275–310.

51 M. Widen, 'Sociotechnical systems ideas as public policy in Norway: empowering participation through worker managed change', *Journal of Applied Behavioural Science*, 22 (1986): 239–55.

52 W. Pasmore, C. Haldeman and A. Shani, 'Sociotechnical systems: a North American reflection on empirical studies in North America', *Human Relations*, 32 (1982): 1179–204; W. Pasmore and J. Sherwood, *Sociotechnical Systems: A Source Book* (San Diego: University Associates, 1978); J. Porras, *Stream Analysis: A Powerful Way to Diagnose and Manage Organizational Change* (Reading, MA: Addison-Wesley, 1987); J. Porras, P. Robertson and L. Goldman, 'Organization development: theory, practice, and research', in *Handbook of Industrial and Organizational Psychology*, 2nd edn, ed. M. Dunnette (Chicago: Rand McNally, 1990).

53 P. Block, *Flawless Consulting* (Austin, TX: Learning Concepts, 1981); P. Block, The Empowered Manager: *Positive Political Skills at Work* (San Francisco: Jossey-Bass, 1987); P. Block, *Stewardship* (San Francisco: Berrett-Koehler, 1994).

54 K. Murrell, 'Organization development experiences and lessons in the United Nations development program', *Organization Development Journal*, 12 (1994): 1–16; J. Vogt and K. Murrell, *Empowerment in Organizations* (San Diego: Pfeiffer and Company, 1990); J. Preston and L. DuToit, 'Endemic violence in South Africa: an OD solution applied to two educational settings', *International Journal of Public Administration*, 16 (1993): 1767–91; J. Preston, L. DuToit and I. Barber, 'A potential model of transformational change applied to South Africa', in *Research in Organizational Change and Development*, 9 (Greenwich, CT: JAI Press, in press).

55 S. Mohrman, S. Cohen and A. Mohrman, *Designing Team-Based Organizations* (San Francisco: Jossey-Bass, 1995); S. Cohen and G. Ledford Jr, 'The effectiveness of self-managing teams: a quasi-experiment', *Human Relations*, 47 (1994): 13–43; G. Ledford and E. Lawler, 'Research on employee participation: beating a dead horse?', *Academy of Management Review*, 19 (1994): 633–6; G. Ledford, E. Lawler and S. Mohrman, 'The quality circle and its variations', in Productivity in *Organizations: New Perspectives from Industrial* and *Organizational Psychology*, eds J. Campbell, R. Campbell and associates (San Francisco: Jossey-Bass, 1988); A. Mohrman, G. Ledford Jr, S. Mohrman, E. Lawler III and T. Cummings, *Large Scale Organization Change* (San Francisco: Jossey-Bass, 1989).

56 D. Cooperrider and T. Thachankary, 'Building the global civic culture: making our lives count', in *Global and International Organization Development*, eds P. Sorensen Jr, T. Head, N. Mathys, J. Preston and D. Cooperrider (Champaign, IL: Stipes, 1995): 282–306; D. Cooperrider, 'Positive image, positive action: the affirmative basis for organising', in Appreciative Management and Leadership, eds S. Srivastva, D. Cooperrider and associates (San Francisco, CA: Jossey-Bass, 1990); D. Cooperrider and S. Srivastva, 'Appreciative inquiry in organizational life', in *Organizational Change and Development*, 1, eds R. Woodman and W. Pasmore (Greenwich, CT: JAI Press, 1987): 129–70.

57 S. Marinos, 'Getting down to business beyond 2000', *The Age* (24 February 1998): 6.

58 C. Rance, 'Recognition for Casey learning system', *The Age* (20 September 1997): 12.

59 A. Hepworth, 'Yearning for more learning', *Australian Financial Review* (5 June 1984): 4.

PART 2

THE ENVIRONMENT OF CHANGE

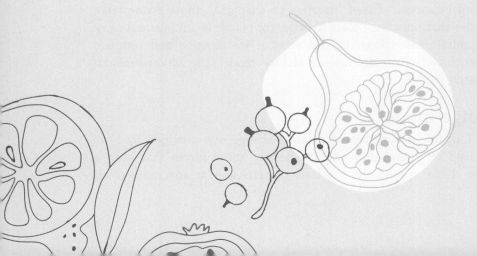

CHAPTER 2

Understanding change

The increasing pace of global, economic and technological development makes change an inevitable feature of organisational life. However, change that happens to an organisation can be distinguished from change that is planned by organisation members. In this book, the term 'change' will generally refer to planned change. Organisation development[1] (OD) is directed at bringing about planned change in order to increase an organisation's effectiveness. It is generally initiated and implemented by managers, often with the help of an OD practitioner from inside or outside the organisation. Organisations can use planned change to solve problems, to learn from experience, to adapt to external environmental changes, to improve performance and to influence future changes.

All approaches to OD rely on some theory about planned change. These theories describe the different stages through which planned change[2] may be effected in organisations and explain the temporal process of applying OD methods to help organisation members manage change. In this chapter, we first describe and compare three major theories of organisation change: Lewin's change model, the action research model, and the positive model. These three approaches, which have received considerable attention in the field, offer different concepts of planned change. Next we present a general model of planned change that integrates the earlier models and incorporates recent conceptual developments in OD. This model has broad applicability to many types of planned change efforts. We then discuss different types of change and how the process can vary according to the change situation. Finally, several critiques of planned change are presented.

THEORIES OF PLANNED CHANGE

Conceptions of planned change have tended to focus on how change can be implemented in organisations.[3] Called 'theories of changing', these frameworks describe the activities that must take place in order for people to initiate and carry out successful organisational change. In this section, we describe and compare three different theories of changing: Lewin's change model, the action research model and the positive model.

Lewin's change model

One of the early fundamental models of planned change was provided by Kurt Lewin.[4] He conceived of change as a modification of those forces that keep a system's behaviour stable; specifically, the level of behaviour at any moment in time is the result of two sets of forces: those striving to maintain the status quo and those pushing for change. When both sets of forces are about equal, current levels of behaviour are maintained in what Lewin termed a state of 'quasi-stationary equilibrium'. To change that state, one can increase those forces pushing for change, decrease those forces that maintain the current state or apply some combination of both. For example, the level of performance of a work group might be stable because group norms maintaining that level are equivalent to the supervisor's pressures for change to higher levels. This level can be increased either by changing the group norms to support higher levels of performance or by increasing supervisor pressures to produce at higher levels. Lewin suggested that modifying those forces that maintain the status quo produces less tension and resistance than increasing forces for change, and consequently is a more effective strategy for change.

Lewin viewed this change process as consisting of three steps, which are shown in Figure 2.1(A):

1   *Unfreezing.* This step usually involves reducing those forces that maintain the organisation's behaviour at its present level. Unfreezing is sometimes accomplished through a process of 'psychological disconfirmation'. By introducing information that shows discrepancies between the behaviours desired by organisation members and those behaviours currently exhibited, members can be motivated to engage in change activities.[5]

2   *Moving.* This step shifts the behaviour of the organisation, department or individual to a new level. It involves the development of new behaviours, values and attitudes through changes in organisational structures and processes.

3   *Refreezing.* This step stabilises the organisation at a new state of equilibrium. It is frequently accomplished through the use of supporting mechanisms that reinforce the new organisational state, such as organisational culture, norms, policies and structures.

Lewin's model provides a general framework for understanding organisational change. Because the three steps of change are relatively broad, considerable effort has gone into elaborating on them. For example, the planning model (developed by Lippitt, Watson and Westley) arranges Lewin's model into seven steps: scouting, entry, diagnosis (unfreezing), planning, action (movement), stabilisation and evaluation, and termination (refreezing).[6] This model remains closely identified with the field of OD, however, and is used to illustrate how other types of change can be implemented. For example, Lewin's three-step model has been used to explain how information technologies can be implemented more effectively.[7]

Action research model

The action research model[8] focuses on planned change as a cyclical process in which initial research about the organisation provides information to guide subsequent action. Then the results of the action are assessed to provide further information that will guide further action, and so on. This iterative cycle of research and action involves considerable collaboration between organisation members and OD practitioners. It places heavy emphasis on data gathering and diagnosis prior to action planning and implementation, as well as careful evaluation of the results after action has been taken.

Action research is traditionally aimed both at helping specific organisations to implement planned change and at developing more general knowledge that can be applied to other settings.[9] Although action research was originally developed to have this dual focus on change and knowledge, it has been adapted to OD efforts in which the major emphasis is on planned change.[10] Figure 2.1(B) shows the cyclical phases of planned change as defined by the action research model. There are eight main steps:

1 *Problem identification.* This stage usually begins when a key executive in the organisation, or someone with power and influence, senses that the organisation has one or more problems that might be alleviated with the help of an OD practitioner. In one case, the quality manager of an electronics plant had been involved with OD before, but it took her almost a year to persuade the plant manager to bring in a consultant.

2 *Consultation with a behavioural science expert.* During the initial contact, the OD practitioner and the client carefully assist each other. The practitioner has his or her own normative, developmental theory or frame of reference and must be conscious of those assumptions and values.[11] Sharing them with the client from the beginning establishes an open and collaborative atmosphere.

3 *Data gathering and preliminary diagnosis.* This stage is usually completed by the OD practitioner, often in conjunction with organisation members. It involves gathering appropriate information and analysing it to determine the underlying causes of organisational problems. The four basic methods of gathering data are interviews, process observation, questionnaires and organisational performance data (unfortunately, often overlooked). One approach to diagnosis begins with observation, proceeds to a semistructured interview and concludes with a questionnaire to measure precisely the problems identified by the earlier steps.[12] When gathering diagnostic information, it is possible that OD practitioners may influence members from whom they are collecting data. In OD, 'every action on the part of the ... consultant constitutes an intervention' that will have some effect on the organisation.[13]

4 *Feedback to key client or group.* Because action research is a collaborative activity, the diagnostic data are fed back to the client, usually in a group or work-team meeting. The feedback step, in which members are given the information gathered by the OD practitioner, helps them to determine the strengths and weaknesses of the organisation or the department under study. The consultant provides the client with all relevant and useful data. Obviously,

FIGURE 2.1 Comparison of planned change models

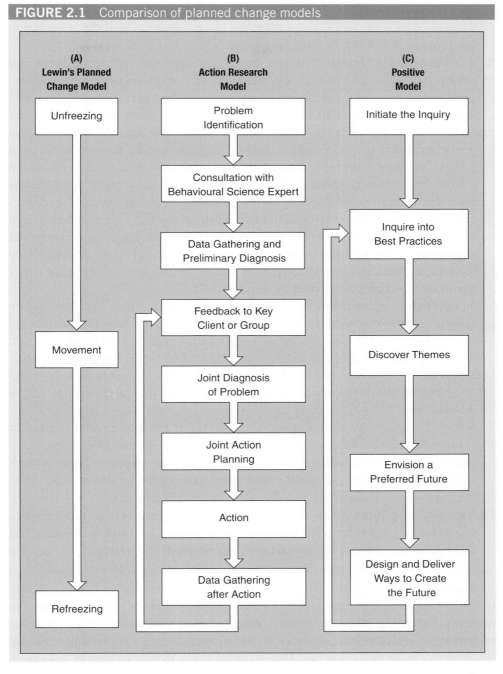

(A)
Lewin's Planned Change Model

Unfreezing

Movement

Refreezing

(B)
Action Research Model

Problem Identification

Consultation with Behavioural Science Expert

Data Gathering and Preliminary Diagnosis

Feedback to Key Client or Group

Joint Diagnosis of Problem

Joint Action Planning

Action

Data Gathering after Action

(C)
Positive Model

Initiate the Inquiry

Inquire into Best Practices

Discover Themes

Envision a Preferred Future

Design and Deliver Ways to Create the Future

Source: Thomas Cummings and Christopher Worley, *Organization Development and Change*, 9th edn, South-Western (with InfoTrac® College Edition Printed Access Card), a part of Cengage Learning Inc. (2009): 25. Reproduced by permission, www.cengage.com/permissions.

the practitioner will protect those sources of information and, at times, withhold data if the group is not ready for the information or if the information would make the client overly defensive.

5 *Joint diagnosis of problem.* At this point, members discuss the feedback and explore with the OD practitioner whether they want to work on identified problems. A close interrelationship exists among data gathering, feedback and diagnosis as the consultant summarises the basic data from the client members and presents the data to them for validation and further diagnosis. An important point to remember, as Schein suggests, is that the action research process is very different from the doctor–patient model, in which the consultant comes in, makes a diagnosis and prescribes a solution. Schein notes that the failure to establish a common frame of reference in the client–consultant relationship may lead to faulty diagnosis or to a communications gap whereby the client is sometimes 'unwilling to believe the diagnosis or accept the prescription'. He believes 'most companies have drawers full of reports by consultants, each loaded with diagnoses and recommendations which are either not understood or not accepted by the "patient".[14]

6 *Joint action planning.* Next, the OD practitioner and the client members jointly agree on further actions to be taken. This is the beginning of the moving process (described in Lewin's change model), as the organisation decides on how best to reach a different quasi-stationary equilibrium. At this stage, the specific action to be taken depends on the culture, technology and environment of the organisation; the diagnosis of the problem; and the time and expense of the intervention.

7 *Action.* This stage involves the actual change from one organisational state to another. It may include installing new methods and procedures, reorganising structures and work designs, and reinforcing new behaviours. These actions typically cannot be implemented immediately, but require a transition period as the organisation moves from the present to a desired future state.[15]

8 *Data gathering after action.* Because action research is a cyclical process, data must also be gathered after the action has been taken in order to measure and determine the effects of the action and to feed the results back to the organisation. This, in turn, may lead to rediagnosis and new action.

Application 2.1 suggests that a conversion model of franchising has to be right from the beginning for a business in a tough economic climate. It demonstrates the necessity for careful planning at the outset, constant monitoring of the business environment and continual review of the appropriateness of the organisational structure as circumstances change. Also, planning needs to take account of the nature of the relationships between participants and ensure adequate consultation occurs between affected parties when change in organisational structure/relationships is being considered.

The conversion model

There are more than 1500 franchise systems in Australia, operating in almost every business sector, and due to the tough economic climate many businesses have been looking at converting their operations to a franchising model...

Franchising often offers a solution for businesses looking to find new ways to expand... However, there are questions to be asked when considering a franchising model. First, can the business be franchised? Usually the answer is yes. In fact, any business that operates under management can be franchised. The second question is: should the business be franchised? Due diligence is required to ensure that a franchise model will deliver the financial return it needs in order to survive. If the answer to the first two questions is yes, then the third question is: how will the business be franchised? That is the most important question and there is no one way to do it.

There are infinite ways to go about modelling a franchise operation. It comes down to understanding the market, evaluating and getting the balance right between the number of system-owned operations and fully franchised operations and then working out the financial structure. This includes how the franchises get their remuneration, whether through royalties, commissions, flat fees or profit share.

How much each franchise is expected to return to the system for management, training, marketing and the other centrally provided services forms the basis for differentiating franchising from other businesses.

... Evaluating the market is vital, as is understanding that not all franchises succeed. Yum!Brands, the largest food franchise operator in the world, has twice tried to enter the Australian market with Taco Bell without success... the key principles of an agreement have to be in place at day one. Every franchise will evolve in terms of marketing and product but it is very hard to make changes to territory or contracts once you are some way down the track.

...the recent high-profile failure of several franchise systems shows the importance of getting the business model right...the collapse of the kitchen appliance retailer Kleenmaid Group, which was placed under the control of liquidators in May owing about $102 million to creditors... Kleenmaid's model was not in the usual mould, they had a very high proportion of company-owned stores. When the bank looked at the business, the franchised stores did far better. In this model the franchisees did not own a share of profit and were on a royalty base. The franchisees were more like sales agents. Unfortunately, when the administrators moved in the operation could not work on a franchise model any longer...

Another example is the case of Samsara, a Brisbane-headquartered Asian furniture retailer. The operation got into difficulty and administrators were appointed in May this year. The company had a complex ownership structure and each of the franchisees had a different agreement with the franchisor. This created confusing and difficult-to-manage arrangements.

However, others have found the establishment of a franchising model has saved their business and promoted growth. Electronics supplier Strathfield Group went into administration earlier this year, and it emerged as a franchised operation, selling off the various stores to franchisee partners and building on the network's established reach. Another successful move to franchising was taken by Ella Baché, which had been a chain of retail outlets. Franchising involved, in many cases, the sale of outlets to the operators plus the addition of franchisee operations in new areas. This gave the operators a greater say in the marketing and structure of the operation.

...the franchising model stands out because it does not suffer as much in downturns. The co-operative nature of marketing and the ability to adapt business-to-market trends gives the model agility for survival. Greater control over suppliers, over pricing, marketing and general flexibility is all done on a scale well beyond a stand-alone business. The network can support individuals when circumstances change.

...the bulky goods retail Clark Rubber, which had many discretionary stock items such as swimming pools and outdoor furnishings... bought out three franchisees in stores that were not in good profitable shape and closed the stores. The franchisor took on more responsibility for the back office and they did the right thing to share the risk. The company adapted the product and services range to match the market and the move paid off. They have had the best four-month start to any year. Two of the stores have reopened.

...in challenging times, the business with a plan and tight financial and management controls will do better, but it is important to note that franchising will not make a bad business better. The fact is that running a franchise is far more complex than running your own stand-alone business. You have to manage your franchisees, who are often independently minded people who are running their own businesses, they are not employees.

Source: Tony Blackie, 'The conversion model', *Business Review Weekly*, June 2009, p. 36.

Critical thinking questions:
1. If you were a consultant engaged by Samsara to improve its business model as a franchised business, how would you apply the action research model outlined above? What are the key issues you would explore?
2. Tony Blackie observes, 'You have to manage your franchisees, who are often independently minded people who are running their own businesses, they are not employees'. What are the implications of this statement for the relationship between the franchisor and the franchisee? How do they impact on your recommendations flowing from your answer to the first question above?

Contemporary adaptations to action research

The action research model underlies most current approaches to planned change and is often identified with the practice of OD. Action research has recently been extended to new settings and applications, and consequently researchers and practitioners have made the requisite adaptations to its basic framework.[16]

Trends in the application of action research include the movement from smaller sub-units of organisations to total systems and communities.[17] In these larger contexts, action research is more complex and political than in smaller settings. Therefore, the action research cycle is co-ordinated across multiple change processes and includes a diversity of stakeholders who have an interest in the organisation.

Action research is also increasingly being applied in international settings, particularly in developing nations in the southern hemisphere.[18] Embedded within the action research model, however, are Western assumptions about change. For example, action research traditionally views change more linearly than Eastern cultures, and it treats the change process more collaboratively than Latin American and African countries.[19] To achieve success in these settings, action research needs to be tailored to fit the organisations' cultural assumptions.

Finally, action research is increasingly being applied to promote social change and innovation.[20] This is demonstrated most clearly in community-development and global social-change projects.[21] These applications are heavily value-laden and seek to redress imbalances in power and resource allocations across different groups. Action researchers tend to play an activist role in the change process, which is often hectic and conflicted.

In view of these general trends, contemporary applications of action research have substantially increased the degree of member involvement in the change process. This contrasts with traditional approaches to planned change where consultants carried out most of the change activities, with the agreement and collaboration of management.[22] Although consultant-dominated change still persists in OD, there is a growing tendency to involve organisation members in learning about their organisation and how to change it. Referred to as 'participatory action research',[23] 'action learning',[24] 'action science'[25] or 'self-design',[26] this approach to planned change emphasises the need for organisation members to learn about it first-hand if they are to gain the knowledge and skills to change the organisation. In today's complex and changing business environment, some argue that OD must go beyond solving particular problems to helping members gain the necessary competence to continually change and improve the organisation.[27]

In this modification of action research, the role of OD consultants[28] is to work with members to facilitate the learning process. Both parties are 'co-learners' in diagnosing the organisation, designing changes and implementing and assessing them.[29] Neither party dominates the change process. Rather, each participant brings unique information and expertise to the situation, and together they combine their resources to learn how to change the organisation. Consultants, for example, know how to design diagnostic instruments and OD interventions, while organisation members have 'local' knowledge about the organisation and how it functions. Each participant learns from the change process. Organisation members learn how to change their organisation, to refine and improve it. OD consultants learn how to facilitate complex organisational change and learning.

The positive model

The third model of change, the positive model, is the promotion of a 'positive' approach to planned change.[30] This model focuses on what the organisation is doing right. It represents an important departure from Lewin's model and the action research process, which are primarily deficit based, focusing on the organisation's problems and how they can be solved so it functions better. This application of planned change helps members understand their organisation when it is working at its best and builds off those capabilities to achieve even better results. This positive approach to change suggests that all organisations are to some degree effective and that planned change should focus on the 'best of what is'.[31] It is consistent with a growing movement in the social sciences called 'positive organisational scholarship', which focuses on positive dynamics in organisations that give rise to extraordinary outcomes.[32] Considerable research on expectation effects supports this positive approach to planned change.[33] It suggests that people tend to act in ways that make their expectations occur; a positive vision of what the organisation can become can energise and direct behaviour to make that expectation come about.

The positive model has been applied to planned change primarily through a process called appreciative inquiry (AI).[34] As a 'reformist and rebellious' form of social constructionism, appreciative inquiry explicitly infuses a positive value orientation into analysing and changing organisations.[35] Social constructionism assumes that organisation members' shared experiences and interactions influence how they perceive the organisation and behave in it.[36] Because such shared meaning can determine how members approach planned change, appreciative inquiry encourages a positive orientation towards how change is conceived and managed. It promotes broad member involvement in creating a shared vision about the organisation's positive potential. Because members are heavily involved in creating the vision, they are committed to changing the organisation in that direction.

The positive model of planned change involves five phases that are depicted in Figure 2.1(C).

1 *Initiate the inquiry.*[37] This first phase determines the subject of change. It emphasises member involvement to identify the organisational issue they have the most energy to address. For example, members can choose to look for successful male-female collaboration (as opposed to sexual discrimination), instances of customer satisfaction (as opposed to customer dissatisfaction), particularly effective work teams, or product development processes that brought new ideas to market especially fast. If the focus of inquiry is real and vital to organisation members, the change process itself will take on these positive attributes.

2 *Inquiry into best practices.*[38] This phase involves gathering information about the 'best of what is' in the organisation. If the topic is organisational innovation, then members help to develop an interview protocol that collects stories of new ideas that were developed and implemented in the organisation. The interviews are conducted by organisation members; they interview each other and tell stories of innovation in which they have personally been involved. These stories are pulled together to create a pool of information describing the organisation as an innovative system.

3 *Discover the themes.* Here, members examine the stories, both large and small, to identify a set of themes representing the common dimensions of people's experiences. For example, the stories of innovation may contain themes about how managers gave people the freedom to explore a new idea, the support organisation members received from their co-workers, or how the exposure to

customers sparked creative thinking. No theme is too small to be represented; it is important that all of the underlying mechanisms that helped to generate and support the themes are described. The themes represent the basis for moving from 'what is' to 'what could be'.

4   *Envision a preferred future.* Members then examine the identified themes, challenge the status quo, and describe a compelling future. Based on the organisation's successful past, members collectively visualise the organisation's future and develop 'possibility propositions' – statements that bridge the organisation's current best practices with ideal possibilities for future organising. These propositions should present a truly exciting, provocative and possible picture of the future. Based on these possibilities, members identify the relevant stakeholders and critical organisation processes that must be aligned to support the emergence of the envisioned future. The vision becomes a statement of 'what should be'.

5   *Design and deliver ways to create the future.*[39] The final phase involves the design and delivery of ways to create the future. It describes the activities and creates the plans necessary to bring about the vision. It proceeds to action and assessment phases similar to those of action research described previously. Members make changes, assess the results, make necessary adjustments and so on as they move the organisation towards the vision and sustain 'what will be'. The process is continued by renewing the conversations about the best of what is.

Yesterday's organisational structure is not necessarily appropriate for today's business environment. Markets change as do client needs. Businesses need to ensure that their structures and skill sets are relevant to contemporary needs. To successfully implement change, it is vital that management is fully consulted and involved in the identification of market opportunities and planning of effective changes to take advantage of those opportunities. Application 2.2 presents an accounting firm, Deloitte, which takes a positive approach to restructure its private client practice in anticipation of economic recovery.

2.2

APPLICATION

Deloitte – positive approach to private practice

The smallest of the big four accounting firms has begun restructuring its private client practice to focus on the investment objectives of cashed-up private business.

'We are going to have a big team that focuses only on private business because I am convinced of the role it is going to play as this recovery emerges,' Deloitte's chief executive officer Giam Swiegers told the *Australian Financial Review*. 'A lot of family businesses are very well cashed up and will require specialist skills.'

Before rolling out the new strategy in June 2009, Deloitte's private-client business was serviced by Deloitte Growth Solutions, which also looked after unlisted smaller companies. Under the changes, the majority of the 58 partners in DGS's Sydney, Melbourne, Parramatta and Canberra offices will join a new practice area to be called Deloitte Private.

...Mr Swiegers said the change followed a two-day conference in early May in Sydney attended by partners from DGS to identify opportunities in the middle market.

>>

... 'Our belief is that, as the economy starts turning, private businesses in Australia are going to be some of the big winners because they have not been under the same scrutiny and same pressures as publicly listed companies,' Mr Swiegers said. 'After two years, we are going to see people who have made very serious money in this country buying real bargains. We are betting a lot of our money on making sure we know how to serve private business.'

Source: Mark Fenton-Jones, 'Deloitte – positive approach to private practice', *The Australian Financial Review*, June 2009, p. 53.

Critical thinking questions:
1. Which of the change models discussed above would be best suited to the Deloitte situation? Why?
2. A vital element in any successful change situation is appropriately managing the interests of the people involved. The article intimates that not all DGS partners will be transferred to the new organisation. What are the considerations you would need to have in mind as you addressed the interests of both groups?

Comparisons of change models

All three models – Lewin's change model,[40] the action research model and the positive model – describe the phases by which planned change occurs in organisations. As shown in Figure 2.1, the models overlap in that their emphases on action to implement organisational change is preceded by a preliminary stage (unfreezing, diagnosis or initiate the inquiry) and is followed by a closing stage (refreezing or evaluation). Moreover, all three approaches emphasise the application of behavioural science knowledge, involve organisation members in the change process and recognise that any interaction between a consultant and an organisation constitutes an intervention that may affect the organisation. However, Lewin's change model differs from the other two in that it focuses on the general process of planned change, rather than on specific OD activities.

Lewin's model and the action research model differ from the positive approach in terms of the level of involvement of the participants and the focus of change. Lewin's model and traditional action research models emphasise the role of the consultant with limited member involvement in the change process. Contemporary applications of action research and the positive model, on the other hand, treat both consultants and participants as co-learners who are heavily involved in planned change. In addition, Lewin's model and action research are more concerned with fixing problems than with focusing on what the organisation does well, and leveraging those strengths.

GENERAL MODEL OF PLANNED CHANGE

The three theories outlined above suggest a general framework for planned change, as shown in Figure 2.2. The framework describes the four basic activities that practitioners and organisation members jointly carry out in organisation development.

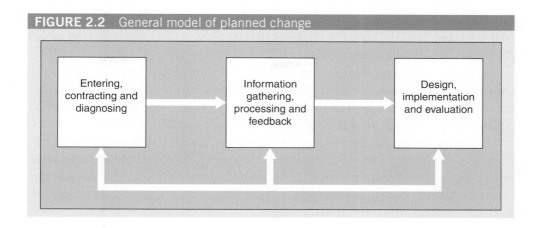

FIGURE 2.2 General model of planned change

The arrows connecting the different activities in the model show the typical sequence of events, from entering and contracting, to diagnosing, to planning and implementing change, to evaluating and institutionalising change. The lines connecting the activities emphasise that organisational change is not a straightforward, linear process, but involves considerable overlap and feedback among the activities. These four major change activities are discussed in more detail in Chapter 5.

Entering and contracting

The first set of activities in planned change concerns entering and contracting. They help managers decide whether they want to engage further in a planned change program and commit resources to such a process. Entering an organisation involves gathering initial data to understand the problems or opportunities facing the organisation. Once this information has been collected, the problems are discussed with managers and other organisation members in order to develop a contract or agreement to engage in planned change. The contract spells out future change activities, the resources that will be committed to the process, and how OD practitioners and organisation members will be involved. In many cases, organisations do not get beyond this early stage of planned change, because disagreements about the need for change surface, resource constraints are encountered or other methods for change appear more feasible. When OD is used in non-traditional and international settings, the entering and contracting process must be sensitive to the context in which the change is taking place.

Diagnosing

In this stage of planned change, the client system is carefully studied. Diagnosis can focus on understanding organisational problems, including their causes and consequences, or on identifying the organisation's positive attributes. The diagnostic process is one of the most important activities in OD. It includes choosing an appropriate model for understanding the organisation, and gathering, analysing and feeding back information to managers and organisation members about the problems or opportunities.

Diagnostic models for analysing problems explore three levels of activities. Organisation problems represent the most complex level of analysis and involve the total system. Group-level problems are associated with departmental and group effectiveness, and individual-level problems involve how jobs are designed.

Gathering, analysing and feeding back data are the central change activities in diagnosis. Chapter 5 describes how data can be gathered through interviews, observations, survey instruments or from archival sources such as meeting minutes and organisation charts. It also explains how data can be reviewed and analysed, and the process of feeding back diagnostic data is described. Organisation members, often in collaboration with an OD practitioner, jointly discuss the data and their implications for change.

Planning and implementing change

In this stage, organisation members and practitioners jointly plan and implement OD interventions. They design interventions to improve the organisation and make action plans to implement them. As discussed in Chapter 6, there are several criteria for designing interventions, including the organisation's readiness for change, its current change capability, its culture and power distributions, and the change agent's skills and abilities. Depending upon the outcomes of diagnosis, there are four major types of interventions in OD. Chapter 7 describes human process interventions at the individual, group and total system levels. Chapter 8 presents interventions that modify an organisation's structure and technology. Chapter 9 addresses human resource interventions that seek to improve member performance and wellness. Chapter 10 describes strategic interventions. These change programs involve managing the organisation's relationship to its external environment and the internal structure and processes necessary to support a business strategy.

Implementing interventions is concerned with managing the change process. It includes motivating change, creating a desired future vision of the organisation, developing political support, managing the transition towards the vision and sustaining momentum for change.

Evaluating and institutionalising change

This last stage in planned change involves an evaluation of the effects of the intervention and management of the institutionalisation of successful change programs. Feedback to organisation members about the intervention's results provides information about whether the changes should be continued, modified or suspended. Institutionalising successful changes involves reinforcing them through feedback, rewards and training.

DIFFERENT TYPES OF PLANNED CHANGE

The general model of planned change describes how the OD process typically unfolds in organisations. In actual practice, the different phases are not nearly as orderly as the model implies. OD practitioners tend to modify or adjust the stages to fit the needs of the situation. Steps in planned change can be implemented in a variety of ways that depend on the client's needs and goals, the change agent's skills and values, and the organisation's context. Therefore, it is clear that planned change can vary enormously from one situation to another.

To understand these differences better, planned change can be contrasted across situations on two key dimensions: the magnitude of organisational change and the degree to which the client system is organised.

Magnitude of change

Planned change efforts can be characterised as falling along a continuum, ranging from incremental changes that involve fine-tuning the organisation to quantum changes that entail fundamentally altering how it operates.[41] Incremental changes tend to involve limited dimensions and levels of the organisation, such as the decision-making processes of work groups. They occur within the context of the organisation's existing business strategy, structure and culture, and are aimed at improving the status quo. Quantum changes, on the other hand, are directed at significantly altering how the organisation operates. They tend to involve several organisational dimensions, including structure, culture, reward systems, information processes and work design. They also involve changing multiple levels of the organisation, from top-level management through departments and work groups to individual jobs.

Planned change has traditionally been applied in situations that involve incremental change. Organisations in the 1960s and 1970s were mainly concerned with fine-tuning their bureaucratic structures by resolving many of the social problems that emerged with increasing size and complexity. In these situations, planned change involves a relatively bounded set of problem-solving activities. OD practitioners are typically contracted by managers to help solve specific problems in particular organisational systems, such as poor communication among members of a work team or high absenteeism among shop floor employees in a production facility. Diagnostic and change activities tend to be limited to these issues, although additional problems may be uncovered and may need to be addressed. Similarly, the change process tends to focus on those organisational systems that have specific problems, and it generally ends when the problems are resolved. Of course, the change agent may be contracted to help solve additional problems.

In recent years, OD has been increasingly concerned with quantum change. As described in Chapter 1, the greater competitiveness and uncertainty of today's business environment have caused a growing number of organisations to drastically alter the way in which they operate. In these situations, planned change is more complex, extensive and long term than when applied to incremental change.[42] Because quantum change involves most features and levels of the organisation, it is typically driven from the top of the organisation, where corporate strategy and values are set. Change agents help senior managers create a vision of a desired future organisation and energise movement in that direction. They also help executives develop structures for managing the transition from the present to the future organisation. This may include, for example, a variety of overlapping steering committees and redesign teams. Staff experts may also redesign many features of the organisation, such as performance measures, rewards, planning processes, work designs and information systems.

Because of the complexity and extensiveness of quantum change,[43] OD professionals often work in teams that consist of members with different yet complementary expertise. The consulting relationship persists over relatively long time periods and includes a great deal of renegotiation and experimentation among consultants and managers. The boundaries of the change effort are more uncertain and diffuse than in incremental change, making diagnosis and change seem more like discovery than problem solving. (Complex strategic and transformational types of change are described in more detail in Chapters 9, 10 and 11.)

It is important to emphasise that quantum change may or may not be developmental in nature. Organisations may drastically alter their strategic direction and way of operating without significantly developing their capacity to solve problems and achieve both high performance and quality of work life. For example, firms may simply change their marketing mix, dropping or adding products, services or customers; they may drastically downsize by cutting out marginal businesses and laying off managers and workers; or they may tighten managerial and financial controls and attempt to squeeze more out of the labour force. On the other hand, organisations may undertake quantum change from a developmental perspective. They may seek to make themselves more competitive by developing their human resources, by getting managers and employees more involved in problem solving and innovation, and by promoting flexibility and direct, open communication. This OD approach to quantum change is particularly relevant in today's rapidly changing and competitive environment. To succeed in this setting, organisations such as Australia Post, the Australian Taxation Office and the Department of Defence are transforming themselves from control-oriented bureaucracies to high-involvement organisations capable of continually changing and improving themselves.

Degree of organisation

Planned change efforts can also vary according to the degree to which the organisation or client system is organised. In overorganised situations, such as in highly mechanistic, bureaucratic organisations, various dimensions such as leadership styles, job designs, organisation structure, and policies and procedures are too rigid and overly defined for effective task performance. Communication between management and employees is typically suppressed, conflicts are avoided and employees are apathetic. In underorganised organisations, on the other hand, there is too little constraint or regulation for effective task performance. Leadership, structure, job design and policy are ill-defined and fail to control task behaviours effectively. Communication is fragmented, job responsibilities are ambiguous and employees' energies are dissipated because of lack of direction. Underorganised situations are typically found in such areas as product development, project management and community development, where relationships among diverse groups and participants must be co-ordinated around complex, uncertain tasks.

In overorganised situations, where historically much of OD practice has taken place, planned change is generally aimed at loosening constraints on behaviour. Changes in leadership, job design, structure and other features are designed to liberate suppressed energy, to increase the flow of relevant information between employees and managers, and to promote effective conflict resolution. The typical steps of planned change – entry, diagnosis, intervention and evaluation – are intended to penetrate a relatively closed organisation or department and make it increasingly open to self-diagnosis and revitalisation. The relationship between the OD practitioner and the management team attempts to model this loosening process. The consultant shares leadership of the change process with management, encourages open communication and confrontation of conflict, and maintains flexibility when relating to the organisation.

When applied to organisations that face problems because of being underorganised, planned change is aimed at increasing organisation by clarifying leadership roles, structuring communication between managers and employees, and specifying job and departmental responsibilities. These activities require a modification of the traditional phases of planned change and include the following four stages:[44]

1 *Identification.* This step identifies the relevant people or groups that need to be involved in the change program. In many underorganised situations, people and departments can be so disconnected that there is uncertainty about who should be included in the problem-solving process. For example, managers of different departments who have only limited interaction with each other might disagree or be confused about which departments should help to develop a new product or service.

2 *Convention.* In this phase, the relevant people or departments in the company are brought together to begin organising for task performance. For example, department managers might be asked to attend a series of organising meetings to discuss the division of labour and the co-ordination required to introduce a new product.

3 *Organisation.* Different organising mechanisms are created to structure the newly required interactions among people and departments. They might include creating new leadership positions, establishing communication channels and specifying appropriate plans and policies.

4 *Evaluation.* In this final step the outcomes of the organisation phase are assessed. The evaluation might signal the need for adjustments in the organising process or for further identification, convention and organisation activities.

By carrying out these four stages of planned change in underorganised situations, the relationship between the OD practitioner and the client system attempts to reinforce the organising process. The consultant develops a well-defined leadership role, which might be autocratic during the early stages of the change program. Similarly, the consulting relationship is clearly defined and tightly specified. In effect, the interaction between the consultant and the client system supports the larger process of bringing order to the situation.

Application 2.3 cautions that Qantas's design-focused strategy may not be as successful as Qantas executives would like it to be, due to a fierce price war between airlines.

2.3

APPLICATION

Ahead in the clouds

Unbearably cramped and excruciatingly boring. That's the reality of international jet travel for the passengers at the back of the plane. The judges of the Australian International Design Awards think locally born master designer Marc Newson may have changed that. On May 29, they awarded his design for Qantas' Airbus A380 economy seat the top gong. Some industry experts believe the high-profile win may help Qantas defend margins on its long-haul routes in the current cutthroat operating environment. If so, it will vindicate the airline's investment in design as a strategy for all seasons, and not just boom times.

Newson's biomorphic economy seat…boasts numbers of innovations, including … the design of the seat's structure which is considerably lighter, leading to fuel and cost savings …

The airline appointed Newson as its creative director in 2003, and he has designed high-profile products, including the Skybed and the Qantas First Lounges in Melbourne and Sydney, as well as every aspect of its A380 fit-out, from the seating plan to its lighting scheme.

… Newson's appointment and Qantas' design strategy was conceived in the heady days of endless economic sunshine. Now the airline is competing in the toughest operating environment in living memory. Will Qantas' design-centric focus help the airline defend its margins, or is it a costly extravagance that will have to be trimmed?

'Our investment in design is a key objective to differentiate ourselves from the rest of the airlines,' Qantas' executive manager of customer and marketing, Lesley Grant, says. '[As part of] our vision to be the world's best premium airline, we are seeking to have a cohesive, end-to-end experience. Integrating design means customers will feel that connection throughout the experience.'

British design consultant Keith Lovegrove is an expert on air carriers' use of design [who] says that an emphasis on design is a way of rendering an ethos of customer care in a visual way, and is crucial to an airline's competitive edge, because it is inimitable. 'The experience

>>

must be one of "this doesn't happen anywhere else, this is unique",' Lovegrove says. He comments: 'This only works if the experience runs through every element of customer service . . .'

Is this competitive edge somewhat blunted in a recession, when travel budgets are slashed and passenger numbers plummet? Lovegrove argues it is just as important to focus on design in a downturn. 'It is a great opportunity to entice some of that core market, however diminished it may be, while all around are slicing their design and marketing budgets. After all, design is marketing,' he says, 'To be visually sheepish in down times is to relinquish market leadership and damage customer confidence.'

Others are not so sure. When the global economy was booming, the design-focused strategy made sense. The International Air Transport Association says that premium tickets make up 7 per cent to 8 per cent of international passenger numbers, but 25 per cent of revenue.

The downturn has devastated the top end of the market. Qantas' passenger volumes at the front of the plane are reportedly down 30 per cent. At the same time, competition has increased and there is a fierce price war on formerly lucrative routes. In April, the airline's chief executive, Alan Joyce, announced it would have to sack about 1750 staff, ground planes and defer new aircraft orders. He cut the carrier's earnings forecast 80 per cent, its second downgrade in five months.

Does a design focus offer any protection to profits in a downturn? Peter Harbison, executive chairman of the Centre for Asia Pacific Aviation, says, 'Right now, price is the blinding light. People tend not to notice what they will be sitting on when they plan a trip.'

Qantas' Grant will not put a figure on any 'design dividend' the airline might earn from proprietary innovations such as the First Class Lounges or its plane seats. 'That's commercially sensitive for us,' she says. All she will reveal is that Qantas is seeing 'strong results' and that customer feedback on both has 'exceeded expectations'.

Nor will Grant comment on whether, in the current economic climate, design work will focus on the experience of its economy rather than business and first-class passengers. 'It's under constant review, with customer feedback and the competitive situation – you have to keep updating, making sure you are relevant,' Grant says.

Winning the Australian International Design of the Year Award will certainly garner some media coverage and a higher degree of consumer awareness about Qantas' new and improved economy seat. Harbison says this may increase Qantas' share of the very long-haul sectors, where comfort – or discomfort – still rates alongside price.

Harbison thinks that strength may be short-lived but whatever happens to Qantas' profits, economy passengers will be the winners. 'Design is highly valuable when it comes to major steps in comfort,' he says. '[But] it is hard to define the value today, when pricing is so important.' But he cautions, 'The great problem always in the airline business is also that imitation only takes a matter of a few months, or a year or so. Then the advantages are neutralised.'

Source: Gina McColl, 'Ahead in the clouds', *Business Review Weekly*, June 2009, pp. 40–1.

Critical thinking questions:
1. What is/are being changed in this example? What is the rationale for those changes?
2. What are the consequential changes flowing from the change/s identified in the first question?

Domestic versus international settings

Developed in Western societies, OD reflects the underlying values and assumptions of these cultural settings, including quality, involvement, and short-term time horizons. Under these conditions, it works quite well. In other societies, a different set of cultural values and assumptions can be operating and make the application of OD problematic. In contrast to Western societies, for example, the cultures of most Asian countries are more hierarchical and status conscious, less open to discussing personal issues, more concerned with 'saving face', and have a longer time horizon for results.[45] These cultural differences can make OD more difficult to implement, especially for practitioners from Western countries; they simply may be unaware of the cultural norms and values that permeate the society.

The cultural values that guide OD practice in Australia or the United States include, for example, equality among people, individuality, and achievement motives. An OD process that encourages openness among individuals, high levels of participation and actions that promote increased effectiveness is viewed favourably. The OD practitioner is also assumed to hold these values and to model them in the conduct of planned change. Most reported cases of OD involve Western-based organisations using practitioners trained in the traditional model, and raised and experienced in Western society.

When OD is applied outside of Western countries (and sometimes even within these settings), the action research process must be adapted to fit the cultural context. For example, the diagnostic phase, which is aimed at understanding the current drivers of organisation effectiveness, can be modified in a variety of ways. Diagnosis can involve many organisation members or include only senior executives, be directed from the top, conducted by an outside consultant or performed by internal consultants, or involve face-to-face interviews or organisational documents. Each step in the general model of planned change must be carefully mapped against the cultural context.

Conducting OD in international settings can be highly stressful on OD practitioners. To be successful, they must develop a keen awareness of their own cultural biases, be open to seeing a variety of issues from another perspective, be fluent in the values and assumptions of the host country, and understand the economic and political context of business in the host country. Most OD practitioners are not able to meet all of those criteria and should consider partnering with a 'cultural guide', often a member of the client organisation, to help navigate the cultural, operational and political nuances of change in that society.

CRITIQUE OF PLANNED CHANGE

Despite their continued refinement, the models and practices of planned change are still in a formative stage of development, and there is considerable room for improvement. Critics of OD[46] have pointed out several problems with the way planned change has been both conceptualised and practised.

Conceptualisation of planned change

Planned change typically has been characterised as involving a series of activities for carrying out effective change in organisations. Although current models outline a general set of steps that need to be followed, considerably more information is needed to guide how those steps should be performed in specific situations. In an extensive review and critique of planned change theory, Porras and Robertson argued that planned change activities should be guided by information about: (1) the organisational features that can be changed, (2) the intended outcomes from making those changes, (3) the causal mechanisms by which those outcomes are achieved, and (4) the contingencies upon which successful change depends.[47] In particular, they noted that the key to organisational change is change in the behaviour of each member and that the information available about the causal mechanisms that produce individual change is lacking. Overall, Porras and Robertson concluded that the information necessary for guiding change is only partially available and that a good deal more research and thinking are needed to fill the gaps.

Knowledge about how the stages of planned change differ across situations is a related area where current thinking about planned change is deficient. Most models specify a general set of steps that are intended to be applicable to most change efforts. The previous section of this chapter showed, however, how change activities can vary, depending on such factors as the magnitude of change and the degree to which the client system is organised. Considerably more effort needs to be expended on identifying situational factors that may require modification of the general stages of planned change. This would probably lead to a rich array of planned change models, each geared to a specific set of situational conditions. Such contingency thinking is sorely needed in planned change.

Planned change also tends to be described as a rationally controlled, orderly process. Critics have argued that, although this view may be comforting, it is seriously misleading.[48] They point out that planned change has a more chaotic quality, often involving shifting goals, discontinuous activities, surprising events and unexpected combinations of changes. For example, managers often initiate changes without clear plans that clarify their strategies and goals. As change unfolds, new stakeholders may emerge and demand modifications that reflect previously unknown or unvoiced needs. These emergent conditions make planned change a far more disorderly and dynamic process than is customarily portrayed, and conceptions need to capture this reality.

Finally, the relationship between planned change and organisational performance and effectiveness is not well understood. OD has traditionally had problems assessing whether interventions are, in fact, producing observed results.

The complexity of the change situation, the lack of sophisticated analyses and the long time periods for producing results have all contributed to a weak evaluation of OD efforts. In contrast, managers have often accounted for OD efforts with post-hoc testimonials, reports of possible future benefits and calls to support OD as the right thing to do.

In the absence of rigorous assessment and measurement, it is difficult to make resource-allocation decisions about change programs and to know which interventions are most effective in certain situations.

Practice of planned change

Critics have suggested that there are several problems with the way planned change is carried out.[49] These concerns are not with the planned change model itself, but with how change takes place and with the qualifications and activities of OD practitioners.

A growing number of OD practitioners have acquired skills in specific techniques such as team building, total quality management, large-group interventions or gain sharing, and have chosen to specialise in those methods. Although such specialisation may be necessary, given the complex array of techniques that make up modern OD, it can lead to a certain myopia. Some OD practitioners favour particular techniques and ignore other OD strategies that might be more appropriate. They tend to interpret organisational problems as requiring the favoured technique. Thus, for example, it is not unusual to see consultants pushing such methods as diversity training, re-engineering, organisation learning or self-managing work teams as solutions to most organisational problems.

Effective change depends upon a careful diagnosis of how the organisation is functioning. Diagnosis identifies the underlying causes of organisational problems, such as poor product quality and employee dissatisfaction. It requires both time and money, and some organisations are not willing to make the necessary investment. They rely on preconceptions about what the problem is and hire consultants with appropriate skills for solving it. Managers may think, for example, that work design is the problem and hire an expert in job enrichment to implement a change program. The problem, however, may be caused by other factors, such as poor reward practices, and job enrichment would be inappropriate. Careful diagnosis can help to avoid such mistakes.

In situations that require complex organisational changes, planned change is a long-term process involving considerable innovation and learning on-site. It requires a good deal of time and commitment and a willingness to modify and refine changes as the circumstances require. Some organisations demand more rapid solutions to their problems and seek 'quick fixes' from experts. Unfortunately, some OD consultants are more than willing to provide quick solutions. They sell pre-packaged programs that tend to be appealing to managers as they typically include an explicit recipe to be followed, standard training materials and clear time and cost boundaries. The quick fixes, however, have trouble gaining wide organisational support and commitment. They seldom produce the positive results that have been advertised.

Other organisations have not recognised the systemic nature of change. Too often, they believe that intervention into one aspect or unit of the organisation will be sufficient to ameliorate the problems. They are unprepared for the other changes that may be necessary to support a particular intervention. For example, at Mono Pumps in Melbourne the positive benefits of an employee involvement program did not begin to appear until after the organisation had redesigned its reward system to support the cross-functional collaboration necessary for solving highly complex problems. Changing any one part or feature of an organisation often requires adjustments in other parts in order to maintain an appropriate alignment. Thus, although quick fixes and change programs that focus on only one part or aspect of the organisation may resolve some specific problems, they generally do not lead to complex organisational change, or increase members' capacity to carry out change.[50]

Application 2.4 suggests that a number of companies in Australia had 'let too many people go' in the economic downturn of the global financial crisis (GFC), although there is likely to be an increase in demand for temporary staff.

2.4

APPLICATION

Contract workers in demand as bosses caught short

The permanent white-collar job market is still deteriorating but the end of the financial year could bring a fillip to contract workers, as companies seek to fill the gaps left by mass redundancies with short-term ad hoc appointments. The chairman of Ambition Group, Nick Waterworth, said businesses were continuing to shed workers, and were extremely reluctant to take on permanent employees.

'We won't see any increase in demand for permanent staff this year but we are likely to see an increase in demand for temp staff from next quarter,' Mr Waterworth said ... 'Once we're into the new financial year, some new budgets will be set and we'll see quite a lot of companies in the private sector who have let too many people go realise they haven't got enough pairs of hands.'

...The demands of end-of-financial year accounting may also result in some short-term job creation. 'Companies will need to draw on temp work to handle the year end but they will not be brave enough to put permanent staff on.' [Mr Waterworth also suggested]... 'We have six months to go before there is any chance of a permanent recovery in the white-collar market.'

The chief executive of Hamilton James & Bruce, Deborah Wilson, said some of her clients were considering taking on new permanent staff once they had their budgets for the 2009 financial year. But on the contract side of Ms Wilson's business, many large clients – including government departments – were seeking to renegotiate preferred supplier agreements to take advantage of the crippled employment market.

There was downward pressure on contractors' wages as these large organisations passed on the pressures of their slashed budgets. [Ms Wilson claimed] 'They'll say, "we have to remove $50 million in costs from the business, and you're part of it".' Some employers are seeking cost reductions of as much as 20 per cent, which means recruiters have to negotiate carefully with contractors about who absorbs the lowered revenues. 'The pain has to be shared,' Ms Wilson said. 'It may be a choice between working at a lower hourly rate or not working at all.'

... Employers were making savings now, but when the turnaround came, those who had screwed down contract rates would face a high turnover of staff as workers left for better pay and conditions. Mr Waterworth said business confidence was low and many employers had salaries on hold, either formally or informally. 'I don't think the fixed-term component of wages is going down but equally there are no drivers for [salaries] to go up,' he said. 'When you talk to senior people running big businesses, there is a great deal of confidence that we're in much better shape than in the early '90s, but, and it is a big but, everybody thinks unemployment will keep rising for another 12 months.'

But despite the illiquid local job market, skills shortages still existed ... Research sponsored by Manpower shows 49 per cent of Australian employers and 32 per cent of employers in the Asia-Pacific region struggle to fill some positions, despite the economic crisis.

Source: Jacqueline Maley, 'Contract workers in demand as bosses caught short', *Australian Financial Review*, June 2009, p. 4.

Critical thinking questions:
1. With the benefit of hindsight, how would you have responded to the global financial crisis?
2. Given a history of downs/ups in the local and international economies, would you have reacted to the GFC any differently to the situation outlined in the application?
3. In managing change, what are the trade-offs between employing permanent and casual staff? Do those trade-offs differ between various industry sectors?

The contingency approach to change management

Australian researchers Dexter Dunphy and Douglas Stace argue that change management should be approached from a situational perspective. Their argument for contingency is as follows:

> [D]ramatically different approaches to change can work in different circumstances ... turbulent times create varied circumstances and demand different responses according to the needs of the situation. What is appropriate for one organisation may not be appropriate for another. So we need a model of change ... that indicates how to carry change strategies to achieve optimum fit with the changing environment.[51]

As a result of some seven years' research into change management techniques in Australia, Dunphy and Stace have derived a model of change that incorporates both 'soft' and 'hard' approaches. The model is a two-dimensional matrix that categorises the scale of change (from fine-tuning OD to corporate transformation (CT)) and the style of management that needs to be employed to facilitate the change (from collaborative to coercive). Four process change strategies or typologies may be identified from these dimensions.[52] See Figure 2.3.

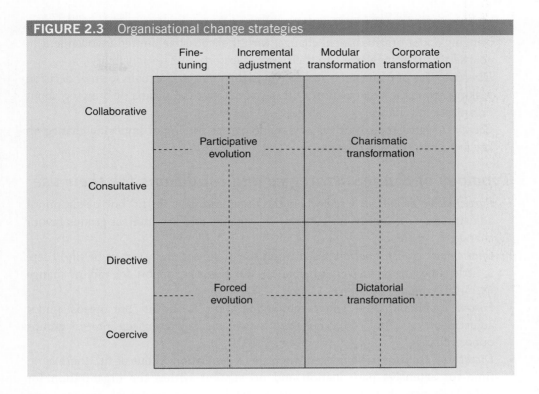

FIGURE 2.3 Organisational change strategies

Scale of change

- *Fine-tuning:* Organisational change that is an ongoing process characterised by fine-tuning of the 'fit' or match between the organisation's strategy, structure, people and processes. Such effort is typically manifested at departmental/divisional levels.
- *Incremental adjustment:* Organisational change that is characterised by incremental adjustments to the changing environment. Such change involves distinct modifications (but not radical change) to corporate business strategies, structures and management processes.
- *Modular transformation:* Organisational change that is characterised by major realignment of one or more departments/divisions. The process of radical change is focused on these subparts rather than on the organisation as a whole.
- *Corporate transformation:* Organisational change that is corporation-wide, characterised by radical shifts in business strategy and revolutionary changes throughout the whole organisation.

Style of management

- *Collaborative:* Widespread participation by employees in important decisions about the organisation's future and about the means of bringing about organisational change.

- *Consultative:* Consultation with employees, primarily about the means of bringing about organisational change, with their possible limited involvement in goal setting that is relevant to their area of expertise or responsibility.
- *Directive:* Use of managerial authority and direction as the main form of decision making about the organisation's future, and about the means of bringing about organisational change.
- *Coercive:* Managers/executives or outside parties forcing or imposing change on key groups in the organisation.

Typology of change strategies and conditions for their use

- *Participative evolution:* Used when the organisation is 'in fit' but needs minor adjustment, or is 'out of fit' but time is available and key interest groups favour change.
- *Charismatic transformation:* Used when the organisation is 'out of fit' and there is little time for extensive participation, but there is support for radical change within the organisation.
- *Forced evolution:* Used when the organisation is 'in fit' but needs minor adjustment, or is 'out of fit', but time is available. However, key interest groups oppose change.
- *Dictatorial transformation:* Used when the organisation is 'out of fit', there is no time for extensive participation and no support within the organisation for radical change, but radical change is vital to organisational survival and fulfilment of the basic mission.

As with any paradigm, Dunphy and Stace's model has created considerable debate. There certainly are positive and negative aspects and issues of resistance, politics, the unpredictability of environment, ethical considerations and the unique characteristics of particular groups.

Summary

Theories of planned change describe the activities that are necessary in order to modify strategies, structures and processes to increase an organisation's effectiveness. Lewin's change model, the action research model and the positive model offer different views of the phases through which planned change occurs in organisations.

Lewin's change model views planned change as a three-step process of unfreezing, movement and refreezing. It provides a general description of the process of planned change. The action research model focuses on planned change as a cyclical process involving joint activities between organisation members and OD practitioners. It involves eight sequential steps that overlap and interact in practice: problem identification, consultation with a behavioural science expert, data gathering and preliminary diagnosis, feedback to key client or group, joint diagnosis of the problem, joint action planning, action, and data gathering after action. The action research model places heavy emphasis on data gathering and diagnosis prior to action planning and implementation, as well as on the assessment of results after action has been taken. In addition, change strategies are often modified on the basis of continued diagnosis, and termination of one OD program may lead to further work in other areas of the organisation. Recent trends in action research include the movement from smaller to larger systems, from domestic to international applications and from organisational issues to social change. As the name suggests, the positive model focuses on all that is good about the organisation. This constructive approach utilises the processes that are working and builds on their strengths.

These theories can be integrated into a general model of planned change. Four sets of activities – entering and contracting, diagnosing, planning and implementing, and evaluating and institutionalising – can be used to describe how change is accomplished in organisations. The general model has broad applicability to planned change; it identifies the steps that an organisation typically moves through in order to implement change and specifies the OD activities necessary for effecting the change.

Although the planned change models describe general stages of how the OD process unfolds, there are different types of change according to the situation. Planned change efforts can vary in terms of the magnitude of the change and the degree to which the client system is organised. When situations differ on these dimensions, planned change can vary greatly. Critics of OD have pointed out several problems with the way planned change has been conceptualised and practised. They point out specific areas where planned change can be improved.

Activities

REVIEW QUESTIONS

1 Identify the people generally responsible for carrying out planned change efforts. What factors will influence who is allocated these responsibilities?

2 In Lewin's model of change, what brings about the proposed change? Explain why variations have to be made, over a period of time, to the original model.

3 Describe the three sequential steps in Lewin's change model. Give a current example where Lewin's model is evident.

4 What is action research and what is the 'first step'? What is the relationship between action research and organisation development?

5 Name the four basic steps in gathering data. What is the purpose of collecting that data?

6 Action research is described as a 'collaborative activity'. What are the key stages when joint client/ OD practitioner action is required?

7 What is the positive model of change? In what circumstances

should it be the preferred approach to OD?

8 What are the four steps involved in the general model of planned change?

9 What are the major problems associated with planned change efforts? Are there any problems that are more prevalent than others?

10 How useful is Dunphy and Stace's model when considering transformational change? What criticisms or reservations do you have about the model?

DISCUSSION AND ESSAY QUESTIONS

1 What is 'planned change' as compared to 'unplanned change'? Give current examples and critically evaluate their appropriateness.

2 This text comments 'Problem identification ... usually begins when a key executive in the organisation, or someone with power and influence, senses that the organisation has one or more problems that might be alleviated with the help of an OD practitioner'. Describe some 'problems' that may indicate the need for OD. What early warning system could be put in place to ensure action before the problem/s escalate and cause major difficulties to the organisation?

3 Describe the major differences between underorganised and overorganised organisations. How would you suggest that these factors be managed?

4 Successfully implementing OD initiatives requires close collaboration between managers and OD practitioners. Describe some of the problems that might arise in the relationship between the two parties and propose ways of foreseeing and mitigating the impact of those issues.

5 What are the positive and negative aspects of Dunphy and Stace's model? How does it take into account such things as resistance, politics, dealing with unforeseen circumstances, ethics, particular group characteristics, and so on? Is there an opportunity to modify the model? How might this be done?

6 Compare and contrast the various models of planned change. Discuss the advantages and disadvantages of each. Develop and explain your 'ideal' model of planned change.

7 The effectiveness of the OD practitioner in successfully implementing OD initiatives is clearly important. If you were hiring an OD practitioner, what qualities and skills would you look for in that person? Why?

SEARCH ME! EXCERCISES

Explore **Search me! management** for relevant articles on understanding change. Search me! is an online library of world-class journals, e-books and newspapers, including *The Australian* and *The New York Times,* and is updated daily. Log in to Search me! through **http://login.cengage.com** using the access card in the front of this book.

Keywords

Try searching for the following terms:

> Action research
> Contingency approach
> Critique of change

> Degree of organisation
> Kurt Lewin
> Magnitude of change

>> *Search tip:*

Search me! management contains information from both local and international sources. To get the greatest number of search results, try using both Australian and American spellings in your searches, e.g. 'globalisation' and 'globalization'; 'organisation' and 'organization'.

Notes

1 Organisation Development Australia, 'Who is ODA? What is ODA on about?', www.odaustralia.org, accessed 10 June 2010.

2 M. F. Broom, Ph.D. and E. W. Seashore, M.A., *The Meta-Model of Planned Change*, www.chumans.com/human-systems-resources/meta-model-planned-change.html, revised February 2009.

3 W. Bennis, *Changing Organizations* (New York: McGraw-Hill, 1966); J. Porras and P. Robertson, 'Organization development theory: a typology and evaluation', in *Organizational Change and Development*, 1, eds R. Woodman and W. Pasmore (Greenwich, CT: JAI Press, 1987): 1–57.

4 K. Lewin, *Field Theory in Social Science* (New York: Harper and Row, 1951).

5 E. Schein, *Process Consultation*, 1 and 2 (Reading, MA: Addison-Wesley, 1987).

6 R. Lippitt, J. Watson and B. Westley, *The Dynamics of Planned Change* (New York: Harcourt, Brace and World, 1958).

7 R. Benjamin and E. Levinson, 'A framework for managing IT-enabled change', *Sloan Management Review* (Summer 1993): 23–33.

8 H. Knill-Griesser, *The Ontario Action Researcher*, Nipising University 2009, www.nipissingu.ca/oar, cited 11 June 2010.

9 A. Shani and G. Bushe, 'Visionary action research: a consultation process perspective', *Consultation*, 6 (Spring 1987): 3–19; G. Sussman and R. Evered, 'An assessment of the scientific merit of action research', *Administrative Science Quarterly*, 12 (1978): 582–603.

10 W. French, 'Organization development: objectives, assumptions, and strategies', *California Management Review*, 12 (1969): 23–34; A. Frohman, M. Sashkin and M. Kavanagh, 'Action research as applied to organization development', *Organization and Administrative Sciences*, 7 (1976): 129–42; E. Schein, *Organizational Psychology*, 3rd edn (Englewood Cliffs, NJ: Prentice-Hall, 1980).

11 N. Tichy, 'Agents of planned change: congruence of values, cognitions, and actions', *Administrative Science Quarterly*, 19 (1974): 163–82.

12 M. Beer, 'The technology of organization development', in *Handbook of Industrial and Organizational Psychology*, ed. M. Dunnette (Chicago: Rand McNally, 1976): 945.

13 E. Schein, *Process Consultation: Its Role in Organization Development* (Reading, MA: Addison-Wesley, 1969): 98.

14 ibid.: 6.

15 R. Beckhard and R. Harris, *Organizational Transitions*, 2nd edn (Reading, MA: Addison-Wesley, 1987).

16 M. Elden and R. Chisholm, 'Emerging varieties of action research: introduction to the special issue', *Human Relations*, 46:2 (1993): 121–42.

17 G. Ledford and S. Mohrman, 'Self-design for high involvement', *Human Relations*, 46:2 (1993): 143–68; B. Bunker and B. Alban, 'The large group intervention – a new social innovation?', *Journal of Applied Behavioral Science*, 28:4 (1992): 473–80.

18 R. Marshak, 'Lewin meets Confucius: a review of the OD model of change', *Journal of Applied Behavioral Science*, 29:4 (1993): 393–415; K. Murrell, 'Evaluation as action research: the case of the Management Development Institute in Gambia, West Africa', *International Journal of Public Administration*, 16:3 (1993): 341–56; J. Preston and L. DuToit, 'Endemic violence in South Africa: an OD solution applied to two educational settings', *International Journal of Public Administration*, 16:11 (1993): 1767–91.

19 D. Brown, 'Participatory action research for social change: collective reflections with Asian nongovernmental development organizations', *Human Relations*, 46:2 (1993): 208–27.

20 D. Cooperrider and S. Srivastva, 'Appreciative inquiry in organizational life', in *Organizational Change and Development*, 1, eds R. Woodman and W. Pasmore (Greenwich, CT: JAI Press, 1987): 129–70.

21 D. Cooperrider and W. Pasmore, 'Global social change: a new agenda for social science?', *Human Relations*, 44:10 (1991): 1037–55.

22 W. Burke, *Organization Development: A Normative View* (Reading, MA: Addison-Wesley, 1987).

23 D. Greenwood, W. Whyte and I. Harkavy, 'Participatory action research as process and as goal', *Human Relations*, 46:2 (1993): 175–92.

24 J. Enderby and D. Phelan, 'Action learning groups as the foundation for cultural change', *Asia Pacific Journal of Human Resources*, 32:1 (1994).

25 C. Argyris, R. Putnam and D. Smith, *Action Science* (San Francisco: Jossey-Bass, 1985).

26 S. Mohrman and T. Cummings, *Self-designing Organizations: Learning How to Create High Performance* (Reading, MA: Addison-Wesley, 1989).

27 P. Senge, *The Fifth Discipline* (New York: Doubleday, 1990).

28 B. Braham Phd, Organizational Development Consultant, 'The inner arts of leadership', www.bbraham.com/ organizational_development_consultant.html, 2006–10.

29 M. Weisbord, *Productive Workplaces* (San Francisco: Jossey-Bass, 1987).

30 D. Cooperrider, 'Positive image, positive action: the affirmative basis for organizing', in *Appreciative Management and Leadership*, eds S. Srivastva, D. Cooperrider and associates (San Francisco, CA: Jossey-Bass, 1990); D. Cooperrider, lecture notes, *Presentation to the MSOD Chi Class*, October 1995, Monterey, CA.

31 Cooperrider and Srivastva, 'Appreciative inquiry in organizational life', op. cit.

32 K. Cammeron, J. Dutton, and R. Quinn (eds), *Positive Organizational Scholarship: Foundations of a New Discipline* (New York: Berrett-Kohler, 2003).

33 D. Eden, 'Creating expectation effects in OD: applying self-fulfilling prophecy', in *Research in Organization Change and Development*, 2, eds W. Pasmore and R. Woodman (Greenwich, CT: JAI Press, 1988); D. Eden, 'OD and self-fulfilling prophecy: boosting productivity by raising expectations', *Journal of Applied Behavioral Science*, 22 (1986): 1–13; Cooperrider, 'Positive image, positive action', op. cit.

34 D. Cooperrider and D. Whitney, 'A positive revolution in change: appreciative inquiry,' in *Appreciative Inquiry: Rethinking Human Organisation Toward a Positive Theory of Change*, eds. D. Cooperrider, P. Sorensen, D. Whitney, and T. Yaeger (Champaign, Ill.: Stipes Publishing, 2000), 3–28; J. Watkins and B. Mohr, *Appreciative Inquiry* (San Francisco: Jossey-Bass, 2001).

35 I. Hacking, *The Social Construction of What?* (Cambridge: Harvard University Press, 1999).

36 P. Berger and T. Luckman, *The Social Construction of Reality* (New York: Anchor Books, 1967); K. Gergen, 'The social constructionist movement in modern psychology,' *American Psychologist*, 40 (1985): 266–5; V. Burr, *An Introduction to Social Constructionism* (London: Routledge, 1995).

37 M. Zion and I. Sadeh, 'Curiosity and open inquiry learning', *Journal of Biological Education*, www.britannica.com/bps/additionalcontent/18/ 27185359/Curiosity-and-open-inquiry-learning, 2007.

38 'Inquiry into disclosure regimes for charities & not for profit organisations', Youth of the Streets, www.youthoffthestreets.com.au/downloads/ inquiry_disclosure_regimes_charitie.pdf, 2008.

39 Dr G. Myszkowski, 'Getting it right: a comparative analysis of two distinct leadership development curriculum designs and programs, www.lorenet.com/ pubs2/eBriefsArchive/Quarter12009/ GettingItRightAComparativeAnalysis/tabid/1175/ language/en-US/Default.aspx, cited 11 June 2010.

40 K. A. S. Bahgel, *A Presentation on Organisational Change Model*, www.scribd.com/doc/6976882/A-Presentation-on-Organizational-Change-Model, 2008, cited 14 June 2010.

41 D. Nadler, 'Organizational frame-bending: types of change in the complex organization', in *Corporate Transformation*, eds R. Kilmann and T. Covin (San Francisco: Jossey-Bass, 1988): 66–83; P. Watzlawick, J.

Weakland and R. Fisch, *Change* (New York: WW Norton, 1974); R. Golembiewski, K. Billingsley and S. Yeager, 'Measuring change and persistence in human affairs: types of change generated by OD designs', *Journal of Applied Behavioral Science*, 12 (1975): 133–57; A. Meyer, G. Brooks and J. Goes, 'Environmental jolts and industry revolutions: organizational responses to discontinuous change', *Strategic Management Journal*, 11 (1990): 93–110.

42 A. Mohrman, G. Ledford Jr, S. Mohrman, E. Lawler III and T. Cummings, *Large-Scale Organization Change* (San Francisco: Jossey-Bass, 1989).

43 C. F. Wordsworth, *Quantum Change Made Easy: Breakthroughs in Personal Transformation, Self-Healing and Achieving the Best of Who You Are* (Arizona, USA: Resonance Publishing, 2007), www.olympus.net/ personal/brewster/PDFs/RRQuantumSample1.pdf.

44 F. Barrett and D. Cooperrider, 'Generative metaphor intervention: a new approach for working with systems divided by conflict and caught in defensive perception', *Journal of Applied Behavioral Science*, 26 (1990): 219–39.

45 G. Hofstede, *Culture's Consequences, Comparing Values, Behaviors, Institutions, and Organizations Across Nations* (Thousand Oaks CA: Sage Publications, 2001).

46 T. G. Cummings and C. G. Worley, *Organization Development & Change*, 2008, http://books.google.com. au/books?id=rdjtPTfkWG8C&pg=PA41&lpg=PA41 &dq=Critics+of+OD&source=bl&ots=4hQgDGc1YE& sig=Yt4tQH1nkQCPn1wWLq1RNLuUIig&hl=en&ei= HvIVTOWdMYTBcZHLwbcM&sa=X&oi=book_result &ct=result&resnum=5&ved=0CC0Q6AEwBA#v=one page&q=Critics%20of%20OD&f=false, cited 13 June 2010.

47 J. Porras and P. Robertson, 'Organization development theory, practice, and research', in *Handbook of Industrial and Organizational Psychology*, 3, 2nd edn, eds M. Dunnette and M. Hough (Palo Alto, CA: Consulting Psychologists Press, 1992).

48 T. Cummings, S. Mohrman, A. Mohrman and G. Ledford, 'Organization design for the future: a collaborative research approach', in *Doing Research That Is Useful for Theory and Practice*, eds E. Lawler III, A. Mohrman, S. Mohrman, G. Ledford and T. Cummings (San Francisco: Jossey-Bass, 1985): 275–305.

49 A. Frohman, M. Sashkin and M. Kavanagh, 'Action research as applied to organization development', *Organization and Administrative Sciences*, 7 (1976): 129–42; S. Mohrman and T. Cummings, *Self-designing Organizations: Learning How to Create High Performance* (Reading, MA: Addison-Wesley, 1989); M. Beer, R. Eisenstat and B. Spector, 'Why change programs don't produce change', *Harvard Business Review*, 6 (November–December 1990): 158–66.

50 Beer, Eisenstat and Spector, 'Why change programs don't produce change', op. cit.

51 D. Dunphy and D. Stace, *Under New Management: Australian Organisations in Transition* (Sydney, McGraw-Hill, 1990): 82.

52 D. Dunphy and D. Stace, 'Strategies for organisational transition', *Centre for Corporate Change*, Paper 002, 1991, AGSM, University of New South Wales.

CHAPTER 3

Leadership and the role of the change agent

This chapter examines the people who perform OD in organisations. A closer look at OD practitioners can provide a more personal perspective on the field, and help us to understand the essential character of OD as a helping profession, involving personal relationships between OD practitioners and organisation members.

Much of the literature about OD practitioners views them as internal or external consultants who provide professional services: diagnosing problems, developing solutions and helping to implement them. More recent perspectives expand the scope of OD practitioners to include professionals in related disciplines, such as industrial psychology and organisation theory, as well as line managers who have learned how to carry out OD in order to change and develop their departments.

A great deal of opinion and some research studies have focused on the necessary skills and knowledge of an effective OD practitioner. Studies provide a comprehensive list of basic skills and knowledge needed by all OD practitioners if they are to be effective.

Most of the relevant literature focuses on people who specialise in OD as a profession and addresses their roles and careers. The OD role can be described in relation to the position of OD practitioners: internal to the organisation, external to it or in a team composed of both internal and external consultants. The OD role can also be examined in terms of its marginality in organisations and where it fits along a continuum from client-centred to consultant-centred[1] functioning. Finally, organisation development is an emerging profession that provides alternative opportunities for gaining competence and developing a career. The stressful nature of helping professions, however, suggests that OD practitioners must cope with the possibility of professional burnout.

As in other helping professions, values and ethics play an important role in guiding OD practice and minimising the possibility of clients being neglected or abused.

WHO IS THE ORGANISATION DEVELOPMENT PRACTITIONER?

Throughout this text, the term 'organisation development (OD) practitioner'[2] refers to at least three kinds of people. The most obvious group of OD practitioners consists of those people who specialise in OD as a profession. They may be internal or external consultants who offer professional services to organisation clients, including top managers, functional department heads and staff groups. OD professionals have traditionally shared a common set of humanistic values,[3] promoting open communications, employee involvement and personal growth and development. They tend to have common training, skills and experience in the social processes of organisations (for example, group dynamics, decision making and communications). In recent years, OD professionals have expanded these traditional values and expertise to include more concern for organisational effectiveness, competitiveness and bottom-line results, and greater attention to the technical, structural and strategic parts of organisations. This expansion is mainly in response to the highly competitive demands that face modern organisations. It has resulted in a more diverse set of OD professionals geared to helping organisations cope with those pressures.[4]

Second, the term 'OD practitioner' applies to people who specialise in fields related to OD, such as reward systems, organisation design, total quality management, information technology or business strategy. These content-oriented fields are increasingly becoming integrated with OD's process orientation, particularly as OD projects have become more comprehensive, involving multiple features and varying parts of organisations. A growing number of professionals in these related fields are gaining experience and competence in OD, mainly through working with OD professionals on large-scale projects and through attending OD training sessions. For example, Australia's 'Big Four' accounting firms have diversified into management consulting and change management. In most cases, these related professionals do not fully subscribe to traditional OD values, nor do they have extensive training and experience in OD. Rather, they have formal training and experience in their respective specialties, such as industrial relations, management consulting, control systems, health care and work design. They are OD practitioners in the sense that they apply their special competence within an OD-like process, typically by having OD professionals and managers help to design and implement change programs. They also practise OD when they apply their OD competence to their own specialties, thus diffusing an OD perspective into such areas as compensation practices, work design, labour relations and planning and strategy.[5]

Third, the term 'OD practitioner' applies to the increasing number of managers and administrators who have gained competence in OD and who apply it to their own work areas. Various reviewers of change management argue that OD applied by managers, rather than OD professionals, has grown rapidly.[6] It has been suggested that the faster pace of change affecting organisations today is highlighting the centrality of the manager in managing change. Consequently, OD must become a general management skill. Along these lines, the Centre for Corporate Change at the Australian Graduate School of Management has studied a number of organisations such as the New South Wales State Library and Woolworths, where managers and employees have become 'change masters'.[7] They have gained the expertise to introduce change and innovation into the organisation.

Managers tend to gain competence in OD by interacting with OD professionals in actual change programs. This on-the-job training is frequently supplemented with more formal OD training, such as the variety of OD workshops offered by the Australian Institute of Management (AIM), Institution of Engineers (IE), Australian Human Resource Institute (AHRI) and others. Line managers are increasingly attending such external programs. Moreover, a growing number of organisations, including Ernst and Young and Ericsson, have instituted in-house training programs for managers to learn how to develop and change their work units. As managers gain OD competence, they become its most basic practitioners.

In practice, the distinction between the three kinds of OD practitioners is becoming blurred. A growing number of managers have moved, either temporarily or permanently, into the OD profession. For example, companies such as Budget trained and rotated managers into full-time OD roles so that they could gain the skills and experience necessary for higher level management positions. Also, it is increasingly common to find managers (for example, David Mallen from MCS Management Consultants and Ann Boland, an independent consultant and psychologist, formerly from Ernst and Young) using their experience in OD to become external consultants, particularly in the employee involvement area. More OD practitioners are gaining professional competence in related specialties, such as business process re-engineering, reward systems,[8] and career planning and development. Conversely, many specialists in these related areas are achieving professional competence in OD. Cross-training and integration are producing a more comprehensive and complex kind of OD practitioner, who has a greater diversity of values, skills and experience than does the traditional OD practitioner.

THE OD PRACTITIONER AS LEADER OF CHANGE

Traditional, hierarchical organisations may once have made complex decisions about the organisation in-house. Changes in a business's competitive environment, as well as issues affecting the global economy, such as the 2009 global financial crisis, can create opportunities for OD practitioners to lead change within organisations.

Generally, in beginning the change process, a member of an organisation or unit contacts an OD practitioner about potential help in addressing an organisational issue.[9] The organisation member may be a manager, staff specialist or some other key participant, and the practitioner may be an OD professional from inside or outside the organisation. Determining whether the two parties should enter into an OD relationship typically involves clarifying the nature of the organisation's problem, the relevant client system for that issue and the appropriateness of the particular OD practitioner.[10] In helping to assess these issues, the OD practitioner may need to collect preliminary data about the organisation. Similarly, the organisation may need to gather information about the practitioner's competence and experience.[11] This knowledge will help both parties determine whether they should proceed to develop a contract for working together.

This section describes the process of engaging an OD practitioner as organisational change agent: (1) clarifying the organisational issue, (2) determining the relevant client, and (3) selecting an appropriate OD practitioner.

Clarifying the organisational issue[12]

When seeking help from OD practitioners, organisations typically start with a presenting problem – the issue that has caused them to consider an OD process. It may be specific (decrease in market share, increase in absenteeism) or general ('we're growing too fast', 'we need to prepare for rapid changes'). The presenting problem often has an implied or stated solution. For example, managers may believe that, because members of their teams are in conflict, team building is the obvious answer. They may even state the presenting problem in the form of a solution: 'We need some team building.'

In many cases, however, the presenting problem is only a symptom of an underlying problem. For example, conflict among members of a team may result from several deeper causes, including ineffective reward systems, personality differences, inappropriate structure and poor leadership. The issue facing the organisation or department must be clarified early in the OD process so that subsequent diagnostic and intervention activities are focused on the right issue.[13]

Gaining a clearer perspective on the organisational issue may require the collection of preliminary data.[14] OD practitioners often examine company records and interview a few key members to gain an introductory understanding of the organisation, its context and the nature of the presenting problem. These data are gathered in a relatively short period of time, typically from a few hours to one or two days. They are intended to provide rudimentary knowledge of the organisational issue that will enable the two parties to make informed choices about proceeding with the contracting process.

The diagnostic phase of OD involves a far more extensive assessment of the organisational issue than occurs during the entering and contracting stage. The diagnosis might also discover other issues that need to be addressed, or it might lead to redefining the initial issue that was identified during the entering and contracting stage. This is a prime example of the emergent nature of the OD process, where things may change as new information is gathered and new events occur.

Determining the relevant client

A second activity involved in entering an OD relationship is the definition of who is the relevant client for addressing the organisational issue.[15] Generally, the relevant client includes those organisation members who can directly impact on the change issue, whether it be solving a particular problem or improving an already successful organisation or department. Unless these members are identified and included in the entering and contracting process, they may withhold their support for, and commitment to, the OD process. In trying to improve the productivity of a unionised manufacturing plant, for example, the relevant client may need to include union officials as well as managers and staff personnel. It is not unusual for an OD project to fail because the relevant client was inappropriately defined.

Determining the relevant client can vary in complexity according to the situation. In those cases where the organisational issue can be addressed in a particular organisation unit, client definition[16] is relatively straightforward. Members of that unit constitute the relevant client. They or their representatives would need to be included in the entering and contracting process. For example, if a manager asked for help in improving the decision-making process of his or her team, the manager and team members would be the relevant clients. Unless they are actively involved in choosing an OD practitioner and defining the subsequent change process, there is little likelihood that OD will improve team decision making.

Determining the relevant client is more complex when the organisational issue cannot readily be addressed in a single organisation unit. Here, it may be necessary to expand the definition of the client to include members from multiple units, from different hierarchical levels and even from outside the organisation. For example, the manager of a production department may seek help in resolving conflicts between his or her unit and other departments in the organisation. The relevant client would transcend the boundaries of the production department because it alone cannot resolve the organisational issue. The client might include members from all departments involved in the conflict as well as the executive to whom all the departments report. If this interdepartmental conflict[17] also involved key suppliers and customers from outside the business, the relevant client might also include members of those groups.

In these complex situations, OD practitioners may need to gather additional information about the organisation in order to determine the relevant client. This can be accomplished as part of the preliminary data collection that typically occurs when clarifying the organisational issue. When examining company records or interviewing personnel, practitioners can seek to identify the key members and organisational units that need to be involved in addressing the organisational issue. For example, they can ask organisation members such questions as: 'Who can directly affect the organisational issue?' 'Who has a vested interest in it?' 'Who has the power to approve or reject the OD effort?' Answers to these questions can help determine who is the relevant client for the entering and contracting stage. The relevant client may change, however, during the later stages of the OD process as new data are gathered and changes occur. If so, participants may have to return to this initial stage of the OD effort and modify it.

Selecting an OD practitioner

The last activity involved in entering an OD relationship is selecting an OD practitioner who has the expertise and experience to work with members on the organisational issue. Unfortunately, little systematic advice is available on how to choose a competent OD professional, whether from inside or outside the organisation. Perhaps the best criteria for selecting, evaluating and developing OD practitioners are those suggested by the late Gordon Lippitt, a pioneering practitioner in the field.[18] Lippitt listed areas that managers should consider before selecting a practitioner, including the ability of the consultant to form sound interpersonal relationships, the degree of focus on the problem, the skills of the practitioner relative to the problem, the extent that the consultant clearly informs the client as to his or her role and contribution, and whether the practitioner belongs to a professional association. References from other clients are highly important. A client may not like the consultant's work, but it is critical to know the reasons for both pleasure and displeasure. One important consideration is whether the consultant approaches the organisation with openness and an insistence on diagnosis or whether the practitioner appears to have a fixed program that is applicable to almost any organisation.

Certainly, OD consulting is as much a person specialisation as it is a task specialisation. The OD professional must have not only a repertoire of technical skills but also the personality and interpersonal competence to be able to use himself or herself as an instrument of change. Regardless of technical training, the consultant must be able to maintain a boundary position, co-ordinating various units and departments and mixing disciplines, theories, technology and research findings in an organic rather than a mechanical way. The practitioner is potentially the most important OD technology available.

Thus, in the selection of an OD practitioner, perhaps the most important issue is the fundamental question: 'How effective has the person been in the past, with what kinds of organisations, using what kinds of techniques?' In other words, references must be checked. Interpersonal relationships are tremendously important, but even con artists have excellent interpersonal relationships and skills.

The burden of choosing an effective OD practitioner should not, however, rest entirely with the client organisation.[19] Organisation development practitioners also bear a heavy responsibility for seeking an appropriate match between their skills and knowledge and what the organisation or department needs. Few managers are sophisticated enough to detect or understand subtle differences in expertise among OD professionals. They often do not understand the difference between consultants who specialise in different types of interventions. Thus, practitioners should help to educate potential clients. Consultants should be explicit about their strengths and weaknesses and about their range of competence. If OD professionals realise that a good match does not exist, they should inform managers and help them find more suitable help.

DEVELOPING A CONTRACT

The activities of entering an OD relationship – clarifying the organisational issue, determining who is the relevant client, and deciding whether the practitioner is appropriate for helping the organisation – are a necessary prelude to developing an OD contract. They define the major focus for contracting, including the relevant parties. Contracting is a natural extension of the entering process and clarifies how the OD process will proceed. It typically establishes the expectations of the parties, the time and resources that will be expended, and the ground rules under which the parties will operate.

The goal of contracting is to make a good decision about how to carry out the OD process.[20] It can be relatively informal and involve only a verbal agreement between the client and OD practitioner. A team leader with OD skills, for example, may voice his or her concerns to members about how the team is functioning. After some discussion, they might agree to devote one hour of future meeting time to diagnosing the team with the help of the leader. Here, entering and contracting are done together in an informal manner. In other cases, contracting can be more protracted and result in a formal document. This typically occurs when organisations employ outside OD practitioners. Government agencies, for example, generally have procurement regulations that apply to contracting with outside consultants.[21]

Regardless of the level of formality, all OD processes require some form of explicit contracting that results in either a verbal or written agreement. Such contracting clarifies the client's and the practitioner's expectations about how the OD process will take place. Unless there is mutual understanding and agreement about the OD process, there is considerable risk that someone's expectations will be unfulfilled.[22] This can lead to reduced commitment and support, to misplaced action or to premature termination of the process.

The contracting step in OD generally addresses three key areas:[23] (1) what each party expects to gain from the OD process; (2) the time and resources that will be devoted to OD; and (3) the ground rules for working together.

Mutual expectations

This part of the contracting process focuses on the expectations of the client and the OD practitioner. The client states the services and outcomes to be provided by the OD practitioner and describes what the organisation expects from the OD process and the consultant. Clients can usually describe the desired outcomes of the OD process, such as decreased turnover or higher job satisfaction. Encouraging them to state their wants in the form of outcomes, working relationships and personal accomplishments can facilitate the development of a good contract.[24]

The OD practitioner should also state what he or she expects to gain from the OD process. This can include the opportunity to try new OD interventions, report the results to other potential clients and receive appropriate compensation or recognition.

Time and resources

To accomplish change, the organisation and the OD practitioner must commit time and resources to the effort. Each must be clear about how much energy and resources will be dedicated to the change process. Failure to make explicit the necessary requirements of a change process can quickly ruin an OD effort. For example, a client may clearly state that the assignment involves diagnosing the causes of poor productivity in a work group. However, the client may expect the practitioner to complete the assignment without talking to the workers. Typically, clients want to know how much time will be necessary to complete the assignment, who needs to be involved, how much it will cost and so on.

Block has suggested that resources can be divided into two parts.[25] Essential requirements are things that are absolutely necessary if the change process is to be successful. From the practitioner's perspective, they can include access to key people or information, enough time to do the job properly and commitment from certain people. The organisation's essential requirements might include a speedy diagnosis or assurances that the project will be conducted at the lowest price. Being clear about the constraints on carrying out the assignment will facilitate the contracting process and improve the chances for success. Desirable requirements are the things that would be nice to have but are not absolutely necessary. They may include access to special resources and written (as opposed to verbal) reports.

Ground rules

The final part of the contracting process involves specifying how the client and the OD practitioner will work together. This includes such issues as confidentiality, if and how the OD practitioner will become involved in personal or interpersonal issues, how to terminate the relationship and whether the practitioner is supposed to make expert recommendations or help the manager to make decisions. For internal consultants, organisational politics make it especially important to clarify issues of how to handle sensitive information and how to deliver 'bad news'.[26] These process issues are as important as the substantive changes to take place. Failure to address these concerns can mean that the client or the OD practitioner has inappropriate assumptions about how the process will unfold.

Application 3.1 presents the story of a business experiencing dramatic growth in Australia, which can present its own difficulties if mismanaged.

Aldi's simple recipe for success

Nearly 10 years ago, Michael Kloeters was living a comfortable life in Germany, working for the Aldi supermarket chain, when his superiors called him in one day. They asked whether he'd like to set up Aldi in Australia. This surprise proposal would change his life.

'For me, it was simply a question of do I want to tackle another challenge. I said yes, but I had a pre-condition, which was to come and have a look at the Australian marketplace,' Kloeters, 51, recalled.

He travelled to Australia, visited several supermarkets and decided he wasn't scared of Woolworths and Coles. He sold his assets in Germany and moved his family to Australia.

The first big test came in 2001 when Aldi opened its first two stores. There are now 172 stores, and there will be 200 by the end of this year. Kloeters says there is potential for 500 along the eastern seaboard.

The privately owned German parent company, Aldi Sud, has ploughed $1.25 billion into Australia and plans to reinvest a further $1 billion during the next three years.

Aldi is an intensely private organisation. Decades ago, the two Albrecht brothers – leading to ALbrecht DIscount – had different ideas about how to run the business. One was hands-on and the other believed in delegation of responsibility.

They got a map of Germany. One of the brothers drew a line and the other had to choose which part of the country he would take. They went on to call the businesses Aldi Nord and Aldi Sud. They are now apparently the richest men in Germany. It's all very amicable, and they go to church together.

The business in Australia is also a secretive affair and is structured through limited partnerships. No profit or loss figures are available.

A couple of years ago, Kloeters was declining to comment on whether the show was profitable. Now, when asked, he says: 'Yes. We have a very viable business and we are now strong enough to go about our business. We're here to stay'.

'People cannot imagine that someone is prepared to live for years without profits.'

More than 1 million customers a week now pass through Aldi's checkouts. Kloeters won't disclose sales figures but says they're somewhere between David Jones and Myer. He says sales are closer to $2 billion than $4 billion.

Talk to him about the way Aldi does business and he frequently uses the word 'simple'. When it comes to products, he says the company's operation is 'very simple'. When it comes to suppliers, he says that when Aldi was setting up here, 'they couldn't believe that life could be so simple'.

'It seems to be quite challenging for people to keep things simple,' he says. What it boils down to is that Aldi tries to keep everything as lean as possible. There is no marketing department, no advertising department, no legal department and no human resources department. There are only 70 people at head office.

'We are hard discounters,' he says. 'We are real discounters who start with brand quality first. And that is absolutely where we start. We always look at the quality first and then we will have a look at who can make that product best for us.'

Aldi's model is simplicity itself. The average size of stores is 836 square metres, compared with about 3500 to 4500 sq m for a conventional supermarket. There are only about 900 products against tens of thousands at Woolworths and Coles.

Almost all the products are Aldi's own brands although there are some exceptions such as Vegemite and Nescafe.

Aldi gets sales figures of all products and then, with the help of independent analysis, gets manufacturers to replicate or improve on the market leaders in each product category.

Often a product at Aldi will be made by the manufacturer that makes the market-leading branded product that sells at a much higher price.

Aldi runs two internal sampling sessions a day and has outside consultants – 'the best Australia has to offer', according to Kloeters – who advise Aldi about product quality.

Aldi prices are between 10% and 40% cheaper than the major chains.

Aldi stores are bare-boned operations, with products left on pallets for customers to pick up and load into a trolley. Some of the products are rarely touched by an Aldi employee's hands. Unit pricing and claimed higher employee pay are other Aldi features.

The company does little press advertising, has no petrol price gimmicks, and doesn't do complex deals with manufacturers.

'They have one discussion with us at our headquarters,' Kloeters says. 'We agree on a plan and stick to it, and no further negotiations are necessary.'

'What we say to the suppliers is, OK, cut out all the crap, tell us what the bottom line will be and we agree on that price. We agree on one price for delivery to our warehouse, end of story. It can't be any simpler than that.'

He says Aldi puts the ball back into the manufacturers' courts, and that must come as a big surprise to those suppliers used to dealing with the market might of Woolworths or Coles.

Kloeters says: 'We ask them, "When do you want us to order? What are the quantities you want us to order? What delivery arrangements suit you best?"'

'We tell them what we need and they tell us what they want and we try and make it work together. Because, at the end of the day, their profit is our profit and vice versa.'

He says manufacturers reacted with astonishment when they were asked to say what suited them. 'At the beginning, they didn't believe us. They couldn't believe that life could be so simple. Seriously, they couldn't believe it.'

Source: Adapted (extract) from Christopher Webb, 'Aldi's simple recipe for success', *The Age*, 26 July 2008.

Critical thinking questions:
1. Do you think Michael Kloeters can be described as an OD practitioner? Why/why not?
2. Aldi's 'lean' approach to head office operations is quite different to other, similar organisations. What implications may this have for an OD practitioner consulting for Aldi?
3. Aldi's rapid growth in Australia may lead to problems requiring the use of an external OD practitioner. What do you think these problems may be? What skills and competencies would the ideal OD practitioner have?

COMPETENCIES OF AN EFFECTIVE ORGANISATION DEVELOPMENT PRACTITIONER

Much of the literature about the skills and knowledge of an effective OD practitioner claims that a mixture of personality traits, experiences, kinds of knowledge and skills can be assumed to lead to effective practice. For example, research on the characteristics of successful change practitioners yields the following list of attributes and abilities: diagnostic ability, basic knowledge of behavioural science techniques, empathy, knowledge of the theories and methods within the consultant's own discipline, goal-setting ability, problem-solving ability, ability to do self-assessment, the ability to see things objectively, imagination, flexibility, honesty, consistency and trust.[27] Although these qualities and skills are certainly laudable, there has been relatively little consensus about their importance in effective OD practice.

Many consulting styles or approaches have been suggested, but each style usually varies according to its underlying character – shaped by the kinds of skills and techniques that the consultants use, the values they bring to their clients and the manner in which they carry out their assignments. Other research also examines the degree of emphasis that the consultant places upon two interrelated goals or dimensions of the change process. Application 3.2 describes a classification that involves the consultant's orientation to the two interrelated dimensions:

1 the degree of emphasis upon effectiveness or goal accomplishment
2 the degree of emphasis upon relationships, morale and participant satisfaction.[28]

3.2

APPLICATION

Consultant styles matrix

Based upon two dimensions – an emphasis on morale and an emphasis on effectiveness – five different types of consultant styles or roles may be identified.

The stabiliser style:

- Maintains a low profile.
- Is a survivalist – follows top management direction.

FIGURE 3.1 Consultant styles

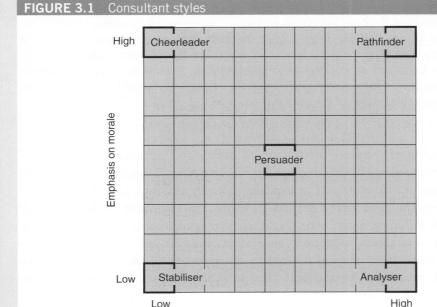

>>

- Has learned to confirm and suppress internal motivations, usually stemming from being situated in a large organisation where development programs may not be highly regarded by top management.

The cheerleader style:

- Chiefly concerned with employee motivation and morale.
- Seeks warm working relationships and in general is more comfortable in non-confrontational situations.
- Assumes that high employee satisfaction equals high effectiveness (evidence, however, contradicts this assumption).
- Avoids open conflict and attempts to maintain harmony by smoothing over differences.

The analyser style:

- Emphasises efficiency over employee satisfaction.
- Is a rationalist – assumes the facts will lead to a solution.
- May be confrontational, usually relying on authority to resolve conflict.
- Is a technical specialist – has the expertise, knowledge and experience to solve specific problems.

The persuader style:

- Tends to be low-risk, focusing on both effectiveness and moral dimensions.
- The persuader is motivated primarily to satisfy; that is, to achieve something that is 'good enough'.
- Expends effort in satisfying differing forces, although the resulting change program may become 'watered down' or weakened.

The pathfinder style:

- Seeks high degree of effectiveness and employee satisfaction, believing problems can be solved through teamwork.
- Is aware that confrontation and conflict may improve effectiveness.
- Uses collaborative problem solving and challenges the underlying patterns of employee behaviour.

Most organisation problems are complex situations and may not be neatly solved by any one particular change, but will depend upon the particular consultant, the nature of the problem and the type of organisation climate that exists. The styles are not mutually exclusive. All consultant styles can be effective and are interrelated. A consultant may use different styles at different times to meet changing client system needs and deal with diverse situations. Frequently, some combination of the types may be applied.

Two ongoing projects are attempting to define and categorise the skills and knowledge required of OD practitioners. In the first effort, a broad and growing list of well-known practitioners and researchers annually update a list of professional competencies. The most recent list has grown to 187 statements in nine areas of OD practice, including entry, start-up, assessment and feedback, action planning, intervention, evaluation, adoption, separation and general competencies. The statements range from 'staying centred in the present, focusing on the ongoing process' and 'understanding and explaining how diversity will affect the diagnosis of the culture' to 'basing change on business strategy and business needs' and 'being comfortable with quantum leaps, radical shifts, and paradigm changes'. The discussion is currently considering additional items related to international OD, large-group interventions and transorganisation skills.

To understand the relative importance of this long list, Worley and his colleagues collected data from 364 OD practitioners.[29] The average respondent had six to 10 years of OD experience, a master's degree, and came from the United States. The results suggested an underlying structure to this list. Twenty-three competencies were generated that reflected both the skills and knowledge necessary to conduct planned change processes and the individual characteristics necessary to be an effective OD practitioner. Similar to other lists, the competencies included the ability to evaluate change, work with large-scale change efforts, create implementation plans and manage diversity. One of the most surprising results, however, was the emergence of 'self mastery' as the most important competence. The results supported the long-held belief that good OD practitioners know themselves and that such knowledge forms the basis of effective practice.

The second project, sponsored by the Organisation Development and Change Division of the Academy of Management, seeks to develop a list of competencies to guide curriculum development in graduate OD programs. So far, more than 40 OD practitioners and researchers have worked to develop two competency lists (shown in Table 3.1). First, foundation competencies are oriented towards descriptions of an existing system. They include knowledge from organisation behaviour, psychology, group dynamics, management and organisation theory, research methods and business practices. Second, core competencies are aimed at how systems change over time. They include knowledge of organisation design, organisation research, system dynamics, OD history, and theories and models for change. They also involve the skills needed to: manage the consulting process; analyse and diagnose systems; design and choose interventions; facilitate processes; develop clients' capability to manage their own change; and evaluate organisation change.

The information in Table 3.1 applies primarily to people who specialise in OD as a profession. For those people, the list of skills and knowledge seems reasonable, especially in light of the growing diversity and complexity of interventions in OD. Gaining competence in those areas may take considerable time and effort, and it is questionable whether the other two types of OD practitioners – managers and specialists in related fields – also need this full range of skills and knowledge. It seems more reasonable to suggest that some subset of the items listed in Table 3.1 should apply to all OD practitioners, whether they are OD professionals, managers or related specialists. These items would constitute the basic skills and knowledge of an OD practitioner. Beyond this background, the three types of OD practitioners would probably differ in areas of concentration. OD professionals would extend their breadth of skills across the remaining categories in Table 3.1; managers would focus on the major management knowledge areas; and related specialists would

TABLE 3.1	Knowledge and skill requirements of OD practitioners	
	Foundation competencies	**Core competencies**

Knowledge	1 Organisation behaviour
	  A Organisation culture
	  B Work design
	  C Interpersonal relations
	  D Power and politics
	  E Leadership
	  F Goal setting
	  G Conflict
	  H Ethics
	2 Individual psychology
	  A Learning theory
	  B Motivation theory
	  C Perception theory
	3 Group dynamics
	  A Roles
	  B Communication processes
	  C Decision-making process
	  D Stages of group development
	  E Leadership
	4 Management and organisation theory
	  A Planning, organising, leading and controlling
	  B Problem solving and decision making
	  C Systems theory
	  D Contingency theory
	  E Organisation structure
	  F Characteristics of environment and technology
	  G Models of organisation and system
	5 Research methods/ statistics
	  A Measures of central tendency
	  B Measures of dispersion
	  C Basic sampling theory
	  D Basic experimental design
	  E Sample inferential statistics
	6 Comparative cultural perspectives
	  A Dimensions of natural culture
	  B Dimensions of industry culture
	  C *Systems implications*
		1 Organisation design: the decision process associated with formulating and aligning the elements of an organisational system, including but not limited to structural systems, human resource systems, information systems, reward systems, work design, political systems, and organisation culture
		  A The concept of fit and alignment
		  B Diagnostic and design model for various subsystems that make up an organisation at any level of analysis, including the structure of work, human resources, information systems, reward systems, work design, political systems and so on
		  C Key thought leaders in organisation design
		2 Organisation research: field research methods; interviewing; content analysis; design of questionnaires and interview protocol; designing change evaluation processes; longitudinal data collection and analysis; understanding and detecting alpha, beta and gamma change; and a host of quantitative and qualitative methods
		3 System dynamics: the description and understanding of how systems evolve and develop over time, how systems respond to exogenous and endogenous disruption as well as planned interventions (for example, evolution and revolution, punctuated equilibrium theory, chaos theory, catastrophe theory, incremental versus quantum change, transformation theory and so on)
		4 History of organisation development and change: an understanding of the social, political, economic and personal forces that led to the emergence and development of organisation development and change, including the key thought leaders, the values underlying their writings and actions, the key events and writings, and related documentation
		  A Human relations movement
		  B NTL/T-groups/sensitivity training
		  C Survey research
		  D Quality of work life
		  E Tavistock Institute
		  F Key thought leaders
		  G Humanistic values
		  H *Statement of ethics*

TABLE 3.1 Knowledge and skill requirements of OD practitioners (*continued*)

	Foundation competencies	Core competencies
	7 Functional knowledge of business and management principles and practice	5 Theories and models for change: the basic action research model, participatory action research model, planning model, change typologies (for example, fast, slow, incremental, quantum, revolutionary); Lewin's model, transition models, and so on
Skills	1 Interpersonal communication; (listening, feedback and articulation) 2 Collaboration/working together 3 Problem solving 4 Using new technology 5 Conceptualising 6 Project management 7 Present/education/coach	1 Managing the consulting process: the ability to enter, contract, diagnose, design appropriate interventions, implement those interventions, manage unprogrammed events and evaluate change process 2 Analysis/diagnosis: the abilities to conduct an inquiry into a system's effectiveness, to see the root cause(s) of a system's current level of effectiveness; the core skill is interpreted to include all systems – individual, group, organisation and multi-organisation – as well as the ability to understand and inquire into oneself 3 Designing/choosing appropriate, relevant interventions: understanding how to select, modify or design effective interventions that will move the organisation from its current state to its desired future state 4 Facilitation and process consultation: the ability to assist an individual or group towards a goal; the ability to conduct an inquiry into individual and group processes such that the client system maintains ownership of the issue, increases its capacity for reflection on the consequences of its behaviours and actions, and develops a sense of increased control and ability 5 Developing client capability: the ability to conduct a change process in such a way that the client is better able to plan and implement a successful change process in the future, using technologies of planned change in a values-based and ethical manner 6 Evaluating organisation change: the ability to design and implement a process to evaluate the impact and effects of change intervention, including control of alternative explanations and interpretation of performance outcomes

concentrate on skills in their respective areas, such as those included in the major management and collateral knowledge areas.

Based on the data in Table 3.1, as well as on more recent studies of OD skills,[30] all OD practitioners should have the following basic skills and knowledge to be effective:

1 *Intrapersonal skills or 'self-management' competence.* Despite the growing knowledge base and sophistication of the field, organisation development is still a human craft. As the primary instrument of diagnosis and change, practitioners often must process complex, ambiguous information and make informed judgements about its relevance to organisational issues.

   The core competency of analysis and diagnosis listed in Table 3.1 includes the ability to inquire into oneself, and it remains one of the cornerstone skills in OD. Practitioners must also have the personal centring to know their own values, feelings and purposes and the integrity to behave responsibly in a helping relationship with others. Bob Tannenbaum, one of the founders of OD, argues that self-knowledge is the most central ingredient in OD practice and suggests that practitioners are becoming too enamoured of skills and techniques.[31] Some recent data support his view. A study of 416 OD practitioners found that 47% agreed with the statement: 'Many of the new entrants into the field have little understanding of or appreciation for the history or values underlying the field'.[32] Because OD is a highly uncertain process that requires constant adjustment and innovation, practitioners need to have active learning skills and a reasonable balance between their rational and emotional sides. Finally, OD practice can be highly stressful and can lead to early burnout, so practitioners need to know how to manage their own stress.

2 *Interpersonal skills.* Practitioners must create and maintain effective relationships with individuals and groups within the organisation to help them gain the competence necessary to solve their own problems. Table 3.1 identifies group dynamics, comparative cultural perspectives and business function as foundation knowledge, plus managing the consulting process and facilitation as core skills. All of these interpersonal competencies promote effective helping relationships. Such relationships start with a grasp of the organisation's perspective and require listening to members' perceptions and feelings to understand how they see themselves and the organisation. This understanding provides a starting point for joint diagnosis and problem solving. Practitioners must establish trust and rapport with organisation members so that they can share pertinent information and work effectively together. This requires being able to converse in the members' own language and to exchange feedback about how the relationship is progressing.

To help members learn new skills and behaviours, practitioners must serve as concrete role models of what is expected. They must act in ways that are credible to organisation members and provide them with the counselling and coaching necessary for development and change. Because the helping relationship is jointly determined, practitioners need to be able to negotiate an acceptable role and to manage changing expectations and demands.

3 *General consultation skills.* Table 3.1 identifies the ability to manage the consulting process and the ability to design interventions as core competencies that all practitioners should possess. OD starts with diagnosing an organisation or department to understand the causes of its problems and to discover areas for further development. OD practitioners need to know how to carry out an effective diagnosis, at least at a rudimentary level. They should know how to engage organisation members in diagnosis, how to help them ask the right questions and how to collect and analyse information. A manager, for example, should be able to work with subordinates to jointly find out how the organisation or department is functioning. The manager should know basic diagnostic questions, some methods for gathering information (such as interviews or surveys) and some techniques for analysing it, such as force-field analysis or statistical means and distributions.

In addition to diagnosis, OD practitioners should know how to design and execute an intervention. They need to be able to lay out an action plan and to gain commitment to the program. They also need to know how to tailor the intervention to the situation, using information about how the change is progressing in order to guide implementation (see Chapter 6). For example, managers should be able to develop action steps for an intervention with subordinates. They should be able to gain their commitment to the program (usually through participation), sit down with them and assess how it is progressing, and make modifications if necessary.

4 *Organisation development theory.* The final basic tool that OD practitioners should have is a general knowledge of OD, as presented in this book. They should have some appreciation for planned change, the action research model and contemporary approaches to managing change. They should have some familiarity with the range of available interventions and the need for assessing and institutionalising change programs. Perhaps most important is that OD practitioners should understand their own role in the emerging field of organisation development, whether as managers, OD professionals or specialists in related areas.

Application 3.3 discusses the implications of generational change.

Y are we leaders?

There can be little doubt that the frugal generation born in the 1920s and who touched the Great Depression were profoundly shaped by their childhood experience with adversity. This generation was raised in an era of hardship. Even with prosperity much later in life the frugals were never comfortable with consumerism: 'why do I need to buy new clothes when my old clothes haven't worn out?' They were even less comfortable with debt.

The frugals reached the peak of their careers over the decade-and-a-half to the early 1980s. It was this generation that managed graduate baby-boomers in the 1970s. And in those offices at that time their depression-based frugal values fizzed and fissured to the fore. The office was hierarchical: steps up the ladder were carefully measured and doled out: bigger office, fancier title, ever closer relationship with 'the boss'. From way down below the boss was revered.

If you accept that the values and the management style of the frugals was shaped by their youthful exposure to adversity, then you must also accept that Gen-Y's leadership will be shaped by their youthful exposure to peace and unfettered prosperity.

Ys are by nature, and/or by [reflection] of their times, both inclusive and participatory; frugals were downright divisive and exclusionary.

Why be deferential and defensive in a world that continually offers opportunity? What Ys value is not the observance of hierarchy and protocol, as did the frugals, but relationships and experience: the former qualities are required to survive war and depression; the latter qualities flourish in happier times.

Beyond the Ys lie the unknown force of millenniums, otherwise known as Generation Z, and [those] who straddle the millennium. The millennium generation are the children of the Xers: they are being raised in households that struggle with HECS and housing debt. Unlike the Ys, the millenniums will experience recession before most enter the professional job market. These straitened circumstances could well make millenniums tougher managers than the softer, older, relationship-driven Ys.

Source: Extract from Bernard Salt, 'Y are we leaders?', *Property Australia*, February 2007.

Critical thinking question:
1. Considering the range of competencies listed in Table 3.1, what advantages may generational change bring to the OD field? What challenges may Gen Y face when entering positions as OD practitioners and change agents?

THE PROFESSIONAL ORGANISATION DEVELOPMENT PRACTITIONER

Most of the literature about OD practitioners has focused on people specialising in OD as a profession. In this section, we discuss the role and typical career paths of OD professionals.

The role of organisation development professionals

Position

Organisation development professionals have positions that are either internal or external to the organisation. Internal consultants are members of the organisation, and may be located in the human resources department or manager. They may perform the OD role exclusively, or th other tasks, such as compensation practices, training or large organisations, such as Mayne Group Ltd, have consulting groups. Their internal consultants typically within the organisation, serving both line and staff depa

External consultants are not members of the clien work for a consulting firm, a university or themselves. Organisa external consultants to provide a particular expertise that is unavailable ini and to bring a different and potentially more objective perspective into the organisation development process.

Table 3.2 describes the differences between these two roles at each stage of the action research process.

During the entry process, internal consultants have clear advantages. They have ready access to and relationships with clients, know the language of the organisation and have insights about the root cause of many of its problems. This allows internal consultants to save time in identifying the organisation's culture, informal practices and sources of power. They have access to a variety of information, including rumours, company reports and direct observation. In addition, entry is more efficient and congenial, and their pay is not at risk. External consultants, however, have the advantage of being able to select the clients they want to work with according to their own criteria. The contracting phase is less formal for internal consultants and there is less worry about expenses, but there is less choice about whether to complete the assignment. Both types of consultants must address issues of confidentiality, risk project termination (and other negative consequences) by the client, and fill a third-party role.

During the diagnosis process, internal consultants already know most organisation members and enjoy a basic level of rapport and trust. But external consultants often have higher status than internal consultants, which allows them to probe difficult issues and assess the organisation more objectively. In the intervention phase, both types of consultants must rely on valid information, free and informed choice, and internal commitment for their success. However, an internal consultant's strong ties to the organisation may make him or her overly cautious, particularly when powerful others can affect a career. Internal consultants also may lack certain skills and experience in facilitating organisational change. Insiders may have some small advantages in being able to move around the system and cross key organisational boundaries. Finally, the measures of success and reward differ from those of the external practitioner in the evaluation process.

A promising approach to having the advantages of both internal and external OD consultants is to include them both as members of an internal–external consulting team.[34] External consultants can combine their special expertise and objectivity with the inside knowledge and acceptance of internal consultants. The

LE 3.2 The differences between external and internal consulting

Stage of change	External consultants	Internal consultants
Entering	• Source clients • Build relationships • Learn company jargon • 'Presenting problem' challenge • Time-consuming • Stressful phase • Select project/client according to own criteria • Unpredictable outcome	• Ready access to clients • Ready relationships • Knows company jargon • Understands root causes • Time efficient • Congenial phase • Obligated to work with everyone • Steady pay
Contracting	• Formal documents • Can terminate project at will • Guard against out-of-pocket expenses • Information confidential • Loss of contract at stake • Maintain third-party role	• Informal agreements • Must complete projects assigned • No out-of-pocket expenses • Information can be open or confidential • Risk of client retaliation and loss of job at stake • Acts as third party, driver (on behalf of client), or pair of hands
Diagnosing	• Meet most organisation members for the first time • Prestige from being external • Build trust quickly • Confidential data can increase political sensitivities	• Has relationships with many organisation members • Prestige determined by job rank and client stature • Sustain reputation as trustworthy over time • Data openly shared can reduce political intrigue
Intervening	• Insist on valid information, free and informed choice and internal commitment • Confine activities within boundaries of client organisation	• Insist on valid information, free and informed choice and internal commitment • Run interference for client across organisational lines to align support
Evaluating	• Rely on repeat business and customer referral as key measures of project success • Seldom see long-term results	• Rely on repeat business, pay raise and promotion as key measures of success • Can see change become institutionalised • Little recognition for job well done

Source: M. Lacey, 'Internal consulting: perspectives on the process of planned change', *Journal of Organizational Change Management*, 8 (1995):76.

two parties can provide complementary consulting skills, while sharing the workload and possibly accomplishing more than either would by operating alone. Internal consultants, for example, can provide almost continuous contact with the client, while their external counterparts can periodically provide specialised services, perhaps on two or three days each month. External consultants can also help train their organisation partners, thus transferring OD skills and knowledge to the organisation.

Although little has been written on internal–external consulting teams, recent studies suggest that the effectiveness of such teams depends on the members developing strong, supportive, collegial relationships. They need to take time to develop the consulting team, confronting individual differences and establishing appropriate roles and exchanges. Members need to provide each other with continuous feedback and to make a commitment to learning from each other. In the absence of these team-building and learning features, internal–external consulting teams can be more troublesome and less effective than consultants working alone.

Marginality

A promising line of research on the professional OD role centres on the issue of marginality.[35] The marginal person is one who successfully straddles the boundary between two or more groups that have differing goals, value systems and behaviour patterns. In the past, the marginal role has always been seen as dysfunctional. Now marginality is seen in a more positive light. There are many examples of marginal roles in organisations: the salesperson, the buyer, the first-line supervisor, the integrator and the project manager.

Evidence is mounting that some people are better at taking marginal roles than others. Those who are good at marginal roles seem to have personal qualities of low dogmatism, neutrality, open-mindedness, objectivity, flexibility and adaptable information-processing ability. Rather than being upset by conflict, ambiguity and stress, they thrive on it. Individuals with marginal orientations are more likely than others to develop integrative decisions that bring together and reconcile viewpoints between opposing organisational groups, and are more likely to remain neutral in controversial situations. Thus, the research suggests that the marginal role[36] can have positive effects when it is filled by a person with a marginal orientation. Such a person can be more objective and better able to perform successfully in linking, integrative or conflict-laden roles.[37]

A study of 89 external OD practitioners and 246 internal practitioners (response rates of 59% and 54%, respectively) showed that external OD professionals were more comfortable with the marginal role than were internal OD professionals. Internal consultants with more years of experience were more marginally oriented than were those with less experience.[38] These findings, combined with other research on marginal roles, suggest the importance of maintaining the OD professional's marginality, with its flexibility, independence and boundary-spanning characteristics.

Emotional demands

The OD practitioner role is emotionally demanding. The importance of understanding emotions and their impact on the practitioner's effectiveness have been evidenced by research and practice support.[39] The research on emotional intelligence in organisations suggests a set of abilities that can aid OD practitioners in conducting successful change efforts.[40] Emotional intelligence refers to the ability to recognise and express emotions appropriately, to use emotions in thought and decisions, and to regulate emotion in oneself and in others. It is, therefore, a different kind of intelligence from problem-solving ability, engineering aptitude or the knowledge of concepts. In tandem with traditional knowledge and skill, emotional intelligence affects and supplements rational thought; emotions help prioritise thinking by directing attention to important information not addressed in models and theories. In that sense, some researchers argue that emotional intelligence is as important as cognitive intelligence.[41]

The importance of emotional intelligence in practice has been supported from OD practitioners' reports. From the client's perspective, OD practitioners must understand emotions well enough to relate to and help organisation members address resistance, commitment and ambiguity at each stage of planned change. Despite the predominant focus on rationality and efficiency, almost any change process must address important and difficult issues that raise emotions such as the fear of failure, rejection, anxiety and anger.[42] OD practitioners can provide psychological support, model appropriate emotional expression, reframe client perspectives and provide resources. OD practitioners must also understand their own emotions. Ambiguity, unfamiliarity or denial of emotions can lead to inaccurate and untimely interventions. For example, a practitioner who is uncomfortable with conflict may intervene to defuse an argument between two managers because of the discomfort he or she feels, not because the conflict is destructive. In such a case, the practitioner is acting to address a personal need rather than intervening to improve the system's effectiveness.

Evidence suggests that emotional intelligence increases with age and experience.[43] Research also supports the conclusion that competence with emotions can be developed through personal growth processes such as sensitivity training, counselling and therapy. It seems reasonable to suggest that professional OD practitioners dedicate themselves to a long-term regimen of development that includes acquiring both cognitive learning and emotional intelligence.

Use of knowledge and experience

The professional OD role has been described in terms of a continuum ranging from client-centred (using the client's knowledge and experience) to consultant-centred (using the consultant's knowledge and experience), as shown in Figure 3.2. Traditionally, OD consultants have worked at the client-centred end of the continuum. OD professionals, relying mainly on sensitivity training, process consultation and team building, have been expected to remain neutral, refusing to offer expert advice on organisational problems. Rather than contracting to solve specific problems, the consultant has tended to work with organisation members to

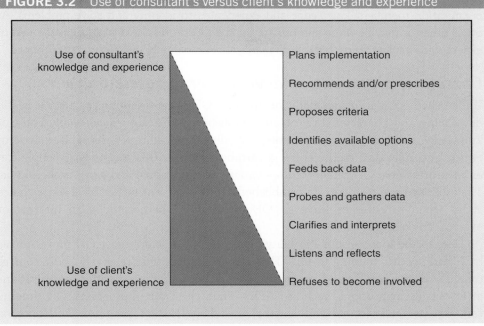

FIGURE 3.2 Use of consultant's versus client's knowledge and experience

Use of consultant's knowledge and experience

Use of client's knowledge and experience

Plans implementation

Recommends and/or prescribes

Proposes criteria

Identifies available options

Feeds back data

Probes and gathers data

Clarifies and interprets

Listens and reflects

Refuses to become involved

Source: Adapted by permission of the authors from W. Schmidt and A. Johnson, 'A continuum of consultancy styles', unpublished manuscript (July 1970): 1.

identify problems and potential solutions, to help them study what they are doing now and to consider alternative behaviours and solutions, and to help them discover whether in fact the consultant and they can learn to do things better. In doing this, the OD professional has generally listened and reflected upon members' perceptions and ideas, and helped to clarify and interpret their communications and behaviours.

With the recent proliferation of OD interventions in the structural, human resource management and strategy areas, this limited definition of the professional OD role has expanded to include the consultant-centred end of the continuum. In many of these newer approaches, the consultant may have to take on a modified role of expert, with the consent and collaboration of organisation members. For example, if a consultant and managers were to try to bring about a major structural redesign, managers may not have the appropriate knowledge and expertise to create and manage the change. The consultant's role might be to present the basic concepts and ideas and then to struggle jointly with the managers to select an approach that might be useful to the organisation and decide how it might be best implemented. In this situation, the OD professional recommends or prescribes particular changes and is active in planning how to implement them. However, this expertise is always shared rather than imposed.

With the development of new and varied intervention approaches, the role of the OD professional needs to be seen as falling along the entire continuum from client-centred to consultant-centred. At times, the consultant will rely mainly on organisation members' knowledge and experiences to identify and solve problems. At other times, it may be more appropriate for the OD professional to take on the role of expert, withdrawing from this role as managers gain more knowledge and experience.

Careers of organisation development professionals

Unlike such occupations as medicine and law, OD is an emerging practice. It is still developing the characteristics of an established profession: a common body of knowledge, educational requirements, accrediting procedures, a recognised code of ethics, and rules and methods for governing conduct. This means that people can enter professional OD careers from a variety of educational and work backgrounds. They do not have to follow an established career path, but rather have some choice about when to enter or leave an OD career and whether to be an internal or external consultant.[44]

Despite the looseness or flexibility of the OD profession, most OD professionals have had specific training in OD. This training can include relatively short courses (one day to two weeks) and programs or workshops conducted within organisations or at outside institutions, such as TAFE's 'Train the Trainer' programs. OD training can also be more formal and lengthy, including master's programs and doctoral training.

As might be expected, career choices widen as people gain training and experience in OD. Those with rudimentary training tend to be internal consultants, often taking on OD roles as temporary assignments on the way to higher managerial or staff positions. Holders of master's degrees are generally evenly split between internal and external consultants. Those with doctorates may join a university faculty and consult part-time, join a consulting firm or seek a position as a relatively high-level internal consultant.

External consultants tend to be older, to have more managerial experience, and to spend more of their time in OD than do internal practitioners. Perhaps the most common career path is to begin as an internal consultant, gain experience and visibility through successful interventions or publishing and then become an external consultant. A field study found that internal consultants acquired greater competence by working with external consultants who deliberately helped to develop them. This development took place through a tutorial arrangement of joint diagnosis and intervention in the organisation, which gave the internal consultants a chance to observe and learn from the model furnished by the external consultants.[45]

There is increasing evidence that an OD career can be stressful, sometimes leading to burnout.[46] Burnout comes from taking on too many jobs, becoming overcommitted and, in general, working too hard. OD work often requires six-day weeks, with some days running up to 15 hours. Consultants may spend a week working with one organisation or department and then spend the weekend preparing for the next client. They may spend 50–75% of their time on the road, living in planes, cars, hotels, meetings and restaurants. Indeed, one practitioner has suggested that the majority of OD consultants would repeat the phrase 'quality of work life for consultants' as follows: 'Quality of work life? For consultants?'[47]

Organisation development professionals are increasingly taking steps to cope with burnout. They may shift jobs, moving from external to internal roles to avoid travel. They may learn to pace themselves better and to avoid taking on too much work.

PROFESSIONAL VALUES

Values have played an important role in OD from its beginning. Traditionally, OD professionals have promoted a set of humanistic and democratic values. They have sought to build trust and collaboration; to create an open, problem-solving climate; and to increase the self-control of organisation members. More recently, OD practitioners have extended those humanistic values to include a concern for improving organisational effectiveness (for example, to increase productivity or to reduce turnover) and performance (for example, to increase profitability). They have shown an increasing desire to optimise both human benefits and production objectives.[48]

The joint values of humanising organisations and improving their effectiveness have received widespread support in the OD profession, as well as increasing encouragement from managers, employees and union officials. Indeed, it would be difficult not to support these joint concerns. But, increasingly, questions have been raised about the possibility of simultaneously pursuing greater humanism and organisational effectiveness.[49] More practitioners are experiencing situations in which there is conflict between the employees' needs for greater meaning and the organisation's need for more effective and efficient use of its resources. For example, expensive capital equipment may run most efficiently if it is highly programmed and routinised; yet people may not derive satisfaction from working with such technology. Should efficiency be maximised at the expense of people's satisfaction? Can technology be changed to make it more humanly satisfying yet remain efficient? What compromises are possible? These are the value dilemmas often faced when trying to optimise both human benefits and organisational effectiveness.

In addition to value issues within organisations, OD practitioners are dealing more and more with value conflicts with powerful outside groups. Organisations are open systems and exist within increasingly turbulent environments. For example, hospitals are facing complex and changing task environments. Australia has long had privately owned hospitals and now public hospitals are being offered to private operators. This means a proliferation of external stakeholders with interests in the organisation's functioning, including patients, suppliers, health insurance funds, employers, the government, shareholders, unions, the press and various interest groups. These external groups often have different and competing values for judging the organisation's effectiveness. For example, shareholders may judge the business in terms of price per share, the government in terms of compliance with Equal Employment Opportunity legislation, patients in terms of quality of care, and ecology groups in terms of hazardous waste disposal. Because organisations must rely on these external groups for resources and legitimacy, they cannot simply ignore these competing values: they must somehow respond to them and try to reconcile the different interests.

Recent attempts to help organisations manage external relationships suggest the need for new interventions and competence in OD.[50] Practitioners must have not only social skills (like those proposed in Table 3.1) but also political skills. They must understand the distribution of power, conflicts of interest and value dilemmas inherent in managing external relationships and be able to manage their own role and values in respect to those dynamics. Interventions promoting collaboration and system maintenance may be ineffective in this larger arena, especially when there are power and dominance relationships between organisations, plus competition for scarce resources. Under these conditions, OD practitioners may need more power-oriented interventions, such as bargaining, coalition forming and pressure tactics.

For example, firms in the tobacco industry have waged an aggressive campaign against efforts of groups such as the Australian Medical Association, the Royal Australasian College of General Practitioners, the Australian Cancer Society and the federal and state governments, to limit or ban the smoking of tobacco products. They have formed a powerful industry coalition to lobby against anti-smoking legislation, and they have spent enormous sums of money sponsoring leading sporting and culture events, conducting public relations and refuting research that purportedly shows the dangers of smoking. These power-oriented strategies are intended to manage an increasingly hostile environment. They may be necessary for the industry's survival. People practising OD in such settings may need to help organisations implement such strategies if they are to manage their environments effectively. This will require political skills and greater attention to how the OD practitioner's own values fit with those of the organisation.

Application 3.4 presents environmental practices for the development of an organisation.

3.4

APPLICATION

Clean green sweep

The toll-free telephone line at Craig Mostyn Group's PPC Linley Valley pork abattoir, 60km east of Perth, fell silent 18 months ago, but this doesn't worry executive director Andrew Mostyn. Quite the contrary. It is his job, in part, to stop that number from ringing. 'There is an 1800 line for people to ring with complaints,' he says. 'We used to get a fair number from neighbours.'

Mostyn co-ordinates his company's response to climate change and as the company moves to reduce its greenhouse gas emissions and recycle water and waste, its operations have become cleaner, neater and less smelly for its neighbours. The dramatic fall in complaints is one immediate benefit. Another is staffing. 'Finding staff is so much easier when you have a good work environment,' Mostyn says.

Craig Mostyn Group – a private company owned by the Mostyn family for three generations – is the winner of the BRW ANZ Excellence in Environmental Practices award. The company's

>>

revenue for 2008–09 was $293.8 million from its three divisions, meat and livestock (pigs), seafood and recycling.

Meat and livestock is a messy, water and energy-intensive business. On three farms – two owned and one leased – the company breeds, grows, slaughters and processes pigs and pig-meat products. It distributes them around Australia and overseas. Its abattoir is the only one in Western Australia accredited for pork exports and the company is responsible for about half of Australia's pork exports to Singapore.

The recycling division renders animal waste – everything that comes from its own and other abattoirs that cannot be sold, such as fat, blood and bones – into tallow and bone meal, sold for animal feed, soaps, detergents and, more recently, biodiesel.

It talks a lot of water – about 260 000 litres a year – to keep the farms and abattoir hygienic and a lot of energy to render 100 000 tonnes of waste each year, including the 10.5 tonnes from its own operations.

The company emits about 25 000 tonnes of greenhouse gases a year but the process of rendering animal waste provides three environmental benefits. First, the rendered waste is not swamping the state's limited landfill. 'One hundred thousand tonnes of waste would fill WA's landfill in weeks,' Mostyn says. Second, animal waste left in landfill produces greenhouse gases. For each metric tonne of CO_2 produced by operating rendering plants, 7.19 metric tonnes of CO_2 are removed from the environment, the American National Renderers Association says. In Craig Mostyn's case, this is a saving of 179 750 tonnes of CO_2 emissions. Finally, the waste is 100 per cent recycled and turned into valuable products.

Andrew Mostyn is the grandson of Robert Mostyn, who founded the company in 1932 with George Craig. He is the only third-generation Mostyn working in the business (the Craig family exited in the 1960s). Andrew's father, Robert Jr, who retired as chairman eight years ago at the age of 72, and his sisters appeared on the BRW Rich 200 list from 1993–96.

The company included a corporate social responsibility segment to its biannual report to shareholders four years ago, but Mostyn says the company was committed to CSR before this. The company's water recycling program does not earn revenue; it costs money. The treated water, which is processed through anaerobic and six aerobic ponds, irrigates the neighbouring 27-hectare golf course of the El Caballo Resort.

The waste business made nearly $100 million in revenue last year. The profit margins for the products of processing animal waste fluctuate widely, with sale prices for tallow and meal ranging from $484 to S968 a tonne. Craig Mostyn exports rendered products to more than 20 countries.

'Rendering is a capital-intensive business,' Mostyn says. 'The [waste] material is cheap and people are reluctant to move to new technology. We have embraced new technology in recent years, and will increase that.'

Source: Kath Walters, 'Clean green sweep', *Business Review Weekly*, 27 August 2009, p. 39.

Critical thinking questions:
1. What characteristics of a successful change agent is exhibited by Andrew Mostyn?
2. What is corporate social responsibility (CSR)? Where is this evidenced in the application?

PROFESSIONAL ETHICS

Ethical issues in OD are concerned with how practitioners perform their helping relationship with organisation members. Inherent in any helping relationship is the potential for misconduct and client abuse. OD practitioners can let personal values stand in the way of good practice; they can use the power inherent in their professional role to abuse organisation members (often unintentionally).

Ethical guidelines

To its credit, the field of OD has always shown concern for the ethical conduct of its practitioners. There have been several articles and conferences about ethics in OD. The School of Management, the Australian Business Ethics Network at the Royal Melbourne Institute of Technology (RMIT) and the St James Ethics Centre conducted a successful one-day symposium on teaching and training in business ethics.[51] In addition, statements of ethics governing OD practice have been sponsored by many professional associations; for example, the Australian Association for Professional and Applied Ethics (AAPAE) comprises academics and professionals across a range of disciplines in a non-partisan and non-profit association, while Corporate Ethics is committed to helping business develop a strategic system that incorporates value and ethics.[52] The accounting industry is just one of many professions that has codes of ethics.[53] Both the Chartered Practising Accountants Australia (CPA Australia) and the Institute of Chartered Accountants in Australia (ICAA) now follow the Code of Ethics for Professional Accountants (APES 110) as issued by the Accounting Professional and Ethical Standards Board (APESB). Visit http://apesb.org.au/ to view the Code.

Ethical dilemmas

Although adherence to statements of ethics helps prevent ethical problems from occurring, OD practitioners can still encounter ethical dilemmas. Figure 3.3 is a process model that explains how ethical dilemmas can occur in OD. The antecedent conditions include an OD practitioner and a client system with different goals, values, needs, skills and abilities. During the entry and contracting phase, there is an intention to address and clarify these differences. As a practical matter, however, it is reasonable to assume that these differences may or may not be addressed and clarified. Under such circumstances, the subsequent intervention process or role episode is subject to role conflict and role ambiguity. Neither the client nor the OD practitioner is clear about his or her respective responsibilities. Each party is pursuing different goals, and each is using different skills and values to achieve those goals. The role conflict and ambiguity can lead to five types of ethical dilemmas: (1) misrepresentation, (2) misuse of data, (3) coercion, (4) value and goal conflict, and (5) technical ineptitude.

Misrepresentation

This occurs when OD practitioners claim that an intervention will produce results that are unreasonable for the change program or the situation. The client can contribute to this problem by portraying inaccurate goals and needs. In either case,

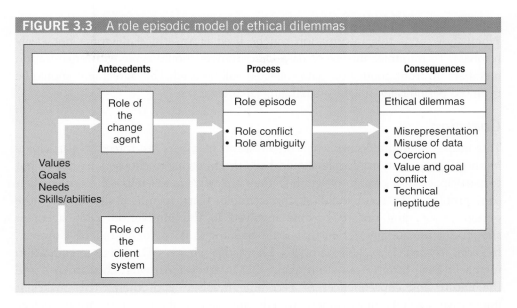

FIGURE 3.3 A role episodic model of ethical dilemmas

Source: L. White and M. Rhodeback, 'Ethical dilemmas in organization development: a cross-cultural analysis', Figure 1, *Journal of Business Ethics*, 11 (1992): 663–70. With kind permission from Springer Science Business Media.

one or both parties are operating under false pretences and an ethical dilemma exists. For example, in an infamous case called 'The undercover change agent', an attempt was made to use laboratory training in an organisation whose top management did not understand it and was not ready for it. The OD consultant sold 'T-groups' as the intervention that would solve the problems that faced the organisation. After the chairman of the business made a surprise visit to the site where the training was being held, the consultant was fired. The nature and style of the T-group was in direct contradiction to the chairman's concepts about leadership.[54] Misrepresentation is likely to occur in the entering and contracting phases of planned change when the initial consulting relationship is being established. To prevent misrepresentation, OD practitioners need to be very clear about the goals of the change effort and to explore openly with the client its expected effects, its relevance to the client system and the practitioner's competence in executing the intervention.

Misuse of data

This occurs when information gathered during the OD process is used punitively. Large amounts of information are invariably obtained during the entry and diagnostic phases of OD; although most OD practitioners value openness and trust, it is important that they be aware of how such data are going to be used. It is a human tendency to use data to enhance a power position. Openness is one thing, but leaking inappropriate information can be harmful to individuals and to the organisation as well. It is easy for a consultant, under the guise of obtaining information, to gather data about whether a particular manager is good or bad. When, how or if this information can be used is an ethical dilemma not easily resolved. To minimise misuse of data, practitioners should agree with organisation members up front about how data collected will be used. This agreement should be reviewed periodically in light of changing circumstances.

Coercion

This ethical dilemma occurs when organisation members are forced to participate in an OD intervention. People should have the freedom to choose whether or not to participate in a change program if they are to gain self-reliance to solve their own problems. In team building, for example, team members should have the option of deciding not to become involved in the intervention. Management should not unilaterally decide that team building is good for members. However, freedom to make a choice implies knowledge about OD. Many organisation members have little information about OD interventions, what they involve and the nature and consequences of becoming involved with them. This makes it imperative for OD practitioners to educate clients about interventions before choices are made as to whether or not to implement them.

Coercion can also pose ethical dilemmas for the helping relationship between OD practitioners and organisation members. Inherent in any helping relationship are possibilities for excessive manipulation and dependency, two facets of coercion. Kelman pointed out that behaviour change 'inevitably involves some degree of manipulation and control, and at least an implicit imposition of the change agent's values on the client or the person he [or she] is influencing'.[55] This places the practitioner on two horns of a dilemma: (1) any attempt to change is in itself a change and thereby a manipulation, no matter how slight; and (2) there exists no formula or method to structure a change situation so that such manipulation can be totally absent. To attack the first aspect of the dilemma, Kelman stressed freedom of choice, seeing any action that limits freedom of choice as being ethically ambiguous or worse. To address the second aspect, Kelman argued that the OD practitioner must remain keenly aware of her or his own value system and alert to the possibility that these values are being imposed upon a client. In other words, an effective way to resolve this dilemma is to make the change effort as open as possible, with the free consent and knowledge of the individuals involved.

The second facet of coercion that can pose ethical dilemmas for the helping relationship involves dependency. Helping relationships invariably create dependency between those who need help and those who provide it.[56] A major goal in OD is to lessen the clients' dependency on consultants by helping them gain the knowledge and skills to address organisational problems and manage change themselves. In some cases, however, achieving independence from OD practitioners can result in the clients being either counterdependent or overdependent,[57] especially in the early stages of the relationship. To resolve dependency issues, consultants can openly and explicitly discuss with the client how to handle the dependency problem, especially what the client and consultant expect of one another. Another approach is to focus on problem finding. Usually, the client is looking for a solution to a perceived problem. The consultant can redirect the energy to improved joint diagnosis so that both are working on problem identification and problem solving. This moves the energy of the client away from dependency. Finally, dependency can be reduced by changing the client's expectation – from being helped or controlled by the practitioner – to focusing on the need to manage the problem. This helps to reinforce the concept that the consultant is working for the client and offering assistance at the client's discretion.

Value and goal conflict

This ethical dilemma occurs when the purpose of the change effort is not clear or when the client and the practitioner disagree over how to achieve the goals. The important practical issue for OD consultants is whether it is justifiable to unilaterally withhold services from an organisation that does not agree with their values or methods. Lippitt suggested that the real question is the following: Assuming that some kind of change is going to occur anyway, doesn't the consultant have a responsibility to try to guide the change in the most constructive fashion possible?[58] The question may be of greater importance and relevance to an internal consultant or to a consultant who already has an ongoing relationship with the client.

Argyris takes an even stronger stand, maintaining that the responsibilities of professional OD practitioners to clients are comparable to those of lawyers or doctors, who, in principle, are not permitted to refuse their services. He suggests that the very least the consultant can do is provide 'first aid' to the organisation as long as the assistance does not compromise the consultant's values. Argyris suggests that if the Ku Klux Klan were to ask for assistance and the consultant could at least determine that the KKK was genuinely interested in assessing itself and willing to commit itself to all that a valid assessment would entail concerning both itself and other groups, the consultant should be willing to help. If the Klan's objectives later prove to be less than honestly stated, the consultant would be free to withdraw without being compromised.[59]

Technical ineptitude

This final ethical dilemma occurs when OD practitioners attempt to implement interventions for which they are not skilled or when the client attempts a change for which it is not ready. Critical to the success of any OD program is the selection of an appropriate intervention, which depends, in turn, on careful diagnosis of the organisation. Selection of an intervention is closely related to the practitioner's own values, skills and abilities. In solving organisational problems, many OD consultants tend to emphasise a favourite intervention or technique, such as team building, total quality management or self-managed teams. They let their own values and beliefs dictate the change method.[60] Technical ineptitude dilemmas can also occur when interventions do not align with the ability of the organisation to implement them. Again, careful diagnosis can reveal the extent to which the organisation is ready to make a change and possesses the skills and knowledge to implement it.

Application 3.5 describes a new social responsibility and ethic guide for companies to report their environmental credentials, so that companies could achieve higher share prices in the long term if they revealed more information about their activities to superannuation funds.

3.5

APPLICATION

Super funds demand to see green credentials

Superannuation funds are urging companies to provide the capital markets with information on a broader range of their activities, including their environmental performance, arguing it will lead to higher share prices in the long run. VicSuper chief executive Bob Welsh said he wanted companies to report on non-financial matters in a more standard way, so investors could make more meaningful comparisons between companies. 'The sooner companies recognise that these issues are going to materially impact their long-term shareholder value, the better position they are going to be in,' Mr Welsh said.

Cbus chief executive David Atkin said super funds had been asking fund managers to include matters such as the impact of climate-change policies in their decision-making. 'Our expectation is our fund managers should be including that framework in their analysis. Climate change, changes in regulation, price of carbon is material. They need to have undertaken modelling,' Mr Atkin said.

Australian Council of Super Investors president Michael O'Sullivan said that while some companies were disclosing such information well, 'there is quite a number who are not reporting at all, or not reporting in a way that's much help to investors'. Mr O'Sullivan said it was clear that good governance, including reporting on environmental risks, 'makes a difference to share price'. 'If you disclose that to your shareholders, it does build confidence,' he said. 'That's what builds sustainable wealth creation through the share price. Ultimately, it reduces your cost of capital.'

The push comes as finance executives from the nation's biggest companies, the Group of 100, and KPMG will this week launch a new guide for companies on dealing with the financial effects and reporting of carbon emissions. It also comes as a new paper, to be released today, argues the current economic climate has made it more important for companies to broaden their reporting.

'Financial modelling by sophisticated capital market players is forced to rely too much on extrapolation, assumptions, industry-based input, and unaudited and inconsistent information,' the paper, by the Institute of Chartered Accountants in Australia (ICAA), finds. 'As such there are gaps in company-specific information and prospects of the business.'

Cannae Capital managing partner Hugh Giddy said there was an increasing focus on so-called environmental, social and governance (ESG) performance of companies, particularly from institutions such as super funds. 'Companies already report in some detail on governance, but with the focus on carbon emissions many companies will need to report on their exposure and strategy to satisfy investors,' Mr Giddy said.

Fund managers say that while there has been a focus on governance matters such as executive remuneration recently, companies should focus increasingly on environmental

>>

issues. 'We've been holding companies to account on governance issues for a long time – how is the board structured, how do you pay your executives? – that's nothing new,' QIC's portfolio manager for Australian equities, Tony Edwards, said. 'There has been more focus on it and generally the quality of governance has improved each year.

'It's more around the environmental and social impacts of companies. There is a lot more awareness. With the emissions trading scheme, with some companies there will be quite significant financial impacts in adhering to this.'

Super funds point to research by Goldman Sachs JBWere analyst Andrew Gray, which has found that companies considered to have good corporate governance tend to outperform that broader ASX 200 index.

'We see the investor community wanting more information,' said the ICAA's general manager of leadership and quality, Lee White. 'It will give Australia a global advantage, no doubt about it. When we talk about attracting money and capital, it's not just in the nationalistic sense; it's really the global flow of money. It's the global investors that will pour the money into Australia.'

The push comes amid broader concerns that investors are forced to rely on inconsistent information in the way companies report.

'The framework of company reporting needs to be seriously looked at and refreshed,' KPMG's head of audit, Peter Nash, said. Mr Nash also supported 'businesses being clear to their stakeholders and shareholders what their key measurement indicators are' but that 'template reporting' for industries would not work.

Investors are also concerned that there is greater consistency in how companies adjust their figures to arrive at so-called 'underlying profits' amid a surge in the number of companies using them to communicate results. These figures are less formal than heavily regulated statutory profits and strip out the recent spike in one-offs such as the asset write-downs that have totalled at least $60 billion since the beginning of the financial crisis.

Mr Nash said there was a 'degree of inconsistency' in what companies stripped out from statutory profit to derive underlying profit.

Mr Giddy said that with the recent spate of asset write-downs, some investors would feel lost without the underlying profit numbers and would base their analysis on what the company put to them. 'Companies do have an incentive in most instances to present as good a picture as they can,' he said.

The Group of 100's national president and OneSteel's chief financial officer, Tony Reeves, said there was transparency in the adjustments to profit figures because statutory and underlying profit were reconciled.

Mr Reeves pointed to an updated guide released earlier this year by the Financial Services Institute of Australia and the Australian Institute of Company Directors that aimed to address concerns with underlying earnings.

AICD chief executive John Colvin said directors were concerned to get their reports to the market right because of the liability they otherwise faced.

Source: Annabel Hepworth and John Kehoe, 'Super funds demand to see green credentials', *The Australian Financial Review*, 8 September 2009, p. 1/10.

Critical thinking questions:
1. Why is it important to build confidence in the governance system within an organisation?
2. 'It's more around the environmental and social impacts of companies.' What does this mean in the context of this application?

Summary

This chapter examined the role of leaders in the change process. This term applies to three kinds of people: individuals specialising in OD as a profession, people from related fields who have gained some competence in OD and managers who have the OD skills necessary to change and develop their organisations or departments. Comprehensive lists exist of core and advanced skills and knowledge that an effective OD specialist should possess, but a smaller set of basic skills and knowledge is applicable for all practitioners, regardless of whether they are OD professionals, related specialists or managers. These include four kinds of background: intrapersonal skills, interpersonal skills, general consultation skills and knowledge of OD theory.

The professional OD role can apply to internal consultants who belong to the organisation undergoing change, to external consultants who are members of universities and consulting firms or are self-employed, and to members of internal–external consulting teams. The OD practitioner's role may be aptly described in terms of marginality and emotional demands. People with a tolerance for marginal roles seem especially adapted for OD practice because they are able to maintain neutrality and objectivity, and develop integrative solutions that reconcile viewpoints between opposing organisational departments. Similarly, the OD practitioner's emotional intelligence and awareness are keys to implementing the role successfully. Whereas, in the past, the OD practitioner's role has been described as falling at the client end of the continuum from client-centred to consultant-centred functioning, the development of new and varied interventions has shifted the role of the OD professional to cover the entire range of this continuum.

Although OD is still an emerging profession, most OD professionals have specific training in OD, ranging from short courses and workshops to graduate and doctoral education. No single career path exists, but internal consulting is often a stepping-stone to becoming an external consultant. Because of the hectic pace of OD practice, OD specialists should be prepared to cope with high levels of stress and the possibility of career burnout.

Values have played a key role in OD, and traditional values promoting trust, collaboration and openness have recently been supplemented with concerns for improving organisational effectiveness and productivity. OD specialists may face value dilemmas in trying to jointly optimise human benefits and organisation performance. They may also encounter value conflicts when dealing with powerful external stakeholders, such as the government, stockholders and customers. Dealing with these outside groups may take political skills, as well as the more traditional social skills.

Ethical issues in OD involve how practitioners perform their helping role with clients. OD has always shown a concern for the ethical conduct of practitioners,

and several ethical codes for OD practice have been developed by the various professional associations in OD. Ethical dilemmas in OD tend to arise around the following issues: misrepresentation, misuse of data, coercion, value and goal conflict, and technical ineptitude.

Activities

REVIEW QUESTIONS

1 Distinguish between an internal and an external change agent. Give examples, or explain particular circumstances, where internal and external change agents have exercised successful change programs.

2 Why is it important to clarify any organisational issues?

3 What are the steps necessary to enter a contract with a change agent?

4 What are the core skills of an OD practitioner? How do you think these skills would differ from those of a practitioner who is known to favour organisation transformation (OT)?

5 What are the advantages and disadvantages of an internal change agent? Compare these with the advantages and disadvantages of an external change agent. Give examples that clearly delineate between the two.

6 Explain what is meant by 'emotional demands' and why is it important to consider in a change process?

7 What is meant by the 'professional ethics' of a change agent? Do you know of any instances where there may be conflict? Explain the circumstances.

DISCUSSION AND ESSAY QUESTIONS

1 'The OD practitioner is the primary leader of change.' Discuss.

2 What are the important considerations that a change leader needs to clarify before entering a change process? What difficulties do you envisage?

3 Discuss the role of the OD practitioner in depth. It would be advisable to interview several change agents to get their varied, or differing, perspectives.

4 Which would be more beneficial for an organisation – an external or an internal change agent? What are the factors that need to be considered

before such a choice is made? What would be the ideal scenario? Explain your answer.

5 'Emotional intelligence increases with age and experience'. Do you agree or disagree? Explain your answer.

6 What type of ethical considerations would confront an OD practitioner and how may they be addressed? Investigate instances where there have been contentious situations and the resolution you would recommend.

7 Debate: 'Burnout is prevalent among change agents.'

SEARCH ME! EXCERCISES

> ▶ Search me! 🖑

Explore **Search me! management** for relevant articles on leadership and the role of the change agent. Search me! is an online library of world-class journals, e-books and newspapers, including *The Australian* and *The New York Times*, and is updated daily. Log in to Search me! through **http://login.cengage.com** using the access card in the front of this book.

Keywords

Try searching for the following terms:
> Code of conduct
> OD practitioner

> Professional ethics
> Professional values

>> Search tip:

Search me! management contains information from both local and international sources. To get the greatest number of search results, try using both Australian and American spellings in your searches, e.g. 'globalisation' and 'globalization'; 'organisation' and 'organization'.

Notes

1 B. B. Grossman PHD, 'MBA Client Centered Consulting (CCC) Overview', www.hsod.net/Client%20Centered%20Consulting.html, cited 12 June 2010.

2 R. James, *Faith-Based Organisational Development (OD) with Churches in Malawi*, INTRAC: International NGO Training and Research Centre, www.intrac.org/data/files/resources/584/Praxis-Note-47-Faith-Based-Organisational-Development-with-Churches-in-Malawi.pdf, cited 13 June 2010.

3 M. Touchstone, *Professional Development: Part 5–Core Humanistic Values*, www.emsresponder.com/print/EMS-Magazine/Professional-Development–Part-5Core–Humanistic-Values/1$12975, cited 12 June 2010.

4 A. Church and W. Burke, 'Practitioner attitudes about the field of organization development', in *Organization Change and Development*, eds W. Pasmore and R. Woodman (Greenwich, CT: JAI Press, 1995).

5 Carlson, Dawn S., Upton, Nancy, Seaman, Samuel, 'The impact of human resource practices and compensation design on performance: an analysis of family-owned SMEs', *Journal of Small Business Management*, www.allbusiness.com/management-companies-enterprises/3897253-1.html, 12 March 2007.

6 Centre for Corporate Change in the Australian Graduate School of Management, The University of NSW and The University of Sydney, www.ccc.agsm.edu.au.

7 Centre for Corporate Change, Working Papers, Nos 005 and 028.

8 E. E. Lawler III and C. G. Worley, 'Winning support for organizational change: Designing employee reward systems that keep on working', www.ibj.ca/view_article.asp?intArticle_ID=619, April 2006.

9 C. Margerison, 'Consulting activities in organizational change', *Journal of Organizational Change Management*, 1 (1988): 60–7; P. Block, *Flawless Consulting: A Guide to Getting Your Expertise Used* (Austin, TX: Learning Concepts, 1981); R. Harrison, 'Choosing the depth of organizational intervention', *Journal of Applied Behavioural Science*, 6:11 (1970): 182–202.

10 M. Beer, *Organization Change and Development: A Systems View* (Santa Monica, CA: Goodyear, 1980); G. Lippitt and R. Lippitt, *The Consulting Process in Action*, 2nd edn (San Diego: University Associates, 1986).

11 L. Greiner and R. Metzger, *Consulting to Management* (Englewood Cliffs, NJ: Prentice-Hall, 1983): 251–8; Beer, *Organization Change and Development*, op. cit.: 81–3.

12 F. Bevilacqua, 'The impact of organisational issues in the development of institutional repositories', University of Parma, www.dspace.org/images/Training_Materials/The%20impact%20of%20organisational%20issues%20in%20the%20development%20of%20institutional%20repositories.pdf, 17 October 2007.

13 Block, *Flawless Consulting*, op. cit.

14 J. Fordyce and R. Weil, *Managing WITH People*, 2nd edn (Reading, MA: Addison-Wesley, 1979).

15 Beer, *Organization Change and Development*, op. cit.; Fordyce and Weil, *Managing WITH People*, op. cit.

16 N. Raab, 'Working with the client consultant relationship: why every step is an "intervention"', *OD Practitioner*, 36 (2004), www.raaborganisationaldynamics.com.au/pdfs/The%20Client%20Consultant%20Relationship%20Why%20Every%20Step%20is%20an%20Intervention.pdf.

17 D. Hamlin, 'Interdepartmental conflict resolution intervention strategy', Berkeley, California, USA, www.helium.com/items/1779621-methods-to-resolve-interdepartmental-team-conflict, cited 18 June 2010.

18 G. Lippitt, 'Criteria for selecting, evaluating, and developing consultants', *Training and Development Journal*, 28 (August 1972): 10–15.

19 Greiner and Metzger, *Consulting to Management*, op. cit.

20 Block, *Flawless Consulting*, op. cit.; Beer, *Organization Change and Development*, op. cit.

21 T. Cody, *Management Consulting: A Game Without Chips* (Fitzwilliam, NH: Kennedy and Kennedy, 1986): 108–16; H. Holtz, *How to Succeed as an Independent Consultant*, 2nd edn (New York: John Wiley and Sons, 1988): 145–61.

22 G. Bellman, *The Consultant's Calling* (San Francisco: Jossey-Bass, 1990).

23 M. Weisbord, 'The organization development contract', *Organization Development Practitioner*, 5:11 (1973): 1–4; M. Weisbord, 'The organization contract revisited', *Consultation*, 4 (Winter 1985): 305–15; D. Nadler, *Feedback and Organization Development: Using Data Based Methods* (Reading, MA: Addison-Wesley, 1977): 110–14.

24 Block, *Flawless Consulting*, op. cit.

25 Ibid.

26 M. Lacey, 'Internal consulting: perspectives on the process of planned change', *Journal of Organization Change Management*, 8:3 (1995): 75–84; J. Geirland and M. Maniker-Leiter, 'Five lessons for internal organization development consultants', *OD Practitioner*, 27 (1995): 44–8.

27 B. Glickman, 'Qualities of change agents' (unpublished manuscript, May 1974); R. Havelock, *The Change Agent's Guide to Innovation in Education* (Englewood Cliffs, NJ: Educational Technology, 1973): 5; R. Lippitt, 'Dimensions of the consultant's job', in *The Planning of Change*, eds W. Bennis, K. Benne and R. Chin (New York: Holt, Rinehart and Winston, 1961): 156–61; C. Rogers, *On Becoming a Person* (Boston: Houghton Mifflin, 1971); N. Paris, 'Some thoughts on the qualifications for a consultant' (unpublished manuscript, 1973); 'OD experts reflect on the major skills needed by consultants: with comments from Edgar Schein', *Academy of Management OD Newsletter* (Spring 1979): 1–4.

28 D. Harvey and D. Brown, *An Experiential Approach to Organization Development*, 5th edn (Englewood Cliffs, NJ: Prentice Hall, 1996): 94–6.

29 C. Worley, W. Rothwell and R. Sullivan, 'Competencies of OD Practitioners', in *Practicing Organization Development*, 2nd edn, eds W. Rothwell and R. Sullivan (San Diego: Pfeiffer, 2005).

30 J. Esper, 'Core competencies in organization development' (independent study conducted as partial fulfilment of the MBA degree, Graduate School of Business Administration, University of Southern California, June 1987); E. Neilsen, *Becoming an OD Practitioner* (Englewood Cliffs, NJ: Prentice-Hall, 1984); S. Eisen, H. Steele and J. Cherbeneau, 'Developing OD competence for the future', in *Practicing Organization Development*, eds W. Rothwell, R. Sullivan and G. McLean (San Diego: Pfeiffer, 1995).

31 B. Tannenbaum, 'Letter to the editor', Consulting Practice Communique, *Academy of Management Managerial Consultation Division*, 21:3 (1993): 16–17; B. Tannenbaum, 'Self-awareness: an essential element underlying consultant effectiveness', *Journal of Organizational Change Management*, 8:3 (1995): 85–6.

32 A. Church and W. Burke, 'Practitioner attitudes about the field of organization development', in *Organization Change and Development*, eds W. Pasmore and R. Woodman (Greenwich, CT: JAI Press, 1995).

33 M. Lacey, 'Internal consulting: perspectives on the process of planned change', *Journal of Organizational Change Management*, 8:3 (1995): 75–84.

34 E. Kirkhart and T. Isgar, 'Quality of work life for consultants: the internal–external relationship', *Consultation*, 5 (Spring 1986): 5–23; J. Thacker and N. Kulick, 'The use of consultants in joint union/management quality of work life efforts', *Consultation*, 5 (Summer 1986): 116–26.

35 R. Ziller, *The Social Self* (Elmsford, NY: Pergamon, 1973).

36 D. W. Puchniak, *The Marginal Role of Hostile Takeovers in Japanese Corporate Governance Remains Unchanged*, www.law.usyd.edu.au/anjel/documents/2010/DelusionsofHostility.pdf, 2010.

37 R. Ziller, B. Stark and H. Pruden, 'Marginality and integrative management positions', *Academy of Management Journal*, 12 (December 1969): 487–95; H. Pruden and B. Stark, 'Marginality associated with interorganizational linking process, productivity and satisfaction', *Academy of Management Journal*, 14 (March 1971): 145–8; W. Liddell, 'Marginality and integrative decisions', *Academy of Management Journal*, 16 (March 1973): 154–6; P. Brown and C. Cotton, 'Marginality, a force for the OD practitioner', *Training and Development Journal*, 29 (April 1975): 14–18; H. Aldrich and D. Gerker, 'Boundary spanning roles and organizational structure', *Academy of Management Review*, 2 (April 1977): 217–30; C. Cotton, 'Marginality – a neglected dimension in the design of work', *Academy of Management Review*, 2 (January 1977): 133–8; N. Margulies, 'Perspectives on the marginality of the consultant's role', in *The Cutting Edge*, ed. W. Burke (La Jolla, CA: University Associates, 1978): 60–79.

38 P. Brown, C. Cotton and R. Golembiewski, 'Marginality and the OD practitioner', *Journal of Applied Behavioural Science*, 13 (1977): 493–506.

39 C. Lundberg and C. Young, 'A note on emotions and consultancy,' *Journal of Organisational Change Management* 14 (2001): 530–8; A. Carr, 'Understanding emotion and emotionality in a process of change,' *Journal of Organisational Change Management*, 14 (2001): 421–36.

40 D. Goleman, *Emotional Intelligence* (New York: Bantam Books, 1995); R. Cooper and A. Sawaf, *Executive EQ: Emotional Intelligence in Leadership and Organisations* (New York: Grosset/Putnam, 1997); P. Salovey and D. Sluyter, eds, *Emotional Development and Emotional Intelligence* (New York: Basic Books, 1997).

41 Goleman, *Emotional Intelligence*.

42 J. Sanford, *Fritz Kunkel: Selected Writings* (Mahwah, N.J.: Paulist Press, 1984) Lundberg and Young, 'Note on emotions', op. cit.; Carr, 'Understanding emotion', op. cit.

43 J. Ciarrochi, J. Forgas and J. Mayer, *Emotional Intelligence in Everyday Life: A Scientific Inquiry* (New York: Psychology Press, 2001).

44 D. Kegan, 'Organization development as OD network members see it', *Group and Organization Studies*, 7 (March 1982): 5–11.

45 J. Lewis III, 'Growth of internal change agents in organizations', PhD Dissertation, Case Western Reserve University, 1970.

46 G. Edelwich and A. Brodsky, *Burn-Out Stages of Disillusionment in the Helping Professions* (New York:

Human Science, 1980); M. Weisbord, 'The wizard of OD: or, what have magic slippers to do with burnout, evaluation, resistance, planned change, and action research?', *The OD Practitioner*, 10 (Summer 1978): 1–14; M. Mitchell, 'Consultant burnout', in *The 1977 Annual Handbook for Group Facilitators*, eds J. Jones and W. Pfeiffer (La Jolla, CA: University Associates, 1977): 145–56.

47 T. Isgar, 'Quality of work life of consultants', *Academy of Management OD Newsletter* (Winter 1983): 2–4.

48 A. Church and W. Burke, 'Practitioner attitudes about the field of organization development', in *Organization Change and Development*, eds W. Pasmore and R. Woodman (Greenwich, CT: JAI Press, 1995).

49 T. Cummings, 'Designing effective work groups', in *Handbook of Organisational Design*, eds P. Nystrom and W. Starbuck (Oxford: Oxford University Press, 1981): 250–71.

50 J. Schermerhorn, 'Interorganizational development', *Journal of Management*, 5 (1979): 21–38; T. Cummings, 'Interorganisation theory and organisation development', in *Systems Theory for Organisation Development*, ed. T. Cummings (Chichester: John Wiley and Sons, 1980): 323–38.

51 www.bf.rmit.edu.au/Aben.

52 www.arts.unsw.edu.au/aapae (accessed 1 November 2006); http://corporate-ethos.com.au (accessed 1 November 2006).

53 D. Grace and S. Cohen, *Business Ethics*, Australian Problems and Cases, 2nd edn (Melbourne: Oxford University Press, 1998): 124–6.

54 W. Bennis, *Organization Development: Its Nature, Origins, and Prospects* (Reading, MA: Addison-Wesley, 1969).

55 H. Kelman, 'Manipulation of human behaviour: an ethical dilemma for the social scientist', in *The Planning of Change*, 2nd edn, eds W. Bennis, K. Bennie and R. Chin (New York: Holt, Rinehart and Winston, 1969): 584.

56 R. Beckhard, 'The dependency dilemma', *Consultants' Communique*, 6 (July–August–September 1978): 1–3.

57 J. Jarvis, President Corporate Coach, *Turning Potential into Performance!*, I:11 (2009), www.themorsegroup.net/newsletters/11Jan09-85JarvisBoss.pdf.

58 G. Lippitt, *Organization Renewal* (Englewood Cliffs, NJ: Prentice-Hall, 1969).

59 C. Argyris, 'Explorations in consulting-client relationships', *Human Organizations*, 20 (Fall 1961): 121–33.

60 J. Slocum, Jr, 'Does cognitive style affect diagnosis and intervention strategies?', *Group and Organization Studies*, 3 (June 1978): 199–210.

CHAPTER 4

Managing resistance and organisational culture

This chapter presents two contentious issues facing change management practitioners. First, resistance to change is an inevitable response to any attempt to alter the status quo but, rather than suppress, negate or discourage resistance, it should be managed and utilised as a resource. This chapter presents an overview of the research on resistance in the context of change management. A basic search through the literature returns a great number of articles, indicating a profound interest in resistance as a relevant – and important – area of focus for academic research and change management practitioners. In this chapter, we aim to outline the various perspectives and theories that have arisen over many years of research. You will see that there is not just one right approach, and some approaches suit certain situations, while a different approach will be appropriate for another situation.

As the general aim of organisational change is to adapt to the environment or to improve performance, either through incremental change or through strategic, transformational change,[1] it is perhaps unsurprising that resistance to change is often cited as the distinguishing feature of a failed change initiative. Individuals and groups will deal with and regard change in different ways depending on the situation.[2]

Second, in worldwide organisations, managers can use change management strategies, especially organisation development (OD), to help firms operate in multiple countries. Referred to as international, global, multinational or transnational corporations, these firms must fit their organisational strategies, structures, and processes to different cultures. Chapter 9 has a more detailed analysis of organisational culture as part of organisation transformation (OT), but OD can help members gain the organisational skills and knowledge needed to operate across cultural boundaries, enhancing organisational effectiveness through better alignment of people and systems with international strategy.

RESISTANCE TO CHANGE: REALITY OR MYTH?

Resistance is an oft misunderstood outcome of change. The increasing rate of change, and uninvited changes in environment determine an organisation's rise and fall.[3] Bruckman's[4] review of relevant literature found that there is no standard definition for resistance to change, and that perhaps the word 'change' is too big a word. Further, not all changes are necessarily worth resisting (who would resist a pay rise, for example).

Bruckman's literature review of why resistance occurs includes:[5]

- Change in the status quo
- Increased fear and anxiety about the consequences of change – real or perceived
- Altering of the way people see the world and calling into question their values and rationality
- Misunderstanding of the change itself
- Mistrust of those leading the change.

It is generally agreed that understanding resistance aids an organisation's response to that resistance.

According to Falkenburg et al.,[6] much of the literature focuses on negative reactions to change, but that more recent studies show this is an oversimplification. Studies suggest that people do not resist change per se, rather they resist the loss of pay or comfort or other benefits. Falkenburg et al. refer to Piderit's structure model of attitudes to change:

> Piderit uncovered three different emphases in conceptualisations of resistance: a cognitive state, an emotional state, and a behavioural or intentional state. The cognitive dimension of an attitude refers to an individual's beliefs about the attitude object. The emotional dimension of an attitude refers to an individual's feelings in response to the attitude object. The intentional dimension is a plan or resolution to take some action.[7]

Heffernan and Smythe[8] note that the research literature recognises that managing resistance is thought to be critical to successful change programs. Employees who are considered willing to initiate and respond positively to change are inherently valued by modern organisations.[9] The literature is divided, however, on whether resistance is positive or negative, whether it hinders or helps change, or whether it exists at all – for example, is resistance just a label or a category that means different things to different people.[10] Organisations that attempt change initiatives often find that the change efforts are stymied by individuals or groups who resist the changes.[11] As such, resistance to change is often cited as the reason for change failure.[12]

Sources of resistance to change

Most approaches to resistance are situation-based, but recent research has focused on the individual difference perspective.[13] What is it about an individual that affects their adaptability to change? A significant amount of research has been conducted into the sources of resistance in individuals. The following table describes many of these sources.

Pardo del Val and Martinez Fuentes[14] conducted a similar study of sources of resistance; however they linked the sources with the stage of the change process.

TABLE 4.1	Six sources of generalised disposition to resist change
1 Reluctance to lose control	• The loss of control is considered a primary cause of resistance. • Control is lost because change is imposed rather than it being self-initiated. • Perspectives of resistance to change that advocate employee involvement in decision making generally focus primarily on loss of control.
2 Cognitive rigidity	• The trait of dogmatism may predict an individual's approach to change. • Dogmatic individuals are characterised by rigidity and closed-mindedness and therefore might be less willing and less able to adjust to new situations.
3 Lack of psychological resilience	• Organisational change can be a stressor, so less resilient individuals may have a lesser ability to cope with change. • Less resilient individuals may be reluctant to change because to change might be to admit past practices were faulty, i.e., loss of face.
4 Intolerance to the adjustment period involved in change	• Resistance due to more work in the short-term. • Resistance may come from those who support the need for change, but are reluctant to go through the adjustment period.
5 Preference for low levels of stimulation and novelty	• Those who prefer a lower level of stimulation may resist change whereas those who are generally innovative show a greater need for novel stimuli. • A weaker need for stimuli may be shown by those who most resist change.
6 Reluctance to give up old habits	• A common characteristic of an individual's resistance to change. • 'Familiarity breeds comfort.'

Source: Adapted from S. Oreg, 'Resistance to change: developing an individual differences measure', *Journal of Applied Psychology*, 88:4(2003): 680–93.

Graetz et al.[15] align responses to change according to certain factors.

Clarke and Clegg[16] propose that because continuous incremental change has been displaced by discontinuous change, organisation environments are less predictable and more complex to manage. Old ways of operating are no longer effective in dealing with the new levels of complexity and require new ways of thinking and practice, especially in the way that organisations manage change. This calls for new paradigms, deconstruction of the old order and development of new assets. Change managers should be mindful that implementing change is complex, and that multiple stakeholders have diverse needs and that no one change implementation strategy is going to satisfy them simultaneously.[17]

TABLE 4.2 Sources of resistance in five groups (adapted from Pardo del Val and Martinez Fuentes's (2003) extension of Rumelt's (1995) five groups)

Source of resistance	The barrier
Formulation stage The formulation stage is where the change strategy is developed	
Perception of the need for change Resistance may form because the initial perception for the need for change is wrong, or misguided.	It may include: • Myopia, or inability of the company to look into the future with clarity • Denial or refusal to accept any information that is not expected or desired • Perpetuation of ideas, meaning the tendency to go on with the present thoughts although the situation has changed • Implicit assumptions, which are not discussed due to their implicit character and which therefore distort reality • Communication barriers that lead to information distortion or misinterpretations • Organisational silence, which limits the information flow with individuals who do not express their thoughts, meaning that decisions are made without all the necessary information.
Low motivation for change	• Direct costs of change • Cannibalisation costs, that is to say, change that brings success to a product but at the same time brings losses to others, so it requires some sort of sacrifice • Cross-subsidy comforts, because the need for a change is compensated through the high rents obtained without change with another different factor, so that there is no real motivation for change • Past failures, which leave a pessimistic image for future changes • Different interests among employees and management, or lack of motivation of employees who value change results less than managers who value them
Lack of creative response	• Fast and complex environmental changes, which do not allow a proper situation analysis • Reactive mindset, resignation or tendency to believe that obstacles are inevitable • Inadequate strategic vision or lack of clear commitment of top management to changes
Implementation stage This is the stage between the decision to change and the regular use of it in the organisation	
Political and cultural deadlocks to change	• Implementation climate and relation between change values and organisational values, considering that a strong implementation climate when the values' relation is negative will result in resistance and opposition to change • Departmental politics or resistance from those departments that will suffer with the change implementation • Incommensurable beliefs, or strong and definitive disagreement among groups about the nature of the problem and its consequent alternative solutions • Deep-rooted values and emotional loyalty • Forgetfulness of the social dimension of changes

TABLE 4.2	Sources of resistance in five groups (adapted from Pardo del Val and Martinez Fuentes's (2003) extension of Rumelt's (1995) five groups) (*continued*)
Source of resistance	**The barrier**
A disparate group of sources of resistance with different characteristics	• Leadership inaction, sometimes because leaders are afraid of uncertainty, sometimes for fear of changing the status quo • Embedded routines • Collective action problems, especially dealing with the difficulty to decide who is going to move first or how to deal with free-riders • Lack of necessary capabilities to implement change – capabilities gap • Cynicism

Source: Adapted from M. Pardo del Val and C. Martinez Fuentes, 'Resistance to change: a literature review and empirical study', *Management Decision*, 41:2 (2003): 148–55.

TABLE 4.3	Drivers of responses to change
Factors	**Indicators**
Economic	• Job loss or job security and impact on self-image • Economic future for family • Reduction of value of existing skills for future promotion • Transfer of organisation or components of the organisation to less costly locations • Vested interests in position, or salary benefits
Uncertainty	• Doubt about the stated benefits of the change • Doubt about ability to undertake new role or tasks • Rumours that destabilise the benefits of the change • Impact on relationships and values
Inconvenience	• Additional load to current role • Relocation of office or home • Loss of security of the familiar • Challenge to familiar routine
Threats to interpersonal relationships	• Status among employees • Threat to work team • Impact on morale of work team • Impact on organisation culture • Impact on social relationships
Impact on internal processes and systems	• Technology • Structure and dependencies • Inadequate communication to explain the change • Impact on resources
Impact on social functions	• Cognitive dissonance or incompatibility with new values • Fear of the unknown

Source: Adapted from F. Graetz, M. Rimmer, A. Lawrence and A. Smith, *Managing Organisational Change* (Milton: Wiley, 2006): 289, with permission from Emerald Group Publishing Limited

What do we mean by 'resistance'?

The term 'resistance' tends to be viewed in the pejorative sense, most likely because it can be difficult to manage. The following section describes the various meanings of resistance as understood by those who study resistance as a key aspect of change management.

Research into resistance to change has occurred over several years, beginning with Lewin who introduced the term as a systems concept (a force affecting managers and employees equally), followed by other interpretations including Dent and Goldberg's suggestion that people do not resist change, rather they resist the impact of change on their personal status quo. More recent research, however, attempts to revisit Lewin's systems approach and critically appraise the interpretations that followed. Waddell, Cummings and Worley[18] describe change as a process that can 'hurt', even if we know that change is inevitable. Regardless of the organisation (even in public sector organisations), change and innovation are required in order to adapt and survive. Pardo del Val and Martinez Fuentes define resistance to change:

> On the one hand, resistance is a phenomenon that affects the change process, delaying or slowing down its beginning, obstructing or hindering its implementation, and increasing its costs. On the other hand, resistance is any conduct that tries to keep the status quo, that is to say, resistance is equivalent to inertia, as the persistence to avoid change. So, inertia and thus resistance are not negative concepts in general, since change is not inherently beneficial for organisations. Even more, resistance could show change managers certain aspects that are not properly considered for the change process.[19]

Erwin and Garman[20] acknowledge that while there has been significant research into resistance to change, there still remains substantial variability in how its 'phenomena' is perceived. Resistance is still studied as either a problem or a positive factor for change.[21]

Ford and Ford[22] revisit the current understanding of resistance and suggest that new avenues of investigation into resistance are possible. They first break the current understanding into three views of resistance: mechanistic, social and conversational.

The mechanistic view:

1 *Resistance is a natural, and everyday phenomenon.* Movement cannot occur without some form of resistance, and in fact, resistance is evidence that something is moving. Ford and Ford[23] liken it to a boat moving through water. It is not exceptional. Things move every day, therefore there is resistance occurring every day. In an organisational context, these researchers identify common incidents of resistance: being late for meetings, forgetting a task, damaging equipment, being confused, complaining, declining requests, delaying the accomplishment of everyday goals.

2 *Resistance is neutral.* Resistance is neither good or bad, positive or negative, beneficial or detrimental.

3 *Resistance is a product of interaction.* The higher the resistance, the bigger the change (returning to the boat analogy – Ford and Ford[24] describe how greater resistance by the water is directly proportionate to how fast the boat motors through it). There are always two sides to the equation.

The social view:

1 *Resistance is exceptional.* Resistance is something extraordinary, and only happens in response to change.

2 *Resistance is detrimental.* This is the pejorative sense of the word 'resistance'. Resistance is seen as detrimental to the success of a change. That all changes are inherently beneficial is implied and should be implemented as planned. Ford and Ford[25] refer here to the notion that an individual can be 'tagged' as resistant, when in fact that individual considers themselves compliant. This is an important factor for the conversational view, mentioned later.

3 *Resistance is 'over there, in them/it'.* The social view refutes the interactive nature of resistance, it belongs over there, that is, resistance is 'in the workers' or the workers are maladjusted. The error of locating it 'over there' is that it implies that resistance is not tied to movement, that the resistance is not caused by pressure elsewhere, that is, from the change itself.

Lastly, the conversational view:

1 *Conversations and change.* This view recognises that organisations are made up of simultaneous, sequential and recursive conversations, undertaken by various networks within the organisation. There are different language communities, different language games and different approaches to texts. Therefore a change agent cannot communicate with the assumption that there is a single language to which everyone has access. They cannot make their own language game dominant over others. The change agent must work within the message recipients' meanings.

2 *Resistance: the construction of a distinction.* The conversational view also recognises that individuals draw boundaries and make distinctions. They assign actions and events into categories of distinctions. Each individual has their own reality. This is an important concept in the 'resistance is positive/negative' debate. What Ford and Ford[26] point out is that each person has a different meaning of resistance, that resistance is therefore not a 'thing' that exists in its own right, it only exists in association with a language, which could be different among individuals. Ford and Ford also point out that the labelling by a person of another individual as resistant is the result of that person making comparisons based on their point of view. They advocate that the change agent should not be asking 'why is this person resisting?', rather 'why do I call that resistance?'

3 *A construct of assertions and declarations.* Conversations are speech acts, and therefore resistance is brought into being through assertion and declaration, not before. If a change agent declares there is resistance, it is because they understand there to be resistance. They are making a pronouncement. It is, in effect, the framing of the word resistance, and how this framing impacts on the change process. Think about how different the change process may be if the label was changed to 'cooperative' or 'compliant'.

The following application describes a proposed major change management program in the Australian Army. The army, like many military organisations, is a traditional command and control structure. Command and control management is increasingly falling out of favour in organisations. Keep Ford and Ford's[27] analysis of resistance in mind while reading the application.

Revamp a sign of 'adaptive army'

In a constantly changing environment, many companies undergo restructuring to improve efficiency. The Australian Army, subject to more demands on its resources than in the past, is participating in that trend and is currently in the process of revising its command structure.

According to Lieutenant General Ken Gillespie, Chief of Army, there are too many headquarter units in the army. This leads to restrictions in access to information and slower decision making than is appropriate in the contemporary environment. As a result a new arrangement, known as the 'Adaptive Army' initiative, is being introduced with completion planned for 2011. The objective is to merge the present headquarter divisions into two; one concentrating on current activities and the other on development and strategic planning. The two divisions will operate alongside the existing Special Operations Command.

The present command structure was initiated by the Hassett review in the early 1970s. However, General Gillespie commented that this arrangement is no longer consistent with the significant changes in ADF command and control structure, inhibits efficient joint operations planning and creates problems in dealing with the increased demands on the army's resources.

General Gillespie also believes the nature of current army operations means it must be capable of working among the people of the area in which it operates, and be able to establish a 'broad relationship with the supported population'. He said achieving this capacity requires the army to develop skills in non-warlike activities as much as in its traditional functions.

Source: Based on Patrick Walters, 'Revamp a sign of "adaptive army"', *The Australian*, 28 August 2008, News Ltd.

Critical thinking question:

1. What type of resistance do you think an OD practitioner would face in a traditional command and control organisation like the Australian Army? How do you think resistance might be overcome in this environment?

Managerial responses to resistance

In predicting where resistance to change will come from, managers should first identify who will win and who will lose from the proposed changes.[28] Change can generate deep resistance in people and in organisations, making it difficult, if not impossible, to implement organisational improvements.[29] At a personal level, change can arouse considerable anxiety about letting go of the known and moving to an uncertain future. Individuals may be unsure whether their existing skills and contributions will be valued in the future. They may have significant questions about whether they can learn to function effectively and to achieve benefits in the new situation. At the organisation level, resistance to change can come from three sources.[30] Technical resistance comes from the habit of following common procedures and the investment cost of resources invested in the status quo. Political resistance can arise when organisational changes threaten powerful stakeholders, such as top executive or staff personnel, and may call into question the past decisions of leaders. Organisation change often implies a different allocation of already scarce resources, such as capital, training budgets and good people. Finally, cultural resistance takes the form of systems and procedures that reinforce the status quo, promoting conformity to existing values, norms and assumptions about how things should operate.

There are at least three major strategies for dealing with resistance to change:[31]

1   *Empathy and support.* A first step in overcoming resistance is to know how people are experiencing change. This can help to identify those who are having trouble accepting the changes, the nature of their resistance and possible ways of overcoming it. Understanding how people experience change requires a great deal of empathy and support. It demands a willingness to suspend judgement and to try to see the situation from another's perspective, a process called 'active listening'. When people feel that those managing change are genuinely interested in their feelings and perceptions, they are likely to be less defensive and more willing to share their concerns and fears. This more open relationship not only provides useful information about resistance but also helps to establish the basis for the kind of joint problem solving that is necessary for overcoming barriers to change.

2   *Communication.* People tend to resist change when they are uncertain about its consequences. Lack of adequate information fuels rumours and gossip, and adds to the anxiety generally associated with change. Effective communication about changes and their likely consequences can reduce this speculation and allay unfounded fears. It can help members realistically prepare for change.

However, communication is also one of the most frustrating aspects of managing change. Organisation members are constantly receiving data about current operations and future plans as well as informal rumours about people, changes and politics. Managers and OD practitioners must think seriously about how to break through this stream of information. One strategy is to make change information more salient by communicating through a new or different channel. If most information is delivered through memos and letters, then change information can be sent through meetings and presentations. Another method that can be effective during large-scale change is to deliberately substitute change information for normal operating information. This sends a message that changing one's activities is a critical part of a member's job.

3   *Participation and involvement.* One of the oldest and most effective strategies for overcoming resistance is to involve organisation members directly in planning and implementing change.[32] Members can provide a diversity of information and ideas, which can contribute to making the innovations effective and appropriate to the situation. They can also identify pitfalls and barriers to implementation. Involvement in planning the changes increases the likelihood that members' interests and needs will be accounted for during the intervention. Consequently, participants will be committed to implementing the changes as it is in their best interests to do so. Implementing the changes will contribute to meeting their needs. Moreover, for people who have strong needs for involvement, the very act of participation can be motivating, leading to greater effort to make the changes work.[33]

How we manage resistance depends as much on the individual change practitioner as it does on established theories of resistance and subsequent recommendations for managing resistance. A consistent finding across much of the research into resistance is that without a clear strategy and well-defined key messages, effective management of change is unlikely.[34] As Ford and Ford[35] point out, resistance is a concept defined within an individual's own paradigm and experience. Therefore it is inevitable that resistance to change continues to be considered a difficulty to overcome in change initiatives.

Calabrese[36] discusses change within a school administration context. He notes that a typical school administrator tasked with changing a school organisation can become fixed in a politically driven change process rather than one based on readiness resulting in change that is temporary. The change in people, therefore, comes about from coercive power although there remains a passive resistance. Calabrese refers to this process as one that never 'captures their soul', and refers to paradigms as a way to understand resistance:

> Paradigms affect personal and collective behaviour. As individuals, we use paradigms to interpret our environment. Our paradigms save us time from analysing every situation. As new situations appear, our minds quickly process these situations against a myriad of paradigms that our minds maintain on active duty. When the new situation conflicts with a paradigm, a warning signal sounds and subconsciously a defensive reaction develops ... The greater the mismatch between the new situation and our existing set of paradigms, the greater the level of resistance.[37]

From here, rigidity, lack of compromise, resentment and anger come in to play. Calabrese builds on a four-step model proposed by Martin Luther King:

1 collection of the facts to determine whether injustices exist
2 negotiation
3 self-purification, and
4 direct action.

The answers to the questions raised in collection of the facts enables the change leader to determine whether anyone is likely to be hurt by the change, or if anyone is likely to benefit to a greater degree from the change.

In the negotiation stage, the change leader brings to the fore the existing paradigms of the organisation, and questions how these are relevant to the organisation currently. The self-purification stage refers to the analysis of one's motives before acting, a kind of self-reflective preparatory stage. In the direct action stage, the change leader responds to opponents through patience and understanding. A failure to take action means that they are complicit with those who resist the change; however it is necessary to note that those who resist are not considered 'enemies', rather, their opposition may stem from fear and reluctance to change. Calabrese uses this model to examine the school administrator as change leader, but it can be argued that it can be used in many other situations.

Another approach is Erwin and Garman's 2010 framework which is intended to be a starting point for practitioners in addressing resistance to change. What this framework lacks, however, is recognition that the need for change may be ill-advised. For example, Erwin and Garman refer to the personality trait of 'predisposition to resist'. Even if an individual has this trait, it nevertheless should be part of the change practitioner's resolve to understand the nature of the resistance rather than simply assigning it as a personality trait issue, a view supported by Ford, Ford and D'Amelio: 'This "change-agent-centric" view presumes that resistance is an accurate report by unbiased observers (change agents) of an objective reality (resistance by change recipients).'[38] Work with many practitioners, who have undertaken study through action learning and research-based leadership and management Masters programs, strongly indicates that it is the adversarial and mixed message approach to resistance that still dominates the implementation of change programs in organisations.[39]

CONCRETE RESPONSES TO CHANGE

Change opponents also play an important and often underappreciated role. Those with day-to-day involvement and detailed knowledge may offer important insights into the proposed changes.[41] In managing a change process, managers should pay attention to broader concerns than that of the change program itself. It is thought that an individual's resistance to change is caused by deep-rooted values that do

TABLE 4.4 Erwin and Garman's (2009)[40] framework for addressing resistance to change

Resistance research findings	Practice guidance for change agents and managers
What is resistance? Resistance to change Individuals may have negative thoughts, feelings and behaviours towards organisational change initiatives	Plan for resistance Anticipate and plan for resistance
How do personality differences influence *resistance*? Predisposition to resist Openness to change	Provide additional support • Identify those inclined toward negative reactions and work to gain their trust. Engage the support of those more open to change. Gain support and help • Select and involve individuals with higher levels of resilience in leading change initiatives.
What are the key concerns and responses to change initiatives? Responses to change Competence	Address individuals' concerns • Recognise and be prepared to respond to concerns about change. • Provide meaningful opportunities for feedback. • Respond to valid resistance; use it for organisational improvement. Provide support and training • Provide adequate support and training in building employee confidence and their capabilities associated with the desired change.
What factors in the change process influence resistance? Communication Understanding Management consistency Participation	Communicate, communicate, communicate • Provide ample, clear and quality communications about change initiatives, associated implications and implementation actions Ensure understanding of the change • Provide clear and appropriate details to ensure individuals understand the change, how it influences them, and what is expected of them. Examine policies and behaviours for consistency • Be certain organisational policies, goals and management actions and behaviours are consistent with change initiatives. Encourage and allow opportunities for participation in the change process • Provide meaningful information about the change to individuals, solicit their input and opinions, and encourage involvement in the decision process. • Provide individuals with the opportunity to participate in the change process including identifying the need to change, and developing and implementing change plans.
How do management relationships and styles influence resistance? Confidence and trust Management styles Employee relationships	Develop confidence and trust • Developing confidence and trust is a long-term endeavour involving gaining buy-in to the value of change and the probability of success; openness to constructive criticism and willingness to revise change plans if appropriate; transparency and clear

TABLE 4.4	Erwin and Garman's (2009)[40] framework for addressing resistance to change (*continued*)
Resistance research findings	**Practice guidance for change agents and managers**
	articulation of the need, benefits, and motivations behind change and that it is best for the organisation. Emphasise more effective management styles
	• Encourage collaboration, facts, and logic in managing while avoiding the use of power and coercion.
	Develop quality manager-employee relationships
	• Assess manager-employee relationships and employee development opportunities to determine how they can be improved in a meaningful way; and follow through with the implementation of those initiatives.

Source: Adapted and summarised version of D. Erwin and A. Garman's framework in 'Resistance to organizational change: linking research and practice', *Leadership & Organisation Development Journal*, 31:1 (2009): 39–56. With permission from Emerald Group Publishing Limited.

not necessarily 'fit' with the organisational culture, or the change program's objectives.[42] Before the change process begins, managers who are acting as change agents need to analyse the organisational culture versus the change objectives, and if they find a disconnect between the two, work to establish a better alignment before the change process starts. Considered another key reason for change failure, organisational silence occurs, in part, when organisation culture does not align with the proposed change's objectives.[43] Silence can be perceived as vagueness and a lack of planning by change agents and top management. The change agent therefore must ensure that the organisation vocalises the change process.

When there is excessive change

Genuine resistance may be the result of too much organisational change. In a study by Falkenburg, Stensaker, Meyer and Haueng, excessive change causes individuals to resist – an expected outcome. The consequences were felt by both organisations and individuals. Managers experienced job rotation, middle managers were unable to function effectively and there were increased organisational inefficiencies.[44] Falkenburg et al. proposed a definition of excessive change that can be summarised as a movement that exceeds that which is normal, proper or reasonable, away from the present state towards a future state.[45]

Managers should be aware of the extent to which change becomes excessive. Excessive change may increase the level of resistance by employees due to 'change-fatigue' and most likely becomes excessive at the middle manager level because this is the level where most implementation activities occur.

> Individuals reacted to excessive change with frustration and anger.
> Some individuals expressed that they experienced stress and physical

and psychological problems ... Employees also expressed feelings of uncertainty resulting from the change: uncertainty about their job, and about their competence and adequacy.[46]

Falkenburg et al. build on an existing framework by Porras and Robertson to manage the effects of excessive change. They found that individuals responded to excessive change in different ways, classified by whether the individual was active or passive in responding to the change. Some individuals worked to support the change: 'the response was active, take-charge, take-over attitude. When faced with

TABLE 4.5	Managing the effects of excessive change
Diagnosis	The first step is to determine if the proposed change is necessary – or is it just change for change's sake? If the proposed change is necessary, limit it to only the necessary parts that are crucial to the organisation's prosperity, or in a difficult climate, an organisation's survival.
Planning	The planning phase involves the creation of discourse through conversations and discussions. The creation of discourse is fundamental to employees' understanding of the reason for change, particularly if it is a major, or complex change. It can be argued that this should occur even when the change is not deemed excessive.
Intervention	The involvement of middle managers is crucial in the formulation and intervention stage. It is the middle managers who carry out the day-to-day operations and are closer to the organisation's internal and external stakeholders. Getting middle managers on board can help to visualise the expected change. Empowering individuals to make decisions may reduce resistance caused by excessive change. However, it is important to be careful when using empowerment and delegation as tools – excessive change can cause increased workload, and with increased workload there is a chance that employees may become paralysed. When this happens, empowerment and delegation may exacerbate an already tenuous situation. Equip individuals and teams with the necessary skills to carry out the change. One of the most basic reasons for resistance is that the individual or group does not feel they have the necessary skills with which to successfully respond to change. The skills are not just technical skills – interpersonal and conflict management skills are just as important.
Evaluation	Ensure employees know that the change process is completed. This can enable a sense of achievement and success. Following on from completion, it can be good practice to initiate a period of stability – free from major change. Build on the successes of the change process to develop the organisation's capacity for change. The perception of excessive change should be minimised to reduce the consequences of excessive change.

Source: Adapted from J. Falkenburg, I. Stensaker, C. Meyer and A. Haueng, 'When change becomes excessive', *Research in Organizational Change and Development*, 15 (2005): 31–62. With permission from Emerald Group Publishing Limited.

many different change programs, or initiatives for new changes, they attempted taking control of the situation', such as calling meetings with their managers, or making decisions themselves. The passive employees followed orders without taking initiative on their own – where the change was probable. Where the change was improbable, the employees were overcome with paralysis and cynicism. According to Falkenburg et al., the most serious behaviour was paralysis because 'employees become paralysed and cannot perform even their daily tasks. People were not unwilling, but unable, to carry through the changes, nor could they carry out the simple, routine tasks that they had always managed previously'. The framework is broken down into four categories of implementation: diagnosis, planning, intervention and evaluation.

Application 4.2 refers to Google's attempt to be more customer conscious within in an environment of competitive and chaotic technological change.

4.2

APPLICATION

Google gets creative in the search for a positive image

Concern among advertising agencies that the formation of an advertising group within Google will put them out of business was addressed by the newly appointed strategic planning director of the company's Creative Lab, Stuart Smith. He said the group intended to work cooperatively with agencies in developing new ideas and products to promote the Google brand.

According to Smith, Google engineers in the past have focused on developing a wide range of products and then modifying them until they find a market. They have not researched market needs and then produced solutions to those identified needs. He sees the new group's role as being able to reverse that approach: first, understand the market, then encourage the creation of initiatives, projects, ideas, products that satisfy its requirements. The Lab will enhance the level of creativity within Google.

An important task for the Lab, he suggested, will be to address community concerns about Google's scale and influence by communicating the positive aspects of the company's activities.

Smith explained that Google's strong commitment to measuring every aspect of its activities may create tension within the company. He explained that creative people 'don't necessarily like to be evaluated in that particular fashion and then an organisation that has always done that and been very successful at it'. However, going into a recession, the group will have to justify its actions.

Source: Based on Simon Canning, 'Google gets creative in the search for a positive image', *The Australian*, 17 November 2008, News Ltd.

Critical thinking question:

1. Imagine you work at Google as an engineer. How would you respond to Google's attempt to 'get more creative' by establishing the Creative Lab? What type of OD interventions do you think would assist Google engineers to accept the change?

Management approaches

Richard Cooke describes six reasons for employees to resist change:[47]

1 Employees may know something that you do not know, which may, in fact, make their resistance not only understandable but even correct.
2 People who are happy with the status quo will fight to protect it.
3 If they can see no clear path between their current state and the new position then they cannot begin to move forwards.
4 If they do not believe they have the necessary skills to be successful in the new order or are heavily invested in the current order then again they will resist.
5 They need to have clear and credible role models of the new behaviours.
6 They need to understand why the change is in their interests. Too many people make the mistake of saying why the company needs this, that and the other, but fail to make the link as to how these things benefit the individuals.

OVERCOMING RESISTANCE TO CHANGE

This chapter emphasises that resistance to change has been maligned by many and should be reconsidered by academics and practitioners alike. If people are to be successful in change management, resistance should be managed constructively and not feared or suppressed. This includes taking a fresh look at what resistance to change can offer the organisation.

The importance of training

Pardo del Val and Martinez Fuentes[48] advocate training as a key aspect in managing change. Often the reason for individual resistance is a lack of understanding and skills in those on whom change is imposed. Change programs imply that new capabilities will be required by employees, and it is by the acquisition of skills that individuals may embrace the change rather than resist. But the need for training does not just apply to those who may resist the change, it is also important to ensure that change agents are equipped with the appropriate skills and competencies. Waddell, Cummings and Worley[49] suggest change agent training encompass the following competencies (first described by Kotter and Schlesinger). These are:

1 *Education and communication*. This may need to be stratified through the organisation depending on department need, group norms within those departments and the capabilities of internal people to facilitate this.
2 *Participation and involvement of individuals and groups*. Even if change agents think they have all the answers, organisation member involvement will minimise resistance.

3 *Facilitation of support*. Participation and involvement of individuals and groups will assist in identifying which groups need priority support.

4 *Negotiation and agreement*. This may be needed if feedback from organisation members indicates the change plan is not feasible or is flawed.

5 *Manipulation and co-option*. This can be used if there are still people resisting the change and the change is systems-driven. Try to avoid this approach.

6 *Explicit and implicit coercion*. Avoid this approach at all costs unless there is the potential of physical risk for employees who do not adapt to the change. There is always a solution![50]

Organisations should also learn from the collective learnings of years of research. Bruckman summarises learnings based on observation of change processes in organisations:[51]

1 Work with the group
2 Confront the fear of change
3 Consider the group's perspective
4 Build trust
5 Avoid manipulating the work group
6 Be willing to compromise
7 Allow group ownership
8 Actions versus words
9 Reward new behaviours
10 Financial rewards rarely reinforce behavioural change
11 Manage the myths and realities
12 Integrity – the most important variable.

THE REFLECTIVE PRACTITIONER

The pressure upon managers is significant, particularly when their time is precious and limited. Any thoughts of change initiatives and planning is given scant regard when rewards are usually based on tangible profitable outcomes. The main characteristics of a successful manager are where he or she has an opportunity to be reflective and where decisions are made based on information that has been carefully considered. This process includes consideration of differing points of view and the contribution of others.[52] This self-reflective regime requires a skilled approach in which participants take an external perspective and judge their actions accordingly. By improving their skills base, individuals can more fully develop their own personal identities and improve their performance in group and organisational activities. Managers should receive organisational support for this professional development and there are many interventions which facilitate this.

In Application 4.3, the effectiveness of team-building exercises depends on pinpointing the needs of individuals as well as their organisations.

All together now

Expect to see an increase in the use of team-building exercises and workshops this year, but beware of following the crowd. 'There is a pick-up in the use of [team building] when there has been hardship or difficulty,' director Henriette Rothschild of management consulting firm Hay Group Australia says.

'In the early '90s after the recession, in the early 2000s after the dotcom crash, and now after the global financial crisis, managers feel they have a disengaged workforce, and they want to take action,' she says.

Team building promises more engaged and motivated staff. 'The sports team is a simple metaphor,' Australian Human Resources Institute national president Peter Wilson says. 'Defenders cannot kick goals, but they put the ball into the hands of those who can. It is all about maximising your strengths and finding your opponent's weaknesses.'

However, what qualifies as 'team building' is broad and subject to fads. Abseiling and other physical challenges have given way to cooking classes and model building. Some practitioners advocate psychological testing, and attempt to discuss real problems – organisational and personal – in teams.

Nonetheless, things can go wrong. Embarrassment and humiliation were the outcome of one team-building workshop in which the facilitator encouraged participants to get personal. 'The facilitator wanted to delve deeper into the personal lives of participants to "open up dialogue for greater bonding",' recounts an executive who prefers not to be named.

'One woman in the group wanted to share how her parents had broken up when she was a child and that had had a profound effect on her. She was weeping as she was telling the group about the circumstances. The others present were ... sympathetic but mortified that this was going on at a work team-building session.

'The facilitator was clearly out of his depth and the issue was left hanging. Others there just did not know how to handle the situation over dinner that night and for the rest of the conference.'

Such outcomes are rare, Wilson says. 'Occasionally people find it threatening or confronting, but that is perhaps 2 or 3 per cent of the total.'

Exact figures on the extent of such problems are difficult to find. Wilson bases his estimate on his own professional experience. However, a Safe Work Australia report in 2008 found that mental stress claims rose 95 per cent from 1997–98 to 2004–05.

So, are disengagement and workplace stress individual problems or organisational issues? The head of RMIT University's Graduate School of Business and Law, John Toohey, reviewed the records of about 100 stress-related claims.

'I plotted the claims back to the presenting problem,' he says. 'A lot were not about individual stress – they were about a lack of confidence in their ability to do the task, too much work, being harassed or bullied, relocated into jobs they were not trained for, and feeling aggrieved.'

Team building may stray from ineffective to dangerous when participants have a pre-existing mental condition. Depression affects one in five Australians, specialist organisation beyondblue says, so most workplaces could expect to have a sufferer.

'There is no literature that team building is a risk factor for relapse [into depression],' beyondblue's clinical adviser, Michael Baigent, says. 'However, any such exercise has the potential to be harmful. Self-disclosure, having to talk about yourself and the way you think is, of itself, quite stressful for a variety of reasons. Also, I would have to say that [team building] is not a recognised treatment [for depression] or a method of preventing depression.'

Sydney consulting firm Challenge Consulting offers team-building services. 'Team building is not new,' its organisational psychologist, Narelle Hess, says. 'It can involve all sorts of activities. We recommend a combination depending on the specific need of the organisation, such as miscommunication in the team or getting individuals to understand their communication styles.'

Challenge assesses participants' individually through one-on-one interviews or surveys. 'We want to be sure what the actual issue is that we are dealing with,' Hess says. Facilitators state clearly the limits of their expertise, halt proceeding if a participant is upset, and offer participants a referral to a qualified professional for follow-up.

Hay Group's Rothschild agrees team building is not a panacea. 'You need to be clear about what is disengaging people.' Before investigating, consultants need to warn their clients that the answer might come as a shock. Rothschild says her organisation does not offer team building, but does help with organisational change and making executives more effective.

'We clarify with managers before we start by asking what they are prepared to hear,' she says. 'There is no point in investigating [disengagement] if they are not prepared to take action.'

Tips for effective team building:

- Clearly identify the problems you are trying to solve.
- Be willing to respond to the answer, even if it is difficult, such as improving resources or sacking a bully.
- Investigate whether team building is an effective solution to some of the problems.
- Prepare participants in advance about the content, and set realistic expectations.
- Create a face-saving mechanism for people who do not want to attend.
- Employers have a duty of care to their employees under occupational health and safety laws. It is therefore the responsibility of all parties to provide employees with a safe workplace.

Source: Kath Walters, 'All together now', *Business Review Weekly*, 21 January 2010.

Critical thinking question:
1. How are team building activities, whether positive or negative, impacting on members in your organisation?

ORGANISATIONAL CULTURE

Because change management theories were developed predominantly by American and Western European practitioners, the practices and methods of change management are heavily influenced by the values and assumptions of those industrialised cultures. Thus, the traditional approaches to planned change may promote management practices that conflict with the values and assumptions of other societies. Will Chinese cultural values, for example, be preserved or defended as an increasing number of European and American organisations establish operations in that country? How should OD be conducted in an Indian firm operating in New Zealand? On the other hand, some practitioners believe that OD can result in organisational improvements in any culture.[53] Despite different points of view on this topic, the practice of OD in international settings can be expected to expand dramatically. The rapid development of foreign economies and firms, along with the evolution of the global marketplace, is creating organisational needs and opportunities for change.

In designing and implementing planned change for organisations operating outside the home country, OD practice must account for two important contingencies: alignment between the cultural values of the host country and traditional OD values, and the host country's level of economic development. Preliminary research suggests that failure to adapt OD interventions to these cultural and economic contingencies can produce disastrous results.[54] For example, several OD concepts, including dialogue, truthfulness and performance management, do not always work in all countries.[55] Dialogue assumes that 'all differences can be bridged if you get people together in the right context'. However, mediation, arbitration or traditional negotiations are more acceptable in some cultures than in others. Similarly, the notion of truthfulness is culturally relativistic and as a value depends on whether you are Australian, Asian, Middle Eastern or from some other culture. Finally, the process and content of performance evaluation can also depend on culture.[56]

OD interventions need to be responsive to the cultural values and organisational customs of the host country if the changes are to produce the kinds of positive results shown in Western cultures, such as the United States.[57] For example, team-building interventions in Latin American countries can fail if there is too much emphasis on personal disclosure and interpersonal relationships. Latin Americans typically value masculinity and a devotion to family, avoid conflict and are status conscious. They may be suspicious of human process interventions that seek to establish trust, openness and equality, and consequently they may resist them actively. The more a country's cultural values match the traditional values of OD, the less likely it is that an intervention will have to be modified.

Cultural context

Researchers have proposed that applying OD in different countries requires a 'context-based' approach to planned change.[58] This involves fitting the change process to the organisation's cultural context, including the values held by members in the particular country or region. These beliefs inform people about behaviours that are important and acceptable in their culture. Cultural values play a major role in shaping the customs and practices that occur within organisations as well, influencing how members react to phenomena having to do with power, conflict, ambiguity, time and change.

There is a growing body of knowledge about cultural diversity and its effect on organisational and management practices.[59] Researchers have identified five key values that describe national cultures and influence organisational customs: context orientation, power distance, uncertainty avoidance, achievement orientation and individualism (Table 4.6).[60]

Context orientation[61]

This value describes how information is conveyed and time is valued in a culture. In low-context cultures, such as Scandinavia and Australia, information is

TABLE 4.6	Cultural values and organisation customs		
Value	**Definition**	**Organisation customs when the value is high**	**Representative countries**
Context	The extent to which words carry the meaning of a message; how time is viewed	Ceremony and routines are common. Structure is less formal; fewer written policies exist. People are often late for appointments.	*High:* Asian and Latin American countries *Low:* Scandinavian countries, United States
Power distance	The extent to which members of a society accept that power is distributed unequally in an organisation	Decision making is autocratic. Superiors consider subordinates as part of a different class. Subordinates are closely supervised. Employees are not likely to disagree. Powerful people are entitled to privileges.	*High:* Latin American and Eastern European countries *Low:* Scandinavian countries
Uncertainty avoidance	The extent to which members of an organisation tolerate the unfamiliar and unpredictable	Experts have status/ authority. Clear roles are preferred. Conflict is undesirable. Change is resisted. Conservative practices are preferred.	*High:* Asian countries *Low:* European countries
Achievement orientation	The extent to which organisation members value assertiveness and the acquisition of material goods	Achievement is reflected in wealth and recognition. Decisiveness is valued. Larger and faster are better. Gender roles are clearly differentiated.	*High:* Asian and Latin American countries, South Africa *Low:* Scandinavian countries
Individualism	The extent to which people believe they should be responsible for themselves and their immediate families	Personal initiative is encouraged. Time is valuable to individuals. Competitiveness is accepted. Autonomy is highly valued.	*High:* Australia, New Zealand *Low:* Latin American and Eastern European countries

Source: Thomas Cummings and Christopher Worley, *Organization Development and Change*, (with InfoTrac® College Edition Printed Access Card) 9th edition, South-Western, a part of Cengage Learning Inc., 2009, p. 617. Reproduced by permission, www.cengage.com/permissions.

communicated directly in words and phrases. By using more specific words, more meaning is expressed. In addition, time is viewed as discrete and linear – as something that can be spent, used, saved, or wasted. In high-context cultures, on the other hand, the communication medium reflects the message more than the words, and time is a fluid and flexible concept. For example, social cues in Japan and Venezuela provide as much, if not more, information about a particular situation than do words alone. Business practices in high-context cultures emphasise ceremony and ritual. For example, knowing how to exchange business cards, participate in a reception, or conducting a banquet in China honours the client and facilitates business relationships. How one behaves is an important signal of support and compliance with the way things are done. Structures are less formal in high-context cultures; there are few written policies and procedures to guide behaviour. Because high-context cultures view time as fluid, punctuality for appointments is less a priority than is maintaining relationships.

Power distance

This value concerns the way people view authority, status differences and influence patterns. People in high power-distance regions, such as Latin America and Eastern Europe, tend to accept unequal distributions of power and influence, and consequently autocratic and paternalistic decision-making practices are the norm. Organisations in high power-distance cultures tend to be centralised, with several hierarchical levels and a large proportion of supervisory personnel. Subordinates in these organisations represent a lower social class. They expect to be supervised closely and believe that power holders are entitled to special privileges. Such practices would be inappropriate in low power-distance regions, such as Scandinavia, where participative decision making and egalitarian methods prevail.

Uncertainty avoidance

This value reflects a preference for conservative practices and familiar and predictable situations. People in high uncertainty-avoidance regions, such as Asia, prefer stable routines over change and act to maintain the status quo. They do not like conflict and believe that company rules should not be broken. In regions where uncertainty avoidance is low, such as in many European countries, ambiguity is less threatening. Organisations in these cultures tend to favour fewer rules, higher levels of participation in decision making, more organic structures and more risk taking.

Achievement orientation

This value concerns the extent to which the culture favours the acquisition of power and resources. Employees from achievement-oriented cultures, such as Asia and Latin America, place a high value on career advancement, freedom and salary growth. Organisations in these cultures pursue aggressive goals and can have high levels of stress and conflict. Organisational success is measured in terms of size, growth and speed. On the other hand, workers in cultures where achievement is less of a driving value, such as those in Scandinavia, prize the social aspects of work, including working conditions and supervision, and typically favour opportunities to learn and grow at work.

Individualism

This value is concerned with looking out for oneself as opposed to one's group or organisation. In high-individualism cultures, such as Australia and the United States, personal initiative and competitiveness are valued strongly. Organisations in individualistic cultures often have high turnover rates and individual rather than group decision-making processes. Employee empowerment is supported when members believe that it improves the probability of personal gain. These cultures encourage personal initiative, competitiveness and individual autonomy. Conversely, in low individualism countries, such as China, Japan and Mexico, allegiance to one's group is paramount. Organisations operating in these cultures tend to favour cooperation among employees and loyalty to the company.

Economic development

In addition to cultural context, an important contingency affecting OD success internationally is a country's level of industrial and economic development. For example, although long considered an industrial economy, Russia's political and economic transformation, and the concurrent increases in uncertainties over infrastructure, corruption, cash flow and exchange rates, has radically altered assumptions underlying business practices. Thus, economic development can be judged from social, economic and political perspectives.[62] For example, it can be reflected in a country's management capability as measured by information systems and skills; decision-making and action-taking capabilities; project planning and organising abilities; evaluation and control technologies; leadership, motivational and reward systems; and human selection, placement and development levels. The United Nations' Human Development Programme has created a Human Development Index that assesses a country's economic development in terms of life expectancy, educational attainment and adjusted real income.

Subsistence economies

Countries such as Pakistan, Nepal, Nigeria, Uganda and Rwanda have relatively low degrees of development and their economies are primarily agriculture-based. Their populations consume most of what they produce, and any surplus is used to barter for other needed goods and services. A large proportion of the population is unfamiliar with the concept of 'employment'. Working for someone else in exchange for wages is not common or understood, and consequently few large organisations exist outside of the government. In subsistence economies, OD interventions emphasise global social change and focus on creating conditions for sustainable social and economic progress.

Industrialising economies

Malaysia, Venezuela, India, Turkey, the Philippines, Iran and the People's Republic of China are moderately developed and tend to be rich in natural resources. An expanding manufacturing base that accounts for increasing amounts of the country's gross domestic product fuels economic growth. The rise of manufacturing also contributes to the formation of a class system including upper-, middle- and low-income groups. Organisations operating in these nations generally focus on efficiency of operations and revenue growth. Consequently, OD interventions address strategic, structural and work design issues.[63] They help organisations identify domestic and international markets, develop clear and appropriate goals, and structure themselves to achieve efficient performance and market growth.

Industrial economies

Highly developed countries, such as Sweden, Japan, France and the United States, emphasise non-agricultural industry. In these economies, manufactured goods are exported and traded with other industrialised countries; investment funds are available both internally and externally; the workforce is educated and skilled; and technology is often substituted for labour. Because the OD interventions described in this book were developed primarily in industrial economies, they can be expected to have their strongest effects in those contexts. Their continued success cannot be ensured, however, because these countries are advancing rapidly to post-industrial conditions. Here, OD interventions will need to fit into economies driven by information and knowledge, where service outpaces manufacturing, and where national and organisational boundaries are more open and flexible.

How cultural context and economic development affect OD practice

The contingencies of cultural context and economic development can have powerful effects on the way OD is carried out in various countries.[64] They can determine whether change proceeds slowly or quickly; involves few or many members; is directed by hierarchical authority or by consensus; and focuses on business, organisational, or human process issues. For example, planned change processes in Russia require more clarity in roles, the development of common understandings, changes in how an organisation's vision is communicated, and the insightful use of symbols and signals.[65] When the two contingencies are considered together, they reveal four different international settings for OD practice, as shown in Figure 4.1. These different situations reflect the extent to which a country's culture fits with traditional OD values of direct and honest communication, sharing power, and improving their effectiveness and the degree to which the country is economically developed.[66]

FIGURE 4.1 The cultural and economic contexts of international OD practice

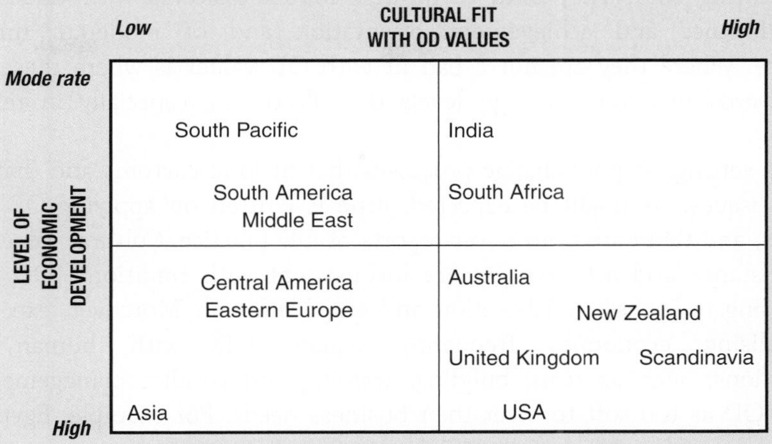

Source: Thomas Cummings and Christopher Worley, *Organization Development and Change*, (with InfoTrac® College Edition Printed Access Card) 9th edition, South-Western, a part of Cengage Learning Inc., 2009, p. 620. Reproduced by permission, www.cengage.com/permissions.

In Figure 4.1, the degree of economic development is restricted to industrialising and highly industrialised regions. Subsistence economies are not included because they afford little opportunity to practise traditional OD; in those contexts, a more appropriate strategy is global social change. In general, however, the more developed the economy, the more OD is applied to the organisational and human process issues described in this book. In less developed situations, OD focuses on business issues, such as procuring raw materials, producing efficiently and marketing successfully.[67] On the other hand, when the country's culture supports traditional OD values, the planned change process can be applied to organisational and human process issues with only small adjustments.[68] The more the cultural context differs from OD's traditional values profile, the more the planned change process will need to be modified to fit the situation.

BHP is an internationally recognised organisation and, as Application 4.4 attests, is well respected.

Low cultural fit, moderate industrialisation

This context is least suited to traditional OD practice. It includes industrialising economies with cultural values that align poorly with OD values, including many Middle East nations, such as Iraq, Iran and the United Arab Republic; the South Pacific region, including Malaysia and the Philippines; and certain Latin American countries, such as Brazil, Ecuador, Guatemala and Nicaragua. These regions are highly dependent on their natural resources and have a relatively small manufacturing base. They tend to be high-context cultures with values of high power distance and achievement orientation and of moderate uncertainty avoidance. Where they are not a bad fit with OD values is where these cultures tend towards moderate or high levels of collectivism, especially in relation to family.

These settings require change processes that fit local customs and that address business issues. As might be expected, little is written on applying OD in these countries, and there are even fewer reports of OD practice. Cultural values of high power distance and achievement are inconsistent with traditional OD activities emphasising openness, collaboration and empowerment. Moreover, executives in industrialising economies frequently equate OD with human process interventions, such as team building, training and conflict management. They perceive OD as too soft to meet their business needs. For example, Egyptian and

---

4.4

APPLICATION

Big on vision

There is a stark contrast between the prosperity the mining industry delivers to Australia and the disdain it generates in society. Without mining, the country would have felt the full force of the global financial crisis, and yet every defeat of a mining proposal is heralded as a victory for mankind. So it is a milestone that BHP Billiton, the world's largest miner, is now also Australia's most respected company.

BHP Billiton is one of Australia's few truly global companies and it has received accolades for its handling of the economic crisis. While its international peers such as Rio Tinto, Anglo American and Xstrata have struggled to repair damaged balance sheets, BHP Billiton has not had to ask shareholders for funds and has continued to pursue growth.

That said, the financial crisis still hurt. Last December, BHP Billiton was forced to withdraw its proposed takeover offer for Rio Tinto that would have formed a $400 billion company after its target's high debt levels became too great a lodestone to bear. BHP Billiton also shut its $2.5 billion Ravensthorpe nickel mine in Western Australia after just a year of operations.

As its chief executive Marius Kloppers had to quietly push under the carpet his vision of a 20-year mining boom heralded in mid-2007. It can be dusted off again once the global recession is well and truly in the past.

Pushing past adversity, whether imposed or self-inflicted, is part of the admiration BHP Billiton inspires. After all, it embraced governance practices in the 1980s to defend against a takeover from the late Robert Holmes a Court that today would likely get its directors thrown in jail. Since then, it has had to sack two chief executives and defend itself against environmental disasters such as the OK Tedi copper mine in Papua New Guinea and Beenup minerals sands debacle in Western Australia. As one chief executive of a large corporation notes: 'They learn from their mistakes – sometimes fairly large ones.'

So why is BHP Billiton so respected? Mostly it has to do with leadership and strategy. The strategy is simple. The company has its suite of chosen minerals and energy commodities such as oil and gas, iron ore, coal and copper, and it is only interested in world-class assets that will

>>

expand its product base. It pursues those assets through exploration agreements with other miners and acquisitions, and it seeks a diversified spread. Some assets will not be developed by the leadership as they do not meet demand requirements even though they are world-class. This is the nature of the company – it sucks in and hoards the assets it needs for long-term plans measured in decades.

Leadership is something that BHP Billiton has developed from the board down. Its soon-to-depart chairman Don Argus is one of a handful of business leaders who could vie for the title of most respected in the country. Argus, in tandem with Kloppers' predecessor, Chip Goodyear, can take a lot of the credit for BHP Billiton's position of respect. Between them, they steered the company out of the wreckage of the 1990s and into the position of the world's top miner.

Notwithstanding the global financial crisis and the bid for Rio Tinto, Kloppers has carried the baton reasonably smoothly since he took on the job in October 2007 and Argus's successor, the former president and chief executive of Ford Motor Company, Jac Nasser, has been well received as the chairman-elect.

An important feature in Kloppers' appointment was that he was hired internally. He had been with BHP since 1993 and he had to compete with external candidates for the job. For an internal candidate to gain appointment, a company must not only have the talent to fill the position but the board also be pleased with the culture and direction of the organisation.

Kloppers has shown he has an uncluttered and thoughtful head on his shoulders. Had he been egocentric, something found too often in chief executives, he may have pushed on with the bid for Rio and, if successful, created a company of incredible size but also one that nevertheless would have destroyed value for BHP Billiton shareholders. 'Ballsy enough to drop the Rio takeover rather than letting ego rule' is how one chief executive responded.

Now that BHP Billiton has had a decade of strong growth and solid leadership, there is an issue that will require vigilance from both Nasser and Kloppers – complacency. It was something on the mind of Wesfarmers chief executive Richard Goyder when he took over from his much-lauded predecessor Michael Chaney in 2005. Managers of successful companies can miss opportunities and stifle initiative if they become too averse to making mistakes. Goyder tackled the spectre of complacency by making a successful bid for Coles, and in the process kept the flame of entrepreneurial spirit in the company burning.

Kloppers has been no slouch in this department. After the merger plan with Rio Tinto was abandoned, he did not crawl away and brood. Instead, he found a way to pursue the jewel in the crown from the would-be merger.

In June, BHP Billiton and Rio announced they had entered a non-binding agreement to put both miners' iron ore assets in the Pilbara region of Western Australia into a joint venture. The synergies from the merger have been estimated at more than US$10 billion. The agreement must be made binding by December 5 or it will lapse, and it requires regulatory approvals before completion and formation mid-next year.

At the time of the announcement, Kloppers said both companies had been looking for a solution to merging the world-class iron ore operations for more than a decade.

BHP Billiton's ability to maintain its position as Australia's most respected company should and will be a challenge. While no rival can threaten in terms of size and market capitalisation, the ability to deliver on its promises will determine its future eligibility for the top position.

In some ways the timing of the global financial crisis may have helped BHP Billiton in managing its asset growth and delivering on its promises. Like all major mining companies, it was under strong pressure from its customers to ramp up production to meet demand, particularly from 2003–08. The global crisis and resulting recession cooled demand and have given BHP Billiton a breather – time to ponder the conditions it needs in future to justify expansion of its assets or bring new mines online.

As the strength of Chinese demand resumes, it is being dampened on a global scale from weakness in developed regions such as Europe and the United States. Yet the Middle Kingdom should provide sufficient growth for BHP Billiton to boost output and seek opportunities.

One area in which the company admits it needs more scale is in oil and gas. Woodside Petroleum has always been considered a natural fit and given the smaller scale of the iron ore joint venture compared with a full merger, BHP Billiton retains the firepower for such a deal.

Source: Damon Firth, 'Big on vision', *Business Review Weekly*, November–December 2009.

Critical thinking question:

1. BHP Billiton has maintained its position under fierce competition and the global economic downturn. What are some of the factors that impacted on the organisation's development and where do you suggest it goes from here?

Filipino managers tend to be autocratic, engage in protracted decision making, and focus on economic and business problems. Consequently, organisational change is slow paced, centrally controlled and aimed at achieving technical rationality and efficiency.[69]

These contextual forces do not influence all organisations in the same way. A recent study of 20 large-group interventions in Mexico suggests that culture may not be as constraining as has been hypothesised.[70] Similarly, in an apparent exception to the rule, the president of Semco S/A (Brazil), Ricardo Semler, designed a highly participative organisation.[71] Most Semco employees set their own working hours and approve hires and promotions. Information flows downward through a relatively flat hierarchy, and strategic decisions are made participatively by companywide vote. Brazil's cultural values are not as strong on power distance and masculinity as in other Latin American countries, and that may explain the apparent success of this high-involvement organisation. It suggests that OD interventions can be implemented within this cultural context when strongly supported by senior management.

High cultural fit,[72] moderate industrialisation[73]

This international context includes industrialising economies with cultures that align with traditional OD values. Such settings support the kinds of OD processes described in this book, especially technostructural and strategic interventions that focus on business development. According to data on economic development and cultural values, relatively few countries fit this context. India's industrial base and democratic society are growing rapidly and may fit this contingency. Similarly, South Africa's recent political and cultural changes make it one of the most interesting settings in which to practise OD.[74]

South Africa is an industrialising economy. Its major cities are the manufacturing hubs of the economy, although agriculture and mining still dominate in rural areas. The country's values are in transition and may become more consistent with OD values. South Africans customarily have favoured a low-context orientation; relatively high levels of power distance; and moderate levels of individualism, uncertainty avoidance and achievement orientation. Organisations typically have been bureaucratic with authoritarian management, established career paths, and job security primarily for Caucasian employees. These values and organisational conditions are changing, however, as the nation's political and governance structures are transformed. Formerly, apartheid policies reduced uncertainty and defined power differences among citizens. Today, free elections and the abolishment of apartheid have increased uncertainty drastically and established legal equality among the races. These changes are likely to move South Africa's values closer to those underlying OD. If so, OD interventions should become increasingly relevant to that nation's organisations.

A study of large South African corporations suggests the directions that OD is likely to take in that setting.[75] The study interviewed internal OD practitioners about key organisational responses to the political changes in the country, such as the free election of Nelson Mandela, abolishment of apartheid and the Reconstruction and Development Program. Change initiatives at Spoornet, Eskom and Telkom, for example, centred around two strategic and organisational issues. First, the political changes opened up new international markets, provided access to new technologies, and exposed these organisations to global competition. Consequently, these organisations initiated planned change efforts to create corporate visions and identify strategies for entering new markets and acquiring new technologies. Second, the political changes forced corporations to modify specific human resources and organisational practices. The most compelling change was mandated affirmative action quotas. At Spoornet, Eskom and Telkom, apartheid was thoroughly embedded in the organisations' structures, policies and physical arrangements. Thus, planned change focused on revising human resources policies and practices. Similarly, organisational structures that had fit well within the stable environment of apartheid were outmoded and too rigid to meet the competitive challenges of international markets. Planned changes for restructuring these firms were implemented as part of longer-term strategies to change corporate culture towards more egalitarian and market-driven values.

Low cultural fit, high industrialisation[76]

This international setting includes industrialised countries with cultures that fit poorly with traditional OD values. Many countries in Central America, Eastern Asia and Eastern Europe fit this description. Reviews of OD practice in those regions suggest that planned change includes all four types of interventions described in this book, although the change process itself is adapted to local conditions.[77] For example, Mexico, Venezuela, China, Japan and Korea are high-context cultures where knowledge of local mannerisms, customs and rituals is required to understand the meaning of communicated information. To function in such settings, OD practitioners must know not only the language but the social customs as well. Similarly, cultural values emphasising high levels of power distance, uncertainty avoidance and achievement orientation foster organisations where roles, status differences and working conditions are clear; where autocratic and paternalistic decisions are expected; and where the acquisition of wealth and influence by the powerful is accepted. OD interventions that focus on social processes and employee empowerment are not favoured naturally in this cultural context and consequently need to be modified to fit the situations.

Japanese and Korean organisations, such as Matsushita, Nissan, Toyota, Fujitsu, NEC and Hyundai, provide good examples of how OD interventions can be tailored to this global setting. These firms are famous for continuous improvement and total quality management (TQM) practices; they adapt these interventions to fit the Asian culture. Roles and behaviours required to apply TQM are highly specified, thereby holding uncertainty to a relatively low level. Teamwork and consensus decision-making practices associated with quality improvement projects also help to manage uncertainty. When large numbers of employees are involved, information is spread quickly and members are kept informed about the changes taking place. Management controls the change process by regulating the implementation of suggestions made by the problem-solving groups. Because these interventions focus on work processes, teamwork and employee involvement do not threaten the power structure. Moreover, TQM and continuous improvement do not alter the organisation radically but produce small, incremental changes that can add up to impressive gains in long-term productivity and cost reduction.

In these cultures, OD practitioners also tailor the change process itself to fit local conditions. Mexican companies, for example, expect OD practitioners to act as experts and to offer concrete advice on how to improve the organisation. To be successful, OD practitioners need sufficient status and legitimacy to work with senior management and to act in expert roles.[78] Status typically is associated with academic credentials, senior management experience, high-level titles or recommendations by highly placed executives and administrators. As might be expected, the change process in Latin America is autocratic and driven downward from the top of the organisation. Subordinates or lower-status people generally are not included in diagnostic or implementation activities because inclusion might equalise power differences and threaten the status quo. Moreover, cultural norms discourage employees from speaking out or openly criticising management. There is relatively little resistance to change because employees readily accept changes dictated by management.

In Asia, OD is an orderly process, driven by consensus and challenging performance goals. Organisational changes are implemented slowly and methodically, so trust builds and change-related uncertainty is reduced. Changing too quickly is seen as arrogant, divisive and threatening. At the China Association for the International Exchange of Personnel, the move from a government bureau to a 'market-facing' organisation[79] has been gradual but consistent. Managers have been encouraged to contact more and more foreign organisations, to develop relationships and contracts, and to learn marketing and organisation development skills. Because Asian values promote a cautious culture that prizes consensus, dignity and respect, OD tends to be impersonal and to focus mainly on work-flow improvements. Human process issues are rarely addressed because people are expected to act in ways that do not cause others to 'lose face' or to bring shame to the group.

High cultural fit, high industrialisation

This last setting includes industrialised countries with cultural contexts that fit well with traditional OD values. Much of the OD practice described in this book was developed in these situations, particularly in the United States.[80] To extend our learning, we will focus on how OD is practised in other nations in this global setting, including the Scandinavian countries – Sweden, Norway, Finland and Denmark – and countries with a strong British heritage, such as Great Britain, Northern Ireland, Australia and New Zealand.

Scandinavians enjoy a high standard of living and strong economic development. Because their cultural values most closely match those traditionally espoused in OD, organisational practices are highly participative and egalitarian. OD practice tends to mirror these values. Multiple stakeholders, such as managers, unionists and staff personnel, are involved actively in all stages of the change process, from entry and diagnosis to intervention and evaluation. This level of involvement is much higher than that typically occurring in the United States. It results in a change process that is heavily oriented to the needs of shop-floor participants. Norwegian labour laws, for example, give unionists the right to participate in technological innovations that can affect their work lives. Such laws also mandate that all employees in the country have the right to enriched forms of work.

Given this cultural context, it is not surprising that Scandinavian companies pioneered sociotechnical interventions[81] to improve productivity and quality of work life. Sweden's Saab and Volvo restructured automobile manufacturing around self-managed work groups. Denmark's Patent Office and Norway's Shell Oil demonstrated how union–management cooperative projects can enhance employee involvement throughout the organisation. In many cases, national governments were involved heavily in these change projects by sponsoring industry-wide improvement efforts. The Norwegian government, for example, was instrumental in introducing industrial democracy to that nation's companies. It helped unions and management in selected industries implement pilot projects to enhance productivity and quality of work life. The results of these sociotechnical experiments were then diffused throughout the Norwegian economy. In many ways, the Scandinavian countries have gone further than other global regions in linking OD to national values and policies.

Countries associated with the United Kingdom tend to have values consistent with a low-context orientation, moderate to high individualism and achievement orientation, and moderate to low power distance and uncertainty avoidance. This cultural pattern results in personal relationships that often seem indirect to Americans. For example, a British subordinate who is told to think about a proposal is really being told that the suggestion has been rejected. These values also promote organisational policies that are steeped in formality, tradition and politics. The United Kingdom's long history tends to reinforce the status quo, and consequently resistance to change is high.

OD practice in the United Kingdom parallels the cultural pattern described above. In Great Britain, for example, sociotechnical systems theory was developed by practitioners at the Tavistock Institute of Human Relations.[82] Applications such as self-managed work groups, however, have not readily diffused through British organisations. The individualistic values and inherently political nature of this culture tend to conflict with interventions emphasising employee empowerment and teamwork. In contrast, the Scandinavian cultures are far more supportive of sociotechnical practice and have been instrumental in diffusing it worldwide.

The emergence of the European Union has served as a catalyst for change in many organisations. Companies such as Akzo Nobel, Unilever, BMW and Credit Lyonnais are actively engaged in strategic change interventions. At L'Oreal, CEO Lindsay Owen-Jones implemented an aggressive strategy of acquiring and integrating cosmetic firms, driving the international business, and building its brand.[83] More limited interventions, such as team building, conflict resolution and work redesign, are being carried out in such organisations as Carrefour and British Telecom.

Summary

Resistance is a complex and misunderstood concept which has often been used as an excuse for the failure of a change process. It is crucial to have a thorough understanding as to the basis and form of resistance such that it may be managed in a constructive manner. By utilising the energy that is involved in contributing to the improvement of the change process, resistance can be perceived as more of a help rather than a hindrance.

In organisations outside the country of origin (the home country), traditional approaches to OD need to be adapted to fit the cultural and economic development context in which they are applied in the country of destination (the host country). This adaptation approach recognises that OD practices may be culture-bound: What works in one culture may be inappropriate in another. The cultural contexts of different geographical regions were examined in terms of five values: context orientation, power distance, uncertainty avoidance, achievement orientation and individualism. This approach also recognises that not all OD interventions may be appropriate in all organisations, or in all cultures.

Activities

Review questions

1 Describe some of the factors that lead to 'resistance'.
2 Summarise the variety of ways in which resistance can be managed.
3 Explain the differences between 'overt' and 'covert' resistance.
4 Discuss the ways in which resistance can have positive or negative impacts on the change management process.
5 What negative consequences could occur if the change management process ignores cultural differences?
6 What does 'cultural context' mean? Give three examples.

Discussion and essay questions

1 Describe ways in which managers can positively and actively manage resistance, and what managers need to understand when undertaking this.
2 Discuss the overall role of the change manager in managing resistance during the change process, and the critical knowledge they and the human resource department need to apply.
3 Do types of resistance differ between types of organisations? Reflect on the type of resistance that might occur in those organisations that are: board-directed, family-owned, governmental and not-for-profit.
4 Which of Kotter and Schlesinger's six competencies can be classified as either 'soft' or 'hard'? Discuss which would be effective in the short term but not for long-term organisational acceptance of the change. List what other competencies are required to create ownership and commitment to make the change last.
5 Compare and contrast the various cultural values. Give examples as evidence of your understanding.

Search me! Excercises

Explore **Search me! management** for relevant articles on managing resistance and organisation culture. Search me! is an online library of world-class journals, e-books and newspapers, including *The Australian* and *The New York*

Times, and is updated daily. Log in to Search me! through http://login.cengage.com using the access card in the front of this book.

Keywords

Try searching for the following terms:

> Nature of resistance
> Organisation culture

> Reflective practitioner
> Responses to resistance

>> *Search tip:*

Search me! management contains information from both local and international sources. To get the greatest number of search results, try using both Australian and American spellings in your searches, e.g. 'globalisation' and 'globalization'; 'organisation' and 'organization'.

Notes

1 M. Pardo del Val and C. Martinez Fuentes, 'Resistance to change: a literature review and empirical study', *Management Decision*, 41:2 (2003): 148–55.

2 A. D. Price and K. Chahal, 'A strategic framework for change management', *Construction Management and Economics*, 24 (2006): 237–51.

3 J. C Bruckman, 'Overcoming resistance to change: causal factors, interventions, and critical values', *The Psychologist-Manager Journal*, 11 (2008): 211–19. Psychology Press, Taylor & Francis Group.

4 ibid.

5 ibid.

6 J. Falkenberg, I. Stensaker, C. Meyer and A. Haueng, 'When change becomes excessive', *Research in Organizational Change and Development*, 15 (2005): 31–62.

7 ibid.: 44.

8 In D. Waddell, T. Cummings and C. Worley, *Organisation Development & Change*, 3rd edn (Australia: Nelson ITP, 2007).

9 S. Oreg, 'Resistance to change: developing an individual differences measure', *Journal of Applied Psychology*, 88:4 (2003): 680–93.

10 J. Ford and L. Ford, 'Resistance to change: a reexamination and extension', *Research in Organizational Change and Development*, 17 (2009): 211–39.

11 S. Oreg, 'Resistance to change: developing an individual differences measure', op. cit.

12 D. Erwin and A. Garman, 'Resistance to organizational change: linking research and practice', *Leadership & Organization Development Journal*, 31:1 (2009): 39–56.

13 S. Oreg, 'Resistance to change: developing an individual differences measure', op. cit.

14 M. Pardo del Val and C. Martinez Fuentes, 'Resistance to change: a literature review and empirical study', op. cit.: 149.

15 F. Graetz, M. Rimmer, A. Lawrence and A. Smith, *Managing Organisational Change* (Milton: Wiley, 2006): 289.

16 T. Clarke and S. Clegg, *Changing Paradigms: The Transformation of Management Knowledge for the 21st Century* (London: Harper Collins, 1998).

17 M. Heffernan and A. Smythe in Waddell, Cummings and Worley, *Organisation Development & Change*, op. cit.

18 Waddell, Cummings and Worley, *Organisation Development & Change*, op. cit.

19 Pardo del Val and Martinez Fuentes, 'Resistance to change', op. cit: 149.

20 Erwin and Garman, 'Resistance to organizational change', op. cit.

21 ibid.

22 Ford and Ford, 'Resistance to change', op. cit.

23 ibid.

24 ibid.

25 ibid.

26 ibid.

27 ibid.

28 Price and Chahal, 'A strategic framework for change management', op. cit.

29 D. Garvin, *Learning in Action* (Cambridge: Harvard Business School Press, 2000).

30 M. McGill, J. Slocum and D. Lei, 'Management practices in learning organizations', *Organizational Dynamics* (Autumn 1993): 5–17; E. Nevis, A. DiBella and J. Gould, 'Understanding organizations as learning systems,' *Sloan Management Review* (Winter 1995): 73–85.

31 J. Dewey, *How We Think* (Boston: D.C. Heath, 1933).

32 C. Argyris and D. Schon, *Organizational Learning II – Theory, Method and Practice* (Mass.: Addison-Wesley).

33 Argyris and Schon, *Organizational Learning II*; Senge, *Fifth Discipline*; P. Senge, C. Roberts, R. Ross, B. Smith and A. Kleiner, *The Fifth Discipline Fieldbook: Strategies for Building a Learning Organization* (New York: Doubleday, 1995).

34 Waddell, Cummings and Worley, *Organisation Development & Change*, op. cit.

35 Ford and Ford, 'Resistance to change', op. cit.

36 R. Calabrese, 'The ethical imperative to lead change: overcoming the resistance to change', *The International Journal of Educational Management*, 17:1 (2003): 7–13.

37 Calabrese, 'The ethical imperative to lead change', op. cit.: 7.

38 Ford, J., Ford, L. and D'Amelio, A. 'Resistance to change: the rest of the story', *Academy of Management Review*, 33:2 (2008): 362–77.

39 M. Heffernan and A. Smythe in Waddell, Cummings and Worley, *Organisation Development & Change*, op. cit.

40 Erwin and Garman, 'Resistance to organizational change', op. cit.

41 Price and Chahal, 'A strategic framework for change management', op. cit.

42 Pardo del Val and Martinez Fuentes 'Resistance to change', op. cit.

43 ibid.

44 Falkenberg, Stensaker, Meyer and Haueng, 'When change becomes excessive', op. cit.

45 ibid.

46 ibid.: 43.

47 Adapted from R. Cooke, 'Deflating resistance to change: or a quick guide to understanding resistance and moving forwards', *Human Resource Management International Digest*, 17:3 (2009): 3–4.

48 Pardo del Val and Martinez Fuentes, 'Resistance to change', op. cit.

49 Waddell, Cummings and Worley, *Organisation Development & Change*, op. cit.

50 M. Heffernan and A. Smythe in Waddell, Cummings and Worley, *Organisation Development & Change*, op. cit.

51 Adapted from Bruckman, 'Overcoming resistance to change', op. cit.: 214.

52 C. Argyris and D. A. Schon, *Organizational Learning 11 – Theory, Method and Practice*, Addison-Wesley OD Series (Reading, MA: Addison-Wesley, 1996); D. Kolb, *Experiential learning: experience as the source of learning and development* (Englewood Cliffs, New Jersey: Prentice Hall, 1984); W. Doyle and J. Young, 'Management development: making the most of experience and reflection', *Canadian Manager* (Fall, 2000): 18–20; I. Gardner and C. Boucher, 'Reflective practice: a meta-competency for Australian allied health managers' (paper presented to Seventh Annual International Conference on Advances in Management, Colorado Springs, 12–15 July 2000).

53 S. Camden-Anders, and T. Knott, 'Contrasts in culture: practicing OD globally', in *Global and International Organization Development*, eds P. Sorensen, T. Head, T. Yaeger and D. Cooperrider (Chicago: Stipes Publishing, 2001).

54 L. Bourgeois and M. Boltvinik, 'OD in cross-cultural Settings: Latin America', *California Management Review*, 23 (Spring 1981): 75–81; L. Brown, 'Is organization development culture bound?' *Academy of Management Newsletter* (Winter 1982); P. Evans, 'Organization development in the transnational enterprise', in *Research in Organizational Change and Development*, vol. 3, eds R. Woodman and W. Pasmore (Greenwich, Conn.: JAI Press, 1989): 1–38; R. Marshak, 'Lewin meets Confucius: a re-View of the OD model of change',

Journal of Applied Behavioral Science, 29 (1997): 400–2; A. Chin and C. Chin, *Internationalizing OD: Cross-Cultural Experiences of NTL Members* (Alexandria, VA: NTL Institute, 1997); A. Shevat, 'Practicing OD with a technology-driven global company', *OD Practitioner*, 33 (2001): 28–35.

55 Shevat, 'Practicing OD', op. cit.

56 R. Kjar, 'A time of transition: lessons in global OD from a successful Japanese firm', *Organization Development Journal*, 25 (2007): 11–17; J. Schmuckler, 'Cross-cultural performance feedback', *OD Practitioner* 33 (2001): 15–20.

57 Evans, 'Organization development', op. cit.: 8–11; Brown, 'Is organization development culture bound?' op. cit.; Bourgeois and Boltvinik, 'OD in cross-cultural settings', op. cit.; W. Ouchi, *Theory Z* (Reading, MA: Addison-Wesley, 1981).

58 E. Schein, *Organization Culture and Leadership*, 2nd edn (San Francisco: Jossey-Bass, 1992); Evans, 'Organization Development', op. cit.: 11.

59 G. Hofstede, *Culture's Consequences* (Beverly Hills, Calif.: Sage Publications, 1980); A. Jaeger, 'Organization development and national culture: where's the fit?' *Academy of Management Journal*, 11 (1986): 178–90; A. Francesco and B. Gold, *International Organizational Behavior*, 2nd edn (Upper Saddle River, N.J.: Prentice-Hall, 2004); R. Hodgetts, F. Luthans and J. Doh, *International Management: Culture, Strategy, and Behavior*, 6th edn (New York: McGraw-Hill, 2005).

60 G. Hofstede, *Culture's Consequences*, op. cit.; E. Hall and M. Hall, 'Key concepts: understanding structures of culture', in *International Management Behavior*, 3rd edn, eds H. Lane, J. DiStefano and M. Maznevski (Cambridge: Blackwell, 2000); F. Kluckhohn and F. Strodtbeck, *Variations in Value Orientations* (Evanston, IL.: Peterson, 1961); F. Trompenaars, *Riding the Waves of Culture* (London: Economist Press, 1993).

61 H. A. von der Gracht, C. R. Vennemann and I. Darkow, 'Corporate foresight and innovation management: a portfolio-approach in evaluating organizational development', Supply Chain Management Institute (SMI), European Business School (EBS), International University Schloss Reichartshausen, EBS Campus Wiesbaden, Soehnleinstrasse 8F, 65201 Wiesbaden, Germany, www.sciencedirect.com/science?_ob=Article URL&_udi=B6V65-4XR5N82-7&_user=10&_cover Date=05%2F31%2F2010&_rdoc=1&_fmt=high&_orig =search&_sort=d&_docanchor=&view=c&_search StrId=1377110543&_rerunOrigin=google&_acct=C00 0050221&_version=1&_urlVersion=0&_userid=10 &md5=576f72925f831ebbf5fb7d51cd9b4335, cited 18 November 2009.

62 J. Sachs, *The End of Poverty* (New York: Penguin Books, 2005); A. Sen, *Development as Freedom* (New York: Anchor Books, 1999); K. Murrell, 'Management infrastructure in the Third World', in *Global Business Management in the 1990s*, ed. R. Moran (New York: Beacham, 1990); S. Fukuda-Parr, N. Woods and N. Birdsall, *Human Development Report 2002* (New York: United Nations Development Program, 2002), www.undp.org.

63 B. Webster, 'Organization development: an international perspective' (unpublished master's thesis, Pepperdine University, 1995).

64 Jaeger, 'Organization development and national culture', op. cit.

65 S. Michailova, 'Contrasts in culture: Russian and Western perspectives in organization change', *Academy of Management Executive*, 14 (2000): 99–112.

66 The dearth of published empirical descriptions of OD in particular countries and organisations necessitates a regional focus. The risk is that these descriptions may generalise too much. Practitioners should take great care in applying these observations to specific situations.

67 W. Woodworth, 'Privatisation in Belorussia: organizational change in the former USSR', *Organization Development Journal*, 3 (1993): 53–9.

68 K. Johnson, 'Estimating national culture and OD values', in Sorensen et al. eds, *Global and International Organization Development*, op. cit.: 329–44; Jaeger, 'Organization development and national culture', op. cit.

69 A. Shevat, 'The practice of organizational development in Israel', in Sorensen et al. eds, *Global and International Organization Development*, op. cit.: 237–41; W. Fisher, 'Organization development in Egypt', in *Global and International Organization Development*, Sorensen et al. eds, *Global and International Organization Development*, op. cit.: 241–9.

70 M. Manning and J. Delacerda, 'Building organization change in an emerging economy: whole systems change using large group methods in Mexico', in *Research in Organization Change and Development*, 14, eds W. Pasmore and R. Woodman (Oxford, England: JAI Press, 2003): 51–97.

71 R. Semler, *Maverick* (New York: Random House, 2001); R. Semler, *The Seven Day Weekend: Changing the Way Work Works* (New York: Penguin Books, 2004).

72 T. F. Yaeger and P. F. Sorensen Jr, 'Strategic organization development: managing change for succcess, Benedictine University', http://lindasharkey.com/Strategic%20OD%20Article.pdf.

73 G. M. Schwarz and G. P. Huber, *Challenging Organizational Change Research*, School of Organization and Management, University of New South Wales, Sydney, NSW 2052, Australia, and McCombs School of Business, Department of Management, University of Texas at Austin, http://jpkc.henu.edu.cn/glxlx/uppic/Challenging%20organizational%20change%20research.pdf.

74 J. Preston, L. DuToit and I. Barber, 'A potential model of transformational change applied to South Africa', in *Research in Organizational Change and Development*, 9, eds R. Woodman and W. Pasmore (Greenwich, Conn.: JAI Press, 1998); G. Sigmund, 'Current issues in South African corporations: an internal OD perspective' (unpublished master's thesis, Pepperdine University, 1996).

75 Sigmund, 'Current Issues', op. cit.

76 Q. Yang, Y. Yu and W. Chen, *Research on Growing-up Mechanism and Fostering of Venture Enterprise Based on Knowledge Management*, January 2009, www.computer.org/portal/web/csdl/doi/10.1109/WKDD.2009.21.

77 Webster, 'Organization development', op. cit.; I. Perlaki, 'Organization development in Eastern Europe', *Journal of Applied Behavioral Science*, 30 (1994): 297–312; J. Putti, 'Organization development scene in Asia: the case of Singapore', in Sorensen et al. eds, *Global and International Organization Development*, op. cit.: 275–84; I. Nonaka, 'Creating organizational order out of chaos: self-renewal in Japanese firms', *California Management Review* (Spring 1988): 57–73; K. Johnson, 'Organizational development in Venezuela', in Sorensen et al. eds, *Global and International Organization Development*, op. cit.: 305–10; Fuchs, 'Organizational development', op. cit.; R. Babcock and T. Head, 'Organization development in the Republic of China (Taiwan)', in Sorensen et al. eds, *Global and International Organization Development*, op. cit.: 285–92; R. Marshak, 'Training and consulting in Korea', *OD Practitioner*, 25 (Summer 1993): 16–21.

78 Johnson, 'Organizational development', op. cit.; A. Mueller, 'Successful and unsuccessful OD interventions in a Venezuelan banking organization: the role of culture' (unpublished master's thesis, Pepperdine University, 1995).

79 M. F. Grace and R. W. Klein, *Facing Mother Nature*, Georgia State University, 2007, www.cato.org/pubs/regulation/regv30n3/v30n3-5.pdf.

80 Webster, 'Organization development', op. cit.; B. Gustavsen, 'The LOM Program: a network-based strategy for organization development in Sweden', in *Research in Organizational Change and Development*, vol. 5, eds R. Woodman and W. Pasmore (Greenwich, Conn.: JAI Press, 1991): 285–316; P. Sorensen Jr, H. Larsen, T. Head and H. Scoggins, 'Organization development in Denmark', in Sorensen et al. eds, *Global and International Organization Development*, op. cit.: 95–112; A. Derefeldt, 'Organization development in Sweden', in Sorensen et al. eds, *Global and International Organization Development*, op. cit.: 113–22.

81 D. Dulany and V. Pellettiere, *Knowledge Management Process: A Socio-Technical Approach*, Aurora University, 2008, www.swdsi.org/swdsi08/paper/SWDSI%20Proceedings%20Paper%20S203.pdf.

82 E. Trist, 'On socio-technical systems', in *The Planning of Change*, 2nd edn, eds W. Bennis, K. Benne and R. Chin (New York: Holt, Rinehart & Winston, 1969): 269–72; A. Cherns, 'The principles of sociotechnical design', *Human Relations*, 19 (1976): 783–92; E. Jacques, *The Changing Culture of a Factory* (New York: Dryden, 1952).

83 R. Tomlinson, 'L'Oreal's global makeover', *Fortune* (15 August 2002), www.fortune.com/fortune/ceo/articles/0,15114,372136,00.html, accessed 18 November 2003.

CHAPTER 5

The process of organisational change

Intervention design, or action planning, derives from careful diagnosis and is meant to resolve specific problems and to improve particular areas of organisational functioning identified in the diagnosis. OD interventions vary from standardised programs that have been developed and used in many organisations to unique programs tailored to a specific organisation or department.

Once diagnosis has revealed the causes of problems or opportunities for development, organisation members can begin planning, and subsequently implementing, the changes necessary for improving organisation effectiveness and performance. A large part of OD is concerned with interventions for improving organisations.

Planned change processes generally start when one or more key managers or administrators sense that their organisation, department or group could be improved or has problems that could be alleviated through organisation development. The organisation might be successful, yet have room for improvement. It might be facing impending environmental conditions that necessitate a change in how it operates. This requires information gathering, processing and feedback. The quality of the information gathered is, therefore, a key part of the OD process. But perhaps the most important step in the diagnostic process – and often 'forgotten' – is feeding back diagnostic information to the client organisation. Although the data may have been collected with the client's help, the OD practitioner is usually responsible for organising and presenting the data to the client. Properly analysed and meaningful data can have an impact on organisational change only if organisation members can use the information to devise appropriate action plans. A key objective of the feedback process is to be sure that the client has ownership of the data. This chapter introduces some basic methods of gathering data and emphasises the importance of gaining accurate and honest feedback before proceeding with the design, implementation and evaluation of change interventions.

This chapter finishes with the final stage of the OD cycle – evaluation and institutionalisation. Evaluation is concerned with providing feedback to practitioners and organisation members about the progress and impact of interventions. Such information may suggest the need for further diagnosis and modification of the change program, or it may show that the intervention is successful. Institutionalisation involves making OD interventions a permanent part of the organisation's normal functioning. It ensures that the results of successful change programs persist over time.

DIAGNOSING ORGANISATIONS

When done well, diagnosis clearly points the organisation towards appropriate intervention activities that will improve organisation effectiveness.

Diagnosis is the process of assessing the functioning of the organisation, department, group or job to discover sources of problems and areas for improvement. It involves collecting pertinent information about current operations, analysing those data and drawing conclusions for potential change and improvement. Effective diagnosis provides the systematic understanding of the organisation necessary for the design of appropriate interventions. Thus, OD interventions derive from diagnosis and include the specific actions intended to resolve problems and improve organisational functioning.

Diagnostic models derive from conceptions about how organisations function and tell OD practitioners what to look for when diagnosing organisations, departments, groups or jobs. They represent a road map for discovering current functioning. A general, comprehensive diagnostic model is presented, based on open systems theory.[1]

What is diagnosis?

Diagnosis is the process of understanding how the organisation is functioning: it provides the information necessary for designing change interventions. It generally follows from successful entry and contracting. The preliminary activities in planned change set the stage for successful diagnosis. They help the OD practitioner and client jointly determine organisational issues to focus on, show how to collect and analyse data to understand them and how to work together to develop action steps.

Unfortunately, the term 'diagnosis' can be misleading when applied to organisations. It suggests a model of organisation change analogous to medicine: an organisation (patient) experiencing problems seeks help from an OD practitioner (doctor); the practitioner examines the organisation, finds the causes of the problems and prescribes a solution. Diagnosis in OD is, however, much more collaborative than such a medical perspective implies. The values and ethical beliefs that underlie OD suggest that organisational members and change agents should be jointly involved in discovering the causes of organisational problems. Similarly, both should be actively involved in developing appropriate interventions and implementing them.

For example, a manager might seek OD help to reduce absenteeism in a department. The manager and consultant might jointly decide to diagnose the cause of the problem by examining company absenteeism records and by interviewing selected employees about possible reasons for absenteeism. Analysis of these data could uncover causes of absenteeism, thus helping the manager and the practitioner to develop an appropriate intervention for reducing the problem.

The medical view of diagnosis also implies something is wrong with the patient and that one needs to uncover the cause of the illness. Where organisations have specific problems, diagnosis is problem-oriented. It seeks reasons for the problems. However, many managers involved with OD are not experiencing specific organisational problems. Rather, they want to improve the overall effectiveness of their organisation, department or group. Here, diagnosis is development-oriented. It assesses the current functioning to discover areas for future development. For example, a manager might be interested in using OD to improve a department already seemingly functioning well. Diagnosis might include an overall assessment of both the task-performance capabilities of the department and the department's impact upon its individual members. This process seeks to uncover specific areas for future development of the department's effectiveness.

In organisation development, diagnosis is used more broadly than a medical definition would suggest. It is a collaborative process between organisation members and the OD consultant to collect pertinent information, analyse it and draw conclusions for action planning and intervention. Diagnosis may be aimed at uncovering the causes of specific problems or directed at assessing the overall functioning of the organisation or department to discover areas for future development. Diagnosis provides a systematic understanding of organisations so that appropriate interventions may be developed for solving problems and enhancing effectiveness.

The need for diagnostic models

To diagnose an organisation, OD practitioners and organisational members need to have some idea about what information to collect and analyse, based on intuitive hunches through to scientific explanations of how the organisations function. Conceptual frameworks used to understand organisations are referred to as *diagnostic models*.[2] They describe the relationships between different features of the organisation, its context and effectiveness. As a result, diagnostic models indicate areas to examine and questions to ask when assessing how an organisation is functioning.

However, all models represent simplification of reality and therefore choose certain features as critical. Focusing attention on those features, to the exclusion of others, can result in a biased diagnosis. For example, a diagnostic model relating team effectiveness to the handling of interpersonal conflict[3] would lead an OD practitioner to ask questions about relationships among members, decision-making processes and conflict-resolution methods. Although relevant, these questions ignore other group issues such as skills and knowledge composition, complexity of tasks performed by the group, and member interdependencies. Thus, diagnostic models must be carefully chosen to address the organisation's presenting problems as well as ensuring comprehensiveness.

Potential diagnostic models are everywhere. Any collection of concepts and relationships that tries to represent a system or explain its effectiveness can potentially qualify as a diagnostic model. Major sources of diagnostic models in OD are the literally thousands of articles and books that discuss, describe and analyse how organisations function. They provide information about how and why certain organisational systems, processes or functions are effective. These studies often concern a specific facet of organisational behaviour, such as employee stress, leadership, motivation, problem solving, group dynamics, job design or career development. They also can involve the larger organisation and its context, including the environment, strategy, structure and culture. Diagnostic models can be derived from that information by noting the dimensions or variables that are associated with organisational effectiveness.

Another source of diagnostic models is the OD practitioner's own experience in organisations. This field knowledge is a wealth of practical information about how organisations operate. Unfortunately, only a small part of this vast experience has been translated into diagnostic models. These more clinical models represent the professional judgements of people with years of experience in organisational diagnosis. They generally link diagnosis with specific organisational processes, such as group problem solving, employee motivation, or communication between managers and employees.

Open systems model

This section introduces systems theory, a set of concepts and relationships that describes the properties and behaviours of things called *systems* – organisations, groups and people, for example. Systems are viewed as unitary wholes composed of parts or subsystems; they serve to integrate the parts into a functioning unit. For example, organisation systems are composed of departments such as sales, manufacturing and research. The organisation serves to co-ordinate the behaviours of its departments so that they function together. The general diagnostic model based on systems theory that underlies most of OD is called the 'open systems model'.

Systems can vary in how open they are to their outside environments. Open systems, such as organisations and people, exchange information and resources with their environments. They cannot completely control their own behaviour and are influenced in part by external forces. Organisations, for example, are affected by such environmental conditions as the availability of raw material, customer demands and government regulations. Understanding how these external forces affect the organisation can help to explain some of its internal behaviour.

Open systems display a hierarchical ordering. Each higher level of system is composed of lower level systems. Systems at the level of society are composed of organisations; organisations are composed of groups (departments); groups are composed of individuals; and so on. Although systems at different levels vary in many ways – in size and complexity, for example – they have a number of common characteristics by virtue of being open systems. These properties can be applied to systems at any level. The following key properties of open systems are described: 1) inputs, transformations and outputs; 2) boundaries; 3) feedback; 4) equifinality; and 5) alignment.

Inputs, transformations and outputs

Any organisational system is composed of three related parts: inputs, transformations and outputs, as shown in Figure 5.1. *Inputs* consist of human or other resources, such as information, energy and materials, coming into the system. They are acquired from the system's external environment. For example, a manufacturing organisation acquires raw materials from an outside supplier. Similarly, a hospital nursing unit acquires information about a patient's condition from the attending doctor. In each case, the system (organisation or nursing unit) obtains resources (raw materials or information) from its external environment.

Transformations are the processes of converting inputs into outputs. In organisations, transformations are generally carried out by a production or operations function that is composed of social and technological components. The social component consists of people and their work relationships, whereas the technological component involves tools, techniques and methods of production or service delivery. Organisations have developed elaborate mechanisms for transforming incoming resources into goods and services. Banks, for example, transform deposits into mortgage loans. Schools attempt to transform students into more educated people. Transformation processes can also take place at the group and individual levels. For example, research and development departments can transform the latest scientific advances into new product ideas.

Outputs are the result of what is transformed by the system and sent to the environment. Thus, inputs that have been transformed represent outputs ready to leave the system. Health insurance funds, such as HCF and Medibank Private,

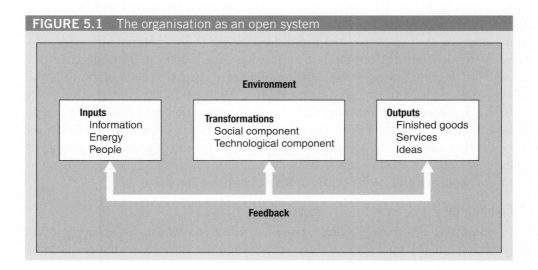

FIGURE 5.1 The organisation as an open system

receive money and medical bills, transform them through the operation of record keeping, and export payments to hospitals and doctors.

Boundaries

The idea of boundaries helps to distinguish between systems and environments. Closed systems have relatively rigid and impenetrable boundaries, whereas open systems have far more permeable ones. Boundaries – the borders or limits of the system – are easily seen in many biological and mechanical systems. Defining the boundaries of social systems is more difficult as there is a continuous inflow and outflow through them. For example, where are the organisational boundaries in the following case? Call centres for various companies may be positioned offshore (for example, mail-order services are being centralised and established in India and will be able to service companies based in Australia and elsewhere). The emergence of the information superhighway and worldwide information networks will continue to challenge the notion of boundaries in open systems.

The definition of 'boundary' is arbitrary, as a social system has multiple subsystems and one subsystem's boundary line may not be the same as that of another. As with the system itself, arbitrary boundaries may have to be assigned to any social organisation, depending on the variable to be stressed. The boundaries used for studying or analysing leadership may be quite different from those used to study intergroup dynamics.

Just as systems can be considered to be relatively open or closed, the permeability of boundaries also varies from fixed to diffuse. The boundaries of a community's police force are probably far more rigid and sharply defined than are those of the community's political parties. Conflict over boundaries is always a potential problem within an organisation, just as it is in the world outside the organisation.

Feedback

As shown in Figure 5.1, feedback is information about the actual performance or the results of the system. However, not all such information is feedback. Only information used to control the future functioning of the system is considered to be feedback. Feedback can be used to maintain the system in a steady state (for example, keeping an assembly line running at a certain speed) or to help the organisation adapt to changing circumstances. McDonald's, for example, has strict feedback processes for ensuring that a meal in one outlet is as similar as possible to a meal in any other outlet. On the other hand, a salesperson in the field may report that sales are not going well and may suggest some organisational change to improve sales. A market research study may lead the marketing department to recommend a change in the organisation's advertising campaign.

Equifinality

In closed systems, there is a direct cause-and-effect relationship between the initial condition and the final state of the system. When the 'on' switch on a computer is pushed, the system powers up. Biological and social systems, however, operate quite differently. The idea of equifinality suggests that similar results may be achieved with different initial conditions and in many different ways. This concept suggests that a manager can use varying forms of inputs into the organisation and can transform them in a variety of ways to obtain satisfactory outputs. Thus, the function of management is not to seek a single rigid solution but rather to develop a variety of satisfactory options. Systems and contingency theories suggest that there is no universal best way to design an organisation. Organisations and departments providing routine services, such as Telstra and Optus's long-distance phone services, should be designed differently from pharmaceutical development groups at Mayne Pharma or GlaxoSmithKline Australia.

Alignment

A system's overall effectiveness is determined by the extent to which the different parts are aligned with each other. This alignment or fit concerns the relationships between inputs and transformations, between transformations and outputs, and among the subsystems of the transformation process. Diagnosticians who view the relationships between the various parts of a system as a whole are taking what is referred to as a 'systemic perspective'.

Fit and alignment refer to a characteristic of the relationship between two or more parts. Just as the teeth in two wheels of a watch must mesh perfectly for the watch to keep time, so too do the parts of an organisation need to mesh for it to be effective. For example, Foster's Group attempts to achieve its goals through a strategy of diversification, and a divisional structure is used to support that strategy. A functional structure would not be a good fit with the strategy as it is more efficient for one division to focus on one product line than for one manufacturing department to try to make many different products. The systemic perspective suggests that diagnosis is the search for misfits among the various parts and subsystems of an organisation.

COLLECTING AND ANALYSING DIAGNOSTIC INFORMATION

Data collection involves gathering information on specific organisational features, such as the inputs, design components and outputs presented above. The process begins by establishing an effective relationship between the OD practitioner and those from whom data will be collected, and then choosing data-collection techniques. Four methods can be used to collect data: questionnaires, interviews, observations and unobtrusive measures. Data analysis organises and examines the information to make clear the underlying causes of an organisational problem or to identify areas for future development. The next step in the cyclical OD process is the feeding back of data to the client system. The overall process of data collection, analysis and feedback is shown in Figure 5.2.

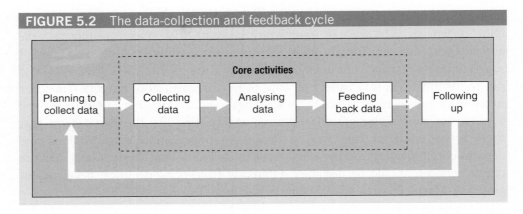

FIGURE 5.2 The data-collection and feedback cycle

Source: D. Nadler, *Feedback and Organization Development* © 1977, p.43. Reprinted by permission of Pearson Education, Inc., Upper Saddle River, New Jersey.

The diagnostic relationship

In most cases of planned change, OD practitioners play an active role in gathering data from organisation members for diagnostic purposes. For example, they might interview members of a work team about causes of conflict among members, or they might survey employees at a large industrial plant about factors that contribute to poor product quality. Before collecting diagnostic information, practitioners need to establish a relationship with those who will provide and subsequently use it. Because the nature of that relationship affects the quality and usefulness of the data collected, it is vital that OD practitioners provide organisation members with a clear idea of who they are, why the data are being collected, what the data gathering will involve and how the data will be used.[4] Answers to these questions can help to allay people's natural fears that the data might be used against them. Such answers also help to gain members' participation and support, which is essential for developing successful interventions.

Establishing the diagnostic relationship between the consultant and relevant organisation members is similar to forming a contract. It is meant to clarify expectations and to specify the conditions of the relationship. In those cases where members have been directly involved in the entering and contracting process, the diagnostic contract will typically be part of the initial contracting step. However, in situations where data will be collected from members who have not been directly involved in entering and contracting, OD practitioners will need to establish a diagnostic contract as a prelude to diagnosis. The answers to the following questions provide the substance of the diagnostic contract:[5]

1   *Who am I?* The answer to this question introduces the OD practitioner to the organisation, particularly to those members who do not know the consultant, but who will be asked to provide diagnostic data.

2   *Why am I here, and what am I doing?* These answers are aimed at defining the goals of the diagnosis and data-gathering activities. The consultant needs to

present the objectives of the action research process and to describe how the diagnostic activities fit into the overall developmental strategy.

3   *Who do I work for?* This answer clarifies who has hired the consultant, whether it be a manager, a group of managers or a group of employees and managers. One way to build trust and support for the diagnosis is to have such persons directly involved in establishing the diagnostic contract. Thus, for example, if the consultant works for a joint labour–management committee, representatives from both sides of that group could help the consultant build the proper relationship with those from whom data will be gathered.

4   *What do I want from you, and why?* Here the consultant needs to specify how much time and effort people will need to give in order to provide valid data, and subsequently to work with these data in solving problems. Because some people may not want to participate in the diagnosis, it is important to specify that such involvement is voluntary.

5   *How will I protect your confidentiality?* This answer addresses member concerns about who will see their responses and in what form. This is especially critical when employees are asked to provide information about their attitudes or perceptions. OD practitioners can either assure confidentiality or state that full participation in the change process requires open information sharing. In the first case, employees are frequently concerned about privacy and the possibility of being punished for their responses. To alleviate concern and to increase the likelihood of getting honest responses, the consultant may need to assure employees of the confidentiality of their information. This may require explicit guarantees of response anonymity. In the second case, full involvement of the participants in their own diagnosis may be a vital ingredient in the change process. If sensitive issues arise, assurances of confidentiality can restrict the OD practitioner and thwart meaningful diagnosis. The consultant is bound to keep confidential the issues that are most critical for the group or organisation to understand.[6] OD practitioners must think carefully about how they want to handle confidentiality issues.

6   *Who will have access to the data?* Respondents typically want to know whether or not they will have access to their data and who else in the organisation will have similar access. The OD practitioner needs to clarify access issues and, in most cases, should agree to provide respondents with their own results. Indeed, the collaborative nature of diagnosis means that organisation members will work with their own data to discover causes of problems and to devise relevant interventions.

7   *What's in it for you?* This answer is aimed at providing organisation members with a clear assessment of the benefits they can expect from the diagnosis. This usually entails describing the feedback process and how they can use the data to improve the organisation.

8   *Can I be trusted?* The diagnostic relationship ultimately rests on the trust that is established between the consultant and those providing the data. An open and

honest exchange of information depends on such trust, and the practitioner should provide ample time and face-to-face contact during the contracting process in order to build this trust. This requires the consultant to actively listen and openly discuss all questions raised by respondents.

Careful attention to establishing the diagnostic relationship helps to promote the three goals of data collection.[7] The first and most immediate objective is to obtain valid information about organisational functioning. Building a data-collection contract can ensure that organisation members provide information that is honest, reliable and complete.

Data collection can also rally energy for constructive organisational change. A good diagnostic relationship helps organisation members to start thinking about issues that concern them, and it creates expectations that change is possible. When members trust the consultant, they are likely to participate in the diagnostic process and to generate energy and commitment for organisational change.

Finally, data collection helps to develop the collaborative relationship necessary for effecting organisational change. The diagnostic stage of action research is probably the first time that most organisation members meet the OD practitioner. It can provide the basis for building a longer-term relationship. The data-collection contract and the subsequent data-gathering and feedback activities provide members with opportunities for seeing the consultant in action and for getting to know her or him personally. If the consultant can show employees that she or he is trustworthy, is willing to work with them and is able to help improve the organisation, then the data-collection process will contribute to the longer-term collaborative relationship so necessary for carrying out organisational changes.

Methods for collecting data

The four major techniques for gathering diagnostic data are questionnaires, interviews, observations and unobtrusive methods. Table 5.1 briefly compares the methods and lists their major advantages and problems. No single method can fully measure the kinds of variables important to OD; each has certain strengths and weaknesses.[8] For example, perceptual measures, such as questionnaires and surveys, are open to self-report biases, such as the respondents' tendency to give socially desirable answers rather than honest opinions. Observations, on the other hand, are susceptible to observer biases, such as seeing what one wants to see rather than what is really there. Because of the biases inherent in any data-collection method, we recommend that more than one method be used when collecting diagnostic data. The data from the different methods can be compared and, if they are consistent, it is likely that the variables are being validly measured. For example, questionnaire measures of job discretion could be supplemented with observations of the number and kinds of decisions that the employees are making. If the two kinds of data support one another, job discretion is probably being accurately assessed. If the two kinds of data conflict, then the validity of the

TABLE 5.1 Different methods of data collection

Method	Major advantages	Major potential problems
Questionnaires	1 Responses can be quantified and easily summarised 2 Easy to use with large samples 3 Relatively inexpensive 4 Can obtain large volume of data	1 Non-empathy 2 Predetermined questions missing issues 3 Overinterpretation of data 4 Response bias
Interviews	1 Adaptive – allows data collection on a range of possible subjects 2 Source of 'rich' data 3 Empathic 4 Process of interviewing can build rapport	1 Expense 2 Bias in interviewer responses 3 Coding and interpretation difficulties 4 Self-report bias
Observations	1 Collects data on behaviour, rather than reports of behaviour 2 Real time, not retrospective 3 Adaptive	1 Coding and interpretation difficulties 2 Sampling inconsistencies 3 Observer bias and questionable reliability 4 Expense
Unobtrusive measures	1 Non-reactive – no response bias 2 High face validity 3 Easily quantified interviews	1 Access and retrieval difficulties 2 Validity concerns 3 Coding and interpretation difficulties

Source: D. Nadler, *Feedback and Organization Development* © 1977, p.119. Reprinted by permission of Pearson Education, Inc., Upper Saddle River, New Jersey.

measures should be examined further – perhaps by employing a third method, such as interviews.

Questionnaires

One of the most efficient ways of collecting data is through questionnaires. Because they typically contain fixed-response questions about various features of an organisation, these paper-and-pencil measures can be administered to large numbers of people simultaneously. Also, they can be analysed quickly, especially with the use of computers, thus permitting quantitative comparison and evaluation. As a result, data can easily be fed back to employees. Numerous basic resource books on survey methodology and questionnaire development are available.[9]

Questionnaires can vary in scope: some measure selected aspects of organisations and others assess more comprehensive organisational characteristics. They can also vary in the extent to which they are either standardised or tailored to a specific organisation. Standardised instruments are generally based on an explicit model of organisation, group or individual effectiveness. These questionnaires usually contain a predetermined set of questions that have been developed and refined over time. The questionnaire includes three items or questions for each dimension; a total score for each job dimension is computed simply by adding the responses for the three relevant items and arriving at a total score from 3 (low) to 21 (high). The questionnaire has wide applicability. It has been used in a variety of organisations with employees in both blue-collar and white-collar jobs.

Several research organisations have been highly instrumental in developing and refining surveys. The Australian Council for Educational Research is a prominent example. Two of the council's most popular measures of organisational dimensions are 'Changing your management style' and 'Team climate inventory'.[10] Other examples include 'Organization change: orientation scale' available from the Australian Institute of Management.[11] In fact, so many questionnaires are available that rarely would an organisation have to create a totally new one. However, because every organisation has unique problems and special jargon for referring to them, almost any standardised instrument will need to have organisation-specific additions, modifications or omissions.

Customised questionnaires, on the other hand, are tailored to the needs of a particular client. Typically, they include questions composed by consultants or organisation members, receive limited use and do not undergo longer-term development. Customised questionnaires can be combined with standardised instruments to provide valid and reliable data focused on the particular issues that face an organisation.

Questionnaires, however, have a number of drawbacks that need to be taken into account when choosing whether to employ them for data collection. First, responses are limited to the questions asked in the instrument. They provide little opportunity to probe for additional data or ask for points of clarification. Second, questionnaires tend to be impersonal, and employees may not be willing to provide honest answers. Third, questionnaires often elicit response biases, such as the tendency to answer questions in a socially acceptable manner. This makes it difficult to draw valid conclusions from employees' self-reports.

Interviews

A second important measurement technique is the individual or group interview. These probably represent the most widely used technique for collecting data in OD. They permit the interviewer to ask the respondent direct questions, and further probing and clarification is possible as the interview proceeds. This flexibility is invaluable for gaining private views and feelings about the organisation and for exploring new issues that emerge during the interview.

Interviews may be highly structured, resembling questionnaires, or highly unstructured, starting with general questions that allow the respondent to lead the way. Structured interviews typically derive from a conceptual model of organisation functioning; the model guides the types of questions that are asked.

Unstructured interviews are more general and include broad questions about organisational functioning, such as:

- What are the major goals or objectives of the organisation or department?
- How does the organisation currently perform with respect to these purposes?
- What are the strengths and weaknesses of the organisation or department?
- What barriers stand in the way of good performance?

Although interviewing typically involves one-to-one interaction between an OD practitioner and an employee, it can be carried out in a group context. Group interviews save time and allow people to build on others' responses. A major drawback, however, is that group settings may inhibit some people from responding freely.

A popular type of group interview is the focus group or sensing meeting.[12] These are unstructured meetings conducted by a manager or a consultant. A small group of 10 to 15 employees is selected, representing either a cross-section of functional areas and hierarchical levels or a homogeneous grouping, such as minorities or engineers. Group discussion is frequently started by asking general questions about organisational features and functioning, an intervention's progress or current performance. Group members are then encouraged to discuss their answers in some depth. Consequently, focus groups and sensing meetings are an economical way of obtaining interview data and are especially effective in understanding particular issues in some depth. The richness and validity of that information will depend on the extent to which the manager or consultant develops a trust relationship with the group and listens to member opinions.

Another popular unstructured group interview involves assessing the current state of an intact work group. The manager or consultant generally directs a question to the group, calling its attention to some part of group functioning. For example, group members may be asked how they feel the group is progressing on its stated task. The group might respond and then come up with its own series of questions about barriers to task performance. This unstructured interview is a fast, simple way of collecting data about group behaviour. It allows members to discuss issues of immediate concern and to engage actively in the questioning-and-answering process. This technique is, however, limited to relatively small groups and to settings where there is trust among employees and managers, and a commitment to assessing group processes.

Interviews are an effective method of collecting data in OD. They are adaptive, allowing the interviewer to modify questions and to probe emergent issues during the interview process. They also permit the interviewer to develop an empathetic relationship with employees, frequently resulting in frank disclosure of pertinent information. Such interviews can only be successful if both parties are prepared to listen.

A major drawback of interviews is the amount of time required to conduct and analyse them. They can consume a great deal of time, especially if the interviewers take full advantage of the opportunity to hear respondents out, and change their questions accordingly. Personal biases can also distort the data. Like questionnaires, interviews are subject to the self-report biases of respondents and, perhaps more importantly, to the biases of the interviewer. For example, the nature of the questions and the interactions between the interviewer and the respondent may discourage or encourage certain kinds of responses. These problems suggest that interviewing takes considerable skill to gather valid data. Interviewers must be able to understand their own biases, to listen and establish empathy with respondents and to change questions to pursue issues that develop during the course of the interview.

Observations

One of the more direct ways of collecting data is simply to observe organisational behaviours in their functional settings. The OD practitioner may do this by casually walking through a work area and looking around or by simply counting the occurrences of specific kinds of behaviours (for example, the number of times a phone call is answered after three rings in a service department). Observation can range from complete participant observation, in which the OD practitioner becomes a member of the group under study, to more detached observation, in which the observer is clearly not part of the group or situation itself and may use film, videotape or other methods to record behaviours.

Observations have a number of advantages. They are free of the biases inherent in self-report data. They put the practitioner directly in touch with the behaviours in question, without having to rely on others' perceptions. Observations also involve real-time data, describing behaviour that is occurring in the present rather than the past. This avoids the distortions that invariably arise when people are asked to recollect their behaviours. Finally, observations are adaptive in that the consultant can modify what she or he is observing according to the circumstances.

Among the problems with observations are difficulties in interpreting the meaning that underlies the observations. Practitioners may need to code the observations to make sense of them, and this can be expensive, take time and introduce bias into the data. Because the observer is the data-collection instrument, personal bias and subjectivity can distort data unless the observer is trained and skilled in knowing what to look for, how to observe, where and when to observe, and how to record data systematically. Another problem concerns sampling. Observers must not only decide which people to observe but also choose the time periods, territory and events in which observations will be made. Failure to attend to these sampling issues can result in highly biased samples of observational data. When used correctly, observations provide insightful data about organisation and group functioning, intervention success and performance.

Unobtrusive measures

Unobtrusive data are not collected directly from respondents but from secondary sources, such as company records and archives. These data are generally available in organisations and include records of absenteeism or tardiness, grievances, quantity and quality of production or service, financial performance and correspondence with key customers, suppliers or governmental agencies.

Unobtrusive measures[13] provide a relatively objective view of organisational functioning. They are free from respondent and consultant biases and are perceived by many organisation members as being real. Moreover, unobtrusive measures tend to be quantified and reported at periodic intervals, permitting statistical analysis of behaviours occurring over time. Examination of monthly absenteeism rates, for example, might reveal trends in employee withdrawal behaviour.

The major problems with unobtrusive measures occur when collecting such information and drawing valid conclusions from it. Company records may not include data in a form that is usable by the consultant. If, for example, individual performance data are needed, the consultant may find that many companies only record production information at the group or departmental level. Unobtrusive data may also have their own built-in biases. Changes in accounting procedures and in methods of recording data are common in organisations; such changes can affect company records independently of what is actually happening in the organisation. For example, observed changes in productivity over time might be caused by modifications in methods of recording production, rather than by actual changes in organisational functioning.

Despite these drawbacks, unobtrusive data serve as a valuable adjunct to other diagnostic measures, such as interviews and questionnaires. Archival data can be used in preliminary diagnosis, indicating those organisational units that have absenteeism, grievance or production problems. Interviews can then be conducted or observations made in those units to discover the underlying causes of the problems. Conversely, unobtrusive data can be used to cross-check other forms of information. For example, if questionnaires reveal that employees in a department are dissatisfied with their jobs, company records might show whether that discontent is manifested in heightened withdrawal behaviours, in lowered quality of work or in similar counterproductive behaviours.

Sampling

Before discussing how to analyse data, the issue of sampling needs to be emphasised. Application of the different data-collection techniques invariably raises the following questions: 'How many people should be interviewed and who should they be?' 'What events should be observed and how many?' and 'How many records should be inspected and which ones?'[14]

In many OD cases, sampling is not an issue. Practitioners simply collect interview or questionnaire data from all members of the organisation or department in question, and so do not have to worry about whether the information is representative of the organisation or unit because all members of the population are included in the sample.

Sampling becomes an issue in OD, however, when data are collected from selected members, behaviours or records. This is often the case when diagnosing organisation-level issues or large systems. In these cases, it may be important to ensure that the sample of people, behaviours or records adequately represents the characteristics of the total population. For example, a sample of 50 employees might be used to assess the perceptions of all 300 members of a department, or a sample of production data might be used to evaluate the total production of a work group. OD practitioners often find that it is more economical and quicker to gather a sampling of diagnostic data than to collect all possible information. If done correctly, the sample can provide useful and valid information about the entire organisation or unit.

Sampling design involves considerable technical detail, and consultants may need to become familiar with basic references in this area or to obtain professional help.[15] The first issue to address is *sample size*, or how many people, events or records are needed to carry out the diagnosis or evaluation. This question has no simple answer: the necessary sample size is a function of size of the population, the confidence desired in the quality of the data and the resources (money and time) available for data collection.

First, the larger the population (for example, the number of organisation members or total number of work outcomes) or the more complex the client system (for example, the number of salary levels that must be sampled or the number of different functions), the more difficult it is to establish a 'right' sample size. As the population increases in size and complexity, the less meaning one can attach to simple measures, such as an overall average score on a questionnaire item. Because the population is composed of such different types of people or events, more data are needed to ensure an accurate representation of the potentially different subgroups. Second, the larger the proportion of the population that is selected, the more confidence one can have about the quality of the sample. If the diagnosis concerns an issue of great importance to the organisation, then extreme confidence may be needed, indicative of a larger sample size. Third, limited resources constrain sample size. If resources are limited but the required confidence is high, then questionnaires will be preferred to interviews because more information can be collected per member per dollar.

The second issue to address is sample selection. Probably the most common approach to sampling diagnostic data in OD is a simple random sample in which each member, behaviour or record has an equal chance of being selected. For example, assume that an OD practitioner would like to randomly select 50 people out of the 300 employees at a manufacturing plant. Using a complete list of all 300 employees, the consultant can generate a random sample in one of two ways. The first method would be to use a random number table in the back of almost any statistics text; the consultant would pick out the employees corresponding to the first 50 numbers under 300 beginning anywhere in the table. The second method would be to pick every sixth name ($300 \div 50 = 6$) starting anywhere in the list.

If the population is complex, or many subgroups need to be represented in the sample, a *stratified sample*[16] may be more appropriate than a random one. In a stratified sample, the population of members, events or records is segregated into a number of mutually exclusive subpopulations. Then, a random sample is taken from each subpopulation. For example, members of an organisation might be divided into three groups: managers, white-collar workers and blue-collar workers. A random sample of members, behaviours or records could be selected from each grouping in order to make diagnostic conclusions about each of the groups.

Adequate sampling is critical when gathering valid diagnostic data, and the OD literature has tended to pay little attention to this issue. OD practitioners should gain rudimentary knowledge in this area and use professional help if necessary.

FEEDING BACK DIAGNOSTIC INFORMATION

As shown in Figure 5.3, the success of data feedback depends largely on its ability to arouse organisational action and to direct energy towards organisational problem solving. Whether or not feedback helps to energise the organisation depends on the content of the feedback data and on the process by which they are fed back to organisation members.

Determining the content of the feedback

Large amounts of data are collected in the course of diagnosing the organisation. In fact, there is often more information than the client needs or could interpret in a realistic period of time. If too many data are fed back, the client may decide that changing is impossible. Therefore, OD practitioners need to summarise the data in ways that are useful for clients, so that they can both understand the information and draw action implications from it.

Several characteristics of effective feedback data have been described in the literature.[17] They include the following nine properties:

1 *Relevant.* Organisation members are more likely to use feedback data for problem solving if they find the information meaningful. Including managers and employees in the initial data-collection activities can increase the relevance of the data.
2 *Understandable.* Data must be presented to organisation members in a form that is readily interpreted. Statistical data, for example, can be made understandable through the use of graphs and charts.
3 *Descriptive.* Feedback data need to be linked to real organisational behaviours if they are to arouse and direct energy. The use of examples and detailed illustrations can help employees gain a better feel for the data.
4 *Verifiable.* Feedback data should be valid and accurate if they are to guide action. Thus, the information should allow organisation members to verify whether the findings really describe the organisation. For example, questionnaire data might

FIGURE 5.3 Possible effects of feedback

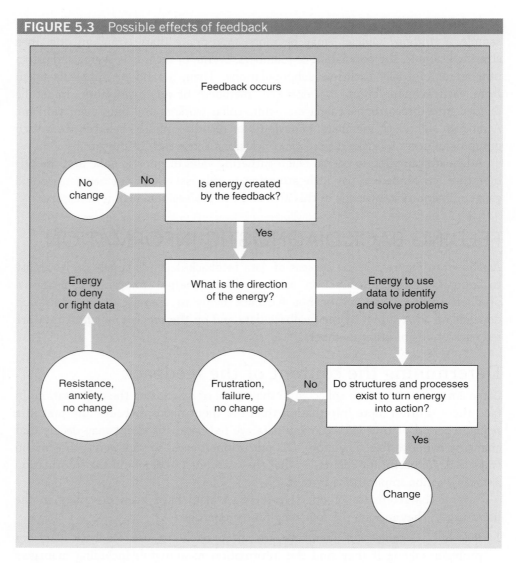

Source: D. Nadler, *Feedback and Organization Development* © 1977, p.146. Reprinted by permission of Pearson Education, Inc., Upper Saddle River, New Jersey.

include information about the sample of respondents as well as frequency distributions for each item or measure. This kind of information can help members verify whether the feedback data accurately represent organisational events or attitudes.

5 *Timely.* Data should be fed back to members as quickly as possible after being collected and analysed. This will help ensure that the information is still valid and is linked to members' motivations to examine it.

6 *Limited.* Because people can easily become overloaded with too much information, feedback data should be limited to what employees can realistically process at any one time.

7 *Significant.* Feedback should be limited to those problems that organisation members can do something about. This will help energise them and direct their efforts towards realistic changes.

8 *Comparative.* Feedback data without some benchmark as a reference can be ambiguous. Whenever possible, data from comparative groups should be provided in order to give organisation members a better idea of how their group fits into a broader context.

9 *Unfinalised.* Feedback is primarily a stimulus for action and should, therefore, spur further diagnosis and problem solving. Members should be encouraged, for example, to use the data as a starting point for more in-depth discussion of organisational issues.

Characteristics of the feedback process

In addition to providing effective feedback data, it is equally important to attend to the process by which that information is fed back to people. Typically, data are provided to organisation members in a meeting or series of meetings. Feedback meetings provide a forum for discussing the data, drawing relevant conclusions and devising preliminary action plans. Because the data might include sensitive material and evaluations of organisation members' behaviours, people may come to the meeting with considerable anxiety and fear about receiving the feedback. This anxiety can result in defensive behaviours aimed at denying the information or providing rationales. More positively, people can be stimulated by the feedback and the hope that desired changes will result from the feedback meeting.

Because people are likely to come to feedback meetings with anxiety, fear and hope, OD practitioners need to manage the feedback process so that constructive discussion and problem solving will occur. The most important objective of the feedback process is to ensure that organisation members own the data. Ownership is the opposite of resistance to change and refers to people's willingness to take responsibility for the data, its meaning and the consequences of using the data to devise a change strategy.[18] If the feedback session results in organisation members rejecting the data as invalid or useless, then the motivation to change is lost and members will have difficulty in engaging in a meaningful process of change.

Ownership of the feedback data is facilitated by the following five features of successful feedback processes:[19]

1 *Motivation to work with the data.* People need to feel that working on the feedback data will have beneficial outcomes. This may require explicit sanction and support from powerful groups so that people feel free to raise issues and identify concerns during the feedback sessions. If they have little motivation to work with the data or feel that there is little chance to use the data for change, the information will not be owned by the client system.

2 *Structure for the meeting.* Feedback meetings need some structure, or they may degenerate into chaos or aimless discussion. An agenda or outline and a

discussion leader can usually provide the necessary direction. If the meeting is not kept on track, especially when the data are negative, ownership can be lost in conversations that become too general. When this happens, the energy gained from dealing directly with the problem is lost.

3 *Appropriate membership.* Generally, people who have common problems and can benefit from working together should be included in the feedback meeting. This may involve a fully intact work team, or groups made up of members from different functional areas or hierarchical levels. Without proper representation in the meeting, ownership of the data is lost because the participants cannot address the problem(s) suggested by the feedback.

4 *Appropriate power.* It is important to clarify the power possessed by the group. Members need to know to which issues they can make necessary changes, on which they can only recommend changes and on which they have no control. Unless there are clear boundaries, members are likely to have some hesitation about using the feedback data for generating action plans. Moreover, if the group has no power to make changes, the feedback meeting will become an empty exercise rather than a real problem-solving session. Without the power to address change, there will be little ownership of the data.

5 *Process help.* People in feedback meetings need help to work together as a group. When the data are negative, there is a natural tendency to resist the implications, deflect the conversation onto safer subjects and the like. An OD practitioner with group process skills can help members stay focused on the subject and improve feedback discussion, problem solving and ownership.

When combined with effective feedback data, these features of successful feedback meetings enhance member ownership of the data. They help to ensure that organisation members fully discuss the implications of the diagnostic information and that their conclusions are directed towards organisational changes that are relevant and feasible.

DESIGNING INTERVENTIONS

The term 'intervention' refers to a set of sequenced planned actions or events that are intended to help an organisation increase its effectiveness. Interventions purposely disrupt the status quo; they are a deliberate attempt to move an organisation or sub-unit towards a different and more effective state. In OD, three major criteria define an effective intervention: (1) the extent to which it fits the needs of the organisation, (2) the degree to which it is based on causal knowledge of intended outcomes, and (3) the extent to which it transfers competence to manage change to organisation members.

The first criterion concerns the extent to which the intervention is relevant to the organisation and its members. Effective interventions are based on valid information about the organisation's functioning. They provide organisation members with opportunities to make free and informed choices; and they gain members' internal commitment to those choices.[20]

Valid information is the result of an accurate diagnosis of the organisation's functioning. It must fairly reflect what organisation members perceive and feel about their primary concerns and issues. Free and informed choice suggests that members are actively involved in making decisions about the changes that will affect them. It means that they can choose not to participate and that interventions will not be imposed upon them. Internal commitment means that organisation members will accept ownership of the intervention and take responsibility for implementing it. If interventions are to result in meaningful changes, management, staff and other relevant members must be committed to implementing them.

The second criterion of an effective intervention involves knowledge of outcomes. Because interventions are intended to produce specific results, they must be based on valid knowledge that those outcomes can actually be produced. Otherwise there is no scientific basis for designing an effective OD intervention. Unfortunately, and in contrast to other applied disciplines, such as medicine and engineering, knowledge of intervention effects is in a rudimentary stage of development in OD. Much of the evaluation research lacks sufficient rigour to make strong causal inferences about the success or failure of change programs. Moreover, few attempts have been made to examine the comparative impacts of different OD techniques. This makes knowing whether one method is more effective than another difficult.

Despite these problems, more attempts are being made to systematically assess the strengths and weaknesses of OD interventions and to compare the impact of different techniques on organisation effectiveness.[21] Many of the OD interventions that will be discussed in this book have been subjected to evaluative research. This research is explored in the appropriate chapters, along with respective change programs.

The third criterion of an effective intervention involves the extent to which it enhances the organisation's capacity to manage change. The values underlying OD suggest that organisation members should be better able to carry out planned change activities on their own after an intervention. They should gain knowledge and skill in managing change from active participation in designing and implementing the intervention. Competence in change management is essential in today's environment, where technological, social, economic and political changes are rapid and persistent.

How to design effective interventions

Designing OD interventions requires careful attention to the needs and dynamics of the change situation and to crafting a change program that will be consistent with the criteria of the effective interventions outlined above. Current knowledge of OD interventions provides only general prescriptions for change. There is little precise information or research about how to design interventions or how they can be expected to interact with organisational conditions to achieve specific results.[22] Moreover, the ability to implement most OD interventions is highly dependent on the skills and knowledge of the change agent. Thus, the design of an intervention will depend to some extent on the expertise of the practitioner.

Two major sets of contingencies that can affect intervention success have been discussed in the OD literature: those having to do with the change situation (including the practitioner) and those related to the target of change. Both kinds of contingencies need to be considered when designing interventions.

Contingencies related to the change situation

Researchers have identified a number of contingencies present in the change situation that can affect intervention success. These include individual differences among organisation members (for example, needs for autonomy), organisational factors (for example, management style and technical uncertainty) and dimensions of the change process itself (for example, the degree of top-management support). Unless these factors are taken into account when designing an intervention, the intervention will have little impact on organisational functioning or, worse, it might even produce negative results. For example, if you are seeking to resolve motivational problems among blue-collar workers in an oil refinery, it is important that you know whether interventions intended to improve motivation (for example, job enrichment) will succeed with the kinds of people who work there. In many cases, having knowledge of these contingencies might result in modifying or adjusting the change program to fit the setting. In applying a reward-system intervention to an organisation, the changes might have to be modified according to whether the company wants to reinforce individual or team performance.

Although knowledge of contingencies is still in a rudimentary stage of development in OD, researchers have discovered several situational factors that can affect intervention success.[23] These include contingencies for many of the interventions reviewed in this book, and they will be discussed in the relevant chapters that describe the change programs. More generic contingencies that apply to all OD interventions follow, including the situational factors that must be considered when designing any intervention: the organisation's readiness for change, its change capability, its cultural context and the change agent's skills and abilities.

Readiness for change

Intervention success depends heavily on the organisation being ready for planned change. Indicators of readiness for change[24] include sensitivity to pressures for change, dissatisfaction with the status quo, availability of resources to support change, and commitment of significant management time. When these conditions are present, interventions can be designed to address the organisational issues uncovered during diagnosis. When readiness for change is low, however, interventions need to focus on increasing the organisation's willingness to change.[25] Application 5.1 describes how organisations should be prepared for the use, and abuse, of technology.

Restaurants learn dark side of social networking

The firings of two Burger King executives over the content of their Web postings are underscoring the very real problems the virtual world brings to the modern workplace.

While the Digital Age has served up numerous business solutions addressing such topics as inventory control, site selection, self-administered employee benefits and the ability to profile guests, it also has ushered in a new era of workplace frictions as the employee's right to communicate is pitted against the employer's need to protect the foodservice brand.

'It's just a host of land mines out there when dealing with e-communication in all of its forms,' said Carolyn Richmond, a labor attorney who mainly represents restaurant employers. She noted the widespread use of digital devices like laptops, multifunctional cell phones and personal digital assistants is unleashing a torrent of litigation between employees, ex-employees and employers over sexual harassment, trademark infringement, breach of contract, confidentiality agreements and defamation.

'I'm increasingly consulting with companies that want to update their Internet policies in their employee handbooks,' Richmond said. 'Some of them are updating it every three to five years because the technology is moving so fast.

'But one thing is for sure: An employee should expect to have zero expectation of privacy in the workplace because, minus California, where there are more restrictions, most places give employers wide latitude to monitor e-mail, phone calls, even to include video surveillance.'

The clash between the employee's right to communicate and the employer's need to protect the brand took a dramatic turn earlier this month when Burger King fired two executives for unauthorized online comments that blasted a tomato farmers advocacy group.

The firings followed confirmation by the company that unsanctioned comments on various public websites had been traced to Steve Grover, the chain's vice president of food safety, quality assurance and regulatory compliance. The comments, made under names other than Grover's, were directed at the Coalition of Immokalee Workers, an advocacy group at odds with Burger King, which has in the past refused to pay a penny more per pound for tomatoes harvested by the group.

In addition to embarrassing the brand, Denise Wilson, a spokeswoman for Burger King, said the employees violated several corporate guidelines, including those forbidding employees from speaking for the company outside of official corporate releases and sharing with outsiders matters dealing with private negotiations.

John Chidsey, BK's chief executive, said: 'I was distressed to learn of the allegations. Neither I nor any of my senior management team were aware of or condone the unauthorized activities in question. BKC maintains a strict code of conduct for our employees and vendors, and we will not tolerate unethical or unlawful behavior.'

Observers said the fact that Burger King was able to trace the posts to Grover is notable, and should send a powerful message to employees who might believe their online messages are anonymous.

Lewis L. Maltby, president of the National Workrights Institute, said there is no such thing as privacy and little legal defense available when employees misuse employers' confidential data or sexually harass colleagues through the Internet.

>>

There's 'not a great deal you can say to support employees who run afoul of their bosses' e-mail and Internet restrictions,' Maltby said. 'If you send messages on work time and your job believes these messages are objectionable, or you spend too much time talking with your girlfriend or keeping up with the Yankees game, you have no legal protection at all if the boss wants to discipline you.'

Maltby added that employers have a right to protect themselves and to ferret out individuals who disseminate derogatory information about a company that could damage its reputation or its dealings. While employers cannot put recording devices in the office lunchroom or record phone conversations without letting employees know about it, the Internet and e-mail use is unrestricted to such eavesdropping thanks to spyware, Maltby said.

Tina Burke said that in her four years as human resources director for the Claim Jumper casual-dining chain, her company has not needed to take action against an employee for spreading proprietary or unflattering information about the chain on the Internet or through e-mails. She added employees know the company's strict policy forbidding misuse of the company's e-mail and computers, particularly relating to sexual harassment.

Burke says the company monitors blogs where employees might post opinions or information the company might find embarrassing or unfounded. In addition, the company is researching a blogging policy.

'But it is such a grey area,' she said. 'We want to balance our employees' right to privacy and free speech with the company's right to protect our reputation.'

Dean Sockett, vice president of Keg Restaurants, a casual-dining chain, said his company has a strict policy outlining what the Internet and the company computers are to be used for during work hours: work.

The policy clearly informs workers that posting recipes as well as gripes about co-workers, customers, vendors or other labor complaints that divulge proprietary information or information that is untrue could be grounds for dismissal.

Calling the BK-Grover imbroglio more a 'public-relations nightmare' than an operational failing or legal threat, Stephen J. Molen, senior account manager of EthicsPoint Inc., a risk assessment consulting firm, encouraged operators to be proactive and monitor employees' communication about company business to outsiders, even if it means cameras and spyware.

Source: Milford Prewitt, 'Restaurants learn dark side of social networking', *Nation's Restaurant News*, 26 May 2008.

Critical thinking questions:
1. The article suggests that today's employees have no right to privacy when they are expressing their opinions or thoughts about their working environment on electronic sites such as MySpace or Facebook. Therefore, do you think an employer has the right to fire or discipline you, if you express unflattering comments about your employer? Discuss.
2. When an employee enters into an employment contract are they also signing away their rights to privacy and their own private life within work hours? Discuss.

Capability to change

Managing planned change requires particular knowledge and skills. These include the ability to motivate change, to lead change, to develop political support, to manage the transition and to sustain momentum. If organisation members do not have these capabilities, then a preliminary training intervention may be needed before members can meaningfully engage in intervention design.

Cultural context

The national culture within which the organisation is embedded can have a powerful influence on members' reactions to change. Thus, intervention design needs to account for the cultural values and assumptions held by organisation members. Interventions may need to be modified to fit the local culture, particularly when OD practices developed in one culture are applied to organisations in another culture.[26] For example, a team-building intervention designed for top managers at an Australian company may need to be modified when applied to its foreign subsidiaries.

Capabilities of the change agent

Many failures in OD result when change agents apply interventions beyond their competence. In designing interventions, OD practitioners should assess their experience and expertise against the requirements needed to implement the intervention effectively. When a mismatch is discovered, practitioners can explore whether the intervention can be modified to fit their talents better, whether another intervention more suited to their skills can satisfy the organisation's needs or whether they should enlist the assistance of another change agent who can guide the process more effectively. The ethical guidelines under which OD practitioners operate require full disclosure of the applicability of their knowledge and expertise to the client situation. Practitioners are expected to intervene within their capabilities or to recommend someone more suited to the client's needs.

Contingencies related to the target of change

OD interventions seek to change specific features or parts of organisations. These targets of change are the main focus of interventions, and researchers have identified two key contingencies related to change targets that can affect intervention success: the organisational issues that the intervention is intended to resolve and the level of organisational system at which the intervention is expected to have a primary impact.

Organisational issues

Organisations need to address certain issues to operate effectively. Figure 5.4 lists these issues along with the OD interventions that are intended to resolve them. It shows four interrelated issues that are key targets of OD interventions:

1 *Strategic issues.* Organisations need to decide what products or services they will provide and the markets in which they will compete, as well as how to relate to their environments and how to transform themselves to keep pace with changing conditions. These strategic issues are among the most critical facing organisations in today's changing and highly competitive environments. OD methods aimed at these issues are called 'strategic interventions'. They are among the most recent additions to OD and include integrated strategic change, transorganisational development and organisation transformation.

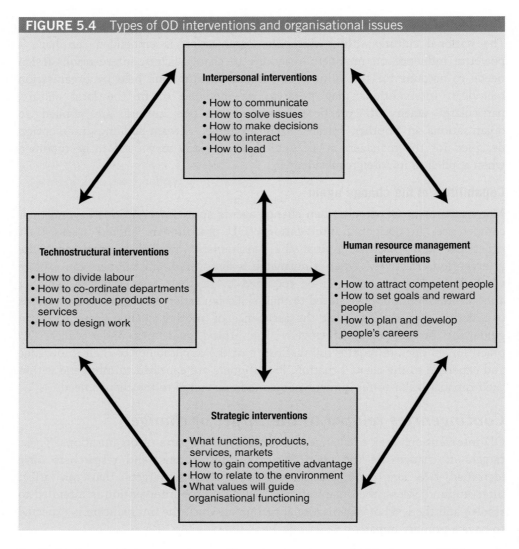

FIGURE 5.4 Types of OD interventions and organisational issues

2 *Technology and structure issues.* Organisations must decide how to divide work into departments and then how to co-ordinate them to support strategic directions. They must also make decisions about how to produce products or services and how to link people with tasks. OD methods for dealing with these structural and technological issues are called 'technostructural interventions'. They include OD activities relating to organisation design, employee involvement and work design.

3 *Human resource issues.* These issues are concerned with attracting competent people to the organisation, setting goals for them, appraising and rewarding their performance and ensuring that they develop their careers and manage stress. OD techniques aimed at these issues are called 'human resource management interventions'.

4 *Interpersonal issues.* These issues have to do with social processes occurring among organisation members, such as communication, decision making, leadership and group dynamics. OD methods focusing on these kinds of issues are called 'human process interventions'; included among them are some of the most common OD techniques, such as conflict resolution and team building.

These organisational issues are interrelated and need to be integrated with each other. The double-headed arrows connecting the different issues in Figure 5.4 represent the fits or linkages among them. Organisations need to match answers to one set of questions with answers to other sets of questions to achieve high levels of effectiveness. For example, decisions about gaining competitive advantage need to fit with choices about organisation structure, setting goals for people, rewarding people, communication and problem solving.

The interventions presented in this book are intended to resolve these different concerns. As shown in Figure 5.4, particular OD interventions apply to specific issues. Thus, intervention design must create change methods appropriate to the organisational issues identified in diagnosis. Moreover, because the organisational issues are themselves linked, OD interventions need to be similarly integrated with one another. For example, a goal-setting intervention that attempts to establish motivating goals may need to be integrated with supporting interventions, such as a reward system that links pay to goal achievement. The key point is to think systematically. Interventions that are aimed at one kind of organisational issue will invariably have repercussions on other kinds of issues. This requires careful thinking about how OD interventions affect the different kinds of issues and how different change programs might be integrated to bring about a broader and more coherent impact on organisational functioning.

IMPLEMENTING CHANGE

Change can vary in complexity from the introduction of relatively simple processes into a small work group to transforming the strategies and organisation design features of the whole organisation.

Overview of change activities

The OD literature has directed considerable attention to managing change. Much of this material is highly prescriptive, offering advice to managers about how to plan and implement organisational changes. Traditionally, change management has focused on identifying sources of resistance to change and offering ways of overcoming them.[27] Recent contributions have been aimed at creating visions and desired futures, gaining political support for them and managing the transition of the organisation towards them.[28]

The diversity of practical advice for managing change can be organised into five major activities, as shown in Figure 5.5. The activities contribute to effective change management and are listed in roughly the order in which they are typically performed. The first activity involves motivating change and includes creating a readiness for change among organisation members and helping them to manage resistance to change. This involves creating an environment in which people accept the need for change and commit physical and psychological energy to it. Motivation is a critical issue in starting change, and there is ample evidence to show that people and organisations seek to preserve the status quo and are willing to change only when there are compelling reasons to do so. The second activity is concerned with creating a vision. The vision provides a purpose and reason for change and describes the desired future state. Together, they provide the 'why' and 'what' of planned change. The third activity involves the development of political support for change. Organisations are made up of powerful individuals and groups that can either block or promote change, and change agents need to gain their support to implement changes. The fourth activity is concerned with managing the transition from the current state to the desired future state. It involves creating a plan for managing the change activities as well as planning special management structures for operating the organisation during the transition. The fifth activity involves sustaining momentum for change so that it will be carried to completion. This includes providing resources for implementing the changes, building a support system for change agents, developing new competencies and skills, and reinforcing the new behaviours necessary for implementing the changes.

Each of the activities shown in Figure 5.5 is important for managing change. Although little research on their relative contributions to change has been conducted, they all seem to demand careful attention when planning and implementing organisational change. Unless individuals are motivated and committed to change, unfreezing the status quo will be extremely difficult. In the absence of vision, change is likely to be disorganised and diffuse. Without the support of powerful individuals and groups, change is likely to be blocked and possibly sabotaged. Unless the transition process is carefully managed, the organisation will have difficulty functioning while it is moving from the current state to the future state. Without efforts to sustain the momentum for change, the organisation will have problems carrying the changes through to completion. Thus, all five activities must be managed effectively if organisational change is to be successful.

Motivating change

Organisational change involves moving from the known to the unknown. Because the future is uncertain and may adversely affect people's competencies, worth and coping abilities, organisation members do not generally support change unless compelling reasons convince them to do so. Similarly, organisations tend to be heavily invested in the status quo, and they resist changing it in the face of uncertain future benefits. Consequently, a key issue in planning for action is how

FIGURE 5.5 Activities contributing to effective change

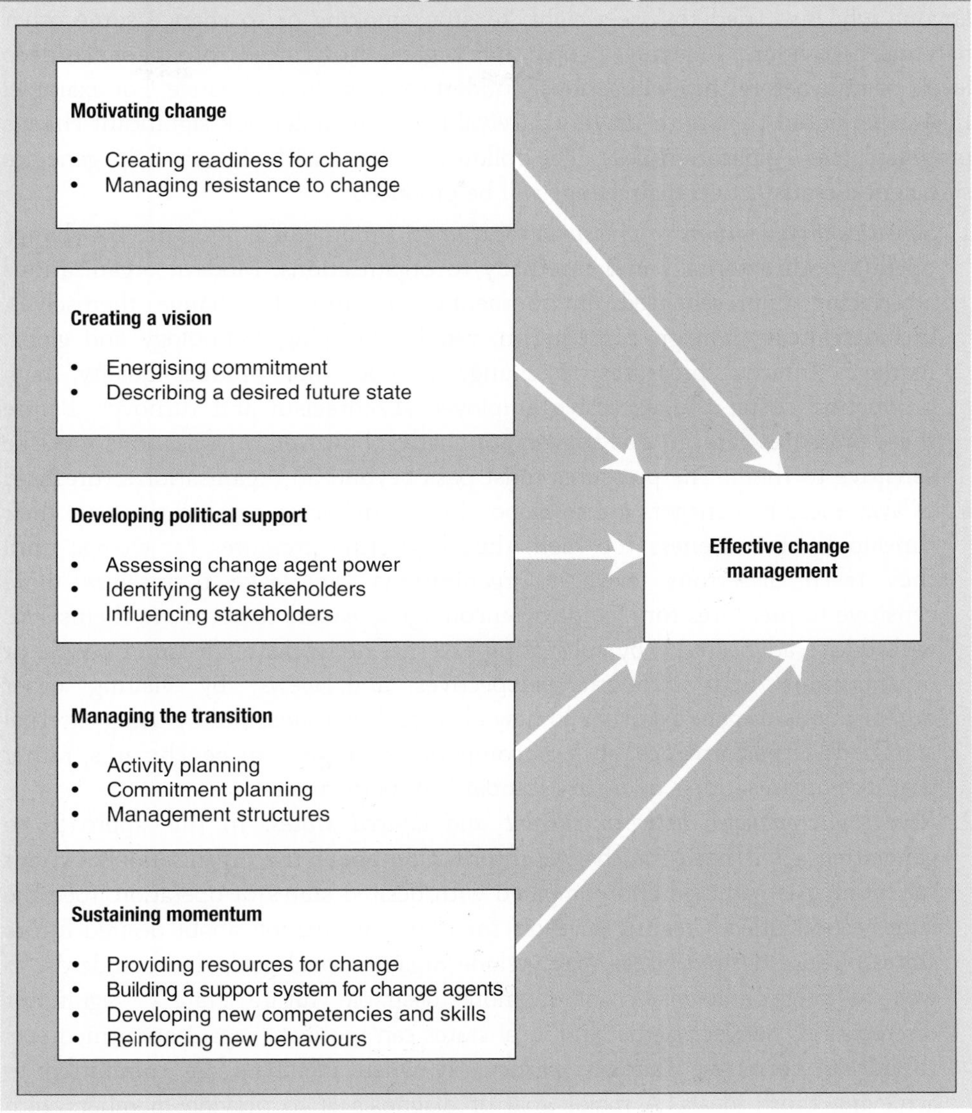

to motivate commitment to organisational change. As shown in Figure 5.5, this requires attention to two related tasks: creating readiness for change and managing resistance to change.

Creating readiness for change

One of the more fundamental axioms of OD[29] is that people's readiness for change depends on creating a felt need for change. This involves making people so dissatisfied with the status quo that they are motivated to try new things and ways of behaving. Creating such dissatisfaction can be rather difficult, as evidenced by anyone who has tried to lose weight, to stop smoking or to change some other habitual behaviour. Generally, people and organisations need to experience deep levels of hurt before they will seriously undertake meaningful change. For example, IBM experienced threats to its very survival before it undertook significant change programs (see Application 5.2). The following three methods can help generate sufficient dissatisfaction that change will be produced:

1 *Sensitise organisations to pressures for change.* Innumerable pressures for change operate both externally and internally to organisations. Modern organisations are facing unprecedented environmental pressures to change themselves, including heavy foreign competition, rapidly changing technology and global markets. Internal pressures to change include poor product quality, high production costs, and excessive employee absenteeism and turnover. Before these pressures can serve as triggers for change, however, organisations must be sensitive to them. The pressures must pass beyond an organisation's threshold of awareness if managers are to respond to them. Many organisations set their thresholds of awareness too high, thus neglecting pressures for change until they reach disastrous levels.[30] Organisations can make themselves more sensitive to pressures for change by encouraging leaders to surround themselves with devil's advocates;[31] by cultivating external networks made up of people or organisations with different perspectives and views; by visiting other organisations to gain exposure to new ideas and methods; and by using external standards of performance, such as competitors' progress or benchmarks, rather than the organisation's own past standards of performance.

2 *Reveal discrepancies between current and desired states.* In this approach to generating a felt need for change, information about the organisation's current functioning is gathered and compared with desired states of operation. (See the later section titled 'Creating a vision' for more information about desired future states.) These desired states may include organisational goals and standards, as well as a general vision of a more desirable future state.[32] Significant discrepancies between actual and ideal states can motivate organisation members to initiate corrective changes, particularly when members are committed to achieving those ideals. A major goal of diagnosis is to provide members with feedback about current organisational functioning so that this information can be compared with goals or with desired future states. Such feedback can energise action to improve the organisation. At Honeywell, Chrysler and Imperial Chemical Industries, for example, balance sheets had reached the point at which it was painfully obvious that drastic renewal was needed.

3 *Convey credible positive expectations for the change.* Organisation members invariably have expectations about the results of organisational changes, and those expectations can play an important role in generating motivation for change.[33] The expectations can serve as a self-fulfilling prophecy, leading

members to invest energy in change programs that they expect will succeed. When members expect success, they are likely to develop greater commitment to the change process and to direct more energy into the kinds of constructive behaviour needed to implement change.[34] The key to achieving these positive effects is to communicate realistic, positive expectations about the organisational changes. Organisation members can also be taught about the benefits of positive expectations and can be encouraged to set credible positive expectations for the change program. Application 5.2 describes the difficulty in determining the future leadership requirements for organisations.

5.2

APPLICATION

Changes at IBM – signing off: Akers quits at IBM under heavy pressure; dividend is slashed – outsiders will lead search for new chief executive to be a 'change-master' – but who'd want this job?

An example of the expanding influence of non-executive directors in the US occurred when IBM Chairman and Chief Executive John Ackers announced he was standing down as CEO. His departure, in response to considerable internal and external pressures, contrasted with his previous repeated assertions that he intended to continue in this role. A search for his replacement will be undertaken by a panel of 7 of the 14 non-executive directors.

IBM's announcement that it was facing record losses indicated a need for radical change. During Ackers' reign its long held principle of not laying off staff was breached when 100 000 employees were dismissed. The chairman of the search panel, James Burke, said finding a new CEO will be difficult because that person must be strong enough to lay off even more staff in order for IBM to achieve the correct size for its workforce in a challenging and rapidly changing market environment.

Reacting to Ackers' decision, Bill Gates, Microsoft Chairman, commented that IBM needed to reorganise its general sales force into specialist groups and recruit a technically knowledgeable CEO.

In addition to Ackers, two other senior IBM executives will be leaving the company, Mr Kuehler, incoming Vice Chairman, and Mr Metz, chief financial officer, allowing the new CEO to restructure senior management to reflect his view of the company's future operations.

Several business commentators were predicting the appointment of an external executive to replace Ackers. They argued that an external recruit would be more capable of identifying and implementing the extent of change necessary to restore IBM's competitive position in the market and profitability.

However, Harvard public policy professor John Pound noted that in addition to forcing the departure of the CEO, the board needs to reform its approach and do things differently in the future too.

Source: Based on Michael W. Miller and Laurence Hooper, 'Changes at IBM – signing off: Akers quits at IBM under heavy pressure; dividend is slashed – outsiders will lead search for new chief executive to be a "change-master" – but who'd want this job?', Staff Reporters, *Wall Street Journal*, 28 January 1993.

Critical thinking questions:
1. What implementations can the board introduce that will make a difference to IBM's profitability? Think about how IBM's landmark announcement to abandon its tradition to never lay off staff will impact on the board's thinking.
2. Why do you think successful change in corporate America has come about with the introduction of having someone 'outside' the business leading the business?

Creating a vision

The second activity for managing change involves creating a vision of what members want the organisation to look like or become. Generally, the vision describes the desired future, towards which change is directed. It provides a valued direction for designing, implementing and assessing organisational changes. The vision can also energise commitment to change by providing a compelling rationale as to why change is necessary and worth the effort. It can provide members with a common goal and challenge. However, if the vision is seen as impossible or promotes changes that the organisation cannot implement, it can actually depress member motivation. For example, Bob Hawke's unfulfilled vision that 'no child will live in poverty' was emotionally appealing, but impossible to achieve. In contrast, John Kennedy's vision of 'putting a man on the moon and returning him safely to the earth' was only just beyond current engineering and technical feasibility. In the context of the 1960s, it was bold, alluring and vivid; it not only provided a purpose, but a valued direction as well.[35]

Creating a vision is considered a key element in most leadership frameworks.[36] Those leading the organisation or unit are responsible for its effectiveness, and they must take an active role in describing a desired future, and energising commitment to it. In many cases, leaders encourage participation in developing the vision in order to gain wider input and support. For example, they may involve subordinates and others who have a stake in the changes. The popular media include numerous accounts of executives who have helped to mobilise and direct organisational change. Although these people are at the senior executive level, providing a description of a desired future is no less important for those who lead change in small departments and work groups. At these lower organisational levels, ample opportunities exist to get employees directly involved in the visioning process.

People's values and preferences for what the organisation should look like, and how it should function, heavily drive the process of developing a vision. The vision represents people's ideals, fantasies or dreams of what they would like the organisation to look like or become.

Unfortunately, dreaming about the future is discouraged in most organisations.[37] It requires creative and intuitive thought processes that tend to conflict with the rational, analytical methods prevalent in organisations. Consequently, leaders may need to create special conditions for describing a desired future, such as off-site workshops or exercises that stimulate creative thinking.

To be effective in managing change, creating a vision addresses two key aspects of organisation change: (1) describing the desired future, and (2) energising commitment to moving towards it.

Describing the desired future

The visioning process is future-oriented. It generally results in a vision statement that describes the organisation's desired future state. Although the vision statement may be detailed, it does not generally specify how the changes will occur. These details are part of the subsequent activity planning that occurs when managing the transition towards the desired future.

A vision statement may include all or some of the following elements that can be communicated to organisation members:

1 *Mission*. Participants often define the mission of their organisation or sub-unit as a prelude to describing the desired future state. The mission includes the organisation's major strategic purpose or reason for existing. It may include specification of the following: target customers and markets, principal products or services, geographic domain, core technologies, strategic objectives and desired public image. A study of the mission statements from 218 Fortune 500 companies showed that the higher financial performers prepared written mission statements for public dissemination.[38] The statements included the companies' basic beliefs, values, priorities, competitive strengths and desired public images. Defining the mission can provide a sound starting point for envisioning what the organisation should look like and how it should operate. In some cases, members may have conflicting views about the mission, and surfacing and resolving those conflicts can help to mobilise and direct energy for the process.

2 *Valued outcomes*. Descriptions of desired futures often include specific performance and human outcomes that the organisation or unit would like to achieve. These valued outcomes can serve as goals for the change process and standards for assessing progress. Valued performance outcomes might include high levels of product innovation, manufacturing efficiency and customer service. Valued human outcomes could include high levels of employee satisfaction, development, safety and job security. These outcomes specify the kinds of values that the organisation would like to promote in the future.

Energising commitment

In addition to describing a desired future, creating a vision includes energising the commitment to change. This aspect of the visioning process is exciting, connected to the past and present, and compelling. It seeks to create a vision that is emotionally powerful to organisation members and which motivates them to change. To achieve excitement for change, organisations often create a slogan or metaphor that captures the essence of the changes. For example, part of Disneyland's return to prominence was guided by the motto, 'Creating a place where people can feel like kids again'. The metaphor of feeling like a kid provided an important emotional appeal to Disney's change effort.

A vision that is clearly linked to the organisation's past and present can also energise commitment to change. It can provide a realistic context for moving towards the future and can enable members to develop realistic goals and maintain a temporal perspective of the 'big picture'. Apple's original vision of 'changing the way people do their work' provides a good example. Many employees had experienced the drudgery of a boring job, an uninspired boss or an alienating workplace. The notion that they could be a part of an organisation that is changing work into something more challenging, creative or satisfying was naturally alluring to many of them.

Finally, a compelling vision can energise commitment to change. By identifying a powerful reason or purpose for the change, the vision can provide meaning to the change activities that members will need to undertake during the transition. Thus, the words used in the vision can encourage behaviour towards the desired future as well as generate feelings of inclusiveness. Conversely, words can constrain people and leave them feeling controlled or manipulated. For example, 'shrewd' and 'creative' both imply innovative behaviour but have different connotations.

Developing political support

From a political perspective, organisations can be seen as loosely structured coalitions of individuals and groups with different preferences and interests.[39] For example, shop-floor workers may want secure, high-paying jobs, while top executives may be interested in diversifying the organisation into new businesses. The marketing department might be interested in developing new products and markets, and the production department may want to manufacture standard products in the most efficient way. These different groups or coalitions compete with one another for scarce resources and influence. They act to preserve or enhance their self-interest while managing to arrive at a sufficient balance of power to sustain commitment to the organisation and to achieve overall effectiveness.

Given this political view, attempts to change the organisation may threaten the balance of power among groups, resulting in political conflicts and struggles.[40] Individuals and groups will be concerned with how the changes affect their own power and influence, and they will act accordingly. Some groups will become less powerful, while others will gain influence. Those whose power is threatened by the change will act defensively and seek to preserve the status quo; for example, they might attempt to present compelling evidence that change is unnecessary or that only minor modifications are needed. On the other hand, those participants who will gain power from the changes will tend to push heavily for them. They may bring in seemingly impartial consultants to legitimise the need for change. Consequently, conflicting interests, distorted information and political turmoil frequently accompany significant organisational changes.

Methods for managing the political dynamics of organisational change are relatively recent additions to OD. Traditionally, OD has tended to neglect political issues, mainly because its humanistic roots promoted collaboration and power sharing among individuals and groups.[41] Today, change agents are increasingly paying attention to power and political activity, particularly as they engage in strategic change that involves most parts and features of organisations. Some practitioners are concerned, however, about whether power and OD are compatible. A growing number of advocates suggest that OD practitioners can use power in positive ways.[42] They can build their own power base to gain access to other power holders within the organisation. Without such access, those who influence or make decisions may not have the advantage of an OD perspective. OD practitioners can use power strategies that are open and above board to get those in power to consider OD applications. They can facilitate processes for examining the uses of power in organisations and can help power holders devise more creative and positive strategies than political bargaining, deceit and the like. They can help power holders to confront the need for change and can help to ensure that the interests and concerns of those with less power are considered. Although OD professionals can use power constructively in organisations, they will probably always be ambivalent and tense about whether such uses promote OD values and ethics or whether they represent the destructive, negative side of power. This tension seems healthy, and it is hoped that it will guide the wise use of power in OD.

As shown in Figure 5.6, managing the political dynamics of change includes the following activities:

1 *Assessing change agent power.* The first task is to evaluate the change agent's own sources of power. The change agent might be the leader of the organisation or department undergoing change, or he or she might be the OD consultant, if professional help is being used. By assessing their own power base, change

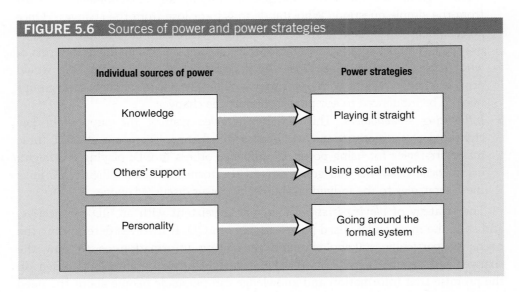

FIGURE 5.6 Sources of power and power strategies

Source: L. Greiner and V. Schein, *Power and Organization Development: Mobilizing Power to Implement Change*, copyright © 1988, p.52. Reprinted by permission of Pearson Education, Inc., Upper Saddle River, New Jersey.

agents can determine how to use it to influence others to support changes. They can also identify areas in which they might need to enhance their sources of power.

Greiner and Schein, in the first OD book written entirely from a power perspective, identified three key sources of personal power in organisations (in addition to one's formal position): knowledge, personality and others' support.[43] Knowledge bases of power include having expertise that is valued by others and controlling important information. OD professionals typically gain power through their expertise in organisational change. Personality sources of power can derive from change agents' charisma, reputation and professional credibility. Charismatic leaders can inspire devotion and enthusiasm for change from subordinates. OD consultants with strong reputations and professional credibility can wield considerable power during organisational change. Others' support can contribute to individual power by providing access to information and resource networks. Others may also use their power on behalf of the change agent. For example, leaders in organisational units undergoing change can call on their informal networks for resources and support. They can encourage subordinates to exercise power in support of the change.

2 *Identifying key stakeholders.* Once change agents have assessed their own power bases, they can identify powerful individuals and groups who have an interest in the changes, such as staff groups, unions, departmental managers and top-level executives. These stakeholders can either thwart or support change, and it is important to gain broad-based support to minimise the risk that a single interest group will block the changes. Identifying key stakeholders can start from the simple question: 'Who stands to gain or lose from the changes?' Once stakeholders have been identified, creating a map of their influence may be useful.[44] The map could show relationships among the stakeholders in terms of who influences whom and what the stakes are for each party. This would provide change agents with information about which individuals and groups need to be influenced to accept and support the changes.

3 *Influencing stakeholders.* This activity involves gaining the support of key stakeholders to motivate a critical mass for change. There are at least three major strategies for using power to influence others in OD: playing it straight, using social networks and going around the formal system.[45] Figure 5.6 links these strategies to the individual sources of power discussed above.

The strategy of *playing it straight* is very consistent with an OD perspective, and so is the most widely used power strategy in OD. It involves determining the needs of particular stakeholders and presenting information as to how the changes can benefit them. This relatively straightforward approach is based on the premise that information and knowledge can persuade people about the need and direction for change. The success of this strategy relies heavily on the change agent's knowledge base. He or she must have the expertise and information necessary for persuading stakeholders that the changes are a logical way to meet their needs. For example, a change agent might present diagnostic data, such as company reports on productivity and absenteeism or surveys of members' perceptions of problems, to generate a felt need for change among specific stakeholders. Other persuasive evidence might include educational material and expert testimony, such as case studies and research reports, demonstrating how organisational changes can address pertinent issues.

The second power strategy, *using social networks*, is more foreign to OD and includes forming alliances and coalitions with other powerful individuals and groups, dealing directly with key decision makers and using formal and informal contacts to gain information. In this strategy, change agents try to use their social relationships to gain support for changes. As shown in Figure 5.6, they use the individual power base of others' support to gain the resources, commitment and political momentum needed for change. This social networking might include, for example, meeting with other powerful groups and forming an alliance to support specific changes. This would probably involve ensuring that the interests of the different parties – for example, labour and management – are considered in the change process. Many union and management quality-of-work-life efforts involve forming such alliances. This strategy might also include using informal contacts to discover key roadblocks to change and gain access to major decision makers that need to sanction the changes.

The power strategy of *going around the formal system* is probably least used in OD and involves deliberately circumventing organisational structures and procedures to get the changes implemented. Existing organisational arrangements can be roadblocks to change, and, rather than taking the time and energy to remove them, working around the barriers may be more expedient and effective. As shown in Figure 5.6, this strategy relies on a strong personality base of power. The change agent's charisma, reputation or professional credibility lend legitimacy to going around the system and can reduce the likelihood of negative reprisals. For example, managers with reputations as 'winners' can often bend the rules to implement organisational changes. Those needing to support change trust their judgement. This power strategy is relatively easy to abuse, however, and OD practitioners should carefully consider the ethical issues and possible unintended consequences of circumventing formal policies and practices.

Managing the transition

Implementing organisational change involves moving from the existing organisation state to the desired future state. This movement does not occur immediately but, as shown in Figure 5.7, requires a transition state during which the organisation learns how to implement the conditions needed to reach the desired future. Beckhard and Harris pointed out that the transition state may be quite different from the present state of the organisation and consequently may

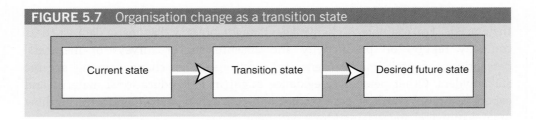

FIGURE 5.7 Organisation change as a transition state

Current state ▷ Transition state ▷ Desired future state

require special management structures and activities.[46] They identified three major activities and structures to facilitate organisational transition:

1 *Activity planning.* This involves making a road map for change, citing specific activities and events that must occur if the transition is to be successful. Activity planning should clearly identify, temporally orient and integrate discrete change tasks and should link these tasks to the organisation's change goals and priorities. Activity planning should also gain top-management approval, be cost-effective and remain adaptable as feedback is received during the change process.

  An important feature of activity planning is that visions and desired future states can be quite general when compared with the realities of actually implementing change. As a result, it may be necessary to supplement them with midpoint goals as part of the activity plan.[47] These represent desirable organisational conditions between the current state and the desired future state. Midpoint goals are clearer and more detailed than desired future states, and so provide more concrete and manageable steps and benchmarks for change. Activity plans can use midpoint goals to successfully provide members with the direction and security for embarkation towards the desired future.

2 *Commitment planning.* This activity involves identifying key people and groups whose commitment is needed for change to occur and deciding how to gain their support. Although commitment planning is generally a part of developing political support (discussed above), specific plans for identifying key stakeholders and obtaining their commitment to change need to be made early in the change process.

3 *Management structures.* Because organisational transitions tend to be ambiguous and to need direction, special structures for managing the change process need to be created. These management structures should include people who have the power to mobilise resources to promote change, the respect of the existing leadership and advocates of change, and the interpersonal and political skills to guide the change process. Alternative management structures include the following:[48]

  • The chief executive or head person manages the change effort.
  • A project manager is given the temporary assignment of co-ordinating the transition.

- The formal organisation manages the change effort in addition to supervising normal operations.
- Representatives of the major constituencies involved in the change jointly manage the project.
- Natural leaders who have the confidence and trust of large numbers of affected employees are selected to manage the transition.
- A cross-section of people representing different organisational functions and levels manages the change.
- A kitchen cabinet representing people whom the chief executive consults and confides in manages the change effort.

Sustaining momentum

Once organisational changes are under way, explicit attention must be directed at sustaining energy and commitment for implementing them.[49] Often, the initial excitement and activity of changing dissipate in the face of the practical problems of trying to learn new ways of operating. A strong tendency exists among organisation members to return to what is well known and learned, unless they receive sustained support and reinforcement for carrying the changes through to completion.

The following four activities can help to sustain momentum for carrying change through to completion:

1 *Providing resources for change.* Implementing organisation change generally requires additional financial and human resources, particularly if the organisation continues day-to-day operations while trying to change itself. These extra resources are needed for such change activities as training, consultation, data collection and feedback, and special meetings. Extra resources are also helpful to provide a buffer as performance drops during the transition period. Organisations can seriously underestimate the need for special resources devoted to the change process. Significant organisational change invariably requires considerable management time and energy, as well as the help of consultants. A separate 'change budget' that exists along with capital and operating budgets can help to identify the resources needed for training members in how to behave differently and for assessing progress and making necessary modifications in the change program.[50] Unless these extra resources are planned for and provided, meaningful change is not as likely to occur.

2 *Building a support system for change agents.* Organisation change can be difficult and filled with tension, not only for participants but also for change agents.[51] Change agents must often provide members with emotional support, yet they may receive little support themselves. They must often maintain 'psychological distance' from others in order to gain the perspective needed to lead the change process. This can produce considerable tension and isolation, and change agents may need to create their own support system to help them cope with these

problems. This typically consists of a network of people with whom the change agent has close personal relationships. These people can provide emotional support and can serve as a sounding board for ideas and problems. They can challenge untested assumptions. For example, OD professionals often use trusted colleagues as 'shadow consultants' to help them think through difficult issues with clients and to offer conceptual and emotional support. Similarly, a growing number of companies, such as Fisher & Paykel and Heinz-Wattie, are forming internal networks of change agents to provide mutual learning and support.[52]

3 *Developing new competencies and skills.* Organisational changes frequently demand new knowledge, skills and behaviours from organisation members. In many cases, the changes cannot be implemented unless members gain new competencies. For example, employee-involvement programs often require managers to learn new leadership styles and new approaches to problem solving. Change agents need to ensure that such learning occurs. They need to provide multiple learning opportunities, such as traditional training programs, on-the-job counselling and coaching, and experiential simulations. This learning should cover both technical and social skills. Because it is easy to overlook the social component, change agents may need to devote special time and resources to helping members gain the social skills needed to implement changes.

4 *Reinforcing new behaviours.* People in organisations generally do those things that bring them rewards. Consequently, one of the most effective ways of sustaining momentum for change is to reinforce the kinds of behaviours needed to implement the changes. This can be accomplished by linking formal rewards directly to the desired behaviours. Desired behaviours can also be reinforced through recognition, encouragement and praise. These can usually be given more frequently than formal rewards, and change agents should take advantage of the myriad of informal opportunities available to recognise and praise changed behaviours in a timely fashion. Perhaps equally important are the intrinsic rewards that people can experience through early success in the change effort. Achieving identifiable, early successes can make participants feel good about themselves and their behaviours, thus reinforcing the drive to change.

EVALUATING ORGANISATION DEVELOPMENT INTERVENTIONS

Evaluation processes consider both the implementation success of the intended intervention and the long-term results it produces. Two key aspects of effective evaluation are measurement and research design. The institutionalisation or long-term persistence of intervention effects is examined in a framework that shows the organisation characteristics, intervention dimensions and processes that contribute to institutionalisation of OD interventions in organisations.

Evaluating OD interventions

Assessing OD interventions involves judgements about whether an intervention has been implemented as intended and, if so, whether it is having desired results. Managers investing resources in OD efforts are increasingly being held accountable for the results. They are being asked to justify the expenditures in terms of hard, bottom-line outcomes. More and more, managers are asking for rigorous assessment of OD interventions and are using the results to make important resource allocation decisions about OD, such as whether to continue to support the change program, whether to modify or alter it, or whether to terminate it altogether and perhaps try something else.

Traditionally, OD evaluation has been discussed as something that occurs after the intervention. This view can be misleading. Decisions about the measurement of relevant variables and the design of the evaluation process should be made early in the OD cycle so that evaluation choices can be integrated with intervention decisions.

There are two distinct types of OD evaluation: one intended to guide the implementation of interventions and the other to assess their overall impact. The key issues in evaluation are measurement and research design.

Implementation and evaluation feedback

Most discussions and applications of OD evaluation imply that evaluation is something done after intervention. It is typically argued that, once the intervention has been implemented, it should be evaluated to discover whether it is producing the intended effects. For example, it might reasonably be expected that a job-enrichment program would lead to higher employee satisfaction and performance. After implementing job enrichment, evaluation would involve assessing whether or not it did actually lead to positive results.

This after-implementation view of evaluation is only partially correct. It assumes that interventions have actually been implemented as intended and that the key problem of evaluation is to assess their effects. In many, if not most, OD programs, however, implementing interventions cannot be taken for granted.[53] Most OD interventions require significant changes in people's behaviours and ways of thinking about organisations, yet interventions typically offer only broad prescriptions for how such changes are to occur. For example, job enrichment calls for adding discretion (freedom of judgement), variety and meaningful feedback to people's jobs. Implementing such changes requires considerable learning and experimentation as employees and managers discover how to translate these general prescriptions into specific behaviours and procedures. This learning process involves much trial and error and needs to be guided by information about whether behaviours and procedures are being changed as intended.[54] Consequently, we should expand our view of evaluation to include both during-implementation assessment of whether interventions are actually being implemented and after-implementation evaluation of whether they are producing expected results.

FIGURE 5.8 Implementation and evaluation feedback

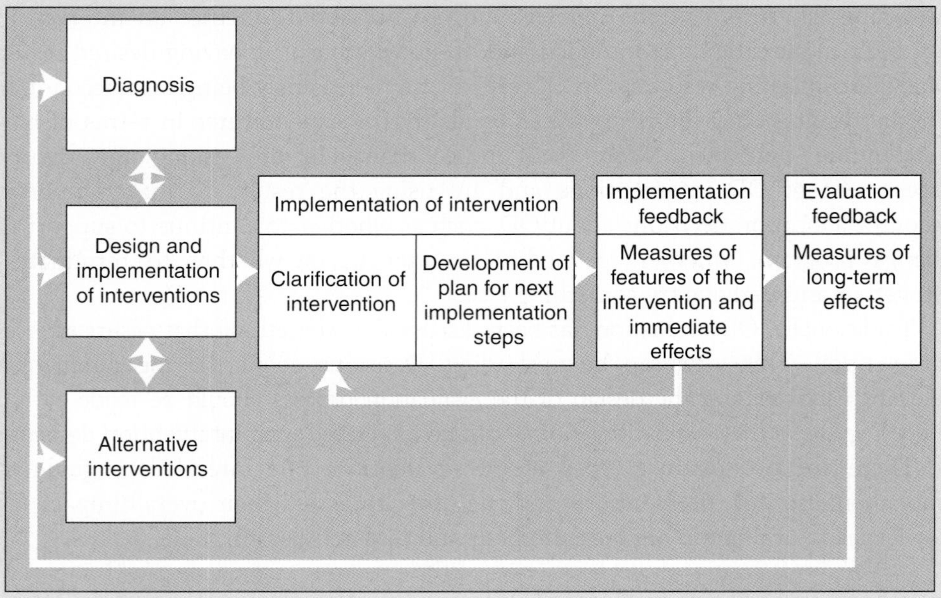

Both kinds of evaluation provide organisation members with feedback about interventions. Evaluation aimed at guiding implementation may be called *implementation feedback*, and assessment intended to discover intervention outcomes might be called *evaluation feedback*.[55] Figure 5.8 shows how the two kinds of feedback fit with the diagnostic and intervention stages of OD. The application of OD to a particular organisation starts with a thorough diagnosis of the situation, which helps to identify particular organisational problems or areas for improvement, as well as likely causes underlying them. Next, from an array of possible interventions, one or more sets are chosen as a means of improving the organisation. This choice is based on knowledge that links interventions to diagnosis and change management. Application 5.3 exhibits an unusual form of feedback which is still of value if it leads to a solution.

5.3

APPLICATION

In the workplace: Division of labour

Our 70-year board chairman took over the job of a dynamic 45-year CEO who joined a competitor. Yesterday, he inquired about some details on how we assign work to people. I told him that we're slowly moving to multi-tasking and are in the process of removing specialized functions in some jobs. Now he wants me to go back to a company-wide approach of 'division of labour' among specialists. Our CEO's request spells big trouble for me as we've gained much with multi-tasking before. Can you help me decipher what's on the mind of my boss? – September Morn.

>>

When you think, really think about it, your concern will start to make you crazy. But first, consider understanding your own behaviour. You appear to have worked hard for the CEO who resigned his job. Probably, you did a lot of job evaluation and process reengineering to arrive at a conclusion that you 'gained much with multi-tasking before.'

But more than anything else, a classic mistake that you should avoid is to compare the style of the two CEOs who may have come from two contrasting worlds. That's one temptation that you should prevent from happening. Needless to say, you have to value diversity – diversity of style, if you will.

Your 70-year-old CEO may be dead wrong with his outdated thinking. Imagine pushing work specialization more in this era of empowerment where the workers are given enough leeway to identify problems, generate solutions, and apply the best idea among them.

So let's have a theoretical review. Division of labour or the resulting job specialization is where each job includes a subset of the tasks required to complete a product or service. Producing an automobile, for instance requires thousands of specific tasks that are subdivided among several hundreds of thousands of workers.

Workers' tasks are also divided vertically so that line supervisors must coordinate work while their workers perform their respective specialized duties. Frenchman Henri Fayol (1841–1925) said that work must be divided into specialized jobs because it potentially increases work efficiency.

In having a specialized function, the workers can master their tasks quickly because work cycles are very short. And less time is wasted changing from one task to another. In addition, job specialization makes it easy to match people with specific aptitudes or skills to the jobs for which they are trained or experienced.

There were other advantages of having a division of labour until multi-tasking came along. It proceeded from job enrichment, empowerment, and participatory management which were popularized by the Japanese who practised it without letup, not to mention their intensity, consistency, and discipline.

Throughout my almost three decades of dealing with CEOs, including toxic bosses, recognizing that the best time for us in management to be objective about a certain practice or policy is during the first six months from any change – including the resignation of one's boss.

This is the best time to question everything before you became part of the problem. If you cannot rock the boat with the new CEO, you are destined to always do what you've always done before.

What I'm saying is – it's really difficult to fathom the mind of your CEO unless you directly deal with the issue. Find out why your CEO is very much against multi-tasking. Then proceed from there. But let it not be said that you did not clear things up with him.

Source: Reylito A. H. Elbo, 'In the workplace: Division of labor', *BusinessWorld*, 12 June 2009, pp. 156–7.
Thomson Learning, www.thomsonrights.com.

Critical thinking questions:
1. Henri Fayol (1841–1925) stated that workers must be divided into specialised jobs because potentially, workers who are specialised in their work will be more efficient and productive. This suggests that the implementation of multi-tasking might be counterproductive to the overall productivity of the firm. Therefore, would 'multi-tasking' be suitable in a modern contemporary work environment: why/why not?
2. The article states: 'if you cannot rock the boat with the new CEO, you are destined to always do what you've always done before.' Why is this statement about feedback and interventions? Think about the behaviours of people when they start a new job, what are they most likely to do and not do. For example, when you started a new job, what was your first day like?

In most cases, the chosen intervention provides only general guidelines for organisational change, leaving managers and employees with the task of translating them into specific behaviours and procedures. Implementation feedback guides this process. It consists of two types of information: data about the different features of the intervention itself and data about the immediate effects of the intervention. These data are collected repeatedly and at short intervals. They provide a series of snapshots about how the intervention is progressing. Organisation members can use this information first to gain a clearer understanding of the intervention (the kinds of behaviours and procedures required to implement it) and, second, to plan for the next implementation steps. This feedback cycle might proceed for several rounds, with each round providing members with knowledge about the intervention and ideas for the next stage of implementation.

Once implementation feedback has informed organisation members that the intervention is sufficiently in place, evaluation feedback begins. In contrast to implementation feedback, it is concerned with the overall impact of the intervention and whether resources should continue to be allocated to it or to other possible interventions. Evaluation feedback takes longer to gather and interpret than implementation feedback. It typically includes a broad array of outcome measures, such as performance, job satisfaction, absenteeism and turnover. Negative results on these measures tell members that either the initial diagnosis was seriously flawed or that the choice of intervention was wrong. Such feedback might prompt additional diagnosis and a search for a more effective intervention. Positive results, on the other hand, tell members that the intervention produced the expected outcomes and might prompt a search for ways of institutionalising the changes, making them a permanent part of the organisation's normal functioning.

An example of a job-enrichment intervention helps to clarify the OD stages and feedback linkages shown in Figure 5.8. Suppose the initial diagnosis reveals that employee performance and satisfaction are low and that an underlying cause of this problem lies with jobs that are overly structured and routinised. An inspection of alternative interventions to improve productivity and satisfaction suggests that job enrichment might be applicable for this situation. Existing job-enrichment theory proposes that increasing employee discretion, task variety and feedback can lead to improvements in work quality and attitudes, and that this job design and outcome linkage are especially strong for employees with growth needs – needs for challenge, autonomy and development. Initial diagnosis suggests that most employees have high growth needs and that the existing job design prevents the fulfilment of these needs. Therefore, job enrichment seems particularly suited to this situation.

Managers and employees now start to translate the general prescriptions offered by job-enrichment theory into specific behaviours and procedures. At this stage, the intervention is relatively broad and needs to be tailored to fit the specific situation. To implement the intervention, employees might decide on the following organisational changes: job discretion can be increased through more participatory styles of supervision; task variety can be enhanced by allowing employees to inspect their job outputs; and feedback can be made more meaningful by providing employees with quicker and more specific information about their performances.

After three months of trying to implement these changes, the members use implementation feedback to see how the intervention is progressing. Questionnaires and interviews (similar to those used in diagnosis) are administered in order to measure the different features of job enrichment (discretion, variety and feedback) and to assess employees' reactions to the changes. Company records are analysed to show the short-term effects on productivity of the intervention. The data reveal that productivity and satisfaction have changed very little since the initial diagnosis. Employee perceptions of job discretion and feedback have also shown negligible change, but perceptions of task variety have shown significant improvement. In-depth discussion and analysis of this first round of implementation feedback help the supervisors gain a better feel for the kinds of behaviours needed to move towards a participatory leadership style. This greater clarification of one feature of the intervention leads to a decision to involve the supervisors in leadership training and so help them to develop the skills and knowledge needed to lead participatively. A decision is also made to make job feedback more meaningful by translating such data into simple bar graphs, rather than continuing to provide voluminous statistical reports.

After these modifications have been in effect for about three months, members institute a second round of implementation feedback to see how the intervention is progressing. The data now show that productivity and satisfaction have moved moderately higher than in the first round of feedback and that employee perceptions of task variety and feedback are both high. Employee perceptions of discretion, however, remain relatively low. Members conclude that the variety and feedback dimensions of job enrichment are sufficiently implemented but that the discretion component needs improvement. They decide to put more effort into supervisory training and to ask OD practitioners to provide on-line counselling and coaching to supervisors about their leadership styles.

After four more months, a third round of implementation feedback occurs. The data now show that satisfaction and performance are significantly higher than in the first round of feedback and moderately higher than in the second round. The data also show that discretion, variety and feedback are all high, suggesting that the job-enrichment interventions have been successfully implemented. Now evaluation feedback is used to assess the overall effectiveness of the program.

The evaluation feedback includes all the data from the satisfaction and performance measures used in the implementation feedback. Because both the immediate and broader effects of the intervention are being evaluated, additional outcomes are examined, such as employee absenteeism, maintenance costs and reactions of other organisational units not included in job enrichment. The full array of evaluation data might suggest that one year after the start of implementation, the job-enrichment program is having the expected effects and so should be continued and made more permanent.

Measurement

Providing useful implementation and evaluation feedback involves two activities: selecting the appropriate variables and designing good measures.

Selecting variables

Ideally, the variables measured in OD evaluation should derive from the theory or conceptual model that underlies the intervention. The model should incorporate the key features of the intervention as well as its expected results.

The job-level diagnostic model suggests a number of measurement variables for implementation and evaluation feedback. Whether or not the intervention is being implemented could be assessed either by determining how many job descriptions have been rewritten to include more responsibility, or how many organisation members have received cross-training in other job skills. Evaluation of the immediate and long-term impact of job enrichment would include measures of employee performance and satisfaction over time. Again, these measures would probably be included in the initial diagnosis, when the company's problems or areas for improvement are discovered.

The measurement of both intervention and outcome variables is necessary for implementation and evaluation feedback. Unfortunately, there has been a tendency in OD to measure only outcome variables while neglecting intervention variables altogether.[56] It is generally assumed that the intervention has been implemented, and attention is directed to its impact on organisational outcomes, such as performance, absenteeism and satisfaction. As argued earlier, implementing OD interventions generally takes considerable time and learning. It must be empirically determined that the intervention has been implemented; it cannot simply be assumed. Implementation feedback[57] serves this purpose, guiding the implementation process and helping to interpret outcome data. Outcome measures are ambiguous unless it is known how well the intervention has been implemented. For example, a negligible change in measures of performance and satisfaction could mean that the wrong intervention has been chosen, that the correct intervention has not been implemented effectively or that the wrong variables have been measured. Measurement of the intervention variables helps to determine the correct interpretation of outcome measures.

As suggested above, the choice of what intervention variables to measure should derive from the conceptual framework that underlies the OD intervention. Organisation development research and theory have increasingly come to identify the specific organisational changes that are necessary for the implementation of particular interventions. These variables should guide not only the implementation of the intervention but also choices about what change variables to measure for evaluative purposes. Additional sources of knowledge about intervention variables can be found in the numerous references at the end of each of the intervention chapters in this book and in several of the books in the Wiley Series on Organisational Assessment and Change.[58]

Institutionalising interventions

Once it has been determined that an intervention has been implemented and is effective, attention is directed at institutionalising the changes: making them a permanent part of the organisation's normal functioning. Lewin described change as occurring in three stages: unfreezing, moving and refreezing. Institutionalising an OD intervention concerns refreezing. It involves the long-term persistence of organisational changes. To the extent that changes persist, they can be said to be institutionalised. Such changes are not dependent on any one person but exist as part of the culture of an organisation: numerous others share norms about the appropriateness of the changes.

How planned changes become institutionalised has not received much attention in recent years. Rapidly changing environments have led to admonitions from consultants and practitioners to 'change constantly', to 'change before you have to' and 'if it's not broke, fix it anyway'. Such a context has challenged the utility of the institutionalisation concept. Why endeavour to make any change permanent, given that it may require changing again soon? However, the admonitions have also resulted in institutionalisation concepts being applied in new ways. Change itself has become the focus of institutionalisation.[59] Total quality management, organisation learning, integrated strategic change and self-design interventions are all aimed at enhancing the organisation's capability for change.[60] In this vein, processes of institutionalisation take on increased utility. This section presents a framework that identifies factors and processes contributing to the institutionalisation of OD interventions, including the process of change itself.

Institutionalisation framework

Figure 5.9 presents a framework that identifies organisation and intervention characteristics and institutionalisation processes affecting the degree to which change programs are institutionalised.[61] The model shows that two key antecedents – organisation and intervention characteristics – affect different institutionalisation processes operating in organisations. These processes in turn affect various indicators of institutionalisation. The model also shows that organisation characteristics can influence intervention characteristics. For example, organisations with powerful unions may have trouble gaining internal support for OD interventions.

Organisation characteristics

Figure 5.9 shows that three key dimensions of an organisation can affect intervention characteristics and institutionalisation processes.

1 *Congruence.* This is the degree to which an intervention is perceived as being in harmony with the organisation's managerial philosophy, strategy and structure; its current environment; and other changes taking place.[62] When an intervention is congruent with these dimensions, the probability is improved

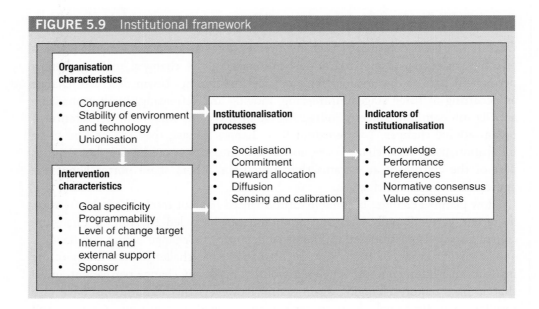

FIGURE 5.9 Institutional framework

that it will be institutionalised. Congruence can facilitate persistence[63] by making it easier to gain member commitment to the intervention and to diffuse it to wider segments of the organisation. The converse is also true. Many OD interventions promote employee participation and growth. When applied in highly bureaucratic organisations with formalised structures and autocratic managerial styles, participative interventions are not perceived as being congruent with the organisation's managerial philosophy.

2 *Stability of environment and technology.* This involves the degree to which the organisation's environment and technology are changing. Unless the change target is buffered from these changes or unless the changes are directly dealt with by the change program, it may be difficult to achieve long-term stability of the intervention.[64] For example, decreased demand for the business's products or services can lead to reductions in personnel, which may change the composition of the groups involved in the intervention. Conversely, increased product demand can curtail institutionalisation by bringing new members on board at a rate faster than they can be effectively socialised.

3 *Unionisation.* Diffusion of interventions may be more difficult in unionised settings, especially if the changes affect union contract issues, such as salary and fringe benefits, job design and employee flexibility. For example, a rigid union contract can make it difficult to merge several job classifications into one, as might be required to increase task variety in a job-enrichment program. It is important to emphasise, however, that unions can be a powerful force for promoting change, especially when a good relationship exists between union and management.

Intervention characteristics

Figure 5.9 shows that five major features of OD interventions can affect institutionalisation processes:

1 *Goal specificity.* This involves the extent to which intervention goals are specific rather than broad. Specificity of goals helps to direct socialising activities (for example, training and orienting new members) to particular behaviours required to implement the intervention. It also facilitates operationalising the new behaviours so that rewards can be clearly linked to them. For example, an intervention aimed only at the goal of increasing product quality is likely to be more focused and readily put into operation than a change program intended to improve quality, quantity, safety, absenteeism and employee development.

2 *Programmability.* This involves the degree to which the changes can be programmed. This means that the different characteristics of the intervention are clearly specified in advance, thus facilitating socialisation, commitment and reward allocation.[65] For example, job enrichment specifies three targets of change: employee discretion, task variety and feedback. The change program can be planned and designed to promote these specific features.

3 *Level of change target.* This concerns the extent to which the change target is the total organisation, rather than a department or small work group. Each level possesses facilitators and inhibitors to persistence. Departmental and group change are susceptible to countervailing forces from others in the organisation, which can reduce the diffusion of the intervention, thus lowering its ability to improve organisation effectiveness. However, this does not necessarily preclude institutionalising the change within a department that successfully insulates itself from the rest of the organisation. This often manifests itself as a subculture within the organisation.[66]

Targeting the intervention to wider segments of the organisation, on the other hand, can also help or hinder change persistence. It can facilitate institutionalisation by promoting a consensus across organisational departments exposed to the change. A shared belief about the intervention's value can be a powerful incentive to maintain the change. But targeting the larger system can also inhibit institutionalisation. The intervention can become mired in political resistance because of the 'not invented here' syndrome, or because powerful constituencies oppose it.

4 *Internal and external support.* Internal support refers to the degree to which there is an internal support system to guide the change process. Internal support, typically provided by an internal consultant, can help to gain commitment to the changes and help organisation members to implement them. External consultants can also provide support, especially on a temporary basis during the early stages of implementation. For example, in many interventions aimed at implementing high-involvement organisations, both external and internal consultants provide support for the changes. The external

consultant typically provides expertise on organisational design and trains members to implement the design. The internal consultant generally helps members to relate to other organisational units, to resolve conflicts and to legitimise the change activities within the organisation.

5 *Sponsor.* This concerns the presence of a powerful sponsor who can initiate, allocate and legitimise resources for the intervention. Sponsors must come from levels in the organisation high enough to control appropriate resources. They must have the visibility and power to nurture the intervention and see that it remains viable in the organisation. There are many examples of OD interventions that persisted for several years and then collapsed abruptly when the sponsor, usually a top administrator, left. There are also numerous examples of middle managers withdrawing support for interventions because top management did not include them in the change program.

Institutionalisation processes

The framework depicted in Figure 5.9 shows five institutionalisation processes operating in organisations that can directly affect the degree to which OD interventions are institutionalised:

1 *Socialisation.* This concerns the transmission of information about beliefs, preferences, norms and values with respect to the intervention. Because implementation of OD interventions generally involves considerable learning and experimentation, a continual process of socialisation is necessary to promote persistence of the change program. Organisation members must focus attention on the evolving nature of the intervention and its ongoing meaning. They must communicate this information to other employees, especially new members. Transmission of information about the intervention helps to bring new members on board and allows participants to reaffirm the beliefs, norms and values that underlie the intervention.[67] For example, employee-involvement programs often include an initial transmission of information about the intervention, as well as the retraining of existing participants and training of new members. These processes are intended to encourage persistence with the program, as both new behaviours are learned and new members introduced.

2 *Commitment.* This binds people to behaviours associated with the intervention. It includes initial commitment to the program, as well as recommitment over time. Opportunities for commitment should allow people to select the necessary behaviours freely, explicitly and publicly. These conditions favour high commitment and can promote stability of the new behaviours. Commitment should derive from several organisational levels, including the employees directly involved and the middle and upper managers who can support or thwart the intervention. In many early employee-involvement programs, for example, attention was directed at gaining the workers' commitment to such

programs. Unfortunately, middle managers were often ignored, resulting in considerable management resistance to the interventions.

3 *Reward allocation.* This involves linking rewards to the new behaviours required by an intervention. Organisational rewards can enhance the persistence of interventions in at least two ways. First, a combination of intrinsic and extrinsic rewards can reinforce new behaviours. Intrinsic rewards are internal and derive from the opportunities for challenge, development and accomplishment found in the work. When interventions provide these opportunities, motivation to perform should persist. Providing extrinsic rewards, such as money, for increased contributions can further reinforce this behaviour. Because the value of extrinsic rewards tends to diminish over time, it may be necessary to revise the reward system to maintain high levels of desired behaviours.

Second, new behaviours should persist to the extent that employees perceive rewards as equitable. When new behaviours are fairly compensated, people are likely to develop preferences for those behaviours. Over time, those preferences should lead to normative and value consensus about the appropriateness of the intervention. For example, many employee-involvement programs fail to persist because the employees feel that their increased contributions to organisational improvements are unfairly rewarded. This is especially true for interventions that rely exclusively on intrinsic rewards. People argue that an intervention that provides opportunities for intrinsic rewards should also provide greater pay or extrinsic rewards for higher levels of contribution to the organisation.

4 *Diffusion.* This refers to the process of transferring interventions from one system to another. Diffusion facilitates institutionalisation by providing a wider organisational base to support the new behaviours. Many interventions fail to persist because they run counter to the values and norms of the larger organisation. Rather than support the intervention, the larger organisation rejects the changes and often puts pressure on the change target to revert to old behaviours. Diffusion of the intervention to other organisational units reduces this counter-implementation strategy. It tends to lock in behaviours by providing normative consensus from other parts of the organisation. Moreover, the very act of transmitting institutionalised behaviours to other systems reinforces commitment to the changes.

5 *Sensing and calibration.* This involves detecting deviations from desired intervention behaviours and taking corrective action. Institutionalised behaviours invariably encounter destabilising forces, such as changes in the environment, new technologies and pressures from other departments to nullify changes. These factors cause some variation in performances, preferences, norms and values. To detect this variation and take corrective actions, organisations must have some sensing mechanism. Sensing mechanisms, such as implementation feedback, provide information about the occurrence of deviations. This knowledge can then initiate corrective actions to ensure that

behaviours are more in line with the intervention. For example, the high level of job discretion associated with job enrichment might fail to persist. Information about this problem might initiate corrective actions, such as renewed attempts to socialise people or to gain commitment to the intervention.

Indicators of institutionalisation

Institutionalisation is not an all-or-nothing concept, but it does reflect degrees of persistence of an intervention. Figure 5.9 shows five indicators that can be used to determine the extent of an intervention's persistence. The extent to which these factors are present or absent indicates the degree of institutionalisation.

1 *Knowledge.* This involves the extent to which organisation members have knowledge of the behaviours associated with an intervention. It is concerned with whether members know enough to perform the behaviours and to recognise the consequences of that performance. For example, job enrichment includes a number of new behaviours, such as performing a greater variety of tasks, analysing information about task performance and making decisions about work methods and plans.

2 *Performance.* This is concerned with the degree to which intervention behaviours are actually performed. It may be measured by counting the proportion of relevant people performing the behaviours. For example, 60% of the employees in a particular work unit might be performing the job-enrichment behaviours described above. Another measure of performance is the frequency with which the new behaviours are performed. In assessing frequency, it is important to account for different variations of the same essential behaviour, as well as highly institutionalised behaviours that only need to be performed infrequently.

3 *Preferences.* This involves the degree to which organisation members privately accept the organisational changes. This contrasts with acceptance that is based primarily on organisational sanctions or group pressures. Private acceptance is usually reflected in people's positive attitudes towards the changes, and can be measured by the direction and intensity of these attitudes across the members of the work unit receiving the intervention. For example, a questionnaire that assesses members' perceptions of a job-enrichment program might show that most employees have a strong positive attitude towards making decisions, analysing feedback and performing a variety of tasks.

4 *Normative consensus.* This focuses on the extent to which people agree on the appropriateness of the organisational changes. This indicator of institutionalisation reflects the extent to which organisational changes have become part of the normative structure of the organisation. Changes persist to the degree that members feel they should support them. For example, a job-enrichment program would become institutionalised to the extent that employees support it and see it as appropriate to organisational functioning.

5 *Value consensus.* This is concerned with social consensus on values that are relevant to the organisational changes. Values are beliefs about how people ought or ought not to behave. They are abstractions from more specific norms. Job enrichment, for example, is based on values promoting employee self-control and responsibility. Different behaviours associated with job enrichment, such as making decisions and performing a variety of tasks, would persist to the extent that employees widely share values of self-control and responsibility.

These five indicators can be used to assess the level of institutionalisation of an OD intervention. The more the indicators are present in a situation, the higher will be the degree of institutionalisation. Further, these factors seem to follow a specific development order: knowledge, performance, preferences, norms and values. People must first understand new behaviours or changes before they can perform them effectively. Such performance generates rewards and punishments, which in time affect people's preferences. As many individuals come to prefer the changes, normative consensus about their appropriateness develops. Finally, if there is normative agreement about the changes reflected in a particular set of values, over time there should be some consensus on those values among organisation members. This developmental view of institutionalisation implies that, whenever one of the last indicators is present, all the previous ones are automatically included as well; for example, if employees normatively agree with the behaviours that are associated with job enrichment, then they also have knowledge about the behaviours, can perform them effectively and prefer them. An OD intervention is fully institutionalised only when all five factors are present.

Summary

This chapter presented an overview of the design, implementation and evaluation of interventions currently used in OD. An intervention is a set of planned activities intended to help an organisation improve its performance and effectiveness. Effective interventions are designed to fit the needs of the organisation, are based on causal knowledge of intended outcomes and transfer competence to manage change to organisation members.

'Designing OD interventions' discussed the selection of the most appropriate intervention, or series of interventions, which is an extremely difficult and sometimes risky venture. It is not only common to use more than one intervention but also tempting often to choose the most familiar, thereby ignoring alternatives that may be more aligned with the needs of the organisation.

It is important to ask two primary questions when considering the multifaceted approach to change management. First, what is the type of change required? Is it behavioural (including people and process), structural, technical or a combination of these? Second, what is the impact of the change process? Will the impact be on individuals, groups or the organisation as a whole? By determining a response to

these questions, it is possible to limit the choices and reduce the confusion that may occur.

'Implementing change' described five kinds of activities that change agents must carry out when planning and implementing changes. The first activity is motivating change, which involves creating a readiness for change among organisation members and managing their resistance. The second activity is about describing the desired future state, which may include the organisation's mission, valued performance and human outcomes, and valued organisational conditions to achieve those results, and creating a vision by articulating a compelling reason for implementing change. The third task for change agents is developing political support for the changes. Change agents must first assess their own sources of power, identify key stakeholders whose support is needed for change, and then devise strategies for gaining their support. The fourth activity concerns managing the transition of the organisation from its current state to the desired future state. This calls for planning a road map for the change activities, as well as planning how to gain commitment for the changes. It may also involve creating special management structures for managing the transition. The fifth change task is sustaining momentum for the changes so that they are carried to completion. This includes providing resources for the change program, creating a support system for change agents, developing new competencies and skills, and reinforcing the new behaviours required to implement the changes.

'Evaluating OD interventions' discussed the final two stages of planned change – evaluating interventions and institutionalising them. Evaluation was discussed in terms of two kinds of necessary feedback. Implementation feedback is concerned with whether the intervention is being implemented as intended, and evaluation feedback indicates whether the intervention is producing expected results. The former is collected data about features of the intervention and its immediate effects, which are fed back repeatedly and at short intervals. The latter is data about the long-term effects of the intervention, which are fed back at long intervals.

Evaluation of interventions also involves decisions about measurement and research design. Measurement issues focus on selecting variables and designing good measures. Ideally, measurement decisions should derive from the theory that underlies the intervention and should include measures of the features of the intervention and its immediate and long-term consequences. Further, these measures should be operationally defined, valid and reliable and should involve multiple methods, such as a combination of questionnaires, interviews and company records.

Research design focuses on setting up the conditions for making valid assessments of an intervention's effects. This involves ruling out explanations for the observed results other than the intervention. Although randomised experimental designs are rarely feasible in OD, quasi-experimental designs exist for eliminating alternative explanations.

Organisation development interventions are institutionalised when the change program persists and becomes part of the organisation's normal functioning. A framework for understanding and improving the institutionalisation of interventions identified organisation characteristics (congruence, stability of environment and technology, and unionisation) and intervention characteristics (goal specificity, programmability, level of change target, internal support and sponsor) affecting institutionalisation processes. It also described specific institutionalisation processes (socialisation, commitment, reward allocation, diffusion, and sensing and calibration) that directly affect indicators of intervention persistence (knowledge, performance, preferences, normative consensus and value consensus).

Activities

REVIEW QUESTIONS

1 What is meant by the term 'intervention'? Identify and give examples of interventions for various situations.

2 Compare and contrast different types of interventions.

3 What/who are the primary targets of change programs? Why is it important that the identification of the primary target be accurate? What could occur if a mistake is made?

4 What does 'interpersonal' refer to? Compare and contrast the interventions that could facilitate interpersonal development.

5 Why do people resist change? In your opinion, is this acceptable? Give reasons.

6 List the means by which resistance may be managed. Should managers consider the ethical component of such management?

7 Which power strategy is most closely aligned with OD's traditional humanistic values? What is the relationship between power and politics?

8 How may you develop political support for the change process?

Was Machiavelli the first OD practitioner? Give reasons.

9 What does 'implementation feedback' try to measure? Is it likely to cover all aspects? Why/ why not?

10 When should you identify the measurement variables to be used for evaluation and feedback? Is there a different perspective that you should consider?

11 Which indicator represents the highest degree of institutionalisation? Is this a good or a bad thing for an organisation?

12 Whose ultimate responsibility is it to measure the outcomes of an OD process?

13 What is 'diagnosis'? How does it relate to medical diagnosis?

14 What is 'equifinality'? What is its application in business?

15 What are the eight questions that need to be answered in establishing a diagnostic contract with an organisation? Can you think of others?

DISCUSSION AND ESSAY QUESTIONS

1 Compare and contrast employee involvement (EI) and quality of work life (QWL) with OD. Under what circumstances are these best used?

2 Explain what an 'intervention' is and how it fits into the OD process. What are the key considerations when deciding on an intervention? What are the inherent dangers in selecting the most appropriate interventions?

3 'The process of evaluating OD interventions are often ignored.' Why would this be the case?

Consider the consequences of this occurring.

4 Some would say that the word 'institutionalising' is an emotive term and should not be used when describing OD. Why is this so? Do you agree? Why/why not?

5 Feedback of diagnostic data collected during an examination of the organisation concerned is considered an important element in a successful OD intervention. Why? What are the characteristics of effective feedback

SEARCH ME! EXCERCISES

Explore **Search me! management** for relevant articles on the process of organisational change. Search me! is an online library of world-class journals, e-books and newspapers, including *The Australian* and *The New York Times*, and is updated daily. Log in to Search me! through **http://login.cengage.com** using the access card in the front of this book.

Keywords

Try searching for the following terms:

> Contingencies
> Data collection
> Design
> Design components
> Diagnosing organisations
> Diagnostic relationship
> Evaluation
> Feedback cycles
> Force-field analysis

> Implementation
> Institutionalisation
> Open systems
> Power
> Readiness for change
> Research design
> Resistance
> Strategic orientation

>> *Search tip:*

Search me! management contains information from both local and international sources. To get the greatest number of search results, try using both Australian and American spellings in your searches, e.g. 'globalisation' and 'globalization'; 'organisation' and 'organization'.

Notes

1 Dr M. Beitler, *From Systems Thinking to Open Systems Theory*, 2008, www.improvementandinnovation.com/ features/articles/systems-thinking-open-systems-theory.

2 D. Nadler, 'Role of models in organizational assessment', in *Organizational Assessment*, eds E. Lawler III, D. Nadler and C. Cammann (New York: John Wiley and Sons, 1980): 119–31; R. Keidel, *Seeing Organizational Patterns* (San Francisco: Berrett-Koehler, 1995); M. Harrison, *Diagnosing Organizations*, 2nd edn (Thousand Oaks, CA: Sage Publications, 1994).

3 A. Corney, *Stanford MBA Teaches Executives How To Master The 'Soft Skills' That Drive Bottom Line Results*, 2006, www.acorn-od.com/files/Andrea_Corney_Speaking_Resume.pdf.

4 S. Mohrman, T. Cummings and E. Lawler III, 'Creating useful knowledge with organizations: relationship and process issues', in *Producing Useful Knowledge for Organizations*, eds R. Kilmann and K. Thomas (New York: Praeger, 1983): 613–24; C. Argyris, R. Putnam and D. Smith, eds, *Action Science* (San Francisco: Jossey-Bass, 1985); E. Lawler III, A. Mohrman, S. Mohrman, G. Ledford, Jr and T. Cummings, *Doing Research That Is Useful for Theory and Practice* (San Francisco: Jossey-Bass, 1985).

5 D. Nadler, *Feedback and Organization Development: Using Data-Based Methods* (Reading, MA: Addison-Wesley, 1977): 110–14.

6 W. Nielsen, N. Nykodym and D. Brown, 'Ethics and organizational change', *Asia Pacific Journal of Human Resources*, 29 (1991).

7 Nadler, *Feedback and Organization Development*, op. cit.: 105–7.

8 W. Wymer and J. Carsten, 'Alternative ways to gather opinion', *HR Magazine* (April 1992): 71–8.

9 Examples of basic resource books on survey methodology include: S. Seashore, E. Lawler III, P. Mirvis and C. Cammann, *Assessing Organizational Change* (New York: Wiley Interscience, 1983); J. Van Mannen and J. Dabbs, *Varieties of Qualitative Research* (Beverly Hills, CA: Sage Publications, 1983); E. Lawler III, D. Nadler and C. Cammann, *Organizational Assessment: Perspectives on the Measurement of Organizational Behaviour and the Quality of Worklife* (New York: Wiley Interscience, 1980); R. Golembiewski and R. Hilles, *Toward the Responsive Organization: The Theory and Practice of Survey/Feedback* (Salt Lake City: Brighton Publishing, 1979); Nadler, *Feedback and Organization Development*, op. cit.; S. Sudman and N. Bradburn, *Asking Questions* (San Francisco: Jossey-Bass, 1983).

10 www.acer.edu.au/index3.html/, accessed 1 November 2006.

11 J. Jones and W. Bearley, 'Organization change: orientation scale', *HRDQ* (King of Prussia, Pennsylvania, 1986).

12 J. Fordyce and R. Weil, *Managing WITH People*, 2nd edn (Reading, MA: Addison-Wesley, 1979); W. Wells, 'Group interviewing', in *Handbook of Marketing Research*, ed. R. Ferder (New York: McGraw-Hill, 1977); R. Krueger, *Focus Groups: A Practical Guide for Applied Research*, 2nd edn (Thousand Oaks, CA: Sage Publications, 1994).

13 T. Armstrong, *Where Have All The O.D. Programs Gone?*, www.odinstitute.org/news0908.htm, 2008.

14 C. Emory, *Business Research Methods* (Homewood, IL: Richard D. Irwin, 1980): 146.

15 W. Deming, *Sampling Design* (New York: John Wiley, 1960); L. Kish, *Survey Sampling* (New York: John Wiley, 1965); S. Sudman, *Applied Sampling* (New York: Academic Press, 1976).

16 H. A. Sánchez, Binbin Lai and M. E. Fayad, *The Sampling Analysis Pattern*, www.hsanchez.net/repository/ hsanchez-sampling-analysis-pattern-uml03.pdf, 2003.

17 S Mohrman, T. Cummings and E. Lawler III, 'Creating useful knowledge with organizations: relationship and process issues', in *Producing Useful Knowledge for Organizations*, eds R. Kilmann and K. Thomas (New York: Praeger, 1983): 61–124.

18 C. Argyris, *Intervention Theory and Method: A Behavioral Science View* (Reading, MA: Addison-Wesley, 1970).

19 D. Nadler, *Feedback and Organization Development: Using Data-Based Methods* (Reading, MA: Addison-Wesley, 1977): 156–8.

20 C. Argyris, *Intervention Theory and Method: A Behavioral Science View*, op.cit.

21 T. Cummings, E. Molloy and R. Glen, 'A methodological critique of 58 selected work experiments', *Human Relations*, 30 (1977): 675–708; T. Cummings, E. Molloy and R. Glen, 'Intervention strategies for improving productivity and the quality of work life', *Organizational Dynamics*, 4 (Summer 1975): 59–60; J. Porras and P. Berg, 'The impact of organization development', *Academy of Management Review*, 3 (1978): 249–66; J. Nicholas, 'The comparative impact of organization development interventions on hard criteria measures', *Academy of Management Review*, 7 (1982): 531–42; R. Golembiewski, C. Proehl and D. Sink, 'Estimating the success of OD applications', *Training and Development Journal*, 72 (April 1982): 86–95.

22 D. Warrick, 'Action planning', in *Practicing Organization Development*, eds W. Rothwell, R. Sullivan and G. McClean (San Diego: Pfeiffer and Co., 1995).

23 Nicholas, 'The comparative impact of organization development interventions', op. cit.; J. Porras and P. Robertson, 'Organization development theory: a typology and evaluation', in *Research in Organizational Change and Development*, 1, eds R. Woodman and W. Pasmore (Greenwich, CT: JAI Press, 1987): 1–57.

24 B. J Weiner, *A Theory of Organizational Readiness for Change, Department of Health Policy and Management*, Gillings School of Global Public Health, University of North Carolina, USA, 2009, www.implementation science.com/content/4/1/67.

25 T. Stewart, 'Rate your readiness for change', *Fortune* (7 February 1994): 106–10.

26 G. Hofstede, *Culture's Consequences* (Beverly Hills, CA: Sage, 1980); K. Johnson, 'Estimating national culture and OD values', in *Global and International Organization Development*, eds P. Sorensfen Jr, T. Head, K. Johnson, N. Mathys, J. Preston and D. Cooperrider (Champaign, IL: Stipes, 1995): 266–81.

27 J. Kotter and L. Schlesinger, 'Choosing strategies for change', *Harvard Business Review*, 57 (1979): 106–14; R. Ricardo, 'Overcoming resistance to change', *National Productivity Review*, 14 (1995): 28–39.

28 M. Weisbord, *Productive Work Places* (San Francisco: Jossey-Bass, 1987); R. Beckhard and R. Harris, *Organizational Transitions: Managing Complex Change*, 2nd edn (Reading, MA: Addison-Wesley, 1987); R. Beckhard and W. Pritchard, *Changing the Essence* (San Francisco: Jossey-Bass, 1991).

29 U. Majer, T. Sauer, *Intuition and the Axiomatic Method in Hilbert's Foundation of Physics*, Universität Göttingen, Germany and California Institute of Technology, Pasadena, USA, 2006, www.springerlink.com/content/ k66217528223r715/.

30 N. Tichy and M. Devanna, *The Transformational Leader* (New York: John Wiley and Sons, 1986).

31 R. Cosier and C. Schwenk, 'Agreement and thinking alike: ingredients for poor decisions', *Academy of Management Executive*, 4 (1990): 69–74.

32 W. Burke, *Organization Development: A Normative View* (Reading, MA: Addison-Wesley, 1987).

33 D. Eden, 'OD and self-fulfilling prophesy: boosting productivity by raising expectations', *Journal of Applied Behavioral Science*, 22 (1986): 1–13.

34 ibid.: 8.

35 P. Senge, *The Fifth Discipline* (New York: Doubleday, 1990).

36 J. Kotter, *Leading Change* (Boston, MA: Harvard Business School Press, 1994); W. Bennis and B. Nanus, *Leadership* (New York: Harper and Row, 1985); J. O'Toole, *Leading Change: Overcoming the Ideology of Comfort and the Tyranny of Custom* (San Francisco: Jossey-Bass, 1995); F. Hesselbein, M. Goldsmith and R. Beckhard, eds, *The Leader of the Future* (San Francisco: Jossey-Bass, 1995).

37 Tichy and Devanna, *The Transformational Leader*, op. cit.

38 J. Pearce II and F. David, 'Corporate mission statements: the bottom line', *Academy of Management Executive*, 1 (1987): 109–15.

39 J. Pfeffer, *Power in Organizations* (New York: Pitman, 1982).

40 D. Nadler, 'The effective management of change', in *Handbook of Organizational Behavior*, ed. J. Lorsch (Englewood Cliffs, NJ: Prentice-Hall, 1987): 358–69.

41 C. Alderfer, 'Organization development', *Annual Review of Psychology*, 28 (1977): 197–223.

42 T. Bateman, 'Organizational change and the politics of success', *Group and Organization Studies*, 5 (June 1980): 198–209; A. Cobb and N. Margulies, 'Organization development: a political perspective', *Academy of Management Review*, 6 (1981): 49–59; A. Cobb, 'Political diagnosis: applications in organization development', *Academy of Management Review*, 11 (1986): 482–96; L. Greiner and V. Schein, *Power and Organization Development: Mobilizing Power to Implement Change* (Reading, MA: Addison-Wesley, 1988).

43 Greiner and Schein, *Power and Organization Development*, op. cit.

44 Nadler, 'The effective management of change', op. cit.; Beckhard and Pritchard, *Changing the Essence*, op. cit.

45 Greiner and Schein, *Power and Organization Development*, op. cit.

46 Beckhard and Harris, *Organizational Transitions*, op. cit.

47 ibid.

48 ibid.

49 M. Otto, International Conference on Renewable Energy in Africa, Making Renewable Energy Markets Work for Africa 16-18 April 2008, United Nations Environment Programme, www.unido.org/fileadmin/media/docum ents/pdf/Energy_Environment/senegal_presentations _day1_paralell2_ws22_starting_point_UNIDO.pdf.

50 C. Worley, D. Hitchin and W. Ross, *Integrated Strategic Change: How OD Helps to Build Competitive Advantage* (Reading, MA: Addison-Wesley, 1996).

51 M. Beer, *Organization Change and Development: A Systems View* (Santa Monica, CA: Goodyear, 1980).

52 R. Hill, T. Bullard, P. Capper, K. Hawes and K. Wilson, 'Learning about learning organisations: case studies of skill formation in five New Zealand organisations', *The Learning Organisation*, 5:4 (1998): 184–92.

53 T. Cummings and E. Molloy, *Strategies for Improving Productivity and the Quality of Work Life* (New York: Praeger, 1977); J. Whitfield, W. Anthony and K. Kacmar, 'Evaluation of team-based management: a case study', *Journal of Organizational Change Management*, 8:2 (1995): 17–28.

54 S. Mohrman and T. Cummings, 'Implementing quality-of-work-life programs by managers', in *The NTL Manager's Handbook*, eds R. Ritvo and A. Sargent (Arlington, VA: NTL Institute, 1983): 320–8; T. Cummings and S. Mohrman, 'Self-designing organizations: towards implementing quality-of-work-life innovations', in *Research in Organizational Change and Development*, 1, eds R. Woodman and W. Pasmore (Greenwich, CT: JAI Press, 1987): 275–310.

55 T. Cummings, 'Institutionalising quality-of-work-life programs: the case for self-design', paper delivered at the Annual Meeting of the Academy of Management, Dallas, TX, August 1983.

56 Cummings and Molloy, *Strategies for Improving Productivity and the Quality of Work Life*, op. cit.

57 D. Waltrip, J. Maniscalco, C. Meinhard and A. Anderson, *Implementation of an Organizational Development Plan to Create a Learning Organization*, Virginia Beach, Virginia, USA, 2006, http://docs.google.com/viewer?a=v&q=ca che:N3qjPtxlbugJ:www.wef.org/WorkArea/linkit.aspx %3FLinkIdentifier%3Did%26ItemID%3D3665+Imple mentation+feedback+in+OD&hl=en&gl=au&pid= bl&srcid=ADGEESjfme07YckDkiskv-_nZoWGf9Hy5u0 LscRwrmqtWDd7se6JbgK9kP_p8yLIo6BtPyT9TDaV ssvQohlFEvRMprQ2ttL5tmPg1O6F6pz-SOAwjHI_-3h IKBW-4f5T5uF-W-9fc0ho&sig=AHIEtbR0dRzMUrS guAQYWJ6B0Jp9hppD7g.

58 P. Goodman, *Assessing Organizational Change: The Rushton Quality of Work Experiment* (New York: John Wiley, 1979); A. Van de Ven and D. Ferry, eds, *Measuring and Assessing Organizations* (New York: John Wiley, 1985); E. Lawler III, D. Nadler and C. Cammann, eds, *Organizational Assessment: Perspectives on the Measurement of Organizational Behavior and Quality of Work Life* (New York: John Wiley, 1980); A. Van de Ven and W. Joyce, eds, *Perspectives on Organizational Design and Behavior* (New York: John Wiley, 1981); S. Seashore, E. Lawler III, P. Mirvis and C. Cammann, eds, *Assessing Organizational Change: A Guide to Methods, Measures, and Practices* (New York: John Wiley, 1983).

59 M. Luppa, T. Luck, E. Brähler, H. H. König, S. G. Riedel-Heller, *Prediction of Institutionalisation in Dementia*, University of Leipzig, Leipzig, Germany, May 2008,

http://content.karger.com/produktedb/
produkte.asp?typ=pdf&file=000144027.

60 D. Ciampa, *Total Quality: A User's Guide for
Implementation* (Reading, MA: Addison-Wesley, 1992); P.
Senge, *The Fifth Discipline* (New York: Doubleday, 1990);
Cummings and Mohrman, 'Self-designing organizations:
towards implementing quality-of-work-life innovations',
op. cit.; C. Worley, D. Hitchin and W. Ross, *Integrated
Strategic Change* (Reading, MA: Addison-Wesley, 1996).

61 This section is based on the work of P. Goodman and J.
Dean, 'Creating long-term organizational change', in
Change in Organizations, ed. P. Goodman (San Francisco:
Jossey-Bass, 1982): 226–79. To date, the framework is
largely untested and unchallenged. Ledford's process
model of persistence (see note 62) is the only other
model proposed to explain institutionalisation. The
empirical support for either model, however, is nil.

62 G. Ledford, 'The persistence of planned organizational
change: a process theory perspective' (PhD dissertation,
University of Michigan, 1984).

63 E. Vigoda, *Internal Politics in Public Administration
Systems: An Empirical Examination of Its Relationship With
Job Congruence, Organizational Citizenship Behavior, and
In-Role Performance*, Public Personnel Management, June
2000, www.allbusiness.com/legal/580916-1.html.

64 L. Zucker, 'Normal change or risky business:
institutional effects on the "hazard" of change in
hospital organizations, 1959–1979', *Journal of
Management Studies*, 24 (1987): 671–700.

65 S. Mohrman and T. Cummings, *Self-Designing
Organizations: Learning How to Create High Performance*
(Reading, MA: Addison-Wesley, 1989).

66 J. Martin and C. Siehl, 'Organizational cultures and
counterculture: an uneasy symbiosis', *Organizational
Dynamics* (1983): 52–64; D. Meyerson and J. Martin,
'Cultural change: an integration of three different views',
Journal of Management Studies, 24 (1987): 623–47.

67 L. Zucker, 'The role of institutionalization in cultural
persistence', *American Sociological Review*, 42 (1977):
726–43.

PART 3

ORGANISATION DEVELOPMENT

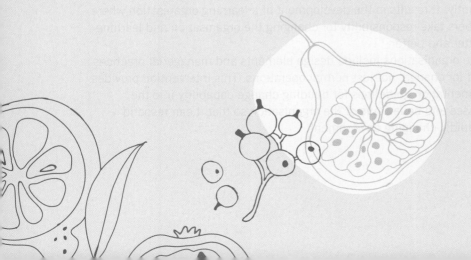

CHAPTER 6

Organisation development and change

This chapter describes interventions that enable organisations to change themselves continually. These change processes are relatively new to OD and are still being developed and refined. They are aimed at the growing number of organisations facing highly turbulent environments, such as businesses in high-technology, entertainment and biotechnology industries, where timing is critical, technological change is rapid and competitive pressures are unrelenting and difficult to predict. In these situations, standard sources of competitive advantage – strategy, organisation design and core competencies – erode quickly and provide only temporary advantage. What is needed are dynamic capabilities[1] built into the organisation that enable it to renew forms of competitive advantage constantly to adapt to a rapidly shifting environment.

Continuous change interventions extend transformational change into a nonstop process of strategy setting, organisation designing and implementing the change.[2] Rather than focus on creating and implementing a particular strategy and organisation design, continuous change addresses the underlying structures, processes and activities for generating new forms of competitive advantage. Thus, the focus is on learning, changing and adapting – on how to produce a constant flow of new strategies and designs and not just on how to transform existing ones.

Self-designing organisations have the capability to alter themselves fundamentally and continuously. Creating them is a highly participative process in which multiple stakeholders set strategic direction, design appropriate structures and processes and implement them. This intervention includes considerable innovation and learning as organisations gain the capacity to design and implement significant changes continually.

Learning organisations are those with the ability to learn how to change and improve themselves constantly. Distinct from individual learning, this intervention helps organisations move beyond solving existing problems to gaining the capability to improve constantly. It results in the development of a learning organisation where empowered members take responsibility for changing the organisation and learning how to do this better and better.

Built-to-change organisations include design elements and managerial practices that are all geared for change, not just normal operations. This intervention provides design and implementation guidelines for building change capability into the structures, processes and behaviours of the organisation so that it can respond continually to a rapidly changing environment.

SELF-DESIGNING ORGANISATIONS

A growing number of researchers and practitioners have called for self-designing organisations that have the built-in capacity to transform themselves continually to achieve high performance in today's competitive and changing environments.[3] Mohrman and Cummings have developed a self-design change strategy that involves an ongoing series of designing and implementing activities carried out by managers and employees at all levels of the organisation.[4] The approach assists members to translate corporate values and general prescriptions for change into specific structures, processes and behaviours suited to their situations. It enables them to tailor changes to fit the organisation and helps them continually adapt the organisation to changing conditions.

The demands of adaptive change

Mohrman and Cummings developed the self-design strategy in response to a number of demands facing organisations having to adapt to turbulent environments. These demands strongly suggest the need for self-design, in contrast to more traditional approaches to organisation change that emphasise ready-made programs and see change as a periodic event. Although organisations prefer the control and certainty inherent in traditional change, the five requirements for adaptive change reviewed below argue against this strategy:

1 Adaptive change generally involves altering most features of the organisation and achieving a fit among them and with the organisation's strategy. This suggests the need for a systematic change process that accounts for these multiple features and relationships.[5]

2 Adaptive change generally occurs in situations experiencing rapid change and uncertainty. This means that changing is never totally finished as new structures and processes will have to be continually modified to fit changing conditions. Thus, the change process needs to be dynamic and iterative, with organisations continually changing themselves.[6]

3 Current knowledge about adaptive change provides only general prescriptions for change. Organisations need to learn how to translate that information into specific structures, processes and behaviours appropriate to their situations. This generally requires considerable on-site innovation and learning as members learn by doing – trying out new structures and behaviours, assessing their effectiveness and modifying them if necessary. Thus, adaptive change calls for constant organisational learning.[7]

4 Adaptive change invariably affects many organisation stakeholders, including owners, managers, employees and customers. These different stakeholders are likely to have different goals and interests related to the change process. Unless the differences are revealed and reconciled, enthusiastic support for change may be difficult to achieve. Consequently, the change process must attend to the interests of multiple stakeholders.[8]

5   Adaptive change needs to occur at multiple levels of the organisation if new strategies are to result in changed behaviours throughout the organisation. Top executives must formulate a corporate strategy and clarify a vision of what the organisation needs to look like to support it. Middle and lower levels of the organisation need to put those broad parameters into operation by creating structures, procedures and behaviours to implement the strategy.[9]

Application stages

The self-design strategy accounts for these demands of adaptive change. It focuses on all features of the organisation (for example, structure, human resources practices and technology) and designs them to support the business strategy. It is a dynamic and an iterative process aimed at providing organisations with the built-in capacity to change and redesign themselves continually as circumstances demand. This approach promotes organisational learning among multiple stakeholders at all levels of the organisation, providing them with the knowledge and skills needed to transform the organisation and continually improve it.

Figure 6.1 outlines the self-design approach. Although the process is described in three stages, in practice those stages merge and interact iteratively over time. Each stage is described below:

1   *Laying the foundation.* This initial stage provides organisation members with the basic knowledge and information needed to get started with adaptive change. It involves three kinds of activities. The first is acquiring knowledge about how organisations function, about organising principles for achieving high performance and about the self-design process. This information is generally gained through reading relevant material, attending in-house workshops and visiting other organisations that have adapted themselves successfully. This learning typically starts with senior executives or with those managing the change process and cascades to lower organisational levels if a decision is made to proceed with self-design. The second activity in laying the foundation involves

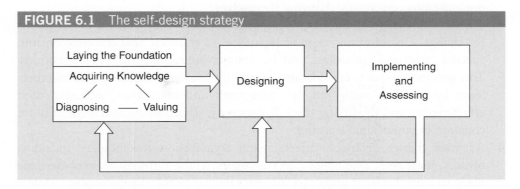

FIGURE 6.1   The self-design strategy

Source: S. Mohrman and T. Cummings, *Self-designing Organizations: Learning How to Create High Performance*, © 1989, p. 37. Reprinted by permission of Pearson Education, Inc., Upper Saddle River, New Jersey.

valuing – determining the corporate values that will guide the change process. These values represent those performance outcomes and organisational conditions that will be needed to implement the corporate strategy. They are typically written in a values statement that is discussed and negotiated among multiple stakeholders at all levels of the organisation. The third activity is diagnosing the current organisation to determine what needs to be changed to enact the corporate strategy and values. Organisation members generally assess the different features of the organisation, including its performance. They look for incongruities between its functioning and its valued performances and conditions. In the case of an entirely new organisation, members diagnose constraints and contingencies[10] in the situation that need to be taken into account in designing the organisation.

2   *Designing.* In this second stage of self-design, organisation designs and innovations are generated to support corporate strategy and values. Only the broad parameters of a new organisation are specified; the details are left to be tailored to the levels and groupings within the organisation. Referred to as 'minimum specification design',[11] this process recognises that designs need to be refined and modified as they are implemented throughout the organisation.

3   *Implementing and assessing.* This last stage involves implementing the designed organisation changes. It includes an ongoing cycle of action learning: changing structures and behaviours, assessing progress and making necessary modifications. Information about how well implementation is progressing and how well the new organisational design is working is collected and used to clarify design and implementation issues and to make necessary adjustments. This learning process continues not only during implementation but indefinitely as members periodically assess and improve the design and alter it to fit changing conditions. The feedback loops shown in Figure 6.1 suggest that the implementing and assessing activities may lead back to affect subsequent activities of designing, diagnosing, valuing and acquiring knowledge. This iterative sequence of activities provides organisations with the capacity to transform and improve themselves continually.

The self-design strategy is applicable to existing organisations needing to change themselves, as well as to new organisations. It is also applicable to changing the total organisation or only some sub-units. The way self-design is managed and unfolds can also differ. In some cases, it follows the existing organisation structure, starting with the senior executive team and cascading downward across organisational levels. In other cases, the process is managed by special design teams that are sanctioned to set broad parameters for valuing and designing for the rest of the organisation. The outputs of these teams are then implemented across departments and work units, with considerable local refinement and modification. Application 6.1 shows how senior lawyers at Blake Dawson lead by example.

6.1

APPLICATION

Meditation in business

We are working harder and longer and becoming more stressed as a result. Intensified global competition, cost cutting, multi-tasking and workforce reductions all combine to create increased uncertainty and pressure on employees. According to an Australian Bureau of Statistics survey in 2008, one in five Australians resorted to stress medication. As well, Medibank Private research revealed that absenteeism and reduced productivity resulting from stress reportedly costs Australia $10.11 billion annually and causes a loss of 3.2 days per worker per year.

Increased stress levels can contribute to a variety of health issues. A survey of 115 000 people found that 13 per cent experienced sleep problems, 10 per cent reported work-related health problems and 39 per cent were reluctant to take time off. The consequences of increased stress are particularly noticeable in a number of business sectors including law enforcement, education, finance, hospitality, transport, retail and marketing.

In response, many leading companies are introducing in-house meditation and yoga programs. A director of a corporate coaching company believes beneficial results can be experienced after just one session of meditation. She says the number of firms utilising meditation is increasing. Other firms are sponsoring voluntary yoga sessions.

A study by Ohio State University suggests a weekly combination of meditation and yoga can lower stress by more than 10 per cent, while Dr Ramesh Manocha, a researcher at the University of Sydney, reported in 2009 that meditation over a period of eight weeks reduced occupational stress by 26 per cent.

Source: Based on G. Jerums, 'The business of meditation', *Sunday Herald Sun*, 14 March 2010.

Critical thinking questions:
1. What are the arguments against this practice in the workplace?

LEARNING ORGANISATIONS

The second continuous change intervention is aimed at helping organisations develop and use knowledge to change and improve themselves constantly. It includes two interrelated change processes: organisation learning (OL) which enhances an organisation's capability to acquire and develop new knowledge and knowledge management (KM) which focuses on how that knowledge can be organised and used to improve performance. Both OL and KM are crucial in today's complex, rapidly changing environments. They can be a source of strategic renewal and can enable organisations to acquire and apply knowledge more quickly and effectively than competitors, thus establishing a sustained competitive advantage.[12] Moreover, when knowledge is translated into new products and services, it can become a key source of wealth creation for organisations.[13] OL and KM are among the most widespread and fastest-growing interventions in OD. They are the focus of an expanding body of research and practice and have been applied in such diverse organisations as the Australian Army, Blake Dawson Waldron, Minter Ellison, McKinsey, Microsoft and Boeing.

Conceptual framework

Like many new interventions in OD, there is some ambiguity about the concepts underlying OL and KM.[14] Sometimes the terms 'organisation learning' and 'knowledge management' are used interchangeably to apply to the broad set of activities through which organisations learn and organise knowledge; other times, they are used separately to emphasise different aspects of learning and managing knowledge. This confusion derives in part from the different disciplines and applications traditionally associated with OL and KM.[15]

OL interventions emphasise the organisational structures and social processes that enable employees and teams to learn and to share knowledge. They draw heavily on the social sciences for conceptual grounding and on OD interventions, such as team building, structural design and employee involvement for practical guidance. In organisations, OL change processes typically are associated with the human resources function and may be assigned to a special leadership role such as chief learning officer.

KM interventions, on the other hand, focus on the tools and techniques that enable organisations to collect, organise and translate information into useful knowledge. They are rooted conceptually in the information and computer sciences and, in practice, emphasise electronic forms of knowledge storage and transmission such as intranets, data warehousing and knowledge repositories. Organisationally, KM applications often are located in the information systems function and may be under the direction of a chief information or technology officer.

There is also confusion about the concept of organisation learning itself, about whether it is an individual- or organisation-level process. Some researchers and practitioners describe OL as individual learning that occurs within an organisation context; thus, it is the aggregate of individual learning processes occurring within an organisation.[16] Others characterise it in terms of organisation processes and structures; they emphasise how learning is embedded in routines, policies and organisation cultures.[17] Snyder has proposed an integration of the two perspectives that treats organisation learning as a relative concept.[18] Individuals do learn in organisations but that learning may or may not contribute to OL. Learning is organisational to the extent that:

- It is done to achieve organisation purposes.
- It is shared or distributed among members of the organisation.
- Learning outcomes are embedded in the organisation's systems, structures and culture.

To the extent that these criteria are met, organisation learning is distinct from individual learning. Thus, it is possible for individual members to learn while the organisation does not. For example, a member may learn to serve the customer better without ever sharing such learning with other members. Conversely, it is possible for the organisation to learn without individual members learning. Improvements in equipment design or work procedures, for example, reflect OL, even if these changes are not understood by individual members. Moreover, because OL serves the organisation's purposes and is embedded in its structures, it stays with the organisation, even if members change.

A key premise underlying much of the literature on OL and KM is that such interventions will lead to higher organisation performance. Although their positive linkage to performance is assumed, the mechanisms through which OL and KM translate into performance improvements are rarely identified or explained. Understanding those mechanisms, however, is essential for applying these change processes in organisations.

Based on existing research and practice, Figure 6.2 provides an integrative framework for understanding OL and KM interventions,[19] summarising the elements of these change processes and showing how they combine to affect organisation performance. This framework suggests that specific characteristics, such as structure and human resources systems, influence how well organisation learning processes are carried out. These learning processes affect the amount and kind of knowledge that an organisation possesses; that knowledge, in turn, directly influences performance outcomes, such as product quality and customer service. As depicted in Figure 6.2, the linkage between organisation knowledge and performance depends on the organisation's competitive strategy. Organisation knowledge[20] will lead to high performance to the extent that it is both relevant and applied effectively to the strategy. For example, customer-driven organisations require timely and relevant information about customer needs. Their success relies heavily on members having that knowledge and applying it effectively in their work with customers.

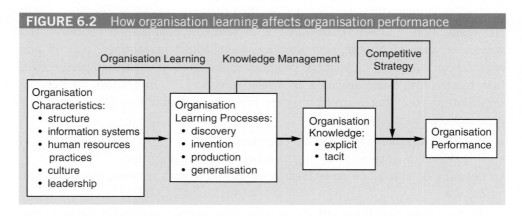

FIGURE 6.2 How organisation learning affects organisation performance

Source: Reprinted by permission of Sage Publications Ltd. from W. Snyder and T. Cummings, 'Organization learning disorders: conceptual model and intervention hypotheses', *Human Relations* 51 (1998): 873–95.
© The Tavistock Institute, 1998.

Figure 6.2 also shows how OL and KM are interrelated. OL interventions address how organisations can be designed to promote effective learning processes and how those learning processes themselves can be improved. KM interventions focus on the outcomes of learning processes, on how strategically relevant knowledge can be effectively organised and used throughout the organisation. Each of the key elements of OL and KM – organisation characteristics, organisation learning processes and organisation knowledge – are described below along with the interventions typically associated with them.

Organisation learning interventions

As shown in Figure 6.2, there are several organisation features that can promote effective learning processes, including structure, information systems, human resources practices, culture and leadership. Consequently, many of the interventions described in this book can help organisations develop more effective learning capabilities.[21] Human resources management interventions – performance appraisal, reward systems and career planning and development – can reinforce members' motivation to gain new skills and knowledge. Technostructural interventions,[22] such as process-based and network structures, self-managing work teams and re-engineering, can provide the kinds of lateral linkages and teamwork needed to process, develop and share diverse information and knowledge. Human process changes, including team building, search conferences and intergroup relations interventions, can help members develop the kinds of healthy interpersonal relationships that underlie effective OL. Strategic interventions, such as integrated strategic change and alliances, can help organisations gain knowledge about their environments and develop values and norms that promote OL.

Characteristics of a learning organisation

OL practitioners have combined many of these interventions into the design and implementation of what is commonly referred to as the 'learning organisation.' It is an organisation 'skilled at creating, acquiring, interpreting, transferring and retaining knowledge and at purposefully modifying its behaviour to reflect new knowledge and insights'.[23] Much of the literature on the learning organisation is prescriptive and proposes how organisations should be designed and managed to promote effective learning. Although there is relatively little systematic research to support these premises, there is growing consensus among researchers and practitioners about specific organisational features that characterise the learning organisation.[24] These qualities are mutually reinforcing and fall into five interrelated categories:

- *Structure.* Organisation structures emphasise teamwork, lesser number of layers, strong lateral relations and networking across organisational boundaries both internal and external to the business. These features promote information sharing, involvement in decision making, systems thinking and empowerment.

- *Information systems.* Organisation learning involves gathering and processing information and, consequently, the information systems of learning organisations provide an infrastructure for OL. These systems facilitate rapid acquisition, processing and sharing of rich, complex information and enable people to manage knowledge for competitive advantage.
- *Human resources practices.* Human resources, including appraisal, rewards and training, are designed to account for long-term performance and knowledge development; they reinforce the acquisition and sharing of new skills and knowledge.
- *Organisation culture.* Learning organisations have strong cultures that promote openness, creativity and experimentation among members. These values and norms provide the underlying social support needed for successful learning. They encourage members to acquire, process and share information; they nurture innovation and provide the freedom to try new things, to risk failure and to learn from mistakes.
- *Leadership.* Like most interventions aimed at continuous change, OL and KM depend heavily on effective leadership throughout the organisation. The leaders of learning organisations actively model the openness, risk taking and reflection necessary for learning. They also communicate a compelling vision of the learning organisation and provide the empathy, support and personal advocacy needed to lead others in that direction.

Organisation learning processes

The organisation characteristics described above affect how well members carry out organisation learning processes. As shown in Figure 6.2, these processes consist of four interrelated activities: discovery, invention, production and generalisation.[25] Learning starts with discovery when errors or gaps between desired and actual conditions are detected. For example, sales managers may discover that sales are falling below projected levels and set out to solve the problem. Invention is aimed at devising solutions to close the gap between desired and current conditions; it includes diagnosing the causes of the gap and creating appropriate solutions to reduce it. The sales managers may learn that poor advertising is contributing to the sales problem and may devise a new sales campaign to improve sales. Production processes involve implementing solutions and generalisation includes drawing conclusions about the effects of the solutions and extending that knowledge to other relevant situations. For instance, the new advertising program would be implemented and, if successful, the managers might use variations of it with other product lines. Thus, these four learning processes enable members to generate the knowledge necessary to change and improve the organisation.

Organisations can apply the learning processes described above to three types of learning.[26] First, *single-loop learning* or *adaptive learning*[27] is focused on improving the status quo. This is the most prevalent form of learning in organisations and enables members to reduce errors or gaps between desired and existing conditions.

It can produce incremental change in how organisations function. The sales managers described above engaged in single-loop learning when they looked for ways to reduce the difference between current and desired levels of sales.

Second, *double-loop learning* or *generative learning*[28] is aimed at changing the status quo. It operates at a more abstract level than does single-loop learning because members learn how to change the existing assumptions and conditions within which single-loop learning operates. This level of learning can lead to transformational change, where the status quo itself is radically altered. For example, the sales managers may learn that sales projections are based on faulty assumptions and models about future market conditions. This knowledge may result in an entirely new conception of future markets, with corresponding changes in sales projections and product development plans. It may lead the managers to drop some products that had previously appeared promising, develop new ones that were not considered before and alter advertising and promotional campaigns to fit the new conditions.

The third type of learning is called *deuterolearning,*[29] which involves learning how to learn. Here learning is directed at the learning process itself and seeks to improve how organisations perform single- and double-loop learning. For example, the sales managers might periodically examine how well they perform the processes of discovery, invention, production and generalisation. This could lead to improvements and efficiencies in how learning is conducted throughout the organisation.

Practitioners have developed change strategies designed specifically for organisation learning processes. Although these interventions are relatively new in OD and do not follow a common change process, they tend to focus on cognitive aspects of learning and how members can become more effective learners. In describing these change strategies, we draw heavily on the work of Argyris and Schon and of Senge and his colleagues because it is the most developed and articulated work in OL practice.[30]

From this perspective, organisation learning is not concerned with the organisation as a static entity but as an active process of sense making and organising. Based on the interpretive model of change, members socially construct the organisation as they continually act and interact with each other and learn from those actions how to organise themselves for productive achievement. This active learning process enables members to develop, test and modify mental models or maps of organisational reality. Called *theories in use*, these cognitive maps inform member behaviour and organising.[31] They guide how members make decisions, perform work and organise themselves. Unfortunately, members' theories in use can be faulty, resulting in ineffective behaviours and organising efforts. They can be too narrow and fail to account for important aspects of the environment; they can be too broad and include erroneous assumptions that lead to unexpected negative consequences. Effective OL can resolve these problems by enabling members to learn from their actions how to detect and correct errors in their mental maps, and thus it can promote more effective organising efforts.

The predominant mode of learning in most organisations is ineffective, however, and may even intensify errors. Referred to as *Model I learning*, it includes values and norms that emphasise unilateral control of environments and tasks and protection of oneself and others from information that may be hurtful.[32] These norms result in a variety of defensive routines that inhibit learning, such as withholding information and feelings, competition and rivalry, and little public testing of theories in use and the assumptions underlying them. Model I is limited to single-loop learning, where existing theories in use are reinforced.

A more effective approach to learning, called *Model II learning*, is based on values promoting valid information, free and informed choice, internal commitment to the choice and continuous assessment of its implementation.[33] This results in minimal defensiveness, with greater openness to information and feedback, personal mastery and collaboration with others and public testing of theories in use. Model II applies to double-loop learning, where theories in use are changed and to deuterolearning, where the learning process itself is examined and improved. There are many examples where organisations work in partnership with educational institutions, as in Application 6.2.

6.2

APPLICATION

Back to school

Corporate education programs enable companies to link the development of their employees to business goals.

Facing intense competition and a protracted skills shortage, Australian organisations are recognising the benefits of investing in the development of their employees and future leaders and many are doing so through education partnerships between universities and corporations...

By aligning corporate education and training programs with corporate goals, organisations not only ensure greater accountability for their investment in corporate education, but they are also directly linking the development of their employees to the development of the organisation.

In a global study of corporate education, more than half, 53 per cent of respondents, consider themselves 'learning organisations'. The concept of the learning organisation has been around since the 1990s, largely due to the work of United States management academic Dr Peter Senge, but it is an area of growing importance as globalisation and increasing competition place renewed pressure on organisations to be innovative and create new opportunities.

Organisations with a strategic approach to corporate education provide a non-threatening environment in which employees can contribute ideas and explore innovative products, services and processes.

Corporate education programs delivered in partnership with a university also benefit from the objectivity university academics can provide both to employees and their projects and to stretching the level of thinking within an organisation.

>>

Other reasons for employer-sponsored corporate education programs include:

- To provide a mechanism to identify and select leaders and enhance employee retention;
- To enhance an organisation's position as an 'employer of choice' to attract and retain the best available talent in a tight labour market;
- To improve an organisation's ability to compete by improving internal communication and understanding; to promote and strengthen the values and culture of an organisation.

Source: Dr. Lindsay Ryan, 'Back to school', *Business Review Weekly*, 21 May 2008.

Critical thinking questions:
1. The relationships between universities and business in Australia are very different compared to the United States. How are they different and what are the advantages of these differing perspectives?
2. Research further the theories espoused by Peter Senge and find examples within your own business areas of interest.
3. What kinds of education programs/projects are available within your organisation or organisations you are familiar with? Do you consider they have been effective? Why/why not?
4. To what extent does your organisation or an organisation you are familiar with, encourage staff to contribute ideas? In your opinion, are those encouragements effective? Why/why not?

Application stages

OL interventions are aimed at helping organisation members learn how to change from Model I to Model II learning. Like all learning, this change strategy includes the learning processes of discovery, invention, production and generalisation. Although the phases are described linearly below, in practice they form a recurrent cycle of overlapping learning activities.

1 *Discover theories in use and their consequences.* This first step involves uncovering members' mental models or theories in use and the consequences that follow from behaving and organising according to them. Depending on the size of the client system, this may directly involve all members, such as a senior executive team, or it may include representatives of the system, such as a cross-section of members from different levels and areas.

OL practitioners have developed a variety of techniques to help members identify their theories in use. Because these theories generally are taken for granted and rarely examined, members need to generate and analyse data to infer the theories' underlying assumptions. One approach is called *dialogue*, a variant of the human process interventions described previously.[34] It involves members in genuine exchange about how they currently address problems, make decisions and interact with each other and relevant others, such as suppliers, customers and competitors. Participants are encouraged to be open and frank with each other, to behave as colleagues and to suspend individual assumptions as much as possible. OL practitioners facilitate dialogue sessions using many of the human process tools, such as process consultation and third-party intervention. As a result, group members are encouraged to inquire into their own and others' ways of thinking, to advocate for certain beliefs and to reflect on the assumptions that led to those beliefs. Dialogue can result in clearer understanding of existing theories in use and their behavioural consequences and enable members to uncover faulty assumptions that lead to ineffective behaviours and organising efforts.

A second method of identifying theories in use involves constructing an *action map* of members' theories and their behavioural consequences.[35] OL practitioners typically interview members about recurrent problems in the organisation, why they are occurring, actions that are taken to resolve them and outcomes of those behaviours. Based on this information, an action map is constructed showing interrelationships among the values underlying theories in use, the action strategies that follow from them and the results of those actions. Such information is fed back to members so that they can test the validity of the map, assess the effectiveness of their theories in use and identify factors that contribute to functional and dysfunctional learning in the organisation.

A third technique for identifying theories in use and revealing assumptions is called the *left-hand, right-hand column*.[36] It starts with each member selecting a specific example of a situation where he or she was interacting with others in a way that produced ineffective results. The example is described in the form of a script and is written on the right side of a page. For instance, it might include statements such as, 'I told Larry that I thought his idea was good.' 'Joyce said to me that she did not want to take the assignment because her workload was too heavy.' On the left-hand side of the page, the member writes what he or she was thinking but not saying at each phase of the exchange. For example, 'When I told Larry that I thought his idea was good, what I was really thinking is that I have serious reservations about the idea, but Larry has a fragile ego and would be hurt by negative feedback.' 'Joyce said she didn't want to take the assignment because her workload is too heavy, but I know it's because she doesn't want to work with Larry.' This simple yet powerful exercise reveals hidden assumptions that guide behaviour and can make members aware of how erroneous or untested assumptions can undermine work relationships.

A fourth method that helps members identify how mental models are created and perpetuated is called the *ladder of inference*, as shown in Figure 6.3.[37] It demonstrates how far removed from concrete experience and selected data are the assumptions and beliefs that guide our behaviour. The ladder shows vividly how members' theories in use can be faulty and lead to ineffective actions. People may draw invalid conclusions from limited experience; their cultural and personal biases may distort meaning attributed to selected data. The ladder of inference can help members understand why their theories in use may be invalid and why their behaviours and organising efforts are ineffective. Members can start with descriptions of actions that are not producing intended results and then back down the ladder to discover the reasons underlying those

FIGURE 6.3 The ladder of inference

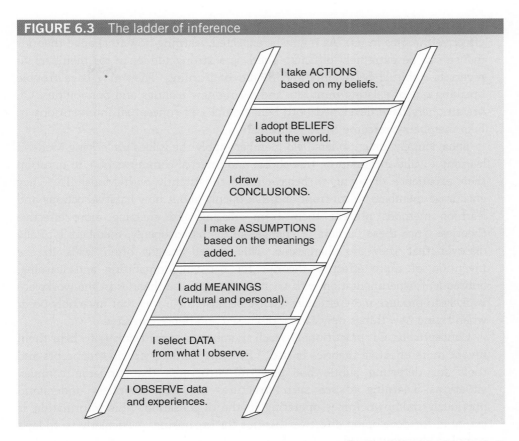

I take ACTIONS
based on my beliefs.

I adopt BELIEFS
about the world.

I draw
CONCLUSIONS.

I make ASSUMPTIONS
based on the meanings
added.

I add MEANINGS
(cultural and personal).

I select DATA
from what I observe.

I OBSERVE data
and experiences.

Source: Cummings/Worley, *Organization Development and Change* (with InfoTrac® College Edition Printed Access Card), 9e © 2009 South-Western, a part of Cengage Learning, Inc. Reproduced by permission www.cengage.com/permissions.

ineffective behaviours. For example, a service technician might withhold from management valuable yet negative customer feedback about product quality, resulting in eventual loss of business. Backing down the ladder, the technician could discover an untested belief that upper management does not react favourably to negative information and may even 'shoot the messenger'. This belief may have resulted from assumptions and conclusions that the technician drew from observing periodic lay-offs and from hearing widespread rumours that the company is out to get troublemakers and people who speak up too much. The ladder of inference can help members understand the underlying reasons for their behaviours and help them confront the possibility that erroneous assumptions are contributing to ineffective actions.

2 *Invent and produce more effective theories in use.* Based on what is discovered in the first phase of this change process, members invent and produce theories in use that lead to more effective actions and that are more closely aligned with Model II learning. This involves double-loop learning as members try to create and enact new theories. In essence, members learn by doing; they learn from

their invention and production actions how to invent and produce more effective theories in use. As might be expected, learning how to change theories in use can be extremely difficult. There is a strong tendency for members to revert to habitual behaviours and modes of learning. They may have trouble breaking out of existing mindsets and seeing new realities and possibilities. OL practitioners have developed both behavioural and conceptual interventions to help members overcome these problems.

Behaviourally, practitioners help members apply the values underlying Model II learning – valid information, free choice and internal commitment – to question their experience of trying to behave more consistently with Model II.[38] They encourage members to confront and talk openly about how habitual actions and learning methods prevent them from creating and enacting more effective theories. Once these barriers to change are discussed openly, members typically discover that they are changeable. This shared insight often leads to the invention of more effective theories for behaving, organising and learning. Subsequent experimentation with trying to enact those theories in the workplace is likely to produce more effective change because the errors that invariably occur when trying new things now can be discussed and hence corrected.

Conceptually, OL practitioners teach members *systems thinking* to help them invent more effective theories in use.[39] Systems thinking provides concepts and tools for detecting subtle but powerful structures that underlie complex situations. Learning to see such structures can help members understand previously unknown forces operating in the organisation. This information is essential for developing effective theories for organising, particularly in today's complex, changing world.

Systems thinking generally requires a radical shift in how members view the world: from seeing parts to seeing wholes; from seeing linear cause–effect chains to seeing interrelationships; from seeing static entities to seeing processes of change. Practitioners have developed a variety of exercises and tools to help members make this conceptual shift. These include systems diagrams for displaying circles of influence among system elements; system archetypes describing recurrent structures that affect organisations; computerised micro worlds where new strategies can be tried out under conditions that permit experimentation and learning; and games and experiential exercises demonstrating systems principles.[40]

3 *Continuously monitor and improve the learning process.* This final stage involves deuterolearning – learning how to learn. As described earlier, learning is directed at the learning process itself and at how well Model II learning characteristics are reflected in it. This includes assessing OL strategies and the organisational structures and processes that contribute to them. Members assess periodically how well these elements facilitate single- and double-loop learning. They generalise positive findings to new or changing situations and make appropriate modifications to improve OL. Because these activities reflect the highest and most

difficult level of OL, they depend heavily on members' capabilities to do Model II learning. Members must be willing to openly question their theories in use about OL; they must be willing to test publicly the effectiveness of both their learning strategies and those of the wider organisation.

Knowledge management interventions

The key outcome of organisation learning processes is organisation knowledge. It includes what members know about organisational processes, products, customers and competitive environments. Such knowledge may be explicit and exist in codified forms such as documents, manuals and databases; or it may be tacit and reside mainly in members' skills, memories and intuitions.[41] Fuelled by innovations in information technology, KM interventions have focused heavily on codifying organisation knowledge so it can be readily accessed and applied to organisational tasks. Because tacit knowledge is difficult if not impossible to codify, attention has also been directed at how such knowledge can be shared informally across members and organisational units.

Knowledge and performance

Organisation knowledge contributes to organisation performance to the extent that it is relevant and applied effectively to the organisation's competitive strategy, as shown in Figure 6.2. Moreover, organisation knowledge is particularly valuable when it is unique and cannot easily be obtained by competitors.[42] Thus, organisations seek to develop or acquire knowledge that distinctly adds value for customers and that can be leveraged across products, functions, business units or geographical regions. For example, Wal-Mart excels at managing its unique distribution system across a wide variety of regional stores. Honda is particularly successful at leveraging its competence in producing motors across a number of product lines, including automobiles, motorcycles, generators, outboard motors and lawn mowers.[43]

Because organisation knowledge plays a crucial role in linking organisation learning processes to organisation performance, increasing attention is being directed at how businesses can acquire and use it effectively. Studies have demonstrated how many Japanese companies and such American companies as Hewlett-Packard and Motorola achieve competitive advantage through building and managing knowledge effectively.[44] These knowledge capabilities have been described as 'core competencies',[45] 'invisible assets'[46] and 'intellectual capital',[47] thus suggesting their contribution to organisation performance. Mohrman and her colleagues have looked at organisations through a knowledge lens.[48] They have shown how businesses can fine-tune their organisation designs so that each design element, such as structure, rewards, work design and managerial processes, contributes to creating and leveraging knowledge for competitive advantage.

There is growing emphasis both in the accounting profession and in many industries on developing measures that capture knowledge capital.[49] For many organisations, the value of intellectual assets far exceeds the value of physical and financial assets; intellectual assets are usually worth three- to four-times tangible book value.[50] Moreover, the key components of cost in many of today's organisations are research and development, intellectual assets and services, rather than materials and labour, which are the focus of traditional cost accounting. Dow Chemical, for example, has developed a process for measuring and managing intellectual capital.[51] The method first defines the role of knowledge in the organisation's business strategy, then assesses current knowledge assets and deficiencies and finally assembles a knowledge portfolio. This process enables Dow to manage knowledge almost as rigorously as it manages its tangible assets. There are examples in the legal profession of a similar strategy to that described in Application 6.3.

6.3

APPLICATION

Knowledge keepers

Managing and sharing legal information is as vital as ever and law firms are finding better ways of delivering these services.

Some of Australia's largest law firms are using the economic downturn to explore new ways of delivering training and providing legal information.

With cost-cutting prevalent among many big firms and redundancies becoming more common in 2009, support services of all kinds are being scrutinised for excess capacity and many non-billing employees are being asked to find better ways to run the business.

In the UK, where thousands of lawyers and support staff have been made redundant, knowledge managers – legal and non-legal staff who support lawyers – have not been spared the axe, while others have had their roles absorbed by business development areas.

But in Australia, where redundancies and the downturn in demand for legal services have been less severe, many knowledge managers have been able to keep their jobs.

Allens Arthur Robinson employs about 60 staff nationally in knowledge management, a mixture of legal and non-legal staff.

'Like any function in a law firm, we are immune,' Allens Arthur Robinson director of knowledge Rachel O'Connor says. 'When there is an economic downturn, people are always looking and asking questions.'

O'Connor says she has spoken to many partners in the past month to remind them of the continuing relevance of knowledge management. 'I'm seeing the economic downturn as a good chance for us to evaluate what we've been doing and how we've been doing it, to ensure that we are providing relevant services to our lawyers,' she says.

Freehills has a knowledge management team of about 100 across its production and print room, library and research and precedent centres. The team was restructured this year to facilitate its new role in managing the firm's intranet.

Freehills chief operating officer Janet Young says it has always been difficult to express the value and return that the firm gets from knowledge management to the partnership. The downturn has caused her to focus on more efficient ways of delivering services to lawyers and is being expressed to lawyers as an essential tool to help them advise their clients.

She says a need to cut costs has meant all areas of the firm need to justify why they should continue to exist as they are.

'Basically, they exist to support our lawyers to support our clients. If we can't draw that link then it's a very valid question as to why do we have them,' Young says.

Sydney firm Marque Lawyers formed in August after the former managing partner of Gadens, Michael Bradley and three other partners, went out on their own. The firm now has 20 lawyers.

One of the former Gadens partners, Damian Sturzaker, says leaving knowledge management to a large team is almost an 'abrogation of responsibility' by the lawyers.

'Once someone becomes a knowledge management professional, they become disconnected from practice and are less able to anticipate what is needed by the professionals who are providing service to the clients,' he says.

Marque holds regular lunchtime seminars in which individual lawyers give presentations on precedents and other new information they use in the course of their work. It also subscribes to online case and legislation services, as well as making use of free sites such as AusLII.

'In a really big firm, you get an email from the knowledge manager asking for your contribution and you just delete it, because there is not that sense of collective responsibility,' Sturzaker says.

'Technology has really allowed a smaller firm to compete quite aggressively with larger firms in that space.'

Source: Alex Boxsell, 'Knowledge keepers', *Business Review Weekly*, 3 June 2009.

Critical thinking questions:
1. This application focuses on law firms. What other industries have similar arrangements?
2. What problems exist with knowledge management and how may they be remedied?
3. In your experience, do knowledge management systems actually contribute to a firm's success or are they essentially a cost item? Why do you hold that opinion?
4. 'In a really big firm, you get an email from the knowledge manager asking for your contribution and you just delete it, because there is not that sense of collective responsibility . . .' How would you respond to this statement?

Application stages

KM interventions are growing rapidly in OD and include a range of change strategies and methods. Although there is no universal approach to KM, these change processes address the essential steps for generating, organising and distributing knowledge within organisations:

1 *Generating knowledge.* This stage involves identifying the kinds of knowledge that will create the most value for the organisation and then creating mechanisms for increasing that stock of knowledge. It starts with examination of the organisation's competitive strategy – how it seeks to create customer value to achieve profitable results. Strategy provides the focus for KM; it identifies those areas where knowledge is likely to have the biggest payoff. For example, competitive strategies that emphasise customer service, such as those found at McKinsey and Nordstrom, place a premium on knowledge about

customer needs, preferences and behaviour. Strategies favouring product development, like those at Microsoft and Hoffman-LaRoche, benefit from knowledge about technology and research and development. Strategies focusing on operational excellence, such as those at Motorola and Chevron, value knowledge about manufacturing and quality improvement processes.

Once the knowledge required for competitive strategy is identified, organisations need to devise mechanisms for acquiring or creating that knowledge. Externally, organisations can acquire other companies that possess the needed knowledge, or they can rent it from knowledge sources such as consultants and university researchers.[52] Internally, organisations can facilitate *communities of practice* – informal networks among employees performing similar work to share expertise and solve problems together.[53] They also can create more formal groups for knowledge generation, such as R&D departments, corporate universities and centres of excellence. Organisations can bring together people with different skills, ideas and values to generate new products or services. Called *creative abrasion*, this process breaks traditional frames of thinking by having diverse perspectives rub creatively against each other to develop innovative solutions.[54]

2   *Organising knowledge.* This phase includes putting valued knowledge into a form that organisational members can use readily. It may also involve refining knowledge to increase its value to users. KM practitioners have developed tools and methods for organising knowledge that form two broad strategies: codification and personalisation.[55]

Codification approaches[56] rely heavily on information technology. They categorise and store knowledge in databases where it can be accessed and used by appropriate members. This strategy works best for explicit forms of knowledge that can be extracted from people, reports and other data sources and then organised into meaningful categories called 'knowledge objects' that can be reused for various purposes. The economic rationale underlying this strategy is to invest once in a knowledge asset and then to reuse it many times. Management consulting firms such as McKinsey and Bain extract key knowledge objects from consulting reports, benchmark data and market segmentation analyses[57] and then place them in an electronic repository for people to use. This enables them to apply knowledge assets across various projects and clients, thus achieving scale in knowledge reuse to grow their business.

Personalisation strategies for organising knowledge focus on the people who develop knowledge and on how they can share it person-to-person. This approach emphasises tacit knowledge, which cannot be codified and stored effectively in computerised information systems. Such knowledge is typically accessed through personal conversations, direct contact and ongoing dialogue with the people who possess it. Thus, KM practitioners have developed a variety of methods for facilitating personal exchanges between those with tacit knowledge and those seeking it. For example, Bain and Company fosters networking among its employees through transferring people across offices, encouraging the prompt return of phone calls from colleagues, brainstorming sessions and cross-functional project teams. Hughes, Microsoft and Time-Life have created 'knowledge maps' that identify valued competencies, skills and knowledge and show people where to go and whom to contact to access them.[58]

3 *Distributing knowledge.* This final stage of KM creates mechanisms for members to gain access to needed knowledge. It overlaps with the previous phase of KM and involves making knowledge easy for people to find and encouraging its use and reuse. KM practitioners have developed a variety of methods for distributing knowledge, generally grouped as three approaches: self-directed distribution, knowledge services and networks and facilitated transfer.[59]

Self-directed distribution methods rely heavily on member control and initiative for knowledge dissemination. They typically include databases for storing knowledge and locator systems for helping members find what they want. Databases can include diverse information such as articles, analytical reports, customer data and best practices. Locator systems can range from simple phone directories to elaborate search engines. Self-directed knowledge transfer can involve either 'pull' or 'push' systems.[60] The former lets members pull down information they need, when they need it; the latter makes knowledge available to members by sending it out to them. Fluor Corporation, for example, placed job requirements and career ladder information on its intranet and let employees access the information on an 'as needed' basis.

Knowledge services and networks promote knowledge transfer by providing specific assistance and organised channels for leveraging knowledge throughout the organisation. KM services include a variety of support for knowledge distribution, such as help desks, information systems and knowledge packages. They may also involve special units and roles that scan the flow of knowledge and organise it into more useful forms, such as 'knowledge departments', 'knowledge managers' or 'knowledge integrators'.[61] Knowledge networks create linkages among organisational members for sharing knowledge and learning from one another. These connections can be electronic, such as those occurring in chat rooms, intranets and discussion databases, or they may be personal, such as those taking place in talk rooms, knowledge fairs and communities of practice.

Facilitated transfer of organisation knowledge involves specific people who assist and encourage knowledge distribution. These people are trained to help members find and transmit knowledge as well as gain access to databases and other knowledge services. They may also act as change agents helping members implement knowledge to improve organisation processes and structures. For example, BP's 'Shared Learning Program' includes dedicated practitioners, called 'quality/progress professionals', who coach employees in best practices and how to use them.[62]

Outcomes of organisation learning and knowledge management

Given the popularity of OL and KM interventions, research about their effects in organisations is growing. The Society for Organisational Learning (SoL: www.solonline.org) at MIT in the United States is engaged in a variety of research efforts that focus on capacity building, dialogue and other aspects of OL processes. For example, Volvo and IKEA applied learning processes in their implementation of environmentally sustainable organisation designs. Other organisations claim considerable success with the ladder of inference, the left-hand/right-hand column tool and systems thinking. The Canadian Broadcasting Corporation used the left-hand/right-hand column to increase collaboration between the English and French radio and TV organisations and to create a new vocabulary for sharing resources. Shani and Docherty reported how OD interventions aimed at designing and implementing organisation learning mechanisms contributed to positive performance outcomes in companies in Israel, Sweden, the United Kingdom and the United States.[63] Studies of transfer of best practices and KM by the American Productivity & Quality Center reveal a number of performance improvements in such companies as Buckman Laboratories, Texas Instruments, CIGNA Property & Casualty and Chevron.[64] Among the reported outcomes were increases in new product sales, manufacturing capacity and corporate profits, as well as reductions in costs, service delivery time and start-up time for new ventures. A study of 40 firms in Europe, Japan and the United States found that in contrast to poorer performing companies, higher performing firms were better at creating, distributing and applying knowledge.[65] A recent study of KM in 131 Korean companies showed that those that combined strategies for managing both internal-oriented tacit knowledge and external-oriented objective knowledge performed the best.[66]

Despite these success stories, there appears to be considerable room for improving OL interventions. A longitudinal analysis of Royal Dutch Shell described its rise and fall as a 'premier learning organisation' and questioned whether such a strategy could be institutionalised.[67] Argyris and Schon state that they are unaware of any organisation that has fully implemented a double-loop learning (Model II) system.[68] Accenture, a pioneer in KM, experienced problems applying a standardised KM system across its global operations primarily because it did not take into account local and regional differences in how knowledge is generated and used.[69] A comprehensive study of KM in 431 US and European firms also suggests that organisations may have more problems implementing KM practices than is commonly reported in the popular media.[70] Only 46% of the companies reported above-average performance in 'generating new knowledge'. Ratings were even lower for 'embedding knowledge in processes, products and/or services' (29%) and 'transferring existing knowledge into other parts of the organisation' (13%). Another study of 31 KM projects across 20 organisations revealed that KM contributed to the fundamental transformation of only three of the firms studied.[71] Many of the companies, however, reported operational improvements in product development, customer support, software development, patent management and education and training. Because many of the existing reports of OL and KM outcomes are case studies or anecdotal reports, more systematic research is need to assess the effects of these popular interventions.

BUILT-TO-CHANGE ORGANISATIONS

One of the newest continuous change interventions involves designing an entire organisation for change and not just for normal operations. Based on extensive action research at the University of Southern California's Center for Effective Organisations, Lawler and Worley have developed a built-to-change (B2C) approach to designing organisations.[72] It is based on the simple fact that most organisations are designed for stability and dependable operations. Their design elements and managerial practices reinforce predictable behaviours aimed at sustaining a particular competitive advantage. Lawler and Worley argue that many change efforts are unsuccessful, not because of human resistance or lack of visionary leadership, but because organisations are designed to be stable. Such built-in stability can be a recipe for failure in rapidly changing environments. In these situations, the ability to change constantly is the best sustainable source of competitive advantage. The B2C intervention helps organisations design themselves for change.

Design guidelines

The B2C intervention includes guidelines such as the following for how organisation design components can be configured to promote change:

- *Managing talent.* B2C designs are geared to selecting, developing and managing the right talent for change. Selection practices seek quick learners who want to take initiative, desire professional growth and thrive on change. Employment contracts specify clearly that change is to be expected and support for change is a condition of employment and a path to success. Rather than specific job descriptions, members are encouraged to discover what needs to be done by frequent goal-setting reviews where tasks are constantly assessed and revised. Training and development are continuous and aimed at supporting change and gaining value-added skills and knowledge.
- *Reward system.* Rewards play a key role in motivating and reinforcing change in B2C organisations. Individual or team bonuses are tied directly to change goals, learning new things and performing new tasks well. This establishes a clear line of sight between rewards and change activities. Bonuses can include one-time rewards given at the end of a particular change effort, or rewards targeted to different phases of the change process. B2C designs also shift the basis of

rewards from jobs to people. Members are rewarded for what they can do, not for the particular job they perform. Because jobs and tasks are continually changing, people are motivated to learn new skills and knowledge, thus keeping pace with change and enhancing their long-term value to the organisation.

- *Structure.* B2C designs emphasise flat, lean and flexible organisation structures that can be reconfigured quickly when the circumstances demand. These organic designs – process, matrix and network structures, for example – put decision making into the hands of those closest to the work and the environment. They enable members to process information, share it with relevant others and make decisions rapidly. Organic designs keep the organisation closely connected with the environment, so that it can detect external changes and create innovative responses to them.

- *Information and decision processes.* In B2C organisations, information and decision making are moved throughout the organisation to wherever they are needed. These performance-based systems ensure that information is transparent and current and that it provides a clear picture of how the organisation is performing relative to its competitors. They enable organisations to make timely and relevant decisions to keep pace with changing conditions.

- *Leadership.* B2C designs stress the importance of shared leadership throughout the organisation. Rather than having the organisation rely on centralised sources of power and control, these designs spread leadership across multiple levels of the organisation. This speeds decision making and response rates because those lower in the organisation need not have to wait for top-down direction. It provides leadership experience and skills to a broad array of members, thus developing a strong cadre of leadership talent. Shared leadership supports continuous change by spreading change expertise and commitment across the organisation. It increases the chances that competent leaders will be there to keep the change process moving forward. Application 6.4 describes the experience of mentoring in a legal company.

6.4

APPLICATION

Maximum rewards

Talent counts for staff of any age and experience at one Adelaide law firm, which is bridging the generation gap between workers.

Its staff has a range of experience, from junior workers fresh from university to masters of the industry, who have more than five decades under their belt.

But the skills at all levels are being appreciated by each generation.

Law firm Duncan Basheer Hannon has 33 solicitors practicing in a variety of corporate, commercial, hospitality and personal injury law, as well as 38 professional and support staff.

Its most experienced consultant, Max Basheer, 82, is still practicing – 58 years after he stared his legal career.

He is in the office five days a week, keeping up a case load and making a point to help less experienced staff...

His willingness to pass on his knowledge is an invaluable asset to solicitor Stella Kassapidis, 24, who has worked at the firm for a year.

She said the move from Flinders University into working full-time in law had been a steep learning curve, but she was grateful for the support of the more experienced staff to help her move forward in her career, both personally and for the company.

The support has included a strong working relationship with Mr Basheer, who made a point from day one to encourage her to seek his guidance if she needed it, she said.

But although Ms Kassapidis is just starting out in the profession, she feels her skills and talents are valued by more experienced staff. '... It's a great place to work and I'm looking to stay here long-term. It's really going to benefit my career....'

General Manager Steve Nollis, 49, has worked at the firm only for a month but said he had been able to bring experience from other fields.

He said the people and culture of the firm attracted him to the position '.... I'm impressed with the diversity of the group, the professionalism of the group and the can-do attitude.'

Source: Cara Jenkin, 'Maximum rewards', *The Adelaide Advertiser*, 13 March 2010. News Limited.

Critical thinking questions:
1. How does this application support the 'built-to-change' intervention definition?
2. What difficulties could you anticipate in such a situation and how may they be avoided?
3. The process outlined above can be described as 'mentoring'. How could a similar approach be applied in a start-up business?

Application stages

Lawler and Worley stress that not all organisations should be built to change, though most could benefit from applying some B2C principles. This intervention is mainly for organisations having problems adapting to complex and rapidly changing environments. For them, the following five initiatives can help the transition to a B2C organisation:

1 *Create a change-friendly identity.* This first stage addresses organisation identity – the established set of core values, norms and beliefs shared by organisation members. Similar to organisation culture, identity is the most stable part of an organisation; it is deep-seated, taken for granted and guides decisions and behaviours like an invisible hand. Organisation identity can promote or hinder the transition to B2C depending on whether it supports change or stability. In many traditionally designed organisations, values and norms reinforce stability and predictability, thus making change difficult. To move towards a change-friendly identity requires surfacing existing values and norms, assessing their relevance to change and making appropriate adjustments. This typically involves highly interactive sessions where relevant stakeholders openly discuss and debate questions about the organisation's identity and how it can be 'reframed' to be more change friendly. Attention is directed at creating values and norms that focus behaviour on the organisation's environment and help members see change

as necessary and natural. To enhance member commitment to a new change-friendly identity, these new or reframed values and norms are placed in the context of important external pressures facing the organisation and what these mean for its effectiveness. The organisation's existing design is also assessed in relation to the new identity and plans are made for changing specific components using the B2C guidelines outlined above.

2 *Pursue proximity.* This step helps the organisation get closer to current and possible future environments. Starting from the organisation's identity, the intervention looks outward to gain a clearer picture of environmental demands and opportunities. Rather than try to predict what's going to happen, attention is directed at developing scenarios of possible and desired future environments. Senior executives commit significant time to thinking about the future and to creating possible paths to future success using various scenario-planning methods. They identify how the organisation's core competencies and capabilities can contribute to making desired futures happen. This is then translated into a robust strategy for what needs to be done to move the organisation and the competitive environment in the desired directions.

3 *Build an orchestration capability.* This stage helps the organisation gain the ability to implement the strategy and to execute change effectively. It first specifies the events and decisions necessary to make the strategy happen, including how new competencies will be developed, if necessary. Then, based on the B2C belief that the ability to change is the key to competitive advantage, attention is directed at building this change capability into the organisation. This involves three related activities. First, change management skills are developed widely in the organisation by hiring people with those skills and by training existing managers and employees to acquire those skills. Second, an organisation effectiveness function is created with competencies in strategic planning, organisation design and change management. This centre of excellence is usually staffed by professionals from the strategic planning and human resources functions; they provide advice and facilitation for planning and executing change in the organisation. Third, organisation members learn how to apply their change capability by engaging in organisational changes and reflecting on that experience. This so-called 'learning by doing' is essential for building an orchestration capability. It provides members with the hands-on experience and reflective learning necessary to hone their change skills in action.

4 *Establish strategic adjustment as a normal condition.* This step involves creating dynamic alignment in implementing strategy, developing new capabilities and fitting organisation design elements to emerging environmental demands. In fast-paced environments, the organisation must continually make strategic adjustments as part of normal operations. It must constantly work at changing and coordinating all of the organisation design elements so that they promote new strategies and capabilities and respond to shifting environmental demands and opportunities. Keys to making strategic adjustment a standard practice

include pushing decision making downward in the organisation, sharing relevant information widely, giving members the relevant skills and knowledge and measuring and rewarding the right things. These 'employee empowerment' practices reinforce the enormous value placed on human resources in B2C organisations; they also provide the structures, talent and systems to support continual change and adjustment.

5 *Seek virtuous spirals.* This last stage involves bringing all of the prior processes together to pursue a series of temporary competitive advantages. This so-called 'hit and run' approach rests on the logic that in turbulent environments, success results from identifying future opportunities, organising to take advantage of them and then moving on to the next opportunity when things change. Because specific sources of competitive advantage do not last long, B2C organisations continually modify their capabilities and designs to take advantage of emerging prospects. They constantly work to balance the short and long runs, to keep close to an unfolding environment, and to sustain dynamic alignment among their design elements and capabilities. When they do this for long periods of time, a virtuous spiral results. The organisation's design and capabilities support a successful strategy, which in turn provides the rewards and motivation to create even better designs and capabilities for newer strategies and so on. In rapidly changing environments, B2C organisations are more capable of seeking and creating virtuous spirals than traditional organisations.

Summary

In this chapter, we presented interventions for helping organisations change themselves continually. These change processes are particularly applicable for organisations facing turbulent environments where traditional sources of competitive advantage erode quickly. Building change capabilities directly into the organisation is essential to constantly renew forms of competitive advantage to keep pace with a rapidly shifting environment.

A self-design change strategy helps an organisation gain the capacity to design and implement its own continuous change. Self-design involves multiple levels of the organisation and multiple stakeholders and includes an iterative series of activities: acquiring knowledge, valuing, diagnosing, designing, implementing and assessing.

Organisation learning and knowledge management interventions help organisations develop and use knowledge to change and improve themselves continually. Organisation learning interventions address how organisations can be designed to promote effective learning processes and how those learning processes themselves can be improved. An organisation designed to promote learning can create a continuous stream of valuable knowledge. Knowledge management focuses on how that knowledge can be organised and used to improve organisation performance.

Built-to-change organisations are designed for change, not stability. They are based on design guidelines that promote change capability in the organisation's talent management, reward systems, structure, information and decision processes and leadership. In a rapidly changing environment, this change capability can be a source of sustained competitive advantage.

Activities

REVIEW QUESTIONS

1 How does organisation learning (OL) differ to individual learning?

2 Explain 'single-loop' and 'double-loop' learning.

3 Identify the steps for the application of knowledge management.

4 Define 'built-to-change'. Give an example of each component.

5 What is the difference between OL and knowledge management? Give an example of each.

6 What are the five requirements for adaptive change?

7 Is it easier to have a self-design strategy for a new business or an existing business? Explain your answer.

8 What is organisation knowledge? Why is it important?

9 What are the series of activities involved in a self-design change strategy?

10 What is a virtuous spiral? What are its benefits?

DISCUSSION AND ESSAY QUESTIONS

1 'When times are tough, the tough get going.' How may this quote be relevant to change management? Discuss.

2 'Self-design change strategies will facilitate optimum competitive advantage.' How may this occur? What difficulties do you envisage?

3 'Organisation learning and knowledge management are one and the same thing.' Do you agree? Why/why not?

4 Is there a conflict between the concept of a built-to-change organisation and the establishment of long-term business goals? What are the implications of pursuit of a built-to-change strategy for investors?

5 The text refers to the use of scenario planning as part of the adaptive process. What are the strengths and weaknesses of this technique given the premise of this chapter that a growing number of organisations are facing highly turbulent environments?

SEARCH ME! EXCERCISES

Explore **Search me! management** for relevant articles on organisation development and change. Search me! is an online library of world-class journals, ebooks and newspapers, including *The Australian* and *The New York Times*, and is updated daily. Log in to Search me! through **http://login.cengage.com** using the access card in the front of this book.

Keywords

Try searching for the following terms:

> Adaptive change
> Built-to-change (B2C) organisations
> Knowledge management

> Learning organisations
> Self-designing organisations

>> Search tip:

Search me! **management** contains information from both local and international sources. To get the greatest number of search results, try using both Australian and American spellings in your searches, e.g. 'globalisation' and 'globalization'; 'organisation' and 'organization'.

Notes

1 D. Teece, G. Pisano and A. Shuen, 'Dynamic capabilities and strategic management', *Strategic Management Journal*, 18 (1997): 509–33.

2 T. Lawrence, B. Dyck, S. Maitlis and M. Mauws, 'The underlying structure of continuous change', *Sloan Management Review*, 47 (2006): 59–66.

3 B. Hedberg, P. Nystrom and W. Starbuck, 'Camping on seesaws: prescriptions for a self-designing organization', *Administrative Science Quarterly*, 21 (1976): 41–65; K. Weick, 'Organization design: organizations as self-designing systems', *Organizational Dynamics*, 6 (1977): 30–46.

4 S. Mohrman and T. Cummings, *Self-Designing Organizations: Learning How to Create High Performance* (Reading, Mass.: Addison-Wesley, 1989); T. Cummings and S. Mohrman, 'Self-designing organizations: towards implementing quality-of-work-life innovations', in *Research in Organizational Change and Development*, vol. 1, eds R. Woodman and W. Pasmore (Greenwich, CT: JAI Press, 1987): 275–310.

5 E. Beinhocker, 'The adaptable organization', *The McKinsey Quarterly*, 2 (2006): 77–87.

6 P. Lawrence and D. Dyer, *Renewing American Industry* (New York: Free Press, 1983).

7 C. Argyris, R. Putnam and D. Smith, *Action Science* (San Francisco: Jossey-Bass, 1985); C. Lundberg, 'On organizational learning: implications and opportunities for expanding organizational development', in *Research on Organizational Change and Development*, vol. 3, eds R. Woodman and W. Pasmore (Greenwich, Conn.: JAI Press, 1989): 61–82; P. Senge, *The Fifth Discipline* (New York: Doubleday, 1990).

8 M. Weisbord, *Productive Workplaces* (San Francisco: Jossey-Bass, 1987); R. Freeman, *Strategic Management* (Boston: Ballinger, 1984).

9 D. Miller and P. Friesen, *Organizations: A Quantum View* (Englewood Cliffs, N.J.: Prentice-Hall, 1984).

10 D. Byman, *Strengthening the Partnership: Improving Military Coordination with Relief Agencies and Allies in Humanitarian Operations* (Santa Monica, CA: Rand, 2000).

11 G. D'Antona and A. Ferrero, *Digital Signal Processing for Measurement Systems: Theory and Applications* (New York: Springer, 2006).

12 T. Lant, 'Organization learning: creating, retaining and transferring knowledge', *Administrative Science Quarterly* (Winter, 2000): 622–43; M. Crossan, H. Lane and R. White, 'An organizational learning framework: from intuition to institution', *Academy of Management Review*, 24 (1999): 522–37; S. Prokesch, 'Unleashing the power of learning: an interview with British Petroleum's John Browne', *Harvard Business Review* (September–October 1997): 147–68; J. C. Spender, 'Making knowledge the basis of a dynamic theory of the firm', *Strategic Management Journal*, 17 (1996): 45–62; R. Strata, 'Organizational learning: the key to management innovation', *Sloan Management Review*, 30 (1989): 63–74.

13 D. Teece, 'Capturing value from knowledge assets: the new economy, market for know-how and intangible

assets', *California Management Review*, 40 (Spring 1998): 55–79.

14 G. Roth, 'The order and chaos of the learning organization', in *Handbook of Organization Development*, ed. T. Cummings (Thousand Oaks, CA: Sage Publications, 2008): 475–97.

15 D. A. Bray, 'Literature review – knowledge management research at the organizational level' (May 2007), available at SSRN: http://ssrn.com/abstract=991169.

16 C. Argyris and D. Schon, *Organizational Learning: A Theory of Action Perspective* (Reading, Mass.: Addison-Wesley, 1978); C. Argyris and D. Schon, *Organizational Learning II: Theory, Method and Practice* (Reading, Mass.: Addison-Wesley, 1996); Senge, *Fifth Discipline*, op. cit.

17 P. Adler and R. Cole, 'Designed for learning: a tale of two auto plants', *Sloan Management Review*, 34 (1993): 85–94; S. Cook and D. Yanow, 'Culture and organizational learning', *Journal of Management Inquiry*, 2 (1993): 373–90; G. Huber, 'The nontraditional quality of organizational learning', *Organization Science*, 2 (1991): 88–115.

18 W. Snyder, 'Organization learning and performance: an exploration of the linkages between organizational learning, knowledge and performance', unpublished Ph.D. diss. (University of Southern California, Los Angeles, 1996).

19 This framework draws heavily on the work of W. Snyder and T. Cummings, 'Organization learning disorders: conceptual model and intervention hypotheses', *Human Relations*, 51 (1998): 873–95.

20 The University of Queensland, *Knowledge in Organisations*, May 2007, www.business.uq.edu.au/display/research/Knowledge+in+Organisations.

21 K. Field, P. Holden and H. Lawlor, *Effective Subject Leadership* (London; New York: Routledge, 2000).

22 M. Kormanik, *Organizational Development (OD) interventions: Managing Systematic Change in Organisations*, April 2009, http://armandojusto.blogspot.com/2009/04/organizational-development-od.html.

23 D. Garvin, *Learning in Action* (Cambridge: Harvard Business School Press, 2000).

24 M. McGill, J. Slocum and D. Lei, 'Management practices in learning organizations', *Organizational Dynamics* (Autumn 1993): 5–17; E. Nevis, A. DiBella and J. Gould, 'Understanding organizations as learning systems', *Sloan Management Review* (Winter 1995): 73–85.

25 J. Dewey, *How We Think* (Boston: D.C. Heath, 1933).

26 Argyris and Schon, *Organizational Learning*, op. cit.; Argyris and Schon, *Organizational Learning II*, op. cit.; Senge, *Fifth Discipline*, op. cit.

27 N. Y. Nikolaev and H. Iba, *Adaptive Learning of Polynomial Networks: Genetic Programming, Backpropagation and Bayesian Methods* (New York: Springer, 2006).

28 D. L. Cooperrider and M. Avital, *Constructive Discourse and Human Organization* (Amsterdam; London: Elsevier JAI, 2004).

29 S. Hall, *Connectivity: Spike Hall's RU Weblog*, June 2004, http://radio-weblogs.com/0106698/2004/06/15.html.

30 Argyris and Schon, *Organizational Learning II*, op. cit.; Senge, *Fifth Discipline*, op. cit.; P. Senge, C. Roberts, R. Ross, B. Smith and A. Kleiner, *The Fifth Discipline Fieldbook: Strategies for Building a Learning Organization* (New York: Doubleday, 1995).

31 Argyris and Schon, *Organizational Learning II*, op. cit.

32 ibid.

33 Argyris and Schon, *Organizational Learning II*, op. cit.; C. Argyris, *Intervention Theory and Method* (Reading, Mass.: Addison-Wesley, 1970).

34 Senge, *Fifth Discipline*, op. cit.

35 Argyris and Schon, *Organizational Learning II*, op. cit.

36 Argyris and Schon, ibid.; Senge et al., *Fifth Discipline Fieldbook*, op. cit.; B. Dumaine, 'Mr. learning organization', *Fortune* (17 October 1994): 147–57.

37 Senge et al., *Fifth Discipline Fieldbook*, op. cit.

38 Argyris and Schon, *Organizational Learning II*, op. cit.; Argyris, *Intervention Theory and Method*, op. cit.

39 Senge, *Fifth Discipline*, op. cit.

40 ibid.

41 M. Polanyi, *The Tacit Dimension* (New York: Doubleday, 1966); I. Nonaka and H. Takeuchi, *The Knowledge-Creating Company: How Japanese Companies Foster Creativity and Innovation for Competitive Advantage* (New York: Oxford University Press, 1995).

42 M. Sarvary, 'Knowledge management and competition in the consulting industry', *California Management Review*, 41 (1999): 95–107; J. Barney, 'Looking inside for competitive advantage', *Academy of Management Executive*, 9:4 (1995): 49–61; M. Peteraf, 'The cornerstones of competitive advantage', *Strategic Management Journal*, 14:3 (1993): 179–92.

43 Snyder, 'Organization learning', op. cit.

44 D. Leonard-Barton, *Wellsprings of Knowledge: Building and Sustaining the Sources of Innovation* (Boston: Harvard Business School Press, 1995); Nonaka and Takeuchi, *The Knowledge–Creating Company*, op. cit.

45 C. Prahalad and G. Hamel, 'The core competencies of the corporation', *Harvard Business Review*, 68 (1990): 79–91.

46 H. Itami, *Mobilizing for Invisible Assets* (Cambridge, Mass.: Harvard University Press, 1987).

47 L. Edvinsson and M. Malone, *Intellectual Capital: Realizing Your Company's True Value by Finding Its Hidden Brainpower* (New York: Harper Business, 1997); T. Stewart, *Intellectual Capital: The New Wealth of Organizations* (New York: Doubleday, 1997); J. Nahapiet and S. Ghoshal, 'Social capital, intellectual capital and the organizational advantage', *Academy of Management Review*, 23 (1998): 242–66.

48 S. Mohrman, S. Cohen and A. Mohrman, 'An empirical model of the organization knowledge system in new product development firms', *Journal of Engineering and Technology Management*, 20 (2003): 7–38; S. Mohrman, 'Designing organizations to lead with knowledge', in *Handbook of Organization Development*, ed. T. Cummings (Thousand Oaks, CA: Sage Publications, 2008): 519–37.

49 Edvinsson and Malone, *Intellectual Capital*, op. cit.; Stewart, *Intellectual Capital*, op. cit.; R. Kaplan and D. Norton, *The Balanced Scorecard* (Boston: Harvard Business School Press, 1996); K. Svieby, *The New Organizational Wealth: Managing and Measuring Knowledge-Based Assets* (San Francisco: Berrett-Koehler, 1977).

50 Edvinsson and Malone, *Intellectual Capital*, op. cit.; C. Handy, *The Age of Unreason* (Boston: Harvard Business School Press, 1991).

51 T. Stewart, 'Intellectual capital', *Fortune* (3 October 1994): 68–74.

52 V. Anand, C. Manz and W. Glick, 'An organizational memory approach to information management', *Academy of Management Review*, 23 (1998): 796–809.

53 E. Wenger, *Communities of Practice: Learning, Meaning and Identity* (Cambridge, Eng.: Cambridge University Press, 1999); J. Brown and P. Duguid, 'Organizational learning and communities of practice: towards a unified view of working, learning and innovation', *Organization Science*, 2 (1991): 40–57.

54 Leonard-Barton, *Wellsprings of Knowledge*, op. cit.; D. Leonard-Barton and S. Sensiper, 'The role of tacit knowledge in group innovation', *California Management Review*, 40 (Spring 1998): 112–32.

55 M. Hansen, N. Nohria and T. Tierney, 'What's your strategy for managing knowledge?' *Harvard Business Review* (March–April 1999): 106–16.

56 M. H. Boisot, I. C. MacMillan and K. Seok Han, *Explorations in Information Space: Knowledge, Agents and Organization* (Oxford: Oxford University Press, 2007).

57 D. Stroud, *The 50-plus Market: Why the Future is Age-neutral When it Comes to Marketing and Branding* (Sterling, VA: Kogan Page, 2005).

58 T. Davenport and L. Prusak, *Working Knowledge: How Organizations Manage What They Know* (Boston: Harvard Business School Press, 1998).

59 C. O'Dell and C. Grayson, *If Only We Knew What We Know* (New York: Free Press, 1998).

60 D. Garvin and A. March, *A Note on Knowledge Management* (Boston: Harvard Business School Publishing, 1997).

61 O'Dell and Grayson, *If Only We Knew*, op. cit.

62 ibid.

63 A. B. Shani and P. Docherty, *Learning by Design: Building Sustainable Organizations* (London: Blackwell, 2003); A.

B. Shani and P. Docherty, 'Learning by design: key mechanisms in organization development', in *Handbook of Organization Development*, ed. T. Cummings (Thousand Oaks, CA: Sage Publications, 2008): 499–518.

64 O'Dell and Grayson, *If Only We Knew*, op. cit.

65 S. Hauschild, T. Licht and W. Stein, 'Creating a knowledge culture', *The McKinsey Quarterly*, 1 (2001): 74–81.

66 B. Choi, S. Poon and J. Davis, 'Effects of knowledge management strategy on organizational performance: a complementarity theory-based approach', *Omega*, 36 (2008): 235–51.

67 E. Boyle, 'A critical appraisal of the performance of Royal Dutch Shell as a learning organization in the 1990's', *The Learning Organization*, 9 (2002): 6–18.

68 Argyris and Schon, *Organizational Learning II*, op. cit.: 112.

69 Y. Paik and D. Choi, 'The shortcomings of a standardized global knowledge management system: the case study of Accenture', *Academy of Management Executive*, 19 (2005): 81–84.

70 R. Ruggles, 'The state of the notion: knowledge management in practice', *California Management Review*, 40 (Spring 1998): 80–9.

71 Davenport and Prusak, *Working Knowledge*, op. cit.

72 E. Lawler and C. Worley, *Built to Change: How to Achieve Sustained Organizational Effectiveness* (San Francisco: Jossey-Bass, 2006); C. Worley and E. Lawler, 'Designing organizations that are built to change', *Sloan Management Review*, 48 (2006): 19–23.

CHAPTER 7

OD interventions: People and process

This chapter discusses change programs relating to organisation development interventions: people and process. These change programs are among the earliest in OD and represent attempts to improve people's working relationships with one another. The interventions are aimed at helping group members to assess their interactions and to devise more effective ways of working together. These interventions represent a basic skill requirement for an OD practitioner. In this chapter, we initially discuss human resource management interventions that are concerned with the management of individual and group performance: goal setting, performance appraisal and reward systems. Later in the chapter we look at human process interventions, aimed at interpersonal relations and group dynamics.

INDIVIDUAL AND GROUP PERFORMANCE

Performance management involves goal setting, performance appraisal and reward systems that align member work behaviour with business strategy, employee involvement and workplace technology.

- *Goal setting.* Describes the interaction between managers and employees in jointly defining member work behaviours and outcomes. Orienting employees to the appropriate kinds of work outcomes can reinforce the work designs and support the organisation's strategic objectives. Goal setting can clarify the duties and responsibilities associated with a particular job or work group. When applied to jobs, goal setting can focus on individual goals and reinforce individual contributions and work outcomes. When applied to work groups, goal setting can be directed at group objectives and reinforce members' joint actions, as well as overall group outcomes. One popular approach to goal setting is called 'management by objectives'.

- *Performance appraisal.* Involves collecting and disseminating performance data to improve work outcomes. It is the primary human resource management intervention for providing performance feedback to individuals and work groups. Performance appraisal is a systematic process of jointly assessing work-related achievements, strengths and weaknesses, but it can also facilitate career development counselling, provide information about the strength and diversity of human resources in the company, and link employee performance with rewards.

- *Reward systems.* Are concerned with eliciting and reinforcing desired behaviours and work outcomes. They can support goal-setting and feedback systems by rewarding the kinds of behaviours required, implementing a particular work design or supporting a business strategy. Like goal setting, rewards systems can be oriented to individual jobs and goals or to group functions and objectives. Moreover, they can be geared to traditional work designs that require external forms of control or to enriched, self-regulating work designs requiring employee self-control. Several innovative and effective reward systems are in use in organisations today.

The personnel or human resource departments of organisations traditionally implement performance management interventions, and personnel practitioners have special training in these areas. Because of the diversity and depth of knowledge required to successfully carry out these kinds of change programs, practitioners tend to specialise in one part of the personnel function, such as performance appraisal or compensation.

A model of performance management

Performance management is an integrated process of defining, assessing and reinforcing employee work behaviours and outcomes.[1] Organisations with a well-developed performance management process tend to outperform organisations that don't have this element of organisation design.[2] As shown in Figure 7.1, performance management includes practices and methods for goal setting, performance appraisal and reward systems, all of which work together to influence the performance of individuals and work groups.

Goal setting specifies the kinds of performances that are desired; performance appraisal assesses those outcomes; and reward systems provide the reinforcers that ensure that desired outcomes are repeated. Because performance management occurs in a larger organisational context, at least three contextual factors determine how these practices affect work performance: business strategy, workplace technology and employee involvement.[3] High levels of work performance tend to occur when goal setting, performance appraisal and reward systems are jointly aligned with these organisational factors.

- *Business strategy.* This defines the goals and objectives that are needed if an organisation is to compete successfully. Performance management needs to focus, assess and reinforce member work behaviours towards those objectives, thus ensuring that work behaviours are strategically driven.
- *Workplace technology.* This affects the decision as to whether performance management practices[4] should be based on the individual or the group. When technology is low in interdependence and work is designed for individual jobs, goal setting, performance appraisal and reward systems should be aimed at individual work behaviours. Conversely, when technology is highly interdependent and work is designed for groups, performance management should be aimed at group behaviours.[5]

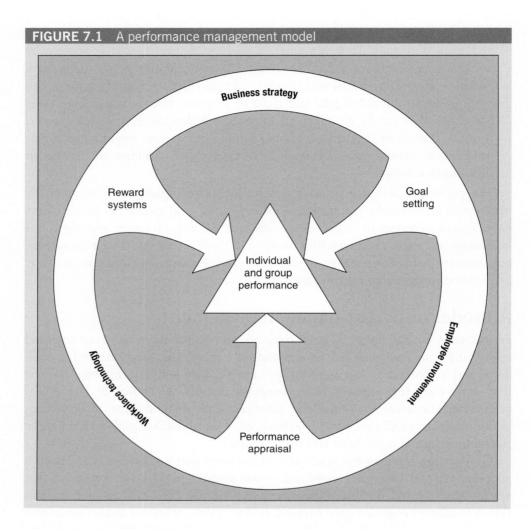

FIGURE 7.1   A performance management model

- *Employee involvement.* Finally, the level of employee involvement in an organisation should determine the nature of performance management practices. When organisations are highly bureaucratic with low levels of participation, goal setting, performance appraisal and reward systems should be formalised and administered by management and staff personnel. In high-involvement situations; on the other hand, performance management should be heavily participative, with both management and employees setting goals and appraising and rewarding performance. In high-involvement plants, for example, employees tend to participate in all stages of performance management. They are heavily involved in both designing and administering performance management practices.

Goal setting

Goal setting involves managers and subordinates in jointly establishing and clarifying employee goals. In some cases, such as management by objectives, it can also facilitate employee counselling and support. The process of establishing challenging goals involves management in the level of participation and goal difficulty. Once goals have been established, how they are measured is an important determinant of member performance.[6] Goal setting can affect performance in at least three ways: it influences what people think and do as it focuses behaviour in the direction of the goals, rather than elsewhere; goals energise behaviour, motivating people to make an effort to reach difficult goals that are accepted; and, finally, goal setting leads to persistence in effort over time when goals are difficult but achievable.

Characteristics of goal setting

An impressive amount of research underlies goal-setting interventions and practices.[7] This research has resulted in identification of two major processes affecting positive outcomes:

1 Establishment of challenging goals
2 Clarification of goal measurement.

Goal setting appears to work equally well in both individual and group settings.[8]

Establishing challenging goals

The first element of goal setting concerns the establishment of goals perceived as challenging, but which are realistic and for which there will be a high level of commitment. This can be accomplished by varying goal difficulty and the level of employee participation in the goal-setting process. Increasing the difficulty of employee goals, 'stretch goals', can increase their perceived challenge and enhance the amount of effort necessary for their achievement.[9] Thus, more difficult goals tend to lead to increased effort and performance, as long as they can be seen to be feasible. Set too high, however, goals may lose motivational potential, and employees will give up when failing to achieve them. Another aspect of establishing challenging goals is to vary the amount of participation in the goal-setting process. Having employees participate can increase motivation and performance, but only to the extent that members set higher goals than those typically assigned to them.

All three contextual factors play an important role in the establishment of challenging goals. First, there must be a clear 'line of sight' between the business strategy goals and the goals established for individuals or groups. Second, employee participation in goal setting is more likely to be effective if employee involvement policies in the organisation support it. Third, when tasks are highly interdependent and work is designed for groups, group-oriented participative goal setting tends to increase commitment.[10]

Clarifying goal measurement

The second element in the goal-setting process involves specification and clarification of the goals. Given specific goals, employees tend to perform higher than when simply told to 'do their best', or when receiving no guidance at all. Specific goals reduce ambiguity about expectations, and focus the search for appropriate behaviours.

To clarify goal measurement, objectives should be operationally defined. For example, employees may agree to increase productivity by 5%, a challenging and specific goal. Clarifying goal measurement also requires that employees and supervisors negotiate the resources necessary for their achievement. These may include time, equipment, raw materials or access to information.

Contextual factors also play an important role in the clarifying process. Goal specification and clarity can be difficult in high-technology settings. The work is often uncertain and highly interdependent. Increasing employee participation in the clarification of goal measurement can give employees ownership of a non-specific but challenging goal. Finally, the process of specifying and clarifying goals is extremely difficult if the business strategy is unclear. Under these conditions, attempting to gain consensus on the measurement and importance of goals can cause frustration and resistance to change.

Application steps

Based on these features of the goal-setting process, OD practitioners have developed specific approaches to goal setting. The following steps characterise those applications:

1 *Diagnosis.* Provides information about the nature and difficulty of specific goals, the appropriate types and levels of participation and the necessary support systems.

2 *Preparing for goal setting.* Typically involves increased interaction and communication between managers and employees, as well as formal training in goal–setting methods.

3 *Setting goals.* Here, challenging goals are established and goal measurement clarified. Employees participate in the process to the extent that contextual factors support such involvement, and because employees are likely to set higher goals than those assigned by management.

4 *Review.* Goal attributes are evaluated to see whether they are energising and challenging, and whether they support the business strategy and can be influenced by the employees.

Management by objectives

A common goal setting form used in organisations is management by objectives (MBO). This method mainly attempts to align personal goals with business strategy by increasing communications and shared perceptions between manager and subordinates, either individually or as a group, or by reconciling conflict.

All organisations have goals and objectives. Often, however, goals are unclearly stated, and managers and subordinates have different perceptions as to what those objectives are. MBO seeks to resolve these differences in perceptions and goals. Management by objectives can be defined as systematic and periodic manager–subordinate meetings designed to accomplish organisational goals by mutual work planning, periodic reviewing of accomplishments and mutual solving of problems arising in the course of getting the job done.

MBO originated in two different backgrounds: organisational and developmental. The organisational root of MBO was developed by Drucker, who emphasised the need to establish objectives in eight key areas: 'market standing; innovation; productivity; physical and financial resources; profitability; manager performance and development; worker performance and attitude; and public responsibility'.[11] Drucker's work was expanded by Odiorne, whose first book on MBO stressed the need for quantitative measurement.[12]

According to Levinson,[13] MBO's second root lies in the work of McGregor, who stressed its qualitative nature, and use for development and growth on the job.[14] McGregor attempted to shift the emphasis from identifying weaknesses to analysing performance in order to define strengths and potentials. He believed this shift could be accomplished by having subordinates reach agreement with their boss on major job responsibilities. Afterwards, they could develop short-term performance goals and action plans for their achievement, allowing self-appraisal of their own performance. Subordinates would then discuss the results of this self-appraisal with their supervisors, thus developing a new set of performance goals and plans. This emphasis on mutual understanding and performance, rather than on personality, would change the supervisor's role from judge to helper, reducing both role conflict and ambiguity. This second MBO root reduces role ambiguity by making goal setting more participative and transactional,[15] as it increases communication between role incumbents and ensures individual and organisational goals are identified and achieved.

An MBO program often goes beyond the one-on-one, manager–subordinate relationship to focus on problem-solving discussions also involving work teams. Setting goals and reviewing individual performance are considered within the larger context of the job. In addition to organisational goals, the MBO process gives attention to individuals' personal and career goals, and tries to make these and organisational goals more complementary. The target-setting procedure allows real (rather than simulated) subordinate participation in goal setting, with open, problem-centred discussions among team members, supervisors and subordinates.

Effects of goal setting

Goal setting appears to produce positive results over a wide range of jobs and organisations. Tested on keypunch operators, logging crews, clerical workers, engineers and truck drivers, it has produced performance improvements of between 11% and 27%.[16] Moreover, four meta-analyses of the extensive empirical evidence supporting goal setting conclude that the proposed effects of goal difficulty, goal specificity and participation in goal setting are generally substantiated across studies and with both groups and individuals.[17] Longitudinal analyses support the conclusion that the profits in performance are not short–lived.[18] A more recent field study, however, failed to replicate the typical positive linear relationship between goal difficulty and performance, raising concern about the generalisability of the method from the laboratory to practice.[19] Additional research has tried to identify potential factors that might moderate the results of goal setting, including task uncertainty, amount and quality of planning, need for achievement, education, past goal successes and supervisory style.[20] Some support for the moderators has been found. For example, when the technical context is uncertain, goals tend to be less specific and people need to engage in more search behaviour to establish meaningful goals.

Performance appraisal

Performance appraisal is a feedback system involving direct evaluation[21] of individual or work group performance by a supervisor, manager or peers. Most organisations use some kind of evaluation system for performance feedback, pay administration and, in some cases, counselling and developing employees.[22] Thus, performance appraisal represents an important link between goal-setting processes and reward systems. One survey of more than 500 companies found 90% used performance appraisal to determine merit pay increases, 87% to review performance and 79% as the opportunity to set goals for the next period.[23]

Abundant evidence, however, indicates that organisations do a poor job in appraising employees.[24] One study found that 32% of managers surveyed rated their performance appraisal process as very ineffective.[25] Application 7.1 provides evidence of outcomes as a result of an appraisal system appropriate for the organisation.

The government of New Zealand issued the following news release:

Wellington City Council's Performance Review Committee has completed its annual review of the performance of Council Chief Executive Garry Poole.

Mr Poole is in his 12th year with the Council and Mayor Kerry Prendergast says he has had another excellent year. 'But he won't be receiving a pay rise this year – at his own request.

'Mr Poole advised us some months ago that he and the Council's leadership team had voluntarily opted not to receive any remuneration increases or bonuses this year as part of Council-wide cost saving measures in response to the recession.

'Such leadership is both admirable and typical of Mr Poole, whose performance this year has again been excellent. The past year has been a difficult one for us as we faced the challenges of the recession head-on.

'Mr Poole and his team had identified two years ago the likelihood of affordability issues and their forward and lateral thinking has helped to mitigate the impact on the organisation and city.'

Ms Prendergast says another highlight of the past year has been the strong focus on engaging with ratepayers and residents in different ways and its obvious success. 'We have just completed our Long-Term Council Community Plan, setting out our priorities and spending for the next 10 years, which is never an easy task.

'Not only did Mr Poole and his team do a splendid job pulling that together, the new pre-engagement tools we employed resulted in 38% of our submissions being from first-time submitters – meaning we successfully reached new people and encouraged them to have their say.'

Mr Poole's remuneration is reviewed annually. It will remain at $387 256 per annum until the next review in July 2010.

Source: Wellington City Council, Wellington, New Zealand, 3 July 2010, www.wellington.govt.nz/news/display-item.php?id=3558.

Critical thinking questions:

1. The Mayor stated: 'Mr Poole advised us some time ago that he and the Council's leadership team had voluntarily opted not to receive any remuneration increases or bonuses this year as part of Council-wide saving measures in response to the recession.' Discuss this statement and think about why the Council's CEO and its leadership would not want to receive their bonuses. Ask yourself: would you do the same?

2. Do you think this type of decision will catch on in the corporate environment? In your answer think about the environmental influences that might have occurred in the Council's management structure and influenced the CEO's thinking.

3. 'Employees are likely to set higher goals than those assigned by management.' If the remuneration freeze applied to all Council staff and not only to senior management, and the Council's targets were met across the board, what impact do you think the freeze might have on employees' willingness to set 'higher goals than those assigned by management' in the future? Why?

As a consequence of problems associated with performance appraisal, increasingly organisations have sought ways of improving the process. Some innovations have enhanced employee involvement, balancing organisational and employee needs, and enlarging the number of raters (supervisors).[26] These newer approaches are being used in organisations such as Levi-Strauss, Intel and Monsanto.

The performance appraisal process

Table 7.1 summarises several common elements of performance appraisal systems.[27] For each element, two contrasting features – representing traditional bureaucratic approaches and newer, high-involvement approaches – are presented. Performance appraisals are conducted for several purposes, including affirmative action, pay and promotion decisions, as well as human resource planning and development.[28] Because each purpose defines what performances are relevant and how they should be measured, separate appraisal systems are often used. For example, appraisal methods for pay purposes are often different from systems

TABLE 7.1	Performance appraisal elements	
Elements	**Traditional approaches**	**Newer approaches**
Purpose	Organisational, legal Fragmented	Developmental Integrative
Appraiser	Supervisor, managers	Appraised, co-workers and others
Role of appraised	Passive recipient	Active participant
Measurement	Subjective Concerned with validity	Objective and subjective
Timing	Periodic, fixed and administratively driven	Dynamic, timely and employee- or work-driven

assessing employee development or promotability. Employees also have several reasons for wanting appraisal, such as receiving feedback for career decisions, getting a raise and being promoted. Rather than expecting a few standard appraisal systems to meet these multiple purposes, the new approaches are more tailored to balance the multiple organisational and employee needs. This is accomplished by actively involving the appraised, their co-workers and managers in assessing the purposes of the appraisal when it takes place, and adjusting the process to fit that purpose. Thus, at one time the appraisal process might focus on pay decisions, another time on employee development and still another on employee promotability. Actively involving all relevant participants can increase the chances that the appraisal's purpose will be correctly identified and understood, and appropriate appraisal methods applied.

The new methods tend to expand the appraiser role beyond managers to include multiple raters, such as the appraised, co-workers and others having direct exposure to the employee's performance. Also known as 360-degree feedback, it is used more for member development than compensation purposes.[29] This wider involvement provides a number of different views of the appraisee's performance. It can lead to a more comprehensive assessment of the employee's performance and increase the likelihood that both organisational and personal needs will be considered. The key task is to find an overall view of the employee's performance that incorporates all the different appraisals. Thus, the process of working out differences and arriving at an overall assessment is an important aspect of the appraisal process. This improves the appraisal's acceptance, accuracy of information and focus on activities critical to the business strategy.

The newer methods also expand the appraisee's role. Traditionally, the employee is simply a receiver of feedback. The supervisor unilaterally completes a form about performance on predetermined dimensions – usually personality traits, such as initiative or concern for quality. The newer approaches actively involve the appraisee in all phases of the appraisal process. The appraisee joins with superiors and staff personnel in gathering data on performance, and identifying training needs. This active involvement increases the likelihood that performance appraisal will include the employee's views, needs and criteria, along with those of the organisation. This newer role increases employees' acceptance and understanding of the feedback process.

Performance measurement is typically the source of many problems in appraisal as it is seen as subjective. Traditionally, performance evaluation focuses on the consistent use of pre-specified traits or behaviours. To improve consistency and validity of measurement, considerable training is used to help raters make valid assessments. This concern for validity stems largely from legal tests of performance appraisal systems and leads organisations to develop measurement approaches, such as the behaviourally anchored rating scale (BARS) and its variants. In newer approaches, validity is not only a legal or methodological issue but also a social issue, and all appropriate participants are involved in negotiating acceptable ways of measuring and assessing performance. Increased participation in goal setting is a part of this new approach. Rather than simply training the supervisor, all participants are trained in methods of measuring and assessing performance. By focusing on both objective and subjective measures of performance, the appraisal process is better understood, accepted and accurate.

The timing of performance appraisals is traditionally fixed by managers or staff personnel and is based on administrative criteria, such as annual pay decisions. Newer approaches now being used increase the frequency of feedback. Although it may not be practical to boost the number of formal appraisals, the frequency of informal feedback can increase, especially when strategic objectives change or when technology is highly uncertain. In these situations, frequent performance feedback is often necessary to ensure appropriate adaptations in work behaviour. The newer approaches increase the timeliness of feedback and allow employees to have more control over their work.

Effects of performance appraisal

Research strongly supports the role of feedback on performance. One study concluded that objective feedback as a means for improving individual and group performance has been 'impressively effective'[30] and has been supported by a large number of literature reviews over the years.[31] Another researcher concluded that 'objective feedback does not usually work, it virtually always works'.[32] In field studies where performance feedback contained behaviour-specific information, median performance improvements were more than 47%, and when the feedback concerned less specific information, median performance improvements were over 33%. In a meta-analysis of performance appraisal interventions, feedback was found to have a consistently positive effect across studies.[33] In addition, although most appraisal research has focused on the relationship between performance and individuals, several studies have demonstrated a positive relationship between group performance and feedback.[34]

Reward systems

Organisational rewards are powerful incentives for improving employee and work group performance. OD has traditionally relied on intrinsic rewards, such as enriched jobs and opportunities for decision making, to motivate employee performance. Early quality-of-work-life interventions were mainly based on the intrinsic satisfaction to be derived from performing challenging, meaningful types of work. Also, OD practitioners have expanded their focus to include extrinsic rewards, such as pay, along with various incentives, such as stock options, bonuses and profit sharing, promotions and benefits. They have discovered that both intrinsic and extrinsic rewards can enhance performance and satisfaction.[35]

OD practitioners are increasingly attending to the design and implementation of reward systems. This recent attention to rewards has derived in part from research into organisation design and employee involvement. These perspectives treat rewards as an integral part of organisations. They hold that rewards should be congruent with other organisational systems and practices, such as the organisation structure, top-management's human-relations philosophy and work designs. Many features of reward systems contribute to both employee fulfilment and organisational effectiveness.

How rewards affect performance

Considerable research has been done on how rewards affect individual and group performance. The most popular model to describe this relationship is the value expectancy theory. In addition to explaining how performance and rewards are related, it suggests requirements for designing and evaluating reward systems.

The value expectancy model[36] posits that employees will expend effort to achieve performance goals that they believe will lead to outcomes that they value. This effort will result in the desired performance goals as long as the goals are realistic, the employees fully understand what is expected of them, and that they have the necessary skills and resources. Ongoing motivation depends on the extent to which attaining the desired performance goals actually results in valued outcomes. Consequently, key objectives of reward-systems interventions are to identify the intrinsic and extrinsic[37] outcomes (rewards) that are highly valued and to link them to the achievement of desired performance goals.

Based on value expectancy theory, the ability of rewards to motivate desired behaviour depends on six factors:

1 *Availability.* For rewards to reinforce desired performance, they must be not only desired but also available. Too little of a desired reward is no reward at all.
2 *Timeliness.* A reward's motivating potential is reduced to the extent that it is separated in time from the performance that it is intended to reinforce.
3 *Performance contingency.* Rewards should be closely linked with particular performances. If the employees succeed in meeting the goal, the reward must be given; if the target is missed, the reward must be reduced or not given. The

clearer the linkage between performance and rewards, the better rewards are able to motivate desired behaviour.

4 *Durability.* Some rewards last longer than others. Intrinsic rewards, such as increased autonomy and pride in workmanship, tend to last longer than extrinsic rewards.

5 *Equity.* Satisfaction and motivation can be improved when employees believe that the pay policies of the organisation are equitable or fair. Internal equity concerns a comparison of personal rewards to those holding similar jobs or performing similarly in the organisation. External equity concerns a comparison of rewards with those of other organisations in the same labour market.

6 *Visibility.* Organisation members must be able to see who is getting the rewards. Visible rewards – such as placement on a high-status project, promotion to a new job or increased authority – send signals to employees that rewards are available, timely and performance-contingent.

Reward-systems interventions are used to elicit and maintain desired levels of performance. To the extent that rewards are available, durable, equitable, timely, visible and performance-contingent, they can support and reinforce organisational goals, work designs and employee involvement.

Reward-system process issues

Process refers to how rewards are typically administered in the organisation. At least two process issues affect employees' perceptions of the reward system:

- who should be involved in designing and administering the reward system
- what kind of communication should exist with respect to rewards.[38]

Traditionally, reward systems are designed by top managers and compensation specialists and then simply imposed on employees. Although this top-down process may result in a good system, it cannot ensure that employees will understand and trust it. In the absence of trust, workers are likely to have negative perceptions of the reward system. There is growing evidence that employee participation in the design and administration of a reward system can increase employee understanding and can contribute to feelings of control over, and commitment to, the plan.

Lawler and Jenkins described a small manufacturing plant where a committee of workers and managers designed a pay system.[39] The committee studied alternative plans and collected salary survey data. This resulted in a plan that gave control over salaries to members of work groups. Team members behaved responsibly in setting wage rates. They gave themselves 8% raises, which fell at the fiftieth percentile in the local labour market. Moreover, the results of a survey administered six months after the start of the new pay plan showed significant improvements in turnover, job satisfaction and satisfaction with pay and its administration. Lawler attributed these improvements to employees having greater information about the pay system. Participation led to employee ownership of the plan and feelings that it was fair and trustworthy.

Communication about reward systems can also have a powerful impact on employee perceptions of pay equity and on motivation. Most organisations maintain secrecy about pay rates, especially in the managerial ranks. Managers typically argue that employees prefer secrecy. It also gives managers freedom in administering pay as they do not have to defend their judgements. There is evidence to suggest, however, that pay secrecy can lead to dissatisfaction with pay and to reduced motivation. Dissatisfaction derives mainly from people's misperceptions about their pay relative to the pay of others. Research shows that managers tend to overestimate the pay of peers and of people below them in the organisation, and that they tend to underestimate the pay of superiors. These misperceptions contribute to dissatisfaction with pay because, regardless of the pay level of a manager, it will seem small in comparison to the perceived pay level of subordinates and peers. Perhaps worse, potential promotions will appear less valuable than they actually are.

Secrecy can reduce motivation by obscuring the relationship between pay and performance. For organisations that have a performance-based pay plan, secrecy prevents employees from testing whether the organisation is actually paying for performance, so employees come to mistrust the pay system, fearing that the company has something to hide. Secrecy can also reduce the beneficial impact of accurate performance feedback. Pay provides people with feedback about how they are performing in relation to some standard. Because managers tend to overestimate the pay of peers and subordinates, they will consider their own pay low and thus perceive performance feedback more negatively than it really is. Such misperceptions about performance discourage those managers who are actually performing effectively.

It is important to emphasise that both the amount of participation in designing reward systems and the amount of frankness in communicating about rewards should fit the rest of the organisation design and managerial philosophy. Clearly, high levels of participation and openness are congruent with democratic organisations. It is questionable whether authoritarian organisations would tolerate either one. Application 7.2 reports on the impact of women in senior positions and the consequences that need to be considered.

7.2

APPLICATION

FT top 50 women in world business

This inaugural ranking comes as the global crisis has turned a spotlight on male domination of the corporate world: would we be better off if more women were in charge? Helen Alexander, first female president of the CBI [Confederation of British Industry], the UK employers' body, says diversity is needed to prevent 'groupthink' by white male boards. And 17 leading businessmen, including the chairmen of Anglo American, BP and Tesco, recently called for faster progress in appointing women to senior positions.

Our report celebrates women business leaders around the world. Their numbers remain tiny; just 3 per cent of Fortune 500 chief executives are women. Across Europe, only 10 per cent of board directors of the biggest companies are female (quotas make Norway the exception, with more than 40 per cent); the numbers are even lower in Asia. This is all the

>>

more surprising given the substantial evidence that a better gender balance has a positive impact on performance. Studies by Catalyst and McKinsey in the US and Europe have found a correlation between the number of women in a company's leadership and the company's profitability.

What about better governance? The collapse of some of the world's biggest banks has been blamed partly on directors' failure to ask tough questions. A study by The Conference Board of Canada found that boards with women directors paid greater attention than all-male boards to audit and risk controls, while a US study showed that boards with more women directors were more assiduous at monitoring areas such as chief executive performance.

And some do preside over deep cultural change. Take Xerox, where women make up one-third of the management team and where Anne Mulcahy recently handed over to Ursula Burns, the first black woman to lead a Fortune 500 company. But a small group of women chief executives – or women on boards – cannot carry all the weight. Change requires willing leadership from the male majority. The financial crisis has, at least, made the business and moral case for change more apparent than ever.

Source: 'FT Top 50 Women in World Business', *Financial Times*, September 25, 2009.

Critical thinking questions:
1. Why do you think that in the twenty-first century articles such as this one are still written? Think about how women are perceived in the modern-day corporate environment.
2. If women had been the majority instead of the minority in the corporate and financial world, do you think the recent global financial crisis would have occurred?
3. 'Studies by Catalyst and McKinsey in the US and Europe have found a correlation between the number of women in a company's leadership and the company's profitability.' What might be the reasons for this correlation? How can companies take best advantage of those skills?
4. In your own experience, what differences, if any, have you found in the approach to managing by a female compared to a male manager?

INTERPERSONAL PROCESS APPROACH

There are many OD interventions that are aimed at enhancing the development and empowerment of individuals within organisations. T-groups and team building are the techniques most often used to improve employees' communication ability, performance and interpersonal skills in an organisational context, although process consultation and third-party intervention can be used under particular circumstances.

- *T-groups*, derived from the early laboratory training stem of OD, are used mainly today to help managers learn about the effects of their behaviour on others.
- *Process consultation* is another OD technique for helping group members to understand, diagnose and improve their behaviour. Through process consultation, the group should become better able to use its own resources to identify and solve interpersonal problems which often block the solving of work-related problems.

- *Third-party intervention* focuses directly on dysfunctional interpersonal conflict. This approach is used only in special circumstances and only when both parties are willing to engage in the process of direct confrontation.
- *Team building* is aimed both at helping a team to perform its tasks better and at satisfying individual needs. Through team-building activities, group goals and norms become clearer. In addition, team members become better able to confront difficulties and problems and to understand the roles of individuals within the team. Among the specialised team-building approaches presented are interventions associated with ongoing teams as well as temporary teams, such as project teams and task forces.

Application 7.3 provides an example of the steps required to make an informed decision regarding the appropriateness of training.

7.3

APPLICATION

Developing an action plan for self-development

My company encourages professional development. How do I decide what training would be the best use of my time and support my career goals?

The advice

Self-development is key to getting ahead in your current organization, as well as increasing your employability if you decide to look elsewhere. Here are some things to think about:

Not just formal training

Successful development involves learning in a variety of ways. Princeton University bases its approach to learning and development on the 70/20/10 formula – 70 per cent of how people learn to be good at what they do occurs on the job, 20 per cent through feedback and role models, and 10 per cent through formal training. Use different approaches in your development plan, including online learning, lunch-and-learn sessions, networking, mentoring programs and workshops. Consider becoming a mentor yourself, as teaching others can often enhance our own knowledge. Taking the time to reflect on what you have done well and how you could improve next time is key to real learning.

Know your strengths

Many of us tend to obsess over 'areas for improvement'. You are much more likely to get a bang for your buck if you build on what you are good at. Of course, you will need to be competent in areas that may not be what you are best suited for. But as a rule, you should focus your development on talents you already have and that represent the best opportunities for growth.

Be selective

Trying to focus on improving too many things at the same time can be confusing and interfere with your ability to do your job well. Identify one or two areas to address, set goals for yourself, and monitor your progress. With success, you can then move on to new areas.

Know your career goals

The best investment of your time will occur if you are clear about your career goals; in other words, what you are developing for. Use any career planning tools your organization provides, as well as self-help books, such as *What Color is Your Parachute?* by Richard Bolles or *What Next? Find the Work That's Right for You* by Barbara Moses, to help clarify your thinking. Use your boss for feedback on your goals and to gain support for your development activities.

Mine the resources
Check what training is available through human resources or online. Some organizations provide learning maps that outline training required for different roles. Welcome coaching from your boss or your peers as you establish and work through your development plan. Seek out opportunities to be involved in special projects or high-profile assignments that will leverage your strengths and create opportunities to get better. Often, companies will subsidize continuing formal education through tuition assistance policies, if that is right for you.

Shine in your current job
The best way to get ahead in your career is to perform well in your job. Organizations are more likely to invest in your development if you consistently get results and demonstrate commitment.

Source: J. Hutcheson, 'Developing an action plan for self-development', *The Globe Mail*, 27 February 2008, p. 2.

Critical thinking questions:
1. Do you think 'self-development is the key to getting ahead in your career'? In your answer, think about your own job (if applicable) – have you thought about self-development? If you don't have, or have never had, a job would you use a career self-development program?
2. As a university student, do you think there are areas of self-development that a student could undertake? Think about areas that you can improve.
3. Have you set yourself an action plan to achieve your career goals? How often do you review that plan and your goals in the light of changing personal and environmental circumstances?
4. Not all companies provide internal training schemes. Apart from university, what other training possibilities suited to you have you observed? How might you measure their appropriateness?

T-groups
As discussed in Chapter 1, sensitivity training, or the T-group, is an early forerunner of modern OD interventions. Its direct use in OD has lessened considerably, but OD practitioners often attend T-groups to improve their own functioning. For example, T-groups can help OD practitioners become more aware of how others perceive them and thus increase their effectiveness with client systems. In addition, OD practitioners often recommend that organisation members attend a T-group to learn how their behaviours affect others, and to develop more effective ways of relating to people.

What are the goals?
T-groups are traditionally designed to provide members with experiential learning[40] about group dynamics, leadership and interpersonal relations. The basic T-group consists of about 10 to 15 strangers who meet with a professional trainer to

explore the social dynamics that emerge from their interactions. Modifications of this basic design have generally moved in two directions. The first path has used T-group methods to help individuals gain deeper personal understanding and development. This intrapersonal focus is typically called an encounter group or a personal-growth group. It is generally considered outside the boundaries of OD and should be conducted only by professionally trained clinicians. The second direction uses T-group techniques to explore group dynamics and member relationships within an intact work group. Considerable training in T-group methods and group dynamics should be acquired before attempting these interventions.

After an extensive review of the literature, Campbell and Dunnette listed six overall objectives common to most T-groups, although not every practitioner need accomplish every objective in every T-group.[41] These objectives are:

1 increased understanding, insight and awareness of one's own behaviour and its impact on others
2 increased understanding and sensitivity about the behaviour of others
3 better understanding and awareness of group and intergroup processes
4 increased diagnostic skills in interpersonal and intergroup situations
5 increased ability to transform learning into action
6 improvements in individuals' ability to analyse their own interpersonal behaviour.

These goals seem to meet many T-group applications, although any one training program may emphasise one goal more than the others.

The results of T-groups

T-groups have been among the most controversial topics in organisation development, and probably more has been written about them than any other single topic in OD. A major issue of concern relates to the effectiveness of T-groups, and their impact on both the individual and the organisation. Campbell and Dunnette reviewed a large number of published articles on T-groups and criticised them for their lack of scientific rigour.[42] Argyris, on the other hand, criticised Campbell and Dunnette, arguing that a different kind of scientific rigour is necessary for evaluating T-groups.[43] Although there are obvious methodological problems, the studies generally support the notion that T-group training does bring about change in the individual back in his or her work situation.[44] Among the most frequently found changes are increased flexibility in role behaviour; more openness, receptivity and awareness; and more open communication, with better listening skills and less dependence on others. However, because the goals of many T-group designs are not carefully spelled out, because there are so many variations in design, and particularly because many of the research designs do not carefully measure an individual's real work climate and culture, the findings are not highly predictable. Further, some individuals do not attend T-group sessions voluntarily, and little knowledge is available about the differences between those who want to attend and those who are forced to attend.

In considering the value of T-groups for organisations, the evidence is even more mixed. One comparative study of different human process interventions showed that T-groups had the least impact on measures of process (for example, openness and decision making) and outcome (for example, productivity and costs).[45] Another comparative study showed, however, that structured T-groups had the most impact on hard measures, such as productivity and absenteeism.[46] The T-groups in this study were structured so that learning could be explicitly transferred back to the work setting. A third comparative study showed that, although T-groups improved group process, they failed to improve the organisational culture surrounding the groups and to gain peer and managerial support in the organisation.[47] Finally, in a meta-analysis of 16 studies, researchers concluded that laboratory training interventions had significant positive effects on overall employee satisfaction and other attitudes.[48]

In his review of the T-group literature, Kaplan concluded that, despite their tarnished reputation, such interventions 'can continue to serve a purpose they are uniquely suited for, to provide an emotional education and to promote awareness of relationships and group process'.[49]

Process consultation

Process consultation (PC) is a general model for carrying out helping relationships in groups.[50] It is oriented to helping managers, employees and groups to assess and improve processes, such as communication, interpersonal relations, group performance and leadership. Schein argues that effective consultants and managers are good helpers, aiding others to get things done and achieve the goals they have set.[51] Process consultation is an approach to performing this helping relationship. It is aimed at ensuring that those who are receiving the help own their problems and gain the skills and expertise to diagnose and solve them themselves. Thus, it is an approach to helping people and groups to help themselves. Schein defines process consultation as 'a set of activities on the part of the consultant that helps the client to perceive, understand and act upon the process events which occur in the client's environment'.[52] The process consultant does not offer expert help in the sense of providing solutions to problems as in the doctor–patient model. Rather, the process consultant observes groups and people in action, helps them to diagnose the nature and extent of their problems, and helps them to learn to solve their own problems.

The stages of process consultation follow closely those described for planned change: entering, defining the relationship, selecting an approach, gathering data and making a diagnosis, intervening, reducing the involvement and terminating the relationship. However, when used in process consultation, these stages are not so clear-cut, because any one of the steps constitutes an intervention. For example, the process consultant has intervened merely by conducting some preliminary interviews with group members. By being interviewed, the members may begin to see the situation in a new light.

Group process

Process consultation deals primarily with five important group processes:

1 communications
2 the functional roles of group members
3 the ways in which the group solves problems and makes decisions
4 the development and growth of group norms
5 the use of leadership and authority.

Communications

One of the process consultant's areas of interest is the nature and style of communication among group members, at both the overt and covert levels. At the overt level, communication issues involve who talks to whom, for how long and how often. By keeping a time log, the consultant can also note who talks and who interrupts. Watching body language and other non-verbal behaviour can also be a highly informative way of understanding communication processes.[53]

At the covert or hidden level of communication, sometimes one thing is said but another meant, thus giving a double message. Luft has described this phenomenon in what is called the Johari window.[54] Figure 7.2, a diagram of the Johari window, shows that some personal issues are perceived by both the individual and others (cell 1). Other people are aware of their own issues, but they conceal them from others (cell 2). In this situation, persons may have certain feelings about themselves or about others in the work group that they do not share

FIGURE 7.2 Johari window

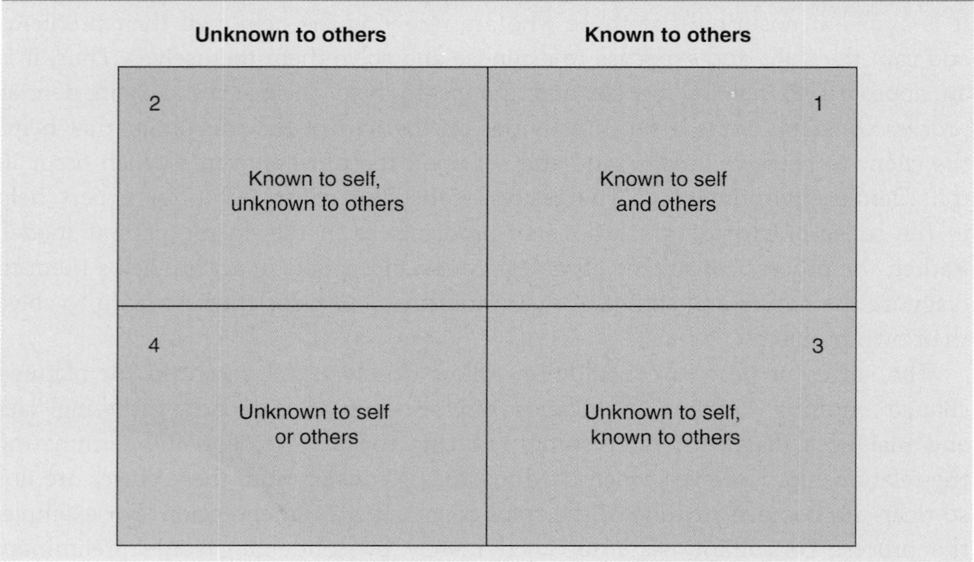

	Unknown to others	Known to others
2	Known to self, unknown to others	Known to self and others **1**
4	Unknown to self or others	Unknown to self, known to others **3**

Source: Adapted from J. Luft, 'The Johari window', *Human Relations Training News*, 5 (1961): 6–7.

with others unless they feel safe and protected; by not revealing reactions that they feel might be hurtful or impolite, they lessen the degree of communication.

Cell 3 comprises personal issues that are unknown to the individual but that are communicated clearly to others. Cell 4 of the Johari window represents those personal aspects that are unknown to either the individual or others. Because such areas are outside the realm of the consultant and the group, focus is typically on the other three cells. The consultant can help people to learn about how others experience them, thus reducing cell 3. Further, the consultant can help individuals to give feedback to others, thus reducing cell 2. Reducing the size of these two cells helps to improve the communication process by enlarging cell 1, the 'self that is open to both the individual and others'.

The climate of the work group can have a great impact on the size of the quadrants in the Johari window, particularly cell 2. Gibb has outlined two basic types of climate: supportive and threatening.[55] Threatening climates (those that put the receiver on the defensive) can be of several types, and for each there is a corresponding supportive climate.

- *Evaluative versus descriptive.* A listener who perceives a statement as evaluative is put on guard. If, on the other hand, the comment is perceived as descriptive and factual, the receiver is more likely to accept the communication.
- *Control versus problem orientation.* One person's attempt to control another increases the latter's defensiveness. Problem orientation, by contrast, is supportive, as it does not imply that the receiver is somehow inferior.
- *Strategy versus spontaneity.* Strategy implies manipulation, whereas spontaneity reduces defensive behaviour.
- *Superiority versus equality.* To the extent that a person assumes a superior role, he or she arouses defensiveness in the other person. Equality is much more likely to result in joint problem solving.
- *Certainty versus provisionalism.* The more dogmatic a person is, the more that defensiveness will be aroused in others. Provisionalism, on the other hand, allows the other person to have some control over the situation and increases the likelihood of collaboration.

Functional roles of group members

The process consultant must be keenly aware of the different roles that individual members take on within a group. Both upon entering and while remaining in a group, the individual must determine a self-identity, influence and power that will satisfy personal needs while working to accomplish group goals. Preoccupation with individual needs or power struggles can severely reduce the effectiveness of a group, and unless the individual can, to some degree, expose and share those personal needs, the group is unlikely to be productive. Therefore, the process consultant must help the group confront and work through these needs.

Two other functions that need to be performed if a group is to be effective are: (1) task-related activities, such as giving and seeking information and elaborating, co-ordinating and evaluating activities; and (2) the group-maintenance function,[56] which is directed towards holding the group together as a cohesive team and includes encouraging, harmonising, compromising, setting standards and observing. Most ineffective groups do little group maintenance. This is a primary reason for bringing in a process observer. The process consultant can help by suggesting that some part of each meeting be reserved for examining these functions and periodically assessing the feelings of the group's members. The consultant's role is to make comments and to assist with diagnosis, but the emphasis should be on facilitating the group's understanding and articulation of its own processes.

Problem solving and decision making

To be effective, a group must be able to identify problems, examine alternatives and make decisions. The first part of this process is the most important. Groups often fail to distinguish between problems (either task-related or interpersonal) and symptoms. Once the group has identified the problem, an OD consultant can help the group analyse its approach, restrain the group from reacting too quickly and making a premature diagnosis, or suggest additional options. The process consultant can help the group understand how it makes decisions and the consequences of each decision process, as well as help diagnose which type of decision process may be most effective in the given situation. Decision by unanimous consent, for example, may sometimes be ideal, but too time-consuming or costly at other times.

Group norms and growth

If a group of people works together over a period of time, it often develops group norms or standards of behaviour about what is good or bad, allowed or forbidden, and right or wrong. There may be an explicit norm that group members are free to express their ideas and feelings, whereas the implicit norm is that one does not contradict the ideas or suggestions of certain members (usually the more powerful ones) of the group. The process consultant can be very helpful in assisting the group to understand and articulate its own norms and to determine whether those norms are helpful or dysfunctional. By understanding its norms and recognising which ones are helpful, the group can grow and deal realistically with its environment, make optimum use of its own resources and learn from its own experiences.[57]

Leadership and authority

A process consultant needs to understand the processes of leadership and how different leadership styles can help or hinder a group's functioning. In addition, the consultant can help the leader to adjust his or her style to fit the situation. An important step in that process is for the leader to gain a better understanding of his or her own behaviour and the group's reaction to that behaviour. It is also important that the leader become aware of alternative behaviours.

Basic process interventions

For each of the five group processes described above, a variety of interventions may be used. In broad terms, these interventions may be of the following types:[58]

1 Process interventions, including:
    * questions that direct attention to interpersonal issues
    * process-analysis periods
    * agenda review and testing procedures
    * meetings devoted to interpersonal processes
    * conceptual inputs on interpersonal-process topics.

    Process interventions are designed to make the group sensitive to its own internal processes and to generate interest in analysing these processes.
2 Diagnostic and feedback interventions, including:
    * diagnostic questions and probes
    * forcing historical reconstruction, concretisation and process emphasis
    * feedback to groups during process analysis or regular work time
    * feedback to individuals after meetings or data-gathering sessions.

    To give feedback to a group, the consultant must first observe relevant events, ask the proper questions, and make certain that the feedback is given to the client system in a usable manner. The process consultant's feedback must be specific, timely and descriptive.
3 Coaching or counselling of individuals or groups to help them learn to observe and process their own data, accept and learn from the feedback process, and become active in identifying and solving their own problems.
4 Structural suggestions pertaining to the following:
    * group membership
    * communication or interaction patterns
    * allocation of work, assignments of responsibility or lines of authority.

When is process consultation appropriate?

Process consultation is a general model for helping relationships, and so has wide applicability in organisations. Because process consultation helps people and groups to own their problems and learn how to diagnose and resolve them, it is most applicable when:[59]

1 the client has a problem but does not know its source or how to resolve it
2 the client is unsure of what kind of help or consultation is available
3 the nature of the problem is such that the client would benefit from involvement in its diagnosis
4 the client is motivated by goals that the consultant can accept and has some capacity to enter into a helping relationship
5 the client ultimately knows what interventions are most applicable
6 the client is capable of learning how to assess and resolve his or her own problem.

Results of process consultation

A number of difficulties arise when trying to measure performance improvements as a result of process consultation. One problem is that most process consultation is conducted with groups that perform mental tasks (for example, decision making) – the outcomes of such tasks are difficult to evaluate. A second difficulty with measuring its effects occurs because, in many cases, process consultation is combined with other interventions in an ongoing OD program. Isolating the impact of process consultation from other interventions is difficult. A third problem with assessing the performance effects of process consultation is that much of the relevant research has used people's perceptions as the index of success, rather than hard performance measures. Much of this research shows positive results, including studies in which the success of process consultation was measured by questionnaires.

Third-party intervention

Third-party intervention focuses on conflicts arising between two or more people within the same organisation. Conflict is inherent in groups and organisations and can arise from a variety of sources, including differences in personality, task orientation and perceptions among group members, as well as competition over scarce resources. To emphasise that conflict is neither good nor bad per se is important. It can enhance motivation and innovation and lead to greater understanding of ideas and views. On the other hand, conflict can prevent people from working together constructively; it can destroy necessary task interactions among group members. Consequently, third-party intervention is used primarily in situations in which conflict significantly disrupts necessary task interactions and work relationships among members.

Third-party intervention varies considerably according to the kinds of issues that underlie the conflict. Conflict can arise over substantive issues, such as work methods, pay rates and conditions of employment; or it can emerge from interpersonal issues, such as personality conflicts and misperceptions. When applied to substantive issues, conflict resolution interventions traditionally involve resolving labour–management disputes through arbitration and mediation. These methods require considerable training and expertise in law and labour relations and are not generally considered to be part of OD practice. When conflict involves interpersonal issues, however, OD has developed approaches that help to control and to resolve it. These third-party interventions help the parties to directly interact with each other, facilitating their diagnosis of the conflict and how to resolve it. That ability to facilitate conflict resolution is a basic skill in OD and applies to all of the process interventions discussed in this chapter. Consultants, for example, frequently help organisation members to resolve the interpersonal conflicts that invariably arise during process consultation and team building.

Third-party consultation interventions cannot resolve all interpersonal conflicts in organisations, and nor should they. Interpersonal conflicts are frequently not severe or disruptive enough to warrant attention. At other times, they may simply burn themselves out without any intervention.

An episodic model of conflict

Interpersonal conflict often occurs in iterative, cyclical stages known as 'episodes'. An episodic model is shown in Figure 7.3. At times, the issues underlying the conflict are latent and do not present any manifest problems for the parties. Something triggers the conflict, however, and brings it into the open. For example, a violent disagreement or frank confrontation can unleash conflict behaviour. Because of the negative consequences of conflict behaviour, the disagreement usually becomes latent again, even though it is still unresolved. Once again, something triggers the conflict, making it overt, and so the cycle continues with the next conflict episode. Conflict has both costs and benefits for the antagonists and for those in contact with them. Unresolved conflict can proliferate and expand. An interpersonal conflict may be concealed under a cause or issue, serving to make the conflict more legitimate. Frequently, the overt conflict is only a symptom of a deeper problem.

The episode model identifies four strategies for conflict resolution. The first three attempt to control the conflict, and only the last approach tries to change the basic issues that underlie it.[60] The first strategy is to prevent the ignition of conflict by arriving at a clear understanding of the triggering factors and thereafter avoiding or blunting them when the symptoms occur. This may not always be functional and may merely drive the conflict underground until it explodes. As a control strategy, though, this method may help to achieve a temporary cooling-off period.

The second control strategy is to set limits on the form of the conflict. Conflict can be constrained by informal gatherings before a formal meeting or by exploration of other options. It can also be limited by setting rules and procedures that specify the conditions under which the parties can interact.

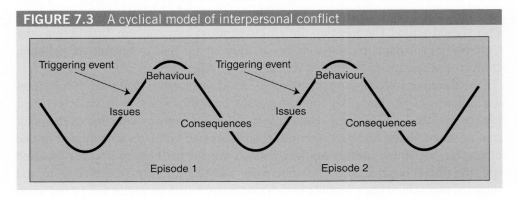

FIGURE 7.3 A cyclical model of interpersonal conflict

Source: R. G. Walton, *Managing Conflict*, 2nd edn © 1987 p.67. Reprinted by permission of Pearson Education, Inc., Upper Saddle River, New Jersey.

The third control strategy is to help the parties cope differently with the consequences of the conflict. The third-party consultant may work with the individuals involved to help them to devise coping techniques, such as reducing their dependence on the relationship, airing their feelings to friends and developing additional sources of emotional support. These methods can reduce the costs of the conflict without resolving the underlying issues.

The fourth method is an attempt to eliminate or resolve the basic issues causing the conflict.

Facilitating the conflict-resolution process

Walton has identified a number of factors and tactical choices that can facilitate the use of the episode model in resolving the underlying causes of conflict.[61] The following ingredients can help third-party consultants achieve productive dialogue between the disputants so that they examine their differences and change their perceptions and behaviours: mutual motivation to resolve the conflict; equality of power between the parties; co-ordinated attempts to confront the conflict; relevant phasing of the stages of identifying differences and of searching for integrative solutions; and open and clear forms of communication and productive levels of tension and stress.

Among the tactical choices identified by Walton are those that have to do with diagnosis, the context of the third-party intervention and the role of the consultant. One of the tactics in third-party intervention is the gathering of data, usually through preliminary interviewing. Group-process observations can also be used. Data gathering provides some understanding of the nature and type of conflict, the personality and conflict styles of the individuals involved, the issues and attendant pressures, and the participants' readiness to work together to resolve the conflict.

The context in which the intervention occurs is also important. Consideration of the neutrality of the meeting area, the formality of the setting, the appropriateness of the time for the meeting (that is, a meeting should not be started until a time has been agreed upon to conclude or adjourn) and the careful selection of those who should attend the meeting are all elements of this context. In addition, the third-party consultant must decide on an appropriate role to assume in resolving conflict. The specific tactic chosen will depend on the diagnosis of the situation.

The third-party consultant must develop considerable skill at diagnosis, intervention and follow-up. The third-party intervener must be highly sensitive to his or her own feelings and to those of others. He or she must also recognise that some tension and conflict are inevitable and that, although there can be an optimum amount and degree of conflict, too much conflict can be dysfunctional for both the individuals involved and the larger organisation. The third-party consultant must be sensitive to the situation and able to use a number of different intervention strategies and tactics when intervention appears to be useful. Finally, he or she must have professional expertise in third-party intervention and must be seen by the parties as neutral or unbiased regarding the issues and outcomes of the conflict resolution.

Team building

Team building refers to a broad range of planned activities that help groups to improve the way they accomplish tasks and help group members to enhance their interpersonal and problem-solving skills. Organisations consist of many permanent and temporary groups. Team building is an effective approach to improving teamwork and task accomplishment in these situations. It can help problem-solving groups make maximum use of members' resources and contributions. It can help members to develop a high level of motivation to carry out group decisions. Team building can also help groups overcome specific problems, such as: apathy and general lack of interest among members; loss of productivity; increasing complaints within the group; confusion about assignments; low participation in meetings; lack of innovation and initiation; increasing complaints from those outside the group about the quality, timeliness and effectiveness of services and products; and hostility or conflict among members.

Equally importantly, team building can facilitate other OD interventions, such as employee involvement, work design, restructuring and strategic change. These change programs are typically designed by management teams and implemented by various committees and work groups. Team building can help these groups design high-quality change programs. It can ensure that the programs are accepted and implemented by organisation members. Indeed, most technostructural, human resource management and strategic interventions depend on some form of team building for effective implementation.

Team building is not clearly differentiated from process consultation in the OD literature. This confusion stems mainly from the fact that most team building includes process consultation: helping the group to diagnose and to understand its own internal processes. However, process consultation is a more general approach to helping relationships than team building. Team building focuses explicitly on helping groups to perform tasks and to solve problems more effectively. Process consultation, on the other hand, is concerned with establishing effective helping relationships in organisations. It is seen as being essential for effective management and consultation, and can be applied to any helping relationship, from subordinate development[62] to interpersonal relationships to group development. Thus, team building consists of process consultation plus other, more task-oriented, interventions.

Dyer has developed a checklist for identifying whether a team-building program is needed and whether the organisation is ready to start such a program (Table 7.2).[63] If the problem is a structural or technical one, an intergroup issue, an administrative mistake or a conflict between only two people, team building would not be an appropriate change strategy.

TABLE 7.2 Team-building checklist

I Problem identification: To what extent is there evidence of the following problems in your work unit?

		Low evidence		Some evidence	High evidence	
1	Loss of production or work-unit output	1	2	3	4	5
2	Grievances or complaints within the work unit	1	2	3	4	5
3	Conflicts or hostility between unit members	1	2	3	4	5
4	Confusion about assignments or unclear relationships between people	1	2	3	4	5
5	Lack of clear goals or low commitment to goals	1	2	3	4	5
6	Apathy or general lack of interest or involvement of unit members	1	2	3	4	5
7	Lack of innovation, risk taking, imagination or taking initiative	1	2	3	4	5
8	Ineffective staff meetings	1	2	3	4	5
9	Problems in working with the boss	1	2	3	4	5
10	Poor communications: people afraid to speak up, not listening to each other or not talking together	1	2	3	4	5
11	Lack of trust between boss and members or between members	1	2	3	4	5
12	Decisions made that people do not understand or agree with	1	2	3	4	5
13	People feel that good work is not recognised or rewarded	1	2	3	4	5
14	People are not encouraged to work together in a better team effort	1	2	3	4	5

Scoring: Add the score for the 14 items. If your score is between 14 and 28, there is little evidence that your unit needs team building. If your score is between 29 and 42, there is some evidence but no immediate pressure, unless two or three items are very high. If your score is between 43 and 56, you should seriously think about planning the team-building program. If your score is over 56, then team building should be the top priority for your work unit.

II Are you (or your manager) prepared to start a team-building program? Consider the following statements. To what extent do they apply to you or your department?

		Low		Medium	High	
1	You are comfortable in sharing organisational leadership and decision making with subordinates and prefer to work in a participative atmosphere	1	2	3	4	5
2	You see a high degree of interdependence as necessary among functions and workers in order to achieve your goals	1	2	3	4	5

TABLE 7.2   Team-building checklist (*continued*)

II Are you (or your manager) prepared to start a team-building program? Consider the following statements. To what extent do they apply to you or your department?

		Low		Medium		High
3	The external environment is highly variable or changing rapidly and you need the best thinking of all your staff to plan for these conditions	1	2	3	4	5
4	You feel you need the input of your staff to plan major changes or develop new operating policies and procedures	1	2	3	4	5
5	You feel that broad consultation among your people as a group in goals, decisions and problems is necessary on a continuing basis	1	2	3	4	5
6	Members of your management team are (or can become) compatible with each other and are able to create a collaborative rather than a competitive environment	1	2	3	4	5
7	Members of your team are located close enough to meet together as needed	1	2	3	4	5
8	You feel you need to rely on the ability and willingness of subordinates to resolve critical operating problems directly and in the best interest of the company or organisation	1	2	3	4	5
9	Formal communication channels are not sufficient for the timely exchange of essential information, views and decisions among your team members	1	2	3	4	5
10	Organisation adaptation requires the use of such devices as project management, task forces or ad hoc problem-solving groups to augment conventional organisation structure	1	2	3	4	5
11	You feel it is important to bring out and deal with critical, albeit sensitive, issues that exist in your team	1	2	3	4	5
12	You are prepared to look at your own role and performance with your team	1	2	3	4	5
13	You feel there are operating or interpersonal problems that have remained unsolved too long and need the input from all group members	1	2	3	4	5
14	You need an opportunity to meet with your people to set goals and develop commitment to these goals	1	2	3	4	5

Scoring: If your total score is between 50 and 70, you are probably ready to go ahead with the team-building program. If your score is between 35 and 49, you should probably talk the situation over with your team and others to see what would need to be done to get ready for team building. If your score is between 14 and 34, you are probably not prepared to start team building.

Source: W. Dyer, *Team Building*, 2nd edn, copyright © 1987 by Addison-Wesley Publishing Company, Inc.

Team-building activities

A team is a group of interdependent individuals who share a common purpose, have common work methods and hold each other accountable.[64] The nature of that interdependence varies, creating the following types of teams:

- groups reporting to the same supervisor, manager or executive
- groups involving people with common organisational goals
- temporary groups formed to do a specific, one-time task
- groups consisting of people whose work roles are interdependent
- groups whose members have no formal links in the organisation but whose collective purpose is to achieve tasks they cannot accomplish as individuals.

Just as there are various types of teams, so there are a number of factors that affect the outcomes of a specific team-building activity: the length of time allocated to the activity; the team's willingness to look at the way in which it operates; the length of time the team has been working together; and the permanence of the team. Consequently, the results of team-building activities can range from comparatively modest changes in the team's operating mechanisms (for example, meeting more frequently or gathering agenda items from more sources) to much deeper changes (for example, modifying team members' behaviour patterns or the nature and style of the group's management, or developing greater openness and trust).

In general, team-building activities can be classified as follows:

- activities relevant to one or more individuals
- activities specific to the group's operation and behaviour
- activities that affect the group's relationship with the rest of the organisation.

The manager role

Ultimately, the manager is responsible for team functioning,[65] even though the team itself must obviously share this responsibility. Therefore, the development of a team group that can regularly stop to analyse and diagnose its own effectiveness and work process is management's task. The manager has the responsibility of diagnosing (with the team) the effectiveness of the team and taking appropriate action if the work unit shows signs of operating difficulty or stress.

However, many managers have not been trained to perform the data gathering, diagnosis, planning and action necessary for them to continually maintain and improve their teams. Thus, the issue of who should lead a team-building session is a function of managerial capability. The initial use of a consultant is usually advisable if a manager is aware of problems, feels that she or he may be part of the problem and believes that some positive action is needed to improve the operation of the unit, but is not exactly sure how to go about it. Dyer has provided a checklist for assessing the need for a consultant (Table 7.3). Some of the questions ask the manager to examine problems and to establish the degree to which the

TABLE 7.3 Addressing the need for a consultant			
Should you use an outside consultant to help in team building?			
		Circle the appropriate response	
1	Does the manager feel comfortable in trying out something new and different with the staff?	Yes	No	?
2	Is the staff used to spending time in an outside location working on issues of concern to the work unit?	Yes	No	?
3	Will group members speak up and give honest data?	Yes	No	?
4	Does your group generally work together without a lot of conflict or apathy?	Yes	No	?
5	Are you reasonably sure that the boss is not a major source of difficulty?	Yes	No	?
6	Is there a high commitment by the boss and unit members to achieving more effective team functioning?	Yes	No	?
7	Is the personal style of the boss and his or her management philosophy consistent with a team approach?	Yes	No	?
8	Do you feel you know enough about team building to begin a program without help?	Yes	No	?
9	Would your staff feel confident enough to begin a team-building program without outside help?	Yes	No	?

Scoring: If you have circled six or more 'yes' responses, you probably do not need an outside consultant. If you have four or more 'no' responses, you probably do need a consultant. If you have a mixture of 'yes', 'no' and '?' responses, you should probably invite a consultant to talk over the situation and make a joint decision.

Source: W. Dyer, *Team Building*, 2nd edn © 1987 by Addison-Wesley Publishing Co., Inc.

manager feels comfortable in trying out new and different things, the degree of knowledge about team building, whether the boss might be a major source of difficulty, and the openness of group members.

Basically, the role of the consultant is to work closely with the manager (and members of the unit) to a point at which the manager is capable of actively engaging in team-development activities as a regular and ongoing part of overall managerial responsibilities. Assuming that the manager wants and needs a consultant, the two should work together as a team in developing the initial program, keeping in mind that: (1) the manager is ultimately responsible for all team-building activities, even though the consultant's resources are available; and (2) the goal of the consultant's presence is to help the manager to learn to continue team-development processes with minimum consultant help or without the ongoing help of the consultant. Thus, in the first stages, the consultant might be much more active in data gathering, diagnosis and action planning, particularly if a one- to three-day off-site workshop is considered. In later stages, the consultant takes a much less active role, with the manager becoming more active and taking on the role of both manager and team developer.

When is team building applicable?

Team building is applicable to a large number of team situations, from starting a new team and resolving conflicts among members to revitalising a complacent team. Lewis has identified the following conditions as best suited to team building:[66]

1 Patterns of communication and interaction are inadequate for good group functioning.
2 Group leaders desire an integrated team.
3 The group's task requires interaction among members.
4 The team leader will behave differently as the result of team building, and members will respond to the new behaviour.
5 The benefits outweigh the costs of team building.
6 Team building must be congruent with the leader's personal style and philosophy.

The results of team building

The research on team building has a number of problems. First, it focuses mainly on the feelings and attitudes of group members. There is little evidence to support the notion that group performance improves as a result of team-building experiences. One study, for example, found that team building was a smashing success in the eyes of the participants.[67] However, a rigorous field test of the results over time showed no appreciable effects on either the team's or the larger organisation's functioning and efficiency. Second, the positive effects of team building are typically measured over relatively short periods. Evidence suggests that the positive effects of off-site team building are short-lived and tend to fade after the group returns to the organisation. Third, team building rarely occurs in isolation. It is usually carried out in conjunction with other interventions that lead to, or result from, team building itself. For this reason, it is difficult to separate the effects of team building from those of the other interventions.[68]

Studies of the empirical literature present a mixed picture of the impact of team building on group performance. One review shows that team building improves process measures (such as employee openness and decision making) about 45% of the time; it improves outcome measures (such as productivity and costs) about 53% of the time.[69] Another review reveals that team building positively affects hard measures of productivity, employee withdrawal and costs about 50% of the time.[70] Still another review concludes that team building cannot be convincingly linked to improved performance. Of the 30 studies reviewed, only 10 attempted to measure changes in performance. Although these changes were generally positive, the studies' research designs were relatively weak, reducing confidence in the findings.[71] One review concluded that process interventions, such as team building and process consultation, are most likely to improve process variables, such as decision making, communication and problem solving.[72]

Boss has conducted extensive research on arresting the potential 'fade-out effects' of off-site team building.[73] He proposes that the tendency for the positive behaviours developed at off-site team building to regress once the group is back in the organisation can be checked by conducting a follow-up intervention called 'personal management interview' (PMI). This is done soon after the off-site team building and involves the team leader – who first negotiates roles with each member and then holds weekly or biweekly meetings with each member to improve communication – to resolve problems and to increase personal accountability.

Buller and Bell have attempted to differentiate the effects of team building from the effects of other interventions that occur along with team building.[74] Specifically, they tried to separate the effects of team building from the effects of goal setting, an intervention aimed at setting realistic performance goals and developing action plans for achieving them. In a rigorous field experiment, Buller and Bell examined the differential effects of team building and goal setting on productivity measures of underground miners. The results show that team building affects the quality of performance, while goal setting affects the quantity of performance. This differential impact was explained in terms of the nature of the mining task. The task of improving the quality of performance was more complex, unstructured and interdependent than the task of achieving quantity. This suggests that team building can improve group performance, particularly on tasks that are complex, unstructured and interdependent.

ORGANISATION PROCESS APPROACHES

This second section of the chapter describes four system-wide process interventions – change programs directed at improving such processes as organisational problem solving, leadership, visioning and task accomplishment between groups – for a major subsystem or for an entire organisation.

- The first type of intervention, the *organisation confrontation meeting*, is among the earliest organisation-wide process approaches. It helps to mobilise the problem-solving resources of a major subsystem or an entire organisation by encouraging members to identify and confront pressing issues.
- The second organisation process approach is called *intergroup relations*. It consists of two interventions: the intergroup conflict resolution meeting and microcosm groups. Both interventions are aimed at diagnosing and addressing important organisation-level processes, such as conflict, the co-ordination of organisational units and diversity. The intergroup conflict intervention is

specifically oriented towards conflict processes, whereas the microcosm group is a more generic system-wide change strategy.

- A third organisation-wide process approach, the *large-group intervention*, has received considerable attention recently and is one of the fastest-growing areas in OD. Large-group interventions get a 'whole system into the room'[75] and create processes that allow a variety of stakeholders to interact simultaneously. A large-group intervention can be used to clarify important organisational values, develop new ways of looking at problems, articulate a new vision for the organisation, solve cross-functional problems, restructure operations or devise an organisational strategy. It is a powerful tool for addressing organisational problems and opportunities and for accelerating the pace of organisational change.
- The final section of this chapter describes a normative approach to OD: Blake and Mouton's Grid® Organization Development. This is a popular intervention, particularly in large organisations. Grid® Organization Development is a packaged program that organisations can purchase and train members to use. In contrast to modern contingency approaches, the Grid proposes that there is one best way of managing organisations. Consequently, OD practitioners have increasingly questioned its applicability and effectiveness in contemporary organisations.

Organisation confrontation meeting

The confrontation meeting is an intervention designed to mobilise the resources of the entire organisation to identify problems, set priorities and action targets, and begin working on identified problems. Originally developed by Beckhard,[76] the intervention can be used at any time, but is particularly useful when the organisation is in stress and when there is a gap between the top and the rest of the organisation (such as a new top manager). General Electric's 'WorkOut' program is a recent example of how the confrontation meeting has been adapted to fit today's organisations.[77]

What are the steps?

The organisation confrontation meeting typically involves the following steps:

1 A group meeting of all involved is scheduled and held in an appropriate place. Usually the task is to identify problems about the work environment and the effectiveness of the organisation.

2 Groups are appointed, with representatives from all departments of the organisation. For example, each group might have one or more members from sales, purchasing, finance, manufacturing and quality assurance.

3 It must be stressed that the groups are to be open and honest and must work hard at identifying problems they see in the organisation. No one will be criticised for bringing up problems and, in fact, the groups will be judged on their ability to do so.

4 The groups are given an hour or two to identify organisation problems. Generally, an OD practitioner goes from group to group, encouraging openness and assisting the groups with their tasks.

5 The groups then reconvene in a central meeting place. Each group reports the problems it has identified and sometimes offers solutions. Because each group hears the reports of all the others, a maximum amount of information is shared.

6 Either then or later, the master list of problems is broken down into categories. This process eliminates duplication and overlap, and allows the problems to be separated according to functional or other appropriate areas.

7 Following problem categorisation, participants are divided into problem-solving groups, whose composition may (and usually does) differ from that of the original problem-identification groups.

8 Each group ranks the problems, develops a tactical action plan and determines an appropriate timetable for completing this phase of the process.

9 Each group then periodically reports its list of priorities and tactical plans of action to management or to the larger group.

10 Schedules for periodic (often monthly) follow-up meetings are established. The formal establishment of such follow-up meetings ensures both continuing action and the modification of priorities and timetables as needed.

Results of confrontation meetings

Because organisation confrontation meetings are often combined with other approaches, such as survey feedback, determining specific results is difficult. In many cases, the results appear dramatic in mobilising the total resources of the organisation for problem identification and solution.

Beckhard cites a number of specific examples in such varying organisations as a food-products manufacturer, a military-products manufacturer and a hotel.[78] Positive results were also found in a confrontation meeting with 40 professionals in a research and development firm.[79] The organisation confrontation meeting is a promising approach for mobilising organisational problem solving, especially in times of low performance.

Intergroup relations interventions

The ability to diagnose and understand intergroup relations is important for OD practitioners as:

* groups must often work with and through other groups to accomplish their goals
* groups within the organisation often create problems and demands on each other
* the quality of the relationships between groups can affect the degree of organisational effectiveness.

Two OD interventions – microcosm groups and intergroup conflict resolution – are described here. A microcosm group uses members from several groups to help solve organisation-wide problems. Intergroup issues are explored in this context, and then solutions are implemented in the larger organisation. Intergroup conflict resolution helps two groups work out dysfunctional relationships. Together, these approaches help to improve intergroup processes and lead to organisational effectiveness.

Microcosm groups

A microcosm group consists of a small number of individuals who reflect the issue being addressed.[80] For example, a microcosm group made up of members who represent a spectrum of ethnic backgrounds, cultures and races can be created to address diversity issues in the organisation. This group, with the assistance of OD practitioners, can create programs and processes targeted to specific problems. In addition to addressing diversity problems, microcosm groups have been used to carry out organisation diagnoses, solve communications problems, integrate two cultures, smooth the transition to a new structure and address dysfunctional political processes.

Microcosm groups work through 'parallel processes', which are the unconscious changes that take place in individuals when two or more groups interact.[81] After two or more groups have interacted, members often find that their characteristic patterns of roles and interactions change to reflect the roles and dynamics of the group with whom they were relating. Put simply, one group seems to 'infect' and become 'infected' by the other groups.

What are the steps?

The process of using a microcosm group to address organisation-wide issues involves the following five steps:

1 *Identify an issue.* This step involves finding a system-wide problem to be addressed. This may result from an organisational diagnosis or may be an idea generated by an organisation member or task force.
2 *Convene the group.* Once an issue has been identified, the microcosm group can be formed. The most important convening principle is that group membership needs to reflect the appropriate mix of stakeholders related to the issue. For example, if the issue is organisational communication, then the group should contain people from all hierarchical levels and functions, including staff groups and unions, if applicable. Following the initial set-up, the group itself becomes responsible for determining its membership. It will decide whether to add new members and how to fill vacant positions. Convening the group also draws attention to the issue and gives the group status. Members also need to be perceived as credible representatives of the problem. This will increase the likelihood that organisation members will listen to, and follow, the suggestions they make.

3   *Provide group training.* Group training focuses on establishing a group mission or charter, working relationships between members, group decision-making norms and definitions of the problem to be addressed. Team-building interventions may also be appropriate. From a group-process perspective, OD practitioners may need to observe and comment on how the group develops. Because the group is a microcosm of the organisation, it will tend, through its behaviour and attitudes, to reflect the problem in the larger organisation.

4   *Address the issue.* This step involves solving the problem and implementing solutions. OD practitioners may help the group to diagnose, design, implement and evaluate changes. A key issue is gaining wider organisation commitment to implementing the group's solutions. The following factors can facilitate such ownership. First, a communication plan should link group activities to the organisation. Second, group members need to be visible and accessible to management and labour. Third, problem-solving processes should include an appropriate level of participation by organisation members.

5   *Dissolve the group.* The microcosm group can be disbanded after the successful implementation of changes. This typically involves writing a final report or holding a final meeting.

The microcosm group intervention derives from an intergroup relations theory developed by Alderfer[82] and has been applied by him to communications and race-relations problems. A dearth of research exists on microcosm groups. This is partly due to the difficulty of measuring parallel processes and associating them with measures of organisational processes.

Resolving intergroup conflict

This intervention is specifically designed to help two groups or departments within an organisation resolve dysfunctional conflicts. Intergroup conflict is neither good nor bad in itself. In some cases, conflict among departments is necessary and productive for organisations. This applies in organisations where there is little interdependence among departments. Here, departments are independent, and conflict or competition among them can lead to higher levels of productivity. In other organisations, especially those with very interdependent departments, conflict may become dysfunctional.[83] Two or more groups may become polarised, and continued conflict may result in the development of defensiveness and negative stereotypes of the other group. It is particularly the case that, when intergroup communication is necessary, the amount and quality of communication usually drops off. Groups become defensive and begin seeing the others as 'the enemy', rather than in either positive or neutral terms. As the amount of communication decreases, the amount of mutual problem solving also falls off. The tendency increases for one group to sabotage the efforts of the other group, either consciously or unconsciously.

What are the steps?

A basic strategy for improving interdepartmental or intergroup relationships is to change the perceptions (perhaps, more accurately, misperceptions) that the two groups have of each other. One formal approach for accomplishing this consists of a 10-step procedure, originally described by Blake and his associates.[84]

1 A consultant external to the two groups obtains their agreement to work directly on improving intergroup relationships. (The use of an outside consultant is highly recommended because without the moderating influence of such a neutral third party, it is almost impossible for the two groups to interact without becoming deadlocked and polarised in a defensive position.)

2 A time is set for the two groups to meet; preferably away from normal work situations.

3 The consultant, together with the managers of the two groups, describes the purpose and objectives of the meeting: the development of better mutual relationships, the exploration of the perceptions the groups have of each other and the development of plans for improving the relationship. The two groups are asked the following or similar questions: 'What qualities or attributes best describe our group?', 'What qualities or attributes best describe the other group?' and 'How do we think the other group will describe us?' Then the two groups are encouraged to establish norms of openness for feedback and discussion.

4 The two groups are then placed in separate rooms and asked to write their answers to the three questions. Usually, an outside consultant works with each group to help the members become more open and to encourage them to develop lists that accurately reflect their perceptions of their own image and of the other group.

5 After completing their lists, the two groups come together again. A representative from each group presents the written statements. Only the two representatives are allowed to speak. The primary objective at this stage is to make certain that the images, perceptions and attitudes are presented as accurately as possible and to avoid the arguments that might arise if the two groups openly confronted each other. Questions, however, are allowed to ensure that both groups clearly understand the written lists. Justifications, accusations or other statements are not permitted.

6 When it is clear that the two groups thoroughly understand the content of the lists, they again separate. By this time, a great number of misperceptions and discrepancies have already been brought to light.

7 The task of the two groups (almost always with a consultant as a process observer) is to analyse and review the reasons for the discrepancies. The emphasis is on solving the problems and reducing the misperceptions.

8 When the two groups have worked through the discrepancies, as well as the areas of common agreement, they meet to share both the identified discrepancies and their problem-solving approaches to those discrepancies.

9   The two groups are then asked to develop specific plans of action for solving specific problems and for improving their relationships.

10   When the two groups have gone as far as possible in formulating action plans, at least one follow-up meeting is scheduled so that the two groups can report on actions that have been implemented, identify any further problems that have emerged and, where necessary, formulate additional action plans.

In addition to this formal approach to improving interdepartmental or intergroup relationships, there are a number of more informal procedures. Beckhard asks each of the two groups to develop a list of what irritates or exasperates them about the other group and to predict what they think the other group will say about them.[85]

Different approaches to resolving intergroup conflict form a continuum varying from behavioural solutions to attitudinal change solutions.[86] Behavioural methods are oriented to keeping the relevant parties physically separate and specifying the limited conditions under which interaction will occur. Little attempt is made to understand or to change how members of each group see the other. Conversely, attitudinal methods – such as exchanging group members or requiring intense interaction with important rewards or opportunities clearly tied to co-ordination – are directed at changing how each group perceives the other. Here, it is assumed that perceptual distortions and stereotyping underlie the conflict and need to be changed to resolve it.

Most of the OD solutions to intergroup conflict reviewed in this section favour attitudinal change strategies. However, these interventions typically require considerably more skill and time than the behavioural solutions. Changing attitudes can be quite difficult in conflict situations, especially if the attitudes are deep-seated and form an integral part of people's personalities. Attitudinal change interventions should be reserved for those situations in which behavioural solutions might not work.

Results of intergroup conflict interventions

Several studies have been done on the effects of intergroup conflict resolution. In his original study, Blake reported vastly improved relationships between the union and management.[87] In a later study, Bennis used Blake's basic design to improve relationships between two groups of State Department officials: high-level administrative officers, and officers in the Foreign Service.[88] Initially, there was much mutual distrust, negative stereotyping, blocked communication and hostility between the two groups: 'Each side perceived the other as more threatening than any realistic overseas enemy.'[89] Although no hard data were obtained, the intervention seemed to improve relationships so that the two groups 'at least understood the other side's point of view'.

Golembiewski and Blumberg used a modification of the Blake design that involved an exchange of 'images' among both organisational units and individuals in the marketing division of a large organisation.[90] An attitude questionnaire was used to make before-and-after comparisons. The results were found to be different for more or less 'deeply involved' individuals or units. In general, the more deeply involved individuals or units (promotion, regions and divisions, and sales) reflected more positive attitudes towards collaboration and had greater feelings of commitment to the success of the entire organisation. Less deeply involved positions or units (such areas as sales training, hospital sales and trade relations) did not show any particular trends in attitudinal changes, either positive or negative.

French and Bell, who used a somewhat similar design, reported that they were able to work successfully with three groups simultaneously.[91] They obtained positive results in their work with key groups in a Native American organisation: the tribal council, the tribal staff and the Community Action Program (CAP).[92] The researchers asked each group to develop perceptions of the other two, as well as of itself, and to share those perceptions in the larger group. The tribal council developed four lists: both favourable and unfavourable items about the tribal staff, a similar list about the CAP, and predictions as to what the staff and CAP, respectively, would say about the council. Once each group had developed its lists, the results were shared in a three-group meeting, and the similarities and dissimilarities in the various lists worked through. According to the researchers, the use of this method reduces intergroup problems and friction while increasing communications and interactions.

Huse and Beer have described positive results arising from periodic cross-departmental meetings, whereby personnel within one department would meet, in sequence, with those from other departments to discuss perceptions, expectations and strong and weak points about one another.[93] In another study, Huse found that bringing representatives of different groups together to work on common work-related problems had a marked effect, not only on relationships among a number of different manufacturing groups but also on the quality of the product, which increased by 62%.[94] The basic tactic in this study was to ensure that representatives of two or more groups worked jointly on each work-related problem.

Based on their experience at TRW Systems, Fordyce and Weil developed a modified approach whereby each group builds three lists: one containing 'positive feedback' items (those things the group values and likes about the other group), a 'bug' list (those things the group dislikes about the other group) and an 'empathy' list (predictions about what the other group's list would contain).[95] When the groups come together, they build a master list of major concerns and unresolved problems, which are assigned priorities and developed into an agenda. When they have completed the task, the subgroups report the results of their discussions to the total group, which then develops a series of action steps for improving the relations between the groups and commits itself to following through. For each action step, specific responsibilities are assigned and an overall schedule developed for prompt completion of the action steps.

In conclusion, the technology for improving intergroup relations is promising. A greater distinction between attitudinal and behavioural changes needs to be made in planning effective intergroup interventions. A greater variety of interventions that address the practical difficulties of bringing two groups together is also necessary. Finally, a better background of knowledge must be developed as to when perceptions and behaviour need to be diverse and when they need to be brought more closely together. Growing knowledge and theory suggest that conflict can be either functional or dysfunctional, depending on the circumstances.[96]

Large-group interventions

System-wide process interventions in the third group are called large-group interventions. These change programs have been variously referred to as 'search conferences', 'open space meetings' and 'future searches'.[97] They focus on issues that affect the whole organisation or large segments of it, such as budget cuts, introduction of new technology and changes in senior leadership. The defining feature of large-group interventions is bringing together large numbers of organisation members (often more than 100) for a two- to four-day meeting or conference. Here, members work together to identify and resolve organisation-wide problems, design new approaches to structuring and managing the organisation or propose future directions for it.

Large-group interventions are among the fastest-growing OD applications. Large-group interventions[98] can vary on several dimensions including purpose, size, length, structure and number. The purposes of these change methods can range from solving particular organisational problems to envisioning future strategic directions. Large-group interventions have been run with groups of fewer than 50 to more than 2000 participants and have lasted between one and five days. Some large-group processes are relatively planned and structured, although others are more informal.[99] Some interventions involve a single large-group meeting, and others include a succession of meetings to accomplish system-wide change in a short period of time.[100]

Despite these differences, large-group interventions have similar conceptual foundations and methods. Large-group interventions have evolved over the past 25 years and represent a combination of open systems applications and 'futuring' and 'visioning' exercises. Open systems approaches direct attention to how organisations interact with, and are shaped by, their environments. A popular method used in large-group interventions is called 'environmental scanning', which involves mapping the pressures placed on the organisation by external stakeholders, such as regulatory agencies, customers and competitors.[101] This analysis helps members devise new ways of responding to, and influencing, the environment. Futuring and visioning exercises guide members in creating 'images of potential' towards which the organisation can grow and develop.[102] Focusing on the organisation's potential rather than on its problems can increase members' energy for change.

What are the steps?

Conducting a large-group intervention generally involves the following three steps:

1 *Preparing for the large-group meeting.* A design team consisting of OD practitioners and several members from the organisation is convened to organise the event. The team generally addresses three key ingredients for successful large-group meetings: a compelling meeting theme, appropriate members to participate, and relevant tasks to address the theme. First, large-group interventions require a compelling reason or focal point for change. Although 'people problems' can be an important focus, more powerful reasons for large-group efforts include impending mergers or reorganisations, responding to environmental threats and opportunities, or proposing radical organisational changes.

A second issue in preparing for a large-group meeting includes inviting relevant people to participate. A fundamental goal of large-group interventions is to 'get the whole system in the room'. This involves inviting as many people as possible who have a stake in the conference theme, and who are energised and committed to conceiving and initiating change. The third ingredient for successful large-group meetings is to have a range of task activities that enable the participants to fully address the conference theme.

2 *Conducting the meeting.* The flow of events in a large-group meeting can vary greatly according to its purpose and the framework adopted. These gatherings, however, tend to involve three sequential activities: developing common ground among participants, discussing the issues and creating an agenda for change. First, participants develop sufficient common ground among themselves to permit joint problem solving. This generally involves team-building activities. One exercise for creating teamwork is called 'appreciating the past'. It asks participants to examine the significant events, milestones and highlights of the organisation's previous 20 years.[103]

Second, members discuss the system-wide issue or theme. To promote widespread participation, members are typically organised into subgroups of eight to 10 people, representing as many stakeholder viewpoints as possible. The subgroups may be asked to address a general question. Subgroup members brainstorm answers to these questions, record them on flipchart paper, and share them with the larger group. The responses from the different subgroups are compared, and common themes identified. The final task of large-group meetings is creating an agenda for change. Participants are asked to reflect on what they have learned at the meeting and to suggest changes for themselves, their department and the whole organisation. Members from the same department are often grouped together to discuss their proposals and to decide on action plans, timetables and accountabilities.

Action items for the total organisation are referred to a steering committee that addresses organisation-wide policy issues and action plans. At the conclusion of the large-group meeting, the departmental subgroups and the steering committee report their conclusions to all participants and seek initial commitment for change.

3 *Follow-up on the meeting outcomes.* Follow-up efforts are vital if the action plans from large-scale interventions are to be implemented. These activities involve communicating the results of the meeting to the rest of the organisation, gaining wider commitment to the changes, and structuring the change process.

Results of large-group interventions

The number of case studies describing the methods and results of large-group interventions has increased dramatically. Large-group interventions have been conducted in a variety of organisations (including Hewlett-Packard and Rockport); around a variety of themes or issues, including natural resource conservation, community development and strategic change; and in a variety of countries, including Pakistan, England and India.[104] Despite this proliferation of practice, however, little systematic research has been done on the effects of large-group interventions. Because these change efforts often set the stage for subsequent OD interventions, it is difficult to isolate their specific results from those of the other changes. Anecdotal evidence from practitioners suggests the following benefits from large-group interventions: increased energy towards organisational change, improved feelings of 'community', ability to see 'outside the boxes' and improved relationships with stakeholders. Clearly, systematic research is needed on this important system-wide process intervention.

Summary

In this chapter, we presented human process interventions aimed at people and processes. In this area of OD – and some would suggest it is the most common form of change management – the chapter begins with the many strategies directed towards improving individual performance and group dynamics. Although there are many interventions that may be appropriate under certain circumstances, a few were selected which are most commonly used: performance appraisal, goal setting, management by objectives (MBO) and reward systems. As these are among the earliest interventions in OD, these change programs also help people to gain interpersonal skills, work through interpersonal conflicts and develop effective groups.

The first interpersonal intervention discussed was the T-group, the forerunner of modern OD change programs. T-groups typically consist of a small number of strangers who meet with a professional trainer to explore the social dynamics that emerge from their interactions. OD practitioners often attend T-groups themselves to improve their interpersonal skills, or recommend that managers attend a T-group to learn more about how their behaviours affect others.

Process consultation is used not only as a way of helping groups become effective but also as a process whereby groups can learn to diagnose and solve their own problems and to continue to develop their competence and maturity. Important areas of activity include communications, roles of group members, difficulties with problem-solving and decision-making norms, and leadership and authority. The basic difference between process consultation and third-party intervention is that the latter focuses on interpersonal dysfunction in social relationships between two or more individuals within the same organisation, and is directed more towards resolving direct conflict between those individuals.

Team building is directed towards improving group effectiveness and the ways in which members of teams work together. These teams may be permanent or temporary, but their members have either common organisational aims or work activities. The general process of team building, like process consultation, attempts to equip a group to handle its own ongoing problem solving. Selected aspects of team building include the family group diagnostic meeting and family group team-building meeting.

The other organisation process interventions do not claim universal success; they work best only in certain situations. The organisation confrontation meeting is a way of mobilising resources for organisational problem solving and seems especially relevant for organisations undergoing stress. The intergroup relations approaches are designed to help solve a variety of organisational problems. Microcosm groups can be formed to address particular issues and use parallel processes to diffuse group solutions to the organisation. The intergroup conflict resolution approach involves a method for mitigating dysfunctional conflicts between groups or departments. Conflict can be dysfunctional in situations in which groups must work together. It may, however, promote organisational effectiveness when departments are relatively independent of each other. Large-group interventions are designed to focus the energy and attention of a 'whole system' around organisational processes such as a vision, strategy or culture. It is best used when the organisation is about to begin a large-scale change effort or is facing a new situation.

Activities

REVIEW QUESTIONS

1   How can you best describe a 'process consultant'?

2   Describe the two major components of group problem solving.

3   What are the basic implications of the model for conflict resolution?

4   In a third party consultation, what skill must the third party develop in order to be successful?

5   The results of team building can be classified into three main areas. What are they?

6 Outline the five forms of intervention. When are they used?

7 What are the characteristics of a system-wide process intervention?

8 Identify the characteristics of intergroup conflict resolution methods.

9 What are the two basic assumptions about managerial behaviour in the management grid?

10 What are the steps involved in improving interdepartmental/intergroup relationships?

11 What are the components of the Johari window?

12 What are the essential characteristics of 'large-scale interventions'?

DISCUSSION AND ESSAY QUESTIONS

1 What is a T-group? Discuss the basic objectives of T-groups. What are their strengths and weaknesses?

2 Describe the similarities and differences between a normative approach, such as Grid® Organization Development, and an organisation confrontation meeting.

3 Discuss the similarities and differences between an organisation confrontation meeting and an intergroup conflict resolution intervention.

4 Outline the steps and processes in Bennis's use of Blake's basic design to improve relationships between two groups of State Department officials: high-level administrative officers, and officers in the Foreign Service. How might they be used in a parallel situation within an organisation? Are they appropriate? What changes, if any, might be required?

5 The text discusses the use of microcosm groups and, as an example, outlines the use of such a group to address diversity issues within an organisation. Could the same or a similar technique be used to resolve incidents of racial intolerance in the general community? If so, how? If not, why not?

SEARCH ME! EXCERCISES

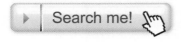

Explore **Search me! management** for relevant articles on OD interventions: people and process. Search me! is an online library of world-class journals, ebooks and newspapers, including *The Australian* and *The New York Times,* and is updated daily. Log in to Search me! through **http://login.cengage.com** using the access card in the front of this book.

Keywords

Try searching for the following terms:
> Conflict
> Development
> Goal setting
> Johari window
> Management by objectives
> Performance management

> Process consultation
> Reward
> Team building

> T-groups
> Third-party intervention

>> *Search tip:*

Search me! management contains information from both local and international sources. To get the greatest number of search results, try using both Australian and American spellings in your searches, e.g. 'globalisation' and 'globalization'; 'organisation' and 'organization'.

Notes

1 A. Mohrman, S. Mohrman and C. Worley, 'High technology performance management', in *Managing Complexity in High Technology Organizations*, eds M. Von Glinow and S. Mohrman (New York: Oxford University Press, 1990): 216–36.

2 D. McDonald and A. Smith, 'A proven connection: performance management and business results', *Compensation and Benefits Review*, 27 (1995): 59–64.

3 J. Riedel, D. Nebeker and B. Cooper, 'The influence of monetary incentives on goal choice, goal commitment and task performance', *Organisational Behaviour and Human Decision Processes*, 42 (1988): 155–80; P. Earley, T. Connolly and G. Ekegren, 'Goals, strategy development and task performance: some limits on the efficacy of goal setting', *Journal of Applied Psychology*, 74 (1989): 24–33; N. Perry, 'Here come richer, riskier pay plans', *Fortune* (19 December 1988): 50–8; E. Lawler III, *High Involvement Management* (San Francisco: Jossey-Bass, 1986); A. Mohrman, S. Resnick-West and E. Lawler III, *Designing Performance Appraisal Systems* (San Francisco: Jossey-Bass, 1990).

4 D. E. Detmer and E. B. Steen, *The Academic Health Centre: Leadership and Performance* (New York: Cambridge University Press, 2005).

5 Mohrman, Mohrman and Worley, 'High technology performance management', op. cit.

6 E. Locke and G. Latham, *A Theory of Goal Setting and Task Performance* (Englewood Cliffs, NJ: Prentice-Hall, 1990).

7 Locke and Latham, *A Theory of Goal Setting*, op. cit.; E. Locke, R. Shaw, L. Saari and G. Latham, 'Goal setting and task performance: 1969–1980', *Psychological Bulletin*, 97 (1981): 125–52; M. Tubbs, 'Goal setting: a meta-analytic examination of the empirical evidence', *Journal of Applied Psychology*, 71 (1986): 474–83.

8 A. O'Leary-Kelly, J. Martocchio and D. Frink, 'A review of the influence of group goals on group performance', *Academy of Management Journal*, 37:5 (1994): 1285–301.

9 S. Tully, 'Why to go for stretch targets', *Fortune* (14 November 1994): 145–58.

10 D. Crown and J. Rosse, 'Yours, mine and ours: facilitating group productivity through the integration of individual and group goals', *Organisation Behaviour and Human Decision Processes*, 64:2 (1995): 138–50.

11 P. Drucker, *The Practice of Management* (New York: Harper and Row, 1954): 63.

12 G. Odiorne, *Management by Objectives* (New York: Pitman, 1965).

13 H. Levinson, 'Management by objectives: a critique', *Training and Development Journal*, 26 (1972): 410–25.

14 D. McGregor, 'An uneasy look at performance appraisal', *Harvard Business Review*, 35 (May–June 1957): 89–94.

15 M. D. Tovey and M. L. Uren, *Managing Performance Improvement* (Frenchs Forest, NSW: Pearson Education, 2006).

16 Locke and Latham, *A Theory of Goal Setting*, op. cit.

17 Tubbs, 'Goal setting', op. cit.; R. Guzzo, R. Jette and R. Katzell, 'The effects of psychologically based intervention programs on worker productivity: a meta-analysis', *Personal Psychology*, 38 (1985): 275–91; A. Mento, R. Steel and R. Karren, 'A meta-analytic study of the effects of goal setting on task performance: 1966–84', *Organisational Behaviour and Human Decision Processes*, 39 (1987): 52–83; O'Leary-Kelly, Martocchio and Frink, 'A review of the influence of group goals on group performance', op. cit.

18 C. Pearson, 'Participative goal setting as a strategy for improving performance and job satisfaction: a longitudinal evaluation with railway track maintenance gangs', *Human Relations*, 40 (1987): 473–88; R. Pritchard, S. Jones, P. Roth, K. Stuebing and S. Ekeberg, 'Effects of group feedback, goal setting and incentives on organisational productivity', *Journal of Applied Psychology*, 73 (1988): 337–58.

19 S. Yearta, S. Maitlis and R. Briner, 'An exploratory study of goal setting in theory and practice: a motivational technique that works?', *Journal of Occupational and Organisational Psychology*, 68 (1995): 237–52.

20 R. Steers, 'Task-goal attributes: achievement and supervisory performance', *Organisational Behaviour and Human Performance*, 13 (1975): 392–403; G. Latham and G. Yukl, 'A review of research on the application of goal setting in organisations', *Academy of Management Journal*, 18 (1975): 824–45; R. Steers and L. Porter, 'The role of task-goal attributes in employee performance', *Psychological Bulletin*, 81 (1974): 434–51; Early, Connolly and Ekegren, 'Goals, strategy development and task performance', op. cit.; J. Hollenbeck and A. Brief, 'The effects of individual differences and goal origin on goal setting and performance', *Organisational Behaviour and Human Decision Processes*, 40 (1987): 392–414.

21 P. J. Davis, *Organisational Development in Local Government: Human Resource Issues and CEOs*, 2006, http://trove.nla.gov.au/work/34480686?selectedversion=NBD40843764.

22 G. Latham and R. Wexley, *Increasing Productivity Through Performance Appraisal* (Reading, MA: Addison-Wesley, 1981).

23 C. Peck, 'Pay and performance: the interaction of compensation and performance appraisal', *Research Bulletin*, 155 (New York: Conference Board, 1984).

24 E. Lawler III, *Pay and Organization Development* (Reading, MA: Addison-Wesley, 1981): 113; Mohrman, Resnick-West and Lawler, *Designing Performance Appraisal Systems*, op. cit.

25 D. Antonioni, 'Improve the performance management process before discounting performance appraisals', *Compensation and Benefits Review*, 26:3 (1994): 29–37.

26 S. Mohrman, G. Ledford Jr, E. Lawler III and A. Mohrman, 'Quality of work life and employee involvement', in *International Review of Industrial and Organizational Psychology*, eds C. Cooper and I. Robertson (New York: John Wiley, 1986); G. Yukl and R. Lepsinger, 'How to get the most out of 360 degree feedback', *Training*, 32:12 (1995): 45–50.

27 Mohrman, Ledford, Lawler and Mohrman, 'Quality of work life and employee involvement', op. cit.

28 E. Huse, 'Performance appraisal – a new look', *Personnel Administration*, 30 (March–April 1967): 3–18.

29 S. Gebelein, 'Employee development: multi-rater feedback goes strategic', *HR Focus*, 73:1 (1996): 1, 4; B. O'Reilly, '360 degree feedback can change your life', *Fortune* (17 October 1994): 93–100.

30 J. Fairbank and D. Prue, 'Developing performance feedback systems', in *Handbook of Organizational Behavior Management*, ed. L. Frederiksen (New York: John Wiley & Sons, 1982).

31 R. Ammons, *Knowledge of Performance: Survey of Literature, Some Possible Applications and Suggested Experimentation*, USAF WADC technical report 5414 (Wright Patterson Air Force Base, Ohio: Wright Air Development Center, Aero Medical Laboratory, 1954); J. Adams, 'Response feedback and learning', *Psychology Bulletin*, 70 (1968): 486–504; J. Annett, *Feedback and Human Behaviour* (Baltimore, MD: Penguin, 1969); J. Sassenrath, 'Theory and results on feedback and retention', *Journal of Educational Psychology*, 67 (1975): 894–9; F. Luthans and T. Davis, 'Behavioural management in service organisations', in *Service Management Effectiveness*, eds D. Bowen, R. Chase and T. Cummings (San Francisco: Jossey-Bass, 1989): 177–210.

32 R. Kopelman, *Managing Productivity in Organizations* (New York: McGraw-Hill, 1986).

33 Guzzo, Jette and Katzell, 'The effects of psychologically based intervention programs', op. cit.

34 D. Nadler, 'The effects of feedback on task group behaviour: a review of the experimental research', *Organisational Behaviour and Human Performance*, 23 (1979): 309–38; D. Nadler, C. Cammann and P. Mirvis, 'Developing a feedback system for work units: a field experiment in structural change', *Journal of Applied Behavioural Science*, 16 (1980): 41–62; J. Chobbar and

J. Wallin, 'A field study on the effect of feedback frequency on performance', *Journal of Applied Psychology*, 69 (1984): 524–30.

35 W. Scott, J. Farh and P. Podsakoff, 'The effects of "intrinsic" and "extrinsic" reinforcement contingencies on task behaviour', *Organisational Behaviour and Human Decision Processes*, 41 (1988): 405–25; E. Lawler III, *Strategic Pay* (San Francisco: Jossey-Bass, 1990).

36 J. Campbell, M. Dunnette, E. Lawler III and K. Weick, *Managerial Behaviour, Performance and Effectiveness* (New York: McGraw-Hill, 1970).

37 I. Brooks, *Organisational Behaviour: Individuals, Groups and Organisation*, 2nd edn, paperback (Prentice Hall, 2002).

38 Lawler, *Pay and Organisation Development*, op. cit.: 101–11.

39 E. Lawler III and G. Jenkins, *Employee Participation in Pay Plan Development* (unpublished technical report to US Department of Labor, Ann Arbor, MI: Institute for Social Research, University of Michigan, 1976).

40 C. Beard and J. P. Wilson, *Experiential Learning: A Best Practice Handbook for Educators and Trainers* (London, Philadelphia: Kogan Page, 2006).

41 J. Campbell and M. Dunnette, 'Effectiveness of T-group experiences in managerial training and development', *Psychological Bulletin*, 70 (August 1968): 73–103.

42 ibid.

43 M. Dunnette, J. Campbell and C. Argyris, 'A symposium: laboratory training', *Industrial Relations*, 8 (October 1968): 1–45.

44 Campbell and Dunnette, 'Effectiveness of T-Group experiences', op. cit.; R. House, 'T-group education and leadership effectiveness: a review of the empirical literature and a critical evaluation', *Personnel Psychology*, 20 (Spring 1967): 1–32; J. Campbell, M. Dunnette, E. Lawler III and K. Weick, *Managerial Behavior, Performance, and Effectiveness* (New York: McGraw-Hill, 1970): 292–8.

45 J. Porras and P. Berg, 'The impact of organization development', *Academy of Management Review*, 3 (April 1978): 249–66.

46 J. Nicholas, 'The comparative impact of organization development interventions on hard criteria measures', *Academy of Management Review*, 7 (October 1982): 531–42.

47 D. Bowers, 'OD techniques and their results in 23 organizations: the Michigan IGL Study', *Journal of Applied Behavioral Science*, 9 (January–February 1973): 21–43.

48 G. Neuman, J. Edwards and N. Raju, 'Organizational development interventions: a meta-analysis of their effects on satisfaction and other attitudes', *Personnel Psychology*, 42 (1989): 461–83.

49 R. Kaplan, 'Is openness passe?', *Human Relations*, 39 (November 1986): 242.

50 E. Schein, *Process Consultation II: Lessons for Managers and Consultants* (Reading, MA: Addison-Wesley, 1987).

51 ibid.: 5–17.

52 ibid.: 34.

53 J. Fast, *Body Language* (Philadelphia: Lippincott, M. Evans, 1970).

54 J. Luft, 'The Johari window', *Human Relations Training News*, 5 (1961): 6–7.

55 J. Gibb, 'Defensive communication', *Journal of Communication*, 11 (1961): 141–8.

56 S. G. Krantz and L. Lee, *Explorations in Harmonic Analysis: With Applications to Complex Function Theory and the Heisenberg Group* (Boston: Birkhauser Verlag, c2009).

57 N. Clapp, 'Work group norms: leverage for organizational change, theory and application', working paper (Plainfield, NJ: Block Petrella Weisbord, no date); R. Allen and S. Pilnick, 'Confronting the shadow organization: how to detect and defeat negative norms', *Organizational Dynamics* (Spring 1973): 3–18.

58 Schein, *Process Consultation; Process Consultation II*, op. cit.

59 ibid.: 32–4.

60 R. Walton, *Managing Conflict: Interpersonal Dialogue and Third-Party Roles*, 2nd edn (Reading, MA: Addison-Wesley, 1987).

61 ibid.: 83–110.

62 J. B. Miner, *Organizational Behavior I. Essential Theories of Motivation and Leadership* (Armonk, N.Y.: M.E. Sharpe, c2005).

63 W. Dyer, *Team Building: Issues and Alternatives*, 2nd edn (Reading, MA: Addison-Wesley, 1987).

64 J. Katzenbach and D. Smith, *The Wisdom of Teams* (Boston: Harvard Business School Press, 1993).

65 M. A. West, *Effective Teamwork: Practical Lessons from Organizational Research* (Malden, MA: BPS Blackwell, 2004).

66 J. Lewis III, 'Management team development: will it work for you?', *Personnel* (July/August 1975): 14–25.

67 D. Eden, 'Team development: a true field experiment at three levels of rigor', *Journal of Applied Psychology*, 70 (1985): 94–100.

68 R. Woodman and J. Sherwood, 'The role of team development in organizational effectiveness: a critical review', *Psychological Bulletin*, 88 (July–November 1980): 166–86.

69 Porras and Berg, 'Impact of organization development', op. cit.

70 Nicholas, 'Comparative impact', op. cit.

71 Woodman and Sherwood, 'The role of team development', op. cit.

72 R. Woodman and S. Wayne, 'An investigation of positive-finding bias in evaluation of organization development interventions', *Academy of Management Journal*, 28 (December 1985): 889–913.

73 R. Boss, 'Team building and the problem of regression: the personal management interview as an intervention', *Journal of Applied Behavioral Science*, 19 (1983): 67–83.

74 R. Buller and C. Bell Jr, 'Effects of team building and goal setting: a field experiment', *Academy of Management Journal*, 29 (1986): 305–28.

75 M. Weisbord, *Productive Workplaces* (San Francisco: Jossey-Bass, 1987).

76 R. Beckhard, 'The confrontation meeting', *Harvard Business Review*, 4 (1967): 149–55.

77 B. Benedict Bunker and B. Alban, 'What makes large-group interventions effective?', *Journal of Applied Behavioral Science*, 28:4 (1992): 579–91; N. Tichy and S. Sherman, *Control Your Destiny or Someone Else Will* (New York: HarperCollins Publishers, 1993).

78 R. Beckhard, *Organization Development: Strategies and Models* (Reading, MA: Addison-Wesley, 1969).

79 W. Bennis, *Organization Development: Its Nature, Origins, and Prospects* (Reading, MA: Addison-Wesley, 1969): 7.

80 C. Alderfer, 'An intergroup perspective on group dynamics', in *Handbook of Organizational Behavior*, ed. J. Lorsch (Englewood Cliffs, NJ: Prentice-Hall, 1987): 190–222; C. Alderfer, 'Improving organizational communication through long-term intergroup intervention', *Journal of Applied Behavioral Science*, 13 (1977): 193–210; C. Alderfer, R. Tucker, C. Alderfer and L. Tucker, 'The Race Relations Advisory Group: An intergroup intervention', in *Organizational Change and Development*, 2, eds W. Pasmore and R. Woodman (Greenwich, CT: JAI Press, 1988): 269–321.

81 Alderfer, 'An intergroup perspective on group dynamics', op. cit.

82 Alderfer, 'Improving organizational communication', op. cit.

83 D. Tjosvold, 'Cooperation theory and organizations', *Human Relations*, 37 (1984): 743–67.

84 R. Blake, H. Shepard and J. Mouton, *Managing Intergroup Conflict in Industry* (Houston: Gulf, 1954).

85 Beckhard, *Organization Development*, op. cit.

86 E. Neilson, 'Understanding and managing intergroup conflict', in *Organizational Behavior and Administration*, eds P. Lawrence, L. Barnes and J. Lorsch (Homewood, IL: Richard Irwin, 1976): 291–305.

87 Blake, Shepard and Mouton, *Managing Intergroup Conflict*, op. cit.

88 Bennis, *Organization Development*, op. cit.

89 ibid.: 4.

90 R. Golembiewski and A. Blumberg, 'Confrontation as a training design in complex organizations: attitudinal changes in a diversified population of managers', *Journal of Applied Behavioral Science*, 3 (1967): 525–47.

91 W. French and C. Bell, *Organization Development: Behavioral Science Interventions for Organization Improvement* (Englewood Cliffs, NJ: Prentice-Hall, 1978).

92 P. D. Howard, *Building and Implementing a Security Certification and Accreditation Program: Official (ISC) Guide to the CAP CBK* (Boca Raton, FL: Auerbach Publications, 2006).

93 E. Huse and M. Beer, 'Eclectic approach to organizational development', *Harvard Business Review*, 49 (1971): 103–13.

94 E. Huse, 'The behavioral scientist in the shop', *Personnel*, 44 (May–June 1965): 8–16.

95 J. Fordyce and R. Weil, *Managing WITH People* (Reading, MA: Addison-Wesley, 1971).

96 K. Thomas, 'Conflict and conflict management', in *Handbook of Industrial and Organizational Psychology*, ed. M. Dunnette (Chicago: Rand McNally, 1976): 889–936.

97 Weisbord, *Productive Workplaces*, op. cit.; M. Weisbord, *Discovering Common Ground* (San Francisco: Berrett Koehler, 1993); B. Benedict Bunker and B. Alban, eds, 'Special issue: large-group interventions', *Journal of Applied Behavioral Science*, 28:4 (1992); H. Owen, *Open*

Space Technology: A User's Guide (Potomac, MD: Abbott, 1992).

98 J. Smythe, *The CEO – The Chief Engagement Officer: Turning Hierarchy Upside Down to Drive Performance* (Aldershot, England; Burlington, VT: Gower, c2007).

99 H. Owen, *Open Space Technology*, op. cit.

100 D. Axelrod, 'Getting everyone involved', *Journal of Applied Behavioral Science*, 28:4 (1992): 499–509.

101 F. Emery and E. Trist, *Towards a Social Ecology* (New York: Plenum Publishing, 1973); R. Beckhard and R. Harris, *Organizational Transitions: Managing Complex Change*, 2nd edn (Reading, MA: Addison-Wesley, 1987).

102 R. Lippitt, 'Future before you plan', in *NTL Manager's Handbook* (Arlington, VA: NTL Institute, 1983): 38–41.

103 Weisbord, *Productive Workplaces*, op. cit.

104 Weisbord, *Discovering Common Ground*, op. cit.

CHAPTER 8

OD interventions: Strategy and structure

This chapter is concerned with interventions that are aimed at organisation and environment relationships. These change programs are relatively recent additions to the OD field that focus on helping organisations to relate better to their environments, and to achieve a better fit with those external forces that affect goal achievement and performance. Practitioners are discovering that additional knowledge and skills, such as competitive strategy, finance, marketing and political science, are necessary to conduct such large-scale change.

Because organisations are open systems, they must relate to their environments if they are to gain the resources and information needed to function and prosper. These relationships define an organisation's strategy and are affected by particular aspects and features of the environment. Organisations have devised a number of responses for managing environmental interfaces. The responses vary from creating special units to scan the environment to forming strategic alliances with other organisations.

The interventions described in this chapter are designed to help organisations to gain a comprehensive understanding of their environments and to devise appropriate responses to external demands. Open systems planning is aimed at helping organisation members to assess the larger environment and to develop strategies for relating to it more effectively. The intervention results in a clear strategic mission for the organisation, as well as action plans for influencing the environment in favoured directions.

The final section is concerned with work design: creating jobs and work groups that generate high levels of employee fulfilment and productivity. This technostructural intervention[1] can be part of a larger employee involvement application, or it can be an independent change program. Work design has been extensively researched and applied in organisations. Recently, organisations have tended to combine work design with formal structure and the support of changes in goal setting, reward systems, work environment and other performance management practices. These organisational factors can help to structure and reinforce the kinds of work behaviours associated with specific work designs.

ORGANISATION AND ENVIRONMENT FRAMEWORK

This section provides a framework for understanding how environments affect organisations and, in turn, how organisations can impact on environments. The framework is based on the concept that organisations and their sub-units are open systems existing in environmental contexts. Environments provide organisations with the necessary resources, information and legitimacy, and organisations must maintain effective relationships with suitable environments if they are to survive and grow. A manufacturing firm, for example, must obtain raw materials so that it can produce its products, and then use appropriate technologies to efficiently produce them, induce customers to buy them, and satisfy the laws and regulations that govern its operations. Because organisations are dependent on environments, they need to manage all the external constraints and contingencies, while at the same time taking advantage of external opportunities. They also need to influence the environment in favourable directions through such methods as political lobbying, advertising and public relations.

In this section, we first describe the different environments that can affect organisations, and then identify those environmental dimensions that tend to influence the organisational responses to those external forces. Finally, we review the different ways in which an organisation can respond to the environment. This material provides an introductory context for describing the various interventions that concern organisation and environment relationships: open systems planning and transorganisational development.[2]

Environments

Organisational environments consist of everything outside organisations that can affect, either directly or indirectly, their performance and outcomes. This could include external agents (such as suppliers, customers, regulators and competitors) and the cultural, political and economic forces in the wider societal and global context. These two classes of environments are called the 'task environment' and the 'general environment', respectively.[3] We will also describe the enacted environment, which reflects members' perceptions of the general and task environments.

The *general environment* consists of all external forces that can influence an organisation or department, and includes technological, legal and regulatory, political, economic, social and ecological components. Each of these forces can affect the organisation in both direct and indirect ways. For example, economic recessions can directly impact on the demand for a company's product. The general environment can also impact indirectly on organisations by virtue of the linkages between external agents. For example, an organisation may have trouble obtaining raw materials from a supplier because a consumer group has embroiled the supplier in a labour dispute with a national union, a lawsuit with a government regulator or a boycott. These members of the organisation's general environment can affect the organisation, even though they have no direct connection to it.

The *task environment* consists of those specific individuals and organisations that interact directly with the organisation and can affect goal achievement. The task environment consists of customers, suppliers, competitors, producers of substitute products or services, labour unions, financial institutions and so on. These direct relationships are the medium through which organisations and environments mutually influence one another. Customers, for example, can demand changes in the organisation's products, but the organisation can attempt to influence customers' tastes and desires through advertising.

The *enacted environment*[4] consists of the organisation's perception and representation of its environment. Weick suggested that environments must be perceived before they can influence decisions as to how to respond.[5] Organisation members must actively observe, register and make sense of the environment before their decisions as to how to act can be made. Thus, only the enacted environment can affect which organisational responses are chosen. The general and task environments, however, can influence whether those responses are successful or ineffective. For example, members may perceive customers as relatively satisfied with their products and may decide to make only token efforts at new-product development. If those perceptions are wrong and customers are dissatisfied with the products, the meagre efforts at product development can have disastrous consequences for the organisation. Consequently, an organisation's enacted environment should accurately reflect its general and task environments if members' decisions and actions are to be based on external realities.

Environmental dimensions

Organisational environments can be characterised along a number of dimensions that can influence organisation and environment relationships. One perspective views environments as information flows and suggests that organisations need to process information in order to discover how to relate to their environments.[6] The key feature of the environment to affect information processing is information uncertainty or the degree to which environmental information is ambiguous. Organisations seek to remove uncertainty from their environment so that they know how best to transact with it. For example, they try to discern customer needs through focus groups and surveys, and they attempt to understand competitor strategies by studying their press releases and sales force behaviours, and by learning about their key personnel. The greater the uncertainty, the more information processing is required to learn about the environment. This is particularly the case when environments are dynamic and complex. Dynamic environments change abruptly and unpredictably, while complex environments have many parts or elements that can affect organisations. These kinds of environments pose difficult information-processing problems for organisations. Global competition, technological change and financial markets, for example, have made the environments of many multinational firms highly uncertain and have severely strained their information-processing capacity.

Another perspective sees environments as consisting of resources for which organisations compete.[7] The key feature of the environment is resource dependence, or the degree to which an organisation relies on other organisations for resources. Organisations seek to manage critical sources of resource dependence, while remaining as autonomous as possible. For example, companies may contract with several suppliers of the same raw material so that they are not overly dependent on one vendor. Resource dependence is extremely high for an organisation when other organisations control critical resources that cannot easily be obtained elsewhere. Resource criticality and availability determine the extent to which an organisation is dependent on other organisations and must respond to their demands, as the 1970s oil embargo by the Organisation of the Petroleum Exporting Countries (OPEC) clearly showed many Australian companies.

These two environmental dimensions – information uncertainty and resource dependence – can be combined to show the degree to which organisations are constrained by their environments and consequently must be responsive to their demands.[8] As shown in Figure 8.1, organisations have the most freedom from external forces when information uncertainty and resource dependence are both low. In this situation, organisations do not need to be responsive to their environments and can behave relatively independently of them. United States automotive manufacturers faced these conditions in the 1950s and operated with relatively little external constraint or threat. As information uncertainty and resource dependence become higher, however, organisations are more constrained

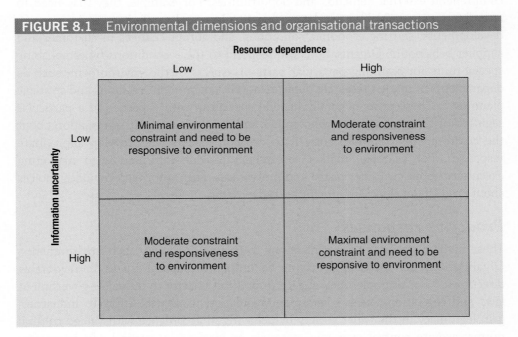

FIGURE 8.1 Environmental dimensions and organisational transactions

Resource dependence

	Low	High
Low	Minimal environmental constraint and need to be responsive to environment	Moderate constraint and responsiveness to environment
High	Moderate constraint and responsiveness to environment	Maximal environment constraint and need to be responsive to environment

Information uncertainty

and must be more responsive to external demands. They must accurately perceive the environment and respond to it appropriately. Modern organisations – such as financial institutions, high-technology businesses and health care facilities – are facing unprecedented amounts of environmental uncertainty and resource dependence. Their very existence depends on their recognition of external challenges and their quick and appropriate responses to them.

Organisational responses

Organisations employ a number of ways of responding to environmental demands. These help to buffer the organisation's technology from external disruptions and to link the organisation to sources of information and resources. Referred to as 'external structures', these responses are generally carried out by administrators and staff specialists who are responsible for setting corporate strategy and managing the environment. Three major external structures are described next.

Scanning units

Organisations must have the capacity to monitor and make sense of their environment if they are to respond to it appropriately. They must identify and attend to those environmental parts and features that are highly related to the organisation's own survival and growth. When environments have high information uncertainty, organisations may need to gather a diversity of information in order to comprehend external demands and opportunities. For example, they may need to attend to segmented labour markets,[9] changing laws and regulations, rapid scientific developments, shifting economic conditions, and abrupt changes in customer and supplier behaviours. Organisations can respond to these conditions by establishing special units for scanning particular parts or aspects of the environment, such as departments of market research, public relations, government relations and strategic planning.[10] These units generally include specialists with expertise in a particular segment of the environment, who gather and interpret relevant information about the environment, communicating it to decision makers who develop appropriate responses. For example, market researchers provide information to marketing executives about customer tastes and preferences. Such information guides choices about product development, pricing and advertising.

Proactive responses

These involve attempts by organisations to change or modify their environments. Organisations are increasingly trying to influence external forces in favourable directions.[11] For example, they engage in political activity to influence government laws and regulations; seek government regulation to control entry to industries; gain legitimacy in the wider society by behaving in accordance with valued cultural norms; acquire control over raw materials or markets by vertical and horizontal integration;[12] and introduce new products and services, using advertising to shape customer tastes and preferences. Although the range of proactive responses is almost limitless, organisations tend to be highly selective when choosing them. The responses can be costly to implement and can appear aggressive, thus evoking countervailing actions by powerful others, such as competitors and the government. For example, Microsoft's dominance in the software industry has drawn heavy scrutiny from the US Justice Department and from competitors. Moreover, organisations are paying increased attention to whether their responses are socially responsible and contribute to a healthy society. The Body Shop, for example, views its business as an important arm of society and devotes a considerable amount of time and corporate resources to charity and pressing social issues. Today, there is much global attention to the ethical and moral implications of organisational behaviours.

Collective structures

Organisations can cope with problems of environmental dependence[13] and uncertainty by increasing their co-ordination with other organisations. These collective structures help to control interdependencies among organisations and include such methods as bargaining, contracting, co-opting and creating joint ventures, federations, strategic alliances and consortia.[14] Contemporary organisations are increasingly turning to joint ventures and partnerships with other organisations in order to manage environmental uncertainty and perform tasks that are too costly and complicated for single organisations to perform. These multi-organisation arrangements are being used as a means of sharing resources for large-scale research and development, for reducing risks of innovation, for applying diverse expertise to complex problems and tasks, and for overcoming barriers to entry into foreign markets. For example, defence contractors are forming strategic alliances to bid on large government projects; organisations from different countries are forming joint ventures to overcome restrictive trade barriers; and high-technology businesses are forming research consortia to undertake significant and costly research and development for their industries. Major barriers to forming collective structures in Australia are the organisations' own drive to act autonomously and government policies that discourage co-ordination among organisations, especially in the same industry. Japanese industrial and economic policies, on the other hand, promote co-operation among organisations, thus giving them a competitive advantage in their responses to complex and dynamic global environments.[15] For example, starting in the late 1950s, the Japanese government provided financial assistance and support to a series of co-operative research efforts among Japanese computer manufacturers. The resulting technological developments enabled the computer firms to reduce IBM's share of the mainframe market in Japan from 70% to about 40% in less than 15 years.

OPEN SYSTEMS PLANNING

Open systems planning (OSP) helps an organisation to systematically assess its task environment and to develop strategic responses to it. Like the other interventions in this book, OSP treats organisations or departments as open systems that must interact with a suitable environment in order to survive and develop. It helps organisation members develop a strategic mission for relating to the environment and influencing it in favourable directions. The process of applying OSP begins with a diagnosis of the existing environment and how the organisation relates to it. It then develops possible future environments, and action plans to bring about the desired future environment. A number of practical guidelines exist to apply this intervention effectively.

Assumptions about organisation–environment relations

Open systems planning is based on four assumptions about how organisations relate, or should relate, to their environment.[16] These include the following:

1 *Organisation members' perceptions play a major role in environmental relations.* Members' perceptions determine which parts of the environment are attended to or ignored, as well as what value is placed on those parts. Such perceptions provide the basis for planning and implementing specific actions in relation to the environment. For example, a production manager might focus on those parts of the environment that are directly related to making a product, such as raw-material suppliers and available labour, while ignoring other, more indirect parts, such as government agencies. These perceptions would probably direct the manager towards talking with the suppliers and potential employees, while possibly neglecting the agencies. The key point is that organisation and environment relations are largely determined by how members perceive the environment and choose to act towards it.

2 *Organisation members must share a common view of the environment to permit co-ordinated action towards it.* Without a shared view of the environment, organisation members would have trouble relating to it. Conflicts would arise about what parts of the environment are important and what value should be placed on different parts. Such perceptual disagreements make planning and implementing a coherent strategy difficult. For example, members of a top management team might have different views on the organisation's environment. Unless those differences are shared and resolved, the team will have problems developing a business strategy for relating to the environment.[17]

3 *Organisation members' perceptions must accurately reflect the condition of the environment if organisational responses are to be effective.* Members can

misinterpret environmental information, ignore important forces or attend to negligible events. Such misperceptions can render organisational responses to the environment inappropriate, as happened to American car makers during the energy crisis of the mid-1970s. They believed that consumers wanted large automobiles and petroleum producers had plentiful supplies of relatively inexpensive petrol. The traditional strategy of manufacturing a high number of large-sized cars was quickly shown to be inappropriate to the actual environment; that is, consumers' growing preference for small, fuel-efficient cars and the decision of OPEC member nations to raise the price of crude oil. Such misperceptions typically occur when the environment exhibits high levels of complexity and unpredictable change. Such turbulence makes understanding the environment or predicting its future difficult.

4 *Organisations can not only adapt to their environment but also create it proactively.* Organisation and environment relations are typically discussed in terms of organisations adapting to environmental forces. Attention is directed to understanding and predicting environmental conditions so that organisations can better react to them. A more proactive alternative is for organisations to plan for a desired environment and then to take action against the existing environment so as to move it in the desired direction. This active stance goes beyond adaptation, because the organisation is trying to create a favourable environment rather than simply reacting to external forces. For example, when Alcoa first started to manufacture aluminium building materials, there was little demand for them. Rather than wait to see whether the market developed, Alcoa entered the construction business and pioneered the use of aluminium building materials. By being proactive, the company created a favourable environment.

Implementation process

Based on these premises about organisation and environment relations, open systems planning can help organisation members to assess their environment and plan a strategy for relating to it. After OSP, they may value differently the complexity of their environment and may generate a more varied range of response strategies.[18] OSP is typically carried out by the top management of an entire organisation, or by the management and key employees of a department. This group initially meets off-site for a two- to three-day period and may have several follow-up meetings of shorter duration. The OD practitioner helps to guide the process. Members are encouraged to share their perceptions of the environment and to collect and examine a diversity of related data. Considerable attention is directed to the communication process itself. Participants are helped to establish sufficient trust and openness to share different views and to work through differences.

OSP starts from the perspective of a particular organisation or department. This point of reference identifies the relevant environment. It serves as the focus of the planning process, which consists of the following steps:[19]

1 *Assess the external environment*[20] *in terms of domains and the expectations that those domains have for the organisation's behaviour.* This step maps the current environment facing the organisation. First, the different parts or domains of the environment are identified. Listing all the external groups that directly interact with the organisation – such as customers, suppliers or government agencies – usually does this. Then each domain's expectations of the organisation's behaviour are assessed.

2 *Assess how the organisation responds to the environmental expectations.* This step assesses the organisation's responses to the environmental expectations identified in step one.

3 *Identify the core mission of the organisation.* This step helps to identify the underlying purpose or core mission of the organisation, as shown by how it responds to external demands. Attention is directed at discovering the mission as it is evidenced in the organisation's behaviour, rather than by simply accepting an official statement of the organisation's purpose. This is accomplished by examining the organisation and those environment transactions identified in steps one and two, and then assessing the values that seem to underlie those interactions. These values provide clues about the actual identity or mission of the organisation.

4 *Create a realistic future scenario of environmental expectations and organisation responses.* This step asks members to project the organisation and its environment into the near future, assuming that there are no real changes in the organisation. It asks what will happen in steps one, two and three if the organisation continues to operate as it does at present.

5 *Create an ideal future scenario of environmental expectations and organisation responses.* Here, members are asked to create alternative, desirable futures. This involves going back over steps one, two and three and asking what members would ideally like to see happen in both the environment and the organisation in the near future. People are encouraged to fantasise about desired futures without worrying about possible constraints.

6 *Compare the present with the ideal future and prepare an action plan for reducing the discrepancy.* This last step identifies specific actions that will move both the environment and the organisation towards the desired future. Planning for appropriate interventions typically occurs in three time frames: tomorrow, six months from now and two years from now. Members also decide on a follow-up schedule for sharing the flow of actions and updating the planning process.

Guidelines for implementing open systems planning

Practitioners who have applied open systems planning offer a number of suggestions for its effective use.[21] These rules of thumb include the following:

1 *Devote sufficient time and resources.* Open systems planning is time-consuming and requires considerable effort and resources. There is much preparatory work

in collecting environmental information, analysing it and drafting reports for group discussion. Also, participants must be given sufficient time to develop healthy interpersonal relationships so that they can discuss the information openly, resolve conflicting viewpoints and arrive at a sufficient consensus to proceed effectively.

2 *Document all steps.* OSP generates considerable information and people can easily lose track of the data. Written reports of the various steps help to organise the diverse information. They can also keep other organisation members informed of the process and can provide them with a concrete focus for reacting to it.

3 *Deal only with key parts of the environment.* The tendency is to collect and examine too much information, losing track of what is important for organisational effectiveness. Mapping out the existing environment should start with an initial scanning that defines broad environmental domains. Only those domains considered important to organisational or departmental functioning are used for the remaining steps of the process.

4 *Follow the steps in order.* In using OSP, people tend to confuse the existing environment with the future environment. They also tend to mix the realistic future with the ideal future. If the steps are systematically followed, the process will logically lead from the present to the realistic future environment and then to the desired future environment.

5 *View planning as process, not outcome.* Probably the key value of OSP is helping organisation members develop an ongoing process for assessing and relating to the environment. While specific plans and action steps are important, they should be viewed as periodic outcomes of a larger process of environmental management.

TRANSORGANISATIONAL DEVELOPMENT

Transorganisational development[22] (TD) is an emerging form of planned change aimed at helping organisations develop collective and collaborative strategies with other organisations. Many of the tasks, problems and issues facing organisations today are too complex and multifaceted to be addressed by a single organisation. Multi-organisation strategies and arrangements are increasing rapidly in today's global, highly competitive environment. In the private sector, research and development consortia allow companies to share resources and risks associated with large-scale research efforts. For example, Sematech involves many large organisations – such as Intel, AT&T, IBM, Xerox and Motorola – that have joined together to improve the competitiveness of the US semiconductor industry. Joint ventures between domestic and foreign companies help to overcome trade barriers and to facilitate technology transfer across nations. For example, the New United Motor Manufacturing, Inc. in Fremont, California, began as a joint venture between General Motors and Toyota to produce automobiles, using Japanese teamwork methods. Recently closed, it was expected to reopen in 2010 as a Tesla–Toyota joint venture. In the public sector, partnerships between government and business provide the resources and initiative to undertake complex urban renewal projects, such as the Docklands project in Melbourne. Alliances among public service agencies in a region – such as the Goulburn rural health services in alliance with the local councils in Albury and Wodonga – can improve the co-ordination of services, promote economies and avoid costly overlap and redundancy.

Transorganisational systems and their problems

Cummings has referred to these multi-organisation structures as transorganisational systems (TSs): groups of organisations that have joined together for a common purpose.[23] TSs are functional social systems midway between single organisations and societal systems. They are able to make decisions and perform tasks on behalf of their member organisations, although members maintain their separate organisational identities and goals. In contrast to most organisations, TSs tend to be underorganised: relationships among member organisations are loosely coupled; leadership and power are dispersed among autonomous organisations, rather than hierarchically centralised; and commitment and membership are tenuous as member organisations attempt to maintain their autonomy while jointly performing.

These characteristics make creating and managing TSs difficult.[24] Potential member organisations may not see the need to join with other organisations. They may be concerned with maintaining their autonomy or have trouble identifying potential partners. Australian companies, for example, are traditionally 'rugged individualists', preferring to work alone rather than to join with other organisations. Even if organisations do decide to join together, they may have problems managing their relationships and controlling joint performances. Because members are typically accustomed to hierarchical forms of control, they may have difficulty managing lateral relations among independent organisations. They may also have difficulty managing different levels of commitment and motivation among members, and sustaining membership over time.

Application stages

Given these problems, transorganisational development has evolved as a unique form of planned change aimed at creating TSs and improving their effectiveness. In laying out the conceptual boundaries of TD, Cummings described the practice of TD as following the stages of planned change appropriate for underorganised systems (see Chapter 2).[25] These stages parallel other process models that have been proposed for creating and managing joint ventures, strategic alliances and interorganisational collaboration.[26] The four stages are shown in Figure 8.2, along with key issues that need to be addressed at each stage. The stages and issues are described next.

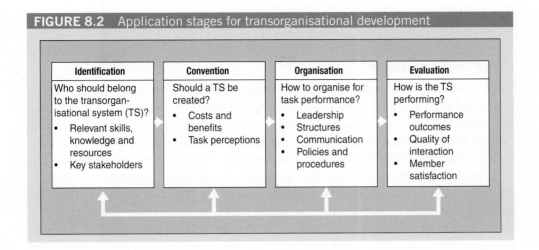

FIGURE 8.2 Application stages for transorganisational development

Identification stage

This initial stage of TD involves the identification of potential member organisations of the TS. It serves to specify the relevant participants for the remaining stages of TD. Identifying potential members can be difficult, because organisations may not perceive the need to join together or may not know enough about each other to make membership choices. These problems are typical when trying to create a new TS. Relationships among potential members may be loosely coupled or nonexistent, and so, even if organisations see the need to form a TS, they may be unsure about who should be included.

The identification stage is generally carried out by one or a few organisations who are interested in exploring the possibility of creating a TS. Change agents work with these organisations to specify criteria for membership in the TS and identify organisations meeting those standards. Because TSs are intended to perform specific tasks, a practical criterion for membership is how much organisations can contribute to task performance. Potential members can be identified and judged in terms of the skills, knowledge and resources that they can bring to bear on the TS task. TD practitioners warn, however, that identifying potential members should also take into account the political realities of the situation.[27] Consequently, key stakeholders who can affect the creation and subsequent performance of the TS are identified as possible members.

During the early stages of creating a TS, there may be insufficient leadership and cohesion among participants to choose potential members. In these situations, participants may contract with an outside change agent who can help them to achieve sufficient agreement on TS membership. In several cases of TD, change agents helped members to create a special leadership group that could make decisions on behalf of the participants.[28] This leadership group comprised a small cadre of committed members and was able to develop enough cohesion among themselves to carry out the identification stage.

Convention stage

Once potential members of the TS have been identified, the convention stage is concerned with bringing them together to assess whether creating a TS is desirable and feasible. This face-to-face meeting enables potential members to mutually explore their motivations for joining, and their perceptions of the joint task. They seek to establish sufficient levels of motivation and of task consensus to form the TS.

Like the identification stage, this phase of TD generally requires considerable direction and facilitation by change agents. Existing stakeholders may not have the legitimacy or skills to perform the convening function, and change agents can serve as convenors if they are perceived as legitimate and credible by the different organisations. In many TD cases, conveners came from research centres or universities with reputations for neutrality and expertise in TD.[29] Because participating organisations tend to have diverse motives and views and limited means for resolving differences, change agents may need to structure and manage interactions to facilitate the airing of differences and arriving at consensus about forming the TS. They may need to help organisations work through differences and reconcile self-interests with those of the larger TS.

Organisation stage

When the convention stage results in the decision to create a TS, members begin to organise themselves for task performance. This involves establishing structures and mechanisms to facilitate communication and interaction among members and to direct joint efforts to the task at hand.[30] For example, members may create a co-ordinating council to manage the TS and they might assign a powerful leader to head that group. They might choose to formalise exchanges among members by developing rules, policies and formal operating procedures. In cases in which members are required to invest large amounts of resources in the TS, such as might occur in an industry-based research consortium, the organising stage typically includes voluminous contracting and negotiating about members' contributions and returns. Here, corporate lawyers and financial analysts play key roles in structuring the TS. They determine how costs and benefits will be allocated among member organisations, as well as the legal obligations and contractual rights of members.

Evaluation stage

This final stage of TD involves assessing how the TS is performing. Members need feedback so that they can identify problems and begin to resolve them. Feedback data generally include performance outcomes and member satisfaction, as well as indicators of how well members are jointly interacting. Change agents, for example, can periodically interview or survey member organisations about various outcomes and features of the TS and feed that data back to TS leaders. Such information can enable leaders to make necessary modifications and adjustments in how the TS is operating. It may signal the need to return to previous stages of TD to make necessary corrections, as shown by the feedback arrows in Figure 8.2.

RESTRUCTURING ORGANISATIONS

Interventions aimed at structural design include moving from more traditional ways of dividing the organisation's overall work – such as functional, self-contained unit and matrix structures – to more integrative and flexible forms, such as process- and network-based structures. Diagnostic guidelines help determine which structure is appropriate for particular organisational environments, technologies and conditions.

Downsizing seeks to reduce costs and bureaucracy by decreasing the size of the organisation. This reduction in personnel can be accomplished by lay-offs, organisation redesign and outsourcing, which involves moving functions that are not part of the organisation's core competence to outside contractors. Successful downsizing is closely aligned with the organisation's strategy.

Re-engineering radically redesigns the organisation's core work processes to give tighter linkage and co-ordination among the different tasks. This work-flow integration results in faster, more responsive task performance. Business process management is often accomplished with new information technology that permits employees to control and co-ordinate work processes more effectively.

Downsizing

Downsizing refers to interventions that are aimed at reducing the size of the organisation.[31] This is typically accomplished by decreasing the number of employees through lay-offs, attrition, redeployment or early retirement, or by reducing the number of organisational units or managerial levels through divestiture, outsourcing, reorganisation or delayering. An important consequence of downsizing has been the rise of the contingent workforce. These less expensive temporary or permanent part-time workers are often hired by the organisations that just laid off thousands of their employees. In many cases, terminated employees become independent contractors or consultants to the organisation that terminated them. Overall cost reduction is achieved by replacing expensive permanent workers with a contingent workforce.

Downsizing is generally a response to several factors, including product or service demand, pressure to focus on short-term profits or budget goals, a major change in organisational strategy and the belief that the slimmer the organisation the better.[32] John Corrigan, the Technical Support Consultant at Chartered Practising Accountants Australia Management Accounting Centre of Excellence,

TABLE 8.1	Advantages, disadvantages and contingencies of the network-based form

Advantages

- Enables highly flexible and adaptive response to dynamic environments
- Creates a 'best of the best' organisation to focus resources on customer and market needs
- Each organisation can leverage a distinctive competency
- Permits rapid global expansion
- Can produce synergistic results

Disadvantages

- Managing lateral relations across autonomous organisations is difficult
- Motivating members to relinquish autonomy to join the network is troublesome
- Sustaining membership and benefits can be problematic
- May give partners access to proprietary knowledge/technology

Contingencies

- Highly complex and uncertain environments
- All sizes of organisations
- Highly uncertain technologies
- Goals of organisational specialisation and innovation
- Worldwide operations

states that cutting costs has been the mantra of business for the past decade or so, but that there is evidence to suggest that the decimation of middle management ranks in organisations has caused a loss of valuable experience and knowledge.[33] This view is supported by Professor Collins of the Australian Graduate School of Management, who says that downsizing in Australia has very negative connotations and that, through downsizing, companies have lost a lot of skills that were really needed.

Application stages

Successful downsizing interventions tend to proceed in the following steps:[34]

1 *Clarify the organisation's strategy.* In this initial stage, organisation leaders specify corporate strategy and clearly communicate how downsizing relates to it.

2 *Assess downsizing options and make relevant choices.* Once corporate strategy is clear, the full range of downsizing options can be identified and assessed. Table 8.2 describes three primary downsizing methods: workforce reduction, organisation redesign and systemic changes. A specific downsizing strategy may use elements of all three approaches.

From around the mid-1980s to today, it has become common for both private and public sector organisations to announce the elimination of thousands of jobs in the quest for quick productivity improvement. For example, in recent years Telstra and the Australian Public Service have each undergone major downsizing efforts involving thousands of employees.

TABLE 8.2 Three types of downsizing tactics

Downsizing tactic	Characteristics	Examples
Workforce reduction	Aimed at headcount reduction Short-term implementation Fosters a transition	Attrition Transfer and outplacement Retirement incentives Buyout packages Lay-offs
Organisation redesign	Aimed at organisation change Moderate-term implementation Fosters transition and, potentially, transformation	Eliminate functions Merge units Eliminate layers Eliminate products Redesign tasks
Systemic	Aimed at culture change Long-term implementation Fosters transformation	Change responsibility Involve all constituents Fosters continuous improvement and innovation Simplification Downsizing: a way of life

Source: K. Cameron, S. Freeman and A. Mishra, *Academy of Management Executive: The Thinking Manager's Source*. Copyright 1991 by Academy of Management (NY). Reproduced with permission of Academy of Management (NY) in the format Textbook via Copyright Clearance Center.

Organisations going through such downsizing have to be concerned about managing the effects of these cutbacks, not only for those who are being made redundant, but also for those who 'survive' – albeit with a reduced level of job security.

Unfortunately, organisations often choose obvious solutions for downsizing, such as lay-offs, that can be quickly implemented. This can produce a climate of fear and defensiveness as members focus on identifying who will be separated from the organisation. It is important to examine a broad range of options and to consider the entire organisation rather than certain areas. This can help to allay fears that favouritism and politics are the basis for downsizing decisions. Moreover, the participation of organisation members in such decisions can have positive benefits. It can create a sense of urgency for identifying and implementing options to downsizing other than lay-offs.

3 *Implement the changes*. This stage involves implementing methods for reducing the size of the organisation. Several practices characterise successful implementation. First, understand that downsizing is best controlled from the top down. Second, identify and target specific areas of inefficiency and high cost. Third, link specific actions to the organisation's strategy. Finally, communicate frequently, using a variety of media.

4 *Address the needs of survivors and those who leave*. When lay-offs occur, employees are generally asked to take on additional responsibilities and to learn new jobs, often with little or no increase in compensation. This added workload

can be stressful, and when combined with anxiety over past lay-offs and possible future ones, it can lead to what researchers have labelled the 'survivor syndrome'.[35] This involves a narrow set of self-absorbed and risk-averse behaviours that can threaten the organisation's survival. Organisations can address these survivor problems with communication processes that increase the amount and frequency of information provided. Communication should shift from explanations about who left (or why) to clarification of where the company is going, including its visions, strategies and goals.

Given the negative consequences typically associated with job loss, organisations have developed a number of methods to help employees who have been laid off. These include outplacement counselling, personal and family counselling, severance packages, office support for job searches, relocation services and job retraining. Each of these services is intended to help employees in their transition to another work situation.

5 *Follow through with growth plans.* Failure to move quickly to implement growth plans is a key determinant of ineffective downsizing.[36] For example, a 1992 study of 1020 human resource directors reported that only 44% of the companies that had downsized in the previous five years had shared details of their growth plans with employees; only 34% had told employees how they would fit into the company's new strategy.[37] These findings suggest that organisations need to ensure that employees understand the renewal strategy.

Results of downsizing

Research on the effects of downsizing has shown mixed results. Many studies have indicated that downsizing may not meet its intended goals, and there is mounting evidence that workforce reduction efforts were carried out in piecemeal fashion and failed to meet the objectives of the organisation.[38] Craig Littler studied 3500 companies across Australia and monitored downsizing patterns: in more than 60% of those companies, the practice of downsizing had not led to any improvement in productivity.[39]

These research findings paint a rather bleak picture of the success of downsizing. The results must be interpreted cautiously, however, as they are subject to at least two major flaws. First, many of the surveys were sent to human resource specialists who might have been naturally inclined to view downsizing in a negative light. Second, the studies of financial performance may have included a biased sample of firms. If the companies selected for analysis had been poorly managed, then downsizing alone would have been unlikely to improve financial performance.

On the positive side, a number of organisations – such as Telstra, General Electric, Motorola, Texas Instruments, Boeing, Chrysler and Hewlett-Packard – have posted solid financial returns after downsizing. Although this evidence contradicts the negative findings described above, recent research suggests that the way in which downsizing is conducted may explain these divergent outcomes.

A study of 30 downsized firms in the automobile industry showed that those companies that had effectively implemented the application stages described above scored significantly higher on several performance measures than had firms that had no downsizing strategy or that had implemented the steps poorly.[40] Anecdotal evidence from case studies of downsized firms also shows that organisations that effectively apply the application stages are more satisfied with the process and outcomes of downsizing than are firms that do not. Thus, the success of downsizing efforts may depend as much on how effectively this intervention is applied as on the size of the lay-offs or the amount of delayering. Application 8.1 is an example of a downsizing exercise where lucrative benefits are offered to employees to encourage staff to leave the organisation.

8.1

APPLICATION

Ford pushes buyout packages: Offers are most diverse, lucrative industry has seen

Responding to increasing competition from imported vehicles, significant losses and the consequences of the global financial crisis, US automotive manufacturers are in the process of laying off large numbers of employees as a part of an industry-wide restructuring program. As industry consultant John A. Casesa commented, 'These companies are trying to do in 24 months what they should have done over the past 24 years'.

Although 80 000 jobs have disappeared for various reasons since 2006, the industry is seeking to further reduce numbers and employ a lower-paid workforce in the future. Even the United Automobile Workers (UAW) union endorses the downsizing program. UAW's Ford Division Vice President, Bob King, is reported as saying that, 'there aren't enough jobs for everybody' as a result of the poor state of the US economy and the domestic manufacturers' loss of market share to imports.

Ford has instituted an aggressive attempt to sign up workers to agree to buyouts through offers of cash payments of $140 000, family college tuition plans and introductions to new external job opportunities. While the company hasn't revealed how many workers it wants to remove, industry observers estimate Ford's objective could be as high as 8000.

Buyouts are also on offer by General Motors to its 74 000 hourly employees and by Chrysler on a regional and plant basis.

Workers seem to recognise the inevitability of the reductions. One employee compared Ford's approach to his experience as a former steel worker. 'We never had this type of opportunity when I was in the steel industry. We knew for years that the industry was in trouble, and one day the doors just shut'.

Source: Based on Bill Vlasic, New York Times News Service, 'Ford pushes buyout packages: Offers are most diverse, lucrative industry has seen', *Corpus Christi Caller-Times*, 28 February 2008. Copyright 2008 Scripps Howard Publishing, Inc. All Rights Reserved.

Critical thinking questions:
1. One of Ford's buyout offers provides employees with four years of tuition up to the value of $15 000, health care and a stipend of 50% of the employee's base salary. Is this a good deal for the employee? Do you think Australian companies would do the same?
2. Does restructuring always have to include 'downsizing' in order to improve profitability and survival of the organisation?

Re-engineering

The final restructuring intervention is re-engineering: the fundamental rethinking and radical redesign of business processes in order to achieve dramatic improvements in performance.[41] Re-engineering seeks to transform how organisations produce and deliver goods and services. Beginning with the Industrial Revolution, organisations have increasingly fragmented work into specialised units, each focusing on a limited part of the overall production process. Although this division of labour has enabled organisations to mass-produce standardised products and services efficiently, it can be overly complicated and difficult to manage, as well as being slow to respond to the rapid and unpredictable changes experienced by many organisations today. Re-engineering addresses these problems by breaking down specialised work units into more integrated, cross-functional work processes. This streamlines work processes and makes them faster and more flexible; consequently, they are more responsive to changes in competitive conditions, customer demands, product life cycles and technologies.[42] As might be expected, re-engineering requires an almost revolutionary change in how organisations design and think about work. It addresses fundamental issues about why organisations do what they do, and why they do it in a particular way.

In radically changing business processes, re-engineering frequently takes advantage of new information technology. Modern information technologies – such as teleconferencing, expert systems, shared databases and wireless communication – can enable organisations to re-engineer. They can help organisations to break out of traditional ways of thinking about work and can permit entirely new ways of producing and delivering products. Whereas new information technology can enable organisations to re-engineer themselves, existing technology can thwart such efforts. Many re-engineering projects fail because existing information systems do not provide the information needed to operate integrated business processes. The systems do not allow interdependent departments to interface with each other; they often require new information to be entered by hand into separate computer systems before people in different work areas can access it.

Re-engineering[43] is also associated with interventions that have to do with downsizing and work design. Although these interventions have different conceptual and applied backgrounds, they overlap considerably in practice. Re-engineering can result in production and delivery processes that require fewer people and layers of management. Conversely, downsizing may require subsequent re-engineering interventions. When downsizing occurs without fundamental changes in how work is performed, the same tasks are simply being performed by a smaller number of people. Thus, expected cost savings may not be realised because lower productivity offsets lower salaries and fewer benefits.

Re-engineering invariably involves aspects of work design, where tasks are assigned to jobs or teams. It identifies and assesses core business processes and redesigns work to account for key task interdependencies running through them.

This typically results in new jobs or teams that emphasise multifunctional tasks, results-oriented feedback and employee empowerment – characteristics associated with motivational and sociotechnical approaches to work design. Regrettably, re-engineering has failed to apply attention to differences in individual people's reactions to work to its own work-design prescriptions. It advocates enriched work and teams, without consideration for the considerable research that shows that not all people are motivated to perform such work.

What are the steps?

Re-engineering is a relatively new intervention and is still developing applied methods. Early applications emphasised the identification of which business processes to re-engineer and technical assessment of the work flow. More recent efforts have extended re-engineering practice to address issues of managing change, such as how to manage resistance to change and how to manage the transition to new work processes.[44] The following application steps are included in re-engineering efforts, although the order may change slightly from one application to another.[45]

1 *Prepare the organisation.* Re-engineering begins with clarification and assessment of the organisation's strategic context, including its competitive environment, strategy and objectives.

2 *Fundamentally rethink the way work gets done.* This step lies at the heart of business process management and involves these activities:
    *   identifying and analysing core business processes
    *   defining their key performance objectives
    *   designing new processes.

    These tasks are the real work of business process management and are typically performed by a cross-functional team that is given considerable time and resources to accomplish them.[46]

3 *Restructure the organisation around the new business processes.* An important element of this restructuring is the implementation of new information and measurement systems. They must reinforce a shift from measuring behaviours, such as absenteeism and grievances, to assessing outcomes, such as productivity, customer satisfaction and cost savings. Moreover, information technology is one of the key drivers of business process management because it can drastically reduce the cost and time associated with integrating and co-ordinating business processes.

    Re-engineered organisations typically have the following characteristics:[47]

    *   Work units change from functional departments to process teams.
    *   Jobs change from simple tasks to multidimensional work.
    *   People's roles change from controlled to empowered.
    *   The focus of performance measures and compensation shifts from activities to results.

- Organisation structures change from hierarchical to flat.
- Managers change from supervisors to coaches; executives change from score-keepers to leaders.

Results from re-engineering

The results from re-engineering vary widely. Industry journals and the business press regularly contain accounts of dramatic business results attributable to re-engineering. On the other hand, a best-selling book on re-engineering reported that as many as 70% of the efforts failed to meet their cost, cycle time or productivity objectives.[48] Despite its popularity, re-engineering is only beginning to be evaluated systematically, and there is little research to help unravel the disparate results.[49]

One evaluation of business process re-engineering examined more than 100 companies' efforts.[50] In-depth analysis of 20 re-engineering projects found that 11 cases had total business unit cost reductions of less than 5% while six cases had total cost reductions averaging 18%. The primary difference was the scope of the business process selected. Re-engineering key value-added processes significantly affected total business unit costs; re-engineering narrow business processes did not. Similarly, performance improvements in particular processes were strongly associated with changes in six key levers of behaviour, including structure, skills, information systems, roles, incentives and shared values. Efforts that addressed all six levers produced average cost reductions in specific processes by 35%; efforts that affected only one or two change levers reduced costs by 19%. Finally, the percentage reduction in total unit costs was associated with committed leadership. Application 8.2 describes how technology can advance re-engineering efforts.

8.2 APPLICATION

2007 Electronic Monitoring and Surveillance Survey: Over half of all employers combined fire workers for e-mail and internet abuse

From e-mail monitoring and Website blocking to phone tapping and GPS tracking, employers increasingly combine technology with policy to manage productivity and minimize litigation, security, and other risks. To motivate compliance with rules and policies, more than one fourth of employers have fired workers for misusing e-mail and nearly one third have fired employees for misusing the Internet, according to the 2007 Electronic Monitoring and Surveillance Survey from American Management Association (AMA) and The ePolicy Institute.

E-Mail and Internet-Related Terminations:
The 28% of employers who have fired workers for e-mail misuse did so for the following reasons: violation of any company policy (64%); inappropriate or offensive language (62%); excessive personal use (26%); breach of confidentiality rules (22%); other (12%).

The 30% of bosses who have fired workers for Internet misuse cite the following reasons: viewing, downloading, or uploading inappropriate/offensive content (84%); violation of any company policy (48%); excessive personal use (34%); other (9%).

>>

Internet, E-Mail, Blogs and Social Networking:

Employers are primarily concerned about inappropriate Web surfing, with 66% monitoring Internet connections. Fully 65% of companies use software to block connections to inappropriate Websites – a 27% increase since 2001 when AMA/ePolicy Institute first surveyed electronic monitoring and surveillance policies and procedures. Employers who block access to the Web are concerned about employees visiting adult sites with sexual, romantic, or pornographic content (96%); game sites (61%); social networking sites (50%); entertainment sites (40%); shopping/auction sites (27%); and sports sites (21%). In addition, companies use URL blocks to stop employees from visiting external blogs (18%).

Computer monitoring takes many forms, with 45% of employers tracking content, keystrokes, and time spent at the keyboard. Another 43% store and review computer files. In addition, 12% monitor the blogosphere to see what is being written about the company, and another 10% monitor social networking sites.

Of the 43% of companies that monitor e-mail, 73% use technology tools to automatically monitor e-mail and 40% assign an individual to manually read and review e-mail.

'Concern over litigation and the role electronic evidence plays in lawsuits and regulatory investigations has spurred more employers to monitor online activity. Data security and employee productivity concerns also motivate employers to monitor Web and e-mail use and content,' said Nancy Flynn, executive director of The ePolicy Institute and author of *The ePolicy Handbook*, 2(nd) Edition (AMACOM, 2008), *E-Mail Rules* (AMACOM 2003), *Instant Messaging Rules* (AMACOM 2004), *Blog Rules* (AMACOM 2006), and other books related to workplace computer use.

'Workers' e-mail and other electronically stored information create written business records that are the electronic equivalent of DNA evidence,' said Flynn, noting that 24% of employers have had e-mail subpoenaed by courts and regulators and another 15% have battled workplace lawsuits triggered by employee e-mail, according to 2006 AMA/ ePolicy research. 'To help control the risk of litigation, security breaches and other electronic disasters, employers should take advantage of monitoring and blocking technology to battle people problems – including the accidental and intentional misuse of computer systems and other electronic resources,' Flynn said.

While only two states, Delaware and Connecticut, require employers to notify employees of monitoring, the majority are doing a good job of alerting employees when they are being watched. Fully 83% inform workers that the company is monitoring content, keystrokes and time spent at the keyboard; 84% let employees know the company reviews computer activity; and 71% alert employees to e-mail monitoring. But are employers doing enough to educate employees on their specific policies?

'Most employees receive policies regarding use of office business tools and privacy issues on the first day of employment, but too often they don't read them. Employers need to do more than hand over a written policy,' says Manny Avramidis, senior vice president of global human resources for AMA. 'They should educate employees on company expectations and offer training on an annual basis.'

Telephone and Voice Mail:

Six percent of employers have fired employees for misuse or private use of office phones. Fully 45% monitor time spent and numbers called, and another 16% record phone conversations. An additional 9% monitor employees' voicemail messages. Most employers notify employees of phone (84%) and voicemail (73%) monitoring.

Video Surveillance:

Almost half (48%) of the companies surveyed use video monitoring to counter theft, violence and sabotage. Only 7% use video surveillance to track employees' on-the-job performance.

Most employers notify employees of anti-theft video surveillance (78%) and performance-related video monitoring (89%).

Global Satellite Positioning and Emerging Surveillance Technology:
Employers who use Assisted Global Positioning or Global Positioning Systems satellite technology are in the minority, with only 8% using GPS to track company vehicles; 3% using GPS to monitor cell phones; and fewer than 1% using GPS to monitor employee ID/Smartcards. The majority (52%) of companies employ Smartcard technology to control physical security and access to buildings and data centers. Trailing far behind is the use of technology that enables fingerprint scans (2%), facial recognition (0.4%) and iris scans (0.4%).

The 2007 Electronic Monitoring and Surveillance Survey is co-sponsored by American Management Association (www.amanet.org) and The ePolicy Institute (www.epolicyinstitute.com). Of the 304 U.S. companies that participated: 27% represent companies employing 100 or fewer workers, 101–500 employees (27%), 501–1,000 (12%), 1,001–2,500 (12%), 2,501–5,000 (10%) and 5,001 or more (12%).

About AMA

American Management Association is a world leader in professional development, advancing the skills of individuals to drive business success. AMA's approach to improving performance combines experiential learning – learning through doing – with opportunities for ongoing professional growth at every step of one's career journey. AMA supports the goals of individuals and organizations through a complete range of products and services, including seminars, Webcasts and podcasts, conferences, corporate and government solutions, business books and research. Organizations worldwide, including the majority of the Fortune 500, turn to AMA as their trusted partner in professional development and draw upon its experience to enhance skills, abilities and knowledge with noticeable results from day one.

About The ePolicy Institute

The ePolicy Institute is dedicated to helping employers limit electronic risks, including litigation, through the development and implementation of written policies and employee training programs. An international speaker and trainer, Executive Director Nancy Flynn is the author of 10 books published in 5 languages. As a recognized authority on workplace e-mail and web usage, Nancy Flynn also serves as an expert witness in e-mail-related litigation. Since 2001, The ePolicy Institute has partnered with AMA on an annual survey of workplace e-mail and Internet policies and procedures. Nancy Flynn is a popular media source who has been interviewed by *Fortune*, *Time*, *Newsweek*, *The Wall Street Journal*, *US News & World Report*, *Business Week*, *USA Today*, *Reader's Digest*, *New York Times*, NPR, BBC, CNBC, CNN, CBS, ABC, NBC, and Fox Business News among others.

Source: Doug Novarro, '2007 Electronic Monitoring & Surveillance Survey: Over half of all employers combined fire workers for e-mail & internet abuse', Business Wire, *Business Review Weekly*, 29 February 2008. With Permission of American Management Association.

Critical thinking questions:
1. As the previous section described employee involvement (EI) is important to workplace productivity. Discuss this point in relation to the article on how employers can work with employees to reduce or prevent email and internet abuse.
2. Do you think it is OK to 'surf the net' and/or 'send and receive personal emails' at work, if you think you are being productive at work?

WORK DESIGN

This section examines three approaches to work design:

- The engineering approach focuses on efficiency and simplification, and results in traditional job and work group designs.
- A second approach to work design rests on motivational theories and attempts to enrich the work experience. Job enrichment[51] involves designing jobs with high levels of meaning, discretion and knowledge of results.
- The third and most recent approach to work design derives from sociotechnical systems methods. This perspective seeks to optimise both the social and the technical aspects of work systems. It has led to the development of a popular form of work design called 'self-managed teams'.

The section describes each of these perspectives. Then, a contingency framework for integrating the approaches is presented, based on personal and technical factors in the workplace. When work is designed to fit these factors, it is both satisfying and productive.

The engineering approach

The oldest and most prevalent approach to work design is based on engineering concepts and methods. It proposes that the most efficient work designs can be determined by specifying the tasks to be performed, the work methods to be used and the work flow between individuals. The engineering approach is based on the pioneering work of Frederick Taylor, the father of scientific management. He developed ways of analysing and designing work and laid the groundwork for the professional field of industrial engineering.[52]

The engineering approach seeks to scientifically analyse the tasks performed by workers so as to discover those procedures that produce the maximum output with the minimum input of energies and resources.[53] This generally results in work designs with high levels of specialisation and specification. Such designs have several benefits: they allow workers to learn tasks rapidly, they permit short work cycles so that performance can take place with little or no mental effort, and they reduce costs as lower-skilled people can be hired and trained easily and paid relatively low wages.

The engineering approach produces two kinds of work design: traditional jobs and traditional work groups. When one person can complete the work, as is the case with bank tellers and telephone operators, traditional jobs are created. They tend to be simplified, with routine and repetitive tasks having clear specifications concerning time and motion. When the work requires co-ordination between people, such as automobile assembly lines, traditional work groups are developed. They are composed of members who perform relatively routine, yet related, tasks. The overall group task is typically broken into simpler, discrete parts (often called jobs). The tasks and work methods are specified for each part, and the different parts are assigned to group members. Each member performs a routine and repetitive part of the group task.

Members' separate task contributions are co-ordinated for overall task achievement through external controls, such as schedules, rigid work flows and supervisors.[54] In the 1950s and 1960s, this method of work design was popularised by the assembly lines of Australian automobile manufacturers, such as GM Holden, and was an important reason for the growth of Australian industry after World War II.

The engineering approach to job design is less an OD intervention than a benchmark in history. Critics of the approach argue that the method ignores the social and psychological needs of workers. They suggest that the increasing educational level of the workforce and the substitution of automation for menial labour point to the need for more enriched forms of work, where people have greater discretion and challenge. Moreover, current competitive challenges require a more committed and involved workforce that is able to make online decisions and develop performance innovations. Work designed with the employee in mind is more humanly fulfilling and productive than that designed in traditional ways. However, it is important to recognise the strengths of the engineering approach. It remains an important work design intervention as its immediate cost savings and efficiency can easily be measured. It is also well understood and easily implemented and managed.

The motivational approach

The motivational approach to work design views the effectiveness of organisational activities primarily as a function of member needs and satisfaction. It seeks to improve employee performance and satisfaction by enriching jobs. This provides people with opportunities for autonomy, responsibility, closure (doing a complete job) and feedback about performance. Enriched jobs can be found in Australia at such companies as Golden Circle Limited and Rupnorth Co-operative Limited, among others.

The motivational approach is usually associated with the research of Herzberg, as well as that of Hackman and Oldham. Herzberg's two-factor theory of motivation proposed that certain attributes of work (such as opportunities for advancement and recognition, which he called 'motivators') help to increase job satisfaction.[55] Other attributes (called 'hygiene' factors, such as company policies, working conditions, pay and supervision) do not produce satisfaction but prevent dissatisfaction. Only satisfied workers are motivated to produce.

Although Herzberg's motivational factors sound appealing, increasing doubt has been cast on the underlying theory. For example, motivation and hygiene factors are difficult to put into operation and measure, making implementation and evaluation of the theory difficult. Important worker characteristics that can affect whether or not people will respond favourably to job enrichment were also not included in the theory. Finally, Herzberg's failure to involve employees in the job enrichment process itself does not sit well with most current OD practitioners. Consequently, a second, well-researched approach to job enrichment has been favoured. It focuses on the attributes of the work itself and has resulted in a more scientifically acceptable theory of job enrichment than Herzberg's model. The research of Hackman and Oldham represents this more recent trend in job enrichment.[56]

A large company may have scope to offer employees motivation through the opportunity to take different positions, and therefore different challenges as illustrated in Application 8.3.

8.3

APPLICATION

Changing landscape. The global financial crisis is a wake-up call for the next generation of professionals, says Ivey business school's associate professor Gerard Seijts

How does the role of managing GenerationY employees differ from managing older generations?

It would be foolish to only look at what generation people fall into and make attributions. Great bosses make an honest effort to understand their people. The challenge is to leverage the unique characteristics, values and skills of people [independent of the category they belong to]. Gen-Y has a different mindset than Gen-X and the other generations. Each generation's attitudes and beliefs are shaped by cultural shifts, influential public personalities, politicians, world shaping events, technological advances and so on. These differences in mindset play out in the workplace and that sets up an interesting dynamic: several generations with different views, attitudes, loyalties and skills. Such differences include relationships with the organisation, relationships with colleagues, work approaches, orientation towards leadership and orientation towards career. A main driver from Gen-Y is to create a life and find work that has a meaning. Work-life balance is a key issue for Gen-Y. Time off the job is important even if it costs a promotion.

What are the main challenges that face today's managers when motivating and setting goals for Generation Y employees?

Employees of the different generations bring different values, attitudes towards work, work styles, job satisfaction criteria, learning styles and levels of commitment to the workplace. The role of the leader is to flex him or herself and find ways to motivate these individuals, understanding that what might work for a Gen-X does not work for Gen-Y. But even two Gen-Yers can be different, so the leader must understand the psyche of the employee and see what truly motivates the employee. Motivational tools, rewards, recognition and retention tools will look different for each employee. A key question is how flexible is the organisation in its policies and practices to adjust to people from the different generations, and to cater to their needs and motivations? Or is a change required for us to become more flexible? This is a key question that organisations need to ask themselves, as success depends on the ability to recruit, retain, engage, manage and develop people.

What effect will the recession have on how Generation Y employees view the workplace/job market?

The recession is going to hit Gen-Y hard. Their sense of loyalty to the organisation will decrease; it was not high to begin with. Remember this is the job-hopping generation. They'll now have to compete with highly experienced people for limited positions. These younger people had high expectations in terms of salary, promotability, significance of projects and perks. All of them [and us] need to adjust our expectations. The criticism that has been levelled against Gen-Y is that they have been brought up as 'being special' and that they are all

>>

'winners'. That mindset might hurt them in the new environment. How well prepared are they in terms of experience and job search skills? The recession is a huge wake-up call for Gen-Y.

How can taking an MBA directly improve the leadership and management skills of today's managers when dealing with the next generation of business executives?
Students need judgment - making sound decisions and thinking about how to implement the lessons. Ivey's motto is think, act and lead. The case-based method allows us to spend significant time on the act and lead aspect. Teaching people skills in the functional areas is relatively straightforward. How to implement decisions is far more difficult, yet decision making and action is the essence of leadership.

Is it worthwhile for graduates who are having a tough time finding a job to embark on an MBA course without several years of management experience behind them?
You will get the most out of an MBA programme if you have several years of experience, two to five years. (EMBA programmes look at candidates with more than 10 years of experience.) Doing the programme is a significant commitment in time and money. Think about how to get the most out of it.

Source: Staff reporter, 'Changing landscape. The global financial crisis is a wake-up call for the next generation of professionals', *South China Post*, 18 March 2009.

Critical thinking questions:
1. Should employers' motivational approach to work design include and consider differences between the mindsets of Gen-Y and Gen-X? In your discussion, think about what you want out of life.
2. If employers have to consider what motivates each generation in relation to work design, do you think universities also should consider how they deliver course content and teaching methods?

The core dimensions of jobs

Considerable research has been devoted to defining and understanding core job dimensions.[57] Figure 8.3 summarises the Hackman and Oldham model of job design. Five core dimensions of work affect three critical psychological states, which in turn produce personal and job outcomes. These outcomes include high internal work motivation, high-quality work performance, satisfaction with the work, and low absenteeism and turnover.

Not all people react in similar ways to job enrichment interventions. Individual differences – such as a worker's knowledge and skill levels, growth-need, strength and satisfaction with contextual factors – moderate the relationships between core dimensions, psychological states and outcomes. 'Worker knowledge and skill' refers to the education and experience levels that characterise the workforce. If employees lack the appropriate skills, for example, increasing skill variety may not improve a job's meaningfulness. Similarly, if workers lack the intrinsic motivation to grow and develop personally, attempts to provide them with increased autonomy may be resisted. (We discuss growth needs more fully in the last section of this chapter.) Finally, contextual factors include reward systems, supervisory style and co-worker

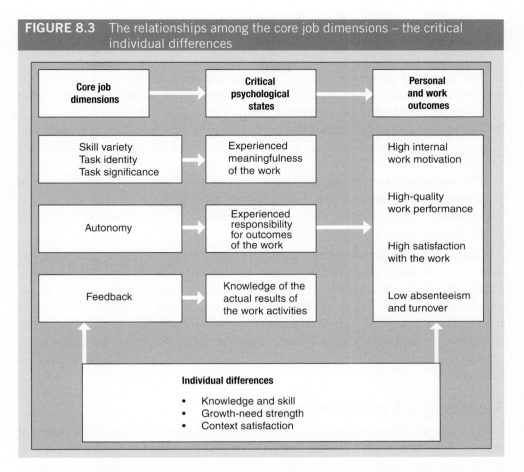

FIGURE 8.3 The relationships among the core job dimensions – the critical individual differences

Source: J. Richard Hackman and Greg R. Oldham, *Work Redesign*, 1st edition, © 1980, p.83. Reprinted by permission of Pearson Education, Inc., Upper Saddle River, New Jersey.

satisfaction. When the employee is unhappy with the work context, attempts to enrich the work itself may be unsuccessful.

Barriers to job enrichment

As the application of job enrichment has spread, several obstacles to significant job restructuring have been identified. Most of these barriers exist in the organisational context within which the job design is executed. Other organisational systems and practices, whether technical, managerial or personnel, can affect both the implementation of job enrichment and the life span of whatever changes are made. At least four organisational systems can constrain the implementation of job enrichment:[58]

1 *The technical system.* The technology of an organisation can limit job enrichment by constraining the number of ways in which jobs can be changed.

Technology may also set an 'enrichment ceiling'. Some types of work, such as continuous process production systems, may be naturally enriched, so there is little more that can be gained from a job enrichment intervention.

2 *The personnel system.* Personnel systems can constrain job enrichment by creating formalised job descriptions that are rigidly defined and that limit flexibility in changing people's job duties.

3 *The control system.* Control systems, such as budgets, production reports and accounting practices, can limit the complexity and challenge of jobs within the system.

4 *The supervisory system.* Supervisors determine to a large extent the amount of autonomy and feedback that subordinates can experience. To the extent that supervisors use autocratic methods and control work-related feedback, jobs will be difficult, if not impossible, to enrich.

Once these implementation constraints have been overcome, other factors determine whether the effects of job enrichment are strong and lasting.[59] Consistent with the contingency approach to OD, the staying power of job enrichment depends largely on how well it fits with and is supported by other organisational practices, such as those associated with training, career development, compensation and supervision. These practices need to be congruent with, and to reinforce, jobs that have high amounts of discretion, skill variety and meaningful feedback.

Results of job enrichment

Hackman and Oldham reported on more than 1000 people in about 100 different jobs in more than a dozen organisations.[60] In general, they found that employees whose jobs were high on the core dimensions were more satisfied and motivated than those whose jobs were low on the dimensions. The core dimensions were also related to such behaviours as absenteeism and performance, although the relationship was not strong for performance. In addition, they found that responses were more positive for people with high growth needs than for those with weaker ones. Similarly, research has shown that enriched jobs are strongly correlated with mental ability.[61] Enriching the jobs of workers with low growth needs or with low knowledge and skills is more likely to produce frustration than satisfaction.

An impressive amount of research has been done on Hackman and Oldham's approach to job enrichment. In addition, several studies have extended and refined Hackman and Oldham's approach to both produce more reliable data[62] and incorporate other moderators, such as the need for achievement and job longevity.[63] In general, research has supported the proposed relationships between job characteristics and outcomes, including the moderating effects of growth needs, knowledge and skills, and context satisfaction.[64] In regard to context satisfaction, for example, research indicates that employee turnover, dissatisfaction and withdrawal are associated with dark offices, a lack of privacy and high worker densities.[65]

Reviews of the job enrichment research also report positive effects. An analysis of 28 studies concluded that the job characteristics are positively related to job satisfaction, particularly for people with high growth needs.[66] Another review concluded that job enrichment is effective at reducing employee turnover.[67] A different examination of 28 job enrichment studies reported overwhelmingly positive results.[68] Improvements in quality and cost measures were reported slightly more frequently than improvements in employee attitudes and quantity of production. However, the studies suffered from methodological weaknesses that suggest that the positive findings should be viewed with some caution. Another review of 16 job enrichment studies showed mixed results.[69] Thirteen of the programs were developed and implemented solely by management. These studies showed significant reduction in absenteeism, turnover and grievances, and improvements in quality of production in only about half of the cases where these variables were measured. The three studies with high levels of employee participation in the change program showed improvements in these variables in all cases where they were measured. Although it is difficult to generalise from such a small number of studies, employee participation in the job enrichment program appears to enhance the success of such interventions.

The sociotechnical systems approach

The sociotechnical systems (STS) approach is the most extensive body of scientific and applied work underlying employee involvement and innovative work designs today. Its techniques and design principles derive from extensive action research in both public and private organisations across a diversity of national cultures. This section reviews the conceptual foundations of the STS approach and then describes its most popular application: self-managed work teams.

Conceptual background

Sociotechnical systems theory was originally developed at the Tavistock Institute of Human Relations in London in the early 1960s and has since spread to most industrialised nations. In Europe, and particularly Scandinavia, STS interventions are almost synonymous with work design and employee involvement. In Canada and the United States, STS concepts and methods underlie many of the innovative work designs and team-based structures that are so prevalent in today's organisations. Intel and Procter & Gamble are among the many organisations applying the STS approach to transform how work is designed and performed. Sociotechnical systems theory is based on two fundamental premises:

- that an organisation or work unit is a combined, social-plus-technical system
- that this system is open in relation to its environment.[70]

Sociotechnical system

The first assumption suggests that whenever human beings are organised to perform tasks, a joint system is operating – a sociotechnical system. This system consists of two independent, yet related, parts: a social part that includes the people performing the tasks and the relationships among them, and a technical part consisting of the tools, techniques and methods for task performance. These two parts are independent of each other by virtue of each following a different set of behavioural laws. The social part operates according to biological and psychosocial laws, whereas the technical part functions according to mechanical and physical laws. Nevertheless, the two parts are related because they must act together to accomplish tasks. Hence, the term 'sociotechnical' signifies the joint relationship that must occur between the social and technical parts, and the word 'system' communicates that this connection results in a unified whole.

Because a sociotechnical system is composed of social and technical parts, it follows that it will produce two kinds of outcomes: products, such as goods and services, and social and psychological consequences, such as job satisfaction and commitment. The key issue is how to design the relationship between the two parts so that these outcomes are both positive (referred to as 'joint optimisation').

Sociotechnical practitioners design work and organisations so that the social and technical parts work well together, producing high levels of product and human satisfaction. This contrasts with the engineering approach to designing work, which tends to focus on the technical component and worries about fitting in people later. This often leads to mediocre performance at high social costs. This also contrasts with the motivation approach that views work design in terms of human fulfilment. This approach can lead to satisfied employees, but inefficient work processes.

Environmental relationship

The second major premise underlying STS theory concerns the fact that such systems are open to their environments. Open systems need to interact with their environments to survive and develop. The environment provides the STS with necessary inputs of energy, raw materials and information, while the STS, in turn, provides the environment with products and services. The key issue here is how to design the interface between the STS and its environment so that the system has sufficient freedom to function while exchanging effectively with the environment. In what is typically referred to as boundary management, STS practitioners attempt to structure environmental relationships to both protect the system from external disruptions and to facilitate the exchange of necessary resources and information. This enables the STS to adapt to changing conditions and to influence the environment in favourable directions.

In summary, sociotechnical systems theory suggests that effective work systems jointly optimise the relationship between their social and technical parts. Moreover, such systems effectively manage the boundary that separates them from, while relating them to, the environment. This allows them to exchange with the environment while protecting themselves from external disruptions.

Self-managed work teams

The most prevalent application of the STS approach is self-managed work teams.[71] Alternatively referred to as 'self-directed work teams', 'self-regulating work teams' or 'high-performance work teams', these work designs consist of members performing interrelated tasks.[72] Self-managed work teams are typically responsible for a whole product or service, or a major part of a larger production process. They control members' task behaviours and make decisions about task assignments and work methods. In many cases, the team sets its own production goals, within broader organisational limits, and may be responsible for support services, such as maintenance, purchasing and quality control. Team members are generally expected to learn many, if not all, of the jobs within the team's control and frequently are paid on the basis of knowledge and skills rather than seniority. When pay is based on performance, team rather than individual performance is used.

Figure 8.4 is a model explaining how self-managed work teams perform. It summarises current STS research and shows how teams can be designed for high performance. Although the model is mainly based on experience with teams that perform the daily work of the organisation (work teams), it also has relevance to other team designs, such as problem-solving teams, management teams, cross-functional integrating teams and employee involvement teams.[73]

The model shows that team performance and member satisfaction follow directly from how well the team functions. This includes how well members

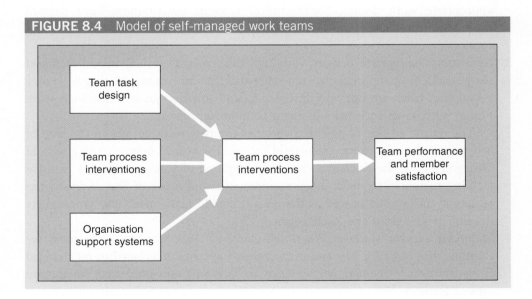

FIGURE 8.4 Model of self-managed work teams

communicate and co-ordinate with each other, resolve conflicts and problems, and make and implement task-relevant decisions. Team functioning, in turn, is influenced by three major inputs:

- team task design
- team process interventions
- organisation support systems.

Because these inputs affect how well teams function and subsequently perform, they are key intervention targets for designing and implementing self-managed work teams.

Application steps

Sociotechnical systems work designs have been implemented in a variety of settings, including manufacturing firms, hospitals, schools and government agencies. Although the specific implementation strategy is tailored to the situation, a common method of change underlies many of these applications. It generally involves high worker participation in the work design and implementation process. Such participative work design allows employees to translate their special knowledge of the work situation into relevant work designs. Because employees have ownership over the design process, they tend to be highly committed to implementing the work designs.[74] STS applications generally proceed in six steps:[75]

1 *Sanctioning the design effort.* In this stage, workers are provided with the necessary protection and support to diagnose their work system and to design an appropriate work design.

2 *Diagnosing the work system.* Knowledge of existing operations (or of intended operations, in the case of a new work system) is the basis for designing an appropriate work design. Sociotechnical systems practitioners have devised diagnostic models applicable to work systems making products or delivering services.

3 *Generating appropriate designs.* Although this typically results in self-managed work teams, it is important to emphasise that, in some cases, the diagnosis may reveal that tasks are not very interdependent and that an individual-job work design, such as an enriched job, might be more appropriate.

   The output of this design step specifies the new work design. In the case of self-managed work teams, this would include the team's mission and goals, an ideal work flow, the skills and knowledge required of team members, a plan for training members to meet those requirements and a list of the decisions the team will make now, as well as the ones it should make over time as members develop greater skills and knowledge.

4 *Specifying support systems.* When self-managed work teams are designed, for example, the basis for pay and measurement systems may need to be changed from individual to team performance to facilitate necessary task interaction among workers.

5 *Implementing and evaluating the work designs.* For self-managing work teams, implementation generally requires considerable training to enable workers to gain the necessary technical and social skills to perform multiple tasks, and to control members' task behaviours. Organisation development consultants often help team members carry out these tasks with a major emphasis on helping them gain competence in this area. Evaluation of the work design is necessary both to guide the implementation process and to assess the overall effectiveness of the design. In some cases, the evaluation information suggests the need for further diagnosis and redesign efforts.

6 *Continual change and improvement.* The ability to continually design and redesign work needs to be built into existing work designs. Members must have the skills and knowledge to continually assess their work unit and to make necessary changes and improvements.

Results of self-managed teams

Research on sociotechnical systems design efforts is extensive. For example, a 1994 bibliography by researchers at Eindhoven University of Technology in the Netherlands found 3082 English-language studies.[76] And, as with reports on job enrichment, most of the published reports on self-managed teams show favourable results.[77]

A series of famous case studies at General Foods' Gaines Pet Food/Topeka plant, the Saab-Scania engine assembly plant and Volvo's Kalmar and Udevalla plants provides one set of positive findings. The Gaines Pet Food plant operated at an overhead rate some 33% below that of traditional plants.[78] It reported annual variable cost savings of US$600 000, one of the best safety records in the company, turnover rates far below average and high levels of job satisfaction. A long-term, external evaluation of the groups at the Gaines plant[79] attributed savings related to work innovation at about US$1 million a year, and, despite a variety of problems, productivity increased in every year but one over a decade of operation. The plant has maintained one of the highest product quality ratings at General Foods since its opening.

Extensive research on self-managing groups has been done by Saab-Scania.[80] The first group was established in 1969, and four years later there were 130 production groups. These groups have generally shown improvements in production and employee attitudes and decreases in unplanned work stoppages and turnover rates. Interestingly, when workers from the United States visited Saab's engine assembly plant, they reported that work was too fast and that lunch breaks were too short.[81] A Saab executive commented that the visitors had not stayed long enough to become completely proficient, causing their complaint that the pace was too fast.

The widely publicised use of self-managing groups at Volvo's automotive plant in Kalmar, Sweden, has also shown positive results.[82] The Kalmar factory opened in

July 1974, and by the following year it was operating at 100% efficiency. As a reference point, highly productive automobile plants normally operate at about 80% of engineering standards. Interviews with workers and union officials indicated that the quality of work life was considerably better than in assembly jobs that they had had in the past. In addition, Volvo's Udevalla plant reported significant quality improvements and higher productivity than in comparable plants.[83]

A second set of studies supporting the positive impact of sociotechnical design teams comes from research comparing self-managed teams with other interventions. For example, probably one of the most thorough assessments of self-managing groups is a longitudinal study conducted in a food-processing plant in the midwest of the United States.[84] Self-managing groups were created as part of an overall revamping of a major part of the plant's production facilities. The effects of the intervention were extremely positive. One year after start-up, production was 133% higher than originally planned, while start-up costs were 7.7% lower than planned. Employee attitudes were extremely positive towards the group design. These positive effects, however, did not result solely from the self-managing design. The intervention also included survey feedback for diagnostic purposes and changes in technology, the physical work setting and management. These kinds of changes are common in self-managing group projects. They suggest that such designs may require supporting changes in other organisational dimensions, such as technology, management style and physical setting, in order to facilitate the development of self-managed teams.

This study also permitted a comparison of self-managing groups with job enrichment, which occurred in another department of the company. Both interventions included survey feedback. The self-managing project involved technological changes, whereas the job enrichment program did not. The results showed that both interventions had similar positive effects in terms of employee attitudes. However, only the self-managing project had significant improvements in productivity and costs. Again, the productivity improvements cannot be totally attributed to the self-managed teams, but were also the result of the technological changes. Although the majority of studies report positive effects of self-managing groups, some research suggests a more mixed assessment.

Designing work for technical and personal needs

This section has described three approaches to work design: engineering, motivational and sociotechnical. However, trade-offs and conflicts among the approaches must be recognised. The engineering approach produces traditional jobs and work groups, and focuses on efficient performance. This approach tends to downplay employee needs and emphasise economic outcomes. The motivational approach strives to design jobs that are stimulating and demanding, and highlights the importance of employee need satisfaction. Research suggests, however, that increased satisfaction does not necessarily produce improvements in productivity.

Finally, the sociotechnical systems approach attempts to optimise both social and technical aspects. Despite this integrative goal, STS has not produced consistent research results.

In this final section, we attempt to integrate the three perspectives by providing a contingency framework that suggests all three approaches can be effective when applied in the appropriate circumstances. Work design involves creating jobs and work groups for high levels of employee satisfaction and productivity. Considerable research shows that achieving such results depends on designing work to match specific factors that operate in the work setting. These factors have to do with the technology for producing goods and services and the personal needs of employees. When work is designed to fit or match these factors, it is most likely to be both productive and humanly satisfying.

Technical factors

Two key dimensions can affect change on the shop floor: technical interdependence, or the extent to which co-operation among workers is required to produce a product or service; and technical uncertainty, or the amount of information processing and decision making that employees must do in order to complete a task.[85] In general, the degree of technical interdependence determines whether work should be designed for individual jobs or work groups. With low technical interdependence and little need for worker co-operation – as, for example, in field sales and data entry – work can be designed for individual jobs. Conversely, when technical interdependence is high and employees must co-operate – as in production processes such as coal mining, assembly lines and software writing – work should be designed for groups composed of people who perform interacting tasks.

The second dimension, technical uncertainty, determines whether work should be designed for external forms of control, such as supervision, scheduling or standardisation, or for worker self-control. When technical uncertainty is low and little information has to be processed by employees, work can be designed for external control, such as might be found on assembly lines and in other forms of repetitive work. On the other hand, when technical uncertainty is high and people must process information and make decisions, work should be designed for high levels of employee self-control, such as might be found in professional work and troubleshooting tasks.

Figure 8.5 shows the different types of work designs that are most effective, from a purely technological perspective, for different combinations of interdependence and uncertainty. In quadrant 1, where technological interdependence and uncertainty are both low, such as might be found in data entry, jobs should be designed traditionally with limited amounts of employee interaction and self-control. When task interdependence is high yet uncertainty is low (quadrant 2), such as work occurring on assembly lines, work should be designed for traditional work groups in which employee interaction is scheduled and self-control is limited. In quadrant 3, where

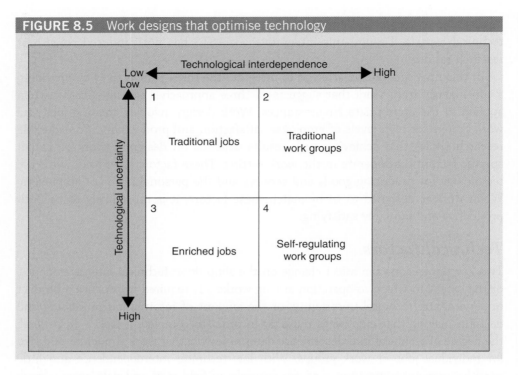

FIGURE 8.5 Work designs that optimise technology

Source: Reproduced by permission from T. Cummings, 'Designing work for productivity and quality of work life', *Outlook*, 6 (1982): 39.

technological interdependence is low but uncertainty is high, as in field sales, work should be structured for individual jobs with internal forms of control, as in enriched jobs. Finally, when both technological interdependence and uncertainty are high (quadrant 4), such as might be found in a continuous-process chemical plant, work should be designed for self-managed teams in which members have the multiple skills, discretion and information necessary to control their interactions around the shared tasks.

Personal-need factors

Most of the research identifying individual differences in work design has focused on selected personal traits. Two types of personal needs can influence the kinds of work designs that are most effective: social needs, or the desire for significant social relationships; and growth needs, or the desire for personal accomplishment, learning and development.[86] In general, the degree of social needs determines whether work should be designed for individual jobs or work groups. People with low needs for social relationships are more likely to be satisfied working on individualised jobs than in interacting groups. Conversely, people with high social needs are more likely to be attracted to group forms of work than to individualised forms.

The second individual difference, growth needs, determines whether work designs should be routine and repetitive or complex and challenging. People with low growth needs are generally not attracted to jobs that offer complexity and challenge (that is, enriched jobs). They are more satisfied performing routine forms of work that do not require high levels of decision making. On the other hand, people with high growth needs are satisfied with work offering high levels of discretion, skill variety and meaningful feedback. Performing enriched jobs allows them to experience personal accomplishment and development.

That some people have low social and growth needs is often difficult for OD practitioners to accept, particularly in view of the growth and social values that underlie much OD practice. It is important to recognise that individual differences do exist, however. Assuming that all people have high growth needs or want high levels of social interaction can lead to inappropriate work designs. For example, a new manager of a clerical support unit was astonished to find the six members using typewriters when a significant portion of the work consisted of retyping memos and reports that were produced frequently, but changed very little from month to month. In addition, the unit had a terrible record for quality and on-time production. The manager quickly ordered new word processors and redesigned the work flow to increase interaction among members. Worker satisfaction declined, interpersonal conflicts increased and work quality and on-time performance remained poor. An assessment of the effort revealed that all six of the staff members had low growth needs and low needs for inclusion in group efforts. In the words of one worker: 'All I want is to come into work, do my job and get my pay cheque.'

It is important to emphasise that people who have low growth or social needs are not inferior to those placing a higher value on these factors. They are simply different. It is also necessary to recognise that people can change their needs through personal growth and experience. OD practitioners need to be sensitive to individual differences in work design and careful not to force their own values on others. Many consultants, eager to be seen on the cutting edge of practice, tend to recommend self-managed teams in all situations, without careful attention to technological and personal considerations.

Figure 8.6 shows the different types of work designs that are most effective for the various combinations of social and growth needs. When employees have relatively low social and growth needs (quadrant 1), traditional jobs are most effective. In quadrant 2, where employees have high social needs but low growth needs, traditional work groups, such as might be found on an assembly line, are most appropriate. These allow for some social interaction but limited amounts of challenge and discretion. When employees have low social needs but high growth needs (quadrant 3), enriched jobs are most satisfying. Here, work is designed for individual jobs that have high levels of task variety, discretion and feedback about results. A research scientist's job is likely to be an enriched one, as is that of a skilled craftsperson. Finally, in quadrant 4, where employees have high social and growth needs, work should be specifically designed for self-managed teams. Such

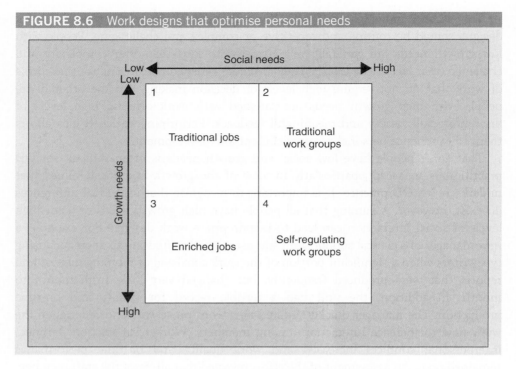

FIGURE 8.6 Work designs that optimise personal needs

Source: Reproduced by permission from T. Cummings, 'Designing work for productivity and quality of work life', *Outlook*, 6 (1982): 40.

groups offer opportunities for significant social interaction around tasks that are both complex and challenging. A team of astronauts in a space shuttle resembles a self-managing work group, as does a group managing the control room of an oil refinery or a group of nurses in a hospital unit.

Meeting both technical and personal needs

Satisfying both technical and human needs to achieve work-design success is likely to occur only in limited circumstances. When the technical conditions of a company's production processes (as shown in Figure 8.5) are compatible with the personal needs of its employees (as shown in Figure 8.6), the respective work designs combine readily and can satisfy both. On General Motors' assembly lines, for example, the technology is highly interdependent, yet low in uncertainty (quadrant 2 in Figure 8.5). Much of the work is designed around traditional work groups in which task behaviours are standardised, and interactions among workers are scheduled. Such work is likely to be productive and fulfilling to the extent that General Motors' production workers have high social needs and low growth needs (quadrant 2 in Figure 8.6).

When technology and people are incompatible – for example, when an organisation has quadrant 1 technology and quadrant 4 worker needs – at least two kinds of changes can be made to design work to satisfy both requirements.[87] One strategy is to change technology or people to bring them more into line with each other. This is a key point underlying sociotechnical systems approaches. For example, technical interdependence can be reduced by breaking long assembly lines into more discrete groups. In Sweden, Volvo redesigned the physical layout and technology for assembling automobiles and trucks to promote self-managed teams. Modifying people's needs is more complex, and begins by matching new or existing workers to available work designs. For example, companies can assess workers' needs through standardised paper-and-pencil tests. The information from these can be used to counsel employees and to help them locate jobs that are compatible with their needs. Similarly, employees can be allowed to volunteer for specific work designs, a common practice in sociotechnical systems projects. This matching process is likely to require high levels of trust and co-operation between management and workers, as well as a shared commitment to designing work for high performance and employee satisfaction.

A second strategy for accommodating both technical and human requirements is to leave the two components alone and to design compromise work designs that only partially fulfil the demands of either. The key issue is to decide to what extent one contingency will be satisfied at the expense of the other. For example, when capital costs are high relative to labour costs (such as is found in highly automated plants) work design is likely to favour the technology. Conversely, in many service jobs where labour is expensive relative to capital, organisations may design work for employee motivation and satisfaction at the risk of short-changing their technology. These examples suggest a range of possible compromises based on different weightings of technical and human demands. Careful assessment of both types of contingencies and of the cost–benefit trade-offs is necessary to design an appropriate compromise work design.

Clearly, the strategy of designing work to bring technology and people more into line with each other is preferable to compromise work designs. Although the latter approach seems necessary when there are heavy constraints on changing the contingencies, in many cases those constraints are more imagined than real. The important thing is to understand the technical and personal factors that exist in a particular situation and to design work accordingly. Traditional jobs and traditional work groups are likely to be successful in certain situations (as shown in Figures 8.5 and 8.6); in other settings, enriched jobs and self-managed teams are likely to be more effective.

Summary

In this chapter we presented interventions aimed at improving organisation and environment relationships. Because organisations are open systems that exist in environmental contexts, they must establish and maintain effective linkages with the environment in order to survive and prosper. Three environments impact on organisational functioning: the general environment, the task environment and the

enacted environment. Only the last of these can affect organisational choices about behaviour, but the first two impact on the consequences of those actions. Two key environmental dimensions affect the degree to which organisations are constrained by their environments and need to be responsive to them: information uncertainty and resource dependence. When both dimensions are high, organisations are maximally constrained and need to be responsive to their environment.

Open systems planning (OSP) helps an organisation to systematically assess its environment and develop strategic responses to it. OSP is based on assumptions about the role of people's perceptions in environmental relations and the need for a shared view of the environment that permits co-ordinated action towards it. It begins with an assessment of the existing environment and how the organisation relates to it and progresses to possible future environments and action plans to bring them about. A number of guidelines exist for effectively applying this intervention.

Transorganisational development is an emerging form of planned change that is aimed at helping organisations create partnerships with other organisations to perform tasks or to solve problems that are too complex and multifaceted for single organisations to carry out. Because these multi-organisation systems tend to be underorganised, TD follows the stages of planned change relevant to underorganised systems: identification, convention, organisation and evaluation.

We then presented interventions aimed at restructuring organisations. Two restructuring interventions were described: downsizing and re-engineering. Downsizing decreases the size of the organisation through workforce reduction or organisational redesign. It is generally associated with lay-offs where a certain number or class of organisation member is no longer employed by the organisation. Downsizing can contribute to organisation development by focusing on the organisation's strategy, using a variety of downsizing tactics, addressing the needs of all organisation members and following through with growth plans.

Re-engineering is the fundamental rethinking and radical redesign of business processes to achieve dramatic improvements in performance. It seeks to transform how organisations traditionally produce and deliver goods and services. A typical re-engineering project prepares the organisation, rethinks how work gets done and finally restructures the organisation around the newly designed core processes.

In the final section we discussed three different approaches to work design. In addition, a contingency framework was described to determine the approach most likely to result in high productivity and worker satisfaction, given certain workplace characteristics. The contingency framework reconciles the strengths and weaknesses of each approach. The engineering approach produces traditional jobs and traditional work groups. Traditional jobs are highly simplified and involve routine and repetitive forms of work. They do not require co-ordination among people to produce a product or service. Traditional jobs achieve high productivity and worker satisfaction in situations that are characterised by low technical uncertainty and interdependence, and low growth and social needs.

Traditional work groups are composed of members performing routine yet interrelated tasks. Member interactions are controlled externally, usually by rigid work flows, schedules and supervisors. Traditional work groups are best suited to conditions of low technical uncertainty, but high technical interdependence. They fit people with low growth needs but high social needs.

The motivational approach produces enriched jobs that involve high levels of skill variety, task identity, task significance, autonomy and feedback from the work itself. Enriched jobs achieve good results when the technology is uncertain but does not require high levels of co-ordination, and when employees have high growth needs and low social needs.

Finally, the sociotechnical systems approach is associated with self-managed teams. These groups are composed of members performing interrelated tasks. Members are given the multiple skills, autonomy and information necessary to control their own task behaviours with relatively little external control. Many organisation development practitioners argue that self-managed teams represent the work design of the 1990s. This is because high levels of technical uncertainty and interdependence are prevalent in today's workplaces and because today's workers often have high growth and social needs.

Activities

REVIEW QUESTIONS

1 What constitutes the organisation's general environment? How would this impact on decisions made by a change agent?

2 Through what strategies do organisations gain 'control' over their environments? What implications does this have for how change is managed?

3 What is associated with a transorganisational system?

Describe its stages and compare and contrast this with the OD process.

4 Describe both downsizing and re-engineering, then compare and contrast them.

5 What are the approaches to work design? Give an example of each.

6 Why are the work design approaches more effective when integrated?

DISCUSSION AND ESSAY QUESTIONS

1 What is open systems planning and what assumptions is it based on? Create a convincing argument for its being accepted as a valid change strategy.

2 How do environmental factors affect the types of interventions that might be carried out in an organisation? What role does the change agent play in determining the most appropriate intervention?

3 'Downsizing has been the most successful change strategy for organisations in a turbulent environment.' Discuss.

4 Self-managed work teams have been in existence for a long period of time and several research reports have commented on their success. Critically evaluate self-managed teams and determine if there are any negative aspects. Give examples where relevant.

Search me! Excercises

Explore **Search me! management** for relevant articles on OD interventions: strategy and structure. Search me! is an online library of world-class journals, ebooks and newspapers, including *The Australian* and *The New York Times,* and is updated daily. Log in to Search me! through **http://login.cengage.com** using the access card in the front of this book.

Keywords

Try searching for the following terms:

> Downsizing
> Environment scanning
> Framework
> Open systems planning

> Re-engineering
> Restructuring
> Transorganisational development
> Work design

>> Search tip:

Search me! management contains information from both local and international sources. To get the greatest number of search results, try using both Australian and American spellings in your searches, e.g. 'globalisation' and 'globalization'; 'organisation' and 'organization'.

Notes

1 N. Pupat, 'The Impact of Organisation Development Intervention on Service Process for Curriculum Development in Assumption University: A Case Study', http://gsbejournal.au.edu/Ph.DOD/1.THE%20IMPACT% 20OF%20ORGANIZATION%20DEVELOPMENT%20 INTERVENTION%20ON%20SERVICE%20PROCESS%20 FOR%20CURRICULUM%20DEVELOPMENT%20IN% 20ASSUMPTION%20UNIVERSITY.pdf.

2 D. M. Boje and M. Hillon, 'Transorganisational development', in ed. Tom Cummings, *Handbook of Organizational Change* (Sage, 2008): 651–4, http:// peaceaware.com/vita/paper_pdfs/ boje%20hillon%20transorg%20ch%2034%202008.pdf.

3 R. Miles, *Managing Complexity in High Technology Organisations Macro Organization Behavior* (Santa Monica, CA: Goodyear, 1980); D. Robey and C. Sales, *Designing Organizations,* 4th edn (Homewood, IL: Irwin, 1994).

4 B. Barker Scott, *Organization Development Primer: Theory and Practice of Large Group Interventions,* June 2009, Faculty Queen's University IRC, IRC Research Program,

http://irc.queensu.ca/gallery/1/dps-odprimer-large-group-interventions.pdf.

5 K. Weick, *The Social Psychology of Organizing,* 2nd edn (Reading, MA: Addison-Wesley, 1979).

6 J. Galbraith, *Competing with Flexible Lateral Organizations,* 2nd edn (Reading, MA: Addison-Wesley, 1994).

7 J. Pfeffer and G. Salancik, *The External Control of Organizations: A Resource Dependence Perspective* (New York: Harper and Row, 1978).

8 H. Aldrich, *Organizations and Environments* (New York: Prentice-Hall, 1979); L. Hrebiniak and W. Joyce, 'Organizational adaptation: strategic choice and environmental determinism', *Administrative Science Quarterly,* 30 (1985): 336–49.

9 Commission of the European Communities, 'On the Active Inclusion of People Excluded from the Labour Market', 2008, Brussels, www.eu2008.fr/webdav/site/ PFUE/shared/import/1016_Ministerielle_Pauvrete/ Recommendation_EC_active_inclusion_EN.pdf.

10 Pfeffer and Salancik, *The External Control of Organizations*, op. cit.

11 Aldrich, *Organizations and Environments*, op. cit.

12 S. Pilsbury and A. Meaney, *Are Horizontal Mergers and Vertical Integration a Problem? Analysis of the Rail Freight Market in Europe*, 2009, www.internationaltransportforum.org/jtrc/DiscussionPapers/DP200904.pdf.

13 K. D. Heath and P. Tiffin, *Context Dependence in the Coevolution of Plant and Rhizobial Mutualists*, April 2007, Department of Plant Biology, 250 Biological Sciences Centre, 1445 Gortner Avenue, University of Minnesota, St Paul, MN 55108, USA, http://ukpmc.ac .uk/articles/PMC2270936;jsessionid=0C9F7D91BE321DE5E7D6638A06311A8D.jvm1.

14 Aldrich, *Organizations and Environments*, op. cit.

15 W. Ouchi, *The M-Form Society: How American Teamwork Can Recapture the Competitive Edge* (Reading, MA: Addison-Wesley, 1984); L. Thurow, *Head to Head: The Coming Economic Battle Among Japan*, Europe and America (New York: William Morrow, 1992).

16 T. Cummings and S. Srivastva, *Management of Work: A Socio-Technical Systems Approach* (San Diego: University Associates, 1977): 112–16.

17 L. Bourgeois, 'Strategic goals, perceived uncertainty and economic performance in volatile environments', *Academy of Management Journal*, 28 (1985): 548–73; C. West Jr and C. Schwenk, 'Top management team strategic consensus, demographic homogeneity and firm performance: a report of resounding nonfindings', *Academy of Management Journal*, 17 (1996): 571–6.

18 J. Clark and C. Krone, 'Towards an overall view of organisation development in the seventies', in *Management of Change and Conflict*, eds J. Thomas and W. Bennis (Middlesex, England: Penguin Books, 1972): 284–304.

19 C. Krone, 'Open systems redesign', in *Theory and Method in Organization Development: An Evolutionary Process*, ed. J. Adams (Arlington, VA: NTL Institute for Applied Behavioral Science, 1974): 364–91; G. Jayaram, 'Open systems planning', in *The Planning of Change*, 3rd edn, eds W. Bennis, K. Benne, R. Chin and K. Corey (New York: Holt, Rinehart and Winston, 1976): 275–83; R. Beckhard and R. Harris, *Organizational Transitions: Managing Complex Change*, 2nd edn (Reading, MA: Addison-Wesley, 1987); Cummings and Srivastva, *Management of Work*, op. cit.

20 The Survey of Employee Engagement, 2009, Institute for Organizational Excellence, 1 University Station D3500 Austin, Texas 78712, www.banking.state.tx.us/exec/surveyooe09.pdf.

21 Jayaram, 'Open systems planning', op. cit.: 275–83; Cummings and Srivastva, Management of Work, op. cit.; R. Fry, 'Improving trustee, administrator and physician collaboration through open systems planning', in *Organization Development in Health Care Organizations*, eds N. Margulies and J. Adams (Reading, MA: Addison-Wesley, 1982): 282–92.

22 Prof. K. V. Bhanu Murthy, *Social Responsibility Standards and Global Environmental Accountability: A Developing Country Perspective*, November 2007, Department of Commerce, Delhi School of Economics, University of Delhi, http://mpra.ub.uni-muenchen.de/2636/1/MPRA_paper_2636.pdf.

23 T. Cummings, 'Transorganizational development', in *Research in Organizational Behavior*, 6, eds B. Staw and L. Cummings (Greenwich, CT: JAI Press, 1984): 367–422.

24 B. Gray, 'Conditions facilitating interorganizational collaboration', *Human Relations*, 38 (1985): 911–36; K. Harrigan and W. Newman, 'Bases of interorganization co-operation: propensity, power, persistence', *Journal of Management Studies*, 27 (1990): 417–34; Cummings, 'Transorganizational development', op. cit.

25 Cummings, 'Transorganizational development', op. cit.

26 C. Raben, 'Building strategic partnerships: creating and managing effective joint ventures', in *Organizational Architecture*, eds D. Nadler, M. Gerstein, R. Shaw and associates (San Francisco: Jossey-Bass, 1992): 81–109; B. Gray, *Collaborating: Finding Common Ground for Multiparty Problems* (San Francisco: Jossey-Bass, 1989); Harrigan and Newman, 'Bases of interorganization co-operation', op. cit.; P. Lorange and J. Roos, 'Analytical steps in the formation of strategic alliances', *Journal of Organizational Change Management*, 4 (1991): 60–72.

27 D. Boje, 'Towards a theory and praxis of transorganizational development: stakeholder networks and their habitats' (working paper 79–6, Behavioral and Organizational Science Study Center, Graduate School of Management, University of California at Los Angeles, February 1982); B. Gricar, 'The legitimacy of consultants and stakeholders in interorganizational problems' (paper presented at annual meeting of the Academy of Management, San Diego, August 1981); T. Williams, 'The search conference in active adaptive planning', *Journal of Applied Behavioral Science*, 16 (1980): 470–83; B. Gray and T. Hay, 'Political limits to interorganizational consensus and change', *Journal of Applied Behavioral Science*, 22 (1986): 95–112.

28 E. Trist, 'Referent organizations and the development of interorganizational domains' (paper delivered at annual meeting of the *Academy of Management*, Atlanta, August 1979).

29 Cummings, 'Transorganizational development', op. cit.

30 Raben, 'Building strategic partnerships', op. cit.

31 W. Cascio, 'Downsizing: what do we know? what have we learned?', *The Academy of Management Executive*, 7 (1993): 95–104.

32 ibid.

33 J. Corrigan, 'Corporate anorexia?', *Australian Accountant*, 67:8 (1997): 50–1.

34 Adapted from Cameron, Freeman and Mishra, 'Best practices in white-collar downsizing: managing contradictions', op. cit.; and R. Marshall and L. Lyles, 'Planning for a restructured, revitalized organization', *Sloan Management Review*, 35 (1994): 81–91.

35 J. Brockner, 'The effects of work layoffs on survivors: research, theory and practice', in *Research in Organization Behavior*, 10, eds B. Staw and L. Cummings (Greenwich, CT: JAI Press, 1989): 213–55.

36 Marshall and Lyles, 'Planning for a restructured, revitalized organization', op. cit.

37 J. Rogdon, 'Lack of communication burdens restructurings', *The Wall Street Journal* (2 November 1992): B1.

38 Kirby, 'Downsizing gets the push', op. cit.

39 ibid.

40 Cameron, Freeman and Mishra, 'Best practices in white-collar downsizing: managing contradictions', op. cit.

41 M. Hammer and J. Champy, *Reengineering the Corporation* (New York: HarperCollins, 1993); T. Stewart, 'Reengineering: the hot new managing tool', Fortune (23 August 1993): 41–8; J. Champy, *Reengineering Management* (New York: HarperCollins, 1994).

42 R. Kaplan and L. Murdock, 'Core process redesign', *The McKinsey Quarterly*, 2 (1991): 27–43.

43 S. Sitalaksmi and Y. Zhu, 'The transformation of human resource management in Indonesian state-owned enterprises since the Asian Crisis', *Asia Pacific Business Review*, 16:1 & 2 (January 2010): 37–57, www.informaworld.com/smpp/content~db=all~content=a920257752.

44 M. Miller, 'Customer service drives reengineering effort', *Personnel Journal*, 73 (1994): 87–93.

45 Kaplan and Murdock, 'Core process redesign', op. cit.; R. Manganelli and M. Klein, *The Reengineering Handbook* (New York: AMACOM, 1994).

46 J. Katzenbach and D. Smith, 'The rules for managing cross-functional reengineering teams', *Planning Review* (March–April 1993): 12–13; A. Nahavandi and E. Aranda, 'Restructuring teams for the reengineered organization', *The Academy of Management Executive*, 8 (1994): 58–68.

47 ibid.

48 Hammer and Champy, *Reengineering the Corporation*, op. cit.

49 Champy, *Reengineering Management*, op. cit.; K. Jensen, 'The effects of business process management on injury frequency', unpublished Master's thesis (Culver City, CA: Pepperdine University, 1993).

50 D. Glew, A. O'Leary-Kelly, R. Griffin, and D. Van Fleet, 'Participation in organizations: a preview of the issues and proposed framework for future analysis', *Journal of Management*, 21:3 (1995): 395–421.

51 U. Hongchatikul, *The Impact of Organizational Development Interventions on Employee Commitment and Motivation and Customer Satisfaction: A Case Study*, http://gsbejournal.au.edu/Journals/5.pdf.

52 F. Taylor, *The Principles of Scientific Management* (New York: Harper and Row, 1911).

53 ibid.

54 T. Cummings, 'Self-regulating work groups: a socio-technical synthesis', Academy of Management Review, 3 (1978): 625–34; G. Susman, *Autonomy at Work* (New York: Praeger, 1976); J. Slocum and H. Sims, 'A typology of technology and job redesign', *Human Relations*, 33 (1983): 193–212.

55 F. Herzberg, B. Mausner and B. Snyderman, *The Motivation to Work* (New York: John Wiley and Sons, 1959); F. Herzberg, 'The wise old Turk', Harvard Business Review, 52 (September–October 1974): 70–80; F. Herzberg and Z. Zautra, 'Orthodox job enrichment: measuring true quality in job satisfaction', *Personnel*, 53 (September–October 1976): 54–68.

56 J. Hackman and G. Oldham, *Work Redesign* (Reading, MA: Addison-Wesley, 1980).

57 A. Turner and P. Lawrence, *Industrial Jobs and the Worker* (Cambridge: Harvard Graduate School of Business Administration, Division of Research, 1965); J. Hackman and G. Oldham, 'Development of the job diagnostic survey', *Journal of Applied Psychology*, 60

(April 1975): 159–70; H. Sims, A. Szilagyi and R. Keller, 'The measurement of job characteristics', *Academy of Management Journal*, 19 (1976): 195–212.

58 G. Oldham and J. Hackman, 'Work design in the organizational context', in *Research in Organizational Behavior*, 2, eds B. Staw and L. Cummings (Greenwich, CT: JAI Press, 1980): 247–78; J. Cordery and T. Wall, 'Work design and supervisory practice: a model', *Human Relations*, 38 (1985): 425–41.

59 Hackman and Oldham, *Work Redesign*, op. cit.

60 ibid.

61 M. Campion, 'Interdisciplinary approaches to job design: a constructive replication with extensions', *Journal of Applied Psychology*, 73 (1988): 467–81.

62 C. Kulik, G. Oldham and P. Langner, 'Measurement of job characteristics: comparison of the original and the revised job diagnostic survey', *Journal of Applied Psychology*, 73 (1988): 426–66; J. Idaszak and F. Drasgow, 'A revision of the job diagnostic survey: elimination of a measurement artifact', *Journal of Applied Psychology*, 72 (1987): 69–74.

63 R. Steers and D. Spencer, 'The role of achievement motivation in job design', *Journal of Applied Psychology*, 62 (1977): 472–9; J. Champoux, 'A three sample test of some extensions to the job characteristics model', *Academy of Management Journal*, 23 (1980): 466–78; R. Katz, 'The influence of job longevity on employee reactions to task characteristics', *Human Relation*, 31 (1978): 703–25.

64 R. Zeffane, 'Correlates of job satisfaction and their implications for work redesign', *Public Personnel Management*, 23 (1994): 61–76.

65 G. Oldham and Y. Fried, 'Employee reactions to workspace characteristics', *Journal of Applied Psychology*, 72 (1987): 75–80.

66 B. Loher, R. Noe, N. Moeller and M. Fitzgerald, 'A meta-analysis of the relation of job characteristics to job satisfaction', *Journal of Applied Psychology*, 70 (1985): 280–9.

67 B. McEvoy and W. Cascio, 'Strategies for reducing employee turnover: a meta-analysis', *Journal of Applied Psychology*, 70 (1985): 342–53.

68 T. Cummings and E. Molloy, *Improving Productivity and the Quality of Work Life* (New York: Praeger, 1977).

69 J. Nicholas, 'The comparative impact of organization development interventions on hard criteria measures', *Academy of Management Review*, 7 (1982): 531–42.

70 E. Trist, B. Higgin, H. Murray and A. Pollock, *Organizational Choice* (London: Tavistock, 1963); T. Cummings and B. Srivastva, *Management of Work: A Socio-Technical Systems Approach* (San Diego: University Associates, 1977); A. Cherns, 'Principles of sociotechnical design revisited', *Human Relations*, 40 (1987): 153–62.

71 Cummings, 'Self-regulating work groups', op. cit.: 625–34; J. Hackman, *The Design of Self-Managing Work Groups*, Technical Report No. 11 (New Haven: Yale University, School of Organization and Management, 1976); Cummings and Srivastva, *Management of Work*, op. cit.; Susman, *Autonomy at Work*, op. cit.; H. Sims and C. Manz, 'Conversations within self-managed work groups', *National Productivity Review*, 1 (Summer 1982): 261–9; T. Cummings, 'Designing effective work groups', in *Handbook of Organizational Design: Remodeling*

Organizations and Their Environments, 2, eds P. Nystrom and W. Starbuck (New York: Oxford University Press, 1981): 250–71.

72 C. Manz, 'Beyond self-managing teams: toward self-leading teams in the work place', in *Research in Organizational Change and Development*, 4, eds W. Pasmore and R. Woodman (Greenwich, CT: JAI Press, 1990): 273–99; C. Manz and H. Sims Jr, 'Leading workers to lead themselves: the external leadership of self-managed work teams', *Administrative Science Quarterly*, 32 (1987): 106–28.

73 Dumaine, 'The trouble with teams', *Fortune* (5 September 1994): 86–92.

74 Weisbord, 'Participative work design: a personal odyssey', *Organizational Dynamics* (1984): 5–20.

75 T. Cummings, 'Socio-technical systems: an intervention strategy', in *New Techniques in Organization Development*, ed. W. Burke (New York: Basic Books, 1975): 228–49; Cummings and Srivastva, *Management of Work*, op. cit.; Cummings and Molloy, *Improving Productivity and the Quality of Work Life*, op. cit.

76 F. van Eijnatten, S. Eggermont, G. de Goffau and I. Mankoe, *The Socio-technical Systems Design Paradigm* (Eindhoven, The Netherlands: Eindhoven University of Technology, 1994).

77 P. Goodman, R. Devadas and T. Hughson, 'Groups and productivity: analysing the effectiveness of self-managing teams', in *Productivity in Organizations*, eds J. Campbell, R. Campbell and associates (San Francisco: Jossey-Bass, 1988): 295–325.

78 R. Walton, 'How to counter alienation in the plant', *Harvard Business Review*, 12 (November–December 1972): 70–81.

79 R. Schrank, 'On ending worker alienation: the Gaines Pet Food plant', in *Humanizing the Workplace*, ed. R. Fairfield (Buffalo, NY: Prometheus Books, 1974): 119–20, 126; R. Walton, 'Teaching an old dog food new tricks', *The Wharton Magazine*, 4 (Winter 1978): 42; L. Ketchum, *Innovating Plant Managers Are Talking About . . .* (International Conference on the Quality of Working Life, Toronto, Canada, 30 August–3 September 1981): 2–3; H. Simon et al., *General Foods Topeka: Ten*

Years Young (International Conference on the Quality of Working Life, Toronto, Canada, 30 August–3 September 1981): 5–7.

80 J. Norsted and S. Aguren, *The Saab-Scania Report* (Stockholm: Swedish Employer's Confederation, 1975).

81 'Doubting Sweden's way', Time (10 March 1975): 40.

82 P. Gyllenhammär, *People at Work* (Reading, MA: Addison-Wesley, 1977): 15–17, 43, 52–3; B. Jönsson, *Corporate Strategy for People at Work – The Volvo Experience* (International Conference on the Quality of Working Life, Toronto, Canada, 30 August–3 September 1981); N. Tichy and J. Nisberg, 'When does work restructuring work? Organizational innovations at Volvo and GM', *Organizational Dynamics*, 5 (Summer 1976): 73.

83 J. Kapstein and J. Hoerr, 'Volvo's radical new plant: the death of the assembly line?', *Business Week*, (28 August 1989): 92–3.

84 W. Pasmore, 'The comparative impacts of sociotechnical system, job-redesign and survey–feedback interventions', in *Sociotechnical Systems: A Source Book*, eds W. Pasmore and J. Sherwood (San Diego, University Associates, 1978): 291–300.

85 T. Cummings, 'Self-regulating work groups: a socio-technical synthesis', *Academy of Management Review*, 3 (1978): 625–34; G. Susman, *Autonomy at Work* (New York: Praeger, 1976); J. Slocum and H. Sims, 'A typology of technology and job redesign', *Human Relations*, 33 (1983): 193–212; M. Kiggundu, 'Task interdependence and job design: test of a theory', *Organizational Behavior and Human Performance*, 31 (1983): 145–72.

86 Hackman and Oldham, *Work Redesign*, op. cit.; K. Brousseau, 'Toward a dynamic model of job–person relationships: findings, research questions and implications for work system design', *Academy of Management Review*, 8 (1983): 33–45; G. Graen, T. Scandura and M. Graen, 'A field experimental test of the moderating effects of growth needs strength on productivity', *Journal of Applied Psychology*, 71 (1986): 484–91.

87 T. Cummings, 'Designing work for productivity and quality of life', *Outlook*, 6 (1982): 35–9.

PART 4

ORGANISATION TRANSFORMATION

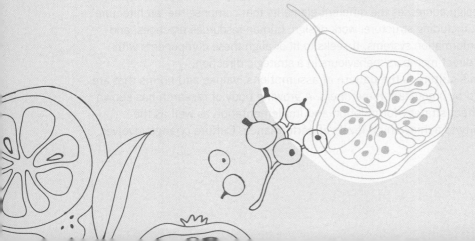

CHAPTER 9

Organisation transformation and change

This chapter presents interventions for transforming organisations – that is, for changing the basic character of the organisation, including how it is structured and how it relates to its environment. These frame-breaking and sometimes revolutionary interventions go beyond improving the organisation incrementally, focusing instead on changing the way it views itself and its environment. They bring about important alignments between the organisation and its competitive environment and among the organisation's strategy, design elements and culture.

Transformational change can occur in response to or in anticipation of major changes in the organisation's environment or technology. In addition, these changes often are associated with significant revision of the organisation's business strategy which, in turn, may require modifying internal structures and processes as well as its corporate culture to support the new direction. Such fundamental change entails a new paradigm for organising and managing organisations. It involves qualitatively different ways of perceiving, thinking and behaving in organisations. Movement towards this new way of operating requires senior executives to take an active leadership role. The change process is characterised by considerable innovation as members discover new ways of improving the organisation and adapting it to changing conditions.

Transformational change[1] is an emerging part of organisation development and there is some confusion about its meaning and definition. This chapter starts with a description of several major features of transformational change. Against this background, three kinds of interventions are discussed: integrated strategic change, organisation design and culture change.

Integrated strategic change[2] is a comprehensive OD intervention aimed at a single organisation or business unit. It suggests that business strategy and organisation design must be aligned and changed together to respond to external and internal disruptions. A strategic change plan helps members manage the transition between the current strategic orientation and the desired future strategic orientation.

Organisation design addresses the different elements that comprise the 'architecture' of the organisation, including structure, work design, human resources practices, and management and information systems. It seeks to fit or align these components with each other so they direct members' behaviours in a strategic direction.

An organisation's culture is the pattern of assumptions, values and norms that are more or less shared by organisation members. A growing body of research has shown that culture can affect strategy formulation and implementation as well as the organisation's ability to achieve high levels of performance. Culture change involves helping senior executives and administrators diagnose the existing culture and make necessary alterations in the basic assumptions and values underlying organisational behaviours.

CHARACTERISTICS OF TRANSFORMATIONAL CHANGE

As the twenty-first century unfolds, a large number of organisations are radically altering how they operate and relate to their environments.[3] Increased global competition is forcing many organisations to downsize or consolidate and become leaner, more efficient and flexible. Deregulation is pushing businesses in the financial services, telecommunications and airline industries to rethink business strategies and reshape how they operate. Public demand for less government intervention and lowered deficits is forcing public sector agencies to streamline operations and to deliver more for less. Rapid changes in technologies render many organisational practices obsolete, pushing businesses to be continually innovative and nimble.

Organisation transformation implies radical changes in how members perceive, think and behave at work. These changes go far beyond making the existing organisation better or fine-tuning the status quo. They are concerned with fundamentally altering the prevailing assumptions about how the organisation functions and relates to its environment. Changing these assumptions entails significant shifts in corporate values and norms and in the structures and organisational arrangements that shape members' behaviours. Not only is the magnitude of change greater, but the change fundamentally alters the qualitative nature of the organisation.

Change is triggered by environmental and internal disruptions

Organisations are unlikely to undertake transformational change unless significant reasons to do so emerge. Power, emotion and expertise are vested in the existing organisational arrangements and when faced with problems, organisations are more likely to fine-tune those structures than to alter them drastically. Thus, in most cases, organisations must experience or anticipate a severe threat to survival before they will be motivated to undertake transformational change.[4] Such threats arise when environmental and internal changes render existing organisational strategies and designs obsolete. The changes threaten the very existence of the organisation as it presently is constituted.

In studying a large number of organisation transformations, Tushman, Newman and Romanelli showed that transformational change occurs in response to at least three kinds of disruption:[5]

1 *Industry discontinuities* – sharp changes in legal, political, economic and technological conditions that shift the basis for competition within an industry.

2 *Product life cycle shifts* – changes in product life cycle that require different business strategies.

3 *Internal company dynamics* – changes in size, corporate portfolio strategy or executive turnover.

These disruptions severely jolt organisations and push them to question their business strategy and, in turn, their mission, values, structure, systems and procedures. Application 9.1. describes an organisation transformation at Reader's Digest.

9.1

APPLICATION

Reader's Digest chief shakes up the empire

Mary Berner has been described as moving at warp speed and that barely does justice to the blur of activity that has been the New Yorker's first year as head of global media behemoth, the Reader's Digest Association Inc.

Announcing only two initiatives would seem to be a slow day for Berner as she races to transform the 86-year-old publishing institution, which is best known for its diminutive flagship title, *Reader's Digest*.

'So, first of all, I changed the whole structure of the company,' is how she starts the conversation about her first 12 months at the helm.

A year on, 26 per cent of the top 200 executives across the world are new. A 'very aggressive' performance management process has been instituted. The European business has been reorganised. 'We did everything very, very quickly. But that's what the company needed,' Berner says. 'It had all the right stuff, the core assets, it just needed to change the culture, to be faster and more decisive.

'So we got the structure right and then we started to focus very, very quickly on "How do we grow the company?" We launched in China just last month. We've launched into Turkey. We launched several new magazines. The idea was to grow the assets and to structure the company with ... a combination of veterans and newer people, so we'd have a new platform for growth and then accelerate global growth. And that's what we're going to do. So we absolutely haven't wasted any time.'

According to an analysis by NDD, *Reader's Digest Australia* is the fourth largest local magazine publisher in terms of sales, with a 3.5 per cent market share from its three magazines, *Australian Reader's Digest*, *HealthSmart* and *Australian Handyman*. A fourth, science and nature bimonthly *Discovery Channel Magazine*, will be added in May. It was launched in November in Singapore, Malaysia, the Philippines, Hong Kong, Taiwan, Thailand, Japan and South Korea.

Berner says the new magazine is already 30 per cent above sales projections.

'And to be a truly modern media company ... there will be a lot more diversification, so we need to continue to grow our brand portfolio. The face of the whole company will look very different in a couple of years.'

Source: Sally Jackson, 'Reader's Digest chief shakes up the empire', *The Australian*, 27 March 2008. News Limited.

Critical thinking questions:
1. What form of disruption stimulated the reorganisation at Reader's Digest?
2. What significant changes have happened at Reader's Digest since this interview? What benefits and difficulties are they now facing?

Change is systemic and revolutionary

Transformational change involves reshaping the organisation's design elements and culture. These changes can be characterised as systemic and revolutionary because the entire nature of the organisation is altered fundamentally. Typically driven by senior executives, change may occur rapidly so that it does not get mired in politics, individual resistance and other forms of organisational inertia.[6] This is particularly pertinent to changing the different features of the organisation such as structure, information systems, human resources practices and work design. These features tend to reinforce one another, thus making it difficult to change them in a piecemeal manner.[7] They need to be changed together and in a co-ordinated fashion so that they can mutually support each other and the new cultural values and assumptions.[8] Ultimately, these changes should motivate and direct people's behaviour in a new strategic direction. They are considered transformational when a majority of individuals in an organisation change their behaviours.[9]

Long-term studies of organisational evolution underscore the revolutionary nature of transformational change.[10] They suggest that organisations typically move through relatively long periods of smooth growth and operation. These periods of convergence or evolution are characterised by incremental changes. At times, however, most organisations experience severe external or internal disruptions that render existing organisational arrangements ineffective. Successful businesses respond to these threats to survival by transforming themselves to fit the new conditions. These periods of total system and quantum changes[11] represent abrupt shifts in the organisation's structure, culture and processes. If successful, the shifts enable the organisation to experience another long period of smooth functioning until the next disruption signals the need for drastic change.[12]

These studies of organisation evolution and revolution point to the benefits of implementing transformational change as rapidly as possible. The faster the organisation can respond to disruptions, the quicker it can attain the benefits of operating in a new way. Rapid change enables the organisation to reach a period of smooth growth and functioning sooner, thus providing it with a competitive advantage over those organisations that change more slowly.

Change demands a new organising paradigm

Organisations undertaking transformational change are, by definition, involved in second-order or gamma types of change.[13] *Gamma change* involves discontinuous shifts in mental or organisational frameworks.[14] Creative metaphors, such as 'organisation learning' or 'continuous improvement', are often used to help members visualise the new paradigm.[15] Increases in technological change, concern for quality, and worker participation have led many organisations to shift their organising paradigm. Characterised as the transition from a 'control-based' to a 'commitment-based' organisation, the features of the new paradigm include leaner, more flexible structures; information and decision making pushed down to the lowest levels; decentralised teams and business units accountable for specific products, services or customers; and participative management and teamwork. This new organising paradigm is well suited to changing conditions.

Change is driven by senior executives and line management

A key feature of transformational change is the active role of senior executives and line managers in all phases of the change process.[16] They are responsible for the strategic direction and operation of the organisation and actively lead the transformation. They decide when to initiate transformational change, what the change should be, how it should be implemented and who should be responsible for directing it. Because existing executives may lack the talent, energy and commitment to undertake these tasks, they may be replaced by outsiders who are recruited to lead the change. Research on transformational change suggests that externally recruited executives are three times more likely to initiate such change than are existing executives.[17]

The critical role of executive leadership in transformational change is clearly emerging. Lucid accounts of transformational leaders describe how executives, such as Richard Branson (Virgin Enterprises), Christine Nixon (former Chief Commissioner of Victoria Police) and Graeme Wood (wotif.com), actively managed both the organisational and personal dynamics of transformational change.[18] The work of Nadler, Tushman and others points to three key roles for executive leadership of such change:[19]

1 *Envisioning*. Executives must articulate a clear and credible vision of the new strategic orientation. They also must set new and difficult standards for performance and generate pride in past accomplishments and enthusiasm for the new strategy.

2 *Energising*. Executives must demonstrate personal excitement for the changes and model the behaviours that are expected of others. Behavioural integrity, credibility and 'walking the talk' are important ingredients.[20] They must communicate examples of early success to mobilise energy for change.

3 *Enabling*. Executives must provide the resources necessary for undertaking significant change and use rewards to reinforce new behaviours. Leaders also must build an effective top-management team to manage the new organisation and develop management practices to support the change process.

Change involves significant learning

Transformational change requires much learning and innovation.[21] Organisational members must learn how to enact the new behaviours required to implement new strategic directions. This typically involves trying new behaviours, assessing their consequences and modifying them if necessary. Because members usually need to learn qualitatively different ways of perceiving, thinking and behaving, the learning process is likely to be substantial and to involve much unlearning. It is directed by a vision of the future organisation and by the values and norms needed to support it. Learning occurs at all levels of the organisation, from senior executives to lower-level employees.

Because the environment itself is likely to be changing during the change process, transformational change rarely has a delimited time frame, but is likely to persist as long as the organisation needs to adapt to change. Learning how to manage change continuously can help the organisation keep pace with a dynamic environment. It can provide the built-in capacity to fit the organisation continually to its environment.

INTEGRATED STRATEGIC CHANGE

Integrated strategic change (ISC) extends traditional OD processes into the content-oriented discipline of strategic management. It is a deliberate, co-ordinated process that leads gradually or radically to systemic realignments between the environment and an organisation's strategic orientation and that results in improvement in performance and effectiveness.[22]

The ISC process was initially developed by Worley, Hitchin and Ross in response to managers' complaints that good business strategies often are not implemented.[23] Research suggests that too little attention is given to the change process and human resources issues necessary to execute strategy.[24] The predominant paradigm in strategic management – formulation and implementation – artificially separates strategic thinking from operational and tactical actions; it ignores the contributions that planned change processes can make to implementation.[25] In the traditional process, senior managers and strategic planning staff prepare economic forecasts, competitor analyses and market studies. They discuss these studies and rationally align the organisation's strengths and weaknesses with environmental opportunities and threats to form the organisation's strategy.[26] Then, implementation occurs as middle managers, supervisors and employees hear about the new strategy through memos, restructuring announcements, changes in job responsibilities or new departmental objectives. Consequently, because participation has been limited to top management, there is little understanding of the need for change and little ownership of the new behaviours, initiatives and tactics required to achieve the announced objectives.

Key features

ISC, in contrast to the traditional process, was designed to be a highly participative process. It has three key features:[27]

1   The relevant unit of analysis is the organisation's *strategic orientation* comprising its strategy and organisation design. Strategy and the design that supports it must be considered as an integrated whole.

2 Creating the strategic plan, gaining commitment and support for it, planning its implementation and executing it are treated as one integrated process. The ability to repeat such a process quickly and effectively when conditions warrant is valuable, rare and difficult to imitate. Thus, a strategic change capability represents a sustainable competitive advantage.[28]

3 Individuals and groups throughout the organisation are integrated into the analysis, planning and implementation process to create a more achievable plan, to maintain the organisation's strategic focus, to direct attention and resources on the organisation's key competencies, to improve co-ordination and integration within the organisation and to create higher levels of shared ownership and commitment.

Application stages

The ISC process is applied in four phases: performing a strategic analysis, exercising strategic choice, designing a strategic change plan and implementing the plan. The four steps are discussed sequentially here but actually unfold in overlapping and integrated ways. Figure 9.1 displays the steps in the ISC process and its change components. An organisation's existing strategic orientation, identified as its current strategy (S_1) and organisation design (O_1), is linked to its future strategic orientation (S_2/O_2) by the strategic change plan.

1 *Performing the strategic analysis.* The ISC process begins with a diagnosis of the organisation's readiness for change and its current strategy and organisation design (S_1/O_1). The most important indicator of readiness is senior

FIGURE 9.1 The integrated strategic change process

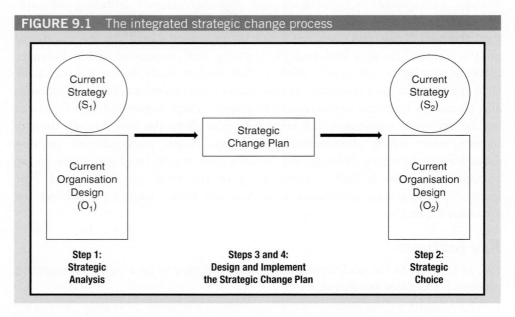

Source: Cummings/Worley, *Organization Development and Change* (with InfoTrac® College Edition Printed Access Card), 9e © 2009 South-Western, a part of Cengage Learning, Inc. Reproduced by permission, www.cengage.com/permissions.

management's willingness and ability to carry out strategic change. Greiner and Schein suggest that the two key dimensions in this analysis are the leader's willingness and commitment to change and the senior team's willingness and ability to follow the leader's initiative.[29] Organisations whose leaders are not willing to lead and whose senior managers are not willing and able to support the new strategic direction when necessary should consider team-building processes to ensure their commitment.

The second stage in strategic analysis[30] is understanding the current strategy and organisation design. The process begins with an examination of the organisation's industry as well as its current financial performance and effectiveness. This information provides the necessary context to assess the current strategic orientation's viability. Porter's model of industry attractiveness[31] and the environmental framework are the two most relevant models for analysing the environment.

Next, the current strategic orientation is described to explain current levels of performance and human outcomes. Several models for guiding this diagnosis exist.[32] For example, the organisation's current strategy, structure and processes can be assessed according to the model and methods. A metaphor or other label that describes how the organisation's mission, objectives and business policies lead to improved performance can be used to represent strategy. 3M Corporation's traditional strategy of 'differentiation' aptly summarises its mission to resolve unsolved problems innovatively, its goal of having a large percentage of current revenues come from products developed in the last five years and its policies that support innovation, such as encouraging engineers to spend up to 15% of their time on new projects. An organisation's objectives, policies and budgets signal which parts of the environment are important and allocate and direct resources to particular environmental relationships.[33] Intel's new product development objectives and allocation of more than 20% of revenues to research and development signal the importance of its linkage to the technological environment.

The organisation's design is described by the structure, work design, information system and human resources system. Other models for understanding the organisation's strategic orientation include the competitive positioning model[34] and other typologies.[35] These frameworks assist in assessing customer satisfaction; product and service offerings; financial health; technological capabilities; and organisational culture, structure and systems.

The strategic analysis process actively involves organisation members. Large group conferences; employee focus groups; interviews with salespeople, customers and purchasing agents; and other methods allow a variety of employees and managers to participate in the diagnosis and increase the amount and relevance of the data collected. This builds commitment to and ownership of the analysis; should a strategic change effort result, members are more likely to understand why and be supportive of it.

2   *Exercising strategic choice.* Once the existing strategic orientation is understood, a new one must be designed. For example, the strategic analysis might reveal misfits among the organisation's environment, strategic orientation and performance. These misfits can be used as inputs for crafting the future strategy and organisation design. Based on this analysis, senior management formulates visions for the future and broadly defines two or three alternative sets of strategies and objectives for achieving those visions. Market forecasts, employees' readiness and willingness to change, competitor analyses and other projections can be used to develop the alternative future scenarios.[36] The different sets of strategies and objectives also include projections about the organisation design changes that will be necessary to support each alternative. Although participation from other organisational stakeholders is important in the alternative generation phase, choosing the appropriate strategic orientation ultimately rests with top management and cannot easily be delegated. Senior executives are in the unique position of viewing a strategy from a general-management position. When major strategic decisions are given to lower-level managers, the risk of focusing too narrowly on a product, market or technology increases.

This step determines the content or 'what' of strategic change. The desired strategy (S_2) defines the products or services to offer, the markets to be served and the way these outputs will be produced and positioned. The desired organisation design (O_2) specifies the organisation structures and processes necessary to support the new strategy. Aligning an organisation's design with a particular strategy can be a major source of superior performance and competitive advantage.[37]

3   *Designing the strategic change plan.* The strategic change plan is a comprehensive agenda for moving the organisation from its current strategy and organisation design to the desired future strategic orientation. It represents the process or 'how' of strategic change. The change plan describes the types, magnitude and schedule of change activities, as well as the costs associated with them. It also specifies how the changes will be implemented, given power and political issues; the nature of the organisational culture; and the current ability of the organisation to implement change.[38]

4   *Implementing the plan.* The final step in the ISC process is the actual implementation of the strategic change plan.[39] This draws heavily on knowledge of motivation, group dynamics and change processes. It deals continuously with such issues as alignment, adaptability, teamwork and organisational and personal learning. Implementation requires senior managers to champion the different elements of the change plan. They can, for example, initiate action and allocate resources to particular activities, set high but achievable goals and provide feedback on accomplishments. In addition, leaders must hold people accountable to the change objectives, institutionalise the changes that occur and be prepared to solve problems as they arise. This final point recognises that no

strategic change plan can account for all of the contingencies that emerge. There must be a willingness to adjust the plan as implementation unfolds to address unforeseen and unpredictable events and to take advantage of new opportunities.

Application 9.2 describes how the Foster's Group is leading its wine division through change while plotting a course for the future.

9.2

APPLICATION

Managing strategic change at Foster's Group

Foster's Group is a leading premium global multi-beverage manufacturer delivering a selection of beer, wine, spirits, cider and non-alcohol beverages.

In April 2008, the Foster's Group initiated a comprehensive strategic and operational review of its Global Wine business due to the disappointing performance of their new wine acquisitions: Beringer and Southcorp. Foster's earnings had deteriorated, its competitive position had weakened and it failed to achieve the required profits on its investment in wine.

The Group's review was headed by then new CEO, Ian Johnston, and overseen by the board. It included a comprehensive study of the structure of the wine industry, business strategy, organisational design, operational capabilities and efficiencies and economic and financial performance.

The review recommended that the wine business be retained but remodelled with major organisational and operational changes to be taken into effect. The business would be divided into Wine and Beer Divisions. This would give the new wine operational leadership team, which was hired to implement the review's outcomes, a clearer focus, organisational simplicity, financial transparency and performance accountability.

To improve the marketing and sales of the wine group, the number of sales people would be increased, leveraging greater sales effectiveness, superior wine product knowledge and better customer support and service to the region. Gradually, global supply operations would be incorporated within their relevant demand regions. This would create autonomous business units comprising sales, marketing, supply and functional support for each region.

A further outcome was that thirty-six non-core vineyards were sold off and three wineries were closed, reconfigured or consolidated in both Australia and California.

Finally, the Review identified a futures strategy to improve outcomes for the business. An 18 month plan was presented to the board detailing a program that focused on improving growth, efficiency and capabilities across the wine group.

Source: 'Managing strategic change at Foster's Group', www.fosters.com.au/mediacentre/ 5935651CF1B34A02A455B1012E357437.htm, accessed 3 February 2010.

Critical thinking questions:
1. Ian Johnston has now had time to establish himself within the company. What significant changes have resulted from his implementation of the review? What problems do you expect will occur and how may they be overcome?
2. The review split the wine and beer divisions. What steps need to be taken to ensure vertical co-ordination?
3. Analyse the emergence of the new strategy in terms of the preceding discussion. Were all steps followed? Do they appear to have been effective?

ORGANISATION DESIGN

Organisation design configures the organisation's structure, work design, human resources practices and management and information systems to guide members' behaviours in a strategic direction. This intervention typically occurs in response to a major change in the organisation's strategy that requires fundamentally new ways for the organisation to function and members to behave. It involves many of the organisational features discussed in previous chapters such as restructuring organisations, work design and performance management. Because they all significantly affect member behaviour, organisation design constructs them to fit with each other so they all mutually reinforce the desired behaviour in the new strategic direction. This comprehensive intervention contrasts sharply with piecemeal approaches that address the design elements separately and thus risk misaligning them with each other and sending mixed signals about desired behaviours. For example, many organisations have experienced problems implementing team-based structures because their existing information and reward systems emphasise individual-based performance.

Conceptual framework

A key notion in organisation design is 'fit', 'congruence' or 'alignment' among the organisational elements.[40] Figure 9.2 presents a systems model showing the different components of organisation design and the interdependencies among them. It highlights the idea that the organisation is designed to support a particular strategy (strategic fit) and that the different design elements must be aligned with each other and all work together to guide members' behaviour in that strategic direction (design fit). Research shows that the better these fits, the more effective the organisation is likely to be.[41]

Most of the design components are reviewed briefly below.

- *Strategy* determines how the organisation will use its resources to gain competitive advantage. It may focus on introducing new products and services (innovation strategy), controlling costs and reducing prices (cost-minimisation strategy), or some combination of both (imitation strategy). Strategy sets the direction for organisation design by identifying the criteria for making design choices and the organisational capabilities needed to make the strategy happen.
- *Structure* has to do with how the organisation divides tasks, assigns them to departments and co-ordinates across them. It generally appears on an organisation chart showing the chain of command – where formal power and authority reside and how departments relate to each other. Structures can be highly formal and promote control and efficiency, such as a functional structure;[42] or they can be loosely defined and flexible and favour change and innovation, such as a matrix, process or network structure.

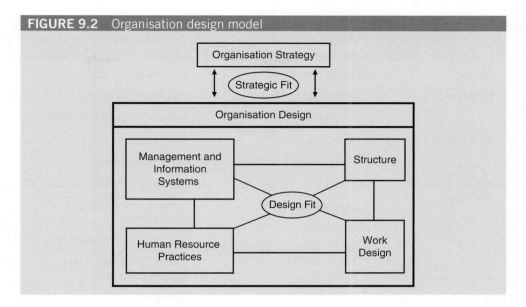

FIGURE 9.2 Organisation design model

Source: Cummings/Worley, *Organization Development and Change* (with InfoTrac® College Edition Printed Access Card), 9e © 2009 South-Western, a part of Cengage Learning, Inc. Reproduced by permission, www.cengage.com/permissions.

- *Work design* specifies how tasks are performed and assigned to jobs or groups. It can create traditional jobs and groups that involve standard tasks with little task variety and decision making or enriched jobs and self-managed teams that involve highly variable, challenging and discretionary work.
- *Human resources practices* involve selecting people and training, developing and rewarding them. These methods can be oriented to hiring and paying people for specific jobs, training them when necessary and rewarding their individual performance. Conversely, human resources practices can also select people to fit the organisation's culture, continually develop them and pay them for learning multiple skills and contributing to business success.
- *Management and information systems*[43] have to do with how employees are led and the nature and kinds of information they are provided to guide their work. Managers can lead through command and control, relying on hierarchical authority and the chain of command; or they can be highly participative and facilitate employee involvement in decision making. Information systems can be highly centralised with limited access and data sharing; or they can be open and distribute copious information throughout the organisation.

Table 9.1 shows how these design components can be configured into two radically different organisation designs: *mechanistic*, supporting efficiency and control and *organic*, promoting innovation and change.[44] Mechanistic designs have been prevalent in organisations for over a century; they propelled organisations into the industrial age. Today, competitive conditions require many organisations to be more flexible, fast and inventive.[45] Thus, organisation design is aimed more and more at creating organic designs, both in entirely new start-ups and in existing businesses

TABLE 9.1 Organisation designs

	Mechanistic design	Organic design
Strategy	Cost minimisation	Innovation
Structure	Formal/hierarchical	Flat, lean and flexible
	Functional	Matrix, process and network
Work design	Traditional jobs	Enriched jobs
	Traditional work groups	Self-managed teams
Human resources practices	Selection to fit job	Selection to fit organisation
	Up-front training	Continuous training and development
	Standard reward mix	Individual choice rewards
	Pay for performance and individual merit	Pay for performance and business success
	Job-based pay	Skill-based pay
Management and information systems	Command and control	Employee involvement
	Closed, exclusive, centralised information	Open, inclusive, distributed information

that reconfigure mechanistic designs to make them more organic. Designing a new organisation is much easier than redesigning an existing one in which multiple sources of inertia[46] and resistance to change are likely to be embedded.

As shown in Table 9.1, a mechanistic design supports an organisation strategy emphasising cost minimisation, such as might be found at Target and McDonald's or other businesses competing on price. The organisation tends to be structured into functional departments with employees performing similar tasks grouped together for maximum efficiency. The managerial hierarchy is the main source of co-ordination and control. Accordingly, work design follows traditional principles with jobs and work groups being highly standardised with minimal decision making and skill variety. Human resources practices are geared towards selecting people to fit specific jobs and training them periodically when the need arises. Employees are paid on the basis of the job they perform, share a standard set of fringe benefits and achieve merit raises based on their individual performance. Management practices stress command and control with power concentrated at the top of the organisation and orders flowing downward through the chain of command. Similarly, information systems are highly centralised, limited in access and do not permit sharing data widely in the organisation. When taken together, all of these design elements direct organisational behaviour towards efficiency and cost minimisation.

Table 9.1 shows that an organic design supports an organisation strategy aimed at innovation such as might be found at 3M, Apple and Intel or other businesses competing on new products and services. All the design elements are geared to getting employees directly involved in the innovation process, facilitating interaction among them, developing and rewarding their knowledge and expertise and providing them with relevant and timely information. Consequently, the organisation's structure tends to be flat, lean and flexible like the matrix, process and network structures. Work design is aimed at employee motivation and decision making with enriched jobs and self-managed teams. Human resources practices focus on attracting, motivating and retaining talented employees. They send a strong signal that employees' knowledge and expertise are key sources of competitive advantage. Members are selected to fit an organisation culture valuing participation, teamwork and invention. Training and development are intense and continuous. Members are rewarded for learning multiple skills, have choices about fringe benefits and gain merit pay based on the business success of their work unit. Management practices are highly participative and promote employee involvement. Information systems are highly open and inclusive, providing relevant and timely information throughout the organisation. In summary, these design choices guide members' behaviours towards change and innovation.

Application stages

Organisation design can be applied to the whole organisation or to a major subpart such as a large department or stand-alone unit. It can start from a clean slate in a new organisation or reconfigure an existing organisation design. To construct the different design elements appropriately requires broad content knowledge of them. Thus, organisation design typically involves a team of change practitioners with expertise in corporate strategy, organisation structure, work design, human resources practices and management and information systems. This team works closely with senior executives who are responsible for determining the organisation's strategic direction and leading the organisation design intervention. The design process itself can be highly participative, involving stakeholders from throughout the organisation. This can increase the design's quality and stakeholders' commitment to implementing it.[47]

Organisation design generally follows the three broad steps outlined below.[48] Although they are presented sequentially, in practice they are highly interactive, often feeding back on each other and requiring continual revision as the process unfolds.

1 *Clarifying the design focus.* This preliminary stage involves assessing the organisation to create the overall framework for design. It starts with examining the organisation's strategy and objectives and determining what organisation capabilities are needed to achieve them. These become the design criteria for making choices about how to configure the design components. Then, the organisation is assessed against these design criteria to uncover gaps between how it currently functions and is designed and the desired capabilities. This gap analysis identifies current problems that the design intervention should address.

It provides information for determining which design elements will receive the most attention and the likely magnitude and time frame of the design process.

2 *Designing the organisation.* This key step in organisation design involves configuring the design components to support the organisation's strategy and objectives. It starts with a broad outline of how the organisation should be structured and how the design components should fit together to form a particular design, usually falling somewhere along the continuum from mechanistic to organic. Senior executives responsible for the overall direction of the organisation typically design this overarching structure. Next, the design process addresses the specific details of the components, which involves generating alternatives and making specific design choices. A broader set of organisational members often participates in these decisions, relying on its own as well as experts' experience and know-how, knowledge of best practices and information gained from visits to other organisations willing to share design experience. This stage results in an overall design for the organisation, detailed designs for the components and preliminary plans for how they will fit together and be implemented.

3 *Implementing the design.* The final step involves making the new design happen by putting into place the new structures, practices and systems. It draws heavily on the methods for leading and managing change and applies them to the entire organisation or subunit and not just limited parts. Because organisation design generally involves large amounts of transformational change, this intervention can place heavy demands on the organisation's resources and leadership expertise. Members from throughout the organisation must be motivated to implement the new design; all relevant stakeholders must support it politically. Organisation designs usually cannot be implemented in one step but must proceed in phases that involve considerable transition management. They often entail significant new work behaviours and relationships that require extensive and continuous organisation learning.

Application 9.3 describes organisation design at Coles supermarkets. It illustrates how the different design elements must fit together and reinforce each other to promote a high-performance organisation.

APPLICATION 9.3

Coles retailer revitalises itself

Coles, Australia's second-biggest retailer, has revitalised itself by revamping its brands, the supply chain and training its managers.

Ian McLeod took over the controls of the supermarket chain, Coles, in mid-2008 and one of his first directives was to ban staff from looking in customers' bags and to take down the signs warning that shoplifting was theft. McLeod was taking Coles into a new direction where the customer is paramount.

The previous management had taken a band aid approach to fixing infrastructure and had shelved training programs for managers. McLeod has a different focus: the band aid approach

>>

had short term savings but ultimately it costs you more and they do not address long term problems. The checkouts do not run efficiently and the customers were spending too long in queues.

McLeod brought in a new management team to transform the company. The company is once more training managers and bureaucracy has been trimmed back with 1500 staff cut from the head office in Tooronga, Melbourne. However, the supermarkets now have an extra 8000 staff. 'Mystery shoppers' are contracted to visit the stores every three months to measure queuing times and management leadership programs have been established.

House brands, which are more profitable as they don't require marketing spend, have been reorganised and restructured. The supply chain has also been revamped. Previously, Coles had trouble keeping its shelves fully stocked due to the supply chain not keeping up with consumer demand, costing the company in lost sales. Distribution centres have been halved from 40 to 20, a decision made by the previous administration, and is now starting to show results with lower costs and delivery effectiveness. Fresh food can be ordered and delivered quickly, reflecting what consumers want in their stores. The end shopping experience is also being altered: softer lighting, wider aisles and lower shelving to make the products more accessible.

The cultural change within Coles was highlighted effectively in the 2009 Victorian bushfires. The Monday after Black Saturday, the board decided to give that week's Friday profits to the Bushfire appeal. Also, the 14 stores within the fire-catchment area were directed to provide the Red Cross and Salvation Army with food, water and toiletries for the fire victims. Huge co-ordination was required but Coles managed to do it in four days. This mammoth effort would have been impossible under the previous administration.

Source: Leon Gettler, 'Coles retailer revitalises itself', *Business Review Weekly*, 14 May 2009, pp. 28–9.

Critical thinking questions:
1. What has been the main focus of the restructure at Coles? Has this focus changed over time?
2. How is Woolworths, the other Australian supermarket giant, responding to these changes? How are the smaller chains responding?
3. What are the three steps in organisation design? Do you see these steps reflected in the article above?

CULTURE CHANGE

The topic of organisation culture is becoming very important to companies and the number of culture change interventions has grown accordingly. Organisation culture is also the focus of growing research and OD application and has spawned a number of best-selling management books starting with *Theory S*, *The Art of Japanese Management* and *In Search of Excellence* and, more recently, *Built to Last* and *Corporate Culture and Performance*.[49] Organisation culture is seen as a major strength of such companies as Intel, PepsiCo, Motorola, Hewlett-Packard and Levi Strauss. A growing number of managers appreciate the power of corporate culture in shaping employee beliefs and actions. A well-conceived and well-managed organisation culture, closely linked to an effective business strategy, can mean the difference between success and failure in today's demanding environments.

Concept of organisation culture

Despite the increased attention and research devoted to corporate culture, there is still some confusion about what the term 'culture' really means when applied to organisations.[50] Martin argues that culture can be viewed from an integrated, a differentiated or a fragmented perspective.[51] The integrated view focuses on culture as an organisationally shared phenomenon; it represents a stable and coherent set of beliefs about the organisation and its environment. In contrast to the integrated perspective, the differentiated view argues that culture is not monolithic but that it is best seen in terms of subcultures that exist throughout the organisation. While each subculture is locally stable and shared, there is much that is different across the subcultures. Finally, the fragmented view holds that culture is always changing and is dominated by ambiguity and paradox. Summarising an organisation's culture from a fragmented viewpoint is somewhat meaningless.

Despite these different cultural views, there is some agreement about the elements or features of culture that are typically measured. They include the artefacts, norms, values and basic assumptions that are more or less shared by organisation members. The meanings attached to these elements help members make sense out of everyday life in the organisation. The meanings signal how work is to be done and evaluated and how employees are to relate to each other and to significant others such as customers, suppliers and government agencies.

As shown in Figure 9.3, organisation culture includes four major elements existing at different levels of awareness:[52]

1 *Artefacts*. Artefacts are the highest level of cultural manifestation.[53] They are the visible symbols of the deeper levels of culture, such as norms, values and basic assumptions. Artefacts include members' behaviours, clothing and language; and the organisation's structures, systems, procedures and physical aspects, such as decor, space arrangements and noise levels. At Nordstrom, a high-end retail department store in the United States, the policy and procedure manual is rumoured to be one sentence, 'Do whatever you think is right'. In addition, stores promote from within; pay commissions on sales to link effort and compensation; provide stationery for salespeople to write personal notes to customers; and expect buyers to work as salespeople to better understand the customer's expectations. By themselves, artefacts can provide a great deal of information about the real culture of the organisation because they often represent the deeper assumptions. The difficulty in their use during cultural analysis is interpretation; an outsider (and even some insiders) has no way of knowing what the artefacts represent, if anything.

2 *Norms*. Just below the surface of cultural awareness are norms guiding how members should behave in particular situations. These represent unwritten rules of behaviour. Norms generally are inferred from observing how members behave and interact with each other. At Nordstrom, norms dictate that it's okay

for members to go the extra mile to satisfy customer requests and it's not okay for salespeople to process customers who were working with another salesperson.

3 *Values.* The next-deeper level of awareness includes values about what ought to be in organisations. Values tell members what is important in the organisation and what deserves their attention. Because Nordstrom values customer service, the sales representatives pay strong attention to how well the customer is treated. Obviously, this value is supported by the norms and artefacts.

4 *Basic assumptions.* At the deepest level of cultural awareness are the taken-for-granted assumptions about how organisational problems should be solved. These basic assumptions tell members how to perceive, think and feel about things. They are non-confrontable and non-debatable assumptions about relating to the environment and about human nature, human activity and human relationships. For example, a basic assumption at Nordstrom is the belief in the fundamental dignity of people; it is morally right to treat customers with extraordinary service so that they will become loyal and frequent shoppers.

In summary, culture is defined as the pattern of artefacts, norms, values and basic assumptions about how to solve problems that works well enough to be

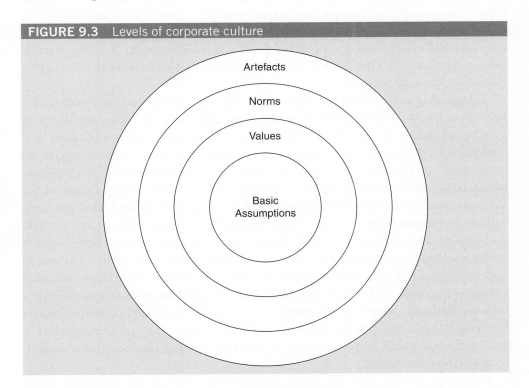

FIGURE 9.3 Levels of corporate culture

Source: Cummings/Worley, *Organization Development and Change* (with InfoTrac® College Edition Printed Access Card), 9e © 2009 South-Western, a part of Cengage Learning, Inc. Reproduced by permission, www.cengage.com/permissions.

taught to others.[54] Culture is a process of social learning; it is the outcome of prior choices about and experiences with strategy and organisation design. It is also a foundation for change that can either facilitate or hinder organisation transformation. For example, the cultures of many companies (for example, IBM, Sony, Disney, Microsoft and Hewlett-Packard) are deeply rooted in the company's history. They were laid down by strong founders and have been reinforced by top executives and corporate success into customary ways of perceiving and acting. These customs provide organisation members with clear and often widely shared answers to such practical issues as 'what really matters around here', 'how do we do things around here' and 'what we do when a problem arises'.

Organisation culture and organisation effectiveness

The interest in organisation culture derives largely from its presumed impact on organisation effectiveness. Considerable speculation and increasing research suggest that organisation culture has both direct and indirect relationships with effectiveness.

Indirectly, culture affects performance through its influence on the organisation's ability to implement change. A particular pattern of values and assumptions that once was a source of strength for a company can become a major liability in successfully implementing a new strategy.[55] Case studies of organisation transformation are full of accounts where the change failed because the culture did not support the new strategy, including AT&T's failed integration of NCR, Daimler-Benz's troubles with Chrysler and Prudential Insurance's difficulties in diversifying into other financial services.

The growing appreciation that culture can play a significant role in implementing new strategy has fuelled interest in the topic, especially in those organisations needing to adapt to turbulent environments. A number of practitioners and academics have focused on helping organisations implement new strategies by bringing culture more in line with the new direction.[56] Indeed, much of the emphasis in the 1970s on formulating business strategy shifted to organisation culture in the 1980s as businesses discovered cultural roadblocks to implementing a strategy. Along with this emerging focus on organisation culture, however, came the sobering reality that cultural change is an extremely difficult and long-term process. Some experts doubt whether large organisations actually can bring about fundamental changes in their cultures; those who have accomplished such feats estimate that the process takes from six to 15 years.[57] For example, Telstra has struggled for years to change from a service-orientated telephone company to a market-orientated communications business. Its industrial conflict is thought to be partly the result of a dramatic shift in culture from a 'public sector' mindset to one that is more conducive to a market-competitive environment.

Indirectly, culture can also affect performance through its influence on an organisation's ability to operate in different countries. Multinationals may face problems doing business in other countries, especially when their corporate culture does not fit with the national culture. For example, Australia Post, in the 1980s had a reputation for being a bureaucratic, stagnant organisation with poor customer service and increasing industrial unrest. The then Federal government, as part of its micro-economic reform agenda, commercialised and corporatised the organisation. Beginning with a commitment from the managing director, cultural change included turning the organisation into a customer service-focused business; building a committed and motivated workforce; increasing productivity and profitability. Australia Post began a culture change intervention that took over 15 years. Its efforts have seen the business transform into a profitable and trusted commercial organisation with improved employee relations.[58]

Multinationals may face problems doing business in other countries, especially when their corporate culture does not fit with the national culture. For example, Starbucks learned this when it had to close 70% of its Australian stores. Australia has an entrenched coffee culture ranging from independents to local brands like Hudsons, which US-styled Starbucks found hard to enter. Customers were accustomed to stronger coffee brews brought in by European immigrants. Starbucks had failed, in part, to comprehend and value the uniqueness of the Australian coffee drinker. This cultural mismatch resulted in Starbucks closing down 61 cafes.[59]

Directly, evidence suggests that, in addition to affecting the implementation of business strategy, corporate culture can affect organisation performance. Comparative studies of Eastern and Western management methods suggest that the relative success of Japanese companies in the 1980s could be partly explained by their strong corporate cultures emphasising employee participation, open communication, security and equality.[60] A study of the productivity of university research departments in the United Kingdom showed a strong relationship between productivity and organisation cultures emphasising teamwork, information flow and employee involvement.[61] Another study of American companies showed a similar pattern of results.[62] Using survey measures of culture and Standard & Poor's financial ratios as indicators of organisational effectiveness, the results showed that companies whose cultures support employee participation in decision making, adaptable work methods, sensible work designs and reasonable and clear goals perform significantly higher (financial ratios about twice as high) than do companies scoring low on those factors. Moreover, the employee participation element of corporate culture showed differences in effectiveness among the companies only after three years; the other measures of culture showed differences in all five years. This suggests that changing some parts of corporate culture, such as participation, should be considered as a long-term investment.

Another study of 207 companies in 22 different industries examined relationships between financial performance and the strength of a culture, the strategic appropriateness of a culture and the adaptiveness of a culture.[63] First, there were no significant performance differences between organisations with widely shared values and those with little agreement around cultural assumptions. Second, there was a significant relationship between culture and performance when the organisation emphasised the 'right' values – values that were critical to success in a particular industry. Finally, performance results over time supported cultures that emphasised anticipating and adapting to environmental change.

These findings suggest that the strength of an organisation's culture can be both an advantage and a disadvantage. Under stable conditions, widely shared and strategically appropriate values can contribute significantly to organisation performance. However, if the environment is changing, strong cultures can be a liability. Unless they also emphasise adaptiveness, the organisation may experience wide swings in performance during transformational change. This line of thought was recently given empirical support.[64] In a study of over 150 large, publicly traded companies from 19 industries, organisations with strong cultures had more reliable performance outcomes – that is, the strength of the culture was related to the predictability of performance. However, when the environment was more uncertain and dynamic, this reliability faded. In stable environments, strong cultures can provide efficiency in decision making and operations. In volatile environments, the strength of the culture can become a weakness if it stunts creativity. Organisations with strong cultures are less able to exploit new environmental opportunities, unless, of course, the culture emphasises innovation and change.

Diagnosing organisation culture

Culture change interventions generally start by diagnosing the organisation's existing culture to assess its fit with current or proposed business strategies. This requires uncovering and understanding the shared assumptions, values, norms and artefacts that characterise an organisation's culture. OD practitioners have developed a number of useful approaches for diagnosing organisation culture. These approaches fall into three different yet complementary perspectives: the behavioural approach, the competing values approach and the deep assumption approach. Each diagnostic perspective focuses on particular aspects of organisation culture and together the approaches can provide a comprehensive assessment of these complex phenomena.

The behavioural approach

This method of diagnosis emphasises the surface level of organisation culture – the pattern of behaviours that produce business results.[65] It is among the more practical approaches to culture diagnosis because it assesses key work behaviours that can be observed.[66] The behavioural approach provides specific descriptions about how tasks are performed and how relationships are managed in an organisation. For example, Table 9.2 summarises the organisation culture of an international banking division as perceived by its managers. In this classic case, the data were obtained from a series of individual and group interviews asking managers to describe 'the way the game is played', as if they were coaching a new organisation member. Managers were

TABLE 9.2 Summary of corporate culture at an international banking division

Relationships	Culture summary
Companywide	Preserve your autonomy
	Allow area managers to run the business as long as they keep the profit budget
Boss–subordinate	Avoid confrontations
	Smooth over disagreements
	Support the boss
Peer	Guard information; it is power
	Be a gentleman or lady
Interdepartment	Protect your department's bottom line
	Form alliances around specific issues
	Guard your turf

Tasks	Culture summary
Innovating	Consider it risky
	Be a quick second
Decision making	Handle each deal on its own merits
	Gain consensus
	Require many sign-offs
	Involve the right people
	Seize the opportunity
Communicating	Withhold information to control adversaries
	Avoid confrontation
	Be a gentleman or lady
Organising	Centralise power
	Be autocratic
Monitoring	Meet short-term profit goals
Appraising and rewarding	Reward the faithful
	Choose the best bankers as managers
	Seek safe jobs

Source: Reprinted from *Organizational Dynamics*, Summer/1981 © 1981, Vol. 10, *Matching Corporate Culture and Business Strategy* by Howard Schwartz and Stanley M. Davis, with permission from Elsevier.

asked to give their impressions in regard to four key relationships (companywide, boss–subordinate, peer and interdepartmental) and in terms of six managerial tasks (innovating, decision making, communicating, organising, monitoring and appraising/rewarding). These perceptions revealed a number of implicit norms for how tasks are performed and relationships managed at the division.

Cultural diagnosis derived from a behavioural approach also can be used to assess the cultural risk of trying to implement organisational changes needed to support a new strategy. Significant cultural risks result when changes that are highly important to implementing a new strategy are incompatible with the existing patterns of behaviour. Knowledge of such risks can help managers determine whether implementation plans should be changed to manage around the existing culture, whether the culture should be changed, or whether the strategy itself should be modified or abandoned.

The competing values approach

This perspective assesses an organisation's culture in terms of how it resolves a set of value dilemmas.[67] The approach suggests that an organisation's culture can be understood in terms of two important 'value pairs'; each pair consists of contradictory values placed at opposite ends of a continuum, as shown earlier in Figure 9.3. The two value pairs are (1) internal focus and integration versus external focus and differentiation and (2) flexibility and discretion versus stability and control. Organisations continually struggle to satisfy the conflicting demands placed on them by these competing values. For example, when faced with the competing values of internal versus external focus, organisations must choose between attending to the integration problems of internal operations and the competitive issues in the external environment. Too much emphasis on the environment can result in neglect of internal efficiencies. Conversely, too much attention to the internal aspects of organisations can result in missing important changes in the competitive environment.

The competing values approach commonly collects diagnostic data about the competing values with a survey designed specifically for that purpose.[68] It provides measures of where an organisation's existing values fall along each of the dimensions. When taken together, these data identify an organisation's culture as falling into one of the four quadrants shown in Figure 9.3: clan culture, adhocracy culture,[69] hierarchical culture and market culture. For example, if an organisation's values are focused on internal integration issues and emphasise innovation and flexibility, it manifests a clan culture. On the other hand, a market culture characterises values that are externally focused and emphasises stability and control.

The deep assumptions approach

This final diagnostic approach emphasises the deepest levels of organisation culture – the generally unexamined, but tacit and shared assumptions that guide member behaviour and that often have a powerful impact on organisation effectiveness. Diagnosing culture from this perspective typically begins with the most tangible level of awareness and then works down to the deep assumptions.

Diagnosing organisation culture at the deep assumptions level poses at least three difficult problems for collecting pertinent information.[70] First, culture reflects the more or less shared assumptions about what is important, how things are done and how people should behave in organisations. People generally take cultural assumptions for granted and rarely speak of them directly. Rather, the company's culture is implied in concrete behavioural examples, such as daily routines, stories, rituals and language. This means that considerable time and effort must be spent observing, sifting through and asking people about these cultural outcroppings to understand their deeper significance for organisation members. Second, some values and beliefs that people espouse have little to do with the ones they really hold and follow. People are reluctant to admit this discrepancy, yet somehow the real assumptions underlying idealised portrayals of culture must be discovered. Third, large, diverse organisations are likely to have several subcultures, including countercultures going against the grain of the wider organisation culture. Assumptions may not be shared widely and may differ across groups in the organisation. This means that focusing on limited parts of the organisation or on a few select individuals may provide a distorted view of the organisation's culture and subcultures. All relevant groups in the organisation must be identified and their cultural assumptions sampled. Only then can practitioners judge the extent to which assumptions are shared widely.

OD practitioners emphasising the deep assumptions approach have developed a number of useful techniques for assessing organisation culture.[71] One method involves an iterative interviewing process involving both outsiders and insiders.[72] Outsiders help members uncover cultural elements through joint exploration. The outsider enters the organisation and experiences surprises and puzzles that are different from what was expected. The outsider shares these observations with insiders and the two parties jointly explore their meaning. This process involves several iterations of experiencing surprises, checking for meaning and formulating hypotheses about the culture. It results in a formal written description of the assumptions underlying an organisational culture.

A second method for identifying the organisation's basic assumptions brings together a group of people for a culture workshop – for example, a senior management team or a cross-section of managers, old and new members, labour leaders and staff.[73] The group first brainstorms a large number of the organisation's artefacts, such as behaviours, symbols, language and physical space arrangements. From this list, the values and norms that would produce such artefacts are deduced. In addition, the values espoused in formal planning documents are listed. Finally, the group attempts to identify the assumptions that would explain the constellation of values, norms and artefacts. Because basic assumptions generally are taken for granted, they are difficult to articulate. A great deal of process consultation skill is required to help organisation members see the underlying assumptions.

Application stages

There is considerable debate over whether changing something as deep-seated as organisation culture is possible.[74] Those advocating culture change generally focus on the more surface elements of culture, such as norms and artefacts. These elements are more changeable than the deeper elements of values and basic assumptions. They offer change practitioners a more manageable set of action levers for changing organisational behaviours. Some would argue, however, that unless the deeper values and assumptions are changed, organisations have not really changed their culture.

Those arguing that implementing culture change is extremely difficult, if not impossible, typically focus on the deeper elements of culture (values and basic assumptions). Because these deeper elements represent assumptions about organisational life, members do not question them and have a difficult time envisioning anything else. Moreover, members may not want to change their cultural assumptions. The culture provides a strong defence against external uncertainties and threats.[75] It represents past solutions to difficult problems. Members also may have vested interests in maintaining the culture. They may have developed personal stakes, pride and power in the culture and may strongly resist attempts to change it. Finally, cultures that provide companies with a competitive advantage may be difficult to imitate, thus making it hard for less successful organisations to change their cultures to approximate the more successful ones.[76]

Given the problems with cultural change, most practitioners in this area suggest that changes in corporate culture should be considered only after other, less difficult and less costly solutions have been applied or ruled out.[77] Attempts to overcome cultural risks when strategic changes are incompatible with the existing culture might include ways to manage around that culture. Consider, for example, a single-product organisation with a functional focus and a history of centralised control that is considering an ambitious product-diversification strategy. The company might manage around its existing culture by using business teams to co-ordinate functional specialists around each new product. Another alternative to changing culture is to modify strategy to bring it more in line with culture. The single-product organisation just mentioned might decide to undertake a less ambitious strategy of product diversification.

Despite problems in changing corporate culture, large-scale cultural change may be necessary in certain situations: if the organisation's culture does not fit a changing environment; if the industry is extremely competitive and changes rapidly; if the company is mediocre or worse; if the business is about to become a very large company; or if the company is smaller and growing rapidly.[78] Organisations facing these conditions need to change their cultures to adapt to the situation or to operate at higher levels of effectiveness. They may have to supplement attempts at cultural change with other approaches, such as managing around the existing culture and modifying strategy.

Although knowledge about changing corporate culture is in a formative stage, the following practical advice can serve as guidelines for cultural change:[79]

1 *Formulate a clear strategic vision.* Effective cultural change should start from a clear vision of the organisation's new strategy and of the shared values and behaviours needed to make it work.[80] This vision provides the purpose and direction for cultural change. It serves as a yardstick for defining the organisation's existing culture and for deciding whether proposed changes are consistent with the core values of the organisation. A useful approach to providing clear strategic vision is the development of a statement of corporate purpose, listing in straightforward terms the basic values that the organisation believes in.

2 *Display top-management commitment.* Cultural change must be managed from the top of the organisation. Senior executives and administrators have to be strongly committed to the new values and need to create constant pressures for change. They must have the staying power to see the changes through.[81] For example, Bob Ansett, the former CEO of Budget Rent-a-Car who was famed for his practice of 'management by walking around', now has a successful career on the management lecture circuit.

3 *Model culture change at the highest levels.* Senior executives must communicate the new culture through their own actions. Their behaviours need to symbolise the kinds of values and behaviours being sought. In the few publicised cases of successful culture change, corporate leaders have shown an almost missionary zeal for the new values; their actions have symbolised the values forcefully.[82] For example, Toyota Australia's implementation of '360-degree performance appraisal' began at the top, giving even the most junior workers a chance to assess the performances of their bosses.

4 *Modify the organisation to support organisational change.* Cultural change generally requires supporting modifications in organisation structure, human resources systems, information and control systems and management styles. These organisational features can help to orient people's behaviours to the new culture.[83] They can make people aware of the behaviours required to get things done in the new culture and can encourage performance of those behaviours. For example, when Ian McLeod became managing director of Coles in 2008, he had a clear brief: refresh the stores, rather than focus on back office operations. He realised that what the company needed was cultural change: better customer service, better supply chains and less bureaucracy (see Application 9.3).

5 *Select and socialise newcomers and terminate deviants.* One of the most effective methods for changing corporate culture is to change organisational membership. People can be selected and terminated in terms of their fit with the new culture. This is especially important in key leadership positions, where people's actions can significantly promote or hinder new values and behaviours. For example, in trying

to change from a car parts and battery company to a leader in electronics, Gould replaced about two-thirds of its senior executives with people more in tune with the new strategy and culture. Jan Carlson of Scandinavian Airlines (SAS) replaced 13 out of 15 top executives in his turnaround of the airline. Another approach is to socialise newly hired people into the new culture. People are most open to organisational influences during the entry stage, when they can be effectively indoctrinated into the culture. For example, companies with strong cultures like Amcor, CSR and Westpac attach great importance to socialising new members into the company's values.

6 *Develop ethical and legal sensitivity.* Cultural change can raise significant tensions between organisation and individual interests, resulting in ethical and legal problems for practitioners. This is particularly pertinent when organisations are trying to implement cultural values promoting employee integrity, control, equitable treatment and job security – values often included in cultural change efforts. Statements about such values provide employees with certain expectations about their rights and about how they will be treated in the organisation. The organisation needs to follow through with behaviours and procedures supporting and protecting these implied rights, or risk violating ethical principles and, in some cases, legal employment contracts. Recommendations for reducing the chances of such ethical and legal problems include setting realistic values for culture change and not promising what the organisation cannot deliver; encouraging input from throughout the organisation in setting cultural values; providing mechanisms for member dissent and diversity, such as internal review procedures; and educating managers about the legal and ethical pitfalls inherent in cultural change and helping them develop guidelines for resolving such issues.

Application 9.4 presents an example of culture change at McDonald's. It illustrates how important cultural principles are used to shape behaviour during a period of organisational growth and how culture can be used to facilitate changes.

9.4

APPLICATION

Culture change at McDonald's

The surprise hit film, *Supersize Me* by Morgan Spurlock, had fast-food chain McDonald's against the ropes. The film had criticised the salt and sugar laden food that McDonald's traditionally served and derided the junk-food culture that went with it.

The chain had hit a period of stagnation during the 1990s which saw the profitability of the restaurant drop in Australia. The introduction of the goods and services tax in 2000 had cut into profits and the 1950s look of McDonald's was starting to look tired in a time of lattes and wraps. The company had to go back to the fundamentals of customer service and work out what and how the consumer wanted to eat.

They found that customers were more interested in health and, consequently, eating habits were changing. This resulted in McDonald's introducing nutritional labelling on products and a

>>

healthier choice menu. Alterations were also made to the traditional menu by reducing the amount of sugar in the buns, reducing salt and modifying the type of oil used in cooking.

McDonald's spent $200 million on this investment program Australia wide. The investment would go into opening 40 restaurants and refurbishing established restaurants so they can offer made-to-order menus and stay open 24 hours. The company wants to offer consumers a range of healthier choices and the opportunity to eat when they want to without wondering about closing times.

Meanwhile, the company also developed a plan for carrying out significant restructures throughout franchise and company owned restaurants. Kitchens were ripped out and replaced, supplier relations were changed and the original processes were revised. Within 12 months, 130 restaurants had been upgraded and were operating profitably again.

In 2008, Australians ate $3 billion worth of McDonald's food, beating projections a year earlier than forecasted. The Australian arm had won significant status on the McDonald's international stage as only one of two countries to try new menus. Whatever is served world-wide, Australians have usually eaten it first.

McDonald's has come a long way towards addressing changing food values.

Source: Jeanne-Vida Douglas/Business Review Weekly/Fairfax.

Critical thinking questions:
1. How did McDonald's transform itself?
2. In your opinion, should McDonald's consider further transformation? Explain your answer.
3. What changes in corporate culture were likely to be involved in this transformation? Would those changes have been difficult to introduce given McDonald's long, historical association with a fast-food, hamburger-based image?

Summary

In this chapter, we presented interventions for helping organisations transform themselves. These changes can occur at any level in the organisation, but their ultimate intent is to change the total system. They typically happen in response to or in anticipation of significant environmental, technological or internal changes. These changes may involve alterations in the organisation's strategy, which, in turn, may lead to changing its design and culture.

Integrated strategic change is a comprehensive intervention for responding to complex and uncertain environmental pressures. It gives equal weight to the strategic and organisational factors affecting organisation performance and effectiveness. In addition, these factors are highly integrated during the process of assessing the current strategy and organisation design, selecting the desired strategic orientation, developing a strategic change plan and implementing it.

Organisation design involves the organisation's structure, work design, human resources practices and management and information systems. It aligns these components with the organisation's strategy and with each other so they mutually direct behaviour to execute the strategy. This results in organisation designs that vary along a continuum from mechanistic to organic, depending on the

requirements of the organisation's strategy. Organisation design typically starts with assessing the organisation to clarify the design focus. Then the design components are configured to support the organisation's strategy. Finally, implementation involves putting the new structures, practices and systems into place using many of the methods for leading and managing change.

Organisation culture includes the pattern of basic assumptions, values, norms and artefacts shared by organisation members. It influences how members perceive, think and behave at work. Culture affects whether organisations can implement new strategies and whether they can operate at high levels of excellence. Culture change interventions start with diagnosing the organisation's existing culture. This can include assessing the cultural risks of making organisational changes needed to implement strategy. Changing corporate culture can be extremely difficult and requires clear strategic vision, top-management commitment, symbolic leadership, supporting organisational changes, selection and socialisation of newcomers and termination of deviants and sensitivity to legal and ethical issues.

Activities

REVIEW QUESTIONS

1 Define 'organisation transformation'. How is it different from organisation development?

2 What are the environmental and internal disruptions that can affect an organisation? Give current examples of each and explain why you selected them as examples.

3 What are the key features of integrated strategic change (ISC) and how do they relate to each other?

4 Explain what is meant by 'organisation design'. What difficulties would you expect if you intended to change an organisation in this manner?

5 Explain the difference between 'mechanistic' and 'organic' design and give examples.

6 Define organisational culture. What are the major elements at different levels of awareness?

7 What is the relationship between 'organisational culture' and 'organisation effectiveness'?

DISCUSSION AND ESSAY QUESTIONS

1 'OT is revolutionary whereas OD is evolutionary.' Discuss.

2 'It is impossible to dramatically change an organisation's culture.' Do you agree or disagree? Explain your answer.

3 Is there one best way to diagnose organisational culture? Argue both sides of the question and provide an informed opinion.

4 It is said that 'diagnosing organisation culture at the deep assumptions level poses at least

three difficult problems for collecting pertinent information'. What are the three difficulties referred to? How might they be addressed?

5 'Cultural change can raise significant tensions between organisation and individual interests, resulting in ethical and legal problems for practitioners.' Discuss.

SEARCH ME! EXCERCISES

Explore **Search me! management** for relevant articles on organisation transformation and change. Search me! is an online library of world-class journals, ebooks and newspapers, including *The Australian* and *The New York Times*, and is updated daily. Log in to Search me! through **www.cengage.com/sso** using the access card in the front of this book.

Keywords

Try searching for the following terms:
> Culture change
> Integrated strategic change
> Organisation culture

> Organisation design
> Transformational change

>> Search tip:

Search me! management contains information from both local and international sources. To get the greatest number of search results, try using both Australian and American spellings in your searches, e.g. 'globalisation' and 'globalization'; 'organisation' and 'organization'.

Notes

1 M. Eyre, *Personal or Organisational Development – Which Matters More?* June 2010, http://ezinearticles.com/?Personal-Or-Organisational-Development—Which-Matters-More?&id=4444368.

2 E. Flamholtz and Y. Randle, *Leading Strategic Change* (Cambridge University Press, 2008), http://assets.cambridge.org/97805218/49470/frontmatter/9780521849470_frontmatter.pdf.

3 L. Bryan and C. Joyce, 'The 21st century organization', *The McKinsey Quarterly* (2005): 24–33.

4 F. Suares and R. Oliva, 'Environmental change and organisational transformation', *Industrial and Corporate Change*, 14 (2005): 1017–41; A. Grove, 'Churning things up', *Fortune* (11 August 2003): 115–18; J. Sorensen, 'The strength of corporate culture and the reliability of firm performance', *Administrative Science Quarterly*, 47 (2002): 70–91; G. Young, 'Managing organizational transformations: lessons from the Veterans Health Administration', *California Management Review*, 43 (2000): 66–82.

5 M. Tushman, W. Newman and E. Romanelli, 'Managing the unsteady pace of organizational evolution', *California Management Review* (Fall 1986): 29–44.

6 ibid.

7 A. Meyer, A. Tsui and C. Hinings, 'Guest co-editors introduction: configurational approaches to organizational analysis', *Academy of Management Journal*, 36 (1993): 1175–95.

8 D. Miller and P. Friesen, *Organizations: A Quantum View* (Englewood Cliffs, N.J.: Prentice-Hall, 1984).

9 B. Blumenthal and P. Haspeslagh, 'Toward a definition of corporate transformation', *Sloan Management Review*, 35 (1994): 101–7.

10 Tushman, Newman and Romanelli, 'Managing the Unsteady Pace', op. cit.; L. Greiner, 'Evolution and revolution as organizations grow', *Harvard Business Review* (July–August 1972): 37–46.

11 A. Husain and A. Khan, *Clarifying Spiritual Values Among Organizational Development Personnel Department of Educational Psychology and Counseling*, Faculty of Education, University of Malaya, Kuala Lumpur, Malaysia, 2009, www.academicjournals.org/ajbm/PDF/pdf2010/Feb/Husain%20and%20Khan.pdf.

12 M. Tushman and E. Romanelli, 'Organizational evolution: a metamorphosis model of convergence and reorientation', in *Research in Organisational Behavior*, vol. 7, eds L. Cummings and B. Staw (Greenwich, Conn.: JAI Press, 1985): 171–222.

13 J. Bartunek and M. Louis, 'Organization development and organisational transformation', in *Research in Organisational Change and Development*, vol. 2, eds W. Pasmore and R. Woodman (Greenwich, Conn.: JAI Press, 1988): 97–134.

14 R. Golembiewski, K. Billingsley and S. Yeager, 'Measuring change and persistence in human affairs: types of changes generated by OD designs', *Journal of Applied Behavioral Science*, 12 (1975): 133–57.

15 J. Sackmann, 'The role of metaphors in organization transformation', *Human Relations*, 42 (1989): 463–85.

16 R. Eisenbach, K. Watson and R. Pillai, 'Transformational leadership in the context of organization change', *Journal of Organizational Change Management*, 12 (1999): 80–89; R. Waldersee, 'Becoming a learning organization: the transformation of the workplace', *Journal of Management Development*, 16 (1997): 262–74; A. Pettigrew, 'Context and action in the transformation of the firm', *Journal of Management Studies*, 24 (1987): 649–70; Tushman and Romanelli, 'Organisational Evolution', op. cit.

17 M. Tushman and B. Virany, 'Changing characteristics of executive teams in an emerging industry', *Journal of Business Venturing*, 2 (1986): 37–49; L. Greiner and A. Bhambri, 'New CEO intervention and dynamics of deliberate strategic change', *Strategic Management Journal*, 10 (Summer 1989): 67–86.

18 N. Tichy and M. Devanna, *The Transformational Leader* (New York: John Wiley & Sons, 1986); M. DuPree, *Leadership Jass* (New York: Doubleday, 1992); Blumenthal and Haspeslagh, 'Corporate transformation', op. cit.; N. Tichy and S. Sherman, *Control Your Destiny or Someone Else Will* (New York: Doubleday, 1993).

19 P. Nutt and R. Backoff, 'Facilitating transformational change', *Journal of Applied Behavioral Science*, 33 (1997): 490–508; M. Tushman, W. Newman and D. Nadler, 'Executive leadership and organizational evolution: managing incremental and discontinuous change', in *Corporate Transformation: Revitalising Organizations for a Competitive World*, eds R. Kilmann and T. Covin (San Francisco: Jossey-Bass, 1988): 102–30; W. Bennis and B. Nanus, *Leaders: The Strategies for Taking Charge* (New York: Harper & Row, 1985); Pettigrew, 'Context and action', op. cit.

20 J. Kouses and B. Posner, *The Leadership Challenge*, 3rd edn (San Francisco: Jossey-Bass, 2002); T. Simons, 'Behavioral integrity as a critical ingredient for transformational leadership', *Journal of Organizational Change Management*, 12 (1999): 89–105.

21 T. Cummings and S. Mohrman, 'Self-designing organizations: towards implementing quality-of-work-life innovations', in *Research in Organizational Change and Development*, vol. 1, eds R. Woodman and W. Pasmore (Greenwich, Conn.: JAI Press, 1987): 275–310.

22 L. Greiner and A. Bhambri, 'New CEO intervention and the dynamics of strategic change', op. cit.

23 C. Worley, D. Hitchin and W. Ross, *Integrated Strategic Change: How Organization Development Builds Competitive Advantage* (Reading, MA: Addison-Wesley, 1996).

24 M. Jelinek and J. Litterer, 'Why OD must become strategic', *Organizational Change and Development*, vol. 2, eds W. Pasmore and R. Woodman (Greenwich, Conn.: JAI Press, 1988): 135–62; A. Bhambri and L. Pate, 'Introduction – The strategic change agenda: stimuli, processes and outcomes', *Journal of Organization Change Management*, 4 (1991): 4–6; D. Nadler, M. Gerstein, R. Shaw and Associates, eds, *Organizational Architecture* (San Francisco: Jossey-Bass, 1992); C. Worley, D. Hitchin and W. Ross, *Integrated Strategic Change: How Organization Development Builds Competitive Advantage* (Reading, MA: Addison-Wesley, 1996).

25 C. Worley, D. Hitchin, R. Patchett, R. Barnett and J. Moss, 'Unburn the bridge, get to bedrock and put legs on the dream: looking at strategy implementation with fresh eyes' (paper presented to the Western Academy of Management, Redondo Beach, Calif., March 1999).

26 H. Mintsberg, *The Rise and Fall of Strategic Planning* (New York: Free Press, 1994).

27 Worley, Hitchin and Ross, *Integrated Strategic Change*, op. cit.

28 P. Senge, *The Fifth Discipline* (New York: Doubleday, 1990); E. Lawler, *The Ultimate Advantage* (San Francisco: Jossey-Bass, 1992); Worley, Hitchin and Ross, *Integrated Strategic Change*, op. cit.

29 L. Greiner and V. Schein, *Power and Organization Development* (Reading, MA: Addison-Wesley, 1988).

30 L. B. Ncube and M. H. Wasburn, *Strategic Analysis: Approaching Continuous Improvement Proactively*, *Review of Business*, 2008, www.entrepreneur.com/tradejournals/article/192353566_3.html.

31 M. Porter, *Competitive Strategy* (New York: Free Press, 1980).

32 Grant, *Contemporary Strategy Analysis*, op. cit.

33 C. Hofer and D. Schendel, *Strategy Formulation: Analytic Concepts* (St.Paul, Minn.: West Publishing, 1978).

34 M. Porter, *Competitive Advantage* (New York: Free Press, 1985).

35 R. Miles and C. Snow, *Organization Strategy, Structure and Process* (New York: McGraw-Hill, 1978); M. Tushman and E. Romanelli, 'Organizational evolution: a metamorphosis model of convergence and reorientation', in *Research in Organizational Behavior*, vol. 7, eds L. Cummings and B. Staw (Greenwich, Conn.: JAI Press, 1985).

36 J. Naisbitt and P. Aburdene, *Reinventing the Corporation* (New York: Warner Books, 1985); A. Toffler, *The Third Wave* (New York: McGraw-Hill, 1980); A. Toffler, *The Adaptive Corporation* (New York: McGraw-Hill, 1984); M. Weisbord, *Productive Workplaces* (San Francisco: Jossey-Bass, 1987).

37 E. Lawler, *The Ultimate Advantage*, op. cit.; M. Tushman, W. Newman and E. Romanelli, 'Convergence and upheaval: managing the unsteady pace of organizational evolution', *California Management Review*, 29 (1987): 1–16; Nadler et al., *Organizational Architecture*, op. cit.; R. Bussell and B. Gale, *The PIMS Principles* (New York: Free Press, 1987).

38 L. Hrebiniak and W. Joyce, *Implementing Strategy* (New York: Macmillan, 1984); J. Galbraith and R. Kasanjian, *Strategy Implementation: Structure, Systems and Process*, 2nd edn (St. Paul, Minn.: West Publishing, 1986).

39 K. Long, *Integrated Strategic Change and What it Can Do For You*, June 2010, http://ezinearticles.com/?Integrated-Strategic-Change-and-What-it-Can-Do-For-You&id=4473574.

40 J. Galbraith, *Organization Design* (Reading, MA: Addison Wesley, 1977); D. Nadler, M. Tushman and M. Nadler, *Competing by Design: The Power of Organizational*

Architecture (New York: Oxford University Press, 1997);
R. Burton, B. Eriksen, D. Håkonsson and C. Snow,
Organization Design: The Evolving State-of-the-Art (New
York: Springer, 2006); A. Kates and J. Galbraith,
*Designing Your Organization: Using The STAR Model To
Solve 5 Critical Design Challenges* (San Francisco: Jossey-
Bass, 2007); J. Galbraith, 'Organization design', in
Handbook of Organization Development, ed. T. Cummings
(Thousand Oaks, CA: Sage Publications, 2008):
325–52.

41 P. Lawrence and J. Lorsch, *Organization and
Environment: Managing Differentiation and Integration*
(Cambridge, MA: Harvard Business School Press,
Revised Edition, 1986); D. Miller, 'Advantage by design:
competing with opportunity-based structures', *Business
Horizons*, 48 (2005): 393–407; J. Roberts, *The Modern
Firm: Organizational Design for Performance and Growth*
(New York: Oxford University Press, 2007); R. Daft,
Organization Theory and Design (Mason, OH: South-
Western, 2006).

42 L. Alvares, L. Silva and M. Soto, *Spatial Dimension of
University Students' Daily Commuting: Greater Valparaiso
Case Study*, 2009, www.scielo.cl/scielo.php?pid=S0718-
83582009000100002&script=sci_arttext&tlng=en.

43 H. Ahmadi and P. Salami, *Application of Information
Systems in Electronic Insurance*, Department of
Agricultural Machinery Engineering, Faculty of
Biosystems Engineering, University of Tehran,
Karaj, Iran, 2010, www.maxwellsci.com/print/
rjit/v2-1-6.pdf.

44 T. Burns and G. Stalker, *The Management of Innovation*
(London: Social Science Paperbacks, 1961).

45 S. Mohrman, J. Galbraith and E. Lawler, eds, *Tomorrow's
Organization: Crafting Winning Capabilities in a Dynamic
World* (San Francisco: Jossey-Bass, 1998); J. Galbraith,
D. Downey and A. Kates, *Designing Dynamic
Organizations: A Handson Guide for Leaders at All Levels*
(New York: AMACOM, 2001); E. Beinhocker, 'The
adaptable corporation', *The McKinsey Quarterly*, 2
(2006): 76–87.

46 M. Moon, 'Bottom-up instigated organization change
through constructionist conversation', *Journal of
Knowledge Management Practice*, 9:4 (December 2008),
www.tlainc.com/articl169.htm.

47 S. Mohrman and T. Cummings, *Self-designing
Organizations: Learning how to Create High Performance*
(Reading, MA: Addison Wesley, 1989); N. Stanford,
Organization Design: The Collaborative Approach
(Burlington, MA: Elsevier Butterworth-Heinemann,
2005).

48 J. Galbraith et al., *Designing Dynamic Organizations*, op.
cit.; Kates and Galbraith, *Designing Your Organization*,
op. cit.; Stanford, *Organization Design*, op. cit.

49 W. Ouchi, *Theory S: How American Business Can Meet
the Japanese Challenge* (Reading, MA: Addison-Wesley,
1979); R. Pascale and A. Athos, *The Art of Japanese
Management* (New York: Simon & Schuster, 1981);
T. Deal and A. Kennedy, *Corporate Cultures* (Reading,
MA: Addison-Wesley, 1982); T. Peters and R. Waterman,
In Search of Excellence (New York: Harper & Row, 1982);
T. Peters and N. Austin, *A Passion for Excellence* (New
York: Random House, 1985); J. Pfeffer, *Competitive
Advantage Through People* (Cambridge, MA: Harvard
Business School, 1994); J. Collins and J. Porras, *Built to*

Last (New York: Harper Business, 1994); J. Kotter and
J. Heskett, *Corporate Culture and Performance* (New York:
Free Press, 1992).

50 J. Martin, *Organization Culture* (Newbury Park, Calif.:
Sage Publications, 2002); D. Meyerson and J. Martin,
'Cultural change: an integration of three different views',
Journal of Management Studies, 24 (1987): 623–47;
D. Denison and G. Spreitser, 'Organizational culture and
organizational development: a competing values
approach', in *Research in Organizational Change and
Development*, vol. 5, eds R. Woodman and W. Pasmore
(Greenwich, Conn.: JAI Press, 1991): 1–22; E. Schein,
Organizational Culture and Leadership, 2nd edn (San
Francisco: Jossey-Bass, 1992).

51 Martin, *Organization Culture*, op. cit.

52 Schein, *Organizational Culture*, op. cit.; R. Kilmann,
M. Saxton and R. Serpa, eds, *Gaining Control of the
Corporate Culture* (San Francisco: Jossey-Bass, 1985).

53 R. W. Clement, *Culture, Leadership, and Power: The Keys
to Organizational Change*, November 2007,
www.rssfeedconverter.com/converterarticles/Culture-
leadership-and-power-the-keys-to-organizational-
change—includes-bibliography.php.

54 Schein, *Organizational Culture*, op. cit.

55 E. Abrahamson and C. J. Fombrun, 'Macrocultures:
determinants and consequences', *Academy of
Management Journal*, 19 (1994): 728–55; B. Dumaine,
'Creating a new company culture', *Fortune* (15 January
1990): 127–31.

56 B. Uttal, 'The corporate culture vultures', *Fortune*
(17 October 1983): 66–72; C.-M. Lau, L. Kilbourne and
R. Woodman, 'A shared schema approach to
understanding organizational culture change', in
Research on Organizational Change and Development,
vol. 14, eds W. Pasmore and R. Woodman (Greenwich,
Conn.: JAI Press, 2003): 225–56.

57 Uttal, 'The corporate culture vultures', op. cit.

58 R. Mules, 'Delivering change at Australia Post',
Businessdate, 13:1, pp 5–7.

59 D. Miletic, T. Arup and D. Emerson, 'Hundreds of jobs
lost as Starbucks shuts 61 shops', *The Age* (30 July
2008).

60 Ouchi, *Theory S*, op. cit.; Pascale and Athos, *Japanese
Management*, op. cit.

61 J. Ryan and J. Hurley, 'An empirical examination of the
relationship between scientists' work environment and
research performance', *R&D Management*, 37 (2007):
345–54.

62 D. Denison, 'The climate, culture and effectiveness of
work organisations: a study of organizational behavior
and financial performance', Ph.D. diss. (University of
Michigan, 1982).

63 Kotter and Heskett, *Corporate Culture*, op. cit.

64 J. Sorensen, 'The strength of corporate culture and the
reliability of firm performance', *Administrative Science
Quarterly*, 47 (2002): 70–91.

65 D. Hanna, *Designing Organizations for High Performance*
(Reading, MA: Addison-Wesley, 1988).

66 H. Schwarts and S. Davis, 'Matching corporate culture
and business strategy', *Organizational Dynamics*
(Summer 1981): 30–48; S. Davis, *Managing Corporate
Culture* (Cambridge, MA: Ballinger, 1984).

67 Denison and Spreitser, 'Organizational culture', op. cit.;
R. E. Quinn, *Beyond Rational Management: Mastering the*

Paradoxes and Competing Demands of High Performance
(San Francisco: Jossey-Bass, 1988); K. Cameron and
R. Quinn, *Diagnosing and Changing Organizational Culture*
(San Francisco: Jossey-Bass, 2006).

68 R. Quinn and G. Spreitser, 'The psychometrics of the
competing values culture instrument and an analysis of
the impact of organizational culture on quality of life', in
Research in Organizational Change and Development, vol.
5, eds R. Woodman and W. Pasmore (Greenwich, Conn.:
JAI Press, 1991): 115–42.

69 Canis W. M. Cheng and Anita M. M. Liu, 'The
relationship of organizational culture and the
implementation of total quality management in
construction firms', *Surveying and Built Environment*,
18:1 (June 2007): 7–16, ISSN 1816-9554,
www.hkis.org.hk/hkis/html/upload/Journal/
jrnl43_0.pdf.

70 Schein, *Organizational Culture*, op. cit.

71 R. Sammuto and J. Krakower, 'Quantitative and
qualitative studies of organizational culture', in *Research
in Organizational Change and Development*, vol. 5,
eds R. Woodman and W. Pasmore (Greenwich, Conn.:
JAI Press, 1991): 83–114; Quinn and Spreitser,
'Psychometrics', op. cit.

72 Schein, *Organizational Culture*, op. cit.

73 E. Schein, *The Corporate Culture Survival Guide* (San
Francisco: Jossey-Bass, 1999).

74 P. Frost, L. Moore, M. Louis, C. Lundberg and J. Martin,
eds, *Organizational Culture* (Beverly Hills, Calif.: Sage,
1985): 95–196; Martin, *Organizational Culture*, op. cit.

75 Meyerson and Martin, 'Cultural change', op. cit.

76 J. Barney, 'Organizational culture: can it be a source
of sustained competitive advantage?' *Academy of
Management Review*, 11 (1986): 656–65.

77 Uttal, 'Corporate culture vultures', op. cit.

78 ibid.: 70.

79 Schein, *Corporate Culture Survival Guide*, op. cit.;
Schwarts and Davis, 'Matching corporate culture',
op. cit.; Uttal, 'Corporate culture vultures', op. cit.;
Davis, *Managing Corporate Culture*, op. cit.; Kilmann,
Saxton and Serpa, *Gaining Control*, op. cit.; Frost et al.,
Organizational Culture, op. cit.; V. Sathe, 'Implications of
corporate culture: a manager's guide to action',
Organizational Dynamics (Autumn 1983): 5–23; B. Drake
and E. Drake, 'Ethical and legal aspects of managing
corporate cultures', *California Management Review*
(Winter 1988): 107–23; K. Cameron, 'A process for
changing organization culture', in *Handbook of
Organization Development*, ed. T. Cummings (Thousand
Oaks, CA: Sage Publications, 2008): 429–45.

80 C. Worley, D. Hitchin and W. Ross, *Integrated Strategic
Change* (Reading, MA: Addison-Wesley, 1996);
R. Beckhard and W. Pritchard, *Changing the Essence*
(San Francisco: Jossey-Bass, 1992).

81 Dumaine, 'Creating a new company culture', op. cit.;
C. O'Reilly, 'Corporations, culture and commitment:
motivation and social control in organizations',
California Management Review, 31 (Summer 1989): 9–25;
Pettigrew, 'Context and action', op. cit.

82 Dumaine, 'Creating a new company culture', op. cit.

83 Tichy and Sherman, *Control Your Destiny*, op. cit.

CHAPTER 10

Change in a chaotic and unpredictable environment

This chapter describes the practice of change management in a chaotic and unpredictable environment which is exhibited in international settings. It presents the contingencies and practice issues associated with change in organisations outside countries of origin (home countries), in worldwide organisations and in global social change organisations. The applicability and effectiveness of change in countries and cultures in countries of destination (host countries) are the subject of intense debate, however. Because many change theories were developed predominantly by Western practitioners, this has heavily influenced the perceptions and practices of change management in places throughout the world. Regardless of good intentions, many errors can be made by implementing strategies that are not congruent with existing cultures and norms. How will South-East Asian countries change when their next generation is being educated by Western universities with differing cultural values and behavioural norms? How would change practices be adapted by Malaysian companies establishing businesses in Australia. Alternatively, there is a body of thought that suggests culture has a significant impact when change theory is internationalised, regardless of its origin.[1] Recognising these current viewpoints, change management in an international setting will quickly become the norm rather than the exception.

There is significant evidence that change interventions need to be adapted before adoption in differing cultural settings otherwise they can cause more damage than success.[2] Therefore as part of the change management process there must be cultural and economic alignment with the values of the country of destination.

CHANGE MANAGEMENT THROUGHOUT THE WORLD

Change management is playing an increasingly important role in global social change. Practitioners using highly participative approaches are influencing the development of evolving countries, providing a voice to underrepresented social classes and bridging the gap between cultures facing similar social issues.

Survey feedback interventions have been used at Air New Zealand and Emirates Airlines (United Arab Republic); work design interventions have been implemented in Gamesa (Mexico); large-group interventions have been used in Vitro (Mexico);

structural interventions have been completed at Neusoft Corporation (China); and merger and acquisition integration interventions have been used at Akzo-Nobel (Netherlands).[3] This international diffusion of OD derives from three important trends: the rapid development of foreign economies, the increasing worldwide availability of technical and financial resources and the emergence of a global economy.[4]

The dramatic restructuring of socialist and communist economies and the rapid economic growth of developing countries are astounding in scope and impact. The US government has estimated that world gross domestic product will grow an average of about 3.1% between 2005 and 2017, from $36.1 trillion to $52.2 trillion. Projected growth rates in East Asia, the Pacific and South Asia remain strong. The European Union is continuing its push for integration through fiscal policies, the admission of new countries and the rationalising of economic standards, while political transformations in the Middle East, China, Russia and South Africa are producing both uncertainty and new growth-oriented economies.

Organisations operating in these rejuvenated or newly emerging economies are increasingly turning to OD practices to embrace opportunities and improve effectiveness. In China, for example, economic reforms are breaking up the 'work units' – operational business units organised with housing, health care, education, food service and other infrastructure organisations – that used to dominate the Chinese economy. As these work units are disbanded so that the operational unit can address 'market facing' issues, the social fabric of China is being severely shocked. A variety of non-governmental organisations (NGOs) have formed to help China develop a 'civil society'. Many of these organisations, such as Global Village of Beijing, Friends of the Earth and the Green Earth Volunteers, are using appreciative inquiry interventions[5] to identify best practices and capacity-building processes. Ways of working together are being developed and networks of these NGOs are coming together to assist the homeless, build environmental awareness and deliver childcare. Other interventions, including work design, survey feedback and leadership development, represent efforts to increase ownership, commitment and productivity in Chinese organisations.

The second trend contributing to OD applications in global settings is the unprecedented availability of technological and financial resources on a worldwide scale. The development of the internet and e-commerce has increased foreign governments' and organisations' access to enormous information resources and fuelled growth and development. The increased availability of capital and technology, for example, was cited as a primary reason for the rise of Chilean companies in the 1980s.[6] Information technology, in particular, is making the world 'smaller' and more interdependent. As organisations outside the United States adopt new technology, the opportunity increases to apply techniques that facilitate planned change. OD interventions can smooth the transition to a new reporting structure, clarify roles and relationships and reduce the uncertainty associated with implementing new techniques and practices.

The final trend fuelling international OD applications has been the emergence of a global economy.[7] The continued growth of China's economy, the spread of terrorism on a worldwide basis and the impact of global warming aptly demonstrate how interdependent the world's markets have become. Many foreign organisations are maturing and growing by entering the global business community. Lowered trade barriers, deregulation and privatisation aid this international expansion. The established relationships and local knowledge that once favoured only a small number of worldwide organisations no longer are barriers to entry into many countries.[8] As organisations expand globally, they are faced with adapting structures, information systems, co-ordinating processes and human resources practices to worldwide operations in a variety of countries.

WORLDWIDE ORGANISATION DEVELOPMENT

An important trend facing many businesses is the emergence of a global marketplace.[9] Driven by competitive pressures, lowered trade barriers and advances in information technologies, the number of companies offering products and services in multiple countries is increasing rapidly. The organisational growth and complexity associated with managing worldwide operations is challenging. Executives must choose appropriate strategic orientations for operating across cultures and geographical locations and under diverse governmental and environmental requirements. They must be able to adapt corporate policies and procedures to a range of local conditions. Moreover, the tasks of controlling and co-ordinating operations in different nations place heavy demands on information and control systems and on managerial skills and knowledge.

Worldwide organisation development applies to organisations that are operating across multiple geographic and cultural boundaries. This contrasts with OD in organisations that operate outside a particular country but within a single cultural and economic context.

Worldwide strategic orientations

Worldwide organisations can be defined in terms of three key facets.[10] First, they offer products or services in more than one country and actively manage substantial direct investments in those countries. Consequently, they must relate to a variety of demands, such as unique product requirements, tariffs, value-added taxes, governmental regulations, transportation laws and trade agreements. Second, worldwide businesses must balance product and functional concerns with geographic issues of distance, time and culture. American tobacco companies, for example, face technological, moral and organisational issues in determining whether to market cigarettes in less-developed countries and if they do, they must decide how to integrate manufacturing and distribution operations on a global scale. Third, worldwide companies must carry out co-ordinated activities across cultural boundaries using a wide variety of personnel, including expatriates, short-term and extended business travellers and local employees. Workers with different cultural backgrounds must be managed in ways that support the overall goals and image of the organisation.[11] The company must therefore adapt its human resources policies and procedures to fit the culture and accomplish operational objectives. From a managerial perspective, selecting executives to head foreign operations is an important decision in worldwide organisations.

How these three facets of products/services, organisation and personnel are arranged enables businesses to compete in the global marketplace.[12] Worldwide organisations can offer certain products or services in some countries and not in others; they can centralise or decentralise operations; and they can determine how to work with people from different cultures (for more detail, see Chapter 4). Despite the many possible combinations of characteristics, researchers have found that two dimensions are useful in guiding decisions about choices of strategic orientation.

As shown in Figure 10.1, managers need to assess two key success factors: the degrees to which there is a need for global integration or for local responsiveness. *Global integration* refers to whether or not business success requires tight co-ordination of people, plants, equipment, products or service delivery on a worldwide basis. For example, Intel's 'global factory' designs chips in multiple countries, manufactures the chips in a variety of locations around the world, assembles and tests the finished products in different countries and then ships the chips to customers. All of this activity must be co-ordinated carefully. *Local responsiveness*, on the other hand, is the extent to which business success is

FIGURE 10.1 The integration–responsiveness framework

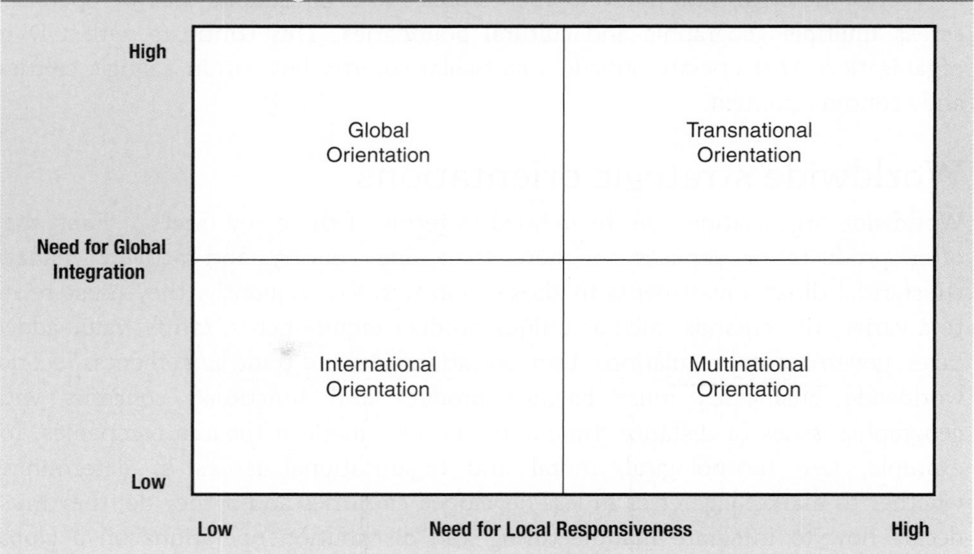

Source: Cummings/Worley, *Organization Development and Change* (with InfoTrac® College Edition Printed Access Card), 9e © 2009 South-Western, a part of Cengage Learning, Inc. Reproduced by permission www.cengage.com/permissions.

dependent on customising products, services, support, packaging and other aspects of operations to local conditions. Based on that information, worldwide organisations generally implement one of four types of strategic orientations: international, global, multinational or transnational. Table 10.1 presents these orientations in terms of a diagnostic framework. Each strategic orientation is geared to specific market, technological and organisational requirements. OD interventions that support each orientation are also included in Table 10.1.

The international strategic orientation

The international orientation exists when the key success factors of global integration and local responsiveness are low. This is the most common label given to organisations making their first attempts at operating outside their own country's markets. Success requires co-ordination between the parent company and the small number of foreign sales and marketing offices in chosen countries. Similarly, local responsiveness is low because the organisation exports the same products and services offered domestically. When an organisation has decided to expand internationally, it has most often determined that:

- other country-markets appear to offer specific advantages large enough to exceed the tangible and intangible costs of implementing a new strategy
- the organisation's products, services and value propositions are sufficiently powerful to counteract the initial disadvantages of operating in a foreign location
- the organisational capabilities exist to extract value from the foreign operations in excess of simpler contracting or licensing of the organisation's technology, products, or services in the foreign location.[13]

Characteristics of the international design

The goal of the international orientation is to increase total sales by adding revenues from non-domestic markets. By using existing products/services, domestic operating capacity is extended and leveraged. As a result, most domestic companies will enter international markets by extending their product lines first into nearby countries and then expanding to more remote areas. For example, most Australian-based companies first offer their products in New Zealand or Europe. After a certain period of time, they begin to set up operations in other countries.

To support this goal and operations strategy, an 'international division' is given responsibility for marketing, sales and distribution, although it may be able to set up joint ventures, licensing agreements, distribution territories/franchises and, in some cases, manufacturing plants. The organisation basically retains its original structure and operating practices. The information system governing the division is typically looser, however. While expecting returns on its investment, the organisation recognises the newness of the venture and gives the international division some 'free rein' to establish an international presence.

TABLE 10.1 Characteristics and interventions for worldwide strategic orientations

Worldwide strategic orientation	Strategy	Structure	Information system	Human resources	OD interventions
International	Existing products Goals of increased foreign revenues	Centralised international division	Loose	Volunteer	Cross-cultural training Strategic planning
Global	Standardised products Goals of efficiency through volume	Centralised, balanced and co-ordinated activities Global product division	Formal	Ethnocentric selection	Career planning Role clarification Employee involvement Senior management team building Conflict management
Multinational	Tailored products Goals of local responsiveness through specialisation	Decentralised operations; centralised planning Global geographic divisions	Profit centres	Regiocentric or polycentric selection	Intergroup relations Local management team building Management development Reward systems Strategic alliances
Transnational	Tailored products Goals of learning and responsiveness through integration	Decentralised, worldwide co-ordination Global matrix or network	Subtle, clan-oriented controls	Geocentric selection	Extensive selection and rotation Cultural development Intergroup relations Building corporate vision

Source: Cummings/Worley, *Organization Development and Change* (with InfoTrac® College Edition Printed Access Card), 9e © 2009 South-Western, a part of Cengage Learning, Inc. Reproduced by permission www.cengage.com/permissions.

Finally, roles in the new international division are staffed with volunteers from the parent company, often with someone who has appropriate foreign language training, experience living overseas or eagerness for an international assignment. Little training or orientation for the position is offered as the organisation is generally unaware of the requirements for being successful in international business.

Implementing the international orientation

Changing from a domestic to an international organisation represents an incremental shift in scope for most organisations and is typically handled as a simple extension of the existing strategy into new markets. Despite the logic of such thinking, the shift is neither incremental nor simple and OD can play an important role in making the transition smoother and more productive. Application 10.1 highlights significant contemporary changes to the domestic marketplace where large homes on small blocks will have a dramatic impact on the gardening business.

10.1

APPLICATION

Backyard bounty

Summer Sunday mornings are simply not what they used to be in suburban Australia. Once broken by the staccato hack and cough of the recalcitrant lawnmower, the call of the currawong is now interrupted, if at all, by the whine of the leaf blower or the angry rattle of the whipper snipper working its way over unruly edges.

The spreads of burnt lawn, the lemon tree in the back and the veggie patch in the corner, have all become endangered as dwellings swell to fill the bulk of ever-decreasing suburban blocks. As a result, the alloy petrol beasts that used to inhabit backyard sheds are being replaced by smaller, electric mowers designed to quietly clip smaller patches of lawn without disturbing the neighbours.

'Twenty years ago all we made were sturdy alloy mowers that were built to last. We still make those mowers for people living on the fringe of the city,' product manager for Briggs and Stratton, Greg Wright, says. The United States company bought Australia's iconic Victa brand of lawnmowers in July 2008.

'There's now demand for smaller electrical mowers in the inner urban areas, as well as other equipment like leaf blowers and whipper snippers,' Wright says. 'At Victa our marketing tag used to be turn grass into lawns, but a few years ago we shifted to the marketing message "great gardens easy".' And it is not just the mowers that are being forced to evolve as living arrangements change.

'Sunday used to be our big day, nurseries were just about the only shops that could trade on Sundays and with nothing else to do it was the day that everyone put aside to do the gardening,' the owner of Tim's Garden Centre, Tim Pickles, says. 'When we first opened the store in 1986 we were flat out just keeping the place stocked, everyone was a keen gardener and everyone wanted to fill their garden with seedlings in the spring.'

>>

After a bull run in the 1980s, Pickles expanded from Campbelltown in Sydney's outer west, opening a second store in the neighbouring suburb of Mount Annan. But the good times didn't last long. From the mid-1990s onwards the nursery and garden centre sector was effectively pincered between shifting demographics and shifts in urban planning. Lot sizes became smaller, houses became bigger, working hours became longer and kikuyu, buffalo and bindies were paved over. More apartments have been erected and multiple town houses have replaced single-family homes.

Pickles' nearest rival, Garden Magic in the nearby suburb of Narellan, closed in 2007. The site was sold and eventually became a Bunnings Warehouse development.

'The two main trends have been an increase in working hours and in the size of the home relative to the block around it,' Tony Hall, the adjunct professor of urban research at Griffith University, says. 'You maximise the floor space, which increases the resale value of the property and because both of you are working full-time and don't get home until dark you don't notice that you have nothing to look out on.'

Hall has mapped the changing landscape of Australian suburbia over two decades and uses aerial footage to demonstrate the difference between older and more recent suburbs. 'There is virtually no space left between or around houses any more, except for tiny strips of lawn and the odd tree,' he says.

The real blow to the nursery and garden sector, however, came in 2002 when successive state governments began to introduce water restrictions as a result of drought. Industry representatives claim the changes were introduced overnight and without consultation, leaving garden centres deserted and overstocked with water-hungry species which were no longer desirable in the average suburban garden.

'There's been a lot of consolidation in recent years and there's probably been close to 1000 smaller nurseries that have either closed or have been sold since the beginning of the drought,' the chief executive of the Nursery and Garden Industry Association, Robert Prince, says. 'Urban encroachment has led to a significant rise in land values in some areas and for some of the older owners selling up was a bit like cashing in their superannuation.'

Despite this consolidation and a dramatic shock when water restrictions were initially introduced, Prince says sales in the garden sector have been growing in recent years, as owners seek to drought-proof their gardens.

Prince believes there are presently more than 20 000 garden-related businesses operating in Australia, and 3000 of these are production nurseries, 6000 garden retailers, with the remainder related landscaping suppliers or garden service companies.

'Despite the drought, Australians still spend more than $6 billion every year at garden retail centres, although now there is more focus on products like water tanks, smaller space veggies, fruit trees that grow in pots and on balconies,' Prince says. 'In some ways the garden centre has become more like the outdoor store, while in other cases what used to be pure hardware stores have developed into garden centres.' Operating more than 15 garden centres in Sydney and Melbourne, Flower Power chief executive John Salmat says the company survived by rapidly diversifying its product line. 'Our business grew at double digits between 2000 and 2004, then froze in 2005,' he says. 'We suffered considerable margin loss and sales loss because we had to simply clear out the stock and start again, concentrating on natives and drought-resistant plants. Plant sales fell by 10 per cent in 2006, 5 per cent in 2007 and then began to recover, but we had to shift into different areas, focus more on the homewares side of the business and keep the business profitable despite the drop in sales.'

Salmat says there is a contradiction at the centre of all large demographic and environmental shifts that have buffeted the garden sector; Australians are still gardening, they're just doing it a little differently to how they once were. 'There has been a flood of cooking-based television shows that have focused on growing your own veggies and fruit, which has brought a younger demographic to our business,' Salmat says. 'It is almost like gardening skipped a generation, but now parents are gardening with their children and gardens are back in fashion.'

With many of the smaller family businesses gone, it is likely to be the large retail chains that take advantage of this. Each of the five new Bunnings stores opened in the past 18 months has a garden centre and in late 2009 the company announced plans to spend $420 million opening 12 new stores across New South Wales in the next three years.

Garden and nursery sales now constitute an important segment for traditional hardware retailers, accounting for 20 per cent of trade through some of the larger stores. Bunnings management is no doubt aware that the decades-long decline in gardening has turned a corner and is hoping to capitalise on this emerging trend.

In August 2009, a survey taken by Newspoll on behalf of the Nursery and Garden Industry Association found 43 per cent of respondents were growing herbs, 44 per cent tended to fruit trees and 63 per cent of respondents were growing vegetables in their suburban gardens. Vegetable, herb and lettuce seedlings now outsell flower seedlings by a factor of three or four in some nurseries, as flower beds are replaced by veggie gardens.

Although they are smaller and less common than they once were, gardens are still seen as valuable by most Australians, with 75 per cent of respondents to the survey saying they believed that plants around their homes improved their health and added value to their home and lifestyle. The industry is even conducting a Green-life Careers campaign designed to attract young people into the sector.

'Starting up a new garden centre would be a challenge these days because of land prices, but there are still opportunities because sales are increasing,' Prince says. 'There are lots of opportunities to supply some of the larger centres with specialist plants or equipment and there is a lot of demand for garden services, because a lot of people really appreciate their garden, but just don't have the time to get out there and do the work.'

Source: Jeanne-Vida Douglas/Business Review Weekly/Fairfax.

Critical thinking question:
1. What are the trends mentioned in Application 10.1? With each trend identify how organisations will need to implement changes to remain competitive.

Strategic planning, technostructural and human resource interventions can help to implement an international orientation. Managers can use integrated strategic change or an organisation redesign process to design and manage the transition from the old strategic orientation to the new one. Environmental scans, competitor analyses and market studies can be done to calibrate expectations about revenue goals and determine the levels of investment necessary to support the division. Team building and large-group interventions, such as search conferences, can aid the process by allowing senior executives to gather appropriate information about international markets, distinctive competencies and culture and then choose a strategic orientation. Similarly, managers can apply technostructural interventions to design an appropriate organisation structure, to define new tasks and work roles and to clarify reporting relationships between corporate headquarters and foreign-based units. Based on these decisions, OD interventions can help the organisation to implement the change.

Managers and staff can also apply human resources management interventions to train and prepare managers and their families for international assignments and to develop selection methods and reward systems relevant to operating internationally.[14] Since these are the organisation's first experiences with international business, OD practitioners can alert key managers and potential candidates for the international assignments to the need for cultural training. Candidates can be directed to outsourced offerings on cross-cultural skills, local country customs and legal/regulatory conditions. OD practitioners can also assist the human resource organisation to design or modify existing compensation and benefits packages, or set up policies around housing, schooling and other expenses associated with the relocation.

This initial movement into the international arena enables domestic organisations to learn about the demands of the global marketplace, thus providing important knowledge and experience with the requirements for success in more sophisticated strategies. OD practitioners should help the organisation set up learning practices and communication systems so that information about international experiences are shared with others, especially senior managers.

The global strategic orientation

This orientation exists when the need for global integration is high but the need for local responsiveness is low. The global orientation is characterised by a strategy of marketing standardised products in different countries. It is an appropriate orientation when there is little economic reason to offer products or services with special features or locally available options. Manufacturers of office equipment, consumer goods, computers and semiconductors, tyres and containers, for example, can offer the same basic product in almost any country.

Characteristics of the global design

The goal of efficiency dominates this orientation. Production efficiency is gained through volume sales and a small number of large manufacturing plants; managerial efficiency is achieved by centralising product design, manufacturing, distribution and marketing decisions. Global integration is supported by the close physical proximity of major functional groups and formal control systems that balance inputs, production and distribution with worldwide demand. Many Japanese companies, such as Honda, Sony, NEC and Matsushita, used this strategy in the 1970s and early 1980s to grow in the international economy. In Europe, Nestlé exploits economies of scale in marketing by advertising well-known brand names around the world. The increased number of microwave and two-income families, for example, allowed Nestlé to push its Nescafé coffee and Lean Cuisine low-calorie frozen dinners to dominant market-share positions in Europe, North America, Latin America and Asia. Similarly, a Korean noodle maker, Nong Shim Company, avoided the 1999 financial crisis by staying focused on efficiency. Yoo Jong Suk, Nong Shim's head of strategy, went against recommendations to diversify and stated, 'All we want is to be globally recognised as a rayon maker'.[15]

In the global orientation, the organisation tends to be centralised with a global product structure. Presidents of each major product group report to the CEO and form the line organisation. Each of these product groups is responsible for worldwide operations. Information systems in global orientations tend to be quite formal, with local units reporting sales, costs and other data directly to the product president. The predominant human resources policy[16] integrates people into the organisation through ethnocentric selection[17] and staffing practices. These methods seek to fill key foreign positions with personnel from the home country where the corporation headquarters is located.[18] Key managerial jobs at Volvo, Siemens, Nissan and Michelin, for example, are often occupied by Swedish, German, Japanese and French citizens, respectively. Ethnocentric policies support the global orientation because expatriate managers are more likely than host-country nationals to recognise and comply with the need to centralise decision making and to standardise processes, decisions and relationships with the parent company. Although many Japanese automobile manufacturers have decentralised production, Nissan's global strategy has been to retain tight, centralised control of design and manufacturing, ensure that almost all of its senior foreign managers are Japanese and have even low-level decisions emerge from face-to-face meetings in Tokyo.

Implementing the global orientation

OD interventions can be used to refine and support the global strategic orientation as well as assist in the transition from an international orientation.

1 *Planned change in the global orientation.* Several OD interventions support the implementation of this orientation. Career planning, role clarification, employee involvement, conflict management and senior management team building help the organisation achieve improved operational efficiency. For example, role clarification interventions, such as job enrichment or goal setting and conflict management, can formalise and standardise organisational activities. This ensures that each individual knows specific details about how, when and why a job needs to be done. As a result, necessary activities are described and efficient transactions and relationships are created. Similarly, Intel has used training interventions to ensure consistent implementation of a variety of company-standard business practices, such as meeting protocols, performance management processes and reporting accountability.

   Senior management team building can improve the quality of strategic decisions. Centralised policies make the organisation highly dependent on this group and can exaggerate decision-making errors. In addition, interpersonal conflict can increase the cost of co-ordination or cause significant co-ordination mistakes. Process interventions at this level can help to improve the speed and quality of decision making and improve interpersonal relationships.

Career planning can help home-country personnel develop a path to senior management by including foreign subsidiary experiences and cross-functional assignments as necessary qualifications for advancement. At the country level, career planning can emphasise that advancement beyond regional operations is limited for host-country nationals. OD can help here by developing appropriate career paths within the local organisation or in technical, non-managerial areas. Finally, employee empowerment can support efficiency goals by involving members in efforts at cost reduction, work standardisation and minimisation of co-ordination costs.

2 *The transition to a global orientation.* In addition to fine-tuning this strategic orientation, OD can help the organisation transition from an international to a global strategic orientation. The organisation's experience with the international strategic orientation has helped to build basic knowledge and skills in international business. The successful transition to a global strategy assumes that managers believe global integration is more important than local responsiveness and that the organisation has strong centralised operating capabilities. If the assessment of either key success factors or the organisation's competencies is inaccurate, implementation will be more difficult and performance will suffer.

The decision to favour global integration over local responsiveness must be rooted in a strong belief that the worldwide market is relatively homogeneous in character. That is, products and services, support, distribution or marketing activities can be standardised without negatively affecting sales or customer loyalty. This decision should not be made lightly and OD practitioners can help to structure rigorous debate and analysis of this key success factor.

In addition to information about the market, organisations must take into account their distinctive competencies when choosing a global strategy. The key organisational and operational competence necessary for success in a global strategy is the ability to co-ordinate a complex, worldwide organisation. The global strategy is facilitated when culture and core competencies are more suited to centralised decision making, when the organisation has experience with supply-chain management and when it is comfortable with enterprise resource and material resource planning processes. Centralisation favours a global orientation because the orientation favours tight, global co-ordination.

Once companies develop a strategic orientation for competing internationally, they create an organisation design to support it. Information like that found in Table 10.1 is useful for designing structures, information systems and personnel practices for specific strategic orientations. OD practitioners can help to design change management programs to implement these features.

The multinational strategic orientation

This strategic orientation exists when the need for global integration is low, but the need for local responsiveness is high. It represents a strategy that is conceptually quite different to the global strategic orientation.

Characteristics of the multinational design

A multinational strategy is characterised by a product line that is tailored to local conditions and is best suited to markets that vary significantly from region to region or country to country. At American Express, for example, charge card marketing is fitted to local values and tastes. The 'Don't leave home without it' and 'Membership has its privileges' themes seen in Australia and the United States had to be translated to 'Peace of mind only for members' in Japan because of the negative connotations of 'leaving home' and 'privilege'.[19]

The multinational orientation emphasises a decentralised, global division structure. Each region or country is served by a divisional organisation that operates autonomously and reports to headquarters. This results in a highly differentiated and loosely co-ordinated corporate structure. Operational decisions, such as product design, manufacturing and distribution, are decentralised and tightly integrated at the local level. For example, laundry soap manufacturers offer product formulas, packaging and marketing strategies that conform to the different environmental regulations, types of washing machines, water hardness and distribution channels in each country. On the other hand, planning activities are often centralised at corporate headquarters to achieve important efficiencies necessary for the worldwide co-ordination of emerging technologies and of resource allocation. A profit-centre control system allows local autonomy as long as profitability is maintained. Examples of multinational corporations include Hoechst and BASF of Germany, IBM and Procter & Gamble of the United States and Fuji Xerox of Japan. Each of these organisations encourages local subsidiaries to maximise effectiveness within their geographic region.

People are integrated into multinational organisations through polycentric or regiocentric personnel policies because these businesses believe that host-country nationals can understand native cultures most clearly.[20] By filling positions with local citizens who appoint and develop their own staffs, the organisation aligns the needs of the market with the ability of its subsidiaries to produce customised products and services. The distinction between a polycentric and a regiocentric selection[21] process is one of focus. In a polycentric selection policy, a subsidiary represents only one country; in the regiocentric selection policy, a slightly broader perspective is taken and key positions are filled by regional citizens (people who might be called Europeans, as opposed to Belgians or Italians, for example).

Implementing the multinational orientation

The decentralised and locally co-ordinated multinational orientation suggests the need for a complex set of OD interventions. When applied to a subsidiary operating in a particular country or region, the OD processes described earlier in the chapter for organisations outside the home country are relevant. The key is to tailor OD to fit the specific cultural and economic context where the subsidiary is located.

1 *Planned change in the multinational orientation.* When OD is applied across different regions and countries, interventions must allow for differences in cultural and economic conditions that can affect its success. Appropriate interventions for multinational corporations include intergroup relations, local management team building, sophisticated management selection and development practices and changes to reward systems. Team building remains an important intervention. Unlike team building for the senior management team in global orientations, the local management teams require attention in multinational organisations. This presents a challenge for OD practitioners because polycentric selection policies can produce management teams with different cultures at each subsidiary. Thus, a program developed for one subsidiary may not work with a different team at another subsidiary, given the different cultures that might be represented.

   Intergroup interventions to improve relations between local subsidiaries and the parent company are also important for multinational companies. Decentralised decision making and regiocentric selection can strain corporate–subsidiary relations. Local management teams, operating in ways appropriate to their cultural context, may not be understood by corporate managers from another culture. OD practitioners can help both groups understand these differences by offering training in cultural diversity and appreciation. They can also smooth parent–subsidiary relationships[22] by focusing on the profit-centre control system or other criteria as the means for monitoring and measuring subsidiary effectiveness.

   Management selection, development and reward systems also require special attention in multinational organisations. Managerial selection for local or regional subsidiaries requires finding technically and managerially competent people who also possess the interpersonal competence needed to interface with corporate headquarters. Because these people may be difficult to find, management development programs can teach the necessary cross-cultural skills and abilities. Such programs typically involve language, cultural awareness and technical training; they can also include managers and staff from subsidiary and corporate offices to improve communications between the two areas. Finally, reward systems need to be aligned with the decentralised structure. Significant proportions of managers' total compensation could be tied to local profit performance, thereby aligning reward and control systems.

2 *The transition to multinational.* Organisation development activities can also help to facilitate the transition from an international to a multinational orientation. Much of the recommended activity in transitioning to a global

orientation applies here as well, except that it must be customised to the issues facing a multinational strategy. For example, the successful transition to a multinational strategy assumes that managers believe local responsiveness is more important than global integration and that the organisation is comfortable with the ambiguity of managing decentralised operations.

The decision to favour local responsiveness over global integration must be made with the same analytic rigour described earlier. In this case, the analysis must support the belief that the worldwide market is relatively heterogeneous in character. That is, that products and services, support, distribution or marketing activities must be customised and localised to drive overall sales. Similarly, the organisation must have the managerial, technical and organisational competence to achieve profit margins from businesses operating around the globe. The multinational strategy is facilitated when culture and core competencies are more suited for decentralised decision making and when the organisation can manage high amounts of ambiguity and complexity.

Once companies develop a strategic orientation for competing internationally, they create an organisation design to support it. Information like that found in Table 10.1 is useful for designing structures, information systems and personnel practices for specific strategic orientations. OD practitioners can help to design change management programs to implement these features.

The transnational strategic orientation

This orientation exists when the need for global integration and local responsiveness are both high. It represents the most complex and ambitious worldwide strategic orientation and reflects the belief that any product or service can be made anywhere and sold everywhere.[23]

Characteristics of the transnational design

The transnational strategy combines customised products with both efficient and responsive operations; the key goal is learning. This is the most complex worldwide strategic orientation because transnationals can manufacture products, conduct research, raise capital, buy supplies and perform many other functions wherever in the world the job can be done optimally. They can move skills, resources and knowledge to regions where they are needed.

The transnational orientation combines the best of global and multinational orientations and adds a third attribute – the ability to transfer resources both within the organisation and across national and cultural boundaries. Otis Elevator, a division of United Technologies, developed a new programmable elevator using six research centres in five countries: a US group handled the systems integration; Japan designed the special motor drives that make the elevators ride smoothly; France perfected the door systems; Germany created the electronics; and Spain produced the small-geared components.[24] Other examples of transnational companies include General Electric, Asea Brown Boveri (ABB), Motorola, Electrolux and Hewlett-Packard.

Transnational companies organise themselves into global matrix and network structures especially suited for moving information and resources to their best use. In the matrix structure, local divisions similar to the multinational structure are crossed with product groups at the headquarters office. The network structure treats each local office, including headquarters, product groups and production facilities, as self-sufficient nodes that co-ordinate with each other to move knowledge and resources to their most valued place. Because of the heavy communication and logistic demands needed to operate these structures, transnationals have sophisticated information systems. State-of-the-art information technology is used to move strategic and operational information throughout the system rapidly and efficiently. Organisational learning and knowledge management practices gather, organise and disseminate the knowledge and skills of members who are located around the world.

People are integrated into transnational companies through a geocentric selection policy that staffs key positions with the best people, regardless of nationality.[25] This staffing practice recognises that the distinctive competence of a transnational business is its capacity to optimise resource allocation on a worldwide basis. Unlike global and multinational businesses, which spend more time training and developing managers to fit the strategy, the transnational business attempts to hire the right person from the beginning. Recruits at any of Hewlett-Packard's foreign locations, for example, are screened not only for technical qualifications but for personality traits that match the company's cultural values.

Implementing the transnational orientation

There are two perspectives on change in a transnational strategy.

1 *Planned change in the transnational orientation.* Transnational companies require OD interventions that can improve their ability to achieve efficient global integration under highly decentralised decision-making conditions. These interventions include extensive management selection and development practices in support of the geocentric policies described above, intergroup relations and development, and communication of a strong corporate vision and culture. Knowledge management interventions help develop a worldwide repository of information that enables members' learning.

Effective transnational businesses have well-developed vision and mission statements that communicate the values and beliefs underlying the organisation's culture and guide its operational decisions. ABB's mission statement, for example, went through a multicultural rewriting when the company recognised that talking about profit was an uncomfortable activity in some cultures.[26] OD processes that increase member participation in the construction or modification of these statements can help members gain ownership of them. Research into the development of corporate credos at the British computer manufacturer ICL, SAS and Apple Computer showed that success was more a function of the heavy involvement of many managers than the quality of the statements themselves.[27]

Once vision and mission statements are crafted, management training can focus on clarifying their meaning, the values they express and the behaviours required to support those values. This process of gaining shared meaning and developing a strong culture provides a basis for social control. Because transnationals need flexibility and co-ordination, they cannot rely solely on formal reports of sales, costs or demand to guide behaviour. This information often takes too much time to compile and distribute. Rather, the corporate vision and culture provide transnational managers with the reasoning and guidelines for why and how they should make decisions.

This form of social control supports OD efforts to improve management selection and development, intergroup relationships and strategic change. The geocentric selection process can be supplemented by a personnel policy that rotates managers through different geographical regions and functional areas to blend people, perspectives and practices. At organisations such as GE, ABB, Coca-Cola and Colgate a cadre of managers with extensive foreign experience has been developed. Rotation throughout the organisation also improves the chances that when two organisational units must co-operate, key personnel will know each other and make co-ordination more likely. The corporate vision and culture can also become important tools in building cross-functional or interdepartmental processes for transferring knowledge, resources or products. Moreover, they can provide guidelines for formulating and implementing strategic change and serve as a social context for designing appropriate structures and systems at local subsidiaries.

2 *The transition to the transnational orientation.* In addition to implementing planned changes that support the development of the transnational orientation, OD can help businesses make the complex transition to a transnational strategy. Although many organisations take on the international orientation, a much smaller number are large enough to become global or multinational. The requirements for successfully operating a transnational orientation – global integration and local responsiveness – are sufficiently restrictive and demanding that only a small fraction of organisations should pursue this strategy. As a result, knowledge about the transition to transnational is still being developed.

Global and multinational organisations tend to evolve into a transnational orientation because of changes in the organisation's environment, markets or technologies.[28] In the global orientation, for example, environmental changes can challenge the logic of centralised and efficient operations. The success of Japanese car manufacturers employing a global strategy caused employment declines in the US car industry and overall trade imbalances. Consumer and government reactions forced Japanese companies to become more responsive to local conditions. Conversely, consumer preference changes can reduce the needs for tailored products and locally responsive management that are characteristic of the multinational strategy. The typical response is to centralise many decisions and activities.

Thus, the evolution to a transnational orientation is a complex strategic change effort requiring the acquisition of two additional capabilities. First, global organisations need to learn to trust distant operations and multinational organisations need to become better at co-ordination. Second, both types of organisations need to acquire the ability to transfer resources efficiently around the world. Much of the difficulty in evolving to a transnational strategy lies in developing these additional capabilities.

In the transition from a global to a transnational orientation, the business must acquire the know-how to operate a decentralised organisation and learn to transfer knowledge, skills and resources among disparate organisational units operating in different countries. In this situation, the administrative challenge is to encourage creative over centralised thinking and to let each functional area operate in a way that best suits its context. For example, if international markets require increasingly specialised products, then manufacturing needs to operate local plants and flexible delivery systems that can move raw materials to where they are needed, when they are needed. OD interventions that can help this transition include training efforts that increase the tolerance for differences in management practices, control systems, performance appraisals and policies and procedures, reward systems that encourage entrepreneurship and performance at each foreign subsidiary, and efficient organisation designs at the local level.

The global orientation strives to achieve efficiency through centralisation and standardisation of products and practices. In the case of organisational systems, this works against the establishment of highly specialised and flexible policies and resists the movement of knowledge, skills and resources. Training interventions that help managers develop an appreciation for the different ways that effectiveness can be achieved will aid the global organisation's move towards transnationalism.[29]

Changes in reward systems can also help the global business evolve. By moving from a highly quantitative, centralised, pay-for-performance system characteristic of a global orientation, the organisation can reward people who champion new ideas and provide incentives for decentralised business units. This more flexible reward system promotes co-ordination among subsidiaries, product lines and staff groups. In addition, the transition to a transnational orientation can be aided by OD practitioners working with individual business units, rather than with senior management at headquarters. Working with each subsidiary on issues relating to its own structure and function sends an important message about the importance of decentralised operations.

Finally, changing the staffing policy is another important signal to organisation members that a transition is occurring. Under the global orientation, an ethnocentric policy supported standardised activities. By staffing key positions with the best people, rather than limiting the choice to just parent-country individuals, the symbols of change are clear and the rewards for supporting the new orientation are visible.

In moving from a multinational to a transnational orientation, products, technologies and regulatory constraints can become more homogeneous and require more efficient operations. The competencies required to compete on a transnational basis, however, may be located in many different geographic areas. The need to balance local responsiveness against the need for co-ordination among organisational units is new to multinational businesses. They must create interdependencies among organisational units through the flow of parts, components and finished goods; the flow of funds, skills and other scarce resources; or the flow of intelligence, ideas and knowledge. For example, as part of Ford's transition to a transnational company, the redesign of the US Tempo car was given to one person in the United Kingdom. He co-ordinated all features of the new car for both sides of the Atlantic and used the same platform, engines and other parts. Ford used teleconferencing and computer links, as well as extensive air travel, to manage the complex task of meshing car companies on two continents.[30]

In such situations, OD is an important activity because complex interdependencies require sophisticated and non-traditional co-ordinating mechanisms.[31] OD interventions, such as intergroup team building or cultural awareness and interpersonal skills training, can help develop the communication linkages necessary for successful co-ordination. In addition, the inherently 'matrixed' structures of worldwide companies and the cross-cultural context of doing business in different countries tend to create conflict. OD interventions, such as role clarification, third-party consultation and mediation techniques, can help to solve such problems.

The transition to a transnational business is difficult and threatens the status quo. Under the multinational orientation, each subsidiary is encouraged and rewarded for its creativity and independence. Transnational businesses, however, are effective when physically or geographically distinct organisational units co-ordinate their activities. The transition from independent to interdependent business units can produce conflict as the co-ordination requirements are worked through. OD practitioners can help mitigate the uncertainty associated with the change by modifying reward systems to encourage co-operation and spelling out clearly the behaviours required for success.

GLOBAL SOCIAL CHANGE

The newest and perhaps most exciting applications of organisation development in international settings are occurring in global social change organisations (GSCOs).[32] These organisations generally are not-for-profit and non-governmental. They typically are created at the grassroots level to help communities and societies address such important problems as unemployment, race relations, sustainable development, homelessness, hunger, disease and political instability. In international settings, GSCOs are heavily involved in the developing nations. Examples include the World Conservation Union (IUCN), the Hunger Project, the Nature Conservancy, the Mountain Forum, International Physicians for the Prevention of Nuclear War and the Asian Coalition for Agrarian Reform and Rural Development (ANGOC). Many practitioners who help create and develop these GSCOs come from an OD background and have adapted their expertise to fit highly complex, global situations. This section describes global social change organisations and how OD is practised in them.

Global social change organisations

Global social change organisations are part of a social innovation movement to foster the emergence of a global civilisation.[33] They exist under a variety of names, including development organisations (DOs), international nongovernmental organisations (INGOs), social movement organisations (SMOs), international private voluntary organisations and bridging organisations.[34] They exist to address complex social problems, including overpopulation, ecological degradation, the increasing concentration of wealth and power, the lack of management infrastructures to facilitate growth and the lack of fundamental human rights. The efforts of many GSCOs to raise awareness and mobilise resources towards solving these problems culminated in the United Nations' Conference on Environment and Development in Rio de Janeiro in June 1992, where leaders from both industrialised and less-developed countries met to discuss sustainable development.[35] More recently, the Kyoto Protocol and the United Nations Global Compact have focused attention on global warming and social responsibility and how countries and organisations can co-operate to address these concerns.

GSCOs have the following characteristics:[36]

- They assert, as their primary task, a commitment to serve as an agent of change in creating environmentally and socially sustainable world futures; their transformational missions are articulated around the real needs of people and the earth.
- They have discovered and mobilised innovative social-organisational architectures that make possible human co-operation across previously polarising or arbitrarily constraining boundaries.
- They hold values of empowerment, or people-centred forms of action, in the accomplishment of their global change mission, emphasising the central role of people as both means and ends in any development process.

- They are globally and locally linked in structure, membership or partnership and thereby exist, at least in identity and practice (maybe not yet legally), as entities beyond the nation-state.
- They are multi-organisational and often cross-sectoral. They can be business, governmental or not-for-profit. Indeed, many of the most significant global change organising innovations involve multi-organisation partnerships bridging sectoral boundaries in new hybrid forms of business, intergovernmental and private voluntary sectors.

GSCOs therefore differ from traditional for-profit businesses on several dimensions.[37] First, they typically advocate a mission of social change – the formation and development of better societies and communities. 'Better' normally means more just (Amnesty International, Hunger Project), peaceful (International Physicians for the Prevention of Nuclear War) or ecologically conscious (Nature Conservancy, the Global Village of Beijing, the Mountain Forum, IUCN, World Wildlife Fund). Second, the mission is supported by a network structure. Most GSCO activity occurs at the boundary or periphery between two or more organisations.[38] Unlike most industrial firms that focus on internal effectiveness, GSCOs are directed at changing their environmental context. For example, Australian Aid International co-ordinated the efforts of large numbers of organisations to address the human needs and consequences of the 2004 Tsunami in South-East Asia. Third, GSCOs generally have strong values and ideologies that justify and motivate organisation behaviour. These 'causes' provide intrinsic rewards to GSCO members and a blueprint for action.[39] The ideological position that basic human rights include shelter has directed Habitat for Humanity to erect low-cost homes in a wide variety of underdeveloped communities. Fourth, GSCOs interact with a broad range of external and often conflicting constituencies. To help the poor, GSCOs often must work with the rich; to save the ecology, they must work with developers; to empower the masses, they must work with the powerful few. This places a great deal of pressure on GSCOs to reconcile pursuit of a noble cause with the political realities of power and wealth. Fifth, managing these diverse external constituencies often creates significant organisational conflict. On the one hand, GSCOs need to create specific departments to serve and represent particular stakeholders. On the other hand, they are strongly averse to bureaucracy and desire collegial and consensus-seeking cultures. The conflicting perspectives of the stakeholders, the differentiated departments and the ideological basis of the organisation's mission can produce a contentious internal environment. For example, the International Relief and Development Agency was created to promote self-help projects in Third World countries using resources donated from First World countries. As the agency grew, departments were created to represent different stakeholders: a fund-raising group handled donors, a projects department worked in the Third World, a public relations department directed media exposure and a policy information department lobbied the government. Each department adapted to fit its role. Fund-raisers and lobbyists dressed more formally, took more moderate political positions and managed less participatively than did the projects departments. These differences were often interpreted in political and ideological terms, creating considerable internal conflict.[40] Sixth, GSCO membership is often transitory. Many people are volunteers and the extent and depth of their involvement varies over time and by issue. Turnover is quite high.

Application 10.2 reports how technology can assist small businesses to consider social networking sites as job agencies to find applications. If small businesses can utilise this medium, GSCOs should also attract the attention of volunteers by this means.

10.2

APPLICATION

DIY recruitment

Social networking sites such as Twitter and LinkedIn can save businesses tens of thousands of dollars, especially when it comes to recruitment. For Sydney information technology company Atlassian, the sites have halved its recruitment bill and attracted job applicants from 55 countries, including from Microsoft in the United States.

A combination of economic factors and the emergence of new technologies has inspired many small and medium enterprises to recruit staff through social media. The shake-up of recruitment companies during the downturn has encouraged many businesses to consider smarter, more affordable ways to find quality staff.

Today Twitter, LinkedIn and Facebook are the preferred social media websites of SMEs in Australia. Each has different benefits: Facebook has huge reach with more than 7 million users in Australia, Twitter is known for its viral marketing capabilities and LinkedIn allows users to target niche groups.

For Atlassian human resources director Joris Lujike, using social networking to find 32 new highly skilled IT engineers is a 'no brainer'. In the past, Atlassian has had difficulty finding the right candidates through traditional recruitment channels.

'We were really limited in the level of expertise that we are able to tap into in Australia,' Lujike says. 'With some of the jobs there are literally only a handful of people who can do them in Australia. Then if you look at companies like Google or IBM, they have millions of dollars to create their reputation. Medium businesses like us don't have that luxury.'

Atlassian's social media strategy needed to be aggressive and different. Merely having a presence on Twitter and LinkedIn and posting job ads on the sites would not suffice. As a sweetener, the company offered a $2000 bonus to people who referred successful applications and a Wotif holiday voucher to new employees to ensure they started fresh in their new jobs. Since then, personal referrals have tripled.

Lujike says the company has offered a $10 000 bonus to employees who successfully refer new applicants and it wants to extend the strategy.

'We wanted four average Aussie guys to be able to stand around at a barbecue and be able to talk about what this medium IT company in Sydney was doing,' he says.

Today, Atlassian estimates that just 6 per cent of its staff has been hired through recruitment agencies. Not wanting to alienate recruitment agencies completely, it has developed a new set of rules for them. Lujike tells recruiters they can submit up to four applicants for each position, but if none is appropriate the recruiter will be wiped from Atlassian's books. If any of the applicants is hired, the recruiter can continue to work with the company.

'The quality of the application is much, much higher when it comes from a referral compared with a recruitment agency or job site,' Lujike says. 'Besides, we would much rather give our own people and people who refer their friends to us, a bonus than pay tens of thousands of dollars to a recruitment company. We've created a great culture of openness and honesty, with no bullshit and no bureaucracy.'

Since Atlassian implemented the strategy, its job application numbers have increased from an average of 30 to 125 for each position. The company has hired 24 employees in six months – a 60 per cent increase on initial forecasts.

This year it will tweak its recruitment strategy to include video uploads on social networking site YouTube as it attempts to hire a new vice-president of engineering – one of the most senior roles in the business. It will also offer overseas applicants perks such as Sydney city tours and a Harbour Bridge climb.

Like Atlassian, intellectual property company Inovia has noticed an improvement in the quality of job applicants since using social networking for recruitment. Recruiting through sites such as LinkedIn and Twitter was initially a cost-saving exercise for Inovia, which has about 30 employees, but it soon became apparent that the company could access better staff this way.

'Social networking is putting the power back into the hands of small businesses and giving them alternative methods for finding good staff,' Inovia chief executive David Nelson says. 'It gives you the opportunity to get referrals for a job – which have a greater degree of success attached to them than just a random person who applies through an ad on an online job website.'

Source: Jane Lindhe, 'DIY recruitment', *Business Review Weekly*, 18–24 February 2010.

Critical thinking questions:
1. What significant changes have resulted from the social networking implementation of Atlassian's strategy? What problems do you expect will occur and how may they be overcome?
2. To what extent do you consider recruitment rates improved due to the use of social media sites compared to the use of incentives for referrals? Without the latter do you believe use of social media sites would have been as effective as reported?
3. What are the implications of this report for traditional recruitment agencies? How can OD assist in addressing those implications?

Application stages

Global social change organisations are concerned with creating sustainable change in communities and societies. This requires a form of change process in which the practitioner is heavily involved, many stakeholders are encouraged and expected to participate and 'technologies of empowerment' are used. Often referred to as 'participatory action research',[41] change processes in GSCOs typically involve three types of activities: building local organisation effectiveness, creating bridges and linkages with other relevant organisations and developing vertical linkages with policymakers.

Building the local organisation

Although GSCOs are concerned primarily with changing their environments, a critical issue in development projects is recognising the potential problems inherent in the GSCO itself. Because the focus of change is their environment, members of GSCOs are often oblivious to the need for internal development. Moreover, the complex organisational arrangements of a network make planned change in GSCOs particularly challenging.

OD practitioners focus on three activities in helping GSCOs build themselves into viable organisations: using values to create the vision, recognising that internal conflict is often a function of external conditions and understanding the problems of success. For leadership to function effectively, the broad purposes of the GSCO must be clear and closely aligned with the ideologies of its members. Singleness of purpose can be gained from tapping into the compelling aspects of the values and principles that the GSCO represents. For example, the Latin American Division of the Nature Conservancy held annual two-day retreats. Each participant prepared a white paper concerning his or her area of responsibility: the issues, challenges, major dilemmas or problems and ideas for directions the division could take. Over the course of the retreat, participants actively discussed each paper. They had broad freedom to challenge the status quo and to question previous decisions. By the end of the retreat, discussions produced a clear statement about the course that the division would take for the following year. People left with increased clarity about and commitment to the purpose and vision of the division.[42]

Developing a shared vision can align individual and organisational values. Because most activities occur at the boundary of the organisation, members are often spread out geographically and are not in communication with each other. A clearly crafted vision allows people in disparate regions and positions to co-ordinate their activities. At the Hunger Project, for example, OD practitioners asked organisation members, 'What is your job or task in this organisation?' The GSCO president responded, 'That is simple. My work is to make the end of hunger an idea whose time has come.' A receptionist answered, 'My task in this organisation is to end hunger. I don't just answer phones or set up meetings. In everything I do, I am working to end hunger.'[43] Because of the diverse perspectives of the different stakeholders, GSCOs often face multiple conflicts. In working through them, the organisational vision can be used as an important rallying point for discovering how each person's role contributes to the GSCO's purpose. The affective component of a GSCO vision gives purpose to members' lives and work.

Another way to manage conflict is to prevent its occurrence. At the Hunger Project, the 'committed listener' and 'breakthrough' processes give GSCO members an opportunity to seek help before conflict becomes dysfunctional. Every member of the organisation has a designated person who acts as a committed listener. When things are not going well or someone is feeling frustrated in their ability to accomplish a goal, they can talk it out with this colleague. The role of the committed listener is to listen intently, to help the individual understand the issues and to think about framing or approaching the problem in new ways. This new perspective is called a 'breakthrough' – a creative solution to a potentially conflictual situation.

Finally, a GSCO's success can create a number of problems. The very accomplishment of its mission can take away its reason for existence, thus causing an identity crisis. For example, a GSCO that succeeds in creating jobs for underprivileged youth can be dissolved because its funding is redirected towards organisations that have not yet met their goals, because its goals change or simply because it has accomplished its purpose. During these times, the vital social role that these organisations play needs to be emphasised. GSCOs often represent bridges between the powerful and powerless, between the rich and poor and between the elite and oppressed, and as such may need to be maintained as legitimate parts of the community.

Another problem can occur when GSCO success produces additional demands for greater formalisation.[44] New people must be hired and acculturated; greater control over income and expenditures has to be developed; new skills and behaviours have to be learned. The need for more formal systems often runs against ideological principles of autonomy and freedom and can produce a profound resistance to change. Employees' participation during diagnosis and implementation can help them commit to the new systems. In addition, new employment opportunities, increased job responsibilities and improved capabilities to carry out the GSCO's mission can be used to encourage commitment and reduce resistance to the changes.

Alternatively, the organisation can maintain its autonomy through structural arrangements. The Savings Development Movement (SDM) of Zimbabwe was a grassroots effort to organise savings clubs, the proceeds of which helped farmers buy seed in volume. Its success in creating clubs and helping farmers lower their costs caused the organisation to grow very rapidly. Leaders chose to expand SDM not by adding staff but by working with the Ministry of Agriculture to provide technical support to the clubs and with the Ministry of Community Development and Women's Affairs to provide training. The savings clubs remained autonomous and locally managed. This reduced the need for formal systems to co-ordinate the clubs with government agencies. The SDM office staff did not grow, but the organisation remained a catalyst, committed to expanding participation rather than providing direct services.[45]

Creating horizontal linkages

Successful social change projects often require a network of local organisations with similar views and objectives. Such projects as creating a civil society in China, turning responsibility for maintenance and control over small irrigation systems to local water users in Indonesia, or teaching leadership skills in South Africa require that multiple organisations interact. Consequently, an important planned change activity in GSCOs is creating strong horizontal linkages to organisations in the community or society where the development project is taking place. The China Brief (www.chinadevelopmentbrief.com), for example, publishes a newsletter describing the activities of different NGOs focused on environmental, child welfare and other issues. Like-minded NGOs can then contact each other and support common interests. Similarly, GSCOs aimed at job development not only must recruit, train and market potential job applicants but also must develop relationships with local job providers and government authorities. The GSCO must help these organisations commit to the GSCO's vision, mobilise resources and create policies to support development efforts.

The ability of GSCOs to sustain themselves depends on establishing linkages with other organisations whose co-operation is essential to preserving and expanding their efforts. Members of GSCOs often view local government officials, community leaders or for-profit organisations as part of the problem. Rather than interacting with these stakeholders, GSCOs often 'protect' themselves and their ideologies from contamination by these outsiders. Planned change efforts to overcome this myopia are similar to the transorganisational development interventions. GSCO members are helped to identify, convene and organise these key external organisations. For example, following the earthquakes in Pakistan in 2005–06, Australian Aid International (AAI) was directed to assist with the migration of thousands of villagers who were displaced from their homes and to establish temporary accommodation. AAI needed to form relationships with other GSCOs concerned with organising the poor or with responding to the disaster. The group also linked up with local churches, universities, charitable organisations and poor urban neighbourhood organisations. It bargained with the government and appealed to the media to assist with donated goods. This activity resulted in a smooth transition of the population from damaged areas to fully equipped temporary accommodation and supplies.[46]

Application 10.3 describes how small businesses will need to ditch at least part of their learned disciplines to match the new conditions during the downturn to prosper in the upturn. As many GSCOs have proven, it is necessary to be responsive to the environment and adapt accordingly.

10.3 APPLICATION

Managing the recovery

Small businesses will need every bit of the nous gained from navigating the downturn to survive the recovery. But not all business strategies from the past year will work in the new one. The pain felt by small businesses in the past year was offset by federal government pump priming and low mortgage interests rates; but the recovery offers no such silver lining.

In 2010, there are no cheques to consumers or tax breaks for small businesses. The first-home-owners' grant is being wound back. Mortgage interest rates are rising. The four biggest

>>

banks have a stranglehold on the mortgage market. Westpac Banking Corporation's decision to increase its variable mortgage interest rate above the Reserve Bank of Australia's official rise in December shows the impact of that market power.

Small business interest rates remain high and credit is so tight that the Australian Chamber of Commerce and Industry called for a review by the Productivity Commission of small business financing. The RBA reduced the cash rate by 425 basis points between August 2008 and May 2009, but interest on small business loans fell by only about 230 points.

The skill for 2010 will be judging when to invest in new products and services, increasing advertising and marketing, upgrading information technology and staff training to capture market share.

In the scramble, some raised investment capital to reassure the banks. Tasmanian training company Esset Group found four private investors in May and suddenly the banks were knocking on the company's door. Last September, the RBA's head of economic analysis, Tony Richards, warned of a housing bubble risk in 2010 because of too few new houses.

For small business owners, many of whom secure their bank debt or overdrafts against their own homes, this is a worry. The RBA's decision to raise interest rates in December was a close call; its next decision might be to keep rates on hold. Low rates and constrained supply have the makings of a bubble. Learning to do without debt will serve small businesses well in 2010. Many will need capital to invest in 2010, but secured bank debt will be expensive and risky. Borrowing against the company debtors may offer a low-risk alternative and the cheapest option.

Staff

Business busted a gut to keep staff during the downturn. The pain of staff shortages was all too fresh in most leaders' minds and many cut back working hours across the board rather than laying off individuals. This left them with latent capacity when needed or so they thought.

Surprisingly, many staff that accepted part-time hours don't want to return to full-time work. Some companies now find their contracts leave them no power to insist. Once again, they are scrambling for talent.

Meanwhile, staff are feeling 'trapped', the general manager of Hay Group Australia and New Zealand, Henriette Rothschild, says. 'Over the last year, there has been a prisoner mentality with staff,' Rothschild asserts.

New markets

While loving existing customers was an effective downturn strategy, grabbing market share is for upturns. The decision on when to move and when to hold back will be one of the toughest of the new year. For those with capital there will still be opportunities to increase market share by buying struggling rivals.

But there are other market opportunities going begging. Despite the downturn, the market for healthy and sustainable products grew by 27 per cent, from $15 billion to $19 billion in the past year, a report by market researcher Mobium Group has found.

Included in the category are products such as organic food, alternative therapies, 'natural' cleaning, health and beauty products, water and energy-saving devices, which have all seen rapid growth. Government pump priming in areas such as roofing insulation and solar hot water contributed strongly to the increase.

Widespread cynicism about greenwashing means companies must shift their green marketing strategies, Mobium director Andy Baker says. Offering carbon credits is out. Products need to provide tangible saving or health benefits. As green becomes mainstream, Baker predicts the market will reach $27 billion by 2012.

Last year's global survey by Boston Consulting Group of 12 000 women in 22 countries, including 480 in Australia, identified a $US5 trillion ($5.6 trillion) market opportunity. Women, the survey found, wanted better service from the investment industry, the car industry, banks, insurers and their doctors.

Source: Kath Walters, 'Managing the recovery', *Business Review Weekly*, January–Feburay 2010.

Critical thinking questions:
1. Investigate the Australian Business Excellence Framework. What other companies have won this award and what change processes did they implement?
2. The article lists a number of challenges and possible responses by business to the economic downturn. What role can OD play in facilitating organisations' reactions to the challenges?

Developing vertical linkages

GSCOs also must create channels of communication and influence upward to governmental and policy-level decision-making processes. These higher-level decisions often affect the creation and eventual success of GSCO activities. For example, the Global Village of Beijing (GVB) is a nongovernmental organisation that raises the environmental consciousness of people in China. GVB leveraged its relationships with journalists and the government to produce a weekly television series on government channels to discuss and promote environmentally friendly practices, such as recycling and to expose the Chinese people to environmental projects in different countries. When the Chinese government proposed new environmental regulations and policies as part of the World Trade Organization admission process, GVB helped assess the proposals.[47] More recently, GVB's founder, Liao Xiaoyi, sat on Beijing's successful 2008 Summer Olympics Committee and drafted a 'green Olympics movement' proposal that addressed concerns about Beijing's pollution.[48]

Vertical linkages[49] can also be developed by building on a strong record of success. The Institute of Cultural Affairs (ICA) is concerned with the 'application of methods of human development to communities and organisations all around the world'. With more than 100 offices in 39 nations, ICA trains and consults with small groups, communities, organisations and voluntary associations, in addition to providing leadership training for village leaders, conducting community education programs and running ecological preservation projects. Its reputation has led to recognition and credibility: it was given consultative status by the United Nations in 1985 and it has category II status with the Food and Agriculture Organization, working relation status with the World Health Organization and consultative status with UNICEF.

Change agent roles and skills

Planned change in GSCOs is a relatively new application of organisation development in international settings. The number of practitioners is small but growing and the skills and knowledge necessary to carry out OD in these situations are being developed. The grassroots, political and ideological natures of many international GSCOs require change agent roles and skills that are quite different from those in more formal, domestic settings. GSCO change agents typically occupy stewardship and bridging roles. The *steward* role derives from the ideological and grassroots activities associated with GSCOs. It asks the change agent to be a co-learner or co-participant in achieving global social change. This type of change is 'sustainable', or ecologically, politically, culturally and economically balanced. Change agents must, therefore, work from an explicit value base that is aligned with GSCO activities. For example, change agents are not usually asked, 'What are your credentials to carry out this project?' Instead, practitioners are asked, 'Do you share our values?' or 'What do you think of the plight of the people we are serving?' Stewardship implies an orientation towards the development of sustainable solutions to local and global problems.

The second role, *bridging*, derives from the grassroots and political activities of many GSCOs. Bridging is an appropriate title for this role because it metaphorically reflects the core activities of GSCOs and the change agents who work with them. Both are mainly concerned with connecting and integrating diverse elements of societies and communities towards sustainable change and with transferring ideas among individuals, groups, organisations and societies.

Carrying out the steward and the bridging roles requires communication, negotiation and networking skills. Communication and negotiation skills are essential for GSCO change agents because of the asymmetrical power bases extant in grassroots development efforts. GSCOs are relatively powerless compared with governments, wealthy upper classes and formal organisations. Given the diverse social systems involved, there often is no consensus about a GSCO's objectives. Moreover, different constituencies may have different interests and there may be histories of antagonism among groups that make promulgation of the development project difficult. The steward and the bridging roles require persuasive articulation of the GSCO's ideology and purpose at all times, under many conditions and to everyone involved.

Application 10.4 proposes that a company's documents are one of its most valuable resources, yet they often are not stored or archived properly and it is the change agent who can identify weaknesses and recommend improvements. Proficient and effective communication requires sophisticated information management and GSCOs can be advantaged by utilising these processes.

Record breakers

Businesses in so-called 'information-rich' professions such as the law spend 20 hours a week tracking down hard-to-find information in their archives as the amount of data and information companies are expected to keep increases – and gets more complicated.

A study reveals that individual records managers spend, on average, more than three hours a week searching for more awkward records. The task is getting bigger as information managers need to track more informal information from internet and mobile sources.

Unless businesses improve access and retrieval for users, they will continue to waste valuable time in searching for records, independent information technology analyst John Brand says, particularly when it comes to compliance requirements, legal discovery and better managing records at a remote location. 'It's only going to get more difficult to manage information, with the evolution of remote and mobile computing technology and enterprise Web 2.0,' Brand says.

The study, commissioned by information infrastructure provider EMC Corporation, found few organisations with documents relating to commitments and obligations made by staff that were recorded properly.

Records managers underestimate the effort required to locate records inside their own organisation, Brand says. 'This is because records managers typically have a narrower view of business records and are often more confident of their own classification and retrieval capabilities,' he says.

However, requests for information don't always involve records managers, as a lot of requests are not official legal discovery orders.

Information requests may be investigative projects where employees are looking for early collections of information that may assist in future legal discovery orders, Brand says.

Sophisticated search tools can cut the time spent searching for records, but most new search tools are still too complex for most employees, Monash University records manager Janet Brennen says.

Brennen has more than 15 years' experience managing records at Monash University, the Department of Justice Victoria, St Vincent's Hospital, Melbourne and the CSIRO.

'Investing resources in good systems up front, training staff in how to use them and ensuring they are well maintained pay dividends later on, but few organisations are willing to commit the required time and money,' Brennen says.

The design efficiency of electronic tools and software of record keeping most often frustrates employees, Record Management Association of Australia chief executive Kate Walker says. 'Poor usability impacts on productivity, contribution of content and therefore access and retrievability,' Walker says.

Records managers and the legal fraternity dispute the type of content that should be recorded and archived as the amount of recordable information grows, Brand says.

The adage 'you don't want to keep lunch orders as records' sums up the relationships between the disciplines. However, in a telling case, lunch orders became critical to an investigation when workers on an oil rig were overcome with food poisoning, Brand says.

The research analysed responses from 60 information governance professionals on the strengths and weaknesses in their organisations' information governance processes.

Source: Dan Hall, 'Record breakers', *Business Review Weekly*, 4 February 2010.

The change agent must also be adept at political compromise and negotiation.[50] Asymmetrical power contexts represent strong challenges for stewardship and bridging. To accomplish sustainable change, important trade-offs often are necessary. The effective change agent needs to understand the elements of the ideology that can and cannot be sacrificed and when to fight or walk away from a situation.

Networking skills represent a significant part of the action research process as applied in GSCO settings. Networking takes place at two levels. First, in the steward role, practitioners bring to the GSCO specific knowledge of problem solving, technologies of empowerment using processes that socially construct and make sense of the surrounding conditions and organisation design.[51] The participants bring local knowledge of political players, history, culture and ecology. A 'co-generative dialogue' or 'collective reflection' process emerges when these two frames of reference interact to produce new ideas, possibilities and insights.[52] When both the practitioner and the participants contribute to sustainable solutions, the stewardship role is satisfied.

But bridging also implies making linkages among individual, group, GSCO and social levels of thought. Ideas are powerful fuel in international grassroots development projects. Breakthrough thinking by individuals to see things in new ways can provide the impetus for change at the group, GSCO, social and global levels. This was demonstrated by U2's Bono and US Treasury Secretary Paul O'Neill during their 2002 visit to Africa to understand and develop solutions to poverty. The change agent in international GSCO settings must play a variety of roles and use many skills. Clearly, stewardship and bridging roles are important in facilitating GSCO accomplishment. Other roles and skills will likely emerge over time. Change agents, for example, are finding it increasingly important to develop 'imaginal literacy' skills – the ability to see the possibilities rather than the constraints and the ability to develop sustainable solutions by going outside the boxes to create new ideas.[53]

Summary

This chapter introduces the perspective that change management is complex and inevitable. It also anticipated the future by examining the practice of international organisation development in defined areas. The prevailing economic situation may strongly favour business-oriented over process-oriented interventions. The process of OD under different conditions was also described, although the descriptions are tentative. As OD matures, its methods will become more differentiated and adaptable.

OD activities to improve international, global, multinational and transnational strategic orientations increasingly are in demand. Each of these strategies responds to specific environmental, technological and economic conditions. Interventions in worldwide organisations require a strategic and organisational perspective on change to align people, structures and systems.

Finally, the OD process in global social change organisations was discussed. This relatively new application of OD promotes the establishment of a global civilisation. Strong ideological positions regarding the fair and just distribution of wealth, resources and power fuel this movement. By strengthening local organisations, building horizontal linkages with other like-minded GSCOs and developing vertical linkages with policy-making organisations, a change agent can help the GSCO become more effective and alter its external context. To support roles of stewardship and bridging, change agents need communication, negotiation and networking skills.

Activities

REVIEW QUESTIONS

1 Identify three significant political and economic changes in the past five years that would require businesses to respond accordingly.

2 Explain the three key facets in worldwide strategic orientation. Give examples that are not in the book.

3 What are the characteristics of the global design? How do these differ from the characteristics of the multinational orientation and transnational design?

4 How are global social change organisations (GSCOs) related to creating sustainable change in communities and societies? What is the role of the change agent in this unusual situation?

5 The text suggests that internal differences within GSCOs can emerge as a result of certain developments. What are they?

6 Can a GSCO play the role of an OD consultant? In what circumstances? How?

7 What are the necessary skills to be an effective OD consultant to a GSCO?

DISCUSSION AND ESSAY QUESTIONS

1 'The process of OD under different conditions, in an international context, is tentative.' Explain what is meant by this. What is your opinion?

2 Why are GSCOs important? How can change agents facilitate their processes?

3 Compare and contrast the strategies for change in worldwide organisations. Is there one best way? Why/why not?

4 'Communication and negotiation skills are essential for GSCO change agents because of the asymmetrical power bases extant in grassroots development efforts.' Discuss.

5 'Interventions in worldwide organisations require a strategic and organisational perspective on change to align people, structures and systems.' What do you see as the elements of such a perspective?

SEARCH ME! EXCERCISES

Explore **Search me! management** for relevant articles on change in chaotic and unpredictable environments. Search me! is an online library of world-class journals, ebooks and newspapers, including *The Australian* and *The New York Times*, and is updated daily. Log in to Search me! through www.cengage.com/sso using the access card in the front of this book.

Keywords

Try searching for the following terms:
> Global social change organisations
> Global strategic orientation
> International strategic orientation
> Multinational strategic orientation
> Transnational strategic orientation
> Worldwide organisation development

>> *Search tip:*

Search me! management contains information from both local and international sources. To get the greatest number of search results, try using both Australian and American spellings in your searches, e.g. 'globalisation' and 'globalization'; 'organisation' and 'organization'.

Notes

1 S. Camden-Anders and T. Knott, 'Contrasts in culture: practicing OD globally', in *Global and International Organization Development*, eds P. Sorensen, T. Head, T. Yaeger and D. Cooperrider (Chicago: Stipes Publishing, 2001).

2 L. Bourgeois and M. Boltvinik, 'OD in cross-cultural settings: Latin America', *California Management Review*, 23 (Spring 1981): 75–81; L. Brown, 'Is organization development culture bound?' *Academy of Management Newsletter* (Winter 1982); P. Evans, 'Organization development in the transnational enterprise', in *Research in Organizational Change and Development*,

vol. 3, eds R. Woodman and W. Pasmore (Greenwich, Conn.: JAI Press, 1989): 1–38; R. Marshak, 'Lewin meets Confucius: a re-view of the OD model of change', *Journal of Applied Behavioral Science*, 29 (1997): 400–2; A. Chin and C. Chin, *Internationalizing OD: Cross-Cultural Experiences of NTL Members* (Alexandria, VA.: NTL Institute, 1997); A. Shevat, 'Practicing OD with a technology-driven global company', *OD Practitioner*, 33 (2001): 28–35.

3 B. Moore, 'The service profit chain – a tale of two airlines', unpublished master's thesis (Pepperdine University, 1999). The other examples come from

fieldwork projects in Pepperdine University's Master of Science in Organization Development program.

4 T. Friedman, *The World is Flat* (New York: Farrar, Straus and Giroux, 2006); T. Peters, 'Prometheus barely unbound', *Academy of Management Executive*, 4 (1990): 70–84; Evans, 'Organization development', op. cit.: 3–23; L. Thurow, *The Future of Capitalism* (New York: Morrow, 1996).

5 D. H. Burger, *The Applicability of Logotherapy as an Organisation Development Intervention*, November 2007, http://ujdigispace.uj.ac.za:8080/dspace/bitstream/ 10210/2541/1/01%20Abstract,cover,statement,acknow ledgements.pdf.

6 C. Fuchs, 'Organizational development under political, economic and natural crisis', in Sorensen et al., eds, *Global and International Organization Development*, op. cit.: 248–58.

7 J. Bhagwati, *In Defense of Globalization* (New York: Oxford University Press, 2004); Friedman, *The World is Flat*, op. cit.

8 'A survey of multinationals: big is back', *Economist*, 24 (June 1995).

9 Dr D. Cole, 'RODC', *Organization Development Journal*, 25:2 (Organization Development Institute, 2007), http://view.fdu.edu/files/futodenablsusbus.pdf.

10 C. Bartlett, S. Ghoshal and J. Birkinshaw, *Transnational Management*, 4th edn (New York: McGraw-Hill, 2004).

11 H. Lancaster, 'Global managers need boundless sensitivity, rugged constitutions', *Wall Street Journal* (13 October 1998): B1.

12 Bartlett, Ghoshal and Birkinshaw, *Transnational Management*, op. cit.; D. Heenan and H. Perlmutter, *Multinational Organization Development* (Reading, MA: Addison-Wesley, 1979); Evans, 'Organisation Development', op. cit.: 15–16; C. Bartlett, Y. Doz and G. Hedlund, *Managing the Global Firm* (London: Routledge, 1990).

13 Bartlett, Ghoshal and Birkinshaw, *Transnational Management*, op. cit.

14 H. Lee, 'Factors that influence expatriate failure: an interview study', *International Journal of Management*, 24 (2007): 403–15; L. Littrell, E. Salas, K. Hess, M. Paley and S. Riedel, 'Expatriate preparation: a critical analysis of 25 years of cross-cultural training research', *Human Resource Development Review*, 5 (September, 2006): 355–89; R. Tung, 'Expatriate assignments: enhancing success and minimizing failure', *Academy of Management Executive* (Summer 1987): 117–26; A. Mamman, 'Expatriate adjustment: dealing with hosts' attitudes in a foreign assignment', *Journal of Transitional Management Development*, 1 (1995).

15 M. Ihlwan, 'Doing a bang-up business', *Business Week* (18 May 1999): 50.

16 A. D. Kodwani, 'Human resource outsourcing: issues and challenges', *The Journal of Nepalese Business Studies*, IV:1 (December 2007), www.nepjol.info/index.php/JNBS/ article/viewFile/1028/1043.

17 J. W. Bernardzon, *Staffing Policies of Swedish MNCs* (January 2010), http://epubl.ltu.se/1402-1552/2010/ 032/LTU-DUPP-10032-SE.pdf.

18 Heenan and Perlmutter, *Multinational Organization Development*, op. cit.: 13.

19 J. Main, 'How to go global – and why', *Fortune* (28 August 1989): 76.

20 Heenan and Perlmutter, *Multinational Organization Development*, op. cit.: 20.

21 M. Rozkwitalska, 'Cultural dilemmas of international management', *Journal of Intercultural Management*, 1:1 (April 2009): 91–9, www.joim.pl/pdf/Rozkwitalska.pdf.

22 S. Dowd, *Nonprofit Merger as an Opportunity for Survival and Growth*, Library Strategies Consulting Group, The Friends of the Saint Paul Public Library, 2009, www.mapfornonprofits.org/vertical/Sites/ %7B876C4FB8-E997-480F-BF5B-AFAA0F113D9D%7D/ uploads/%7B71BC22A6-931B-45AF-84EC- 8F9A07113E70%7D.PDF.

23 Thurow, *The Future of Capitalism*, op. cit.

24 A. Borrus, 'The stateless corporation', *Business Week* (14 May 1990): 101–3.

25 Heenan and Perlmutter, *Multinational Organisation Development*, op. cit.: 20.

26 T. Stewart, 'A way to measure worldwide success', *Fortune* (15 March 1999): 196–8.

27 Evans, 'Organization development', op. cit.

28 J. Galbraith, *Designing the Global Corporation* (San Francisco: Jossey-Bass, 2000); C. Bartlett and S. Ghoshal, 'Organizing for worldwide effectiveness: the transnational solution', *California Management Review* (Fall 1988): 54–74.

29 R. Sanders, 'In the twilight of two states: the "German House" in Tekmok, Kazakhstan', *Antrhopological Notebooks*, 15:1: 37–47, ISSN 1408-032X, © Slovene Anthropological Society 2009, Max Planck Institute for Social Anthropology, www.drustvo-antropologov.si/AN/ PDF/2009_1/Anthropological_Notebooks_XV_1_ Sanders.pdf.

30 Main, 'How to go global', op. cit.: 73.

31 Evans, 'Organization development in the transnational enterprise', op. cit.

32 P. McMichael, *Development and Social Change: A Global Perspective* (Thousand Oaks, CA: Pine Forge Press, 2007); L. Brown and J. Covey, 'Development organizations and organization development: toward an expanded paradigm for organization development', in *Research in Organizational Change and Development*, vol. 1, eds R. Woodman and W. Pasmore (Greenwich, Conn.: JAI Press, 1987): 59–88; P. Tuecke, 'Rural international development', in *Discovering Common Ground*, ed. M. Weisbord (San Francisco: Berrett-Koehler, 1993).

33 P. Freire, *Pedagogy of the Oppressed* (Harmondsworth, England: Penguin, 1972); D. Bornstein, *How to Change the World: Social Entrepreneurs and the Power of New Ideas* (New York: Oxford, 2004); T. Kidder, *Mountains Beyond Mountains* (New York: Random House, 2003); H. Perlmutter and E. Trist, 'Paradigms for societal transition', *Human Relations*, 39 (1986): 1–27; F. Westley, 'Bob Geldof and Live Aid: the affective side of global social innovation', *Human Relations*, 44 (1991): 1011–36; D. Cooperrider and W. Pasmore, 'Global social change: a new agenda for social science', *Human Relations*, 44 (1991): 1037–55; H. Perlmutter, 'On the rocky road to the first global civilization', *Human Relations*, 44 (1991): 897–920; E. Boulding, 'The old and new transnationalism: an evolutionary perspective', *Human Relations*, 44 (1991): 789–805; P. Johnson and D. Cooperrider, 'Finding a path with a heart: global social change organizations and their challenge for the field of organizational development', in *Research in Organizational Change and Development*, vol. 5, eds R. Woodman and W. Pasmore (Greenwich, Conn.: JAI Press, 1991): 223–84.

34 D. Cooperrider and T. Thachankary, 'Building the global civic culture: making our lives count', in Sorensen et al. eds, *Global and International Organization Development*, op. cit.: 282–306; Brown and Covey, 'Development organizations', op. cit.

35 E. Smith, 'Growth vs. environment', *Business Week* (11 May 1992): 66–75.

36 D. Cooperrider and J. Dutton, eds, *Organizational Dimensions of Global Change* (Newbury Park, Calif.: Sage Publications, 1999): 12.

37 L. Brown, 'Bridging organizations and sustainable development', *Human Relations*, 44 (1991): 807–31; Johnson and Cooperrider, 'Finding a path', op. cit.; Cooperrider and Thachankary, 'Building the global civil culture', op. cit.

38 L. D. Brown and D. Ashman, 'Social capital, mutual influence and social learning in intersectoral problem solving in Africa and Asia', in Cooperrider and Dutton, eds, *Organisational Dimensions of Global Change*, op. cit.: 139–67.

39 F. Westley, 'Not on our watch', in Cooperrider and Dutton, eds, *Organisational Dimensions of Global Change*, op. cit.: 88–113.

40 Brown and Covey, 'Development organisations', op. cit.

41 P. Reason and H. Bradbury, eds, *The SAGE Handbook of Action Research*, 2nd edn (Newbury Park, CA: Sage Publications, 2007).

42 Johnson and Cooperrider, 'Finding a path', op. cit.: 240–1.

43 ibid.: 237.

44 S. Md Nordin, *The Impact of Formalization and Centralization on Organizational Communication: A Study on a Highway Concessionaire in the Klang Valley*, Malaysia, ANZCA09 Communication, Creativity and Global Citizenship. Brisbane, July 2009, www.cpe.qut.edu.au/conferences/2009/anzca/proceedings/Nordin_Halib_Ghazali_ANZCA09.pdf.

45 M. Bratton, 'Non-governmental organisations in Africa: can they influence public policy?' *Development and Change*, 21 (1989): 81–118.

46 www.aai.org.au/.

47 Personal communication with members of the Global Village of Beijing, 28 March 2000.

48 Bornstein, *How to Change the World*, op. cit.; L. Brown and J. Covey, 'Action research for grassroots development: collective reflection and development NGOS in Asia' (presentation at the Academy of Management, Miami, 1990).

49 M. U. Dimelu and A. C. Anyanwu, 'Linkage behavior and practices of agencies in the agricultural innovation transfer sub system in Southeastern Nigeria: issues for agricultural extension policy', *Journal of Agricultural Extension*, 12:2 (December 2008), Department of Agricultural Extension, University of Nigeria, Nsukka, http://ajol.info/index.php/jae/article/viewFile/47046/33429.

50 R. Saner and L. Yiu, 'Porous boundary and power politics: contextual constraints of organisation development change projects in the United Nations organisations', *Gestalt Review*, 6 (2002): 84–94.

51 D. Cooperrider and S. Srivastva, 'Appreciative inquiry in organizational life', in *Research in Organizational Change and Development*, vol. 1, eds R. Woodman and W. Pasmore (Greenwich, Conn.: JAI Press, 1987): 129–69; Cooperrider and Dutton, *Organisational Dimensions of Global Change*, op. cit.

52 Brown and Covey, 'Action research', op. cit.; M. Elden and M. Levin, 'Cogenerative learning: bringing participation into action research', in *Participatory Action Research*, ed. W. Whyte (Newbury Park, Calif.: Sage Publications, 1991): 127–42.

53 E. Boulding, *Building a Global Civic Culture: Education for an Interdependent World* (Syracuse, N.Y.: Syracuse University Press, 1988).

CHAPTER 11

Competitive and collaborative strategies

This chapter describes transformation interventions that help organisations implement strategies for both competing and collaborating with other organisations. These change programs are relatively recent additions to the OT field. They focus on helping organisations position themselves strategically in their social and economic environments and achieve a better fit with the external forces affecting goal achievement and performance. Practitioners are discovering that additional knowledge and skills in such areas as marketing, finance, economics, political science and complexity theory are necessary to implement these significant interventions.

Organisations are open systems and must relate to their environments. They must acquire the resources and information needed to function, and they must deliver products or services that customers value. An organisation's strategy – how it acquires resources and delivers outputs – is shaped by particular aspects and features of the environment. For example, cigarette manufacturers faced with increasing regulation and declining demand in New Zealand and Australia increased distribution to other countries and diversified into other industries, such as foods, beverages and consumer products. Thus, organisations can devise a number of competitive and collaborative responses for managing environmental interfaces. Competitive responses – such as creating or clarifying mission statements and goals, developing new strategies or creating special units to respond to the environment – help the organisation to outperform rivals. Collaborative responses, such as forming strategic alliances with other organisations and developing networks, seek to improve performance by joining with others. These often result in dramatic and chaotic change which is called organisation transformation (OT).

The OT interventions described in this chapter help organisations gain a comprehensive understanding of their environments and devise appropriate responses to external demands. The chapter begins with an elaboration of the organisational environments; then two categories of interventions are described: competitive strategies and collaborative strategies.

Competitive strategies[1] include integrated strategic change, mergers and acquisitions. Integrated strategic change is a comprehensive OT intervention aimed at a single organisation or business unit. It suggests that business strategy and organisation design must be aligned and changed together to respond to external and internal disruptions. A strategic change plan helps members manage the transition between the current strategic orientation and the desired future strategic orientation.

Mergers and acquisitions represent a second strategy of competition. These interventions seek to leverage the strengths (or shore up the weaknesses) of one organisation by combining with another organisation. This complex strategic change involves integrating many of the interventions previously discussed in this text, including human process, technostructural and human resource management interventions. Research and practice in mergers and acquisitions strongly suggest that OT practices can contribute to implementation success.

Collaborative strategies include alliances and networks. Alliance interventions – including joint ventures, franchising and long-term contracts – help to develop the relationship between two organisations that believe the benefits of co-operation outweigh the costs of lowered autonomy and control. These increasingly common arrangements require each organisation to understand its goals and strategy in the relationship, build and leverage trust, and ensure that it is receiving the expected benefits. Finally – and building on the knowledge of alliances – network development interventions are concerned with helping sets of three or more organisations engage in relationships to perform tasks or to solve problems that are too complex and multifaceted for a single organisation to resolve. These multi-organisation systems abound in today's environment and include research and development consortia, public–private partnerships and constellations of profit-seeking organisations. They tend to be loosely coupled and non-hierarchical, and consequently they require methods different from most traditional OD interventions that are geared to single organisations. These methods involve helping organisations recognise the need for partnerships and the development of co-ordinating structures for carrying out multi-organisation activities.

ENVIRONMENTAL FRAMEWORK

The framework is based on the concept that organisations and their sub-units are *open systems*[2] existing in environmental contexts. Environments can be described in two ways. First, there are different types of environments consisting of specific components or forces. To survive and grow, organisations must understand these different environments, select appropriate parts to respond to, and develop effective relationships with them. A manufacturing firm, for example, must understand raw materials markets, labour markets, customer segments and production technology alternatives. It then must select from a range of raw material suppliers, applicants for employment, customer demographics and production technologies to achieve desired outcomes effectively. Organisations are thus dependent on their environments. They need to manage external constraints and contingencies, and take advantage of external opportunities. They also need to influence the environment in favourable directions through such methods as political lobbying, advertising and public relations.

Second, several useful dimensions capture the nature of organisational environments. Some environments are rapidly changing and complex, and so require organisational responses different from those in environments that are stable and simple. For example, breakfast cereal manufacturers face a stable market and use well-understood production technologies. Their strategy and organisation design issues are radically different from those of software developers, which face product life cycles measured in months instead of years, where labour skills are rare and hard to find, and where demand can change drastically overnight.

In this section, we first describe different types of environments that can affect organisations. Then we identify environmental dimensions that influence organisational responses to external forces. This material provides an introductory context for describing two kinds of interventions – competitive strategies and collaborative strategies – that represent ways organisations can change dramatically as a response to their environments.

Environmental types and dimensions

Organisational environments are everything beyond the boundaries of organisations that can indirectly or directly affect performance and outcomes. There are two classes of environments: the general environment and the task environment; plus the enacted environment, which reflects members' perceptions of the general and task environments.

The *general environment* consists of all external forces that can influence an organisation, including technological, legal and regulatory, political, economic, social and ecological components. The *task environment*[3] consists of the specific individuals and organisations that interact directly with the organisation and can affect goal achievement: customers, suppliers, competitors, producers of substitute products or services, labour unions, financial institutions and so on. The *enacted environment*[4] consists of the organisation members' perception and representation of its general and task environments. Only the enacted environment can affect which organisational responses are chosen. The general and task environments, however, can influence whether those responses are successful or ineffective.

Environments also can be characterised along dimensions that describe the organisation's context and influence its responses. The key dimension of the environment affecting information processing is *information uncertainty*, or the degree to which environmental information is ambiguous. Another key dimension is *resource dependence*, or the degree to which an organisation relies on other organisations for resources. These two environmental dimensions can be combined to show the degree to which organisations are constrained by their environments and consequently must be responsive to their demands.

Organisations must have the capacity to monitor and make sense of their environments if they are to respond appropriately. Organisations employ a number of methods to influence and respond to their environments, to buffer their technology from external disruptions, and to link themselves to sources of information and resources. OT practitioners can help organisations implement competitive and collaborative responses.

The two types of interventions discussed in this chapter derive from this environmental framework. Competitive interventions, such as integrated strategic change and mergers and acquisitions, focus on sets of administrative and competitive responses to help an individual organisation improve its performance. Collaborative interventions, such as alliances and networks, utilise a variety of collective responses to co-ordinate the actions of multiple organisations.

COMPETITIVE STRATEGIES

These interventions are concerned with choices organisations can make to improve their competitive performance. They include integrated strategic change and mergers and acquisitions. Competitive strategies use a variety of responses to better align the organisation with pressing environmental demands. To establish a competitive advantage, organisations must achieve a favoured position vis-à-vis their competitors or perform internally in ways that are unique, valuable and difficult to imitate.[5] Although typically associated with commercial firms, these competitive criteria can also apply to not-for-profit and governmental organisations. Activities that are unique, valuable and difficult to imitate enhance the organisation's performance by establishing a competitive advantage over its rivals.

- *Uniqueness.* A fundamental assumption in competitive strategies is that all organisations possess a unique bundle of resources and processes. Individually or in combination, they represent the source of competitive advantage. An important task in any competitive strategy is to understand these unique organisational features. For example, resources can be financial (such as access to low-cost capital), reputational (such as brand image or a history of product quality), technological (such as patents, know-how or a strong research and development department) and human (such as excellent labour–management relationships or scarce and valuable skill sets). Bill Gates's knowledge of IBM's need for an operating system on the one hand and the availability of the disk operating system (DOS) on the other hand represent a powerful case for how resources alone can represent a unique advantage.

  An organisation's processes – regular patterns of organisational activity involving a sequence of tasks performed by individuals[6] – use resources to produce goods and services. For example, a software development process combines computer resources, programming languages, typing skills, knowledge of computer languages and customer requirements to produce a new software application. Other organisational processes include new product development, strategic planning, appraising member performance, making sales calls, fulfilling customer orders and the like. When resources and processes are formed into capabilities that allow the organisation to perform complex activities better than others, a distinctive competence or 'hedgehog concept' is identified.[7] Collins found that a key determinant in an organisation's transition from 'good to great' was a clear understanding and commitment to the one thing an organisation does better than anyone else.

- *Value.* Organisations achieve competitive advantage when their unique resources and processes are arranged in such a way that products or services either warrant a higher-than-average price or are exceptionally low in cost. Both advantages are valuable according to a performance–price criterion. Products and services with highly desirable features or capabilities, although expensive, are valuable because of their ability to satisfy customer demands for high quality or some other performance dimension. BMW automobiles are valuable because the perceived benefits of superior handling exceed the price paid. On the other hand, outputs that cost little to produce are valuable because of their ability to satisfy customer demands at a low price. Hyundai automobiles are valuable because they provide basic transportation at a low price. BMW and Hyundai are both profitable, but they achieve that outcome through different value propositions.

- *Difficult to imitate.* Finally, competitive advantage is sustainable when unique and valuable resources and processes are difficult to mimic or duplicate by other organisations.[8] Organisations have devised a number of methods for making imitation difficult. For example, they can protect their competitive advantage by making it difficult for other businesses to identify their distinctive competence. Disclosing unimportant information at trade shows or forgoing superior profits can make it difficult for competitors to identify an organisation's strengths. Organisations also can aggressively pursue a range of opportunities, thus raising the cost for competitors who try to replicate their success. Finally, organisations can seek to retain key human resources through attractive compensation and reward practices, thereby making it more difficult and costly for competitors to attract such talent.

The success of a competitive strategy depends on organisation responses that result in unique, valuable and difficult-to-imitate advantages. This section describes two OT interventions that can assist individual organisations in developing these advantages and managing strategic change.

Integrated strategic change

Integrated strategic change (ISC) is a recent intervention that extends traditional OD processes into the content-oriented discipline of strategic management. Discussed more fully in Chapter 9, ISC is a deliberate, co-ordinated process that leads gradually or radically to systemic realignments between the environment and a business's strategic orientation, and that results in improvement in performance and effectiveness.[9]

The ISC process was developed in response to managers' complaints that good business strategies often are not implemented. Implementation occurs as middle managers, supervisors and employees hear about the new strategy through memos, restructuring announcements, changes in job responsibilities or new departmental objectives. Consequently, because participation has been limited to top management, there is little understanding of the need for change and little ownership of the new behaviours, initiatives and tactics required to achieve the announced objectives.

Mergers and acquisitions

Mergers and acquisitions (M&As) involve the combination of two organisations. The term *merger* refers to the integration of two previously independent organisations into a completely new organisation, while *acquisition* involves the purchase of one organisation by another for integration into the acquiring organisation. M&As are distinct from the strategies of collaboration described later in this chapter because at least one of the organisations ceases to exist. The stressful dynamics associated with M&As led one researcher to call them the 'ultimate change management challenge'.[10]

M&A rationale

Organisations have a number of reasons for wanting to acquire or merge with other organisations, including diversification or vertical integration; gaining access to global markets, technology or other resources; and achieving operational efficiencies, improved innovation or resource sharing.[11] As a result, M&As have become a preferred method for rapid growth and strategic change. In 2002, for example, over 6900 M&A deals worth $458.7 billion were conducted in the United States; globally, over 23 500 deals worth $1.4 trillion were registered according to the Dealogic market research firm.[12] Some examples of large transactions are Oracle and Peoplesoft, HP and Compaq, AOL and Time/Warner, Chrysler and Daimler-Benz, Ford and Volvo, and Boeing and McDonnell Douglas. Despite M&A popularity, they have a questionable record of success.[13] Among the reasons commonly cited for merger failure are inadequate due diligence processes, the lack of a compelling strategic rationale, unrealistic expectations of synergy, paying too much for the transaction, conflicting corporate cultures and failure to move quickly.[14]

M&A interventions typically are preceded by an examination of corporate and business strategy. *Corporate strategy* describes the range of businesses within which the organisation will participate, while *business strategy* specifies how the organisation will compete in any particular business. Organisations must decide whether their corporate and strategic goals should be achieved through strategic change, such as ISC, a merger or acquisition, or a collaborative response, such as alliances or networks. Mergers and acquisitions are preferred when internal development is considered too slow, or when alliances or networks do not offer sufficient control over key resources to meet the organisation's objectives.

In addition to the OT issues described here, M&As are complex strategic changes that involve legal and financial knowledge beyond the scope of this text. OT practitioners are encouraged to seek out and work with specialists in these other relevant disciplines. The focus here is on how OT can contribute to M&A success.

India outsourcing offers future vision

Amid the bustle of north Mumbai, the headquarters of Pangea3, one of India's biggest legal outsourcers, is enough to give a European corporate lawyer the heebie-jeebies.

Unlike the slick environs of Europe's legal precincts, the street outside is busy with scavengers picking through the morning garbage, while hawkers throng in the sidestreets.

Inside, the scene is just as alien – more reminiscent of the bridge of the Starship Enterprise than of a traditional London law firm.

Hardly anybody is wearing a suit, there are no private offices and there is not a wood-panelled boardroom in sight. Instead, an army of young Indian graduates, largely from the country's top law and engineering schools, sits before a barrage of computer terminals.

Many are working on legal documents digitally accessed from the servers of blue-chip Western clients via intercontinental fibre-optic cables.

Others are engaged in research for litigation to be fought out in US courtrooms, or analysing patent filings registered by British companies.

Most striking, perhaps, are the giant perspex tubes that tower above the large open-plan office. Accessible via spiral staircases, they contain raised meeting rooms.

Together with the fingerprint scanners that operate the locks on the doors, they lend the premises a sci-fi feel.

This may be fitting: if Sanjay Kamlani, the firm's co-chief executive (and one of the few workers wearing a tie) is right, this is the future of the corporate legal profession.

It is a vision that could radically change Britain's legal business.

Much of the work that Pangea3 and similar firms deal with, such as drafting derivatives contracts or conducting due diligence for mergers and acquisitions, was once the preserve of trainees and associates at big City law firms. Some of those firms racked up annual revenue of more than £1 billion during the boom years, in part by billing out teams of junior lawyers at up to £300 an hour for even the most routine tasks.

However, those firms, in a drive to cut costs, are beginning to send that sort of work to cheaper locations, such as India, South Africa and the Philippines.

A recruit at a magic-circle firm in London can expect a starting salary of about £60 000 ($105 650), rising to more than £90 000 at the best-paid firms, but Pangea3 can pay a good Indian law graduate as little as Rs350 000 ($8275) a year.

That sort of cost saving has proved compelling since the economic downturn and demand for Indian outsourcers is soaring.

Studies suggest as many as 10 000 lawyers in India are working for outsourcers, and total revenue in the sector is expected to double this year to $US1 billion ($1.12 billion) and rise to $US4 billion within five years.

Pangea3's turnover doubled last year, and a similar increase was likely this year, Mr Kamlani said. The company's investors include Sequoia, the venture capital group that backed Google. Its clients include several leading Wall Street banks.

Although the drive to outsource legal work began with banks and big companies that saw an opportunity to reduce the time their internal lawyers spent handling routine matters, law firms have also embraced it as they seek drastic cuts in costs.

Most of the City of London's leading firms are believed to have at least explored the possibility of sending work overseas or to cheaper locations in Britain, and several have established pilot schemes.

Among magic-circle firms, Allen & Overy has used providers in India for matters such as reviewing documents, and Clifford Chance has established a centre in Delhi that is growing and expected to employ 30 lawyers this year.

Mr Kamlani said he had been visited by several big City firms.

'Attitudes are changing,' he said. 'We are being visited by some of the most senior managing partners in the UK. They are thinking strategically about how to make their businesses more dynamic.'

Sam Waller, a senior manager in the consulting division of accounting firm Deloitte, said law firms were responding to pressure from clients to reduce fees.

'Clients themselves have successfully outsourced parts of their businesses, so they don't see why law firms shouldn't do the same,' he said.

The commercial legal market was shaken by the downturn and many senior partners expect the double-digit growth of the boom years will not return for some time. Instead, the sector is reshaping itself. Some top firms expect they will have to be leaner to retain profitability, with fewer associates for each partner. They plan to focus exclusively on high-end work for which clients will continue to pay top rates, while less valuable work will be farmed out.

That will have consequences for junior lawyers, for whom long hours trawling through documents has been an integral part of their training. They are already under fire after a wave of redundancies and salary freezes.

Legal technology consultant Richard Susskind said clients were no longer prepared to subsidise the training of junior lawyers by paying high fees. Law firms may have to cut salaries to remain competitive, he said.

Source: Rhys Blakely, Mumbai, Alex Spence, 'India outsourcing offers future vision',
© *The Times*, January 15, 2010, nisyndication.com.

Critical thinking questions:
1. What is the greatest impact on businesses with this type of outsourcing arrangement? If training is no longer valued, whose role is it to prepare employees for such a transition?
2. What do you think will be the future of such an organisation? Explain your answer with examples.

Application stages

Mergers and acquisitions involve three major phases as shown in Table 11.1: precombination, legal combination and operational combination.[15] OT practitioners can make substantive contributions to the precombination and operational combination phases.

Precombination phase

This first phase consists of planning activities designed to ensure the success of the combined organisation. The organisation that initiates the OT change must identify a candidate organisation, work with it to gather information about each other, and plan the implementation and integration activities. The evidence is growing that precombination activities are critical to M&A success.[16]

1 *Search for and select candidate*. This involves developing screening criteria to assess and narrow the field of candidate organisations, agreeing on a first-choice

TABLE 11.1 Major phases and activities in merger and acquisitions

Major M&A phases	Key steps	OD and change management issues
Precombination	• Search for and select candidate • Create M&A team • Establish business case • Perform due diligence assessment • Develop merger integration plan	• Ensure that candidates are screened for cultural as well as financial, technical and physical asset criteria • Define a clear leadership structure • Establish a clear strategic vision, competitive strategy and systems integration potential • Specify the desirable organisation design features • Specify an integration action plan
Legal combination	• Complete financial negotiations • Close the deal • Announce the combination	
Operational combination	• Day 1 activities • Organisational and technical integration activities • Cultural integration activities	• Implement changes quickly • Communicate • Solve problems together and focus on the customer • Conduct an evaluation to learn and identify further areas of integration planning

candidate, assessing regulatory compliance, establishing initial contacts and formulating a letter of intent. Criteria for choosing an M&A partner can include leadership and management characteristics, market-access resources, technical or financial capabilities, physical facilities and so on. OT practitioners can add value at this stage of the process by encouraging screening criteria that include managerial, organisational and cultural components, as well as technical and financial aspects. In practice, financial issues tend to receive greater attention at this stage, with the goal of maximising shareholder value. Failure to attend to cultural and organisational issues, however, can result in diminished shareholder value during the operational combination phase.[17]

Identifying potential candidates, narrowing the field, agreeing on a first choice and checking regulatory compliance are relatively straightforward activities. They generally involve investment brokers and other outside parties who have access to databases of organisational, financial and technical information. The final two activities – making initial contacts and creating a letter of intent – are aimed at determining the candidate's interest in the proposed merger or acquisition.

2 *Create an M&A team.* Once there is initial agreement between the two organisations to pursue a merger or acquisition, senior leaders from the

respective organisations appoint an M&A team to establish the business case, oversee the due diligence process and develop a merger integration plan.[18] This team typically comprises senior executives and experts in such areas as business valuation, technology, organisation and marketing. OT practitioners can facilitate formation of this team through human process interventions, such as team building and process consultation, and help the team establish clear goals and action strategies. They also can help members define a leadership structure, apply relevant skills and knowledge, and ensure that both organisations are represented appropriately. The group's leadership structure, or who will be accountable for the team's accomplishments, is especially critical. In an acquisition, an executive from the acquiring organisation is typically the team's leader. In a merger of equals, the choice of a single individual to lead the team is more difficult, but essential. The outcome of this decision and the process used to make it form the first outward symbol of how this strategic change will be conducted.

3 *Establish the business case.* The purpose of this activity is to develop a prima facie case that combining the two organisations will result in a competitive advantage that exceeds their separate advantages.[19] It includes specifying the strategic vision, competitive strategy and systems integration potential for the M&A. OT practitioners can facilitate this discussion to ensure that each issue is fully explored. If the business case cannot be justified on strategic, financial or operational grounds, the M&A should be revisited or terminated, or another candidate should be sought.

Strategic vision represents the organisations' combined capabilities. It synthesises the strengths of the two organisations into a viable new organisation.

Competitive strategy describes the business model for how the combined organisation will add value in a particular product market or segment of the value chain, how that value proposition is best performed by the combined organisation (compared with competitors) and how it will be difficult to imitate. The purpose of this activity is to force the two organisations to go beyond the rhetoric of 'these two organisations should merge because it's a good fit'.

Systems integration specifies how the two organisations will be combined. It addresses how and if they can work together. It includes the following key questions: Will one organisation be acquired and operated as a wholly owned subsidiary? Does the transaction imply a merger of equals? Are lay-offs implied and, if so, where? On what basis can promised synergies or cost savings be achieved?

4 *Perform a due diligence assessment.* This involves evaluating whether the two organisations actually have the managerial, technical and financial resources that each assumes the other possesses. It includes a comprehensive review of each organisation's articles of incorporation, stock option plans, organisation charts and so on. Financial, human resources, operational, technical and logistical inventories are evaluated along with other legally binding issues. The

discovery of previously unknown or unfavourable information can halt the M&A process.[20]

Although due diligence assessment traditionally emphasises the financial aspects of M&As, this focus is increasingly being challenged by evidence that culture clashes between two organisations can ruin expected financial gains.[21] Thus, attention to the cultural features of M&As is becoming more prevalent in due diligence assessment. The scope and detail of due diligence assessment depends on knowledge of the candidate's business, the complexity of its industry, the relative size and risk of the transaction, and the available resources. Due diligence activities must reflect symbolically the vision and values of the combined organisations. An overly zealous assessment, for example, can contradict promises of openness and trust made earlier in the transaction. Missteps at this stage can lower or destroy opportunities for synergy, cost savings and improved shareholder value.[22]

5 *Develop merger integration plans.* This stage specifies how the two organisations will be combined.[23] It defines integration objectives; the scope and timing of integration activities; organisation design criteria; Day 1 requirements; and who does what, where and when. The scope of these plans depends on how integrated the organisations will be. If the candidate organisation will operate as an independent subsidiary with an 'arm's-length' relationship to the parent, merger integration planning need only specify those systems that will be common to both organisations. A full integration of the two organisations requires a more extensive plan.

Merger integration planning starts with the business case conducted earlier and involves more detailed analyses of the strategic vision, competitive strategy and systems integration for the M&A. For example, assessment of the organisations' markets and suppliers can reveal opportunities to serve customers better and to capture purchasing economies of scale. Examination of business processes can identify: best operating practices; which physical facilities should be combined, left alone or shut down; and which systems and procedures are redundant. Capital budget analysis can show which investments should be continued or dropped. Typically, the M&A team appoints subgroups composed of members from both organisations to perform these analyses. OT practitioners can conduct team-building and process-consultation interventions to improve how those groups function.

Next, plans for designing the combined organisation are developed. They include the organisation's structure, reporting relationships, human resources policies, information and control systems, operating logistics, work designs and customer-focused activities.

The final task of integration planning involves developing an action plan for implementing the M&A. This specifies tasks to be performed, decision-making authority and responsibility, and timelines for achievement. It also includes a process for addressing conflicts and problems that will invariably arise during the implementation process.

Legal combination phase

This phase of the M&A process involves the legal and financial aspects of the transaction. The two organisations settle on the terms of the deal, register the transaction with and gain approval from appropriate regulatory agencies, communicate with and gain approval from shareholders, and file appropriate legal documents. In some cases, an OT practitioner can provide advice on negotiating a fair agreement, but this phase generally requires knowledge and expertise beyond that typically found in OT practice.

Operational combination phase

This final phase involves implementing the merger integration plan. In practice, it begins during due diligence assessment and may continue for months or years following the legal combination phase.[24] OT implementation includes the three kinds of activities described below.

1   *Day 1 activities*. These include communications and actions that officially start the implementation process. For example, announcements may be made about key executives of the combined organisation, the location of corporate headquarters, the structure of tasks, and areas and functions where lay-offs will occur. OT practitioners pay special attention to sending important symbolic messages to organisation members, investors and regulators about the soundness of the merger plans and those changes that are critical to accomplishing strategic and operational objectives.[25]

2   *Operational and technical integration activities*. These involve the physical moves, structural changes, work designs and procedures that will be implemented to accomplish the strategic objectives and expected cost savings of the M&A. The merger integration plan lists these activities, which can be large in number and range in scope from seemingly trivial to quite critical. For example, Westpac's acquisition of the Bank of Melbourne involved changing Bank of Melbourne's employee uniforms, the signage at all banks, marketing and public relations campaigns, repainting buildings and integrating the route structures, among others. When these integration activities are not executed properly, the M&A process can be set back.

3   *Cultural integration activities*.[26] These tasks are aimed at building new values and norms in the combined organisation. Successful implementation melds both the technical and cultural aspects of the combined organisation.

The OT literature contains several practical suggestions for managing the operational combination phase.[27] First, the merger integration plan should be implemented sooner rather than later, and quickly rather than slowly. Integration of two organisations generally involves aggressive financial targets, short timelines and intense public scrutiny.[28] Moreover, the change process is often plagued by culture clashes and political fighting. Consequently, organisations need to make as many changes as possible in the first hundred days following the legal combination phase.[29]

Quick movement in key areas has several advantages: it pre-empts unanticipated organisation changes that might thwart momentum in the desired direction; it reduces organisation members' uncertainty about when things will happen; and it reduces members' anxiety about the M&A's impact on their personal situation. All three of these conditions can prevent desired collaboration and other benefits from occurring.

Second, integration activities must be communicated clearly and in a timely fashion to a variety of stakeholders, including shareholders, regulators, customers and organisation members. M&As can increase uncertainty and anxiety about the future, especially for members of the involved organisations who often inquire: Will I have a job? Will my job change? Will I have a new boss? These kinds of questions can dominate conversations, reduce productive work and spoil opportunities for collaboration. To reduce ambiguity, organisations can provide concrete answers through a variety of channels including company newsletters, email and intranet postings, press releases, video and in-person presentations, one-on-one interaction with managers, and so on.

Third, members from both organisations need to work together to solve implementation problems and to address customer needs. Such co-ordinated tasks can clarify work roles and relationships, and they can contribute to member commitment and motivation. Moreover, when co-ordinated activity is directed at customer service, it can assure customers that their interests will be considered and satisfied during the merger.

Fourth, organisations need to assess the implementation process continually to identify integration problems and needs. The following questions can guide the assessment process:[30]

- Have savings estimated during precombination planning been confirmed or exceeded?[31]
- Has the new entity identified and implemented shared strategies or opportunities?
- Has the new organisation been implemented without loss of key personnel?
- Was the merger and integration process seen as fair and objective?
- Is the combined company operating efficiently?
- Have major problems with stakeholders been avoided?
- Did the process proceed according to schedule?
- Were substantive integration issues resolved?
- Are people highly motivated (more so than before)?

Mergers and acquisitions are among the most complex and challenging interventions facing organisations and OT practitioners.

COLLABORATIVE STRATEGIES

In the previous section, we explored strategies of competition: OT interventions that helped individual organisations cope with environmental dependence and uncertainty by managing their internal resources to achieve competitive advantage and improve performance. Organisations also can cope with environmental pressures by collaborating with other organisations. This section discusses collaborative strategies where two or more organisations agree to work together to achieve their objectives. This represents a fundamental shift in strategic orientation because the strategies, goals, structures and processes of two or more organisations become interdependent and must be co-ordinated and aligned.

The rationale for collaboration is discussed first. Then we describe the process of forming and developing alliances and networks. *Alliance interventions*[32] focus on the relationship between two organisations, while *network interventions* involve three or more organisations. As the number of organisations increases, the scope and complexity of the problems and issues that need to be addressed increase. Alliances can be building blocks for networks, however, and the lessons learned there can be applied to the development of network arrangements. Application 11.2 identifies government departments' desire to adopt smart online technology to improve communication.

11.2

APPLICATION

Virtual conferencing – is your organisation game?

The [Federal] Government's push for greater use and returns from adopting smart online technological solutions is well documented. Initially driven from a cost perspective, the debate has rapidly broadened to espousing many other benefits, including the increasingly critical ease and effectiveness of employee engagement. The benefits of adopting collaborative technologies (technology that permits individuals to participate in real-time, conferencing, learning and collaboration using the tools they already possess, such as a PC and internet access) can be quantified. For example significantly less need to travel, reduced telecommunications costs, more effective and more frequent collaboration and potentially improved work–life balance.

Yellow Edge has been distributing one such technology in the Australian market for almost five years. Elluminate Live is a Canadian developed technology, widely considered the leading online conferencing, collaboration and learning product in the world. Elluminate Live has consistently been included in the Gartner Group's Visionaries Quadrant for Web conferencing. According to Gartner, 'real time collaboration support is becoming a primary requirement, after email, for efficient enterprise communications.' 'Web conferencing not only allows people to collaborate virtually and share information, it also provides facilities to record and capture formal or ad hoc collaborative interactions for later tracking and reuse.

'As organisations develop their collaborative strategies from a technical and people perspective, web conferencing penetration rates will increase because of the cost savings and productivity improvements web conferencing brings,' he said.

Andy Gregory, chief executive of Yellow Edge said, 'while we already have over 100 customers in Australia, including many of our leading universities, we are now very excited about the opportunities offered to government more broadly.' Recently adopted to support the interface between the business sector and the NSW Government, Elluminate Live would appear to 'tick all the boxes' in meeting the outcomes sought by the Rudd Government in respect of efficiencies in addition to fundamentally improving the public

>>

sectors' ability to network and collaborate. 'There is not a single organisation in the Australian government who would not derive great benefit from adopting Elluminate Live. The technology is proven, the business benefits are readily quantifiable and the broader benefits, for example, facilitating meaningful, efficient work-from-home arrangements, are there to be exploited. It is a low risk way of taking a significant leap forward in exploiting innovative technology.' For those organisations who have already invested heavily in video-conferencing, Elluminate Live greatly increases the benefits that can be derived through this communication medium. Using Elluminate's video conferring solution (VCS), video conferencing infrastructure is extended to the desktop, proving a flexible, interactive environment that includes chat, whiteboard, application and desktop sharing, file transfer and document presentation.

Source: 'Virtual conferencing – is your organisation game?', *Canberra Times*, 1 December 2009, © Andy Gregory, Yellow Edge Performance Architects.

Critical thinking question:

1. The successful use of technology in this circumstance is dependent upon other businesses being similarly equipped. What would be the problems when this is not the case? What would be your recommendation/s?

Collaboration rationale

More and more, organisations are collaborating with other organisations to achieve their objectives. These collaborative strategies can provide additional resources for large-scale research and development; spread the risks of innovation; apply diverse expertise to complex problems and tasks; make information or technology available to learn and develop new capabilities; position the organisation to achieve economies of scale or scope; or gain access to new, especially international, marketplaces.[33] For example, pharmaceutical firms form strategic alliances to distribute non-competing medications and avoid the high costs of establishing sales organisations; businesses from different countries form joint ventures to overcome restrictive trade barriers; and high-technology firms form research consortia to undertake significant and costly research and development for their industries.

More generally, however, collaborative strategies allow organisations to perform tasks that are too costly and complicated for single organisations to perform.[34] These tasks include the full range of organisational activities, including purchasing raw materials, hiring and compensating organisation members, manufacturing and service delivery, obtaining investment capital, marketing and distribution, and strategic planning. The key to understanding collaborative strategies is recognising that these individual tasks must be co-ordinated with each other. Whenever a good or service from one of these tasks is exchanged between two units (individuals, departments or organisations), a *transaction* occurs. Transactions can be designed and managed internally within the organisation's structure, or externally between organisations. For example, organisations can acquire a raw materials provider and operate these tasks as part of internal operations or they can collaborate with a raw material supplier through long-term contracts in an alliance.

Economists and organisation theorists have spent considerable effort investigating when collaborative strategies are preferred over competitive strategies. They have developed frameworks, primarily transaction cost theory and agency theory, that are useful for understanding the interventions described in this chapter.[35] As a rule, collaborative strategies work well when transactions occur frequently and are well understood. Many organisations, for example, outsource their payroll tasks because the inputs (such as hours worked, pay rates and employment status), the throughputs (such as tax rates and withholdings) and the outputs occur regularly and are governed by well-known laws and regulations. Moreover, if transactions involve people, equipment or other assets that are unique to the task, then collaboration is preferred over competition. For example, Microsoft works with a variety of value-added resellers, independent software vendors, and small and large consulting businesses to bring its products to customers ranging in size from individual consumers to the largest business enterprises in the world. An internal sales and service department to handle the unique demands of each customer segment would be much more expensive to implement and would not deliver the same level of quality as the partner organisations. In general, relationships between and among organisations become more formalised as the frequency of interaction increases, the type of information and other resources that are exchanged become more proprietary, and the number of different types of exchanges increases.[36]

Cummings has referred to groups of organisations that have joined together for a common purpose, including alliances and networks, as *transorganisational systems* (TSs).[37] TSs are functional social systems existing intermediately between single organisations on the one hand and societal systems on the other. These multi-organisation systems can make decisions and perform tasks on behalf of their member organisations, although members maintain their separate organisational identities and goals. This separation distinguishes TSs from mergers and acquisitions.

In contrast to most organisational systems, TSs tend to be underorganised: Relationships among member organisations are loosely coupled; leadership and power are dispersed among autonomous organisations, rather than hierarchically centralised; and commitment and membership are tenuous as member organisations act to maintain their autonomy while jointly performing. These characteristics make creating and managing TSs difficult.[38] Because members typically are accustomed to hierarchical forms of control, they may have difficulty managing lateral relations among independent organisations. They also may have difficulty managing different levels of commitment and motivation among members and sustaining membership over time.

Alliance interventions

An alliance is a formal agreement between two organisations to pursue a set of private and common goals through the sharing of resources, including intellectual property, people, capital, technology, capabilities and physical assets.[39] Alliances are an important strategy for such organisations as Corning Glass, Federal Express, IBM and Starbucks. The term *alliance* generally refers to any collaborative effort between two organisations, including licensing agreements, franchises, long-term contracts and joint ventures. Franchising is a common collaborative strategy. Companies such as McDonald's, Jim's Mowing and Holiday Inn license their name and know-how to independent organisations that deliver the service and leverage the brand name for marketing. A *joint venture* is a special type of alliance where a third organisation, jointly owned and operated by two (or more) organisations, is created. Joint ventures between domestic and foreign companies, such as Fuji Xerox, can help overcome trade barriers and facilitate technology transfer across nations.

Application stages

The development of effective alliances generally follows a process of strategy formulation, partner selection, alliance structuring and start-up, and alliance operation and adjustment.

1 *Alliance strategy formulation*. The first step in developing alliances is to clarify the business strategy and understand why an alliance is an appropriate method to implement it. About one-half to two-thirds of alliances fail to meet their financial objectives, and the number-one reason for that failure is the lack of a clear strategy.[40] For example, Collins found that alliance success was heavily influenced by the alignment of the partner to the company's 'hedgehog concept'.[41] If the organisation understood its passion, distinctive capabilities and economic drivers, it was more likely to develop alliances that supported its strategy. Thus, it is important to pursue alliances according to a 'collaboration logic'.[42] The alliance must be seen as a more effective way of organising and operating than: developing new capabilities to perform the work in-house; acquiring or merging with another organisation; or buying the capabilities from another organisation in a transactional relationship.

2 *Partner selection*. Once the reasons for an alliance are clear, the search for an appropriate partner begins. Alliances always involve a cost–benefit trade-off; while the organisation typically gains access to new markets or new capabilities, it does so at the cost of yielding some autonomy and control over its activities.

   Similar to identifying merger and acquisition candidates discussed previously, this step involves developing screening criteria, agreeing on candidates, establishing initial contacts and formulating a letter of intent. A good alliance partnership will leverage both similarities and differences to create competitive advantage. Compatible management styles or cultures, goals, information technologies or operations are important similarities that can smooth alliance formation and implementation. However, different perspectives, technologies, capabilities and other resources can complement existing ones and be good sources of learning and value in the partnership. These differences can also be a source of frustration for the alliance. OT practitioners can add value at this stage of the process by ensuring that the similarities and differences among potential alliance partners are explored and understood. In addition, the way the alliance begins and proceeds is an important ingredient in building trust, a characteristic of successful alliances explored more fully in the next step.

3 *Alliance structuring and start-up.* Following agreement to enter into an alliance, the focus shifts to how to structure the partnership and build and leverage trust in the relationship. First, an appropriate governance structure must be chosen and can include medium-to-long-term contracts, minority equity investments, equal equity partnerships or majority equity investments. As the proportion of equity investment increases, the costs, risk and amount of required management attention also increase.[43] In general, partners need to know how expenses, profits, risk and knowledge will be shared.

Second, research increasingly points to 'relational quality' as a key success factor of long-term alliances.[44] Alliances shift the nature of the relationship from the simple exchange of goods, services or resources with no necessary expectation of a future relationship to one where there is a clear expectation of future exchange. The parties in the relationship must act in good faith to ensure the future. This requires trust – 'a psychological state comprising the intention to accept vulnerability based upon positive expectations of the intentions or behaviour' of another business or individual representing the organisation. It implies an expectation that the organisation will subordinate its self-interest to the 'joint interest' of the alliance under most conditions.[45]

Trust can increase or decrease over the life of the alliance. Early in the alliance formation process, it can serve as an initial reservoir of comfort and confidence based on perceptions of the organisation's reputation, prior success and other sources. These same factors can also contribute to a lack of initial trust. Trust can be increased or decreased by new assessments of the other's capabilities, competence and ethical behaviour. OT practitioners can assist in this initial start-up phase by making implicit perceptions of trust explicit and getting both parties to set appropriate expectations.[46] During the structuring and start-up phase, trust can increase through direct activities as a function of the number, frequency and importance of interactions; differences between expectations and reality; the nature of mistakes and how they are resolved; and attributions made about partners' behaviour.

4 *Alliance operation and adjustment.* Once the alliance is functioning, the full range of OT interventions described in this text can be applied. Team building, conflict resolution, large-group interventions, work design, employee involvement, strategic planning and culture change efforts have all been reported in alliance work.[47] OT practitioners should pay particular attention to

helping each partner in the alliance clarify the capabilities contributed, the lessons learned and the benefits received.

Diagnosing the state of the alliance and making the appropriate adjustments is a function of understanding whether the environment has changed in ways that make collaboration unnecessary, whether partner goals and capabilities have changed the nature of the relationship and interdependence, and whether the alliance is successfully generating outcomes. The long-term success of the Fuji Xerox joint venture, for example, has been due to the willingness and ability of the two organisations to adjust the relationship in terms of ownership, profit sharing, new product development responsibilities and market access.[48] Application 11.3 gives an Australian example of how the legal system is entering into internal expansion strategies.

11.3

APPLICATION

Hands across the globe

Australian law firms say they have boosted revenue by as much as 10 per cent with work referred to them through memberships of international legal networks.

These formal alliances allow member firms in different countries to share cases and deals, refer clients and even benchmark performance against each other. For clients it means that their local law firm can tap expertise in jurisdictions where they might otherwise be inexperienced.

Lex Mundi is one of the largest global legal networks, with 160 member firms across 100 countries. Most of the members are in the United States and the United Kingdom, but exclusive membership rights are also given to smaller regional jurisdictions, such as Australia.

Clayton Utz, Australia's fifth-largest firm by staff number, is the local member of Lex Mundi. Mergers and acquisitions partner Simon Truskett says the exclusivity of the network is the main reason for paying the $50 000 annual membership fee.

'It really is quite modest when you consider we generate 10 per cent of our business in international services and bilateral firms in other jurisdictions,' he says.

The 2009 BRW Top 30 Law Firms survey shows that Clayton Utz earned $490.7 million during the 2008–09 financial year.

The firm is also a member of the Pacific Rim Advisory Council. Truskett, who is to become its chairman in late 2011, says the more people you know the better. The US, UK, Japanese and Canadian markets are the source of the highest number of referrals, but India and China are also growing. 'Five years ago we did very little in China, but now it's quite a substantial sum.'

In addition to creating leads, Lex Mundi firms meet four times a year to exchange best practice techniques in the areas of management and business development.

Mergers and acquisitions is the strongest source of inbound referral work for Clayton Utz, along with big projects and infrastructure.

'They're significant sources of the work we do offshore ... we do the projects offshore on a fly in, fly out basis. We've recently advised on a high-speed rail project in Taiwan. International arbitration is another significant area of work we get purely through being members of the network,' Truskett says.

>>

TressCox Lawyers partner Alistair Little says the firm joined the American Law Firms Association in 1996 and now 'makes back the fees 10 times over'. While unwilling to specify the annual membership fee, Little says the business earns 'hundreds of thousands' in revenue from the membership each year. Referrals are tracked by member firms and submitted to the Chicago head office.

'The ALFA alliance is quite valuable. There's no direct competition so people are frank about issues they face and how they deal with them. There's an enormous degree of personal interaction between members – we're not just a name on a list. I genuinely know the representatives in places like Mexico, Paris and Hong Kong ... I've had dinner at their houses,' he says.

One of the most common referrals from ALFA member firms are start-up companies entering the Australian marketplace, or companies with a small domestic operation who want to expand or take over a new business, Little says.

Multinational M&A work, often incorporating as many as 15 network firms advising on the matter, is also common. 'They all get together around the world to run on the one sale and run it out of Paris or London.'

Most of the referrals come from other Australian firms and New Zealand. Many also stem from the US, UK, Europe and Asia, but also the most unlikely of places.

'We've certainly had some large matters from comparatively small cities in the US, like the one from Roanoke, Virginia. It dealt with a travelling ice show visiting Australia that was involved in a nasty vehicle accident. We worked hand in hand with the Virginia firm to make sure the case was represented. It was several tens of thousands,' he says.

Many Australian firms, including most of the top-tier, have taken a different tack and prefer to open their own office networks rather than rely on alliance partners.

Allens Arthur Robinson has 11 offices in the Asia region that earn 10 per cent of its revenue, while Mallesons Stephen Jacques earns 12 per cent of its revenue from its four Asian offices.

Nonetheless, most other local law firms say the high cost of running their own overseas network just isn't worth it.

Source: Judith Tydd, 'Hands across the globe', *Business Review Weekly*, 4 March 2010.

Critical thinking questions:
1. What are the advantages and disadvantages of entering into the type of alliance described in the application?
2. Choose another industry and explain if there is a possibility for such a relationship to be entered into there.

Network interventions

Networks involve three or more organisations that have joined together for a common purpose, and their use is increasing rapidly in today's highly competitive global environment. In the private sector, research and development consortia, for example, allow companies to share resources and risks associated with large-scale research efforts. Networks among airlines with regional specialisations can combine to provide worldwide coverage, while Japanese *keiretsu*, Korean *chaebols* and Mexican *grupos* can enable different organisations to take advantage of complementary capabilities among them. In the public sector, partnerships between government and business provide the resources and initiative to undertake complex urban renewal projects that promote economies, and avoid costly overlap and redundancy.[49]

Managing the development of multi-organisation networks involves two types of change: (1) creating the initial network, and (2) managing change within an established network. Both change processes are complex and not well understood. First, the initial creation of networks recognises their underorganised nature. Forming them into a more coherent, operating whole involves understanding the relationships among the participating organisations and their roles in the system, as well as the implications and consequences of organisations leaving the network, changing roles or increasing their influence. Second, change within existing networks must account for the relationships among member organisations as a whole system.[50] The multiple and complex relationships involved in networks produce emergent phenomena that cannot be fully explained by simply knowing the parts. Each organisation in the network has goals that are partly related to the good of the network and partly focused on self-interest. How the network reacts over time is even more difficult to capture and is part of the emerging science of complexity.[51]

Creating the network

OT practitioners have evolved a unique form of planned change aimed at creating networks and improving their effectiveness. In laying out the conceptual boundaries of network development, also known as *transorganisation development*,[52] Cummings described the practice as following the phases of planned change appropriate for underorganised systems.[53] Due to their significance and the fact that they exemplify the fine line between organisation transformation (OT) and organisation development (OD), the four stages are shown again in Figure 11.1, along with key issues that need to be addressed at each stage, and are described below.

1 *Identification stage*. This initial stage of network development involves identifying existing and potential member organisations best suited to achieving their collective objectives. Identifying potential members can be difficult because organisations may not perceive the need to join together or may not know enough about each other to make membership choices. These problems are typical when trying to create a new network. Relationships among potential members may be loosely coupled or nonexistent; thus, even if organisations see the need to form a network, they may be unsure about who should be included.

The identification stage is generally carried out by one or a few organisations interested in exploring the possibility of creating a network. OT practitioners work with these initiating organisations to clarify their own goals, such as product or technology exchange, learning or market access, and to understand the trade-off between the loss of autonomy and the value of collaboration. Change agents also help specify criteria for network membership and identify

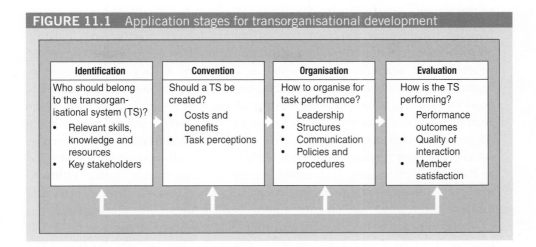

FIGURE 11.1 Application stages for transorganisational development

Identification	Convention	Organisation	Evaluation
Who should belong to the transorganisational system (TS)? • Relevant skills, knowledge and resources • Key stakeholders	Should a TS be created? • Costs and benefits • Task perceptions	How to organise for task performance? • Leadership • Structures • Communication • Policies and procedures	How is the TS performing? • Performance outcomes • Quality of interaction • Member satisfaction

organisations meeting those standards. Because networks are intended to perform specific tasks, a practical criterion for membership is how much organisations can contribute to task performance. Potential members can be identified and judged in terms of the skills, knowledge and resources that they bring to bear on the network task. Practitioners warn, however, that identifying potential members also should take into account the political realities of the situation.[54] Consequently, key stakeholders who can affect the creation and subsequent performance of the network are identified as possible members.

An important difficulty at this stage can be insufficient leadership and cohesion among participants to choose potential members. In these situations, OT practitioners may need to adopt a more activist role in creating the network.[55] They may need to bring structure to a group of autonomous organisations that do not see the need to join together or may not know how to form relationships. In several cases of network development, change agents helped members create a special leadership group that could make decisions on behalf of the participants.[56] This leadership group comprised a small cadre of committed members and was able to develop enough cohesion among members to carry out the identification stage. The activist role requires a good deal of leadership and direction. For example, change agents may need to educate potential network members about the benefits of joining together. They may need to structure face-to-face encounters aimed at sharing information and exploring interaction possibilities.

2 *Convention stage*. Once potential network members are identified, the convention stage is concerned with bringing them together to assess whether formalising the network is desirable and feasible. This face-to-face meeting enables potential members to explore mutually their motivations for joining and their perceptions of the joint task. They work to establish sufficient levels of motivation and task consensus to form the network.

Like the identification stage, this phase of network creation generally requires considerable direction and facilitation by OT practitioners. Existing stakeholders may not have the legitimacy or skills to perform the convening function, and practitioners can serve as conveners if they are perceived as legitimate and credible by the attending organisations. However, change agents need to maintain a neutral role, treating all members alike.[57] They need to be seen by members as working on behalf of the total system, rather than as being aligned with particular members or views. When practitioners are perceived as neutral, network members are more likely to share information with them and to listen to their inputs. Such neutrality can enhance change agents' ability to mediate conflicts among members. It can help them uncover diverse views and interests and forge agreements among stakeholders. OT practitioners, for example, can act as mediators, ensuring that members' views receive a fair hearing and that disputes are equitably resolved. They can help to bridge the different views and interests, and achieve integrative solutions. In many cases, practitioners came from research centres or universities with reputations for neutrality and expertise in networks.[58] Because participating organisations tend to have diverse motives and views and limited means for resolving differences, change agents may need to structure and manage interactions to facilitate airing of differences and arriving at consensus about forming the network. They may need to help organisations work through differences and reconcile self-interests with those of the larger network.

3 *Organisation stage.* When the convention stage results in a decision to create a network, members then begin to organise themselves for task performance. This involves developing the structures and mechanisms that promote communication and interaction among members and that direct joint efforts to the task at hand.[59] It includes the organisations to be involved in the network and the roles each will play; the communication and relationships among them; and the control system that will guide decision making and provide a mechanism for monitoring performance. For example, members may create a co-ordinating council to manage the network and a powerful leader to head it. They might choose to formalise exchanges among members by developing rules, policies and formal operating procedures. When members are required to invest large amounts of resources in the network, such as might occur in an industry-based research consortium, the organising stage typically includes voluminous contracting and negotiating about members' contributions and returns. Here, corporate lawyers and financial analysts play key roles in specifying the network structure. They determine how costs and benefits will be allocated among member organisations as well as the legal obligations, decision-making responsibilities and contractual rights of members. OT practitioners can help members define competitive advantage for the network as well as the structural requirements necessary to support achievement of its goals.

4 *Evaluation stage*. This final stage of creating a network involves assessing how the network is performing. Members need feedback so that they can identify problems and begin to resolve them. Feedback data generally include performance outcomes and member satisfactions, as well as indicators of how well members are interacting jointly. Change agents can periodically interview or survey member organisations about various outcomes and features of the network, and feed that data back to network leaders. Such information will enable leaders to make necessary operational modifications and adjustments. It may signal the need to return to previous stages in the process to make necessary corrections, as shown by the feedback arrows in Figure 11.1.

Managing network change

In addition to developing new networks, OT practitioners may need to facilitate change within established networks. Planned change in existing networks derives from an understanding of the 'new sciences', including complexity, nonlinear systems, catastrophe and chaos theories. From these perspectives, organisation networks are viewed as complex systems displaying the following properties:[60]

1 The behaviour of a network is sensitive to small differences in its initial conditions. How the network was established and formed – the depth and nature of trust among the partners, who was selected (and not selected) to be in the network, and how the network was organised – play a key role in its willingness and ability to change.

2 Networks display 'emergent' properties or characteristics that cannot be explained through an analysis of the parts: 'Given the properties of the parts and the laws of their interaction, it is not a trivial matter to infer the properties of the whole.'[61] The tools of systems thinking and the understanding of emergence in complex systems is still being developed and applied.[62]

3 A variety of network behaviours and patterns, both expected and unexpected, can emerge from members performing tasks and making decisions according to simple rules to which everyone agreed. This is amply demonstrated in Senge's 'beer game' simulation where a retailer, a wholesaler and a brewery each acts according to the simple rule of maximising its own profit. Participants in the simulation routinely end up with enormous inventories of poor-selling beer, delayed deliveries, excess capacity and other problems. Without an understanding of the 'whole' system, the nature of interdependencies within the system, and timely and complete information, each part – acting in its own self-interest – destroys itself.[63] Apparently random changes in networks may simply be chaotic patterns that are not understood. These patterns cannot be known in advance but represent potential paths of change that are the result of the complex interactions among members in the network.

The process of change in complex systems such as networks involves creating instability, managing the tipping point and relying on self-organisation. These phases roughly follow Lewin's model of planned change. Change in a network requires an unfreezing process where the system becomes unstable. Movement in the system is described by the metaphor of a 'tipping point' where changes occur rapidly as a result of information processing. Finally, refreezing involves self-organisation. The descriptions below represent rudimentary applications of these concepts to networks; our understanding of them is still in a formative stage.

1 *Create instability in the network.* Before change in a network can occur, relationships among member organisations must become unstable. A network's susceptibility to instability is a function of members' motivations for structure versus agency.[64] *Structure* refers to the organisation's expected role in the network and represents a source of stability. All things being equal, network members tend to behave and perform according to their agreed-upon roles. For example, most routine communications among the network members are geared towards increasing stability and working together. A manufacturing plant in Nike's network is expected to produce a certain number of shoes at a certain cost with certain features. Nike headquarters in Beaverton, Oregon, has planned for its plant to behave this way. On the other hand, *agency* involves self-interest which can create instability in the network. Each member of the network is trying to maximise its own performance in the context of the network. Changes in member goals and strategies, the ratio of costs and benefits in network membership and so on can affect the willingness and ability of members to contribute to network performance. When a plant in Nike's network grows to a sufficient size, it may decide to alter its role in the network. As the ratio of agency to structure increases, the instability of the network rises, thus enabling change to occur.

   OT practitioners can facilitate instability in a network by changing the pattern of communication among members. They can, for example, encourage organisations to share information. Technology breakthroughs, new product introductions, changes in network membership or changes in the strategy of a network member all represent fluctuations that can increase the susceptibility of the network to change. Another important aspect of changing the pattern of information is to ask who should get the information. Understanding and creating instability is difficult because the nature of members' connectedness also influences the system's susceptibility. Some organisations are more connected than others; most organisations are closely connected to several others, but relatively unconnected to many. This makes creating a sense of urgency for change difficult. Diagnosis of the relationships among member organisations can provide important information about organisations that are central to network communications.[65]

2 *Manage the tipping point.* Although instability provides the impetus and opportunity for change, the direction, type and process of change are yet to be determined. An unstable network can move to a new state of organisation and performance or it can return to its old condition. At this point, network members, individually and collectively, make choices about what to do. OT practitioners can help them through this change period. Recent studies suggest the following guides for facilitating network change:[66]

a *The law of the few.* A new idea, practice or other change spreads because of a relatively few but important roles in the network. Connectors, 'mavens' and salespeople help an innovation achieve sufficient awareness and credibility throughout the network to be considered viable. *Connectors* are individuals who occupy central positions in the network and are able to tap into many different network audiences. They have 'Rolodex' power; they are quickly able to alert and connect with a wide variety of people in many organisations. *Mavens* are 'information sinks'. They passionately pursue knowledge about a particular subject and are altruistically willing to tell anyone who is interested everything they know about it. The key to the maven's role is trust. People who speak to mavens know that they are getting unbiased information; that there is no 'hidden agenda' – just good data. Finally, *salespeople* are the champions of change and are able to influence others to try new ideas, do new things or consider new options. Thus, the first key factor in changing a network is the presence of communication channels occupied by connectors, mavens and salespeople. OT practitioners can fill any of these roles. They can, if appropriate, be mavens on a particular subject and act as a source of unbiased information about a new network practice, aspects of interpersonal relationships that network members agree is slowing network response, or ideas about information systems that can speed communication. Less frequently, OT practitioners can be connectors, ensuring that any given message is seeded throughout the network. This is especially true if the change agent was part of the network's formation. In this case, the practitioner might have the relationships with organisations in the network. Thus, networking skills, such as the ability to manage lateral relations among autonomous organisations in the relative absence of hierarchical control, are indispensable to practitioners of network change. Change agents must be able to span the boundaries of diverse organisations, link them together and facilitate exchanges among them.[67] The OT practitioner can also play the role of salesperson. Although it is in line with the 'activist' role described earlier in the practice of network creation, it is not a traditional aspect of OT practice. The wisdom of having a change agent as the champion of an idea rather than a key player in the organisation network is debatable. The change agent and network members must understand the trade-offs in sacrificing the OT practitioner's neutrality for influence. If that trade-off is made, the change agent will need the political competence to understand and resolve the conflicts of interest and value dilemmas inherent in systems made up of multiple organisations, each seeking to maintain autonomy while jointly interacting. Political savvy can help change agents manage their own roles and values in respect to those power dynamics.

b *Stickiness.* The second ingredient in network change is stickiness. For a new idea or practice to take hold, the message communicated by the connectors, mavens and salespeople must be memorable. A memorable or sticky message is not a function of typical communication variables, such as frequency of the message, loudness or saliency. Stickiness is often a function of small and seemingly insignificant characteristics of the message, such as its structure, format and syntax, as well as its emotional content, practicality or sequencing with other messages. OT practitioners can also help network members develop sticky messages. Brainstorming alternative phrases, using metaphors to symbolise meaning or enlisting the help of marketing and communications specialists can increase the chance of developing a sticky message. Since the ingredients of stickiness are often not obvious, several iterations of a message's structure with focus groups or different audiences may be necessary to understand what gets people's attention.

c *The power of context.* Finally, a message must be meaningful. This is different from stickiness and refers to the change's relevance to network members. The source of meaning is in the context of the network. When network members are feeling pressure to innovate or move quickly in response to a customer request, for example, messages about new cost-cutting initiatives or new and exciting information systems that will allow everyone to see key financial data are uninteresting and can get lost. On the other hand, a message about how a new information system will speed up customer communication is more likely to be seen as relevant. When OT practitioners understand the network's current climate or 'conversation', they can help members determine the appropriate timing and relevance of any proposed communication.[68]

When the right people communicate a change, and present and package it appropriately, and distribute it in a timely fashion, the network can adopt a new idea or practice quickly. In the absence of these ingredients, there is not enough information, interest or relevance, and the change stalls.

3 *Rely on self-organisation.* Networks tend to exhibit 'self-organising' behaviour. Network members seek to reduce uncertainty in their environment, while the network as a whole drives to establish more order in how it functions. OT practitioners can rely on this self-organising feature to refreeze change. Once change has occurred in the network, a variety of controls can be leveraged to institutionalise it. For example, communication systems can spread stories about how the change is affecting different members, diffusing throughout the network or contributing to network effectiveness. This increases the forces for stability in the network. Individual organisations can communicate their commitment to the change in an effort to lower agency forces that can contribute to instability. Each of these messages signifies constraint and shows that the different parts of the network are not independent of each other. Application 11.4 provides evidence that organisations that are innovative and rely on organic growth are more likely to survive a chaotic economic environment.

11.4

APPLICATION

Organic growth is back

Creating organic growth has a higher priority for the nation's chief executives than mergers and acquisitions in 2010, business advisory firm thinkGROWTH says.

The firm's Growth Insights survey of 60 chief and senior executives of Australian companies shows that organisations that give precedence to innovation and organic growth will be better placed to capture greater market share in the wake of the economic crisis.

More than 50 per cent of respondents describe their companies' approach to organic growth management as ad hoc or basic, and only 37 per cent claim any sophistication at all.

The respondents consistently identified their capabilities across important growth factors as merely at or below average.

And thinkGROWTH managing director Mike Kaye says the global economic fallout has changed the landscape for business growth in Australia.

'The M&A frenzy, which fuelled last decade's stock market growth, has faded and been replaced by a battle-hardened market more wary of acquisition strategies and financial engineering,' he says.

Kaye believes the economic fallout forced many businesses into a state of paralysis, with stages of recovery comparable to the personal grief cycle.

'Companies start out in shock, simply watching as demand falls away, before turning to short-term measures such as substantial cost reduction. After realising they're not going to shrink to greatness, the focus returns to growth and innovation, albeit still too slowly for some. Only this time, when they get there, they find that M&A skills alone don't prepare them for the road ahead,' Kaye says.

Source: Judith Tydd, 'Organic growth is back', *Business Review Weekly*, 11 March 2010.

Critical thinking questions:
1. What is the 'personal grief cycle' and how does it compare with the description in the application?
2. Is the focus on M&A a fad or a fashion? Why/why not? Explain your answer.

Summary

In this chapter, we presented interventions aimed at implementing competitive and collaborative strategies. Organisations are open systems that exist in environmental contexts and they must establish and maintain effective linkages with the environment to survive and prosper. Three types of environments affect organisational functioning: the general environment, the task environment and the enacted environment. Only the last environment can affect organisational choices about behaviour, but the first two impact on the consequences of those actions. Two environmental dimensions – information uncertainty and resource dependence – affect the degree to which organisations are constrained by their environments and the need to be responsive to them. For example, when information uncertainty and resource dependence are high, organisations are maximally constrained and need to be responsive to their environments.

Integrated strategic change is a comprehensive intervention for responding to complex and uncertain environmental pressures. It gives equal weight to the strategic and organisational factors affecting organisation performance and effectiveness. In addition, these factors are highly integrated during the process of assessing the current strategy and organisation design, selecting the desired strategic orientation, developing a strategic change plan and implementing it.

Mergers and acquisitions (M&A) involve combining two or more organisations to achieve strategic and financial objectives. The process generally involves three phases: precombination, legal combination and operational combination. The M&A process has been dominated by financial and technical concerns, but experience and research strongly support the contribution that OT practitioners can make to M&A success.

Collaborative strategies are a form of planned change aimed at helping organisations create partnerships with other organisations to perform tasks or to solve problems that are too complex and multifaceted for single organisations to carry out. Alliance interventions describe the technical and organisational issues involved when two organisations choose to work together to achieve common goals.

Network development interventions must address two types of change. First, because multi-organisation systems tend to be underorganised, the initial development of the network follows the stages of planned change relevant to underorganised systems: identification, convention, organisation and evaluation. Second, the management of change within a network also must acknowledge the distributed nature of influence and adopt methods of change that rely on the law of the few, the power of context and the stickiness factor.

Activities

REVIEW QUESTIONS

1 What is the difference between 'open' and 'closed' systems?

2 There are three types of environments to consider when designing an OT change process. What are they? (Give examples.)

3 What is the difference between general and task environments? Give three examples of each.

4 The two environmental dimensions – information uncertainty and resource dependence – can be barriers to successful change. How may they be managed?

5 Distinguish between competitive and collaborative strategies. What type of environment would be beneficial for each?

6 Select two of the competitive strategies. After explaining the characteristics of each, compare and contrast them.

7 Explain what is integrative strategic change and give current examples.

8 Why would an organisation choose to merge rather than acquire another company?

9 Explain the difference between mergers and acquisitions. Why is this significant when considering a change process?

10 What is meant by transorganisational systems? Give four current examples.

11 What are the advantages and disadvantages of alliances? Give examples where appropriate.

12 What would the problems be if managers network change?

13 Are networks the current fad or fashion in management theory? Why or why not?

Discussion and essay questions

1 'Some environments are rapidly changing and complex, and so require organisational responses different from those in environments that are stable and simple.' Do you agree with this statement? Why/why not?

2 Explain the importance of the activities (uniqueness, value and difficulty to imitate) in enhancing an organisation's performance. Choose an organisation that you are familiar with and describe how these activities give it a competitive advantage.

3 Investigate further Cummings's transorganisational systems (TSs)

theory. How does this theory differ significantly from other change approaches? How would OT interventions assist organisations that intend to enter such an arrangement?

4 'Competitive strategies are not appropriate for not-for-profit or governmental organisations.' Do you agree with this statement? Explain your answer.

5 'In collaborative strategies, as the numbers of organisations increase, the scope and complexity of the problems and issues that need to be addressed increase.' Discuss.

Search me! Excercises

Explore **Search me! management** for relevant articles on competitive and collaborative strategies. Search me! is an online library of world-class journals, ebooks and newspapers, including *The Australian* and *The New York Times*, and is updated daily. Log in to Search me! through www.cengage.com/sso using the access card in the front of this book.

Keywords

Try searching for the following terms:
> Acquisition
> Collaborative strategies
> Competitive strategies
> Environmental framework
> Merger
> Network organisations

>> *Search tip:*

Search me! management contains information from both local and international sources. To get the greatest number of search results, try using both Australian and American spellings in your searches, e.g. 'globalisation' and 'globalization'; 'organisation' and 'organization'.

Notes

1 K. Barnes and D. Francis, Ph.D, *The OD Practitioner as Facilitator of Innovation*, OD Network Conference, Copyright © 2006 B. Kim Barnes and David Francis. All rights reserved. www.odnetwork.org/events/conferences/conf2006/documents/PS-05-3.pdf.

2 R. V. Aguilera, *An Organizational Approach to Comparative Corporate Governance: Costs, Contingencies, and Complementaries*, May 2007, Department of Business Administration and Institute of Labor and Industrial Relations, University of Illinois at Champaign-Urbana, Illinois, USA, www.business.uiuc.edu/aguilera/pdf/os-spec-06-1222%20revised%20final%2001may2007.pdf.

3 S. Miller and A. Kirlik, 'Modeling the task environment: ACT-R and the lens model', Proceedings of the Human Factors and Ergonomics Society 50th Annual Meeting – 2006, University of Illinois, Aviation Human Factors Division, Savoy, Illinois, USA, www.humanfactors.illinois.edu/Reports&Papers PDFs/humfac06/Modeling%20the%20Task%20Environment.pdf.

4 S. Schick Case and T. Thatchenkery, 'Leveraging appreciative intelligence for positive enactment in times of uncertainty: a case study of a small investment firm', *American Journal of Economics and Business Administration*, 2:2 (2010): 147–52, Weatherhead School of Management, Organizational Behavior, Case Western Reserve University, Cleveland and Ohio School of Public Policy, George Mason University, Arlington, Virginia, www.scipub.org/fulltext/ajeba/ajeba22147-152.pdf.

5 J. Barney, *Gaining and Sustaining Competitive Advantage* (Reading, MA: Addison-Wesley, 1996).

6 R. Nelson and S. Winter, *An Evolutionary Theory of Economic Change* (Cambridge, MA: Belknap Press, 1982).

7 P. Selznick, *Leadership in Administration* (New York: Harper & Row, 1957); M. Peteraf, 'The cornerstones of competitive advantage: a resource-based view', *Strategic Management Journal*, 14 (1993): 179–92; J. Collins, *Good to Great* (New York: HarperCollins, 2001).

8 R. Grant, *Contemporary Strategy Analysis*, 4th edn (Malden, MA: Blackwell, 2001); Barney, *Competitive Advantage*, op. cit.

9 L. Greiner and A. Bhambri, 'New CEO intervention and the dynamics of strategic change', *Strategic Management Journal*, 10 (1989): 67–87.

10 T. Galpin and D. Robinson, 'Merger integration: the ultimate change management challenge', *Mergers and Acquisitions*, 31 (1997): 24–9.

11 M. Marks and P. Mirvis, *Joining Forces: Making One Plus One Equal Three in Mergers, Acquisitions, and Alliances* (San Francisco: Jossey-Bass, 1998).

12 G. Dixon, 'Merger and acquisition activity in Canada, world continues to decline in 2002', *The Canadian Press* (6 January 2003), www.factiva.com, accessed 12 June 2003.

13 A variety of studies have questioned whether merger and acquisition activity actually generates benefits to the organisation or its shareholders, including M. Porter, 'From competitive advantage to corporate strategy', *Harvard Business Review* (May–June 1978): 43–59; 'Merger integration problems', *Leadership and Organization Development Journal*, 19 (1998): 59–60; 'Why good deals miss the bull's-eye: slow integration, poor communication torpedo prospects for creating value', *Mergers and Acquisitions*, 33 (1999): 5; T. Brush, 'Predicted change in operational synergy and post-acquisition performance of acquired businesses', *Strategic Management Journal*, 17 (1996): 1–24; P. Zweig with J. Perlman, S. Anderson and K. Gudridge, 'The case against mergers', *Business Week* (30 October 1995): 122–30. The research includes: an A. T. Kearney study of 115 multibillion-dollar global mergers between 1993 and 1996 where 58% failed to create 'substantial returns for shareholders', measured by tangible returns in the form of dividends and stock price appreciation; a Mercer Management Consulting study of all mergers from 1990 to 1996 where nearly half 'destroyed' shareholder value; a PriceWaterhouseCoopers study of 97 acquirers that completed deals worth $500 million or more from 1994 to 1997 and where two-thirds of the buyer's stocks dropped on announcement of the transaction and 'a year later' a third of the losers still were lagging the levels of peer-company shares or the stock market in general; and a European study of 300 companies that found that planning for restructuring was poorly thought-out and underfunded. Similarly, despite the large amount of writing on the subject, a large proportion of firms involved in mergers have not understood the message that post-merger integration is the key to success. For example, in the A. T. Kearney study, only 39% of the cases had set up a management team in the first 100 days and only 28% had a clear vision of corporate goals when the acquisition began.

14 Zweig et al., 'Case against mergers', op. cit.

15 Marks and Mirvis, *Joining Forces*, op. cit.; R. Ashkenas, L. DeMonaco and S. Francis, 'Making the deal real: how GE capital integrates acquisitions', *Harvard Business Review* (January–February 1998); B. Brunsman, S. Sanderson and M. Van de Voorde, 'How to achieve value behind the deal during merger integration', *Oil and Gas Journal*, 96 (1998): 21–30; A. Fisher, 'How to make a merger work', *Fortune* (24 January 1994): 66–70; K. Kostuch, R. Malchione and I. Marten, 'Post-merger integration: creating or destroying value?', *Corporate Board*, 19 (1998): 7–11; A. Kruse, 'Merging cultures: how OD adds value in mergers and acquisitions' (presentation to the ODNetwork meeting, San Diego, CA, October 1999); M. Sirower, 'Constructing a

synergistic base for premier deals', *Mergers and Acquisitions*, 32 (1998): 42–50; D. Jemison and S. Sitkin, 'Corporate acquisitions: a process perspective', *Academy of Management Review*, 11 (1986): 145–63.

16 Ashkenas, DeMonaco and Francis, 'Making the deal real', op. cit.; G. Ledford, C. Siehl, M. McGrath and J. Miller, 'Managing mergers and acquisitions' (working paper, Center for Effective Organizations, University of Southern California, Los Angeles, 1985).

17 Ledford et al., 'Managing mergers and acquisitions', op. cit.; B. Blumenthal, 'The right talent mix to make mergers work', *Mergers and Acquisitions* (September–October 1995): 26–31; A. Buono, J. Bowditch and J. Lewis, 'When cultures collide: the anatomy of a merger', *Human Relations*, 38 (1985): 477–500; D. Tipton, 'Understanding employee views regarding impending mergers to minimize integration turmoil' (unpublished master's thesis, Pepperdine University, 1998).

18 Marks and Mirvis, *Joining Forces*, op. cit.; Ashkenas, DeMonaco and Francis, 'Making the deal real', op. cit.

19 Sirower, 'Constructing a synergistic base', op. cit.; Brunsman, Sanderson and Van de Voorde, 'How to achieve value', op. cit.

20 Sirower, 'Constructing a synergistic base', op. cit.

21 Ledford et al., 'Managing mergers and acquisitions', op. cit.

22 S. Elias, 'Due diligence', 1998, www.eliasondeals.com/duedilig.html.

23 Brunsman, Sanderson and Van de Voorde, 'How to achieve value', op. cit.

24 Ashkenas, DeMonaco and Francis, 'Making the deal real', op. cit.

25 Ashkenas, DeMonaco and Francis, 'Making the deal real', op. cit.; Brunsman, Sanderson and Van de Voorde, 'How to achieve value', op. cit.

26 K. V. Maarten Van Craeni and J. Ackaert, *Transnational Activities and Social-cultural Integration of Moroccan and Turkish Descendants in Flemish Belgium*, Paper to be presented at the XXVI IUSSP International Population Conference, Marrakech (Morocco), 27/09 – 02/10/10, http://iussp2009.princeton.edu/download.aspx?submissionId=90999.

27 Galpin and Robinson, 'Merger integration', op. cit.

28 ibid.

29 Ashkenas, DeMonaco and Francis, 'Making the deal real', op. cit.

30 Kostuch, Malchione and Marten, 'Post-merger integration', op. cit.

31 This application was developed by Michael Krup. His contribution is gratefully acknowledged.

32 H. M. Krumholz, E. H. Bradley, B. K. Nallamothu, H. H. Ting, W. B. Batchelor, E. Kline-Rogers, A. F. Stern, J. R. Byrd and J. E. Brush Jr, 'A campaign to improve the timeliness of primary percutaneous coronary intervention door-to-balloon: an alliance for quality', *J Am Coll Cardiol Intv* (2008), http://interventions.onlinejacc.org/cgi/content/full/1/1/97.

33 A. Tsai, *A Note on Strategic Alliances*, 9-298-047 (Boston: Harvard Business School, 1997); B. Gomes-Casseres, *Managing International Alliances: Conceptual Framework*, 9-793-133 (Boston: Harvard Business School, 1993); J. Bamford, B. Gomes-Casseres and M. Robinson, *Mastering Alliance Strategy* (New York: John Wiley and Sons, 2002).

34 Aldrich, *Organizations and Environments*, op. cit.

35 O. Williamson, *Markets and Hierarchies* (New York: Free Press, 1975); O. Williamson, *The Economic Institutions of Capitalism* (New York: Free Press, 1985); J. Barney and W. Ouchi, *Organizational Economics* (San Francisco: Jossey-Bass, 1986); K. Eisenhardt, 'Agency theory: an assessment and review', *Academy of Management Review*, 14 (1989): 57–74.

36 P. Kenis and D. Knoke, 'How organisational field networks shape interorganisational tie-formation rates', *Academy of Management Review*, 27 (2002): 275–93.

37 T. Cummings, 'Transorganisational development', in *Research in Organisational Behaviour*, vol. 6, eds B. Staw and L. Cummings (Greenwich, CT: JAI Press, 1984): 367–422.

38 B. Gray, 'Conditions facilitating interorganisational collaboration', *Human Relations*, 38 (1985): 911–36; K. Harrigan and W. Newman, 'Bases of interorganisation co-operation: propensity, power, persistence', *Journal of Management Studies*, 27 (1990): 417–34; Cummings, 'Transorganizational development', op. cit.

39 A. Arino, J. de la Torre and P. Ring, 'Relational quality: managing trust in corporate alliances', *California Management Review*, 44 (2001): 109–31; M. Hitt, R. Ireland and R. Hoskisson, *Strategic Management* (Cincinnati, OH: South-Western College Publishing, 1999).

40 Bamford, Gomes-Casseres and Robinson, *Mastering Alliance Strategy*, op. cit.

41 Collins, *Good to Great*, op. cit.

42 Gomes-Casseres, 'Managing international alliances', op. cit.; J. Child and D. Faulkner, *Strategies of Co-operation: Managing Alliances, Networks, and Joint Ventures* (New York: Oxford University Press, 1998).

43 Bamford, Gomes-Casseres and Robinson, *Mastering Alliance Strategy*, op. cit.

44 A. Arino, J. de la Torre and P. Ring, 'Relational quality', op. cit.

45 C. Rousseau, S. Sitkin, R. Burt and C. Camerer, 'Not so different after all: a cross-discipline view of trust', *Academy of Management Review*, 23 (1998): 395.

46 M. Hutt, E. Stafford, B. Walker and P. Reingen, 'Case study defining the social network of a strategic alliance', *Sloan Management Review*, Winter (2000): 51–62.

47 Marks and Mirvis, *Joining Forces*, op. cit.; Child and Faulkner, *Strategies of Cooperation*, op. cit.

48 K. McQuade and B. Gomes-Casseres, *Xerox and Fuji-Xerox*, 9-391-156 (Boston: Harvard Business School, 1991).

49 R. Chisholm, *Developing Network Organizations* (Reading, MA: Addison-Wesley, 1998).

50 D. Watts, *Six Degrees* (New York: W.W. Norton and Co., 2003).

51 S. Strogatz, 'Exploring complex networks', *Nature*, 410 (March 2001): 268–76.

52 P. Berthon, L. Pitt, D. Nel, E. Salehi-Sangari and A. Engstrom, 'The biotechnology and marketing interface: functional integration using mechanistic and holographic responses to environmental turbulence', *Journal of Commercial Biotechnology*, 14 (July 2008): 213–24, www.palgrave-journals.com/jcb/journal/v14/n3/full/jcb200812a.html.

53 Cummings, 'Transorganizational development', op. cit.; C. Raben, 'Building strategic partnerships: creating and managing effective joint ventures', in *Organizational*

Architecture, eds Nadler et al. (San Francisco: Jossey-Bass, 1992): 81–109; B. Gray, *Collaborating: Finding Common Ground for Multiparty Problems* (San Francisco: Jossey-Bass, 1989); Harrigan and Newman, 'Bases of interorganisation co-operation', op. cit.; P. Lorange and J. Roos, 'Analytical steps in the formation of strategic alliances', *Journal of Organizational Change Management*, 4 (1991): 60–72; B. Gomes-Casseres, 'Managing international alliances', op. cit.

54 D. Boje, *Towards a Theory and Praxis of Transorganizational Development: Stakeholder Networks and Their Habitats* (working paper no. 79-6, Behavioral and Organizational Science Study Center, Graduate School of Management, University of California, Los Angeles, February 1982); B. Gricar, *The Legitimacy of Consultants and Stakeholders in Interorganizational Problems* (paper presented at annual meeting of the Academy of Management, San Diego, CA, August 1981); T. Williams, 'The search conference in active adaptive planning', *Journal of Applied Behavioural Science*, 16 (1980): 470–83; B. Gray and T. Hay, 'Political limits to interorganisational consensus and change', *Journal of Applied Behavioural Science*, 22 (1986): 95–112.

55 Cummings, 'Transorganizational development', op. cit.

56 E. Trist, *Referent Organizations and the Development of Interorganizational Domains* (paper presented at annual meeting of the Academy of Management, Atlanta, August 1979).

57 Cummings, 'Transorganizational development', op. cit.

58 ibid.

59 Raben, 'Building strategic partnerships', op. cit.; C. Baldwin and K. Clark, 'Managing in an age of modularity', in *Managing in the Modular Age*, eds R. Garud, A. Kumaraswamy and R. Langlois (Malden, MA: Blackwell Publishing Ltd., 2003): 149–60.

60 P. Anderson, 'Complexity theory and organisation science', *Organisation Science*, 10 (1999): 216–32.

61 H. Simon, 'The architecture of complexity', in *Managing in the Modular Age*, eds R. Garud, A. Kumara-swamy and R. Langlois (Malden, MA: Blackwell Publishing Ltd., 2003): 15–37.

62 Senge, *The Fifth Discipline*, op. cit.; B. Lichtenstein, 'Emergence as a process of self-organising: new assumptions and insights from the study of non-linear dynamic systems', *Journal of Organisational Change Management*, 13 (2000): 526–46.

63 Senge, *The Fifth Discipline*, op. cit.

64 Watts, *Six Degrees*, op. cit.

65 P. Monge and N. Contractor, *Theories of Communication Networks* (New York: Oxford University Press, 2003).

66 This section relies on information in M. Gladwell, *The Tipping Point* (Boston: Little, Brown, 2000).

67 B. Gricar and D. Brown, 'Conflict, power, and organisation in a changing community', *Human Relations*, 34 (1981): 877–93.

68 P. Shaw, *Changing Conversations in Organisations: A Complexity Approach to Change* (London: Routledge, 2002).

PART 5

THE FUTURE OF CHANGE MANAGEMENT

12 *Future directions: Change in a global setting*

CHAPTER 12

Future directions: Change in a global setting

The field of organisation change continues to grow, especially with organisation development (OD) where new methods and interventions are being applied, more complex and rigorous research is being conducted and organisations from more diverse countries and cultures are becoming involved. However, with organisation transformation (OT), as explained in previous chapters, it is far more difficult to predict and plan as organisations are generally in a chaotic and/or volatile environment.

With this renewed focus or intent on organisational planning, and the desire for a smooth transition in the change process, predicting the future can be a risky business. On the other hand, the field of OD is also maturing and it is useful to look at the forces influencing how change is likely to evolve. This knowledge can enable OD practitioners, researchers and managers to more readily affect a relevant OD future. The chapter first identifies three trends within the OD field that are pushing it towards different futures. The implications of these trends are discussed. The chapter then describes trends in the larger context within which OD operates, including economic, workforce, technology and organisation trends. It concludes with a discussion of how these trends are likely to influence future OD practice.

TRENDS WITHIN ORGANISATION DEVELOPMENT

In updating his OD bibliography, Glenn Varney noted that much of the recent writings in OD had focused more on the status of the field than on evaluations of practice or research on the processes of change.[1] In support of that observation, reviews of the literature, conversations within Internet listservs and the diversity in OD education and training opportunities suggest three trends occurring within OD – characterised as traditional, pragmatic and scholarly.[2] Each trend has a different vision of what OD can and should be and although they are presented separately, they are not mutually exclusive or independent. On the contrary, the future of OD will no doubt emerge from their integration. Figure 12.1 summarises the trends and their likely implications for the future of OD.

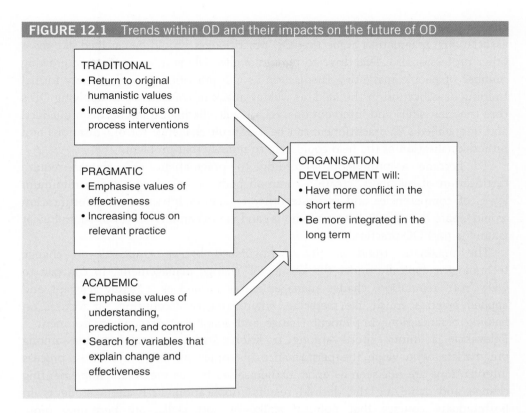

FIGURE 12.1 Trends within OD and their impacts on the future of OD

Source: Cummings/Worley, *Organization Development and Change* (with InfoTrac® College Edition Printed Access Card), 9e © 2009 South-Western, a part of Cengage Learning, Inc. Reproduced by permission www.cengage.com/permissions.

Traditional

The first trend has to do with increasing calls for a return to OD's traditional values and practices. Championed by the National Training Laboratories (NTL) and others, traditionalists argue that OD should be driven by long-established values of human potential, equality, trust and collaboration. The major objective of OD should be to promulgate these root values through interventions that humanise work, organisations and society; help employees balance work and family life; promote diversity and spirituality at the workplace; and champion the self-actualisation of organisation members.[3] Thus, traditionalists propose that OD should do what is 'right' by assuring that organisations promote positive social change and corporate citizenship.[4]

A strong focus on process interventions also characterises the traditional trend. OD's key purpose, according to this view, is to ensure that organisational processes are transparent, possess integrity, treat people with dignity and serve diverse stakeholders. Thus, OD's primary goal is to help organisations create such processes; whether they subsequently lead to performance outcomes is of secondary importance.

Pragmatic

The second trend within OD is related to increasing demands for professionalisation of the field and an emphasis on relevance. Championed by the change management practices at large consulting firms and some OD professional associations, pragmatists argue that OD practitioners should be certified like most other professionals.[5] This drive to professionalise OD is in response to a growing number of people marketing themselves as OD practitioners without any formal training or education in the field, as well as a lack of consistency in applying OD's core theories, skills and interventions. As a result, distinguishing between qualified and unqualified OD practitioners can be a difficult challenge for organisations and professionalisation of the field could help to remedy that problem.[6]

To become a profession, according to pragmatists, OD should require certification of members, create a common body of knowledge, define minimum levels of competencies and institute other regulatory infrastructure. Certification would create boundaries between who is (and is not) an OD professional and what is (and is not) OD practice.

The pragmatic trend is also distinguished by an emphasis on change technologies, typically under the banner of 'change management'. In contrast to OD's 'soft' reputation, change management is viewed as a highly relevant and applied practice, much like medicine, engineering or accounting.[7] It focuses on helping organisations implement change and adapt to turbulent environments.[8] Relevance, a minor chord among traditionalists, is a major theme among pragmatists, who value the performance outcomes of OD work. Thus, process interventions are not seen as ends in themselves but as means for implementing change and achieving the desired results. Application 12.1 alerts students in postgraduate courses that political skills, or soft skills, are becoming more important in the business world.

12.1

APPLICATION

Political savvy just one of five skills MBAs need on board

For all their claims to distinctiveness, the core structure of most Australian MBAs is surprisingly similar and has changed little through the years.

Core subjects typically include accounting, finance, marketing, economics, strategy and organisational behaviour. There are important managerial competencies, however, that are less evident in a traditional MBA curriculum. Based on observations of, and discussions with, hundreds of senior executives through the years, here are five key skills managers do well to acquire.

- Political skills: Perhaps no activity is as condemned, but widely practised, as organisational politics. Organisational politics has acquired a bad reputation in many quarters, but mastering political skills such as influencing, lobbying and building coalitions of interest is essential for any effective executive. Organisational politics needs to be rescued from its pejorative associations and seen as the essential managerial skill it is.
- Taking advice: While decisiveness is rightly celebrated in business, very few critical business decisions are made by an individual alone. As a result, managers need to recognise when they need advice, know how to find good advisers and be able to recognise and act on good advice when they get it. This ability to draw on the expertise of others

becomes more important as the scope of a manager's role grows, as a successful manager will outgrow their original functional knowledge.

- Personal productivity: A good senior manager's time is highly leveraged and having an extra hour or so a week available through superior personal productivity can be invaluable for the organisations they lead. This, of course, has been recognised by the market. There is a bewildering array of personal productivity tools, techniques and systems available to the time-pressed executive. Finding their way through this maze of options can be time consuming in itself.
- Communication: Whether the organisational context is a new strategic initiative, a substantial turnaround or simply the ongoing effort to ensure effective execution, the maxim 'you can never over-communicate' is one you will hear repeatedly from senior executives. The ability to shape, craft, convey and sell a credible message to a wide range of people through a wide variety of media and forums is a rare and valued commodity.
- Hiring decisions: As the scope of an individual manager's role grows, commented Amazon's Jeff Bezos, 'how I can run my business' decisions increasingly become decisions about 'who can run this business for me'. Perhaps no class of decisions a senior manager makes is as important as the key appointments they make. Through these decisions a manager casts a long shadow – for better or worse – across the affected parts of the organisation.

How can these skills fit into the traditional MBA curriculum? Criticising MBA curriculums is something of a periodic sport among business commentators, sometimes leading to bestselling books such as Mark McCormack's *What They Still Don't Teach You at Harvard Business School* (a successor to a work more than a decade earlier) and Henry Mintzberg's *Managers, not MBAs*.

Like educators everywhere, business schools have the problem of accommodating disparate demands for curriculum additions with the reality that contact hours and staff resources are limited. The traditional MBA curriculum, after all, has some real benefits.

Studying a wide range of subjects can help in understanding how different line functions contribute to the organisation, as well as provide different analytical frameworks through which to view complex business problems.

Notionally, at least, a generalist approach prepares the MBA student for a wide variety of management roles, something that appeals to the student (who values the career flexibility implied) and the institution (which values the greater student numbers a generalist program can bring in).

Nonetheless, mutual satisfaction, or even complacency, between staff and students should not stymie sensible innovations in curriculum and learning methods.

Source: Mike Riddiford, 'Political savvy just one of five skills MBAs need on board',
The Australian, 30 September 2009. News Limited.

Critical thinking questions:
1. How do the managerial skills listed above relate to OD?
2. Is it possible to create a certification process for accrediting competent change agents? Discuss both perspectives and justify your answer.
3. Is the maxim 'You can never overcommunicate' always correct? What are the associated conditions required to make it appropriate?
4. Politics, as the article intimates, can be seen as destructive in an organisation. Have you observed politics in play in business? Was it being used for good or bad? Why?

Scholarly

The third trend within OD is connected with the increasing number of people making research contributions to our understanding of change. Championed by universities and applied research centres, such as USC's Center for Effective Organisations and MIT's Society of Organization Learning, and the Centre for Corporate Change in the Australian Graduate School of Management at the University of New South Wales and the Centre for Workplace Culture Change at RMIT University, scholars propose a 'research agenda' for OD that includes (1) how multiple contexts and levels of analysis affect organisational change; (2) the inclusion of time, history, process and action in theories of change; (3) the link between change processes and organisation performance; (4) the comparative analysis of international and cross-cultural OD interventions; (5) the study of receptivity, customisation, sequencing, pace and episodic versus continuous change processes; and (6) the partnership between scholars and practitioners in studying organisational change.[9]

The scholarly perspective focuses on understanding, predicting and controlling change. It is far less concerned about how OD is defined, what its values are, how it is practised, or whether an OD practitioner is involved except as potential explanations for change success. OD is just one of several ways organisations can be changed. Unlike traditionalists and pragmatists, scholars are concerned with creating valid knowledge and with generalising conclusions about how change occurs, how it is triggered, under what conditions it works well and so on. Similar to the traditional and pragmatic trends, however, the scholarly trend is connected to the actors involved in change; its favoured methodology is action research but from a more distant and detached perspective than the other two trends.

Implications for the future of OD

These three trends are likely to have important consequences for OD's future. In the short term, advocates of each view will likely continue on their separate paths with periodic and perhaps intense conflicts among them. In the longer term, however, there should be increasing attempts at reconciling these differences and generating a more integrative view of OD.

OD will have more conflicts in the short term

Current views and debates about OD values and professionalisation are likely to continue at least in the near term. The traditional and pragmatic trends hold different and often conflicting views of how the field should evolve. Traditionalists fear that OD is becoming too corporate and may unwittingly collude with powerful stakeholders to promote goals that are inconsistent with OD's social responsibility[10] and humanistic values.[11] For example, corporate strategies can concentrate wealth and ignore cultural diversity. Technology can isolate people and alienate them. The traditionalists, therefore, advocate a stronger focus on the central values of the field. Pragmatists, on the other hand, worry that relying too heavily on traditional values will reinforce OD's 'touchy-feely' orientation. They argue that focusing on human potential exclusively will doom OD to irrelevance in today's highly competitive organisations. Thus, in the short term, the battle over values within the field is likely to continue.

Symbolic of the struggle, no fewer than three formal projects are under way to clarify OD's values. Each effort is championed by a different institutional sponsor, relies on a different set of OD practitioners and argues that their results will clarify this important issue for the field. The ongoing conflict in the field is therefore likely to continue and may become even more intense as additional values, such as environmental sustainability and economic equality, enter the OD field.

OD is also likely to face more disagreement over professionalisation. The debate over values discussed above demonstrates how difficult it will be to gain agreement about standards, competencies, enforcement mechanisms and oversight. Unless a groundswell of support for a common set of OD values emerges, judgements about qualifications will likely become caught up in conflicts between the traditional and the pragmatic perspectives. Several prior attempts to professionalise the field or to accredit practitioners have had limited success and provide ample evidence of the difficulty of resolving such differences.

OD will become more integrated in the long term

Despite the conflicts likely to continue in the short run, there is considerable common ground among the diverse trends within OD and the emergence of a more integrated view of the field seems likely in the long term. For example, both the traditional and the pragmatic trends agree that applying behavioural science to organisations can improve effectiveness and increase member satisfaction. Both trends believe that knowledge and skill should be transferred to a client system and all three trends believe that a body of theory and practice underlies the process of change in organisations.

Given OD's history, its long-term future is likely to be some blend of practitioner values in use (traditional trend), professional change practice (pragmatic trend) and change theory (scholarly trend). The field is not likely to be completely pragmatic and ignore its values base; there is little likelihood that it will return to its purely traditional roots and be irrelevant to business; and the subject of change is too important and personal to be left to research alone. A more limited integration is also problematic. A pragmatic and research-driven OD would be cold and impersonal; a traditional and research-driven field would be naïve and irrelevant to economic realities; and a traditional and pragmatic-driven OD would be intuitive and non-cumulative. An integration of the three trends, on the other hand, will assure that OD has moral purpose, drives sustainable bottom lines and represents a healthy balance of art and science.

A set of integrated values, including participation and effectiveness but recognising the tension between them, will drive the traditional and pragmatic trends to exploit the common ground in theory and practice. For example, the theories of change underlying traditional action research; positive scholarship and practice; contemporary approaches[12] to change, such as network models, complexity and chaos theories; and the evolution of underorganised systems can be integrated. The practical benefits of traditional objective approaches and the traditional values reflected in a social constructionist view, hold promise for a new view of OD.

This integrated view will challenge the field to redefine existing views of work, competition, culture and organisations. OD cannot view systems only as objects with inertia, structure, resistance and permanence, but as social processes produced, maintained and changed through conversations that are flexible, aspirational and changeable.[13] A positive view of organisations and their members' potential aligns well with the traditional trend and supports values of basic human rights, social responsibility, democracy and environmental sustainability.[14] This view of organisations also supports the pragmatic trend; it recognises the importance of economic viability, the time value of activity and the opportunities that growth conveys. If carefully applied, an integrated objective and socially constructed perspective can be an influential voice in OD's future.

TRENDS IN THE CONTEXT OF ORGANISATION DEVELOPMENT

The field of OD is evolving, but so too is the context within which OD is applied. As summarised in Figure 12.2, several interrelated trends are affecting the context within which OD will be applied in the near future. They concern various aspects of the economy, the workforce, technology and organisations. In some cases, the trends will directly affect OD practice. Technology trends, such as Internet portals, voice over the Internet and wireless networks, will no doubt influence how OD practitioners communicate with organisation members, facilitate teams and manage change. Other trends, such as the increasing concentration of wealth, represent important contextual forces that will indirectly affect OD through their interaction with other trends.[15]

The economy

Researchers and futurists have described a variety of economic scenarios; there is substantial agreement that the world's economy is in the midst of a transition from the industrial age that characterised much of the twentieth century.[16] Although these scenarios differ in their particulars, they all fit under the rubric of globalisation and many of the same trends are identified as drivers, including technology, workforce and organisation, which will be discussed separately.

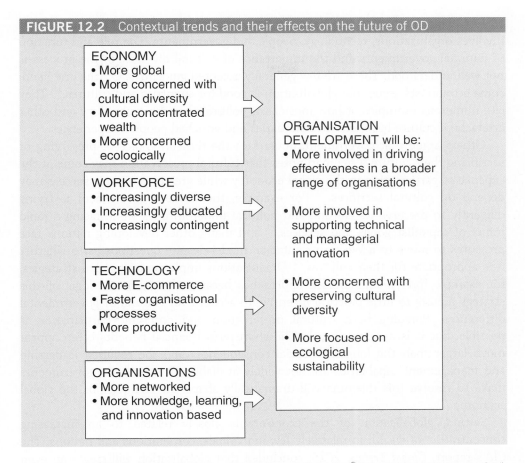

FIGURE 12.2 Contextual trends and their effects on the future of OD

ECONOMY
• More global
• More concerned with cultural diversity
• More concentrated wealth
• More concerned ecologically

WORKFORCE
• Increasingly diverse
• Increasingly educated
• Increasingly contingent

TECHNOLOGY
• More E-commerce
• Faster organisational processes
• More productivity

ORGANISATIONS
• More networked
• More knowledge, learning, and innovation based

ORGANISATION DEVELOPMENT will be:
• More involved in driving effectiveness in a broader range of organisations

• More involved in supporting technical and managerial innovation

• More concerned with preserving cultural diversity

• More focused on ecological sustainability

Source: Cummings/Worley, *Organization Development and Change* (with InfoTrac® College Edition Printed Access Card), 9e © 2009 South-Western, a part of Cengage Learning, Inc. Reproduced by permission www.cengage.com/permissions.

The fall of the Berlin Wall, the end of apartheid, the breakup of the former Soviet Union, the creation of the European Union, terrorist attacks in many different countries and the emergence of the Chinese and Indian economies are key events in the transition to a global economy. Organisations from around the world are increasingly able to shift their manufacturing from high- to low-labour-cost countries, execute international mergers and acquisitions and build worldwide service businesses. Today, almost any product or service can be made, transported and bought anywhere in the world. Globalisation can help companies reduce costs, gain resources, expand markets and develop new products and practices more quickly.

The emergence of a global economy is well under way, but the promise and rationalisation of that process is far from complete.[17] The initial steps towards globalisation have fuelled real price decreases in many consumer products, provided employment for people in less-developed nations and driven revenue growth in a variety of industries. However, the transition to a global economy is for the most part unmanaged, accompanied by increasing concern over its social and environmental consequences.[18] This raises troublesome questions about three key issues: *cultural diversity*, *income distribution* and *environmental sustainability*.

First, transitioning to a global economy is a complex and daunting process that involves organisations, technology, people and governments. The role and function of national governments and the importance of cultural diversity in the process is not well understood. There are few generally accepted guidelines. On the one hand, some economists argue that globalisation is good for countries and cultures.[19] They cite numerous examples of how music, art, political thought, technology and other artefacts of culture have crossed boundaries and enriched people's experiences.

Others argue that governments must face the difficult choice of preserving or sacrificing their culture. Friedman notes that cultural preservation may come at the expense of participation in the global economy while greater economic success may depend on cultural sacrifices.[20] For example, the Chinese government is trying diligently to preserve its cultural and political underpinnings while facing a rapid influx of capitalist goods and services,[21] and many other developing nations face pressures to move to a Western capitalism model despite questions as to whether it is appropriate for their cultures.[22] Organisations implementing global strategies, for example, prefer standardised approaches because the economic logic of this strategy admits to little practical incentive to account for cultural or governmental differences. Pursuing both cultural preservation and economic participation is possible, but it is a complex task. The short-term financial benefits often appear much larger than the long-term social consequences and the required leadership and management capabilities are not widely available. The decisions governments make to resolve this dilemma will dramatically shape the character of the global economy.

Second, globalisation of the economy is closely related to an increasing concentration of wealth in relatively few individuals, corporations and nations. The CIA's report, *Global Trends, 2015*, concluded that globalisation will create an even wider gap between regional winners and losers than exists today. [Its] evolution will be rocky, marked by chronic volatility and a widening economic divide ... deepening economic stagnation, political instability and cultural alienation. [It] will foster political, ethnic, ideological and religious extremism, along with the violence that often accompanies it.[23]

Consider the following:

- US Census data confirms that the share of total income accounted for by the top 20% of households increased from about 43% to over 51% between 1975 and 2005, while the bottom 20% of households saw their share drop from 4% to 3%.[24]

- Using a conservative measure of CEO pay, the Economic Policy Institute estimated that in 2005 the average CEO in the United States earned 262 times the pay of the average worker, the second highest ratio in the 40 years of their data collection. (Other estimates have put the ratio as high as 431:1 for 2004.) To put this in perspective, a CEO earned more in a day than the average worker did in a year.[25]

- The 793 billionaires in 2006 represent an increase of 103 people between 2005 and 2006. Representing about 0.00001% of the world's population, their net worth of $2.6 trillion accounts for about 19.5% of the US gross domestic product.[26]
- Of the world's 6.2 billion people, 5.2 billion live in low- and moderate-income countries and survive on about $3 a day.[27]

The concentration of wealth may be a natural outcome of capitalism facing imperfectly competitive markets, but it can also contribute to misallocation of resources, environmental degradation and short-term thinking.[28] For example, the financial markets' focus on quarterly earnings can skew decision-making criteria to delay preventive maintenance or safety initiatives, postpone implementation of necessary environmental-protection equipment, or forgo important long-term capital investments. The concentration of wealth can also contribute to social conflict driven by fears that the wealthy will act in their own self-interest at the expense of those who are financially less fortunate. The history of the WTO provides visible examples, such as the cancellation of the 2003 meetings in Cancun, Mexico because developing nations banded together against developed countries who were accused of not listening to requests for modifications in trade agreements.

Third, there are increasingly clear warnings that the ecosystem can no longer be treated as a factor of production and that success cannot be defined as the accumulation of wealth and material goods at the expense of the environment. There are strong pressures to fuel economic growth, for example, by exploring and developing oilfields in sensitive and protected areas such as the Arctic National Wildlife Refuge. Yet, sport-utility vehicle (SUV) demand remains strong despite concerns over inefficient fuel consumption. If SUVs complied with the same fuel-economy standards as ordinary cars, the United States would save 1 million barrels of oil a day, more than the Arctic National Wildlife Refuge could produce at peak volumes.[29] These concerns arise in part from the proliferation of capitalism, but also from the growing realisation that free and open markets can have negative unintended consequences for the global ecosystem.

The conclusions from the Intergovernmental Panel on Climate Change suggest that industrialisation is not a controversial but a probable cause of global warming.[30] Several traditional organisations, such as BP and Royal Dutch/Shell, are reversing long-held opinions about their contribution to environmental decay by setting aggressive goals to reduce greenhouse gases.[31] However, many developing economies, including China, the Philippines and Mexico, continue to operate with loose environmental controls. As a result, there are more calls for change in the values underlying capitalism – from consumption to investment, from open to mindful markets and from wealth accumulation as an end in itself to an examination of the return on living capital.[32] Some observers note that such value shifts are already under way in many nations and organisations. For example, traditional business models that assume labour scarcity and natural resource abundance are being tempered by models that emphasise the abundance of knowledge and the scarcity of natural resources. A number of companies, including IKEA, Interface, Honda, S.C. Johnson and Hewlett-Packard, have altered their operations and practices radically to reduce emissions, waste and environmental degradation and to increase sustainability, profits and customer satisfaction.

The workforce

The workforce is becoming more diverse, educated and contingent. Organisations, whether they operate primarily in their home country or abroad, will need to develop policies and operating styles that embrace the changing cultural, ethnic, gender and age diversity of the workforce.

The workforce is also becoming more educated. The 2006 US Census data, for example, reported that 84.1% of adults over 25 years of age have completed high school and that 27% have a bachelor's or higher degree. Both numbers represent similar proportions compared to 2002 but significant increases compared to 2000. A more educated workforce is likely to demand higher wages, more involvement in the decision-making process and continued investment in knowledge and skills. For example, the rate of change in information systems technology requires IT professionals to continually update their knowledge and skills to remain competent. In response, organisations are increasing their training and management development budgets significantly.[33] Many organisations, such as Motorola, Capital One, Boeing and Harley-Davidson, have invested in corporate universities and corporate–university partnerships and many others have policies outlining the minimum hours of technical and managerial training that each employee will receive yearly. Application 12.2 proposes that we should be more accommodating of diverse views and build mechanisms for the story to be told.

12.2

APPLICATION

Creativity can come from anyone, so let's look beyond the elite

Australia has a rich bohemian tradition: the postmodern subcultures of the 1980s and 90s, punk and hippy countercultures of the 70s and 60s, back to the Angry Penguins, the *Bulletin* bards of the late 19th century and Marcus Clarke's dandyish clubs in the 1860s and 70s.

Bohemia has great value for artists, not least as a stimulating space to nurture transgressive art. It is where unknown young artists make contacts and generate a buzz in the city. It is an escalator of social mobility, merging at one end with the demimonde and deviant and at the other with the bourgeois customer and political class. Bohemian pastimes of intense conversation, showing off, dining, drinking and drugging enhance networks and creativity. Being a bohemian is a licence to take risks.

While such formations cannot be controlled, governments and managements can enable some of them and they can certainly be damaged or destroyed, to the detriment of creativity in the community.

Late 20th-century managerial models – beloved of the Australia Council and government film funders – that seek to account for and control all assets actually destroy creativity.

>>

For me the role of the state and public intervention is to encourage diversity of channels of production and distribution and ensure a fair democratic spread of cultural capital. Further, the state should encourage, within public and private institutions, those intangible networks that build cultural capital and audiences.

A new cultural renaissance will not be built by bureaucrats subsidising elitism or picking winners to entertain us, but by entrepreneurs and public institutions bold enough to harness the diverse creative energy in the community, from suburban garages to inner-city garrets.

Social democrats in state and federal government and the public arts bodies need to avoid Keating-era notions that divide artists from the rest of us as a special caste and instead ask, 'How can we spread creativity around?'

I am critical of the persistent romantic idea of the artist-hero and of the disconnection of Australian arts from contemporary working-class life. We need to counter the dichotomy of artist and philistine masses with an appreciation of the creativity of popular cultural forms, craft skills and the role of audiences in creating value for art.

In place of the passive arts consumer I want to emphasise the idea of all people as creative producers.

I don't mean a Wayne's World of amateurism, but genuine, democratic talent-scouting: a 21st-century version of the approach *The Bulletin* took in the 1890s, scouring the bush and the back lanes looking for poets and artists, which led to the discovery of the likes of Henry Lawson, Banjo Paterson and Norman Lindsay.

It was the magazine's carnivalesque disruption of expectation and its topsy-turvy mockery of authority – the blending of genres, use of cartoons and humour, self-conscious parody of the media and blurring of readership and contributors – that made it subversive. The best Australian culture erupts when media enfranchise passionate communities and become clearing houses for new ideas and styles, as happened again with early 70s cinema, Nation Review, Double Jay, inner-city post-punk pop and even Countdown.

Today's managers need to consider the relationship of content producers and distributors to their audiences. Australian arts discourse, enamoured of the artist-hero or star, does not pay audiences sufficient regard.

Audiences not only add value by the way they make sense of art, but are also a source of ideas and aesthetic innovation: the suburbs are much weirder, more interesting and diverse than gatekeepers and programmers obsessed with a mythical mainstream could ever imagine.

One of the drivers in youth's passion for digital mobile phones is that they can use them to contribute to their self-made cultures. Out in the suburbs young people are assembling multi-identities from the material surrounding them as they grow up: the immigration experience, family, religion and politics, sexual options, global television, the Internet, blogs, music culture and the neighbourhood.

Cultural diversity – ethnic, lifestyle, regional, religious – is the great narrative of contemporary Australian life but, apart from a few examples, it makes barely a ripple in our media or art. The clash and fusion of cultures in the suburbs is a new wellspring of hybrid art, just as cubism, jazz and rock rolled out of the cities in the 20th century.

At present far too many of our filmmakers, journalists and artists come from well-off, upper-middle-class backgrounds via elite institutions such as universities, the Australian Film Television and Radio School and the National Institute of Dramatic Art. The trick is to keep these arts finishing schools and Australia Council grants at the apex of the pyramid, but to build on a base of democratic creativity fostered through the public education system.

Veteran art historian Bernard Smith asked this of the Blue Poles-smitten Whitlam government back in the 70s and it is even more relevant today when cultural industries are becoming economic powerhouses.

The great Australian cricketers and swimmers arose from a vibrant participation of all kids in school and local team sport. Smith reckoned everyone is an artist, just as we can all play sport and recommended that government intervention go into energising arts instruction in state schools, including fine art, creative writing, music and so on.

Most kids love to draw, paint, sing and tell jokes, but their natural talent and inclination gets knocked out of them as they move through high school. 'If your object is excellence,' Smith observed, 'you begin with a broad base: elitism fails because it insists upon a narrow base; its apex fails to reach the limits of the possible.'

Source: Dr. Tony Moore, 'Creativity can come from anyone, so let's look beyond the elite', *The Australian*, 18 June 2009. News Limited.

Critical thinking questions:
1. 'If your object is excellence you begin with a broad base: elitism fails because it insists upon a narrow base; its apex fails to reach the limits of the possible.' What do you understand this to mean? Give examples to support your interpretation.
2. Can education stifle creativity? Explain your answer.
3. What are the implications of this application for successful OD? Why?

Finally, the continued high rate of downsizings, re-engineering efforts and mergers and acquisitions is forcing the workforce to become more contingent and less loyal. The US Bureau of Labor Statistics reports that contingent and 'alternative arrangement' workers, including temporary and contract employees, freelancers, independent professionals and consultants, made up between 12.4% and 14.8% of the workforce in 2005.[34] The implicit psychological contract that governs relationships between employers and employees is being rewritten with new assumptions about long-term employment and rewards in exchange for commitment and loyalty. For example, a study by the National Association of Temporary and Staffing Services in the United States found that 90% of companies use temporary help.[35] Other studies have suggested that the personnel supply services industry, about 90% of which is involved in providing contingent employees, will be among the top five fastest-growing industries. One article noted that the contingent staffing industry doubled in size between 2002 and 2007 and would grow to about $200 billion in 2010.[36]

Technology

By almost any measure, information technology is a significant and increasingly common fact of life. An estimated 150.9 million worldwide Internet users in 1998 grew to 605.6 million in 2002.[37] In 2007, according to an Internet World Stats estimate, more than 1.24 billion people were on the Internet and of those, 37% were in Asia.[38] The Internet is the backbone of a global economy and although the technology sector has suffered financial setbacks, few people doubt it's importance.

At the core of information technology is e-commerce, an economy that knows no boundaries.[39] E-commerce involves using automatic teller machines, buying games on your mobile phone, buying and selling products and services over the Internet and selling advertising space. This range of activities makes estimating the size of the e-commerce market difficult. For example, one study estimated that worldwide online retail sales grew 22% to $143.2 billion for 2005 while the US Census Bureau estimated that US online retail sales for 2006 grew about 20% to $119 billion.[40]

Two types of e-commerce seem particularly relevant to OD's future: business-to-consumer and business-to-business. The business-to-consumer market garners much attention and awareness because it is how the public participates in e-commerce. This market, which includes e-tailers such as Amazon.com and eBay.com, is expected to grow in the United States from $172 billion in 2005 to over $329 billion by 2010.[41] In these businesses, OD must help to create and implement novel business models. Dell Computer, for instance, sells custom-made computers to consumers and businesses, but it started out as a mail-order company advertising in the back of magazines. More than 25% of its computer sales come through the Internet. The shift in organisation structures, labour skill sets, work designs and work processes in the transformation from a mail-order business to an e-commerce leader represents the kind of change that many organisations will face and the challenges OD practitioners must meet.

The organisational issues in the business-to-business market are even more complex. A good example of the implications and potential of this market is the global automobile industry's creation of an online store. In February 2000, the major automakers jointly addressed escalating costs and gross inefficiencies of their supply chain to create Covisint, a business that aimed to leverage the power and potential of the Internet to solve industry-specific business problems in real time. Today, Covisint supports over 266 000 users, representing more than 30 000 organisations in over 96 countries in the global automotive industry. In addition, Covisint has moved into the health care industry and supports over 15 000 users, representing more than 450 North American health systems, commercial payers, physician groups/practices, home health agencies, third-party administrators, extended care facilities and home medical equipment providers. Covisint migrates an entire industry's supply chain on to the Internet and re-engineers radically the way businesses interact with each other. Web-based transactions are replacing the inefficient phone, mail and face-to-face sales call processes that dominated these industries.

In addition to providing the infrastructure for e-commerce, technology is also changing and enabling a variety of organisational processes. Technologies, such as SAP or PeopleSoft, drive changes in how information and work processes are co-ordinated and managed; they also require modification in the way productivity is measured. For example, the implementation of enterprise resource systems and supply-chain management programs must integrate with existing work processes and the competencies of organisation members. This requires adjustments in the entire sociotechnical system and how it interfaces with customers, suppliers, regulators and other stakeholders.

Finally, we are gaining a clearer picture of the way technology affects productivity. For example, for years, economists were puzzled by a 'productivity paradox'. Despite a 30-year, $2 trillion investment in computers and technology, productivity rose very slowly during the 1980s and early 1990s. But in 1999, productivity rose 2.9% in the United States (and 5% in the last six months of 1999), nearly twice the 1.5% average annual gains seen since the early 1970s. The biggest gains were in manufacturing, but service businesses such as transportation, trade and finance also started to see a payoff from new technology investments. This productivity lag apparently resulted from the relatively long time it took for organisations to adopt the new technology and learn how to apply it.[42] For example, Countrywide Home Loans, one of the largest mortgage lenders in the United States, began experimenting with technology solutions in the late 1980s. The benefits of technology investment did not pay off until a 1997 implementation of an automated information system in its customer service centre helped reduce the average cost per call from $4 to less than $0.60 on more than 20 000 calls per day. The increased productivity has not cost jobs; Countrywide nearly doubled its workforce between 1996 and 1999. Application 12.3 is an example of where the IT sector has taken advantage of the economic climate to implement change.

Staying power

Many managers who started the senior stage of their careers after 1991 are seeing the signs of serious downturn for the first time. However, the IT industry went through its own nightmare just seven years ago during the dotcom bust.

Battle-hardened senior managers in the IT sector welcome the new era of fiscal constraint as an opportunity to fast track the introduction of more efficient technologies.

While some expect to lose a small amount of business as projects are placed on hold or cancelled, most are predicting growth as the corporate sector looks for technologies to increase productivity in tough times.

'The important thing to remember about a downturn is that it represents a challenge for the incumbents and a tremendous opportunity for the businesses which can present themselves as an alternative,' the managing director of security and data protection software vendor Sophos, Rob Forsyth, says.

'It's a bit Darwinian really – times like this cause great stress and hardship but they also lead to great technical innovation,' Forsyth says. 'And it's those companies that are most able to focus on the customer and respond to their needs despite what's happening in the background that will succeed.'

It is more than just bravado. In the past two years, technologies such as process automation, remote systems management and server and storage virtualisation, have enabled service-focused IT companies to remove much of the capital expenditure associated with the adoption of new technologies by offering many as managed services rather than projects.

At the same time, technologies once confined by price to large companies and government departments have been retooled, repriced and focused on the small-to-medium end of town. As a result, the IT industry is riding a wave of demand for inexpensive productivity tools.

>>

Vigabyte is a case in point. A spin-off from website-hosting outfit SmartyHost, the Vigabyte product allows clients to expand or decrease the processing services they need through a website, whereas most hosting firms require their staff to respond to client needs manually. The Vigabyte tool cuts the client's costs associated with datacentre services and reduces the host's response time to its clients' requirements.

At the other end of the scale, the managing director of IBM Australia and New Zealand, Glen Boreham, is concerned about how the financial crisis in the United States will affect the local economy. But he sees it as an opportunity for the IT industry and for Australia's services sector.

'The current downturn is a challenge, but we should also focus on the opportunities that exist for the Australian economy to provide services into Asian markets,' Boreham says. 'Up until now, a lot of the focus has been on the emerging middle class in Asia as a consumer of manufacturing goods, but they will also need to consume services we are perfectly placed to provide.'

Source: Jeanne-Vida Douglas, 'Staying power', *Business Review Weekly*, 23 October 2009.

Critical thinking questions:
1. Under what circumstances can organisations in the IT industry survive the economic downturn? Why have some other industries been victims of the downturn?
2. In the Application, two companies have responded differently to the downturn. Why is this the case? Is one more likely to be successful?
3. The article refers to capital savings achievable through outsourcing of services. What are the benefits and disadvantages to small business of outsourcing? Why?

Organisations

The final trend likely to shape OD's future involves the increasingly networked and knowledge-based nature of organisations. The interventions described in this book help organisations become more streamlined and flexible, more capable of continuously improving themselves in response to economic and other trends, and more effective. A large proportion of organisations are not aware of these practices, however, and still others resist applying them.[43] Despite the attention to them in the business press, only a small percentage of organisations use self-managed work teams, are organised into networks, successfully manage strategic alliances or have organisation learning programs. But these organisations are harbingers of the future and they will invent entirely new, entrepreneurial structures capable of exploiting new ideas and technologies quickly.

Clearly, organisations are becoming more networked and rely on collaborative strategies and allow single organisations to partner with other organisations to develop, manufacture and distribute goods and services.[44] More than any other organisation form, networks hold the promise of realising the economic opportunities presented by globalisation without the negative social consequences of large multinational corporations.[45] Large organisations that gain economies of scale in manufacturing, distribution and marketing can also become rigid and slow and indifferent to unintended social and environmental consequences. These latter outcomes can be disastrous in today's rapidly changing environments and cannot be easily remedied in the future. Networks, on the other hand, enable small organisations to access the advantages of scale and scope traditionally reserved for large organisations. Small, focused organisations that perform particular tasks with excellence can align with organisations that have complementary resources and expertise. These networks are highly adaptable and can disband and reform along different task or market lines as the circumstances demand. To succeed, organisations are learning how to assess quickly whether they are compatible with network partners and whether the joint product/service is successful. They are gaining competence to form and end networks swiftly, thus enabling them to exploit product/market opportunities rapidly and to 'fail quickly' when the network is unproductive.[46] Because each network node (organisation) is small and local, resident cultures and ecosystems are more likely to be preserved.

Finally, in an organisational world that is technically enabled, fast-paced and networked, there will be a premium placed on learning and knowledge management. This increasingly important source of organisational capability and competitive advantage will require unprecedented amounts of innovation and co-ordination. Multiple stakeholders representing a diversity of interests will come together to envision a shared future and to learn how to enact it.

Because this process typically leads into uncharted waters, both organisational members and OD practitioners will be joint learners, exploring new territory together. Moreover, implementing new organisational innovations will require significant amounts of experimentation as members try out new ways of operating, assess progress and make necessary adjustments. In essence, they will learn from their actions how to create a new strategy, organisation or product/service. Such collaborative learning is capable of implementing radically new possibilities and ways of functioning that could not be envisioned beforehand. It is a process of *innovation*, not of detection and correction of errors. In turn, the new structures and systems will increase feedback and information flow to the organisation, thereby improving its capacity to learn and adapt to a rapidly changing environment. They will transcend both internal and external organisational boundaries, remove barriers to learning and facilitate how employees acquire, organise and disseminate knowledge assets.

Implications for the future of OD

The definition and practice of OD in the future will depend on the forces within OD as well as the economic, workforce, technological and organisation trends outlined above. Although a variety of scenarios are possible, we have chosen to present a likely and positive picture.[47] Figure 12.2, shown earlier, summarises this view.

Organisation development played a powerful role in organisation and social change in the 1960s and 1970s. A set of shared values, including involvement and participation and a complementary set of practices, such as team building and survey feedback, shaped the way leaders and managers designed and operated organisations. Together, these integrated values and practices improved both human and economic outcomes.[48] Application 12.4 asks the question, has anything changed?

12.4

APPLICATION

Problem of a familiar hue

Over lunch, the service manager of a mid-sized software company relates an involved story about a dispute he is having with one of the company's salesmen. At the end of his story, apropos of nothing, the manager adds a final observation about the protagonist: 'He's Jewish.'

Sitting in a train, a young office worker tells her mate a gossipy tale about a workplace feud and notes in conclusion: 'I probably shouldn't say this, but he's Greek and they're apparently worse than the Italians.'

This week, I was presented with anecdotal evidence that some companies, despite a desperate shortage of skilled staff, avoid employing overseas skilled migrants because they are 'too hard' to manage.

Multicultural Australia makes much of being a 'tolerant' society, which is a curious boast. Tolerance hardly suggests the passionate embrace of ethnic and cultural diversity. The evidence of that is all around us.

A management consultant tells of an 'icon' Australian company which decided to introduce a program aimed at employing more Aborigines. The company already employed some indigenous Australians, but did not know how many.

As part of the initiative, the company distributed a questionnaire to its employees which required them, among other things, to indicate if they were Aboriginal. Many indigenous employees declined to reveal themselves, fearing the reaction of their workmates and supervisors. They were concerned that they would be ostracised by their workmates because they would be seen to be receiving special privileges. Some of those who did indicate their Aboriginality have since complained that this is exactly what happened.

Many employees assume that diversity will manage itself, but the reality is that workplaces, like the wider community, are at best superficially at ease with difference.

Prejudice, however latent or dormant, has a way of manifesting itself when least expected. The 2005 Cronulla riots in Sydney reminded us of that, as more recently did the Alice Springs hostel manager who refused accommodation to a group of young indigenous women because she said they frightened Asian tourists.

Ethnic, cultural and religious sensitivity in Australian business is an urgent priority. The challenge is not so much new as it is heightened. It reflects the changing face of Australian society, the impact of globalisation and the bitter divides that have stemmed from the threat of terrorism.

This is an issue on which business can and must lead the way and every indication is that there is a long way to go.

Source: Leo D'Angelo Fisher, 'Problem of a familiar hue', *Business Review Weekly*, 20 March 2008.

Critical thinking questions:
1. How may OD interventions assist with the recognition and successful inclusion of cultural diversity in the workplace?
2. Identify some of the issues associated with cultural diversity in the workplace.
3. What is meant by 'reverse discrimination'? What impact would this have on an organisation?

Recognising the powerful influence that shared values and supportive practices can have, OD in the future will support a policy of 'responsible progress'. Responsible progress begins with an economist's definition of an effective system, integrates traditional OD and more recent effectiveness values and promotes a set of practices to actualise those values. Economists traditionally define progress and economic health in terms of the development of products and services that make society better off, the ability to put scarce resources to their most efficient use, the capacity to support full employment and the equitable distribution of rewards in relation to the risks people take in productive enterprise. Although few people would argue with these criteria, the trends discussed above suggest that there have been important unintended consequences of promoting those goals. For example, global warming and the concentration of wealth cannot be the metrics by which society is judged as 'better off'. The traditional criteria of progress either ignore the environment and cultural diversity or make untenable assumptions about the market's ability to account for them.

Responsible progress addresses that gap by defining a policy that supports economic success and innovation, promotes efficiency and progress, but incorporates cultural diversity and environmental sustainability to produce a more balanced view of effectiveness. It supports a set of traditional and effectiveness-related values as well as practices that reflect today's and tomorrow's organisations. The responsible progress policy asserts that individuals, organisations and countries can pursue economic and personal success through open innovation that leverages and nurtures cultural diversity and the environment.[49] It defines a vision, strategy and future path for OD.

OD will work to shape a global economy populated with flexible, innovative, networked and environmentally responsible organisations that thrive on cultural diversity.[50] As an important influence of this world vision, OD is more likely to develop interventions that drive effectiveness in a broader range of organisations, support technological and managerial innovation, preserve cultural diversity and advocate environmentally sustainable practices.

OD will be more involved in driving effectiveness in a broader range of organisations

Responsible progress affirms that all forms of organisations should have the opportunity to be successful. It suggests, however, that success cannot be achieved at the expense of cultural diversity and the environment. When OD lacks the shared values and applied focus of responsible progress, success can lead to cultural assimilation and environmental damage. The changing context of OD, in particular the economic and organisational trends, suggest that planned change in the future should be as concerned with effectiveness as it is with traditional values of participation and workplace democracy. It will also be applied to a more diverse client base.

Traditionally, OD focused on large business organisations, but three other types of organisations increasingly will become targets of planned change: *small entrepreneurial start-ups*, *government organisations* and *global social change organisations*. Small, entrepreneurial start-ups are an important and underserved market for OD. Many of these organisations are at the forefront of the technology trends cited earlier. Because they are operating on scarce, expensive and finite venture capital, time is their most valuable asset and the one most critical to their success. As a result, entrepreneurial firms generally have a clear action orientation, little perceived need to reflect and learn and few structures and systems to guide behaviours and decisions.[51] This is a context that can be well served by fast, flexible change processes orienting new people quickly to the business strategy, integrating them rapidly into new work roles, increasing the efficiency of work processes and helping founders and key managers think about how the market, competitors and technology are changing. OD can help entrepreneurs to gain the needed competence to address such matters.

Economic, workforce, technological and organisation trends are also pushing government organisations to become more efficient, flexible and networked. Consequently, government is increasingly applying OD interventions such as strategic planning, employee involvement and performance management, and it is expected that the demand for change management expertise in the public sector will grow. Moreover, governments will become more proactive in managing the effects of global economic development. Public–private partnerships, a form of collaborative strategy, are also likely to flourish. They will require the assistance of OD practitioners who are sensitive to the differences between these two types of organisations and to the demands the partnerships will be under, such as environmental protection, corporate citizenship and taxation.

Similarly, the increasing concentration of wealth and globalisation of the economy will create a plethora of opportunities for OD to assist developing countries, disadvantaged citizens and the environment. In China, for example, as the government continues to break up the old 'work unit' structure and creates market-facing enterprises, the need for NGOs to take over delivery of social services is likely to increase. For example, as discussed in Chapter 10, the Global Village of Beijing has begun campaigns to involve the Chinese people in pro-environment practices and to develop leaders for other NGOs; the China Brief has catalogued NGOs and provided a forum for their communication; the Chinese Association for NGOs (CANGO) provides capacity-building services to help NGOs become more effective; and the World Wildlife Fund (WWF) is partnering with corporations to initiate environmentally friendly policies in China. OD can help these organisations achieve their objectives, manage their resources and improve their functioning through such interventions as team building, strategic planning and alliance building.

Not only will OD be applied to a broader range of organisations, it also will be more concerned with effectiveness than in the past. A large portion of the interventions described in this text were developed in the 1950s and 1960s with the primary aim of increasing participation in organisational processes. As the global economy and information technology enable and push for faster, more flexible organisations, the ability to manage change continuously will become a key source of competitive advantage in all types of organisations. This suggests that OD practices will become more embedded in the organisation's normal operating routines. OD skills, knowledge and competencies can and should become part of the daily work of managers and employees.[52] This will diffuse change capabilities throughout the organisation rather than limit them to a special function or role. It will permit faster and more flexible reactions to challenges faced by the organisation. In addition to embedding OD skills in managerial roles, OD interventions themselves will be integrated into core business processes, such as product development, strategic planning and supply-chain management. This should provide a closer linkage between OD and business results.

This does not mean that the role of the professional OD practitioner will disappear. Professionals will be needed to help organisation members gain change management competencies.[53] Small, entrepreneurial firms will need specialised assistance in bringing on new members rapidly and organising their efforts. Organisations involved in strategic alliances, mergers and acquisitions will need professional help managing inter-organisational interfaces, integrating diverse corporate cultures and co-ordinating business practices. OD professionals will also be needed to assist in the implementation of new technologies, particularly knowledge management practices. As supported by the contingent workforce trends, the demand for skilled OD practitioners is likely to increase rather than decrease. For example, there is some anecdotal evidence to suggest that as line and senior managers learn more about the knowledge and skills associated with OD practice, their requests for assistance in formulating change processes increase. Managers will look more frequently for help in leading and facilitating organisation change.

OD's ability to influence responsible progress will grow as it becomes more concerned with effectiveness and more embedded in a broader range of organisations. As OD demonstrates its ability to solve problems or help the organisation to be more agile and responsive to opportunities, it will become easier to suggest that leaders consider the environmental and cultural implications of their innovations. The promise and purpose of responsible progress encourages such a balanced view of success. Moreover, OD practitioners could begin influencing leaders to consider leveraging cultural and environmental resources to accelerate innovation and effectiveness. OD practitioners can help leaders make policy and implement actions that drive performance by leveraging cultural diversity and recognising how the environment can improve the long-term health of the organisation, its people and the planet.

OD will be more involved in supporting technological and managerial innovation

According to the responsible progress policy, innovation is the primary driver of economic success. Innovation helps to create new products, services and the processes to manufacture and distribute them (technological innovation) and the methods and activities necessary to govern and organise systems towards some goal (managerial innovation). Although technological innovation gets most of the attention in the research and business press, Hamel has recently argued that managerial innovation may be more important.[54] He argues that organisations are still managed and operated according to rules and principles laid down before World War I. If the future of organisation effectiveness hinges more on managerial innovation than technological innovation, there is a clear opportunity for OD. The 'open innovation' models of Chesbrough and the 'built to change' (B2C) principles from Lawler and Worley represent two such sets of new management principles.[55] But there is much more that can be done. In the future, OD will be more involved in shaping technological and managerial innovation[56] according to the principles of responsible progress.

There is little doubt about the pervasive influence of technological innovation on organisations. Increases in the speed with which data and information can be manipulated will drive the rate of new product and service development and the organisational changes needed to support those developments. The extent to which technology allows information to be shared within and between organisations will increase the speed and complexity of innovation, co-ordination and other decision-making processes. The amount of information that can be stored and accessed greatly enhances the potential quality of decisions and actions, and the sheer amount of information that research, practice and experience generates is threatening to overwhelm our ability to make sense of it.

In general, these trends will shorten product, organisation and industry life cycles. Pressures to reduce the cycle time of innovation and the OD activities that support them are also likely to increase. OD practitioners must be mindful of opportunities to quicken the pace of innovation and to simultaneously remain aware of the practices and processes that cannot be hurried.

For example, innovation is likely to be more synchronous (anytime, anywhere) as well as more virtual and less face-to-face. In global organisations, innovation occurs in a variety of locations, cultures and time zones. OD interventions that support innovation, such as team building, employee involvement and knowledge management, will have to be planned and implemented in ways that encourage contributions from a variety of stakeholders at times that are convenient or at times when creative ideas emerge. Social networking technology, such as instant messaging, Facebook, MySpace and knowledge management systems can enable organisation members to make these contributions at any time they are ready. In addition, groupware technologies allow members to discuss issues in chat rooms and portals, in Web and videoconferences and in the more traditional telephone conference. For example, in 2003 IBM's CEO Lou Gerstner used these technologies to lead a vigorous discussion of corporate values, a process they called Values Jam, which involved organisation members from around the world.

Using these technologies to exchange ideas, develop technologies or discuss implementation will produce different types of group dynamics from those found in face-to-face meetings. OD practitioners will need to be comfortable with this technology and to develop virtual facilitation skills that recognise these dynamics. In many cases, a more structured and assertive approach will be necessary to ensure that all members have an opportunity to share their ideas. The effect of these technically mediated exchanges on work satisfaction, productivity and quality is not yet known. In addition, processes of visioning, diagnosis, data feedback and action planning will have to be re-engineered to leverage new information technologies.

In addition, innovation processes will be adapted to ensure that members have more information at their fingertips. For example, organisation intranets provide members with an information channel that is richer, more efficient, more interactive and more dynamic than such traditional channels as newsletters and memos. Thus, intranets can provide a timely method to collect data on emerging technologies, to monitor progress on a development project or organisation change and to involve members in key decisions.

These same technologies can also support increased innovation speed by processing a wide variety of inputs in as little as a few hours. In coming years, technological advances in groupware and Web conferencing will increasingly be used to bring more people together faster than ever before. In short, there is real potential to reduce dramatically the time required to perform many OD practices.

Despite the enablement of increased innovation speed, there are physical, psychological, cultural and environmental limits to reductions in the innovation and change cycle. It is not realistic to expect new product development and other forms of innovation to be instantaneous.[57] For example, managers often want product development to occur more rapidly or managerial innovations to be implemented more quickly. Announcing a technological breakthrough, drug formulation or new method of operating is one thing, but its implementation often takes longer than expected because of cultural values, environmental concerns or other unforeseen obstacles. A new organisation chart or a new vision and values statement hung on members' office walls often gives the illusion that change has occurred, but the working relationships, process improvements and other aspects of fully implementing new technologies or organisations often take longer than expected. Similarly, most organisation members are not capable of dropping a well-known and understood set of behaviours one day and picking up a new set of behaviours the next with the same level of efficiency. Members can face a steep learning curve when they are asked to change their routines and thus there are likely minimums with respect to the speed of change in individual behaviour.

The impact that technical and managerial innovation can have on an organisation's effectiveness is immense. They are key drivers in economic and social progress. Without the invisible hand of responsible progress to guide OD practitioners and the organisations they serve, however, they also contain the possibility of great harm to cultures and the environment. To fulfil the promise of responsible progress, innovation must not only support economic success, but must do so in ways that do not standardise or homogenise world cultures. Innovation must also unfold in ways that do not harm the environment. OD practitioners can help organisations increase their innovative activity and raise the questions of diversity and environment as the process unfolds.

OD will become more concerned with preserving cultural diversity

As organisations and the economy become more global, it is clear that the recent growth of OD practice in international and cross-cultural situations will continue. This is a necessary but not sufficient step towards responsible progress.

Responsible progress assumes that the practice of OD is capable of working effectively across cultures. However, we know relatively little about planned change processes in cross-cultural settings. Traditionally, OD has been practised in organisations within specific cultures: British-trained OD practitioners helped British organisations in Great Britain; Mexican OD practitioners helped Latin American organisations; and so on. But the current trends clearly point to the need for OD applications that work across cultures. Team-building interventions need to be modified to help a team composed of Americans, Indians, Chinese, Koreans and French Canadians who have never met face-to-face but are charged with developing a new product in a short period of time. The merger-and-acquisition process needs to be adapted to help a Japanese company and a US company implement a new organisation structure that honours both cultures. Because the number of organisations operating in multiple countries is growing rapidly, opportunities for OD in these situations seem endless: interorganisational and network relationships between subsidiaries, operating units and headquarters organisations; team building across cultural boundaries; working out global logistics and supply-chain processes; implementing diversity-centric values in ethnocentric cultures; designing strategic planning exercises at multiple levels. Moreover, OD is likely to find increased opportunities in global social change organisations (GSCOs) that are often part of an international network. Alliance development processes and network structure interventions adapted for cross-cultural contexts have yet to be developed and will have important applications in the future.

However, working across cultures or with multiple cultures is not the same as pursuing progress and innovation while preserving or even leveraging cultural diversity. Organisations today and in the future will operate in multiple countries, governments and cultures. A single-minded pursuit of financial success can – consciously or unconsciously – undermine local cultures in service of greater efficiency, increased speed or higher market shares. Developing and implementing business models and organisation designs that operate globally but support local cultures will require significant managerial innovation. This is the promise and challenge of responsible progress. On the other hand, responsible progress does not suggest that preserving cultural diversity is an end in itself. If OD truly believes in diversity, then diversity must be a strategy that fuels innovation and economic progress. Biological diversity has always been the source of adaptation in nature and the seeds of organisational responsiveness and successful change are in the innovative possibilities that exist when multiple viewpoints, values and beliefs are heard and nurtured over time.

OD will focus more on environmental sustainability

OD will become increasingly concerned with environmental sustainability. This will be true no matter the status of responsible progress. Limits to the world's ecosystem, including its capacity to absorb population growth, function with a depleted ozone layer and operate with polluted waters, provide serious challenges to the traditional business model. New concepts, frameworks and philosophies, including the Coalition for Environmentally Responsible Economics (CERES) principles, ISO 14000, The Natural Step and natural capitalism, represent opportunities to make environmental sustainability a more deliberate and intentional value of OD. The natural capitalism model,[58] for example, suggests that business strategies built around the productive use of natural resources can solve environmental problems at a profit.[59] Most sustainability models go beyond environmental concerns to promote a multidimensional view called the *triple bottom line*. In line with responsible progress, the triple bottom line proposes that organisation change and globalisation should be guided by the economic, social and environmental values that are added or destroyed. These three values provide a framework for measuring and reporting corporate performance. These values also guide how organisations go about minimising harm or maximising benefits through their decisions and actions to achieve innovation and effectiveness. This involves being clear about the company's purpose and taking into consideration the needs of all stakeholders – shareholders, customers, employees, business partners, governments, the environment, local communities and the public.

OD interventions to promote environmental sustainability are just being developed. The Natural Step, for example, proposes a set of guidelines for development and a process of change that aligns with an OD perspective.[60] It begins with a simple premise: current economic models that are based on the assumption of growth cannot reconcile the increasing demand for and decreasing supply of finite and fundamental natural resources. The sooner this incompatibility is recognised and addressed, the larger the number of available and socially acceptable solutions. The Natural Step utilises four 'system conditions' to guide an organisation's strategic decisions: (1) substances from within the earth must not systematically increase in the ecosphere, (2) substances produced by society must not systematically increase in the ecosphere, (3) the physical ability of nature to renew itself must not be diminished and (4) the basic human needs of all people need to be met with fairness and efficiency. Implementing these guidelines starts with building organisational awareness and knowledge of sustainability concepts and conducting a baseline assessment. Then a vision and strategic plan are created and necessary changes are supported one at a time.

Environmental sustainability interventions represent important and growing influences on global organisations. More and more organisations on the path to globalising their businesses or rationalising their existing worldwide strategies are including sustainability as one of their values. IKEA, InterfaceFLOR and Motorola, among others, provide positive examples of alternative business models in practice. InterfaceFLOR, a manufacturer of carpet products, has made it their mission to ensure that every creative, manufacturing and building decision takes them 'towards a zero environmental footprint'.[61]

In the short run, environmental sustainability is likely to be a constraint on economic success and innovation. Most organisation leaders and members hold assumptions about management and innovation that do not account for the environment in decision making. Responsible progress challenges these beliefs and the largely uncontested value of growth. As demonstrated by models of natural capitalism, the trick will be to see sustainability not as a cost or constraint, but as an ingredient and opportunity. OD practitioners in the future will become well versed in helping organisation members see this possibility and fostering innovation that honours the environment.

Summary

In this concluding chapter, we described three trends within OD and four trends driving change in the OD context. The future of OD is likely to be the result of the interactions among the traditional, pragmatic and scholarly trends as well as how the global economy evolves, technology develops, workforces engage and organisations structure themselves. To be relevant, OD practitioners and the field as a whole must act together to influence the future they prefer or adjust to the upcoming future. Moving OD towards rigour and relevance requires more than simple extensions of existing theory and practice. OD's ability to contribute to an organisation's success, to shape globalisation or unite the trends within OD will depend on its ability to generate new and more powerful interventions that draw on new models and integrated values in pursuit of responsible progress. This places OD in stark contrast to organisation transformation (OT), which is responsive and reactive to external forces with often unpredictable consequences. Our hope is that this text will be able to inform and equip the reader with the skills, knowledge and value awareness necessary to shape the future, whether it be with an OD or OT focus.

Activities

REVIEW QUESTIONS

1 Define what is traditional, pragmatic and scholarly in the OD context. Give an example of each.
2 Technology has often been accused of being the primary cause of uncontrolled change. Do you agree? Why/why not?
3 What are the four 'system conditions' which should guide an organisation's strategic decisions?
4 What is meant by the term 'triple bottom line' and how would this influence decisions made regarding change management?
5 What is meant by 'diversity'? Give examples from your experience, where there have been changes made as a result of diversity.
6 What are the types of e-commerce seen as relevant to OD? Why are they relevant?
7 What are the intercultural implications of responsible progress?
8 What is the 'Natural Step'? What are its basic principles?

DISCUSSION AND ESSAY QUESTIONS

1 Identify three trends within OD. What implications do they have for the future?
2 Compare and contrast the drivers for change and how they are likely to relate to environmental forces. Create a scenario for the year 2020 and how businesses should be prepared.
3 'Governments must face the difficult choice of preserving or sacrificing their culture'. What is meant by this? Give two examples and formulate an informed opinion.
4 'Responsible progress' calls on business to have regard to a variety of considerations when planning change. Is there a tension between that concept and shareholders' expectations that business will seek to maximise returns? If there is a tension, how might it be ameliorated?
5 Managers face many challenges in formulating change processes. Name four and explain why they are significant.
6 Globalisation is resulting in increasing internationalisation of businesses. What are the primary cultural issues that face managers as a result of globalisation and how might they be dealt with?

SEARCH ME! EXCERCISES

Explore **Search me! management** for relevant articles on change in a global setting. Search me! is an online library of world-class journals, ebooks and newspapers, including *The Australian* and *The New York Times*, and is updated daily. Log in to Search me! through **www.cengage.com/sso** using the access card in the front of this book.

Keywords

Try searching for the following terms:
> Trends in organisation development
> Global future for organisation development

>> *Search tip:*

Search me! management contains information from both local and international sources. To get the greatest number of search results, try using both Australian and American spellings in your searches, e.g. 'globalisation' and 'globalization'; 'organisation' and 'organization'.

Notes

1 G. Varney, Personal conversation, Academy of Management Conference, Seattle, Wash., 1 August 2003. For Varney's OD bibliography, see www.cba.bgsu.edu/mod/html/od_bibliography.html.

2 C. Worley and A. Feyerherm, 'Reflections on the future of organisation development', *Journal of Applied Behavioral Science*, 39 (2003): 97–115.

3 J. Milliman, J. Ferguson, D. Trickett and B. Condemi, 'Spirit and community at Southwest Airlines: an investigation of a spiritual values-based model', *Journal of Organisational Change Management*, 12 (1999): 221–33; W. Gellerman, M. Frankel and R. Ladenson, *Values and Ethics in Human Systems Development* (San Francisco: Jossey-Bass, 1990); D. Jamieson and W. Gellerman, 'Values, ethics and OD practice', in *The NTL Handbook of Organization Development and Change*, eds B. Jones and M. Brazzel (San Francisco: Pfeiffer, 2006).

4 S. Gopalakrishna, 'Editor's Introduction: linking theory and practice', *Organization Management Journal*, 5 (2008): 3–5, School of Management, New Jersey Institute of Technology, Newark, NJ 07102, USA, www.palgrave-journals.com/omj/journal/v5/n1/full/omj20082a.html.

5 C. Weidner and O. Kulick, 'The professionalization of organisation development: a status report and look to the future', in *Organisational Change and Development*, vol. 12, eds W. Pasmore and R. Woodman (Oxford, England: JAI Press, 1999); A. Church, 'The professionalization of organisation development: the next step in an evolving field', in *Organisational Change and Development*, vol. 13, eds R. Woodman and W. Pasmore (Oxford, England: JAI Press, 2001): 1–42.

6 L. Forcella, 'Marketing competency and consulting competency for external OD practitioners' (unpublished master's thesis, Pepperdine University, 2003).

7 N. Worren, K. Ruddle and K. Moore, 'From organizational development to change management: the emergence of a new profession', *Journal of Applied Behavioral Science*, 35 (1999): 273–86; H. Hornstein, 'Organisational development and change management: don't throw the baby out with the bath water', *Journal of Applied Behavioral Science*, 37 (2001): 223–26; M. Davis, 'OD and change management consultants: an empirical examination and comparison of their values and interventions' (unpublished doctoral dissertation, The George Washington University, 2002).

8 J. McCann, J. Selsky and J. Lee, 'Building agility, resilience and performance in turbulent environments', 32:3 (2009), Jacksonville University, University of South Florida Polytechnic and The University of Tampa, www.agilityconsulting.com/uploads/HRPS-BuildingAgility.pdf.

9 A. Pettigrew, R. Woodman and K. Cameron, 'Studying organisational change and development: challenges for future research', *Academy of Management Journal*, 44 (2001): 697–714.

10 J. M. Suárez del Toro R and G. Lau, Organizational Development Support Plan 2009–2010, International Federation Red Cross and Red Crescent Societies Context 'Building the capacity of our member National Societies is the first priority for both the Governing Board and for myself', www.ifrc.org/docs/appeals/annual09/MAA0000609p.pdf.

11 J. Ernst van Aken, 'Design science and organization development interventions, aligning business and humanistic values', *The Journal of Applied Behavioral Science*, 43:1 (2007): 67–88, Eindhoven University of Technology, http://jab.sagepub.com/cgi/content/abstract/43/1/23.

12 J. Trullen and J. M Bartunek, 'What a design approach offers to organization development', *The Journal of Applied Behavioral Science*, 43:1 (2007): 23–40, http://jab.sagepub.com/cgi/content/abstract/43/1/23.

13 P. Berger and T. Luckman, *The Social Construction of Reality* (New York: Anchor Books, 1967); K. Gergen, 'The social constructionist movement in modern psychology', *American Psychologist*, 40 (1985): 266–75; D. Cooperrider, 'Positive image, positive action: the affirmative basis for organizing', in *Appreciative Management and Leadership*, eds S. Srivastva, D. Cooperrider and Associates (San Francisco: Jossey-Bass, 1990).

14 S. Benn and E. Baker, *Advancing Sustainability Through Change and Innovation: A Coevolutionary Perspective*, Online publication date 7 December 2009, www.aries.mq.edu.au/publications/other/Business_and_Industry/advancing_sustainability.pdf.

15 C. Worley and A. McCloskey, 'A positive vision of OD's future', in *The NTL Handbook of Organization Development and Change*, eds B. Jones and M. Brazzel (San Francisco: Pfeiffer, 2006); B. Nixon, 'The big issues – the challenge for OD practitioners', *OD Practitioner*, 34

(2002): 16–19; K. Eisenhardt, 'Has strategy changed?' *Sloan Management Review*, 43 (2002): 88–91.

16 D. Bell, *The Coming of Post-Industrial Society: A Venture in Social Forecasting* (New York: Basic Books, 1973); A. Toffler, *The Third Wave* (New York: William Morrow, 1980); D. Korten, *When Corporations Rule the World* (West Hartford, Conn.: Kumarian Press; San Francisco: Berrett-Koehler, 1995); L. Thurow, *The Future of Capitalism* (New York: William Morrow, 1996); The International Forum on Globalization, *Alternatives to Economic Globalization* (San Francisco: Berrett-Koehler, 2002).

17 T. Friedman, *The World is Flat* (New York: Farrar, Straus and Giroux, 2006).

18 A. Chua, *World on Fire* (New York: Anchor Books, 2003); Eisenhardt, 'Has strategy changed?', op. cit.; The International Forum on Globalization, *Alternatives to Economic Globalization*, op. cit.; D. Cooperrider and J. Dutton eds, *Organizational Dimensions of Global Change: No Limits to Cooperation* (Thousand Oaks, CA: Sage Publications, 1999); J. Perkins, *Confessions of an Economic Hit Man* (San Francisco: Berrett-Koehler Publishers, 2004).

19 J. Bhagwati, *In Defense of Globalization* (New York: Oxford University Press, 2004); T. Cowen, *Creative Destruction* (Princeton, N.J.: Princeton University Press, 2002).

20 T. Friedman, *Lexus and the Olive Tree* (New York: Anchor Books, 2000).

21 *The Economist*, 'America's fear of China', *The Economist* (19 May 2007): 9–10; T. Carrel, 'Beijing: new face for the ancient capital', *National Geographic*, 197 (2000): 116–37.

22 International Forum on Globalization, *Alternatives to Economic Globalization*, op. cit.

23 Central Intelligence Agency, *Global Trends, 2015* (Langley, VA.: Central Intelligence Agency, 2000) as cited in The International Forum on Globalization, *Alternatives to Economic Globalization* (San Francisco: Berrett-Koehler, 2002).

24 U. Berliner, 'Haves and have-nots: income equality in America', NPR website, www.npr.org/templates/story/story.php?storyId = 7180618, accessed 4 October 2007.

25 L. Mishel, 'CEO-to-worker pay imbalance grows', Economic Policy Institute website snapshot for 21 June 2006, www.epinet.org/content.cfm/webfeatures_snapshots_20060621, accessed 4 October 2007; J. Sahadi, 'CEO pay: sky high gets even higher', CNNMoney.com, accessed 4 October 2007.

26 J. Sahadi, 'Number of billionaires surges', CNNMoney.com, http://money.cnn.com/ 2006/03/09/news/newsmakers/billionaires_ forbes/index.htm, accessed 4 October 2007.

27 The data here was collected from the World Bank website: www.worldbank.org/data, accessed 20 October 2003.

28 Thurow, *Future of Capitalism*, op. cit.; Korten, *When Corporations Rule*, op. cit.; N. Mankiw, *Principles of Economics* (Fort Worth, Tex.: Dryden Press, 1997).

29 C. Murphy, 'The next big thing', *FSB* (June 2003): 64–70.

30 IPCC, 'Summary for policymakers', in *Climate Change 2007: The Physical Science Basis. Contribution of Working Group I to the Fourth Assessment Report of the Intergovernmental Panel on Climate Change*, eds S. Solomon, D. Qin, M. Manning, Z. Chen, M. Marquis, K. B. Averyt, M. Tignor and H. L. Miller (Cambridge University Press: Cambridge, UK and New York, NY, USA, 2007); U. McFarling, 'Climate is warming at steep rate study says', *Los Angeles Times* (23 February 2000): A1.

31 J. Guyon, 'A big oil man gets religion', *Fortune* (6 March 2000): F87–89.

32 Thurow, *Future of Capitalism*, op. cit.; Korten, *When Corporations Rule*, op. cit.

33 R. Rivera and A. Paradise, 'State of the industry report', American Society of Training and Development, 2006.

34 Data from a Department of Labor report titled 'Contingent and Alternative Employment Arrangements, February 2000' found at www.bls.gov/news.release/conemp.nr0.htm, accessed 5 October 2007.

35 R. Melchionno, 'The changing temporary work force', *Occupational Outlook Quarterly* (Spring 1999), www.bls.gov/opub/ooq/1999/Spring/art03.pdf, accessed 13 November 2003.

36 M. Goldsmith, 'The contingent workforce', *Business Week* (23 May 2007), www.businessweek.com/print/careers/content/may2007/ca20070523_580432.htm, accessed 5 October 2007.

37 Information gathered at http://cyberatlas.internet.com/, accessed 4 October 2003.

38 Data from www.internetworldstats.com/stat.htm, accessed 5 October 2007.

39 P. Drucker, 'Beyond the information revolution', *Atlantic Monthly* (October 1999): 47–57.

40 E. Burns, 'Online retail sales grew in 2005', 5 January 2006, report www.clickz.com/3575456/, accessed 6 October 2007 and U.S. Census data from www.census.gov/mrts/www/data/html/07Q2table1.htm, accessed 5 October 2007.

41 C. Johnson, 'US eCommerce: 2005 to 2010', www.forrester.com/research/document/exerpt/0,7211,37626,00.html, accessed 5 October 2007.

42 E. Sanders, 'Tech-driven efficiency spurs economic boom', *Los Angeles Times* (22 February 2000): A-1.

43 G. Colvin, 'Managing in the info era', *Fortune* (6 March 2000): F6–F9.

44 Institute for the Future, '21st century organisations: reconciling control and empowerment', www.iftf.org, accessed 4 December 1999; J. Child and D. Faulkner, *Strategies of Cooperation: Managing Alliances, Networks and Joint Ventures* (New York: Oxford University Press, 1998); J. Bamford, B. Gomes-Casseres and M. Robinson, *Mastering Alliance Strategy* (New York: John Wiley & Sons, 2002).

45 M. Piore and C. Sabel, *The Second Industrial Divide* (New York: Basic Books, 1984); D. Watts, *Six Degrees* (New York: W.W. Norton and Co., 2003); C. Huxham, *Managing to Collaborate* (Oxford: Routledge, 2005).

46 From remarks of Kirby Dyess, vice president for business development, Intel, in a speech at Pepperdine University's MSOD alumni conference, Watsonville, Calif., July 1999.

47 This section draws heavily from Worley and McCloskey, 'A positive vision', op. cit., but we were also influenced by J. Wirtenberg, L. Abrams and C. Ott, 'Assessing the field of organization development', *Journal of Applied Behavioral Science*, 40 (2004): 465–79; J. Wirtenberg,

D. Lipsky, L. Abrams, M. Conway and J. Slepian, 'The future of organisation development: enabling sustainable business performance through people', *Organisation Development Journal*, 25 (2007): 11–27; R. Marshak, 'Organization development as a profession and a field', in *The NTL Handbook of Organization Development and Change*, eds B. Jones and M. Brazzel (San Francisco: Pfeiffer, 2006).

48 A. Kleiner, *The Age of Heretics* (New York: Doubleday, 1996).

49 H. Chesbrough, *Open Innovation* (Boston: Harvard Business School Press, 2005).

50 *Managing Cultural Diversity*, Produced by the Australian Multicultural Foundation Designed by Robert Bean Consulting 2010, http://amf.net.au/library/file/MCD_Training_Program_Presentation.pdf.

51 K. Chee, 'Strategic and organization development challenges faced by high-technology startup chief executive officers' (unpublished master's thesis, Pepperdine University, 1999).

52 N. Tichy, 'The death and rebirth of organizational development', in *Organization 21C*, ed. S. Chowdhury (Upper Saddle River, N.J.: Financial Times Prentice Hall, 2002): 155–74.

53 R. Gupta, E. Hardman, G. Neumann and W. Katz, *Project Management Competency Review August 2009*, www.ibsa.org.au/Portals/ibsa.org.au/docs/reports/Final_Report_Stage_1_Project_Management_Standards.pdf.

54 G. Hamel, *The Future of Management* (Boston: Harvard Business School Press, 2007).

55 Chesbrough, *Open Innovation*, op. cit.; E. Lawler and C. Worley, *Built to Change* (San Francisco: Jossey-Bass, 2006).

56 S. Zhang, 'The reasons for emergence of born global firms – taking China as an example', 4:8 (August 2009), www.ccsenet.org/journal/index.php/ijbm/article/viewFile/3353/3021.

57 C. Worley and R. Patchett, 'Myth and hope meet reality: the fallacy of and opportunities for reducing cycle time in strategic change', in *Fast-Cycle Organisation Development*, ed. M. Anderson (Cincinnati, OH: South-Western College Publishing, 2000); C. Worley, T. Cummings and P. Monge, 'A critique, test and refinement of the punctuated equilibrium model of strategic change' (working paper, Pepperdine University, 1999).

58 K. V. Mally, 'Linking socio-economic development and environmental pressures', *Dela* 27 (2007): 149–62, www.ff.uni-lj.si/oddelki/geo/publikacije/dela/files/Dela_27/08_vintar.pdf.

59 A. Lovins, L. Lovins and P. Hawken, 'A road map for natural capitalism', *Harvard Business Review* (May–June, 1999): 145–58; information on the Natural Step can be found at www.naturalstep.org.

60 H. Bradbury and J. Clair, 'Promoting sustainable organisations with Sweden's Natural Step', *Academy of Management Executive*, 13 (1999): 63–74.

61 www.interfaceflor.com.au/Sustainability/Innovations.aspx.

PART 6

INTEGRATIVE CASE STUDIES

Case Study

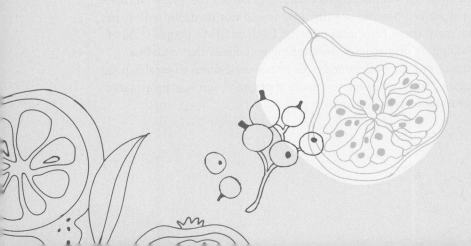

CASE STUDY 1

Balanced and blended leadership at IBM

Simon Woodley, Ranel R. Juanta and Jessica Clayden

Introduction

IBM is an organisation that has gone through tumultuous change over the course of its long history. In all of its major organisational change efforts, strong leadership can be observed at the helm. This case study explores the role that strong and effective leadership has had in driving IBM through various changes.

Leadership models are examined in four major areas of change at IBM including Lou Gerstner's famous turnaround in the early 1990s; the drive for constant innovation; two significant culture shifts; and a specific project to improve IBM's hardware supply chain.

Key change projects at IBM

Lou Gerstner and the turnaround

Background

With its earliest beginnings at the start of the twentieth century, IBM consolidated its technological presence to become the iconic American business that we know through the development of the mainframe computer in the 1950s.[1] For 30 years, the company grew by exploiting the success and massive worldwide footprint of its mainframe systems but it failed to take account of the changing computer marketplace during the 1980s with the shift to Unix and PC based computer hardware.[2] When Lou Gerstner took the role of CEO in 1993, the company was expected by many to fail.[3]

Defining change

A significant part of the problem at IBM was the presiding culture that opposed change. Gerstner defined eight principles as defining priorities for a new culture – see Table C.1 – but describes how these principles would not be useful unless he, as the leader, could 'instil these principles into the DNA of IBM's people'.[4] All of the principles are 'visionary' in nature – overarching guidelines that could be applied to any business unit or work process. Gerstner used them to establish the vision for the company, and took steps to ensure that the vision was propagated and implemented throughout the company.

TABLE C.1	Eight principles of change
1	The marketplace is the driving force behind everything we do
2	At our core, we are a technology company with an overriding commitment to quality
3	Our primary measures of success are customer satisfaction and shareholder value
4	We operate as an entrepreneurial organisation with a minimum of bureaucracy and a never-ending focus on productivity
5	We never lose sight of our strategic vision
6	We think and act with a sense of urgency
7	Outstanding, dedicated people make it all happen, particularly when they work together as a team
8	We are sensitive to the needs of all employees and to the communities in which we operate

Source: L. V. Gerstner Jr, *Who Says Elephants Can't Dance?: Leading a Great Enterprise through Dramatic Change* (New York: HarperCollins Publishers, 2002): 201–2.

Direction and coercion

The changes enacted at IBM during Lou Gerstner's tenure fall clearly into the category of 'turnaround' as defined by Stace and Dunphy.[5] As shown in Table C.2, a turnaround requires directive or even coercive leadership,[6] and this was demonstrated by Gerstner.

In his first meeting with senior staff, he immediately started to break the IBM mould by 'setting an initial agenda'[7] for his staff using a commander approach.[8]

TABLE C.2 Approaches to corporate change

	Fine-tuning	Incremental adjustment	Modular transformation	Corporate transformation
Collaborative				
Consultative	Taylorism (avoiding change)	Developmental transitions (constant change)	Charismatic transformations (inspirational change	
Directive		Task-focused transitions (constant change)	Turnarounds (framebreaking change)	
Coercive				

Source: D. Stace and D. Dunphy, *Beyond the Boundaries: Leading and Re-creating the Successful Enterprise*, 2nd edn (Roseville, NSW: McGraw-Hill Book Company Australia, 2001): 109.

In other words, he was the one setting the direction. Old frames of reference were broken when Gerstner split up the personal kingdoms of IBM's territorial chiefs, insisting that duplication of effort by geographically separate divisions of IBM was no longer acceptable.

Gerstner combined the directive and coercive approaches to rewrite the IBM corporate culture and to develop its strategic positioning.[9] Enacting the strategic repositioning also required another layer of leadership. Much like the way Jack Welch at GE began with directive and coercive styles but later built in a consultative model once the new culture was installed,[10] IBM developed its Business Leadership Model to work within the new IBM culture and structure.[11] This model provided managers and executives at all levels with a common language and process to formulate strategy and was driven by the line managers, rather than from the top.[12]

Constant innovation

Leadership enabling e-business

One of the results of Gerstner's turnaround was IBM's reinvention as an innovative e-business powerhouse. Internal political hurdles were overcome by a combination of strong and visionary leadership and keen strategic insight into the potential of the internet. Charismatic elements to the leadership helped to create a shared vision, set a common direction and inspired staff to volunteer additional time to the company. A shared e-business vision spread across IBM, propagating a culture of innovation through the entire company.

With the vision in place, new corporate structures enabled innovation to flow from the bottom up[13] and were supported by the CEO. The new structures provided the environment in which innovation could prosper and included a fully engaged senior executive team, direct lines of communication to the executives and the charismatic promotion of new internet strategies to other staff by self-appointed e-business evangelists.[14]

Projects for continuous change

Continuous innovation is not an optional strategy for IBM, it is a part of its daily business environment within the global marketplace.[15] One methodology that it has implemented for managing ongoing change has been to identify a 'Change Diamond'. The facets of the Diamond are:

1 Real Insights, Real Actions
2 Solid Methods, Solid Benefits
3 Better Skills, Better Chance
4 Right Investment, Right Impact.[16]

The program resulted in an 80% success rate on change management and projects. Significantly, it was determined that the Change Diamond framework had

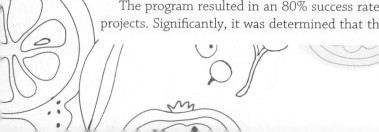

a critical requirement of strong leadership engagement as well as empowerment to employees for change management success to be attained.

Studies in innovation

In a recent study on 'Innovation' conducted by IBM, CEOs, executives and public sector leaders from around the world were interviewed to gain insight into the views and approach of other companies.[17] Among other findings, the unprecedented pace and breadth of technological change was deemed an opportunity for business and technology integration which significantly benefited customer satisfaction, speed and flexibility.

Within this accelerating rate of change, the majority of innovative ideas materialised from outside the organisation; however, the most significant ideas came from employees. This required a consultative style of leadership within IBM to ensure that new ideas were capitalised on.[18] The study supports Hardy on innovation, who says that reflecting on problems and creating an environment supportive of imaginative thinking causes future solutions to flourish.[19] IBM applied the findings to support company innovation by nurturing ideas through external knowledge.

Defining a new culture

Leadership to refine corporate values

A strong culture is core to IBM's corporate identity, with staff known as 'IBMers'[20] and distinct IBM 'lingo' used.[21] A significant part of Gerstner's turnaround of IBM was to recreate the culture as mentioned above. His successor, Sam Palmisano, continued this work and refined Gerstner's eight principles of behaviour core to IBM down to three, via a consultative approach with staff at all levels:[22]

1 dedication to every client's success
2 innovation that matters – for the company and for the world
3 trust and personal responsibility in all relationships.

Appropriate behaviours were upheld and nurtured within the company through this consistent and combined top-down and bottom-up approach to communicate and apply values. Although a bottom-up approach was used to define the final three principles, it was very important that leaders reinforced and gave recognition to the principles.

Leadership of systemic change

The 1990s turnaround and the cultural refinement were systemic changes for IBM that affected every unit within the company and changed the way that staff and divisions interacted with each other.[23]

IBM applied a systemic leadership approach to drive a new culture of inclusion, to break down traditional barriers and to involve all levels in the planning and decision-making process (Yaun 2006).[24] This inclusive approach shaped the corporate culture that underpinned IBM's transformation from a products and services company to a hardware, software and services company with global services divisions.

Forty per cent of IBM staff do not report to a physical office and for them, the corporate intranet '*is* the company'.[25] Free flowing and shared information generates dialogue and questioning and enriches a learning culture. The communication that is driven by leadership at all levels of the company, including electronic communications, is therefore a key to shaping the culture of IBM.

Interestingly, Wing reports that as a result of technology and inspired by employee feedback, acceptance of online company-wide discussions via the IBM intranet – blogging – has provided a new form of collaboration, diffusion of knowledge across business units, organisational intervention and cultural change which is supported by management.[26]

Improving the supply chain

In 1993, IBM experienced dramatic declines in all key business measurements which sparked management into remedial actions and efforts. It was identified that each supply chain step was significantly longer and brought with it associated higher costs which provoked the leadership at IBM to embark on a re-engineering of the organisation and development of the market management process.[27]

The less than satisfactory performance of IBM's hardware supply chain in the 1990s led it to review its processes, identifying 24 'performance improvement initiatives' to be tackled.[28] The first approach at this was driven by management; however, they failed to integrate their findings across the 24 initiatives, resulting in a lack of information across the supply chain about whether the changes were making a real difference.[29]

This failure was followed up with the appointment of a team of non-management, expert staff from across the areas of the supply chain to negotiate and co-ordinate change efforts across the whole chain.[30] Although the change effort was still driven by management (directive approach), a consultative approach was now integrated with this to maximise usage of the knowledge held by staff and to work across the normal structural lines of the organisation.

The co-ordinated approach enabled IBM to view and take into account the inter-connected relationship between IT and knowledge systems, people, processes, and the prioritisation of change through an integrated decision-making process, adding value to all stakeholders.[31] According to Carmichael (1997, p. 103) 'the new processes, systems, tools, and measurements are simply ways of encouraging and supporting major culture and behaviour change'.[32]

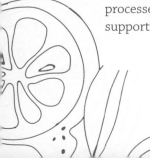

Review questions

1 Is there a common thread in what is required of leadership to effect transformational change? If so, what is it?

2 Some considered the breaking up of the territorial kingdoms at IBM to be draconian. Do you think this was necessary?

3 Identify the positive and negative forces for change evident in this case study.

Notes

1 L. V. Gerstner Jr, *Who Says Elephants Can't Dance?: Leading a Great Enterprise through Dramatic Change* (New York: HarperCollins Publishers, 2002).

2 ibid.

3 ibid.

4 ibid.: 203.

5 D. Stace and D. Dunphy, *Beyond the Boundaries: Leading and Re-creating the Successful Enterprise*, 2nd edn (Roseville, NSW: McGraw-Hill Book Company Australia, 2001).

6 ibid.

7 Gerstner, *Who Says Elephants Can't Dance?*, op. cit.: 22.

8 F. Graetz, M. Rimmer, A. Lawrence and A. Smith, *Managing Organisational Change*, 2nd edn (Milton, Qld: John Wiley & Sons Australia, Ltd, 2006).

9 J. B. Harreld, C. A. O'Reilly III and M. L. Tushman, 'Dynamic capabilities at IBM: driving strategy into action', *California Management Review*, 49:4 (2007): 21–43.

10 Graetz et al., *Managing Organisational Change*, op. cit.

11 Harreld, O'Reilly and Tushman, 'Dynamic capabilities at IBM', op. cit.

12 ibid.

13 G. Hamel, 'Waking up IBM', *Harvard Business Review*, 78:4 (2000): 137–46.

14 ibid.

15 H. H. Jorgensen, L. Owen and A. Neus, 'Stop improvising change management!', *Strategy & Leadership*, 37:2 (2009): 38–44.

16 ibid.

17 M. Chapman, 'Building an innovative organization: consistent business and technology integration', *Strategy & Leadership*, 34:4 (2006): 32–8.

18 Stace and Dunphy, *Beyond the Boundaries*, op. cit.

19 B. Hardy, 'Linking trust, change, leadership and innovation', *KM Review*, 10:5 (2007): 18–23.

20 See p. 16, D. Yaun, 'Driving culture change by consensus at IBM', *Strategic Communication Management*, 10:3 (2006): 14–17.

21 Gerstner, *Who Says Elephants Can't Dance?*, op. cit.: 197–8.

22 Yaun, op. cit.: 16.

23 Gerstner, *Who Says Elephants Can't Dance?*, op. cit.; Graetz et al., *Managing Organisational Change*, op. cit.

24 Yaun, 'Driving culture change by consensus at IBM', op. cit.

25 M. Wing, 'Enabling collaboration at IBM', *Strategic Communication Management*, 9:5 (2005): 4.

26 ibid.

27 D. Carmichael, 'IBM's journey towards a market-driven process-managed business model', *Journal of Market-Focused Management*, 2:1 (1997): 99–103.

28 See p. 1004, S. McLaughlin, R. A. Paton and D. K. Macbeth, 'Managing change within IBM's complex supply chain', *Management Decision*, 44:8 (2006): 1002–19.

29 ibid.

30 ibid.

31 ibid.

32 Carmichael, 'IBM's journey towards a market-driven process-managed business model', op. cit.: 103.

CASE STUDY 2

Miwatj executive leadership and management development: Strengthening the professional skills of Indigenous managers in remote Australia

Zane Ma Rhea
Monash University

Introduction

The dilemmas for executive training and organisational development practitioners working with Indigenous businesses and service organisations and international industries employing Indigenous Australians in remote communities are common ones for the remote populations of the world: rapid technological change, increasingly metropolitan-centric education and training provision, and the integration of the national economy into the global economy have reduced the capacity of most training organisations to deliver high-quality executive face-to-face programs to non-traditional cohorts. There are an estimated 460 000 Indigenous Australians. About 70% live in metropolitan, urban and rural situations and 30% in remote and very remote Australia.[1] All are disadvantaged across all socioeconomic indicators, and according to official statistics improvements in Indigenous socioeconomic status in the last decade have been slow or stagnant, both in absolute and relative terms.[2] In remote areas of Australia, which is the focus of this case study, the conditions in which Indigenous people live pose a complex of policy issues to the nation. In a first world country, conditions for Indigenous Australians have been likened to those of the fourth world.[3]

Miwatj Management Development, the case study being presented, was a highly successful three-module executive leadership and management development program that was developed for Indigenous current and future managers in the Miwatj region of North East Arnhem Land (see the map at Appendix A). The word *Miwatj* is a Yolŋu word for 'morning side' and refers to the fact that this is the most easterly part of the Top End.[4] The speakers of the Yolŋu languages (collectively named Yolŋu Matha) are recognised as the traditional owners of this region of Australia and are known as the Yolŋu people.

The Miwatj Management Development Program (MMDP) aimed to enhance the capacity of Yolŋu and other Indigenous managers of organisations, both public and private, in the Miwatj region (North East Arnhem Land) to develop sustainable

business and service activities through the provision of managerial competencies relevant to leading and managing projects, organisations and communities in the area. Planned outcomes of the program were: (1) to improve the sustainability of organisations by enhancing the skills of local Yolŋu and other Indigenous managers; (2) to identify commercial and service improvement opportunities within participants' communities; (3) to assist Yolŋu organisations to develop networks with government and non-government organisations; and (4) to develop and improve the strategic planning, financial and management skills of the participants. This highly successful program has now evolved into a broader program, offering top-quality face-to-face executive leadership and business management training, particularly for underskilled Indigenous managers across Australia. MMDP was delivered by the Aurora Project, which is working with the Australian Graduate School of Management, the Faculty of Education, Monash University, and has support from Rio Tinto, two Commonwealth Government Departments, Indigenous Community Volunteers and a number of philanthropic organisations.[5]

Context of the case study

This case study considers that there are two interrelated factors which have brought the current position of Indigenous peoples living in remote Australia to the forefront of debate about locally available skilled employment: the considerable interest by global industries, such as the mining industry, in accessing and developing mineral resources in these remote locations concurrent with the legal recognition in Australia that Indigenous peoples in remote locations hold rights to their lands that have not been extinguished with the settlement of Australia. These rights recognise the involvement of Indigenous traditional owners in complex negotiations, and in this context a significant Indigenous services sector has emerged. While some effort has been made to employ local Indigenous traditional owners, such as with the Yolŋu people involved in this program, the skill base is commonly underskilled or so low that there are limited jobs and career paths available to them. Instead, there are many non-Yolŋu Indigenous and non-Indigenous people running these organisations, competing for the leadership and economic opportunities potentially also present for local Yolŋu people.

Indigenous corporate leadership development

In 1992, an historic legal decision recognised that a period of continuous occupancy gave Indigenous groups a legitimate claim to land ownership [*Mabo vs Queensland (No.2)*]. This decision, and the Native Title legislation that followed, profoundly changed the direction and scope of relations between the Australian Federal and State legal jurisdictions, global industries and Indigenous peoples in remote Australia.[6] It is now recognised in law and practice in Australia that Indigenous people who have established claim over their lands have the right to derive direct benefit from development of resources beyond that which the

Australian government would previously have exercised: the right to exclusive control of the development of such resources on behalf of all Australian people.[7] It is the existence of these Indigenous rights that brings to the forefront the way that Indigenous people living in remote Australia are being brought into the Australian and global economies, highlighting the need for economically sustainable communities with access to the same levels of health, education, housing and welfare provision as are available to Australians living in urban and rural locations. Debates about the sustainable employment of Indigenous people in locations where there continues to be little or no viable economic base except that deriving from the presence of large-scale industries, such as mining companies operating for defined periods of time in a location (the fate of whose continued operation is highly dependent on the global economy), directly links to the role of education in enabling and preparing Indigenous peoples to maximise economic benefit though the presence of such activities on their lands.

The need for partnership

Aboriginal leaders have highlighted that with the increased expansion of non-Indigenous interests into remote Australia, Indigenous peoples in these locations have lost access to their traditional lands and waterways[8] and have been increasingly drawn into mainstream Australia, creating a dependency on welfare payments and other government distributed benefits in the absence of local viable economies or the infrastructure to develop them.[9] Pearson argues that capability development and incentives are essential to creating meaningful lives for Indigenous people. Real work, such as is made possible through negotiation with local mining operations, is a central part of his framework for economic sustainability for remote Indigenous communities. From the outset, the MMDP aligned itself with these ideas and developed its program to ensure the sustainability of its work in partnership with Yolŋu people.

According to some analysts, a neo-liberal approach to Indigenous employment especially in the mining industry in remote Australia has also become significant.[10] The mining industry, in making agreements with Indigenous traditional owners, has negotiated a range of employment, education and training opportunities as part of such agreements. Lawrence argues that as the public and private sector – that is, governments and the mining industry – are increasingly coming together to co-ordinate solutions to the problem of welfare dependency and changing frameworks and are developing new policies to address Indigenous underemployment and unemployment, they are also transforming traditional Aboriginal people into 'job ready subjects'. These agreements 'implicitly contain an element of coercion', reflecting the goals of neo-liberal government.[11] Altman and Dillon argue that:

> The challenge facing public policy makers is to devise a program that addresses the
> gap in commercial development and land management on Indigenous land in a way

that recognises the existence of both market failure and parallel state failure. Such a program must build on the comparative advantage of Indigenous landowners in local economies and ensure they share a proportion of the risks, while overcoming the structural constraints facing landowners in relation to access to finance.[12]

Despite the debates that have been conducted publicly about whether remote Indigenous communities have a right to be supported to achieve economic sustainability or that these communities are being forced into the world of work and the cash economy, these two positions have one thing in common: the premise that increased participation and retention of Indigenous people in high-quality education and training is critical to increasing and developing Indigenous leadership in the workforce.[13] MMDP aimed to deliver such a high-quality program to address this critical need. Taylor provides an example from the Northern Territory of the serious nature of the problem and the critical need to support Indigenous traditional owners to become managers and corporate leaders. He says:

> Indigenous employment in the mainstream labour market is trending downwards along with the overall level of labour force participation, while the income gap between Indigenous and other Territory residents is widening. Given projected expansion of the working age population, the numbers in work need to rise just to keep the already low employment rate from falling further. The Northern Territory has a serious economic development problem – around one fifth of its resident adult population remains impoverished, structurally detached from the labour market, and ill-equipped to engage with it.[14]

The case for Indigenous manager development

The capacity of remote Indigenous communities to take up the opportunities presented by the agreements made with mining companies is presently extremely low. Demographic and socioeconomic data suggest that radical intervention is needed by communities, training providers and government partners to enable the effective delivery of appropriate education to develop human resource capacity. Human resource costs are significant for any business in such remote locations because of the need to fly in staff, particularly managerial staff, to maintain the functioning of the business. While it makes good business sense to build the capacity of the local community to take up opportunities in the mines, and the associated service industries that develop around these big operations, there are significant problems to overcome.

Pearson[15] provides alarming statistics about the state of the problem, focusing on far north Queensland where there are substantial mining interests and agreements with Indigenous traditional owners in place (see, for example, the WCCCA Agreement at www.atns.net.au). Pearson notes that:

> Employment is very low and there are very few 'real' jobs. Only around 14% of Indigenous Australians receive an income from paid employment in the real economy (rather than through the Community Development Employment Programs – CDEP).

Incomes are low. The average personal income is around 60% of the Australian average.[16]

Education outcomes are very low. There are very low rates of attendance and secondary school completion. One Cape York statistic shows that of Year 7 students, only 6% will complete Year 12.[17]

Pearson, an Indigenous leader in Australia, is actively involved with others to develop a leadership and policy framework that will, among other things, lead to the development of effective and appropriate education and training programs for Indigenous people to enable them to create a better future for themselves and their families. He says,

> We need to build the capabilities of Cape York people so that they are in a position to exercise meaningful choices. We have been doing considerable work on this issue in Cape York, for example, looking to pilot innovative methods of service delivery in education and health that devolve real responsibility to the community level.[18]

Key factors in workforce participation in the Miwatj region

In North East Arnhem land, there are some variations to the scene painted above by Pearson for Cape York. A review of some key factors reveal the starkly differing profile of workforce participation between Indigenous and non-Indigenous people in this region. In this case study, of the approximately 8000 people living in the region 52.9% are Indigenous.

Weekly income

As Figures C2.1 and C2.2 show, Indigenous people are overrepresented in weekly earnings of less than $400.

Therefore, even though the majority of people living in the region are Indigenous, there are significantly fewer Indigenous people in the workforce and of those that are, there are fewer than non-Indigenous people undertaking the higher paid jobs, a number of which are middle and senior managerial positions.

In order for Indigenous people to be able to gain employment or to avoid relegation to an unskilled or underskilled job, and indeed to be employed in higher-paying jobs, they need high levels of education and formal qualifications.

Schooling and formal qualifications

As Figures C2.3 and C2.4 show, significantly fewer Indigenous people living in the Miwatj region hold post-school formal qualifications and only six hold postgraduate qualifications. Many have not attended school beyond Year 8. By comparison, many non-Indigenous people living in the region have attended up to Year 12 at school and a significant number have a post-school qualification.

About 2400 (63.2%) of the non-Indigenous and 800 (18.7%) of the Indigenous people reported that they were working. Therefore, even though Indigenous people are in the majority in the region, they hold only one third of the available jobs.

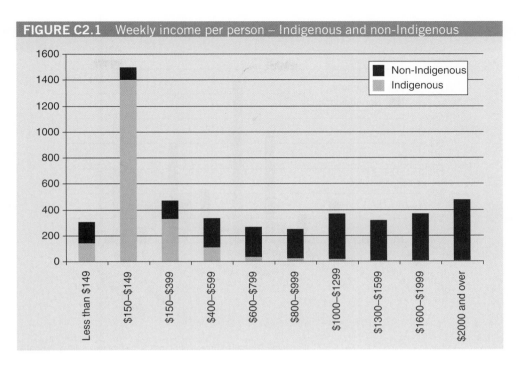

FIGURE C2.1 Weekly income per person – Indigenous and non-Indigenous

Source: Australian Bureau of Statistics © Commonwealth of Australia.

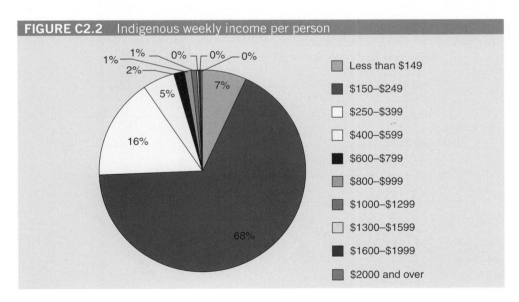

FIGURE C2.2 Indigenous weekly income per person

Source: Australian Bureau of Statistics © Commonwealth of Australia.

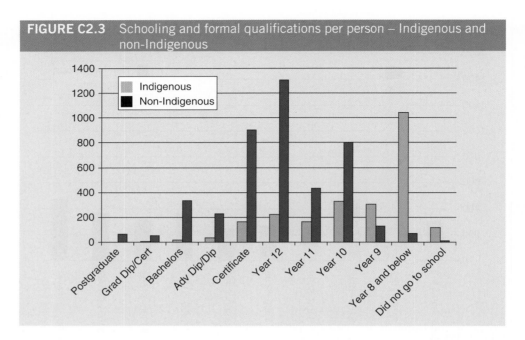

FIGURE C2.3 Schooling and formal qualifications per person – Indigenous and non-Indigenous

Source: Australian Bureau of Statistics © Commonwealth of Australia.

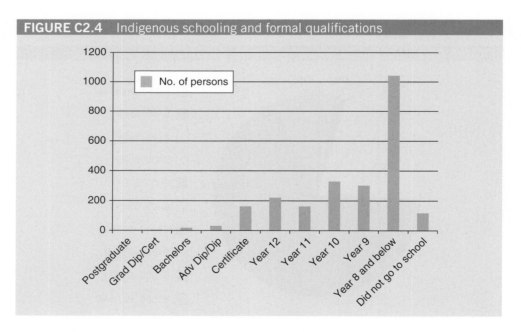

FIGURE C2.4 Indigenous schooling and formal qualifications

Source: Australian Bureau of Statistics © Commonwealth of Australia.

Of relevance to the MMDP, an estimated 18.7% of the Indigenous adults in the Miwatj region are working.[19] The above statistics suggest that those who are employed are in lower paying jobs and have fewer formal post-school qualifications than their non-Indigenous peers.

Employment sector

The predominant employer for Indigenous people in the region is local government. Of the 494 local government jobs, 422 (85.4%) were held by Indigenous people, with short-term contracts and a revolving door of Indigenous people also cycling through the much smaller number of available jobs in the Commonwealth (62 of which 15, or 24.2%, were held by Indigenous people) and Territory Governments (299 of which only 31, or 10.4%, were held by Indigenous people). (See Figures C2.5 and C2.6.)

Interestingly though, there are 346 Indigenous people employed in the private sector even though this only represents 14.5% of the total job pool (n=2386). For the Indigenous population, though, it is the second-highest employer, accounting for 42.5% of jobs reported by Indigenous people. This is an important factor when considering the viability of an executive manager development program in a remote location because it suggests that Indigenous people are employed in the private sector and in administrative jobs potentially requiring ongoing management skills development. This was borne out in the consultation process when many potential Indigenous applicants spoke of the difficulty of becoming

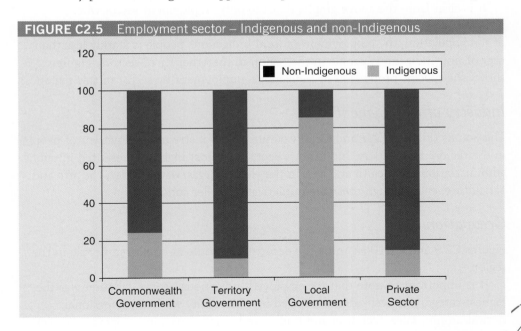

FIGURE C2.5 Employment sector – Indigenous and non-Indigenous

Source: Australian Bureau of Statistics © Commonwealth of Australia.

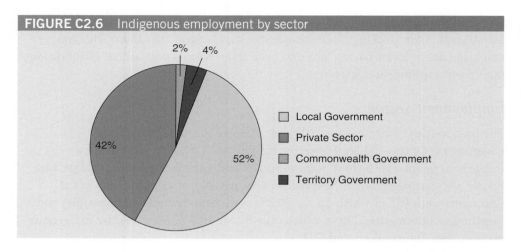

FIGURE C2.6 Indigenous employment by sector

- Local Government
- Private Sector
- Commonwealth Government
- Territory Government

2%   4%

42%

52%

Source: Australian Bureau of Statistics © Commonwealth of Australia.

sufficiently qualified to take on the key leadership roles in organisations and businesses in the area. Key industry and government stakeholders also reported that they found many of the Indigenous applicants to be underskilled in the professional requirements of the middle and senior manager jobs and they were happy to become involved in designing a program that would meet the needs of their present and future staff.

It is clear from the above graphs that the only employment sector where Indigenous people dominate is in Local Government. While representing over half of the population, the employment of local Indigenous people is starkly less than that of non-Indigenous people in the region in the other three sectors. Figure C2.6 shows the specific proportion of Indigenous employment by sector in this region.

Industry of employment

The graphs (Figures C2.7 and C2.8) examine the industry of employment of people in the region. By industry, Indigenous people are most highly represented in public administration and health and also in the electrical/gas/water trades, the arts and agriculture, even though these are numerically smaller cohorts.

Occupation

Figures C2.9 and C2.10 examine the occupation profile of employed people in the region.

It is important to note that for employed Indigenous people, labourer was the highest category of occupation, followed by community worker, professional, clerical/admin, sales, technical and trades, and, finally, machinery operator/driver. For non-Indigenous people the profile was different: technical/trades, professional, community, clerical/admin, machinery operator/driver, manager and, finally, sales.

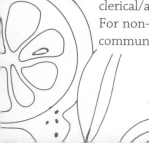

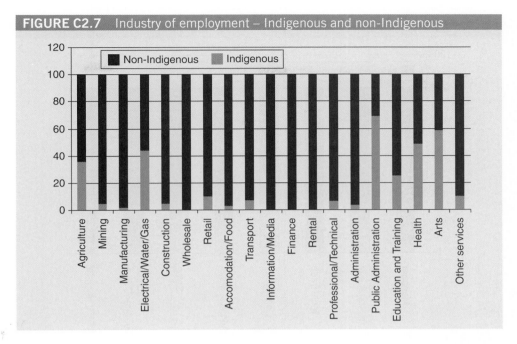

FIGURE C2.7 Industry of employment – Indigenous and non-Indigenous

Source: Australian Bureau of Statistics © Commonwealth of Australia.

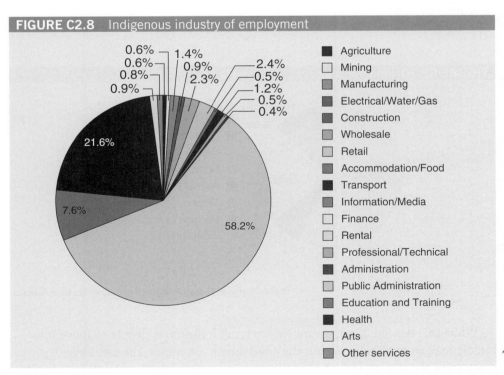

FIGURE C2.8 Indigenous industry of employment

Source: Australian Bureau of Statistics © Commonwealth of Australia.

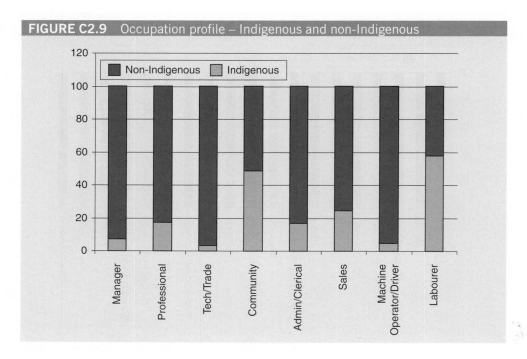

FIGURE C2.9   Occupation profile – Indigenous and non-Indigenous

Source: Australian Bureau of Statistics © Commonwealth of Australia.

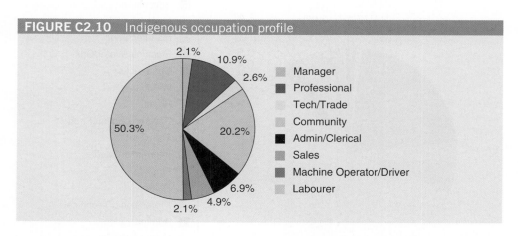

FIGURE C2.10   Indigenous occupation profile

Source: Australian Bureau of Statistics © Commonwealth of Australia.

While this has led to opportunities for some Indigenous people to move into middle manager positions within the government job sector, the service sector supporting the mining industry, or the non-government Indigenous services sector (in areas such as health, childcare and homelands management), few hold senior

leadership positions and there are even fewer Indigenous people working in senior positions in the private sector.

Employment level

In terms of employment level, non-Indigenous people hold 87.8% of the full-time jobs in the region and Indigenous people, in the reverse, hold 60.3% of the part-time jobs (see Figures C2.11 and C2.12).

For Indigenous people, 32% are employed full-time and 68.1% are employed part-time (see Figure C2.12).

Because middle and senior management and leadership positions are predominantly full-time jobs, it is evident that many Indigenous people are not going to be able to take senior leadership positions without working full-time.

With organisations such as Rio Tinto bringing their international business practices into these small communities, they are able to require that local businesses can demonstrate a commitment to Indigenous employment and have, as part of their agreements, been supporting the development of Yolŋu controlled businesses.

Even so, the poverty trap continues, with few Yolŋu people being sufficiently skilled to take up leadership and management positions, instead being clustered in the lower unskilled or underskilled pool of labour in part-time positions, with lower

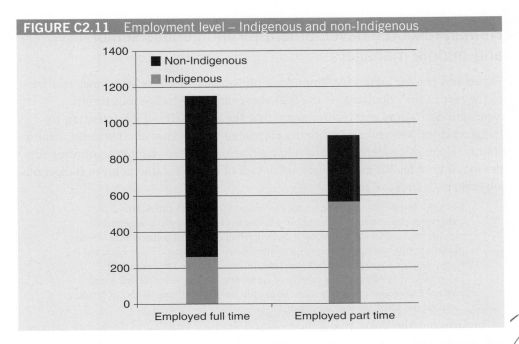

FIGURE C2.11   Employment level – Indigenous and non-Indigenous

Source: Australian Bureau of Statistics © Commonwealth of Australia.

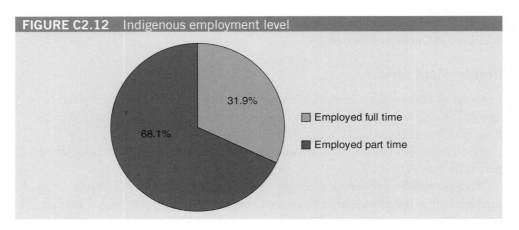

Source: Australian Bureau of Statistics © Commonwealth of Australia.

pay and in a small range of industries such as public administration, health and some trades. As Langton argues,

> The poverty trap is a universal experience throughout the world, both in rural communities and in those that became urbanized in the last half century. It is therefore unlikely that any one strategy alone could alter the circumstances of communities living in historical poverty. Rather, a combination of interventions, based in sound research and designed and implemented in collaboration with the people intended to benefit, are required.[20]

Human resource development for Indigenous senior and middle managers

Taylor and Hunter argue that 'Improving Indigenous education outcomes relative to the rest of the population is the best way to increase Indigenous income expectations'.[21] Gray and Hunter argue that the probability of job retention for Indigenous job seekers is significantly correlated to educational attainment, health status, region of residence, and having been arrested, these factors accounting for the majority of labour market success (or lack of it) among unemployed Indigenous job seekers.[22] Langton says:

> Despite a few positive developments, the education status of the Australian Indigenous population is catastrophic. Closing the education gap is essential to capacity building in the hundreds of dysfunctional Aboriginal communities whose plight is manifestly unnecessary in a wealthy developed nation. Education is the key to creating the Aboriginal leaders, teachers, professionals and self-sufficient individuals of the future. It is capable of expanding opportunities for full social, political and economic participation. Education has a central role to play in building social capital and a sense of belonging.[23]

In Australia, the Vocational Education and Training (VET) and university sectors are charged with the responsibility of skilling the future Australian workforce. For many young Indigenous people living in remote communities, the VET sector has

been a more accessible option than a university qualification. Indigenous enrolments almost doubled between 1994 and 1998 but by 2008 enrolments were beginning to fall. While Indigenous people comprise approximately 2% of Australia's total population, around 4% of all clients aged 15–64 undertaking publicly funded vocational programs in 1998 were Indigenous. However, the weaknesses in the simple 'education equals employment' argument are several. One is the failure of the general provision of education aimed at work readiness and employment to target strategically and purposefully the relevant locales, age and gender cohorts, their social and health characteristics, and actual employment opportunities.

The most serious flaw in the provision of training in remote locations is that substandard 'training' is too often a substitute for proper education. The successful participants in such programs achieve one or more non-transportable and non-articulated certificates that do not provide them with stated industry requirements. If such certificates are non-transportable, the 'qualification' will not be recognised in another state or territory jurisdiction or across industries. If the certificates are non-articulated, they do not permit the holder to enrol in a more advanced course in a similar field without further study. Moreover, often these 'training' programs are based on the assumption that training leads automatically to employment.

The MMDP began with a partnership approach. Analysis of available data and in discussion with Yolŋu traditional owners, local industries, businesses and service organisations were undertaken in the 'Discovery Phase' of the work. Like any organisational development strategy, developing a tailored, high-quality executive leadership and manager development course was going to require strong trust-based partnerships between the program deliverers and the local Indigenous people. Ma Rhea (2009, p. 18) argues that 'there are now many best practice examples of successful economic arrangements being made between big business and indigenous communities and indigenous service organisations (see for example UN Global Compact's (2007) Enhancing Partnership Value and Agreements, Treaties, and Negotiated Settlements). These partnerships recognise the potential and actual economic strengths of indigenous people and are the way of the future'.[24]

Conclusion

In the 1990s, Geoff Clark said, 'We've had more training than the clowns in the Moscow circus. We want jobs', and this sentiment can be heard throughout the Aboriginal world. In some remote communities, mining companies are working through organisations such as the Aurora Project in conjunction with AGSM and Monash University to develop suitably tailored programs such as MMDP. There is emerging anecdotal evidence that this approach is having a positive effect on outcomes. This evidence was incorporated into the development of the MMDP after extensive consultation among the stakeholders.

This case study suggests that the absence of appropriate and effective executive leadership and management training has been a contributing factor to few

Indigenous people being employed in executive leadership and management positions in remote locations in Australia. The key learnings from the MMDP have been:

1 That meaningful partnership with key local Indigenous traditional owners, Indigenous organisations, bureaucrats, and local industries and businesses has been an essential 'success' ingredient

2 That face-to-face delivery of the program and ongoing mentoring over years rather than days have been essential

3 That locally relevant content is vital

4 That for these type of programs to be sustainable, a 'train-the-trainer' partnership with local Indigenous workplace trainers needs to be included

5 Programs delivered in remote locations need to be well resourced and supported to ensure that high-quality training occurs.

The challenge for programs such as MMDP is to deliver high-quality, effective and appropriate skills development to enable Indigenous people in remote locations to develop the executive leadership and management skills to take up business opportunities and challenges, and to build sustainable economic futures for themselves, their families and their communities.

Review questions

1 What is the business case for providing high-quality executive leadership and management programs in remote locations in Australia?

2 Think about the statistics presented in this case study and discuss what aspects of organisational development would need to be considered in the 'data gathering' stage.

3 Consider the chapters on organisational change and think about human resource development: what elements would need to be included in an executive leadership and management program to be delivered in a remote Australian location?

4 Consider the chapters on strategic planning: what would the key 'success' measurements be?

5 Are there new skills or knowledge that an organisational development practitioner needs to work in this sort of environment? What might some of these skills be?

6 How prepared would you be to meet the challenges posed in this case study?

Appendix A: Indigenous Settlement pattern in Eastern Arnhem Land or Miwatj region, Northern Territory

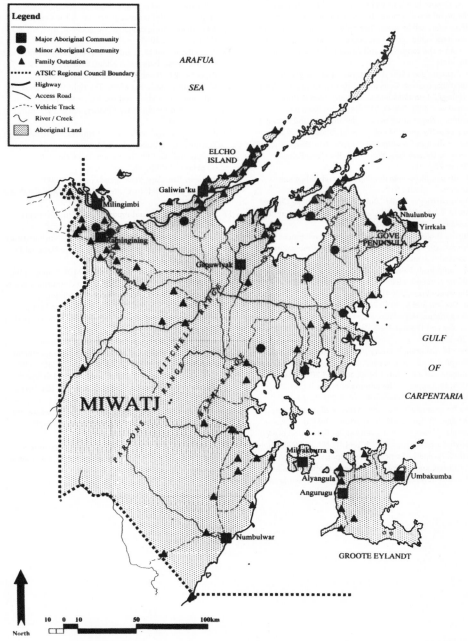

Source: Map adapted from NT, Maps NT 1996; Professor P. Memmott, University of Queensland.

Notes

1 For the purposes of this paper, the employment issues relating to Indigenous people living in both remote and very remote locations will be discussed together using the broad term 'remote'. In particular instances, the distinction will be drawn between the two categories of remoteness but for the purposes of analysis the authors consider the conditions and issues to be substantially the same.

2 J. Altman, 'Economic development and Indigenous Australia: contestations over property, institutions and ideology', *Australian Journal of Agricultural & Resource Economics*, 48:3 (2004): 513–34; Z. Ma Rhea and T. Seddon, 'Negotiating nation: globalization and knowing', in D. Coulby and E. Zambeta (eds), *Globalization and Nationalism in Education: World Education Yearbook 2005*. London, UK and New York, USA: RoutledgeFalmer, 2006): 252–71.

3 J. Altman, 'Economic development and Indigenous Australia', op. cit.: 517.

4 Buku-Larrnggay Mulka, Buku-Larrnggay Mulka Centre: About Yirrkala Art, 2009, www.yirrkala.com/about.html, accessed 5 January 2010.

5 Aurora Project, Miwatj Management Development Project, 2009, www.auroraproject.com.au/miwatj.htm, accessed 5 January 2010.

6 M. Langton, L. Palmer, M. Tehan and K. Shain, *Honour Among Nations?*, Melbourne, Australia: Melbourne University Press, 2004).

7 M. Dodson and L. Strelein, 'Australia's nation building: renegotiating the relationship between Indigenous peoples and the state', *UNSW Law Journal*, 24:3 (2001): 826–39.

8 ibid.; M. Langton, *A Treaty Between Our Nations? Inaugural Professorial Lecture*, 2001, at www.Indigenous.unimelb.edu.au/lecture1.html, accessed 20 January 2004; M. Langton, 'The nations of Australia', in *Balayi: Culture, Law and Colonialism*, vol. 4 (2002): 29–33.

9 See for example N. Pearson, 'When welfare is a curse', *The Age*, 23 April 2004; N. Pearson, 'The Cape York agenda', *Viewpoint*, 30 November 2005, www.cyi.org.au/viewfile.aspx?article=P72E16K2471BN33Z1PIN&file=the%20cape%20york%20agenda.pdf.

10 A. Crawley and A. Sinclair, 'Indigenous human resource practices in Australian mining companies: towards an ethical model', *Journal of Business Ethics*, 45 (2003): 361–73.

11 R. Lawrence, 'Governing Warlpiri subjects: Indigenous employment and training programs in the Central Australian mining industry,' *Geographical Research*, 43:1 (March 2005): 40–8.

12 J. C. Altman and M. C. Dillon, 'A profit-related investment scheme for the Indigenous estate', CAEPR Discussion Paper No. 270 (Canberra: CAEPR, ANU, 2004).

13 M. Langton and Z. Ma Rhea, 'The right to the good life: Indigenous education and the ladder to prosperity', in H. Sykes (ed.) *Perspectives* (Sydney, Australia: Future Leaders, 2009).

14 J. Taylor, 'Indigenous economic futures in the Northern Territory: the demographic and socioeconomic background', CAEPR Discussion Paper No. 246 (Canberra: CAEPR, ANU. 2003): vi.

15 Pearson, 'The Cape York agenda', op. cit., 2005.

16 Internal Cape York Institute analysis and ABS Catalogue 1379.0.55.001.

17 Education Queensland report on transition support supplied to Cape York Institute.

18 Quote from Noel Pearson, Director, Cape York Institute for Policy and Leadership, Address to the National Press Club, Canberra, 30 November 2005.

19 CDATA statistics selected for the MMDP demographic profile from ABS, 2006 Population and Housing Census.

20 M. Langton, 'Accelerated education: addressing education gaps and the "whole of life" crisis facing Australian Indigenous youth,' *Australian Prospect* (Easter 2004): 1–24.

21 J. Taylor and B. H. Hunter, 'The job still ahead: economic costs of continuing Indigenous employment disparity' (Commonwealth of Australia: ATSIC 1998).

22 M. C. Gray and B. H. Hunter, 'Indigenous Job Search Success', CAEPR Discussion Paper No. 274 (Canberra: CAEPR, ANU, 2005): vi.

23 Langton, 'Accelerated education: addressing education gaps and the "whole of life" crisis facing Australian Indigenous youth,' 2004, op. cit.: 1.

24 See p. 18 in Z. Ma Rhea, 'Indigenising international education', *Business Journal of International Education in Business*, 2: 2 (2009): 15–27.

CASE STUDY 3

National Australia Bank: Cultural change program

Jessica Stein and Vanessa Grzinic

National Australia Bank Limited (NAB) was first established as a public limited company in 1858.[1] Today, NAB is the major Australian franchise of the NAB Group of financial services which has businesses in the United Kingdom, New Zealand, the United States and Asia.[2] The NAB Group has almost 40 000 employees and more than 450 000 shareholders[3] and has recently been listed 'within the top thirty most profitable banks in the world'.[4]

In 2004, NAB was at the centre of a major scandal after four traders took part in fictitious trades that enabled their department to report an 'AUD 37 million profit, when its real position was an AUD 5 million loss'.[5] Then, 'in an effort to recoup the losses, and contrary to the Bank's policy', the traders gambled heavily on unhedged positions, anticipating an increasing US dollar that never materialised.[6] When the scandal was eventually uncovered by junior employees, the traders had recorded losses of $360 million.[7]

NAB suffered greatly in the aftermath of the scandal.[8] Aside from financial losses, arguably the greatest impact was the prescribed and voluntary organisational change experienced over the following six years, specifically in relation to NAB's organisational culture. Immediately following the scandal, the bank lost the majority of its key personnel, including its chairman, CEO, chief financial officer, head of corporate and institutional banking, head of markets and head of risk management.[9] Newly appointed executives immediately called NAB's organisational culture into question, describing it as too 'profit driven',[10] 'too big, too old, too male, too full of ex-CEOs and too many insiders'.[11]

Culture in the context of change

Organisational culture is loosely defined as 'a set of norms and values that are widely shared and strongly held throughout the organisation'.[12] It influences the way employees relate to each other, customers, shareholders and business partners.[13]

In the context of organisational change, corporate culture is often utilised by scholars and change management experts as a significant precursor, enabler or influencer.[14] As noted by Levin and Gottlieb, 'most organisation change efforts require some degree of cultural shift'.

In analysing the changes to NAB's culture implemented following the scandal, it is important to understand the various perspectives of culture conveyed in theory. Many perspectives exist in academic literature;[15] however Keleman and Papasolomou identify three main perspectives: integration, differentiation and ambiguity.[16]

> *Integration perspective:* The most widely used perspective of organisational culture is the integration perspective.[17] According to the integration perspective, 'culture is clear, measurable and pervasive and (represents) a consensus within the entire organisation'.[18] From the integrative view, culture manifests itself across the organisation in quite tangible and visible ways.[19] Culture can be reflected in a variety of mediums such as 'business strategies, performance targets and metrics, management practices, formal and informal rules that govern behaviour, traditions, stories and manifestations'.[20]

> *Differentiation perspective:* The differentiation perspective considers culture to be an amalgamation of a collection or combination of cultures 'that meet within an organisation's boundary'.[21] In essence, the differentiation perspective focuses on inconsistencies as the nucleus of culture; culture is viewed as a collection of manifestations, some of which may be contradictory. In recognising these inconsistencies, the various initiators of culture can be identified, both internal and external.[22]

> *Ambiguity perspective:* The ambiguity perspective follows neither the integrative or differentiate views, instead suggesting that 'relationships among culture manifestations are characterised by a lack of clarity as well as paradox and ambiguity'.[23] Individuals may share certain views or values, yet may differ on others. Likewise, from the ambiguity perspective, employees may agree with certain management of some issues, yet 'at other times they may be indifferent, ignorant or in total opposition to the dominant managerial line'.[24] Many academics view this as a more realistic perspective of culture.

Cultural problems at NAB

Much of the blame for NAB's 2004 crisis was immediately attributed to a lack of accountability on behalf of its senior management and board.[25] Maiden (2004) traces these issues back to a culture fomented over the years by disconnected board members who lacked 'an understanding of the principles and the laws of corporate governance and accountability'.[26] In the wake of the 2004 controversy, Jain and Thomson observed that a 'lack of team spirit, distrust and inability to accept alternative points of view' had created factions within the Board,[27] and that these factions led to ineffective communication, resulting in the creation of a lax and unquestioning culture. These unfavourable cultural traits were transferred down through the entire organisation as leaders at all levels reinforced these behavioural and cultural norms.[28]

Poor governance practices were attributed to a 'lack of transparency in operations'.[29] In an early speech by incoming CEO John Stewart, he described NAB as an organisation without 'clear accountabilities and responsibilities' where a good news culture predicated the ability for bad news to be recognised and properly addressed.[30]

NAB's culture was also described by many critics as profit focused, once again stemming from the attitude of Board members and senior management.[31] It was this culture that encouraged increased risk taking in the trading activities in 2004. Dellaportas et al. go so far as to suggest that 'sacrifices in ethical behaviour were acceptable in the name of profits'.[32] 'Profit is king' was said to be an expression commonly relayed by NAB staff members in interviews investigating the 2004 crisis.[33]

In his speech, John Stewart highlighted the importance of addressing this culture in implementing change following the scandal: 'You can see how by improving the culture of the organisation we can make quite a difference'.[34] Ironically, the very shortfalls in NAB's culture that incoming CEO, John Stewart, intended to correct were also NAB's biggest obstacles in implementing a successful change program, not least of which was a top-down culture that was breeding mistrust, lack of ownership and lax employees.[35]

In implementing effective cultural change, the organisation needed to identify its core cultural levers in order to both overcome its key cultural constraints to change within NAB, as well as reverse the culture that that 'enabled the deception to arise and continue for a substantial period'.[36]

Cultural change at NAB

In recognising the ability of leaders to influence change, NAB first readjusted its key priorities to reflect a client-focused organisation as opposed to a profit-driven one.[37] NAB's new key priorities were stated as 'investment in our people, culture and reputation'[38] and its complementing strategic priority 'Differentiating through culture and reputation for the benefit of our people, customers and communities'.[39]

NAB's priorities were then reflected in various mission statements, visions and strategic objectives in order to create visible manifestations of its desired culture. These tangible demonstrations of culture were not just applied to NAB but to its entire portfolio of financial institutions within the NAB Group. The new overarching belief for NAB was now that the way in which results were achieved was just as important as the results themselves.[40]

One of the most tangible change initiatives implemented by management post the 2004 scandal was the 2006 relaunch of the NAB brand with a new logo. The new branding of NAB was aimed at reconnecting the organisation with a public who had lost faith in it in the wake of the trading crisis.[41] The new brand was carefully launched by NAB senior executives to coincide with the Melbourne 2006

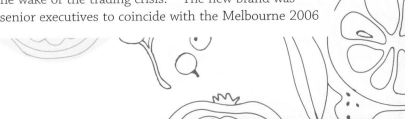

Commonwealth Games, of which the organisation was a top-tier sponsor. NAB capitalised on the cross-promotional opportunities that this presented, highlighting the complementary cultures that existed in both NAB and the international sporting event.[42] This included a focus on community development, a youthful brand and collaborative, 'team-orientated' structures.[43]

Preceding NAB's brand relaunch, CEO John Stewart moved the entire Victorian workforce into its new Docklands headquarters 'in time to assist restructuring'.[44] In the first instance, it represented the gathering of more than 3500 employees from across the state to be 'under the one roof to work more effectively and collaboratively'.[45] However, the building was intended to convey many important cultural messages about NAB:

> *Horizontal integration:* The actual architecture of the building aimed to present a traditional tower, lying on its side. This aimed to represent the traditional 'vertical hierarchy (of NAB), giving way to horizontal integration'.[46]
>
> *Transparency of operation:* A design feature of the new development was the excessive number of windows and open spaces within the building. This aimed to project the open and honest corporate principles of NAB.[47]
>
> *Collaboration:* NAB's new headquarters were developed with no individual offices, intended to represent the corporate principles of teamwork and the breaking down of barriers to communication. In a press release following the launch of the new building, NAB claimed that the internal design was aimed at fostering communication between all levels of employees.[48]

Review questions

1 List one strength and weakness for each cultural perspective described in this case study.

2 Complete a force field analysis using Kurt Lewin's change management model, clearly illustrating the driving and restraining forces for change in a force field diagram.

3 Which cultural change perspective was adopted by NAB during its change program?

4 What would be your future recommendations to the CEO or HR team at NAB?

Notes

1 A. Jain and D. Thomson, 'Corporate governance, board responsibilities, and financial performance: the National Bank of Australia', *Corporate Ownership and Control*, 6:2 (2008): 99–113.

2 National Australia Bank Group, 'Corporate social responsibility report', 2005, www.nabgroup.com, viewed 10 May 2010.

3 ibid.

4 Jain and Thomson, 'Corporate governance, board responsibilities, and financial performance', op. cit.: 99.

5 Jain and Thomson, 'Corporate governance, board responsibilities, and financial performance', op. cit.: 104; S. Dellaportas, B. J. Cooper and P. Braica, 'Leadership, culture and employee deceit: the case of the National Australia Bank', *Corporate Governance*, 15:6 (2007): 1442–52.

6 Dellaportas, Cooper and Braica, 'Leadership, culture and employee deceit', op. cit.: 1447.

7 Dellaportas, Cooper and Braica, 'Leadership, culture and employee deceit', op. cit.

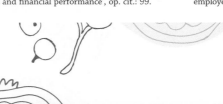

8 Dellaportas, Cooper and Braica, 'Leadership, culture and employee deceit', op. cit.: 1448.

9 Jain and Thomson, 'Corporate governance, board responsibilities, and financial performance', op. cit.

10 Dellaportas, Cooper and Braica, 'Leadership, culture and employee deceit', op. cit.: 1442.

11 Jain and Thomson, 'Corporate governance, board responsibilities, and financial performance', op. cit.: 108.

12 J. B. Sorenson, 'The strength of corporate culture and reliability of firm performance', *Administrative Science Quarterly*, 47 (2002): 70–91.

13 U. Fairbairn, 'HR as a strategic partner: culture change as an American Express case study', *Human Resource Management*, 44:1 (2005): 79–84.

14 F. Graetz, M. Rimmer, A. Lawrence and A. Smith, *Managing Organisational Change*, 2nd edn (Brisbane: John Wiley & Sons Australia, Ltd, 2006); I. Levin and J. Gottlieb, 'Realigning organisation culture for optimal performance: six principles and eight practices', *Organisation Development Journal*, 27:4 (2009): 31–46; C-J. Shieh and I-M. Wang, 'The study of relationships between corporate core competence, management innovation and corporate culture', *International Journal of Organisational Innovation* (2008): 395–411.

15 Dellaportas, Cooper and Braica, 'Leadership, culture and employee deceit', op. cit.; Levin and Gottlieb, 'Realigning organisation culture for optimal performance: six principles and eight practices', op. cit.; Shieh and Wang, 'The study of relationships between corporate core competence, management innovation and corporate culture', op. cit.

16 M. Keleman and I. Papasolomou, 'Internal marketing: a qualitative study of culture change in the UK banking sector', *Journal of Marketing Management*, 23:7–8 (2007): 745–767.

17 Shieh and Wang, 'The study of relationships between corporate core competence, management innovation and corporate culture', op. cit.

18 Dellaportas, Cooper and Braica, 'Leadership, culture and employee deceit', op. cit.: 1443.

19 Keleman and Papasolomou, 'Internal marketing', op. cit.

20 Levin and Gottlieb, 'Realigning organisation culture for optimal performance: six principles and eight practices', op. cit.: 32.

21 Keleman and Papasolomou, 'Internal marketing', op. cit.: 750.

22 Shieh and Wang, 'The study of relationships between corporate core competence, management innovation and corporate culture', op. cit.

23 Keleman and Papasolomou, 'Internal marketing', op. cit.: 750.

24 ibid.

25 M. Flinch, 'NAB and the art of corporate renewal', 2006, www.humanresourcesmagazine.com.au/articles/8f/0c03fc8f.asp, viewed 2 May 2010.

26 As cited in Jain and Thomson, 'Corporate governance, board responsibilities, and financial performance', op. cit.: 103.

27 Jain and Thomson, 'Corporate governance, board responsibilities, and financial performance', op. cit.: 103.

28 Dellaportas, Cooper and Braica, op. cit.: 1445.

29 Jain and Thomson, 'Corporate governance, board responsibilities, and financial performance', op. cit.: 103.

30 Dellaportas, Cooper and Braica, 'Leadership, culture and employee deceit', op. cit.: 1451.

31 Dellaportas, Cooper and Braica, 'Leadership, culture and employee deceit', op. cit.

32 Dellaportas, Cooper and Braica, 'Leadership, culture and employee deceit', op. cit.: 1447.

33 Dellaportas, Cooper and Braica, 'Leadership, culture and employee deceit', op. cit.

34 Dellaportas, Cooper and Braica, 'Leadership, culture and employee deceit', op. cit.: 1451.

35 Flinch, 'NAB and the art of corporate renewal', op. cit.; F. Graetz et al., *Managing Organisational Change*, op. cit.

36 Dellaportas, Cooper and Braica, 'Leadership, culture and employee deceit', op. cit.: 1450.

37 Jain and Thomson, 'Corporate governance, board responsibilities, and financial performance', op. cit.

38 Author Unknown, 'Strategy update', *National Australia Bank*, 2009, 12 March 2010.

39 ibid.

40 S. Fagg, 'Inside NAB's cultural nightmare', 2005, www.humanresourcesmagazine.com.au/articles/61/0c036061.asp, viewed 2 May 2010.

41 Flinch, 'NAB and the art of corporate renewal', op. cit.

42 Flinch, 'NAB and the art of corporate renewal', op. cit.

43 'Australian focus underpins NAB strategy', *National Australia Bank ASX Announcement*, 12 March 2009.

44 S. Drake and G. Brawn, 'National @ Docklands', 2005, www.architecturemedia.com, viewed 10 March 2010.

45 National Australia Bank, 'National Australia Bank officially opens new flagship Docklands Complex', 2004, www.nab.com.au, viewed 10 May 2010.

46 Drake and Brawn, 'National @ Docklands', op. cit.

47 National Australia Bank, 'National Australia Bank officially opens new flagship Docklands Complex', op. cit.

48 National Australia Bank, 'National Australia Bank officially opens new flagship Docklands Complex', op. cit.

CASE STUDY 4

IBM Australia: Managing diversity through organisational culture

Ramanie Samaratunge & Nilupama Wijewardena
Department of Management, Monash University

> Think of culture as the DNA of an organization – invisible to the naked eye but
> critical in shaping the character of the workplace.
>
> Tom Davenport, Academic Director, Process Management Research, Babson College[1]

Organisational culture

Organisational culture is part and parcel of organisational life, one in which
new members must be socialised in, in order for them to be not only accepted
by existing members but also to effectively function within the organisation.
Organisational culture is 'intangible and difficult to measure'[2] and unique to each
and every organisation. It is also the product of influence and shaping by
successive generations of members passing through that organisation. While
definitions on organisational culture abound in the literature, it typically relates to
the 'complex set of values, beliefs, assumptions, and symbols that define the way in
which a firm conducts its business'.[3] Culture defines how organisational members
think, behave and relate to each other as well as outsiders within the organisational
context. It specifies the procedures and policies for conducting business operations,
reporting and handling conflict, initiating innovation and how lines of power and
authority flow. It is also the sum of tangible logos and artefacts existing within
organisations and the shared stories and myths among members.[4] It spells out the
dos and don'ts, the acceptable and the unacceptable, the rights and the wrongs of
the organisation that members consciously and unconsciously adhere to. Having a
well-designed and managed organisational culture can spell the difference between
success and failure as ultimately it has an impact on the overall bottom line. A
strong culture, where organisational members have a clear idea about what is
required of them and a clear sense of the objectives being pursued has been likened
to an 'invisible asset'. A weak culture on the other hand 'may be less effective, less
productive and [a] less satisfying place to work in'.[5]

This case study focuses on the use of culture as a means of aiding
organisational change. Given the fact that organisational culture is a vast area of
study, here we limit our focus to the area of diversity management within the
workplace and explain how diversity can be managed through organisational
culture. We argue that managing diversity is part of organisational culture.

The case study takes IBM Australia as a test case to examine how it has successfully designed and incorporated diversity management practices within its organisational culture to meet the challenges in its external business environment. We believe that diversity management is a timely topic to address given the increasing diversity of the workforce. If left unmanaged by organisations it can adversely impact on employee satisfaction and organisational performance. IBM has been chosen as the company to be examined due to its global presence and diverse workforce, innovative culture and forward thinking practices.

Research has shown the beneficial impact a strong organisational culture can have on organisational performance and employee job satisfaction. Similarly culture aids the change process within organisations. Change is an ever-present fact of life and therefore unavoidable. Organisations must successfully deal with change in order to not just succeed in business but continue in business as well. While some changes such as organisational restructuring and downsizing are within the control of management, the changes that occur in the external environment are mostly unanticipated and beyond the control of managers. Changes such as economic upheavals, changing consumer attitudes and preferences, improvements in technology, natural or man-made disasters, or increases in competition pose threats to organisational profitability and survival and must be dealt with in a timely and efficient manner. All organisations must carry out internal changes as a response to the external changes that occur in the environment. The ultimate objective of these organisational change programs is to increase organisational performance in terms of efficiency and effectiveness as well as increase employee satisfaction. Changes within an organisation may be made to its structure, people or technology. Of these three, the hardest to change are the people. Newspapers and the electronic media are replete with stories of strikes, dissent and frustration vented by employees opposed to the implementation of change within their organisations. It is in this regard that organisational culture becomes very critical because people are an important part of culture. By changing culture, organisations change their people. Therefore, it is impossible to successfully implement organisational change programs without first changing the organisational culture.

Managing diversity is fast becoming an important issue for organisations given rapidly changing demographics within countries and increases in global migration. More and more women with varying educational qualifications and experience levels are joining the workforce and threatening the predominantly male-dominated workplaces that existed a few decades ago. Retirement ages of employees are also rising and companies are finding a growing number of employees in different age groups. People with special needs and disabilities have also entered the workforce. Due to these reasons companies are now faced with the challenge of including, managing and catering to the unique needs of these diverse groups. Global labour mobility is also on the rise as many countries have relaxed their immigration policies with the aim of attracting large numbers of skilled and semi-skilled workers in to their economies. In Australia, skilled migration has resulted in an increase in the proportion of the Australian population born overseas from 23.1% to 23.9% during the period 2001 to 2006.[6] It is also estimated that within the next two decades 'twenty-five per cent of the Australian population will be of Asian origin'.[7] As a result, multicultural societies within national economies are posing a challenge to companies in terms of attracting, hiring and retaining suitable staff. Companies are also more inclined to expand their business operations overseas and thereby are coming in to greater contact with different cultures, attitudes and value systems. It is becoming increasingly clear that companies no longer can afford to ignore the issue of diversity in business dealings.

With the growing diversity of the workforce, companies are faced with the dilemma of managing diversity issues in their workplaces or face the consequences of loss of profitability and employee satisfaction. The external environment has put pressure on companies to change the way they direct the diverse groups within their organisations. Diversity is part of the organisational culture. By incorporating and effectively managing the diversity strategies within their organisational culture, companies can successfully implement the diversity programs and derive the maximum benefit to the organisation as well as its employees.

IBM: Company overview

International Business Machines Corporation (IBM) had its humble beginnings in the United States in the early part of the twentieth century as the Computing-Tabulating-Recording Company, which was formed with the merging of the Tabulating Machine Company, the International Time Recording Company and the Computing Scale Company of America in 1911. In 1924, the company's name was changed to International Business Machines Corporation (IBM) and since then the company has expanded into an iconic multinational corporation with business operations spanning 174 countries around the world. It started off with the production of commercial scales, time clocks, butcher scales and a primitive assortment of punch card tabulators[8] but during the 1950s, under the helm of Thomas J. Watson Jr, company changed its business operations to the development and commercialisation of electronic computer technologies. Watson, Jr is credited with transforming IBM into a modern corporation in the 1950s and by the 1960s it was considered the world's leading high-tech firm.[9] The 1970s and 1980s saw the company further expanding its innovative product line from magnetic strip technology to establishing the status of the PC as a basic necessity of life. Today IBM is one of the world's largest Information Technology (IT) companies with a workforce of 399,409 employees[10] worldwide and global revenues of US$95.8 billion.[11] It specialises in providing business consulting and technology services. It is also one of the world's largest IT research organisations, investing US$6 billion each year in national research.[12] The award of three Nobel Prizes in physics to five IBM researchers is a sound testament of the quality and impact of its research and scientific discovery. With almost a century of expertise in pioneering and revolutionising the global IT industry through its innovative information handling product lines, cutting-edge research and development ventures and global consultation services, IBM remains inventive and original and is expected to continue to thrive.

Organisational culture at IBM

The secret to IBM's phenomenal achievements can be attributed to its innovative culture and management practices grounded in core values. The company has been successful in facing harsh global changes such as the Great Depression and two world wars by holding fast to its vision and values.[13] IBM has relied not just on its product innovation strategies but its social innovation strategies as well to promote diversity and corporate social responsibility in its policies. During 1914 to 1945, which marked the initial period of IBM's business operations, the company's belief system was still being formed, tested and put to work. During this time these beliefs helped the company to maintain itself through many struggles and also achieve a position of leadership and prominence within its industry and American businesses. From 1946 to the present day, IBM's well-grounded beliefs helped the company make drastic technological changes and achieve a high rate of growth.[14] IBM's philosophy stems from three basic beliefs, namely, respect for the individual, provide the best customer service and aim for superiority in everything they do. Much of the groundwork for a strong culture at IBM was laid down during the time of Watson, Jr, who not only created and institutionalised professional corporate management practices but also converted the tacit IBM philosophy and behaviours into formal policies and programs. He was skilled at adapting to changing times, which was a valuable skill the company used to get through the many environmental hazards it has had to face during its long operational existence.

It is difficult to envision one single universal IBM culture that can be seen in all IBM companies worldwide due to it being an international corporation with operations carried out in such diverse markets as Thailand, Brazil, Israel, Singapore and Hungary. The different national, regional, cultural and linguistic distinctions that exist in each region undoubtedly mould the organisational cultures of those particular IBM organisations operating in those regions. However, there are some key characteristics of culture that pervade all IBM organisations around the world. These characteristics are the recognition and encouragement of innovation and risk taking, attention to detail, outcome orientation, people orientation, team orientation, aggressiveness and stability.[15] Adhering to these seven key IBM characteristics has paved the way for IBM to achieve a higher number of high-tech innovations, focus on quality and goal achievement, empower its employees and create talented cross-functional teams. Such managerial values and beliefs embedded within IBM's organisational culture have been attributed to the sustained superior financial performance of IBM and such other companies.[16] Looking from the employees' perspective, Marcus Abeyta states that the culture at IBM is supportive and that employees find working at IBM to be a healthy and pleasant experience. Therefore there is very little dissent among IBM employees.[17]

Diversity policies and practices at IBM

IBM has addressed the issues of diversity from the early as the 1950s when such issues were mainly unheard of. Its commitment to diversity issues is echoed in the then CEO, Watson, Jr's, statement: 'It is the policy of IBM to hire people who have personality, talent and background necessary to fill a given job, regardless of race, colour or creed.'[18]

IBM's diversity policy has helped the company to discover new perspectives, make use of diverse knowledge and experience and thereby come up with innovative ideas, suggestions and methods. Through its diversity framework, IBM aims to achieve the following:

Creation of a work/life balance
Advancement of women
Integration of people with a disability.

Under its formal diversity policy IBM focused on opportunities for women, minorities and the disabled many years before such considerations became the norm. During 1935, IBM recruited 25 women who were college seniors to its Systems Service and thereby paved the way for women to enter into professional careers. Eight years later the first woman Vice President was appointed at IBM. In the same year, as part of its commitment to helping people with disabilities, a training centre for 600 disabled people was opened by IBM. IBM was also instrumental in initiating a three-month leave of absence policy in 1956, 37 years before such policy was mandated by legislation. The company has moved through different phases of diversity management starting with Diversity 1.0 which came into effect during the 1950s. Under this phase the company addressed issues of maternity leave, Equal opportunities for employees and PhD scholarships for minorities and women throughout the 1960s and 1970s. Later the company moved to Diversity 2.0 in the 1990s with the aim of removing barriers and understanding regional communities and the differences between these communities. Today IBM focuses on Diversity 3.0 in which individual differences are treated as a competitive advantage for innovation, and improvement of customer service is achieved by building diversity teams.

Thanks to the policies in place for the advancement of women's opportunities and rights, the company was named as the sixth ranking company in 2010 by the National Association of Female Executives.[19] In 2010 DiversityInc ranked IBM as the No. 1 company for global diversity for 'its training, employee groups and strong cultural values across all boards'.[20] In 2009, IBM was awarded the NGLCC Pinnacle

Award for its support and endeavours in managing diversity issues and initiatives.[21]

IBM continues to grow in the twenty-first century and today employs people from diverse countries and backgrounds. IBM employees come from organisations with different organisational values and cultures.[22] Therefore it has faced the issue of building an organisational culture that values diversity and social inclusion at IBM, to not only further attract new employees but also to develop and retain its existing workforce. IBM's diversity program grew as a response to this environmental challenge.

Diversity policies and practices at IBM Australia

Any change management program within an organisation must have the essential ingredients of the company's readiness to embrace the change, commitment, management support, employee involvement, implementation and feedback for it to be successful. The following discussion on the company's diversity program will show how well IBM Australia has adhered to these steps in managing its diversity strategies.

The impetus for diversity strategies at IBM Australia has come about through the company's corporate strategies such as respecting the individual, through legal requirements of the Anti-Discrimination Act and Racial Discrimination Act and taking into consideration the business case for diversity. IBM Australia's biannual Employee Opinion Survey in 2001 acted as the foundation for understanding the need for managing cultural diversity at IBM Australia. The survey findings showed that individual employee satisfaction differed among different ethnic groups and that their cultural background had an impact on how an employee felt about IBM. Taking the findings from this study, IBM Australia developed a business case for managing diversity at its offices on the following lines:

> Given the changing demographics in the population of Australia in terms of an ageing population and shortage of skilled workers, IBM Australia recognised the need to maximise all opportunities for employees or miss out on attracting talent and business opportunities.

> IBM, being a global corporation, required its employees to recognise and act on global opportunities. IBM Australia recognised that having a diverse workforce made this a much easier task as a diverse workforce facilitated gaining access to global markets.

> Given the international customer base of IBM, the company needed to attract and retain employees with bilingual or multilingual skills. Proficiency in languages other than English are highly valued skills when it comes to servicing customers in non-English speaking countries. At the moment, IBM's IT Helpdesk in Brisbane mainly caters to Japanese clients.

> IBM Australia has moved from a limited 'Face-time culture' of 9–5 Monday to Friday workdays, national/regional markets and bricks and mortar offices to

a 'Results-oriented culture' of 24x7 workdays, global marketplaces and virtual offices. This expansion and explosion of business operations worldwide has left many IBM employees feeling disconnected with the workplace. Therefore a need has arisen to help IBM employees feel included within the larger IBM organisation.

These factors, which represent the demands made on the company by the external environment, played a decisive role in making a sound business case for managing diversity at IBM Australia. As a means of addressing these issues, IBM Australia decided to embrace diversity and create a culture of inclusion for all its employees, improve the focus on all employees and thereby realise the different talents of employees and make IBM Australia a desirable place to work in.

Managing the diversity program at IBM Australia

IBM Australia's diversity program has been established around the objectives of gaining a competitive advantage by attracting and retaining the best employees, participating fully in a diverse and global marketplace and increasing business effectiveness through diversity and teaming. Therefore, the company has moved away from simply 'complying with diversity issues' to managing 'diversity as business leverage'. By examining the various challenges in the external environment that posed threats to the company's survival, the company has been successful in planning, executing and evaluating its formal diversity program. At the planning stage, understanding the changing business climate and data collection as outlined above helped to identify the need for a diversity program within the company. Next the company gained the support of its most senior management by creating the Diversity Council. The business case for diversity management was also explained to the line managers as aiding the performance of the company, and due to their positive impact on profitability, managers were more inclined to readily embrace diversity practices. This ensured greater commitment for the diversity program from management at IBM Australia.

The main aims of the diversity program have been recognised as the advancement of women, integration of people with a disability, maintaining work/life balance and cultural acceptance and awareness. There are also strategies in place at IBM to address Gay Lesbian Bisexual & Transgender (GLBT) issues and cross-generational issues. With these aims in place, suitable infrastructure to implement these strategies was next developed. The infrastructure at IBM Australia included creating an information hub for managers and employees, creating Diversity Networking Groups and Team rooms, developing support infrastructure through business functions, and further developing and communicating diversity policies and practices. At the implementation stage, employees and managers are briefed on the company's diversity strategies and how to execute them. Profiles of exemplary employees and diversity success stories are published for other staff members' benefit. IBM Australia also conducts the People Management Awards as a means of rewarding desired behaviour.

Feedback on the diversity strategies is obtained by analysing complaints, Diversity target measurement, asking for open feedback and Diversity Brand recognition. Such feedback helps the company to evaluate the progress and success of its diversity program and make further changes if necessary. There is also a Work Life Survey done every three years to obtain information on work/life issues of employees.

Groups in charge of diversity at IBM Australia

Apart from the HR personnel at IBM Australia, the people in charge of diversity management in the company fall into two groups. The first group is the Diversity Council, chaired by the CEO of IBM Australia. The Council is responsible for advancing and valuing differences among employees and their contributions to the organisation. The Council exercises its responsibilities by increasing employee and management awareness about diversity issues and promoting the effective use of IBM's diverse workforce. It mainly functions through developing the key initiatives of employee attraction, recruitment, retention and awareness strategies around diversity issues. The Diversity Council has also been instrumental in holding a series of cultural diversity employee roundtables. These face-to-face meetings of employees have resulted in gathering valuable and practical ideas for increasing awareness of cultural diversity at IBM Australia. Some simple ideas drawn from these meetings, which started as pilot projects, have been implemented into full-fledged training programs on cultural diversity.

The second group involved in diversity management at IBM Australia are Diversity Contact Officers. They are permanent employees working at IBM Australia who themselves are from diverse backgrounds. They represent IBM Australia's diverse workforce and include employees with such diverse characteristics as disabilities and different sexual orientations. They are volunteers trained as work/life balance coaches and aid the diversity management program by exchanging information relating to diversity and helping to integrate disabled people into IBM's workforce.

Cultural diversity education and awareness at IBM Australia

Staff and managers at IBM Australia are made aware of the company's diversity program by using the 'Individual Professional Development' approach and the 'General Staff Awareness' approach.

Under the Individual Professional Development approach individual managers or members of multicultural teams are made aware of their own cultural biases and prejudices. They are also given sensitivity to different cultural values and attitudes. Two programs conducted under this approach are the Shades of Blue and

QuickViews programs. Shades of Blue helps managers engaged in cross-cultural business transactions and/or are supervising multicultural teams to develop cross-cultural competence. QuickViews provides managers with necessary and accessible information on such topics as culture and management, and culture and business to help them effectively carry out business dealings with clients and colleagues from other countries.

Under the General Staff Awareness approach, the understanding of all staff regarding the different cultures within IBM Australia is raised. As a means of achieving this end, the company publishes a diversity calendar showing various dates of cultural significance to clients and staff, has a floating holiday program in place where staff members can exchange a public holiday for a significant cultural holiday and celebrate the Chinese New Year for Sydney staff.

Recommendations

It is clear from the preceding discussion that the diversity program at IBM Australia has been well planned and executed. Managing diversity issues at IBM Australia has been done as a need for complying with legislation and as a business case. This has enabled the company to increase its profitability by accessing new markets and expanding its client base. At the same time the company has been able to adhere to and comply with current legislation such as the Equal Employment Opportunity laws that promote a diversity climate. This has been a great boost to the company's public image as well as helped improve staff morale and commitment to the company. However, there are a few key areas that need to be addressed for the diversity program to be fully integrated into the system.

1 Diversity management must become part of IBM Australia's business strategy. At the moment it is only implemented as a business case and IBM Australia has yet to incorporate it as a business strategy. Such a step would ensure greater company-wide commitment and recognition of the importance of diversity practices.

2 There is a need to embed diversity strategies in IBM Australia's performance management. Stronger senior leadership could allow for more proactive diversity programs that extend beyond legal compliance and there is a need for greater integration of diversity management with performance measures.

Conclusion

Organisational culture is a fundamental and inherent part of any organisation. It helps to determine organisational performance and employee satisfaction and aids organisational change. Diversity management, being a part of organisational culture, is coming to the forefront of management issues due to the changing face of society. This case study looked at how diversity issues are being managed at IBM in general and at IBM Australia in particular. The case study concludes that

diversity issues at IBM Australia have come about as a result of adhering to the company's corporate strategies, compliance with relevant legislation and as a business case. It has been well planned and executed. However there is still a need for the diversity program at IBM Australia to be made a part of the company's business strategy and embed it in the company's performance management.

Review questions

1 Why is managing diversity such an important issue for today's business organisations?

2 What are the consequences for business organisations of not managing diversity issues in their organisations?

3 Do you think that the cost of planning and implementing an organisational diversity program is justified given the benefits of its outcomes? Give reasons for your answer.

4 Imagine that you are working on an assignment with a team of people from different cultural backgrounds. What challenges are you likely to face in carrying out the assignment and how do you propose to overcome them?

5 What other organisations do you know of that have successfully used diversity strategies? What are those strategies?

6 How can a cultural awareness training program be useful to managers in charge of multicultural teams?

7 How can a cultural awareness training program be useful for employees in an organisation with a multicultural workforce?

8 What are the problems that are likely to occur in an organisation having a diverse workforce (in terms of age, sex, ethnicity, sexual orientation etc) but lacking in an effective diversity management program?

9 What are the characteristics of an effective diversity program?

Notes

1 S. J. M. Reger, *Can Two Rights Make a Wrong? Insights from IBM's Tangible culture Approach* (Upper Saddle River, NJ: IBM Press Pearson PLC, 2006).

2 C. Carnall, *Managing Change in Organizations* (Essex, England: Pearson Education Limited, 2007): 308.

3 J. B. Barney, 'Organizational culture: can it be a source of sustained competitive advantage', *Academy of Management Review*, 11:3 (1986 July): 656–65.

4 Carnall, *Managing Change in Organizations*, op. cit.

5 Carnall, *Managing Change in Organizations*, op. cit.: 318.

6 Department of Immigration and Citizenship, 2008.

7 Y. Fujimoto, 'The experience of Asian expatriates in Australia', *Journal of Doing Business Across Borders*, 3:1 (2003): 24.

8 T. J. Watson Jr, *A Business and Its Beliefs: The Ideas that Helped Build IBM*, New York: McGraw-Hill, 2003).

9 www.ibm.com/us/en/.

10 2009 figures taken from http://www.ibm.com/ibm/us/en/.

11 2009 figures taken from http://www.ibm.com/ibm/us/en/.

12 Notes from presentation on 'Diversity @ IBM' by K. Nicolson, Diversity Manager IBM Australia & New Zealand held at Monash University, Australia, 10 October 2006.

13 www.ibm.com/us/en/.

14 Watson, op. cit.

15 M. Abeyta, *Organizational Culture* (Tonalli Group LLC, 2006).

16 Barney, 'Organizational culture', op. cit.

17 Abeyta, op. cit.

18 K. Nicolson, 'Cultural diversity, IBM style', *Human Resources Leader* (2010).

19 www.nafe.com/web?service=direct/1/ViewArticlePage/dlinkFullArticle&sp=S3061&sp=5117.

20 www.diversityinc.com/article/7652/The-DiversityInc-Top-10-Companies-for-Global-Diversity/.

21 www.nglcc.org/node/10839.

22 Notes from presentation on 'Management of Change Diversity @ IBM Australia & New Zealand' by K. Nicolson, Diversity Manager, IBM Australia & New Zealand held at Monash University, Australia, 21 September 2004.

CASE STUDY 5

A new look for Convoy

Dr Dorothy Wardale
Curtin Graduate School of Business

Part 1

Convoy is a medium-sized transport and logistics company in South Australia. It employs 300 people at its head office and approximately 700 contractors who are on the road, but occasionally visit the head office. It is relatively traditional and mechanistic in its organisational structure and operating style. Convoy's CEOs are long-lasting; the recently retired CEO held the position for 18 years. He was especially well regarded by customers, industry and government alike.

On his appointment, the new CEO, Charles Walton, wanted to create a different image for the company. He wanted the customer's first impression to be an attractive mix of long-standing expertise and innovative service delivery. Recognising that there were many components to creating a new corporate image, especially at a time of economic downturn, Charles felt that the refurbishment of Convoy's head office would provide a 'quick win'.

A refurbishment had been on-and-off the Executive Group's agenda for the past six years. The Executive had recognised that a refurbishment would be good for staff morale and to support a modern business image. However, the current building was functioning effectively at a business level. It was also heritage listed and had asbestos in the ceiling of the main foyer, which together created a raft of obstacles to overcome. Furthermore, Charles knew from previous experience that change involving the look and feel of a familiar workspace could be as confronting for some people as a major restructure.

During the previous six years, the task of refurbishment had passed from one General Manager (GM) to the next. Each one had commissioned either the in-house engineers or a consultant to undertake various tasks: heritage impact reports had been written, two different architectural firms had drawn up plans, interior designers had provided advice and, of course, the staff all had their opinion on what should be done to improve the building. A wealth of engineering and finance information existed for the potential project.

During his review of the information, Charles also found that the 300 staff within the building did not have a staff room. Historically, there had been 'tea ladies' but as they retired they were not replaced. All that was available for the staff were the cubicle-kitchens where the tea ladies had prepared their trolleys. Charles decided this needed to change too – along with the public face of a refurbishment, he also wanted his staff to feel valued and he knew the importance of informal social networking to an effective organisation. He was, however, conscious of not being seen to spend money unnecessarily in his new role.

After a particularly depressing meeting with his Executive, Charles was heading down in the lift to grab a coffee. He bumped into Debra Lamar, who was employed as the Organisational Development Manager. She had been introduced to him when he first arrived and they had spoken informally on several occasions. When he asked her how her job was going she responded by explaining that while she was enjoying it, she would like more of a challenge. The lift reached its destination; they got out, spoke for a minute more, then said their goodbyes.

Driving home that night Charles reflected on his frustration with the Executive Group meeting; the slow, cautious way in which decisions were made, and his desire to get some quick wins to stake out his claim as a CEO who cared for his staff and who was going to build an innovative company.

The next day he set up a meeting with Debra, James the maintenance engineer, Kim his Executive Assistant (EA), and Leila the social club co-ordinator. One of the GMs, George, was invited to sponsor the project and he agreed, reluctantly. The brief was to revitalise the building to make it a better place for staff with a more contemporary feel for client visitors. No budget was mentioned, no time line indicated, and the 'team' seemed a strange mix of people to put into what was essentially a construction project. Debra was appointed project leader. In her personal life, she loved renovating and so the challenge was within her scope of interest. The CEO left them to get on with the task and to report their progress to the next monthly Executive Group meeting.

Debra called a team meeting the next day and asked the members to bring any documents, or links to documents, they knew of that related to the history of the refurbishment. Enthused, she and a staff trainer went to a floor of the building that was little used, containing just some old equipment stored there with piles of promotional materials and HR records. Together they dreamed up a state-of-the-art learning and development complex and meeting room. Realising that money was an issue they even considered how they might rent the space to other organisations; the suburb in which Convoy was located had few conference or meeting facilities and organisations typically resorted to pubs and hotels for meeting space.

Over the next few weeks the Refurb Team gathered documents, existing plans, cost estimates and a variety of opinions from staff regarding the project. Debra sorted through the various plans and tallied up a cost estimate; a full refurbishment of the ground floor alone came to $1.3 million! This included removing all the asbestos in the foyer while maintaining the heritage listed aspects of the building. It also included relocating a temporary cafe into a courtyard that could be enclosed. Debra and Kim discussed the costs and decided they should not even present the plan to the Executive Group, as it would certainly be rejected. Debra informally ran the ideas past the George, the GM sponsor, and he agreed that it would not happen with that price tag. He wasn't sure how much the company would invest, but it certainly wouldn't be $1.3 million.

The Refurb Team met again. They thrashed out what was possible, what really needed to be done and tried to second-guess what the Executive Group would be prepared to pay. It was a small team and everyone was helpful in their own way:

James, the Senior Maintenance Engineer, could be relied on to give, or find, good advice. He also had significant discretionary power over how he spent a large budget. As much of the proposed work could be classified as maintenance, it could be paid for from the engineering department's cost centre.

Leila, the long-term employee who was also head of the social committee, had insights into the machinations of the organisation that others did not. She was also good at thinking of alternative ways to achieve a desired result. Her reputation was as a somewhat difficult person, who worked to rule. However, she provided a positive and grounding influence on the team.

Kim, the Executive Assistant, was thorough and had an excellent understanding of what the CEO and Executive Group would pass or reject. She had worked in the organisation as the CEO's EA for the past 15 years.

Debra was new to the organisation. She was good at keeping the energy of the group up and she loved both a challenge and refurbishing. She felt that if the budget was going to be inadequate then goodwill, clever ideas and people might get the job done instead.

There was also George, the sponsor. He was a fairly cynical and detail-oriented person, more comfortable dealing with facts than with people and certainly not interested in Charles's new image for the organisation. When Debra told him of the $1.3 million price tag, George breathed a sigh of relief, thinking the project likely to be shelved for yet another financial year – by then it would be given to another GM. This was the end of week three of the project.

Review questions

1 Discuss the potential enablers and barriers for the refurbishment project.

2 What recommendations would you provide to the Refurb Team to advance their project, given the culture of Convoy and the poor economic climate?

3 What advice would you offer Charles Walton, the new CEO, to help him reach his corporate goal?

Part 2

Debra called the team together for a quick meeting at beginning of the fourth week. She outlined the feedback from George regarding the $1.3 million price tag. She stressed that the project could still be done but they had to think differently about the way to achieve it. The team confirmed their enthusiasm but weren't sure of the way forward: they didn't have a budget, they didn't have a supportive sponsor and the project was in addition to their already full-time roles. They agreed to take a couple of options to the next Executive Group meeting the following week to gauge the feelings of the entire Executive Group, not just George.

James had to leave to pick up his children and Leila needed to get back to finish off a bit of work, but Kim and Debra kept chatting about what could be done to refurbish the building without breaking the bank. They took the lift to the foyer and started brainstorming ideas. After a short while they agreed that the foyer could look much more contemporary if a lot of the clutter was removed. They could also have a feature wall painted, the cafe relocated out of immediate sight from people entering the building, install a couple of plasma screens and make the existing ill-matching signage consistent. They then visited the near-vacant floor, proposed as a conference centre and meeting room, and applied the same 'declutter with a lick of paint' philosophy to their thinking.

The next day Debra drew up floor-plan sketches of what the two floors might look like. She ran them by Kim, asked James to confirm the costs, and checked with Leila (who knew the café's history and was co-ordinator of the social committee that ran it) if the idea would work.

Debra and Kim then discussed the merit of asking the CEO for his opinion. As a hierarchical organisation, it was not considered appropriate to ask the CEO unless the request went through the sponsor, George. But feeling that George may not present their ideas favourably, Kim suggested she mention them to the CEO informally. She also planned to ask what he considered to be the most important aspect of the refurbishment. From this 'chat', she discovered that a staff amenities room was the number one priority for Charles.

The team then agreed to formally advance three options at the next Executive Group meeting:

1 Dream Renovation (option 1). Including an architecturally redesigned foyer, newly located cafe in its own covered courtyard that could double as a staff room, with a cost estimate of $1.3 million. This option did not include meeting or conference room facilities.

2 Dream Renovation (option 2). As above but with the cafe located in an existing section of the building. The initial advantage to this plan was the reduced cost. However, it required that a department be relocated, disturbing staff and adding construction costs. The total cost was also likely to be $1.3 million.

3 The 'declutter and tidy-up' option (option 3). Delivering a new look for the foyer, a new staff amenities room, relocation of the cafe to an accessible but

less visually imposing spot, an additional meeting and conference room (that included a plan for conference equipment once the business climate became buoyant). Cost unknown, but guess-timated at below $250 000.

A nervous Debra presented the three options to the Executive. Kim was in the room as the EA, taking the minutes. As a group, they discussed the options. When the third option was presented it was couched in terms of being an inexpensive 'tidy-up'. If expense was an issue, then the third option would create a new look and could be improved as more finances became available. The third option would create one large indoor staff amenities area and, for a small additional cost, a second staff amenities area could be created outside in an unused courtyard.

The General Managers were shocked at the figures and even more surprised to find that the third option had not been costed. They were initially going to send Debra away to work on refining the costs for each of the options: developing options within options; costs within costs. They couldn't say what budget they had, but they thought that anything over $1 million would be too much. They discussed needing more information and more time before they could make a decision.

Then Charles spoke up. He gently chatted about the cost of the first two options being out of the question in the current economic climate. He suggested, therefore, that there was little point in directing the Refurb Team's efforts into further exploring the costs and alternatives for those options. He discussed with his GMs how important it was for him to see the staff have an amenities area. He suggested that he'd really like to see some changes made and that if the team could explore low-cost alternatives within the third option that it would be favourably received. Executive agreed to the Refurb Team presenting costed options within the third option.

Debra and the team then met to discuss the outcomes of the Executive Group's meeting. It was soon realised that Kim's ease of access to the CEO and informal conversations with him had prepared Charles for the third option. That same relationship had also provided the Refurb Team with vital information on the CEO's priorities – which they could then explore by presenting not one, but potentially two staff amenity areas. It also became clear that if this project was going to be achieved, the informal networks might have to be used further.

Debra and Kim drew up more detailed sketches for the staff amenities area, the staff courtyard, a meeting room to accommodate 50 people and a revamped foyer and cafe. They consulted an interior designer, until they realised that she was not good at thinking outside of the box (nor without a large budget). Instead, they engaged a colour consultant from a paint distributer who gave excellent advice and whose entire fee would be refundable if paint was purchased.

James assigned one of his staff to complete the cost estimates. As James also had access to the maintenance budget he could advise the team on what he could cover under general repairs and maintenance. He had an excellent knowledge of the heritage issues for the building and his network of contacts were delighted to

sign off on the ultimate plans for the foyer. James also commissioned a report on the asbestos in the foyer ceiling, the outcome of which allowed any work in foyer to be carried out provided the ceiling space remained undisturbed. This meant that the foyer ceiling could not be painted nor the light fittings changed; but it did mean the rest of the project could go ahead.

Leila continued to come up with clever strategies for resolving problems, not the least of which was relocating the cafe and the cafe staff (who didn't like the initial idea). Leila communicated and consulted with them daily, listened to their ideas and drew up plans. She also convinced them that the area they were moving to would be better ergonomically for them. And eventually, when the weekend for their move arrived (near the end of the project) she and Debra met the staff on-site with the removalists and reconfigured the cafe several times until the cafe manager was happy.

Debra had the advantage of being fairly new to Convoy and therefore could plead ignorance of some of the politics and protocols that existed. One such example involved the HR Manager, who for years had felt he had ownership of the foyer. At one time the HR Department had been located next to the foyer and the HR Manager had agreed to ensure the foyer looked tidy, but he had eventually turned it into a part of his empire. In addition, he used the potential meeting floor as a store room for promotional material and archiving of HR records. Debra was the only one on the team who could deal with these facts at face value. She made comments such as, 'Alan we're going to revamp the foyer. Do you have any suggestions as to what you'd like to see in it?' or, 'The CEO is keen for us to create floor space for meeting rooms and a staff room. I've noticed you've got a bit of material there and some archived documents. We found a spot in the basement that is secure. Perhaps you'd like to check it out first and then we'll happily relocate them for you . . .'

Each team member realised they had easy access to at least one of the GMs and Kim also had access to the CEO. Each member then informally kept 'their' GM informed of the progress of the group. The team spoke enthusiastically about the project as if it were going to happen. They took the GMs, the CEO and other interested staff on the refurbishment journey with them.

At the second Executive Group meeting another three options were tabled. Each was under $250 000. Each provided for an indoor and outdoor staff amenity area, a contemporary looking foyer and a large meeting/conference room. One option included gathering together an existing computer, data projector, tables and chairs to fit out the meeting room (bringing the cost of creating the room to $2000, including the removal of old partitions and carpet cleaning).

Each of the GMs was now onboard and there were no surprises this time. Each GM felt they had influenced the Refurb Team with their comments, and each suggested they had existing projects and funds that could be redirected for the day or a week to cover the refurbishment costs without a clear budget item being expended. Debra and Kim suggested they go shopping in the January sales for

furniture to fit out the staff amenities area. The CEO offered to pay for the furniture from his discretionary fund. Leila revealed the social club had some surplus funds and would pay for the relocation of the cafe provided it was given permission to sell to the general public. The office electrician had a reliable supplier that could sell and install the plasma televisions for near-cost. Overall, the support and assistance the Refurb Team received was outstanding.

Debra kept a record of all costs. In the end, the entire project was completed in five months and for $130 000 – around one-tenth of the original estimate of the foyer alone. The goodwill and informal networks, the sharing of enthusiasm and taking people on the journey with the team were what made it work.

Review questions

1 Critically review the steps that the Refurb Team took to achieve a successful project outcome.

2 Compare the interpersonal interventions taken by the team with respect to the relevant chapter of this book.

3 The approach taken by the Refurb Team seemed counter to the organisation's culture. Why did it work?

CASE STUDY 6

Kenworth Motors*

It began with a telephone call, as did so many of my engagements. The person calling identified himself as Robert Denton, the plant manager of Kenworth Motors' Seattle truck manufacturing operations. Denton said he'd gotten my name from Charles Wright, a client of mine in Seattle. Charlie is the OD manager for a major timber products company. I'd been doing several projects with Charlie's group of internal consultants for the past three years and occasionally served as the OD group's consultant. Denton noted that Charlie and he were members of the same sailing club. He went on to say that when, as someone relatively new to Seattle, he'd asked Charlie if he knew any consultants, Charlie had spoken highly of me. I remember thinking that Charlie probably wouldn't have mentioned me unless he thought I could be useful to Denton. My trust in Charlie's competence and judgment was very high.

Denton went on to explain that he'd been the plant manager for only eight months, that things seemed to be going well, but that he had a gnawing sense that things could be better. I must have murmured something appropriate because Denton invited me to visit him and become acquainted with his operation.

I was both flattered by and interested in Denton's invitation. After all, I thought to myself, it's nice to be wanted, a consulting engagement might come out of it, I always wanted to get behind the gate of the Kenworth plant and Denton sounded like a basically smart guy and nice besides. However, reality intruded into my thoughts, as it often does.

Thoughts on the road

I reminded Denton that I lived across the state in Spokane and added that I had limited time available in the short run. I noted that I had plans to visit Seattle in three weeks and could see him then, otherwise it might not be for a month. Denton sounded almost eager as he agreed to a 10 a.m. appointment on April 11.

The drive westward from Spokane across the state of Washington on Interstate 90 begins with several hours of boring highway. I had purposely put off thinking about my appointment with Robert Denton until I was on the road. As the interstate stretched out over the rolling sagebrush hills and chequered wheat fields, I turned my thoughts to Kenworth Motors and Denton. Uppermost in my mind was that I was about to talk with a man I knew little about, consult with a firm I knew very little about and I had no focused agenda. What should I say and do?

*Source: Craig C. Lundberg, Cornell University.

As the miles went by, I envisioned several alternative scenarios for my upcoming appointment with Robert Denton, the plant manager of the truck manufacturing division of Kenworth Motors Corporation. I saw his office in several possible ways. It could be spartan and centrally located to the production floor. It could be conventionally furnished but of a fair size. It could be large. It might even be opulent. It could be personalised with mementos of career, hobbies or family. It might be far from the production floor, or even in a separate building. The more I tried to envision Denton's office, the more alternatives came to mind. So I focused on Denton, trying to imagine him from the voice cues on the telephone – not old, probably fit, probably clean shaven. Again the futility of trying to imagine came home to me.

What did I think I knew? I didn't know much beyond a handful of facts about his title and his job tenure, the fact that he knew Charlie, believed things were generally going OK at the plant and had some vague notion something wasn't quite right. I also had the distinct impression he had been fairly eager to talk with me – after all, he'd initiated calling me and had quickly settled for an appointment convenient to me.

What did I really want to accomplish when I met with Denton? The more I considered this question, the more I pared down my answers. At minimum, it seemed for me a low-cost situation – a couple of hours of my time, perhaps some impressions of me that would be communicated to Charlie (though I believed Charlie and I had a relationship of mutual respect and trust based on a lot of shared work). On the other hand, there was potentially a lot to gain – perhaps another consulting job, perhaps more visibility and reputation in Seattle, which would be good for my business.

I decided I couldn't plan for our meeting in much detail; about all I could reasonably do was to be true to the posture I found to be useful in situations like this. I had to be myself, be as real as possible. I see myself as a curious, friendly person who basically likes others. I also know I can be bold and thought I might have to be to get the conversation going, to help Denton become clear as to why we were talking together, and to clarify my role.

I also wanted to leave our meeting with a decision to either go forward or not. While I didn't mind investing a little time, my time was valuable. I also felt strongly, as I always do, that I didn't want to work with anyone who I didn't basically like as a person or who didn't seem to genuinely want to do some real work. Seeing the Cascade Mountains on the horizon, I began to feel easier. I'd be myself, whatever happened. Only one question nagged: Could Denton and I connect swiftly enough so there would be time to push for clarity in our possible work relationship?

Making contact

At the Kenworth plant, the uniformed guard at the plant gate checked his clipboard, slipped around my car and copied down my licence plate number.

Returning to my open window, he pointed ahead to a one-storey brick building attached to the multi-storeyed plant and told me I could park in the space in front and then go inside and identify myself to the receptionist.

The floor of the wide hallway inside the double glass doors of the office building was freshly waxed. Framed photographs of trucks and large buildings lined the walls. A middle-aged woman in a suit looked up from her desk and smiled. After I identified myself, she led me down a side corridor to an alcove and informed the secretary there who I was and that I was there to see Mr Denton. She then turned to me, smiled again and wished me a good day. The seated secretary told me Mr Denton was expecting me, but was on the telephone. She gestured toward a bank of chairs and asked me to wait. As I sat down, I observed the corridor traffic, busy but quiet. I settled back to wait.

About 10 minutes later, a man of medium height and build wearing a sports jacket over an open-collared shirt came through the door behind the secretary and walked directly to me. He extended his hand, smiled, introduced himself as Bob Denton and motioned me into his office.

The office was larger than I expected. It was panelled and a large Persian rug was centred on the floor. At one end were a clean desk with side chairs and a table full of papers behind it. At the other side of the office were a couch and two stuffed chairs around a low coffee table. Drapes framed one large window that looked out on the parking lot. Denton asked if I wanted coffee, and I said I did. He went to the door and asked the secretary to bring us both coffee and added we were not to be disturbed. While waiting for the coffee, we sat on the two stuffed chairs and made small talk. He asked about my drive across the state; I asked about the framed sailing prints on the wall and whether he'd been sailing lately. We chatted about the Sonics, the Kingdome and the coming World's Fair in Vancouver. After our coffee arrived, I asked him to tell me about his plant and products.

Denton spoke excitedly for 10 or 12 minutes on a wide range of topics – the daily production rate of 23 trucks, the cost of a truck, the sales order backlog, some equipment updating just finished, his coming to this job from a plant in the Midwest, his spending a lot of time lately with the next year's budget, and so forth. My impression of Denton was that he was highly involved in his work. He spoke rapidly but clearly with enthusiasm. Finally, he leaned back, smiled, and said, 'Well, I've been going on, haven't I?' I remember thinking I liked Denton's ease and his willingness to talk about his plant and himself. I'd already learned a lot about the plant and his job without more than looking interested. Denton certainly did seem likable, and he was younger and more casual than I expected.

Getting down to business

I clearly recall my response to Denton's question. 'Actually, I've appreciated your sharing all this background with me. I've always been curious about this plant. Years ago, I had a part-time job when I was in college and used to deliver some

industrial supplies in this end of town and always wanted to know what happened in this plant. All I could see from the road were those lines of big shiny trucks. It's nice to know they're built with care. But you asked for this meeting, Bob. Remember you told me that while things were going well here you sensed something wasn't quite right. Can you tell me a little more now?'

'Not really. I know the plant is doing fine. I feel pretty much on top of my job. I like what I'm doing here very much. My department heads – all nine of them – are all good people. All but two have been here quite a while. They're dependable, damn good at what they do, get along fine and basically are good managers', he said.

'I get along good with everyone. I go out in the plant every day and circulate around. Things are moving smoothly. My two newer managers – one runs our purchasing and inventory, the other is in personnel – couldn't be working out better. Yet some things nag at me that I can't put my finger on. I guess it boils down to some crazy notion I have that while we get along fine and work together well, we haven't jelled together as a team quite like I'd hoped.'

I bombarded Denton with questions, trying to find something that didn't hang together or might indicate a problem. No matter what I asked about – from union relations to accounts receivable, from engineering-production relations to turnover figures – Denton's responses were consistently factual and full, and everything seemed to be in remarkably good shape.

I caught myself from going on with more questions. Instead I said, 'Bob, everything I've been asking about tells me you're OK. Maybe things here really are OK. Maybe you've just got some apprehension that things couldn't be that good. After all, you've been here long enough to really know. While there is some chance that you're not well informed, and some things aren't so hot, the odds are against it. About all I can suggest is whether you might want someone like me to independently confirm how things are going.' Denton smiled as if to himself and replied, 'Hmm, maybe, what would you suggest?'

'What's usually done in situations like this, if there is the interest and if there is the money to pay for it, is to engage someone like me to spend a few days interviewing a sample of managers and other key staff people to see what might turn up.'

'From what you've heard so far, do you think that makes sense here?' Denton asked.

'Frankly, I don't know. It might be worth it to you just to learn things really are OK. What usually happens, however, is that I do find out about something that could be improved. After all that's what I'm supposed to be good at, finding problems. One way or another, Bob, the mere fact I was here would have some impact. The word would spread pretty fast that some outsider was snooping around. What impact that might have I can't say. If things really are OK, my presence might mean little. If there are real problems, my being here would probably create some tensions, it could raise expectations that something would be done about them, and it could even cause problems.'

Denton nodded, 'I see what you mean. If you came in, it would cost me some bucks, it would have some risks in how my people reacted; one way or another I'd have to do something.' He paused and then went on. 'Well, to tell the truth, I don't want to upset things if they're OK, but just finding out whether they are or not appeals to me. Isn't there some other way to do this?'

Bob Denton seemed to me to be open to some minimal work by me. He'd responded as I'd hoped to my candour about the risks of some conventional diagnostic snooping. He'd really seemed to pay attention to what I'd said, and I was beginning to like him and was intrigued with the situation. At times like this, my thought processes seem to jump into high gear. After all, a careful response was called for and there were a number of considerations to factor in. The things I recall noting to myself went like this: apparently some minimal motivation on Bob's part; my real lack of information about the Kenworth situation; my own schedule for the coming months – which was pretty full; my intuition that probably nothing major was wrong with Bob and his managers; and that whatever I proposed had to be of modest cost.

Let's have a retreat

I said to Bob: 'Let me sketch out one idea that comes to mind. We could do a modest retreat. You, your department managers, and I could meet away from here for a couple of days, say on a weekend, to jointly explore how things are going. At minimum, I see several probable outcomes from such a meeting: everyone would get somewhat better acquainted with one another; we'd know better if there were serious issues to tackle; we'd have the experience of jointly going through problem identification; and you'd get a sense of whether or not your team was open to working with an outsider like myself.'

I paused and went on: 'Such a meeting would be relatively efficient. It wouldn't take time away from work, and it wouldn't cost an arm and a leg.' Bob nodded, sipped his coffee and looked at me intently. 'OK', he said, 'I can see your points. Just what would we be doing?'

Seeing Bob's interest as well as warming to the idea myself, I went on to outline a retreat. I suggested doing it at a country club or lodge within a few hours' drive of Seattle. This setting was to provide a symbolic break from the customary business environment, and because it would cost everyone weekend time and the company the expense of travel, food and lodging, it would show Bob's seriousness about the event. I then suggested we begin with cocktails and dinner on a Friday evening, work all day Saturday with appropriate breaks, and conclude by noon Sunday. Again, Bob nodded. He then asked, 'But what would we do? What would you charge?'

I did some quick calculations and responded, 'As for my fee, I'd have to bill you for a minimum of three days at my daily rate of $___ per day, and travel expenses – assuming Kenworth would provide food and lodging. As for what we'd actually do, that's more difficult to say exactly. Frankly, while I have several ways to get us started, I'd need to play it by ear. In general, it would be my responsibility to see we talked straight and a lot with one another to surface our concerns both big and small. I'm afraid you'd have to trust me on this.' I said this last couple of sentences with some trepidation, knowing from my experience that most managers would want much more clarity, but I needed to know how Bob was viewing me.

I was surprised at what happened next. Denton quickly agreed to have a retreat weekend as I'd outlined. We also selected a weekend a month-and-a-half away. He would find a site and let me know. In addition, we agreed he would use the phrase 'a communications workshop' when he informed participants. Glancing at my watch as I left Denton's office, I saw it was just 11:30.

Review questions

1 How well did the OD consultant prepare for the meeting with Denton? Would you have done anything differently?

2 In the discussion between the OD consultant and Denton, what was effective and ineffective about the consultant's behaviour?

3 How effective was the contracting process described in the last part of the case? What is the scope and clarity of the agreement?

4 How would you design the upcoming retreat?

CASE STUDY 7

Lincoln Hospital: Third-party intervention*

Soon after the election of a new chief of surgery, the president of Lincoln Hospital faced a crisis. Lincoln, a 400-bed for-profit hospital in the south-western United States, was experiencing severe problems in its operating room (OR). Forty per cent of the OR nurses had quit during the previous eight months. Their replacements were significantly less experienced, especially in the specialty areas. Furthermore, not all could be replaced; when the crisis came to a head, the OR was short seven surgical nurses.

Also, needed equipment often was not available. On several occasions, orthopaedic surgeons had already begun surgery before they realised the necessary prosthesis (for example, an artificial hip, finger joint, or knee joint) was not ready, or was the wrong size, or had not even been ordered. Surgery then had to be delayed while equipment was borrowed from a neighbouring hospital. Other serious problems also plagued the OR. For example, scheduling problems made life extremely difficult for everyone involved. Anaesthesiologists often were unavailable when they were needed, and habitually tardy surgeons delayed everyone scheduled after them. The nursing shortage exacerbated these difficulties by requiring impossibly tight scheduling; even when the doctors were ready to begin, the scheduled nurses might still be occupied in one of the other operating rooms.

The surgeons were at odds among themselves. Over 30 of them were widely regarded as prima donnas who considered their own time more valuable than anyone else's and would even create emergencies in order to get 'prime time' OR slots – for which, as often as not, they were late. Worst of all, however, the doctors and nurses were virtually at war. Specifically, Don, the new chief of surgery, was at war with Mary, the veteran OR director; indeed, he had campaigned on a promise to get her fired.

Lincoln's president was faced with a difficult choice. On the one hand, he needed to satisfy the physicians, who during the tenure of his predecessor had become accustomed to getting their way in personnel matters by threatening to take their patients elsewhere. The market was, as the physicians knew, increasingly competitive, and the hospital was also faced with escalating costs, changes in government regulations, and strict Joint Commission on Accreditation of Hospitals standards. Could the president afford to alienate the surgeons by opposing their newly chosen representative – who had a large practice of his own?

*Source: R. Wayne Boss, University of Colorado; Leslee S. Boss, Organization Research and Development Associates; Mark W. Dundon, Sisters of Providence Hospital.

On the other hand, could he afford to sacrifice Mary? She had been OR director for 13 years, and he was generally satisfied with her. As he later explained:

> Mary is a tough lady, and she can be hard to get along with at times. She also doesn't smile all that much. But she does a lot of things right. She consistently stays within her budget. . . .

Furthermore, whereas Don had long been an outspoken critic of the hospital and was generally distrusted by its administrators, Mary was loyal, a strict constructionist who adhered firmly to hospital policies and procedures:

> She is supportive of me, of the hospital, and of our interests. She doesn't let the doctors get away with much. She has been an almost faultless employee for years, in the sense that she comes to work, gets the job done, never complains, and doesn't make any waves. I really don't understand the reason for the recent problems. I trust her and want to keep her. It would be extremely difficult to replace her.

The last point was a key one; a sister hospital had spent almost three years unsuccessfully trying to recruit an OR director.

After talking with both nurses and doctors, the president decided not to fire Mary. Instead, he told both Mary and Don that they must resolve their differences. They were to begin meeting right away and keep on meeting, however long it took, until they got the OR straightened out.

The results were predictable. Neither party wanted to meet with the other. Mary thought the whole exercise was pointless, and Don saw it as a power struggle that he could not afford to lose. The president, who wanted an observer present, chose Terry, the new executive vice president and chief operating officer. Mary didn't know Terry very well so she asked that her boss, the vice president of patient services, sit in. Don, who 'didn't trust either Mary or her boss as far as he could throw them', countered with a request for a second of his own, the vice president for medical services. When the meeting finally occurred, it quickly degenerated into a free-for-all, as Don and Mary exchanged accusations, hotly defended themselves, and interpreted any interventions by the three 'observers' as 'taking sides'.

Diagnosis

At this point, Lincoln's president called me. We negotiated a psychological contract, where the president shared the above historical information, described the problem as he saw it, and identified his expectations of me and for the project. I, in turn, articulated my expectations of the president. We then agreed to take no steps until I had interviewed both Don and Mary.

Later that afternoon, Don expressed his anger and frustration with the hospital administration and, most of all, with Mary:

> I don't want to have anything to do with this lady. She is a lousy manager. Her people can't stand to work with her. We don't have the equipment or the supplies that we need. The turnover in the OR is outrageous. The best nurses have quit, and their replacements don't know enough to come in out of the rain.. . . All we want is

to provide quality patient care, and she refuses to let us do that. She doesn't follow through on things.

He particularly resented Mary's lack of deference.

> Mary's behaviour is so disgraceful it is almost laughable. She shows no respect whatsoever for the physicians.. . . She thinks she can tell us what to do and order us around; and I am not going to put up with it any longer. When I agreed to take this job as chief of surgery, I promised my colleagues that I would clean up the mess that has plagued the OR for years. I have a mandate from them to do whatever is necessary to accomplish that. The docs are sick and tired of being abused, and I am going to deal with this lady head on. If we got rid of her, 95 per cent of our problems would go away. She has just gone too far this time.

In his cooler moments, Don admitted that Mary was only partly to blame for the OR's problems, but he still insisted she must be fired, if only to prove to the doctors that the hospital administration was concerned about those problems, and that something was being done.

Observation: I am always a bit suspicious about the objectivity of someone who has reached the conclusion that someone must be fired. There is almost always something else that is going on that requires more investigation.

Mary was both angry and bewildered. She saw herself as fair and consistent in dealing with doctors and nurses:

> Things had gone relatively well until six months ago. At that time, some of the orthopods started scheduling surgeries and then cancelling them at the last minute, which, in turn, fouled up the schedule for the rest of the doctors. When I called them on it, Don went on a rampage. He is the leader of the pack, and now he has blood in his eyes. I have tried to talk with him about it, but he won't listen.

And just as Don's assessment echoed, in an exaggerated form, the doctors' perception of Mary as an exceptionally strong-willed woman, Mary's assessment of Don echoed his reputation among the orthopaedic nurses and hospital administrators, who feared and distrusted his quick temper and sharp tongue:

> Not only that, but I find his filthy mouth very offensive. I am not going to cooperate with him when he behaves like that. Nobody else talks to me that way and gets away with it. Nobody, I won't put up with it. As long as he behaves that way, it is a waste of time to meet with him. I am sure that I am doing things that bother him, and I want the OR to run as smoothly as possible. But there is no way we can deal with these problems unless we can sit down and talk about them without being abusive.

Clearly, both Mary and Don had strong needs to control other people's behaviour, while remaining free of control themselves. It is significant that each used the word *abuse* to describe the other's behaviour. They did respect each other's technical abilities, but morally, Mary saw Don as 'an egotistical jerk', and he saw her as a 'rigid, petty tyrant'. Neither trusted the other, thus, each was inclined to misconstrue even unintentionally negative comments – an especially disastrous state of affairs in the gossipy environment at Lincoln, where surgeons, nurses, and administrators were quick to relay, and amplify, the signals of hostility.

It was obvious from these initial interviews that Don and Mary were largely contributing to the OR problems; but it was also obvious that many others had a stake in the outcome of their battle. I therefore went on to interview the surgical head nurses, the vice presidents for patient services and medical services, the executive vice president, the president, and 25 physicians.

The vice presidents and the surgical head nurses agreed with the president: Mary might not be the hospital's most personable manager, but she was a good one. Her conservative, tenacious, no-nonsense style had earned the trust of administrators and the respect of OR nurses, as well as some physicians. As one nurse asserted: 'Good OR managers are hard to find and certainly Lincoln is far better off with Mary than without her'.

The doctors, in general, supported Don, though some of them had reservations. At one extreme, an anaesthesiologist began with a classic disclaimer:

> Now, I want you to know that I don't have any problems with Mary, personally. In fact, I really like her. We have been friends for years, and we get along just great.

Nevertheless, he was convinced the OR problems were '100 per cent Mary's fault. I have no doubt about that'. Furthermore, although he claimed to be, as an anaesthesiologist, 'a completely neutral third party in this whole business', he clearly shared Don's assumption that Mary's job as an OR manager was to keep the surgeons happy:

> Her people hate her. She is a lousy manager. She just can't work with the MDs. Surgeons are a rare breed, and there is no changing them. You have got to get someone in there who can work with them and give them what they want.

His conclusion echoed Don's: 'She ought to be fired, if for no other reason than to prove that something is being done to address the problems in the OR'.

Observation: I am always leery of someone who says, 'It is all her fault'. When someone is blamed for 100 per cent of the problem, it usually evidences either denial or a cover-up. There may be a completely innocent party in an emotionally charged conflict, but I have never met one. Emotionally charged conflicts are always power struggles, and it takes two parties to play that game.

A less enthusiastic partisan, a surgeon who was a 10-year veteran of the Lincoln OR, was very conscious of the way expectations such as those expressed by Don and the anaesthesiologist were apt to be viewed by others in the medical community:

> Quite frankly, I am embarrassed to admit that I am a surgeon in this town; by doing so, I am automatically branded as an egotistical dimwit. With only a few exceptions, those guys are a group of conceited, narcissistic technicians who are so caught up with themselves that they have no clue about what is going on around them. Some of them are bullies, and they push the rest of us around because we don't have the patient census they do.

His assessment of blame was correspondingly more moderate than the anaesthesiologist's: 'A lot of people would like you to think that this problem is one sided, and that Mary is totally responsible for this mess. But that isn't true'. And while

he supported Don, whom he described as reasonable and willing to listen to logic, his principal wish was to avoid personal involvement: 'I am glad he is fighting this battle. I won't. The thought of getting caught between him and Mary scares me to death'.

This last wish was vividly elaborated by another surgeon, who also highlighted the general perception of Mary as a strong personality:

> I don't mess with Mary at all. I'm not stupid. It's true that I don't like some of the things that she does. Sometimes she is just plain ornery. But I also am not willing to take her on. In fact, at this point, I will do whatever she wants, whenever she wants it. If the other docs are smart, they won't mess with her either. They can talk big in their meetings, but if they have any sense, they won't mess with that lady. She controls too many of the resources I need to do my job. So far she has been very helpful, and she has gone out of her way to do me some favours. I don't want to mess that up. I think it is great that Don is willing to take her on, and I wish him success. That way, if she wins, it will be him that gets beat up, not me.

The high turnover among OR nurses was a particularly sore point among the surgeons in general, whose frustration was explained by Don:

> I don't think the administration has a clue as to how urgent this matter really is. It takes at least five years for a surgical nurse to gain the necessary skills to be useful. In the last two months, we have lost some of the best nurses I have ever worked with in my life. As a result, I had to start the training process all over again. It has seemed like I've been working with a group of student nurses! This turnover has cut my productivity by more than 50 per cent.

Most of the doctors blamed the high turnover on the nursing managers' inability to retain qualified personnel, whereas the managers blamed it on the doctors' verbal abuse. And in fact, a significant number of doctors were widely regarded by some of their peers as well as by the nurses as impatient, intolerant perfectionists who demanded far more of others than they did of themselves.

From the extended interviews, it was obvious that while Mary had greater credibility with the hospital administration and Don had more backing from the doctors, each had a certain amount of power over the other's constituency: Mary controlled the surgeons' working conditions, while Don controlled a significant portion of the hospital's patient flow. The OR problems could not be resolved without genuine cooperation from both of them – especially from Don, who was outside the formal hierarchy of the hospital and could not be coerced by the president.

I met again privately with each of them to determine whether they were honestly committed to improving their working relationship. Both were sceptical about the possibility of real change but said they were willing to do everything they could to help, as long as their own basic values were not violated. Each defined the kind of help he or she was willing to accept from me and the circumstances under which that help was to be given.

Intervention

Only at this point did actual third-party facilitation intervention begin. I used a design that included perception sharing, problem identification, contracting, and follow-up meetings. At their first formal meeting together with me and the three vice presidents who acted as observers, Mary and Don began by writing answers to three questions:

1 What does he or she do well?
2 What do I think I do that bugs him or her?
3 What does he or she do that bugs me?

The very process of writing things down was helpful. It gave them time to get used to this explicitly confrontational situation before either of them had a chance to 'pop off' at the other, and it forced an element of rationality into an emotionally charged situation. Also, the questions required specific answers concerning behaviours, not subjective generalisations about personalities. Listing specific behaviours made each of them realise that at least some of the things they disliked about the other could be changed.

They then explained these responses orally, in the order shown in Figure C7.1 Because of their mutual hostility, I thought it safer to require that at first they address their remarks only to the third party, not to each other. Each, however, was required to hear the other's presentation so each would understand the other's perceptions. And because both were guaranteed an uninterrupted speech, each was more likely to listen to the other. Taking up the positive perceptions first helped. As Don later explained:

> I was stunned to hear her say those positive things, particularly the part about me taking care of her family. For a long time, I had seen her as my enemy, and I expected only the worst. I was amazed that she had so much respect for me. As a result, many of my negative feelings for her began to leave. It is really tough to stay angry at someone who says so many nice things about you. I also found that I was much more willing to listen to what I do that bugs her. Somehow, criticism is always easier to take when it is accompanied by something positive.

It also helped that before making any accusations against each other, they were required to examine their own behaviour. As Mary acknowledged, neither had ever taken the time to figure out specifically how he or she might be causing problems for the other:

> It had never really occurred to me that I may be doing something that caused Don to react that way. Vaguely, I suspected that I may be doing something that he didn't like, but I was hard pressed to identify what it was. I really had to stand back and say to myself, 'What is it that I am doing that is making this working relationship go sour?' I had spent so much time concentrating on what he was doing that bugged me that I hadn't looked at myself.

The oral discussion of this question made it obvious that neither was intentionally causing problems for the other, making both parties less hypersensitive to imaginary insults. Also, because both were much harder on themselves than they were on each other, the milder criticisms they did subsequently direct at each other were not nearly as offensive as they would otherwise have been.

FIGURE C7.1 Participant Responses to Three Questions in the Third-Party Facilitation Model

1 What does Mary admire about Don and think he does well?
- He is very concerned about patient care.
- I admire him for his skills as a surgeon. I would have no problem sending a member of my family to him.
- He is interested and wants to work out issues that we have with each other.
- He can be very gentle and considerate at times.
- He is well respected for his skills by his peers and by the OR nursing staff.

2 What does Don admire about Mary and think that she does well?
- She is honest in her work.
- She has met my needs in orthopaedics in getting us the instruments and equipment we need.
- She has a lot of external pressures on her and she has handled them well.
- She deals well with the various groups that are pulling at her: patients, staff, administration, physicians.
- She manages the overall picture very well in the OR.

3 What does Don think he does that bugs Mary?
- I am impatient. (Mary agrees)
- I am demanding of personnel in surgery, but everyone can't always get what they want, when they want it. (Mary disagrees)
- She is uncertain as to how much I am willing to support her this coming year. (Mary agrees)
- I am not the best listener. (Mary agrees)

4 What does Mary think she does that bugs Don?
- I don't listen to him. (Don agrees)
- I appear defensive at times. (Don agrees)
- I respond to some directives in a very detailed manner. (Don agrees)

5 What does Mary do that bugs Don?
- She is difficult to communicate with. I can talk to her, but I am not sure that she is listening.
- She doesn't assume the responsibility for some specific problems, such as not being able to do an operation without a full set of prostheses available.
- She doesn't effectively manage the personnel that she supervises in OR. Specifically, there is a great deal of disruption going on. And there are also morale problems, particularly as they relate to their trust of her and her trust of them in the OR.

6 What does Don do that bugs Mary?
- He generalises and is not very specific with examples, even when questioned.
- The staff labels him as a whiner, in terms of 'nothing is ever right', his complaining, etc. This also relates to laying out problems and then walking away.
- He sometimes says one thing but means another – and gives mixed messages. An explanation of this is my asking him how things are going, he says fine, but then I find out that he has problems later in the day.
- I do not feel a full measure of support from him, and that bugs me.
- He doesn't always listen to my concerns.

The next step was to identify specific problems for Mary and Don to address. They wrote their responses to question three on a sheet of newsprint, assigning vectors to represent the relative seriousness of the problem. Some of the most serious problems could be resolved immediately; others were going to take longer, but at least Don and Mary now knew what their priorities had to be.

Finally, it became possible for them to agree on specific behavioural changes that might help. Don and Mary each defined what they wanted from the other and negotiated what they themselves were willing to undertake; I moderated the meeting and wrote down the decisions. (At the end of the meeting, Don, Mary, and the three observers each received a copy of these commitments.) Because Mary and Don were interdependent, either could easily have sabotaged the other's efforts. Therefore, in defining each action item, I reminded them to specify responsibilities for both parties:

- What will Don (Mary) do to resolve this problem?
- What will Mary (Don) do to help the other succeed?

This technique made both parties jointly responsible for resolving each problem and thus changed the whole dynamic of the relationship – from mutual isolation to collaboration, from denial of responsibility to acceptance of responsibility, and from a focus on problems to a focus on solutions.

During the next year, I had four more meetings with Don, Mary, and the three vice presidents. Before each meeting, I interviewed each participant privately. At the beginning of each meeting, the participants gave general reports on what was going on, between Mary and Don and in the OR in general. In particular, I asked the two to list positive events and specific behaviours on each other's part that they appreciated. They then reviewed the commitments they had made during the previous meeting. In almost every case, both Mary and Don had kept these commitments, thus building a basis of trust for further commitments during the latter part of the meeting. Where they had not kept the commitments, plans were made to ensure follow-through before the next meeting.

Review questions

1 If you had been called by Lincoln's president to help resolve the problems described in the case, how would you have carried out the contracting and diagnosis stages? What would you have done differently from what the OD consultant did?

2 Is third-party intervention an appropriate intervention in this case? Other possible OD interventions?

3 How effective was the third-party intervention? Next steps?

CASE STUDY 8

Ben & Jerry's (A): Team development intervention*

'Two real guys', Ben Cohen and Jerry Greenfield, head Ben & Jerry's Homemade Inc., an independent ice cream producer that has gained market share and public approbation against industry competitors Häagen-Dazs (made by Pillsbury), Frusen Glädjé (made by Kraft) and Steve's. The story of the founders has a romantic, antiestablishment quality to it that reads like a new-age entrepreneur's dream.

The 'boys', childhood friends, each dropped out of college in the late '60s, worked at odd jobs for a time and together opened a small ice cream scoop shop in Burlington, Vermont, in 1978 with scant know-how (they learned ice-cream making through a $5 correspondence course) and less capital (they started with $12 000 – a third of it borrowed). But they had something else going for them: a combination of old fashioned values and newfangled ideas.

Neither Ben nor Jerry had any intention of becoming businessmen. From the start, however, both were committed to making the best ice cream possible and to having fun while doing it. More than this, these 'self-styled Vermont hippies', as the press calls them, were committed to the simple notion that business draws from the community and is obliged to give something back to it. In the early days, this meant giving away ice cream to loyal customers and worthy charities. As the company grew to sales of near $50 million, B&J's embraced what it calls a social mission to improve the quality of life – not only of employees, but also locally, nationally and internationally – and to do so in an innovative and upbeat way.

The economics of B&J's show fast-track growth over the past several years characteristic of very successful start-up companies (see Figure C8.1 from the 1988 annual report). Sales doubled annually from 1984 to 1986 and increased nearly 50 per cent from 1987 to 1988. The company is today the super-premium market leader in Boston and New York City and distributes its products in grocery stores and mom-and-pop convenience outlets in Florida, the West Coast and parts of the Midwest. Some 80 franchises operate scoop shops in these markets, and the company's 'pints' manufacturing facility and headquarters in Burlington have become Vermont's second-largest tourist attraction with over 600,000 visitors annually.

In addition to expanding this facility, B&J's recently built a novelty plant in Springfield, Vermont, to manufacture ice-cream brownie bars and stick pops and

*Source: Philip H. Mirvis, Boston University.

FIGURE C8.1 Annual Report 1988: A report to shareholders, customers, community members, suppliers and employees

Five Year Financial Highlights (in thousands except per share data)
Summary of Operations:

	Year Ended December 31				
	1988	1987	1986	1985	1984
Net sales	$47 561	$31 838	$19 954	$9 858	$4 115
Cost of sales	33 935	22 673	14 144	7 321	2 949
Gross profit	13 627	9 165	5 810	2 537	1 166
Selling, delivery and administrative expenses	10 655	6 774	4 101	1 812	822
Operating income	2 972	2 391	1 709	725	344
Other income (expense) – net	(274)	305	208	(31)	(13)
Income before income taxes	2 698	2 696	1 917	694	331
Income taxes	1 079	1 251	901	143	118
Net income	1 618	1 445	1 016	551	213
Net income per common share[1]	$0.63	$0.56	$0.40	$0.28	$0.12
Average common shares outstanding[1]	2579	2572	2565	1991	1724

Balance Sheet Data:

	1988	1987	1986	1985	1984
Working capital	$5 614	$3 902	$3 678	$4 955	$676
Total assets	26 307	20 160	12 805	11 076	3 894
Long-term debt	9 670	8 330	2 442	2 582	2 102
Stockholders' equity[2]	11 245	9 231	7 758	6 683	1 068

[1]The per share amounts and average shares outstanding have been adjusted for the effects of all stock splits, including stock splits in the form of stock dividends.
[2]No cash dividends have been declared or paid by the company on its capital stock since the company's organisation and none are presently contemplated.

leased space to house its marketing, franchising, promotion and art departments. Today, over 350 people work at B&J's. Production runs around the clock, staffed by a few dairy experts and many more offbeat people who gravitated to the company because of competitive wages, its funky image and its social mission. Among the production staff is a team of handicapped employees who have distinct and important responsibilities.

The product side of B&J's blends what *Time* magazine calls 'incredibly delicious' ice cream. The story goes that Ben has deficient taste buds, so products have to be particularly pungent to stir his palate. This means 'double-fudge' and 'big-chunk' add-ins to the ice cream. Funky flavours, like 'Cherry Garcia', an assortment of T-shirts, Vermont 'cow' paraphernalia and wacky promotions all make word-of-mouth marketing the key to B&J's commercial success. And, yes, the founders insist on having fun. At annual meetings, Jerry, trained in carnival tricks, uses a sledgehammer to break a cement block over the stomach of the mystical 'Habeeni Ben Coheeni'.

It is, however, the social mission of B&J's that most distinguishes it from corporate America. The good works of the company are many and range from regular donations to community and social action groups to a commitment to buy only Vermont-based cream from area dairy cooperatives. B&J's embraces socially responsible marketing and has proposed to 'adopt a stop' in the New York subway system (which the company would clean and maintain in lieu of advertising) and begun an innovative joint venture with the Knowledge Society in the Soviet Union.

Recently, the company introduced 'Peace Pops' as part of the '1% for Peace Campaign'. This effort is aimed at encouraging other businesses to join a movement urging the government to devote one per cent of the defence budget explicitly to peaceful purposes. A new product featuring Brazilian nuts obtained at above-fair-market price from native Brazilians is further evidence of the founders' social commitments.

Innovating Inside of B&J's

Ben and Jerry have been at the edge of innovation since the company went public. Rather than seeking venture capital to expand the business, they drew up a stock prospectus on their own and sold shares to Vermonters door to door. One in every 100 Vermont families bought in to the tune of $750 000. When Häagen-Dazs tried to pressure shopkeepers to keep 'Vermont's finest' off their shelves, Ben and Jerry started a grass-roots campaign against Pillsbury replete with bumper stickers (What's the Doughboy afraid of?) and a one-person picket line (Jerry) at the Pillsbury headquarters.

Ben and Jerry have tried to introduce this same funky and socially responsible orientation inside the company. The company's mission and many of its policies and practices (see Figure C8.2) reflect the upbeat and caring values of the founders. A policy of 'linked prosperity' ensures that 7.5 per cent of pre-tax profits go to good works and five per cent is returned to employees via profit sharing. The salary ratio between the top paid and least paid in B&J's is set at five to one. This means, if managers want to earn more, they have to increase the base wage throughout the company.

Employees come in all shapes and sizes. Most are young (under 30) and many have responsibilities well beyond their experience. It is a matter of pride to all that B&Jer's can speak, act and dress 'like themselves'. Still, the work is demanding and the pace frenetic. The production room is often awash in cream, and the freezer

FIGURE C8.2 Ben & Jerry's Mission and Operating Principles

Ben & Jerry's, a Vermont-based ice-cream producer, is dedicated to the creation and demonstration of a new corporate concept of linked prosperity. The company has three central missions and several key operating principles.

Three Missions

Product Mission: To make, distribute and sell the finest quality all natural ice cream and related products in a wide variety of innovative flavours made from Vermont dairy products.

Economic Mission: To operate the company on a sound financial basis of profitable growth, increasing value for our shareholders and creating career opportunities and financial rewards for our employees.

Social Mission: To recognise the central role that business plays in the structure of society by seeking innovative ways to improve the quality of life for a broad community – local, national and international.

Operating Principles

Linked Prosperity: 'As the company prospers, the community and our people prosper'. 7.5% of pretax profits go to the Ben & Jerry's Foundation for distribution to community groups and charities. Five per cent of profits are put into a profit-sharing plan. Five to one salary ratio between top management and entry-level production workers. To raise top pay, raise the bottom up.

Community Development: 'Business has the responsibility to give back to the community'. Donations of ice cream by request to all Vermont non-profit organisations. Leveraged assistance where B&J will help non-profits stage fund-raisers selling Vermont's finest ice cream.

Ownership Perspective: 'Everybody is an owner'. Employee stock ownership, stock grants and stock purchase plan. All-company 'town meetings' monthly.

Integrity: 'Two real guys'. All natural products. Commitment to Vermont Dairy Cooperatives. 'What you see is what you get'. People can speak, act and dress as they wish.

Work Hard/Have Fun: 'Bend over backwards'. Pledge to meet orders, satisfy customers, make things right for people. 'If it's not fun, why do it?' Company celebrations. Jerry's Joy Committee to spread joy in the workplace.

Human Activism/Social Change: 'A model for other businesses'. One per cent for Peace Campaign. Socially responsible marketing. Joint ventures in Israel and Moscow to spread goodwill.

crew works in chilling conditions. There is nothing akin to market research in the company, demand is fluid and unpredictable and when I first arrived on the scene, the franchising and sales managers weren't communicating with each other and neither paid attention to the marketing director.

In 1987, it became evident to Ben and Jerry, as well as to managers and employees, that the company's external image – of funk, fun and love – was out of sync with the atmosphere inside the company. The company was always short on ice cream and long on hours, pressure and problems. The author was commissioned to work with the founders and board of directors and with the management and work force of the company to undertake organisational development and bring people, functions, aspirations and directions together.

Entry

Henry Morgan, former dean of the School of Management at Boston University and board member at B&J's, contacted me about this project. Henry comes from a long line of New England activists deeply committed to the improvement of the human condition. His family lineage traces to Hawaii where ancestors were missionaries, and Henry has had a career as an entrepreneur, management innovator and social investor. In addition to his membership on B&J's board, he is active on other boards and is a leader in the Council of Economic Priorities' efforts to promote corporate social responsibility.

Entry through Henry, however, posed some risks. For example, like Henry, I was an outsider coming into B&J's where the emphasis, to this point, had been on 'home-grown' innovation. Ben, Jerry and Jeff Furman, an attorney and long-time B&J's counsel, had crafted the company's innovative employment and investment policies. It was unclear to me what these three really wanted from an OD program. Was I being brought in to get management 'aligned' behind the founders' guiding precepts as a phone conversation with Ben intimated? Or were the precepts themselves open to question and modification via management and employee input? If so, did it require an outsider to stimulate this re-examination? Or was I being set up?

To complicate matters, there was a division in the board of directors. Ben, Jerry and Jeff were rather more 'far out' in their aspirations for the company, particularly in comparison to the more conservative general manager, Fred 'Chico' Lager. The former anticipated an outpouring of good vibes once 'people power' was unleashed. Chico had more everyday concerns: feuding between management, unclear lines of authority and responsibility, a lack of operational control. More specifically, as an example, a freezer door was broken and neither the freezer, nor maintenance, nor production managers claimed ownership of the problem or took responsibility to see that it was fixed. That, to him, was symptomatic of an undeveloped organisation.

Finally, there was the matter of defining OD. Neither Ben nor Jerry nor the board had any inkling about what OD is and what OD people do. I had to educate them about the field and make some kind of action proposal. This would mean getting to know people, getting a handle on their hopes and their problems and learning something about the ice cream business and conditions in the marketplace. Where to start? I went to a board meeting to check out members' hopes for organisation development and what they wanted from me.

First Board Meeting

Ben:

I want our people to love their work and have positive feelings about the company. Love, soul, kindness, consideration, generosity, fairness, heart.

Jerry:

I want a feeling of togetherness and family feeling ...I'd like staff to feel it was their company.

Jeff:

I'd like to see spirit and energy to make a difference in the world … plant seeds of new and different possibilities of looking at our culture and world. Not corporate America.

Chico:

Something special and unique that is making new ground, that will be studied and appreciated in years to come.

Henry:

More open communication, listening at the top. More buy-in to shared values. Showing respect for the individual.

Merritt:

Awakened enthusiasm, accomplishment, high morale.

At this first meeting, I asked board members to state their vision of the ideal organisation and hopes for the OD effort. Ben and Jerry talked of peace, love, family feeling and good vibes. Jeff was on a different wavelength: He articulated a political vision where B&J would be an exemplar of a radical new kind of organisation. Chico spoke about innovativeness and excellence, without the radical chic or global emphasis. Henry's hopes were addressed to better human relations and human resource management. Merritt, another businessman cum board member, expressed similar sentiments.

I had the board members write their visions on sheets of paper, and then together we burned them to symbolise how energy and togetherness could transform things. Some chanting added to the ritual. It must have seemed a bit hokey to the board, but I have my own preferences and style of doing things and wanted to illustrate my own offbeat inclinations. In any case, Ben had offered me a wizard's hat to signify his vision of my role. The fire trick fitted the costuming.

That night, however, I had some misgivings. It was clear that, when pressed, neither Ben, nor Jerry, nor any board member save Chico would provide the day-to-day leadership needed to move development through the organisation. On the contrary, the founders wanted to hand off the responsibility to Chico and his to-be-formed management team. My job was to help bring that team into being and to ensure that the team took leadership of B&J's business and social missions. It was also to help bring the work force together in as-yet-undefined ways.

Should I start my work at the top? I had an inkling that the board was not aligned behind any one definition of Ben & Jerry's. However, the board was not, at this time, asking for assistance with its work nor could the members openly talk about problems within the group. The problems, in board members' eyes, rested within the organisation. That made Chico and his team the natural focus of intervention. Chico, at this time, had 20 managers reporting to him, with responsibilities ranging from running the manufacturing plant to handling orders for T-shirts and other B&J paraphernalia.

Still, I worried whether OD would directly reach the work force. If I worked from the top down, it might take months (years) to have a direct bearing on people's work lives. The production workers were full of ideas, I was told, and eager to become more involved. Maybe some form of quality-of-work-life program was in order wherein employees could take active responsibility for problem solving in their own areas of responsibility. My question: Were managers and supervisors ready for this?

The next step was to do some fact-finding in the company. I arranged with Chico to conduct interviews with all of his 20 managers, tour the plant, talk with production workers and sales personnel, and generally sniff around. That would lead to a diagnosis of the organisation and an action proposal.

Diagnosis

Three months of interviews with key managers and staff at B&J's showed the following areas of strength and concern in the company:

Strengths:

High commitment to the company and its mission.
Norms of honesty and straightforwardness.
Smart and articulate management.
High interest in growth and learning.
Founders and general manager as role models.

The interviews affirmed the positive public side of B&J's: Managers and employees were wholly dedicated to the company. Many of the managers had left successful jobs in other companies to come to B&J's because of its funky atmosphere, freewheeling style, and socially responsible orientation. Some had taken salary cuts to come aboard. The managers were smart and each had his or her own view of how the company should develop. These views, taken together, pointed to a more participatory style of management with people charged with higher levels of responsibility. This would require more training, of managers and supervisors, in both technical and managerial areas. They would also need to get organised – with more clarity about who was doing what and why.

The interest was there. Everybody I spoke with was eager to learn more and get better at their jobs. The commitment was also there. Many professed deep feelings of connection to Ben and Jerry and were inspired by the chance to take 'their company' and run it. They also looked to Chico to teach them the ins and outs and looked forward to working closely with him as part of the 'management team'.

Concerns:

People and systems not keeping pace with growth.
Lack of clear structure, roles and teamwork.
Lack of common mission, direction, priorities.
People are stretched to the limit.
Founders and general manager are both company's greatest strength and greatest weakness.

The roster of concerns shows that Ben & Jerry's was under-organised for handling the challenges posed by rapid growth in the market place and work force.

Interviewees talked about the absence of clear goals and agreed-to priorities, problems of communication and coordination, tasks half-finished and new initiatives begun, then dropped. No one had the time to get on top of things or ensure follow-through.

Furthermore, the interviewees depicted the founders and general manager as both the company's greatest strength and its greatest weakness. To this point, Ben and Chico had access to the most relevant information and called most of the shots. But conflicts between the two were legend. Ben would push for better quality, faster flavour development, funkier ads and promotions, while Chico would urge pragmatism, shuffle priorities, mediate tensions and hawk expenses.

These two titans seemed to be omniscient: They handled hot problems and made all the right moves. But nobody knew how they worked things out or got things done. It was plain enough, however, that the to-be-formed management would have to set more of the direction, solve more of the problems and develop systems for control and follow-through if participatory management and decentralisation were to be accomplished. Furthermore, they would have to get closer to one another personally and develop more trust and confidence in one another, if family feeling and pride of ownership were to prevail.

Thus I pitched the OD effort at helping the board of directors to clarify the company's mission and to cede operating responsibilities to management. In turn, the board was to empower managers to run the company in a strong, unified and responsible fashion. There were pragmatic issues to address: the managers did not see themselves as a team nor had they worked together to formulate goals and establish roles and responsibilities.

There were also matters of principle on the agenda: many managers had no prior experience leading a company so dedicated to social responsibility. Several, frankly, did not fully buy into socially oriented company policies, including the active association of the company with the 1% for Peace Campaign and the salary ratio of five to one between the highest and lowest paid members of the corporation. A few were chafing at the mandate of the founders to have 'fun' at work while still achieving record rates of production at superior quality standards.

Teambuilding Via a Retreat

The 20 managers and Chico went to an offsite retreat where all were blindfolded and roped together in their three work-related clusters and then charged with locating three inner tubes symbolically lashed together maybe 75 yards away. The members of each cluster shouted out instructions or demanded them, took stabs at leading and then pulled back in frustration, while the other groups stumbled along vainly searching for the 'goal'. One group finally located the tubes, then cheered for their own success and chided the other groups. This experience provided a window into current dynamics in the company and led us to examine teamwork, competition and cooperation during the rest of the retreat.

Thereafter, the managers climbed ropes, worked on problem solving initiatives, and trekked in the out of doors, all in the service of finding new ways to work with one another. One evening they talked about their personal lives and values through the medium of 'mind maps'. Everyone recorded on a silhouette the persons and events that had most shaped their character, how they wanted to be thought of in the company and by their peers, and what mark they wanted their life to leave behind. Several spoke of their scarring experiences in Vietnam, their poignant efforts to cope with family trials, the impact their mothers, fathers and now their spouses and children had on them. Many cried. There were hugs and cheers.

The next evening, the clusters had the opportunity to put on skits about their part of the organisation. The manufacturing cluster drew from a popular game show to show their peers the 'jeopardy' involved in making high-volume, high-quality foodstuffs. The marketing and sales group selected a member to wear the beard of one of the founders and joined him in songs and dance about the foibles of competing with less socially responsible companies and the seeming folly of having fun at work.

The search for the inner tubes was repeated at the end of the retreat. The groups quickly joined forces with the others to analyse the problem, work out a plan, figure out roles and responsibilities, and establish procedures to stay in touch with one another. They reached the goal in one third of the time. The retreat concluded with each attendee selecting a 'totem' to represent his or her experiences and developing a personal action plan to be implemented in the months ahead.

Why Teambuilding?

My reasons for recommending teambuilding to launch the OD effort at B&J's were threefold. First, it was crucial for managers to begin to think of themselves as managers and as members of a management team. Many of the managers at B&J's were truly supervisors, who worked alongside employees and focused only on the work going on in their own area of responsibility. To cope with growth, it was essential for them to begin to plan, set priorities and coordinate efforts with one another. This meant they had to operate like real managers and become a management team.

Second, the managers would be assuming new responsibilities heretofore in the hands of the founders and general manager. I thought it important for them to see how much they had in common and how much affinity they had with the founders' vision of the enterprise. Teambuilding provides a good medium for self-disclosure and helps people to open up about who they are and what they believe in. The mind maps and skits were designed such that people could see how they were all in this together. Needless to say, lashing them together to search for an inner tube was a more literal translation of the message.

Finally, managers had to collectively commit to taking on new responsibilities and learn new methods for working together. The several exercises at the retreat

were aimed at educating them in group management and problem- solving skills. The ropes course, in turn, emphasised the importance of personal courage and peer support in tackling the unknown. The managers left the retreat closer and charged up about running the show.

However, the rationale for beginning OD with teambuilding was rather traditional and conservative in character. Many OD proponents eschew the top-down approach to development and work simultaneously at many levels in a company. Work teams and worker-management committees are starting points for OD in many organisations. The aim is to get as many people as possible, as soon as possible, involved in organisational improvement. The risk with going company-wide with OD from the start is managerial resistance. Frankly, in this case, I didn't think managers were ready to respond to group problem-solving initiatives by their subordinates and teams. They were not conversant with techniques like brainstorming, force field analysis and contingency planning – requisites for team leaders. Nor were they ready, in my judgment, to cede responsibility as they were just assuming more of it. Instead, my proposal was to go slow, get management organised and built into a team and then push OD downward.

Follow Up: Goals and Responsibilities

This began months of teambuilding with the newly created management group (see Figure C8.3). Each working cluster was charged with developing a mission statement for its area of responsibility. The cluster groups met several times to

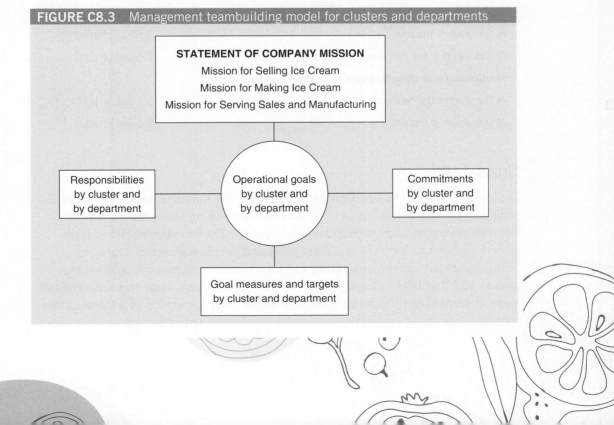

FIGURE C8.3 Management teambuilding model for clusters and departments

STATEMENT OF COMPANY MISSION
Mission for Selling Ice Cream
Mission for Making Ice Cream
Mission for Serving Sales and Manufacturing

Operational goals by cluster and by department

Responsibilities by cluster and by department

Commitments by cluster and by department

Goal measures and targets by cluster and department

translate these into operating goals. The manufacturing group, for example, focused on improving production capacity and quality. Managers from the freezer, production, distribution and maintenance departments then analysed work flow, identified their respective responsibilities, and made commitments to one another to maximise capacity and ensure quality standards. The marketing group, in turn, formed a steering committee to bring franchising and sales together and developed a system to control competing pressures on the art department.

In turn, managers also met with their work groups to gather input and incorporate suggestions. In that way, at least, employees were kept abreast of developments and had a chance to be involved. A safety committee was created, staffed by managers and workers, to address a broad range of concerns throughout the plant and headquarters facility.

Several meetings were held to coordinate cluster goal setting. At one session, managers drew pictures illustrating the degree of alignment between functions and the overall vision of the company. One artist depicted the founders as the sun, the functions as orbiting planets, and the market as a streaking comet. Others used stick figures to show the company coming together, people cheering and craziness all around.

What resulted from these sessions was a series of cluster goal statements, an action agenda for the next year focused on tasks and goals, and closer interpersonal and work relationships. Did teambuilding make a difference? Managers rated themselves as much more of a team and the functions say they are far more aligned:

Understanding of the Goals and Direction of Your Department?	
At the start of the process:	3.5 out of 10.0
At this point in the process:	7.5 out of 10.0
Relationship with Other Members of the Management Team?	
At the start of the process:	5.1 out of 10.0
At this point in the process:	7.5 out of 10.0

Cross-Talk

Despite the progress in organising management, the founders worried whether the funk and fun was being lost in all of this business. There was a heated debate between managers and the founders over growth. The founders hoped to limit growth in order to keep the company small and people connected. Managers pointed out that existing marketing and franchise commitments would require growth and that B&J's simply could not stiff its customers. Back and forth the talk went. It seemed as though the managers had become something of a threat to the founders, who were having trouble letting go of promised authority.

Ben and Jerry then took the initiative to 'lift up' the cluster goals into a unifying statement of the company's economic, product and social mission. To air differences, the newly formed management team and founders then met to examine their differences. Before the meeting, Ben had said publicly that management 'wasn't weird enough' and expressed worry that the company's social mission was being sacrificed to growth. The managers first chafed at his inference that they weren't interested in the social mission. Then they took his concerns to heart. Each member of the management team came to the meeting wearing a mask bearing the likeness of either Ben or Jerry and buttons saying 'We are weird'.

Together, managers and board members talked over issues of trust and relative powers with the founders, fleshed out how management and the board would work together, and made a pact that the company would remain committed to high quality production, good works and fun.

Following the session, several actions were initiated to bring neglected aspects of the mission statement to life. A 'Joy Committee' was established to ensure that spirit was kept alive in the company. It hosted lunches, sponsored social events and launched several happenings throughout the company. Employees were encouraged to take a more active part in the Ben & Jerry's Foundation and contribute directly to charitable giving. Finally, a budget committee was created to formulate B&J's first one-year plan.

Review questions

1 Team building is typically used in OD to loosen up an over-organised system that is too rigid and bureaucratic. In this case, team building was aimed at providing structure to an under-organised system. In doing a diagnosis, what factors are important to consider in determining whether a company or team is over- or under-organised? What are the implications for planning an OD intervention?

2 Is team building a good way to launch an OD effort in this case? Other approaches?

3 What next steps would you recommend?

CASE STUDY 9

Sharpe BMW*

Tom Dunn was the newly appointed service manager for Sharpe BMW, a Grand Rapids, Michigan, BMW dealership. After the previous service manager left, the service department's revenues and the dealership's customer satisfaction index (CSI) ratings fell. In an effort to correct these problems, Bob Deshane, the service director of the dealership, submitted a new plan to owner George Sharpe. The plan called for a change in the way service technicians were compensated. Upon approval by the owner, Deshane handed the plan to Dunn and asked him to implement it.

As Dunn looked at the new plan, he realised that in implementing the plan he was going to initiate a major change in the service department. He wondered what specific steps he could take to ensure that the new plan achieved the results that he and his organisation were hoping for.

The Automotive Dealership Industry

According to the National Automobile Dealers Association (NADA), profits from the sale of new vehicles accounted for 29% of total dealership profits in 1998. Typically, new vehicle sales were a break-even proposition for dealerships. However, in 1998, due to strong new unit sales, good expense control and increased productivity, profitability reached its highest level in ten years. Used vehicle sales contributed 24% of overall profits in 1998. This was a slight improvement since the more than 40% plunge in profits in 1995 and the subsequent slow recovery. NADA attributed the improved used vehicle sales profitability to the increased willingness of financial institutions to lend money at attractive rates for purchase of used vehicles. Total service and parts profits rose 5% in 1998, reaching a record high. Service and parts department profits accounted for 47% of overall dealer profits. NADA forecast a growth in service and parts revenue even as dealers continued to compete with an increased number of independent service outlets and quick-lube centres. To maintain customer satisfaction, franchised dealers invested heavily in the parts and service operations, primarily by adding service bays and carrying a larger inventory of parts. NADA estimated that in 1998, 60% of dealership service departments offered evening and/or weekend hours and were, on an average, open for business 53 hours a week. Figure C9.1 breaks down the components of dealerships' service

*Source: This case was prepared by Professor Ram Subramanian from Grand Valley State University for classroom discussion. It is not intended to illustrate either effective or ineffective handling of a managerial situation. Reprinted by permission from the Case Research Journal. Copyright 2002 by Ram Subramanian and the North American Case Research Association. All rights are reserved.

FIGURE C9.1 Dealerships' Service Sales (in billions of dollars)

	1997	1998	% Change
Service labour sales			
Customer mechanical	$10.54	$11.14	5.7%
Customer body	3.77	3.68	−2.3
Warranty	5.13	5.27	2.6
Sublet	2.73	2.73	0.0
Internal	3.41	3.5	2.6
Other	1.72	1.8	4.7
Total service labour	$27.31	$28.13	3.0%

Source: National Automobile Dealers Association.

revenue, and Figure C9.2 provides a financial profile of the dealership's service and parts operation.

Sharpe BMW

Sharpe BMW was part of the Serra Automotive Group, which was a family of nineteen automobile dealerships in the states of Michigan, Ohio, Georgia, Tennessee, Colorado and California. Sharpe BMW was the only BMW dealership in the group, with the other dealerships selling a wide range of automobiles manufactured primarily by General Motors and Ford.

FIGURE C9.2 Profile of the Dealership's Service and Parts Operation

	Average dealership
Total service and parts sales	$ 2 845 520
Total gross profit as percentage of service and parts sales	44.0%
Total net profit as percentage of service and parts sales	5.7%
Total number of repair orders written	9 847
Total service and parts sales per customer repair order	$ 174
Total service and parts sales per warranty repair order	$ 203
Number of technicians (including body shop)	11.4
Number of service bays (excluding body shop)	16.3
Total parts inventory	$ 221 300
Average customer mechanical labour rate	$ 55

Source: National Automobile Dealers Association.

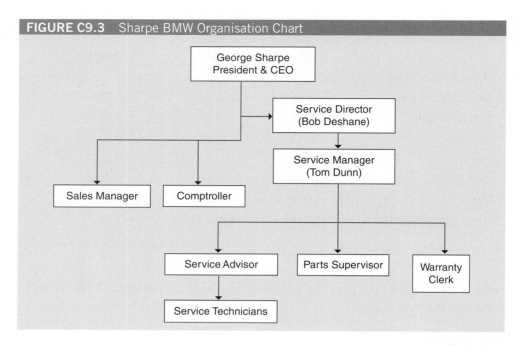

FIGURE C9.3 Sharpe BMW Organisation Chart

George Sharpe
President & CEO

Service Director
(Bob Deshane)

Service Manager
(Tom Dunn)

Sales Manager

Comptroller

Service Advisor

Parts Supervisor

Warranty Clerk

Service Technicians

Source: Sharpe BMW.

Sharpe BMW was the only Grand Rapids BMW dealer (Figure C9.3 contains the dealership's organisation chart). The two closest BMW dealers were in Kalamazoo (located fifty miles southwest of Grand Rapids) and Lansing (about seventy miles east of Grand Rapids). According to Dunn, neither of the two was as big as Sharpe BMW. He had this to say about competing for service jobs in the market area:

> We offer pick-up and drop-off service to those customers who live far away. The service is also extended to whoever purchases a vehicle from us. To some customers, we have a 'virtual' service department. They never see the inside of the service department – their cars are always picked up and brought back to them. This feature is used as a heavy sales tool to lure business from the Kalamazoo and Lansing dealers.

Service departments are an integral part of the revenue stream for auto dealerships. Deshane put the importance of service departments in the proper perspective:

> The average auto dealership service department maintains about an 82 per cent absorption rate. This means that the profit from the service department pays 82 per cent of all of the dealership's overhead. Good service departments are closer to 100 per cent, leaving all dollars from car sales as pure profit. We currently fall between the average and 100 per cent.

Service Department Repairs

Sharpe BMW's service department had grown sizeably in the last three years, primarily by increasing sales of vehicles to local customers and by aggressively seeking business from the Kalamazoo and Lansing areas. When the BMW dealership was first opened, its service department shared facilities with a Buick

dealership that was also part of the Serra group. As BMW service revenues grew, a separate and dedicated service facility was built.

In Sharpe BMW's service department, two types of jobs were performed. The first type, 'customer pay,' occurred when the customer paid for the repair, after the warranty period expired on the car. For customer pay jobs, the customer was charged BMW's hourly labour rate of $69 times the number of hours specified by the *Mitchell Guide to Car Repairs* – a standard guide used by most major car dealerships. The *Guide* listed average time per repair for most types of automotive repair work. For example, the repair time to replace a water pump on a 1993 BMW 740i, according to the *Guide*, was 3.5 hours. The customer, thus, was charged $69 times 3.5 hours, or $241.50. This was the charge to the customer regardless of the actual time to do the repair. At Sharpe BMW, the technician who performed the repair job was paid his hourly wage rate times the *Guide*'s time for the job. For example, a technician making $13 an hour would make 13 times 3.5 hours, or $47.25, for that job.

When the vehicle was still covered by warranty, BMW paid the dealership for the repair work, known as 'warranty pay'. BMW had its own flat-rate book in which average hours for a specific job were often much lower than that listed in the *Mitchell Guide.* For example, the water pump repair was a 2.1-hour job for BMW. Repairing a water pump while the car was covered by warranty generated revenues of $69 times 2.1 hours, or $144.90, for the dealership, and $13 times 2.1 hours, or $27.30, for the technician. Service technicians' compensation, thus, depended upon whether they were working on a customer pay or a warranty pay job. Figure C9.4 provides an illustration of a service technician's pay for the two types of jobs.

FIGURE C9.4	Example of Calculation of Average Weekly Pay for Service Technician

In both examples, it is assumed that the only service job performed by the technician is replacement of a water pump on a 1993 BMW 740i, and that it takes the technician two actual hours to finish the job. In a forty-hour week, the service technician performs twenty such jobs.

Example 1: Customer pay/warranty split: 12/8 jobs

Repair time per the *Mitchell Guide* is 3.5 hours
Repair time per BMW is 2.1 hours

Technician's compensation for 12 customer pay jobs	12 × 3.5 = 42 hours
Technician's compensation for 8 warranty jobs	8 × 2.1 = 16.8 hours
Total compensation	58.8 hours × $13 per hour = $764.40

Example 2: Customer pay/warranty split: 8/12 jobs

Technician's compensation for 8 customer pay jobs	8 × 3.5 = 28 hours
Technician's compensation for 12 warranty jobs	12 × 2.1 = 25.2 hours
Total compensation	53.2 hours × $13 per hour = $691.60

Source: Sharpe BMW and case writer's estimates.

Customer Satisfaction Index

BMW surveyed all its customers, both when they bought cars and when they went to the dealership for warranty repairs. Only scores from customers who went to a dealer for warranty repairs, however, formed the CSI score for the dealership. A total of eight questions on the CSI survey were for service jobs (see Figure C9.5), of which one ('Satisfaction with work performed') related to the technician performing the repair. The others related to the function of the service manager and other dealer personnel who interacted with the customer.

Dunn had this to say about CSI:

> CSI is extremely important to dealers. It governs their flexibility with the manufacturer and is compared regionally and nationally with other dealers. BMW rewards the dealer financially the higher its CSI score is. It can also affect delivery of cars. For example, BMW is to introduce a new sports activity vehicle (SAV). If the dealer's overall CSI (a weighted score with 40 per cent weight for sales CSI and 60 per cent for service CSI) is below the standard, they will not receive any SAVs for the first year of production. In most cases, if your CSI is okay, as a manager you can do no wrong. Revenues are important, but I would rather be called into a meeting where revenues were low than one in which CSI was low. Ninety-one per cent is the industry average CSI score (while our peer group of ten Midwest BMW dealerships had a 92.1 average last year) and about the minimum allowable score that Sharpe will tolerate. Our dealership's score in the last year was below the peer-group and the national average.

Since the previous service manager left, both service department revenues and CSI ratings declined. The average CSI score for the previous year (before Dunn's appointment) was 88 and the scores for the three most recent months were 90.4, 86 and 88. Deshane, the service director, identified the problem in the service department to be the differential rate of compensation paid to technicians for the

---

FIGURE C9.5   Customer Satisfaction Index Questions: Warranty Repair Orders

1 *Ease of obtaining a service appointment.*
2 *Greeted promptly when vehicle dropped off.*
3 *Respectful and courteous treatment.*
4 *Vehicle ready at time promised.*
5 *Waited on promptly at vehicle pick up.*
6 *Paperwork completed/accurate at pick up.*
7 *Explanation of service work performed.*
8 *Satisfaction with work performed.*

The questions are rated on the following scale:

Excellent	100 points
Good	80 points
Fair	60 points
Poor	0 points

Source: Sharpe BMW.

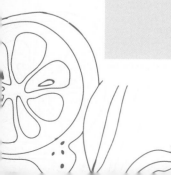

two types of jobs. While customer pay repair work paid the technician more, the dealership's CSI score depended on the quality of the warranty work.

Dunn summed up his feelings about the CSI:

> The dealership can't change the questions on the CSI, nor ask BMW to consider certain questions only for bonus purposes. In short, we have very little control over the index. I don't like some questions, but what I really don't like about the CSI is that if a customer responds 'good' to any question, we get a score of only 80, which would really hurt us. To maintain our ratings, the customer has to rank us 'excellent' (worth 100 points) on the majority of questions. BMW contracts with an independent agency, Sky Allend, to administer the survey over the telephone. All automobile manufacturers have CSI ratings, but we really can't compare them even within the Serra Group because the questions are very different for each manufacturer. We can only compare our performance with other BMW dealers.

Service Technicians' Labour Market

Good technicians were difficult to recruit and retain. According to Dunn:

> Experience and certification determine the qualifications of service technicians. The state of Michigan requires that a technician be state-certified in the area in which he or she does repair work on a vehicle. For example, a technician would need to be state-certified in HVAC to do air-conditioning work or have a certification in brake repair to do brake work. Certification is received via passing written tests administered by the Secretary of State. Some technicians receive additional certification through ASE [Automotive Service Excellence]. These certifications are much more difficult to achieve and carry weight when negotiating hourly wage. Repair shops boast often that ASE-certified technicians perform repairs.

After talking about auto service technicians in general, Dunn spoke about technicians employed by BMW dealers:

> To work at a dealership such as BMW, a technician would go regularly to school for training. Usually one to two times a year, the technician would go, at the dealer's expense, to Chicago for training that would range from two to five days at a time. The complexity of repairs and the specific tools and computer equipment that are needed to repair BMWs highlight the need for proper schooling. The manufacturer requires that dealer technicians attend a certain amount of schooling each year. The cost of educating technicians is expensive for the dealer. Yes, for BMW it would require a lot of training and time until a new hire could perform to the level of the person being replaced. The technician also knows this. Good technicians can quit one job and get another at least equally as good the same day. Unfortunately, this makes discipline and loyalty a problem.

At Sharpe BMW, a service technician's typical weekly workload was 60:40 in favor of customer pay jobs. The dealership paid higher wages than those in aftermarket repair outlets such as Sears and Montgomery Ward's. In addition, Sharpe BMW tried to decrease technician turnover by emphasising factory training, as well as access to BMW's repair hotline, the latest equipment and ongoing training. According to Dunn, all automobile dealerships faced the problem of disparity between customer pay and warranty pay wages for technicians, and to date, neither individual dealerships nor the NADA had attempted a systematic response to this problem. Aftermarket repair shops that were not associated with a manufacturer had an advantage over dealerships because they did not have the disparity problem between customer pay and warranty pay jobs, and paid their technicians a single standard hourly wage rate.

The New Plan

Deshane's plan called for a monthly bonus to be paid to a service technician if the technician's individual CSI rating were above 91%. Since each technician's repairs were linked to a CSI report, an individual technician's repair effectiveness could be easily determined. The bonuses ranged from 2% to 3% of the hourly pay. Four technicians were employed by the dealership. Two were senior and had obtained ASE certification in a number of areas, one was ASE-certified in a small number of areas, and the fourth, the least experienced technician, had no ASE certification. Deshane summed up his proposed bonus plan in the following words:

> Though this does not seem to be a significant amount of bonus money paid, it is a radical change for Sharpe BMW and one that is not very common in the industry. The bonus plan shows dealer commitment to CSI results.

Dunn's Challenge

Dunn had worked his entire career in the auto service industry. After college, he worked as a manager of a tyre store, after which he managed a small automotive repair shop. He then joined the Serra Group, where he worked as a service manager at the group's other dealerships before his present position. While at Serra, Dunn completed his MBA at a nearby regional university. At Sharpe BMW, Dunn's pay was tied to the CSI ratings. His bonus was based on the dealership achieving the national average score of 91 and increased till the score hit 93, when it reached its maximum level of 20% of basic pay.

Dunn had worked for Deshane earlier, who had handpicked him for the current job because of his favourable impression of him. Dunn maintained that he had an excellent working relationship with both Sharpe and Deshane. In addition, he felt that the entire service department worked as a team and that he shared a positive rapport with the service technicians.

As Dunn read the details of the new plan, he realised that the plan neatly dovetailed with the charge that management had given him when he was hired: to improve the dealership's CSI rating and increase the service department's revenues. Given his charge and the possibility that the new plan (even though it had a marginal economic benefit to the technicians) would help him achieve it, he wanted to make sure that the new plan was implemented effectively. He realised that the new plan involved bringing a change in the service department and that organisational change situations had to be handled carefully. He had informally talked about the bonus plan to two of his service technicians.

Peter Jackson* was a level-one technician – the highest level a technician could achieve in the automotive service industry. He had worked five years with Sharpe and over twenty years in the industry. Jackson felt that the bonus was in the right direction, in that it did show that management was more understanding of how hard technicians worked. He told Dunn that the amount of the bonus was not enough, however, and that he could make more money by working fast on warranty work.

Jack Sycamore* was a level-two technician with three years of tenure at Sharpe and twenty years overall in the industry. He was more optimistic about the bonus plan. He felt that though the CSI score depended on too many things beyond his control, it did show that management was doing something beyond a pat-on-the-back or a thank-you. It did make him more satisfied to know that money was attached.

Dunn realised that his job was made more difficult by the fact that the bonus money that technicians would get from the plan was meagre. There was no guarantee that the plan would be successful upon implementation and that everyone would be happy. Dunn knew that both Sharpe and Deshane would measure the success of the plan by the improvement in the dealership's overall CSI scores.

Tom Dunn knew that the new bonus plan was important to his career. The automotive dealership industry had wrestled with the differential-pay problem without finding a solution to it. This might be his chance to have an impact, both in the dealership as well as in his industry, by providing a solution to this recurring problem. But to achieve that, Dunn realised that he had to carefully implement the bonus plan.

He had given this issue a great deal of thought. What if the plan does not result in improved CSI scores? Will the fault be ascribed to the plan or, as seemed more likely, to its implementation?

Review questions

1 What do you see as the pros and cons of the proposed bonus plan?
2 Based on the information in the case, prepare an implementation plan for Dunn to follow.

*Disguised name.

CASE STUDY 10

Fourwinds Marina*

Jack Keltner had just completed his first day as general manager of the Fourwinds Marina. It was mid-August and though the marina slip rentals ran until October 30, business always took a dramatic downturn after Labor Day. It would be unwise to change any of the current operations in the next three weeks, but he would have to move swiftly to implement some of the changes he had been considering, and at the same time would have the better part of a year to develop and implement some short-range and long-range plans that were sorely needed if the marina was to survive.

The day before, Jack had been called in by Sandy Taggart, president of the Taggart Corporation, owners of the Fourwinds Marina and the Inn of the Fourwinds. Leon McLaughlin had just submitted his resignation as general manager of the marina. McLaughlin and Taggart had disagreed on some compensation McLaughlin felt was due him. Part of the disagreement concerned McLaughlin's wife, who had been hired to work in the parts department but had spent little time there due to an illness.

McLaughlin had been the fifth manager in as many years that the marina had been in operation. He had fifteen years of marine experience before being hired to manage the marina. His experience, however, consisted of selling and servicing boats and motors in Evansville, Indiana, not in marina management. He took pride in running a 'tight ship' and felt that the marina had an excellent chance to turn around after some hard times. It was fairly easy to keep the marina staffed because the resort atmosphere was so attractive, and his goal was to have the majority of the staff on a full-time basis year-round. Even though the marina is closed from November until April there is a considerable amount of repair work on boats needed during those months. McLaughlin was told when hired that he had a blank cheque to get the marina shaped up. This open policy, however, was later rescinded. He and his wife have a mobile home near the marina, but maintain a permanent residence in Evansville. For the most part he put in six full days a week, but had an aversion to working on Sunday. McLaughlin was an effective organiser, but weak in the area of employee and customer relations.

Keltner had no experience in marina management, but was considered a hard worker willing to take on tremendous challenges. He had joined the Taggart Corporation after four years as a CPA for Ernst and Young, the accounting firm. Functioning as controller of the corporation, he found that there was a tremendous

*Source: This is a classic case in the strategic management literature. Copyright 1974 by W. Harvey Hegarty, Indiana University, and Harry Kelsy, Jr., California State College. Reprinted with permission.

volume of work demanded, necessitating late hours at the office and a briefcase full of work to take home with him most evenings. At this point, Keltner lived in a small community near the marina, but still had to commute frequently to the home office of the Taggart Corporation in Indianapolis, an hour and a half drive from Lake Monroe. He had indicated that he hoped to move the offices to Lake Monroe, site of the marina and inn, as soon as possible. Handling the accounting for the marina, the inn, and the other Taggart Corporation interests could be done effectively at the marina. The inn and the marina comprise 90% of the corporation.

Much of the explanation for the heavy workload lay in the fact that there had been virtually no accounting system when he first joined Taggart. He had, however, set up six profit centres for the marina and generated monthly accounting reports.

The other principal investors involved in the Taggart Corporation besides Sandy (A. L. Taggart III) were William Brennan, president of one of the state's largest commercial and industrial real estate firms, and Richard DeMars, president of Guepel-DeMars, Inc., the firm that designed both the marina and the inn.

Sandy Taggart is a well-known Indianapolis businessman who is Chairman of the Board of Colonial Baking Company. This organisation is one of the larger bakeries serving the Indianapolis metropolitan area and surrounding counties. He did his undergraduate work at Princeton and completed Harvard's A.M.P. program in 1967. He is an easygoing man and appears not to let problems upset him easily. He maintains his office at the Taggart Corporation in Indianapolis, but tries to get to the marina at least once every week. He kept in daily contact with Leon McLaughlin, and continues to do the same with Keltner. He enjoys being a part of the daily decision making and problem solving that goes on at the marina and feels that he needs to be aware of all decisions due to their weak financial position. Taggart feels current problems stem from a lack of knowledge of the marina business and lack of experienced general managers when they began operation some six years ago. He also admits that their lack of expertise in maintaining accurate cost data and controlling their costs hurt them, but feels Keltner has already gone a long way in correcting this problem.

Keltner has been intimately involved in the operation and feels that at a minimum the following changes should be made over the next twelve-month period.

1. Add eighty slips on E, F, and G docks and put in underwater supports on these docks to deter breakage from storms. Cost $250 000–300 000. Annual profits if all slips are rented: $75 000+.
2. Add a second employee to assist the present secretary-receptionist bookkeeper. This will actually be a savings if the Indianapolis office is closed. Savings: $300+/month.
3. Reorganise the parts department and put in a new inventory system. Cost: $3000. Savings: $2500–3000/year.
4. Keep the boat and motor inventory low. Boat inventory as of mid-August is approximately $125 000. It has been over $300 000.

5 Reduce the workforce through attrition if a vacated job can be assumed by someone remaining on the staff.

6 Use E, F, and G for winter storage with the improved and more extensive bubbling system. Profits to be generated are difficult to estimate.

7 Light and heat the storage building so repair work can be done at night and in the winter. Cost will be $12 000, which he estimates probably would be paid for from the profits in two winters.

Each of these changes would add to the effectiveness and profitability of the marina operation, and that was his prime concern. The operation of the inn was under the control of another general manager, and functioned as a separate corporate entity. Keltner was responsible only for the accounting procedures of the inn.

As he reviewed the structure, background, and development of the inn and the marina, he realised the problems that faced him in his new role of general manager—and at the same time controller of Taggart Corporation. Managing the marina was a full-time, seven-day-a-week job, particularly during the season. The questions uppermost in his mind were 1) what would be the full plan he would present to Taggart for the effective, efficient, and profitable operation of the marina, and 2) how would it be funded? The financial statements presented a fairly glum picture, but he had the available backup data to analyse for income per square foot on most of the operations, payroll data, etc., as well as the knowledge he had gleaned working with the past general managers and observing the operation of the marina. (See Figure C10.3 and Tables C10.1/C10.2 for the organisational structure and financial statements of the marina.)

Background Data on Fourwinds Marina

The Setting

The Fourwinds Marina and the Inn of the Fourwinds are located on Lake Monroe, a manmade reservoir over ten thousand acres in size nestled in the hills of southern Indiana. Both facilities are owned and operated by the Taggart Corporation, but are operated as totally distinct and separate facilities. They cooperate in promoting business for each other.

The inn occupies some 71 000 square feet on 30 acres of land. It is designed to blend into the beautifully wooded landscape and is constructed of rustic and natural building materials. It is designed to appeal to a broad segment of the population with rooms priced from $21 to $33 for a double room. The inn is comprised of 150 sleeping rooms, singles, doubles, and suites, and has meeting rooms to appeal to the convention and sales meetings clientele. The largest meeting room will seat 300 for dining and 350 for conferences. Recreation facilities include an indoor-outdoor swimming pool, tennis courts, sauna, whirlpool bath, a recreation room with pool tables, and other games. Additional facilities include two dining rooms and a cocktail lounge. The inn is open year-round with heavy seasonal business in the summer months.

It is the first lodge of its nature built on state property by private funds. By virtue of the size of its food service facilities (in excess of $100 000 per annum) it qualifies under Indiana State Law for a license to serve alcoholic beverages on Sunday.

A brief description of the Pointe is also in order as its development promises a substantial boost to the marina's business. The Pointe, located three miles from the marina, consists of 384 acres on the lake. It is a luxury condominium development designed to meet the housing needs of primary and secondary home buyers. Currently seventy units are under construction. Twenty of these have been sold and the down-payment has been received on eighty more. These condominiums range from $25 000 to $90 000, with an average price of $60 000. Approval has been secured for the construction of 1900 living units over a seven-year period. The development has a completed eighteen-hole golf course. Swimming pools and tennis courts are now under construction. The Pointe is a multimillion-dollar development by Indun Realty, Inc., Lake Monroe Corporation, and Reywood, Inc. Indun Realty is a wholly owned subsidiary of Indiana National Corp., parent firm of Indiana National Bank, the state's largest fiduciary institution.

The Fourwinds Marina occupies four acres of land and is one of the most extensive and complete marinas of its type in the United States. It is comprised of the boat docks, a sales room for boats and marine equipment, an indoor boat storage facility, and marine repair shop (see Figure C10.1).

There are seven docks projecting out from a main connecting dock that runs parallel to the shore line. The seven parallel docks extend out from 330 to 600 feet into the lake at a right angle to the connecting dock. The centre dock houses a large building containing a grocery store, snack bar, and restrooms, and a section of docks used as mooring for rental boats.

At the end of the dock is an office for boat rental, five gasoline pumps, and pumping facilities for removing waste from the houseboats and larger cruisers.

The three docks to the right of the centre dock (facing toward the lake) are docks A, B, and C and are designed for mooring smaller boats—runabouts, fishing boats, etc. A bait shop is on A dock. A, B, and C slips are not always fully rented. The three docks to the left are the prime slips (E, F, G) and are designed for berthing houseboats, large cruisers, etc.[1] There are a total of 460 rentable slips priced from $205 to $775 for uncovered slips and $295 to $1125 for covered slips per season (April 1–October 30). Seventy-five per cent of all the slips are under roof and are in the more desirable location, hence they are rented first. Electric service is provided to all slips, and the slips on E and F docks have water and trash removal provided at no extra cost. To the left of the prime slips are 162 buoys, renting for $150 per season. This rental includes shuttle boat service to and from the moored craft. Buoys are not considered to be a very profitable segment. The buoys shift and break loose occasionally, requiring constant attention. Time is required to retrieve boats that break loose at night or during storms.

Lake Monroe, the largest lake in Indiana, is a 10 700-acre reservoir developed by the U.S. Army Corps of Engineers in conjunction with and under the jurisdiction

FIGURE C10.1 General Layout of the Marina

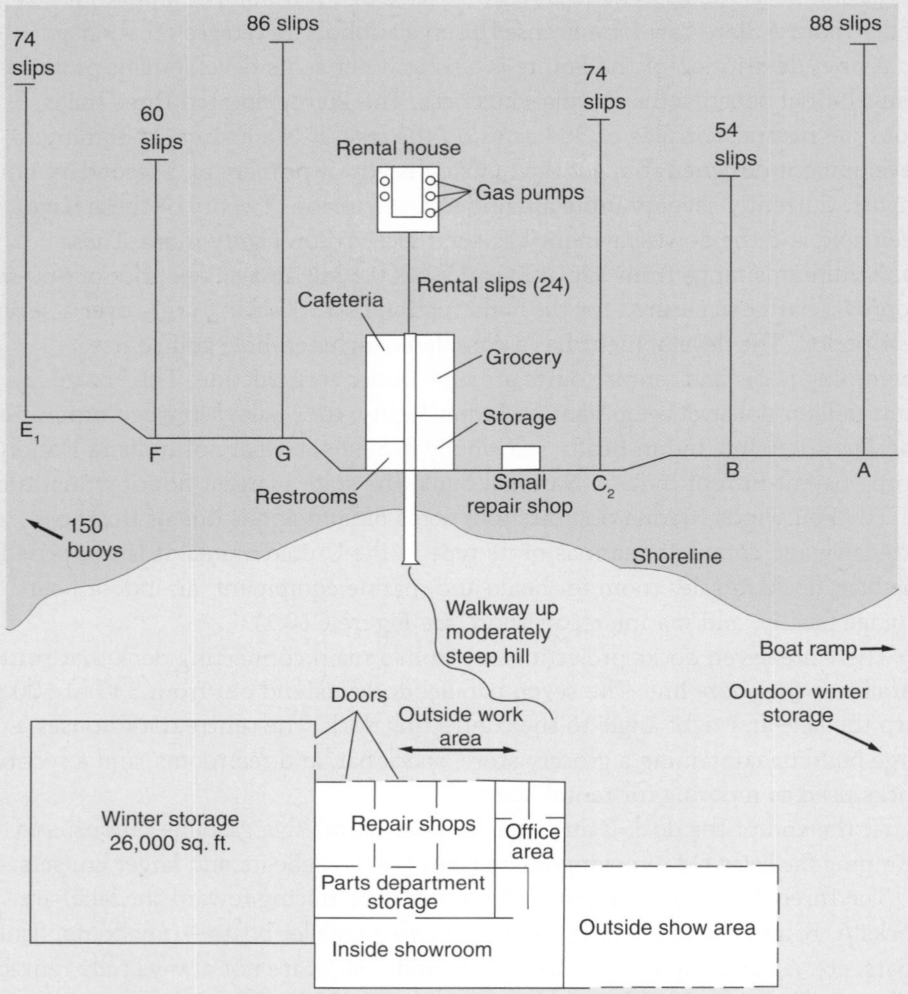

E, F, and G range from 15' × 34' to 18' × 50'. About two-thirds of these slips are covered.
A, B, and C slips range from 9' × 18' to 12' × 32'. Over 80% of these slips are covered.

of the Indiana Department of Natural Resources. With the surrounding public lands (accounting for some 80% of the 150-mile shore line) the total acreage is 26 000. It is a multipurpose project designed to provide flood control, recreation, water supply, and flow augmentation benefits to the people of Indiana.

The reservoir is located in the southwestern quadrant of the state, about nine miles or a fifteen-minute drive southwest of Bloomington, Indiana, home of Indiana University, and a ninety-minute drive from Indianapolis. The Indianapolis metropolitan area has a population of over one million with some $3.5 billion to spend annually. It is considered a desirable site for future expansion by many of the nation's top industrial leaders, as reported in a recent *Fortune* magazine survey. The city is the crossroads of the national interstate highway system, with more interstate highways converging here than in any other section of the United States. Its recently enlarged airport can accommodate any of the jet aircraft currently in operation, and is served by most of the major airlines. The per capita effective buying income is $4264 as contrasted with $3779 for the United States as a whole, with almost half of the households falling in the annual income bracket of $10 000 and above. While approximately 75% of the customers of the marina for boat dockage, etc., come from the Indianapolis area, it is estimated that there is a total potential audience of some 2.9 million inhabitants within a 100-mile radius of Bloomington (see Figure C10.2).

The thirty-four acres of land on which the Fourwinds complex is located are leased to the corporation by the state of Indiana. In 1968 a prospectus was distributed by the Indiana Department of Natural Resources asking for bids on a motel and marina on the selected site. Of the eight to ten bids submitted, only one other bidder qualified. The proposal submitted by the Taggart Corporation was accepted primarily based on the economic strength of the individuals who composed the group, as well as the actual content of the bid.

The prospectus specified a minimum rental for the land of $10 000. Taggart Corporation offered in their bid a guarantee of $2000 against the first $100 000 in marina sales and income and 4% of all income over that amount. For the inn, they guaranteed $8000 against the first $400 000 of income plus 4% of all room sales and 2 per cent of all food and beverage sales over that amount.

An initial lease of thirty-seven years was granted to Taggart with two options of thirty years each. At the termination of the contract, all physical property reverts to the state of Indiana and personal property to Taggart. The entire dock structure is floating and is considered under the personal property category.

Prior to tendering a bid, the corporation visited similar facilities at Lake of the Ozarks, Lake Hamilton in Hot Springs, and the Kentucky Lakes operations.

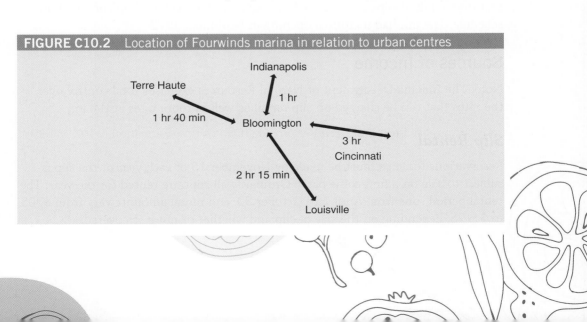

FIGURE C10.2 Location of Fourwinds marina in relation to urban centres

FIGURE C10.3 Organisation chart for Fourwinds marina

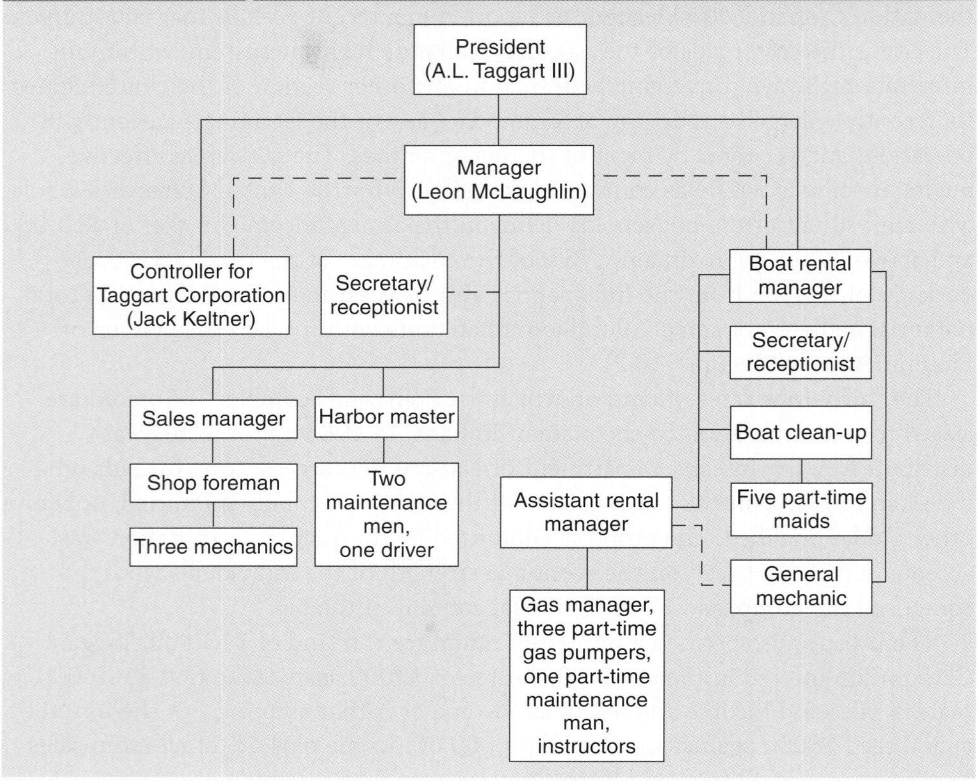

They received a considerable amount of information from the Kentucky Lakes management.

Construction of the initial phase of the marina began in May 1969 and the first one hundred slips were opened in August under a speeded-up construction schedule. The inn had its formal opening in November 1972.

Sources of Income

Note: The Indiana Department of Natural Resources exercises total control over the rates that can be charged on slip rental as well as room rates at the inn.

Slip Rental

Reservations for slips must be made by November 15 of each year or the slip is subject to sale on a first-come basis. Ordinarily all slips are rented for the year. The rental period runs from April 1 to October 30, and rental amounts vary from $205 to $1125, depending on the size of slip and whether or not it is covered.

TABLE C10.1 Profit and Loss Statement (Fiscal Year Ending March 31, 1974)		
REVENUE		
Sale of new boats	$774 352	
Sale of used boats	179 645	
Sale of rental boats	17 051	
Total Sales		$ 971 048
Other Income		
Service and repair	$128 687	
Gasoline and oil	81 329	
Ship store	91 214	
Slip rental	174 808	
Winter storage	32 177	
Boat rental	99 895	
Other income		608 110
Total Income		$ 157 9158
EXPENSES		
Fixed Costs		
Cost of boats	$798 123	
Cost of repair equipment	56 698	
Ship store costs	64 405	
Cost of gasoline	51 882	
Boat rental costs	8 951	
Total Fixed Costs		$ 980 059
Operating Expenses		
Wages and salaries	$228 154	
Taxes	23 725	
Building rent	58 116	
Equipment rent	8 975	
Utilities	18 716	
Insurance	25 000	
Interest on loans	209 310	

REVENUE		
Advertising	30 105	
Legal expenses	19 450	
Bad debt expenses	8 731	
Miscellaneous	39 994	
Total Operating Expenses		670 321
Total Costs		$1 650 380
Operating Loss		$ 71 222
Depreciation		122 340
TOTAL LOSS[1]		$ 193 562

TABLE C10.1 Profit and Loss Statement (Fiscal Year Ending March 31, 1974) (continued)

[1]This represents the total operating loss of the Fourwinds Marina in the fiscal year ending March 31, 1974. Fourwinds sold a subsidiary in 1973 (boat sales firm in Indianapolis), on which they wrote off a loss of $275 580.

Buoy Rental

One hundred and sixty-two buoys are rented for the same April 1 to October 30 season at a rate of $150. Shuttle boat service for transporting boat owners to and from their craft moored at the buoy area is operative twenty-four hours a day. It is not a scheduled service, but operates as the demand occurs. This requires the primary use of a runabout and driver. The charge for the service is included in the buoy rental fee for the season. As long as the buoy field is in existence, the shuttle service must operate on a twenty-four-hour basis in season.

Boat Storage – Winter

It is more expensive to remove a boat from the water than to allow it to remain moored at the dock all winter. The prime rate for storage is based on the charge for storage in the covered area of the main inside storage building. This area is not heated or lighted so repair work cannot be done in this building. An investment of about $12 000 would afford lighting and spot heating to overcome this drawback. When boats are stored, they are not queued according to those needing repair and those not needing service. As a result, time is lost in rearranging boats to get to those on which work must be performed. The storage facility is not utilised in the summer months. The addition of lights in the facility would allow display of used boats for sale, which are currently stored out of doors. Rates for storage charges are:

   100 per cent base rate – inside storage
   70 per cent of base rate – bubbled area of docks covered
   60 per cent of base rate – bubbled area of docks open
   50 per cent of base rate – open storage areas out of water

TABLE C10.2 Balance Sheet (March 31, 1974)

ASSETS		Less depreciation		LIABILITIES	
Current Assets				**Current Liabilities**	
Cash	$ 31 858			Accounts payable	$ 89 433
Accounts receivable	70 632			Intercompany payables	467 091
New boats	199 029			Accrued salary expense	8 905
Used boats	60 747			Accrued interest expense	20 383
Parts	53 295			Accrued tax expense	43 719
Ship store	2 471			Accrued lease expense	36 190
Gas/oil	2 626			Prepaid dock rental	178 466
Total Current Assets	$ 420 928			Boat deposits	4 288
				Current bank notes	177 600
Fixed Assets				Mortgage (current)	982 900
Buoys and docks	$ 984 265	$315 459		Note payable for floor plan	225 550
Permanent buildings	201 975	17 882		Note on rental houseboats	71 625
Office furniture	3 260	704		Notes to stockholders	515 150
Houseboats	139 135	15 631		Dealer reserve liability	13 925
Work boats	40 805	7 987		Total Current Liabilities	$2 835 225
Equipment	72 420	38 742			
	$1 441 860	$396 396		Long-term note on houseboats	117 675
Net Fixed Assets		$1 045 464		Common stock – 1000 shares at par value $1/share	1 000
Other Assets				Retained earnings deficit	–990 105
Prepaid expense		$ 2 940		Loss during year ending March 31, 1974 [1]	–469 142
Deferred interest expense		25 231			
		$ 28 261			
Total Assets		$1 494 653		**Total Liabilities**	$1 494 653

[1] Loss during year ended March 31, 1974, is composed of an operating loss of $71 222 plus depreciation of $122 340, and a write-off loss of a sold subsidiary of $275 580.

Storage rate is computed by the size of the boat. A six-foot-wide boat has a rate of $7. This is multiplied by the boat length to determine the total rate. So a twenty-foot-long boat seven feet wide would cost $140. Last winter the storage facility was filled. One hundred boats were stored, with the average size somewhat larger than the seven by twenty example given above. This rate does not include charges (approximately $75) for removing the boat from the water and moving it to either inside or outside storage areas. In the past there has been vandalism on the boats stored in the more remote areas of the uncovered, out-of-water storage. The marina claims no responsibility for loss, theft, or damage.

Boat and Motor Rental

Available equipment is up-to-date and well maintained. It consists of:

15 houseboats – rental Monday to Friday $300; Friday to Monday $300
10 pontoon boats – hourly rental $20 for 3 hours; $35 for 6 hours
6 runabouts for skiing – $15–$20 per hour
12 fishing boats – $12 for 6 hours; $18 for 12 hours

Maximum hourly rental is thirteen hours per day during the week and fifteen hours per day on Saturday and Sunday (the rental rate does not include gasoline).

It is not uncommon to have all fifteen houseboats out all week long during the height of the season. (Season height is from Memorial Day weekend to Labor Day weekend.) Pontoons are about 50 per cent rented during the week. Utilisation of runabouts is 50 per cent, while fishing boats is approximately 40 per cent. The man who operates the boat and motor rental for the marina has a one-third interest in all of the boat rental equipment. The marina holds the balance. Funds for the purchase of the equipment were contributed on the same one-third to two-thirds ratio. Net profits after payment of expenses, maintenance, depreciation, etc., are split between the two owners according to the same ratio. The area utilised by the rental area could be converted to slips in the $500 range as a possible alternative use for the dock space. Rental income after expenses, but before interest and depreciation, was slightly less than $20 000 last season.

Small-Boat Repair Shop

A small-boat repair shop is located between C and D docks. It is well equipped with mechanical equipment and a small hoist for removing small boats from the water for repair at the docks. This facility is currently standing idle. One qualified mechanic could operate it.

Grocery Store

The grocery store is subleased and is effectively operated. Prices are those expected at a small grocery catering to a predominantly tourist clientele. Income on the leased operation is approximately $500/month.

Snack Bar

The snack bar is operated by the Inn of the Fourwinds and returns a 5 per cent commission to the marina on food sales. Currently it is felt that the manager of the snack bar is not doing a reliable job in operating the unit. The snack bar is sometimes closed for no apparent reason. Food offered for sale includes hot sandwiches, pizza, snack food, soft drinks, milk, and coffee. Prices are high and general quality is rated as good.

Gasoline Sales

Five pumps are located around the perimeter of the end of the centre dock. They are manned thirteen hours per day, from seven a.m. to eight p.m., seven days a week. The pumps for the removal of waste from the houseboats and other large craft are located in this area. It takes an average of five minutes to pump out the waste and there is no charge. These gasoline pumps are the only ones available on the lake, permitting access from the water to the pump.

Boat and Boat Accessory Sales Room

A glass-enclosed showroom occupying approximately 1500 square feet of floor space is located at the main entrance to the marina property. Major boat lines Trojan Yacht, Kingscraft, Burnscraft, Harris Flote Boat, and Signa, as well as Evinrude motors, are offered for sale. In addition, quality lines of marine accessories are available. The sales room building also houses the executive offices of the marina and the repair and maintenance shops. Attached to the building is the indoor storage area for winter housing of a limited number of boats. Last year total boat sales were $971 048. The boat inventory has been reduced from last year's $300 000, removing some lines while concentrating on others that offered higher profit on sales.

Fourwinds Marina is the only operation in the state that stocks the very large boats. It is also the only facility in Indiana with large slips to accommodate these boats. With E, F, and G slips filled and a waiting list to get in, selling the larger, more profitable boats has become nearly impossible.

Marina Docking Area Facts

Dock Construction

The entire section is of modular floating construction. Built-in smaller sections that can be bolted together, the construction is of steel frameworks with poured concrete surfaces for walking upon and plastic foam panels in the side for buoyancy. In the event of damage to a section, a side can be replaced easily, eliminating repair of the entire segment of dock. Electrical conduits and water pipes are inside the actual dock units. The major damage to the plastic foam dock segments comes from ducks chewing out pieces of the foam to make nests, and from gasoline spillage that literally 'eats' the plastic foam. An anti-gas coating is available. Damage from boats to the dock is minimal. The docks require constant attention. A maze of cables underneath the sections must be kept at the proper tension or the dock will buckle and break up. Three people are involved in dock maintenance. If properly maintained, the docks will have twenty to thirty more years of use. Original cost of the entire dock and buoy system was $984 265.

Winter Storage

Winter storage can be a problem at a marina located in an area where a freeze-over of the water occurs. It is better for the boat if it can remain in the water. Water affords better and more even support to the hull. By leaving the craft in the water, possible damage from hoists used to lift boats and move them to dry storage is avoided. These factors, however, are not common knowledge to the boat owner and require an educational program.

A rule of the marina prohibits any employee from driving any of the customers' boats. Maintaining a duplicate set of keys for each boat and the cost of the insurance to cover the employee are the prime reasons for this ruling. This means, however, that all boats must be towed, with possibility of damage to the boats during towing.

Bubbling Process

To protect boats left in the water during the winter season, Fourwinds Marina has installed a bubbling system. The system, simple in concept, consists of hoses that are weighted and dropped to the bottom of the lake around the individual docks and along a perimeter line surrounding the entire dock area. Fractional horsepower motors operate compressors that pump air into the submerged hose. The air escaping through tiny holes in the hose forces warmer water at the bottom of the lake up to the top, preventing freezing of the surface (or melting ice that might have frozen before the compressors were started). The lines inside the dock areas protect the boats from being damaged by ice formations, while the perimeter line prevents major damage to the entire dock area from a pressure ridge that might build up and be jammed against the dock and boats in high wind.

Review questions

1 What are the marina's strengths, weaknesses, opportunities, and threats?

2 How would you describe the marina's strategy and organisation, and what do you think of Keltner's list of actions?

3 Assume Keltner asked you for some help in thinking through the changes. Where would you start, whom would you involve, and what might you propose?

Notes

1 E, F, and G are the most profitable slips and are fully rented. There is a waiting list to get into these slips.

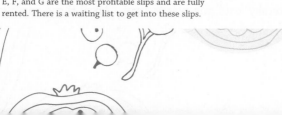

CASE STUDY 11

B. R. Richardson Timber Products Corporation*

Jack Lawler returned to his desk with a fresh cup of coffee. In front of him was a file of his notes from his two visits to the B. R. Richardson Timber Products Corporation. As Lawler took a sip of coffee and opened the file, he was acutely aware that he had two tasks. In a week, he was to meet with the company president, B. R. Richardson, and the industrial relations officer, Richard Bowman, to make a presentation on his findings with regard to the lamination plant and his recommendations for what might be done. Lawler knew he had a lot of preparation to do, starting with a diagnosis of the situation. It wouldn't be easy. Taking another sip from his mug, he leaned back in his chair and recalled how this project had begun.

Making a Proposal

It was about 2:30 p.m. when the office intercom buzzed. Lawler's secretary said there was a Richard Bowman calling from Papoose, Oregon. Lawler knew that Papoose was a small community about a hundred and fifty miles south, a town with three or four lumber mills lying in the mountain range of western Oregon. When Lawler picked up his telephone, Bowman introduced himself as being in charge of industrial relations for the B. R. Richardson Timber Products Corporation. He was calling because a friend of his in a regional association for training and development persons had recommended Lawler, and Bowman had heard of Lawler's management training and consulting reputation. Bowman said he was searching for someone to conduct a 'motivation course' for the blue-collar employees of the lamination plant. Morale in the plant was very low, there had been a fatality in the plant a few months before, and the plant manager was 'a bit authoritative'. Given the gravity of the plant situation, Bowman wanted to conduct the course within the next few months.

Lawler asked if the plant manager was supportive of the course idea. Bowman replied that he hadn't asked him but had gotten approval from B. R. Richardson, the founder and president of the firm. Lawler then stated that he really didn't have enough information on which to design such a course nor enough information to determine whether such a course was appropriate. He suggested a meeting with

*Source: Printed by permission of Craig C. Lundberg, Cornell University. Events described are not intended to illustrate either effective or ineffective managerial behaviour.

Bowman and Richardson the next week; he would be able to stop by Papoose in the late afternoon on his way home from another engagement. Bowman immediately accepted his proposal and gave Lawler directions.

Taking another sip of coffee, Jack Lawler continued to reminisce, visualising the road winding past two very large lumber and plywood plants and over a small hill, and recalling his first sight of the B. R. Richardson Timber Products Corporation. It was much smaller than its neighbours, consisting of a one-storey office building, a medium size lumber mill, open storage yards, an oblong, hangar-like structure, dirt connecting roads, lumber and log piles seemingly scattered around, and cars and pickup trucks parked at random. The office building entryway was panelled with photographs showing the company buildings as they had changed over many years.

Bowman greeted Lawler, led him to a carpeted and panelled conference room, and introduced him to Ben Richardson. 'BR' was a man in his late fifties, dressed in western apparel. The subsequent conversation was one in which the company as a whole was outlined and information was presented about the plant workers. Lawler described his preferred ways of working (essentially, diagnosis before training or other action). BR and Bowman shared their concerns that the plant manager, Joe Bamford, was getting out the work but wasn't sensitive to the workers. Bowman then took Lawler on a tour of the lamination plant. The meeting ended cordially, with Lawler promising to write a letter in a few days in which he would outline his thoughts on going forward.

Jack Lawler opened the file in front of him on his desk and smiled as he found the copy of the letter he had sent:

Mr. Richard Bowman

B. R. Richardson Timber Corporation

PO Box 66

Papoose, Oregon

Dear Mr. Bowman:

When I departed from your office about a week ago, I promised a letter outlining my thoughts on some next steps regarding the laminating plant. Let me sketch some alternatives:

1   One is for me to put you in touch with someone in your immediate region who could design and/or present the 'motivation' course for the laminating workers that you originally had in mind.

2   Second is for me to be engaged as a consultant. Recall the experience I described with the plywood plant in northern California in which I facilitated an approach called 'action research'. You'll remember that it basically involved a process wherein the concerned parties were helped to identify non-controlled problems and plan to overcome them. This would begin with a diagnosis conducted by myself.

3   Third, you'll also recall that I teach part-time at State University. This relationship leads to two ways graduate students might become involved:

I believe I could get a colleague in personnel management training to create a student team to design and conduct the motivation course.

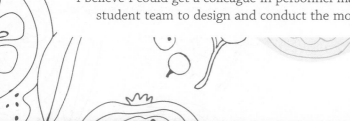

I can have a student team in my change seminar do a diagnosis of the
laminating plant and provide you with their analyses and recommendations.

I believe I was clear during my visit that I think a diagnosis is needed first,
regardless of next steps. When you and Mr. Richardson have thought about these
alternatives, give me a call. I'll be prepared to outline what I see as the costs of
alternatives 2 and 3.

Thanks for the opportunity to visit. I enjoyed meeting you and beginning to learn
about your company.

Sincerely,

Jack Lawler

Partner

Oregon Consulting Associates

Visiting the Plant

Lawler remembered that six weeks went by before Bowman called. He had shown
Lawler's letter to B. R. Richardson, and they agreed that a more adequate diagnosis
was probably a useful first step. Bowman was quite clear that Richardson did not
want to invest much money but also wanted Lawler's expertise. In the ensuing
conversation, Bowman and Lawler worked out an initial plan in which he would
utilise several of his graduate students in a one-day visit to the company to gather
information. Lawler would then analyse it and make a presentation to BR and
Bowman. The use of the graduate students would substantially reduce his time as
well as provide the students with some useful experience. They agreed that he
would bill for three days of his time plus the expenses incurred when he and the
students visited.

The next week when Lawler went to campus to teach his evening seminar called
'The Management of Change' at the Graduate School of Business, he shared with
the class the opportunity for some relevant fieldwork experience. He and four
students could do the observing and interviewing in one day by leaving very early
in the morning to drive to Papoose and arriving home by mid-evening. The
information gained would be the focus of a subsequent class in which all seminar
participants performed the diagnosis. When he asked his seminar who was
interested in the information-gathering day, six students volunteered. When
particular dates for the trip to Papoose were discussed, however, most of the six
had conflicting schedules. Only Mitch and Mike, two second-year MBA students,
were available on one of the days that Lawler's schedule permitted.

Having constituted the field team, Lawler suggested that the seminar invest
some time that evening in two ways. He wanted to share with the class some
information he had gained on his first visit to B. R. Richardson Timber and
suggested that the class could help prepare Mitch and Mike for the experience in
the field. He then drew an organisation chart on the blackboard that showed the

various segments of the corporation and the lamination business, including the personnel and main work groups. He further drew a layout of the laminating plant on the board. Figures C11.1 and C11.2 show these sketches.

While doing this, Lawler spoke of his understanding of the technology, work flow, and product of the laminating plant as follows:

> It's a family-held corporation. It's composed of four small companies, divisions really, three in Papoose – a logging operation, a lumber mill, and the laminating plant – and

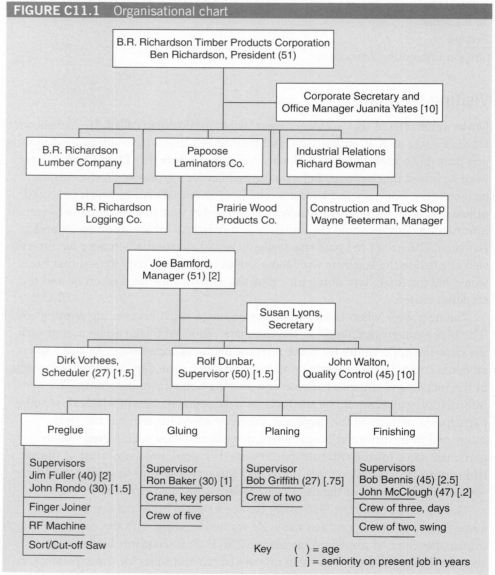

FIGURE C11.1 Organisational chart

B.R. Richardson Timber Products Corporation
Ben Richardson, President (51)

Corporate Secretary and Office Manager Juanita Yates [10]

- B.R. Richardson Lumber Company
- Papoose Laminators Co.
- Industrial Relations Richard Bowman

- B.R. Richardson Logging Co.
- Prairie Wood Products Co.
- Construction and Truck Shop Wayne Teeterman, Manager

Joe Bamford, Manager (51) [2]

Susan Lyons, Secretary

- Dirk Vorhees, Scheduler (27) [1.5]
- Rolf Dunbar, Supervisor (50) [1.5]
- John Walton, Quality Control (45) [10]

Preglue
Supervisors
Jim Fuller (40) [2]
John Rondo (30) [1.5]
Finger Joiner
RF Machine
Sort/Cut-off Saw

Gluing
Supervisor
Ron Baker (30) [1]
Crane, key person
Crew of five

Planing
Supervisor
Bob Griffith (27) [.75]
Crew of two

Finishing
Supervisors
Bob Bennis (45) [2.5]
John McClough (47) [.2]
Crew of three, days
Crew of two, swing

Key   ( ) = age
       [ ] = seniority on present job in years

FIGURE C11.2 Laminating plant

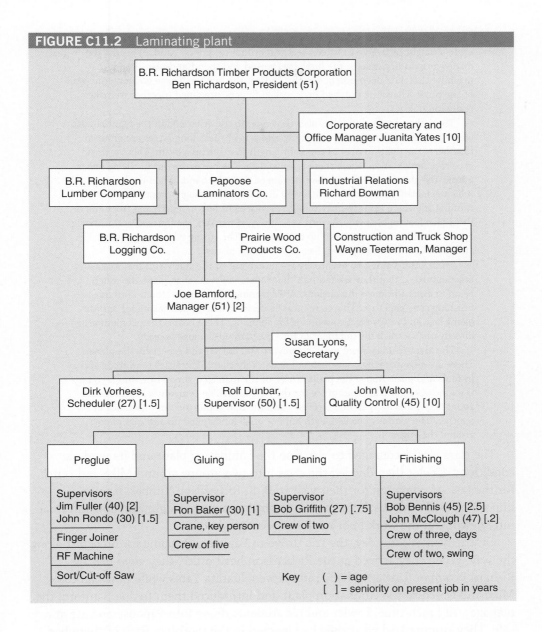

B.R. Richardson Timber Products Corporation
Ben Richardson, President (51)

Corporate Secretary and
Office Manager Juanita Yates [10]

B.R. Richardson
Lumber Company

Papoose
Laminators Co.

Industrial Relations
Richard Bowman

B.R. Richardson
Logging Co.

Prairie Wood
Products Co.

Construction and Truck Shop
Wayne Teeterman, Manager

Joe Bamford,
Manager (51) [2]

Susan Lyons,
Secretary

Dirk Vorhees,
Scheduler (27) [1.5]

Rolf Dunbar,
Supervisor (50) [1.5]

John Walton,
Quality Control (45) [10]

Preglue

Supervisors
Jim Fuller (40) [2]
John Rondo (30) [1.5]

Finger Joiner

RF Machine

Sort/Cut-off Saw

Gluing

Supervisor
Ron Baker (30) [1]

Crane, key person

Crew of five

Planing

Supervisor
Bob Griffith (27) [.75]

Crew of two

Finishing

Supervisors
Bob Bennis (45) [2.5]
John McClough (47) [.2]

Crew of three, days

Crew of two, swing

Key   ( ) = age
         [ ] = seniority on present job in years

a mill over in eastern Oregon. The head office, the mill, and the lam plant are on the edge of Papoose, which is a very small logging town about six or seven miles from the interstate highway. The lam plant looks like a long airplane hangar, the type with a curved roof. Rich Bowman took me on a tour, safety helmet on, and explained the activities as we went along.

Now, the end products are long, laminated wood roof trusses or beams like you sometimes see in supermarkets and arenas. These are built up out of many layers of two-by-fours, two-by-sixes and two-by-eights glued together end to end and then

side to side. So in one end of the plant come lift trucks of lumber, which is stacked up to a height of twelve to fifteen feet. According to orders – and all beams are made to customer order – the lumber is sorted and then hand-placed on a machine that cuts deep notches in the ends of the lumber. These go along one wall of the plant where the notched ends, called fingers, are glued together to make really long pieces.

These then go on along the roller conveyor, to the other end of the plant almost, where they are cut to the correct length, and sets of these long pieces are grouped together – the right number of the right length to make up a beam. This set then goes to a work station where there is a metal jig. The pieces are put in the jig one at a time, the glue is applied and they are tapped down by hand. When the beam is fully assembled, clamps are put on every little way. This rough, clamped beam, running anywhere from twenty to, say, seventy-eight feet in length and from one to three-plus feet high, obviously very, very heavy, is marked, then picked out of the jig by two small hoists and stacked up to cure (dry). The curing piles have cross sticks and must be fifteen to eighteen feet high in some places.

These beams cure and eventually are picked out of the stack with the hoists and manoeuvred so that they are fed into the planer, which is set to plane the rough beam to exact thickness dimensions. After planing, the beam is stored until the finishing crew gets to it. This crew cuts the beam to length, patches minor surface blemishes, and wraps plastic around it for shipping. These beams then sometimes go directly onto a truck for shipment or into the yard until a load is ready.

The plant is noisy from saws, conveyors and hoists, and especially the planer. There are glue drippings, sawdust and ends everywhere. The aisles tend to disappear in tools and piles. Above the plant offices of the manager, supervisor, and secretary is a lunchroom and another office for the scheduler. The company's head office is about fifty yards away in one direction and the mill about the same distance in another. The yard is gravelled, with lumber of all kinds piled up and cars parked around the edges.

The class was encouraged to visualise the laminating plant and its working conditions. Lawler then divided the class into two groups around Mike and Mitch for the task of preparing for their visit to B. R. Richardson Timber. It was important to clarify what information might be usefully sought and how informal interviewing on the work floor might be accomplished.

On the next Wednesday, the trio drove to Papoose, stopping for breakfast along the way. When they arrived at the Richardson head office, they were met by Richard Bowman. Lawler initially interviewed Juanita Yates while Bowman took Mike and Mitch to the lamination plant and introduced them to Joe Bamford, the manager. At lunch time, Lawler and his students drove into Papoose and ate at a cafe. They summarised what they had learned in the morning. Each of them had been jotting some notes, and Lawler encouraged even more. He reminded Mike and Mitch that they would dictate their information during the drive home but that notes were needed as cues. At 4:30 p.m., the three met at Bowman's office, turned in their safety helmets, thanked him and left. The first hour of the drive was filled with the sharing of anecdotes from each other's day. After a dinner stop, they took turns in the back seat dictating their notes.

Reviewing the Notes

Jack Lawler's reverie was broken by the office intercom. His secretary announced a long-distance telephone call from a potential client. After the call, Jack turned his attention to the Richardson file. He realised that his forthcoming meeting with Ben Richardson and Richard Bowman would take place before his graduate seminar met to diagnose the laminating plant situation, and so he had best get to work himself. He decided to review the notes he and his students had created.

Jack's Notes

Current Lam schedule: Breakout crew 2:00 a.m. to 12:00 noon. Finish end 3:30 a.m. on. Joe typically works 7:00 a.m. to 6:00 p.m.

Ben Richardson (Juanita): 'In the beginning he was very authoritarian, still is somewhat. Seen as a perfectionist'. 'Not quite a workaholic'. 'Has been, for several years, politically active – that is to say, locally'. 'When there is a cause, he throws his energies and resources behind it'. Example, workers' compensation is currently a thorn in his side, and he has encouraged Rich to fight. 'In the last few years, Ben has listened a little more and seems slightly more open'. The last couple of years has had consultant Chuck Byron from Eugene, who has pushed the idea of a management team. Rich is the first real outsider hired as a professional. Ben has a 'conservative philosophy'. Will not have safety meetings on company time. Appreciates and rewards loyalty and dedication. Example, December 1978 Christmas party – a couple of twenty-year men were given $1000 cheques and plane tickets to Hawaii for themselves and families – it surprised everybody.

Who's influential (Rich): Juanita Yates, office manager and secretary, has been with Ben ten years. When Ben is away, he calls her once or twice a day. Second-most influential is Wayne Teeterman, also ten years with Richardson. Heads construction and truck shop. Formerly ran the sawmill. Ben's ear to the mill. Rich is a distant third in influence. Mostly via Nita. 'Ben sees Joe, manager of lam plant, as an enigma – almost canned him a couple of times'. However, Joe is seen as dedicated, mostly because of the long hours put in.

Overall business pretty good (Rich): 'Ben keeps thinking the other shoe will drop one of these days'. 'Ben used to be able to predict the lumber market. This is getting more difficult'. Right now the economy is stable enough regarding lumber and lumber products. Richardson mill sales of clear-cut high grade are pretty much cutting to order. Laminating plant growing ever since it was started. It's very profitable, busy, and active – probably has the largest margin of all Richardson companies.

Laminating plant (Rich): Laminating plant has six- to seven-week delivery dates now.

Timber purchases (Rich): Timber purchases from Forest Service and BLM. One to two year's cutting is now available. Last year needed to cut only half of year's sales because of fortunate other purchases. Last year, half of timber requirements were from private ground. 'Costs of cutting, however, go up, and it makes Ben nervous'.

Laminating plant lumber (Rich): 'Approximately 70% of laminating plant lumber purchased outside – 30% from Richardson mill'. This material is in the middle of the quality range. Outside purchases are primarily from Oregon companies – Weyerhaeuser, Bohemia, Georgia-Pacific, and smaller ones. Joe does the purchasing for lam plant. 'He likes to do this'.

Recent changes (Juanita): 'Turnover has consistently been high and continues. For the company as a whole it is around 72 to 76%. In the lam plant there was 100% turnover last year' (among operators). 'Right now this year it is down 50%'.

Rolf (Juanita): Rolf was formerly industrial relations manager. A year ago April, he was appointed supervisor in the lam plant. Rolf's predecessor in lam plant ineffectual; gone from company. Rolf did not do a good job with personnel. Fatality in lam plant happened two months before Rolf went down there. It was in the breakdown area – several people quit at that time. There has been a constant concern for the height of stacking in the lam plant. 'Joe has had a positive impact on morale – started a softball team in a community league'.

Reward system (Juanita): 'Nine paid holidays, hourly wage, liberal vacation plan, life insurance, no pension, no bonus except for those people who report directly to Ben (Nita, Wayne, Joe, and Rich). Joe has not had a bonus yet'.

Incentives for safety: Joe and Rolf have introduced incentives for safety. Competition for groups about lost time. Joe gave a fishing outfit last month for the first time that a safety target was met.

Hiring (Rich): Hiring was traditionally done by division managers. At present, Rich has taken over that. He now goes into background more deeply.

Interaction with middle management (Rich): Normally when Ben is in Papoose, he and Joe interact a couple times a week, which is about the same as Ben interacts with other division or company managers.

Ben's style (Juanita): 'He focuses on a problem. He will write a list and go over it with the manager item by item. Pretty much forcing his way. Later, he will pull out that list to check up with'. He often wants Rich to play intermediary between top management and the lam plant. Rich tries to resist.

Rolf (Rich): 'Fairly introverted, basically a nice guy. He finds it hard to be tough. Doesn't think he could do Joe's job'. His folks were missionaries.

Dirk (Rich): 'His goal is to get into sales. Ben has given okay, and he is supposed to look into local sales. Joe has agreed but has not given Dirk time to do any of this. Dirk probably has no long-run commitment to the company'. He has a degree in forestry.

John Walton (Juanita): In charge of quality control. 'Very loyal to the company. Very dedicated to quality. Member of national organisation. Never gets very

distressed. Seems well liked by crews. Not afraid to pitch in when they are a man short or behind'.

Jim Fuller (Rich): 'Ben doesn't like him'. Had EMT training recently sponsored by the companies. Ben questions Jim's commitment. Jim gets into lots of community activities, has been a disc jockey on Sunday mornings, and is very active in community organisations with youth. 'Not perceived as a real strong leadership type, but knowledgeable and pretty well liked in the lam plant'.

John Rondo (Rich): 'Dedicated, works hard. Pushes the men, too. Ben sees him as having future management promise'. From an old logging family in the area. 'Much more leadership oriented'.

Ron Baker (Rich): Gluing supervisor. 'Business-like, could be sour. Likes to impress others'.

John McClough (Rich): 'Failing as a finishing supervisor. Originally from California. Worked in Roseburg area as carpenter; does excellent work by himself. He is a flop and probably won't last much longer'.

Bob Bennis (Rich): Finishing supervisor. 'Not really a pusher'. 'Time has made him knowledgeable about the work'. 'Willing to be directed'. He has had a number of family conflicts and has been in financial trouble. 'Overall, a nice guy'.

Bob Griffith (Rich): Planer. Came to Richardson out of the service. Started in gluing, then in breakdown, then gluing. Finally, planer's job opened up, and he took it. 'Still learning the job. Generally a good worker; some question about his leadership'.

Supervisors summary (Rich): 'In general, the supervisors all kind of plod along'.

Jim Fuller (Juanita): Is lam plant safety committee representative.

General reputation in community (Rich): 'Not good from employees' point of view. Matter of turnover, accidents, and the fatality. Seems to be turning around somewhat over the last year. The company, as a whole economically, has a successful image. It's made money, survived downturns, and so forth'.

Summer: During summer, fill-ins are hired for vacationers – sometimes college or high school students. The supervisor spots are filled in by key men on the crew.

Communication: Bulletin board outside of lam office has safety information, vacation schedule, and production information. Blackboard in lunchroom has jokes, congratulations, etc.

Reports: Daily production is scheduled by Dirk. Daily report from lam plant to office is compared against that. Production and lam's information reported daily. Joe keeps records on productivity by lam plant area. This duplicates Susan's records. Quality control turns in three sheets a day: on finger-joint testing, glue spread and temperature, and finished-product tests. Also Walton keeps cumulative information on block shear (where a core is drilled and stressed) and de-lamination tests made (where product is soaked and then stressed).

Records: A few years ago, 18 000 board feet was the high for pre-glue. May 9, daily was 16,406 board feet. Swing shift is consistently higher than the day shift pre-glue. Gluing, Ben expects 30 000 feet. On May 9, it was 27,815 feet.

Overtime (Juanita): 'Is approximately 6% over the year. Right now lam plant is higher than that'.

April (Juanita): Bids for the month were $8 166 000. Orders received for the month were $648 600. Shipped in April: $324 400. When $400 000 is shipped, that is an excellent month, according to Nita. Joe does all the bidding. Sue actually may do the calls, however. 'The margin is significantly higher than the sawmill or planing mill'.

History of lam plant (Juanita): 'In 1968 Wayne Lauder started it. He had lots of prior experience'. 'The property that Richardson stands on had just been purchased. Wayne came to Joe with a proposition. Ended up with Wayne having stock in the Papoose Laminators Company'. Original crew was eight to ten men. 'In fact Wayne taught Ben all Ben knows about the laminating plant'. 'Got into lamination business at a very good time'. 'In the early days, there were no accidents and no turnover'. 'Wayne had hired old friends, largely married family types'. 'Walton is the only one left from those days'. In the spring of 1973, Wayne went to South Africa on a missionary call. Between then and Joe, there have been four managers and four or five supervisors. Ben has an image of Wayne that successive managers cannot live up to. Joe, in Ben's eyes, has done better than anyone since Wayne. The supervisor's job was started under Wayne; since then it is not clear what they do. At one time, there was an experiment to move the lam office up to the main office so that the supervisor was forced to see the manager up there. This did not work. With Joe, the office moved back to the plant.

Sue (Juanita): Secretary in lam plant. Now hand-extending the data. Could use a computer. It is programmed; she has computer skills. 'Computer never used for lam bidding since Sue came two years ago'. Phone coverage is awkward. To get copies of things means Sue has to come to the office.

Market conditions: Market conditions have been good since Joe became manager.

Joe's ability (Juanita): Highly questioned around planning. Example: 'Sue away; he knew it beforehand; it was a day he wanted to be away. This left the head office trying to get someone to cover for the phone'. 'Clearly sales is Joe's strong area. Get excellent reports back from customers. But Joe doesn't follow up, so payables are very weak. We still haven't got a ninety-day payment and are likely to ship the next load to the customer anyway'.

Lack of communication (Juanita): 'Lack of communication with us about cash flow is another weak spot of Joe's. Lack of supervision over key people like Sue and Rolf. Seems to just let them go. Certainly doesn't supervise them. Sue gets to set her

own hours'. Example offered by Nita of mis-bidding because Sue didn't get the bid back to the customer. 'Joe just wasn't aware of the timing – hadn't planned for it'. Another example: 'Sue runs out of invoice paper, which means we have to scurry around'.

Sue's wages (Juanita): 'At one time, Sue was all riled up about wages and upset the secretaries in the main office. She got no pay increase last year. Ben upset. Joe went to bat for her. Joe almost put his job on the line for her'.

Sue's performance (Juanita): 'Sue does sloppy work. Not very efficient. Poor letters; late; missing deadlines. Joe allows or accepts, or perhaps doesn't know'. Nita is supposed to be responsible for Sue on quality matters. In general, to make sure that her backup is there. 'Sue now works ten to fifteen hours a week overtime'. Nita cannot see the reason for this.

Rolf's attitude (Rich/Juanita): Rolf's attitude changing. Seems more cooperative to both Rich and Nita. Nita thinks Rolf is a very intelligent man. Neither are clear exactly on what Rolf does. Company policy is to send out invoices each workday and that invoices should be sent and dated on the day shipped. Sue doesn't send them.

After Wayne, a lot of lam workers were hippies, had long hair, etc. Part of that is the reason why Rich now hires. Why is Ben down on Jim Fuller? Nita says because of time lost with accidents. 'Ben knows his family and all about the radio station. Doesn't think he is committed to the lumber company. There have been financial problems, too. There were garnishments in the past. He's quit or been laid off, or was fired about three years ago. Some things stick in Ben's throat. Now Jim is out of debt; they sold the home and moved; his wife works; they do an awful lot of volunteer work at the school. Ben sees this and wonders why he can't give that energy to the company'.

John Rondo (Juanita): From a local logging family. He is a nephew of Butch (someone from a logging company). 'Notorious redneck'. Once called Ben from a bar when he was drunk and swore to Ben about his pay cheque. 'Ben doesn't forget those things'.

Sue hired by Joe: Does all the paperwork in the lam plant. Doesn't really have to interact with any of the men except Joe. Takes care of the purchase orders, invoices, and daily records.

Glue used in lam plant: Twenty-two thousand pounds at 60 cents per pound; that's about $13 000 a month.

Maintenance man: Leon replacing rails and turning chair at pre-glue. 'Had help until noon. Don't know where they took off to'. It's really a two-person job. Also said that they're probably six to eight months overdue with this job.

Hoists: Planer and helper talking at break that it is awkward and sometimes have to wait either on the finish end or breakdown side of planing because of competition

for hoists. Believe the roof could hold more hoists. Can't understand why Ben won't spring for a couple of more hoists on each side. In the lunchroom, the planer was coaching a breakdown/finish helper on how to undo clamps efficiently. Says that the 'whole operation has to be speeded up'. 1:05 p.m. – lunchroom. The planer approaches Joe: 'Can we get off a little early? We've been working lots of ten-hour days'. Joe responds, 'If you get that 57 job done, maybe we'll see'. As Joe turns to leave, the other finish man, who helps the planer, says, 'Hey, Joe, I want to talk to you later'. Joe says, 'Okay'. The man turns to me and says, 'He thinks we should be working harder. I want to tell him what's what'.

Rolf put in lam plant by Ben: Probably consulted with Joe, but still he did it.

Goals for lam plant (Rich): Joe and Ben both have some goals in their heads, of course, and talk on occasion. 'Probably not very systematically written down'.

Jim Fuller, pre-glue supervisor: Swing shift now. Three men work directly under him. First work position is a lumber grading cut-off saw. A nineteen- to twenty-year-old tends to work here. 'You need a big reach'. Then there is a cut-off saw that feeds a finger-joiner cut. Then the ends are glued. 'Young men tend to be in this position, too. Need to have a lot of manual dexterity and a sense of rhythm'. Then there is the radio frequency curing machine. It gives an eight- to ten-second jolt at 109; then the hardest job comes along. The lumber is stopped, set to length, and cut three inches longer than order and then put in stacks on rollers. 'You need to visually check ahead, grade lumber, and everything else'. This position has to be communicated back up to pre-glue line for amount.

Production scheduling (Rich/Jim): 'Rolf is so-called production supervisor. However, if Joe has his druthers, he'd do that, too'. Supposed to have orders from Joe to Dirk to Jim. Needs to be scheduling. This mostly happens, but sometimes he gets a message from Joe himself. Actually Jim says, 'Both Rolf and Joe more or less equally give me orders'. Jim confirms that the majority of materials come from external sources and suppliers. He thinks Joe is a 'sharp bargainer'. 'If he can save $100 per thousand on eight- or ten-footers, he may buy them. Of course, this means they have to do a lot more cutting and gluing'. Somehow it's known that thirty thousand feet a day per shift is what the lam plant is to produce. It takes two pre-glue shifts to get that. A few years ago, Jim reports, a production quota for the plant was eighteen to twenty thousand feet per day. 'Joe is really production-minded, a real pusher'.

Asking about problems (Jim): He quickly responds with 'confusion' and elaborates that it has to do with scheduling. 'Sometimes Dirk has to work on the line and get inaccurate figures, or we don't get them in time'. Nonetheless, he thinks Dirk is a good man and tries hard. Another problem has to do with stacking. There is not enough room to handle items where beams are curing, particularly in the finishing area. He makes a big point about the difference between architectural and other grades. There are 15% of the former in general, but it takes more layout space in the finish end to handle it.

The most inexperienced crew, in Jim's opinion, is in the breakdown area (unclamping beams for planing). There seems to be a bottleneck around the planer. 'The crew tries hard but is somewhat inexperienced. His helpers couldn't care a damn'. Planing is to a tolerance of plus or minus 1/16-inch. He gives an example of large beams for Los Angeles that were over-planed, and those beams now sit in the yard until they can be worked into some later order for someone.

Another problem, according to Fuller, has to do with Paul, an electrician who works under Wayne. Has strong sawmill preference. Can never find him. For example, the RF machine is only half rebuilt. 'People who do this work for Wayne will probably never get it done'.

Age of workers (Jim): Mostly young – 'means that they don't really care about working, aren't very responsible. They take off when they feel like it; hence, there is a lot of personnel being shuffled around. Both Walton and Dirk, and even Joe, pitch in sometimes, not that this makes it really more efficient'. 'Personnel is shuffled too much'. Fuller gives an example. He was hit by a beam and was off for seven weeks. Jay replaced him. There was stacking in the breakdown area on the main two. Jay tried to move a ceiling air hose; it came back; two top beams fell and 'snuffed him out just like that'. Maintenance men have to fill in on lines, too. This cuts into maintenance being done on time. The whole program is behind. It's sort of down to what Fuller calls 'band-aid work'. Also, major replacements are done poorly. Example: glue area where pipes come right down in the middle of the pre-glue line when they should have been run down the wall. Bruce did this.

Ben's approach (Jim): 'Ben used to visit the laminating plant twice a week a few years ago. I haven't seen Ben through here for more than a month now. Ben likes to use a big-stick approach'. He gives example of Ben looking at maintenance work in gluing shop and insisting that the millwright come in on Saturday to get it done, 'or else'.

Those who report to Ben: Rich, industrial relations; Wayne, construction; Juanita, who is secretary and office manager; and managers of three companies. Richardson Lumber, which has 110 employees, was founded in 1951. Papoose Laminators started in 1968, and Prairie Wood Products started in about 1976, with forty-five employees. There is a logging company, too, which is for buying.

Mitch's Notes

Jack, Mike, and I arrive at B. R. Richardson. We enter through the main building into the office and are seated in a conference room located at the back of the main office, which is located up on a hill overlooking the rest of the plant.

Rich enters; after formal introductions, proceeds to talk about Joe, or I should say, describes Joe.

Describes Joe in the following way. Says that Joe is aware the training program was a possibility. Stated that Joe had had military experience, that he (Joe) believes he knows about management, that there are some possible resentful feelings toward our intrusion upon the plant, that he is aware of us and the fact that we are from State University.

Rich, Mike, and I leave the main office and go down to the plant to be introduced to Joe.

Rich introduces us to Joe by saying that we are with Jack and that we are down looking around at the plant, etc. – seemed awkward. Communication not straightforward. Not a lot of eye-to-eye contact. Rich is leaning up against the wall; he looks uncomfortable and leaves rather abruptly.

Joe immediately questions us as to what we are doing, why we are here, and what we are looking for. My perception is that he is resentful. In talking to Joe, I perceive that he felt the workers were good, that with the proper knowledge of the task they could lead themselves. He also stated they were 'multi-capacity' – that 'they had many functions which they performed', and that it wasn't that specialised down on the floor. He mentioned that his functions were bidding, managing, and engineering. He made a comment toward work team functions ('work team crap'), and then he corrected himself. He also remarked that 'theories come and theories go'.

At one point, Joe stressed the use of communication as a tool in management. He showed Mike and me a little exercise and seemed to be impressed with it.

In looking on the walls of his office, he had approximately five awards or merits for leadership or worker participation.

His assistant Rolf had a desk right next to his, which was in an office off the side of the secretarial room serving as the entrance to his building.

Joe's background included working in many plants, primarily in forestry – that is my understanding. He said he preferred working at B. R. Richardson's mainly because it was a 'small and non-political plant'. He likes leadership, and he enjoys working there. He stated, as we were walking through the plant, that he felt a high degree of frustration about the plant because the size was too small at times and the seasonal rush (which is beginning right now as of May) for summer building puts a crunch on things. He stated that production is up 10% from last year; that there have been scheduling problems – they received some wood in February, and it wasn't until May that they could use it and laminate it and get it out the other side, so it's been stacked taking up space. He stated that if they fall behind, they have no chance to catch up and that they are working at full capacity right now.

Later on that afternoon, I went back and talked to Joe. I asked him what his specific duties were. He replied in the following way: His duties were to take orders, to plan the shipping, to make bids on orders, and to manage the plant. His typical day was to arrive about 7:00 to 7:15 a.m., to look over the plant, to look at the new orders of the day, and to take care of any emergencies. Lately, he stated that he was making engineering drawings. When asked if this was common, he said it usually was done by the customers, but he felt it was a service he could render them. He stated, 'It's foolishness because it takes too much time'. However, he continued to work on that project. He stated that he liked the work, that he didn't mind long hours. When asked about the scheduling, he said that after he makes a bid and fills the order, it goes to Dirk, who schedules the work to be done, which goes to Ron, who is either in pre-glue or the gluing operation. I'm not sure, but I felt he was talking about the gluing operation. And he stated that Ron's job was very specific, that he had to coordinate the people to get the wood clamped up, to get the glue on, and to get it organised in a rather specified manner. (I think it is interesting to check Ron's description that I include later on.)

My personal comment on Joe is that he seemed very friendly with the workers, that it was a buddy-buddy relationship. At one time, we were in the lunchroom with Joe, and he was talking openly about the problems of the shop; it was kind of like 'we all suffer through this too, don't we?' He seemed to enjoy his work, he likes to work hard, he was proud of the fact that production was up, he was supportive of the men down there, and he was also apprehensive of Mike's and my presence. I think it is interesting to note the roles that Mike and I took. Mike took the role of a person interested in design, more or less, and I took the role, as I stated to Joe, that I was interested in seeing what it was like to be a manager in this situation and to learn any knowledge he might have to offer. Many times during our encounter, he asked me what my background was and also about what I wanted to do when I got through school. He seemed very interested in my studies and my goals.

Joe's secretary, while I did not talk to her, seemed to play an important role in the organisation. At one point, I was talking to Joe when the secretary answered the phone and interrupted our conversation to tell Joe about a possible bid. Joe then made the bid based on the board footage, and the secretary questioned him on this bid, at which point Joe thought a minute and said, 'Yeah, I want to keep the bid the way it is'. The secretary then asked him, 'Are you sure?' and Joe said, 'Yes', at which point the secretary completed the preliminary parts of the bid over the phone.

At one point when we were walking through the plant with Joe, I made mental notes on safety aspects of the plant – this was something in question. Some of the things I noted are as follows.

There seemed to be many metal spacers or clamps by the glue section. This section wasn't in use, so I don't know if this was normal or not. It was very crowded and difficult to walk around. As we walked through the plant, I saw at least two different types of band saws with no guarding whatsoever – a very dangerous situation in my opinion. There were no safety signs around the plant – at least not outside the lunchroom. One worker did not have a safety helmet on. I also noticed that the safety helmets that they gave us were of very low quality. I base this on past experience in wearing them; they were the cheapest I have seen. I did see a safety insignia on one gentleman's lunch box. (I wonder how they meet OSHA standards.) Also because of the crowdedness of the facility, it was very difficult to move around, and with things going on, I could see how it would be difficult not to get hurt. The workers at one point asked Joe about another worker (I think his name was Bob). It seems that Bob was going down the highway and was reaching for a speaker wire and hit the centre rail on Highway I-5 and totalled his truck. He seemed to be okay with a mild concussion. The workers were very concerned. A group of about three of them asked Joe how Bob was doing.

I had a chance to talk to Ron, the team leader in gluing. His comment about his job was that there were long hours, that these were typically ten or more per day, and that he received overtime for the long hours provided that in total they were over forty hours per week. Each hour over the forty minimum would be paid at 1.5 times the normal rate. For Ron, the normal rate was about $8 an hour, $12 an hour overtime. His comments about his job and his attitude toward the plant were 'sweatshop', 'Richardson won't spend money', and 'everyone's worked at BR's at one time or another before'. 'They have plans for expansion of the plant, but they don't want to spend the money on it'. At one point, he said he didn't really know what he was doing in terms of how to be a supervisor, how to be a leader. When I questioned him some more, he really didn't know what the supervisor did, in this case Rolf. He had just finished his first year, as far as experience on the job.

Ron had a major complaint about his job in that the glue person also had to prepare the glue and was responsible for getting all the boards and clamps in the right direction. He seemed to think maybe an extra glue prepare person would help. It seems to be a major job for him. There seemed to be quite a bit of dissatisfaction about Rolf in his mind. He stated that when overtime or a certain amount of board footage was needed to meet a quota, this created work unrest, which led to accidents. He said that Rolf was always the one who initiated or told the workers that they had to work overtime. When asked about the death that had occurred, he stated that everybody was pretty upset about it, that it was bound to happen. I asked him what happened that day. He said that a guy got hurt, and yet management still wanted them to work even after the guy died. This seemed to upset Ron.

Ron mentioned that they (the workers) had a softball team; that he felt frustrated about it because he couldn't always play because the games were at six or seven o'clock and many times they were working until late in the evening trying to make a quota. He also stated that accidents were very high around here, that it was not uncommon to get a finger smashed or something, and that management didn't seem to care too much. He stated that he liked Joe, the manager, that he was okay but that he was maybe more production-oriented than necessary. He stated that the work is very hard and the need for better methods is evident. He stated that most men had bad backs, hernias, and broken fingers or toes, and he seemed to be kind of embarrassed. He did state that they had medical insurance.

Ron stated that one of the biggest causes of unrest, he felt, was due to overtime, and his own personal frustration was that in a year he had obtained probably the highest vertical level on the management structure, that of supervisor.

He stated that the next job would probably be to take Joe's job. He said that wouldn't happen, so there seems to be a lack of job mobility in his eyes. He stated that workers do almost anything, any task at any time; that what needs to be done, needs to be done, and they do it. He also stated that in the summertime, when it is warmer, the metal building that they work in gets really hot, and it's not uncommon for men to lose five or more pounds in one shift, which would be in an eight-hour period. When asked if it was possible to ventilate the building a little bit more, he said it would be hard, that even if they could, management wouldn't spend the money to do it.

Ron said he didn't have enough time for his home life. He also stated that Rolf and Joe, who were the supervisor and manager, would come out and help when they had the time. He said they would actually end up losing a half-hour of production time that way and would be better off if they would just stay in their offices. Ron seemed to express a great amount of displeasure with Rolf, and he said most of the workers agreed that Rolf was a 'thorn'. When Rolf would give orders, men would get upset and throw things around, and this would cause accidents. When asked about new members, he said they don't last more than a couple of days, and very rarely do they last over a year. Ron stated that one of the jobs they gave new workers was to bang beams in the gluing job with a weight that was on a pole that is picked up and bounced up and down off the wood. It weighed anywhere from forty-five to one hundred pounds; very gruelling work. He laughed a little bit and said that they usually hurt their back the first day, and it takes them a couple of weeks to learn how to do it, to learn the right technique, but he said 'there is no other way to learn the job, other than just jumping up there and doing it'.

My own personal opinion of Ron was that while somewhat upset at the conditions down there, he was dedicated, he did enjoy his role as a leader, and he was looked up to by the fellow workers. He mentioned at one time that the record of total board footage was broken by his crew, and he seemed very proud of that fact. He did not seem to think that any of our suggestions would make any waves around there, that 'I would not be listened to'. He was enjoyable to talk to, and he was more than willing to help me obtain the information I needed.

Marty, who like Ron has been there for over a year, was 'key person' of the glue team. However, Ron acted as the leader. They seemed to be good friends and went home together that afternoon. Marty had been there the longest. He had stated that the work is hard, that there are long hours, and that he had been right next to the man who was killed. He stated that he was no more than three to six feet from his friend (I guess he was his friend) when it happened. He was the one to fill out the accident report for the police and insurance people. He stated that they wanted to stop work and that the plant, and he didn't say specifically who, didn't want to shut down but wanted to complete the work that was started. It seemed that most of the workers there did not want to work that day. That was the extent of my talking to Marty.

When the workers were leaving, it seems they had set up a bet for a keg of beer if the planer Griffith could plane all the beams that were set out in front of him, which from the comments of the men, was quite a chore. But Griffith seemed pretty confident that he could get the work out. He did say that he was looking to go to pharmacy school as soon as he got his hernia fixed, and when asked about the hernia, he said he got it some time ago. He said he got it working while picking up some stuff in the plant. Again, this seemed to be common.

I had a chance to talk to a couple of the pre-glue persons; there is a total of three. I believe Jack had talked to the leader, and I talked to the two workers. They pretty much agreed that a union would be nice; however, BR, the owner, would not allow one to come in. He said, 'Work long hours, or you get fired'. There seemed to be a lot of stress as far as meeting their quota, and they could not go home until they met the quota for the day. They stated that the job was okay, but that they didn't have much time for their families. One said, 'I go home, I sleep, I get up, I go to work and I go back home and go to sleep again'. When asked about their salary, he stated that they're paying, in his opinion, 60 cents per hour lower than the unions around here, and he said further, 'The unions will get a 65-cent-per-hour raise, and we'll get a 45-cent-per-hour raise'.

I also had a chance to talk to some of the guys in the finish area. This seemed to be a typical eight-hour shift that consisted primarily of watching the beams run through the planer. They go back and clean it up so that it can be packaged and shipped out. One man's biggest complaint was that he was upset about the lunch-break change, which he stated was initiated by Rolf. It consisted of taking their one-hour lunch break and cutting it down to a half-hour. He stated that Rolf felt production would be increased by cutting down the lunch break. He seemed upset about this. I don't know his name. He lived five blocks away from the plant and didn't have time to go home to eat and then come back (on a half-hour break). He seemed to have a high degree of resentment toward Rolf, and he had no knowledge of what Rolf does.

I had an opportunity to meet with John, the quality-control man. He seemed like a very nice man. No real quotes. He was just there for a few minutes. He had had an eye operated on: I guess a new lens was put in. He seemed to talk with Joe very well. When I asked Joe about John, Joe stated John was officially to report to him; however, John reported to Rich, and that worked out for the best because quality control should really be removed from production somewhat. Joe seemed to see no conflict in that.

Mike's Notes

Mitch and I had a morning interview with Joe. Some of the quotes on management style were: 'I don't know about this work team crap, oops, stuff', 'Theories come and theories go', 'I believe in giving my workers explicit instructions; perceptions differ, and you have to be sure they understand', and

'I didn't like the politics of larger plants I've worked in'. Also, Joe mentioned frustration over the lack of plant space. To a worker he mentioned, 'You are frustrated, aren't you, Bill?'

During our tour, Joe set a brisk pace. He seemed to have quite a competent manner.

When Rich approached Joe about taking Mitch and me under his wing for a tour, I think Rich was intimidated by Joe. Rich had his back against the wall sideways to Joe, and he shifted his eyes from Joe to Mitch and me during the conversation.

Joe was more than a bit curious in regard to our plant visit objective. I said it was for a class project. Joe replied, 'Oh, then it's theory'. I explained we covered all the theories equally. Another quote from Joe: 'A day's production lost is a day lost', delivered with a hint of frustration and impatience.

Joe's office contained numerous good-worker awards. One prominent sign contained a message roughly to the effect that 'I am right in the end'. My impression of the plant – there were no safety glasses on the workers. One worker had no helmet; there were no band-saw safety devices. Seemed pretty lackadaisical. During our initial interview with Joe, Darrell, a truck driver, was in the office. He talked good-naturedly with Joe, and he seemed to like Joe in general. Later on in the day I had an interview alone with Dirk. Dirk is the scheduler. Dirk has a master's in forestry from the University of Washington. Dirk mentioned that he spends half his time filling in various positions. He says one of the major problems is the transition between shifts. This is in regard to mistakes. One of Dirk's quotes: 'There is no communication between shifts. Mainly people don't want to take the blame for mistakes'. During the course of the interview, Dirk's manner was fidgety; he moved around a bit, but he seemed fairly open. A quote from Dirk: 'The men change jobs so much that it is hard to train them. Everyone has to know what is needed in beams'. This implies that workers weren't really trained well enough to know what was needed in beams. 'Production people go home after the quota'. That was his perception of the amount of overtime worked. 'Repairs after gluing are costly and difficult. Double checking is needed before they are glued together. Average beam is six thousand board feet, or approximately $840. I currently have seventy-five bastard beams I have to find a home for'. Then Dirk went on to an example of mistakes made. A tape cloth shrunk two inches. They used this tape for quite some time before they finally found the mistake. He also mentioned there were frequent mix-ups between the $\frac{13}{4}$-inch and $\frac{11}{4}$-inch strips for laminated beams. Dirk's quote on the workers: 'A few are incompetent; they just get soft warnings. Management should be harder on them'.

Item on bidding or posting for jobs: seniority or ability (whoever they think will do best) decides who gets the job. On the workers: Morale is low. Safety and overtime are the main causes. On Rich, industrial relations: 'The only contact I've had with him is when he came down and asked about people'. I asked, 'Who, what people?' and Dirk said, 'I'd rather not say'. On safety, he mentioned there are no physicals required. Later on in the interview, I asked why he didn't try to change things, seeing as he has a master's and seems to have his head together. Dirk mentioned, 'Go up the line. Joe would listen'. I said, 'Listen?' and Dirk said, 'Yeah, Joe would listen'. At this point, Bruce, a bubbling and brassy guy who is a millwright in charge of special-projects maintenance, came in. The interview with Dirk was about thirty minutes under way; the next twenty minutes I spent with Dirk, he mentioned Ben Richardson, the president. I asked, 'Do men like to see BR?' Dirk responded, 'No, BR is bad news in the laminating plant'. He also mentioned that in the year he has been there, BR had been down to the laminating plant only five times.

Item from Bruce: 'I've had thirty projects in the year I've been here; I only finished one. Joe keeps jerking me around. As I get something operating but not all the kinks out, I'm on to something else'. Bruce also mentioned that he is on emergency call every other week. He splits it with the other maintenance person.

The beam stacks before and after planing were mentioned as being in terrible disarray. Bruce mentioned that the Roseburg plants had a computer and a big yard with designated areas to organise their stacks. He said that this company should take a bulldozer and knock out the field to expand the outside stack area.

Item from Bruce: 'Antiquated machinery. Maintenance is costly and time-consuming'. Bruce commented on BR: 'Joe thinks labour is cheap; we don't have that many benefits. An example of BR's attitude: one of his right-hand men got in a flap over the 3:30 a.m. shift parking down here instead of in the muddy, rutted parking lot an eighth of a mile up the road. Christ, they had a Caterpillar running up there, and they didn't even smooth it out. Anyway, this guy tells Rolf, the super, if these guys are too lazy to walk down from the workers' parking lot, they can go work somewhere else'. This was mentioned right in front of some of the men. Bruce went on to say, 'It really makes us feel wanted'. I then asked who was this guy, BR's right-hand man, and Bruce said, 'I don't want to say.... What the hell, I'm quitting this heap in a while anyway. It was Wayne Teeterman, BR's special-projects director'. During most of Bruce's spiel, Dirk appeared to be quite happy with what Bruce was saying; I'm sure he was glad he didn't have to say it himself.

It was mentioned that the sawmill didn't have a lunchroom, so the laminated plant felt favoured. Also, Rolf mentioned that the bathroom was one of the best in BR's operations.

Bruce on Rolf: 'He, Rolf, is a nice guy. Nobody respects him, though'.

Dirk and Bruce mentioned that there are only six or seven men who have made it ten years in all of BR's five companies.

Dirk on Joe: 'Joe does too much. He keeps it all in his head. He is efficient. It would take two people to replace him. He's overworked, he doesn't like the hours, and he's just trying to keep his job'. Bruce concurred on the above points.

Bruce: 'Stacks of beams are too high. Two of them fell last week. Damned near got me and another guy'. I noted that the accidental death last year and its details were repeated to me three times during the day.

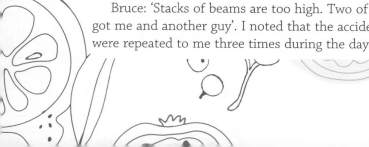

Bruce mentioned that he recently organised a softball team. 'The first thing this plant has ever had. It's hard practising and playing games with all the overtime. We went to BR to ask him for $700 to start it up. He gave us $250. There's fourteen teams in our league, and the minimum anyone else has gotten is $700'.

Dirk mentioned that the workers peak out at $8 an hour after one year. He seemed to think that money was a big motivating factor.

In response to my query why there was no union, Bruce and Dirk mentioned that hearsay has it that when union representatives came, BR said, 'Fine, if you want a union, I'll just close the place down'.

Dirk: 'Communication is the main problem. Joe schedules some changes, and I never hear about them'.

Bruce, on the foremen meetings with BR: 'Hell, the foremen will have their say, and in the end BR will stand up and say, 'This is the way it's going to be because I pay the checks'.

About five minutes before the session ended, Joe came in and with a friendly greeting said, 'There you are', to Bruce and indirectly to Dirk. Dirk got up as if getting ready to go back to work. Bruce stalled. Bruce then said that he didn't know how BR made any money on the operation. Dirk giggled lightly and nodded his head.

In the afternoon, I spent an hour and a half to two hours with Rolf, the superintendent. About an hour of this talking was Rolf trying to prove his competence by divulging intricate, technical and totally useless details of the plant. I got some tasty stuff anyway, and here it is:

Me: 'What does Joe do?'

Rolf: 'So doggone many things, I don't know'. Then he went on to mention he is a general manager in charge of scheduling and raw materials procurement and to rattle off two or three more. I said, 'What's your working relationship with Joe?' Rolf said, 'I implement his schedules. Dirk, the head of the finishing and planing department, and I get Joe's schedules. Joe will skip me whenever he wants to make changes – goes right to planing and finishing. Then I have to go see what's going on'. I asked him if he thought it would be more efficient if Joe went through him. Rolf said, 'No, we get along well. Joe saves time by going directly to the workers. We spend a lot of time after the shift going over and discussing what happened and planning for the next day and weeks ahead'.

Rolf mentioned that there are often schedule changes when customers' trucks pick up their orders. I wondered if maybe they could get tougher with the customers, and Rolf said, 'No, we'd lose them'.

Rolf mentioned that the company deals with brokers, not contractors. He said that customers sometimes cancel their orders.

On Bruce's idea of bulldozing a pasture to expand finish-beam storage, Rolf said that in the winter it was tough enough to keep the field clear with the current area.

Rolf on equipment: 'BR gives us the junkiest stuff to work with'. He went on to mention one particular piece of machinery that has four wheels and five feet of

clearance (I don't know what it is called): 'It has no brakes and no shut-off; you have to idle it to kill it'.

On Joe: 'Joe's good; he and I go to bat for the guys'.

Me: 'You must have a pretty little bat; I hear BR is a tough guy to get through to'.

Rolf: 'Yeah, he picks his battles'.

On Dirk: 'Effective, will improve with time; he doesn't always see the opportunities for utilising stock beams. He has his master's degree in glue technology'.

On John: 'Quality control marginal'. That's all he said.

On Nita, BR's secretary: 'She doesn't always use her power right'.

On Sue, Joe's secretary: 'She does the work of two people. Has lots of customer respect; they often comment on her'.

On Joe: 'He's too intelligent for the job. I don't know why he does not get something better. I guess he likes to work'.

On Rich: 'Rich does his job well'.

On the workforce: 'There are three types of guys. One is eight to five and a paycheque – never volunteers or does anything extra – 50% of the workforce. Second are the ones who use workers' compensation to get time off all the time; this is 20%. Workers' compensation is the biggest deterrent to an effective workforce', he went on to comment. 'And third, the ones who try, 30%'.

Rolf mentioned that 15 to 20% of the work hours were spent trying to unsort the beam piles, pre- and post-planer.

Rolf mentioned that architectural beams, 7 to 12% of the output, took three times as long to process as the plain beams.

On Joe again: 'Joe does a good job of scheduling and customer relations'.

On BR: 'BR is secretive; he should keep the guys informed'.

Rolf often has to juggle men around on their tasks and catches a lot of flak for this. I asked his criteria for deciding which men would go on which jobs. They were (1) how well the man will do the job and (2) how easy it is to replace him at his original task.

Rolf said overtime is a big problem. It's necessary to go through the jobs in order. Men never know how long they'll have to work. Lock-ups have to be finished. He mentioned that a good lock-up will take an hour, a bad one, one and a half to two hours. (A lock-up is essentially gluing and clamping the beam into a form.)

Rolf said he used to spend three hours a day on the glue crew. He doesn't do this any more; he has a good crew. Eighty per cent of the glue crew are good workers, in Rolf's opinion. He mentioned that two of the bad ones quit because they didn't want overtime. Also, Rolf noted that it was possible to avoid overtime by scheduling good or easy lock-ups. This was done when the glue crew had been putting in too much overtime.

Rolf stated that the overall problem with the operation was that everyone knows that 'BR doesn't give a shit about them'. I asked him if there was anything he liked about working for the company, and he said, 'I like working for Joe'. We ended the interview with Rolf saying, 'Overall, it's not a bad place to work; the cheque don't bounce'.

Preparing the Diagnosis

Jack Lawler leaned back in his chair and stretched. It had all come back. Now he needed a plan for working. It seemed that the first step was to determine what ideas, models, or theories would be useful in ordering and understanding the information he had. Then he would have to do a diagnosis and, finally, think about what to say to Ben Richardson and Richard Bowman. After buzzing his secretary to say that he didn't want to be interrupted, Lawler rolled up his sleeves and began to work.

Review questions

1 How would you assess Jack Lawler's entry and contracting process at B. R. Richardson? Would you have done anything differently?

2 What theories or models would you use to make sense out of the diagnostic data? How would you organise the information for feedback to Ben Richardson and Richard Bowman? How would you carry out the feedback process?

3 What additional information would you have liked Jack Lawler and his team to collect? Discuss.

Index